FASCICULUS MORUM
A Fourteenth-Century Preacher's Handbook

FASCICULUS MORUM
A Fourteenth-Century Preacher's Handbook

Edition and Translation by
Siegfried Wenzel

THE PENNSYLVANIA STATE UNIVERSITY PRESS
University Park and London

This publication has been supported by the National Endowment for the Humanities, a federal agency which supports the study of such fields as history, philosophy, literature, and languages; and the School of Arts and Sciences at the University of Pennsylvania.

PA
8310
.F35
E5
1989

Library of Congress Cataloging-in-Publication Data

Fasciculus morum. English & Latin.
Fasciculus morum : a fourteenth-century preacher's handbook / edition and translation by Siegfried Wenzel.
p. cm.
Text in English & Latin; notes in English.
Bibliography: p.
Includes index.
ISBN 0-271-00642-0
1. Preaching—England—Handbooks, manuals, etc. 2. Deadly sins—Handbooks, manuals, etc.
3. Christian literature, Latin (Medieval and modern)—Translations into English. 4. Christian poetry, English (Middle)—Modernized versions. 5. Christian literature, Latin (Medieval and modern)
6. Christian poetry, English (Middle) 7. Franciscans—England—Manuscripts. I. Wenzel, Siegfried.
II. Title.
PA8310.F35E5 1989
251—dc19
88–5809

Contents

Acknowledgments

Insofar as the present edition and translation is the result of a long project which included a study published in 1978 (*Verses in Sermons: "Fasciculus morum" and Its Middle English Poems*), my debts and gratitude recorded in the earlier book apply here as well. I am now further indebted to the Dean and Chapter of Canterbury Cathedral for permission to use Literary Manuscript D.14 as base text for this edition. The Beinecke Library has, once again, graciously loaned me some relevant photostatic material for an extended time. A grant from the National Endowment for the Humanities, together with a generous leave of absence from the University of Pennsylvania, allowed me to undertake and complete the translation. And Mr. Philip Winsor, Senior Editor of the Penn State Press, has been cheerfully dedicated to seeing this book, despite its complicated setup and length, come into print. To all these I give my warmest thanks.

List of Abbreviations

CC	Corpus Christianorum series latina.
CSEL	Corpus scriptorum ecclesiasticorum latinorum.
EETS	Early English Text Society.
EETS, ES	Early English Text Society, Extra Series.
FM	*Fasciculus morum.*
GR	Oesterley, Hermann, ed. *Gesta Romanorum* (Berlin, 1872; repr. Hildesheim: Georg Olms, 1963). Quoted by item number.
In	Walther, Hans. *Initia carminum ac versuum medii aevi posterioris latinorum* (Göttingen, 1959). Quoted by item number.
MGH	Monumenta Germaniae historica.
PG	J.-P. Migne (ed.). *Patrologiae cursus completus . . . Series Graeca.* 161 vols. (Paris, 1857ff.).
PL	J.-P. Migne (ed.). *Patrologiae cursus completus . . . Series Latina.* 221 volumes (Paris, 1844ff.).
Prov	Walther, Hans. *Proverbia sententiaeque latinitatis medii aevi,* 6 vols. (Göttingen, 1963–1967). Quoted by item number.
RL XIV	Carleton Brown (ed.). *Religious Lyrics of the XIVth Century.* Second edition, rev. by G. V. Smithers (Oxford, 1952).
SC	*Sources chrétiennes*
Verses	Siegfried Wenzel. *Verses in Sermons. "Fasciculus morum" and Its Middle English Poems* (Cambridge, Mass., 1978).
VP	*Vitas Patrum,* ed. Rosweyde, PL 73–74.

Biblical books are quoted according to the Authorized Version, but I have used "Cant." for the Song of Solomon.

Introduction

MANUSCRIPTS AND TEXTUAL RELATIONS

Fasciculus morum, an extensive treatise on the seven deadly sins and their opposed remedial virtues, apparently of Franciscan authorship and written as an aid in preaching, has been preserved in 28 known manuscripts. These will be designated by the following sigla:[1]

A   London, British Library, MS Additional 6716, fols. 1–58. First half of the fifteenth century.

B1   Oxford, Bodleian Library, MS 187 (S.C. 2090), fols. 124–209v. Mid-fifteenth century.[2]

B2   Oxford, Bodleian Library, MS 332 (S.C. 2243), fols. 107v–182v. Late fourteenth century.

B3   Oxford, Bodleian Library, MS 410 (S.C. 2305), fols. 1–92v. Fifteenth century.

B4   Oxford, Bodleian Library, MS 687 (S.C. 2501), fols. 1–71v. Early fifteenth century.

C   Cambridge, University Library, MS Dd.10.5, fols. 13–173v. Late fifteenth century.

Co   Oxford, Corpus Christi College, MS 218, fols. 4–219v. End of fourteenth century.

CC   Canterbury, Cathedral Library, MS D.14, fols. 1–222. Third quarter of the fifteenth century.[3]

D   Durham, University Library, MS Cosin V.iv.2, fols. 1–89v. Written in 1477.

E   Edinburgh, University Library, MS 82, fols. 4–274. Fifteenth century.

Et   Eton, Eton College, MS 34, part ii, fols. 5–88. Written in 1443.[4]

Go1   Cambridge, Gonville and Caius College, MS 71, fols. 13–92v. Fifteenth century.

Go2   Cambridge, Gonville and Caius College, MS 364, fols. 1–153v. Ca. 1400.

H   London, British Library, MS Harley 1316, fol. 1–100v. Fifteenth cen-
         tury.
Jo   Cambridge, St. John's College, MS 159, fols. 34–186v. Late fifteenth
         century.
L1   Oxford, Bodleian Library, MS Laud Misc. 111 (S.C. 1550), fols. 49–
         176v. Beginning of fifteenth century.
L2   Oxford, Bodleian Library, MS Laud Misc. 213 (S.C. 1045), fols. 1–186.
         Fifteenth century.
L3   Oxford, Bodleian Library, MS Laud Misc. 568 (S.C. 1117), fols. 1–109.
         Fifteenth century.
Li   Oxford, Lincoln College, MS 52, fols. 1–172. Beginning of fifteenth
         century.
LC   Lincoln, Cathedral Library, MS 44 (A.2.13), fols. 156–228v. Fifteenth
         century.
M   Madrid, University, Library of the Faculty of Law, MS 116^{20}.3, fols. 1–
         139. Mid-fifteenth century.
Mo   New York, Pierpont Morgan Library, MS 298, fols. 2–98v. The section
         containing *FM* was written in Oxford in or before 1412.[5]
Pe   Cambridge, Peterhouse, MS 213, fols. 1–104v. Fifteenth century.
R   Oxford, Bodleian Library, MS Rawlinson C.670 (S.C. 12514), fols. 7–
         150v. First half of the fifteenth century.
Sp   Spalding, Lincs., Spalding Gentlemen's Society, MS M.J.B.14 (*olim*
         Maurice Johnson No. LIV), fols. 1–165. Fifteenth century.
V   Vatican, MS Ottoboni 626, fols. 1–104. Late fourteenth century.[6]
W1   Worcester, Cathedral Library, MS F.19, fols. 161–229. Early fifteenth
         century.
W2   Worcester, Cathedral Library, MS Q.3, fols. 2–166v. Fifteenth century.[7]

The treatise regularly consists of a prologue ("Frater predilecte ac sodalis preelecte, quia Scriptura . . .") and seven *partes* or *particulae* (beginning "Ut enim habetur in Regula beati patris Francisci . . ."). In several copies, the treatise is accompanied by a list of chapters or an alphabetical subject index ("Tabula") as well as a series of outlines for 42 sermons for the Sundays from 1 Advent to Trinity and for the major feasts of this period. These additional matters, however, occur irregularly, in various combinations, and in different sequences and loca- tions. In the following discussion, they are excluded from consideration, and the analysis of *FM* and its textual history will be limited to the treatise proper.

Of the extant copies, at least five (CC, H, Jo, L1, W1) are defective through substantial loss of leaves, and two others (A, D) are highly abbreviated or condensed versions. H, A, and D have been disregarded in the following anal- ysis.

The 25 "full" texts fall into several major, textually clearly distinct groups, which will be designated by letters r to z.[8]

Group x: B2, Pe

This group forms a version of *FM* in which many stories, *exempla*, and even similes present in w, y, and z are either abbreviated or entirely omitted. Sometimes a story is simply omitted; at other times it is shortened and summarized; and at still other times it is referred to without retelling. On occasion, the story is omitted while its moralization has been preserved (e.g., the three classical tales in III.xxii). Now and then the resulting gap in the exposition is bridged by a sentence or phrase peculiar to x. A good example of this whole situation is the story about the tyrant Dionysius, which illustrates how envious people find easy excuses to justify their immoral acts. In the edited text (from CC), it is introduced and begun as follows:

[1] Et tamen mirum est quia quicquid per invidiam faciunt ad dampnum proximi, satis tamen aperte se excusare sciunt, quod non faciunt hoc propter invidiam aut malum sed propter bonum alterius, sicut se excusavit Dionisius Syracusanus templa deorum suorum expoliando. Unde narrat beatus Ieronimus . . . (III.i.79–83).

B2 introduces the story in the same way, but instead of telling it at some length gives a one-sentence summary:

Et tamen . . . alterius. Et hic nota quod Dionisius tyrannus se excusavit quando intravit templum et abstulit anulum, barbam, et clamidem (fol. 122).

After the story has been told, it is moralized by applying Dionysius's three thefts to three "contemporary" social abuses:

Revera spiritualiter ita est de istis invidis. Si enim sit aliqua domus religiosorum . . . Set de istis excusacionibus invidis et falsis dicitur Iohannis 15 . . . (text, III.i.97–138).

Again, B2 summarizes the entire moralization in one brief sentence, which follows immediately after "clamidem":

Et sic nota quando aliqui accipiunt aliquid a viris ecclesiasticis, mercatoribus, et vicinis et pauperibus, se excusant. Sed de istis excusacionibus . . . (fol. 122).

The inference that x is a redaction of the text represented in w (on which the edited text is based) by means of deliberate and wholesale omission of material is further strengthened by lines in which this process of abbreviation has led to syntactic incoherence, as for instance:

[2] *Text:* Ut ait Tullius libro 1 *De officiis.* Unde de modestia Titi imperatoris legitur quod in morte sua non recoluit ullum factum quod esset puniendum excepto uno, quod tamen nulli innotuit, eo quod omnia modeste egit prout erant agenda. Ad has ergo partes temperancie . . . (V.xxxiv.80–84).

B2: Ubi ait Tullius. Ad has ergo partes . . . (fol. 170vb).

B2 seems to stand closer to the archetype of x than Pe (which has many eyeskips), and it is paleographically earlier than Pe. But the two MSS seem to be collateral rather than linear descendants.

Group y: B3, L2

The text of this group is significantly different from the other groups in that it occasionally excludes some material or words it differently. In the moralized *exemplum* of Dionysius cited above [1], for example, this group gives the story itself as well as the moralization (against x), but the text of the moralization differs significantly from that of groups w and z. Thus, the first theft is moralized as follows:

[3] *Text:* Revera spiritualiter ita est de istis invidis. Si enim sit aliqua domus religiosorum de qua annonam optant habere, numquam cessabunt clamare: "Rustici illi sunt nimis pingues; oportet quod laxentur." Unde vel mittent suos ribaldos et equos ad morandum, vel ipsimet venient cum maxima comitiva ad maneria sua vel domum propriam, et illam expensis nimium excessivis excoriant et depauperant. Si ergo abbas, prior, vel alius prelatus offerat alicui tali dextrarium, palefridum, sive maximam summam pecunie, ut scilicet ab huiusmodi inceptis desistant, videtur eis quod huiusmodi iuste lucrantur, eo quod eis offertur, et dicunt quod ibi nulla est invidia. Quod falsum est, quia nisi eorum voluntatem haberent, numquam ex nimia invidie malicia cessarent tales innocentes destruere. Dicunt eciam tales quando vident in bonis Ecclesie sic ecclesiasticos habundare: "Ut quid, inquiunt, tanti rustici tanta bona occupant, rege indigente et terra blado, pecunia, et aliis diviciis carere? Si enim talia haberemus, in nulla causa aut necessitate neque terram in desolacione dimitteremus." Set hoc est falsum, quia quicquid faciunt aut dicunt est per invidiam, eo quod fertilius est illis quam sibi (III.i.97–113).

In contrast, B3 reads:

Moraliter sic est de invidis aliquibus invidentibus possessionibus religiosorum, a quibus annonam habere optant, si eos plene privare non possunt, dicentibus quia sunt nimis pingues, oportet quod laxentur, statimque excogitant vias quibus eos diffament, bona eorum devastent, regi eos accusent, ipsique eos frequentent cum turba nimis gravi, quousque ut desistant preces et precia non modica habeant a predictis. Hii sunt qui auferunt anulum dicendo ipsum esse libenter oblatum et cum magnis precibus (fol. 27).

Such shortening and stylistic tightening is quite characteristic of group y, which otherwise follows the text of group w. The changes are not as drastic as those in group x, nor do they affect the substance of the treatise's material as widely as the omissions in x; on the other hand, they are more extensive and substantial than is the variation found among subgroups of w.

It would seem that y stands farther removed from the original form of *FM* than w. The greater elegance in the y version of Example [3] is less characteristic of the style of *FM* in general than is the more diffuse development in w. Another illustration may be found in the discussion of the love of one's neighbor. Here, w introduces the chapter with a twofold division, which is followed by a discriminating explanation of the biblical injunction to love one's neighbor "as yourself" (Matt. 22.39). In y, the latter is totally omitted, and the preceding division takes a form that differs substantively from w:

[4] *Text:* Circa autem dilectionem et caritatem quas erga proximum habemus sciendum quod ipsa consistit primo in naturali fraternitate, ipsum caritatiue edocendo et a malis defendendo; secundo in temporali necessitate, ipsum pro posse tantum in indigenciis supportando (III.viii.1–4).

B3: Circa caritatem erga proximum sciendum quod ipsa in duobus consistit, videlicet in naturali fraternitate que proximum docet et defendit, et in spirituali que proximum cum indiget compatitur et condescendit (fol. 21v).

In context, y's distinction between *naturalis* and *spiritualis fraternitas* seems to make less sense than w's differentiation. Further support for the argument that w is closer to the original than y derives from the English verses (which are fully represented in group y): they show evidence that the verbal material of w has in y been linguistically updated.[9]

B3 and L2 are extremely close to each other. Individual variants are minor in character, usually less significant than variants between MSS in other groups.

Group z: C, Co, Li, (E)

The text of this group is consistently longer or more expanded than that of x, y, and w. The nature of z's expansions can be seen in the extracts reproduced below, from CC (edited) and C. Here z quotes Scripture verbatim instead of merely referring to it (lines 17–39, etc.); completes quotations (62–65, etc.); adds doctrinal material (84–90) and authorities (Ovid in 108–109, church fathers in 155–71 and 189–92, the Bible in 134–38); clarifies statements (10–11); and offers smaller differences in vocabulary (58–60) and syntax (90–93). The question arises whether the fuller version of group z is the original, which has been abbreviated in the other groups (x, y, and w), or whether conversely z is an expanded redaction of the other groups (in the following designated as o), particularly of w.

An answer can be derived from analyzing the passage in VI.ii in which *FM* discusses the species of gluttony. I reproduce, in parallel columns, a representative text of o, on the basis of MS CC as edited in this book, and an edited transcription from MS C, the representative of group z.

[5]

o = MS CC	z = MS C
Eius autem species in hiis versibus connotantur:	[fol. 135v] Eius autem species in hiis versibus continentur:
Prepropere, laute, nimis ardenter, studiose.	Prepropere, laute, nimis, ardenter, studiose.
Sic Ionathas, populus, Sodomita, Seyrque sacerdos.	5 Sic Ionathas, populus, Sodomita, Seirque, sacerdos.

Prima species est prepropere, hoc
est, tempore indebito et extra horam,

sicut
fecit Ionathas,

de quo Regum 14,

pro
quo maledictionem patris incurrit et
morti addictus est.
          Nec tamen ultra comedit
nisi   quod summitate
virge in melle intinxit. Quid ergo
de gulosis dicendum est qui
diebus abstinencie ieiunia frangunt, et
hoc non tantum bis vel ter in die,
set de vespere usque ad mediam noctem?
Revera iuxta propheciam Ysaie 5 merces
talium
               est hec: "Ve, ve, qui
surgitis mane ad ebrietatem sectandam
et vinum potandum usque ad vesperam."

Prima vero species est prepropere, hoc
est, horam comedendi preveniendo propter
impacienciam expectandi tempus debitum.
10   Et est tempus debitum in diebus ieiunio-
rum hora undecima vel meridies. Exemplum de Ionatha, qui ante tempus assignatum a Saul patre suo comedit et ideo
adductus est ad mortem et maledictus a
15   patre suo, ut patet 1 Regum 14, ubi
dicitur: "Adiuravit Saul populum dicens,
'Maledictus vir qui comederit panem usque
ad vesperam donec ulciscar de inimicis
meis,' et non manducavit universus populus
20   panem. Omneque terre vulgus venit in
saltum in quo erat mel super faciem agri.
Ingressus itaque populus saltum et apparuit fluens mel nullusque applicuit
manum ad os suum. Timebant enim populus
25   iuramentum. Porro Ionathas non audierat
cum adiuraret pater eius populum, exten-
ditque summitatem virge quam habebat in
manu et intinxit in favo mellis et convertit manum suam ad os suum, et illumi-
30   nati sunt oculi eius. Respondens unus de
populo ait: 'Iureiurando astrinxit pater
tuus populum dicens, Maledictus qui
comederit panem hodie. Defecerat autem
populus.' Dixit autem Ionathas: 'Turba-
35   vit pater meus terram. Vidistis ipsi
quia illuminati sunt oculi eo quod gus-
taverim paululum de melle isto. Quanto
magis si comedisset populus de preda
inimicorum suorum,' " etc. [T]um ergo Io-
40   nathas malediccionem patris incurrit et
morti addictus est, ut patet historiam
intuenti, nec tamen ultra comedit nisi
modicum mel quod cum summitate virge
de favo suscepit. Quid dicemus de
45   gulosis qui contra preceptum Dei in
diebus abstinencie ieiunia frangunt, et
hoc non tantum bis vel ter in die comedendo, set eciam per totam noctem ad
tabernas sedendo? Revera, excommunica-
50   cionem et malediccionem Dei patris incurrunt, dicente Domino Ysaie 5: "Ve qui
consurgitis mane ad ebrietatem sectandam
et potandum usque ad vesperam ut vino
estuetis. Cithara et lira et timpano et
55   tibia et vinum in conviviis, et opus D[o-
mi]ni non respicitis nec opera manuum

Istud ergo
"ve" hortatur precavendum
Ecclesiasticus:
"Cogitavi in corde meo abstrahere vinum a carne mea."

Nam per nimiam
gulam vini
adquiritur corporis corrupcio. Nam
corpus corrumpit quicquid infunditur,
sicut vas corruptum liquorem reddit
fetidum aliquatenus ei infusum, quod per
exitum gustus
aperte
probatur;   Ioelis 2:
"Ululate
qui bibitis vinum in dulcedine;
perit enim ab ore vestro."

Inde enim est quod
plus fetet os gulosi quam maximus
fimarius,   iuxta illud
Apocalipsis 9: "Ascendit fumus putei
abissi ut fumus fornacis magne."

O quam abhominabile et mirabile
quod voluptas gutturis, que tanti
hodie estimatur, vix duorum digitorum
habet latitudinem, nec durat delectacio nisi quantum durat transitus ille!

Unde Proverbiorum 23: "Ne intuearis
vinum quando flavescit cum splenduerit
in vitro;   ingreditur enim blande"
—ecce pacificus ingressus—"set in
fine mordebit ut coluber," etc.

Secunda species est nimis laute
pasci,

---

eius consideratis," scil. pauperes Christi necessitatem pacientes. Quam malediccionem videns Salomon ex ebrietate et
60 nimio potu provenire dixit, Eccles. 2:
"Cogitavi in corde [fol. 136] meo abstrahere a vino carnem meam ut animum meum
transferrem ad sapienciam devitaremque
stulticiam donec viderem quid esset
65 utile filiis hominum." Nam per nimiam
ingluviem vini vel cuiuslibet alterius
potus adquiritur corporis corrupcio. Et
corruptum corrumpit quicquid infunditur,
sicut vas corruptum liquorem reddit
70 fetidum aliquatenus ei infusum quod per
exitum gustus ut per anelitum et eructa-
ciones et ceteras egestionem apercius
comprobatur. Unde Joelis 1 dicitur:
"Expergiscimini ebrii et flete et ululate
75 omnes qui bibitis vinum in dulcedine,
quoniam periit ab ore vestro." Valde
enim corruptum est vas quod quocumque
modo abluatur omnia infusa corrumpit, et
tale est corpus humanum. Inde est quod
80 plus fetet os gulosi quam magnus cumilus
fumantis fimarii vel sterquilinii. Unde
Apoc. 9 dicitur: "Ascendit fumus putei
sicut fumus fornacis magni." Et ideo
nimirum si ebriosi et gulosi modernis
85 diebus maximas paciantur egritudines.
Unde Ecclesiastici 37 dicitur: "In
multis enim escis erit infirmitas." Et
sequitur: "Propter crapulam multi perierunt. Qui autem abstinens est adiciet
90 vitam." O quam admirabile et abhominabile est quod voluptas gutturis tantum
hodie estimatur, quod vix duorum digitorum habet latitudinem, nec durat delectacio nisi quantum durat transitus cibi
95 vel potus per os et guttur. Quod videns
Sapiens dixit Prov. 23: "Ne intuearis
vinum quando flavescit cum splendiderit
in vitro color eius. Ingreditur blande"—ecce placens ingressus—"set in
100 novissimo mordebit ut coluber, et sicut
regulus venena diffundet"—ecce exitus
dolorosus.

Secunda species est nimis laute,
105 idest cibaria diversa preciosa et delicata extra status sui exigenciam inqui-

sicut fuit de populo Israel, ut
patet Numeri 11, ubi dicitur quod cum
haberent in deserto copiam manne omne
delectamentum habentis, adhuc optabant

substanciam carnis, porra, pepones,
et huiusmodi. Et ideo de istis
Psalmista ait: "Adhuc esce eorum
erant in ore ipsorum, et ira Dei ascendit super eos."

Tercia species est nimis ardenter
et nimis avide comedere, sicut fecerunt
Sodomite, quorum ruina ab ocio et nimia
habundancia incepit. Unde

ex hoc
pro-
prie accidit crapula, scilicet quando
quis sumit plus quam possit bene et
congrue digerere. Per quod contingit
frequenter vomitum facere; Ysaie
28:

"Omnes mense eorum replete
sunt vomitu."

Quarta species gule est
nimis studiose
cibaria preparare,

rendo. Contra quod dicit Ovidius:
     Est virtus placitis abstinuisse
     cibis.
110 Isto modo fecerunt filii Israel qui cum
     haberent in deserto copiam manne omne
     delectamentum et omne saporem suavitatis
     in se habentis, exquesierunt alia ciba-
     ria dicentes: "Quis dabit nobis ad
115 vescendum carnes? Recordamur piscium
     quos comedebamus in Egipto gratis. In
     mentem nobis veniunt cucumeres et pepo-
     nes, porrique et cepe et alia," ut ha-
     betur Numeri 11. Isti sunt de quibus
120 dicit Psalmista: "Adhuc esce eorum
     erant in ore ipsorum, et ira Dei ascen-
     dit super eos." Nam vidit Dominus mur-
     muracionem eorum, misit eis coturnices
     quorum "carnes adhuc erant in dentibus
125 eorum, nec defecerat huiusmodi cibus.
     Et ecce furor Domini concitatus in popu-
     lum percussit eum plaga magna nimis," ut
     dicitur Numeri 11.

130   Tercia species est nimis, idest
     nimium comedere, sicut eciam fecerunt
     Sodomite, quorum ruina ab ocio et nimia
     habundancia incepit. Unde dicitur Eze-
     chielis 16: "Ecce, hec fuit iniquitas
135 Sodome: superbia, saturitas panis, et
     habundancia, et ocium ipsius et filiarum
     eius; et manum egeno et pauperi non
     porrigebant," etc. Ex tali vero habun-
     dante saturitate et superfluitate pro-
140 prie accidit crapula. Et est crapula
     cum quis sumit plus quam possit bene et
     congrue diger[er]e. Per quod contingit
     frequenter vomitum facere, Unde Ysaie
     28 dicitur: "A vino erraverunt, in
145 ebrietate nescierunt, videntem ignorave-
     runt iudicium. Omnes enim mense replete
     sunt vomituum sordiumque."

         Quarta species [fol. 136v] gule est
150 studiose, scilicet quando quis nimis
     curiose cibaria sua preparare facit.
     Pro qua redarguuntur filii Hely, 1 Regum
     2, qui carnem crudam rapiebant ut sibi
     eam laucius prepararent. Unde Grego-
155 rius: "Ex eo filiorum Hely culpa subor-
     ta est, quia puer crudas carnes quereret"

quas curacius exhiberet." Isidorus de
tali studio dicit: "Tota die epulas
ruminat ad explendum gulam, vespere
160 autem delicias parat. Iste miserabilior
est brutis animalibus que ruminant post
sumpcionem cibi, iste vero ante per
studium et solicitudinem laucius prepa-
randi. Et sepe contingit delicate pas-
165 tos magis egrotare. Querunt cocum qui
callide et delectabiliter sciat ventrem
implere; postea necessario querunt me-
dicum, qui sciat eum evacuare. Habent
enim divites custodem sui corporis,
170 habent eciam custodem rerum suarum;
custodem vero anime pauci vel nulli."

Quinta species gule est ardenter,
idest nimia aviditas vel cupiditas come-
175 dendi voraciter more canino. Que redar-
guitur in Esau qui pre fame se iam mori-
entem reputavit, ut habetur Gen. 25, ubi
dicitur: "Coxit autem Iacob pulmentum.
Ad quem cum venisset Esau de agro las-
180 sus, ait, 'Da michi de coccione hac rufa
quia opido lassus sum.' Cui dixit Iacob: 'Vende michi primogenita tua.'
Ille respondit: 'En morior. Quid proderunt primogenita?' Ait Iacob: 'Iura
185 ergo michi.' Iuravit Esau et vendidit
primogenita, et sic ac[c]epto pane et
lentis ediculo comedit et bibit et abiit
parvipendens quod primogenita vendidis-
set." Ubi dicit Gregorius: "Esau pri-
190 mogenitorum gloriam perdidit, quia pro
magno estu desideriorum lenticulam concupivit." Et ideo precipit Sapiens
Ecclesiastici 37: "Noli avidus esse in
omni epulacione et non te effundas super
195 omnem escam," etc.

Iste enim quinque species gule
ponuntur a beato Gregorio in libro *Mora-*
lium et patent in versu predicto,
200 Prepropere, laute, nimis, ardenter,
studiose.

Left-column glosses:

sicut fecit Seyr aut Esau, de quo
Genesis 25 legitur quod

propter edulium lentis
                                    vendidit
primogenita sua, quod avidissime
comedit.

The discussion of the species of gluttony is especially appropriate for our
analysis because the topic itself is an ancient one: it was given classical form by
Gregory the Great, in *Moralia* XXX.xviii.60 (PL 76:556–67), who established
the number (five) and kinds of species the vice has as well as the biblical figures

that exemplify them. This "common tradition" of the topic can be found in medieval literature continually after Gregory, including the important *Summa vitiorum* by Peraldus (with which *FM* shares much material in its part on gluttony). Similarly common from the early thirteenth century on are the two hexameters that list the species and the biblical figures; they occur in Richard Wetheringsette,[10] Peraldus[11] (only the first line), and many other texts. In light of this strong common tradition, the listing and treatment of only *four* species in o comes as a surprise and suggests the possibility of error. On the ground of this possible error and of the general characteristic of o to give a shorter, sparser text than z, one may think of o as a redaction of z. Since in the passage under discussion there is nothing to suggest an eyeskip or error by homeoteleuton, it might seem that the omission of the fifth species is the result of a general tendency to abbreviate the fuller text of z: in making a selection, the putative redactor skipped from 151 to 176 and thereby inadvertently omitted the fifth species.

However plausible this view may be, it is, however, countered by the following argument. If o has omitted any species at all, it is not the fifth, *ardenter* (where the putative skip occurs). The species of *ardenter* is in fact present in o's third species; here the two groups discuss different species of gluttony (*nimis ardenter* against z's *nimis*, 130), even though both use the same material to develop the third species. In other words, the difference between z and o in this passage, and the reason for o's surprising number of four species, is not simply omission of material on the part of o. Further, if one compares the species of gluttony and their order as they are listed in the opening hexameter and then developed in z and in o, the following picture emerges:

hexameter: prepropere — laute — nimis — ardenter — studiose;
z: 1. prepropere; 2. laute; 3. nimis; 4. studiose; 5. ardenter;
o: 1. prepropere; 2. (nimis) laute; 3. (nimis) ardenter; 4. (nimis) studiose).

It is evident that in its development, z has changed the order of species 4 and 5 that had been established by the hexameter, whereas o has preserved that order but omitted the original third species.

This suggests very strongly that the passage in o with its four species is not the result of a redactor's lapse who skipped the fifth species of z, but rather of a writer's mistaken interpretation of the opening hexameter, which he developed *modo suo* with otherwise traditional material. Careful inspection of o's text shows that the original author indeed misread the opening hexameter: in contrast to the "common tradition," he divided the five terms of the first hexameter into four species, apparently reading *nimis* as an adverbial modifier of *laute* or of *ardenter*. The same faulty division was then applied to the references in the second hexameter—an error easy to understand when one considers the peculiar syntax of *Seyrque sacerdos*. It is equally possible that the author of o did not understand the reference of *sacerdos*, hence found only four biblical figures in the second hexameter, and consequently divided the first line also into four species. In either case, his error is not omission of a species in the process of copying but misunderstanding or misinterpretation of the Latin verses.

This analysis establishes z as a redaction of o. In the passage analyzed, the redactor of z—besides quoting scriptural authorities more extensively, adding new material and authorities, clarifying statements, and making smaller lexical and syntactic changes—also brought the entire discussion of "the species of gluttony" in line with the "common tradition." The result of this analysis parallels that of an *exemplum* and its moralization I have presented in an earlier discussion.[12]

That group z is an expansion of the original text of *FM* can be further argued from an analysis of the English verses in *FM*.[13] In general, z lacks these verses consistently (but not individual English words and phrases). But its handling of Verse 26/27, which is integral to the Latin context, shows that the text of z must derive from a version of *FM* with English verses. The same inference can be drawn from other cases of the same nature. At VII.vii.62, the text speaks of four "contradictoria" which, in w and y, are specified with English sentences as follows:

[6] Et ideo, ut videtur, iam propter istud peccatum tam commune verificantur quatuor contradictoria, scilicet:

> That lawe hath noo ryȝte . . .

Group z simply omits "scilicet" and the following English, thereby creating incoherence in thought. Similarly, when in w and y the second and following "contradictoria" are taken up, the English is repeated. Group z, instead, recasts the paragraph:

[7] Nota ulterius quod luxuria prohibita est, quia ex ea multa mala provenerunt. Nam diluvium Noe provocavit . . . (C, fol. 157)

and eight more biblical figures follow. This is clearly an expansion of the biblical figures of *Minnesklaven* (text: VII.vii.103–110), but the connection with the "contradictoria" has been lost. Similar incoherence caused by the loss of an English verse or saying that is integral to the text occurs at IV.iv.87 (where the Lady Fortune verses are replaced by a Latin saying attributed to Seneca) and at III.xxiii.17–19, where the *nemo*-joke of the English is completely lost:

[8] Dixit nauta ad socium suum: "Ecce, vis mirum audire?" Et alius quasi de illo non curans sed subridendo hoc modo respondit: "Transeamus hinc." (C, fol. 59)

Final proof that z represents an expanded redaction of w derives from a longer addition to the discussion of the proper confessor, in V.xi. After the paragraph on the seven kinds of priest who may hear confession and give absolution (36–66), z continues with further canonical material on the same subject. Part of it repeats in substance a point made earlier. But more importantly, the scribe of Co began to copy the added material and then stopped in mid-sentence with the remark: "etc. De ista materia nota *Pupillam oculi*, parte V, capitulo 6, per totum" (fol. 110v). The entire addition can indeed be found in exactly the place referred to, verbatim and in precisely the same order, except for three or four sentences which bridge extracted passages or summarize a longer paragraph in the quoted source. *Pupilla oculi* was published in 1384. Hence, the relative dates of groups z (post-1384) and w (shortly after 1300, see below) confirm what the nature of the respective texts already suggests: that the direction of revising *FM* went from w to z. The note in Co also establishes an approximate date for the redaction present in group z: after 1384 and before the end of the century (the date of Co).

The characteristics of group z call for some further remarks. The expansions of original material, particularly biblical quotations or mere references, can on occasion be quite long and even amount to a retelling of an entire biblical story. Further, the added illustrative material ranges from biblical and other quotations to exegetical commentary, Latin verses, and even entire stories not found elsewhere in *FM*. Among the added stories, the following are of note: the king who never laughed (replacing I.xiv.86–88; cf. Tubach 4994); the lecherous cleric Oliver, seen by his servant to deny Christ (at V.xiii.137; a variant of the Udo story, Tubach 5015); Saint Erkenwald (V.xv.40); several stories from *Vitae Patrum* and Gregory (V.xx); the archbishop of York and his chaplain who neglects his duty as executor and does not believe in dream warnings (V.xxiv.47; Tubach 1930); the poor monastery that lacked Date and Dabite (V.xxvi.19; Tubach 1438); dragon and unicorn (V.xxix.77; Tubach 5022, "Barlaam"); the two scholars at Toledo who study magic (V.xxx.161; from Caesarius); three stories from the lives of Saints Gregory, Benedict, and Eligius (V.xxx.169); a version of Christ as the pilgrim-lover-knight according to "Tremegistus" (V.xxxv.69); the reply a young man gives his father when he objects to his joining a monastery (V.xxxv.148); the houses of personified virtues (V.xxxv.158; from Alexander Nequam); the woman condemned by drunken king Philip (V.xxxvii.40); Plato controlling his anger against his servant (ibid., 94); and the vision of the Virgin with dainties in a dirty dish (VII.xiv.4–5, repeated from I.i; Tubach 3077).

Among the longer additions of primarily doctrinal material in group z, the following are particularly noteworthy: (a) the third occasion of Christ's weeping (at III.xiii.51); (b) eleven more *mirabilia* of the Eucharist (V.ii.69); (c) canonical material on the question what priest one may or must confess to (V.xi.36–66; see above); (d) discussion of prayer, including its impediments (V.xvii–xviii and xx); (e) discussion of heresy and excommunication (V.xxx.169); (f) description and allegorization of the *pictura* of Pan, i.e., Nature (V.xxxvi.56); (g) the usefulness of fasting, and the various liturgical fasts—a long addition making up five new chapters, which are present only in this group and E (following VI.vi); (h) development of the sin against nature, as against the stated refusal to discuss it (VII.xi.2–3); (i) the six leaves of the lily, i.e., aspects of chastity, which are here fully developed, against the remark that "three will suffice" (VII.xvii.50).

In some cases, z substitutes different quotations for those found in the other groups. And further, the two stories that are repeated in w (Dionysius the temple thief, III.i.81–96; and the shepherd and Mercury, III.vi.38–45) are not fully repeated in z; at their second occurrence, z merely introduces them and then refers to their earlier appearance.

Beyond this increase in bulk, group z shows some other tendencies that distinguish it from the other groups. First of all, it is a more "scholarly" version, in that biblical quotations are usually given complete and with correct identification, and that the sources of its additional material are likewise identified correctly. As a consequence, z mentions many more authorities by name than do w, x, and y, including some "modern" ones, such as: Alexander (Nequam), Hugh de Vienne, Jacques de Vitry, John of Abbeville, John Beleth, the *Oculus moralis*, a *Tabula autentica*, William of Auxerre, etc. Occasionally, z even names the (or a) source for material also in w.x.y; thus the story of the Weeping Bitch (VII.vi.70–93) is here attributed to Petrus Alphonsi. Another tendency is to update references and material. Beside the important addition on the Church's teaching concerning the proper confessor, discussed above, z "updates" single English words and other references. Some examples are:

[9] Incantatores, qui artem suam verbis excercent, Anglice *tilsters* (V.xxx.6–7); C: *sothseggers* (fol. 115).

[10] Apud *eluenlond*, ubi iam, ut dicunt, manent illi athlete fortissimi, scilicet Onewyn et Wad et ceteri (V.xxx.65–66); C: rex Arturus cum suis militibus (fol. 116v).

Group w: r, s, t, u, v

The remaining 18 "full" MSS form a group in which, despite innumerable variant readings—unique or shared—no member shows the extensive variation found in groups x, y, and z. Each member of this group has its own readings, yet on the basis of important shared variants it is possible to establish several subgroups, as shown in the following examples.

(a) In comparing the faithful keeping of the Ten Commandments to the work of a reliable copyist, the author of *FM* speaks about the products of a bad scribe, which must be examined carefully before one pays for them (III.vii.137–138). The following variants occur:

[11] antequam sibi reddat mercedem ne in aliquo defraudetur. Spiritualiter . . .

v (B4.CC.E.Jo.Mo.R.Sp.W1); s (B1.L3.LC)

antequam sibi reddit mercedem ne in aliquo defraudetur. Revera spiritualiter . . .

u (Go2.L1)

antequam sibi reddat mercedem ne in aliquo fraudetur. Spiritualiter . . .

x (B2.Pe)

antequam sibi reddat mercedem. Spiritualiter . . .

t (Et.W2); z (C.Co.Li)

antequam sibi detur pecunia. Moraliter . . .

y (B3.L2)

antequam satisfaciat. Spiritualiter . . .

r (Go1.V)

omitted in M.

The subgroups exemplified in this passage are in general confirmed by
extensive recension of the collated text. Nonetheless, the given example is somewhat unusual in its neatness, for usually one or more subgroups are split, with
their members affiliating themselves with different groups. The following cases
can give an indication of the changing patterns; at the same time, they will serve
to demonstrate several scribal processes that account for the great amount of
variation found in the surviving copies of *FM*.

(b) In illustrating how to love God with one's whole soul, *FM* tells a story
from the *Life of Saint Godric* in which the ailing saint struggles with the devil.
The story is omitted in M and summarized in group x, but elsewhere appears
with only minor variations. It begins:
[12] Unde legitur in *Vita sancti Goderici* quod cum esset solus iacens infirmus
    astitit ei diabolus clam ignitam hastam super eum vibrans (III.vii.42–44).
Of interest is the following phrase with its variants:
    clam ignitam hastam: r, s, and CC.Jo.Mo.R.Sp.W1.
    telam ignitam   : B4.
    telam igneam   : W2.
    telum igneum   : z and Et.
    clamans horribiliter ignitam hastam: u.
    clamans ignitamque hastam: E.
    om M; *different text* x.
The grouping is much as in example [11], but here B4 is outside group v, and
group t is split.

Analysis of the variants in example [12] further reveals several features of the text's evolution. First, the word *clam* was evidently misread as *telam*. The latter, understood as some kind of weapon ("shaft"), caused the suppression of the now tautological *hastam*. Other scribes, however, realized that the word for "shaft" is *telum* and consequently emended the form. Second, the readings with *clamans* for *clam* may suggest that the latter could be the result of scribal corruption. This suggestion gains force from the fact that the source of the story indeed speaks of the devil's loud shouting. But before rushing to the tempting conclusion that u and E have the original reading of *FM*, it is well to weigh the reverse possibility, that u and E have emended the text in the direction of the source. Reasons to believe this to be the case are (a) that there is little if any evidence elsewhere that u and E stand closer to the archetype of *FM* than other groups, and (b) that such "peculiar" or even "erroneous" readings vis-à-vis their possible sources are very frequent in the work, in stories as well as elsewhere. In other words, the reading *clam* may very well be original (i.e., the reading of the archetype of all MSS) and reflect either a particular form or manuscript of the Saint Godric story used by the author of *FM*, or else a mistake, whether authorial or scribal, at the beginning of the text's history.

The greater authority of the MSS with *clam* becomes obvious a few words beyond the analyzed text. In threatening Saint Godric, the devil says: "Te medium secturus adveni" ("I have come to cut you in half"). This is the reading preserved in r, s, y, and E.R (and further in CC with *secaturus*, and in Go2 with *scissurus*). This text, too, became corrupted, perhaps because scribes had difficulty with the future participle *secturus* and the expected but missing preposition *per* before *medium*. In any event, the texts have preserved a stage "te medium securus adveni" (Jo.W1), which then appears to have been reinterpreted as "te moriturum securus agnovi" (z and Et, L1; with *medium* in W2; with *meum* in Sp).[14] Notice that in comparison with the earlier example, group u is here split.

(c) Like a tinker, who does not care for unblemished vessels of gold and silver but rather rejoices over earthen pots that are fractured or in pieces, an envious person, "when he sees some breakage caused by vice, he soon turns his attention to it and tells of it and makes it worse" ("si aliquam fracturam vicii viderit, mox applicando recitat et dupplicat," III.ii.42–43). The gerund *applicando*, though the verb is later used again with the same meaning of "directing one's attention" (III.v.68), was evidently not understood; hence the following variants:

[13] applicando: x, y, and B4.CC.Mo.R.W2.
      ampliando: r, s, and Et.
      amplicando: W1.
      amplificando: Sp.
      applaudendo: u and E.Li.M.
      applaudendo vel applicando: C.Co.

Applicando is the *difficilior lectio* and must be original, whereas forms with *ampl-* (creating tautology with the following *dupplicat*) and *applaudendo* surely would seem to be scribal attempts at making sense. The variants, again, reveal a number of subgroups as well as a split in group z and the possibility of contamination in C.Co.

(d) A person who listens to a slanderer without stopping him is like someone who watches wild dogs tear someone else and does not scare them away but rather cheers them on: "Certe crudelis est audiens detrahentem si ipsum non corripiat . . . set et si ministrat salciamentum hillaris vultus sine qua pro certo talis morcellus insipidus esset detractoribus" (III.iii.48–51). The "sauce of a cheerful face" is part of a continuing metaphor, but the unusual word for "sauce"—I suspect originally *salsam*—was misread as *falsam*, which then gave rise to a number of different readings with initial *f* (some of course different expansions of a contraction for *falsam*):

[14] salsam: y and B2.B4.E.Go2.M.
       salciamentum: CC.
       falsam: R.Mo.W1.
       faciem: s and Go1.Li.Pe (on erasure).
       falcem (?):   Sp.
       flammam: V.
       faciem . . . pro falso: t (W2 with salsa) and C.Co.
       salsam idest faciem: L1.
Here again several subgroups are split: r, u, x, and z.

(e) Finally, envy is compared to a stone (*beloculus*), which the devil uses as a grinding-stone. People who turn this stone are those who always instigate others to evil (III.ii.16):
[15] qui hunc lapidem vertunt: t and B2.B4.CC.E.Mo.R.W1.

This sentence follows somewhat abruptly upon the point that, as a grinding-stone that grinds steel suffers damage to itself, so envious people hurt themselves. The sudden transition may explain why *hunc*, most probably abbreviated as *hc̄*, was misread as *habent*:
       qui habent lapidem vertunt: y and Pe,
and the resulting ungrammatical text was then variously "emended" or reinterpreted:
       qui habent lapidem virtutum: Go2.
       qui habent lapidem: Sp.
       qui habent lapidem et vertunt: r and C.Co.

qui habent lapidem et vertunt illum: s and L1.

qui non habent lapidem set vertunt illum: Li.

Shared errors and distinctive readings, thus, establish a number of subgroups within group w.

Subgroup r: Go1 and V   The close relation between Go1 and V, and their difference from other MSS of group w, is established by their reading *gulsogth* where all other MSS have *jaunes* or *jaundeys* (III.ii.23). Other distinctive errors are *pelle* against *pelve* or *plene* (III.ii.31); *lapidem* against *lampadem* (III.iii.64); *quedam avis* against *quoddam animal vivens* (III.v.66–67); the addition of *et secundus plura* (III.viii.46, after *plura*); and many more. V seems farther removed from the archetype than Go1. Moreover, Go1 has been extensively corrected; in a sample of 500 lines, there are at least six occasions where an original omission or eyeskip in the group has been corrected marginally. These corrections also suggest some relation of Go1 to Et or u (and z).

Subgroup s: B1, L3, and LC   These three MSS agree in a number of distinctive readings, some of which are clearly errors, such as: omission of *set oculus talis est albus in circuitu quando* (III.ii.7), with the following *ubique* replaced by *quia* (B1.LC) or *que* (L3); *exposuit* for *expuit* (III.iii.86–87, both times); omission of *persequitur* (III.iv.6); *me* for *te* (required by the following *dixeris*; III.iv.10); *conveniencior* for *melior* (III.v.10; the quoted source has *fidelior*); and others.

Within the group, B1.L3 seem to be more closely affiliated: e.g., *carnes crudas* against *fratres* (LC and all others; III.iii.47). Finally, L3 has more peculiar and corrupt readings than B1, such as *lacerantur* for the required *lacerari* in the passage just quoted, and a unique eyeskip in III.iv.62–63 (*hoc est . . . iurare*). At the same time, the group occasionally shares a peculiar reading with Jo and Sp.

Subgroup t: Et and W2   The two MSS share a number of small errors and peculiar readings that set them apart from the other witnesses in w. Some examples are: *subiectorum* for *obiectorum* (III.v.67); *aurem/aures* for *faciem* (III.iii.61); *preponunt* for *pretulerunt* (III.v.21; *preposuerunt* in z); addition of *quia per quod homo peccat per hoc et torquetur* (III.iii at 82; apparently a dislocated repetition of III.iii.89); *gaudebit sive gaudet* for *gaudet/gaudeat* (III.viii.9); and others. The two manuscripts are collateral descendants, since each has individual variants and eyeskips.

More important is the fact that group t shares a very large number of distinctive readings with C and Co (or group z). These range from small omissions, such as *libidinis* at III.vii.115 (the sinful "beast" killed by the string of the commandment not to commit adultery), to uniquely correct readings, such as

adulterine voluptatis for *adulterium/adulterii et voluptatis* in the same passage
(where t and z follow the quoted source), and further to all kinds of variants and
small additions, which often involve syntactic restructuring. From the numerous
cases I select three examples which are especially striking for what they reveal
about larger manuscript relations.

First, love of one's neighbor is enjoined by natural law as well as by Christ's
commandment:

[16] secundum legem nature precipitur: Hoc facias alii quod tibi vis fieri. "Sed
hoc est preceptum meum," dicit Christus, "ut diligatis invicem"
(III.viii.37–39).

Aside from very minor scribal variations, the substance of these two quotations
occurs in all MSS except M (omitted), group y (summarized), and L1 (second
quotation omitted). But groups t and z insert a hexameter between the two
sentences, and z then restructures the now-third sentence and adds a fourth one.
Thus, after *fieri*:

t: Unde poetice dicitur: "Quod tibi vis fieri, michi fac; quod non tibi,
noli."—"Sed hoc est preceptum meum [*add* dicit Dominus W2] ut diligatis
invicem" (Et, fol. 22v).

C: Poetice dicitur: "Quod tibi vis fieri, michi fac; quod non tibi, noli." Sed
ut dicit Dominus Iohannis 5: "Hoc est preceptum meum ut diligatis invicem." Teneris ergo tam ex lege nature quam gracie proximum tuum
diligere (fol. 37v).

Second, in the story of the knight who out of love for Christ visited the
Holy Land and, after his death, was found to bear the inscription in his heart,
"Quem quesivi, hic inveni," etc. (III.vii.60–70), the discovery is introduced as
follows:

[17] Cum ergo et eius cor quidam aperuissent.

Group t has the following substitution:

Cum ergo ad cor eius appropinquaverunt (Et, fol. 21v).

C and Co, however, read as follows:

Et cum homines hoc [i.e., his death] viderunt et eum nudaverunt ut eum
sicut moris est sepelirent, apperuerunt [Co: aperierunt] corpus eius, et cum
ad cor appropinquaverunt . . . (C, fol. 36).

The third example concerns the moralized story about the Lernaean Hydra,
in III.vi.38–45. The edited text reads thus:

[18] Narrant autem poete quod in Lerna palude erat quidam serpens qui solo
flatu omnem infecit aerem, unde homines transeuntes intoxicabantur. Cum
autem quidam pastor quodam serto coronatus illesus pertransisset et hoc
alius pastor didicisset quod virtute eius serti sic evasisset, rapuit sertum ab
eo et statim alius mortuus est. Quod cum audisset Mercurius, deus eloquencie, a raptore certum abstulit et ad pastorem mortuum accessit, in cuius ore
flores sigillatim de illo posuit, unde tandem virtute unius a morte surrexit.

In contrast, in t and C.Co the story takes the following form:

> Narrant enim poete quod in Larma palude Archadie latuit immane monstrum, scilicet quidam serpens septem capitum aerea corrumpens. Quem multi frustra nitentes perimere interierunt, dum in locum [abscisi] capitis septem succresserunt [C: succreverunt]. Demum Hercules coronam indutus ex odoriferis floribus contextam, ut vitaret odore florum corrupcionem et fetorem serpentis, dimicans cum hac ydra victus fuerit Hercules et evulsa est sibi corona, ita quod Hercules pene defecit. Cuius rei misertus Mercurius et superveniens illis addidit ad os Herculis duos flores odoriferos et ignem. Quo facto in vires pristinos Hercules est reversus et serpentem superavit (Et, fol. 21).

This is, of course, a very different version of the story, whose beginning is one of the labors of Hercules, the slaying of the Lernaean Hydra (Et quotes "Metamorphoses libro 9, capitulo 10" before the cited text). It should be pointed out that L1 also begins the story like t but after the first sentence follows w.

While the form of this story establishes a relationship between group t and C.Co, it also reveals a good deal about the textual history of *FM* itself. The tale about the shepherd or Hercules is moralized, and fable and moralization occur in the following combinations:

(a) Fable of shepherd   -   moralization: v (-CC.M).r.s.u.y.Li.
(b) Fable only referred to   -   moralization: x.
(c) Fable of Hercules   -   moralization: t.C.Co.
(d) Fable omitted   -   moralization omitted: CC.M.

Now, the moralization is virtually the same in all three patterns that contain it (a–c). Although the Hercules version (c) identifies the first shepherd, moralized as "vir iustus," with Hercules (in C.Co only!), and glosses the *sertum* with "idest coronam" (again, C.Co only), its further moralization has *two* shepherds, and the second steals the wreath from the first, just as in form (a), instead of Hydra knocking the crown off Hercules' head, as she does in the *fable* as told in (c). In other words, in (c) the moralization does not fit the fable it moralizes, in contrast to (a). This surely means that form (a) of both fable and moralization is original, and that at some point in the history of *FM* a scholarly scribe who was more familiar with the labors of Hercules (or perhaps with *Ovidius moralizatus*) than the author of *FM* substituted a more "classical" beginning of the fable.

To return to group t: even though C and Co are thus unmistakably and closely affiliated with t, two points must be stressed. One is that, however striking some readings shared by t.C.Co against all other MSS may be (as in the just-discussed case), the expansions and longer additions we found to be characteristic and distinctive of group z are considerably greater in substance and number than readings shared by C.Co and t. Such genuinely distinctive readings of z are not shared by t (or any other subgroup of w). Examples of such distinctive z readings would be the sentence beginning "Teneris ergo . . ." in Example [16], and the fuller retelling of the burial preparation for the knight in Example [17]. The second point is that the distinctive readings of z occur in all *three* MSS of the group (C, Co, and Li), whereas many of the readings discussed here occur in t and only C.Co (against other subgroups of w). This observation suggests that group z, while it characteristically contains much unique material present in all three MSS, is made up of two MSS (C.Co) that derive from a text of group t, and a third MS (Li) that derives from a text or group other than t (see further below), all three, however, showing the same distinctive z readings.

Group t further shares some peculiar readings with group x, though these occur only sporadically. A good example is the following:

[19] Text: Set utinam multi illorum nichil facerent a tergo, sicut speculum nichil representat a tergo; set quod peius est, ibi detrahunt, menciuntur, derident, et cachinnant. (III.v.62–64)

t, C, Co: Sed *iam*, quod peius est, *tales a tergo in absencia* detrahunt, menciuntur, derident, et cachinnant. Sed utinam multi eorum nichil facerent a tergo, sicut *nec* speculum *aliquid* representat a tergo! (C, fol. 35)

x: Sed utinam multi eorum nichil facerent a tergo, sicut *nec* speculum *aliquid* representat—sed *iam*, quod peius est, *tales a tergo in absencia* detrahunt, menciuntur, derident, et cachinnant. (B2, fol. 124)

Here, x stands between v and z; it shares the (more difficult) word order of v, but has the additional *iam* of t.C.Co as well as its substitution *tales a tergo in absencia* for *ibi* (misread as *isti*?) and *nec . . . aliquid* for *nichil*. Such features are typical of readings x.t.C.Co against other witnesses, though such grouping does not occur very frequently.

Finally, t.C.Co on occasion also share a peculiar reading with L1, as in the following case:

[20] Posito quod abstuleris a proximo bona temporalia, rogo quis te absolveret sine restitucione? Revera, si unde haberes, nullus vivens (III.viii.39–41).

Groups t and z as well as L1 add *nec papa* (C.Co: nec ipse papa; Li: nec eciam ipse papa). The addition—that not even the pope can give absolution if the penitent will not make restitution though he is able to do so—is a legal point which may have entered the text from a marginal note. In z it clearly becomes more rhetorical.

Subgroup u: Go2 and L1   These two MSS share a moderate number of minor omissions and additions as well as peculiar readings. Some typical examples are: omission of *detrahens* at III.iii.40; addition of *pastor* to *alius* at III.vi.42; substitution of *sibi* for *ibi* at III.ii.45; use of first-person plural for second-person singular in the verb forms of III.vii.7–10; and others. More noteworthy are the reading *clamans horribiliter* . . . in Example [12] above, and the displacement of English verse 21 from III.vii.76 to the end of the paragraph (line 83). L1 has considerably more unique readings than Go2, including many longer omissions; but in turn Go2 has omissions of its own.

The group occasionally shares an important distinctive reading with M. Thus, in III.vii.109–116, it combines the members of the two sets instead of listing them separately (see variant note). Similarly, at III.viii.58, u and M omit the sentence *Bene volo diligere amicum.* Here and there u shares a reading with E, though these cases are less striking than u.M.

Much more important is the fact that a very large number of u readings are shared by Li, so that the latter must be considered a member of this group. Some examples are: omission of *pulcherime* (III.vi.35) and of *assistentibus* (III.iv.55); addition and change in the following sentence:

[21] Text: Ipsi vero libenter auscultando prout dicunt accipiunt, et sic una cum illis . . . (III.iii.29)

u and Li: Ipsi vero libenter *audiunt et* ascultando prout dicunt accipiunt, et sic *simul* cum illis . . . ;

and a large number of substitutions, of which two cases will suffice:

[22] Text: habeat [*var* habeant] semper (III.ii.47)

u and Li: habeant eternaliter, scilicet invidiam

[23] Text: Est ergo murmur oblocucio indebito modo facta (III.iii.3)

u and Li: De primo est sciendum quod murmur est oblocucio pravo modo facta.

While in many cases Li shares the distinctive reading of u, in others it agrees with Go2 only while L1 follows the remainder of w or another group, as in the sentence "plus fecit quam noverit cogitare" (III.i.130), which shows the following variants:

[24] noverit] poterit Go2.Li; noverat R; cognovit W2; scivit Et; novit vel scivit C.Co.

In other words, Li is more closely affiliated with Go2 (though not linearly descended from it) than with L1. At the same time, Li has the readings which distinguish group z, i.e., the latter's peculiar expansions and longer additions. As we have noted above, Li is descended from a different group than are C and Co; this group is u, and more precisely a manuscript close to Li.

Subgroup v: B4.CC.(E).Jo.M.Mo.R.Sp.W1 This subgroup comprises the remaining "full" manuscripts of w (as well as H, insofar as the preserved text allows us to judge it). Within this subgroup, one can discern various further groupings; for instance, W1 and B4 share a number of errors or peculiarities. But such patterns are very inconsistent and minor in nature and frequency.

E holds a peculiar place in the manuscript transmission. While it shares readings with various individual manuscripts or groups (particularly with u, and with u and Li), these readings are not very significant and not sufficiently consistent to determine clear affiliation. However, from V.xiii on E has all the additional material of z. It is, thus, evidently the product of two different exemplars.

I would consider subgroup v to be textually prior, that is, to stand closer to the archetype, than subgroups r, s, t, and u. This inference is drawn from analysis of such variations as have been illustrated in examples [11]–[15] above. In these, and in many other cases, v gives the better reading, while the variants of the other witnesses can be shown to be the result of scribal corruption. In addition, v is *relatively* consistent, in contrast to the shifting patterns and affiliations found in the other subgroups. This does not mean that v always has the superior and presumably original reading. In many cases, v's text makes less sense than that found in another subgroup or individual MS. But in light of the process of scribal emendation to be discussed in the following section, the better reading may in fact be the result of correction. Looked at in its totality, therefore, the text preserved in v is likely to reflect the original text of *FM* most directly.

HISTORY OF THE TEXT

The analysis and classification of the surviving manuscripts, and the comparison of the groups which have thus been established, allows us to draw the following tentative picture of the textual history of *FM*. According to various indications I have analyzed elsewhere, the original form of *FM* (as best represented in v) was composed shortly after 1300.[15] Though this date is no more than a strong probability, nothing in the textual history of *FM* would seem to contradict it.

Textual comparison reveals that, like so many other utilitarian texts originating at that time, the original copy of *FM* must have contained a large amount of abbreviation and suspension, which caused scribes the usual difficulties. Also, it is very likely that the frequent divisions and distinctions throughout the work were originally written in columns (still preserved in B1, Mo, W1, and others). Where such distinctions consisted of two or even three parallel columns, careless scribes occasionally copied the text column by column instead of line by line; the outcome can be seen, for example, in III.vii.109–116. As a result of the layout and the highly abbreviated state of the original copy, the text underwent, in the process of successive copying, the kind of corruption that is apparent in any late medieval work whose reproduction was not carefully supervised.

On the other hand, the received text of *FM* continued to "live," in the sense of being subjected to various redactions: in one form, it was shortened by exclusion of illustrative material (group x); in another, it was substantially rephrased (group y); and in yet another, it was considerably expanded (group z). Even in the fifteenth century, at least two copyists adapted the text to their needs, by different forms of extraction (A and D). Part of the expansion in group z, as we have seen, was to bring what seemed to the scribes as oddities in line with familiar texts, especially in the case of pious tales, whether classical or otherwise. Such a continuing "life" of a late medieval text is, again, not unparalleled. What happened to *FM* can similarly be found in the history of William Flete's *De remediis contra temptaciones* or Walter Hilton's *Scale of Perfection*.[16]

But even when they were simply "copying" *FM*, scribes clearly felt very free to emend the received text, that is, to correct apparent corruptions in their exemplars. Such emendations appear in practically all surviving manuscripts, whether as corrections over erasures or as additions in the margins or between the lines. Consequently, the current state of variation among the surviving manuscripts has been caused not only by the normal process of scribal corruption (misreading, eyeskips, dittography, etc.) but also by scribal attempts at emendation, whether with or without recourse to a second exemplar.

The example of R is particularly instructive in this respect. The manuscript shows much evidence of correction in various forms, and in fact in the upper right corner of fol. 52 a note occurs stating "co. usque huc" (at III.xvi.68), evidently meaning "corrected up to here." Yet despite this note, further corrections continue to appear throughout the manuscript and are especially pronounced on fols. 68–76 and 99v–104. My examination of these corrections has not revealed a consistent pattern of readings that would point to a particular MS or group consulted for these corrections. On the contrary, in many instances R's general tendency to follow B1, Mo, and W1 is directly contradicted by corrections that set its text apart from this group. In addition, several of its peculiar corrections appear also only in E (a good example occurs at I.x.88; see variant note); and still others are not found in any surviving witness. A strong impression emerges that the scribe of R very often emended his received text according to his own light.

SELECTION OF THE BASE MANUSCRIPT

In choosing an editorial method and selecting a base manuscript, I assume it to be desirable to present a text of *FM* that is as close to the original form of the work as possible. Given the number of extant MSS, their complex relations, the length of the text's history, and the process of scribal emendation just discussed, it seems extremely difficult, if not impossible, to reconstruct the hypothetical archetype for all extant MSS. On the other hand, given the fact that the work exists in at least four different redactions (i.e., groups w, x, y, and z), it would be highly impractical to present a text based on one manuscript and accompanied by a complete corpus of variants. It seems therefore logical to select a manuscript from a group which reflects the state of the text closest to the original version.

For the reasons that have emerged from the analysis given above, that group is certainly w, and within w, most probably subgroup v.

Several members of subgroup v are automatically excluded from qualifying as base text: E, because of its derivation from two ancestors; Jo, because it is defective and generally full of eyeskips and poor readings; and M, because of its Ibericisms and omission of material.[17] The remaining candidates, therefore, are B4, CC, Mo, R, Sp, and W1. It might be possible to construct a hypothetical archetype of this small group; but in light of the very fluid relations of these witnesses with other members of w, the value of the construct would remain questionable. Alternatively, a good solution might be to select the "best" manuscript and present it as it stands. Unfortunately, none of the six manuscripts is good enough to be reproduced without editorial correction. Hence I have decided to select a base manuscript and correct its readings in the light of several control texts.

My main criterion for this selection is the number (and, secondarily, quality) of unique readings, i.e., of variants that are peculiar to each individual manuscript. The relative number of unique variants of all sorts except changed word order in these six manuscripts changes slightly in various parts of *FM*. Analysis of 100 lines from part III and 100 lines from part VII, with respect to individual variants, gives the following ranking: CC (27), Mo (35), R (46), W1 (55), B4 (92), Sp (103); this relative ranking holds for all parts of *FM*. My choice for the base manuscript, therefore, is CC.

CC is a rather undistinguished paper manuscript of 236 leaves plus a parchment bifolium, written in brown ink, in one column, by one hand of the third quarter of the fifteenth century, in a Secretary script. Its written space is 153x90 mm. Probably eight leaves have been lost at its beginning. It contains only *FM* with a subject index, which ends incomplete in the section on "Versus." Marginalia are scarce, but it has a normal amount of headings and rubrics. There is no decoration, and red is used very sparingly. Blank spaces have been left for larger chapter initials. The owner's name, Richard Turner, appears several times on fols. 222 and 237, in a sixteenth-century hand. On fol. 133v, at the discussion of the proper confessor (V.xi.36–66), appears a marginal note, "A ware þe ffrer," in a Secretary hand but perhaps different from the text hand. The text contains many English words and phrases but only four of the English verses edited in *Verses*. The papermark is a glove crowned by a star.[18]

There are three drawbacks to selecting CC as the base manuscript: it is a relatively late manuscript; it lacks a substantial amount of text at the beginning; and it lacks all but four of the English verses. Nonetheless, the late date itself is no significant handicap, especially since CC is textually closely related to Mo, R, and W1. We know that Mo—the witness that on the whole is textually closest to CC—was copied at Oxford by 1412, that is, at a date not much later than the earliest surviving copy of *FM*. W1 apparently was likewise copied at Oxford, though at a later date than Mo. The intial loss in CC is regrettable, but it can be made up from another manuscript. More serious is the relative absence of the English verses. On this ground alone, R or W1 (or any other MS that has more or less the complete set of English verses) would be preferable. After lengthy experimentation with R and W1, however, I have come to the conclusion that R's text—in many ways a good candidate—is impractical to use as base text because many of its "corrections" are emendations introduced by its scribe and not attested in any extant MS (see History of the Text, above). Since my aim is to give a representative text, this state would require a very large amount of emendation in my critical text accompanied by a large corpus of variants. Conversely, the absence of English verses in CC can be easily remedied by inserting the respective verses from R.

In favor of CC is, first of all, the fact that its unique readings are usually not the result of unintelligent copying leading to plain blunders (as it is very much the case in B4, W1, and other members of v, and often in Mo and R). Further, in many instances CC agrees with Mo (a relatively good text) against R and W1, and there is some evidence that the text of CC.Mo is closer to the archetype than that of R.W1. A good example is the Charter of Christ at II.vii.84–98. Here R and W1 have several additions that appear to be the result of padding: "Filius Dei Patris *omnipotentis*" (line 85), "Marie *matris et* virginis" (line 85), and "reddendo . . . *quolibet die*" (line 91). The following edition, therefore, is based on CC in conjunction with Mo, R, and W1, which are used as control texts.

EDITORIAL PRINCIPLES

The following edition reproduces the text of *FM* as found in CC. Abbreviations are silently expanded, and capitalization and punctuation are normalized according to modern practice. The spellings of CC have been preserved except that I normalize the *u/v* distinction and regularly print *Iesus*, etc., for *Ihesus*, etc., or abbreviated forms. On two or three occasions CC's spelling has been emended where a confusion with homographs is possible and where the correct spelling is attested by variants in O (e.g.: sedat:cedat; iaceat: iaciat). Words that are normally found in abbreviated or suspended forms are expanded according to the full form as found in CC; where CC, on different occasions, uses two different spellings, I follow the full form where it is given and expand abbreviated forms as follows:

spelling: apud, aput   abbreviated form expanded to apud
          velud, velut   velud
          tamquam, tanquam   tamquam
          imp-, inp-   imp-

comp-, conp-	comp-
set, sed	set
parte, particula	parte

The abbreviation "q.d.," occasionally spelled out *quasi dicat* or *quasi diceret*, has been expanded as the syntax seemed to demand. I have interpreted the usually abbreviated forms referring to biblical books, when accompanied by a chapter number, as being in the genetive case, even where in several cases the chapter number is lacking (for example, "Matthei" at I.ix.148). In these cases CC has a blank space for the missing chapter number, and the three control texts nearly almost also lack the expected chapter number. Lacunae in CC (I.i to I.vii; and passages in III.i) are supplied from Mo. The English verses, with introductory and concluding phrases in Latin if such occur, are supplied from R unless otherwise noted.

The text of CC is emended only where CC's reading is patently wrong (in its sense, not grammar[19]) and diverges from subgroup v. Material added to CC appears in [brackets], emendations of material in CC in ⟨angle brackets⟩. Omissions of material from the edited text are signaled by °. Added material is usually taken from Mo.

The corpus of variants registers:

(a) All cases where CC has been followed while all three control texts (O) agree against it. Where only two control texts agree against CC (whether CC is followed by the third control text or not), normally no variant is given, except in cases of particular textual or semantic interest.

(b) The reading of CC where it has been emended.

(c) All material in CC that has been omitted from the edition, except material canceled in CC and marginalia.

In other words, where material appears within brackets in the text but is not accompanied by a variant, such material is missing from CC but present in all three control texts. When such material occurs only in two or one control texts, this information will be found in the corpus of variants. Further, material omitted in the edition (signaled by °) is registered in the variants, with the word before ° serving as the lemma. And lastly, any variant note registers the textual state of all four manuscripts. The text to the right of the lemma is, with one of two exceptions, unedited, that is, given without punctuation and capitalization.

Occasionally, the corpus of variants will register readings from outside CC and the control texts, when such readings may throw some light on problematic passages. Also, here and there the corpus contains some editorial suggestion about apparently corrupt readings in w and elsewhere. In such cases, the following manuscripts have been drawn on as representative of their respective groups: Go1 (group r), B1 (s), Et (t), Go2 (u), B2 (x), B3 (y), and Co (z). Where the text contains Franciscan or fraternal references (I.i.1; IV.xii.55; V.xx.88–89;

VII.xix.55–56; and V.vii.158) and references to Coventry (II.vi.76 and V.xiv.71), the readings of all 25 full manuscripts have been recorded.

The chapter divisions, chapter numbering, and titles are editorial (though not without base in CC and the control texts).

In order to save space, the following sigla have been used in the corpus of variants: C for CC; O for Mo.R.W1; M for Mo; and W for W1. In two or three cases where all manuscripts readings are recorded I have used "Cambridge" for the original siglum C and "Madrid" for M.

In the accompanying translation I have tried to render *Fasciculus morum* into a readable modern English that still remains fairly close to the medieval Latin. Where Middle English verses in the original render a preceding Latin verse more or less closely, I have translated the Latin and then merely quoted the beginning of the Middle English verse. Middle English verses that are only loosely based on preceding Latin material, or that are not based on any Latin material present, have been translated into modern English here. For biblical and classical names I have adopted the normal modern spelling; the same holds for the names of biblical books, though the translation preserves the book and chapter numbers (including erroneous references) as these appear in the Latin. I have omitted the "etc." which in the base manuscript frequently closes a chapter. Likewise, the device of closing a quotation with "Hec X" has been omitted in the translation.

Finally, in the source notes following the translation I have identified the sources of quotations as far as possible. Evidently, the author of *Fasciculus morum* relied to some extent on such collections of authorities as can be found in the *Legenda aurea* (e.g. III.xiii; V.xix) or John of Wales's *Breviloquium* (e.g., V.xv; V.xxxiv; V.xxxvii; VII.xviii). This background of the work calls for further research. To facilitate it, I have occasionally indicated such major intermediary sources in the headnotes to individual chapters of the source notes, which, however, cannot claim to be comprehensive.

NOTES

1. These manuscripts are more fully described, and the entire work, its organization, purpose, popularity, date, and authorship, are discussed in Siegfried Wenzel, *Verses in Sermons. "Fasciculus morum" and Its Middle English Poems* (Cambridge, Mass., 1978). This study will henceforth be referred to as *Verses*.

2. My earlier account of the scribal hands in the volume has been corrected by Alan J. Fletcher in *MAe* 50 (1981), 311.

3. For a fuller description see below, section "Selection of Base Manuscript," and note 18.

4. See Ker, *Medieval Manuscripts*, 2:662–664; and Peter J. Lucas, "William Gybbe of Wisbech: A Fifteenth-Century English Scribe," *Codices manuscripti* 11 (1985), 41–64.

5. To the cross references to *FM* which the scribe of this manuscript, Johannes

Sintram, made elsewhere (see *Verses*, p. 22) can be added Leeds, University Library, MS Brotherton 102; see Ker, *Medieval Manuscripts*, vol. 3 (Oxford, 1983), p. 64.

6. See Neil R. Ker, "Cardinal Cervini's Manuscripts from the Cambridge Friars," in: *Xenia medii aevi historiam illustrantia oblata Thomas Kaeppeli, O.P.*, ed. Raymundus Creytens and Pius Künzle, Storia e letteratura 141 (Rome, 1978), 1:51–71, esp. 58; repr. with addenda in Neil R. Ker, *Books, Collectors and Libraries: Studies in the Medieval Heritage*, ed. Andrew G. Watson (London, 1985), pp. 437–458.

7. To the references to *FM* in medieval booklists, bequests, and the like given in *Verses*, pp. 23–25 and 41–45, the following can be added: A copy of the work is mentioned in a Norwich will; see Norman P. Tanner, *The Church in Late Medieval Norwich 1370–1532* (Toronto, 1984), p. 40 and n. 305; a "Fasciculum pauperculum viciorum et virtutum in septem partes diuisum" appears in an early fifteenth-century booklist from the Benedictine abbey of Saint Mary in York (Dublin, Trinity College MS 207, fol. 22v). *FM* is claimed as the source of some added material in the revisions of John Mirk's *Festial*, in Susan Powell, *The Advent and Nativity Sermons from a Fifteenth-Century Revision of John Mirk's Festial*, Middle English Texts 13 (Heidelberg, 1981).

8. The following recension is based on complete collation of III.i.97–III.viii.61 and of shorter passages throughout *FM*.

9. *Verses*, pp. 111–114

10. *Summa brevis*, London, BL MS Royal 4.B.viii, fol. 235.

11. *Summa vitiorum* II.ii.3.

12. *Verses*, pp. 29–34.

13. *Verses*, p. 110.

14. B4 has "te medium scindam quia novi."

15. *Verses*, pp. 26–34. Since publication of my study, attention has been called to some probable borrowings from *FM* in Oxford, Bodleian Library, MS Barlow 24, and the extensive use in that MS of the name "Selk"; see Alan J. Fletcher, " 'I Sing of a Maiden': A Fifteenth-Century Sermon Reminiscence," *N&Q* 223 (1978), 107–108; Susan Powell, "Connections between the *Fasciculus Morum* and Bodleian MS Barlow 24," *N&Q* 227 (1982), 10–14; and Fletcher, "The Authorship of the *Fasciculus Morum*: A Review of the Evidence of Bodleian MS Barlow 24," *N&Q* 228 (1983), 205–207. It does not seem at all clear what implications for the date of composition of *FM* the borrowings and the occurrence of "Selk" may hold.

16. See the studies by Benedict Hackett, Eric Colledge, and Noel Chadwick, "William Flete's *De Remediis contra Temptaciones* in its Latin and English Recensions: The Growth of a Text," *MS* 26 (1964), 210–230; and S. S. Hussey, "Editing the Middle English Mystics," in: *Spiritualitaet heute und gestern . . . 1982*, Analecta Cartusiana 35 (Salzburg, 1983), 2:160–173.

17. For example, the following substitutions: *Ulixbone* (Lisbon) for London and Coventry (II.vi.76); *bestiones* for *babeweis* (V.xvii.00); *Galeco* for *Wallico* II.vi.102); *greyes* for *greges* (III.vii.118); etc. Cf. also the addition "palefridum vel mullam" (III.i.103), and the frequent confusion of initial *b* and *v*.

18. Very much like Nr. 47 in Edward Heawood, "Sources of Early English Paper Supply," *The Library*, fourth series, 10 (1930), 282–307, found in works dated 1462–1503. For a collation of CC, see Neil R. Ker, *Medieval Manuscripts in British Libraries*, vol. 2 (Oxford, 1977), p. 281.

19. Particularly noticeable, throughout group v, is the uncertainty about verb forms. Especially the present subjunctive and future forms (in the third conjugation) are frequently confused and inconsistent, and certainly wrong in comparison with classical (and even normal medieval) Latin grammar.

FASCICULUS MORUM

Prologus

[[M, f. 2] Frater predilecte ac sodalis preelecte, quia Scriptura
attestante Proverbiorum 18: "Frater qui adiuvatur a fratre quasi civitas
firma," vestram fraternalem caritatem ac michi caram fraternitatem supra
petram Domini positam et fundatam toto cordis conamine operisque iuvamine
5   stabili⟨re⟩ peroptans et firmare, ad vestram peticionem fasciculum pauperculum viciorum et virtutum ad vestrum solacium et utilitatem simplicium e
diversis tractatibus collegi et hic modulo meo inserui. In quo si quid
minus utile inveneritis, meam insipienciam arguatis. Scio enim et protestor
in omni sapiencia et doctrina, prout scribitur Apocalipsis 3, quod "miser"
10   sum "et miserabilis, pauper et cecus." Pro illis vere que placent et valent,
aliis regraciari et laudare curetis.

*In C the text of Prologus to I.vii.13 has been lost due to a loss of evidently eight leaves.
This section is here edited from M. I have collated M closely with R and W (which begins
only at I.iii.51), and I have emended the text of M (indicated by angle brackets) only
where the sense evidently demands it. Authorities for the emendations are given in the
corpus of variants. Occasionally readings of R and W are cited where these are of textual
interest. Material omitted from M is indicated by °. In reproducing M, I have preserved
its peculiar (German) spellings but silently omitted repeated words and phrases. 5 sta-
bilire] stabiliter M.R. Only B3 reads clearly stabilire. The infinitive seems demanded by
the syntax, as object, together with firmare, of peroptans. Instead of firmare many MSS
read firmiter (corrected from firmare in Go1), evidently in an attempt to correlate the form
with stabiliter.*

Prologue

Most beloved brother and companion, dear above all others: Since as Holy Scripture testifies in Proverbs 18 that "a brother who is helped by his brother is like a strong city," I desire, with the greatest effort of my heart and the aid of my work, to build up and strengthen your brotherly love and beloved brotherhood that is placed and founded upon the rock of Our Lord, I have, at your request, collected from various treatises and woven together as well as I could a small and unpretentious bundle of vices and virtues, to comfort you and to help the unlettered. If you find in it anything of little use, you must blame my own lack of wisdom, for I know and acknowledge that, as is said in Revelation 3, in wisdom and learning I am "wretched and miserable, poor and blind." But for the things that please and are helpful, give thanks and praise to others!

2–3 Prov. 18.19.   **9–10** Rev. 3.17.

PARS I

De superbia

I.i   DE PECCATIS IN GENERALI

Ut enim habetur in *Regula* beati patris Francisci et ⟨eciam⟩ statutum
est alibi, tenemur populo denunciare et predicare vicia et virtutes, penam
et gloriam cum brevitate sermonis. Ideo a descripcione viciorum est incho-
andum, et in virtutibus terminandum, primo in generali, secundo in specia-
5   li. Set quia septem considero vicia capitalia et septem oppositas virtutes,
tractatus igitur iste *Fasciculus morum* nominatur, et per septem particulas
dividatur, in quarum unaquaque precedente vicii descripcione sequitur virtus pro fine, tamquam extirpatrix cuiuscumque mali, nam cuius finis bonus,
⟨ipsum totum⟩ bonum.
10   Circa ergo descripcionem viciorum sive peccatorum in generali est
sciendum quod quedam sunt venialia et quedam mortalia. Veniale autem peccatum, secundum Augustinum, est minor amor Dei, utpote quando nimis diligitur
aliqua creatura set tamen minus quam Creator; nam si eque aut magis dilige-
retur creatura quam Creator, omnino mortale diceretur. Est igitur peccatum
15   aversio ab incommutabili bono ad bonum commutabile; hoc est, peccatum est
aversio voluntatis a Deo qui omnino immutabilis est, ad aliquid mutabile et
transitorium peragendum, quod non vult Deus nec sibi placet. Mortale autem
peccatum, secundum Augustinum *Contra Faustum*, "est dictum, factum, aut
concupitum quod fit contra legem Dei." Et dicit "dictum" propter peccatum
20   oris; "factum" propter peccatum operis; et "concupitum" propter peccatum
cordis. Nam sicud hospes per ianitorem ad ostiarium et sic ad domum intro-
ducitur, sic peccatum a corde ad os, ab ore ad factum, set prochdolor de
facto ad dyabolum demandatur.
    Et dicitur mortale eo quod spiritualiter hominem mortuum reddit. Nam
25   sicud mortui temporaliter cum vivis non communicant, sic spiritualiter
mortui per peccatum de beneficiis Ecclesie neque militantis neque triumphantis nullatenus participant. Et ideo omnia eorum opera quoad vitam eter-

PART I

Pride

I.i SINS IN GENERAL

As is said in the *Rule* of blessed Father Francis and has also been decreed elsewhere, we are held to show and preach to the people, in short words, the vices and virtues, punishment and glory. Hence we must begin with the description of the vices and end with the virtues, first in a general way and then in particular. But since I consider seven chief vices and seven virtues that are opposed to them, this treatise is entitled *Fasciculus morum* and divided into seven parts. In each of them, after the description of a vice there follows in the end a virtue, as a force that uproots every evil; for that whose end is good is itself wholly good.

As regards the description of vices or sins in general, we should know that some sins are venial and others mortal. According to Augustine, venial sin is a diminished love of God, namely when some creature is loved too much, yet still less than the Creator—for when a creature is loved as much or even more than its Creator, this love would be considered plainly a mortal sin. "Sin" is a turning away from the unchangeable good to some changeable good; that is to say, sin means turning away our desire from God, who is altogether unchangeable, to something changeable, and to some transitory action which God does not wish us to do and which does not please him. Mortal sin, according to Augustine in *Against Faustus*, "is any word, deed, or desire which is contrary to God's law." By "word" he refers to sin of the mouth, by "deed" to sin in deed, and by "desire" to sin in the heart. For just as a guest is led by the doorkeeper to the gate and thus into the house, so sin proceeds from the heart to the mouth, from the mouth to the deed, and lastly—alas—from the deed to the devil.

And sin is called mortal because it renders man spiritually dead. For as people that are literally dead have no relation with the living, so those who are spiritually dead through sin have no share whatsoever in the benefits of

nam consequendam supervacua dinoscuntur. Est ergo notandum quod sicud
nequaquam aliquis vere loqueretur, ambularet, aut huiusmodi que sunt pro-
30 prietates vite perageret sine vita, sic nec quis in mortali existens nequaquam efficaciter orat, ieiunat, aut cetera opera vite spiritualis peragit
sine confessione et penitencia. Dicit Bernardus in *Epistula ad Sophiam*:
"Absque enim confessione iustus iudicatur ingratus et peccator mortuus
reputatur." Unde peccatorem reprehendens Psalmista ait: "Peccatori autem
35 dixit Deus: 'Quare tu enarras iusticias meas?'" quasi diceret: Sicud ferculum regi presentatum in vase fetido muscis et culicibus deturpato offenderet, revera sic oraciones et alia bona offerendo in corde fedo ac peccatis
pleno. Unde narratur de quodam clerico lubrico set in officio Dei et Beate
Virginis satis devoto, quomodo Beata Virgo sibi apparuit portans liquorem
40 dulcissimum in vase fetido et sordido, offerens ei ad bibendum. Cum ipse
respondit quod propter fetorem vasis non potuit, respondit Virgo Beata:
"Sic michi oraciones vestre nec filio meo placent, dum vas a quo procedit
sit corruptum."
    Et tamen hic notandum est quod bona in mortali peccato [M, f. 2v]
45 facta ad tria valere solent: primo ad augmentum gracie, ut a peccato redeat; secundo ut bona temporalia uberius possideat; tercio ut penas in
inferno levius sustineat. Et ideo qui oraciones dicere vel et elemosinas
vel alia opera bona ⟨facere⟩ peroptat, primo iuxta consilium beati Bernardi
debet a seipso incipere et misereri anime sue, ne regnet peccatum mortale
50 in suo corpore. Quid ergo prodest bona facere et a peccato non cessare?
Revera sicud de edificante una manu patet et alia destruente; unde Ecclesiastici 34: "Unus edificans et alius destruens, quid prodest illis nisi
labor?" quasi diceret: nichil.
    Igitur caveant peccatores, quia Christum capud omnium peccando amit-
55 tunt et potestati totaliter inimicorum se exponunt. Sicud contingit ⟨in⟩
exercitu regis ubi ex adverso bella imminent mortalia: submisso principe
cum vexillo omnes sui exponuntur mortis periculo. Sic certe homines adversus demonum potestates bellantes Christum ⟨principem⟩ habent dum armis
virtutum et bone vite viriliter resistunt se submittunt, quorum vexillum
60 peccatum mortale est.
    Et ideo huiusmodi peccatum est tam Deo quam angelis odiosum, proprio
subiecto perniciosum, dampnum proximo et venenosum, et omni creature contu-
meliosum. Nam omnis creatura natura propria admonet hominem ad Dei cognicionem et debitam subieccionem. Cum ergo peccator eorum doctrinam respuit,
65 certum est quod omnis creatura in ⟨ultimo⟩ vindictam sumet, sicud hactenus
visum est. Nam de ipso terre elemento patet quando apperiens os suum illos
peccatores Dathan et Abiron absorbuit, Numeri ⟨16⟩; de aqua patet in diluvio Noe, Genesis 7; similiter de igne, Genesis ⟨19⟩, qui impios Pentapoly
incendit, et similiter Regum de igne quinquagenarios devorante; de aere

the Church, whether militant or triumphant. And thus all their works turn out to be completely vain with respect to gaining eternal life. And we should note that just as nobody could properly speak, walk, or do any of the things that are proper aspects of life if he is not alive, so nobody can with any spiritual benefit pray, fast, or engage in any other deeds of the spiritual life without previous confession and penance. Bernard says in his *Letter to Sophia*: "With- out confession the just man is judged to be graceless, and the sinner is held to be dead." Therefore the Psalmist reproaches the sinner and says: "To the sinner God has said, 'Why do you tell my deeds of justice?' " as if he were saying: just as a dish that is offered to the king in a dirty bowl full of flies and gnats, so will prayers and other good deeds give offense if they are offered in a heart that is dirty and full of sins. There is a story about a cleric who was lustful and yet very devout in the worship of God and the Blessed Virgin. The Blessed Virgin appeared to him, carrying a sweet drink in a dirty dish and offered it to him to drink. As he said that he could not do so because of the stench of the dish, the Blessed Virgin replied: "Just so do your prayers not please me nor my son as long as the vessel from which they come is tainted."

Yet it should be noted at this point that good deeds performed in mortal sin are still of value for three things: first, for an increase of grace, so that the sinner may return from his sin; second, that he may obtain temporal goods more fully; and third, that he may endure his pains in hell more easily. And so, whoever wants to pray or give alms or do other good works should, on the advice of Blessed Bernard, first begin with himself and have mercy on his own soul, that no mortal sin reign in his body. For what is the use of doing good and not ceasing to sin? It is just like building with one hand and tearing down with the other. Ecclesiasticus 34: "One builds up and the other tears down—what is the use of it?" as if to say, none.

Let therefore sinners beware, for by sinning they lose Christ, the head of all things, and give themselves totally into the power of their enemies. Thus it happens in the king's army when deadly combat threatens: when the leader has fallen with his banner, all soldiers are in danger of death. Likewise, cer- tainly, men who fight against the power of demons have Christ as their leader as long as they withstand manly with the weapons of their virtues and their good life and subject to these the demons, whose banner is mortal sin.

And in this fashion sin is hateful to God and the angels, harmful for the sinner himself, hurtful and poisonous for his neighbor, and an offense to all creation. For every creature by its own nature admonishes man to know God and to subject himself properly to him. But when the sinner refuses to accept their teaching, all creation will certainly punish him in the end, as has been seen before our time. This is true of the element earth, when it opened its mouth and swallowed the sinners Dathan and Abiram, Numbers 16; it is true of

70   similiter patet de plagis Egypti, de grandine cadente ac tenebris. Item de
      nocivis animantibus ad sensum patet tota die; de angelis patet in plerisque
      locis, tam de bonis quam de malis; et de corporibus supercelestibus patuit
      Iosue 10, ubi dicitur quod sol et luna steterunt ⟨spacio⟩ unius diei,
      pugnante Iosue contra inimicos pro filiis Ysrael. Ne ergo Deus ipse per
75   suas creaturas pro peccatis de nobis sicud de predictis vindictam capiat,
      caveamus, iuxta illud metrice dictum:

> Qui tetigit, tetigit; tu desine vivere prave.
> Si feriat, feriat; ° virga secunda cave.

> [[He þat hem reuen, hoe reuen ful sore.
80 > Amende þy lyf and synne no more,
> Lest he eft so ryue þe.
> þat þou be war, I rede þe.]]

Et hec generaliter ad presens dicta sufficiunt.

---

1 in . . . Francisci] in regulis sanctorum patrum Et.L3.Pe.W2 *and* Camb.Dd.10.15; *add*
nostri B3.L2.Sp; *om* patris B1.Jo; *om* R (*eyeskip*); *manuscript defective* C.W. *All full
manuscripts recorded.*   eciam] B1; ecce M.Go2; *longer om* R; ecclesie B2.Go1.   **4** se-
cundo] ac postea R *and others*.   **7** dividatur] dividitur R.   **9** ipsum totum] R; ipse quoque
M.   **32** et penitencia] previa R.   **40** fetido et] *om* R.   **47** levius] leviores *after* penas
R.   **48** vel alia opera bona] *om* R. facere] R; *om* M.   **55** in] R; *om* M.   **58** principem] R;
principum M.   **59** se] *thus in* M.R; et demones illis Co.Go1.   **65** in ultimo] R *corr from*
inutilis; inutilis M.   **67** 16] R *and source*; 10 M.   **68** 19] R; 9 M.   **69** de igne] 4 capitulo
R.   **73** spacio] R; *om* M.   diei] *add* iubente deo R.   **78** feriat(2)] *add* a *interl* M.   **79–
82** He . . . þe] *text from* R. *Verse 1, in* B3.E.Go2.Jo.L1.L2.Li.LC.R.Sp.

I.ii   DE DIFFINICIONE SUPERBIE

      Nunc in speciali ad vicia et virtutes procedamus, ita quod cuicumque
vicio se semper opponat virtus contraria illud extirpans et confundens, ut
dictum est. Et primo et principaliter de superbia et humilitate, secundo de
ira et paciencia et mititate, tercio de invidia et caritate, quarto de
5   avaricia et paupertate, quinto de accidia et ocupacionis ⟨agilitate⟩, sexto
de gula et sobrietate, septimo de luxuria et castitate.
      Circa enim superbiam hoc modo procedam: primo, que est eius diffinicio
et proprietas; secundo, unde progreditur eius iniquitas; tercio, quare sit
detestanda; quarto, que sunt eius membra numeranda.
10   Dico ergo primo quod superbia quantum ad eius diffinicionem est amor

water, as in Noah's flood, Genesis 7; of fire also, which burned the godless
people of Pentapolis, Genesis 19, and similarly devoured the quinquagenarians,
in the Book of Kings; it is likewise true of the air, as in the plagues of
Egypt, when hail fell and darkness came. The same we can observe every day
with respect to harmful animals; it is true of the angels, both the good and
the evil ones, as reported in various places; and it was true of the celestial
bodies, as we are told in Joshua 10 that upon God's command the sun and the
moon stood still for one day while Joshua was fighting against his enemies for
the children of Israel. Let us beware, then, lest God himself take vengeance
on us for our sins with the help of his creatures, as he took vengeance in the
cases just mentioned; according to the poem:

> He who has struck will strike again;
>> Your sinful life repair;
> If he hurts you, bear well the pain:
>> His future rod beware!

> He þat hem reuen, hoe reuen ful sore . . . .

And these general remarks suffice for now.

1–3 Saint Francis, *Regula bullata* 9; ed. Esser, p. 234.   **11–14** Augustine, *De perfectione iustitiae hominis* VI.15 (PL 44:298).   **18–19** Augustine, *Contra Faustum* XXII.27
(CSEL 25:621).   **33–34** Bernard, *Ep. 113, Ad Sophiam* 4 (7:290).   **34–35** Ps. 49.16.
38–43 Tubach 3077. Also in Bromyard, "Confessio," C.VI.3; Brinton, sermons 32, 48,
77, and 96 (pp. 130, 214, 350, and 443); *Spec. laicorum*, No. 361.   **48–50** Cf. Bernard,
Ad cleros de conversione XVI.29 (4:104– 105); or *De gradibus humilitatis* IV.13–14
(3:26–27).   **52–53** Ecclus. 34.28.   **66–67** Num. 16.1–3.   **67–68** Gen. 7.10–24.   **68–
69** Gen. 19.24–29.   **69** 2 Kings 1.9–12.   **69–70** Exod. 7–12.   **73–74** Josh. 10.13.

I.ii   THE NATURE OF PRIDE

Now let us turn to the vices and virtues in particular, so that each vice
is opposed by its contrary virtue which overcomes and uproots it, as was said
earlier. Thus we speak first and foremost of pride and humility, second of
wrath and patience and meekness, third of envy and charity, fourth of avarice
and poverty, fifth of accidia and swift busyness, sixth of gluttony and soberness, and seventh of lust and chastity.

Concerning pride I shall proceed as follows: first I shall indicate what
its nature and character is; second, where its wickedness comes from; third,
why it should be detested; and fourth, what its members are.

First, then, I say that by definition pride is the love of one's own

proprie excellencie, cuius potissimum proprietas est quod retrahit Deum ab homine.

⟨Et⟩ istius peccati quatuor sunt species. Prima species est quando quis bonum quod habet, a seipso id habere estimat. Set contra istud dicitur
15   Ad Corinthios 4: "Quid habes quod non accepisti, aut quid inde gloriaris?" quasi dicat: Gloriaris supervacue; neque temporalia neque naturalia neque gratuita, set tantum, o superbe, de te habes peccata. Nam sicud vitrum, quantumcumque fuerit perspicuum et dyaphonum, de se tamen non gignit lucis radium set a sole accipit beneficium, sic nec homo nisi de gracia divina
20   mediante aliquid boni operatur. Et ideo Bernardus super illud Canticorum 1, "Oleum effusum": "Quis, inquit, tam insanus affuit ut aliunde quam a Deo aliquid habere presumat? Nemo, inquit, adeo sane ut Phariseus agit gracias." [M, f. 3] Et subdit: "O Pharisee, putas quod tu habes aliquid quod non accepisti? Nichil, inquit, et ideo graciam referto largitori."
25   Secunda species est cum quis bonum quod habet a Deo sibi datum pro meritis propriis putat. Contra quam Romanorum 11 scribitur: "Ergo gracia non est gracia," nam si hominibus daretur pro meritis eorum, que gracia Dei erit? Utique nulla. Sicud si paterfamilias solvat operario quod meruit, in hoc certe sibi nullam graciam facit; revera sic contumeliam facit Creato-
30   ri, quando liberatissimum datorem reputat venditorem, dum ea que Dominus dat credit suis meritis emere.

Tercia species est quando quis iactat se habere quod non habet. Contra quam Apocalipsis 3 angelo Laodicie dicitur. Qui cum gloriabatur se esse divitem, locupletem, et huiusmodi, audivit angelum sibi dicentem: "Scio
35   opera tua, quia neque frigidus neque calidus." Et sequitur: "Nescis quia miser es et miserabilis, pauper et cecus."

Quarta species est quando quis, despectis ceteris, appetit singulariter videri et habere quod non habet. Contra quam Ysaie 33 dicitur: "Ve qui spernis, nonne sperneris?"

---

5 agilitate] R; angelice M.   13 Et] R; est M.   19 accipit] *add* lucis R.

I.iii   DE SUPERBIA CORDIS

Circa progressum istius peccati est sciendum quod ⟨a tribus⟩ progreditur, videlicet a corde, ore, et opere, sicud prius diffinivit Augustinus *Contra Faustum*, "Peccatum mortale" supra, capitulo primo.

superiority, and its most outstanding characteristic is that it takes God away from man.

This sin has four branches. The first occurs when someone who has some good believes that he has it from himself. Against this is written in Corinthians 4: "What do you have which you have not received, and why do you take pride in it?" as if to say: you take pride in vain, O proud man, for neither temporal gifts nor natural ones nor those of grace do you have from yourself, but only your sins. For just as glass, however clear and transparent it may be, does yet not produce a ray of light of itself but receives it as a gift from the sun, thus man works no good except with the help of divine grace. And so Bernard says in commenting upon this verse from Canticles 1, "As oil poured out": "Who was so insane that he would presume to have anything from anywhere else but God? No one in his right mind gives thanks as the Pharisee did." And he adds: "O Pharisee, do you believe you have anything that you have not received? You have nothing, and therefore give thanks to the giver!"

The second branch occurs when someone believes that the good he has from God was given him for his own merits. Against this is written in Romans 11: "Thus grace is not grace," for if it were given to men for their merits, what grace of God would there be? Surely none. If an employer pays his worker what he has earned, he is not being gracious toward him. Likewise, a proud person commits an offense against his Creator when he thinks of the most generous giver as if he were a tradesman and believes that what the Lord gives he is buying with his own merits.

The third branch occurs when someone brags of having what he does not have. This branch is referred to in the words to the angel of Laodicea, in Revelation 3. As he gloried in being rich and wealthy and so on, he heard the angel saying: "I know your works, that you are neither cold nor hot"; and afterwards: "You do not know that you are wretched and miserable, poor and blind."

The fourth branch occurs when someone despises other people and wants to appear unique and to have what he does not have. Against this branch is said in Isaiah 33: "Woe to you who despise; will you not be despised?"

---

15 1 Cor. 4.7. **21** Cant. 1.2. **21–24** Bernard, *Super Cantica* XIII.ii.2 (1:69). **26–27** Rom. 11.6. **33–36** Rev. 3.15–17. **38–39** Isa. 33.1.

I.iii   PRIDE OF HEART

It should be known that this vice comes from three sources, namely one's heart, mouth, and deed, as Augustine defined earlier, in his sentence on mortal sin from *Against Faustus* quoted above in chapter 1.

Circa superbiam cordis tamen est primo sciendum quod illa committitur,
5   secundum Crisostomum, quando quis tacitis omnibus exterioribus ambicioni-
bus ad alciorem dignitatem intrinsecus anhelat, sicud fecit ipse de quo Ysaie
14: "In celum conscendam, supra astra celi ° exaltabo solium meum, et similis ero Altissimo." In corde dixit illa, idest in mente, et non ore, quia
organo caruit. Et ideo dici potest peccatum inexcusabile, unde Augustinus:
10   "Superbis angelis non pepercit Deus; quanto magis nec tibi, putredo et
vermis?" Nam qui oppidis impugnat, quomodo tugurio parcet? Similiter qui
armatis ad pugnandum se coniungit, quomodo inermibus se ingerere formida-
ret? Et ideo summopere nobis cavendum est ne cogitaciones inique in cordibus nostris ascendant, quas dyabolus in cordibus fidelium que "terrena
15   meditantur" nititur horis cotidianis immittere, ut in illis sibi locum re-
quiei valeat perlucrari. Sicud quando aliquis princeps magnus quocumque
proponit hospitari, premittit nuncium, ubi recipitur descendit, certe sic
dyabolus vanas et miseras premittit cogitaciones in cordibus hominum, quasi
diceret: "Qui vos rec⟨i⟩pit, me recipit." Et ideo si eius suggestionibus
20   adquiescamus, "tamquam leo rugiens" irruit in nos; set si ei resistamus,
tamquam ⟨muscam⟩ ipsum effugare possumus et in omnibus actibus vincere,
iuxta illud metrice dictum:

Hostis non ledit nisi cum temptatus obedit.
Est leo si cedit; si non, quasi musca recedit.

25   [[þe fende oure foe ne may vs dere,
But ȝyffe we bowen hym for fere.
He is a lyon bote þou with-stond
And ferde as a flye ȝyf þou ne wonde.]]

Et ideo ⟨faciamus⟩ sicud bonus miles qui contra hostes suos imperter-
30   ritus accedit, donec pre confusione devicti ruant et erubescencia discedant. Sicud fecit beatus Martinus qui dixit: "Ego, inquit, signo crucis non
clipeo protectus aut galea, hostium cuneos penetrabo securus." Sic tu,
miles Christi, contra dyabolum pugnaturus signo crucis et cogitacionibus
sanctis te armare non ⟨fingas⟩, quia scriptum est: "Cogitacio sancta serva-
35   bit te." Clypeum eciam crucis anteponas, ut cum cogitaciones magnas inferre
hostis non desinit, omni sollicitudine resistere conamini, donec confusus
recedat. Et pre ceteris Christo cor tuum dare non resistas. Ipse enim dixit
Proverbiorum 23: "Fili, prebe michi cor tuum." Avis enim predalis et generosa plus de preda non querit set cor mundatum; sic nec Christus de preda
40   quam suo precioso sanguine redemit. Unde Augustinus: "De sinu, inquit,
Patris descendit" in cor Virginis tamquam avis generosa, que non querit ni
si corda. Et ideo bene dicit Crisostomus: "Si, inquit, Deus peteret elimo

With respect to pride of heart we must know, first, that according to Chrysostom one commits this sin when, hiding all external ambitions, one gasps for a higher position in one's heart. Thus did he who in Isaiah 14 says: "I shall climb to heaven, I shall exalt my seat beyond the stars of heaven, and I shall be like the Most High." He said this in his heart, that is, his mind, and not in his mouth, because he did not have the latter organ. Therefore this sin may be called unforgivable; whence Augustine writes: "God did not spare the proud angels; how much less will he spare you, who are dirt and a worm?" For how will he that assaults cities spare a hut? And how should he that joins battle with armed opponents be afraid of engaging the weaponless? Therefore we must be keenly on guard that no wicked thoughts rise in our hearts, which the devil tries to implant every hour of the day in the hearts of those faithful who think of earthly things, in order to gain in them a place of rest for himself. Just as a great prince sends before him a messenger wherever he wishes to lodge and alights where he is received, so the devil sends before him vain and miserable thoughts into men's hearts, as if he were saying: "Who receives you, receives me." If we then acquiesce in his suggestions, he falls upon us "roaring like a lion"; but if we resist him, we can put him to flight like a fly and overcome him in all his actions, as the poems says:

> The foe hurts none of those he tempts
> > But him who soon obeys.
> A lion is he if you yield;
> > Else like a fly he flees.

> þe fende oure foe ne may vs dere. . .

Therefore let us act like the good soldier who advances fearlessly against his enemies until they fall overcome by confusion and yield with shame. Thus acted Blessed Martin, who said: "Protected by the sign of the cross, not by shield or helmet, I shall safely penetrate the battlelines of my enemies." Thus you, soldier of Christ, when you are to fight against the devil, do not hesitate to arm yourself with the sign of the cross and with holy thoughts, for it is written: "Holy thoughts will save you." Also put the shield of the cross before you so that, as long as our enemy does not desist from injecting his exalted thoughts, we may endeavor to resist with all eagerness until he is confounded and retreats. And above all else, do not desist from giving your heart to Christ. For he himself has said in Proverbs 23: "Son, lend me your heart." A noble bird of prey takes nothing else from its prey but its clean heart, and Christ does not deal otherwise with his prey whom he has redeemed with his precious blood. Therefore Augustine says: "From the Father's bosom he descended into the heart of the Virgin, like a noble bird that seeks nothing

sinam, posset se pauper excusare; si oraciones, mutus; si peregrinaciones,
claudus. Set quod non habet homo non querit. Set quod omnis homo habet,
45   hoc est cor, illud querit et optat." Hec ille. Et ⟨ideo⟩ pre ceteris circumstanciis magis [M, f. 3v] est timenda superbia cordis. [[Unde Anglice:

The synne of pryde nys noȝt in schroud,
But in herte þat is to proude.

"Let þin herte helde and hit þe schal lyke," quod Hendyng.]]
50   Secundum autem Anshelmum, *De similitudinibus*, sic est de corde hominis
sicud est de molendino quod dominus tradidit servo suo custodiendum ut in
eo tantum annonam suam molet, scilicet frumentum, ordeum, et huiusmodi, et
inde sibi victum acquirat. Cui aliquis inimicus invidet et insidiatur quod,
si aliquando illud vacuum invenerit, aut harenam proicit quod illud dissi-
55   pet, aut picem que conglutinat, aut paleam quod nimis occupat. Spiritualiter hoc molendinum est cor hominis continue molens sine quiete aliquid
cogitando, quod traditum ⟨est⟩ cuilibet ⟨nostrum⟩ a Domino Deo ut in illo
mole⟨mus⟩ cogitaciones puras de Deo et fructuosas proximo. Quod si vacuum
a dyabolo aliquando inventum fuerit, statim nititur illud replere ad dissi-
60   pandum per arenam, scilicet ire et invidie, aut per picem glutinantem gule
et luxurie, aut per paleam occupantem superbie et avaricie. Et sicud rota
molendini volvendo aquam spargit, sic dyabolus per ocium cogitaciones hominum. Et ideo summo opere est cor a vanis cogitacionibus et dyaboli temptacionibus et decepcionibus custodiendum.
65   Nam sensibiliter videmus quod conservacio maxime civitatis aut terre
totaliter aliquando dependet in defensione unius passus, qui si ab hostibus
occupetur, tota ista civitas aut terra est sicud capta; et e converso si a
domino illius terre viriliter defendatur passus iste, tota terra manet secura. Revera totus homo est quasi una terra, quia de lymo terre factus est,
70   ut habetur Genesis 1. Unde istius terre defensio totaliter consistit in
conservacione unius passus, scilicet cordis; nam quicquid inferant hostes
spirituales, scilicet caro, mundus, aut dyabolus, nullum erit periculum si
non intrent per istum passum; set capto illo ab illis, perditur tota terra.
In cuius figura Ioab volens interficere Absolon infixit tres lanceas in cor
75   eius, 2 Regum 18. Revera sic si adversarius noster dyabolus, quem intelligo
per Ioab, poterit istas tres lanceas, scilicet superbie, avaricie, et
luxurie, in cordibus nostris infingere per consensum, statim de morte nostra spirituali certus est. Et ideo bene dicitur Proverbiorum 4: "Omni custodia serva cor tuum, quoniam ab ipso vita procedit."
80   Unde narratur quod quidam vir sollicitus valde de statu suo, utrum scilicet deberet salvari vel dampnari, ⟨sicud⟩ quondam solus transivit super

but the heart." And Chrysostom says fittingly: "If God were to look for alms, the poor man would have an excuse; if for prayers, the dumb man would have an excuse; if for pilgrimages, the lame would have an excuse. But he does not look for what man does not have. Rather, he looks for and desires what every man has, namely a heart." Therefore, pride of heart must be feared more than all other aspects of this sin. Therefore in English:

> The sin of pride does not in clothes reside
> But rather in a heart that's full of pride.

"Let your heart bow down, and you will be pleased," says Hending.

According to Anselm in his book of *Similitudes*, it is with man's heart as it is with the mill that a master has given to his servant for safekeeping so that he may grind in it only his harvest of grain, that is, wheat, barley, and the like, and thereby gain his livelihood. Some enemy is envious and schemes against him. When he finds the mill standing empty, he pours sand into it which ruins it, or pitch which stops it up, or straw which keeps it running too much. Spiritually speaking, this mill is man's heart, which grinds without rest in constant thought, and which each of us has been given by God our Lord so that we may grind in it pure thoughts about God that are fruitful for our neighbor. If the devil finds it standing empty, he at once tries to fill it with sand, that is, with wrath and envy, to ruin it; or with the pitch of gluttony and lust to stop it up; or with the straw of pride and avarice to keep it too busy. And as the mill-wheel scatters water when it turns, so does the devil scatter man's thoughts in idleness. Therefore it is mandatory that we protect our heart against idle thoughts and against the devil's temptations and wiles.

For we see with our own eyes that sometimes the safety of a large city or country depends entirely on holding a single pass. If the latter is occupied by the enemies, the whole city or country is practically taken; and conversely, if that pass is being firmly defended by the lord of that country, the entire country remains safe. Indeed, man is like a country, because he was made from the mud of the earth, as we find in Genesis 1. The defense of that country lies entirely in keeping one single pass, namely our heart, for whatever our spiritual enemies, that is, the flesh, the world, and the devil, may advance against it, there will be no danger as long as they do not enter through that pass. But if the latter is taken, the whole country is lost. As a type of this we have Joab, who, when he wanted to kill Absalom, stuck three spears into his heart, 2 Kings 18. Similarly, if our enemy the devil, whom I understand by Joab, manages to stick these three spears of pride, avarice, and lust in our hearts with our consent, he is at once sure of our spiritual death. And thus

hoc ⟨Deum⟩ rogans ut sibi dignaretur revelare, apparuit sibi quidam in forma humana causam sue tristicie querens; qui cum sibi intimasset ait: "Si,
inquit, vis salvari, oportet te tria necessario habere et illa Deo offerre,
85   scilicet lunam novam, solis rotunditatem, et quartam partem rote." Et hiis
dictis disparuit. Iste ergo tristior effectus eo quod solem et lunam habere
nequit. Apparuit quidam angelus Dei dicens quod verum dixit ⟨homo⟩ ille set
alio modo, et ideo ⟨non diffideret⟩, quia dyabolus fuit volens eum in desperacionem adduxisse. Cum ergo quesisset ab angelo intellectum dicti sui,
90   respondit: "Per novem lunam, inquit, intellexit hanc litteram C, eo quod
habet duo cornua ad modum nove lune; per rotunditatem solis hanc litteram
O, et per quartam partem rote hanc litteram R, que est quarta littera huius
diccionis 'rote.' Coniunge ergo has tres litteras simul et fiet hoc verbum
cor, quod si Deo cum omni puritate custodieris et dederis, revera salvabe-
95   ris." Si ergo a dyabolo vel alio inimico invasus fueris, cogita illud Psalmi: "In Domino speravit cor meum et adiutus sum."

Unde narratur in *Vitas Patrum* quod venit frater quidam ad abbatem
Pastorem dicens: "Multe cogitaciones veniunt in mente mea et quasi pericli-
tor in eis." Et eiecit eum senex in ⟨aere nudo⟩ dicens: "Expande sinum tuum
100   et apprehende ventum." Et ille: "Non possum." Et senex: "Non prohibere poteris ne cogitaciones mentem intrent; set tuum est resistere et illis non
consentire, et sic mereri." Hec ille. Principiis ergo obsta, hoc est, quando in corde occurrunt levia et venialia resistas illis, ne ibi radicantur
et maiora introducant et mortalia, ad modum quo parvuli latrunculi in domum
105   per foramen inmissi apperiunt hostia et fenestras per quas intrant ⟨maio-
res⟩ et forciores ut spoliant et occidant ibidem inhabitantes. In cuius
figura legitur 4 Regum 5 quod latrunculi Syrie captivam duxerunt filiam
Ysrael. Expone ut placet.

---

1 a tribus] R; *canc and replaced by* superbia *interl* M.   **7** celi] *add* et M.   **10** superbis an-
gelis] superbo angelo R.   **19** recipit] R; recepit M.   **21** muscam] R; musca M.   **25–
28** þe . . . wonde] *text from* R. *Verse 2, in* B3.D.E.Go2.Jo.L1.L2.Li. LC.R.Sp.
29 faciamus] R; *om* M.   **34** fingas] R; *corrected to* desperas set confidenter te (*marg*)
singnans M.   **35** magnas] magicas R.   **44–45** quod(2) . . . cor] quia omnino cor habet
homo R.   **45** ideo] R; *om* M.   **46–49** Unde . . . Hendyng] *text from* R. *Verse 3, in*
E.Go1.Go2.L1.Li.LC.R.Sp.V. *In* R *the phrase* quod hendyng *appears after line 47.*
50 Anshelmum] W *begins here.*   **57** est] R.W; *om* M.   nostrum] R.W; nostro M.
58 molemus] moletur M.W; molere R.   **81** sicud] R.W; secundum M.   **82** Deum] R;
diu M.W.   **87** Dei] ei R.W.   homo] R.W; *erased and replaced by* qui in forma humana
tibi comparuit *marg* M.   **88** non diffideret] R.W; ut diffideres *on erasure* M.   **99** aere
nudo] R.W *and source*; aeris medio M.   **105–106** maiores] R.W; amores M (*thus frequently*).

it is well said in Proverbs 4: "Guard your heart with all safekeeping, because from it comes your life."

Whence the story is told that a man who was very concerned about his condition, that is, whether he would be saved or damned, was once walking by himself and asking God to grant him some revelation. Then someone in human shape appeared to him and asked him why he was so sad. When the man told him his thoughts, the other said: "If you want to be saved, you must needs have three things and offer them to God: the new moon, the circle of the sun, and the fourth part of a wheel." With these words he disappeared. As the man now became only sadder because he could not have the sun and the moon, an angel of God appeared to him and said that the other person had spoken the truth but allegorically, and that he should not lose heart, because it had been the devil who wanted to lead him to despair. Then this man asked the angel for the meaning of that message, and the angel replied: "By the new moon he meant the letter C, because it has two horns like the new moon; by the circle of the sun, the letter O; and by the fourth part of a wheel, the letter R, which is the fourth letter of the word *rota*, 'wheel.' Put the three letters together and you get the word COR, 'heart.' If you safekeep this in all purity and give it to God, you will inded be saved." Therefore, if you are attacked by the devil or any other enemy, think on the word of the Psalm: "My heart has hoped in the Lord, and I have been helped."

Whence a story is told in *The Lives of the Fathers* that a brother came to Abba Pastor and said: "Many tempting thoughts come to my mind and I am in danger of perishing in them." The desert father sent him out into the raw air and said: "Open your chest and catch the wind." He answered: "I can't." So the desert father said: "Neither can you prevent thoughts from entering your mind; but it is your task to resist and not give in to them, and thus to earn your reward." Therefore, "resist in the beginning"; that is, when slightly tempting and excusable thoughts rise in your heart, you must withstand them lest they strike root and bring after them more serious and gravely sinful ones, in the same way as thieving children slip into a house through cracks and then open doors and windows through which bigger and stronger thieves enter in order to steal and to kill the inhabitants. A type of this can be found in 4 Kings 5, that the little thieves of Syria have led the daughter of Israel away as a captive. Explain this as you wish.

2–3 Cf. *FM* I.i.17–21.   7–8 Isa. 14.13–14.   10–11 Cf. Bernard, *Super Cantica* LIV.iv.8 (2:107).   14–15 Cf. Phil. 3.19.   19 Matt. 10.40.   20 1 Pet. 5.8.   23–24 *Prov* 11230C and *Verses*, p. 137. Compare also *The Owl and the Nightingale*, lines 402–408 (ed. Stanley, London, 1960). The idea evidently comes from Gregory, *Moralia* V.xxii.43 (PL 75:702).   31–32 Cf. *Leg. aurea*, p. 742.   38 Prov. 23.26.   40–42 Cf. *Meditationes piissimae* III.8 (PL 184:490).   50–64 Ps.-Anselm, *Liber de similitudinibus* 41 (PL

I.iv   DE SUPERBIA ORIS

Secundo considerandum est de superbia oris, que in tribus specialiter
consistit, scilicet in multiloquio, in vaniloquio, in maliloquio. Primum enim
cavendum est, quia sicud ubi multum [M, f. 4] est de palea et parum de grano,
et ubi multum est de foliis et parum de fructu, sic ubi verba plurima, accidit
5   frequenter est egestas et penuria, hoc est defectus bonarum virtutum. Nam
ut dicitur Ecclesiastici ⟨20⟩ capitulo: "Qui multis verbis utitur, ledit
animam suam," quia in multiloquio non deerit peccatum. [[Et ideo dicitur:

      Who-so spekyth oft
      Of þyng þat is vn-wrest,
10   þou hit seme soft
      When he spekyth mest,
      He schal hit heren on loft
      When he wenyth lest.

Et ideo: "Let þy tonge rest and þe schall nouȝt rewe," quod Hendyng.]] Unde
15 Proverbiorum dicitur: "Qui inconsideratus est ad loquendum, senciet mala."
Dicit enim sapiens ille Catho:

      Virtutem primam esse puta compescere ligwam. °

Secundo vaniloquium est cavendum ne forte per hoc labatur in peiora,
quia qui spernit modica paulatim decidat. Nam iuxta Bernardum, sicud ab una
20 scintilla parva magna comburitur patria, sic a levitate vaniloquii multa
proveniunt obstacula virtutum; et tamen quod dolendum est iuxta Psalmistam,
"vana locuti sunt," etc. Caveant ergo tales quia ut habetur Matthei 12: "De
omni verbo ocioso quod locuti fuerint, homines reddent racionem." Intollerabile utique foret preposito qui per multa tempora servierat domino, si in
25 ultimo die sue deposicionis de minimo grano responderet et necessario.
Quanto magis difficile erit in die iudicii de minimo verbo ocioso Deo reddere racionem. Unde illud Iob 40: "Que breviter locutus ⟨sum⟩, respondere
quid possum?" quasi dicat, nescio.
Tercio cavendum est de maliloquio, quia iuxta Apostolum Corinthiorum,
30 "corrumpunt bonos mores colloquia mala." Modicum eciam fermenti totam

159:621). **69–70** Gen. 2.7. **74–75** 2 Sam. 18.14. **78–79** Prov. 4.23. **80–95** The story appears in additions to or expansions of Odo of Cheriton, such as MS Harley 219, fol. 14v. Also in Bromyard, "Cor," C.X.15; Harley 7732, fol. 15v; MS Royal 8.F.vi, fol. 13v (and other copies of *Convertimini*); Cambridge, MS Trinity College 42, fol. 17. All these are later than *FM*. **96** Ps. 27.7. **97–102** *VP* V.55 (PL 73:922). **107–108** 2 Kings 5.2.

I.iv   PRIDE OF MOUTH

In the second place we must consider pride of mouth, which consists in three specific vices: speaking too much, speaking idly, and speaking ill. The first must be avoided because just as where there is much straw and little grain, and where there is much foliage and little fruit, so where there are many words there is often poverty and need, that is, lack of good virtues. For as it is written in Ecclesiasticus 20, "he who uses many words hurts his soul," for when one speaks, too much sin will not be far. Therefore it is said:

> Whoever speaks oft
> Of others's defects,
> They may seem soft
> As he glibly dissects,
> But he'll hear them aloft
> When he least expects.

And likewise: "Give your tongue rest, and you won't regret it," says Hending. Whence in Proverbs 15 it is said: "He who is thoughtless in his speech will suffer evil." For the wise man Cato says:

> Consider that the first among
> All virtues is to hold your tongue.

Next, speaking idly must be avoided lest through it we should slip into worse sins, for he who does not take modest things seriously gradually comes to ruin. According to Bernard, as from a small spark a large country can burn down, so from thoughtless idle speech many obstacles can arise against the virtues; and yet, as we must lament, according to the Psalmist: "They have spoken idle words," etc. Let such people beware, for Matthew 12 tells us: "Of every idle word that men say they will render an account," etc. It surely would be unbearable for an overseer who had served his master for a long time to have to give an account of even the smallest grain on the last day of his stewardship. How much harder will it be to give God an account of the smallest idle word on Doomsday! Therefore Job 40 declares: "What can I answer, who have spoken lightly?"—as if he were saying: I do not know.

massam corrumpit, et una veneni gutta multos inficit cum fuerit diffusa. Secundum ergo ⟨Anselmum⟩ maxime custodienda est ligwa, quia per ipsam omnia mala consuluntur et prestantur. Et ideo ad designandum quod bene deberet
custodiri, posita est quasi in carcere et murus dencium ante eam atque
35 labia pro antemuralibus. Ephesiorum 4 dicitur: "Omnis sermo malus non
procedat de ore vestro." [[Unde bene Anglice dicitur:

> Se and here and holde þe stylle,
> ȝefe þou wolte lyue and haue þy wylle.]]

Unde legitur de quodam sene angelos vidente letantes quando de Deo loqueba-
40 tur; quando vero de mundanis, quasi maculatos et manus stercoratas ad ora
ponentes. Quod intelligens tribus annis portabat lapidem in ore ut ⟨disce-
ret⟩ taciturnitatem. Unde beato Archemio fuit dictum: "Si vis salvari,
fuge, tace, quiesce," etc.

---

6 20] R.W; 2° M.   **7–13** Et ideo . . . Hendyng] *text from* R. *Verse 4, in* B3.E.Go1.
Go2.L1.L2.Li.LC.R.V.W1.   **17** ligwam] M *has the following unique addition*: Nam
apud homines esse sapiens reputatur qui ? rigmam sequentem: Si sapiens fore vis, hec
serva que tibi mando—Quid dicas vel ubi, cui, cur, quot, quomodo, quando.   **27** brevi-
ter] leviter R.   sum] R *interl*; *om* M.W.   **30** mala] prava R.W.   **32** Anselmum] R.W;
augustinum M.   **36–38** Unde . . . wylle] *text from* R. *Verse 5, in* B3.E.Go1.Go2.Jo.
L1.L2.Li.LC.R.V.W1.   **41–42** disceret] R, *corr from* diceret; *om* M; diceret W.
42 dictum] R *adds the unique Verse 6.*

I.v   DE SUPERBIA OPERIS

Tercio de superbia operis sequitur, que specialiter consistit in
vestura, in sciencia, in pulcritudine, in potencia et dignitate, in generis
nobilitate.
Primum autem est cavendum quia sicud parum habet latro gloriari ad
5 patibulum ductus de corda qua debet suspendi—prout habetur Luce 16 de
divite induto purpura et bisso et tamen sepultus in inferno—, revera sic
nec homo de vestibus pulcherrimis in hac vita, et post vestibus iocunditatis privari; Ecclesiastici 11: "In vestimento ne glorieris." Et ideo Bernardus ait: "Inter omnia animalia pauperior nascitur ⟨homo⟩, set nunquam
10 pauperior quam vivit; nam de pratis et pascuis habet victum, et de ovibus
et capris indumentum, ac de stercoribus vermium procedit generositas hominum, scilicet in vestura. O ergo, homo (ait ipse), redde singula singulis,
et certe nudus eris." Hec ille. Dicit tamen Augustinus vestes dignas non

Third, speaking ill must be avoided because, according to the Apostle in
Corinthians, "wicked conversations corrupt good manners." Also, a little yeast
taints all the dough, and one drop of poison when it spreads infects many
people. For according to Anselm our tongue must be guarded most closely, for
through it all sorts of evil counsel and help are given. For that reason, in
order to show that it must be well guarded, our tongue is, as it were, put in a
prison, with a wall of teeth before it, and lips as a rampart. Ephesians 4
says: "Let no evil speech whatever come out of your mouth." And so it is well
said in English:

> See and hear and hold thee still
> If thou wouldst live and have thy will.

Thus we read about a desert father who saw the angels rejoicing when he was
talking about God; but when he talked about worldly matters, they were, so to
speak, stained and put dung-covered hands to their mouths. When he understood
the vision, he carried a stone in his mouth for three years to learn silence.
And to Blessed Arsenius it was said: "If you want to be saved, flee, keep
silence, and be still."

6–7 Ecclus. 20.8.   **15** Prov. 13.3.   **17** *Disticha Catonis* I.3.   **19–20** Cf. Jerome, *Ep.*
127 10 (CSEL 56:153).   **22** Ps. 11.3.   **22–23** Matt. 12.36.   **27–28** Job 39.34.   **30** 1
Cor. 15.33.   **32–33** Similarly in Peraldus, *Summa vitiorum* IX.ii.22.   **35–36** Eph.
4.29.   **39–43** Tubach 245 and 4627; *VP* III.36 and V.7 (PL 73:762 and 865). See *Verses*,
p. 140.

I.v   PRIDE OF DEED

In the third place we speak of pride in deed, which consists especially in
clothes, knowledge, beauty, power and rank, and noble lineage.

The first must be avoided because, just as a thief who is being led to the
gallows has little reason to be proud of the rope with which he will be hanged
—as we see it in the rich man of Luke 16 who is clothed in purple and fine
linen and is finally buried in hell—, so indeed must man not take pride in his
beautiful clothes in this life and be afterwards spoilt of the clothes of his
rejoicing; Ecclesiasticus 11: "Do not take pride in your dress." Bernard says:
"Man is born the poorest of all animals, but he is never poorer than when he
lives; for he gets his food from fields and meadows, his clothing from sheep
and goats, and his nobility, that is, in his dress, from the excrement of worms.
O man, return each to their owners and you will surely be naked!" And
Augustine says that it is not clothes that are worthy of blame but their mis-

⟨esse⟩ vituperio set istorum abusionem, ita quod non debemus vestibus pla-
15 cere set moribus. Set hoc non intendunt iste fatue mulieres que in solempnitatibus vestibus luxuriosis tam in capite quam in corpore ad peccatum
excitandum se ornant. Et ideo sicud custos porcorum qui illos dispersos
vult congregare unum facit clamare et statim alii conveniunt, sic revera
dyabolus quando suos intendit congregare unam de filiabus suis facit cla-
20 mare ac ⟨precedente campana⟩, scilicet *tabour*, tripudiando coreas ducere,
et statim alie conveniunt. In cuius figura in Apocalipsis 14 dicitur ⟨quod⟩
sextus angelus tuba cecinit, "et vidi equos," scilicet mulieres ornatas,
"et ⟨qui⟩ sedebant super eos habebant loricas igneas," scilicet igne concupiscencie inflammatas. Expone. Et ideo, ut michi videtur, corpus sic vane
25 indutum bene assimilatur feretro, quod primo ornatur cum super illud iacet
corpus mortuum; certe sic corpus sine virtutibus superflue ornatum, quod
est feretrum anime, designat ibi animam mortuam ⟨iuxta Apostolum⟩: "Anima
vivens ⟨in⟩ deliciis mortua est." Unde Bernardus: "Magna, inquit, abusio
est ancillam dominari et dominam ancillari," quod facit cum corpus extra
30 perornatur et intus ⟨anima⟩ virtutibus spoliatur et arma dyaboli et eius
signa circumquaque ⟨deferuntur⟩.

Unde legitur in *Vitis Patrum* de quodam ⟨sancto⟩, quomodo transiens per
quandam civitatem vidit quendam [M, f. 4v] demonem a latere sedentem atque
ridentem. Cumque eum adiurasset ut causam sui risus intimaret, respondit:
35 "Vidi, inquit, socium meum sedentem super caudam illius mulieris, et cum
illa cepisset huc atque illuc per vicos discurrere, evulsus est ille et in
fovea proiectus."

Item sicud multum displiceret regi si videret vexillum capitalis inimici in supremo loco sui castri ad eius opprobrium elevatum, revera sic
40 displicet Deo vexillum dyaboli explicatum in peplis et in coronis deauratis
in capitibus multorum fixum et vexillum eius ab eo remotum, scilicet signum
thau, idest crucis humilitatis in frontibus earum, per quod pre ceteris
signis expellitur et confunditur dyabolus. In signo cuius in baptismo et
confirmacione ac ceteris sacramentis, similiter et in oracione bona incipi-
45 enda, signum crucis imponitur ad dyabolum specialiter expugnandum.

Unde narrat Vincencius in *Speculo hystoriali* si lupus velit hominem
invadere et homo ponat signum aliquod inter eos, quod statim lupus timet
fraudem, eo quod credit illud erectum esse ad sui captivitatem, et fugit.
Revera sic nos: Quando dyabolus per superbiam nos invadit corde, ore, et
50 opere, elevemus signum sancte crucis supra turrim frontis nostri vel pocius
memoriam ipsius crucifixi in cordibus nostris, et fugiet sine mora. Ab ista
ergo superbia in abusione vestimentorum caveamus. Dicit enim Ambrosius:
"Horret, inquit, Deus actor omnium cum corpus mulieris a se factum videt
ornamentis vane vel metallis obligatum. Quanto (inquit) hominibus videtur
55 splendida, tanto magis a Deo despicitur." Hec ille. In cuius signum Iudith

use, for we must not please with our clothes but with our good morals. But such is not the intention of those foolish women who on feast days wear luxurious clothes on their heads and bodies in order to excite men to sin. As the swineherd who, when he wants to gather his scattered swine, makes one of them squeal and then the others come quickly together, thus the devil, when he wants to round up those who belong to him, makes one of his daughters call out and, tripping behind a bell, that is a "tabour," lead the dance, and at once all the others come together. A type of this is found in Revelation 14: The sixth angel blew the trumpet, "and I saw horses," that is, dressed-up women, "and those who sat on them had fiery armor," that is, burning with the fire of lust. Explain this. Therefore it seems to me that a body thus idly dressed is like a bier, which is dressed up when a dead body lies on it; surely in the same way a body that is needlessly dressed up without having any true virtues is the soul's bier and indicates that the soul is dead, according to the Apostle: "The soul that lives in delights is dead." And Bernard says: "It is a great abuse when the servant-girl is the mistress and the mistress a servant-girl," which happens when the body is decorated outside and the soul within is despoiled of virtues, and the weapons of the devil and his banners are carried about everywhere.

In *The Lives of the Fathers* we read of a saint who, as he was walking through some city, saw a demon sitting by the way and laughing. When he conjured him to tell him why he was laughing, the demon replied: "I just saw my companion sitting on the train of that woman, and when she started to walk this way and that through the streets, he was tossed off and thrown in the ditch."

Further, just as the king would be much displeased if he saw the banner of his arch-enemy raised to his shame in the highest place of his castle, thus God will be displeased to see the devil's banner unfolded in fine robes and raised on the gold crown on the heads of many people, whereas God's own banner is taken down by the devil, that is, the Thau, the sign of the cross of humility on their foreheads, with which above all other signs the devil is driven out and confounded. In order to indicate that, the sign of the cross is made in baptism, in confirmation, and in the other sacraments, and likewise at the beginning of a good prayer, especially in order to drive out the devil.

Therefore Vincent tells us in his *Mirror of History* that when a wolf wants to attack a man, and the man puts up some sign between himself and the wolf, the latter begins to fear some trick because he thinks the sign has been put up to capture him, and he flees. In the same way, when the devil attacks us through pride in heart, mouth, and deed, let us raise up the sign of the cross on the tower of our forehead or better still remember the Crucified himself in our hearts, and the devil will flee without delay. Therefore let us avoid such pride in the misuse of clothes. For Ambrose says: "God, the Creator of all things, shudders when he sees a woman's body, that was made by him, vainly

oratura pro populo induit se cilicio, capitulo 9; Hester eciam oratura
deposuit vestes regias, capitulo 14; Daniel eciam dicit se faciem suam ut
oraret in sacco et cinere posuisse, capitulo 9; rex quoque Ninive sacco
indutus sedit in cinere et fecit clamare ut operirentur saccis tam homines
60   quam iumenta et clamarent ad Dominum in fortitudine, Ione 3 capitulo; et
cetera huiusmodi satis patent scripturam sacram intuenti. Nec tamen ornatus
honestus nec secundum modum status et patrie usus prohibetur, set tantum
ille qui reddit hominem elevatum et superbum et ad cetera peccata inclina-
tum.
65   Secundo ° superbia operis in sciencia consistens similiter est cavenda, ne cum quidam illam habent ut alios instruant, ne illis assimilarentur
in sciencia abscondunt. Contra quos Sapiencie 6 dicitur: "Ponam in lucem
scienciam illius et ⟨non⟩ preteribo veritatem neque cum invidia tabescente
iter habebo." Lux enim sui communicacione amplius clarescit atque iocundius
70   et lacius diffunditur, set absconsione minuitur et deterioratur. Revera sic
sapiencia hominis et sciencia. Unde sicud qui lucernam datam indigentibus
aut in domo habitantibus aut in tenebris ambulantibus abscondit, certum est
quod datori lucis iniuriosus existeret, sic certe in proposito. Ad hoc enim
Deus ordinavit lucernas, idest in Ecclesia sua doctos sapiencia et scien-
75   cia, non ut lucem sibi datam abscondant, set ut ipsam gratis omnibus commu-
nicantes luceant et aperte demonstrent. Et ideo ipse dicit Luce 11: "Nemo
⟨accendit⟩ lucernam et in abscondito ponit, set super candelabrum ut qui
ingrediuntur," etc.
        Tercio de superbia pulchritudinis dico quod nec in corporis formosita-
80   te est superbiendum vel gloriandum. Dicitur Proverbiorum 31: "Fallax gracia
et vana est pulcritudo," etc. Illud enim satis convenienter dicitur vanum
quod statum suum diu servare non potest, sicud corporis formositas. Et ideo
bene comparatur flori ⟨desciduo⟩ et cadenti, qui ad tempus ⟨virescit⟩,
postea marcessit, et tandem totaliter evanescit; Iacobi 1: "Flos decidit et
85   ⟨decor⟩ vultus eius deperiit." Similiter sicud folium in arbore prius
virescit, postea in lutum cadit, tercio a bestiis conculcatur, et quarto
putrescit et ad arborem nunquam redit, revera sic pulchritudo hominis
floret in iuventute, arescit in senectute, cadit in morte, conculcatur in
sepulchro a bestiis et hominibus quantum ad corpus, a demonibus quantum ad
90   animam, nec unquam eadem formositas ad idem corpus redibit; Ysaie 14:
"Detracta est ad inferos superbia tua, concidit cadaver corpus tuum; subter
te sternetur tinea, et operimentum tuum vermis." Ecce, karissimi, licet
enim vita hominis florida fuerit, post mortem tamen vilis et despecta
invenitur. Nam qui sibi salutavit in vita capucio deposito et genibus
95   flexis, tunc super cervicem [M, f. 5] et nasum figit pedem, nec ⟨rememora-
bitur⟩ quantumcumque nobilis; Malachie ultimo: "Calcabis impios cum fuerit
cinis sub planta pedum vestrorum."

fettered with ornaments and metals. The more beautiful she appears to men, the more she is despised by God." This is prefigured by Judith, who put on sackcloth when she was about to pray for her people, chapter 9; by Esther also, who took off her regal garments when she was about to pray, chapter 14; Daniel, too, says he put his face in sackcloth and ashes in order to pray, chapter 9; and the king of Nineveh put on sackcloth and sat in ashes and let it be announced that both men and animals be covered in sackcloth and call to the Lord with strength, Jonah 3; and other figures of this kind will occur if one reads the Scripture. However, clothing that is decent and in accordance with one's state and the customs of one's country is not condemned, but only such as makes a person arrogant and proud and prone to other sins.

Next, pride of deed which lies in knowledge must be similarly avoided. People who have knowledge to teach others must not hide it in order to avoid becoming their equals in knowledge. Against them is written in Wisdom 6: "I shall place his knowledge in the light and will not pass by the truth, nor will I walk with consuming envy." For by communicating itself the light makes things brighter and is diffused more widely and joyfully, but by being hidden it dwindles and loses brightness. The same is true of man's wisdom and knowledge. A person who has received a lamp but hides it from those who need it, whether they live in the house or wander in darkness, would surely commit an offense against him who has given him the lamp. The same is true in the matter under discussion. For God has established lamps, that is, people in his Church who are learned in wisdom and knowledge, not that they should hide the light given them but that in sharing it freely with all people they should let it shine forth and show it openly. God himself says in Luke 11: "No one lights his lamp and hides it, but rather puts it on a candlestick so that those who enter," etc.

Third, concerning pride in one's beauty, I say that one must not exalt or take pride in the beauty of one's body. It is said in Proverbs 31: "Grace is deceitful and beauty is vain," etc. For that is properly called "vain" which cannot keep its condition for long, such as the beauty of our body. Therefore the latter is like a fading and wilting flower which flourishes for a while and then withers and finally vanishes altogether; James 1: "The flower has wilted, and the splendor of his face has gone." As a leaf on a tree first grows green, then falls in the mud, thirdly is trampled upon by wild animals, and fourthly rots away and never returns to the tree, just so does man's beauty flower in youth, dry up in old age, fall in death, and get trampled on in the grave by wild animals and men with respect to the body, and by the devils with respect to the soul, and the same beauty will never return to the same body; Isaiah 14: "Your pride is brought down to hell, your carcass is fallen down; under you shall the moth be strewed, and worms shall be your covering." Behold, beloved: though a man's life was flourishing, after his death it is found

Quarto dico non superbiendum in potencia et dignitate. Nam qui in ista
gloriatur, similis puelle est pauperrime que in estate in ludo puellarum
100   regina constituitur mutuatis ornamentis ab aliis. Que circumspiciens in
dignitate tali, status pristini oblita, regnare veraciter se credit et
ideo alias contempnit coetaneas; set die advesperante, cum quelibet vestimenta sua receperit, que prius regina apparebat iam pauper et nuda remanebit. Sic revera mundani in potencia et dignitate gloriantes statum humane
105   miserie obliti gaudent, rident, et huiusmodi; set die mortis appropinquante, que nox dici potest respectu vite presentis, cum mundo reddiderit que
ab illo mutuavit, sine potencia et dignitate, nudus et pauper remanebit.

Quod bene figuratum erat Machabeorum 9 de Anthiocho, qui pre nimia
eius ⟨superbia⟩ videbatur sibi fluctibus maris imperare, montes in statera
110   appendere, et tamen consumptus vermibus et fetore expiravit. Item ut habetur Danielis 4 quod Nabuchodonosor qui dignitatem et honorem a Deo sibi
datam ex propria virtute putabat redundare, dicendo: "Nonne hec est Babylon, civitas magna, quam ego edificavi in domum meam et in robore fortitudinis mee et gloria decoris mee?" Et ecce, "cum adhuc esset sermo in ore
115   eius, vox de celo irruit dicens: 'Tibi dicitur, Nabuchodonosor rex, regnum
tuum transiet a te et ab omnibus eicient te; cum bestiis et feris habitacio
tua erit.' " Quod eadem hora factum est. Et ideo bene dicitur in Psalmo:
"Homo cum in honore esset non intellexit; comparatus est iumentis insipien-
tibus et similis factus est illis."
120   Revera sic contingit quandoque de modernis, quod propter ⟨eventus⟩
fortuitos despiciunt minores et ⟨credunt⟩ dignitatem habitam ex propriis
meritis evenire. Set caveant, quia procul dubio aliter continget de eis;
sicud contingit de milvis et cornicibus quas capiunt pueri et excecant, et
postea in altum volare cogunt, que miserabiliter volant hinc inde, in altum
125   erigunt usque pre cecitate collo fracto mortue cadunt. Revera sic superbia
mundi. Cum enim aliquos tales aliqua fortuna ⟨ceperit⟩, spiritualiter statim oculos cordis excecat, sic quod in altum dignitatis volantes et statum
pristinum obliviscentes quasi inoppinate cadunt et animam eterne ⟨dampnaci-
oni⟩ exponunt. Ecclesiastici 11: "Multi potentes oppressi sunt valde, et
130   gloriosi traditi sunt in manus alienorum." Et in Psalmo: "Deiecisti, Domine, dum allevarentur," etc. Et Ecclesiastici 10: "Hodie rex est et cras
morietur." Igitur contra istud peccatum pre ceteris considerandum est quod
Christus natus est de pauperibus; similiter Saul electus in regem post se-
quelam asini patris sui, Regum 10; similiter David de custodia ovium, Regum
135   16. Et ideo in dignitate non est gloriandum, set super omnia Deo regraci-
andum.

Quinto eciam de generis nobilitate non est gloriandum, quia dicitur Malachie 2: "Nonne unus est pater omnium vestrum?" Quare unusquisque ergo
contempnit fratrem suum? Non enim fecit Deus unum hominem aureum et
140   alium luteum, set omnes de eadem materia equaliter creavit, ut sic in eadem

to be vile and despised. For he who used to greet you in life by taking off his hood and bending his knees, then puts his foot on your skull and nose, nor will the dead be remembered, however noble he may have been; Malachi near the end: "You shall tread down the wicked when they shall be ashes under the sole of your feet."

Fourth, I say that one must not take pride in one's power and rank. He who does so is like that very poor girl who in summertime, in a game among girls, is made their queen by borrowing fine clothes from her playmates. As she looks around her in that dignity, she forgets her former condition and believes herself truly to be a queen and thus despises her playfellows. But when evening comes and each of the girls has taken back her own clothes, she who first appeared to be the queen will now remain poor and naked. In the same way, worldly people who take pride in their power and rank and forget the condition of human misery, will rejoice and laugh and the like; but when the day of death approaches, which can be called night in relation to our present life, as they give back to the world what they had borrowed from it, they will remain without power and rank, naked and poor.

This was prefigured in Antiochus, of Maccabees 9, who thought in his excessive pride he could command the flood of the sea and weigh mountains in his scale, and yet he died eaten by worms and in stench. Likewise, in Daniel 4, Nebuchadnezzar thought that the rank and honor which God had given him came from his own power, and he said: "Is this not Babylon the great city, which I have built to be my house, by the strength of my power and in the glory of my excellence?" And lo, "while the word was still in his mouth a voice came down from heaven and said: 'To you, O king Nebuchadnezzar, it is said: Your kingdom shall pass from you, and they shall cast you out from among men; your dwelling shall be with cattle and wild beasts.'" Which happened in that selfsame hour. Thus it is fittingly said in the Psalm: "While man was in his honor and did not understand, he was compared to the brute beasts and made like them."

Thus it sometimes happens to our contemporaries: because of some good fortune they look down on lower-class people and think the rank they hold comes from their own merits. But let them beware, for beyond doubt it will turn out differently; as it happens with kites and crows which boys catch and blind and then force to fly aloft, so that they fly miserably hither and thither and climb up high until in their blindness they fall down dead with their necks broken. Thus also the pride of this world. When it catches such people with some good fortune, it spiritually blinds the eyes of their heart so that they fly up to a high position and forget their former condition, but then they unexpectedly fall and send their soul to eternal damnation. Ecclesiasticus 11: "Many mighty ones have been overcome, and those full of glory have been given into the hands of strangers." And in the Psalm: "You have cast them down, Lord, when they were lifted up," etc. And Ecclesiasticus 10: "A king is today, and tomorrow he shall die." Against this sin we should foremost keep in mind

caritate permanentes equales a primeva creacione se intelligant omnes esse.
Nonne de eodem genere est furfur et farina, ex eadem radice procedit pungens spina atque rosa, et ex eadem arbore fructus dulcis et corruptus?
Revera sic magni et parvi, divites et ⟨pauperes⟩ ex una materia et pari
145 forma creantur, quamvis fortuna quosdam erigit et quosdam deicit; Sapiencie
6: "Pusillum et magnum ipse fecit et equalis est ei cura de omnibus." Unde
Gregorius: "Omnes, inquit, homines equaliter natura genuit; culpa hominem
homini prefecit." Et ideo qui querunt propter parentelam honorari et preferri, similes sunt statuis ⟨depictis⟩ que ad tempus in ecclesiis honoran-
150 tur et postmodum in igne comburuntur. Unde illud Malachie ultimo: "Ecce
dies Domini veniet succensa quasi caminus, ⟨et⟩ erunt omnes superbi et
iniquitatem facientes sicud stipula: inflammabit eos." Ab huiusmodi ergo
superbia caveamus, quia precedente [M, f. 5v] enim superbia semper pro fine
sequitur confusio, prout metrice dicitur:

155   Si tibi copia, si sapiencia formaque detur,
          Sola superbia destruit omnia si comitetur.

[[Anglice sic:

          Pruyde þat is ouergart
          Algate haþ vnquart
160   At þe latter ende.
          For when pryde goþ byfore,
          Schame sewyth euermore,
          Wende hou he wende.]]

2–3 in pulcritudine . . . nobilitate] *corr evidently in light of the sections in this chapter*
M; in potencia, in nobilitate, in generis dignitate R.W.   **9** homo] R.W; *om* M.   **14** esse]
R.W; *om* M.   istorum] istarum R.   **20** precedente campana] R.W; precedentem campanam M.   **21** quod] R.W; *om* M.   **23** qui] R.W; *om* M.   **27** iuxta Apostolum] R.W;
om M.   **28** in] R.W; *om* M.   **29** facit] fit R.   **30** anima] R.W; *om* M.   **31** deferuntur]
W; defertur M; dominantur R.   **32** sancto] R.W; *om* M.   **33** sedentem] stantem R.W.
34 intimaret] indicaret R.W.   **41** fixum] infixum R.W.   **45** imponitur] imprimitur
R.W.   **48** captivitatem] capcionem R.W.   **65** Secundo] *add* de M.   **68** non] R.W; *om*
M.   **77** accendit] R; abscondit M.W.   **79** de . . . pulchritudinis] *om* R.W.   **83** desciduo] R.W; deciso M *corr.*   virescit] R.W; crescit M.   **85** decor] *interl* R.W; *om* M.
91 corpus] *om* R.W.   **95–96** rememorabitur] remurmurabit M; remurmerabitur R; rememorabit W.   **107** pauper] *add* et miser R.W.   **109** superbia] R.W; potencia *marg* M.
114 mee] mei R.   **118–119** insipientibus] *added on erasure* M; *om* R.W.   **120** eventus]
R.W; eventos M.   **121** credunt] R.W; credent M.   **126** ceperit] R *corr from* ceperint;
ceperint M.W.   **128–129** dampnacioni] R.W; dampnacionis M.   **144** pauperes] R.W;
pauperi M.   **149** depictis] *corr from* despectis R; despectis *and marg* pictis M; despectis
W.   **151** et] R.W; *apparently expuncted and replaced by* ibi M.   **157–163** Anglice . . .
wende] *text from* R. *Verse 7, in* B3.D.E.Go1.Go2.L1.L2.Li.LC.R.V.W1.

that Christ was born of poor parents; similarly, Saul was elected king after following his father's ass, Kings 10; and David was called from keeping the sheep, Kings 16. Thus we should not take pride in our rank but for all things give thanks to God.

Fifth, we should also not take pride in the nobility of our blood, for in Malachi 2 it is written: "Is not one the father of all?" Why, therefore, does everyone look down on his brother? God did not make one man from gold and another from mud; rather, he created all alike from the same substance, so that all might live in the same love and perceive that on the basis of their original creation they are all equal. Do not bran and flour come from the same grain? Do not the pricking thorn and the rose grow out of the same root? Does not sweet and rotten fruit grow on the same tree? Likewise, the great and the small, the rich and the poor are created from the same substance and in like shape, even though fortune raises some and flings down others; Wisdom 6: "He has made the small and the great and has equal care for all." Therefore says Gregory: "Nature has created all men alike; it is sin that has set one man over the other." Therefore, those who seek to be honored and put ahead because of their lineage are like painted statues which are worshiped in churches for a while and then are burned in fire. Whence Malachi says in the end: "Behold, the day of the Lord will come burning like an oven, and all that are proud and have done wickedness will be like stubble: it will set them on fire." Therefore let us avoid such pride, for always pride goes before and shame follows after, as it is expressed in the following verses:

> If many riches you possess,
>   Wisdom and great beauty,
> Pride alone destroys it all
>   If it accompany.

In English thus:

> Pruyde þat is ouergart . . .

---

6 Luke 16.19–31. **8** Ecclus. 11.4. **17–21** Also in *Tabula exemplorum*, pp. 96–97. **21–24** Rev. 9.13–17. **24–27** Also in *Tabula exemplorum*, No. 138(b) and note. **27–28** 1 Tim. 5.6. **28–29** *Meditationes piissimae* III.8 (PL 184:490). **32–37** Cf. Tubach 1660; also in Peraldus, *Summa vitiorum* VI.iii.14. **38–43** Also ibidem. **55–56** Jth. 9.1. **56–57** Cf. Esther 4.2–3. **57–58** Dan. 9.3. **58–60** Jon. 3.6–9. **67–69** Wisd. 6.24. **76–78** Luke 11.34. **80–81** Prov. 31.30. **84–85** James 1.11. **91–92** Isa. 14.11. **96–97** Mal. 4.3. **108–110** 2 Macc. 9.8–10. **111–117** Dan. 4.26–30. **117–119** Ps. 48.13. **129–130** Ecclus. 11.6. **130–131** Ps. 72.18. **131–132** Ecclus. 10.12. **133–134** 1 Sam. 9. **134–135** 1 Sam. 16. **138** Mal. 2.10. **146** Wisd. 6.8. **147–148** Gregory, *Moralia* XXVI.xxvi.46 (PL 76:376). **150–152** Mal. 4.1. **155–156** *Prov* 29238 and *Verses* p. 142.

I.vi   DETESTACIO SUPERBIE

Sequitur iam tercio quare spiritualiter est detestanda superbia. Ubi
respondetur primo quia habitaculum anime subruit et confundit. Secundum
enim Philosophum libro 3 *Metheororum* terremotus fit ex vento in ventre
terre exagitato, ex ⟨quo⟩ terra necessario movetur; ad ⟨cuius⟩ nimirum
5   motum nonnunquam ruunt palacia, prosternuntur edificia. Sic superbia in
anima quasi quidam ventus est interclusus et agitatus in terra. Dum illa
⟨que⟩ per humilitatem stabilis et quieta esse deberet vehementer et perni-
ciose se commovet, in ea Christi habitaculum subruit et funditus destruit.
Unde Ysydorus *De summo bono*, libro 1, capitulo 38: "Qui, inquit, inflatur
10   superbia, a vento ⟨pascitur⟩." Et non tantum hoc set eciam Christi habitaculum, idest animam fidelem, simpliciter perimit.

Secundum enim Rabanum *De naturis rerum* et Ysydorum *Ethimologiarum*
12 est quedam aspis, prester nomine, que quem percusserit enormi corpulencia
⟨necat⟩. Sic spiritus superbie dum quempiam in anima suo ⟨veneno⟩ inficit,
15   confestim interimit; unde Deuteronomii 32: "Venenum aspidum insanabile."

Item si miles aliquis regem dominum suum armis ipsis ab eo receptis ad
eius inimicum se transferens hostiliter impugnaret, nonne iuste ingratus et
iniuriosus diceretur? Sic in proposito superbus ⟨graciis⟩ a Deo sibi datis pro
armis ipsum Deum superbiendo impugnat; Iob 15: "Tetendit adversus Deum
20   manum suam et contra Omnipotentem est roboratus." Unde Gregorius ait:
"Scio, inquit, omnia vicia a Deo fugiunt, sola superbia semper se opponit."

Et nota quod superbia est detestanda quia nocet oculis anime sicud
fumus oculis corporis. Et bene assimilatur fumo, nam sicud fumus in ymo
densatur et ⟨sursum⟩ elevatus adnichilatur, sic superbus in sui reputacione
25   est magnus set in futuro adnichilatur. Psalmista: "Vidi impium superexalta-
tum;" et sequitur: "Quemadmodum fumus deficient." Similiter ex igne oritur
set lucis heredem non constituit; sic superbia de natura bona est orta,
sicud tinea de veste, vermis de fructu, rubigo de auro, et tamen illud de
⟨quo⟩ oritur ⟨corrumpit⟩ et consummit. Similiter quanto alcius ascendit,
30   tanto cicius cadet.

---

4 quo] R; qua M.W.   cuius] R.W; quod M.   **7** que] R *interl*; *om* M.W.   **10** pascitur]
R.W; *om* M.   eciam] *add* ipsum R.W.   **14** necat] R; necatur M.W.   veneno] feneno M
(*a characteristic habit of M*).   **15** 32] *add* dicitur R.W.   **18** graciis] R.W; gratus M.
21 Scio] cum *corr* R.   **24** sursum] R.W; rursum M.   **26** et sequitur] *om* R.W.   **29** quo]
R.W; *om* M.   corrumpit] R.W; corrumpitur M.

I.vi   WHY PRIDE MUST BE SCORNED

In the third part we ask why pride must be despised in our mind. The
answer is, first, because it destroys and demolishes the dwelling-place of the
soul. According to the Philosopher, in Book 3 of his *Meteorology*, an earthquake is caused by the violent movement of wind in the bowels of the earth, by
which the earth is shaken; at whose strong movement often palaces fall down and
large buildings are flattened. Pride in our soul is similarly like a wind that
is shut up and violently moved in the earth. When the soul, which should
remain stable and quiet in humility, is in violent and harmful commotion, it
overturns and completely destroys Christ's dwelling-place in it. Therefore
Isidore says in *On the Highest Good*, book 1, chapter 38: "He who is swollen
with pride feeds on wind." And not only that, but he simply ruins Christ's
dwelling-place itself, that is, the faithful soul.

According to Rabanus in *The Nature of Things* and Isidore in *Etymologies*,
12, there is a certain asp called prester which, when it strikes, kills with an
enormous swelling. Thus the spirit of pride kills at once whomever it infects
with its poison in his soul. Hence in Deuteronomy 32 it is said: "The poison
of asps is fatal."

Further, if a knight were to go over to the enemy and fight against the
king his lord with the same weapons that he had received from his king, would
it not be just to call him ungrateful and criminal? In the same fashion, in
being proud the proud person fights against God with the help of the graces God
has given him as weapons; Job 15: "He has stretched out his hand against God
and mounted his strength against the Almighty." Wherefore Gregory says: "I
know that all vices flee before God, pride alone always withstands him."

And notice that pride must be despised because it harms the eyes of the
soul, as smoke harms the eyes of the body. It is fittingly likened to smoke
because as smoke condenses near the ground and evaporates when it rises up, so
the proud person is great in his own estimation, but in the future he comes to
nothing; the Psalmist declares: "I have seen the wicked highly exalted"; and
further: "They shall come to nothing, like smoke." Similarly, smoke is born of
fire but does not inherit light; likewise pride is born from a good substance,
just as a moth from clothing, a worm from fruit, and tarnish from gold, and yet
it spoils and consumes what it is born of. Similarly, the higher smoke rises,
the swifter it will fall.

3–5 Aristotle, *Meteorologica* II.viii (365b).   **9–10** Isidore, *Sent.* II.xxxviii.4 (PL
83:639).   **12–14** Isidore, *Etym.* XII.iv.16; Rabanus, *De universo* VIII.3 (PL 111:231).
15 Deut. 32.33.   **19–20** Job 15.25.   **25–26** Ps. 36.35, 20.

I.vii   DE MEMBRIS SUPERBIE

Demum ad membra superbie procedendum est, eo quod capud membra secuntur sicud discipuli magistrum. Set advertendum quod eius membra quatuor
sunt ⟨consideranda⟩, videlicet ypocrisis simulacio, inobediencie usurpacio,
vane glorie captacio, iactancie elevacio.

5   Ypocrite autem similes sunt trutannis qui cum accessus hominum intel-
ligerint, labia movent sanctitatem ⟨pretendentes⟩, ut cicius a transeuntibus aliquid accipiant, set cum pertransierint in dissolucionem prorumpun-
tur. Revera sic ypocrite in conspectu hominum orant, ieiunant, et huiusmodi
⟨faciunt⟩ ut ab hominibus videantur; set in latibulo faciunt omnia contra-
10   ria, nam orant clamorose ut ab hominibus audiantur, set revera cor dissonat
longe ab ore; Ysaie 29: "Populus hic labiis me honorat, cor autem eorum
longe," etc.

Et nota quod tria oriuntur mala ex] [C, f. 1] oracione clamorosa:
primum quod sic orans Deum ubique esse non credit nec abscondita cordis
15   audire, quod est hereticum dicere; secundum est quod oraciones mittit ad
aures hominum, a quibus deridetur; et tercium malum est quod alium iuxta
illum perfecte orare volentem impedit. Et ideo iuxta illud Matthei: "Cum
oraveris, intra cubiculum tuum," etc. Nam Deus non verborum set cordis est
auditor, iuxta illud metrice:

20   Non vox set votum, non musica cordula set cor,
               Non clamor set amor sonat in aure Dei.

[Anglice sic:

          Ne monnes steuen but gode wylle,
          No murthe of mouth but herte stylle,
25   No cry but love no þer bere
          Nys murthe ny song God to here.]

Unde Crisostomus *Super Mattheum*, omelia 19: "Si, inquit, oraciones nostras
non audimus qui petimus, quomodo ut audiamur a Deo rogamus?" Hec ille. Et
ideo humiliter sine aliqua ypocrisi insistendum est orando cum publicano
30   qui stetit a longe et descendit iustificatus a Domino, et non cum Phariseo
qui fuit reprobatus, Luce 9. Nam sicut sagittator primo ad terram se inclinat ut sagittam alcius emittat, sic qui orat prius se humiliare debet, quia
iuxta Sapientem Ecclesiastici 35: "Oracio humiliantis nubes penetrat."
Exemplum de Chananea que per humilitatem veniam optinuit dum se catellis
35   comparavit, Matthei 15. Unde Crisostomus: "Orans, inquit, nichil novum
faciat quod homines appetunt nec voce clamet nec manus expandet nec impru-

I.vii   THE MEMBERS OF PRIDE

Finally we must turn to the members of pride, for the members follow their head as the disciples their master. Notice that four members of pride must be considered: the deceit of hypocrisy, the practice of disobedience, the clutching of vainglory, and the arrogance of boasting.

Hypocrites are like fake beggars who, when they have noticed someone coming, move their lips in pretended holiness, in order to receive something from the passersby, but when they are gone they dissolve into laughter. Thus in the sight of men hypocrites pray, fast, and do similar works that they may be seen by people; but in secret they do all the opposite, for they pray aloud that they may be heard by people, but in fact their heart is far from their mouth. Isaiah 29: "This people honors me with their lips, but their heart is far from me," and so on.

And notice that three evils arise from noisy prayer. The first is that a person who prays in this way does not believe that God is everywhere and hears what lies hidden in man's heart, which is heretical to maintain. Second, he sends his prayers to the ears of men who laugh at him. Third, he hinders another person near him who wants to pray in a fitting way. According to Matthew: "When you pray, go into your chamber," etc. For God hears not words but the heart, as in the verse:

> Not your voice but your vow,
> Not stringed music but your heart,
> Not shouting but your love
> Sounds in the ear of God.

In English thus:

> Ne monnes steuen . . .

Therefore Chrysostom comments in *On Matthew*, homily 19: "If we do not hear our own prayers, we who say them, how do we ask God to hear us?" We must beseech him humbly without hypocrisy and pray with the Publican who stood from afar and went away justified, not with the Pharisee who was reprimanded, Luke 9. As an archer first bends to the earth so that he can shoot his arrow higher, the person who prays must first humble himself, for according to the wise man, Ecclesiasticus 35, "the prayer of a humble person penetrates the clouds." We have as an example the woman of Canaan who through her humility obtained grace when she compared herself to the little dogs, Matthew 15. Therefore Chrysostom says: "Let the person who prays not do anything novel which pleases people, nor

denter oculos ad celum tollat." Hec ille. Sit ergo oracio tua in abscondito,
ut Pater tuus, etc.

 Secundum membrum superbie est contemptus sive inobediencia exterior,
40 que secundum diffinicionem Crisostomi est vicium ex propria voluntate
proveniens hominem Deo et suo superiori inobedientem reddens. Et a propria
voluntate ⟨recedendum est⟩ tamquam a via pessima. Unde Bernardus in sermone
De lepra Naaman: "Quid, inquit, odit Deus aut quid punit nisi propriam
voluntatem? Cesset ergo (dicit ipse) propria voluntas, et iam non erit
45 infernus." [Nam "ipsa est," prout dicit in sermone *De cena Domini*, "qui in
potestate redigit tenebrarum et nos subicit mortis imperio."] Unde legitur
Regum 23: "Factus est sermo Domini ad virum Dei dicens: 'Quia non obediens
fuisti ori Domini set comedisti panem et bibisti aquam in loco contra
preceptum Domini, etc., non [f. 1v] infertur cadaver tuum in sepulcrum
50 patrum tuorum.' Et percussus est a leone in via et cadaver eius proiectum
est in itinere." Unde Bernardus: "Maximum est, inquit, vicium quo angelus
amisit celum, Saul regnum, Salomon amorem Dei," etc.

 Tercium membrum est vana gloria que semper Deum inpugnat, sicut miles
regi aut filius patri ingratissimus dicitur si contra illum pugnaret in
55 armis ab eo receptis, vel filius cum bonis collatis contra patrem, etc.
Gregorius: "Qui accepta bona sibi arrogat, suis contra Deum donis pugnat."

 Quartum membrum est iactancia, que detestanda est, que non differt
multum a vana gloria. Et est quando quis laudando facta propria aut dicta
ostendit se habere quod non habet, puta in sciencia, in fortitudine, et
60 cetera. Contra quam ait Christus in Mattheo: "Attendite ne iusticiam
vestram faciatis coram hominibus ut videamini ab eis; alioquin mercedem,"
etc. Set opera que sunt per iactanciam magnificata et publicata iuste sunt
a mercede frustrata. Unde Christus concludit: "Amen, dico vobis, receperunt
mercedem suam."

65 Et hec de superbia et eius membris sufficiant.

---

3 consideranda] R.W; considerata M. 5–6 intelligerint] intellexerint *corr* R.B2.B3.Co.
Go1.Go2.; intelligerent W. 6 pretendentes] R.W; precedentes M. 9 faciunt] R.W; faciant M. 13 oracione] C *begins here. For editorial principles, see Introduction.*
15 est(2)] *om* O. 17 Et ideo] *om* O. 18 tuum etc.] *om* O. 19 metrice] *om* O. 22–
26 Anglice . . . here] *text from* R. *Verse 9, in* B3.E.Go1.Go2.Jo.L1.L2.Li.LC.R.Sp.V.
W1. 28 audiamur] audiantur M; audiat R.W. 39 Secundum] *add* autem O. 42 rece-
dendum est] non recedentem C. 53 membrum] vicium O. 55 etc.] unde O. Gre-
gorius] *add* in moralibus R.W; *add* moralium M. 58 quis] aliquis O. 60 cetera]
huiusmodi O. 63 Unde Christus concludit] dicitur in mattheo *after* vobis R.W; *om* M.
65 sufficiunt] sufficiant O.

cry out loud, nor stretch out his hands, nor turn up his eyes to the sky like a fool." Therefore, let your prayer be in secret, that your father, etc.

The second member of pride is open contempt or disobedience, which after a definition by Chrysostom is a vice that comes from self-will and renders man disobedient to God and to his superior. Therefore one must withdraw from self-will as from a most dangerous path. Whence Bernard says in his *Sermon on the Leprosy of Naaman*: "What does God hate or punish if not self-will? Let self-will cease, and there will be no hell." For it is self-will, as he says in his *Sermon on the Last Supper*, that leads us into the power of darkness and subjects us to the rule of death. Whence we read in Kings 23: "The word of the Lord came to the man of God saying: 'Because you have not been obedient to the Lord but have eaten bread and drunk water in a place against the Lord's commandment, etc., your dead body will not be brought into the sepulcher of your fathers.' And he was killed by a lion and his body was cast in the way." Therefore Bernard says: "It is the greatest vice, by which the angel lost heaven, Saul his kingdom, Solomon the love of God," and so forth.

The third member is vainglory, which always struggles against God; just as a knight is called most ungrateful to his king if he fights against him with the weapons he has received from him, or a son is most ungrateful to his father if he fights against him with the goods the latter has bestowed on him, etc. Gregory says: "He who claims for himself the goods he has received fights against God with God's own gifts."

The fourth member to be detested is boasting, which does not much differ from vainglory. It occurs when someone by praising his own deeds or words shows off as if he had what he does not really have, such as knowledge, strength, and the like. Against this vice Christ said in Matthew: "See to it that you do not work your justice before men to be seen by them; otherwise you shall not have a reward," etc. But good deeds that are blown up and publicized through boasting are justly deprived of their reward. And therefore Christ concludes: "Amen, I say unto you, they have received their reward."

And this much should be sufficient about pride and its members.

11–12 Isa. 29.13.   **13–17** Cf. Ps.-Chrysostom, *Opus imperfectum*, hom. 13 (PG 56:710).   **17–18** Matt. 6.6.   **20–21** *Prov* 18723 and *Verses*, p. 143.   **27–28** Chrysostom, *In Matthaeum*, hom. 19, 3 (PG 57:276).   **29–31** Luke 18.10–14.   **33** Ecclus. 35.21.   **34–35** Matt. 15.22–28.   **35–37** Ps.-Chrysostom, *Opus imperfectum*, hom. 13 (PG 56:709).   **37–38** Cf. Matt. 6.6.   **43–45** Bernard, *In Resurrectione*, sermo 3, 3 (5:105).   **45–46** Bernard, *De diversis*, sermo 11, 2 (6.1:125), quoting Col. 1.13.   **47–51** Cf. 1 Kings 13.20–24.   **60–62** Matt. 6.1.   **63–64** Matt. 6.2.

I.viii   DE HUMILITATE

[N]unc autem expleta parte superbie cum suis membris et oblectamentis offert se domina Humilitas econtra tamquam istorum expugnatrix ac bonorum reparatrix. Ipsa enim est radix et fundamentum omnis boni. Circa quam sic intendo procedere: primo videre qualis est et quare imitanda; secundo, qui-
5   bus est humiliandum; tercio, que introducunt humilitatem; et quarto, que sit merces humiliancium.

Dico ergo primo quod humilitas est voluntaria mentis inclinacio et proprie excellencie contemptus.

Est igitur humilitas sic decripta imitanda, primo quia sue angustie
10   est paciens tolleratrix; ut matrona a viro suo iniuriose tractata pacienter sustinet ne virum dignum vituperio reddat, et si forte vituperio ex verberibus lesio foris appareat, illam caute dissimulat [f. 2] asserens se aliunde tale malum incurrisse. Ecclesiastici 2 dicitur: "Aurum et argentum in igne probantur," etc. Unde Augustinus: "Beati, inquit, humiles qui, etsi
15   quando fieri solet ut iniustas audiant increpaciones, amplius se Christo humilient et minus se audire quam meruerunt proclamant." Secundo, quia mala sua recogitans est bonorum morum occultatrix, sicut pavo aspiciens pedes turpissimos caudam suam dimittit lucentem. Unde Luce 18: "Publicanus a longe stans noluit levare oculos ad celum set percuciens pectus suum ait:
20   'Deus, propicius,' " etc. Et sequitur: "Amen dico vobis, descendit hic iustificatus in domum suam, quia omnis qui se exaltat, humiliabitur," etc. Tercio, quia operum Christi crebra inspectrix et assecutrix. Ad modum quo aquila contra solem irreverberatis oculis respicit, sic vere humilis opera Christi qui est sol iusticie, Ysaie 66: "Ad quem aspiciamus nisi ad humi-
25   lem," scilicet Christum, ut eum imitemur, scilicet quomodo se Patri humiliavit—cui erat equalis in deitate—in assumpcione humane nature; Philippensium 2: "Qui cum in forma Dei esset," etc. Quomodo se eciam humiliavit parentibus in voluntaria subiectione; Luce 2: "Erat subditus illis." Et tercio erat humilis peccatoribus, quia "usque ad mortem," ut sic sibi
30   humiliemus animas nostras, pro peccatis primo corde conterendo, secundo ore confitendo, et tercio opere satisfaciendo. Et de istis quere in titulo "De confessione."

Si ergo sic fecerimus, se habebit Christus erga nos sicut leo ad hominem, qui secundum Rabanum micior est captivis et prostratis quam erectis
35   et dominantibus. Certe sic Christus erga humiles magis quam superbis, nam humilibus parcit et superbis [resistentibus lacerat et perimit; Osee 13: "Occurram ei quasi ursa raptis catulis et disperdam quasi leo." Unde Ysidorus: "Descende, inquit, ut ascendas, humilia te ut exalteris, ne exaltatus humilieris." Et nota: Si quis enim vellet ascendere montem pre-
40   eminentem, necesse est ipsum inclinare, ne forte si erectus ascenderet

I.viii   HUMILITY

After the section on pride and its members and false pleasures has been
completed, Lady Humility now rises against them to overcome them and to
restore the good qualities. For she is the root and foundation of every good.
In treating humility I plan to proceed as follows: first we shall see what it is
and why it should be practiced; second, to whom we must humble ourselves;
third, what things lead to humility; and fourth, what the reward of people who
humble themselves is.

First, then, I say that humility is the voluntary lowering of our mind and
contempt for our own superiority.

Humility as thus defined must be practiced, first because it patiently
endures its troubles; just as a wife who is mistreated by her husband suffers
it patiently so that she may not cause her husband to become worthy of public
shame, and if perhaps, to his shame, some external lesion from his beating can
be seen on her, she carefully dissimulates saying she took such an injury
elsewhere. In Ecclesiasticus 2 it is said: "Gold and silver are tried in the
fire," and so forth. Whence Augustine says: "Blessed are the humble who, if it
sometimes happens that they hear unjust accusations against them, humble themselves further before Christ and declare they hear less than they have deserved." Humility must be striven for secondly because it reflects on its
shortcomings and hides its good qualities, like the peacock which, seeing that
its feet are most vile, forgets about its splendid tail. Therefore in Luke 18:
"The Publican, standing afar off, would not lift his eyes up to heaven but
striking his breast said: 'Lord, have mercy on me,' " etc. And then follows:
"Amen, I say to you, this man went down into his house justified, because
everyone that exalts himself will be humbled," etc. Third, humility must be
striven for because it frequently meditates on and follows Christ's deeds. As
the eagle looks at the sun with unblinking eyes, just so does a truly humble
person look at Christ's deeds, who is the sun of justice. Isaiah 66: "To whom
shall we look if not to the humble one," that is, Christ, that we may follow
him, that is, in the way he has humbled himself before the Father—whose equal
he was in divinity—by assuming human nature; Philippians 2: "Who, while he
was in the form of God," etc. Further, in the way he humbled himself before his
parents in voluntary submission; Luke 2: "He became subject to them." And in
the third place he humbled himself before sinners "even unto death," so that we
might humble our souls before him, first by having contrition of heart for our
sins, second by confession of mouth, and third by satisfaction in deed. On
these matters see under the title "On Confession."

If we do this, Christ will act toward us as the lion does toward humans;
according to Rabanus, he is gentler to people who are prostrate and captives
than to those who stand upright and are domineering. Certainly, in the same

posset descendere eiectus; ita certe cum humilitate celum ascenditur, sicud
cum superbia ad inferos proicitur. In cuius figura, ut habetur 1 Regum 14,
Ionathas ascendit clivum montis "reptans manibus et pedibus, et armiger
eius post eum;" sic Christus in celum manibus et pedibus cruci affixis et
45   capite inclinato, cuius armiger verus humilis est quia humilitatem sue
vite, passionis, et ⟨mortis⟩ vere sequitur. Vas enim non impletur aqua de
puteo nisi inclinetur aut profunde mergatur; sic nec homo gracia Dei nisi
humilietur. Ecclesiastici ultimo: "Inclinavi modicum animam et accepi sapienciam." "Quanto ergo ⟨maior⟩ es, humilia te in omnibus et invenies gra-
50   ciam."]

1 membris et] *om* O.   4 procedere] *add* videlicet O.   5 est] sit O. et] *om* O.   14 etc.]
homines vero acceptabiles in camino humiliacionis O.   16 humilient] humiliant O.
17 pedes] *add* suos O.   20 Deus propicius] domine miserere mei O.   21 humiliabitur]
om O.   26 deitate] divinitate O.   29 erat humilis] se humiliavit O.   31 et] *om* O.
quere] *add* infra O.   35 dominantibus] dominativis O.   36 superbis resistentibus] M.W;
superbos resistentes R.   36–50 resistentibus . . . graciam] resistit C; *text from* M.
46 mortis] R.W; morte M.   49 maior] amor M.

I.ix   QUIBUS EST HUMILIANDUM: DEO

[S]equitur quibus sit humiliandum. Ad quod respondetur quod dupplici-
ter, scilicet spiritualiter et corporaliter, hoc est, tam Deo quam homini,
sicut fecit ipsemet Christus, qui primo Deo Patri obedivit dicens: "Non mea
voluntas set tua fiat." Docuit eciam matri Ecclesie obedire quando assumpto
5   f[l]agello de funiculis eiecit vendentes et ementes de templo [f. 2v] dicens: "Domus mea domus oracionis vocabitur." Et ideo debetis eam revereri
et sibi humiliari. Tercio eciam docuit hominibus humiliari quando neque
regi neque regine set Ioseph lignifabri et matri paupercule erat subditus,
Luce 2.
10   Set quia dicitur magis oportet Deo obedire quam hominibus, ideo Deo
tamquam patri qui fecit nos et non ipsi nos precipue debemus obedire, et
hoc secundum nature processum, quia filii magis obediunt patri quam aliis.
Set ipse est pater noster precipuus tripliciter: primo generaliter per
creacionem, secundo specialiter per gracie adopcionem, et tercio singulari-
15   ter per nature nostre incarnacionem. Et ideo bene dicitur et vocatur in
oracione dominica "Pater noster," in signum quod pre ceteris sibi debemus

way Christ will be more gentle to the humble than to the proud, for the former
he spares, but the proud who resist him he tears to pieces and destroys; Hosea
13: "I will confront him like the bear whose cubs have been taken away and will
disperse him like the lion." Therefore Isidore says: "Step down so that you
may climb up; humble yourself that you may be exalted, lest by exalting yourself you be humbled." Notice: if someone wants to climb a steep mountain, he
must needs bend down, lest by walking erect he might fall off; thus one surely
climbs to heaven with humility, just as through pride one is flung to hell. As
a type of this, according to 1 Kings 14, Jonathan climbed the slope of the
mountain "crawling on hands and feet, and his squire behind him." Thus Christ
climbed to heaven, with his hands and feet nailed to the cross and his head
bent down; his squire is the truly humble person who sincerely follows the
humility of Christ's life, passion, and death. For a vessel is not filled with
water from a well unless it is lowered and deeply immersed; likewise man is not
filled with God's grace unless he humbles himself. At the end of Ecclesiasticus: "I have bent my soul a little and have received wisdom." Therefore, the
greater you are, humble yourself, and you will find grace.

13–14 Ecclus. 2.5.   **18–20** Luke 18.13–14.   **24–25** Cf. Isa. 66.2.   **27** Phil. 2.6.
28 Luke 2.51.   **29** Phil. 2.8.   **31–32** *FM* V.   **34–35** Rabanus, *De universo* VIII.1 (PL
111:217).   **37** Hos. 13.8.   **38–39** Isidore, *Synonyma* II.21 (PL 83:850).   **43–44** 1 Sam.
14.13.   **48–49** Ecclus. 51.21.   **49–50** Ecclus. 3.20.

I.ix   HUMBLING ONESELF BEFORE GOD

Next we ask before whom one must humble oneself. To which we reply that
we must do so in two ways, namely spiritually and bodily, and that means before
God as well as before man, as Christ himself did, who first obeyed his Father
saying: "Not my will be done but yours." He further taught us to obey our
mother the Church, when he took a scourge made of ropes and drove those who
were selling and buying from the temple, saying: "My house shall be called a
house of prayer." Therefore you should hold the Church in reverence and humble
yourselves before it. And thirdly he taught us to humble ourselves before men,
as "he was subject," Luke 2, not to king or queen but to Joseph, a carpenter,
and his poor mother.

But since, as is said in Acts, it is more important to obey God than men,
we should, in the right order of nature, obey God first of all as our father
who has made us and not we ourselves, for children obey their father more than
anyone else. But he is our father above any other in three ways: first in
general by creating us, second more specifically by adopting us in his grace,
and thirdly quite uniquely by becoming one of us in taking on human nature.

obedienciam, reverenciam, et honorem. Unde Augustinus: "Vocatur, inquit,
Christus novi testamenti 'Pater noster qui es in celis'. Antiquitus eciam
dicebatur 'Dominus' respectu servorum; servi enim fuimus tunc per pecca-
20   tum. Set iam dicitur 'Dominus' per graciam." Iuste ergo a nobis veneratur
et hoc corde, ore, et opere. Semper enim ipse tamquam pius pater gaudet de
bono; ⟨et si ei⟩ deliquerimus, propter hoc visa contricione in corde et
audita gracie postulacione in ore, ad graciam recipit sperans emendam vite
nostre et satisfactionem de commissis. In cuius figura, quando filius
25   prodigus bona sua dissipasset vivendo luxuriose, statim ut dixit "Pater,
peccavi in celum et coram te," pater osculatus est eum. Et ideo attende hoc
quod dicit Petrus Ravennatensis: "Quare, inquit, moramini in peccatis,
quare non redimus ad patrem? Non enim dicit pater iste filio prodigo, 'Ubi
fuisti? Ubi sunt que tecum optulisti?' Non, 'Quare tantam gloriam in tantam
30   turpitudinem commutasti?' Set continuo ait: 'Proferte stolam primam,' quia
delicta non vidit vis amoris." Hec ille. Sic ergo faciamus nos cum omnia
tempora in malis dissipamus. Redeamus cum humilitate ad Patrem et dicamus
sicut ille dixit: "Pater, peccavi in celum et coram te. Iam non sum dignus
vocari filius tuus, sicut Petrus crucifixus, Paulus occisus, Laurencius
35   assatus, [f. 3] Bartholomeus excoriatus; et tamen mediante tua misericordia
permaxima fac me sicut unum de numero salvandorum." Et hiis auditis procul
dubio ad osculum pacis te recipiet [nec extorquetur a te quo fuisti, set
pocius sinum sue misericordie tibi aperiet et ad veniam te recipiet] indilate. In cuius signum affixus in patibulo brachia expandit ut te amplecte-
40   tur, et capud inclinans ut te ad penitenciam vocaret; Proverbiorum 1:
"Vocavi vos et renuistis, expandi manus meas et non fuit qui aspiceret."
      Et adverte: Christus enim pater noster benedictus facit ad modum
nobilium qui aves suas avolantes reclamant. Cumque voces eorum obaudierint
aves, reclamatorium suum faciunt sanguinolentum carne cruda apposita, ut
45   visa carne cicius descendunt domestice. Revera sic Christus clamavit ut
dispersos per peccatum congregaret, at illi vocem eius non audientes,
pietate maxima motus crucem ascendit manus et corpus cruentatum et sanguine
conspersum ostendens, ut sic visa eius passione redirent cicius et a peccato cessarent. Set timeo quod contingit de multis sicut de ave saciata, que
50   nec ad clamorem nec ad ⟨re⟩clamatorium volunt venire, hoc est non minus
propter Christi compassionem cessant peccare. Unde Osee dicitur: "Effraym
quasi avis avolavit." "Effraym" enim frugifer interpretatur et signat eos
qui propter habundanciam frugum ac ceterarum rerum temporalium ab
obsequiis divinis fugiunt.
55   Et ideo consulo quod faciamus sicut pueri faciunt disciplinabiles et
discreti, qui cum se senciunt aliquid contra precepta paterna deliquisse,
assumunt sibi virgam et vadunt ad patrem petentes misericordiam, et prepa-
rent se totaliter ad disciplinam et patris voluntatem; quod videns pater
pietate motus rigorem omnino tollit aut saltem in bona parte compescit. Sic

Therefore he is rightly called and named "our Father" in the Lord's Prayer, as a sign that we owe him obedience, reverence, and honor before anyone else. Whence Augustine says: "The Christ of the New Testament is called 'Our Father who art in heaven.' In olden times he was also called 'Lord' with respect to his slaves, for then we were slaves through sin; but now he is called 'Lord' through grace." Therefore it is right that we should worship him, and that in heart, mouth, and deed. For he always rejoices at the good in us like a loving father; and if we have sinned, when he sees remorse for that in our heart and hears the prayer for grace from our mouth, he receives us to his grace and hopes that we may amend our life and make restitution for our sins. A type of this is the Prodigal Son, who wasted his goods in loose living; as soon as he cried, "Father, I have sinned against heaven and before you," his father kissed him. Therefore listen to what Peter of Ravenna says: "Why do you dwell in your sins, why do we not return to our Father? For that father does not say to his prodigal son: 'Where have you been? Where are the goods you took with you? Why have you exchanged so much honor for such vileness?' Rather, he said at once: 'Bring forth the first robe,' for the power of love has not seen his crimes." Let us therefore do the same if we have wasted all our time in wickedness. Let us return to our father in humility and say as the Prodigal Son did: "Father, I have sinned against heaven and before you. I am no longer worthy to be called your son, as Peter, who was crucified, Paul, who was killed, Lawrence, who was grilled, or Bartholomew, who was flayed; and yet, through your exceedingly great mercy make me one of the number of those that will be saved." And when God hears this, he will without doubt receive you to the kiss of peace and will not force you to confess where you have been but rather open his merciful heart and accept you into his forgiveness without delay. As a sign of this he opened his arms when he hung on the cross that he might embrace you, and bowed down his head that he might call you to penance; Proverbs 1: "I called you and you refused; I stretched out my hand and there was none that regarded me."

   And notice: Christ our blessed father does as noblemen do who recall their hunting birds from their flight. When the birds do not listen to their voices, they put some blood on their recall with raw meat, so that the birds may see the meat and fly down tamely. In the same way Christ called out that he might gather those who were scattered far through sin. But when they did not hear his voice, he was moved by the deepest pity and climbed onto the cross, showing his bleeding hands and his body covered with blood all over, so that in seeing his suffering they might quickly return and leave their sin. But I fear that with many people it goes as it does with the sated bird that will not come either at his call or to his recall—that is, they do not in the least leave their sin out of compassion for Christ. Therefore in Hosea it is said: "Ephraim has flown away like a bird." "Ephraim" means fruitful and indicates those who for their wealth of fruits and other temporal goods flee from God's service.

60   certe Pater celestis, cum delicta recognoscimus et preterita deplangimus et
     plangenda deserimus, aut penam omnino tollit aut ita mitigat quod parum aut
     nichil gravat.
         Nam de tanta misericordia existit pater noster Christus quod [f. 3v]
     si crucifigere vel interficere eum vellemus, tamen si contriti veniam
65   humiliter peterimus, remitteret et ad graciam reciperet. Unde refert Vale-
     rius libro 3, capitulo 3, de quodam patre divite filium habente qui conti-
     nue quasi in mortem patris machinavit, aliquando ad occidendum et aliquando
     ad intoxicandum, et cetera huiusmodi. Quod pater intelligens et ab uxore
     bona fide veritatem didicisset, scilicet quod filius suus esset et non
70   alterius, quodam die dictum filium secum duxit in campum et extracto gladio
     ° eciam in manibus filii tradito hiis verbis illum allocutus est: "Fili mi,
     quid contra te demerui? Ulterius ° in mortem patris tui ne machineris. Ecce
     paratus sum; modo ergo pro voluntate tua occide me." Quo audito naturaliter
     abhorruit filius necem patris et cum eiulatu magno et lacrimis ad pedes
75   patris provolutus veniam postulabat. Quem pater suscipiens et dulciter
     amplexans in signum pacis reconciliacionis osculum dedit, nec ultra talia
     cogitare filius temptatus est. Spiritualiter autem loquendo per istum
     patrem benedictum intelligo Christum, qui non solum unicum filium ⟨habet⟩
     ingratum set multos, ut timeo, qui multociens insurgunt in eum ut eum
80   iterum interficerent, quando scilicet per superbiam, avariciam, gulam, et
     huiusmodi in hospicium cordis diabolum introducunt, qui intrat ad modum
     latronum ut Christum, qui ibidem habitare deberet, quantum in eis est
     expellunt et occidunt, et non tantum sic set aliquando per intoxicaciones
     falsorum iuramentorum et conspiracionum et huiusmodi, etc. Quod videns
85   pater noster Christus huiusmodi filium in campum deducit, quando scilicet
     illum ad memoriam reducit ostendens sibi quot bona pro eo fecit, quanta pro
     eo sustinuit. Que quidem beneficia enumerans beatus Augustinus in quodam
     sermone sic ait: "Cogor, inquit, racionibus ipsum, idest Deum Patrem, super
     omnia diligere, a quo me video omnia pignora recepisse. Dedit autem michi
90   esse et preesse, vivere et bene vivere, corpus cum sensibus, animam [f. 4]
     cum viribus, mundum cum contentis, Filium cum tormentis, dona cum sacra-
     mentis, virtutes cum incrementis, et huiusmodi. Respice, queso (inquit Augus-
     tinus), universum mundum et considera si quid in ipso sit quod tibi non
     serviat. Omnis enim natura sic cursum suum ad hunc finem dirigit, ut tuis
95   obsequiis famuletur." Hec ille. In hunc ergo campum, scilicet beneficiorum
     memoratorum, cum Pater celestis quemlibet nostrum tamquam filium [ingra-
     tum] introduxerit, primo dat gladium in manibus, idest iudicium racionis, quod
     ad modum gladii dividere habet inter istius patris Christi gratitudinem et
     nostram ingratitudinem, et tunc ait sic: "Fili mi, quid feci tibi aut in
100 quibus molestavi te? Responde michi." Quo audito, revera, si fuerimus per
     testimonium matris Ecclesie vere filii Dei ad vitam eternam predestinati,

Therefore I counsel that we act like obedient and sensitive children who, when they perceive that they have failed against their father's commands, take a rod and go to their father and ask for his mercy, fully ready to be disciplined and to receive their father's will. When their father sees that, he is moved by pity and lays aside all severity or at least softens it to a large extent. Thus, if we acknowledge our failings and weep for our past sins and leave what we weep about, our heavenly Father surely lays aside our punishment altogether or else softens it so that it hurts us little or not at all.

For our father has such great mercy that, even if we wanted to crucify and kill him, yet if we were contrite and humbly asked for his forgiveness, he would forgive and take us back into his grace. Whence Valerius in book 3, chapter 3, tells of a rich father who had a son that continuously plotted his father's death, sometimes by murder, sometimes by poison and the like. When his father learned that and had ascertained from his wife the truth in good faith, namely that the boy was his own son and not someone else's, he took that son with him into the country some day, drew out his sword, placed it into his son's hands, and spoke to him as follows: "My son, what wrong have I done against you? Do not plot any more for your father's death. Look, I am ready; kill me now if you want to." When the son heard this, he naturally shrank in horror from murdering his father; with loud wailing and tears he threw himself at his father's feet and prayed for forgiveness. Then his father raised him up, embraced him sweetly, and gave him a kiss of reconciliation as a sign of peace. And the son was no longer tempted to such thoughts. Spiritually speaking, by this blessed father I understand Christ, who has not only one ungrateful son but many, as I fear, who often rise against him to kill him again, namely when through their pride, avarice, gluttony, and other sins they bring the devil into the house of their heart, who enters as thieves do, so that they, as much as they can, expel and murder Christ, who should live there, and they plot this not only in the way described but sometimes through the poison of false oaths, conspiracies, and the like. When Christ our father notices this, he takes such a son into the country, that is, he refreshes his memory and shows him how much good he has done for him, how much he has suffered for him. In a sermon blessed Augustine lists these benefits and says: "I am forced by these reasons to love him above all things, that is, God the Father, from whom I realize I have received all these love-pledges. For he gave me being and being ahead, life and living well, my body with its senses, my soul with its powers, the world with all it contains, his Son with his sufferings, his gifts with the sacraments, the virtues with their growth, and so on. Look at the whole universe, I ask (says Augustine), and see if there is anything in it which does not serve you: for all nature directs its course to the purpose of obeying your will." When our heavenly father has led one of us as his ungrateful son into this country, that is, the recollection of his benefits, he first

mox compassione promoti veniam postulare non cessemus. Quo facto, nulli
dubium sit quin ipse qui proditori suo Iude osculum non negavit, pacem
nobis et concordiam non negabit indilate.

105   Item si tanta fuerit erga patrem nostrum Christum transgressio quod
eius misericordiam postulare formidamus, faciamus enim tunc sicut ille qui
regi ⟨terre⟩ tantam indignacionem incurrit quod coram ipso accedere non
audet ad eius graciam quoquo modo postulandum. Talis enim tunc accedit
latenter ad reginam aliquod exe⟨nn⟩ium premittens ut dominum regem pro eo

110   roget et deprecetur; deinde vadit ad comites et barones similia faciens;
deinde ad familiam liberam; et postremo ad pedi⟨tes⟩ qui sunt in palacio
inferiores, unumquemque iuxta statum suum in aliquo respiciens, ad quorum
omnium instanciam non potest in conspectu regis pati repulsum. Revera sic
ex parte illa faciendum est cum patrem Christum offendimus et eius veniam

115   et misericordiam postulare formidamus. Primo matrem misericordie, celi et
terre reginam, adeamus aliquas specialitates orando loco exe⟨nn⟩ii sibi
premittentes, scilicet vigilando, ieiunando, orando, et elemosinas largiendo. Quo facto certe ipsa ad modum pie [f. 4v] matrone occurret inter ⟨te⟩
et patrem Christum volentem te verberare pro delicto tuo, et pallium inter

120   te et virgam proiciet. Et revera omnem penam tollet vel saltem pro maxima
parte compescet, ita ut liberi sine gravamine recedere poterimus. Et tunc
dicat unusquisque sic: "Maria, mater gracie, mater misericordie, tu nos ab
hoste protege," etc.

           [Mary, moder of grace, we cryen to þe,
125   Moder of mercy and of pyte,
           Wyte vs fro þe fendes fondyng
           And helpe vs at oure last endyng;
           And to þy sone oure pes þou make,
           þat he on vs no wreche take.
130   Alle þe halewen þat aren in heuen,
           To ȝow I crye with mylde steuen.
           Helpe þat Cryst my gult forȝeue,
           And I wol him serue whyl þat I leue.]

    Et postea accedendum est ad comites et barones istius regis, hoc est ad
135   apostolos Christi qui cum summo iudice iudicabunt fines terre, ut et ipsi
pro te interpellant; deinde ad milites, ad armigeros, scilicet martires et
confessores, et similiter ad domicellas de camera regine, etc., dicendo:
"Omnes sancti, orate pro me ad Christum." [Tandem pauperes pedites sunt
placandi per elemosinarum largicionem, ut et ipsi pro nobis ad Christum

140   intercedant.] Et certe si sic fecerimus, ad istorum peticionem Christus
pater veniam concedet pro peccatis. Est autem hic notandum quod si predic-

puts his sword in his hands, that is, his rational judgment which like a sword can sharply distinguish between the gratitude of this father, Christ, and our ingratitude. And then he says thus: "My son, what have I done to you or in what have I offended you? Answer me." When we hear this, if indeed we are truly God's children after the testimony of our mother the Church and predestined for eternal life, we will soon be driven by compassion and not cease to pray for mercy. After which, let there be no doubt that he who did not deny his traitor, Judas, a kiss will not deny us peace and reconciliation without delay.

Further, if our offense against our father Christ should be so great that we are afraid to pray for his mercy, let us do as he does who causes the king of his land such great indignation that he does not dare come before him in order to ask for his grace in whatever form. Such a person goes secretly to the queen and sends her some gift so that she may pray and intercede with the king her lord for him; then he goes to the counts and barons and does likewise; next to the king's household; and finally he goes to the lower footsoldiers in the palace paying his respect to each of these with some gift according to his rank. When all of them make their prayer, he cannot possibly suffer rejection from the king. Indeed, thus should we do when we have offended Christ our father and are afraid to pray for his mercy. First let us go to the Mother of Mercy, the Queen of Heaven and Earth, and send her as a gift something special, such as waking, fasting, prayer, or almsgiving. At this she will certainly, like a loving mother, hasten to come between you and Christ your father who wants to chastise you for your failing, and she will stretch her mantle between you and his rod. And he will surely relinquish all punishment or at least soften it to a large extent, so that we will go free without grief. And then everyone should say: "Mary, Mother of Grace, Mother of Mercy, protect us from the fiend," etc.

> Mary, mother of grace, we cry to thee,
> Mother of mercy and of pity.
> Shield us from our en'my's tempting,
> And help us at our own last ending.
> And with thy son our peace thou make,
> That he on us no vengeance take.
> All you saints in heaven high,
> With gentle voice to you I cry.
> Help that Christ my sin forgive,
> And I will serve Him while I live.

After that you should go to the counts and barons of this king, that is, to Christ's apostles, who will judge all the earth with the highest judge, so that

tis modis Christo patri humiliaverimus animas nostras, maximum honorem sibi facimus.

Set timeo quod sunt nonnulli de filiis suis qui non inmerito "bastardi"
145 vocantur; ipsum ad tempus cum reverencia et humilitate honorant sicut
fecerunt Iudei in die Palmarum. Tunc enim illum primo honorabant eius
[discipuli] suis preceptis obediendo, Matthei: "Cum autem discipuli fecerunt sicut preceperat illis Iesus." Set econtra inhonoraverunt eum feria
sexta die Parasceves ab eo fugiendo, quia "relicto eo fugerunt," vel si
150 precipere vellet, non erat cui loqui posset. Et certe sic dehonoratur ab homine quando ab eius obediencia fugimus eius precepta contempnentes. Maximum enim dedecus aliquis regi faceret si edictum suum servare contempneret;
Romanorum 1: "Quid in lege gloriaris," scilicet te Christianum esse confitendo ac Dei filium esse, "et per prevaricacionem legis Deum inhonoras?"
155 Ideo dicitur Ecclesiastici 7: "Honora Deum ex tota anima tua."

Secundo honorabant eum turbe obviam sibi procedendo, ut patet Iohannis
21; et certe sic adhuc honoratur per veram cordis contricionem. Et tamen
postea ipsum inhonorabant de civitate eiciendo; Iohannis 9: "Baiulans sibi
crucem exivit." Sic multi spiritualiter [f. 5] obviantes ei per mundam
160 vitam sibi obviant in die Pasche, set post cito per peccatum eum turpiter
eiciunt. Nonne falsi hospites et prodiciosi dicuntur qui, recepto domino
suo et maxime patre, si statim post superinducerent inimicos suos capitales
qui ipsum exire compellerent? Revera sic hic. Exemplum et signa habemus 2
Regum 15 de Absolon, qui cum David patrem offenderat, postea fuit reconci-
165 liatus, scilicet per confessionem et satisfactionem, set post procuravit
mortem patris reducendo sua peccata. Unde ipsum de civitate eiecit nudis
pedibus et discooperto capite.

Tercio honorabant eum Iudei vestimenta sua in via sternendo, ut patet
Matthei. Per que intelligo bona temporalia, iuxta illud beati Gregorii:
170 "Que, inquit, sunt ista temporalia nisi quedam corporis indumenta?" Quando
enim huiusmodi bona sternuntur in via, hoc est pauperibus in via Dei ince-
dentibus distribuuntur, tunc honoratur Deus. Nam dicit Matthei 25: "Quod
uni de minimis meis fecistis," etc. Et ideo dicitur Proverbiorum 3: "Honora
Deum de tua substancia." Non enim dicit "de aliena," quod faciunt tales qui
175 spoliant pauperes ut inde faciant suas elemosinas. Set econtra isti Iudei
inhonoraverunt eum feria sexta quando eum propriis vestibus spoliabant.
Certe sic faciunt usurarii et raptores qui pauperes spoliant bonis suis
iniuste; Iob 24: "Nudos dimittunt homines vestimenta tollentes."

Quarto honorabant cum virgis et ramis viam decorando, ut patet in
180 Matthei 21. Sic et nos cum virgis discipline et ramis penitencie debemus
sibi obviare. Set econtra feria sexta cum virgis eum flagellabant. Sic
certe post Pascha multi quasi illum flagellant, quando vacando peccatis et
deliciis virgam discipline quam in Quadragesima portabant a se proiciunt.

they too may intercede for you; then to the knights and squires, that is, the martyrs and confessors, and likewise to the ladies of the queen's chamber, and so forth, and say to them: "All you saints, pray to Christ for me." And finally the poor footsoldiers should be appeased with generous alms, so that they also may intercede for us before Christ. And surely if we have done this, Christ our father will grant us forgiveness for our sins at their prayer. And it should be noted here that if we humble our souls before Christ our father in the ways mentioned, we will pay him the highest honor.

But I fear that there are many of his children who with good reason are called bastards. For a while they honor him with all reverence and humility, as did the Jews on Palm Sunday. For then, in the first place, his disciples honored him by obeying his commands; Matthew: "His disciples went and did all things as Jesus had ordered them." But in contrast, on Good Friday they dishonored him by fleeing from him, for "they left him and fled," and if he wanted to give them an order, there was none to whom he could speak. Certainly, thus he is dishonored by man when we flee from obeying him and despise his commandments. One would do one's king the greatest dishonor if one were to despise observing his command; Romans 1: "Why do you take pride in the Law," that is, when you profess to be a Christian and a child of God, "and dishonor God by breaking the Law?" Therefore it is said in Ecclesiasticus 7: "Honor God from your whole soul."

In the second place, the crowds honored him when they met him on the way, as narrated in John 21; and thus he is still honored by true contrition of heart. And yet later on they dishonored him by casting him out of the city; John 9: "Carrying his cross he went out of the city." Likewise, many meet him on his way spiritually on Easter Sunday by their pure life, but soon thereafter they cast him out shamefully through their sin. Do we not call those people false hosts and traitors who first receive their lord and, above all, their father and then right away let in his deadly enemies who force him to leave? So likewise in this case. Of this we have a good example and type in Absalom, in 2 Kings 15: after he had offended his father David, he was afterwards reconciled, that is, by confession and penance; but later he sought to kill his father, namely by bringing back his sins. For that he drove him out of the city with naked feet and bare head.

In the third place, the Jews honored him by spreading their garments in his way, as Matthew tells us. By these garments I understand temporal goods, after the saying of Blessed Gregory: "What else are these temporal goods than garments of our body?" When such goods are spread in the way, that is when they are given to the poor who walk in God's way, then God is honored. For he says in Matthew 25: "What you have done to the least of my brothers," etc. And thus it is said in Proverbs 3: "Honor God with your possessions." He does not say, "with other people's possessions," which is what those people do who rob

185 Set caveat, quia certe virga sic proiecta vertetur in colubrum, ut habetur
Exodi 4, hoc est, in penam eternam. Et ideo dicitur in Psalmo: "Apprehen-
dite disciplinam ne quando irascatur Dominus et pereatis," etc.

Quinto illum honorabant [f. 5v] salvatorem confitendo dicentes: "Osanna
in excelsis," idest, obsecro salva. Quod fit per fidem et spem. Tunc enim
honoratur Deus quando homo proprie opinioni contradicit credendo Deo
190 et spem suam in illo ponendo. Non enim facit michi honorem qui non credit
michi de pariete quod est albus nisi videat; tunc enim non credit michi set
sibi. Sic qui credit Deo de hoc quod vidit, facit Deo honorem, set non
talem sicut si sibi credat de non visis, iuxta illud: "Quia vidisti me,
Thomas, credidisti. Beati qui non viderunt," etc. Sic qui credit secundum
195 fidem Ecclesie quod in albedine panis est verum corpus Christi; et de isto
modo honorandi dicitur Ad Romanos 3: "Deus autem paciencie et solacii det
vobis idipsum sapere," ut sitis concordes in fide. Set econtra ipsum inhonorabant fidem eius ac ipsum abnegando; unde qui prius clamabant "Osanna,"
postea clamabant: "Alios salvos fecit; seipsum salvum facere non potest."
200 Et hoc modo inhonorant Deum infideles et heretici, etc.

Sexto modo ipsum honorabant laudando et cum laudibus ipsum suscipiendo. Unde dicitur quod "turba que preibat et que sequebatur clamabant Osanna"; et hoc modo iam laudatur in Ecclesia. Set ibi cavendum est ne sit
discordia in laudibus et officiis Ecclesie, hoc est, quod os non discordat
205 a corde, nec e contrario; sicut illi de quibus Ysaie 25: "Populus iste hic
me labiis honorat, cor autem eorum longe est a me." Set econtra feria sexta
ipsum inhonorabant dicentes: "Vath [qui] destruit templum Dei," etc.; sic
modo fatui filii et periurantes faciunt, de quibus dicitur 2 Regum 2: "Per
vos nomen Dei blasphematur inter gentes."
210 Septimo autem ipsum honorabant regiam dignitatem sibi attribuendo
dicentes: "Benedictus qui venit in nomine Domini, rex Israel," sicut iam
faciunt boni et sancti dicentes: "Soli Deo honor et gloria." Set econtra
fecerunt feria sexta dicentes: "Non habemus regem nisi Cesarem." Et hoc
modo iam faciunt superbi [f. 6] sibi quasi regiam [dignitatem usurpando. Et
215 certe tales filii Dei non sunt, nam ipse dicit: "Vos," scilicet superbi, "ex
patre dyabolo estis," Iohannis 8. Patet ergo quomodo aliqui Deum honorant
et similiter inhonorant.

Si ergo vestigia Christi sequi optamus, eodem modo oportet quod in
seipso contumelias recipiat sicud honores. Et ecce hystoria ad hoc. Legitur
220 in *Gestis Romanorum* quod si aliquis strenuus foret in civitate qui trina
vice pro civitate pungnasset et vicisset, quod triplex honor sibi debebatur: primo quod sederet in curru deaurato et quatuor equi albi ipsum trahe-
rent per civitatem; secundo quod inimici eius ad dictum currum afflicti
ligarentur; tercio quod duceretur ad templum Iovis et ibi tunica dei sui
225 indueretur. Set ne de hiis superbirent, tria opprobria eadem die et tempore

the poor and from that give their alms. But in contrast on Good Friday these
Jews dishonored him when they despoiled him of his own garments. Thus do
usurers and robbers act who unjustly despoil the poor of their goods; Job 24:
"They leave men naked by taking their garments."

In the fourth place, they honored him by decorating his way with twigs and
branches, as Matthew 21 tells us. Thus should we also meet him with the twigs
of mortification and the branches of penance. But in contrast on Good Friday
they scourged him with rods. Thus do many people as it were scourge him after
Easter when they give themselves to sins and pleasures and throw away the rod
of mortification which they were carrying during Lent. But let them take heed
lest the rod thus thrown away turn into a serpent, as happened in Exodus 4,
that is, into eternal punishment. Therefore it is said in the Psalm: "Take
upon yourselves mortification so that the Lord may not be angry and you perish," etc.

In the fifth place they honored him by proclaiming him as their Savior
when they said: "Hosanna in the highest," which means: "I pray, save us." This
is done through faith and hope. For God is honored when man goes against his
own understanding and believes in God and puts his hope in him. A person does
me no honor if he does not believe me that a wall is white unless he sees for
himself, for then he does not believe me but his own eyes. Just so, a person
who believes God in things which he can perceive does God honor, but not the
same as when he believes him in things which he does not perceive, according to
that word: "Because you have seen me, you have believed, Thomas; but blessed
are they who have not seen," etc. This applies to him who, according to the
faith of the Church, believes that under the white color of bread is the true
body of Christ. And of this way of honoring God it is said in Romans 3: "The
God of patience and of comfort grant you to be of one mind one toward another,"
that you may be unanimous in faith. By contrast they dishonored him by denying
their faith in him and denying himself, whence those who first shouted "Hosanna" later on shouted: "He has saved others, but he cannot save himself." And
it is in this fashion that the infidels and heretics dishonor God.

In the sixth place they honored him with singing praise and by receiving
him with praises. Whence it is written that "the crowd that went before and
after him cried 'Hosanna,'" and in this fashion he is still praised in the
Church. But here we should take heed lest there be any discord in the praise
and offices of the Church, that is, that the mouth may not disagree with the
heart or vice-versa, so that it may not be with us as it was with those of whom
Isaiah 25 says: "This people honors me with their lips, but their heart is far
from me." In contrast, on Good Friday they dishonored him saying: "Vah, he who
destroys the temple of God," etc.; as now his foolish children and perjurers
do, of whom it is written in 2 Kings 2: "By you the name of God is blasphemed
among the Gentiles."

sustinerent: primum, quod servus quidam rurissime condicionis iuxta eum
sederet equalis honoris cum eo; secundum, quod hic servus eum colaphizaret
dicens, "Nothos olitos," idest cognosce teipsum; ⟨tercium⟩, quod illo die
inimici eius contra ipsum dicerent ⟨impune⟩ quicquid vellent. Revera,
230   karissimi, spiritualiter loquendo quilibet nostrum est in cottidiana pungna
cum carne propria, mundo, et dyabolo. Unde si istos vicerimus, triplex
honor debetur nobis: primo scilicet quod sedebimus in curru deaurato, per
quem intelligo laudem humanam et bonam famam, ⟨per quam⟩ quasi per currum a terra elevamur. Set si currus ille bene disponatur, oportet quod habeat
235   quatuor rotas, scilicet amorem Dei et proximi, similiter humilitatem in
prosperis [M, f. 8v] et pacienciam in adversis. Nam rota, que est figura
circularis et perfectissima, finem non habet. Sic certe iuxta Apostolum Ad
Corinthios: "Caritas numquam excidit." Per quatuor equos albos intelligo
quatuor virtutes cardinales, scilicet iusticiam, prudenciam, fortitudinem,
240   temperanciam. Si ergo currus iste per istos equos ducatur, idest una cum
quatuor rotis predictis, tunc primus honor satis patebit. Secundus honor
erit scilicet quod inimici ligati erunt, scilicet caro, mundus, et demon;
quoniam si ipsi viderint nos sic in perfectione permanere, quasi ex dolore
et invidia confusi ligantur et vincantur, et sic de bonis nostris torquen-
245   tur. Tercius honor ⟨erit⟩ quod debet indui tunica Dei, hoc est per totum
circumdari compassione mortis Christi. Set ne de hiis honoribus superbia-
mus, tria opprobria sustinemus: primo servus vilis, scilicet caro nostra,
iuxta nos velis nolis sedebit; secundo ipsa caro colaphizet animam nostram,
quia iuxta Apostolum "caro concupiscit," etc.; tercio inimici nostri nos
250   accusabunt.
    Patet ergo ex predictis quomodo debemus primo Deo nos humiliare tam-
quam patri.

---

6 vocabitur] est O.   **8** lignifabri] lignifabro O.   **10** quia] *add* prout O.   dicitur] actuum
O.   **11–12** et hoc] *om* O.   **13** tripliciter primo] *om* O.   **14** specialiter] spiritualiter O.
et] *om* O.   **17** obedienciam] *om* O.   **22** et si ei] nec sibi C; nec si M.   **29** optulisti] tulisti
O.   **32** dissipamus] dissipavimus O.   humilitate] *add* et reverencia M.W; *add* et paciencia R.   **33** dixit] *om* O.   **36** auditis] *add* ipse O.   **43** eorum] illorum O.   **50** recla-
matorium] viri clamatorium C.   **59** rigorem] rigiditatem O.   **65** peterimus] peteremus
O.   **67** machinavit] machinantem O.   et] *om* O.   **68** cetera] *om* O.   **70** gladio] *add* alio
interl C.   **72** Ulterius] *add* non *canc* ut *interl* C; *add* non M.W; *add* enim R.   **74** abhor-
ruit] exhorruit O.   **78** habet] scilicet C.   **79** ingratum] *add* et degenerem O.   **81** diabo-
lum] latere M.W; latenter R.   intrat] intrant O.   **84** etc.] *om* O.   **94** sic] *om* O.
100 quibus] quo O.   **106** enim tunc] *om* O.   **107** regi terre] regi terreni C; regis terreni
corr R.   **108** tunc] *om* O.   **109** exennium] exemium C.   **111** pedites] pedicas C.
113 repulsum] repulsam R.   **116** exennii] exemii C.   **117** et] *om* O.   **118** te] se C.
119 tuo] *om* O.   **122** dicat unusquisque sic] dices O.   **124–133** Mary . . . leue] *text
from* R. *Verse 10, in* B3.E. Go1.Go2.Jo.L1.L2.LC.R.V.W1.   **136** ad(2)] et O.   **137** ad]
om O.   etc. dicendo] et dicatis O.   **138** orate pro me ad Christum] et sancte dei inter-
cedite pro nobis M; *om* R.W.   **145** cum] *add* omni O.   **149** die] *om* O.   **164** offenderat]

But in the seventh place they honored him by giving him royal dignity when they said: "Blessed is he who comes in the name of the Lord, the king of Israel"; so do the good and the saints nowadays when they say: "To God alone be honor and glory." But on Good Friday people did the opposite by saying: "We have no king except Caesar." Nowadays proud people do just that when they, as it were, assume royal dignity for themselves. Certainly, these are not children of God, for he himself says in John 8: "You," that is, proud people, "are from your father the devil." Thus it is evident how people honor God and likewise dishonor him.

If we then wish to follow in Christ's footsteps, we must in the same way as he did accept for ourselves reproaches as well as honors. A story relevant to this occurs in *The Deeds of the Romans*, where it is reported that if there was a hardy champion in the City who had fought for it and won a victory three times, he deserved a threefold honor: first, he was to sit in a golden chariot and four white horses were to draw him through the City; second, his enemies were in their defeat to be bound to his chariot; and third, he was to be led to the temple of Jupiter and there clothed in the cloak of his god. But that he should not be too proud in these honors, he was to suffer threefold shame on the same day: first, a slave of the lowest class was to sit next to him in equal honor; second, this slave was to strike him and say, "Gnothi seauton," that is, "Know thyself"; and third, on that day his enemies could with impunity say anything they wanted against him. In truth, dearly beloved, spiritually speaking each one of us is in daily battle against his flesh, the world, and the devil. If we overcome these, we deserve a threefold honor. First, we shall sit in a golden chariot, by which I understand men's praise and good reputation, through which we are raised from the earth as if in a chariot. But in order to be well made, this chariot must have four wheels, that is to say, the love of God and of our neighbor, together with humility in prosperity and patience in adversity. For a wheel, which is round and of the most perfect shape, has no end; thus, according to the Apostle in Corinthians, "charity never ends." By the four white horses I understand the four cardinal virtues, that is, justice, prudence, strength, and moderation. If therefore this chariot is drawn by these horses and has the four wheels mentioned above, the first honor is evident. The second honor will be that our enemies will be bound, that is, the flesh, the world, and the devil; for when these see that we live thus in perfection, they are overcome by grief and envy and are, as it were, bound and fettered and derive torture from our well-being. The third honor will be that he must put on the cloak of God, that is, he must completely wrap himself in compassion for Christ's death. But that we may not become proud of these honors, we shall suffer a threefold shame; first, a lowborn slave, that is, our flesh, will sit next to us willy-nilly; second, the same flesh will strike our soul, for according to the Apostle, "the flesh lusts," and so on; and third, our enemies will accuse us.

add per quem intelligo peccatorem O.   **165** satisfactionem] penitenciam RW; *add* in quadragesima M.W.   set] et O.   **166** sua] scilicet O.   **169** beati] *om* O.   **172** dicit] *add* in O.   **25**] *om* O.   **173** uni de] *om* O.   **174** aliena] alia O.   **175** isti Iudei] *om* O. **176** eum(2)] illum O.   vestibus] vestimentis O.   **184** caveat] caveant O.   **194** Sic] sicud O.   **195** in] sub O.   **199** postea clamabant] iam clamant O.   **200** etc.] *om* O.   **205** iste] *om* O.   **207** sic] sicud O.   **208** filii] falsi O.   dicitur] *om* O.   **211** in nomine Domini] *om* O.   **214** dignitatem . . . per (I.x.17)] *one leaf mutilated* C; *text taken from* M.   **228** tercium] R; tercio M.W.   **229** impune] R.W; impie M.   **233** per quam] R.W; *om* M. **245** erit] R; *om* M.W.

I.x   HUMILIANDUM ECCLESIE

Secundo eciam ⟨humiliari⟩ debemus Ecclesie Dei, que est mater nostra. Nam sicud mater temporalis et carnalis primo puerum portat et parit, deinde ipsum lavat et balneat, deinde induet, fovet, et pascit, et tandem in lectis secum quiescere facit, revera sic Ecclesia militans mater nostra. Primo
5 ad huius hostium portamur et ibi pompis dyabolicis renunciamus et Christum induimus. Postea ibi in ipsa baptismatis unda abluimur et mundamur et a peccato originali sanctificamur. Deinde in ipsa corpore et sanguine Christi pascimur et potamur. Tandem appropinquante vite termino cum ipsa et iuxta ipsam corpora nostra requiescunt. Et merito Ecclesie tamquam matri nostre
10 spirituali debemus ⟨nos⟩ totaliter humiliare pre ceteris, maxime scilicet illa que sua sunt sine fraude solvere, hoc est decimas et oblaciones.

Et adverte: decime enim ⟨omnium⟩ datori de iure naturali debentur; nam iustum ⟨est⟩ ut ille qui dat totum, partem recipiat; Paralipomenon ultimo: "Tua sunt omnia, Domine, et de manu tua accepimus quod dedimus tibi." Deus
15 enim precepit illas ⟨dari⟩, ut patet Exodi 22: "Decimas, inquit, et primicias non tardabis offerre." Et ideo illas fideliter non solventes] [C, f. 7] per prophetam excommunicavit, Malachie 3: "Quia, inquit, non reddidistis decimas et primicias, idcirco in fame et penuria maledicti estis."

Et nota quod vita decimas recipiencium non est discucienda, cuiusmodi
20 sunt rectores, vicarii, et prelati, sive bene vivant sive male, quia non illis set Deo solvunt. Ipsi enim non sunt nisi "dispensatores ministeriorum Dei," ut dicit Apostolus. Et ideo quomodo illa expenderunt, durissimum

Therefore, from all these things it is evident how we must first humble ourselves before God as our father.

3–4 Luke 22.42. **6** Matt. 21.13. **8–9** Luke 2.51. **10** Acts 5.29. **25–26** Luke 15.18. **27–31** Cf. Petrus Chrysologus, *Sermo 3* 4 (CC 24:29). **41** Prov. 1.24. **51–52** Hos. 9.11. **66–77** Tubach 4485, from Valerius, V.ix.4. **99–100** Cf. the Improperia of the Good Friday liturgy. **103** Cf. Matt. 26.49–50. **146–217** Peraldus, *Summa vitiorum* VI.iii.39 (pride), has a similar pattern, though it is attributed to Bernard. **147–148** Cf. Matt. 21.6. **149** Matt. 26.56. **153–154** Rom. 2.23. **155** Ecclus. 7.33. **156–157** John 12.12–13. **158–159** John 19.17. **164–167** 2 Sam. 15. **168–169** Matt. 21.8. **172–173** Matt. 25.40. **173–174** Prov. 3.9. **178** Job 24.7. **179–180** Matt. 21.8. **181** Cf. Matt. 27.26; John 19.1. **184–185** Cf. Exod. 4.3. **185–186** Ps. 2.12. **187–188** Mark 11.9–10 (cf. Matt. 21.9). **193–194** John 20.29. **196–197** Rom. 15.5. **199** Matt. 27.42. **202–203** Mark 11.9. **205–206** Isa. 29.13. **207** Matt. 27.40; Mark 15.29. **211** Matt. 21.9. **213** John 19.15. **215–216** John 8.44. **220–229** Tubach 5084, a very widespread *exemplum*. Also in Bromyard, "Tribulacio," T.V.36; Holcot, *In Sapienciam* lect. 164; Brinton, sermons 7, 36, and 106 (pp. 18–19, 152, and 488). **238** 1 Cor. 13.8. **249** Gal. 5.17.

I.x HUMBLING ONESELF BEFORE THE CHURCH

In the second place we must humble ourselves before the Church, who is our mother. Just as a mother in this world and in the flesh first carries a child and gives birth to it, then washes and bathes it, next clothes, nurses, and feeds it, and at last brings it to rest with her in bed, so does our mother, the Militant Church. First we are carried to its door and there renounce the devil and his pomp and put on Christ. Next we are washed there in the water of baptism and are cleansed and purified of Original Sin. Then we are given the Body and Blood of Christ to eat and to drink in the Church. And at last, when the end of our life approaches, our bodies rest with her and beside her. Therefore we must rightly humble ourselves totally before the Church as our spiritual mother, primarily by giving her without cheating what belongs to her, namely tithes and other offerings.

Notice that tithes are owed to the giver of all things by natural law, for it is just that he who gives everything receive back a part; at the end of Chronicles: "Yours, O Lord, are all things, and from your hand we have received what we have given you." God has commanded to give tithes, as is clear from Exodus 22: "Do not delay to offer tithes and the first fruits." And those who do not faithfully offer them he has excommunicated through the prophet, in Malachi 3: "Because you have not rendered tithes and first fruits, you are cursed with hunger and need."

And notice that the life of those who receive tithes, such as pastors, vicars, and prelates, is not to be examined by those who render tithes, whether

compotum in extremo iudicio persolvent. Si quis ergo retrahit scienter vel
fraudem facit solvendo decimas et oblaciones Deo et Ecclesie debitas, sac-
25 rilegium committit, quia non homini set Deo fraudem facit, et per consequens excommunicatus est tam a Deo quam a communi iure, ut patet 17,
questione 4, quam eciam a statutis Ecclesie Anglicane. Et ideo si tales
inventi fuerint aliqui, ecclesiastica carebunt sepultura. Nichil enim ad
dantes sive recipientes, quibus non dant set committunt loco Dei ad bene
30 custodiendum et dispensandum fideliter, sive boni fuerint sive mali, set
semper considerant quod Deus ipse cui dant bonus est et suavis, iuxta illud
Psalmi: "Et reddens unicuique iuxta opera sua." Unde Augustinus: "Sicut,
inquit, infirmitas medici non impedit effectum medicine et virtutem, sic
nec iniquitas sacerdotis effectum sacramenti." Opus ergo operatum est semper
35 mundum, quamvis opus operans sit inmundus. "Nichil ergo (inquit Augustinus) a bono maius vel a malo minus sacrum in altari conficitur, quia sunt verba
Redemptoris et non sacerdotis;" set bonus ad sui et populi salutem conficit,
malus autem ad populi salutem et sui ipsius dampnacionem, iuxta illud
Apostoli Corinthiorum: "Qui manducat corpus Domini indigne," etc.
40 Et ideo quando decimas damus, consideremus [quod] Deo, non homini,
debitum solvimus, et hoc specialiter propter decimi angelorum ordinis
perditi restauracionem. Unde Augustinus: "Si non decimaveris, non decima-
beris," quasi diceret: nisi decimas Deo et Ecclesie debitas fideliter sine
fraude persolveris, ad decimum ordinem angelorum pervenire non [f. 7v]
45 poteris. Absit ergo ut decimando, offerendo malum pro bono commutaveris
quia forte non diligis recipientem, set sicut Deus renovavit bona et ut ad
manum venerit offerendum est, quia dicit Dominus per prophetam: "Maledictus homo qui habet masculum in grege et offert debilem Deo."
Et nota secundum Raymundum [Distinccione 16] quod quadruplex remunera-
50 cio fideliter decimancium est: prima est habundancia fructuum, secunda est
sanitas corporum, tercia est indulgencia peccatorum, et quarta premium regni celorum. De duabus autem primis dicit Augustinus 16, questione 1, Decime: "Si decimam, inquit, dederis semper fideliter, non solum habundanciam
fructuum recipies, set et sanitatem corporis consequeris." Item ibidem pro
55 duabus aliis: "Qui, inquit, premium eternum aut indulgenciam peccatorum
desiderat promereri, reddat fideliter decimam, et de novem partibus resi-
duis studeat elemosinam dare pauperibus." Hec ille.
Unde narratur de Ancelmo vidente diabolum in horreo semipleno, qui de-
cimavit iterum et vix nova pars post in horreo poterat intrare. Narratur
60 eciam quod beatus Ignacius vidit semel diabolum super horreum suum sedentem; qui admirans a ministris suis quesivit si recte decimassent. Et accessit unus dicens quod septem garbas de decima, ut horreum impleret, ibidem
reposuit. Quo audito accessit vir sanctus ad horreum adiurans diabolum
quare ibi sederet. Qui respondit se in huiusmodi iurisdictionem habere. [Et

they lead a good life or a wicked one, because tithes are not given to them but to God alone. They are only "dispensers of the mysteries of God," as the Apostle says, and therefore will have to give a very close account in the Last Judgment on how they have spent them. Therefore, if anyone in any way knowingly withholds or cheats in giving tithes or offerings that he owes to God and the Church, he commits a sacrilege, because he cheats not man but God and is consequently excommunicated by God and by common [Church] law, as is stated in *Causa* 17, question 4, as well as by the statutes of the English Church. If any are found to be in this condition, they will not receive ecclesiastic burial.

Thus they must not look at the recipients, for they do not give their offering but only commit it to them in God's place for safekeeping and faithful distribution, whether they are good or evil; and they should always consider that God himself, to whom they give, is good and gentle, according to the Psalmist: "He renders each according to his deeds." Therefore Augustine says: "As the physician's illness is no obstacle against the effect and power of his medicine, thus is the wickedness of a priest no obstacle to the efficacy of a sacrament; the work performed is always pure, even it the performer of the work may be impure. For if a good priest celebrates it," says Augustine, "the sacrament of the altar does not become greater, nor does it become less if celebrated by a bad priest, because the words [of consecration] are the Redeemer's and not the priest's. Yet a good priest celebrates for his own and the people's salvation, a bad one to the people's salvation and his own damnation, after the Apostle in Corinthians: 'Who eats my body unworthily,' etc."

Thus, when we give tithes, let us consider that we pay our debt to God, not to man, and this particularly for the restoring of the tenth order of angels that was lost. Whence Augustine: "If you have not given a tenth, you will not become a tenth," as if he were saying: unless you render the tenth owed to God and the Church faithfully without cheating, you will not be able to come to the tenth order of the angels. Far be it, then, that in giving tithes you render evil for good because perhaps you do not like the recipient; but you must offer just as God has renewed your goods and as they come to hand, for the Lord says through the prophet: "Cursed be the man who has a male in his flock and offers God a weakling."

And notice that according to Raymundus, Distinction 16, those who give tithes faithfully have a fourfold reward, namely, abundance of crops, health of their body, forgiveness of sins, and the kingdom of heaven. Concerning the first two Augustine declares, in Distinction 16, question 1, *Decime*: "If you have always given your tithe faithfully, you will not only receive an abundance of crops but also have health of your body." And concerning the last two he says in the same place: "He who wishes to gain eternal reward or forgiveness of his sins must give his tenth faithfully and from the other nine parts try to give alms to the poor."

65 ille:] "Tu, inquit, potestatem et vires tuas excerce." At ille summitatem
    domus asportavit, et supercecidit ignis infernalis et residuum domus com-
    bussit. Hoc autem non contingit propter quantitatem bladi detenti, set
    propter inobedienciam Ecclesie factam.
         Caveamus igitur, et maxime timore excommunicacionis quam quis incurrit
70 male decimando. Et [si] forte dic⟨a⟩tur: "Quid habeo curare de excommunica-
    cione talis rectoris vel vicarii et cetera?" respondeo quod sic iuste ex-
    communicatus separatur a bonis omnibus que fiunt in Ecclesia Dei universa,
    tam [f. 8] de die quam de nocte, in missis, in matutinis, horis, vigiliis,
    oracionibus, ieiuniis, et ceteris; huiusmodi homines a congregacione fide-
75 lium separantur et membrum diaboli efficiuntur, ac eius potestati totaliter
    relinquuntur dum perseverant pro eterno igne cruciandi, sicut lignum omni
    viriditate carens igni terreno committitur. Unde Augustinus: "Omnis, in-
    quit, Christianus effectus prophanus Sathane potestati traditur, sicut fur
    incarceratori cruciandus," etc.
80   [I]nsuper et ipsam matrem [Ecclesiam] debemus et tenemur devote reve-
    reri absque vaniloquiis et dissolucionibus, propter que divinum obsequium
    poterit impediri quoquo modo. Sicut enim boni et devoti de omnibus bonis
    que fiunt in Ecclesia participant, sic tales dissoluti officium Dei quoquo
    modo impedientes [illius] beneficio carent. Nam ipsi, quantum in eis est,
85 faciunt de domo Dei speluncam latronum, et domum oracionis domum taberne
    aut negociacionis. Et adverte: Si aliquis infans infra claustrum uteri
    materni palam loqueretur, pro demoniaco reputaretur; quanto magis [qui] in
    utero matris Ecclesie, ubi verum corpus Christi efficitur, garulat in vanum
    et eius officium impedit. Unde refert Cassiodorus quod apud Egiptum in
90 solempnitatibus quas vocant Senax⟨e⟩s a cunctis prebetur silencium, in
    tantum quod preter illum qui psallit nullus adesse videtur quousque omnia
    consummantur; non enim emittitur sputum, non tussis intersonat, non oscita-
    cio sompni, nullus gemitus, nullaque suspiria, nulla eciam vox preter
    psallentis auditur aut sonus, nisi forte ex excessu mentis quis modo suo
95 submisse quid devotum evaporat. Hec ille. Si ergo illi infideles sic hono-
    rant ecclesiam suam prophanam, quanto magis nos Christiani tenemur Eccle-
    siam Dei et eius officium venerari et non impedire; Thobie 3: "Numquam cum
    ludentibus me miscui, neque cum hiis qui in levitatibus ambulant participem
    me prebui." Et ideo iuxta consilium Sapientis, Ecclesiastici 7: "Non te
100 reputes in multitudine indisciplinatorum, [f. 8v] quia ve dissolutis cor-
    de." Nam tales de malis levioribus interdum ad graviora procedunt, sicut
    latro de pedibus ad patibulum, deinde ad infernum.

---

1 humiliari] R.W; humiliare M.   3 induet] ut decet R; decet W.   5 huius] eius *corr*
R.W.   9 Et] *add* ideo R.W.   10 nos] R.W; *om* M.   12 omnium] R.W; omni M.
13 est] R.W; *om* M.   15 dari] R.W; dare M.   17 per] C *full text resumes*.   20 prelati]

There is a story about Anselm, who saw a devil in his half-filled barn. When he tithed again, the new part would hardly fit into the barn. It is also reported that blessed Ignatius once saw a devil sitting on his barn. He wondered and asked his servants if they had tithed correctly. One of them came and said he had put down seven sheaves from the tenth in order to fill the barn. When the saintly man heard this, he went to the barn and conjured the devil to tell him why he was sitting there. He replied that he had jurisdiction over the barn. And Ignatius said: "Exercise your power and might!" And the devil carried off the top of the building, and fire from hell fell on it and burned the rest of the building to the ground. However, this did not happen because a certain amount of grain had been withheld, but rather because of the disobedience that had been shown to the Church.

Let us therefore beware, especially for fear of incurring excommunication on account of false tithing. And if anyone should say: "What do I care about being excommunicated by such a pastor or vicar, etc.?" I answer that anyone who is thus justly excommunicated becomes separated from all good works that are done in the universal Church, both by day and at night, in masses, matins, hours, vigils, prayers, fastings, and other works; such people are separated from the communion of the faithful and become a member of the devil and are totally given over into his power as long as they persevere, to be punished in the eternal fire, just as a piece of wood that is no longer green is put into material fire. Wherefore Augustine says: "Every Christian who has been expelled from the Church is given into the power of Satan, as a thief is given to the jailer for punishment."

In addition, we must and are obliged to pay devout reverence to our mother the Church without any idle talk and levity which could in any way detract from the divine service. Just as good and devout people share in all the good works that are done in the Church, so do dissolute people who in any way hinder God's worship lack that benefit. For such people make of God's house a den of thieves, and of the house of prayer a tavern and shop, as much as it lies in their power. And notice: if a child in his mother's womb were to speak openly, it would be considered possessed; how much more does this apply to a person who chatters idly and disturbs the service in the womb of our mother the Church, where the true Body of Christ comes into being? Cassiodorus reports that among the Egyptians, in the solemn service they call Synaxes, all keep absolute silence, so much so that besides the one who recites the psalms no one else seems to be present until the service is completed; no one spits or coughs or yawns or sighs or sobs, no voice is heard except that of the person who recites the palms, no noise except that perhaps someone in ecstasy quietly emits some pious sound in his manner. If therefore those infidels honor their pagan church so much, how much more must we Christians revere the Church of God and its service, and not disturb it; Tobit 3: "Never have I joined myself with them

add ceteri ab illis qui solvunt O.   **21** ministeriorum] *thus* C.O.   **24** decimas] *add* primicias O. oblaciones] *add* quoquo modo O.   **26** a Deo quam] *om* O.   **32** iuxta] secundum O.   **36** vel] nichil O.   **38–39** illud Apostoli] apostolum O.   **39** Domini] meum O. **40** quando] cum O.   **41** specialiter] spiritualiter M.W.   **50** est(1)] *add* scilicet O.   **51** et] *om* O.   **51–52** premium regni] regnum R; regna M.W.   **59** poterat] potuit O.   **61** suis] *om* O. Et] *om* O.   **65** tuas] *om* O.   **67** contingit] contigit O.   **70** dicatur] dicitur C. **71** talis] *add* iusticiatus talis puta O; *in* R iusticiatus *has been corrected to* rustici.   vel] aut O.   **72** universa] universalis O.   **73** in(2)] *om* O.   **74** homines] ac eciam O. **75** separantur] separatur O.   efficiuntur] efficitur O.   **76** relinquuntur] relinquitur O. perseverant] perseverat O.   cruciandi] cruciandum R; cruciandus M.W.   **80** Ecclesiam] *interl* R, *also in* Co.Go2; *om* C.M.W.B1.B2.B3. Et.Go1.   **87** qui] R; *om* C.M.W. **88** efficitur] conficitur *corr from* efficitur R (*with* E).   **90** Senaxes] senaxos C.   **91– 92** omnia consummantur] omnino consummatur O.   **92** enim] *om* O.

I.xi   HUMILIANDUM PARENTIBUS

[N]unc autem de humilitate et obediencia erga hominem est sciendum quod ad hoc tenemur si sequaces Christi esse velimus. De eo vero dicitur Luce 2: "Erat subditus illis," scilicet Christus Marie et Ioseph; per quod innuitur quod parentibus humiliari et obedire debemus, iuxta illud Exodi:

5   "Honora patrem et matrem, ut sis longevus super terram." Sicut enim paterfamilias certum pactum facit cum opifice ut opus suum consummet, set ut melius et subtilius illud perficiat robam vel aliquid tale de sua curialitate repromittit; revera sic Christus parentes honorantibus legem extendit, set ut melius illa exequatur vitam longiorem repromittit in terris et vitam

10   eternam in celis. Ecclesiastici 3 dicitur: "Qui honorat patrem, vita vivet longiori"; set econtra dicitur ibidem: "Quam male fame est qui dereliquerit patrem, et est maledictus a Deo qui exasperat matrem." Multum enim tenemur recordari que et quanta passi sunt pro nobis parentes pariendo, nutriendo, fovendo, pascendo, omnia necessaria inveniendo, quando nos ipsos iuvare

15   neque scivimus neque valuimus.

Set timeo quod hoc male hodie perpenditur ab ingratis, quia Michee 7 dicitur: "Filius contumeliam facit patri et filia consurgit adversus matrem et nurus contra socrum suam, et inimici hominis domestici eius." Et bene patuit de Absalon, Regum 15, qui patrem suum persecutus est usque ad mor-

20   tem. Similiter filius Nabugodonosor propter desiderium hereditatis ne pater

that play; neither have I made myself partaker with them that walk in lightness." And thus, according to the counsel of the wise man, in Ecclesiasticus
7, "Do not number yourself among the multitude of the disorderly, for woe to
the dissolute of heart." For such people sometimes fall from slight offenses
into more grievous ones, as a thief progresses from the stocks to the gallows
and thence to hell.

---

14 1 Chron. 29.14.   **15–16** Exod. 22.29.   **17–18** Cf. Mal. 3.8–9.   **21–22** 1 Cor.
4.1.   **26–27** Gratian II.16.1.65 (1:783–784). In England, excommunication for neglect
in tithing is mentioned at least as early as the Council of Westminster of 1138: *Councils
and Synods with Other Documents Relating to the English Church*, vol. I, ed. D. White-
lock, M. Brett, and C. N. L. Brooke (Oxford, 1981), p. 778; for later decrees, see vol. II,
ed. Powicke and Cheney (Oxford, 1964), pp. 13, 75, etc.   **32** Ps. 61.13.   **35–37** Paschasius Radbertus, *De corpore et sanguine Domini* 4; cf. Gratian II.1.1.77 (1:385).   **39** 1
Cor. 11.29.   **42–43** Cf. Caesarius, *Sermo 33* 2 (CC 103:144–145).   **47–48** Mal. 1.14.
49–57 Raymundus, *Summa* I.xv.16 (p. 137).   **52–57** Augustine, *Sermo 219 de tempore*,
as quoted in Gratian II.16.1.66 (1:784).   **58–59** Tubach 488; see also *Spec. laicorum* 174
and note.   **59–67** See Tubach 489 (Saint Udalric).   **85–86** Cf. Matt. 21.13.   **89–
95** John Cassian, *De institutis coenobiorum* II.x.1 (CSEL 17:25).   **97–99** Tob. 3.17.
99–101 Ecclus. 7.17.

I.xi   HUMBLING ONESELF BEFORE ONE'S PARENTS

Now we turn to humility and obedience before man, and we should realize
that we are obliged to practice this if we wish to be followers of Christ. For
of him is written in Luke 2: "He was subject to them," that is, Christ to Mary
and Joseph; which indicates that we must be humble before and obey our parents,
according to Exodus: "Honor your father and mother that you may live long on
earth." Just as the head of a household makes a firm contract with a builder
to do his work, but out of courtesy promises him a coat or something like it so
that he may do his job better and with greater care, so has Christ given his
law to those who honor their parents, but in order for them to carry it out
better, he has promised them a longer life on earth and eternal life in heaven.
In Ecclesiasticus 3 it is said: "He who honors his father will live a longer
life"; and conversely, in the same place: "What bad reputation does he have who
abandons his father; and he who angers his mother is cursed by God." We must
often call to mind what and how much our parents have suffered for us in giving
us life, nursing us, caring for us, feeding us, and finding what is necessary
for us when we neither knew how nor were able to help ourselves.

But I fear that nowadays this is hardly taken into consideration by ungrateful people, for in Micah 7 it is said: "The son causes his father shame
and the daughter rises against her mother, the daughter-in-law against her
mother-in-law, and a man's housemates are his enemies." This could be clearly

iterum regnaret, ipso mortuo cadaver eius in frustra concidit et particulariter illa pedibus vulturum ligavit ut ipse illa asportantes in eternum non
convenirent.

Et ideo tales bene possunt dici catelli canum qui in iuventute matrem
25   secuntur [f. 9] et ab ipsis lactantur et nutriuntur, set quam cito maiores
efficiuntur et dentes acutos habuerint et possunt ossa corrodere sicut
mater, tunc statim si os in medium proiciatur, illud arripiunt festinanter
et eciam insiliunt in illo, nec plus parcent patri aut matri quam alteri
cani. Sic multi filii et filie ingrati in iuventute satis obtemperant
30   parentibus, set facti adulti si aliquid ab illis possunt lucrari et auferre,
non plus parcunt illis quam aliis.

Contra quos Ambrosius in suo *Exameron* narrat quod ciconia tante pietatis est erga parentes quod, deposita parentis potencia et per longevum
senectutis plumis nudati, circumstant soboles pennis propriis fovendo ac
35   cibo collato de proprio labore pascere non omittunt, et inde senes parentes
sublevantes alarum suarum fulcimento ad volandum exercent et ad pristinos
usus dissueta membra reducunt. Hec ille. Quis ergo nostrum senem parentem,
qui tantum nos dilexit in iuventute, ⟨humeris⟩ inposuit sicut avis ille?
Vel quis patrem infirmum vel eciam decrepitum levare, fovere, alere non
40   fastidit, etc.? "Quis est hic et laudabimus eum." Revera timeo quod valde
pauci.

Narratur eciam de upupa, que est avis silvestris, quod cum earum parentes senio fuerint excecati, querit iuxta mare lapidem preciosum et apponit oculis suis et visum recipiunt. Non sic hodie; set si aliquis horum
45   unum perdiderit oculum propter aliquam substanciam paternam, timeo quod
vellent plures ingrati quod ambo oculi eruerentur et morti traderentur.
Similiter est de matre. Nonne videmus tota die quomodo filius matrem vetulam ad terciam partem ponit eciam terre peioris, et pro ista totaliter
optinenda integre mortem eius affectat? Et sic genitricis sue, que tot
50   dolores parturiendo pro eo sustinuit, quantum amorem nutriendo sibi ostendit,
modo pascendo, [f. 9v] modo lavando, modo amplexando, modo osculando,
modo "episcopum" vel "regem" vocando, et cetera huiusmodi, obliviscitur et
quasi alienam reputat eam. Contra quos dicitur Proverbiorum 53: "Audi patrem qui genuit te, et ne contempnas cum senuerit mater tua." In Deuterono-
55   mio enim legitur quod cum populus venerat in terram promissionis, statuerunt sex viros ad benedicendum eos qui legem servaverunt, et sex econtra ad
maledicendum transgressoribus, et semper respondit omnis populus "Amen."
Et inter alia dixerunt: "Qui patrem et matrem non honorant sint maledicti," et
respondit omnis populus, "Amen."

60   Et si queratur causa quare liberi sunt ita ingrati, revera responderi
potest: propter defectum correctionis et castigacionis dum fuerunt iuvenes;

seen in Absalom, Kings 15, who persecuted his father until his death. Similarly, the son of Nebuchadnezzar, in his desire to inherit the kingdom and not to let his father reign again, cut his father's body into pieces after his death and tied the pieces to the feet of vultures who were to carry them off so that they would never again come together.

Therefore such people may be called sons of bitches, who in their youth follow their mother and are nursed and fed by her, but as soon as they grow older and have sharp teeth and can gnaw bones like their mother, they quickly snatch a bone that is thrown in their midst and jump on it and have no more regard for their father or mother than for any other dog. In the same way, many ungrateful sons and daughters are very obedient to their parents in their youth, but after they have become adults, if they can gain or rip off anything from them, they have no more regard for them than for anyone else.

To their reproach Ambrose reports in his *Exameron* that the stork has such great care for its parents that when their parents' strength has faded and they have lost their feathers because of old age, their offspring stand around them and warm them with their own feathers and do not neglect to feed them with food they have gathered by their own labors, and then they raise their aged parents with the help of their own wings and incite them to fly and to reemploy their unused wings in their former use. Which of us has ever put his aged parent, who has loved us so much in our youth, on his own shoulders as that bird does? Or who has never tired of raising, taking care of, and nourishing his weak or ailing father? "Who is this, and we shall praise him?" Indeed, I fear, very few.

It is also reported that the hoopoe, a bird of the forest, when its parents in their old age have gone blind, seeks a precious stone by the seaside and puts it on their eyes, and they regain their sight. It is not thus nowadays, but if any of them lost one eye, many ungrateful people, I fear, would that, in order to gain their father's possession, their fathers lost both eyes and would die. The same applies to their mothers. Do we not see every day that a son puts his aged mother on the third part, and that a bad piece of land, and then in order to have that part wholly for himself wishes for her death? And thus he forgets his mother who endured so many pains in bringing him into the world, forgets how much love she has shown him, now feeding him, now washing him, now cuddling him, now kissing him, now calling him "bishop" and "king" and such, and he acts as if she were a stranger. In reproach of such people Proverbs 53 says: "Listen to your father who has begotten you, and do not despise your mother when she is grown old." For in Deuteronomy we read that when the people had come into the Promised Land, they placed six men to bless those who kept the Law and six against them to curse those who had broken it, and all the people always answered "Amen." And among other things they

et ideo, quod in iuventute incaute didicerunt, in senio ad usum ducunt. Dicitur enim communiter: "Quod nova tcsta capit, inveterata sapit." Et metrice dicitur sic:

65   Qui non assuessit virtutibus dum iuvenescit,
            A viciis nescit discedere quando senescit.

[Anglice:

            Woso woneþ hym noʒt to goude furst in hys youth,
            Unthewes to leve were to hym in his elde wel uncouþe.]

70   Unde Proverbiorum 22: "Adolescens iuxta viam suam cum senuerit non recedet ab ea." Cera enim mollis de facili recipit sigilli inpressionem, non sic autem cum fuerit indurata; similiter virga de facili flectitur, non sic cum crescit in arborem magnam; certe sic melius et facilius instruuntur filii in iuventute quam in senectute. Vestis autem si bene formatur in principio
75   decens est, si vero male vix ad bonam formam umquam devenire potest; revera sic est de doctrina et correctione puerorum. Et ideo dicitur in Proverbiis: "Qui diligit filium assiduet ei flagella," quia "confusio patris est filius indisciplinatus." "Qui docet filium, laudabitur." [Unde Anglice dicitur:

            Chasteʒ ʒoure chyldren quyl þay ben yonge,
80   Of lokyng, of dede, of speche, of tonge.
            For if ʒe lett hem be to bold,
            þay wol yow greve when þay ben old.
                  Lef chyld lore behoueth, quod Hendyng.]

       Unde narratur de quodam divite unicum filium habente, quem tantum
85   fatue dilexit quod pro nullo defectu illum corripere aut castigare voluit. Tale quidem tandem commisit factum quod pater illum redimere non potuit. Ille ergo assumpto patre in fugam et visis virgis in suo itinere [f. 10] [tradidit] unam patri dicens sibi: "Plica istam virgam, pater"; et fecit levissime. Tradidit eciam sibi maiorem, et fecit similiter. Cum autem sibi
90   tradidisset maximam virgam et illam plicare non potuisset, dicit patri: "Sicut, inquit, leviter plicasti tenerem virgam, sic me in iuventute castigare potuisses; set modo non potes." Et extracto gladio patrem occidit. Unde Proverbiorum: "Qui parcit virge odit filium."
       Similiter narrat Boicius *De disciplina scolarium* de quodam ducto ad
95   suspendium et a patre osculum petente, osculando nasum patris amputavit, quia eum in iuventute non castigavit. Et pro isto nota supcrius dc honore Deo debito in principio istius capituli, etc.

said: "Cursed are those who do not honor their father and mother," and the
whole people answered, "Amen."

And if anyone should ask for the reason why children are so ungrateful,
one can indeed answer: for lack of correction and chastising in their youth;
what they have badly learned in their youth, they make into a habit during old
age. For it is commonly said: "What a young head learns, an old one knows."
And in verse:

> He who of virtuous life in youth
>   Will not a custom make,
> Will not be able in his age
>   His vices to forsake.

In English:

> Woso woneþ him noȝt . . .

Whence in Proverbs 22: "A young man according to his way, even when he is
old he will not depart from it." For soft wax takes the form of the seal easily,
but not so when it has hardened; likewise, a young shoot bends easily, but not
so when it has grown into a large tree. In the same way one's children are
better and more easily taught in their youth than in old age. If a dress is
well cut in the beginning, it will fit well, but if it is cut badly, it will
hardly ever get the right shape; thus is it also with the teaching and correction of children. And therefore it is said in Proverbs: "He who loves his son
chastises him frequently," because "an ill-taught son is the confusion of his
father." "He who instructs his son shall be praised." Whence it is said in
English:

> Chastise your children while they're young,
> In looks, in deed, in speech, in tongue;
> For if you let them grow too bold,
> They'll give you grief when they are old.

"A dear child wants teaching," as Hending says.

There is a story about a rich man who had an only son whom he loved so
foolishly that he would not correct or chastise him for any failing. The boy
finally committed such a crime that his father could not save him. But when
the son had taken his father in flight and saw some rods on his way, he gave
one to his father and said: "Bend this," and he did so most easily. Then he
gave him a larger one, and his father did the same. But when he gave him the
largest rod and his father could not bend it, he said to his father: "As you

---

9 illa exequatur] illam exequantur O.   **11** set] et O.   **27** tunc] *om* O.   **29** obtemperant]
add patri et M.W; *add* se *corr* R.   **32** suo] *om* O.   **38** humeris] ut super humeros C.
40 etc.] *om* O.   **46** oculi] *om* O.   **53** dicitur] *om* O.   **56** eos] illos O.   **61** fuerunt] sunt
O.   **62** didicerunt] didicerint O.   **63** communiter] *om* O.   **67–69** Anglice . . . uncouþe]
text from E. *Verse 11, in* B3.E.L1.L2. LC.W1.   **76** in] *om* O.   **78–83** Unde . . . Hen-
dyng] *text from* R. *Verse 12, in* B3.E. Go1.Jo.L1.L2.LC.R.Sp.V.W1.   **86** quidem] quid
O.   factum] *om* O; crimen B1.Et.   **88** virgam pater] *om* O.   **95** patris] eius O.   **97** etc.]
om O.

I.xii   DE FRAGILITATE VITE

[S]equitur [de hiis] que veram inducunt humilitatem, per que pessimum
vicium superbie potest extirpari et ab eius veneno ab omnibus hominibus
caveri. Et sunt quatuor. Primum est proprie fragilitatis consideracio,
secundum est mortalis vite abbreviacio, tercium est tremenda iudicii mani-
5   festacio, et quartum est reproborum iusta dampnacio.

Circa primum est sciendum secundum Gregorium quod custos humilitatis
est recordacio proprie fragilitatis. Nec mirum, nam secundum quod legitur
Genesis 1, " 'formavit Deus hominem de limo terre,' que est ceteris elemen-
tis indignior. Planetas autem et stellas fecit de igne, flatus et vent⟨o⟩s
10   de aere, pisces et aves ex aqua, set homines et iumenta de terra. Considerans ergo homo aquatica se vilem inveniet; considerans aerea se viliorem
agnoscet; set considerans ignea se vilissimum reputabit nec se parificabit
celestibus nec audebit se preferre terrenis quia parem cum iumentis seipsum
inveniet. Hominum enim et iumentorum unus introitus, et equa utriusque
15   condicio; de terra simul exorta sunt et in terram simul revertentur. Iob:
'Comparatus sum luto et assimilatus sum faville et cineri.' Lutum enim
efficitur ex aqua et pulvere utroque manente, et cinis ex ligno [f. 10v] et
igne utroque deficiente. Quid ergo, lutum, superbis? Quid, cinis, gloriaris?" Dicit enim Bernardus: "Unde superbis, homo, fili terre, pater vermi-
20   bus, frater ⟨ta⟩lparum? Tuum robur infirmitas, tue divicie paupertas, honor
tuus dedecus, gaudium tuum luctus. Si (inquit) vires in iuventute, si

have bent the tender switch easily, so could you have chastised me in my youth; but now you cannot do so any longer." And he pulled out his sword and killed his father. Therefore Proverbs says: "He who spares the rod hates his son." In a similar vein Boethius reports in his *Instruction for Scholars* of someone who was being led to the gallows. He asked his father for a kiss and bit off his nose, because the latter had not chastised him in his youth. And on this matter notice what was said earlier about the honor we owe to God, in the beginning of this chapter.

---

3 Luke 2.51.   **5** Exod. 20.12.   **10–11** Ecclus. 3.7.   **11–12** Ecclus. 3.18.   **17–18** Mic. 7.6.   **19–20** 2 Sam. 15.   **32–37** Ambrose, *Exameron* V.16 (CSEL 32.1:181).   **40** Ecclus. 31.9.   **42–44** See Thorndike 2:422.   **53–54** Prov. 23.22.   **55–59** Deut. 27.11–16.   **63** *Prov* 25948; frequently quoted.   **65–66** *Prov* 24381 and *Verses* p. 145.   **70–71** Prov. 22.6.   **77** Ecclus. 30.1.   **77–78** Ecclus. 22.3.   **78** Ecclus. 30.2.   **85–93** Tubach 4488 (only *FM*).   **94** Prov. 13.24.   **95–97** Tubach 3488. Also in Bromyard, "Ab infancia," A.III.19; John of Wales, *Communiloquium*; Gerson's French sermons, ed. Mourin, p. 409 and n. 10. See also Lutz Röhrich, *Erzählungen des späten Mittelalters*, vol. II, Nr. viii.

I.xii   THE BRITTLENESS OF LIFE

Now we turn to the things that can bring us true humility, with which the evil vice of pride may be uprooted and with which all men may be able to guard against its poison. There are four. The first is consideration of our own frailty; the second, the shortness of this mortal life; the third, the appearing of the terrible judgment; and the fourth, the just condemnation of the wicked.

Concerning the first we must know that, according to Gregory, the guardian of humility is remembrance of our own frailty. This is no wonder, for as we read in Genesis 1, " 'God made man from the mud of the earth,' which is the least noble of all the elements; for he made the planets and stars from fire, breezes and winds from air, fishes and birds from water, but men and cattle from earth. Therefore, when man looks at the sea animals, he will find that he is despicable; when he looks at the animals of the air, he will find that he is even more so; but when he looks at the creatures of fire, he will deem himself the most contemptible; he will not put himself on the same level as the heavenly bodies, nor will he dare think of himself more highly than the creatures of the earth, for he will find that he is equal to land animals, for men and land animals have the same beginning and the same condition: together they have sprung from earth, and together they will return to earth. Job: 'I am like mud and like ashes.' For mud is composed of water and dust, which both remain in it, and ashes are composed of wood and fire, which lose their characteristics.

flores in prosperitate, si fulges pulcritudine, si viges sapiencia, si
splendes eloquencia—status tamen iuventutis in senectute proscribitur,
adversitas prosperitatem excludit, modica febris pulcritudinem expellit,
25 oblivio sapienciam, mors eloquenciam. Considera ergo, o homo, qualem te
fecit Deus et disce humiliari!" Hec ille. O esca vermium, o massa pulveris,
o vapor vanitatis, cur sic extolleris? Ignoras penitus utrum cras vives;
fac bene igitur quamdiu poteris. Si ergo consideres, o homo, quid per os,
quid per nares, quid per ceteros meatus corporis egreditur, numquid vilius
30 sterquilinio invenies te? Certe sic. Ergo humiliemus nos quia pauperes,
quia viles, quia ad bene operan⟨dum⟩ inpotentes; faciles enim sumus ad
seducendum et fragiles ad resistendum. Si temptemus facere bonum, defici-
mus; si conemur resistere malo, deicimur. "Arbores ergo et herbas," dicit
Bernardus, "investiga et considera, quia ille de se producunt frondes et
35 flores, et tu de te lendes et pediculos et huiusmodi; ille eciam de se
fundunt vinum, oleum et balsama, et tu de te stercus, urinam, et sputum. Ad
quid ergo (dicit ipse) philateria dilatas magnificans fimbrias vestimentorum? Dives enim ille qui indutus erat purpura et bisso sepultus est in
inferno." Hec ille. Et ideo dicit beatus Gregorius: "Mens sancti viri
40 semper dolore et fletu afficitur considerando bene ubi fuit, quia in peccato; ubi est, quia in miseria; ubi non est, quia in nulla gloria; ubi erit,
quia in iudicio ubi timendum erit de vindicta." [Et ideo dicitur Anglice
sic:

        Wreche mon, why art þou prowde
45   þat art of erthe maket?
        Hedure ne brouȝtest þou no schroude,
        But pore þou come and naket.
        When þy soule is faren out,
        þy body with erthe yraket,
50   þat body þat was so ronke and loude
        Of alle men is hated.]

Unde legitur in *Gestis Alexandri* [f. 11] quod cum vellet capere quandam
civitatem, cives basiliscum unum super muros eius posuerunt, qui plures
de excercitu Alexandri solo visu interfecit. Cuius causam cum ignorasset
55 Alexander, dicit ei Aristoteles quod parasset quendam armigerum audacem qui
scuto largo se operiret et illud inponeret inter ipsum et serpentem, atque
coram illo speculum magnum et politum ante serpentem poneret. Quo facto
proprio visu interfectus est. Spiritualiter autem per istam civitatem
intelligo celum; per Alexandrum illud capere volentem quemlibet fidelem;
60 illi autem qui nobis ingressum negant aliquando cives erant, quia angeli
mali qui, ut melius nos defendant ab ingressu, serpentem in sublimi faci-

Why therefore are you proud, O mud; whence do you derive your glory, O ashes?"
For Bernard says: "On what basis are you so proud, O man, son of the earth,
father of worms, brother of moles—your strength is weakness, your wealth
poverty, your honor shame, and your joy mourning. If you sprout in your youth,
if you bloom in prosperity, if you shine in beauty, if you flourish with
wisdom, if you sparkle with eloquence—still your youthful condition is banished in old age, adversity shuts out your prosperity, a little fever drives
away your beauty, failing memory your wisdom, death your eloquence. Therefore
consider, O man, what God has made you and learn to be humble!" O food for
worms, lump of dirt, cloud of vanity, why do you exalt yourself thus? Since
you hardly know if tomorrow you will be alive, do good while you can. For if
you consider, O man, what comes out of your mouth, your nose, and the other
passages of your body, will you not find that you are worse than a dungheap?
Certainly so. Therefore let us become humble, for we are poor, vile, and
powerless to do good deeds; we are easy to be seduced and weak to offer resistance. If we try to do good, we fail; if we attempt to resist evil, we are
overthrown. "Study and consider the trees and herbs," says Bernard, "for they
produce leaves and blossoms of their own, but you by yourself bring forth fleas
and lice and the like; they flow with wine, oil, and balm, but you with faeces,
urine, and spit. Why, then, do you broaden your philacteries and enlarge the
hems of your garments? For the rich man that was clothed in purple and fine
linen was buried in hell." And for the same reason Gregory says: "The mind of
a saintly person is always touched by grief and weeping when he considers where
he was—in sin; where he is—in misery; where he is not—in glory; where he
will be—in judgment and fear of vengeance." Therefore it is said in English
as follows:

> Wretched man, why are you proud
>   Who only are made of earth?
> To this life you brought no shroud
>   But naked you came and in dearth.
> When your soul has left its hold,
>   Your body is covered with dirt,
> That body that once was strong and bold
>   All people will desert.

Whence it is reported in *The Deeds of Alexander* that when Alexander wanted
to capture a certain city, its citizens set a basilisk on its walls, who killed many
from Alexander's army by his look alone. As Alexander did not understand
the cause, Aristotle told him to get a brave soldier ready who was to cover
himself with a broad shield and hold it between himself and the serpent, and to
put before himself a large, well-polished mirror in the face of the serpent.

unt, qui omnes solo visu interficit. Qui quidem serpens mundus est, qui
postquam aliquem sublimaverit et ex nimia dilectione bona mundi respicit et
detinet, quasi in illis omnino mortuus videtur, eo quod per illa impeditur
65   ne vitam eternam considerent. Quid ergo faciendum est? Revera speculum
consideracionis proprie, de qua dictum est, inter nos et illam delectacionem
erigendum est, quam diligenter si perspexerimus totum venenum mundi
et eius infectio avaricie moritur et adnichilatur.

---

2 hominibus] *add* potest O.   **5** et] *om* O.   **9** autem] enim O.   ventos] ventus C.
18 Quid(2)] unde O.   **20** talparum] culparum C.   **27** Ignoras] ignorans O.   vives] vix-
eris O.   **30** sterquilinio . . . sic] sterquilinium invenies quasi diceret non O.   **31** operan-
dum] operantes C.M.   **36** balsama] balsamum O.   **39** beatus] *om* O.   **42** ubi timendum
erit] timendus M.W; timens R.   **42–51** Et ideo . . . hated] *text from* R. *Verse 13, in*
B3.E.Go2.L1.L2.LC.R.Sp.W1.   **55** dicit] dixit O.   parasset] pararet O.   **56** operiret]
cooperiret O.   **61–62** faciunt] statuunt O.   **65** considerent] consideret M.W; desideret
R.

I.xiii   DE MEMORIA MORTIS

[S]ecundo humilitatem inducit memoria mortis, de qua Ieronimus ait:
"Facile, inquit, contempnit omnia qui se cogitat moriturum." "Memorare
novissima tua," iuxta consilium Sapientis, "et in eternum non peccabis."
Unde metrice dicitur:

5   Non aliter melius poterit caro viva domari
            Mortua qualis erit quam semper premeditari.

[Anglice sic:

            þe flesches lust may þou nou3t o-lyue bettur quenche
            Bote aftur þy deth which þou be3 euermore beþenche,]

10   scilicet quam breve erit tempus et quam incertum, et quam vile est corpus
mortuum, quia iuxta Iob: "Homo natus de muliere, brevi vivens tempore,
repletur multis miseriis," etc. [Anglice:

            Mon iboren of wommon ne lyueth but a stounde.
            In wrechednes and in wo ben his dayes iwounde.
15   He spryngus out as blossome and sone falles to grounde,
            And wendes away as schadewe þat no wey is ifounde.]

This being done, the basilisk was killed by its own look. Spiritually speaking, by that city I understand heaven; by Alexander, any believer who wishes to capture it; but those who deny us the entrance are former citizens, that is, the evil angels, who in order to better deny us entrance place a serpent on the top who kills everyone by its mere look. This serpent is the world. After it has lifted someone on high and he gazes at wordly goods and keeps them with great love, he seems to be totally dead in them, because he is prevented by them from thinking of eternal life. What then shall we do? Indeed, we must put up the mirror of self-knowledge, of which we spoke earlier, between ourselves and that delight; if we look at that with eagerness, all the poison of the world and its infection with avarice dies and comes to nothing.

6–19 Innocent III, *De miseria* I.2. **8** Gen. 2.7. **16** Job 30.19. **19–28** Widespread commonplaces; similarly in *Meditationes piissimae* III.8 (PL 184:490). **28–30** Ibid., III.7 (PL 184:489). **30–32** Cf. Bernard, *In adventu Domini*, sermo 7, 1 (4:196). **33–36** Innocent III, *De miseria* I.8. **36–39** Ibid., II.37. **37–38** Cf. Matt. 23.5. **38–39** Cf. Luke 16.19–22. **52–58** Tubach 495; and see F. Pfister, *Münchener Museum* 1 (1912), 264–265.

I.xiii   MEDITATING ON DEATH

In the second place it is meditation on death that brings us humility, of which Jerome says: "He who thinks of himself as about to die easily despises everything." "Remember your last things," after the counsel of the wise man, "and you will not sin in eternity." Whence it is said in a poem:

> There is no other way nor better
> Our lustful flesh well to subject
> Than always on its future nature
> When dead it will be to reflect.

In English thus:

> þe flesches lust . . .

namely, how short and uncertain time is and how vile our mortal body, for according to Job: "Man born of woman, living a short time, is filled with many miseries," etc.; in English:

> Man born of woman lives no more than an hour.
> In wretchedness and woe his days are wound.
> He blossoms and soon fades like a flower,
> And away like a shadow that nowhere is found.

Nam cum magno labore agitatur et cum dolore terminatur. Et tunc quod in
vita erat hominibus amabile, erit in morte illis odiosum [f. 11v] et abhominabile.
20   Nam sicut candela quando extinguitur lumen non ministrat assistentibus, set certe quod homines solet confortare fetet pessime, revera sic est
de homine cum moritur, quia corpus quod vivendo diversos confortabat post
mortem illis cedet in horrorem, iuxta illud:

          Vilior est humana caro quam pellis ovina:
25   Cum moriatur ovis, aliquid valet illa ruina,
          Extrahitur pellis et scribitur intus et extra;
          Cum moriatur homo, moritur simul caro et ossa.

Unde Bernardus: "Cum homo, inquit, moritur, nasus frigescit, facies pallescit, nervi ac vene rumpuntur, cor in duas partes dividitur. Nichil est
30   horribilius cadavere illius: in domo non dimittitur ne familia moriatur, in
aqua non proicitur ne inficiatur, in aere non suspenditur ne ille corrumpatur; set tamquam venenum pestiferum in fovea proicitur ne amplius appareat,
terra circumdatur ne fetor ascendat, firmissime calcatur ne iterum assur-
gat, set ut terra in terram maneat et amplius visus hominis illud non aspi-
35   ciat." [Unde Anglice dicitur:

          Was þer neuer caren so lothe
          As mon when he to put goth
             And deth has layde so lowe.
          For when deth drawes mon from oþur,
40   þe suster nul not se þe brother,
             Ne fader þe sone iknawe.]

Ideo dicit [Beda] quod mortis memoria humilitatis est victoria.
     Cogitemus ergo temporis brevitatem, mortis securitatem, et amicorum
instabilitatem, et simus semper parati, quia revera dies est certissima set
45   omnino incognita. Nescimus si media nocte an gallicantu an mane veniat,
quia sicut umbra cum declinat, ablatus est homo de medio; et sicut navis
pertransit aquam fluctuantem, cuius cum preterit non est invenire eius
vestigium, sic et nos nati desinimus esse. Quia ergo hec mors communis est
omnibus, ideo dicitur quod omnibus superveniet una captivitas.
50   Unde narratur quod Alexander in quadam epistola quesivit ab Aristotele
magistro suo quatuor questiones subscriptas. Prima fuit hec: Quid est illud
quod quanto longior est vel alcior, tanto cursior et brevior est? Et respondit quod vita hominis. [f. 12] Secunda hec fuit: Quid est illud de quo
plus capis, tanto ponderosi⟨us⟩ est? Et respondit quod corpus mortuum

For he is saddled with hard work and ends with pain. And whatever was love-
worthy to men during their life will then be hateful and abhorrent in death.

For as a candle when it is blown out no longer gives light to those present, but rather what used to bring men comfort smells very badly, just so is it
with a man when he dies, for his body which gave comfort to many people while
he was alive turns into something horrible after death. According to the poem:

> Man's flesh is viler than the skin of sheep.
> When sheep are dead, their skin still has some use,
> For it is pulled and writ upon, both sides.
> But with man's death both flesh and bones are dead.

Whence Bernard says: "When a man dies, his nose grows cold, his face turns
pale, his nerves and veins break, his heart splits in two. Nothing is more
abhorrent than his corpse: it is not left in the house lest his family die; it
is not thrown into the water lest it become polluted; it is not hung in the air
lest it become tainted; but it is thrown in a ditch like deadly poison so that
it may not be seen any further, it is surrounded with earth so that its stench
may not rise, it is firmly trodden down so that it may not rise again but stay,
earth in earth, and the eyes of man shall not behold it any further." Whence
it is said in English:

> Never was there carrion so loath
> As man when to his grave he goeth,
>   And death has laid him low.
> For when death draws a man from another,
> A sister will not see her brother,
>   Nor father his son know.

And therefore Bede declares that to think upon death is the triumph of humility.

Let us therefore keep in mind how brief time is, how certain death, and
how unstable our friends, and let us always be prepared, for the day is most
certain though completely unknown. We do not know if death comes at midnight
or at cockcrow or in the morning, for man is taken from our midst like a
shadow when it fades; and as a ship sails over the flowing sea, whose track
cannot be found once it has gone by, thus we, too, begin to cease being when we
are born. Since thus death is common to all, it is said that one and the same
captivity will come to all.

Therefore it is reported that Alexander in a letter asked of his teacher
Aristotle the following four questions. The first was this: What is that which
the longer and taller it is, the shorter and smaller it becomes? And Aristotle

55 postquam anima ab illo fuerit ablata. Tercia questio fuit hec: Quid est hoc
quod quanto propinquius est, tanto remocius est? Et repondit breviter quod
amici defuncti. Quarta questio fuit: Quid est hoc quod quanto lacius est,
tanto strictius est? [Et] respondit quod bona defuncti, que cum fuerint
largissim⟨e⟩ inter amicos et executores defuncti dispersa, strictissimam
60 partem miser defunctus inveniet.

[Unde narratur de clerico Parisius commorante famoso et divite, qui in
memoriam mortis sue ipso vivente fecit fieri sepulcrum suum; supra pro epi-
taphio fecit depingi ymaginem sui ipsius ⟨quasi morientis⟩, ad cuius pedes
eciam depinxit genus nummorum decurrencium in ⟨illa⟩ civitate aut terra. Ad
65 caput autem et ex utraque parte dicte ymaginis fecit depingi suos executores
suas manus sic extendentes, unam scilicet versus pecuniam et aliam versus
socios. Quorum primus dixit in Gallico:

De ceo mort sumus executors,
Mais de co money quei from nus?

70 Secundus sic:

Pren ta part et ieo la moye,
Ly mort n'ad cure de monoye.

Tercius sic:

Kyke noster dyner achatera,
75   Ceo mort issi le quitera.

In Anglico sic primus:

We ben executors of þis dede,
But of þis mone what is oure rede?

Secundus:

80   Take to þe and I to me,
þe dede kepes of no mone.

Tercius:

By vs oure dyner who-so wol,
þe dede schal quyten al þe fulle.]

replied: man's life. The second question: What is that which the more you take
from it, the heavier it becomes? And he answered: our dead body after the soul
has been taken from it. The third question: What is that which the nearer it
is, the more remote it becomes? And he said briefly: our dead friends. And
the fourth question: What is that which the broader it is, the narrower it
becomes? And he replied: the goods of the dead, because when they are most
widely distributed among the friends and executors of the dead person, the
latter, poor man, will find his part to be the narrowest.

There is a story about a cleric that lived in Paris and was famous and
rich, who during his lifetime had a tomb built for himself in memory of his
death. Instead of an epitaph he had made on it a picture of himself as if
dying, at whose feet he represented some money of the kind that was current in
that city or country. But at his head and at either side of this image he had
his executors depicted with their hands extended, that is, one pointing toward
the money and the other toward his companions. The first of them said in
French: "We are the executors of this dead man. What shall we do with his
money?" The second: "You take your part and I take mine. This dead man doesn't
care about money." And the third: "Who will buy our dinner? This dead man
here will pay for it." In English, the first said:

> We ben executors . . .

The second:

> Take to þe . . .

And the third:

> By vs oure dyner . . .

Because of all these things we must know that in the word *Mors*, "death,"
there are four letters which stand for four words and the qualities of anyone's
death. To the letter *M* corresponds the following sentence: Death is a marvelous mirror. Second, to the letter *O*: Death is a clock. Third, to the letter
R: Death is a raping robber. And fourth, to the letter S: Death is a summoner
on his circuit.

First, then, I say that death is like a mirror because in it all men are
seen without differences, the rich as well as the poor, the old as well as the
young; in the same way, death spares no one. According to authoritative writers, and as is obvious to one's sight, in a mirror there is an elevation on
one side called "boss" and a concavity on the other; if one looks into the side

85   Unde est sciendum quod in isto verbo "mors" sunt quatuor littere co-
      respondentes quatuor verbis et proprietatibus mortis cuiuslibet hominis.
      Nam pro ista littera M hec proposicio corespondet: Mors est mirum speculum;
      secundo pro ista littera O corespondet hec proposicio: Mors est orologium;
      tercio pro ista littera R corespondet hec proposicio: Mors est raptor [ra-
90   piens]; quarto pro ista littera S corespondet hec proposicio: Mors est
      sitator circuiens.
      Primo ergo dico quod mors assimilatur speculo eo quod in illo videntur
      omnes, tam divites quam pauperes, tam senes quam iuvenes, indifferenter;
      revera sic mors nulli parcit. Secundum enim auctores et sicut ad sensum
95   patet, in speculo ex una parte est quedam eminencia que vocatur "booce,"
      et una concavitas ex alia parte; tunc qui respicit ubi est illud booce apparet
      ulterius extra speculum, set qui respicit ex alia parte tunc apparet ulte-
      rius citra speculum, idest inter te et illud. Spiritualiter per istud booce
      intelligitur pompa mundi et superbia, que mortem videre non vult quia extra
100   ponitur; set per aliam partem speculi, scilicet concavitatem, intelliguntur
      humiles quibus apparet ulterius citra speculum, idest ante mortem. Nam ipsi
      considerant bene mundi decepcionem et propriam fragilitatem, [quo eciam
      tendunt,] et quod omnia concludit mors.
      Unde narratur de quadam muliere filium pariente, que cum misisset pro
105   quodam philosopho querens fortunam pueri, respondit quod bene viveret quo-
      usque proprium vultum in speculo respiceret, [f. 12v] set illo viso statim
      moreretur. Tandem accidit quod ille puer siciens descendit ad quendam fon-
      tem, in quo cum seipsum vidisset statim expiravit. Expone sic: Fons iste
      est consideracio proprie vite, per quam erga mundum homo moritur.
110   Secundo mors assimilatur orilogio, cuius officium est religiosos exci-
      tare ad orandum Deum; set pigri audita prima pulsacione expectant secundam
      et sic sompno gravati, ut frequenter, illam non audiunt. Et causa est quia
      in principio non excuciunt pigriciam, unde ab officio absentantur, et ideo
      postea per prelatum puniuntur. Set quia orologia habent diversos cantus,
115   ideo istius orologii mortis cantus est: "Memorare novissima tua et in
      eternum non peccabis." [Anglice sic:

            Haue mynde on þyn ende,
            And euer fro synne þou myght wende.]

      Set, quod dolendum est, pauci habent hunc canticum aut attendunt, et ⟨si⟩
120   quando aliqui audiunt et per pigriciam dormientes, a Deo tandem punientur.
      Tercio mors assimilatur raptori. Nam sicut talis distribuit bona rapta
      ad libitum et sibi ipsi reservat quod magis diligit, sic certe mors. Nam
      ipsa animam dat Deo aut diabolo prout in vita meruit, bona temporalia ami-
      cis, corpus vermibus, et cetera omnia ut sibi placet.

where the boss is, one's image appears beyond the mirror, but if one looks into
the other side, the image appears in front of the mirror, that is, between
oneself and the mirror. Spiritually speaking, this "boss" indicates the pomp
of the world and pride, which does not want to see death because it puts it
outside the mirror; but the other side of the mirror, its concavity, indicates
humble people who see their image in front of the mirror, that is before their
death, for these keep well in mind the treachery of the world, their own
frailty, where they are going, and that death is the end of all things.

There is a story about a woman who bore a son. When she sent for a
philosopher asking him about the boy's fortune, he replied that he would be
fine until he saw his own face in a mirror, but once he saw his face he would
die right away. Later on it happened that this boy got thirsty and went to a
fountain; when he saw himself there, he died at once. Expound as follows: this
fountain is the meditation on one's life, through which man dies to the world.

Second, death is likened to a clock, whose function it is to wake people
of religion for their prayer to God. Now, the lazy ones hear the first stroke
and wait for the second, and they become so heavy with sleep that often they do
not hear it. This is because they do not shake off their laziness in the beginning, wherefore they are absent from the Office and later on are punished by
their superior. But since clocks have different voices, the song of the clock
of death is as follows: "Remember your last things and you will not sin in
eternity." In English:

> Haue mynde on þyn ende . . .

But it is deplorable that few hear or pay attention to this song, and if they
sometimes hear it and thus sleep in their laziness, they will in the end be
punished by God.

Third, death is likened to a robber. For just as a robber distributes among
his companions at his will the goods that have been robbed and keeps for
himself what he likes most, thus death does too. For it gives the soul either
to God or to the devil, as man has deserved it in his life, his temporal goods
to his friends, the body to the worms, and all the rest as he pleases.

Fourth, death is likened to a summoner. As a summoner carries letters or
a staff as a sign of his office, thus death carries as his staff an acutely
painful arrow. Therefore, according to the ancients Death was depicted as a
knight sitting on horseback and carrying a squared shield. In its first quarter was a grinning ape, as a sign that after death a man's executors laugh at
him and spend his goods at their pleasure. In the second quarter a raving lion
was painted, for as a lion when he catches his prey roars horribly, at whose
roaring the other animals stand still, and he, having made a circle with his
tail, takes his prey as he pleases—just so death arrests all around him as he

125   Quarto mors assimilatur sitatori. Et sicut citator portat litteras aut
        virgam in signum sui officii, sic mors portat loco virge sagittam acutissime
        pene. Et ideo secundum antiquos mors depingebatur ad modum militis in
        equo sedentis et scutum quadratum baiulantis. In cuius primo quarterio fuit
        una simea cachinnans, in signum quod post mortem executores illum deluden-
130   tes expendunt bona sua ad placitum eorum. In secundo quarterio depingebatur
        leo rapiens, quia sicut leo quando capit predam horribiliter clamat, ad cuius
        clamorem cetera animalia sistunt gradum, et sic facto circulo cum cauda
        rapit ut placet, revera sic mors [f. 13] omnes per circuitum arestat ut
        placet et devorat. In tercio quarterio erat quidam sagittarius, in signum
135   quod ultimus ictus quem homo portabit est mors. Set in quarto erat quidam
        scriptor, in signum quod omnia facta scribentur et coram Deo recitentur,
        sive bona sive mala, post mortem hominis. Iste ergo citator mors primo ci-
        tat ad mortem in iuventute, secundo attachiat in fortitudine adolescencie,
        tercio incarcerat in senectute per debilitates naturales, et quarto secun-
140   dum veredictum duodenarii coram Deo iusticiario prout meruerunt vite vel
        morti iudicentur. "O ergo mors, quam amara," etc.

7–9 Anglice . . . beþenche] *text from* R. *Verse 14, in* B3.E.Go1.Jo.L1.L2.LC.R.V.
W1.   **10** quam(2)] *om* O.   **12** repletur . . . miseriis] *om* O.   **12–16** Anglice . . .
ifounde] *text from* R. *Verse 15, in* B3.Go2.Jo.L1.L2.LC.R.W1.   **35–41** Unde . . . ik-
nawe] *text from* R. *Verse 16, in* B3.E.L1.L2.LC.R.W1.   **42** Beda] *blank* C.   **50** fuit] est
O.   **53** fuit] est O.   **54** ponderosius] ponderosior C.   **59** largissime] largissima C.   **61–
84** Unde . . . fulle] *om* C. *Since* M *lacks the French and English verses, the text has here
been supplied from* R.   **63** quasi morientis] M.W; *om* R.   **64** illa] M.W; *om* R.   **77–
84** We ben . . . fulle] *text from* R. *Verse 17, in* B1.B3.E.Go1.Go2.Jo.L1.L2.L3.Li.LC.
R.Sp.V.W1.   **85** Unde] *add* pro omnibus istis O.   **86** hominis] *om* O.   **89–90** rapiens]
add et O.   **95** et] *om* O.   **97** ulterius] *thus* C.O *and others here and in the following lines*;
vultus B1.E.   **102** et] *om* O.   **108** sic] *om* O.   **115** est] *add* iste O.   **116–118** Anglice . . . wende] *text from* R. *Verse 19, in* B3.E.G1. Jo.L1.L2.LC.R.Sp.V.W1.   **119** si]
sic C.   **120** et] *add* sic O.   **121** rapta] *add* sociis O.   **125** Et sicut] sicut enim O.   **129–
130** deludentes] deridentes O.

I.xiv   DE IUDICIO

        [T]ercio dico quod humilitatem inducit tremenda iudicii manifestacio,
        de quo Ieronimus sic ait: "Quocienscumque, inquit, de die iudicii cogito,
        toto cor⟨pore⟩ contremisco, quia sive comedo sive bibo aut quicquid aliud
        egero, semper videtur in auribus meis tuba illa sonare: 'Surgite mortui,
5   venite ad iudicium.' " Nam sicut latro propter scelus incarceratus delibera-
        cionem expectans de adventu iudicis valde timet, sic debet quilibet Christi-
        anus in carcere peccati detrusus diem iudicii et Deum iudicem summe time-
        re, prout dicitur Corinthiorum 5: "Omnes vos manifestari oportet coram

pleases and devours them. In the third quarter was an archer, as a sign that
the last blow man will bear is death. But in the fourth quarter was a scribe,
as a sign that all deeds will be written down and read out before God, the good
as well as the evil ones, after man's death. This summoner Death first summons
us to death in our childhood; then he seizes us in the strength of our youth;
next he puts us in prison in our old age through our natural debility; and
finally we will be sentenced before God our justicer after the verdict of our
jury, to life or death as we have deserved it. Therefore: "O death, how bitter," etc.

---

2 Jerome, *Ep. 53* XI.3 (CSEL 54:465).   **2–3** Ecclus. 7.40.   **5–6** *Prov* 17219a and
Verses p. 148. The passage in Gregory on which the verse is based may be *Moralia*
XVI.lxix.83 (PL 75:1162).   **11–12** Job 14.1.   **24–27** *Prov* 33353; *In* 20331.   **28–
29** On the "Signs of Death," see *FM* VII.xix.   **61–84** Tubach 4896 (only *FM*).   **104–
108** Probably the myth of Narcissus: Ovid, *Met.* III.   **115–116** Ecclus. 7.4.   **141** Ecclus. 41.1.

I.xiv   THE DAY OF JUDGMENT

In the third place I say that the fearful revelation of the Judgment also
leads to humility. About it Jerome says: "Every time I think about the day of
judgment, I tremble in my whole body, for whether I eat or drink or do anything
else, always that trumpet seems to sound in my ears: "Rise, you dead, and come
to your judgment!" For as a thief who is put in prison for his crime and waits
for the sentence is much afraid of the coming of his judge, thus should every
Christian who has been thrown into the prison of sin fear above all the day of
judgment and Christ his judge, for as it is said in Corinthians 5: "You must all

tribunali Christi, ut recipiat unusquisque prout gessit," etc. Item scribi-
10 tur 3 capitulo: "Iudicabo te iuxta vias tuas et imponam tibi omnia scelera
tua et non parcet oculus meus et non miserebor, etc. Et scies quia ego
Dominus percuciens." Et Aggei dicitur capitulo 3: "Movebo pariter [celum et
terram] et subvertam solium regnorum et convertam fortitudinem gencium et
convertam quadrigam et ascensorem eius." Unde Ieremie 4 dicitur: "In die
15 illa, dicit Dominus, peribit cor regum et principum, et obstubescent sacerdotes, et prophete consternabuntur." Ecce quod iudicium illud magnum tale
erit quod pro indifferenti nullus [f. 13v] latebit set unusquisque de
factis suis reddet racionem, sicut pastor de agno minimo. Nos siquidem nunc
cum arguimur, dicit Ieronimus, multas pretendimus excusaciones, set tunc
20 obmutescemus nec dabitur locus audiendi, ubi nos accusabunt nostre consciencie. Unde Bernardus: "Veniet, inquit, veniet dies iudicii, ubi plus
valebunt opera bona quam auri pondera, consciencia pura quam verba dura,
ubi iudex donis non flectetur, nec precibus placabitur, ubi nil prodesse
poterint Aristotelis argumenta, quando filius mulieris iudicabit fines
25 terre." "Quis ergo non timet," dicit Ieronimus, "⟨illud examen⟩ in quo idem
erit accusator, advocatus, et iudex? Accuset enim cum dicet, 'Esurivi et
non dedistis michi manducare,' etc.; advocabit cum dicet, 'Quod minimis
meis fecistis, michi fecistis;' set iudicabit cum infert, 'Ite maledicti,'
etc." Unde versus:

30   Quantus erit luctus cum iudex dixerit, "Ite,"
        Tantus erit fructus cum dixerit ipse, "Venite."

    Dicunt enim naturales quod turbo per suam maximam violenciam quandoque
quercum maximam eradicat et quandoque hominem in sublime elevat, et nescit
utrum in plano vel in foveam cadat; revera sic erit de ira Dei; Ieremie 13:
35 "Ecce turbo dominice indignacionis egredietur," cui nullus resistere potest
quantumcumque potens quin in ira conterit et subvertit. Et ideo hic in vita
ista de hoc cogitemus et ipsum placare pro posse nostro curemus; modo enim
est satis benignus et misericors ad prestandum; non sic autem tunc, set
omnem iusticiam excercebit.
40   Unde ut videtur est modo et erit tunc de Deo sicut de sole in suis
signis. Secundum astronomos aliqua sunt signa solis maioris efficacie et
aliqua maioris austeritatis et duricie; quia signum Virginis est secundum
aliquos mitissimum et signum Leonis austerissimum, et sic de aliis. Inter
que [f. 14] transit sol sicut rex aut magnus dominus annuatim de castro ad
45 castrum, de manerio ad manerium. Ymaginando ergo de Christo, qui est verus
sol iusticie, videtur quod primo intravit signum Libre, sicut in suum castrum de circumstanciis ibidem ordinandis; in antiqua lege [reddebat ut
videtur] bonum pro bono, malum pro malo, quia "oculum pro oculo et dentem
pro dente," secundum legem talionis, iuxta illud: "Qua mensura mensi fueri-

be manifested before the judgment seat of Christ, that everyone may receive according as he has done," etc. In Ezekiel 3 is written: "I shall judge you according to your ways and all your crimes, and my eye will not spare you, and I shall have no mercy, etc. And you shall know that I am the Lord that strike." And in Haggai 3 it is said: "I will move both heaven and earth, and I will overthrow the throne of kingdoms and will destroy the strength of the Gentiles, and I will overthrow the chariot and him that rides in it." Whence in Jeremiah 4 it is said: "In that day, says the Lord, the heart of kings and princes shall perish, and the priests shall be astonished and the prophets shall be amazed." Behold what a great judgment it will be, so that no one will be able to hide as if it were none of his business, but everyone will render an account of his deeds, as a shepherd of his smallest sheep. When we are accused now, says Jerome, we put forth many excuses; but then we shall fall silent and have no chance to be heard when our consciences will accuse us. Therefore Bernard says: "It will come, the day of judgment will come, when your works will weigh more than weights of gold, a pure conscience more than hard words, when the judge cannot be bent by gifts or placated with prayers, when the proofs of Aristotle will avail nothing, when the son of a woman shall judge the whole earth." "Who then will not be afraid," says Jerome, "of that examination in which prosecutor, defense lawyer, and judge will be the same person? For he will accuse when he says: 'I have been hungry and you have not given me to eat', etc.; he will speak in our defense when he says: 'What you have done to the least of mine, you have done to me'; but he will judge when he enjoins: 'Go, you cursed ones,' " etc. As it is said in verse:

> As great as the sorrow will be when the judge says, "Go!"
> So great will the reward be when the same says, "Come!"

Natural philosophers say that a whirlwind sometimes uproots a mighty oak through its enormous violence, and sometimes it carries a man aloft and he does not know if he falls on level ground or in a ditch; thus it will be with God's wrath. Jeremiah 13: "Behold, the whirlwind of the Lord's indignation shall come forth," for no one, no matter how strong he is, can keep God's wrath from tearing and pounding him to pieces. Therefore let us meditate on this now in this life and try to placate him as much as we can, for now he is very benign and merciful to give us a chance; but not so later, when he will exercise complete justice.

Therefore it seems that it is now and will then be with God as it is with the sun in the signs of the zodiac. According to the astronomers, some signs through which the sun moves are more benign and others more austere and harsh. For according to some, the sign of Virgo is most mild and the sign of Leo most severe, and similarly with the other signs. The sun passes through them as a king or great lord who every year travels from castle to castle, from manor to

50   tis, remecietur vobis." Set iam de illo signo sive castro Libre amotus est
     et venit in castrum Virginis, quando ad consolacionem humani generis natu-
     ram nostram infra castrum castissime Virginis et matris eius suscipere dig-
     natus est. Unde sicut quando sol est in signo Virginis, ista inferiora me-
     lius disponuntur et micius tractantur, sic existente Christo cum ista
55   Virgine Maria, que semper illum pro nobis interpellat ac eius furorem
     contra nos pro peccatis mitigare non cessat, securi esse possumus de venia
     et gracia si velimus, ipso cum illa durante, ° ad illam confidenter recur-
     rere. Caveamus igitur, quia in illo castro Virginis et gracie morabitur per
     totum tempus vite nostre, ut quantumcumque fecerit peccator in vita et
60   misericordiam pecierit, concedet; ipse enim dicit: "Convertimini ad me,
     quia nolo mortem peccatoris set ut convertatur et vivat." Cum ergo amotus
     fuerit ab illo signo Virginis, transit ad signum Leonis; tunc ulterius non
     est gracia speranda, ut predictum est, set tunc per iram iusti iudicii
     sicut leo circuit "querens quem devorat," nullique parcens set omnibus
65   reddens secundum opera sua.
         Unde de isto die pulcre scribit Ieronimus *Ad Eliodorum Epistula prima*,
     dicens sic: "Veniet, inquit, dies illa quando hoc corruptum et mortale cor-
     pus induet incorrupcionem et inmortalitatem. Beatus tunc servus quem Domi-
     nus vigilantem invenerit. Tunc enim ad vocem tube pavebit terra cum populo,
70   [f. 14v] et tunc gaudebit regnaturus cum Domino, ⟨lugubre mundus rugiet,
     tribus ad tribum pectora feriet,⟩ potentissimi reges nudo latere palpita-
     bunt, tunc [se exhibebit cum prole sua Venere ignis Iupiter, adducetur cum
     stulticiis discipulis Platonis,] argumenta Aristotelis non proderunt. Tu
     autem rusticanus et pauper exultabis et ridebis et dices: "Ecce crucifixus
75   Deus meus!" Hec Ieronimus.
         De isto ergo iudicio cogitabat Dionisius magnus, de quo narratur quod
     cum argueretur semel a quodam super tristiciam vultus quam semper ostende-
     bat cum alii gauderent, fecit illum poni in quodam loco deaurato et mensam
     optimis cibariis repletam ante eum; supra capud eius gladium acutissimum et
80   maximi ponderis cum filo gracillimo [pependit], et subtus pedes eius prunas
     ardentes substituit, et quatuor lanceas acutissimas apposuit illum paratas
     perforare. Quo facto sibi dixit: "Comede et cum aliis gaude." Qui respondit:
     "Quomodo, inquit, hoc facere possem cum videam mortem meam ubique im-
     minere?" Cui Dionisius: "Sic, inquit, est michi cotidie sicut tibi hodie.
85   Tantum enim timeo iudicem superius rigidum et subtus ignem inferni et cete-
     ra quod gaudere non possum." Ad idem nota narracionem de rege Grecie, qui
     cum esset sic interrogatus a germano suo, fecit eum capi sicut dampnatum,
     etc.

---

3 corpore] corde C.   4 sonare] resonare O.   7 timere] *add* quia O.   9 Item] *longer om*
M; ezechielis *interl* R; *om* W.   10 capitulo] *om* O.   14 convertam] subvertam O.   4 di-

manor. If we apply this to Christ, who is the true sun of justice, it seems
that he first entered the sign of Libra as if he were entering his castle in
order to put it in order; in the Old Law, as it seems, he rendered good for
good, evil for evil, "an eye for an eye and a tooth for a tooth," according to
the law of retaliation, after these words: "By the same measure that you measure with, it will be measured to you." But now he has left that sign or
castle of Libra and has come to the castle of Virgo, when to the consolation of
mankind he deigned to assume our nature within the castle of the most chaste
Virgin, his mother. When the sun is in the sign of Virgo, things here below
are under a good and benevolent influence; just so, as long as Christ is with
the Virgin Mary, who always intercedes for us before him and never ceases to
mitigate the wrath he has against us for our sins, we can be assured of his
grace and forgiveness if we will go confidently to her while he is with her.
But let us beware: he will remain in that castle of Virgo and of grace as long
as we live, so that, whatever a sinner has done in his life, if he begs for
mercy, Christ will grant it, for he himself says: "Turn to me, for I do not
want the sinner's death but that he repent and live." But when he has moved
away from the sign of Virgo, he passes on to the sign of Leo, and then we can
no longer hope for grace, as was said earlier, but then he goes about in the
wrath of a just judgment like a lion, "seeking whom he may devour" and sparing
no one but rendering to all according to their deeds.

    With respect to that day Jerome speaks beautifully in his *First Letter to
Eliodorus* and says: "That day will come when this corrupt, mortal body puts on
incorruption and immortality. Happy then the servant whom the Lord finds
watching. For then the earth with all mankind will tremble at the voice of the
trumpet, and he who shall reign with the Lord will rejoice, the world will howl
in grief, tribe will beat its breast against tribe, kings, once most powerful,
will shiver with naked flanks, fiery Jupiter will show itself with its offspring Venus, the disciple of Plato will be brought forth with his stupidities,
and Aristotle's arguments will avail nothing. But you, a poor peasant, will
exult and laugh and say: 'Behold, the Crucified, my God!' "

    It is of that judgment that the mighty Dionysius was thinking, of whom it
is reported that once when he was criticized by somebody for always looking
glum while others were rejoicing, he had his critic put in a golden room with a
table full of the best food set before him, but above his head he hung a sharp
and heavy sword on a hair-thin string, and beneath his feet he put burning
coals and set four sharp lances ready to pierce him. When this was arranged he
told him: "Eat and rejoice with the others." His critic then replied: "How can
I do so when I see death threatening me from all sides?" And Dionysius said to
him: "Thus I feel all the time as you do today. For I fear the stern judge
above and the fire of hell below and the other things so much that I cannot
rejoice." On this matter also notice the story about the king of Greece who

citur] *om* O.   **23** flectetur] flectitur O.   placabitur] placatur O.   **24** prodesse poterint]
proderint M; proderunt *corr* R.W.   **25** illud examen] in suo exameron C.   **26** erit] est O.
dicet] dicit O.   **27** dicet] dicit O.   **34** Dei] *add* in die iudicii O.   **37** nostro] *om* O.
48 et] *om* O.   **57** durante] *add* et C.   **59** nostre] *om* O.   **62** transit] *om* O.   **64** devorat]
devoret O.   **66** scribit] ait O.   **69** invenerit] invenit O.   **70–71** lugubre . . . feriet] et
tunc C.   **71** potentissimi] *add* quondam O.   **72–73** se exhibebit . . . Platonis] *om* C.
The entire quotation is much corrupted in O. RW *omit* tunc *and read* exibebitur . . . ignitus iupiter . . . suis stulticiis . . . *See source note.*   **77** tristiciam] tristicia O.   **77–
78** ostendebat] ostendit O.   **79** supra] *add* vero O.   **87** dampnatum] *add various corrupted forms of* sub buccina O.

I.xv   DE PENIS REPROBORUM

[Q]uarto inducitur humilitas considerando reproborum iustam dampnacionem. Sicud scolaris trutannus attendens discipline flagellum cum diligencia
excercet studium, et latro considerans patibulum dimittit latrocinium, sic
superbus considerans Domini verba diffinitiva in iudicio: "Ite maledicti,"
5   etc., sequitur exemplum humilitatis. Maxima enim pena est malorum intueri
gaudia electorum. Unde Gregorius: "Quis putas tunc erit meror et tristicia
cum separabuntur mali a consorcio iustorum et sanctorum et tradentur in
potestate demonum divina visione carentes?" Revera secundum Crisostomum:
"Siquis in mille iehennis esset positus sine culpa, nichil esset tale quale
10   est ab illa gloria [f. 15] excedere et divina visione carere, ⟨odio⟩ haberi
a Christo, et ° audire: 'Non novi vos.' " Tales enim tunc dicent
illud Sapiencie 9: "Erravimus a via veritatis." Set certe caveant quia
nimis tarda est eorum penitencia, sicut est de latrone qui primo penitet ad
pedem patibuli; sic eciam expectavit dives ille quousque venit ad infernum
15   penitere, ubi dixit: "Pater Habraham, miserere mei." Iste enim patrem
vocavit in penis cuius filius non erat in terris, et a Lazaro peciit
ministrari in pena cui numquam ministravit in vita. ⟨Sic⟩ isti qui de bonis
dicunt: "Hii sunt quos aliquando habuimus in derisum," etc. Unde dicit
Gregorius: "Sic acrius, inquit, dolebunt miseri videntes gloriam quam
20   amiserunt et boni amplius gloriantur videntes penam quam evaserunt, quia ut

was asked a similar question by his brother and had him captured like a condemned criminal, and so forth.

2–5 Ps.-Jerome, *Regula monacharum* 30 (PL 30:417), from Jerome, *Ep. 66* 10 (CSEL 54:660).   **8–9** 2 Cor. 5.10.   **10–12** Ezek. 7.8–9.   **12–14** Hag. 2.22.   **14–16** Jer. 4.9.   **21–23** Bernard, *Ep. 1* 7 (7:6).   **23–25** Cf. below, line 73.   **25–29** Innocent III, *De miseria* III.19.   **26–27** Matt. 25.40–42.   **27–28** Matt. 25.40.   **28** Matt. 25.41.   **30–31** *Prov* 23647; 30991a. Very widespread.   **35** Jer. 23.19.   **48–49** Exod. 21.24, etc.   **49–50** Matt. 7.2.   **60–61** Ezek. 33.11.   **64** 1 Pet. 5.8.   **67–75** Jerome, *Ep. 14* 11 (CSEL 54:61): "Veniet, veniet illa dies, qua corruptivum hoc et mortale incorruptionem induat et immortalitatem. Beatus servus, quem Dominus invenerit vigilantem. Tunc ad vocem tubae pavebit terra cum populis, tu gaudebis. Iudicaturo Domino lugubre mundus immugiet; tribus ad tribum ferient pectora; potentissimi quondam reges nudo latere palpitabunt; exhibebitur cum prole sua vere tunc ignitus Iuppiter; adducetur et cum suis stultus Plato discipulis; Aristoteli argumenta non proderunt. Tunc tu rusticanus et pauper exultabis, ridebis et dices: 'Ecce crucifixus Deus meus, ecce iudex.' "   **76–86** "Sword of Damocles (!)": Tubach 4994; also in Bromyard, "Homo," H.I.22; Brinton, sermons 18, 25, 76, and 101 (pp. 74, 99, 347, and 464); Grisdale, pp. 33–34. Derived from Cicero, *Tusculanae disputationes* V.21.   **86–88** "Trumpet of Doom": included in Tubach 4994; see *Gesta Romanorum* 143.

I.xv   THE PUNISHMENT OF THE WICKED

In the fourth place, humility is brought about by considering the just damnation of the wicked. Just as a lazy schoolboy who has his eyes on the rod of punishment pursues his studies with diligence, and as a thief who thinks of the gallows abandons his thieving, thus the proud person who reflects on the words which the Lord will proclaim in judgment: "Go hence, you cursed ones," and so on, follows the way of humility. The greatest pain for the wicked is to see the joys of the elect. Therefore Gregory says: "What do you think will be the grief and mourning when the wicked are taken away from the company of the good or the saints and handed over into the power of the devils, where they will lack the vision of God?" In truth, according to Chrysostom, "if one were put in a thousand hells without guilt, this would be nothing like failing to reach that glory and losing the sight of God, being hated by Christ, and hearing his words: "I do not know you." Such people will then exclaim the words written in Wisdom 9: "We have erred from the way of truth." But let them beware: their remorse comes too late, as in the case of a thief who begins to repent when he stands at the foot of the gallows; just so did that Rich Man wait with his repentance until he came to hell, where he said: "Father Abraham, have pity on me." He called him "father" in his punishment whose son he had never been on earth, and he begged that Lazarus should help him in his pain whom he never helped in his life. So it will go with those who say of the

dicitur Iob 24: 'Transibunt ab aquis nivium ad calorem nimium.' " O quam
cruenti erunt oculi qui tot effundent lacrimas quot habet occeanus guttas,
et tamen tota illa aqua minimam sintillam ignis inferni extinguere non
valebit, testante Augustino et dicente: "Quanto, inquit, naturalis ignis
25   distat a picto, tanto distat ignis inferni a naturali. Cuius (dicit ipse)
tanta erit violencia quod si in ipso influeret universitas aquarum, ipsum
nec ad momentum extingueret." Ille ergo ignis maximum fumum generat, et
fumus tantus necessario magnum fletum provocat, set fletus ille ignem
fortificat et fervescere facit, sicut faber acuit lentum ignem aquam
30   spergendo in illo. Et tunc mortem appetunt qui mori non possunt. Unde
Gregorius: "O, inquit, mors, quam dulcis eris quibus tam amara fuisti." Hec
ille. Unde Apocalipsis dicitur: "Desiderabant mori et fugiet mors ab
illis." Sicut animalia non evellunt radicitus herbas comedendo, summitates
solummodo capiunt ut iterum crescant, [f. 15v] sic dampnati quasi morte
35   depascuntur, et tamen iterum ad mortem reviviscunt. Sicut videmus quod
ioculator equum suum mactat, excoriat, ac mortuum similat, et post
reviviscere facit, sic demones per penas animam quasi mactant et iterum
reviviscere faciunt, etc.

---

7 et] vel O.   9 in . . . culpa] decem milia ponat gehennas O.   esset(2)] *om* O.   10 odio]
apparently hodie C.   11 et] *add* forte cras C.   audire] *add* quoniam O.   Tales] *om* O.
13 eorum] *om* O.   16 non] numquam O.   17 Sic] sicut C; similiter W.   21 nivium] nivis
M.R; nimis W.   32 Desiderabant] desiderabunt R.W.   38 etc.] *om* O.

I.xvi   DE MERCEDE HUMILIUM

[C]irca mercedem humilium est sciendum quod triplex merces veris humilibus qui predictis [modis] se humiliant et superbiam extirpant attribuitur:
prima in oracione exaudicio; secunda in tribulacione consolacio; tercia
est eternalis beatificacio.
5   De primo dicitur Ecclesiastici 35: "Oracio humiliantis se nubes penetrat," quia iuxta illud [Psalmorum]: "Respexit Dominus in oracionem humilium et non sprevit," etc. Nam sic est de humilitate sicut de scala Iacob
quam vidit celos attingentem, cuiusmodi sunt tres gradus, scilicet subdere
propter Deum superiori, pari, et minori; et certe cum hac scala capitur
10   castrum sine resistencia. Similiter sicut ostium humile intrare non potes
nisi inclinato capite, nec lapidem in altum proicere nisi brachio inclinato, nec ludens in alto salire nisi incurvato corpore, sic certe vere humi-

good: "These are the people whom we formerly held in contempt," etc. Whence Gregory says: "Thus the wicked will suffer more keenly when they behold the glory they have lost, and the good will rejoice more fully when they see the punishment they have escaped, for as it is said in Job 24: 'From icy water they will pass to extreme heat.' " How bloody will the eyes be which shed as many tears as there are drops in the ocean, and yet all that water cannot quench the least spark of hellfire, as Augustine witnesses when he says: "As unlike natural fire is to painted fire, so is the fire of hell unlike natural fire. It will burn with such vehemence that, if all the waters there are were to flow into it, they would not extinguish the least bit of it." For that fire causes an enormous smoke, and that smoke of necessity causes weeping, but that weeping increases the fire and makes it burn the more, just as a blacksmith heats up a slow fire by sprinkling water on it. And then they will desire death yet cannot die; whence Gregory exclaims: "O death, how sweet will you be to those to whom you have been so bitter." Therefore it is written in Revelation: "They longed for death, and death will flee from them." Animals, when they feed, do not pull up plants by their roots but only take their tops so that they may grow again; in the same way the damned are, as it were, fed upon by death, and yet they grow afresh for death. We observe that a juggler kills his horse, flays it, and pretends that it is dead, and then he makes it come alive again; in the same way devils kill the soul through their punishments as it were and make it come alive again.

---

4 Matt. 25.41.   6–8 *Meditationes piissimae* III.10 (PL 184:491).   9–11 Chrysostom, *In Matthaeum*, hom. 23, 8 (PG 57:317).   12 Wisd. 5.6.   15 Luke 16.24.   18 Wisd. 5.3. 21 Cf. Job 24.19.   31 Innocent III, *De miseria* III.12.   32–33 Rev. 9.6.

I.xvi   THE REWARD OF THE HUMBLE

Concerning the reward of humble people, we must know that to the truly humble who in the aforesaid manners humble themselves and eradicate pride a threefold reward is given: first, the fulfillment of their prayer; second, comfort in tribulation; and third, eternal bliss.

Of the first is said in Ecclesiasticus 35: "The prayer of one who humbles himself pierces the clouds," for according to the Psalm verse, "the Lord has looked on the prayer of the humble and has not scorned it," etc. For true humility is like the ladder Jacob saw, which reached to the skies; it has three steps, namely, to submit oneself for God's sake to a person of higher standing, or of equal rank, or of a lower one; and surely, with this ladder a castle may be captured without resistance. In similar fashion, just as one cannot go through a low gate without bending one's head, nor throw a stone up high

lis quanto humilius se inclinat tanto alcius ad gaudii perfectionem ascendit; Iacobi 4: "Humiliamini in conspectu Domini, et exaltabit vos."
15   Secundum premium est in tribulacione consolacio, sicut pie matris presencia filio egrotanti est consolacio maxima; Corinthiorum 7: "Qui consolatur humiles, consolatus est vos Deus." Arbores autem quanto magis fructificant, tanto magis inclinantur; sic perfectus humilis quanto magis in bonis
operibus crescit, tanto magis humiliatur et in tribulacione consolatur;
20   Iudith 8: "Expectemus humiles consolacionem eius."
        Tercium premium eterna gloria est et celi gaudia; Proverbiorum: "Humi-
lis spiritu suscipit gloriam." Unde Augustinus *De verbis Domini*, sermone
39: "Si, inquit, vis [f. 16] capere celcitudinem, cape humilitatem." Dicit
enim Christus Matthei 4: "Sinite parvulos venire ad me, talium est enim
25   regnum celorum." Ibi enim cum venerimus, eum facie ad faciem sicuti est in
natura nostra filius Dei, una cum beatissima matre eius et omnibus sanctis
videbimus; ubi nullus alteri incognitus, nullus ab alio separatur, nulla
servilis subiectio, nulla tristicia, nichil compaciendum, nichil despicien-
dum, set pax interminabilis, amicicia indissolubilis. Ibi eciam rex est
30   veritas, lex est caritas, et merces iocunditas. Quid plura? Certe, quod
"oculus non vidit nec auris audivit nec in cor hominis ascendit, que preparavit Deus diligentibus se," sicut dicitur Corinthiorum 2. Ad quam nos perducat per veram humilitatem Iesus Christus. Amen.
        Et hec de superbia et humilitate cum suis membris ad presens dicta
35   sufficiunt, et sic terminatur prima particula istius libelli.

---

6 Psalmorum] *om* C.W.   **7** de] *add* vera O.   sicut] *add* est O.   **12** alto] altum O.
14 Domini] dei O.   **30** quod] *om* O.

without bending one's arm, nor in a game jump high without bending one's body—
thus likewise a truly humble person, the lower he bends, the higher he climbs
to perfect joy; James 4: "Humble yourselves in the sight of God and he will
raise you up."

The second reward is comfort in tribulation, as the presence of his loving
mother is the greatest comfort for her sick child; Corinthians 7: "God who comforts the humble, has comforted you also." For the more heavily trees are
laden with fruit, the more they bend down; thus, the more a perfect, humble
person grows in good works, the more humble he becomes and is comforted in
tribulation; Judith 8: "Let us in humility wait for his consolation."

The third reward is eternal bliss and the joy of heaven; Proverbs: "The
humble of spirit receives bliss." Whence Augustine says in Sermon 39 of *On the
Words of the Lord*: "If you want to gain the height, gain humility." For Christ
says in Mark 4: "Let the children come to me, for theirs is the kingdom of
heaven." When we get there, we shall see him face to face as he is in our
nature, the Son of God, together with his most blessed mother and all the
saints; where no one will be unknown to the other and no one is separated from
the other; there will be no slavish submission, no sadness, nothing to feel
pity for, nothing to be scorned, but peace without end and friendship that
never dissolves. For there truth is king, charity law, and joy the reward.
What more? Surely, "eye has not seen, nor ear has heard, nor has it entered
the heart of man what things God has prepared for those that love him," as is
said in Corinthians 2. To which Jesus Christ may lead us through true humility. Amen.

And these things that have been said about pride and humility and their
members suffice for now, and thus ends part 1 of this book.

5–6 Ecclus. 35.21.   6–7 Ps. 101.18.   7–8 Cf. Gen. 28.12.   14 James 4.10.   16–17 2
Cor. 7.6.   20 Jth. 8.20.   21–22 Prov. 29.23.   23 Augustine, *Sermo 117* 17 (PL
38:671).   24–25 Mark 10.14.   31–32 1 Cor. 2.9.

PARS II

De ira

II.i   QUID SIT IRA

[Q]uia mater crudelis parere solet filiam sevissimam, ideo in ista
secunda particula agitur de ira, tamquam de principali filia pessime matris
superbie; cuius condicio principalis est cito accendi, et numquam mitigari
potest donec per vindictam voluntatis irascibilis totaliter consummatur, ad
5   modum quo ignis cui ligna sicca administrantur de levi accenditur nec
cessat, quantum in eo est, donec omnia destruantur. Unde circa istam iram
sic intendo procedere et videre primo que sit eius proprietas, secundo que
mala facit eius iniquitas, tercio que sunt eius membra, quarto quare omnino
est detestanda.
10   Circa primum est sciendum secundum Gregorium libro 5 *Moralium* quod
aliquando dicitur ira per zelum et aliquando per vicium. Prima est quando
animus turbatur propter malum, iuxta illud Psalmi: "Irascimini et nolite
peccare." Set ira per peccatum, de qua hic intenditur, est secundum Augustinum "voluntas irrefrenata semper ulciscendi et numquam miserendi," [f.
15   16v] sicut patet supra exemplo de igne.

II.ii   MALA QUE IRA FACIT

Circa autem mala que facit eius iniquitas est sciendum quod primo
[anima], que est ymago Dei in homine, [per illam] exterminatur, sicut aqua
turbida non representat formam ymaginis sicut facit aqua limpida et clara.
Unde legitur in *Vitas Patrum* de quodam sene qui posuit denarium in cipho

PART II

Wrath

II.i THE NATURE OF WRATH

Since a cruel mother usually gives birth to a savage daughter, in this
second part we deal with wrath, as the chief daughter of that wicked mother,
pride. Its main character is to be quickly inflamed, and it can never be
mitigated until it has spent itself by totally venting its irascibility, just
as a fire that is given dry sticks is easily kindled and cannot stop of itself
until all the sticks are burnt. Therefore I plan to deal with wrath in the
following way: to see first what its nature is, second what evil consequences
its wickedness has, third what its members are, and fourth why it should be
totally condemned.

Concerning the first point we must know that according to Gregory, in book
5 of his *Morals*, wrath is sometimes considered as zeal and sometimes as a vice.
The former occurs when one's mind is disturbed on account of some evil; according to the Psalm: "Be angry and sin not." But the kind of wrath which is a
sin, with which we are dealing here, is according to Augustine "the unbridled
desire always to get vengeance and never to have pity," as we saw above in the
example of fire.

---

11 Cf. Gregory, *Moralia* V.xlv.82 (PL 75:726).   **12–13** Ps. 4.5.   **14** Cf. Augustine, *De
civitate Dei* XIV.15 (CC 48:438) or *Sermo 58* vii.8 (PL 38:396).   **15** *FM* II.i.3–6.

II.ii THE EVIL CONSEQUENCES OF WRATH

Concerning the evil consequences which its wickedness has, we must know
first that the soul, which is the image of God in man, is destroyed by it, just
as turbulent water does not hold the shape of a reflection in the same way as
clear and still water does. Whence we read in *The Lives of the Fathers* about a

5   pleno aqua clara, et videns ymaginem illius dixit fratri suo: "Sic apparet
ymago Dei in tranquillis cordibus." Quo dicto aqua[m] movit et ymago denarii disparuit, et dixit: "Sic deletur ymago Dei in turbatis cordibus." Hec
ille, etc.

    Secundo impedit animam ab influencia divine gracie, sicut aer turbidus
10 impedit splendorem et irradiacionem solis. Unde Gregorius libro 5 *Moralium*:
"Per iram, inquit, lux veritatis amittitur, quia cum iracundia confusionis
tenebras [menti] incutit, huic Deus radium sue cognicionis abscondit." Hec
ille.

    Tercium malum est quod sibi subiectum membrum diaboli facit. Ieremie
15 6: "Crudelis est et non miserebitur." Contra dicit Augustinus: "Non meretur
misericordiam qui eam proximo negat." Et ideo tales merito peiores possunt
dici diabolo. Diabolus enim instigator malorum peccata dum perpetrantur
commemorat; cum vero per penitenciam delentur, omnino illa ignorat, et
Christus remittit sua gracia. Exemplum de illo de quo narrat Gregorius, qui
20 postquam homagium fecerat diabolo et eius carecteres in manu sua recep⟨e-
ra⟩t, postea contritus et confessus et penitencia recepta evanuerunt carac-
teres nec illum diucius diabolus pro suo agnovit. Ezechielis 18: "Si impius
egerit penitenciam, omnium iniquitatum eius non recordabor, dicit Dominus."
Multo forcius ergo nec diabolus. Nam demones ad mensuram reddunt malum
25 pro malo nec ultra meritum punire possunt nec unum pro peccatis alterius; set
certe iracundi pro unico verbo mille reddunt et pro una alapa in facie
mergunt arma mortifera in corpore, et non in illum qui dedit alapam [f. 17]
tantum, set secundum suum posse totam progeniem destruere nititur. Patet
ergo quod peiores sunt diabolo. Dicitur autem metrice sic:

30   Impedit ira animum ne possit cernere verum, etc.

---

19 narrat] *add* beatus O. **20–21** receperat] recepit C. **22** diucius] *om* O. **28** nititur]
nitetur M; nituntur R; nitentur W. **30** etc.] *om* O.

II.iii DE MEMBRIS IRE

[C]irca eius membra est sciendum quod duo sunt specialiora, scilicet
odium et vindicta; nam multi sunt hodie qui se armis materialibus vindicare

desert father who put a denarius in a bowl full of clear water, and as he saw
its image he said to his brother: "Thus does the image of God appear in tran-
quil hearts." After saying that he moved the water, and the image of the
denarius disappeared, and he said: "Thus is the image of God destroyed in
troubled hearts."

Second, wrath obstructs God's grace from flowing into the soul, as turbulent air obstructs the brightness and radiance of the sun. Therefore, Gregory
says in book 5 of *Morals*: "Through wrath the light of truth is lost, for when
anger injects the darkness of confusion into the mind, God withholds from it
the ray of his knowledge."

The third evil is that wrath makes a person who suffers from it a member
of the devil. Jeremiah 6: "He is cruel and will take no pity." Against such a
person Augustine says: "He deserves no mercy who denies it to his neighbor."
Those people may rightly be said to be worse than the devil; for the devil, who
instigates evil, remembers sins as long as they are being committed; but when
they are wiped away through penance, he forgets them altogether, and Christ
forgives them in his grace. As an example we have the case of a person of whom
Blessed Gregory reports that, after he had sworn fealty to the devil and had
received his marks in his hand, when he later on felt remorse and confessed and
received his penance, the marks disappeared and the devil no longer recognized
him as his own. Ezekiel 18: "If the wicked does penance, I will not remember
all his iniquities, says the Lord." Much less, then, will the devil remember
them. For the devils return evil for evil in like measure and cannot give
punishment beyond what is deserved, nor can they punish one person for the sins
of another. But wrathful people, in truth, return a thousand words for one,
and for one blow in the face they thrust deadly weapons into the body, and not
just into the one alone who gave the blow, but they try to destroy his entire
offspring if they can. Thus it is evident that they are worse than the devil.
On this we have the following saying in verse:

Anger blocks our mind from seeing what is true.

4–8 Cf. *Speculum laicorum* 349; also in Bromyard, "Paciencia," P.IV.9.   **11–13** Gregory, *Moralia* V.xlv.78 (PL 75:724).   **15** Jer. 6.23.   **15–16** Cf. Augustine, *Sermo 58* v–
vii (PL 38:395–96) or *En. in Ps. 102* 11–14 (CC 40:1461–1465).   **19–22** Tubach
2414.   **22–23** Ezek. 18.21.   **30** *Prov* 11566, etc.; from *Disticha Catonis* II.iv.2.

II.iii   THE MEMBERS OF WRATH

Concerning its members we should know that there are two in particular,
namely hate and revenge. For many people today cannot take their revenge with

non possunt, et ideo odium per iram induratam in corde retinent. Set nota
quod duplex est odium, scilicet virtuosum et viciosum. De primo dicit Au-
5   gustinus: "Perfectum odium, inquit, est quod nec iusticia nec sciencia ca-
ret, hoc est si propter vicia homine⟨s⟩ non oderis, nec vicia propter homines diligis. Recte ergo in malis odimus maliciam et diligamus creaturam,
ut nec propter vicium creatura dampnetur nec propter naturam vicium dilige-
tur." Et alibi: "Sic, inquit, diligendi sunt homines, ut eorum non diligan-
10 tur errores; quia aliud est amare (dicit ipse) quod facti sunt, et aliud
odisse quod faciunt." Et iterum: "Omnis peccator in quantum peccator non
est diligendus; set omnis homo in quantum homo diligendus est propter Deum,
Deus autem propter seipsum."
De malo autem odio et vicioso similiter dicit Augustinus in quodam
15 sermone: "Si, inquit, irasci fratri non licet sine causa aut dicere ['racha'
aut dicere] 'fatue,' multo magis non licet aliquid tenere in odium, per
quod odium in indignacionem convertaris," nam huiusmodi odium hominem
assimilat diabolo. Est enim [naturale] odium inter homines et serpentes
sicut inter equos et griphones, lupos et canes; unde serpenti a Deo dictum
20 est, Genesis 3: "Inimicicias ponam inter te et mulierem." Igitur qui hominem odit serpentini generis est, ac per hoc diabolo assimilatur, qui est
maledictus; et talis ergo a Domino cum serpente maledicitur. Et ideo talis
ira et odium potest per illum ventum designari de quo Iob 1: "Qui irruit a
regione deserti et concussit quatuor angulos domus et oppressit liberos."
25 Sic ira et odium [cum in domum] anime irruit, quatuor eius affectiones, [f.
17v] scilicet quatuor virtutes, corrumpit et quicquid boni in ea nascitur
destruunt, quoniam sine caritate bona non prosunt.
Secundum autem membrum ire est vindicta, quam qui in proximis excercent et iniuste et ultra debitam mensuram (quod non facit diabolus, ut dic-
30 tum est), non homines set pocius bestie, idest vastie, feroces esse videntur. Unde Crisostomus de Herode loquens sic ait: "Sicut, inquit, fera bestia per naturalem asperitatem si ab alico fuerit vulnerata suam naturalem
crudelitatem duplicis doloris infundit, unde quasi ceca furore iam non aspicit vulnerantem set quicquid ante oculos eius occurrerit, sive homo sive
35 alterum animal, quasi auctorem vulneris sui dilacerat, sic (dicit ipse)
Herodes a magis illusus iram suam super parvulos innocentes infudit."
Unde tales similes sunt iunipero, cuius natura ⟨est⟩ secundum Ysidorum, *Ethimologiarum* libro 17, capitulo 7, quod per annum observat ignem,
si prune ex proprio cinere fuerint cooperte. Certe sic est de multis qui sub
40 cinere ac velamine proprie malicie ignem sic servant iracundie quod aliquando per plures annos semper expectant oportunitatem vindicandi. Et ideo
tales communiter in proprio furore confunduntur, sicut patet sub figura
Exodi 28 de Pharaone cum suis in Mari Rubro submersis filios Israel iniuste
persequendo; similiter de Sampsone a Philisteis illuso, ulcionem expeciit

material weapons and therefore retain hatred through hardened anger in their hearts. But notice that there are two kinds of wrath, one virtuous, the other a vice. Of the first Augustine says: "Just anger is not devoid of either justice or knowledge, namely, when you neither hate men because of their vices, nor love vices because of human beings. For it is right for us to hate evil in wicked men yet to love the created human being, so that the created being should not be condemned because of his vice, nor should a vice be loved for the sake of man's nature." And elsewhere he says: "Men should be loved in such a way that one does not love their mistakes; for it is one thing to love what has been created in them, another to hate what they do." And again: "No sinner, insofar as he is a sinner, must be loved; but every human being, insofar as he is human, must be loved for God's sake, but God for himself."

Of the evil and vicious kind of wrath, however, Augustine says likewise in a sermon: "If it is not permitted to be angry with one's brother without cause, or to call him 'racha' or 'fool,' much less is it right to nurse hatred whereby one turns hatred into indignation," for such hatred makes a man like the devil. There is a natural hatred between men and snakes, as there is between horses and griffins, wolves and dogs; whence God said to the serpent, in Genesis 3: "I will put enmity between you and the woman." Therefore, anyone who hates a human being has the nature of the serpent, and by this he becomes like the devil, who has been cursed; and thus a person who hates is cursed by God together with the serpent. Such anger and hatred may therefore be indicated by the wind of which Job 1 speaks: it "came from the side of the desert and shook the four corners of the house, and it fell upon the children." Thus when anger and hatred come upon the house of our soul, they overthrow its four affects, that is, the four virtues, and destroy whatever good comes to life in it, because no good is of any value without charity.

The second member of wrath is revenge. Whoever practices that against his neighbor both unjustly and beyond due measure (which even the devil does not do, as has been said), seems to be not human but a wild beast. Therefore Chrysostom speaks of Herod as follows: "When a wild beast is wounded by some- one, out of its natural defensive fierceness it makes its natural cruelty twice as painful, and, as it were, blind with fury no longer looks for the one who has wounded it but instead tears to pieces whoever comes into its sight, be it man or another animal, as if it were the cause of its wound; so did Herod vent his wrath on innocent children when he had been fooled by the Magi."

Such people are like the juniper, whose nature it is, according to Isi- dore, *Etymologies*, book 17, chapter 7, to keep a fire alive for a year if the glowing coals are covered with its own ashes. Surely, the same is true of many people who keep the fire of wrath alive under the ashes or the cover of their own wickedness and who through many years still wait for an opportunity to take vengeance. Such people are commonly confounded in their own wrath, as is shown

45   et seipsum cum aliis occidit, Iudicum 26; similiter de Aman, qui suspensus
     est in patibulo quod pro Mardocheo paraverat, Hester 7.
         Unde talis inordinatus appetitus vindicte assimilat bene iracundum
     hominem lapidi magneti, cuius natura est trahere ferrum, et ille qui magis
     est attractivus, magis habet de natura [sua]. Unde recitat Augustinus *De*
50   *civitate*, libro 21, capitulo 4, se vidisse magnetem sub quodam vase argen-
     teo teneri, qui ferrum ipsi vasi appensum miro modo [f. 18] attraxit. Spi-
     ritualiter ergo loquendo per magnetem iram considero, per ferrum autem vin-
     dictam intelligo. Solet enim per ferrum vindict⟨a⟩ sumi; trahit ergo ira
     ferrum, nam lancee, gladii, et omnia genera armorum extrahuntur per iram.
55   Et ideo ira est talium origo. Et quanto quis magis est iratus et maioris
     potencie, tanto plus trahit de ferro. Videmus enim quod plures lanceas et
     loricas trahit comes quam baro, et baro quam miles, et sic de singulis. Set
     aliquando contingit iuxta casum [Augustini] et naturam istius lapidis quod
     si aliquis simplex aliquem magnum offenderit, sive iuste sive iniuste,
60   postea [tamen] instat pro gracia habenda et mittit munera et exennia, et
     certe talis magnetem cooperit quasi sub vase argenteo, ne scilicet talis
     dominus ferrum trahat contra eum pro vindicta. Set aliquando contingit quod
     magnes diabolica est sub isto vase qui movit lapidem, hoc est magnus ribal-
     dus qui est consiliarius talis domini, semper illum instigans ad malum et
65   dicens ⟨quod si esset sicut⟩ ipse, propter omnia dona alterius et exennia
     non dimitt[er]et quin vindica⟨re⟩t se de illo; unde hoc modo non obstante
     vase argenteo attrahit ferrum. Unde timeo quod dicere possum illud Deutero-
     nomii 8: "⟨Hoc modo⟩ est terra cuius lapis ferrum est."
         Unde tales bene assimilantur cuidam alteri lapidi "albeston" dicto,
70   qui "semel accensus numquam extinguitur." Sic nec tales iracundi hiis
     diebus remittunt offensum sine vindicta, etc.

---

3 et ideo] *om* O. induratam] induratum O.   **4–5** Augustinus] *add* pro sermone M; *add*
prosperi 65 R.W.   **6** homines] hominem C.   **7** diligis] diligas O.   **8** naturam] creaturam
M.R.   **16** magis non licet] minus fas O.   **20** est(1)] esse probatur O.   **21** et(1)] ille
serpens antiquus apocalipsis 12 O.   **25** Sic] nam O.   cum in domum anime] anime C;
cum in animam M.   **27** destruunt] destruit M.W. *Notice that* R *has the related verbs* irruit
and corrumpit *in the plural.*   **33** duplicis doloris infundit] duplicat doloris M; duplicat
causa doloris R; duplicat dolorem W.   **34** quicquid] quicumque O.   **36** infudit] *add* hec
ille O.   **37** est] talis C.   **42** tales] *add* ut O.   **50** 4] 10 O.   **53** vindicta] vindicte C.
sumi] assumi O.   **55** est] *add* omnium O.   magis est iratus] iratus forcior est M.R; iratus
forcioris W.   **60** gracia] *add* sua O.   **65** quod si esset sicut] credens sic esse C.   **66** vin-
dicaret] vindicabit C.   **68** Hoc modo] hermon C.M.   **71** etc.] *om* O.

II.iv   DE DETESTACIONE IRE

[R]estat igitur iam quarto ostendere quare est ira omnino detestanda:
revera quia directe vadit contra preceptum Dei et eius voluntatem ubique

typologically in Exodus 28 by Pharaoh, who unjustly persecuted the children of
Israel and drowned with his army in the Red Sea; similarly by Samson, who, when
he was tricked by the Philistines, craved vengeance and killed himself with the
others, according to Judges 26; and similarly by Haman, who was hanged on the
gallows he had prepared for Mordecai, Esther 7.

Such an unruly desire for vengeance easily makes a wrathful man like a
magnet, which by its nature attracts iron, and the more magnetic it is, the
greater is its attractive power. Augustine in *The City of God*, book 21,
chapter 10, says he once saw a magnet held underneath a silver bowl, and the
magnet, in wonderful fashion, attracted a piece of iron that was placed in the
silver bowl. Spiritually speaking, by the magnet I understand anger, by the
iron, revenge, for iron is usually interpreted as symbolizing revenge; wrath
draws iron, because through wrath lances, swords, and all kinds of weapons are
drawn out. And thus wrath is the ground for all such things, and the more
wrathful a person is and the more powerful, the more iron he attracts. For we
see that a count attracts more lances and armor than a baron, and a baron more
than a knight, and so on. But it sometimes happens as it does in the instance
reported by Augustine, according to the nature of this stone: if a simple
citizen has offended some magnate, whether rightly or wrongly, but then asks
him for grace and sends him gifts and presents, he certainly covers that magnet
as it were with a silver bowl, so that such a lord may not draw his iron in
vengeance against him. But it sometimes happens that there is a diabolical
magnet under the bowl which moves the stone, that is, a great scoundrel who is
counselor to that lord and who always instigates him to evil, saying that if *he*
were in the lord's place, he would not for all those gifts and presents refrain
from taking revenge; and in this way he attracts the iron despite the silver
bowl. Therefore I fear that I can say the words of Deuteronomy 8: "Such is the
land whose stone is iron."

Such people are also like another stone called "asbestos," which, once it
has been ignited, can never be extinguished. In similar fashion, such wrathful
people in our days do not forgive any offense without taking revenge.

5–9 Prosper, *Sententiae* 65 (PL 45:1865).   **9–11** Ibid., 2 (1859).   **11–13** Ibid., 267
(1881).   **15–17** Augustine, *De sermone Domini in monte* I.x.26 (PL 34:1242).   **20** Gen.
3.15.   **23–24** Job 1.19.   **31–36** Ps.-Chrysostom, *Opus imperfectum*, hom. 2 (PG
56:644).   **37–39** Isidore, *Etym.* XVII.vii.35.   **43–44** Exod. 14.19–31.   **44–45** Judg.
16.   **45–46** Esther 7.10.   **49–51** Augustine, *De civitate Dei* XXI.4 (CC 48:763–764).
68 Deut. 8.9.   **69–70** Cf. Isidore, *Etym.* XVI.iv.4.

II.iv   HOW TO DETEST WRATH

In the fourth place, it remains to show why wrath should be totally
rejected: because it goes directly against God's commandment and his will when

clamantis et dicentis: "Estote misericordes, sicut et Pater vester misericors est." Unde Bernardus: "Facilius est, inquit, enarrare stellas celi,
5   pisces maris, et folia nemorum, quam misericordiam Dei certe estimare; quia
secundum Psalmistam: 'Miseraciones [f. 18v] eius super omnia opera eius.' "
Nam ipsa qualescumque peccatores cum corde veniam petent⟨es⟩ ad graciam
recipit, sicut patet de Thasi meretrice, propter cuius pulcritudinem multi
substanciam perdiderunt, multi sanguinem effuderunt, et quamplures vitam
10   amiserunt, et tamen reducta ad compunctionem et penitenciam misericordiam
et graciam consecuta est. Nota eciam de milite qui mortem patris remisit
alteri militi in Parasceve pro amore illius qui illo die pro humano genere
mortuus est: qui cum simul ad crucem honorandam et oblaciones offerendas
ivissent, crucifixus brachiis dissolutis illum qui misericordiam fecit
15   amplexatus est, et vocem pro venia ibidem audivit. Idem eciam patet de beato Paulo, de Magdalena, et de beato latrone, etc. Unde Bernardus super illud
"Nolo mortem peccatoris": "Qualiscumque, inquit, necessitas te ad penitenciam duxerit, nec peccati quantitas nec vite enormitas nec operis brevi-
tas excludit a venia, dum vera sit contricio cordis, confessio oris, et sa-
20   tisfactio operis." Unde ibidem Bernardus ait: "O bone Iesu, inquit, non
horruisti latronem confitentem, non lacrimantem peccatricem, non supplican-
tem Chananeam, non deprehensam adulteram, non negantem discipulum Petrum,
non persecutorem Paulum, non impios crucifixores; quomodo ergo de tua misericordia desperarem?" quasi diceret, nullo modo, quia "maius gaudium erit
25   in celo super uno peccatore penitenciam agente," etc. Hec ille.
     Et nota quod hec misericordia divina tam dulcis et benigna habet duos
pessimos armigeros, quia ex una parte presumpcionem sive magnam fiduciam
peccandi ex nimia confidencia de Dei misericordia, ex alia parte desperacionem de venia pro peccatis.
30   Contra igitur primum, scilicet fiduciam magnam peccandi, ait Dominus
Ysaie 36: "Super quem habes fiduciam," peccandi magnam [f. 19] suple, "quia
recessisti a me peccando?" Ideo Proverbiorum 10: "Spes impiorum peribit."
Et nota quod illud vicium tria genera hominum sequuntur: primo ypocrite,
qui pessime confidunt in simulat[ori]a vanitate; Iob 8: "Spes ypocrite
35   peribit, non placebit in corde suo, quia sicut tele ar⟨ane⟩arum fiducia
eius." Secundo superbi illud sequuntur ex sua fortitudine et potestate,
contra quos Amos scribitur 6: "Ve qui confidunt in monte Samarie," hoc est
in sublimitate et arrogancia vel diviciis et habundancia, sicut cupidi et
avari. Tercio luxuriosi in carnali voluptate, contra quos Ieremie 17:
40   "Maledictus homo qui confidit in homine ponens carnem brachium suum," hoc
est appetendo carnales voluptates. Caveamus ergo a tali presumpcione peccandi ex confidencia misericordie Dei. Est ergo de Deo erga peccatores
sicut de aquila et cornice. Cornix autem persequitur aquilam, que est rex
avium, set illa magnitudine animi et sua curialitate dissimulat; quod

he calls out and says, "Be merciful as your Father is merciful." Whence
Bernard declares: "It is easier to count the stars of heaven, the fish in the
sea, and the leaves of the forests, than for you to appraise God's mercy, for
according to the Psalmist, 'his mercies are above all his works.' " God's mercy
receives into his grace any sinners that ask from their heart for his forgiveness, as is seen in Thais, the prostitute: on account of her beauty many
men lost their possessions, many shed their blood, many lost their lives; yet
when she was led to remorse and penance, she obtained mercy and grace. Notice
also the story about the knight who on Good Friday forgave another knight the
death of his father, out of love for him who died on that day for all mankind.
When the two knights went together to worship the cross and bring their offerings, the Crucified detached his arms and embraced the one who had acted so
mercifully, and he then heard a voice speaking of forgiveness. The same is
true of Blessed Paul, of Magdalene, of the Good Thief, and of others. Therefore, in commenting on the verse "I do not want the death of the sinner,"
Bernard says: "Whatever plight may lead you to penance, neither the number of
your sins nor the wickedness of your life nor the short time you have to do
good bars you from God's forgiveness, as long as you have true contrition of
heart, confession of mouth, and satisfaction in deed." Whence Bernard says in
the same place: "O good Jesus, you did not turn in horror from the thief who confessed, the sinful woman who wept, the woman of Canaan who implored you, the
adulteress who was caught, your disciple Peter when he denied you, or Paul, who
persecuted the Church, or the ruthless men who crucified you. How then should
I despair of your mercy?"—as if he were saying, not at all; for "there is
greater joy in heaven over one sinner who repents," and so forth.

But notice that this divine mercy, so sweet and benign, has two very evil
squires: on one hand, presumption or sinning with confidence that stems from
overly relying on God's mercy; on the other hand, despair of receiving forgiveness for one's sins.

Against the former, that is, sinning with overconfidence, the Lord says in
Isaiah 36: "In whom do you trust," add: overly in your sin, "that you are
revolted from me?" Similarly Proverbs 10: "The hope of the godless will perish." Three kinds of people follow this vice. First, hypocrites, who trust
most wickedly in outward show; Job 8: "The hope of the hypocrite shall perish,
it shall not please him in his heart, for his trust shall be like spiderwebs."
Second, the proud follow that vice, on account of their strength and power,
against whom is written in Amos 6: "Woe to those who trust in Mount Samaria,"
that is, in high estate and arrogance, or riches and wealth, as covetous and
greedy men do. Third, lechers follow it in their carnal lust, against whom is
written in Jeremiah 17: "Cursed is the man who trusts in man and makes flesh
his arm," that is, who desires carnal pleasures. Let us therefore beware of
thus sinning in confidence of God's mercy. God's attitude toward sinners is

45 videns cornix ex hoc audacior effecta inportune persequitur, unde aquila
nimium fatigata et irritata ad ultimum cornicem inpetuose arripit et dilacerat. Revera sic Christus peccatores tales nisi desistant ⟨a⟩ mala confidencia in peccando, ad ultimum occidit. Narratur eciam de quodam tali pre-
sumente peccare forte per luxuriam; cum autem super hoc argueretur a quodam
50 clerico sancto, respondit: "Deus enim ita bene mortuus est pro me sicut pro
te; non ergo plus perdet me quam te. Ideo tantum confido de eius misericordia quod si sibi dicere possem ante mortem hec tria verba, 'Miserere mei,
Deus,' salvus ero." Accidit quodam die cum transivit quendam pontem et
cespitare incepit deorsum, tunc predicta tria verba oblitus est; in quorum
55 loco hec tria dixit: "Ore ascent a deables." Sic ergo patet quod non est
peccandum sic presumptuose ex confidencia misericordie Dei, ut scilicet
quis credat sibi misericordiam dari sive bene fecerit sive non, eo quod
Deus [f. 19v] nichil vult perdere vel dampnare quod redemit; verum est
certe quantum in eo est, set quilibet talis hoc modo peccando·seipsum per-
60 dit et dampnat. Et ideo quilibet cupiens veram spem et confidenciam habere,
primo commissa delicta considerat et corrigat, secundo studeat bona facere
et continuat. Nam contra presumentes dicitur Ecclesiastici 5: "Non dicas
peccavi," etc.; et sequitur: "Non adicias peccatum super peccatum dicens,
'Misericordia Dei magna est, super multitudinem peccatorum meorum misere-
65 bitur,' set ⟨converti ad eum ne tardes et⟩ ne differas de die in diem, subito
enim veniet ⟨ira⟩ eius et in tempore vindicte disperdet te." Hec ibi.
    Ut ergo nec diffidas nec presumas, set spem veram et fiduciam habeas,
oportet ut tres partes prudencie caucius consideres: et primo de preteritis
considera mala que commisisti, bona que omisisti, et quam pauca bona egis-
70 ti; secundo de presenti cave ne corruas, et age bona que omisisti et res-
taura; et tercio de futuro vide ne residives ad prohibita, et ne disconti-
nues bene incepta.
    Est eciam hic advertendum quod sicut de Dei misericordia non est pre-
sumendum, ut dictum est, sic nec de eius misericordia est nullatenus despe-
75 randum. Dicit enim Augustinus: "Peccatum, inquit, cum desperacione necessario salute privetur." Nam secundum Ambrosium magis peccat homo desperando
quam peccat perpetrando. Et ideo Ieronimus *Super Psalmos* dicit quod Iudas
plus Deum offendit quando seipsum suspendit quam quando eum tradidit. Et
ideo dicitur Proverbiorum 24: "Ne desperaveris in die angustie." Unde
80 Bernardus super illud Genesis "Maior est iniquitas mea," etc.: "Mentiris,
inquit, o Chayn, quoniam sicut scintilla ignis in medio maris, sic misericordia Salvatoris ad maliciam omnis hominis."
    Et nota quod istud peccatum ex tribus solet provenire: primo ex pusil-
lanimitate, scilicet quando quis considerat penas pro peccatis debitas,
85 puta vero pro mortali peccato septem [f. 20] annos penitere et huiusmodi,
quod videns vel audiens peccator fit pusillanimis, et sic lassus et despe-

similar to the relationship between the eagle and the crow. The crow pursues
the eagle, who is king of the birds, but the latter pays no heed in his great-
heartedness and courtesy. When the crow sees that, it becomes even more daring
and pursues him, until the eagle gets too tired and annoyed and finally catches
the crow with violence and tears it to pieces. Thus will Christ likewise kill
sinners in the end if they do not give up their wicked confidence while they
sin. There is another story about such a person who confidently sinned in
lechery. When he was taken to task by some holy churchman, he answered: "God
has died for me as well as for you; therefore he won't damn me any more than he
will you. So, I trust so much in his mercy that as long as I can say these
three words 'Have mercy, Lord' before I die, I shall be saved." It happened
that one day when he crossed a bridge and began to reel off backwards, he
forgot his three words and instead said: "Devil take it." Thus it is clear
that one must not sin in presumption, by trusting in God's mercy and believing
that one will receive it whether one has lived well or not because God will not
lose or condemn what he has redeemed. The latter is certainly true insofar as
it depends on God, yet anyone who sins in this way loses and condemns himself.
Therefore, whoever wishes to have true hope and trust must first reflect on the
sins he has committed and correct them, and then apply himself to doing good
and continue in this. For against the presumptious is said in Ecclesiasticus
5: "Do not say, 'I have sinned,' " etc. And later: "Do not add sin upon sin,
saying, 'God's mercy is great, he will have mercy on the multitude of my
sins' "; rather, "do not delay to turn to him and do not defer from day to day,
for his wrath shall come on a sudden, and in the time of vengeance he will
destroy you."

So that you may neither lose heart nor be overconfident, but instead have
true hope and trust, it is necessary to reflect carefully on the three parts of
prudence: first on the past, remembering what evil you have done, what good you
have left undone, and how few good things you have accomplished; second on the
present, paying attention that you do not fall, doing the good you have not
done, and making restitution; and third on the future, looking out that you do
not slide back into what is forbidden or give up the good you have begun.

And we should further notice that, just as we must not be overconfident of
God's mercy, as has been shown, we must likewise in no way despair of it. For
Augustine says: "Sin with despair will of necessity forego salvation." According to Ambrose, a man sins more gravely by despairing than by committing an
evil. And Jerome, in his commentary on the Psalms, says that Judas offended
God more when he hanged himself than when he betrayed him. Therefore it is
said in Proverbs 24: "Do not despair on the day of distress." And Bernard
comments on the verse "My iniquity is greater," etc., from Genesis, as follows:
"You lie, Cain, because in comparison with the Savior's mercy the malice of any
man is like a spark of fire in the middle of the sea."

rans penitenciam non aggreditur; secundo provenit ex ipsius peccati enormi-
tate, ut pro peccato contra naturam; tercio provenit ex difficultate vitandi
peccatum quod habet ex consuetudine, eo quod secundum Philosophum "con-
90   suetudo est altera natura." Quod bene figuratum erat 1 Regum 23 ubi dicitur: "David desperabat fugere a facie Saul, eo quod ipse cum viris suis
cingebat David ad modum corone." Iste enim Saul diabolum signat, et viri
eius suggestiones prave que cingunt David, idest animam peccatricem, ut
quasi videatur sibi non posse per penitenciam evadere, et sic desperat,
95   iuxta illud Iob 7: "Desperavi, nequaquam ultra vivam," idest meritum gracie
et penitencie vix accipiam.
      Non sic, set contra diabolum et eius temptaciones viriliter resistemus
et Deus iuvabit iuxta illud:

      Cessa, condono; pugna, iuvo; vince, corono.

100   Proverbiorum 3: "Ne paveas repentino terrore et irruentes potencias impiorum, quia Dominus tecum adiutor fortis." Ecce narracio. Refert Diascorides
hec de Trinitate quod quondam fuerunt duo iuriste sci⟨vi⟩les, nobiles, et
fortes, quorum unus fortitudinem suam circa meretrices ° et alias fatui-
tates, ° scienciam ⟨vero⟩ circa falsas causas consumpsit. Accidit autem
105   quadam [nocte], ut simul dormirent, apparuit Pater celestis isti qui sic
gracias sibi a Deo datas fatue consumpserat, dicens ei: "Surge et veni ad
iudicium, quia in me peccasti cui potencia attribuitur, fortitudine tua
tibi per me data pessime abutendo; dampnaberis." Quo audito horribiliter
clamavit in tantum quod socium suum evigilavit. Qui cum quesisset quid sibi
110   esset, totaliter sibi narravit. Ipse vero illum confortans dixit: "Non est
curandum de visionibus nocturnis et huiusmodi illusionibus." Et iterum
dormierunt. Quo facto secunda vice apparuit Christus Filius Dei sibi dicens
sicut ⟨Pater⟩: "Surge, para te ad iudicium. In me, inquit, similiter peccasti [f. 20v] qui sum sapiencia Patris, pessime in falsis causis sapiencia
115   tua abutendo quam a me recepisti; et ideo dampnaberis." Unde territus evi-
gilando horribilius clamavit quam prius. Cui socius: "Et quid tibi modo
est?" Et omnia sibi narravit que viderat a Filio Dei. Cum autem socius a
desperacione illum allicere non posset, tandem tanquam sciens et prudens
quod dampnari non deberet non obstantibus huiusmodi visionibus, hoc exem-
120   plum proposuit: "Si tres, inquit, homines unam hereditatem participantes
coniunctim et divisim, ita quod unus sine aliis nec duo illorum sine tercio
dictam hereditatem elongare possent, si ergo unus vel duo hoc facere vellent, nonne lex contra illos aperte staret?" Qui respondens dixit quod sic.
"Sic omni modo," dixit socius, "est in proposito. Pater et Filius et Spiri-
125   tus Sanctus hereditatem celestem coniunctim et divisim optinent cum eadem
iusticia et potestate; si ergo Pater vel Filius elongare illam hereditatem

Notice that this sin usually comes from three causes. First from faint-
heartedness, when a sinner thinks of the punishment that is due to his sins,
such as doing seven years of penance for a mortal sin and the like; when he
sees or hears that, the sinner loses heart, and in this torpor and despair does
not take up his penance. Second, it comes from the gravity of the sin itself,
as from a sin against nature. And third it comes from the difficulty of avoid-
ing a sin one commits out of habit, because according to the Philosopher,
"habit is our second nature." This was well prefigured in 1 Kings 23, where it
is said that "David despaired of fleeing from the face of Saul, because he and
his men encompassed David like a crown." Saul stands for the devil, and his
men for evil thoughts which encompass David, that is, the sinner's soul, so
that it may seem to him that he cannot evade them through penance, and then he
despairs, according to Job 7: "I have despaired, I shall not live any longer,"
that is to say, I shall hardly receive the reward of mercy and of penance.

Let us not do thus, but rather withstand the devil and his temptations
manly, and God will help us according to the lines:

> Cease, and I forgive;
> Fight, and I help;
> Win, and I crown you.

Proverbs 3 says: "Be not afraid of sudden fear, nor of the power of the wicked
falling upon you, for the Lord will be with you as a strong helper." Behold
the following story. Diascorides reports about the Trinity that once there
were two noble and strong civil lawyers. One of them used his physical
strength on whores and other follies, and his learning in unjust lawsuits. As
both were asleep one night, it happened that the Heavenly Father appeared to
the one who had thus foolishly spent the gifts he had received from God and
said to him: "Get up and come to your judgment. You have sinned against me
whose mark is power. You have badly misused the strength I have given you.
You shall be condemned." When the lawyer heard this, he gave a horrified cry
so that he woke his companion. When the latter asked him what was the matter,
he told him all. But his companion comforted him and said: "Don't pay any
attention to nocturnal visions and such illusions!" And they went back to
sleep. Then Christ, the Son of God, appeared to him and said, as the Father
had done: "Get up, prepare yourself for your judgment. You have likewise sinned
against me who am the Father's wisdom, by badly misusing in unjust lawsuits the
wisdom you have received from me; and therefore you shall be condemned." Again
the lawyer woke up in terror and cried out even more horrified than he was
earlier. His companion asked: "And what is it now?" And he told him all that
he had seen from the Son of God. Since his companion could not talk him out of
his despair, yet knowing in his prudence that he would not be condemned in spite

a te voluerit, [cui in baptismo virtute sanguinis Christi ascriptus es,]
sine assensu Spiritus Sancti, certum est quod hoc non possent. Et ideo,
quamvis Pater et Filius a te istam hereditatem elongare voluerint, eo prout
130 dicunt absusus es tam potencia Patris tibi data quam eciam sapiencia Filii,
expecta quousque Spiritus Sanctus, cui attribuitur clemencia et bonitas,
veniat; et cum venerit ille, statim illum adiura propter suam magnam clemenciam quod te adiuvare dignetur facere misericordiam inter Patrem et
Filium et te reparare promitt[end]o vite correctionem; et si sic feceris,
135 manucapio quod benedictam hereditatem optinebis." Quo dicto in spiritu
confortatus est.

Ergo para te, o peccator, ad eius misericordiam petendam et non despe-
res, quia ipsum prompciorem invenies ad dandum quam tu ad petendum; pro
magno enim offenditur et pro minimo reconciliatur; Sapiencie 6: "Exiguo
140 conceditur misericordia." "Petite ergo et accipietis." Unde legitur in
Gestis Britonum quod erat quidam rex in hoc regno nomine [f. 21] Cassibila-
nus habens cognatum nomine Androgeum, inter quos erat maxima discordia
pro morte cuiusdam armigeri, ut patet in historia. Unde in tantum crevit discordia quod ⟨omnes terras⟩ quasi in Cancia, idest omnes homines, destruxerat
145 flamma et ferro. Accidit postea quod Iulius Cesar graviter concepit contra
istum regem et [multum cognato suo Androgeo afficiebatur, unde regem]
debellans conpulit ad fugam. Qui cum vidisset non posse resistere, timens
eius potestatem et offensam, litteras misit ad cognatum cui tot mala intu-
lerat, eius misericordiam et graciam petens, recognoscendo quod cognatus
150 eius erat, rogans eciam quatenus inter ipsum et imperatorem foret pacis
mediator. Quibus visis et intellectis, sic nunciis respondit: "Non est
ergo, inquit, princeps iste timendus qui tempore belli est mitis ut agnus
et tempore pacis ferox ut leo." Et addidit: "Licet tamen graciam vel misericordiam erga me in nullo meruit, eum tamen reconciliabo si potero. Suffi-
155 cit enim michi pro iniuria michi facta quod rex in terra sua meam graciam
humiliter imploret." Et sic imperatorem et regem pacificavit. Moraliter:
Isti duo cognati sunt Filius Dei et homo, inter quos erat discordia et
semper erit quando peccatis consentit; nam in tantum persequitur tunc homo
Filium Dei quod quantum in ipso est iterum vult eum crucifigere, quia qui
160 facit illud propter quod Filius Dei mortuus est, hoc est peccatum, quantum
in ipso est iterum Filium Dei morti tradit et crucifigit, iuxta illud Ad
Hebreos 6: "Rursum crucifigentes in semetipsis Filium Dei." Ex qua causa
summe offenditur summus imperator Pater celestis. Quid ergo faciendum est?
Revera oportet quod talis sic peccans a cognato suo Christo petat graciam
165 et misericordiam, et si sic fecerit, non desperet quin illa gracia ex corde
humili petita quoad eum pro sufficienti vindicta reputabit[ur] et culpam
remittet, quo facto pacem inter imperatorem suum Patrem celestem et illum
re- [f. 21v] formabit.

of these visions, he then put the following case to him: "Imagine that three men jointly own an inheritance in equal shares, so that no one could sell it without the other two, nor could two of them do so without the third. If one or two of them wanted to do that, would not the law be openly against them?" He answered that this was so indeed. Then his companion said: "Thus it is in your case. The Father, the Son, and the Holy Spirit hold joint ownership of the heavenly inheritance, with equal right and power. If therefore the Father or the Son wanted to take it from you for which you were given a claim in baptism, by the power of Christ's blood, they certainly could not do so without the consent of the Holy Spirit. Therefore, even though the Father and the Son may want to take it from you, because as they say you have misused the Father's power that you were given as well as the Son's wisdom, wait till the Holy Spirit comes, to whom belong clemency and goodness. And when he comes, implore him at once that because of his great clemency he may help you to achieve mercy between the Father and the Son and to restore yourself, by promising him that you will amend your life. If you do that, I give you my pledge that you will gain your blessed inheritance." By this saying the lawyer was comforted in his mind.

Therefore prepare yourself, O sinner, to ask for his mercy and do not despair, for you will find him more ready to give than you are to ask. It takes much to offend God, but little to make peace with him; Wisdom 6: "To him that is little, mercy is granted." "Ask and you shall receive." Whence we read in *The Deeds of the Britons* that there was a king in this realm called Cassibelanus, who had a relative by the name of Androgeus. Between them was a very great enmity on account of the death of some squire, as history tells us. This enmity grew so great that it destroyed nearly all the lands in Kent, that is, all the people, by fire and sword. Then it happened that Julius Caesar was gravely moved against the king and kindly disposed toward his relative Androgeus, and he fought against the king and forced him to flee. When the latter saw that he could not withstand Caesar and was in fear of his power and attack, he sent letters to his kinsman on whom he had inflicted so many evils and asked for his mercy and good grace in recognition that he was his relative, and begged him further to make peace between himself and the emperor. When Androgeus had seen and read the letters, he replied to the messenger: "One rightly should not fear a prince who in time of war is mild like a lamb and in peace fierce like a lion." Then he added: "Although he has deserved no grace or mercy from me whatsoever, I will yet try to reconcile him with Caesar if I can. I am satisfied, for the injury he has done to me, that the king in his own land is humbly begging for my grace." And thus he made peace between the emperor and the king. Morally speaking, these two relatives are the Son of God and man, between whom there was great enmity and ever will be as long as man gives in to sin, for in that case man pursues the Son of God so much that, if it were

Et ideo qui eius timet vindictam ad eius misericordiam fugiat, sicut
170   fecit quidam miles qui propter culpam suam per imperatorem Romanorum morti
adiudicatus est. Quo audito miles appellavit. Cumque imperator admirasset
cui appellaret, cum non esset in terris aliquis superior illo, respondit
miles: "Necesse, inquit, est cuicumque imperatori et regi non tantum habere
tronum iusticie set eciam tronum misericordie. Unde si in trono iusticie
175   sim dampnatus, ad tronum misericordie appello, que est superior locus et
virtus in principe." Quo audito ait imperator: "Ad misericordiam, inquit,
appellasti, et ipsa te a morte liberabit." Revera sic esse necessario oportet de Christo imperatore nostro, cuius oculi, iuxta Psalmistam, "sunt super timentes eum et in eis qui sperant in misericordia eius." Unde Augusti-
180   nus: "Quid, inquit, misericordius intelligi valet peccatori [eternis tormentis dampnato et unde se redimet non habenti, quam Deum] audire dicere
Patrem: 'Accipe Filium meum unigenitum et da pro te,' ac eciam ipsum Filium
dicere: 'Tolle et redime te,' etc." Unde Apostolus Ad ⟨Titum⟩ 3: "Non ex
operibus iusticie que fecimus nos, set secundum suam misericordiam salvos
185   nos fecit," etc.

---

5 et] *om* O. estimare] estimares O.   **7** petentes] petentibus C.M.   **13** qui cum] quomodo
M.W; quando R.   **15** pro venia] de venia pro peccatis O.   **16** et] *om* O.   **18** operis] temporis M.R.   **19** et] *om* O.   **23** non(2)] nec O.   **24** erit] est O.   **25** etc.] quam supra mil-
ibus penitenciam non indigentibus O.   **35** aranearum] arenarum C.   **42** ergo] enim O.
46 arripit] *add* interimit et O.   **47** a] ex C.   **49** hoc] *om* O.   **51** clerico sancto] fratre
O.B1.B3.Go.Go2; clerico E; *om* Et.Co.   **52** possem] possum O.   **53** Deus] *add* quod
O.   **55** dixit] *add* submergendo M.W; R *adds* submergendo *before* deorsum.   Ore . . .
deables] pereo sine spe M.   **56** sic] *om* O. Dei] divine O.   **62** dicas] dixeris O.
64 super multitudinem] multorum M.W; multitudinis R.   **65** converti . . . et] converte
ad eum et ne tardas vel C; converti ad eum R.   **66** ira] dies C.   **75–76** necessario] certa
mors est necessario desperantis M; certa mors est nemo desperans R.W.   **76** privetur]
fruetur O.   **85** vero pro] pro uno M; uno R.W.   **86** quod . . . fit] quodammodo vadit
peccator O.   **95** 7] *add* capitulo O.   **99** corono] *add* unde illud M.W; *add* unde R.
101 fortis] *add* et O.   **102** sciviles] scioles C.   **103** meretrices] *add* consumpsit C.
103–104 fatuitates] *add* et alius C.   **104** vero] suam C.   **113** Pater] prius C.   **117** Dei]
om O.   **124** Sic . . . est] omnino dixit socius sic O.   **126** vel] et O.   hereditatem] *om*
O.   **127** voluerit] voluerint O.   **129** hereditatem] *om* O.   voluerint] vellent O.
132 veniat] venerit O.   **133** facere misericordiam] concordiam O.   **140** accipietis] *add*
quia in eo impetrabitis M; *add* quia in eo peccabit R.W.   **144** omnes terras] *thus* R.B1.E,
et al.; omnis terra C.M.W.   quasi] *add* que fuerant M.W; que fuerant R.   idest omnes
homines] *om* O.   **151** intellectis] perlectis M.R; auditis W.   **152** ergo] *om* O.   iste] *add*
iuste O.   **154** humiliter imploret] conspicio humiliter implorare O; R *has brought the syntax in line by correcting* rex *to* regem.   **157** erat] *add* magna O.   **161** et crucifigit] *om*
O.   Ad] *om* O.   **162** in semetipsis] sibimetipsis O.   **166** reputabitur] *thus in*
B4.E.Go1.Et *and others*; reputabit C.O.   **167** suum] O *have* summum *before* imperatorem.   **172** illo] eo O.   **180** valet] videlicet O.   **183** Tolle] *add* me M.R.   Titum] thi
C.

in his power, he would crucify him again; for if one does that for which the
Son of God has died, namely sin, one hands the Son over to death and crucifies
him again in as much as lies in one's power, according to Hebrews 6: "Crucifying the Son of God again in themselves." By this we cause the greatest offense
to the highest emperor, our Heavenly Father. What then is to be done? Indeed,
it is necessary that such a sinner ask his relative, Christ, for grace and
mercy. And if he has done so, he should not distrust that the grace he has
asked for with humble heart might not be reckoned sufficient retribution before
God, and that God might not remit his sin. With this, Christ will reestablish
peace between the emperor, his Heavenly Father, and the sinner.

Therefore, if you fear his vengeance, flee to his mercy, as a certain
knight did who was condemned to death by the Roman emperor on account of his
guilt. When the knight heard this, he appealed, and as the emperor wondered to
whom he might be appealing since there was no one higher than himself on earth,
the knight answered: "Every emperor and king must of necessity have not only a
throne of justice but also a throne of mercy. Therefore, if I am condemned in
the throne of justice, I appeal to the throne of mercy, which is the higher
place and virtue in a prince." Hearing this, the emperor said: "You have
appealed to mercy, and mercy will free you from death." It will of necessity
be likewise with Christ our emperor, whose eyes, according to the Psalmist,
"are on those who fear him and on those who hope for his mercy." Whence
Augustine says: "What more merciful word is there to hear for the sinner who is
condemned to eternal punishments and has nothing whereby he may save himself,
than God the Father's saying: 'Take my Only-begotten Son and give him for
yourself' and likewise the Son's saying: 'Take me and save yourself,' etc."
Therefore, the Apostle says in his letter to Titus, 3: "Not by the works of
justice which we have done, but according to his mercy he has saved us."

3–4 Luke 6.36.   **6** Ps. 144.9.   **8–11** Cf. *Leg. aurea*, pp. 677–679.   **11–15** Tubach
1375. The hero of this widespread story is Saint John Gualbertus.   **17** Ezek. 33.11.   **17–
20** Cf. Bonaventure, *De sanctis apostolis Petro et Paulo*, sermo 2, 1 (9:550), where this
quotation is attributed to Augustine.   **20–25** Cf. Bernard, *Super Cantica* XXII.iii.8
(1:134).   **24–25** Cf. Luke 15.7.   **31–32** Isa. 36.5.   **32** Prov. 10.28.   **34–36** Job 8. 13–
14.   **37** Amos 6.1.   **40** Jer. 17.5.   **62–63** Ecclus. 5.4   **63–66** Ecclus. 5.5–6, 8–9.
75–76 Augustine, *En. in Ps. 50* 5 (CC 38:602).   **76–77** Cf. Augustine, *Sermo 20* 1 (PL
38:138).   **79** Cf. Prov. 24.10.   **80** Gen. 4.13.   **81–82** A commonplace attributed to different authorities; apparently based on Augustine, *En. in Ps. 143* 8 (CC 40:2079).   **89–
90** Aristotle, *Rhetorica* I.xi.3 (1370a).   **91–92** 1 Sam. 23.26.   **95** Job 7.16.   **99** *Prov*
2690.   **100–101** Prov. 3.25–26.   **101–136** Tubach 2862.   **139–140** Wisd. 6.7.
140 John 16.24.   **141–156** Geoffrey of Monmouth, *Historia regum Britanniae* IV.viii–
ix (pp. 313–318).   **162** Hebr. 6.6.   **170–177** Tubach 3268.   **178–179** Ps. 32.18.
183–185 Titus 3.5.

II.v   DE PACIENCIA

[E]xpleta igitur parte ire cum suis miseriis, iam secundo loco in ista
secunda particula tractandum est de paciencia, que se aperte offert ad
illam expugnandam. Circa quam sic procedam: primo quid sit et a quo sumitur; secundo in quibus necessaria et quibus comparatur; tercio de eius
5   membris et quomodo terminatur.
Dico igitur primo quod paciencia est virtus que in prosperis non elevatur nec in adversis frangitur, illatasque iniurias equanimiter tollerans,
proximis compaciens, et nullum dispendium optans. Et hec paciencia sic dif-
finita principaliter a Christo sumitur exemplum, cuius paciencia in tribus
10   consideratur. Et primo in dulci responsione erga inimicos, Iohannis 8:
"Quem queritis?" ut sic exemplariter [f. 22] nos respondeamus in adversis,
quia Ecclesiastici 6 dicitur: "Verbum dulce multiplicat amicos et mitigat
inimicos, sicut aqua frigida ollam bullientem." Secundo consideratur in
moderata correpcione, sicut patet ⟨Matthei⟩ 26 ubi dixit discipulis suis:
15   "Qui intingit mecum [manum] in parapside," etc.; sic et tu, iuxta illud Ad
Galatas 6, "argue, obsecra, increpa in omni paciencia et doctrina," et hec
contra protervos. Tercio in benigna admissione, sicut quando dixit Matthei
26: "Amice, ad quid venisti?" ad ostendendum quod sic nos qui sumus firmio-
res debemus infirmorum debilitatem sustinere et compassionis benignitatem
20   proximis indigentibus impendere, etc.

---

6 igitur] ergo O.   **8** nullum] nullis M.R.   **14** Matthei] iohannis C.   **19** et] *add* sic O.
20 etc.] *om* O.

II.vi   DE PACIENCIE NECESSITATE

[A]d sciendum autem in quibus necessaria est paciencia per quam voluntatem Dei perficiemus eciam ut illius imitatores simus, adverte quod in
quatuor necessaria est: primo in adversitate inimicorum, secundo in correpcione superiorum, tercio in amissione bonorum, quarto in infirmitate diver-
5   sorum.
Contra enim adversitatem inimicorum qui dura verba et duriora verbera
nobis inferunt, si pacienter sustineamus, est de nobis sicut de illis qui
tempore guerre contra ictus machinelli ponunt culcitras vel fenum vel aliquod huiusmodi molle, ne muri et turres dissolventur; Proverbiorum 12:
10   "Responcio mollis frangit iram." Arbor enim nucis quanto magis verberatur
et percutitur uno anno, tanto magis fructificat alio anno; sic verus paciens per opprobria magis fructificat virtutes [producendo], sicut patet de
filiis Israel qui quanto magis opprimebantur tanto magis crescebant. Et

II.v   THE NATURE OF PATIENCE

After finishing the part on wrath and its wretchedness, in the second
place in this second part we now deal with patience, which offers itself openly
to overcome the vice. About which I shall proceed as follows: first, what it
is and from where it is derived; second, in what situations it is necessary and
to what things it can be compared; and third, what its members are and to what
end it leads.

First, then, I say that patience is the virtue of not becoming exalted in
good fortune or broken by ill fortune; it bears inflicted injuries with equanimity, has pity on fellow men, and wishes no harm. This patience, as it has
been defined, takes its example from Christ, whose patience may be seen in
three things. First, in answering his enemies gently, as in John 18: "Whom do
you seek?" We should answer in the same manner in our adversity, for in
Ecclesiasticus 6 it is written: "A sweet word multiplies friends and appeases
enemies," as cold water appeases the bubbling pot. Second, in censuring others
with moderation, as Christ did in Matthew 26 when he said to his disciples: "He
who dips his hand with me in the dish," etc. Thus you, too, should, according
to Galatians 6, "reprove, entreat, rebuke in all patience and doctrine," which
is said against vehement people. And third, in accepting others with gentle-
ness, as when Christ said in Matthew 26: "Friend, what have you come for?" In
this he showed that we who are stronger should thus bear the frailty of the
weak and show gentle compassion to our needy fellowmen.

---

11 John 18.4.   **12–13** Ecclus. 6.5.   **15** Matt. 26.23.   **16** 2 Tim. 4.2.   **18** Matt. 26.50.

II.vi   THE NEED FOR PATIENCE

In order to know when patience is necessary, through which we shall fulfill God's will even to the point of becoming his imitators, notice that we
need this virtue particularly in four situations: in the adversity we suffer
from our enemies, in correction from our superiors, in the loss of our goods,
and in bearing various kinds of infirmity.

If we patiently endure adversity from our enemies who inflict on us hard
words and harder strokes, we will be like those who in time of war put up
cushions or straw or anything soft of this kind against the battering rams, so
that their walls and towers may not be broken down; Proverbs 12: "A soft answer
breaks wrath." The more a nut-tree is beaten and shaken in one year, the more
fruit it bears the next; thus a person who is truly patient under insults bears
more fruit in bringing forth virtues, as can be seen in the children of Israel:
the more they were oppressed, the more numerous they grew. Therefore the truly

ideo verus paciens auro bene comparatur, quod quanto magis tunditur, tanto
15   magis dilatatur; [sic ille qui per iniuriam atteritur et contunditur, in
paciencia dilatatur;] unde in Psalmo: "In tribulacione dilatasti me." Maximus enim honor est militi si ensis eius in bello frangatur, equus prosternitur et occiditur, et tamen ipse vicit et non devincitur. Et pravus miles
qui nimis atteritur [f. 22v] et inimico sine aliqua percussione redditur.
20   Sic vir inpaciens nullas iniurias valens sustinere set subito in iram
prorumpitur, nullam mercedem a Deo optinere meretur. Et ideo Proverbiis
dicitur: "Coronaberis si sustinueris pacienter." Et debemus iniurias sustinere. Quando autem aliquando tibi accidit aliqua adversitas vel iniuria ab
inimico, delibera bene penes te si sis culpabilis aut non; si sic, revera
25   iniuste conqueris quia forte plura meruisti quam sustines; si non, ecce
quid dicit Christus Matthei: "Beati qui persecucionem paciuntur propter
iusticiam." Et ideo narratur de quodam philosopho ab uxore maledicto et
summe irritato per verba, quem cum ipsa vidit in nullo sibi respondere, vas
aqua repletum super capud suum effudit; quo facto cum paciencia dixit:
30   "Bene, inquit, scivi quod communiter post ventum sequitur pluvia."
     Secundo necessaria est paciencia in superiorum correpcione. Sicut bos
qui semper trahit ad illam partem qua stimulatur, sic paciens humiliter
tendit gressus ad stimulum superioris et ad eius correctionem voluntatem
suam inclinat. Et ideo bene comparatur testudini, quam cum tetigeris statim
35   cornua sua retrahit et abscondit; sic certe paciens et humilis cum tangitur
a superiori per correpciones paternales inclinando capud retrahit et abscondit cornua superbie et impaciencie; Genesis 1: "Audivi, Domine, vocem
tuam et abscondi me," etc.
     Tercio necessaria est in amissione bonorum temporalium, sicut fecit
40   Iob, de quo legitur quod cum amisisset totam substanciam pacienter respondit: "Dominus dedit, Dominus abstulit; sicut Domino placuit," etc. Unde
legitur in *Vitas Patrum* de quodam sene a quo quidam raptor asinum suum
abstulit et dedit ei similiter alapam, qui pacienter sustinens aliam maxil-
lam prebuit atque, ut asinum melius duceret, tradidit capisterium. Unde ex-
45   iens demon hanc vocem [f. 23] emisit dicens: "A sola paciencia victus sum."
Et ideo talis bene comparatur adamanti qui secundum Ysidorum nulli cedit
materie sicut ferro nec igne frangitur nec umquam incalescit, unde "adamas"
Grece, "vis indomita" Latine dicitur; set [dum sic invictus fuerit ferri
ignisque contemptor,] tamen sanguine yrcino ⟨maceratur⟩. Revera sic verus
50   paciens nulla vi ferri aut ignis iniuriarum frangitur aut dissolvitur, et
tamen amore sanguinis Christi Iesu statim ad compassionem emollitur; Romanorum 12: "Noli vinci a malo set vince in bono malum."
     Quarto necessaria est in infirmitate, quod est vinculum Christi, per
quod quos amat castigat. Sicut pia mater filium quem vidit ad aquam vel ad
55   ignem appropinquare unde periculum posset imminere, sic Pater celestis filium quem diligit castigat aliquando per infirmitatem ut caveat ab igne vel

patient person can be compared to gold: the more it is beaten, the wider it
spreads; thus a man who is worn thin and beaten in his injuries grows greater
in his patience; as the Psalm says: "When I was in distress, you have enlarged
me." To a knight it is the greatest honor if his sword breaks in battle, his
horse is felled and killed, and yet he himself has won and is not overcome; and
wretched is the knight who gets beaten too much and is handed over to the enemy
without striking a single blow. Thus an impatient person who cannot endure any
injuries but at once breaks into anger does not deserve to receive any reward
from God. Therefore it is said in Proverbs: "You shall be crowned if you
suffer patiently." And you have to endure injuries. But whenever you suffer
any adversity or injury from an enemy, ask yourself within if you have any
fault or not; if so, you complain unjustly, for you may have deserved more than
you actually suffer; but if not, then behold what Christ says in Matthew:
"Blessed are they who suffer persecution on account of justice." And so, a
story is told about a philosopher who was cursed by his wife and highly annoyed
by her words; when she saw that he would not answer her a single word, she
poured a pot of water over his head; whereupon he said with all patience: "I
knew well that normally after a storm comes rain."

   In the second place patience is necessary when we are corrected by our
superiors. As an ox that always pulls in the direction in which he is driven,
thus a patient person humbly directs his steps after the goading of his superior and bends his will under his superior's correction. Therefore he may be
compared to the snail which, if you touch it, at once pulls in its horns and
hides; thus also a patient and humble person, when he is touched by his superior through fatherly corrections, bows his head and withdraws and hides his
horns of pride and impatience; Genesis 1: "I heard your voice, Lord, and hid
myself."

   In the third place patience is necessary when we lose temporal goods, as
Job did, of whom we read that when he lost all his belongings he said patiently: "The Lord has given, the Lord has taken away; as it has pleased the Lord,"
etc. Hence we read in *The Lives of the Fathers* of a hermit from whom a thief
took his donkey, giving him a blow in the face. The hermit endured this patiently, offered him the other cheek, and gave him the bridle so that he could
lead the donkey away more easily. Whereupon a demon went out of the robber
with a loud cry and said: "By patience alone have I been overcome." Such a
patient person can be compared to a diamond. According to Isidore, it is
harder than any other material, such as iron, cannot be broken by fire, and
never heats up; whence it is called *adamas* in Greek, *vis indomita*, "untamed
power" in Latin. But while it thus resists iron or fire unabated, it yet
becomes weakened by the blood of a goat. Similarly, a patient person cannot be
broken or dissolved by the iron or fire of injuries, and yet out of love for
the blood of Jesus Christ he will grow soft in compassion; Romans 12: "Be not
overcome by evil, but overcome evil with good."

aqua peccati. Unde facit Dominus cum illis sicut faciunt pueri cum captis
avibus, qui ne avolarent partem pennarum illarum auferunt. Iste enim penne
per quas plures avolarent a voluntate Christi, si illis permitteretur, sunt
60 divicie et potencie; et ideo aufert unam per paupertatem et aliam per
infirmitatem. Si enim rex Francie abstulisset a rege Anglie aliquod castrum
et rex de amissione illius ipsum obsideret et oppugnaret donec ipsum opti-
neret, nonne hoc esset signum quod multum illud castrum diligeret si muros
non prosterneret? Per istum regem Francie intelligo diabolum, qui abstulit
65 castrum anime a Christo, rege nostro Anglie; set ne Christus illam amittat,
ex nimio amore quem habet ad illam non statim muros prosternit corporis per
⟨mortem⟩, set immittendo infirmitates illam lucratur. Et ideo contra infirmitatem non est murmurandum, quia videmus quod puer verberatus, si plorat,
provocat magistrum ad duriora; sic est de Christo. Unde Ysidorus in *Solilo-*
70 *quio*: "Qui, inquit, in [f. 23v] flagellis murmurat, Deum contra se plus
incitat." Hoc ergo bene consideravit beatus Paulus qui dixit: "Libenter
gloriabor in infirmitatibus meis."
       Et adverte causam, ut michi videtur, quare Christus iuste corpus per
infirmitates affligit, et specialiter illorum quos diligit. Pono casum
75 sicut frequenter contigit in istis magnis villis inter mercatores, sicut
London et Coventre, quod sunt duo socii in lucro et amissione bonorum equaliter participantes; si ergo alicui deberent aliquod debitum quod solvere
non possent, et unus illorum clam vellet recedere et socium in briga relinquere, si tunc maior civitatis hoc perciperet [et] illum detineret donec
80 cum socio debitum solveret, nonne esset signum magne fidelitatis et dilectionis erga alium? Revera sic. Cum ergo corpus et anima sint in deliciis
socii et in peccatis, videmus quod caro si posset vellet clam inpune recedere et totum debitum anime relinquere, quod esset iniustum. Et ideo maior
noster Christus, ex dilectionis affectione quam habet ad animam, capit
85 corpus et detinet et infirmitates inmittit et sic partem sibi contingentem
de debito solvere cogit. Et ideo dicit Gregorius: "Ante tempus, inquit,
solve, ne pro debito astringaris." Videmus eciam quod aliquando proximus
fideiussor punitur pro debito alterius quod manucepit, in tantum quod
aliquando pro illo vadia eius accipiuntur, aliquando incarceratur, quod
90 nequaquam fieret si verus debitor acquietaret. Revera sic in proposito.
Necessitate compulsa anima pro corporis debito punietur vel torquetur, nisi
hic corpus debitum solvat pro peccatis, quod facit quando per infirmitates
affligitur. Et conveniencius est quod caro ancilla hic parum puniatur quam
anima domina in eternum dampnetur. Non igitur murmurare debemus contra
95 Christum propter infirmitates per [f. 24] quas Deus quasi temptat nos, quia
dicit Sapiens: "Beatus vir qui suffert temptacionem, quoniam cum probatus
fuerit," etc.
       Set timeo quod est de aliquibus sicut de nautis qui tempore tranquillo
ludunt ad taxillos nec cogitant de periculo, set exorta tempestate clamant

In the fourth place patience is necessary in sickness, which is the fetter
of Christ with which he binds those whom he loves. As an anxious mother restrains her child whom she sees nearing water or fire where some danger might
threaten, so does the Heavenly Father sometimes tie down a son he loves through
some sickness, so that he may be held back from the fire or water of sin.
Hence the Lord does to them what boys do to birds they have caught: to prevent
them from flying away, they pull out part of their feathers. The feathers with
which many people would fly away from Christ's will if they could are wealth
and power; and these Christ takes away, the first through poverty, the second
through sickness. If the king of France took some castle from the king of
England, and the latter besieged him because of this loss and made war on him
until he had regained the castle—would it not show that he loves that castle
very much if he did not raze its walls? By the king of France I understand the
devil, who has taken the castle of our soul from Christ, that is, our king of
England; but in order not to lose that soul, Christ, out of the deep love he
has for her, does not at once raze the walls of the body in death, but wins her
by sending sickness. Therefore, we must not grumble against sickness, for we
see that a boy who weeps when he is chastised provokes his teacher to even
harder punishment; the same is true of Christ. Whence Isidore says in his
Soliloquy: "He who grumbles when he is punished stirs God even more against
himself." Blessed Paul had this in mind when he wrote: "Gladly will I glory in
my infirmities."

Listen to the reason why, as I think, Christ justly sends sickness to the
body, and especially of those whom he loves. I set the case that has often
happened among merchants in these large cities, such as London and Coventry,
that two partners share equally in their profit and loss. Now, if they owe
someone a debt which they could not pay, and one of them wanted to disappear
secretly and leave his partner in the lurch, if in this case the mayor of the
city were to notice this and were to detain him until he payed his debt together with his partner—would this not be a sign of great faithfulness and love
toward the other merchant? Yes, indeed. Now, since body and soul are partners
in delights and sins, we see that the flesh, if it could, would like to steal
away without punishment and leave all his debt with the soul. This would be
quite unjust. Therefore, our mayor, Christ, out of his love for our soul,
takes the body and restrains it and sends it infirmities, and thus he forces it
to pay the part of the debt which belongs to it. And therefore says Gregory,
"Pay your debt before your time is up, lest you be bound for it." We also
observe that sometimes the nearest person who has given security is punished
for someone else's debt for which he had given his pledge, so that for that
debt sometimes his security is taken from him and sometimes he is put in jail,
which would not happen if the real debtor were paying up. To the point: out of
necessity the soul will be punished or tormented for the debt of the body
unless the body pays its debt for its sins here, which it does when it is

100 ad Deum et ad sanctos et vota faciunt; set a periculo liberati omnia tra-
dunt oblivioni. Sic aliqui cessante infirmitate nichil faciunt quod promiserunt. Sicut narratur de quodam Wallico qui in periculo maris promisit
Beate Virgini unum cereum ita magnum sicut [malum] navis, set inde evaso
dixit ipsam non habere pro eo maiorem candelam quam posset ad lectum illu-
105 minare.

Et nota hic quod hec bona facit infirmitas inmissa per Deum: primo
spem in Deum firmat iuxta illud Iob 13: "Eciam si occiderit me, in ipso
sperabo." Unde legitur in *Vitas Patrum* quod quidam senex frequenter egrota-
bat, et contigit ipsum anno uno non egrotare; quapropter prorupit in lacri-
110 mas dicens: "Dereliquit me Deus nunc et non visitavit me!"

Secundo facit hominem contempnere ista inferiora et appetere celestia;
sicut puer in scolis verberibus vexatus plus desiderat repatriare quam ille
qui omnino relinquitur proprie voluntati. Unde Gregorius: "Sancti, inquit,
temporalem penam lucrum reputant, quia per hanc futuram penam et eternam
115 evadere non formidant." Unde Aristoteles in *Problematibus*, particula 35,
problemate 4, querit causam quare corpora sunt frigidiora in estate quam in
hyeme, cum estas sit naturaliter calida et hyemps frigida; si corpora
nostra tangantur, quare frigidiora reperiuntur in estate quam in hyeme et e
contrario? Et respondit dicens quod sudor et humectacio plus infrigidant
120 corpora quam calefaciunt, set in tali tempore calido maxime eveniunt su-
dores; vel dicit ipse: ponatur quod sudor non eveniat, fiet tamen exalacio
calidi insensibiliter [f. 24v] et naturaliter. Commentator autem dicit sic:
"Illud, inquit, maxime verificatur in me: video enim quod pulices super me
proiecte in estate fugiunt propter frigiditatem non parvam, set in hyeme
125 accedunt. Set ut michi videtur, verior solucio est quod in estate poris
apertis calor exiit quasi congaudens suo consimili, set in yeme per circum-
stans frigus calor repercutitur ad interiora corporis et ibi manet. Et hec
est vera causa quare fontes sunt frigidiores in estate quam in hyeme." Revera sic hic per estatem intelligo prosperitatem, per yemem vero adversi-
130 tatem. Sicut ergo calor exterior calorem interiorem extrahit ad se, sic
prosperitas seculi amorem hominis qui ad Deum debet dirigi, set certe in
yeme adversitatis, hoc est in infirmitate et huiusmodi, calorem caritatis
detinet et includit in se, quod satis probatur quod infirmitas facit plus
hominem Deum diligere, mundum contempnere, et celestia eciam appetere
135 quam facit prosperitas aut sanitas.

Tercio lascivos domesticat. Sicut magister qui discipulum insolentem
per aures accipit et ferula manum percutit, et tandem verberat ut eum in-
tencius intelligat, sic Christus magister noster, etc.

---

3 quatuor] *add* specialiter O.   8 machinelli] magenelli M.W; magni olli R; mangenelli
B1.E *and others*.   11 percutitur] excutitur O.   13 magis(1)] *om* O.   16 unde in Psalmo]
psalmista O.   38 etc.] *om* O.   41 sicut . . . placuit] *om* O.   42 suum] *om* O.   43 ei] *om*

afflicted with infirmities. And it is better that the flesh, the handmaiden,
be punished here a little than that the soul, its mistress, be damned in
eternity. Therefore we must not grumble against Christ on account of infirmities by which God, as it were, tries us, for the wise man says: "Blessed is the
man who endures temptation, for when he has been proved," etc.

But I fear that with some people it goes as it does with sailors who in
calm weather play dice and have no thought of danger, but when a storm comes
call to God and the saints and offer vows; yet when they are out of danger,
they forget all about these things. In the same way, some people fail to make
good their promises when their sickness is over. There is a story about a
Welshman who, in danger at sea, promised the Blessed Virgin a candle as tall as
the mast of his ship; but when he had escaped the danger, he said that on his
account she would not get anything bigger than a bedside candle.

And notice that sickness sent by God has the following good effects.
First, it strengthens one's hope in God, according to Job 13: "Even if he
should kill me, I will hope in him." For which we read in *The Lives of the
Fathers* that a hermit was frequently ill, and that one year it happened that he
did not fall ill; whereupon he burst out weeping and said: "Now God has forsa-
ken me and has not visited me."

Second, it causes man to scorn these worldly values and desire heavenly
ones, just as a boy in school who is flogged desires more intently to go home
than he who is totally left to his own will. Whence Gregory says: "The saints
consider temporal affliction a gain, for through it they hope to go free of
future and eternal pain." Whence Aristotle in his *Problems*, part 35, problem
4, asks the reason why bodies are colder in winter than in summer, since summer
is hot by nature and winter cold; if one touches bodies, why are they found to
be colder in summer than in winter and vice-versa? And he answers by saying
that sweat and humidity produce more coolness in our bodies than the latter
receive heat, and in summertime we sweat very much; and even if there is no
sweat, yet our bodily heat evaporates insensibly and naturally. Aristotle's
commentator explains as follows: "This is certainly shown to be true in me, for
I notice that the fleas that fall on me in summer flee because of the great
coolness of my body, but in winter they all come. However, I think there is a
better answer: In summer, when the pores are open, the body heat goes out as if
it were rejoicing with what is its like, but in winter the body heat is driven
back into the body by the surrounding cold and stays there. And this is the
true cause why fountains are colder in summer than in winter." Now, by "summer" I understand prosperity and by "winter" adversity. As the external heat
draws out the body's heat to itself, just so worldly prosperity draws to itself
man's love which ought to be directed to God; but in the winter of adversity,
that is, in sickness and such, it retains the fire of love and closes it within
itself. The truth of this is shown in that sickness makes man love God, scorn
the world, and desire heaven more than does prosperity or health.

O.   **47** sicut] nec M; ut R.W.   igne] igni O.   **49** maceratur] frangitur C.   **54** vidit] videt
O. ad(2)] *om* O.   **60** unam] *add* christus O.   **67** mortem] amorem C.   **68** plorat] ploret
O.   **69–70** Soliloquio] *add* 27 O.   **74** specialiter] *om* O.   **76** London et Coventre] *om*
x.y.Jo.; *story om* B4.; lond' ebor' et huiusmodi Co; london ebor' norwic' coventr' et
huiusmodi Li; london colcestr' et huiusmodi Cambridge; london norwic' coventr' et
huiusmodi Go2; vlixbone etc. Madrid. *All full manuscripts recorded.*   **82** in] *om* O.
84 ex] *add* quadam O.   **91** punietur vel] *om* O.   **94** domina] *om* O.   igitur] ergo O.
100 ad(2)] *om* O.   **103** unum] *om* O.   malum] M *garbles the phrase*: cereum sicud magnum navis.   **104** maiorem] *om* O.   **104–105** illuminare] illuminari O.   **121** fiet] fiat
O.   **126** consimili] simili O.   **135** facit] *add* eciam O.   **137** et(1)] *om* O.   **138** etc.] *om*
O.

II.vii   DE MEMBRIS PACIENCIE

[C]irca autem membra paciencie sciendum quod ista sunt compassio
proximi et pietas, pax cordis et tranquillitas.

De compassione autem et pietate erga proximum dicit Ieronimus: "Deus,
inquit, vult quod alterius angustias ut tuas sentire habes; et sicut tibi
5   velles subveniri, sic propter Deum proxim⟨o⟩ in necessitate subvenias."
Ovis naturali instinctu quando consortem suam in fervore solis vel frigidi-
tatis conspicit iacere circa fetum laborantem, umbram sibi facit contra
calorem et contra frigus interponit seipsam, ut sic adiuta ad pascua con-
surgat. Revera sic ex compassione tenetur homo proximo in necessitate
10   compati et pro posse iuvare; sicut [f. 25] Christus fecit, qui tantum
compaciebatur humano generi quod tandem ut illud ab omni labe curaret
mortuus est, sicut inferius patebit quando agitur de dilectione et compassione Christi erga hominem, et similiter de eius passione. Quia satis
concordat cum ista materia, et ideo transeo.

15   De pace autem cordis, quod est secundum membrum virtutis paciencie,
est sciendum secundum Augustinum quod illa est "serenitas mentis, tranquillitas animi, simplicitas cordis, vinculum amoris"; "nec ad hereditatem Christi pervenire poteris qui testamentum pacis nolueris servare." Nam si in
Ecclesia militante excommunicantur qui testamentum temporale impediunt,
20   multo magis qui impediunt sive dirimunt testamentum Christi, quod est pax.
Ipse enim Christus rector Ecclesie triumphantis discipulis suis illam
legavit dicens, Iohannis 14: "Pacem meam do vobis, pacem meam relinquo
vobis."

Est autem sciendum quod ad veram pacem servandam necesse est facere
25   sicut quando aliquod castrum inpugnatur ab aliquo magno, cui dominus castri
non poterit resistere nisi securius ordinaverit de castro et maxime ab
intra: necessarium est ° primo ut consideret utrum in castro sint aliqui

Third, sickness cools down lustful people. As a teacher who takes an
insolent student by his ears, lashes his hand with a switch, and finally gives
him a flogging so that he may pay more attention, so does Christ our teacher.

---

10 Prov. 15.1.   **16** Ps. 4.2.   **26–27** Matt. 5.10.   **27–30** Jerome, *Adversus Iovinianum*
I.48 (PL 23:291), from Classical sources.   **37–38** Gen. 3.10.   **41** Job 1.21.   **42–
45** Conflation of Tubach 4810 and 3364 with *VP* V.14 (PL 73:956–957).   **46–49** Isidore,
Etym. XVI.xiii.2.   **52** Rom. 12.21.   **70–71** Isidore, *Synonyma* I.29 (PL 83:834).   **71–
72** 2 Cor. 12.9.   **96–97** James 1.12.   **102–105** Also in Bromyard, "Penitencia,"
P.VII.75.   **107–108** Job 13.15.   **108–110** *VP* VII.xx.2 (PL 73:1045).   **113–115** Perhaps Gregory, *Moralia* XXVI.xxi.37 (PL 76:370–371) and elsewhere, quoting Phil.
1.21.   **116–122** Aristotle, *Problemata* XXXV.4 (964b–965a).

II.vii   THE MEMBERS OF PATIENCE

Regarding the members of patience we must know that these are compassion
and pity with our neighbor, peace and tranquillity of heart.

Of compassion and pity for our neighbor Jerome says: "God wants that you
feel another person's worries as if they were your own; and just as you would
wish to be helped, so you should help your neighbor in his need for God's
sake." When a sheep sees its mate lying in the heat of the sun or in the blast
of cold concerned about its offspring, out of its natural instinct it places
itself so as to give shade against the heat or shelter against the cold, so
that its mate is protected and rises to feed. In the same way, a human being
must, out of compassion, have pity on his neighbor in his need and help him as
much as possible. Christ acted this way, who had such pity for mankind that in
the end he died in order to heal it from all disgrace, as will be shown further
on when we deal with Christ's love and compassion for man, and likewise with
his Passion. That is quite pertinent to the present topic, so I pass it for
now.

About peace of heart, which is the second member of the virtue of patience, we must know that according to Augustine it is "serenity of the mind,
tranquillity of the soul, singlemindedness of heart, and the bond of love";
"and no one can come to the inheritance of Christ who will not keep his testament of peace." If in the Militant Church people are excommunicated who block
the carrying out of a temporal testament, much more so will this be the case
with those who thwart the last will of Christ, which is peace. For he, the
ruler of the Triumphant Church, gave it to his disciples when he said, in John
14: "My peace I give to you, my peace I leave to you."

But we must know that in order to keep true peace it is necessary to act
in the same manner as one acts when a castle is attacked by a powerful lord:
the castle's owner cannot resist against him unless he carefully puts his

pacem illius perturbantes; secundo si quos tales invenerit, debet eos extra
castrum suum eicere et de illo iusticiam facere; tercio debet castrum suum
30 fortiter munire, ita scilicet quod non habent necesse extra illud ire;
quarto debet ipsum firmum et clausum tenere. Revera sic ex parte ista, quia
enim vulgariter dicitur: "Bonum castrum bene custodit qui cor suum bene
custodit."

Ideo ad veram pacem cordis habendam est necessario primo frequens
35 cordis et consciencie discussio, ut scilicet diligenter consideretur si
quid est in corde quod eius pacem perturbat, quod fit quando homo considerat vilitatem peccati et conteritur de eodem. Ideo Ysaie 1 dicitur: "Red-
ite, prevaricatores, ad cor." Secundo debet tale quid eicere per confessionem et iusticiam facere per satisfactionem, quia dicitur in Psalmo: [f. 25v]
40 "Non est pax ossibus meis a facie peccatorum meorum." Tercio debet
castrum illud bene munire et instaurare per voluntariam paupertatem, que
mundum et eius avariciam contempnit nec querit refectionem nisi in solo Deo
et que necessaria sunt, quia Iohannis 14 dicitur: "In mundo pressuram, in
me pacem habebitis." Paciencia enim cordis castrum ⟨munit⟩ armis et ciba-
45 riis ° quando lapides duros, hoc est ° angustias et tribulaciones, convertit in cibum; ideo de paciente dicitur: "Saturabitur opprobriis." Quarto
necessarium est illud firmum et clausum tenere, quod facit quando sensus
hominis restringuntur ab illicitis; sensus enim sunt quasi porte cordis,
per quos hostes ingredi possunt. Qui autem pacem perturbant maxime in illo
50 sunt carnales concupiscencie, prout dicitur Iacobi 4: "Unde bella et lites
in vobis? Nonne ex concupiscenciis que militant in membris vestris?" Intrat
igitur "mors per fenestras." Et ideo bene dicitur Luce 4: "Cum fortis
armatus," scilicet armis paciencie, "custodit atrium suum," scilicet cor
cum sensibus firmiter clausum, "revera in pace sunt omnia."

55 Set timeo quod multi veram pacem dissimulant addentes falsam pacem, de
quibus Ieremia dicitur: "Dicunt pax, pax, et non est pax." Unde tales sunt
similes cani feroci qui cauda applaudit homini ut eum subtilius mordeat;
similiter lupo famelico qui ludit cum lepore ut strangulat. Unde dicit
Beda: "In summa pace, inquit, natus est Christus ut illam summe dilligere
60 ostenderet; in sua enim nativitate pax erat in universa terra testante
angelo qui dixit: 'Gloria in excelsis Deo et in terra pax hominibus bone
voluntatis.'"

Et ideo caveant pacis perturbatores ne illis eveniat sicut semel
contigit de duobus talibus. Narratur enim de duobus vicinis [f. 26] in
65 proximo manentibus et in continua lite per⟨severa⟩ntibus, qui nulla racione
possent concordar⟨i⟩. Imo suo confessori responderunt se cicius in inferno
sine fine permansuros quam alter alteri condonaret. Cum igitur cito post
una vice simul subito mortui sunt, et iste sacerdos Deum devote rogasset de
illorum statu scire, cito ductus est in spiritu per angelum ad quendam
70 locum ubi vidit quendam fornacem sulphure et pice bullientem, a quo surre-

castle in order, and especially its conditions inside. First he must diligently see whether there are any people in the castle who disturb its peace;
second, if he finds any, he must expel them from the castle and do justice to
them; third, he must fortify his castle, so that there is no need to go outside; and fourth, he must keep it strong and closed. All this applies to us,
for the proverb says: "He keeps a good castle who guards his heart well."

Thus, in order to have true peace of heart, the first thing needed is
frequent examination of one's heart and conscience, that is, to see diligently
if there is anything in one's heart which disturbs its peace. This is done by
reflecting on the wickedness of sin and repenting. Therefore Isaiah 1 says:
"Return, O sinners, to your heart." Next one must expel any such matter
through confession and do justice through satisfaction, for in the Psalm it is
said: "There is no peace for my bones in the face of my sins." Third, one must
fortify and repair that castle through voluntary poverty, which scorns the
world and its greed and seeks no refreshment other than in God and the things
that are needed, for John 14 says: "In the world you will have distress, in me,
peace." For patience provides the castle of our heart with arms and food when
it turns hard stones, that is, anxieties and tribulations, into food; for which
it is said that the patient person "feeds on reproaches." And in the fourth
place it is necessary to keep our castle firm and closed, which happens when
one's senses are withdrawn from illicit things, for our senses are, as it were,
the gates of our heart through which our enemies can enter. But those who most
disturb its peace inside are fleshly desires, as is said in James 4: "Whence
are these wars and strife among us? Are they not from our lusts that war in our
members?" For death enters "through the windows." And therefore it is well
said in Luke 4: "When a strong man armed," that is, with the arms of patience,
"keeps his court," that is, his heart firmly closed with its senses, "in truth
all things are in peace."

But I fear that many people simulate true peace and put on false peace,
about whom Jeremiah says: "They say, 'Peace, peace,' and there is no peace."
Such people are like a fierce dog who wags his tail at a man so that he can
bite him more easily; or like a hungry wolf who plays with a rabbit in order to
strangle it. Wherefore Bede says: "Christ was born at the moment of greatest
peace, to show that he loved it above all else; for at his birth there was peace
in the whole world, as the angel testified when he said: 'Glory to God in
the highest, and on earth peace to men of good will.' "

Therefore, let the disturbers of peace beware that they may not experience
what two such people once did. For there is a story about two neighbors who
lived close to each other and were constantly at strife, who could in no way
come to an agreement. Even to their confessor they said they would rather stay
in hell forever than that one should forgive the other. Soon thereafter they
both died together. When their confessor devoutly prayed to God that he might
learn about their condition, he was led in the spirit by an angel to a place

xerunt duo homines terribiles cum gladiis ignitis invicem confligentes et
seipsos in frustra conscindentes, que quidem demon colligens in fornacem
reiecit; quo facto post bullicionem cito surrexerunt iterum et sicut dicitur supra secundo et tercio fecerunt. Tunc dixit sibi angelus: "Isti sunt
75   illi duo vicini qui numquam pacem in terris habuerunt, set locum istum
cicius elegerunt," etc. Non sic, karissimi, set cum Ecclesia Dei clamemus:
"Da pacem, Domine, in diebus nostris." Quia certe si vera pax fuerit inter
vos, revera tunc sequitur pro suo fine illa Dei benedictio que dicitur
Matthei: "Beati pacifici, quoniam filii Dei vocabuntur."
80   Et certe sicut habetur Ad Galatas: "Si filius et heres per Deum,"
quasi diceret, qui per veram pacienciam et pacem filii Dei fuerunt, "per
ipsum Deum et heredes erunt regni celestis." Illud autem satis care pro
nobis emit a Patre et per hanc cartam confirmavit:
      "Sciant presentes et futuri, omnes qui sunt in celo et in terra ac in
85   inferno, quod ego Christus, Filius Dei Patris et Marie Virginis, verus Deus
et homo, pro hereditate mea ° iniuste et prodiciose a meis ablata diuque
sub manu adversarii detenta teste toto mundo in stadio pugnavi, adversarium
devici, victoriam optinui, et hereditatem meam iuste recuperavi, seisinam
in Parasceves cum heredibus meis accepi, habendum et tenendum in longitu-
90   dine et in latitudine [f. 26v] in eternum secundum quod dispositum est a
Patre libere et quiete, annuatim, et continue reddendo Deo Patri cor mundum
et animam puram. In cuius rei testimonium hanc presentem cartam sanguine
proprio conscripsi, legi, et per totum mundum publicavi, sigillumque divinitatis mee apposui, cum testimonio Patris et Filii et Spiritus Sancti; nam
95   hii tres unum sunt qui testimonium dant in celo. Scripta, lecta, confirma-
ta, et generi humano tradita feria sexta Parasceves supra montem Calvarie,
publice et aperte, in eternum duratura, anno a creacione mundi 5⟨2⟩32."
Quam nobis concedat Iesus Christus. Amen.
      Quia ergo illa in parte que de humilitate supra dicta sunt ad virtutem
100 paciencie reduci possunt et e contrario, ideo hec dicta ad presens de ira
et paciencia sufficiunt. Et sic terminatur secunda pars principalis istius
libelli.

---

1 paciencie] *add* est O.   4 sentire habes] sentire O; sencias B1.B2; sentire debeas Go;
sustineas Et.Co.   5 proximo] proximum C.   13 Quia satis] satis enim O.   14 et] *om*
O.   18 poteris . . . nolueris] poterit . . . noluerit M.R; poterint . . . noluerint W.   ser-
vare] observare O.   20 impediunt sive] *om* O.   22 meam(2)] *om* O.   26 poterit] potest
O.   27 est] *add* eciam C. ut] *add* diligenter O.   29 suum] *om* O.   37 de eodem] *om* O.
44 munit] vincit C.   44–45 cibariis] *add* repletum C.   45 est] *add* quando C.
55 pacem(2)] *om* O.   56 dicitur] *om* O.   65 perseverantibus] permanentibus C.   66 con-
cordari] concordare C.   68 sacerdos] *om* O.   devote] devocius O.   72 conscindentes]
concidcntes M; conscidentes R.W.   quidem] quidam O.   86 mea] *add* detenta C.   95
unum] *om* O.   97 5232] 5432 C.

where he saw a cauldron boiling with sulphur and pitch; from it rose two
horrible men who fought with each other with fiery swords and cut each other
into pieces, which a demon then picked up and threw back into the cauldron; and
after being boiled they soon rose again and did a second and third time what
has been described. Then the angel said to the priest: "These are the two
neighbors who never had peace on earth but rather chose this place," etc. Let
us not act this way, dearly beloved, but call out with God's Church: "Give
peace, O Lord, in our days!" For surely, if there is true peace among us, that
blessing from God will follow in the end which is mentioned in Matthew: "Blessed are the peacemakers, for they shall be called children of God."

And surely, as we find in Galatians, "if a son, also an heir through God";
as if to say: those who were God's sons through true patience and peace, "will
through God also be heirs of the kingdom of heaven." For he bought that
kingdom very dearly for us from the Father, and he confirmed it through the
following charter:

"Let all present and to come, all who are in heaven, on earth, and in
hell, know that I, Christ, Son of God the Father and of the Virgin Mary, true
God and man, have fought before the whole world in the arena for my inheritance
that was taken from me unjustly and by treason and kept for a long time in the
hand of my enemy. I have overcome my enemy, gained the victory, and rightly
recovered my heritage; and on Good Friday I have taken possession of it with my
heirs, to have and to hold, in length and in breadth, forever, as it has been
disposed by my Father, freely and in peace, yearly and always, by giving God
the Father a clean heart and a pure soul. In witness thereof I have written
this present charter with my own blood, read it and published it through the
whole world, and sealed it with the seal of my divinity, with the witness of
the Father, Son, and Holy Spirit, for these three are one, who give witness in
heaven. Written, read, confirmed, and given to mankind on Good Friday on
Mount Calvary, publicly and openly, to last forever, in the year 5232 after the
Creation of the world." May Jesus Christ grant us that. Amen.

Since what has been said above in the part on humility can also be applied
to the virtue of patience, and vice-versa, these remarks on wrath and patience
will suffice for the moment. And thus ends the second chief part of this book.

16–18 Augustine, *Sermo supposititius 97* (PL 39:1931).   **22–23** John 14.27.   **32–
33** Frequently quoted in sermons. See Bernard, *In assumptione Beatae Mariae*, sermo 2,
3 (5:233) and *De diversis*, sermo 82, 2 (6.1:322).   **37–38** Isa. 46.8.   **40** Ps. 37.4.   **43–
44** John 16.33.   **46** Lam. 3.30.   **50–51** James 4.1.   **52** Jer. 9.21.   **52–54** Luke
11.21.   **56** Jer. 6.14.   **61–62** Luke 2.14.   **64–76** Tubach 2509. Also in Bromyard,
"Pax," P.IV.27. For other occurrences taken from *FM* see *Verses*, pp. 43–44.   **77** Antiphon used at Vespers, see F. Procter and C. Wordsworth (eds.), *Breviarium ad usum insignis ecclesiae Sarum* (Cambridge, 1879), 1:xi and mcccxxxv.   **79** Matt. 5.9.   **80–
82** Gal. 4.7.   **84** Cf. Mary Caroline Spalding, *The Middle English Charters of Christ*
(Bryn Mawr, 1914), esp. pp. 95–96.

PARS III

De invidia

III.i   QUID SIT INVIDIA

[S]equitur iam tercio principaliter ostendere de invidia, que filia
diaboli est karissima sua vestigia imitando, scilicet bonum impediendo et
malum promovendo. Pater enim terrenus filium sibi similiorem et corpore et
moribus plus diligit ceteris. Revera sic diabolus, pater invidie, quos
5   noverit per invidiam diligencius imitari plus diligit et appreciatur; set
post quos hic plus diligit, intollerabilius cruciabit. Unde circa illam
maledictam filiam diaboli, scilicet invidiam, de qua dicitur "vos ex patre
diabolo estis et eius desideria perficitis," sic intendo procedere: Primo
videre quid sit invidia et quibus comparatur; secundo, que sunt eius membra
10 et quare detestatur.

Est ergo invidia contristacio aliene felicitatis et exultacio alterius
ruine et adversitatis. Set revera istud est diabolicum, quia iuxta Apostolum,
Romanorum 12, humanum est "gaudere cum gaudentibus et flere cum flen-
tibus." Set e converso miser talis invidus alienum bonum facit suum [ma-
15 lum]. Et ideo bene comparatur monti Ethne, qui plus nocet sibi [f. 27] ipsi
quam alicui alteri. Unde metrice dicitur:

   Nil aliud nisi se valet ardens Ethna cremare.
   Sic se, non alios, invidus igne coquit.

Fertur enim in libro *De naturis animalium* quod naturalis inimicicia
20 est inter draconem et elephantem, et ideo cum simul pugnant, draco cum
cauda sua circumvolvit tibiam eius et prosternit, ita quod surgere non
potest. Draco iste invidus est qui cum nititur bonos devincere, si a parte
antecedente proficere non potest, statim a tergo per caudam ° detractionis
et diffamacionis eum suffocare et prosternere non desistit.
25   Unde, ut michi videtur, bene de talibus exponi potest illud Apocalipsis 16, "Vidi, et ecce de ore draconis tres spiritus inmundi exibant ad

PART III

Envy

III.i WHAT ENVY IS

We continue, in the third part, to treat of envy, which is the most precious daughter of the devil because it follows his footsteps by hindering good and promoting evil. An earthly father loves that son more than others who is more like him in his body and behavior. Thus also the devil, the father of envy, loves and esteems those more whom he knows to follow him more eagerly in envy. But later on he will torture those more unbearably whom he now loves more. Therefore, with respect to that cursed daughter of the devil, envy, of whom is said "you are from your father, the devil, and do his will," I intend to proceed as follows: first to see what envy is and what things it can be compared to; and second what its members are and why it must be shunned.

Envy, then, is sadness about someone else's happiness and glee about someone else's ruin and adversity. Surely, such an emotion is diabolical, for according to the Apostle, Romans 12, it is human "to rejoice with those who rejoice and to weep with those who weep." But an envious wretch, in contrast, makes someone else's good into an evil for himself. Therefore, he can be compared to Mount Etna, which does more harm to itself than to anyone else, as is said in the verse:

> Nought else but itself is flaming Etna able to burn.
> Just so the envious man cooks himself, not others, on fire.

The book *On the Nature of Animals* reports that there is natural enmity between the dragon and the elephant; when they fight with each other, the dragon wraps his tail around the elephant's leg and makes him fall so that he cannot rise again. This dragon is the envious person who, when he wants to bring down good people and cannot succeed from in front, at once tries to strangle them from behind with the tail of backbiting and defamation and thus to make them fall.

modum ranarum, facientes signa ⟨et procedentes⟩ ad reges congregare illos
in prelium." Rane enim, sicut scitis, sunt animalia saltancia, horribilia,
in paludibus habitancia, contra ventos et tempestates crocitancia. Et bene
30   signant tales invidos, qui quasi continue de loco ad locum saltant explo-
rantes ubi melius venenum suum evomere possunt. Set magis habitant in
paludibus quam in aliis locis amenis, eo quod talis invidus plus gaudet de
aqua tribulacionis et desolacionis proximi quam de amenitate sue prosperitatis et gaudii. Crocitant eciam naturaliter rane contra tempestates et
35   pluvias. Nam quando invidus tempestatem ruine, diffamacionis, et desolacionis proximi audierit, statim os eius aperitur clamans et crocitans, atque
addens mala que poterit. Set adverte quod in figura istarum "exibant tres
spiritus inmundi de ore draconis," ad designandum quod tres sunt condiciones pessime in invido que ad malum proximi continue ex eius ore exeunt.
40   Prima condicio est quod libenter dicet bona de proximo set mala intencione,
ut scilicet audientes credant ipsum diligere de quo loquitur, ut sic postea
non habeatur suspectus eciam si dicat mala, [f. 27v] set quod hoc facit pro
sui correctione, amore, et caritate. Secunda condicio est quod quando mala
loqui intendit, hoc modo incipiet: "Revera, inquiet, penitet me quod ali-
45   quid contra eum me dicere oportet, videre vel audire, et tamen bene scio
quod talia commisit et talia." Tercio condicio est hec, secundum Augustinum, quod primo illum quem intendit diffamare et in fama denigrare, commen-
dabit ut ei cicius credatur. Set istud est vicium secundum eum periculosis-
simum, eo quod non potest remitti sine debita satisfactione et restitucione
50   fame, quod non potest forte quia frequenter contingit quod illi quibus
talia de proximo narrant postea numquam videbunt. Unde de isto vicio Sapiencie 2 scribitur: "Invidia diaboli mors intravit in orbem terrarum."
      Set forte dicis: "Numquam per invidiam diffamacio, bonorum destruccio,
aut mors hanc terram intravit." Palpate, dico, et videte. Credo enim quod
55   nisi invidia fuisset, non fuisset talis terra in mundo. Nonne vidimus—set
absit quod umquam in eternum iterum videamus—, si aliquis bene fuerit cum
rege vel alio magno, quod tanta fiet invidia aliorum quod numquam cessabunt
malum loqui et dicere quia proditor est, regnum decipiet, et huiusmodi,
quousque ad mortem esset adductus? Nonne hoc vidimus? Et quod verum hoc
60   sit, testificare poterimus. Si eciam loquamur de minoribus hominibus, nonne
inter illos regnat invidia? Rogo, videte. Volo quod hic sit unus simplex
nesciens leges aut brigas fovere, vivens in innocencia et simplicitate,
habens unam carucam terre aut acram aut saltem aream edificatam in villa
ubi manet, quam desiderat potencior eo quia forte iacet prope domum aut
65   terras eius. Si igitur iste simplex illud sibi vendere aut committere
noluerit, rogo quid faciet? Nonne ballivos et hundredos ad⟨ibit⟩ et eum
indictabit quod fur est et homicida aut proditor civitatis aut regni? Per
quod sic ad terram iniuste deveniet vel simplicem istum suspendi [f. 28]

Whence it seems to me that one can apply to such people the words of Revelation 16: "I saw, and behold three unclean spirits issued from the dragon's mouth like frogs, working signs and going to the kings of the earth to gather them for battle." Frogs, as you know, are animals that jump, are horrible to look at, live in swamps, and croak against storms and bad weather. They can well symbolize envious people who, as it were, constantly jump from place to place and see where they can spit out their venom best. But they live in swamps rather than in other, pleasant places, because an envious person takes greater pleasure in the turbid water of his neighbor's tribulation and anxiety than in the pleasure of his prosperity and joy. Furthermore, frogs by nature croak at the coming of storms and rain. For when an envious person hears of the storm of his neighbor's ruin, loss of reputation, or anxiety, he at once opens his mouth and cries out, croaks, and adds whatever evil he can. But notice that under the biblical image of these frogs "three unclean spirits issued from the moth of the dragon," to show that in an envious person there are three very evil characteristics which constantly issue from his mouth to the harm of his neighbor. The first is that he will gladly speak well of his neighbor but with an evil intention, namely that his hearers should think he loves the person of whom he speaks, so that later on he may not sound suspect when he says evil things, but rather as if he were doing this for that person's correction and out of love. The second characteristic is that, when he intends to say bad things, he will begin as follows: "Alas, I am sorry that I must say, see, or hear anything bad about him; but I know for sure that he has done such and such." The third characteristic, according to Augustine, is that he will first praise the person whose reputation he plans to ruin and denigrate, so that he will be more readily believed. But his, according to Augustine, is a most dangerous vice, because it cannot be forgiven without making due satisfaction and restoring the person's good reputation, which the detractor perhaps cannot do because it often happens that he will never again see the people whom he has told such things about his neighbor. Therefore it is written in Wisdom 2 about this vice: "Through the devil's envy death has entered the world."

But perhaps you say, "Never has slander, the destruction of goods, or death through envy entered *this* country." Consider, I say, and look closely. I believe that, if it were not for envy, there would be no country like ours in the world. Do we not see—but God forbid that ever until eternity we should see it again!—that if someone has been in favor with the king or another great lord, the envy of others will grow so much that they will never cease from speaking evil and saying, "He is a traitor, he will deceive the reign," and so forth, until he is led to his death? Do we not see this? And we could testify that this is true. Further, if we are to speak about the humbler classes, does not envy rule among them? Look, I pray. Suppose there is a simple man who does not know the law or how to start a lawsuit, who lives in innocence and

faciet. Sicut talis tyrannus semel cuidam simplici dixit propter terram
70   ⟨suam: "Voveo, inquit, Deo, terram illam⟩ michi dabis aut vendes aut permu-
tabis, vel tu facies *a mow on the moone*," hoc est, tu eris suspensus per
collum, etc.

Set caveant tales, quia de talibus vere dixit Christus: "Vos ex patre
diabolo estis." Et ideo dicit Augustinus: "Invidia, inquit, cunctas vir-
75   tutes eradicat et concremat, animamque perdicioni tradit et ipsam diabolo
associat." Et ideo dicit Gregorius: "Dum invidi augmenta aliene prosperitatis inspiciunt, aput semetipsos anxius afflicti cordis ⟨sui⟩ peste moriuntur."

Et tamen mirum est quia quicquid per invidiam faciunt ad dampnum
80   proximi °, satis tamen aperte se excusare sciunt, quod non faciunt hoc
propter invidiam aut malum set propter bonum alterius, sicut se excusavit
Dionisius Syracusanus templa deorum suorum expoliando. Unde narrat beatus
Ieronimus in quadam epistola ad Paulinum quod quidam Dionisius nomine
templum deorum intrans, videns statuam quandam extenso brachio manum pro-
85   tendentem, cuius digitum anulus aureus ambiebat. Habebat eciam hec statua
barbam auream, ac clamide aure[a] erat induta. Quod videns Dionisius ille
tyrannus, primo anulum de manu statue abstulit et super digitum suum posuit. Secundo barbam abrasit et penes se abscondit. Tercio a clamide illam
exuit et secum asportavit. Cumque super hoc quidam sapiens et fidelis illum
90   arguisset, hoc modo se excusavit: "Anulum, inquit, accepi eo quod illum
michi liberaliter optulit, in cuius signum manum cum brachio curialiter sua
gracia protendit. Barbam abstuli, quia verecundum est filio esse b⟨a⟩rbatum
[et] patrem inberbem. (Erat enim tunc Exculapius, pater eius, inberbis.)
Clamidem vero asportavi auream, quia nimis ponderosa est in estate et nimis
95   frigida in yeme, et sic [f. 28v] clamidem meam dedi sibi laneam pro utroque
tempore satis sibi aptam."

Revera spiritualiter ita est de istis invidis. Si enim sit aliqua domus
religiosorum de qua annonam optant habere, numquam cessabunt clamare:
"Rustici illi sunt nimis pingues; oportet quod laxentur." Unde vel mit-
100   te[n]t suos ribaldos et equos ad morandum, vel ipsimet venient cum maxima
comitiva ad maneria sua vel domum propriam, et ill⟨a⟩m expensis nimium
excessivis excoriant et depauperant. Si ergo abbas, prior, vel alius prelatus offerat alicui tali dextrarium, palefridum, sive maximam summam pecunie, ut scilicet ab huiusmodi inceptis desistant, videtur eis quod huiusmo-
105   di iuste lucrantur, eo quod eis offertur, et dicunt quod ibi nulla est
invidia. Quod falsum est, quia nisi eorum voluntatem haberent, numquam ex
⟨nimia⟩ invidie malicia cessarent tales innocentes destruere. Dicunt eciam
tales quando vident in bonis Ecclesie ⟨sic⟩ ecclesiasticos habundare: "Ut
quid, inquiunt, tanti rustici tanta bona occupant, rege indigente et terra
110   blado, pecunia, et aliis diviciis carere? Si enim talia haberemus, in

simplemindedness. He owns one carucate of land or an acre or perhaps a built-up lot in the village where he lives, which is coveted by someone more powerful than he is, perhaps because it lies close to the latter's house or lands. If the lower-class citizen does not want to sell or make over his property, what I pray will his more powerful neighbor do? Will he not go to the bailiffs or the hundred-court and accuse him of being a thief or murderer or traitor to his town or the realm? This way he will come injustly to the land or have that lower-class citizen hanged, just as such a tyrant once said to a peasant for the sake of the latter's land: "I swear to God," he said, "you will either give, sell, or swap that land with me, or else 'grin at the moon,'" that is to say, you will at once be hung by your neck.

But let such people beware, for in truth Christ said of them: "You are from your father, the devil." And thus Augustine says: "Envy uproots and burns all the virtues; it gives the soul over to perdition and makes it a companion of the devil." And Gregory says: "When the envious see an increase in someone else's wealth, they become tormented in themselves and die from the plague in their own heart."

And yet it is a wonder that whatever they do out of envy to their neighbor's harm, they yet know how to excuse themselves quite openly that they are not doing such a thing out of envy or ill-will, but rather for the benefit of the other person, just as Dionysius of Syracuse rationalized his plundering the temple of his gods. Blessed Jerome tells in a letter to Paulinus that a certain Dionysius entered a temple of the gods where he saw a statue stretching out its hand from its extended arm, on whose finger was a gold ring. This statue also had a gold beard and was clothed in a gold cloak. When the tyrant Dionysius saw that, he first took the ring from the statue's hand and put it on his own finger. Next he shaved off the beard and hid it on himself. Thirdly he took off the cloak and carried it away with him. When a wise and faithful man confronted him on this, he rationalized as follows: "I took the ring because the statue generously offered it to me, since it courteously and graciously stretched out its hand and arm. I took away its beard because it is shameful for a son to be bearded while his father is beardless. (For at that time Aesculapius, his father, was beardless.) But its gold cloak I carried away because it is too heavy in summer and too cold in winter, and thus I gave the statue my own cloak of wool, which is very suitable for both seasons."

Thus it goes spiritually with the envious. For if there is any religious house from which they want to get an annual rent, they will never stop shouting: "Those peasants are pretty fat; they ought to be relieved." Hence they will either send their menials and horses to stay there or they will come themselves to their manors or house with a very large retinue and skin and impoverish it by exorbitant expenses. When the abbot, prior, or another prelate then offers one of them a charger or a saddle horse or a large sum of money, so

nulla causa aut necessitate neque terram in desolacione dimitteremus." Set
hoc est falsum, quia quicquid faciunt aut dicunt est per invidiam, eo quod
fertilius est illis quam sibi.

   Secundo, si sit aliquis iuvenis mercator in aliqua civitate extraneus,
115   forte de pauperibus extractus, sciolus tamen et providus et in omni prosperitate constitutus, quem intelligo per barbam auream—nonne statim alii de
villa oriundi sibi invidebunt dicentes: "Unde sibi tot divicias congregare?
Non potest esse quod bene sit." Et sic ex precogitata invidia ponent talem
in officio aliquo per quod, velit nolit, in arriragium cadet et sic bona
120   sua perdet et pau- [f. 29] perrimus deveniet. Super quo si arguantur, dicunt quod hoc fecerunt pro salute anime sue, ad deponendum avariciam et
superbiam de novo in eo inceptam. Et sic barbam prosperitatis abradere non
desistunt. Set caveant, quia maledicti et non excusati sunt huiusmodi
barbitonsores, quia nimis prope radunt maxillas.

125   Tercio pono quod sit iuxta aliquem talem aliquis simplex vel pauper,
qui habet loco clamidis porcionem terre, ut predictum est, per quam indigenciis suis cooperitur, sicut corpus clamide deaurato. Velit igitur nolit,
cum tali magno invido commutabit pro clamide lanea, hoc est, pro precio
minori, nisi velit confundi. Et si super hoc arguatur, quare sic pauperem
130   decepit, respondet statim quod pro eo plus fecit quam noverit cogitare, eo
quod sibi dedit pro illa terram sibi viciniorem, et per consequens sibi est
apcior tam in estate quam in yeme.

   Set de istis excusacionibus invidis et falsis dicitur Iohannis 15:
"Excusacionem non habent de peccato." Et nota de invidia Saulis contra
135   David postquam prostravit Goliam, Regum 18; similiter de invidia fratrum
Ioseph erga eum sine merito, Genesis 37; similiter de invidia Philistinorum
erga Sampsonem pro sua fortitudine, Iudi⟨cum 16⟩; similiter de invidia
Babiloniorum contra Danielem, Danielis 9, et huiusmodi.

   Sic ergo patet quid est invidia, quia pessima filia diaboli, de pros-
140   peritate proximi dolens et de malo gaudens. [Et ideo sic Anglice possum
dicere, ut michi videtur:

          Sithen þis world was ful of onde,
          Trewth and love has leyn in bonde.
          Wherfore, þou Lord þat art aboue,
145   Lethe þat bonde and sende vs loue.]

---

5 diligencius] solicicius O.   7 dicitur] *om* O.   8 perficitis] perficietis O.   **14–15** malum]
om v; *text* B1.E *and others*.   **15** ipsi] *om* O.   **16** Unde ⟨   ⟩ dicitur] versus O.   **23** ante-
cedente] ante O; *add* et aperte O.   caudam] *add* draconis idest C.   **27** et procedentes] ad
procedent C.   **31** magis] plus O.   **36** et] *om* O.   **41** diligere] *add* alium O.   **55** non . . .

that they will desist from their undertaking, it looks to them as if they have earned it by right because it is offered to them, and they claim that there is no envy in this. All of which is false, for unless they have their will, they would never, in the great malice of their envy, refrain from destroying these innocent people. For when churchmen thus appear to have plenty of church goods, they say: "Why do these peasants have so many goods while our king is in need and our country lacks grain, money, and other riches? If we had those possessions, we would not leave king and country desolate in any conflict or need." But this is false, for whatever they do or say is motivated by envy, since these goods are more profitable to others than to themselves.

Second, if there is a young merchant, a stranger in some town, perhaps come from poor stock yet smart and flourishing in prosperity—which I understand by the gold beard—, will not at once other townspeople rise up and become envious of him and say: "How come he can gather so many riches for himself? These things cannot be right!" And thus, in their envious scheming, they will put such a man in some office where, willy-nilly, he will fall into arrears and thereby lose his goods and become poor. When they are accused of this, they say that they have done this for the salvation of his soul, to put down the greed and pride that have recently grown in him. And thus they do not refrain from shaving off the beard of prosperity. But let them beware, for barbers of this type are cursed and not excused, because they shave too close.

Third, let us suppose that next to such an envious person lives a simple or poor man who, instead of the cloak, has a piece of land, as was said earlier, with which he covers his needs just as the body is covered with a golden cloak. Willy-nilly, he will exchange it with the envious person of greater rank for a woolen cloak, that is, for a lower price, lest he be totally ruined. And if the great man is taken to task for thus cheating the poor, he will at once reply that he has done more for him than he could imagine, because for that piece of land he has given him one that is closer and therefore more suitable for him in summer and winter.

But with regard to such envious and false excuses it is said in John 15: "They have no excuse for their sin." And notice the envy of Saul against David after he overcame Goliath, Kings 18; similarly the envy which the brothers of Joseph held against him without cause, Genesis 37; likewise the envy of the Philistines against Samson on account of his strength, Judges 16; and again the envy of the Babylonians against Daniel, Daniel 9, and similar cases.

Thus it is clear what envy is like, the most evil daughter of the devil, which grieves at the prosperity of one's neighbor and rejoices at his harm. And thus I can say in English, as it seems to me:

> Since envy spread o'er the world its reign,
> Truth and love in bonds have lain.

mundo] talis terra(*interl*) tante quantitatis(*corr*) non fuisset in mundo R *and similarly*
M.W.   **57** fiet] fuit M.W; sit R.   **60** testificare] estimare M.R.   **63** aut(2)] vel O.
66 adibit] adhibet C.   **67** est] *om* O.   **68** quod] *add* vel O.   **70** suam . . . illam] tuam
venio quam C.   **72** etc.] immediate O.   **77** sui] sue C.   **80** proximi] *add* faciunt C.   fa-
ciunt] *om* O.   **81** malum] *add* hoc dicunt aut faciunt O.   **85** eciam] *add* et O.   **91** sua]
sui O.   **92** barbatum] berbatum C.   **96** sibi] *om* O.   **101** illam] illum C.   **107** nimia]
minima C.   eciam] enim O.   **108** vident] videntur M.W; videtur R.   sic] sicut
C.M.W.   ecclesiasticos] ecclesiasticus O.   **109** inquiunt] *om* O.   **110** carere] carente
Et.Go1.Go2.Co *and others*.   haberemus] *add* regem *here or after* necessitate: B1.B4.
L3.Go2 *and others*.   **124** nimis] *add* de O.   **131–132** est apcior] apciorem O.   **134** Et]
pro huiusmodi ergo invidia O.   **137** Iudicum 16] iudith 10 C.   **140–145** Et . . . loue]
text from R. *Verse 20, in* B3.E.Go2.L1.L2. LC.R.W1.

III.ii   QUIBUS INVIDIA COMPARATUR

[S]ecundo, circa comparacionem invidie est sciendum quod bene comparatur
cuidam lapidi nomine beloculus, qui secundum Ysidorum 16 *Ethimologiarum* est
similis oculo animalis, qui albus est in circuitu et niger in medio. Set ut
michi videtur bene potest dici oculus diaboli. Beel est nomen demonis, sic-
5   ut patet Danielis 14 et Luce 11. [f. 29v] Unde convenienter lapis ille
signat invidum, quia maxima occasio invidie surgit ab illis que videntur.
Set oculus talis est albus in circuitu quando videt in proximo ubique
bonum, et tamen in medio niger est, hoc est in corde inde tristatur. Unde
est oculus valde infirmus qui nichil boni potest videre sine dolore, iuxta
10   illud Ecclesiastici 14: "Nequam est oculus invidi." De illo ergo lapide
beloculo, ut michi videtur, facit sibi diabolus lapidem molarem, quo scilicet utuntur fabri, cuius natura est quod omne quod ei opponitur corrodit et
minuit. Revera sic invidus bonum quod videt in proximo studet quomodo posset corrodere et minuere. Et tamen sicut videmus quod huiusmodi lapides non
15   corrodunt ferrum sine sui lesione, certe sic nec invidus, imo primo nocet
sibi ipsi. Set illi qui hunc lapidem vertunt sunt tales pokerelle semper ad
malum instigantes dicendo: "Expelle talem vel talem de domo aut civitate.
Unde sibi tantum ditari, pro fortitudine aut sciencia tantum laudari? Verecundum valde est tibi ut ipse sic laudes tibi debitas impediat." Et tamen,
20   ut communiter, tales miseri quicquid de malo erga proximum machinantur, in
seipsos retorquetur; Ecclesiastici 27: "Qui statuit lapidem proximo, offendit."

Secundo comparatur invidia cuidam infirmitati que vocatur *jaundys*, que
oritur ex inordinato calore epatis. Unde et in dextro latere ubi epar iacet
25   maxime est istius infirmitatis molestia. Revera sic molestia invidorum non
est in sinistra parte, per quam adversitas designatur, quia non dolent invidi de adversitate proximi, set de prosperitate, que intelligitur per dex-

Therefore, O Lord, who art above,
Loosen those bonds and send us love!

7–8 John 8.44.   **13–14** Rom. 12.15.   **17–18** *Prov* 16669; *In* 11776.   **19–22** Pliny,
Hist. naturalis VIII.xi.32 and VIII.xii.33.   **26–28** Rev. 16.13–14.   **52** Wisd. 2.24.
61–72 For a tale similar to this moralization, see English *Gesta Romanorum*, pp. 386–
387.   **73–74** John 8.44.   **74–76** Ps.-Augustine, *Ad fratres in eremo*, sermo 18 (PL
40:1264).   **82–96** Tubach 4614. Also in: Bromyard, "Rapina," R.I.22 ; Holcot, *In Sapientiam*, lect. 176; CUL MS Kk.4.24, fol. 188. The Jerome reference may be to *Ep. 85*,
which contains a reference to Dionysius.   **134** John 15.22.   **134–135** 1 Sam. 18.6–9.
135–136 Gen. 37.   **136–137** Judg. 16.   **137–138** Dan. 6.

III.ii   WHAT THINGS ENVY CAN BE COMPARED TO

In the second place, with regard to similitudes for envy, notice that the
vice can well be compared to a stone called *beloculus*, which according to
Isidore, *Etymologies*, 16, is like the eye of an animal, which is white all
around and black in the middle. But I think it may well be called the devil's
eye. For Bel is the name of a demon, as is shown in Daniel 14 and Luke 11.
For this reason that stone fittingly symbolizes an envious person, because the
greatest occasion for envy arises from things that one sees. Such an eye is
white all around because the envious person sees the good everywhere in his
neighbor, and yet it is black in the middle because he is thereby saddened in
his heart. Hence such an eye is very sick, for it cannot see any good without
pain, according to Ecclesiasticus 14: "The eye of the envious is wicked."
From this stone *beloculus*, as it seems to me, the devil makes for himself a
grindstone, such as craftsmen use, whose nature it is that it gnaws off and
diminishes everything one holds against it. Thus, indeed, the envious person
strives to gnaw off and diminish as much as he can the good that he sees in his
neighbor. And yet we observe that such stones do not gnaw off iron without
hurting themselves. This is also true of an envious person: above anything
else he causes harm to himself. But those who turn the grindstone are those
pokerels who always instigate evil and say, "Drive this man or that from his
house or the town. How come he is getting so rich, or is being so much praised
for his strength or knowledge? It is shameful for you that he should interfere
with praises that belong to you." Nonetheless, it usually happens that whatever evil these wretches devise against their neighbor will return to themselves; Ecclesiasticus 27: "He who sets a stone for his neighbor will stumble
on it."
    Second, envy can be compared to a sickness called jaundice, which arises
from the disordered heat of the liver; whence the discomfort of this disease is

tram. Et ideo sunt similes Hely, qui non potuit videre lumen Domini donec extingueretur, etc. [Unde poeta:

30   Invidus alterius rebus marcessit opimis.]

Tercio bene comparatur urso cum pelve excecato. Sic invidus in mente de bono proximi. Unde Ecclesiastici 25: [f. 30] "Excecavit vultum suum sicut ursus." Videmus enim ⟨quod⟩ ursus diebus festivis magis trahitur per vicos, et torquetur verberibus, et a canibus laceratur. Sic invidus videns
35   honorem proximi, per quem intelligo diem festivalem, etc.
     Quarto bene comparatur reparatori vasorum, qui dicitur *a tynker or a sprongbolle*, qui transiens per domos et villas hinc et inde ⟨ubi⟩ pulcra vasa aurea, argentea, enea, et lignea aspicit, de illis non curat nec sibi de aliquo placet. Set cum viderit ollam, cacabum, patellam, ciphum, aut
40   discum dilaceratum et confractum, statim gaudet et inde sperat sibi aliquid lucrari. Sic revera invidus mundum perambulans gesta bonorum dissimulat nec sibi placent set dampnat. Set si aliquam fracturam vicii viderit, mox applicando recitat et dupplicat; Ecclesiastici 11: "Bonum in malum convertens insidiatur et in electis ponit maculam." Absit ergo quod umquam in
45   celum veniat invidus talis, eo quod ibi nimis torque[re]tur de gaudiis sanctorum, set vadat ad infernum, ut ibi discat gaudere de tormentis miserorum, et quod illis proprium est, habeat semper, etc.

---

2 Ethimologiarum] *add* capitulo 2 O.   **4** Beel] *add* autem M.W; *add* id R.   **6** ab] de O.
7 videt] vidit O.   **8** corde] *add* sua O.   **9** qui] quia O.   **27** proximi] *add* que per sinistram partem intelligitur O.   **29** etc.] regum O.   **29–30** Unde . . . opimis] *text from* R.
33 quod] quando C.   **34** et(1)] *om* O.   **35** etc.] *om* O.   **36** comparatur] *add* cuidam O.
a] *om* O.   **36–37** or a sprongbolle] vel glodier R.W; vel kesseler M.   **37** ubi] ibi C.
47 etc.] *om* O.

III.iii   DE MURMURE ET DETRACTIONE

[T]ercio circa membra invidie est sciendum quod quatuor sunt sibi propria, scilicet murmur et detractio, mendacium et adulacio.
     Est ergo murmur oblocucio indebito modo facta contra Deum vel proximum. De quo Ecclesiasticus: "Susurro et bilinguis maledictus." Propter hoc

greatest on the right side, where the liver is situated. Thus the discomfort
for envious people is not on the left side (which symbolizes ill fortune),
because the envious do not suffer pain from their neighbor's ill fortune but
rather from his prosperity (which is understood by the right). Therefore they
are like Eli, who was unable to see the light of the Lord before it went out,
and so forth. Hence the poet says:

The envious shrink in weight as their neighbors grow fat in riches.

Third, envy can be easily compared to a bear that has been blinded with a
basin. Thus is an envious person mentally blinded by his neighbor's good.
Whence Ecclesiasticus 25 states: "He has blinded his face like a bear." We
see that on feast days a bear is more violently dragged through the villages,
tormented with beatings, and torn by the dogs. Thus is the envious person
tormented when he witnesses his neighbor's honor, which I understand by the
feast day.

Fourth, envy can be compared to the man who repairs household vessels and
is called a "tinker" or "bowlfixer." Passing through houses and villages, when
he sees here and there vessels of gold, silver, brass, and wood, he pays no
attention, nor do they please him at all. But when he sees a jar, cooking pot,
bowl, cup, or plate that is cracked or in pieces, he is at once joyful and
expects to make some money from it. Thus, an envious person wanders through
the world and keeps quiet about the deeds of the good, nor do these please him,
but he condemns them. But when he sees some breakage caused by vice, he turns
to it right away and tells of it and makes it worse; Ecclesiasticus 11: "He
lies in wait and turns good into evil, and on the elect he lays a blot." Far
be it, therefore, that such an envious person should ever come to heaven, for
there he would be too much tormented by the joys of the saints; but let him go
to hell, where he may learn to rejoice over the torments of the wretches and
have forever what belongs to them!

2–3 Isidore, *Etym.* XVI.x.9.   5 Dan. 14.2–21; and Luke 11.15–19.   10 Ecclus.
14.8.   21–22 Ecclus. 27.29.   28–29 1 Sam. 3.2–3.   30 Horace, *Ep.* I.ii.57.   32–
33 Ecclus. 25.24.   43–44 Ecclus. 11.33.

III.iii   GRUMBLING AND BACKBITING

In the third place, regarding the members of envy we must know that it has
four: grumbling, backbiting, lying, and flattery.

Grumbling is railing in an improper way against God or one's neighbor. Of
it is said in Ecclesiasticus: "The whisperer and the double-tongued is accur-

5   vicium Maria soror Moysi percussa est lepra, ut patet Exodi 1. Similiter
Dathan et Abyron fuerunt a terra absorti, Exodi. Similiter filii Israel ab
igneis serpentibus percussi et pro maiori parte deperditi, Numeri 14. Unde Ad
Corinthios dicitur: "Neque adinvicem murmuraveritis sicut quidam murmu-
raverunt et perierunt." Unde Gregorius: "Regnum, inquit, celorum nullus qui
10 murmurat [f. 30v] accipit, et nemo qui accipit murmurare potest." Hec ille.
     Circa autem detractionem est sciendum quod ille detractor dici potest
qui alieno crimine delectatur aut continue bonum in malum convertens. Et
certe talis impie facit eo quod quantum in ipso est uno flatu tres animas
interficit: Primo illum de quo detrahit, quia ipsum scandalizat et diffa-
15 mat, et sic quasi spiritualiter occidit; secundo audientem illum, quia
facit eum male sentire de proximo et iniuste scandalizare. Unde dicit
Bernardus: "Qui, inquit, detrahit aut detrahentem libenter audit, quis
horum dampnabilior fuerit, non facile dixerim. Nam secundum Augustinum
numquam esset detractor si non esset auditor." Hec ille. Et terci⟨o⟩ [cer-
20 tum] est quod animam propriam falsa de proximo absente detrahendo detractor
dampnat. Et ideo, ut michi videtur, tales detractores ac maledicti diffamatores sunt sicut latrones qui fideles transeuntes spoliant, de quorum
societate unus vel duo passum explorabunt, qui cum audierint aliquos venientes faciunt quoddam signum ⟨vel hutando vel in pugno sibilando⟩. Quo
25 audito conveniunt omnes socii et fideles capiunt, ligant, spoliant, et
mactant. Revera sic est inter detractores et eorum auditores. Nam aliqui
latenter explorabunt quasi in passu facta proximorum, que cum viderint in
minimo deviare ⟨a⟩ vero, statim convocant socios et peius quam est narrant.
Ipsi vero libenter auscultando prout dicunt accipiunt et sic una cum illis
30 bonam famam proximi dilaniant, per quod semetipsos cum illis participes in
detractionis crimine efficiuntur. Bene ergo in antiqua lege precipiebatur,
scilicet Levitici 19: "Non maledices coram surdo nec coram ceco pones
offendiculum." Ad litteram valde enim innaturale et impium esset maledicere
surdo, cum ipse [f. 31] non audiat nec possit cavere. Secundum ergo *Glosam*,
35 surdo maledicere est absenti detrahere. Homo autem absens minus potest
audire detrahentem quam si surdus esset, quia quandoque surdus audit ex
alto clamore, set absens non, quia forte distat per decem miliaria vel amplius, et ideo detrahentem audire non potest quantumcumque clamaverit; et
ideo si absenti maledicit, contra legem facit, et per consequens maledictus
40 est. Similiter talis detrahens "coram ceco ponit offendiculum," dum alium
ipsum audientem qui non habet noticiam persone de quo detrahitur scandalizat, et facit malum de quo omnino nescit, set cecus est credere et
tenere.
     Et ideo Sapiens dicit: "Cum detractoribus ne commiscearis, quia repen-
45 te veniet perdicio eorum." Quia secundum Augustinum tales bona diminuunt,
mala exaggerant, indifferenciam pervertunt, scilicet in malum. Et ideo rogo
nonne crudeles dicerentur illi qui viderint fratres canibus lacerari et

sed." On account of this vice Miriam, the sister of Moses, was stricken with
leprosy, as can be seen in Exodus 1. Similarly, Dathan and Abiron were swallowed by the earth alive, in Exodus. Similarly, the children of Israel were
struck by fiery serpents and died for the most part, Numbers 14. Wherefore it
is said in the Letter to the Corinthians: "Neither do you murmur, as some of
them murmured and were destroyed." And Gregory says: "No one who grumbles
receives the kingdom of heaven, and no one who receives it can grumble."

About backbiting we must know that we can call "backbiter" a person who
takes pleasure in someone else's sin and constantly turns good into evil. Such
a person surely acts very wickedly, because as much as it is in his power he
kills three souls with one breath: first the one of whom he speaks ill, because
he ruins his reputation and defames him and thereby, as it were, kills him
spiritually; second, the one who hears him, because he causes him to think ill
of his neighbor and wrongly to be scandalized. Therefore says Bernard: "The
person who backbites and the person who willingly listens to him—which of them
is more blameworthy is hard to say. For according to Augustine there would
never be a backbiter if there were not an audience." And third, a backbiter
who says wrong things about his neighbor *in absentia* surely damns his own soul.
Therefore, I think that such backbiters and cursed spoilers of good names act
like thieves who plan to rob citizens on their way. One or two of them watch
the road, and when they hear someone coming they give a sign by hooting or
whistling in their fist. When their companions hear this, they all come together and catch the travelers, bind them, despoil them, and kill them. This
applies well to backbiters and their audience. For some people will secretly
watch out for their neighbors' deeds, as if they were watching the road, and if
they see them get off the true path even a little bit, they call their companions together and tell them worse things than there actually are. But the
latter willingly listen and take in whatever they say; and thus together with
the backbiters they tear their neighbor's good name to pieces and make themselves partners in the crime of detraction with them. But in the Old Law, that
is, in Leviticus 19, this was forbidden: "You shall not curse the deaf or put
an obstacle before the blind." It would be literally quite unnatural and
wicked to curse a deaf person since he cannot hear or beware. But according to
the *Gloss*, to "curse the deaf" means to speak ill of an absent person. An
absent person can hear a backbiter even less than if he were deaf, for sometimes a deaf man understands from loud shouting. But not a person that is
absent, who may be ten miles away or more and cannot hear his detractor, however much he may shout; and thus his detractor "curses" an absent person and
acts against the Law and consequently is cursed himself. Such a backbiter similarly "puts an obstacle before the blind" as he causes scandal to his lis-
tener, who has no knowledge of the person he is speaking ill of and thus
commits an evil without knowing it but is "blind" in the way he believes and
accepts it.

ipsos non exterrent set pocius canibus applaudent? Certe crudelis est
audiens detrahentem si ipsum non corripiat cum carnes crudas proximi audie-
50   rit lacerare, set et si ministrat salciamentum hillaris vultus sine qua pro
certo talis morcellus insipidus esset detractoribus; Ecclesiastici 28:
"Sepi aures tuas spinis et noli audire linguam nequam."
   Fatui ergo detractores et diffamatores miserrimi facere deberent sicut
facit formica, de qua Proverbiorum 6 dicitur: "Vade ad formicam et disce
55   sapienciam." Cuius natura talis est, quod si cadaver mortuum ⟨invenerit⟩ ex
una parte corruptum et ex ⟨alia⟩ integrum, a corrupto recedit et ad integrum se convertit, quasi putredinem fugiens et mundiciam diligens. Revera
sic debemus nos. Si enim proximum viderimus ex una parte integrum, hoc est
in bona vita, et ex alia [f. 31v] corruptum, hoc est cum aliquo defectu
60   notabili, semper ad meliorem partem trahere debemus et non nimis leviter
mala indicare; Ecclesiastici 19: "Iustus inclinat faciem suam et fingit se
non videre quasi ignoranter." Set semper detractor ad malam partem se
inclinat. Et sunt similes vespertilioni, cuius natura est quod quando videt
lampadem aut cereum accensum, semper querit lumen extinguere. Revera sic
65   detractor lumen bone fame in proximo, etc.; Proverbiorum 24: "Abhominacio
hominum detractor."
   Dicunt eciam philosophi quod sub lingua canis nascitur quedam vermis,
que cum creverit et se movere ceperit, mox dolore alienatur canis a sensu
et rapidus devenit. Et hoc totum est ex acutissimo veneno illius vermis.
70   Unde aperto ore currit protensa lingua salivam venenosam emittens. Per quod
quicquid momorderit, inficit, in tantum quod alii canes non audent illi
appropinquare, set ipso viso fugiunt. Revera sic movente verme malicie sub
lingua detractoris insanus devenit, hoc est non sanus, quia illa que in
proximo sane deberet interpretari protensa lingua venenum infundit malicie,
75   per quod quantum in illo est proximum occidit. Et ideo iuxta concilium
beati Ieronimi tali est resistendum et in nullo est sibi dare auditum nisi
dis⟨plicencie⟩. Dicit enim Ieronimus: "Sicut, inquit, sagitta emissa in
⟨duram⟩ materiam revertitur ad mittentem, sic detractio emissa ad hominem
solidum et bonum, statim revertitur ad detractorem." Nam quando detractor
80   videt quod verba displiciunt auditori, illico conticescit et quasi confusus
recedit; Proverbiorum 25: "Ventus aquilo dissipat pluvias, et facies tristis linguam detrahentem."
   Unde narratur de quodam detractore qui morte preventus simulavit se
velle confiteri set non fecit [f. 32] et mortuus est. Contigit postea quod
85   quidam sibi notus ipsum vidit in forma horribili valde, linguam habentem
igneam ab ore usque ad terram dependentem, quam continue corrosit et expuit
et iterum resumpsit et expuit, et tercio et quarto. Quod cum alius quesisset, "Quid est hoc?" respondit: "Quia, inquit, in detractionibus dum vixi
applaudebam, sic crucior," quia per quod peccat homo, per istud torquetur,
90   etc.

Therefore the Wise Man says: "Do not mingle with backbiters, for their destruction will come suddenly." For according to Augustine, such people diminish what is good, blow up what is evil, and turn into evil what is indifferent. Shall those, I ask, not be called cruel who when they see their brothers being torn by dogs do not drive the dogs away but rather cheer them on? Just so a person is cruel who listens to a backbiter and does not correct him when he hears him tear at the raw flesh of his neighbor, but in addition offers him the sauce of a smiling face, without which surely such a bite would have no taste for the backbiters; Ecclesiasticus 28: "Hedge your ears with thorns and do not listen to an evil tongue."

Thus, these foolish backbiters and most wretched destroyers of a good name should do as the ant does, of which Proverbs 6 says: "Go to the ant and learn wisdom." When it finds a dead body that is partly decayed and partly whole, it naturally turns away from what is decayed and goes to what is whole, as if it were fleeing from decay and looking for purity. We should do the same; when we notice that our neighbor is partly whole, that is, living a good life, and partly decayed, that is, tainted with some fault that is noteworthy though perhaps unknown to him, we should direct our attention to his better part and not point to his faults too lightly; Ecclesiasticus 19: "The just man turns away his face and pretends he does not see, as if he ignored it." But a backbiter always turns to the part that is spoilt. Such people are like a bat: when it sees a lighted lamp or candle, it naturally tries to extinguish the light. Thus the backbiter tries to blow out the light of good reputation in his neighbor; Proverbs 24: "The detractor is the abomination of men."

The philosophers say a certain worm develops under the tongue of a dog, which when it grows and begins to move, causes the dog almost to lose its mind out of pain and become rabid. And all this happens through the powerful poison of that worm. Then the dog runs about with open mouth, his tongue hanging out, and drips poisonous saliva. Whatever he bites, he infects with this poison, so that other dogs do not dare come near him but run away as soon as they see him. Similarly, when the worm of malice moves underneath the tongue of a backbiter, he becomes insane, that is, not reasonable, because with his tongue hanging out he pours his malicious poison into the acts of his neighbor which he should interpret reasonably and thus, in as much as he can, kills his neighbor. Therefore, according to the advice of blessed Jerome, such a person must be resisted, and one must show him no willingness to listen but only a sign of displeasure. For Jerome says: "As an arrow shot against a hard substance flies back at the archer, thus backbiting that is directed to a solid and good person comes at once back to the backbiter." For when a backbiter notices that his words displease his hearer, he shuts up and draws back in confusion; Proverbs 25: "The north wind drives away the rain, and a sad face a backbiting tongue."

A story is told about a backbiter who, prevented by death, pretended that

1 sunt] considero O.   **2** scilicet] que sunt O.   **4** maledictus] *add* multos enim turbant pacem habere volentes O.   **12** aut] ac O.   **19** tercio] tercium C.   **22** qui . . . spoliant] fideles transeuntes spoliare intendentes O.   **24** vel . . . sibilando] ut cum pugno sibilando vel per signum vocando C.   **28** a] at C.M.W.   **31** crimine] crimini O.   Bene ergo] cum igitur O.   **32** coram(1)] *om* O.   **38** et ideo] *om* O.   **39** si] sibi O.   maledicit] *add* et O.   **43** tenere] *corr to* intendere R.   **46** indifferenciam] indifferencia y.L3.Et *and some others*.   pervertunt] pervertant O.   **50** si] sibi O.   salciamentum] falsam (*for* salsam?) O.   **55** invenerit] fuerit C.   **56** alia] una parte C.   **60** notabili] *add* forte inconsiderato O.   **65** etc.] *om* O.   **67** quedam] quidam O.   **68** que] qui O.   mox] *add* ex O.   **71** illi] illum O.   **72** movente] *add* se O.   **74** infundit] infudit O.   **76** est(2)] *om* O.   **77** displicencie] discipline C.   **78** duram] duratam C.   **89** per istud] inde O.   **90** etc.] *om* O.

III.iv   DE MENDACIO

Circa autem mendacium est sciendum quod propter tria ut communiter homines menciuntur, scilicet vel ut noceant, vel ut gaudeant, vel ut utile faciant. Primum enim est semper mortale, quod faci⟨u⟩nt fidem negantes contra precepta Dei directe se erigentes, sicut dicere quod simplex forni-
5   cacio non est peccatum et huiusmodi. Et similiter quando quis mendaciter persequitur hominem ad mortem, vel lucrando per iuramentum intend⟨it⟩ alium decipere, sicut faciunt aliquando mercatores. Secundum est ex libidine, iocoso scilicet, quando quis mentitur ut ⟨provocet audientes⟩ ad risum. Et sic aliquando est mortale, aliquando veniale. Tercium est pro utilitate
10   futura, ut si⟨quis⟩ intendens alium interficere et querat a te, "Vidistine talem?" et dixeris, "Non novi," vel huiusmodi, tantum sub intencione vitam illius conservandi et similiter pro pudicicia et castitate servanda et huiusmodi. Dicunt aliqui quod tale mendacium semper est veniale nisi ex accidente aliud in mente evenerit quod ore non profert, quia sic potest
15   esse mortale, set semper pro indifferente illud est mortale per quod homo diffamatur iniuriose et maxime si tale mendacium affirmatur cum periurio.

Et hic adverte quod scienter menciens cum periurio primo obligat se diabolo, et quando cum manu librum tangit vel rem sacram, tunc per illam manum retinet eum diabolus donec ad penitenciam redeat; et in tantum quod
20   cum cibum capit, de manu diaboli capit; similiter si se signet aut huiusmo- di faciat, totum de manu diaboli est. Unde Proverbiorum 6. "Defixisti [f.

he wanted to confess, but he did not do so and died. Later it happened that someone who had known him saw him in a frightening shape with a very long tongue of fire hanging from his mouth down to the earth, which he constantly gnawed off and spat out and took back again and spat out, and thus a third and fourth time. When the other man asked him what this meant, he replied: "Because I approved with pleasure of speaking ill while I was alive, I am being thus tortured"; for by what a man sins, by that he is punished.

---

4 Ecclus. 28.15.   **5** Num. 12.10.   **6** Num. 16.1–33.   **6–7** Num. 21.5–7.   **8–9** 1 Cor. 10.10.   **9–10** Gregory, *In Evangelia*, hom. 19, 4 (PL 76:1156).   **13–14** Cf. Bernard, *De diversis*, sermo 17, 4 (6.1:153).   **17–19** Bernard, *De consideratione* II.xiii.22 (3:430). **19** Cf. Peraldus, *Summa vitiorum* IX.ii.6, but without "Augustinus."   **32–33** Lev. 19.14.   **32–43** Cf. Peraldus, loc. cit.   **44–45** Prov. 24.21–22.   **52** Ecclus. 28.28. **54–55** Prov. 6.6.   **61–62** Ecclus. 19.24.   **65–66** Prov. 24.9.   **67–72** Pliny, *Hist. nat.* XXIX.32.   **77–79** Cf. Jerome, *Ep. 52, Ad Nepotianum*, 14 (CSEL 54:438).   **81– 82** Prov. 25.23.   **83–90** Tubach 4907. Add: Bromyard, "Detraccio," D.VI.29; Grisdale, pp. 39ff.; BL MS Royal 7.D.i, fol. 122.   **89** Wisd. 11.17.

III.iv   LYING

About lying we must know that men commonly lie for three reasons, namely in order to do harm, or for enjoyment, or for a useful purpose. The first is always a mortal sin. This is done by people who speak against the faith and directly deny God's commandments, as when they say that fornication is not a sin and the like; likewise when someone by lying sends a man to his death, or when in business he intends to deceive someone by his oaths, as merchants sometimes do. The second kind of lying is for fun, as when one lies in order to provoke his audience to laughter. Sometimes this is a mortal sin, sometimes venial. The third kind is for some future good purpose, such as: if someone plans to kill another man and he asks you, "Have you seen him?" and you say, "I don't know him" or something like it, with the intention to save his life, and similarly in order to preserve modesty and chastity and for other such motivations. Some people say that such a lie is always venial, except if something else comes into one's mind which the mouth does not pronounce, for then it can be a mortal sin. But such a lie, instead of morally neutral, is always a mortal sin if a person is thereby defamed, and especially if such a lie is affirmed with an oath.

And one should notice here that a person who knowingly lies with perjury first of all commits himself to the devil; and when he touches the Book or some sacred object with his hand, by this hand the devil holds him until he returns to penance, to the extent that when he takes food, he takes it from the devil's

32v] apud extraneum manum tuam, illaqueatus es verbis oris tui, et similiter captus propriis sermonibus." Et secundo abnegat bona que continentur in
libro vel fiunt in Ecclesia, sicut missas, oraciones, et cetera bona.

25   Tercio, quantum in se est, nititur Deum adducere ad falsum testificandum,
quia secundum Augustinum iurare est Deum testem adducere, et quantum in
illo est, magis gravat Deum et ledit inponendo sibi malum culpe quam Iudei
Christum occidendo et inponendo malum pene. Et ideo Christus conquerendo
alloquitur talem secundum illud Psalmi: "Existimasti inique quod ero tui

30   similis, arguam te et statuam contra [te] faciem tuam." Et quarto, talis
omni die in omni ecclesia ab omni sacerdote et clerico officium dicente
excommunicatur, cum dic⟨un⟩t illud Psalmi: "Maledicti qui declinant a
mandatis tuis." Set ista sunt mandata Dei, scilicet: "Non assumes nomen Dei
tui in vanum," et istud: "Non falsum testimonium dices"; set periurans

35   directe et proterve contra ista duo facit; ergo, etc.

Unde peiores sunt diabolo, qui omnia mala permissus audet facere per
Deum, tamen non audet iurare. Peiores eciam dici possunt quam Iudas, qui
Christum vendidit pro triginta denariis. Set hodie tales ipsum vendunt pro
tribus obolis et minus. Unde dicunt quidam si super [hoc] arguantur: "Non

40   possum aliter merces meas vendere, nec alii volunt mihi credere, nisi
iurem." Set caveant tales, quia menciuntur aperte.

Et ecce quid accidit Londoniis. Narravit quidam Lumbardus nomine
Hubertus de Lorgo, qui sepultus est Londoniis inter Fratres Predicatores,
quod habuit quendam armigerum, qui in omni verbo ita horribiliter iuravit

45   per Christi membra, sicut per cor, oculos, dentes, et vulnera simul omnia
combinando, quod horror erat audire. Qui tandem infirmatus vidit in extasi
quandam dominam pulcherrimam cameram intrantem et puerum dulcissimum
crudelissime vulneratum in ulnis portantem. Cui ille: "Karissima domina,
inquit, [f. 33] est iste filius tuus?" Et illa lugubri voce, "Ita, inquit, filius

50   meus est." Et ipse: "Quis, inquit, eum sic tractavit, maxima pena esset
dignus sic innocentem vulnerare." Quo audito ipsa quasi irruens in eum
dixit: "Tu, inquit, maledicte, es ille qui sic filium meum per iuramenta
tua [eciam] quamplura falsa dilacerasti. Et ipse tamen erit iudex tuus qui
dixit tibi, 'Fiat tibi sicut petisti.' " Et hiis dictis disparuit illa. Et

55   ille ad se reversus clamavit et assistentibus rem gestam narravit. Et addidit dicens: "Ego, inquit, ibo ad demones." Et hiis dictis protinus expiravit.

Et tamen adverte quod iura aliquando permittunt hominem iurare, sicut
patet in hiis versibus:

60   Lex et fama, fides, reverencia, caucio dampni,
Defectus veri tibi dant iurare licenter.

hand; likewise, if he crosses himself or does something of this sort, it all is done from the devil's hand. Therefore it is said in Proverbs 6: "You have engaged fast your hand to a stranger; you are ensnared with the words of your mouth and caught with your own words." In the second place, he denies all the good that is contained in the Book or that is done in the Church, such as Masses, prayers, and other good things. In the third place, he tries to bring God to a false testimony inasmuch as he can, for according to Augustine, to swear is to bring God as a witness; and inasmuch as lies in him, he burdens and hurts God by laying sin on him even more than the Jews did by killing Christ and laying punishment on him. And therefore Christ laments and addresses such a person in the words of the Psalm: "You have thought unjustly that I should be like you; I will reprove you and set myself against your face." And in the fourth place, the perjurer is excommunicated every day, in every church, by every priest and cleric who recites the Office, when they say the words of the Psalm: "Cursed are those who turn from your commandments." These are God's commandments: "Do not use God's name in vain," and: "Do not give false witness." But a perjurer acts directly and impudently against these two; therefore, etc.

Hence perjurers are worse than the devil, who with God's permission dares commit every evil but does not dare to swear. They may further be said to be worse than Judas, who sold Christ for thirty denarii. But nowadays perjurers sell him for three obuli and less. Whence some say, if they are accused of this: "I cannot sell my wares otherwise; people won't believe me unless I swear." But let such perjurers beware, for they lie openly.

Lo, what happened in London. A certain Lombard by the name of Hubert de Lorgo, who is buried among the Dominicans in London, reported that he had a squire who, whenever he spoke, swore terrible oaths by Christ's members, such as his heart, eyes, teeth, and all wounds together, that it was awful to hear him. At last, when he was ill, he saw in a vision a most beautiful lady enter his room, carrying in her arms the sweetest child, who was most cruelly wounded. "Dearest lady," he said, "is this your son?" And she answered with somber voice: "Yes, this is my son." And he replied: "Whoever has mistreated him thus would be worthy of the greatest punishment, wounding an innocent child this way." When she heard this, she turned to him sharply and said: "You, wretch, are the one who have thus torn my child through your oaths, which often were even false. And now he will be your judge who has said to you, 'May it happen to you as you have said.' " And with these words she disappeared, whereas the squire, returning to his senses, cried out and told those present what had happened. And then he added: "I shall go to the devils." And with these words he expired at once.

You should note, however, that the law does allow a person to swear on certain occasions, as is stated in these verses:

Primo per legem possumus iurare, hoc est dictu, lex aliquando permittit
iurare, sicut patet Deuteronomii 6: "Per nomen illius iurabis," supple: si
iurare contingat. Et alibi: "Iurabis autem est est, non non, quia quod
65   amplius est, a malo est." Et tamen secundum Augustinum, licet licitum sit
iurare, omne iuramentum est periculosum; et ideo semper cavendum et timendum ne forte trahat ad periurium, quia quacumque de causa iuraverit homo,
ipse quasi funem in colle ponit et se periculo astringit. Hec ille. Secundo, pro fama iuratur conservanda vel purganda; Ecclesiastici 41: "Curam
70   habe de bono nomine," etc. Tercio, fides permitt⟨i⟩t iuramentum, ut astru-
antur simplices fidem stabiliter credendam. Similiter ut melius servetur
status Ecclesie. Sic iurant religiosi et votum faciunt, ⟨ut patet 14,
questione 2 *Super prudencia*⟩. Quarto, propter Dei reverenciam et honorem,
ut quando fit in iuramento fidelis protestacio divine maiestatis. Unde
75   dicitur vulgariter: "Qui bene iurat, bene credit." Quinto, caucio dampni,
ut scilicet res tua indempnis servetur vel amissa recuperetur, quia secundum Apostolum Ad Hebreos 6: "Omnis [f. 33v] contraversie eorum finis est
iuramentum." Sexto, defectus veri, ne veritas periclitatur, etc.

---

3 faciunt] faciant C.   6 intendit] intendendo C.   8 provocet audientes] proni ad audiendum C.   9 est(1)] *om* O.   10 siquis] sicut C.   12 conservandi] servare O.   18 et
quando] *om* O.   tunc] et O.   20 signet] signat O.   23 abnegat] *add* omnia O.   que] qui
O.   32 dicunt] dicit C.   34 tui] *om* O.   40 alii] aliter O.   47 et puerum] puerumque O.
53 quamplura] quampluries O.   54 petisti] dixisti O.   65–66 licet . . . ideo] cum omne
iuramentum sit periculosum licitum est iurare est tamen O.   68 ipse] *om* O.   70 permit-
tit] permittat C.   71 servetur] conservetur O.   72–73 ut . . . prudencia] etc C. *Instead of*
14 questione 2, O *read* q.t.   76 ut] *om* O.   78 defectus] *add* verbi O.   ne] scilicet O.
etc.] *om* O.

III.v   DE ADULACIONE

Circa adulacionem quarto et ultimo est sciendum quod de ea sic ait
Bernardus: "Pessimus, inquit, vulpis est occultus detractor, set non minus
blandus adulator." Et ideo dicit Ieronimus: "Adulatores, inquit, tamquam
inimicos cave, quorum sermones sunt super oleum molles, set ipsi sunt
5   iacula." Cuius condiciones describens quidam dicit: "Adulator, inquit,

God's Law itself, and your good name,
Our faith, too, and God's honor,
The threat of harm, endangered truth—
These give you leave to swear.

First, we may swear on account of the Law, that is to say, the Law allows us to swear on certain occasions, as is clear from Deuteronomy 6: "You shall swear by his name," add: if it is necessary to do so. And elsewhere: "You shall swear yes, yes, no, no; what is over and above these, is of evil." Yet according to Augustine: even if it is permissible to swear, every oath is dangerous; hence one must always beware and fear lest one fall into perjury, because for whatever reason a man swears, he ties a rope around his neck and binds himself to danger. Second, one may swear in order to preserve or purge one's good name; Ecclesiasticus 41: "Take care of a good name," etc. Third, faith allows giving an oath in order to strengthen the simple in their faith. Likewise, in order to better preserve the order of the Church; in this way, the religious swear and make a vow, as is shown in Causa 14, question 2, *Super prudencia*. Fourth, one may swear in order to render God worship and honor, as when in an oath one faithfully acknowledges God's majesty. Hence it is commonly said: "He who swears well, believes well." Fifth, one may swear in order to prevent harm, that is, in order to keep what belongs to you unharmed or to recover something that has been lost, for according to the Apostle's Letter to the Hebrews 6: "An oath is the end of all their controversy." And sixth, one may swear because of the lack of true words, that is to say, when truth is in danger.

21–23 Prov. 6.1–2. **26** Augustine, *Sermo 180* III.3 (PL 38:973). **29–30** Ps. 49.21. **32–33** Ps. 118.21. **33–34** Exod. 20.7 and 20.16. **42–57** Tubach 5103. Add: Brinton, Sermons 43, 80, and 81; Bromyard, "Iuramentum," I.XII.29; English *Gesta Romanorum* pp. 409ff.; the sermons of Robert Ripon, British Library, MS Harley 4894, fol. 100; Chartham, fol. 271; *Dives and Pauper*, III.11; BL MS Harley 2247, fol. 69v; Bodl. MS Greaves 54, fol. 94v. **60–61** Also in *Spec. laicorum*, p. 90. Englished in Grimestone, No. 94. **63** Deut. 6.13. **64–65** Cf. Matt. 5.34–37. **65–68** Cf. *Sermo 180* III.3 (PL 38:973) or *De sermone Domini in monte* I.xvii.51 (CC 35: 56–59). **69–70** Ecclus. 41.15. **72–73** Gratian II.14.2.1 (1:734). **77–78** Heb. 6.16.

III.v FLATTERY

In the fourth and last place, concerning flattery, we must know that Bernard writes: "A hidden backbiter is a most wicked fox, but a bland flatterer is not any less evil." And therefore Jerome says: "Beware of flatterers as if they were your enemies. Their words are smoother than oil, but they are darts." Someone else describes the nature of a flatterer as follows: "He

fortiter laudat quicquid laudaveri⟨s⟩, mutat sentenciam si tu mutaveris,
⟨in risus⟩ solvitur in quos te solveris, pluit lacrimas cum ipse plueris."
Hec ille. Unde, quod dolendum est, sic adulacio et dolus regnant hiis
diebus quod "in omnem terram exivit sonus eorum et in omnes fines terre
10   verba eorum." Unde Gregorius in *Registro*: "Nullus, inquit, tibi melior
potest esse ad concilium quam qui te fideliter et non tua diligit." Set
quia iam secundum omnem cursum amoris non diligo te propter te set propter
tua, ° certe:

Rara fides ideo quia multi multa locuntur.

15   Tales ergo hodie diliguntur a magnis dominis eo quod semper loquuntur eis
placencia, iuxta illud Ysaie 3: "Loquimini nobis placencia," etc. Set
contra hoc dicitur Ysaie 5: "Ve qui dicitis bonum malum" et e contrario,
"ponentes tenebras lucem et amarum dulce" et e contrario. Ve ergo adulatoribus qui dicunt perverso, "Bonus es," et iniusto, "Iustus es." Nec mirum
20   si sint maledicti, quia sunt similes pessimis Iudeis qui latronem Baraban
Christo pretulerunt. Ve eciam secundo illis ponentibus tenebras lucem,
idest pessimum peccatum factum optimum. Ve eciam tercio illis ponentibus
dulce amarum, idest veritatem convertendo in falsitatem. Set caveant tales
qui nimis credunt huiusmodi adulatoribus, ne illis eveniat sicut evenit
25   Roboam filio Salomonis, qui spreto concilio senum et sapientum fecit secundum concilium iuvenum adulancium et perdidit decem tribus [f. 34] et quasi
totum regnum suum, ut patet 3 Regum 12. Nam plus nocet, secundum *Glosam*,
lingua adulatoris quam gladius persecutoris: tantum vult dicere quod multi
sunt invincibiles persecucione et tamen vincuntur modica adulacione. Et
30   causa est quia adulacio multa facit que Deus facere non potest, scilicet
quod malus sit bonus et falsus fidelis, et quod peccatum sit bonum, et quod
falsitas sit veritas, et huiusmodi. Que omnia facit adulacio, prout supra
dicit Ysaias. Et ideo Salomon, qui fuit sapientissimus, sprevit Deum verum
et coluit ydola uxorum suarum, 3 Regum 11.
35   Unde, ut michi videtur, deus ille quem colunt adulatores potest sic
depingi, videlicet cum capite et cauda mureligi et corpore draconis. Et
certe bene. Nam sicut catus nulli rei tantum blanditur tam capite quam
cauda sicut muri, non quia amat set ut decipiat, similiter nullum corpus
est ita venenosum sicut corpus draconis, eo quod eius anelitus tantum aerem
40   inficit per quod homo interficitur, sic adulator habet mel in ore et fel in
° corde, ⟨sicut habetur in istis metris:

Multis annis iam transactis
Rara fides est in factis.

praises eagerly whatever you praise, changes his mind when you change yours, bursts out laughing when you do, and sheds tears when you weep." Therefore, flattery and guile reign so much nowadays—which is frightful—that "their sound has gone forth into all the earth, and their words to the ends of the whole world." Hence Gregory says in his *Register*: "No one can give you better advice than a person who loves you, not your possessions." But since, in the common ways of love, I do not love you for your sake but for the sake of your possessions, surely,

> Trust is rare, for many men speak many things.

For such people are nowadays beloved by great lords, because they always say what pleases them, according to Isaiah 3: "Speak unto us pleasant things," and so forth. But against this it is said in Isaiah 5: "Woe to you that call evil good," and vice-versa, "you that put darkness for light and bitter for sweet," and vice-versa. Woe therefore to flatterers who say to a wicked person, "you are good," and to an unjust one, "you are just." No wonder that they are cursed, for they are like the evil Jews who preferred the thief Barabbas to Christ. Woe also to those who "put darkness for light," that is, a wicked sin for a good deed. And woe thirdly to those who "put sweet for bitter," that is, who turn truth into falsehood. But let those people beware who trust such flatterers overmuch, that it may not go with them as it did with Rehoboam, the son of Solomon, who scorned the advice of the elders and the wise and acted on the counsel of young flatterers: he lost ten tribes and nearly his entire kingdom, as is stated in 3 Kings 12. For according to the *Gloss*, a flatterer's tongue does more harm than the sword of the persecutor, which means that many are invincible in persecution and yet are overcome with a little flattery. The reason is that flattery achieves many things that God cannot do, namely, that a bad person be good, a false one trustworthy, a sin a virtue, falsehood truth, and the like. Flattery does all this, as Isaiah said above. And because of this vice Solomon, who was most wise, scorned the true God and worshipped the idols of his wives, in 3 Kings 11.

Therefore I think the god whom flatterers worship can be depicted as follows: with the head and tail of a cat and the body of a dragon. This fits very well, because just as a cat allures no one else with its head and tail so much as a mouse—not because it loves it but wants to deceive it—; and just as no body is as poisonous as that of the dragon, because its breath infects the air that it kills a man—just so does a flatterer have honey in his mouth and gall in his heart, as one finds in these verses:

> For many years that have gone by
> Rarely can trust be put in deeds;

Mel in ore, verba lactis,
45   Fel in corde, fraus in factis.⟩

Unde bene sibi convenit dicta pictura, eo quod primo ore decipit et cauda,
hoc est in posterum, mordet, et tandem sui flatu hominem totaliter occidit
quantum in eo est, et hoc aliquando spiritualiter et aliquando corporaliter.
50   Et ideo, non obstante illa pictura, videtur michi quod sic depingi
posset ipsemet ad modum vage meretricis cuilibet equaliter applaudentis cum
dulci poculo in una manu et speculum in alia. Nam sicut meretrix est mulier
vaga iuxta Sapientem, "non consistens dom⟨i⟩ pedibus," sic certe adulator
vagabundus discurrit de loco ad locum sine quiete querens quem melius
55   poterit decipere cum dulci poculo in manu, hoc est cum factis, signis, et
verbis in exteriori apparatu sanctissimus. Set adverte quod non incongrue
tenet spe- [f. 34v] culum in manu, vultus hominum ostendens, quia certe
sicut tot gestus, tot vultus hominis apparent gaudii aut desolacionis in
speculo quando ponitur ante faciem eius. Set quando ponitur speculum a
60   tergo vel a latere, nichil apparet. Revera sic adulator in presencia hominum gaudet cum gaudente et flet cum flente, set in absencia nichil quasi
curat de eo. Set utinam multi illorum nichil facerent a tergo, sicut speculum nichil representat a tergo; set quod peius est, ibi detrahunt, menciuntur, derident, et cachinnant.
65   Et ideo huiusmodi adulator bene potest comparari cuidam animali dicto
Gamaleon, de quo Ysidorus *Ethimologiarum* libro 12 dicit quod est quoddam
animal vivens in aere, cuius color variatur ad variacionem obiectorum
quibus applicatur. Revera sic adulator: quando applicatur ad bonos, quantum
potest sibi nititur assimilari, et similiter ad malos quando illis applica-
70   tur, iuxta illud Ad Corinthios: ["Nos revelata facie speculantes in eandem
ymaginem transformamur," scilicet] gaudentes cum gaudentibus et e contrario. Et ideo sunt similes ventilogio, qui ad flatum cuiuslibet venti se
convertit et quasi cum capite blanditur.
Sic ergo patet de invidia et eius membris, de qua sic ait Gregorius:
75   "Invidia, inquit, est arbor cuius radix est superbia, truncus malivolencia,
rami rancor et odium, folia adulacio, detractio, et mendacium, flores
pallor et macies, fructus dolor et gaudium, hoc est dolor de proximi prosperitate et gaudium de eius adversitate."

2 Pessimus] pessima O.   6 laudaveris] laudaverit C.M.W.   7 in risus] risu C.   13 tua]
add et C.   15–16 semper . . . placencia] nolunt a sanctis et fidelibus super delicta argui
O.   16 etc.] *add* videte vobis errores hoc est dicunt tales permitte nos errare O.   26 et(1)]
om O.   31 et(2)] *om* O.   sit(2)] *om* O.   et quod] *om* O.   32 sit] *om* O.   40 habet] est O.
in(2)] *add* cauda idest in C.   41–45 sicut . . . factis] etc C. *Text from* M.   47 sui] suo
O.   53 domi] domum C.   61 et] *om* O.   62 illorum] eorum O.   64 et] *om* O.

Honey in mouth and words of milk,
But gall in heart and fraud in deeds.

For this reason, the aforementioned picture fits the flatterer very well, for
he first deceives with his face and bites with his tail, that is, from behind,
and at last he kills a man entirely with his breath in as much as he can, and
this in part spiritually, in part bodily.

And thus, without denying the first picture, I think a flatterer can
further be depicted as a wandering whore who plays up to everyone with a sweet
cup in one hand and a mirror in the other. For as a whore, according to the
Wise Man, is a wandering woman "who cannot stay at home," thus certainly the
flatterer runs restlessly from place to place and seeks whom he can best
deceive, with a sweet cup in his hand, that is, with deeds, signs, and words in
his appearance that make him look like a saint. But notice that not unfittingly she holds a mirror in her hand, which shows the faces of men; because
when a mirror is held before a man's face, so many features and faces of men
appear in it, whether of joy or of sorrow, but when it is held behind or on the
side, nothing appears in it. In the same way, when a flatterer is in one's
presence, he rejoices with the rejoicing and weeps with the weeping, but when
he is away, he does not give a hoot. But would that flatterers would do nothing
from behind, as a mirror shows no image from behind—but alas, many of
them speak ill from behind, lie, laugh, and deride.

Such a flatterer can therefore be compared to an animal called chameleon.
In book 12 of the *Etymologies* Isidore says that this is an animal which lives
in the air, whose color changes after the color of the things which it is next
to. Thus the flatterer, when he is with good people, tries to make himself
like them as much as he can, and similarly with wicked people when he is in
their company, according to Corinthians: "Beholding with open face, we are
transformed into the same image," that is to say, we rejoice with those who rejoice, and vice-versa. Such people are like the weathervane which turns with
every breeze and, so to speak, flatters with its head.

This, then, is the nature of envy and its members, of which Gregory speaks
as follows: "Envy is a tree, whose root is pride, its trunk ill-will, its
branches rancor and hatred, its leaves flattery, backbiting and lies, its
blossoms pallor and emaciation, and its fruit grief and joy," that is to say,
grief at one's neighbor's good fortune and joy at his ill luck.

2–3 Bernard, *Super Cantica* LXIII.ii.4 (2:163).   3–5 Cf. Ps.-Jerome, *Ep. 148, Ad Ce-
lantiam* 17 (PL 22:1212).   5–7 The thought occurs in Jerome, *Ep. 22* 24 (CSEL 54:176);
the same wording in Holcot, *Moralitates* 43.   9–10 Rom. 10.18.   10–11 Gregory, *Re-
gistrum* I.33 (CC 140:41).   14 *Disticha Catonis* I.xiii.2.   16 Isa. 30.10.   17 Isa.
5.20.   25–27 1 Kings 12.6–24.   33–34 1 Kings 11.1–10.   42–45 *Prov* 15,497; *In*
11,396. Englished in Grimestone, No. 60. See also *RL XIV*, p. 346.   50–52 Cf. Holcot,
Moralitates 43. See Liebeschütz, p. 54 and pl. 19.   53 Prov. 7.11.   61 Cf. Rom.
12.15.   66–68 Isidore, *Etym.* XII.ii.18.   70–71 2 Cor. 3.18.

III.vi   DE CARITATE

[N]unc ad virtutem caritatis est advertendum, que in omnibus pessime invidie cum suis sequacibus se obicit et contrariatur. Nam quantum invidia ista in malis, tantum ista caritas in bonis delectatur. Et ideo pugil fortissimus contra illam et hostes antiquos, quos constanter aggreditur,
5   pugnat, prosternit, et devincit. Unde de illa sic [f. 35] intendo procedere: primo ostendere quid sit et quomodo diffinitur; secundo in quibus consistit et firme stabilitur; tercio que illam impediunt unde elongatur; quarto quomodo requiritur et recuperatur.

Circa primum est sciendum quod secundum Iohannis 14 dicitur: "Deus
10   caritas est." Ex quo ergo Deus caritas est sequitur quod nullum vicium permittitur cum ea. Et hoc est quod illam describ⟨ens⟩ Apostolus Ad Corinthios 13 dicit: "Caritas, inquit, paciens est," scilicet contra vicium iracundie; "benigna est," contra vicium invidie sibi opponens; "non inflatur," contra superbiam, que quasi vesica turgescit; "non est ambiciosa," contra cupidi-
15   tatem, que semper [circa] terrena animum ambit et anhelat; "non irritatur," contra accidiam, que bonam occupacionem pervertit; "non querit que sua sunt," contra gulam, hoc est, que ventri placent et abstinencie displicent; "non cogitat malum," contra luxuriam, que secundum Ieronimum cum cor hominis apprehendit, nichil aliud quam lasciviam cogitare permittit; "non
20   gaudet super iniquitate proximi," contra detractores, periuros, adulatores, et huiusmodi; "set gaudet veritati," ne scilicet periclitetur per falsitatem, etc. Secundum autem Augustinum caritas est dulce vinculum quo solo Deus ligatur, cuius dulcedo tanta est quod si eius minima gutta in infernum caderet, tota eius amaritudo in dulcedinem verteretur. Et ideo Hugo *De*
25   *laude caritatis* dicit quod qui caritatem habuerit, non tantum diabolum vincere potest—qui nichil tantum timet sicut illam, quia neque ieiunia neque vigilias neque elemosinas; et hoc quia illam in celo servare contempsit—set eciam ipsum Deum, in quo omnia et per quem omnia. Unde ait Hugo: "O, inquit, caritas, maximam vim habes; tu enim sola Deum trahere potuisti
30   ad terras. O, inquit, quam forte est istud vinculum tuum, quo et Deus ligari potuit et homo ligatus tuis vinculis vincula iniquitatis dirupit." Hec ille. [Unde et apud poetas pro virtute caritatis fuit hoc solempne proverbium, scilicet, "Amor vincit omnia, quia vicit Pana." Pana autem apud illos fingebatur deus omnium vel deus tocius, quem tamen dicunt ipsi captum
35   et devictum amore cuiusdam puelle pulcherime nomine Siringe, ad modum quo nos dicimus Christum Filium Dei devictum amore nature humane.

Certum est ergo quod inter omnes virtutes ista est maioris potestatis et efficacie, et hoc probatur per talem poesim. Narrant autem poete quod in Lerna palude erat quidam serpens qui solo flatu omnem infecit aerem, unde
40   homines transeuntes intoxicabantur. Cum autem quidam pastor quodam serto coronatus illesus pertransisset et hoc alius pastor didicisset quod virtute

III.vi   CHARITY

Now we turn to the virtue of charity, which in every respect opposes
wicked envy with its followers and goes against it. For as much as envy delights in evil, so much does charity delight in good. And thus it is a most
valiant fighter against envy and our ancient foes, whom it continually con-
fronts, combats, overthrows, and defeats. About this virtue I shall proceed as
follows: first I shall show what it is and how it is defined; second, what it
consists in and is firmly established by; third, what things hinder it and
drive it away; and fourth, how it is regained and recovered.

Concerning the first point we should know that according to John 14, "God
is love." Since God is charity, it follows that no vice may exist with it.
Therefore, when the Apostle describes it in Corinthians 13, he says that "Charity is patient," namely against the vice of wrath; "it is benign," opposing
itself to the vice of envy; "it is not puffed up," against pride, which swells
like a bladder; "it is not ambitious," against greed, which always makes the
mind circle around and thirst for earthly goods; "it does not become irri-
tated," against sloth, which undoes one's activity in good deeds; "it does not
seek its own," against gluttony, which seeks what pleases the stomach and
displeases abstinence; "it does not think evil," against lechery, which according to Jerome, when it grips man's heart, does not let it think of anything
else but lust; "it does not rejoice in its neighbor's wickedness," against
backbiters, perjurers, flatterers, and the like; "but it rejoices in truth," so
that it may not be put in jeopardy by falsehood, and so on. According to
Augustine, charity is a sweet bond by which alone God is bound, and its
sweetness is so great that if the smallest drop of it fell into hell, all its
bitterness would be turned into sweetness. Therefore, Hugh, in describing the
virtue in his book *The Praise of Charity*, declares that he who has charity can
overcome not only the devil—who fears nothing, not fasting or waking or almsgiving, so much as charity, and this because he scorned to practice it in
heaven—but even God himself, in whom and through whom all things have their
being. Therefore Hugh says: "O charity, you hold the greatest power, for you
alone could draw God to earth. Oh, how strong is your bond by which God could
be bound, and man, when he was bound with your bonds, broke the bonds of evil."
For which reason the poets of old had this solemn proverb about the virtue of
love: "Love conquers all, for it has conquered Pan." For among them Pan was
thought to be the god of all things or the god of everything; yet they say that
he was captured and overcome by love for a most beautiful girl named Syrinx,
just as we say that Christ, the Son of God, was overcome by love for human
nature.

Therefore it is certain that among all the virtues charity has the most
power and effectiveness, and this is proven by the following fable. The poets
tell us that in the swamp of Lerna there was once a serpent who with its breath

eius serti sic evasisset, rapuit sertum ab eo et statim alius mortuus est.
Quod cum audisset Mercurius, deus eloquencie, a raptore certum abstulit et
ad pastorem mortuum accessit, in cuius ore flores sigillatim de illo po-
45 suit, unde tandem virtute unius a morte surrexit. Revera spiritualiter
loquendo: In ista palude fallacis mundi est iste serpens antiquus, ex cuius
flatu et malicia omnes fere transeuntes inficiuntur. Quod considerans vir
iustus sertum sibi facit de floribus mellifluis bonarum virtutum, quarum
virtute a malicia diaboli illesus pertransit. Si ergo a casu contigerit per
50 alium inimicum sertum hoc auferri, per quod spiritualiter quasi morimur,
revera hoc audito statim venit Mercurius, idest Christus, qui deus est
omnis eloquencie, sapiencie, et sciencie, et dictum sertum bonarum virtutum
reducit, et diversis floribus illius per os cordis illud reficit, quia modo
floribus humilitatis, modo floribus pietatis, modo floribus castitatis, et
55 sic de singulis. Unde si ad plenum virtute istorum non revixerit, tandem
apponit florem caritatis, ex cuius contactu, si bene de illo gustaverit,
mox ad vitam revertitur.] Ex quibus omnibus sequitur quod illa sit maioris
[f. 35v] virtutis et potencie omnium aliarum virtutum et mater et domina
iuxta illud Apostoli Ad Corinthios 13: "Nunc autem manent fides, spes, et
60 caritas, tria hec; maior autem horum est caritas," etc.

5–6 procedere] *add* scilicet O.   **9** dicitur] *om* O.   **10** Deus] *add* ipse O.   **11** describens]
describit O.   **22** etc.] hec ille O.   autem] *om* O.   **25** dicit] illam describens intendit O.
57 Ex . . . illa] eo quod ipsa O.   **60** etc.] *om* O.

III.vii   IN QUIBUS CARITAS CONSISTIT: DILECTIO DEI

[C]irca secundum est sciendum quod caritas consistit et stabilitur in
dileccione Dei et proximi, ita ut Deus ipse diligatur propter se et propter
nostram necessitatem, et proximus propter amorem suum, "sicut te ipsum. In
hiis enim duobus," iuxta illud Matthei 22, "° universa lex pendet et pro-
5 phete," quia unum sine alio veraciter diligi non potest. Et ideo qui implet
ista mandata, certe implet totam sacram Scripturam et omnes leges Dei.
[Probacio: Si enim primo veraciter Deum diligis, tunc non habebis deos
alienos, non assumes nomen Dei in vanum, non violabis Sabbatum, etc. Si
autem diligis proximum, tunc non committes homicidium, furtum, falsum
10 testimonium, nec concupisces uxorem proximi, nec aliquo modo mecaberis.

alone infected the air so that men who passed by were poisoned. But when a
shepherd who wore some wreath on his head passed by without getting hurt,
another shepherd understood that he had escaped the danger by virtue of that
wreath, and he took the wreath from him and the first shepherd died at once.
When Mercury, the god of eloquence, heard this, he took the wreath from the
thief, went to the dead shepherd, and put flowers from it into his mouth, one
by one, until he at last rose from death by the virtue of a single flower. In
spiritual terms: In the swamp of this deceitful world lives the ancient serpent
by whose breath and malice nearly all who pass by are infected. A just man who
reflected on this made for himself a wreath of honey-sweet flowers of good
virtues, by whose virtue he passed without being hurt by the devil's malice.
But if it perchance happens that this wreath is taken away by another enemy, so
that we as it were die spiritually, indeed Mercury comes as soon as he hears of
it, that is, Christ, who is God of all eloquence, wisdom, and knowledge, and
brings the wreath of good virtues back and heals him with its different flowers
through the mouth of his heart, now with flowers of humility, now of piety, now
of chastity, and thus with all separate virtues. When he then has not yet
fully revived through their virtue, he finally gives him the flower of charity;
as soon as he receives that, if he tastes of it well, he returns to life. From
this it follows that charity has greater virtue and power than all the other
virtues and is their mother and mistress, according to the Apostle in Corinthians 13: "But now remain faith, hope, and charity, these three; but charity
is the greatest of them," and so on.

9–10 1 John 4.8.   **12–22** 1 Cor. 13.4–6.   **29–31** Hugh of Saint Victor, *De laude caritatis* (PL 176:974).   **32–35** Cf. Virgil, *Eclogues* X.69, and Servius's commentary on
Eclogue II.31 (pp. 23–24).   **38–45** See the discussion in the Introduction, pp. 18–19.
59–60 1 Cor. 13.13.

III.vii   THE LOVE OF GOD

Concerning the second point, we must know that charity consists and is
established in the love of God and the love of our neighbor, so that God is
loved for his own sake and for our need, and our neighbor for the sake of God's
love, "as yourself. For in these two," according to Matthew 22, "depends the
whole law and the prophets," because one of them cannot be truly loved without
the other. And thus, he who fulfills these commandments certainly fulfills all
of Holy Scripture and all the laws of God. This can be proven as follows: if
you first truly love God, you will have no other gods, you will not take God's
name in vain, you will not violate the Sabbath, and so forth. And if you love
your neighbor, you will not commit murder or theft, give false witness, covet

Sequitur ergo: qui implet ista mandata, implet totam Scripturam et omnes
leges Dei.]
    Primo ergo circa dilectionem et caritatem erga Deum est sciendum quod
ipsa specialiter stabilitur et consistit in duobus et magis laudabilis
15 ostenditur, scilicet primo quando a nobis tanquam pater amando pre ceteris
humilius honoratur, secundo quando eius voluntas quoad precepta diligencius
a nobis observatur. Circa ergo dilectionem et caritatem quam Domino facimus, ipsum humilius laudando, est sciendum quod ipsa consistit in tribus,
videlicet si ipsum laudando et honorando diligamus toto corde, tota anima,
20 et tota mente. Istud enim precipitur Matthei ⟨22⟩: "Diliges Dominum Deum
tuum ex toto corde," etc.
    Nam primo ex toto corde ipsum diligere debemus secundum beatum Augus-
tinum tripliciter: primo ut toto intellectu sine errore, secundo ut supra
eum nichil diligamus, neque mundum neque ea que in mundo sunt, iuxta illud
25 Augustini: "Deus, inquit, meus, cor meum creatum est a te, et ideo non
habet requiem nisi ⟨in⟩ te"; tercio ut per eius dileccionem omnia temporalia evacuemu⟨s⟩. Unde Bernardus: "Deum ex toto corde diligere est ut a
propria concupiscencia sit homo abstractus et illectus." Unde dicit Cipria-
nus: "Nichil ita securum sicut ille qui nichil preter Christum appetit
30 possidere." [f. 36] Unde legitur in *Vita beati Ignasii* quod tantum in corde
dilexit Deum quod cum captus esset ab infidelibus et flagellatus ut Christum Iesum negaret, quem semper in ore et corde habuit, cum igitur sibi
dixissent: "Desine Christum Iesum nominare, aut variis penis interibis,"
respondit: "Non possum aliquo modo silere quod in corde meo gesto conscrip-
35 tum." Cumque illum flagellassent usque ad mortem, ait unus: "Videamus si
verum sit quod vivens dixit." Et ecce, aperientes cor suum invenerunt in
medio cordis litteris aureis hec verba conscripta: "Iesus est amor meus."
    Secundo diligendus est Christus ex tota anima. Et hoc propter tria:
primo ut per fidem sibi adhereamus; secundo ut eius voluntati in minimo non
40 resistamus; tercio ut per illam dilectionem omnis mundana delectacio et
diabolica prudencia evitetur. Et certe, si sic illum diligamus, neque mundi
blandicias neque diaboli malicias timere oportet. Unde legitur in *Vita
sancti Goderici* quod cum esset solus iacens infirmus, astitit ei diabolus
clam ignitam hastam super eum vibrans, ex cuius ore quasi ignis de fornace
45 exibat, duosque cubitos inter oculos in latitudine habebat, et dixit illi:
"Ecce, ego demonum princeps te medium secaturus adveni; meis usque huc
satellitibus illusisti, set modo michi non illudes." Ad quam vocem vir Dei
viriliter surrexit qui ante per quindecim dies surgere non valebat per se,
et ait: "In nomine Iesu, fuge, tu demon maledicte! Quid frustra contra me
50 furis? Defensorem enim habeo Dominum Iesum Christum, quem ex tota anima
per verum amorem et caritatem continue amplector. Et ideo omnes minas tuas
contempno." Quo audito occurrit minister eius tremebundus et aspexit quomo-

your neighbor's wife, or commit adultery in any fashion. Therefore it follows
that he who fulfills these commandments fulfills all of Scripture and all the
laws of God.

First, then, about love and charity toward God, we must know that this
virtue consists and is established especially in two things and is shown to be
most praiseworthy, namely when God is humbly honored by us and loved before all
other things as our father, and when his will, shown in the commandments, is
followed by us with all eagerness. The love and charity we give to God by
praising him in humility consists, we must know, in three things: to love him
with praise and honor with our whole heart, our whole soul, and our whole mind.
This we are commanded to do in Matthew 22: "You shall love the Lord your God
with your whole heart," etc.

First, then, we must love God with our whole heart. According to Blessed
Augustine, we do this in three things: first, with our whole intellect without
error; second, by not loving anything more than him, not the world or the
things that are in the world, according to Augustine's words: "My God, my
heart has been created by you, and thus it has no rest other than in you"; and
third, by despising all earthly things for his love. Whence Bernard says: "To
love God with our whole heart is to be withdrawn and detached from self-will."
And Cyprian writes: "Nothing is as safe as the man who desires to possess
nothing beside Christ." Thus we read in *The Life of Blessed Ignatius* that this
saint loved God so much in his heart that when he was captured by the infidels
and scourged so that he should deny Jesus Christ, he had his name always in his
mouth and heart. When they said to him: "Stop naming Christ Jesus, or else
you will die with many pains," he replied: "I can in no way hide in silence
what I carry written in my heart." After they had scourged him to death, one
of them said: "Let us see if it was true what he said when he was alive." And
lo, as they opened his heart, they found written in it with golden letters
these words: "Jesus is my love."

Second, Christ must be loved with our whole soul. And this for three
reasons: first, that we may adhere to him in faith; second, that we may not
oppose his will in the least; and third, that through this love all worldly
pleasure and the devil's shrewdness may lose their strength. For surely, if we
love him in this way, we need not fear either the attractiveness of the world
or the evil intentions of the devil. The *Life of Saint Godric* reports that
when the saint lay alone in his sickness, the devil stood by him secretly and
shook a fiery lance above him; from his mouth came fire as if from a furnace,
and his eyes were set two cubits apart; and he said to him: "I, the prince of
the devils, have come to cut you in half; until now you have tricked my helpers, but me you shall not trick now." At this voice the man of God stood up
manly, who for a fortnight was unable to rise by himself, and said: "In Jesus'
name, be gone, cursed demon! Why do you rage against me in vain? I have as my

do hoc certamen inter eos duravit a prima hora diei usque ad horam terciam.
Et ter per illud nomen [f. 36v] Iesum [diabolum] superavit. Unde in omni
55   tribulacione nostra Iesum in anima habeamus et ab illis liberabimur.
   Tercio diligendus est Deus ex tota mente, et hoc triplici racione:
primo scilicet ut sensus nostri ad eum vadant; secundo, ut illum oblivioni
nullatenus tradamus; et tercio, ° ne ab eius amore retrahamur. Et revera,
si sic ubicumque et quacumque morte preventi fuerimus, ipsum inveniemus,
60   sicut contigit de quodam milite devoto ad Christum querendum peregre profecto. Qui cum omnia loca ubi Christus in terra conversatus est visitasset,
venit tandem ad locum ubi Christus celos ascendit, ibique cum lacrimis in
huiusmodi prorupit verba: "O, inquit, dulcissime Iesu, tu scis quomodo in
terris te quesivi toto corde, tota anima, et tota mente [te] pre ceteris
65   diligens et concupiscens, nec scio locum ubi fuisti et non fui. Quia ergo
iam nescio locum alium in terris ubi te ulterius querere possum, hic rogo
me suscipere digneris." Et hiis dictis cadens in terra obdormivit in Domino. Cum ergo et eius cor quidam aperuissent, ecce scripta invenerunt litteris aureis in medio cordis hec verba: "Quem quesivi hic inveni, Iesum
70   amorem meum."
   Hiis igitur tribus modis illum diligere pre ceteris debemus et tenemur
ex precepto evangelii, et primo toto corde considerando quomodo ⟨per⟩misit
cor suum pro nobis perforari, secundo in anima considerando quomodo suam
animam pro suis amicis Deo Patri commendavit, tercio in mente considerando
75   quomodo sua mentali intencione omnes salvare peroptavit.

         [Loue God þat loued the,
         þat for þe tholed deth on tree
            And broght þe oute of helle.
         Loue hym with hert, sowle, and þoght
80   þat þe now has wel derre boght
            þen any tonge con telle.]

   Et de ista dilectione pertinen⟨te⟩ ad laudem et honorem sibi debitum nota
supra, de honore Deo debito, etc.
   Secundo dilectio nostra et caritas erga Deum consistit in suorum
85   observacione mandatorum, iuxta illud Iohannis 14: "Si quis diligit me,
sermonem meum servabit," hoc est, precepta mea. Quorum primum est: Non
adorabis Deum [f. 37] alienum, hoc est neque solem neque lunam neque aliquam creaturam pro Deo, set ipsum solum Deum qui regnat in celis debes
honorare, quia ut dicitur Deuteronomii 6: "Deus tuus unus est." Et istum
90   solum tenemur honorare sicut satis dicitur supra, particula prima, de
honore divino et humilitate erga eum, etc. Secundum preceptum est: Non
accipias nomen Dei tui in vanum, scilicet iurando et periurando, de quo

protector the Lord Jesus Christ, to whom I cling steadfastly with my whole soul
through true love and charity. And thus I scorn all your threats." Hearing
this, his servant ran to him trembling and saw how this struggle between them
lasted from the first to the third hour of the day. And the saint overcame the
devil through the name of Jesus three times. Therefore, in every tribulation
we should have Jesus in our soul, and we will be freed from it.

Third, God must be loved with our whole mind, and this for three reasons:
first, that all our senses may be directed to him; second, that we may never
forget him; and third, that we may not be drawn away from his love. If we are
in such a state, wherever and in whatever form we meet death, we shall find
God, as it happened to a devout knight who had gone on a pilgrimage in search
of Christ. He had visited all the places where Christ had walked on earth and
finally came to the spot where Christ ascended into heaven. There he burst out
with tears in these words: "O sweetest Jesus, you know how I have sought you
on earth with my whole heart, soul, and mind, loving you and wanting you before
anything else; nor do I know any place where you have been and I have not, and
thus I know of no other place on earth where I can seek you further. I ask you
then that you will take me to you here." And when he had said this, he fell to
the ground and died in the Lord. But when they opened his heart, they found
these words in golden letters in the middle of his heart: "Whom I have loved I
have found, Jesus my love."

We must therefore love him above all in these three ways and are held to
do so by the commandment of the Gospel: first, considering with our whole heart
how he let his heart be pierced for us; second, considering in our soul how he
commended his soul to God the Father for his friends; and third, considering in
our mind how he desired in his mind to save all men.

> Love God, him who has first loved thee,
> Who suffered death upon the tree,
>   And brought thee out of hell.
> Love him with heart and soul and thought,
> Who thee with greater price has bought
>   Than any tongue can tell.

Regarding this love that is part of the praise and honor due to God, notice the
earlier discussion of the worship that we owe to God, etc.

Second, our love and charity for God consists in keeping his commandments,
according to John 14: "If anyone loves me, he will keep my word," that is, my
commandments. The first of them is: "You shall not worship a strange god,"
that is, neither sun nor moon nor any creature in God's place, but only God
himself who reigns in heaven, for as it is said in Deuteronomy 6: "Your God is
one." And we are held to honor him alone, as is well shown above, in the first

nota supra, capitulo de mendacio et periurio. Tercium preceptum est: Memento quod diem Sabbati sanctifices, hoc est, ab omni opere servili cessabis,
95   quasi diceret: non arabis, non metes, et cetera huiusmodi. Et non tantum hoc, set ab opere vilissimi peccati pre ceteris cessabis et Deo vacabis. De quo nota post, particula quinta de accidia. Quartum est: Honora patrem et matrem, pro quo nota particula prima, capitulo de honore parentum. Quintum est: Non occides, pro quo nota supra, particula secunda de ira. Sextum est:
100 Non furtum facies, pro quo nota supra, particula tercia, capitulo primo. Septimum est: Non falsum testimonium dices, pro quo nota supra particula tercia de periurio. Octavum est: Non concupisces rem proximi tui, pro quo nota particula quarta de cupiditate et avaricia. Nonum et decimum sunt hec: Non concupisces uxorem proximi tui et Non mechaberis, pro quibus nota
105 particula septima de luxuria et particula de avaricia. Unde iuxta concilium evangeliste, "Si vis ad vitam ingredi, serva mandata."

   Circa tamen ipsa est sciendum secundum Augustinum *De decem cordis* quod decalogus est psalterium decem cordarum; quas cordas cum tetigeris manu, idest opere compleveris, effectum per illa mox consideres. Tacta prima per
110 quam unus Deus colitur, secunda de accipiendo nomen Dei in vanum, tercia de Sabati observacione, quarta de honore parentum, quinta scilicet "non mechaberis," sexta "non occides," septima "non furtum facies," octava de falso testimonio, nona de concupiscencia rerum proximi, decima de [f. 37v] concupiscencia uxoris proximi, et cadit bestia supersticionis, heretici erroris,
115 mundani amoris, impietatis, libidinis, crudelitatis, rapacitatis, falsitatis, cupiditatis, adulterium voluptatis. "Citharista ergo," dicit Augustinus, "et venator, tange cordas et occidis bestias, et non singulas, set greges interficis bestiarum. Nam multa capita sub capitibus istis in singulis cordis occides, et sic cantum novum cum amore et non timore cantabis."
120 Hec ibi.

   Unde pro istis preceptis servandis fac doctrinam Christi, Exodi 25: "Inspice, inquit, et fac secundum exemplar quod tibi monstratum est." Ad litteram autem exemplar istorum preceptorum ostensum est. Primo erat in monte Syna Moysi et in tabulis lapideis conscriptum et non in ligneis cum
125 cera molli, ad designandum quod firmiter starent et observarentur et non nimis de facili evellerentur. Set adverte: Videmus enim quod aliquando datur scriptori exemplar, ut illa que in illo continentur in aliud volumen seu pergamenum transferat nichil addendo vel minuendo—quia ut communiter scriptores non sunt scioli ad libros corrigendos, addendo vel minuendo nisi
130 errant. Et tamen hiis non obstantibus scriptor falsus quando conducitur secundum numerum linearum aut punctorum que sunt in exemplari, adhuc tamen aliquando transiliit, quia sperat quod sua falsitas non statim deprehendetur. Set postquam sibi fuerit satisfactum, non curat tunc nisi parum, quamvis eius falsitas denudetur. Unde contingit frequenter quod talis

part on the honor we owe to God and our humility before him, and so forth. The second commandment is: "You shall not take God's name in vain," that is, by swearing and committing perjury; on this, see above in the chapter on lying and perjury. The third commandment is: "Remember to hallow the Sabbath," that is, to cease from all servile work, as if he were saying: you shall not plow or reap, and so forth. And not only this, but you must cease from the wicked work of sin and devote yourself to God. On this see further below, in part 5, on sloth. The fourth commandment is: "Honor your father and mother," on which see above, part 1, the chapter dealing with the honor due to our parents. The fifth is: "You shall not kill"; see above, part 2, on wrath. The sixth is: "You shall not steal"; see above, part 3, chapter 1. The seventh is: "You shall not give false witness"; see above, part 3, on perjury. The eighth is: "You shall not covet your neighbor's good"; see part 4, on covetousness and avarice. And the ninth and tenth commandments are: "You shall not covet your neighbor's wife" and "You shall not commit adultery"; see part 7 on lechery and the part on avarice. Thus, after the advice of the evangelist: "If you wish to enter into life, keep the commandments."

About the commandments we should know that according to Augustine, *On the Ten Strings*, the decalogue is an instrument of ten strings; when you touch these strings with your hand, that is, carry them out in deed, you will soon notice their effect. By touching the first, one God is worshipped; the second is about taking God's name in vain; the third about keeping the Sabbath; the fourth about honoring our parents; the fifth, "you shall not commit adultery"; the sixth, "you shall not kill"; the seventh, "you shall not steal"; the eighth, about giving false witness; the ninth, about coveting your neighbor's goods; and the tenth, about coveting your neighbor's wife. And thus falls the beast of superstition, of heretical error, of worldly love, impiety, lust, cruelty, rapaciousness, falsehood, covetousness, adultery, and carnal desire. "You, stringplayer and hunter," says Augustine, "touch these strings, and you kill the beasts, not one by one but whole flocks. For with single strings you will kill many that go together under these headings; and thus you will sing a new song with love and without fear."

In order to keep these commandments, follow Christ's teaching; Exodus 25: "Look and do according to the exemplar that was shown to you." An exemplar of these commandments has been literally shown. The first was shown to Moses on Mount Sinai, and it was written on stone tablets, not on wooden ones with soft wax, to indicate that they should stand firmly and be kept and not be easily erased. But notice: We see that sometimes an exemplar is given to a scribe so that he may transfer its contents into another volume or piece of parchment, without adding or subtracting anything—for scribes are usually not sufficiently learned to correct books by adding or subtracting anything without making mistakes. And yet, in spite of this, a faulty scribe, when he is guided by the

135 scriptor non est dignus mercede, set pocius dignus pena, quia pergamenum
    omnino est perditum in quo scripsit. Et ideo, qui prudens est diligenter
    examinat opus scriptum antequam sibi reddit mercedem, ne in aliquo defrau-
    detur. Spiritualiter loquendo: Omnes Christiani dicuntur scriptores [f. 38]
    et debent mandata divina transcribere in tabulis cordis, secundum illud
140 Exodi 34: "Scribe in tabulis verba federis." Sumus ergo omnes scriptores
    Domini iuxta illud Ysaie 44: "Hec scribet in manu sua Domino." Exemplar
    autem fidelissimum tradidit nobis Deus Pater, quia Filium suum incarnatum.
    In illo ergo legere debemus scribenda ut non addamus neque minuamus. Deute-
    ronomii: "Non addetis ad verbum quod ego loquor vobis, nec auferetis ⟨ex
145 eo," etc.⟩ Sic enim scribitur Iohannis 13: "Exemplum dedi vobis, ut quemad-
    modum ego feci," etc. Set timeo quod multi sunt falsi scriptores, quibus
    merces promittitur si bene scribant, set tamen credunt decipere, unde
    mirabiliter transiliunt. Nam forte satis bene scribunt primam lineam istius
    exemplaris, que est de Deo vero, et transiliunt secundam, que est de periu-
150 rio. Scribunt enim forte lineam de furto et omittunt aliam, scilicet de
    adulterio, et sic de aliis. Unde propter falsitatem eorum non sunt digni
    premio set pena dignissimi, quia perdunt volumen in quo scribunt, scilicet
    cor suum, ita quod nulli usui est aptum, et forsan hoc facere audent, quia
    non statim opus eorum per diligentem amorem et ferventem caritatem non
155 examinatur. Set consulo quod caveant. Non enim vult Deus defraudari. Et ideo
    omnia que scripta sunt in exemplari, diligenter et fideliter transumant,
    quia Exodi 2 dicitur: "Moyses et Aaron fecerunt omnia signa que scripta
    sunt." Et Apocalipsis ultimo dicitur: "Si quis diminuerit de verbis legis
    huius, auferat Deus partem eius de ⟨libro⟩ vite."
160   Unde hec precepta continentur in hiis versibus:

        Unum crede Deum. Ne iures falsa per ipsum.
        Sabbata sanctifices. Tibi sint in honore parentes.
        Non occisor eris, fur, mechus, testis iniquus.
        Non violas nuptam nec rem cupias alienam.

165   [Take no God but oon in heuen.
           Neme nouȝth his name in ydel steuen.
           Loke ryȝt wel þyn halyday.
           þy fadur and moder þow worshyp ay.
           Loke þou be no monsleere.
170   Of fals wytnes noo berere.
           þou shalt do no lecherye,
           Ni no þefthe of felonye.
           þin neyȝborus godes þou ne wyll.
           Ny wyf ne douȝter for to spylle.]

number of lines or points in his exemplar, still sometimes skips material; he
hopes that his fault will not be detected, and once he has been paid, he cares
but little if his fault is found out. Thus it happens often that such a scribe
is not worth his pay but rather deserves punishment, for the parchment on which
he has written is completely wasted. Therefore, if you are smart, you examine
carefully what has been written before you pay him, so that you do not get
cheated. In spiritual terms: All Christians are said to be scribes who must
transcribe God's commandments on the tablets of their hearts, according to
Exodus 34: "Write the words of the covenant upon tablets." For we all are
scribes of the Lord, after Isaiah 44: "He shall write with his hand, To the
Lord." Now, God the Father has given us a very faithful exemplar, his Son in
human flesh. In him we must read what we ought to write, without adding or
subtracting anything; Deuteronomy: "You shall not add to the word I speak to
you, neither shall you take away from it," etc. For it is written in John 13:
"I have given you an example, so that as I have done," etc. But I fear that
many are faulty scribes, to whom a reward is promised if they copy well, but
they still try to cheat and skip in the most breathtaking way. For perhaps
they write out the first line of their exemplar quite well, the one about the
true God, but then they skip the second, about committing perjury. They write
perhaps the line about theft, but omit the next one, about adultery. And so
with the others. Therefore, because of their cheating they do not deserve a
reward but very much a punishment, because they ruin the codex in which they
write, that is, their heart, so that it is of no further use; and perhaps they
dare to do so because their work is not at once examined through eager love of
God and fervent charity. But I advise them to beware. God will not be
cheated. They should therefore copy all that is written in their exemplar
carefully and faithfully, for in Exodus 2 it is said: "Moses and Aaron did all
the signs that have been written." And at the end of Revelation is said: "If
anyone should take away from the words of this law, may God take away his part
from the book of life."

Hence these commandments are contained in the following verses:

> Believe in God alone, take not his name in vain.
> Observe the holy day, give honor to your parents.
> Commit not murder, theft, adult'ry, or false witness.
> And do not ever lust for others' wife or goods.

> Take no God . . .

3–4 Matt. 22.39–40.   **20–21** Matt. 22.37.   **22ff.** See *Glossa* on Rom. 13.9 (PL
191:1508). The expansions "sine errore," etc., are likewise scholastic commonplaces,
apparently deriving from Alcuin, *Sermo 108* 4 (PL 39:1960); see, for instance, Innocent

2 et(1)] *add* dileccione O.   **4** 22] *add* tota idest C.   **20** et] *om* O. 22] 13 C.   **26** in] a C.
27 evacuemus] evacuemur C.   **30** beati] sancti O.   **32** igitur] ergo C.   **35** Cumque]
cum O.   **41** evitetur] enervetur O.   **46** secaturus] secturus O.   usque huc] hucusque O.
57 ut] *add* omnes O.   tercio] *add* ut C.   **62** milite] *add* anglico et O.   **64** et] *om* O.   **67–
68** terra . . . Domino] terram expiravit O.   **68** quidam] *om* O.   **71** igitur] ergo O.
72 permisit] promisit O.   **74** animam] *om* O.   **76–81** Loue . . . telle] *text from* R. *Verse
21, in* B3.E.Go1.Go2. Jo.L1.L2.LC.R.Sp.V.W1.   **82** pertinente] pertinens C.   **83** su-
pra] *add* particula prima O.   etc.] capitulo O.   **86** mea] *om* O.   **88** debes] *om* O.   **89** is-
tum] illum O.   **90** dicitur] docetur O.   **93** supra] *add* particula ista O.   **98** nota] *add*
supra O. de . . . parentum] 10 O.   **103** avaricia] *add* capitulo O.   **104** et] *om* O.
105 et . . . avaricia] satis O.   **109** idest] et O.   **109–116** Tacta . . . voluptatis] *this material may have originally been written in two columns, to read* tacta prima . . . colitur et
cadit bestia supersticionis, *etc.; thus in* L1.Go2.   **118** istis] hiis O.   **127** illa] ea O.
129 addendo] *add* scilicet O.   **130** errant] errent O.   **137** reddit] reddat O.   **138–
139** Omnes . . . debent] christiani debent esse scriptores et O.   **142** suum] *add* unigenitum O.   **144–145** ex eo etc.] etc ex eo C.   **150** forte] forsan O.   **154** amorem] *add*
ad deum O.   **159** libro] ligno C.   **164** violas] alii O.   **165–174** Take . . . spylle] *text
from* R. *Verse 22, in* B1.B3.E.Go1.Jo.L2.L3.LC.R.V.W1.

III.viii   DE DILECTIONE PROXIMI

[f. 38v] [C]irca autem dilectionem et caritatem quas erga proximum
habemus sciendum quod ipsa consistit, primo in naturali fraternitate, ipsum
caritatiue edocendo et a malis defe⟨nd⟩endo; secundo in temporali necessitate, ipsum pro posse tantum in indigenciis supportando. Set adverte:
5   Qu⟨ando⟩ precipitur Matthei 22: "Diliges proximum tuum sicut teipsum," non
intendit ibi precipere proximum sic diligere quod in omnibus substanciis
uxori, filiis, et similibus sit equalis. Non, certe, set siquis habundave-
rit in diviciis, in scienciis, et viribus, et proximus sibi in fortuna
fuerit similis, tunc sicut de sua gaudeat et de contrario doleat, et sup-
10   portando faciat sicut vellet sibi fieri, quia iuxta Apostolum Romanorum 12:
"gaudere cum gaudentibus et flere," etc. Secundum Ysidorum autem, *Ethimologiarum* 17, capitulo 5, vitis dicitur quia per vices se nectunt vicinisque
arboribus crepitando religentur. E[s]t enim vitis arbor in se debilis set
natura flexibilis, que quasi quibusdam brachiis quicquid ⟨com⟩prehendit
15   stringit. Revera sic et nos flexibiles esse debemus per mutuam caritatem
affligentes amplectentes et in indigenciis supportantes, quia satis in
natura sumus debiles, ut seipsum unusquisque tantum iuvat sine proximi
auxilio.
    Et ideo in vinculo pacis colligari debemus, ut iuxta Apostolum Romano-
20   rum 5: "Unanimes uno ore honorificemus Deum," et ideo iuxta illud Ephesiorum 4: "Sollicite servare ⟨uni⟩tatem spiritus." Hoc autem est signum speciale quod Deum fideliter diligamus, si proximum nostrum qui est eius ymago

III, *Sermo de uno martyre* (PL 217:616–617).   **25–26** Augustine, *Confessiones* I.i.1 (CC
27:1).   **27–28** Cf. Bernard, *Super Cantica* XX.v.7 (1:119).   **30–37** Cf. *Leg. aurea*, p.
157.   **42–54** See the two lives of Saint Godric edited by J. Stevenson, Surtees Society 20
(1847), pp. 199–200.   **60–70** Tubach 2497. Add: BL MS Royal 7.D.i, fol. 78v; *Tabula
exemplorum*, No. 311; J. G. Bougerol, "Les sermons dans les *Studia* des Mendiants," in
Le Scuole degli Ordini Mendicanti (secoli XIII–XIV), Atti del XVII Covegno di Studi,
Todi . . . 1976 (Todi, 1978), pp. 277–78. In some MSS of *FM* this knight is an English-
man (cf. O!); in one of the earliest versions of the story he is French (Etienne de Bourbon).
The motif of "letters in his heart" perhaps entered the story by conflation with the similar
story about Saint Ignatius above. The letters are absent in earlier versions, or else replaced
by a cross.   **85–86** John 14.23.   **90–91** *FM* I.ix.   **93** *FM* III.iv.   **97** *FM* V.i–iv.
98 *FM* I.ix.   **99** *FM* II, passim.   **100** *FM* III.i.53ff.   **101–102** *FM* III.iv.   **103** *FM* IV,
passim.   **105** *FM* VII and IV, passim.   **106** Matt. 19.17.   **107–120** Augustine, *Sermo 9*
13 (CC 41:132–134). See also *Glossa* on Rom. 13.7–10 (PL 191:1509).   **122** Exod.
25.40.   **140** Cf. Exod. 34.27–28.   **141** Isa. 44.5.   **144–145** Deut. 4.2.   **145–146**
John 13.15.   **157–158** Cf. Exod. 4.10–31.   **158–159** Rev. 22.19.   **161–164** *In* 19669
and 9121.

III.viii   LOVE OF OUR NEIGHBOR

Regarding the love and charity we have toward our neighbor, we must know
that it lies, first, in natural brotherhood, by which we teach our neighbor in
charity and defend him from evil; and second, in help of his temporal needs, by
which we support him in his needs as much as we can. But notice that when
Matthew 22 commands us to "love your neighbor as yourself," Scripture does not
intend to command that we should love our neighbor so that in respect to all
our belongings he be the equal to our wife, children, and the like. Certainly
not. But if someone has plenty of wealth or knowledge or strength, and his
neighbor is in a similar fortunate state, then he should rejoice as if those
riches were his own; and if it is otherwise, he should commiserate with him and
by supporting him do what he would wish to have done to himself, for according
to the Apostle in Romans 12 we should "rejoice with those who rejoice and
weep," etc. According to Isidore, *Etymologies*, 17, chapter 5, the vine is so
called because they support each other mutually and fasten themselves onto
neighboring trees by climbing on them. For the vine is a treelike plant that
is weak by itself but flexible and binds, as it were with arms, whatever it
encircles. Thus should we also be flexible and embrace each other in mutual
charity and support each other in our needs; for by nature we are indeed too
weak for each one to help himself without the help of his neighbor.

Therefore, we must be bound in the bond of peace, so that after the Apostle's
words in Romans 5, "we shall praise God together with one mouth"; and
according to Ephesians 4, "careful to keep the unity of the Spirit." That is a

integre diligamus. Est enim proximus noster frater spiritualis, quia eundem
patrem habemus, Deum, et eandem matrem, Ecclesiam; Matthei 23: "Unus est
25   pater vester." Si ergo Christus sit pater omnium nostrum, certum est quod
omnes eius filii sumus; si autem filii, certe et heredes regni celorum. Si
ergo summe diligeres fratrem tuum carnal⟨em⟩ qui tecum divideret hereditatem, et si plures haberes fratres, et omnes de [f. 39] hereditate tecum
participarent, unde quanto plures tanto minor erit porcio tua, et tamen
30   omnes bene diligeres—nonne multo magis teneris diligere fratres tuos
spirituales, idest proximos, qui tecum hereditatem celestem non divident
set unusquisque capiet totam, quia participacio secundum Bernardum in
idipsum est?
     Debes ergo ipsum diligere et nullo modo offendere nec opere nec verbo.
35   Constat enim quod nullo modo velles quod sinistra dicerentur de te nec in
absencia tua nec in presencia, licet essent vera. Quare ergo vis talia de
proximo audire et seminare, cum tamen secundum legem nature precipitur: Hoc
facias aliis quod tibi vis fieri? "Set hoc est preceptum meum," dicit
Christus, "ut diligatis invicem." Et adverte: Posito quod abstuleris a
40   proximo bona temporalia, rogo quis te absolver⟨e⟩t sine restitucione?
Revera, si unde haberes, nullus vivens. Set defamare proximum est gravius
dampnum quam auferre temporalia, quia iuxta Sapientem: "Melius est nomen
bonum quam divicie multe." Ergo nemo potest eum absolvere nisi famam resti-
tuat. Set hoc non potest aliqua racione, nam tu primus diffamator proximum
45   diffamando alia apposuisti que prius non fuerunt, et auditor alteri narrans
plura, et tercius plurima, et sic in infinitum. Quomodo ad illa revocanda,
ad quod teneris, devenires? Quasi diceret, nullo modo. Cave ergo et dilige
proximum in Deum, nec aliquem, sive sit pauper sive quantumcumque simplex,
in contemptum habebis. Non enim fecit Deus ab inicio unum hominem aureum,
50   de cuius genere sunt omnes nobiles et divites, et alium luteum, de quo
omnes ignobiles et pauperes. Set secundum Gregorium omnes homines natura
genuit equales, set culpa, dicit ipse, hominem homini prefecit. Quare ergo
unu⟨s⟩ se reputat superiorem aliis? Exemplis enim racionabilibus ostenditur
omnem hominem esse eiusdem condicionis. Videmus quod de eodem grano et
55   est [f. 39v] furfur et farina delicatissima, ex eadem radice spina pungens et
rosa demulcens, ex eadem arbore fructus dulcis et putridus. Forte dicis
michi: "Quomodo possem diligere meum inimicum qui tot mala michi fecit?
Bene volo diligere meum amicum." Respondeo quod quantum teneris diligere
amicum in Deum, tantum teneris diligere inimicum propter Deum. Ipsemet
60   Deus precipit per evangelistam: "Diligite eos qui persecuntur vos." Et alibi:
"Orate pro persequentibus et calumpniantibus vos. Si ergo (di⟨c⟩it ipse
Christus) tantum diligitis eos qui vos diligunt, quam mercedem habebitis?
Nonne (dicit ipse) publicani hoc faciunt?" Quasi diceret, sic. "Diligite
ergo (dicit ipse) inimicos vestros, benefacite hiis qui od⟨er⟩unt vos"; et
65   certe, [si] sic, celum lucratus es.

special sign that we love God faithfully: when we love our neighbor fully, who
is God's image. For our neighbor is our spiritual brother, since we have the
same father, God, and the same mother, the Church; Matthew 23: "Your father is
one." If therefore Christ is the father of us all, it is certain that we all
are his children; but if children, then surely also heirs of the kingdom of
heaven. Now, if you love your brother in the flesh very much, who will share
your inheritance with you, and if, in case you have several brothers and they
all take their share of your inheritance, so that the more brothers there are,
the smaller your own portion will be, yet you love all of them well—should you
then not love your spiritual brothers even more, that is, your neighbors, who
will not divide the heavenly inheritance with you but each one will receive all
of it, for according to Bernard "sharing" there will be full possession?

Thus you must love him and not offend him in any way in deed or word. You
certainly would not want that people said anything harmful about you, whether
you are absent or not, even if it were true. Why, then, do you want to hear
such things about your neighbor and spread them, while the law of nature tells
you to do to others as you want it done to yourself? "But this is my commandment," says Christ, "that you love one another." And notice: Let us assume
you took some worldly goods from your neighbor. I ask you: who would absolve
you without your making restitution? Indeed, no one alive, if you have the
means. But ruining your neighbor's good name is a greater harm than taking his
worldly goods, for according to the Wise Man, "a good name is better than many
riches." Therefore, no one can absolve him unless he brings back his good
name. But this cannot be done in any way; for when you began to defame your
neighbor, you added things that were not there in the first place, and the
person who hears you has added more when he told this to someone else, and the
third even more, and so *ad infinitum*. How will you manage to revoke all these
things, as you are required to do? There is no way. Therefore, beware and love
your neighbor in God and hold no one in contempt, even if he is poor or somewhat simple. For God did not, in the beginning, make one man of gold, from
whom all noblemen and rich people are descended, and another from clay, from
whom the lower classes and the poor have sprung. Rather, according to Gregory,
nature created all men equal, whereas it is sin, as he says, that has put one
man before another. Why then does one person think he is superior to the
others? That all human beings are of the same condition can also be shown by
natural examples that speak to our reason. For we see that from one and the
same grain come bran and the finest flour, from one and the same root the
prickly thorn and the sweet-smelling rose, and from one and the same tree sweet
and rotten fruit. But perhaps you tell me: "How could I love my enemy who has
done me so many evils? My friend I will love well!" I answer that as much as
you are held to love your friend in God, so much are you held to love your enemy
for God's sake. God himself has commanded through the evangelist: "Love
those who persecute you." And elsewhere: "Pray for those who persecute and

Et nota: malus proximus sive inimicus tuus est quasi virga Dei per
quam castigat electos et bonos, quam virgam, nisi se correxerit, comburet
in igne inferni, et tunc letabitur iustus cum viderit vindictam, sicut puer
letatur cum pater suus comburet virgam de qua fuit punitus et solebat
70   verberari. Et tamen propter preceptum oportet ipsum inimicum hic diligere.
Non debes imputare equo set equitanti, non baculo set percucienti malum
quod habes. Sic nec imputabis inimico malum quod per eum habes et pateris,
set diabolo, cuius instrumentum est malus homo et cuius mandato malum tibi
fit; Psalmista: "Inmisit per angelos malos," scilicet malum quod habes, et
75   non per hominem. Et adverte: Quantumcumque fuerit proximus malus, si tamen
voluerit bonus effici, bonus potest esse et sanctus. Exemplum de beato
Paulo, de beata Magdalena, et huiusmodi; et tamen isti sunt sancti qui
propter Deum postea corpora sua tradiderunt penis et morti. Sic certe
potest et proximus quantumcumque malus; Luce 15: "Maius gaudium est in celo
80   de [uno] peccatore [f. 40] penitenciam agente quam de nonaginta novem
iustis," quia "ubi habundavit," ut dicit Apostolus Ad Romanos, "iniquitas,
superhabundavit et gracia."

Et ideo proximus est omnino diligendus in natura sua, sicut in corpore
et anima. Nam sicut diligit ipse Deus, Sapiencie 11: "Diligis omnia que fe-
85   cisti et nichil odisti eorum que creasti." Set mores si sint boni, diligendi sunt; sin autem, nequaquam. Unde Augustinus: "Debemus, inquit, in proximo diligere illud quod natura plantavit et non quod vicium deformavit."

Unde narratur de tribus sociis ad mensam cuiusdam magni positis,
quibus in fine prandii tria poma apponebantur, sicud largitur in yeme
90   fructus *pur deynte*, quorum singula aliquantulum in una parte putrida erant.
Unus ergo istorum trium pomum suum accepit et comedit totaliter, scilicet
corruptum cum integro. Et cito post tantam sensit abhominacionem quod illud
oport⟨ui⟩t expuere. Unde gulosus reputabatur. Quod videns alius de pomo suo
noluit gustare; unde ineducatus dicebatur. Set tercius accepit pomum suum
95   et separavit corruptum ab integro, et quod bonum erat et sanum gustavit,
reliquum reiecit; unde iste curialis dicebatur. Revera sic istis diebus
aliqui sic fatue diligunt [quod] quicquid fecerint illi quos diligunt, sive
bene sive male, in nullo displicet. Et certe tales sumunt corruptum cum
integro. Set certe ille amor non valet, quia cum venerint ad propriam
100 conscienciam in fine, velint nolint, propter abhominacionem corrupti facti
oportet totum illum amorem expellere. Alii autem sunt qui tantum alios
detestantur quod quicquid [fecerint], sive bene sive male, omnia displicent. Et ille totum pomum, idest totam vitam proximi, abicit. Et hic nulla
dilectio apparet set odium apertissimum. Set certe sunt alii qu⟨i⟩ quicquid
105 vident in proximo de bono accipi- [f. 40v] unt et gaudent, malum vero
abiciunt et detestantur. Et certe isti tantum caritative et ordinate diligunt; Ieremie 15: "Si separaveris preciosum a vili, quasi os meum eris."

slander you. If you therefore love only those that love you," says Christ, "what reward will you have? Do not (he says) the publicans do so also?" as if he were saying, yes indeed. "Therefore love your enemies (he says), do good to those that hate you," and certainly, if you do that, you have earned heaven.

Notice that an evil neighbor or your enemy is like a rod with which God chastises his elect and good people; if the rod does not amend itself, God will burn it in the fire of hell, and then the just man will rejoice when he sees vengeance, as a child rejoices when his father burns the rod with which he used to be punished and beaten. Nonetheless, at the present point we must love our enemy, for the sake of God's commandment. You must not blame the evil you suffer on the horse but the rider, not on the stick but on him who strikes you. Likewise, do not blame your enemy for the evil you receive and suffer through him, but rather the devil, whose tool a wicked person is and by whose order evil comes to you; the Psalmist says: "He sent by evil angels," namely the evil you suffer, and not by man. And notice that however bad your neighbor may have been, if he wanted to become good, he could be good and saintly. We have the proof in Blessed Paul, Blessed Magdalene, and others; these are saints who later in life for God's sake gave their bodies over to pains and death. Your neighbor could do the same, however evil he is; Luke 15: "There is greater joy in heaven over one sinner who does penance than over ninety-nine just"; for as the Apostle says in Romans 6: "Where sin abounded, grace did abound more."

Therefore, our neighbor is to be loved in his entire being, that is, in his body and his soul. For thus does God himself love him; Wisdom 11: "You love all things that you have made, and you hate none of those that you have made." But our neighbor's actions we should love if they are good; if not, then we should not love them. As Augustine declares: "We must love in our neighbor what nature has planted there, not what vice has deformed."

There is a story about three companions who were invited to the table of a nobleman. At the end of the meal they were offered three apples, as in winter fruit is served for dessert. Each one was partially spoiled. Then one of the three companions took his apple and ate it all up, the spoiled part with the whole. Soon thereafter he felt such a revulsion that he had to spit it out. For that he was considered a glutton. The second chap, when he saw this, did not want to taste his apple at all; and for that he was reckoned unmannered. But the third took his apple and cut the spoiled part from what was whole; the latter he ate, the rest the threw away; and for that he was said to be a gentleman. In similar fashion, some people nowadays love so foolishly that whatever those whom they love do, be it good, be it evil, it never displeases them at all. Certainly, such people take the spoiled part with the whole. But such love is no good, for when they gain the proper insight in the end, because of their revulsion to the spoiled part they willy-nilly must give up that love altogether. Others there are who detest other people so much that whatever

Secunda dilectio et caritas erga proximum in ⟨necessariorum⟩ supportacione est, qua scilicet iuxta beatum Gregorium afflictis et indigentibus
110   compati[mur] et pro posse iuvamus. Et si queras que est illa, respondeo
quod modo mortuos sepelire, modo infirmos pascere et curare, sicut fecit
sanctus Thobias; modo eciam pauperes hospitare, sicut fecit beata Martha;
modo nudos vestire, sicut fecit beatus Martinus, et cetera huiusmodi. Et
ista dicuntur opera misericordie. Unde Iohannis [canonica], capitulo 3:
115   "Qui habuerit substanciam huius mundi et vid[er]it fratrem necessitatem
habere et clauserit viscera sua ab eo, quomodo caritas Dei manet in illo?"
Quasi diceret, nullo modo. Ergo oppositum: Qui subvenerit proximo indigen-
ti, modo dando, modo accomodando, modo remittendo, certe perfecta [caritas]
manet in illo, sicut habetur secundum Iohannem ⟨canonica⟩ ubi supra: "Deus
120   caritas est, et qui manet in caritate, in Deo manet et Deus in eo."

Est igitur hic advertendum quod, ut michi videtur, pro operibus misericordie septem genera hominum per septem genera messium non incongrue
possunt significar⟨i⟩. Nam per triticum, de quo panis suavior fit, designantur contemplativi, qui intendunt interiori dulcedini devocionis, de quo
125   Luce ⟨10⟩: "Porro unum est necessarium;" et in exteriori dulcissime infor-
ma⟨cioni proximo⟩, modo docendo ad bonum, ° modo reducendo a malo, et
cetera huiusmodi. Secundo dico quod per siliginem, de quo fit panis pauperum, intelliguntur illi qui exercent se in illo opere misericordie quibus dicitur: "Esurivi et dedistis michi," etc. Per ordeum, de quo fit potus, intel-
130   liguntur illi ° quibus dicitur: "Sitivi et dedistis michi bibere." Per
pisas, que habent formam rotundam et levem, intelli- [f. 41] guntur illi
quibus dicitur: "Hospes eram, et collegistis me." Tales indifferenter circumquaque hospites recipiunt. Per avenas, de quibus fit gruellus infirmorum, intelliguntur illi quibus dicitur: "Infirmus fui," etc. Set per ves-
135   cas, Anglice *vacches*, intelliguntur illi quibus dicitur: "In carcere fui."
Nam sicut istud granum [est] intollerabilius ad gustandum, sic carcer ad
sustinendum. Et ideo omnibus istis dicetur in ultimo die illud Matthei:
"Venite, benedicti patris mei, percipite [regnum]," etc.

Set timeo quod plures qui dictis modis caritatis et dileccionis inten-
140   dere deberent, caritatem simulant, qui non de se set sua, sicut multi
iuvenes desponsant bona vetularum et non corpora. Unde menciuntur amici
mendaces dicentes quod ex caritate diligunt, quia non diligunt nisi sicut
canis ossa propter carnem, qui consumptis carnibus dimittit in luto nec
plus curat de illis. Sic certe filii mendaces diligunt bona et non corpora.
145   Et ideo certe tales induunt in morte formam inimici, nam expoliant quos
⟨dixerunt se⟩ dilexisse in vita omnibus bonis suis, iuxta illud:

Finita vita fini⟨t⟩ amicus ita.

they have done, be it good, be it evil, it displeases them altogether. And
these throw the entire apple away, that is, their neighbor's entire life. In
this there is no love but only open hatred. But truly, there are still others
who accept and rejoice in whatever good they find in their neighbor, but what
there is evil they reject and detest. These alone love with true and well-
ordered charity; Jeremiah 15: "If you will separate the precious from the
vile, you will be as my mouth."

The second kind of love and charity toward our neighbor consists in supporting him in the things he needs. Through this charity, according to blessed
Gregory, we have pity on the afflicted and needy and help them as much as we
can. And if you ask what such charity is, I answer: now it is to bury the
dead, now to feed and care for the sick, as the saintly Tobit did; now to give
the poor shelter, as did Blessed Martha; now to clothe the naked, as did
Blessed Martin; and other such works. These are called the deeds of mercy.
Whence John says in chapter 3 of his Epistle: "He who has the substance of
this world and sees his brother in need and shuts up his bowels from him, how
does the love of God abide in him?" as if he were saying: in no way. Therefore, on the contrary, he who helps his needy neighbor, whether by giving or
putting him at ease or forgiving him, surely in such a person is perfect
charity, according to Blessed John in the Epistle quoted above: "God is love,
and he who abides in love, abides in God, and God in him."

We should notice here that, as it seems to me, in order to illustrate the
deeds of mercy we may fittingly liken seven kinds of people to seven kinds of
harvests. Wheat, from which sweet bread is made, symbolizes the contemplative,
who strive after the inner sweetness of devotion, of which Luke 10 says: "But
one thing is necessary"; and they are intent on giving their neighbor the
sweetest kind of guidance, now by teaching him the way toward the good, now
leading him back from evil, and so forth. Second I say that rye, from which
the bread of the poor is made, symbolizes those who practice that work of mercy
indicated in the words: "I was hungry and you have given me," etc. Barley,
from which a beverage is made, symbolizes those to whom is said: "I was
thirsty and you gave me to drink." Peas, which are round and light, symbolize
those to whom is said: "I was a stranger and you have taken me in." Such
people entertain guests without discrimination. Oats, from which gruel for the
sick is made, symbolize those to whom is said: "I was sick," and so on. But
vetches, in English *vaccches*, symbolize those to whom is said: "I was in
prison." For just as this grain is unbearable to the taste, so is the prison
unbearable to live in. And thus, to all of these the words of Matthew will be
said on the last day: "Come, you blessed of my Father, possess the kingdom."

But I fear that many people who ought to practice these manners of charity
and love simulate charity by not loving people but their possessions, just as

Et ideo est de talibus sicut de pomerio fructuoso, quia tempore fructus
diligenter custoditur et frequenter visitatur, set ablatis fructibus sine
150   custodia relinquitur. Revera sic est de ficta caritate. Dum enim aliquis
talis mundanus fictus amicus ab aliquo desiderat dilectionem, simulat,
blanditur, adulatur. Set habito optento, ⟨dicunt illud Anglicum:

> Now ich haue þat I wyle,
> Goddus grame on þy byle.⟩

155   Set certe, illa non est perfecta caritas, set ista, de quo Proverbiorum 16
dicitur: "In omni tempore diligit qui amicus est."
     Et ideo quicquid facit homo sine caritate, "nichil prodest," secundum
Apostolum, Corinthiorum 13. Nam sicut campana sine flabello non placet
audientibus, et sicut [f. 41v] corpus nudum sine vestimento quantumcumque
160   honestum vile apparet, et sicut lampas clarissima sine oleo et igne non
lucet, et sicut sompnus sine requie corpus attenuat et debilitat—sic omnia
opera coram Deo sine caritate vilia sunt et nichil prosunt; Corinthiorum
13: "Si tradidero corpus meum ita ut ardeam, vel distribuero omnem substanciam in cibos pauperum, caritatem autem non habuero, nichil michi prodest."
165   Et ideo est de multis sicut de pueris parvis qui in estate et temporibus
amenis modo suo faciunt sibi molendinos de lignis in aquis, set quia supervacua sunt, ideo nichil molant nisi ventum et aquam. Similiter faciunt sibi
fornaces de pulvere et argillo et ibi cum sole dequoquant panes, similiter
in furno eiusdem materie pandoxant, et tamen in posterum omnia dissipant,
170   quia nichil eis prodest neque ad comedendum neque ad bibendum. Unde vacuo
ventre domum redeuntes omnia diei opera irrita sunt et cassa. Revera sic
hodie multi ad modum molendini, in quo volvuntur et revolvuntur in curis
secularibus laborantes, et hoc a mane usque ad vesperam, hoc est a principio vite usque ad senectutem vel ad mortem. Set quia omnia fiunt sine
175   caritate, nichil prodest ad vitam.

---

1 quas] quam O.   3 defendendo] deferendo C.   4–5 Quando] quoniam C.   14 compre-
hendit] apprehendit C.   16 in] om O.   20 Unanimes] add vero O.   21 unitatem] veritatem C.   26 heredes] add scilicet O.   27 carnalem] carnaliter C.   29 erit] foret O.
38 aliis] alii O.   40 absolveret] absolverit C.   45 alia] aliqua O. et] add ille O.   46 plu-
rima] plura O. ad] add omnia O.   53 unus] unum C.   54 et] om O.   58 meum] om O.
60 precipit] precepit O.   61 dicit] dixit C.   64 oderunt] odiunt C.   67 virgam] add in
fine O.   69 cum] quando O.   71 non(2)] nec O.   73 Quantumcumque] add enim O.
76 bonus effici] om O.   79 Maius] plus O.   81 iustis] bonis O. ut] om O. Ad] om O.
85 creasti] fecisti O.   87 illud] om O.   90 in] ex O.   93 oportuit] oportet C.   96 di-
cebatur] add tantum O. istis] hiis O.   104 qui] quod C.   108 necessariorum] intimorum
C.   116 habere] pacientem O.   119 canonica] capitulo C.   121 igitur] ergo O.

many young men marry the goods of older women and not their bodies. Wherefore worldly friends lie when they say that they love "out of charity," for they love only as a dog loves bones just for the meat on them; when he has eaten the meat, he leaves the bones in the dirt and no longer cares for them. Thus do deceitful children love their parents' goods but not their persons. And when death comes, they change into an enemy, for they take away all the goods from those they said they loved during their life, after the proverb:

> End of life, end of friend.

Therefore it is with them as it is with an orchard: when the fruit is ripening, it is carefully guarded and frequently inspected, but when the fruit has been harvested, it is left without guard. Just so does it go with feigned charity. For when such a worldly false friend wants to be loved by someone, he pretends and coaxes and flatters. But after they have gained their desire, they say that English proverb:

> Now that I have got my will,
> May God's curse fall on thy bill.

But surely this is not perfect charity; rather, that of which Proverbs 16 says: "He who is a friend loves at all times."

And thus, whatever a person does without charity "is of no avail," according to the Apostle in Corinthians 13. For just as a bell without a clapper gives no pleasure to those who hear it, and just as a naked body without clothes, however attractive, appears shameful, and just as a polished lamp without oil and fire does not give light, and just as sleep without rest wears and weakens the body—just so are all works without charity vile before God and of no use; Corinthians 13: "If I give my body to be burned, or distribute all my goods to feed the poor, but have no charity, it profits me nothing." And thus it goes with many people as it does with small boys who, in fair summertime, after their fashion build themselves wooden water-mills, but as these are empty, they grind nothing but wind and water. Likewise they build themselves stoves of dirt and clay and cook food in the sun, and similarly they bake bread in ovens of the same material; yet in the end they throw it all away, for it is no good for eating or drinking. Then they go home with an empty stomach and all their day's work has been in vain and lost. Many people nowadays likewise turn and turn like water-mills when they work hard in secular pursuits, from morning till evening, that is, from the beginning of their lives till their old age or death. But as they do everything without charity, it is of no use to them for eternal life.

123 significari] significare C.W; assignare M.   **124** quo] *add* dicitur O.   **125** 10] 4 C.R.   **125–126** informacioni proximo] informatum primo C; informacione proximo W.   **126** bonum] *add* secundo *interl* C.   **129** et . . . michi] *om* O.   **130** illi] *add* de C.   Sitivi . . . bibere] nudus fui et cooperuistis me O.   **137** ultimo die] ultimis diebus O.   **139** timeo] *add* michi O.   **140** de se] desiderant hominem M *corr*.   **145** expoliant] spoliant O.   **146** dixerunt se] dilexerunt sic C.   **147** finit] finitur C.   **148** quia] quod O.   **152–154** dicunt . . . byle] etc C. *Text from* R. *Verse 23, in* B1.B3.E.Go1.Go2.Jo. L2.L3. LC.R.Sp.V.W1.   **155** illa] ista O.   **158** flagello M; batillo R.   **172** quo] qua M; aqua *corr* R.   **174** fiunt] faciunt O.

III.ix   QUE CARITATEM IMPEDIUNT

[E]x predictis ergo patet quid sit caritas et in quibus consistit. Iam ergo dicendum est que illam impediunt. Et revera breviter respondetur quod mundi cupiditas et avaricia, que includitur in corde hominis per ista duo, meum et tuum. Dicunt enim isti reges et principes, "Illud regnum est meum,
5   non tuum." Econtra dicit alius, "Hoc falsum est. Imo est meum, non tuum." Et sicut est de istis, sic est de residuo populo in aliis. Unde hec est causa quare caritas impeditur, elongatur, et destruitur. Unde tot clades et bella, [f. 42] tot pugne et pericula, tot casus et infortunia, tot ambiciones superbie, tot falsitates invidie, tot crudelitates malicie, non
10   tantum inter regna verum eciam in civitatibus, villis, domibus, et super omnia in cordibus hominum oriuntur. Et ideo, ut michi videtur, non tantum verificatur modo illud Osee, capitulo 4: "Non est veritas, non est misericordia, non est sciencia Dei in terra," etc., "set maledictum, mendacium, homicidium, furtum, adulterium, et cetera inundaverunt super terram, et
15   sanguis sanguinem tetigit," set eciam illud Ieremie 5: "Renuerunt accipere disciplinam"; et sequitur: "Pauperes sunt et stulti," supple mundani, "ignorantes viam Domini et iudicium Dei sui. Ibo ergo ad optimates et loquar eis, et ecce ipsi magis fregerunt iugum et vincula rumpunt. Idcirco percussit eos leo de silva, et lupus ad vesperam vastabit illos." Hec ille.
20   Iam ergo palpate et videte si non verificetur prophecia hec hiis diebus. Et timeo quod sic. Qui enim magis pecatores quam potentes? Qui magis malefactores quam scientes, scilicet quam viri ecclesiastici qui sciunt viam Domini et iudicium Dei? Ubi rogo superbia, ubi avaricia, ubi luxuria, ubi rapine, homicidia, blasphemie, et huiusmodi? Nonne in scienti-
25   bus et potentibus? Isti ergo fregerunt iugum Domini et legem [Dei], scilicet fidelitatis, religionis, et ordinis contra ordinacionem et voluntatem Dei. Ruperunt eciam vincula, scilicet caritatis Dei et proximi, Deum non timentes nec hominem reverentes. Et ideo certe tandem percuciet eos leo, de quo Petri 5: "Adversarius vester tamquam leo rugiens circuit querens quem
30   devoret." Et non tantum hoc, set "lupus [ad vesperam vastabit illos," ille

5 Matt. 22.39.   **11** Rom. 12.15.   **11–15** Isidore, *Etym.* XVII.v.2.   **20** Cf. Rom. 15.6.   **21** Eph. 4.3.   **24–25** Matt. 23.9.   **26** Rom. 8.17.   **38–39** John 15.12.   **43–44** Prov. 22.1.   **51–52** Gregory, *Moralia* XXVI.xxvi.46 (PL 76:376).   **60–64** Cf. Matt. 5.44–47.   **74** Ps. 77.49.   **79–81** Luke 15.7.   **81–82** Cf. Rom. 5.20.   **84–85** Wisd. 11.25.   **86–87** Cf. Augustine, *En. in Ps. 100* 5 (CC 39:1410).   **88–96** Tubach 318 (only *FM*).   **107** Jer. 15.19.   **109–110** Cf. Gregory, *Moralia* X.vi.8 (PL 75:922–923).   **112** Cf. Tob. 1–2; and Luke 10.40.   **113** Cf. *Leg. aurea*, pp. 741–742.   **115–116** 1 John 3.17.   **119–120** 1 John 4.16.   **125** Luke 10.42.   **129–138** Matt. 25.34–36.   **147** *Prov* 22027, line 2.   **156** Prov. 17.17.   **157** 1 Cor. 13.3.   **163** 1 Cor. 13.3.

III.ix   OBSTACLES TO CHARITY

From what has been said, then, it is clear what charity is and consists in. Now we have to speak of what hinders it. And that, in brief, is worldly cupidity and avarice, which is enclosed in man's heart by the two words "mine" and "thine." For our kings and princes say, "This realm is mine and not yours," and another contradicts: "Wrong. It is mine, not yours." And as it goes with them, so it goes with the rest of the people in other matters. For this reason charity is hindered, driven far away, and destroyed. Hence so many disasters and wars arise, so many fights and dangers, so many falls and misfortunes, so much proud ambition, envious falsehood, and malicious cruelty, not only between realms but also in cities, towns, houses, and above all in the hearts of men. Therefore it seems to me that now not only the word of Hosea 4 has come true: "There is no truth, there is no mercy, there is no knowledge of God in the land," etc., "but cursing, lying, killing, theft, adultery, and other evils have overflowed the earth, and blood has touched blood," but also the word of Jeremiah 5: "They have refused to receive correction"; and what follows: "These are poor and foolish," add: worldly people, "who do not know the way of the Lord and the judgment of their God. I will go therefore to the great men and will speak to them, and behold these have altogether broken the yoke and have burst the bonds. Wherefore a lion out of the wood has slain them, and a wolf in the evening will spoil them."

Look and see if this prophecy has not come true in our days. I fear it has. For who are greater sinners than our political leaders? Who are greater evildoers than our learned men, that is, our churchmen who know the way of the Lord and the judgment of God? Where, I ask, is pride, avarice, lechery, extortion, manslaughter, blasphemy, and the like? Is it not among those who have knowledge and power? They "have broken the yoke" of the Lord and the law of God, namely that of faithfulness, religion, and order, against God's disposition and will. They have also "broken the bonds," namely of the love of God and their neighbor, by not fearing God or having respect for man. And therefore, certainly the lion will at last strike them of whom Peter 5 says: "Your

scilicet lupus] rapax [diabolus] ad vesperam mortis rapiet eos ad infernum
iuxta illud Iob 21: "Ducunt in [f. 42v] bonis dies suos et in puncto ad
inferna descendunt."

35 Unde michi videtur quod vita talium mundanorum bene comparatur li-
ne⟨e⟩, cuius extrema sunt duo puncta, scilicet nasci et mori. Quicquid ergo
acceperit homo inter puncta, ut dicunt philosophi, divisibile est, set cum
ad punctum venerit, non est ulterius divisio, quia tantum unitas manet.
Revera sic in proposito. Quamcumque horam acceperis de vita peccatoris,
quanta est iudicari et dividi bene potest, eo quod quanta; tunc enim sic in
40 alia potest dividi et ab illa separari; ad vitam bonam potest eciam penitere et satisfacere, et huiusmodi. Set certe, cum pervenerit ad punctum,
idest ad mortem, non est ulterius divisio, ut patet.

Ex dictis ergo patet quod avaricia et cupiditas impediunt caritatem,
de quibus diffusius tractatur particula 4, capitulo 1, ubi agitur de avari-
45 cia. Et ideo hic pertranseo.

Si quis ergo cupit invenire amorem fidelem unde sibi coronam cum
floribus preciosissimis et mellifluis sibi parare voluerit, vadat ad cor
suum, et si [ibi] ista quatuor invenerit sine fictione vel falsitate, certe
illum lucratus est, scilicet: si diligat Deum super omnia et animam habeat
50 sine peccato postea; si tercio proximum diligat amicum in Deum, et quarto
inimicum propter Deum.

[Loue God ouer alle þyng,
Sethen þy-selfe withouten synnyng.
Sethen þi frend as kynde þe teches.
55 After þy fo withouten wreche.]

Et certe sic faciens inveniet quadrifolium istius veri amoris. [Set timeo
quod dicere possum:

Trewe loue among men þat most is of lette
In hattes, in hodes, in porses is sette.
60 Trewe loue in herbers spryngeth in May,
Bote trewe loue of herte went is away.]

---

3 ista duo] istas duas vectes O.   6 populo] populi O.   9 falsitates] *add* et O.   crudeli-
tates] *add* et O.   12 4] *corr from* 3 C; 3 O.   31 ad(2)] in O.   34–35 linee] lineo C.   39–
40 in alia] malicia O.   44 particula] parte O.   46 cum] tanquam O.   49 habeat] *om* O.
50 diligat] *om* O.   52–55 Loue . . . wreche] *text from* R. *Verse 24, in* B3.E.Go1.Go2.
Jo.L1.L2.LC.R.Sp.V.W1.   56 istius] illud O.   56–61 Set . . . away] *text from* R. *Verse
25, in* B3.E.Go1.Go2.Jo.L1.L2. LC.R.Sp.V.W1.

enemy goes about like a roaring lion seeking whom he may devour." And not only this, but "the wolf in the evening will spoil them," namely that rapacious wolf, the devil, will in the evening of death carry them off to hell, according to Job 21: "They spend their days in wealth, and in a moment they go down to hell."

For this reason it seems to me that the life of such worldlings can well be compared to a line, whose ends are two points, namely birth and death. Whatever space one takes between these points is divisible, as the philosophers say, but when one comes to the point, no further division is possible, because then only a unity remains. This applies to the present topic. Whatever hour you take in the life of a sinner, and however long it is, it can be judged and divided because of its extension, for then wickedness can be divided and separated from it, and the sinner can convert to the good life and make satisfaction, and the like. But certainly once the sinner arrives at the endpoint, that is, at his death, no further division is possible, as is obvious.

From what has been said, it is clear that charity is blocked by avarice and cupidity. These are dealt with more extensively in part 4, chapter 1, on avarice. Therefore I pass on now.

Whoever wishes to find a true love from which he may want to make himself a wreath as of precious and honey-sweet flowers, let him go to his own heart, and if he there finds the following four without pretense or falsehood, he has gained that wreath: if he loves God above all and afterwards keeps his soul without sin; thirdly, if he loves his neighbor and friend in God, and fourthly his enemy for the sake of God.

> Love God above all other things,
> Yourself next without sin,
> And next your friend as nature wants,
> Your en'my then without sting.

And if he does so, he will certainly find the quatrefoil of true love. But I fear that I can say:

> True love among men, which most is forsaken,
> To hats and hoods and purses is taken.
> True love in arbors blossoms in May,
> But true love of heart has all gone away.

12–15 Hos. 4.1–2. **15–19** Jer. 5.3–6. **29–30** 1 Pet. 5.8. **30** Jer. 5.6. **32–33** Job 21.13. **44–45** *FM* IV.

III.x DE PASSIONE CHRISTI

[R]estat ergo iam quarto et ultimo videre quomodo hec caritas sic elon-
gata et quasi deper⟨d⟩ita poterit inveniri et recuperari. Revera hoc modo:
Si ⟨enim⟩ homo diligenter attenderet et penes se iugiter deliberaret qualem
caritatem Christus nobis ostendit, non tantum in sua benedicta incarnacione
5   verum eciam in sua crudeli passione, a qua nichil audibile, nichil visibile
vel intelligibile vel terribile illum trahere potuit, quin pro nobis mortem
[f. 43] subire vellet ut nos ab eterna morte et diaboli potestate liberaret. Voluit ergo Christus permaximam caritatem qua non esset maior nobis
ostendere, quando animam suam pro nostra redemptione Deo Patri optulit et
10 corpus suum morti humilissime et sine culpa exposuit, iuxta illud Iohannis
15: "Maiorem ⟨hac⟩ dilectionem nemo habet ut animam suam ponat quis pro
amicis suis." Igitur, si hanc caritatem tam mente quam corde discutere
velimus, revera si veri filii [Dei] fuerimus, caritatem sic elongatam
naturaliter reperiemus. Dicitur vulgariter: "Ego diligentes me diligo." Set
15 Christus prius dilexit nos, ut dicitur Apocalipsis 1, "et lavit nos a
peccatis nostris in sanguine suo." Ista ergo passio quam pro nobis sustinuit ad perfectam caritatem reducet. De qua sic intendo procedere, scilicet
primo quare sanguinem suum fudit; secundo quo die passus est, et quomodo,
et ubi; tercio qua hora, qua etate, et quo tempore; quarto de quibus
20 accusabatur et quociens illusus; quinto de misterio et virtute crucis sue.

   Circa primum est sciendum quod primo sanguinem suum fudit ut esset
peccatoribus in auxilium et remedium contra hostes spirituales et peccata temporalia carnalia. Unde notandum quod maximum remedium est eius sanguinis
effusio eo quod inducit peccatorem ad dolorem contricionis, ad pudorem
25 confessionis, et ad laborem satisfactionis. In cuius signum legimus quod in
Christi passione petre scisse sunt, idest dura corda in contricione; aper-
taque monumenta, in confessione; et tercio multa corpora sanctorum surrexerunt, in satisfactione; de quibus post, parte 5, dicetur.

   Et nota quod in sua passione maximum bellum pro genere humano contra
30 eius hostes assumpsit, quod quidem bellum bene figura- [f. 43v] batur in
bello quod accepit David contra gigantem Goliam Philisteum, ut patet Regum
17. Nam ille David, qui manu fortis interpretatur, bene designat Christum,
athletam fortissimum, qui crucem pro baculo accepit, ut illum Goliam gigantem, idest diabolum, devinceret. Qui quidem baculus crucis figuram habuit
35 bellatoris baculi, qui bipennis dicitur eo quod in summitate habet duo
cornua, de quo Abacuch 3 dicitur: "Et cornua in manibus eius." Set adverte:
Sicut enim videmus inter homines quod quando unus nobilis alium intendit
debellare, non expectat insultus adversarii, set ut celebrior habeatur
victor[ia] locum eius requirit quem debellare disponit, revera sic Christus
40 pugil noster sciens habitaculum demonum inimicorum nostrorum esse in aere

III.x   ON CHRIST'S PASSION

In the fourth and last place it remains to see how this charity, when it
has been driven away and is almost completely lost, may be found again and
recovered. Verily thus: if man would diligently consider and intently weigh
within him what love Christ has shown us, not only in his blessed incarnation
but also in his cruel Passion, from which nothing could hold him back that he
might hear or see or understand or fear so that he would not want to suffer
death for us in order to free us from eternal death and the power of the devil.
For Christ wanted to show his exceedingly great love, than which there is none
greater, when he offered his soul to God the Father for our redemption and gave
his body most humbly and without guilt over to death, after the word of John
15: "Greater love than this no man has, that a man lay down his life for his
friends." Therefore, if we were to reflect on this love intently with our mind
and heart, if indeed we are true children of God, we shall naturally find that
love again that has been driven away. There is a common saying: "I love those
that love me." But Christ has loved us first, as is said in Revelation 1, "and
has washed us from our sins in his blood." This Passion, then, which he
suffered for us will lead us back to perfect love. I will treat of it as
follows: first, why he shed his blood; second, on what day, how, and where he
suffered; third, at what hour, what age, and what time; fourth, by whom he was
accused and how much he was taunted; and fifth, of the mystery and power of his
cross.

Concerning the first point we should know that he shed his blood in the
first place that it might be a help to sinners and a remedy against our spiritual enemies and fleshly sins. Notice that shedding his blood is a very strong
remedy because it leads the sinner to the sorrow of contrition, to the shame of
confession, and to the labor of satisfaction. In token of which we read that
at Christ's Passion the rocks, that is, hardened hearts, were cleft in contrition; the graves were opened, in confession; and finally many bodies of saints
arose, in satisfaction. Of these things we shall speak later, in part 5.

Notice also that in his Passion he undertook a great war for mankind
against its enemies, which is prefigured in the war that David took upon
himself against the Philistine giant Goliath, as is recorded in Kings 17.
David, whose name means "strong of hand," stands for Christ, the very strong
champion, who took upon himself the cross as a staff so that he might overcome
that giant Goliath, that is, the devil. The staff of the cross looks like the
staff of a warrior that is called *bipennis*, a double-edged battle-ax, because
it has two points at its end; Habakkuk 3 says of it: "And horns in his hands."
But notice: among men, when one nobleman plans to fight another, he does not
wait for his enemy's attacks but, in order to gain victory more quickly,
marches to his opponent's place; thus our champion, Christ, knowing that our

caliginoso, ideo ut illos tamquam in loco proprio eos et aereas potestates
debellaret, voluit super crucem per quam illos devicit in aere elevari.
  Que quidem victoria bellicosa pro nostra reparacione contra diabolum a
Christo facta bene figuratur Hester 10 in sompno Mardochei, ubi dicitur
45 quod "fons parvus crevit in flumen magnum," ubi eciam dicitur quod Mardocheus vidit super illum fontem duos magnos dracones simul pugnare, et draco
draconem superabat. Unde postea sompnum exponens ait quod illi dracones
fuerunt Aman et Mardocheus. O beatum sompnum nostre reparacionis et auxi-
lii! Spiritualiter autem loquendo fons ille parvus sanguis Christi erat,
50 adhuc infra carnem et cutem inclusus; set certe crevit in flumen magnum
quando lancea eius aperiebat latus et continuo exivit sanguis et aqua, et
non tantum hoc set quando per manus, pedes, et totum corpus eius sanguis
efflu[x]it et ebullivit. Super isto ergo fonte pugnaverunt duo dracones,
[f. 44] idest duplex amor Christi, qui ex una parte ad propriam vitam, ex
55 alia vero ad nostram salutem [se] extendit, quorum unus amor erat naturalis
et alius gratuitus. Amor autem naturalis, quem scilicet Christus ad vitam
propriam habuit, magnus fuit, et merito. Nam sapiens quisque tantum amat
rem quantum valet; set eius vita fuit optima; necessario ergo illam diligere oportebat. Set certe amor gratuitus quem habuit ad animas nostras fuit
60 fortis valde et durus. Et ideo [isti] duo amores tam vehementer pugnabant
in Christi passione quod, quando inter se collidebant, sudorem sanguinis
expresserunt. Et tamen amor gratuitus amorem naturalem tandem superavit, in
tantum quod cicius mori elegit pro genere humano quam proprio corpori parcere. Unde Bernardus: "Numquam, inquit, dedisset se pro me nisi secundum
65 aliquid plus dilexisset me quam se." Et tamen nota quod in ista pugna nulla
fuit in Christo contrarietas culpam inducens, quia utrumque amorem sive
voluntatem voluntati Patris subiecit, dicens illud Matthei: "Non mea voluntas set tua fiat." Et factum est ita. Nam Aman, qui fuit secundus a rege,
idest Christus Filius Dei, qui est secunda persona in Trinitate, suspensus
70 est in patibulo. Mardocheus vero, per quem intelligo naturam humanam vel
hominem qui eterno suspendio fuerat adiudicatus, in graciam regis susceptus
est, idest Patris omnipotentis, et factus secundus a rege quando natura
nostra Filio Dei unita sedit autem a dextris Dei tanto excellencior angelis
effectus, etc.
75   Igitur inspecta erga nos tam ferventissima caritate, iustum est et
quiddam naturale ipsum ex toto corde reamare, dicente beato Augustino:
"Respice, inquit, vulnera pendentis, sanguinem morientis, cicatrices resur-
gentis, precium tradentis, commercium redimentis. Et [f. 44v] hec quantum
valeant pensate et in statera caritatis appendite, ut totus sit ipse nobis
80 fixus in corde qui totus pro nobis fuit fixus in cruce." Hec ille. Et [ad]
hanc caritatem ⟨semper amandam⟩ licet exclamare cum Apostolo: "Et qui non
amat Dominum nostrum Iesum Christum, anathema sit," etc.

enemies the devils have their dwelling place in this dark air, and wanting to
fight them and the powers of the air so to speak in their own camp, wished to
be raised into the air on the cross on which he would defeat them.

That victory in battle, won over the devil for our redemption by Christ,
is prefigured in the dream of Mordecai, Esther 10, where it is said that "a
small wellspring grew into a large river," and that Mordecai saw two large
dragons fight together at the wellspring, and one dragon overcame the other.
When he later explained his dream, he said that these dragons were Haman and
Mordecai. O blessed dream about our redemption and help! For spiritually
speaking, that small wellspring was the blood of Christ, still shut in between
flesh and skin; but it certainly grew into a large river when the spear opened
his side and immediately there came out blood and water, and not only this, but
his blood flowed and welled out through his hands and feet and whole body. At
that fountain two dragons were fighting, that is, the twofold love of Christ,
which on one hand longed for his own life, but on the other for our salvation;
the former love belonged to nature, the latter to grace. His natural love,
that is, the love Christ had for his own life, was great, and justly so, for
any wise person loves an object as much as it is worth, and Christ's life was
of the greatest value, therefore he had to love it of necessity. But certainly
the love of grace which he had for our souls was very strong and firm. And
thus these two loves fought so violently during Christ's Passion that, when
they clashed, they drove forth a sweat of blood. Yet finally the love of grace
overcame the love of nature, so that Christ chose rather to die for mankind
than to spare his own body. Whence Bernard says: "He would never have given
himself for me, had he not, in some way, loved me more than himself." But
notice that in this battle within Christ there was no conflict that would bring
guilt with it, for he submitted both loves or wills to the will of his Father,
saying the words in Matthew: "Not my will but yours be done." And so it was
done. For Haman, who was second to the king—that is, Christ, the Son of God,
who is the second person in the Blessed Trinity—was hanged on the gallows.
Mordecai, by whom I understand human nature or man who had been sentenced to
eternal death, was received into the grace of the king, that is, of the Almighty Father, and made second to the king, when our nature, united with the
Son of God, sits at God's right hand, raised higher than the angels.

Therefore, when we see such burning love for us, it is right and only
natural for us to love him back from our whole heart; as Blessed Augustine
says: "Behold his wounds as he hangs on the cross, his blood as he is dying,
his scars as he rises from death, the price he is paying, and his bargain as he
redeems us. Weigh how much these are worth and place them in the scales of
love, so that he may be wholly enclosed in our heart who for us was wholly put
on the cross." To love this love always, one may cry out with the Apostle:
"If any man does not love our Lord Jesus Christ, let him be anathema," etc.

Secundo, Christus passus est et sanguinem eius fudit pro nobis, ut nos
ad eius amorem et caritatem alliceret. Exemplum: Aliquando enim datur cani
85   venatico sanguis alicuius prede ad lambendum, ut levius alliciatur ad se-
quendum. Revera sic nobis sanguis Christi; Psalmista: "Intinguatur pes
tuus," idest affectio tua, "in sanguine," scilicet Christi, "ut sic illum
per caritatem avidius sequaris.
    Absit ergo quod sibi ingrati simus, sicut fuit quidam amico [suo], de
90   quo hic narratur. Unde narrat Virgilius *Eneydos*, et similiter commentator
super Alexandrum Magnum, libro 5 et 6, de Enea quomodo in amore cuiusdam
puelle nimium exarsit in tantum ut seipsum pro ipsa depauperando humiliaret
[atque] eam ditando exaltaret. Quod et factum est. Accidit ergo quadam die
quod [cum] de quodam bello pro ea rediret vulneribus sauciatus, vix semivi-
95   vus evasit. Accessit ergo ad eam tamquam ad t⟨u⟩ciora refugia confidenter,
eo quod tantum illam pre ceteris dilexisset et seipsum depauperando eam
exaltasset. Set ipsa tanquam ingrata portas seravit et aditum constanter
sibi negavit. Quo facto secundum ⟨Ovidium⟩ *Methamorphoseos* ei sic scripsit
infortunium suum allegans:

100   Cerne cicatrices veteris vestigia pugne.
            Quesivi proprio sanguine quicquid habes.

            [Beholde myne woundes, how sore I am dyȝth,
            For all þe wele þat þou hast I wan hit in fyȝt.
            I am sore woundet, behold on my skyn.
105   Leue lyf, for my loue let me comen in.]

Spiritualiter loquendo iste miles Eneas Christus est, qui istam puellam,
scilicet animam humanam, in tantum dilexit quod [ut] ipsam exaltaret et
ditaret, nostram naturam assumens pau- [f. 45] per devenit atque ⟨pro⟩ ea
contra hostem humani generis bellum fortissimum aggressus est. Ubi tam
110   horribiliter sauciatus [est] quod, ut dicitur Ysaia: "A planta pedis usque
ad verticem capitis non est in e⟨o⟩ sanitas." A quo conflictu vix vivus
evadens ad portam anime ⟨pro⟩ qua tanta passus est secur[i]us accessit ut
ipsa pre ceteris amore et compassione mota ipsum in tali necessitate conso-
laretur et refocillaret. Pulsat ergo ut ingresssum habeat, prout dicitur
115   Apocalipsis 3: "Ecce sto ad ostium et pulso." Quid plura? Revera fortissime
ibi clamat illud Canticorum: "Aperi michi, soror mea, amica mea, columba
mea." Set certe, ut timeo, tanquam ingrata et tanti beneficii immemor
portas anime, que sunt amor, compassio, et huiusmodi affectiones bone,
obser⟨ando⟩ fortiter claudit, dum scilicet peccando sic ingrate illum
120   excludit. Set certe hoc non obstante ipse tamquam gratissimus et fidelissimus
cessare pulsando non desistit et clamare, ["Beholde myn woundes," etc.]

Christ suffered and shed his blood for us secondly that he may draw us to his love and charity. As an example: a hunting dog is sometimes given the blood of some prey to lick so that he may be more easily drawn to the chase. In the same manner we are given the blood of Christ; as the Psalmist has it: "That your foot may be dipped," that is, your affect, "in the blood" of Christ, that you may follow him more eagerly in love.

Far be it, then, that we be ungrateful to him, as someone once was ungrateful to his friend, of whom the following story is told. Virgil reports in the *Aeneid*, and likewise the commentator on Alexander the Great, books 5 and 6, how Aeneas burned so much with love for a girl that he would humble himself by becoming poor for her sake and exalt her with rich gifts. And this he did. Some day it happened that, as he returned greatly wounded from fighting a battle for her, he came back hardly alive. He went to her confidently as to a safe refuge, because he had loved her more than anyone else and had exalted her by becoming poor. But in her ingratitude she shut her doors and steadfastly denied him entrance. Upon this he wrote to her his mishap in the words of Ovid's *Metamorphoses* and told her:

> Behold my wounds, which traces are of ancient fight.
>   Whate'er thou hast, I gained it with my blood.
>
> Behold my wounds, my painful plight.
> All the wealth you own I won in fight.
> I am sorely wounded, behold my skin.
> Dear life, for my love let me now come in.

Spiritually speaking, this knight Aeneas is Christ, who loved this girl, man's soul, so much that in order to make her rich and noble he took on him our nature and became poor and entered a fierce war for her sake against the enemy of mankind. In it he was so terribly wounded that, as Isaiah says, "From the sole of his foot to the top of his head there is no soundness in him." As he issued from this war hardly alive, he confidently approached the door of the soul for whom he had suffered so much, so that she, moved above all else by love and compassion, might comfort and refresh him in his need. Then he knocks that he may be let in, as is said in Revelation 3: "See, I stand at the gate and knock." What else? Indeed, there he calls out loudly the words of Canticles: "Open, my sister, my friend, my turtledove." But alas, I fear that, ungrateful and forgetful as she is of all his favors, she firmly shuts the doors of the soul, which are love, compassion, and similar good sentiments; this the soul does when she ungratefully locks him out by committing sin. Yet nonetheless, as a most gracious and faithful knight he does not cease to knock and to cry: "Behold, my wounds," and so forth. O, human soul, blush then, and

O igitur, anima humana, erubesce, et iuxta Psalmistam: "Aperite portas
iusticie," idest anime affectiones erga Deum et eius beneficia, que tam
fortiter per peccatum sunt serate, et hoc per claves contricionis, confes-
125   sionis, caritatis, et amoris. Et certe, si sic, tunc introibit rex glorie
dicens istud Psalmi: "Hec requies mea in seculum seculi, hic habitabo
quoniam elegi eam."
        Tercio passus est et sanguinem suum fudit, ut profugos et exules ad
terram pacis revocaret. Quod bene figuratum erat Numeri 35, ubi dicitur:
130   "Debuerat enim profugus usque ad mortem pontificis in urbe residere," et
sequitur: "Exules et profugi ante mortem pontificis nullo modo in urbes
suas reverti non poterant," set prout scribitur Iosue 10: "Tunc revertetur
homicida et ingredietur civitatem et domum suam de qua [f. 45v] fugerat."
Spiritualiter autem loquendo homicida erat primus parens, qui se et nos
135   usque ad mortem vulneravit, qui tunc fugit de civitate et domo sua quando
paradisum reliquit veniens in hanc vallem miserie. Set in morte Christi
summi pontificis audacter redire potuit omni timore sublato. Et causa est
quia timor gladii post ipsum evaginati ipsum ad fugam impulit; Genesis 3:
"Eiecit Adam et collocavit [ante] paradisum voluptatis Cherubyn et flammeum
140   gladium." Set per mortem Christi ablatus est timor talis, quia sanguis
habet flammam extinguere. Et sicut dicitur naturaliter sanguis calidus
habet aciem gladii hebetare, et ideo sanguis Christi in morte recenter
effusus gladium flammeum reddit inutilem; Psalmista: "De gladio maligno
eripe me." Sublato igitur omni timore ad patriam celeriter revertendum est;
145   Ieremias: "Revertere, virgo Israel, revertere ad civitates tuas."
        Quarto sanguinem suum fudit, ut nos a morbo culpe lavaret. Docuit enim
sicut bonus medicus et formam talem reliquit, ut quantumcumque spirituali
infirmitate detinemur, sanguinem minuere et ita sanari. Christus enim
minutus ad nostrum exemplum fuit, tamen non eo modo quo solent homines,
150   scilicet tantum in brachio, verum eciam in toto corpore, quia ut dicitur
Ysaia: "A planta pedis usque ad verticem," etc. Et certe suum benedictum
corpus satis erat calidum dum ad columpnam tam fortiter erat cesum; similiter firmiter ligatum, quia cum clavis fortissimis manibus et pedibus cruci
firmiter affixum; similiter profunde percussum, quia cum lancea in latere
155   usque ad cor perforatum. Et defuit sibi omne solacium quod solet minutis
exiberi. Nobiles enim et religiosi in locis amenis et secretis minuuntur,
et tunc laucius illis ministratur. Set revera ipse palam coram omnibus in
monte [f. 46] Calvarie exponebatur et felle acetoque potabatur, ut sic nos
pro eius amore et propria salute sanguinem nostrum spiritualiter minuamus,
160   hoc est, ut ab operibus illicitis ad que per carnalitatem sanguinis nostri
movemur abstineamus, quia ut dicit Bernardus: "Probus miles non senciet sua
cum benigni ducis intuebitur vulnera." Similis ergo factus est Christus
pellicano, qui proprios pullos cum irascitur interficit, set post compas-

according to the Psalmist, "Open the gates of justice," that is to say, the
soul's affections for God and his favors, which are so firmly shut through sin,
and do so with the keys of contrition, confession, love, and charity. When you
do this, the King of Glory will surely enter and speak the words of the Psalm:
"This is my rest for ever and ever; here will I dwell, for I have chosen it."

In the third place, Christ suffered and shed his blood so that he might
call back the fugitives and exiles to the land of peace. This was fittingly
prefigured in Numbers 35, where it is said: "The fugitive ought to have stayed
in the city until the death of the high priest," and afterwards: "The banished
and fugitives before the death of the high priest may by no means return into
their own cities," but as it is written in Joshua 10: "Then shall the manslayer return and go into his own city and house from where he had fled."
Spiritually speaking, the "manslayer" was our first parent, who wounded himself
and us to the death; he fled from "his own city and house" when he left paradise and came to this valley of misery. But after Christ our high priest's
death he could bravely return, leaving all fear behind. The reason for this is
that fear of the sword that was drawn out of its sheath behind him compelled
him to flee; Genesis 3: "He cast out Adam and placed before the paradise of
pleasure Cherubim and a flaming sword." But this fear has been taken away
through Christ's death, because blood has the power to quench fire. And as
warm blood is said to have the natural power to dull the sharpness of a sword,
thus Christ's blood, when it was newly shed in his death, rendered the flaming
sword useless; as the Psalmist says: "From the malicious sword deliver me."
Therefore we should swiftly return to our home leaving all fear behind us;
Jeremiah: "Return, O virgin of Israel, return to your cities."

In the fourth place, Christ shed his blood so that he might wash us from
the sickness of guilt. For he taught as a true physician and left the pre-
scription that, however much we are in the grips of a spiritual illness, we are
to be bled and thus healed. For Christ was bled as an example for us, yet not
in the same way that other men practice, that is, in the arm alone, but rather
in his entire body, for as is said in Isaiah: "From the sole of his foot to
the top," etc. And his blessed body was certainly well heated when he was
fiercely scourged at the column; likewise, it was tightly bound, because it was
tightly nailed to the cross by its hands and feet; and likewise, a deep inci-
sion was made, because it was pierced in its side with a spear to his very
heart. But the consolation which is wont to be shown to people who are bled,
he went totally without. Noblemen and religious are bled in pleasant and
secret surroundings and receive better food and drink. But Christ was openly
put to show before all men on Mount Calvary and was given gall and vinegar to
drink, so that we should let our blood spiritually in the same way for his love
and our own salvation, that is, we should abstain from sinful deeds to which we
are moved by the fleshly nature of our blood; for as Bernard says: "A brave

sione motus corpus suum usque ad cor rostro perforat, ex cuius sanguine
165 aspersi reviviscunt. Revera sic peccatores spiritualiter mortuos Dei offen-
cione per compassionem tamen motus, quia non vult mortem peccatoris, effun-
dendo sanguinem cordis sui benedicti ad vitam gracie reconciliavit. Unde
Augustinus ad Severinum: "Fortis, inquit, ut mors dilectio, que ipsam
mortem mori fecit ⟨in morte⟩ Redemptoris." Et sequitur: "Agnoscat (inquit
170 Augustinus) homo quantum valeat et quantum debeat. Et dum precium suum
recogitat, servilis esse omnino desistat. Reus itaque est (dicit ipse) non
parvi precii set eciam sanguinis dulcissimi Christi, qui animam maculat et
violat sic Christi sanguine emundatam." Hec ille.
   Set timeo michi quod est de multis sicut de filio frenetico, qui
175 quanto plus pia mater eius infirmitatem deplorat, tanto magis ipse in risum
et cachinnaciones prorumpit nichil matri compaciendo. Revera sic Christo
pro peccatoribus lacrimas fundente et sanguinem [minuente], ipsi non tantum
sicut ingrati sue passionis obliti, verum eciam tamquam frenetici ipsum
derident et blasphemant, membratim cum iuramentis horribilibus ipsum divi-
180 dentes et ei pro sua passione, quam tantum pro nobis sustinuit, improperan-
tes. Unde ipse per Psalmistam [ait]: "Retribuebant michi mala pro bonis et
odium pro dilectione mea." Contra quos nota satis supra, capitulo 3. [f.
46v] Non sic, karissimi, set cum universis creaturis passioni sue compati
debemus. Sol enim sibi compaciens in sua morte radios suos retraxit, terra
185 mota est, petre scisse sunt, monumenta aperiebantur, et ob compassionem
[corpora] sanctorum surrexerunt, ut patet Matthei.
   Narrat autem Ovidius in epistolis suis quod iuvenis quidam nomine
Achoncius amorem cuiusdam virginis habere volens, quam cum de amore frequenter rogasset ipsam difficilem reperit supra modum. Quod ipse moleste
190 ferens istam cautelam excogitavit. Accepit unum pomum pulcherrimum et in
illo quoddam obligatorium scripsit de nupciis cum ea contrahendis, cogitans
et sperans quod si ipsa obligatorium illud perlegeret, quod ex tunc tenere-
tur sponsalia secum contrahere, vi scilicet illius lecture. Fuit ergo forma
scripture talis:

195   Iuro tibi sane per mistica sacra Dyane
          Me tibi nupturam sponsam comitemque futuram.

[Anglice sic:

          By dedes of Dayne I swere to the
          Her-aftur to take and wedde the.]

200 Istud ergo pomum in quodam loco ubi ipsa continue conversabatur, scilicet
in templo Dyane dei sui, proiecit, ut ibi eam nullo modo lateret, set

soldier does not feel his wounds when he sees those of his generous leader."
Thus Christ became like the pelican, who kills his own offspring when he gets
angry, but afterwards, moved by compassion, he pierces his own body to his
heart with his beak, and his offspring, sprinkled with his blood, come to life
again. In the same way, by shedding the blood of his blessed heart Christ has
brought sinners back to the life of grace after they had spiritually died by
offending God, because he was moved in his compassion since he "does not want
the death of the sinner." Therefore Augustine says to Severinus: "Love is as
strong as death, for it made death itself die in the death of the Redeemer."
And Augustine says further: "Let man know what he is worth and how much he
owes; and when he thinks of his value, let him altogether stop being a slave.
For he is guilty, not of a little money, but of the sweet blood of Christ when
he stains his soul and violates it after it has thus been washed in the blood
of Christ."

But I fear that with many people it goes as it does with a deranged child:
the more his loving mother worries about his illness, the more he laughs and
roars without any feeling for his mother. In the same way, when Christ sheds
his tears and is bled for the sake of sinners, the latter not merely forget his
Passion like ungrateful people, but like deranged persons laugh at him and
blaspheme by tearing him to pieces with their horrible oaths and by taunting
him for the Passion he suffered for us. Whence he says through the Psalmist:
"They repaid me evil for good and hatred for my love." Notice what has been
said above in chapter 3 against such people. We must not act thus, beloved,
but instead have compassion with his suffering, together with all creation.
For at his death the sun had compassion and withdrew its rays, the earth
quaked, rocks were split, tombs opened up, and the bodies of the saints rose,
as is reported in Matthew.

In his *Letters* Ovid tells us that a young man called Acontius was in love
with a maiden; though he had asked her often for her love, he found her to be
unusually difficult. In his frustration he came up with the following trick.
He took a very beautiful apple and wrote in it a marriage vow, thinking and
hoping that if she read out the vow aloud, she would thereby be held to marry
him, that is, by virtue of her reading it. The writing therefore was as
follows:

>   I swear to you, by the holy rites of Diana,
>   That I will be your wedded spouse and your wife.

In English:

>   By dedes . . .

inventam scripturam perlegeret. Quod et factum est. Scriptura ergo perlec-
ta, statim habuit conscienciam quod cum illo contrahere necessario oporte-
ret. Nichilominus tamen omnino non consensit. Set tandem febribus afflicta
205   celitus sibi litteris missis ad consensum compulsa est et dicto iuveni
nupsit. Moraliter virgo anima humana est; amator Pater celestis, de quo
Sapiencie 11 dicitur: "Parcis omnibus, Domine, quoniam tua sunt omnia qui
amas animas." Multis ergo modis cogitavit amator iste quomodo amorem istius
virginis, scilicet anime humane, ad se posset allicere, nunc per beneficia,
210   nunc per promissa, in veteri lege, eciam et in statu legis nature. Tandem
hac cautela usus est: Cum ipsam expertus esset tam multipliciter repugnan-
tem, accepit enim pomum pulcherrimum, [f. 47] ° scilicet Christum filium
eius incarnatum, in cuius corpore obligatorium quoddam scripsit quando
corpus suum benedictum plagis multiplicibus quasi magnis parvisque litteris
215   manifestis sculpi et perscribi permisit. Et certe hec scriptura in se continet
quoddam obligatorium de nupciis contrahendis inter Deum et animam
tam magnum et efficax quod inpossibile est illud legere quod in hoc pomo
dicto modo perscribitur, quin statim ad eius dilectionem assenciat et
maximam conscienciam habeat nisi veraciter diligat illum qui tot signa sibi
220   dilectionis ostendit. Proverbiorum 12: "Est qui promittit et quasi gladio
pungitur consciencia." Rogo quid potuit fecisse ut amorem tuum alli⟨ceret⟩?
Nonne tam corpus quam animam pro te exposuit? Secundum enim quosdam
anima humana sita est in sanguine, et ideo secundum Ieronimum totum
sanguinem suum fudit Christus ut animam pariter pro nobis dedisse ostenderet.
225   Secundum alios situatur anima in cerebro, et ideo in capite multipliciter passus
est. Secundum vero alios in corde, et ideo per medium cordis voluit lancea-
ri. Unde Ieronimus: "Dedi dilectam animam," ad vere dilectionis insinuacio-
nem ut nos ipsum eatenus diligamus, quia ipse prius dilexit nos et animam
suam tradidit pro nobis. Set quia plerique quamvis dicta consciencia cum
230   ipso contrahere deberemus resistimus tamen opere illud implere, ideo certe
ut frequenter compellit nos per febres mundane tribulacionis vexari, per quod
quasi necessitamur illum amare. Ad hoc enim habemus figuram Luce 4 de
Christo veniente in domum Symonis, ubi socrus Symonis tenebatur magnis
febribus, quibus cum [f. 47v] Christus imperasset et eam dimisissent,
235   surrexit continuo et ministrabat illis. Christus autem multis hominibus
tribulaciones mittit, per quas melius erudientur Christum invocare, et
illis transactis sibi ardencius per amorem ministrare. Patet ergo quomodo
istud pomum, scilicet Christus Filius Dei incarnatus, fuit multiplicibus
plagis ascriptus quasi cum quodam obligatorio, ut cum eo contrahamus et
240   firmiter diligamus. Quod quidem pomum in tot locis repositum est ut nos
omnino latere non potest, nam in omni ecclesia fidelium representatur ut ab
omnibus legi potest. Dicitur ergo Danielis 5: "Qui legerit hanc scripturam
et eius interpretacionem manifestam michi fecerit, purpura vestietur."

This apple he threw in a place where she always stayed, namely the temple of
Diana, her god [sic], so that she could in no way overlook it but should find
the writing and read it. And so it happened. But when she had read out the
writing, she understood at once that she must of necessity marry him. Nonetheless, she did not agree at all. But in the end, after being attacked by fever
and having received letters from heaven, she was compelled to consent and
married the young man. Morally interpreted, that maiden is the soul of man;
her lover, our heavenly Father, of whom is said in Wisdom 11: "You spare all,
O Lord, because all things are yours, who love souls." This lover thought of
many ways how he might draw the love of this maiden, that is, the soul, to
himself—now by gifts, now by promises, both in the Old Law and in the state of
natural law. In the end he used this trick: Since he found that she rejected
him so much, he took a very beautiful apple, namely Christ his Son made flesh,
in whose body he wrote a promise when he allowed his blessed body to be carved
and inscribed with many wounds as with so many large and small clear letters.
This inscription indeed contains a promise of marriage between God and the
soul, a promise so great and powerful that it is impossible to read what is
thus written in this apple without consenting at once to his love and realizing
fully that one must love him who has shown so many signs of love. Proverbs 12:
"There is one who promises, and the conscience is pricked as if with a sword."
What more, I ask, could he have done to attract your love? Did he not offer
his body and soul for you? According to some writers, the soul of man resides
in his blood; and thus, according to Jerome, Christ shed all his blood in order
to indicate that he was likewise giving his soul for us. According to others,
the soul resides in the brain; and therefore Christ suffered much injury to his
head. But according to yet others it resides in the heart; and thus Christ
wanted to be pierced with a spear through the middle of his heart. Whence
Jerome says: "I gave my beloved soul," to show his true love, so that we might
love him in like manner, for he loved us first and gave his soul for us. But
since many of us, although we should marry Christ after the voice of our
conscience, resist doing so in fact, he frequently compels us to suffer the
fevers of worldly tribulation, through which, as it were, we must of necessity
love him. We find a type of this in Luke 4, when Christ came to the house of
Simon, where Simon's mother-in-law was held by a strong fever; Christ commanded it and the fever left her, and she got up at once and served them. Christ
sends many people tribulations through which they are taught the better to call
on Christ, and when the tribulations are over, to serve him more fervently in
love. Thus we see how this apple, that is, Christ, the Son of God made flesh,
was inscribed with manifold wounds as if with a marriage vow, so that we may
marry and firmly love him. That apple has been put in so many places that we
absolutely cannot overlook it, for it is present in every church of the faithful, so that it can be read by everyone. For in Daniel 5 it is said: "Whoever

245 Quinto passus est et sanguinem suum fudit, ut diabolum ab empcione
nostra excluderet °. Ipse diabolus decipiendo genus humanum illud a primis
parentibus citra de⟨bit⟩um precium empserat, quasi pro uno pomo minimi
valoris. Set adverte. Videmus enim ad sensum: illi cicius conceditur qui
plus offert; set Christus plus optulit et dedit quam diabolus, quia non
tantum unum pomum set simul et semel corpus et animam, ut sic per suam
250 mortem amaram et diram de dura et crudeli diaboli potestate nos liberaret.
Et per consequens sui sumus et non diaboli filii. Super quod cartam firmis-
simam nobis reliquit. Et nota quod carta conscripta sanguine vehementer
solet importare securitatem et magnam ⟨generare⟩ admiracionem; set huiusmodi carta[m] scripsit nobis in cruce quando "speciosus forma pre filiis
255 hominum" corpus suum benedictum extendit, sicut pergamenarius ad solem
pergamenum explicare videtur. Sic Christus manibus et pedibus in cruce
affixus corpus suum ad cartam scriben- [f. 48] dam exposuit; clav⟨o⟩s eciam
in manibus habuit pro calamo, sanguinem preciosum pro encausto. Per hanc
cartam hereditatem amissam nobis restituit, prout superius, parte 2, capi-
260 tulo 6, est expressum.
    Et non tantum hoc, set ubi prius a nostra hereditate fuimus exules,
modo cum Psalmista dicere possumus: "Hereditate possideamus sanctuarium
Dei." Et certe, tunc dissolvit cyrographum quod cum diabolo primi parentes
pupigerunt, de quo dicit Augustinus: "Eva, inquit, a diabolo peccat⟨um⟩
265 mutuavit, cyrographum scripsit, fideiussorem invenit, [unde usura peccati
in posteritate eius crevit." Tunc enim Eva a diabolo peccatum mutuavit
quando contra preceptum Dei pessime diaboli suggestioni consensit; cirographum scripsit quando manum ad pomum porrexit; fideiussorem invenit] quando
Adam peccato consentire fecit. ⟨Et sic⟩ usura posteritati sue crevit. Set
270 certe Christus istam servitutem omnino delevit quando in cruce totum corpus
suum pro carta nobis reliquit. Dicit ergo Christus:

In cruce sum pro te. Cur peccas? Desine pro me.
Desine, do veniam; dic culpam, retraho penam.

[Anglice sic:

275 I honge on cros for loue of the.
Lef þy synne for loue of me.
Mercy aske, amende þe sone,
And I forȝyf þe þat is mysdone.]

Sic ergo patet primo quare Christus pro nobis sanguinem suum fudit.

1 ergo] autem O.   2 deperdita] depertita C.   3 enim] vero C.   9 quando] qua O.
11 hac] caritatem ac C; hanc M.   12 caritatem] add iugiter O.   18 et] om O.   34 idest]
hoc est O.   71 susceptus] receptus O.   73 sedit] sedet O.   74 etc.] om O.   75–76 et

shall read this writing and shall make its meaning known to me, shall be
clothed with purple."

And in the fifth place, Christ suffered and shed his blood so that he
might exclude the devil from purchasing us. By his trick the devil had bought
mankind from our first parents for less than its regular price—as it were, for
an apple of very little value. But notice: we see everyday that he who offers
more obtains the goods more easily. But Christ offered and gave more than the
devil: not just an apple but his body and soul all together, that he might thus
free us from the devil's hard and cruel power through his bitter and terrible
death. As a result, we are his children and not the devil's. On that exchange
he left a most reliable charter for us. Notice that a charter that is written
in blood carries with it extreme reliability and produces much admiration.
Just such a charter did Christ write for us on the cross when he who was
"beautiful above the sons of men" stretched out his blessed body, as a
parchment-maker can be seen to spread a hide in the sun. In this way Christ,
when his hands and feet were nailed to the cross, offered his body like a
charter to be written on. The nails in his hands were used as a quill, and his
precious blood as ink. And thus, with this charter he restored to us our
heritage that we had lost, as was explained above, in the sixth chapter of part
2.

And not only this, but whereas once we were banished from our inheritance,
we can now say with the Psalmist: "Let us possess the sanctuary of God for an
inheritance." And there he certainly destroyed the contract which our first
parents made with the devil, of which Augustine says: "Eve borrowed sin from
the devil, wrote out a contract, and found a person to give security, from
which the interest of her sin grew for her posterity." For Eve borrowed sin
from the devil when she most wickedly consented to the devil's suggestion
against God's commandment; she wrote out a contract when she stretched out her
hand for the apple; she found a person to give security when she caused Adam to
consent to sin; and in this fashion the interest grew for her offspring. But
truly Christ canceled this servitude totally when he left his whole body for us
on the cross as a charter. For Christ says:

> I am on the cross for you. Why sin? Cease for my sake!
> Cease, and I give you grace; confess, and I spare your pain.

In English:

> I honge on cros for loue of the . . .

And thus our first point is dealt with, why Christ shed his blood for us.

11–12 John 15.13.   **14** Prov. 8.17.   **15–16** Rev. 1.5.   **31–32** 1 Sam. 17.   **36** Hab.
3.4.   **44–48** Esther 10.5–7; 11.5–11.   **51** Cf. John 19.34.   **67–68** Matt. 26.42; or

quiddam] et quid M.W; inquit (*corr*) et R.   **81** semper amandam] superandam C.R; servandam W.   **Et**] *om* O.   **87** scilicet] *om* O.   **89** quidam] quedam M; quedam puella *interl* R.   **93** quadam] quodam O.   **94** quod cum] quod C; cum O.   **95** tuciora] tuiciora
C.   **98** Ovidium] eundem C.   **102–105** Beholde . . . in] *text from* R. *Verse 26, in*
B3.D.E.Go1.Jo.L2.LC.R.Sp.W1.W2; *variant in* V.   **107** ut] *om* C.O.   **108** pro] per
C.   **111** eo] ea C.   **112** pro] de C.   **119** obserando] observande C.R.   **121** Beholde . . . etc.] *om* O; soror mea columba mea aperi me M. *Text from* R.   **122** igitur]
ergo O.   **132** non] *om* O.   **139** ante] *om* C.O. *The quotation is garbled in various
forms.*   **144** me] *add* etc O.   igitur] ergo O.   **151** etc.] capitis non est in eo sanitas O.
164 suum] *om* O.   **169** in morte] idest mortem C.   **188** habere volens] *om* O.   **191–
192** teneretur] *add* ipsa O.   **197–199** Anglice . . . the] *text from* R. *Verse 28, in*
B3.D.E.Go1.Go2. L1.L2.LC.R.Sp.V.W1.   **204** consensit] assensit O.   **205** compulsa]
pulsa O.   **206** virgo] *add* illa O.   **208** cogitavit] excogitavit O.   **212** pulcherrimum] C
repeats et in illo . . . scriptura talis (*lines 190–194*).   **214** multiplicibus] multipliciter
O.   **221** alliceret] allidet C.   **225** alios] aliquos O.   **226** alios] aliquos O.   **229** plerique]
plerumque R.W.   **235** multis] multas O.   **239** ascriptus] conscriptus O.   **245** ex-
cluderet] *add* et C.   **246** debitum] deletum C.   **251–252** firmissimam] securissimam
O.   **253** generare] regenerare C.   **256** pergamenum] pellem omnibus membris extensis
O.   **257** affixus] affixis O.   clavos] claves C.   **258** Per hanc] et sic per O.   **259** heredi-
tatem] *add* nostram O.   **264** peccatum] peccata O.   **269** Et sic] etc C.   **271** reliquit] dereliquit O.   **274–278** Anglice . . . mysdone] *text from* R. *Verse 29, in* B3.Go2.Jo.L2.
LC.R.Sp.W1.W2.   **279** Christus] *om* O.

III.xi   QUO DIE, LOCO, ET MODO CHRISTUS PASSUS EST

[A]d maiorem autem huius ⟨rei⟩ securitatem habendam, de confectione
huius carte ostendit secundo quo die fuit scripta, quo modo, et in quo
loco. Et nota quod dies fuit feria sexta, que Anglice dicitur *Fryday*. Et
merito mutatur i in e, ut ita dicatur *Freday*, quia in illo die, ut dictum
5   est, de servitute diaboli nos eripuit et liberos ad celestia regna reddidit. In quo autem die primus homo fuit creatus, et eodem die tamquam dominus terrarum in paradiso collocatus, et tercio eodem die pro peccato ab
illo expulsus ac multiplici miserie adiudicatus. Similiter isto die fuit
angelus Marie missus et Filius Dei incarnatus. Unde versus:

10   Salve, festa dies, que vulnera nostra coherces.
         Est Adam factus et eodem ⟨tempore⟩ lapsus.
         Angelus est missus, et passus in cruce Christus.

Est ergo hec dies secundum Psalmistam "quam fecit Dominus; exultemus et
letemur in ea," quia in illa salvatum fuit genus humanum a morte eterna. °
15   [f. 48v] [C]irca modum autem passionis sue et istius carte confeccionis
est sciendum quod pessimi Iudei ipsum fecerunt portare lignum de domo
iudicii fere usque ad montem; ubi pre nimia eius lassitudine quemdam Symonem Syrenensem crucem fecerunt baiulare. Dicunt tamen aliqui sancti et

rather Luke 22.42.   **72–80** Cf. Augustine, *De sancta virginitate* LV.56 (PL 40:428).
81–82 1 Cor. 16.22.   **86–87** Ps. 67.24.   **100–101** Ovid, *Amores* III.viii.19–20.   **110–111** Isa. 1.6.   **115** Rev. 3.20.   **116–117** Cant. 5.2.   **122–123** Ps. 117.19.   **126–127** Ps. 131.14.   **130–132** Num. 35.28, 32.   **132–133** Josh. 20.6.   **139–140** Gen. 3.24.   **143–144** Ps. 143.10–11.   **145** Jer. 31.21.   **151** Isa. 1.6.   **168–171** The thought occurs in *En. in Ps. 51* 1 (CC 39:624).   **181–182** Ps. 108.5.   **184–186** Cf. Matt. 27.45–53.   **187–206** Ovid, *Heroides* XX–XXI.   **207–208** Wisd. 11.27.   **220–221** Prov. 12.18.   **227** Jeremiah (!) 12.7.   **232–235** Luke 4.38–39.   **242–243** Dan. 5.7.   **254–255** Ps. 44.3.   **259–260** *FM* II.vii, near end.   **262–263** Ps. 82.13.   **264–266** Cf. *Leg. aurea*, pp. 230–231.   **272–273** For other occurrences of the Latin hexameters, see *Verses*, pp. 164–65.

III.xi   THE DAY, PLACE, AND MANNER OF CHRIST'S PASSION

In order to have a firmer understanding of this matter, we will in the second place show on what day this charter was written, in what fashion, and in what place. Know then that the day was the sixth day of the week, which in English is called *Friday*. And the letter *i* may justly be changed to *e*, so that it is called *Freeday*, for on that day, as we have said, Christ delivered us from the devil's servitude and made us free for his heavenly kingdom. On that day also the first human being was created, and on the same day he was placed in paradise as lord of all lands, and thirdly on the same day he was driven from it for his sin and sentenced to manifold misery. In like fashion, on the same day the angel was sent to Mary and the Son of God was made flesh. Thus we have these verses:

> Hail, festal day, comprising all our wounds.
> On it was Adam made, and on this day he fell.
> Sent was the angel then, and on his cross Christ died.

According to the Psalmist, "this is the day which the Lord has made; let us be glad and rejoice in it," for on this day mankind was saved from eternal death.
    With respect to the manner of his suffering and of the making of this

devoti quod dum lignum illud ponderosum crucis portavit super humeros,
20　mater eius fere dolore suffocata sequebatur, filium suum videre festinans;
per semitam in campum sibi occurrit, ubi mater in filium et filius in
matrem tam dolorosos aspectus iniecerunt quod ambo pre dolore consternati
in terram quasi mortui ceciderunt. Et dicunt, hec erat causa quare Symonem
Syrenensem crucem portare coegerunt. Dolorosa autem hec erat visio quando
25　mater ⟨proprium⟩ filium, quem veraciter scivit esse Deum, prius sputis
abhominabilibus conspui, colaphis cedi, asperrime flagellari, et iam crucem
ad propriam mortem baiulare sic coartari ⟨vidit⟩. Que quidem crux quia in
proporcione quoad foramina clavorum corpus suum excedebat, super illam
ipsum posuerunt ad terram suppinum, ligantes ad manus et pedes cordas for-
30　tissimas membratim corpus extraxerunt, ut sic ruptis venis et nervis brachia et pedes ad dicta foramina adequabant, ubi affixus et extensus ipsum
de terra elevaverunt super crucem, et sic horribili impetu corpus cum cruce
elevatum in profundam terram infixerunt. Que pena, ut dicunt sancti, omnia
priora excedebat. ⟨Bene⟩ ergo potest Christus dicere illud ⟨Trenorum⟩: "O
35　vos omnes qui transitis per viam," etc.

　　　　　[A, ʒe men þat by me wendenn,
　　　　　Abydes a while and loke on me,
　　　　　ʒef ʒe fyndenn in any ende
　　　　　Suche sorow as here ʒe se on me.]

40　　Et certe omnes pene predicte non tantum illum gravant sicut ingratitudo hominis, quem tantum dilexit et diligit. Et ideo quidam devotus hominem
ingratum loco Christi sic redarguit:

　　　　　Homo (inquit), vide quid pro te pacior,
　　　　　Si est dolor sicut quo crucior.
45　　　　　Ad te clamo qui pro te morior.
　　　　　[f. 49] Vide penas quibus afficior.
　　　　　Vide clav⟨o⟩s quibus confodior.
　　　　　Cum sit dolor tantus exterior,
　　　　　Set interior tamen planctus gravior,
50　　　　　Dum tam ingratum te experior.

　　　　　[Byholde, mon, what I dree,
　　　　　Whech is my payne, qwech is my woo.
　　　　　To the I clepe now I shal dye.
　　　　　By-se the wel, for I mot go.
55　　　　　Byholde þe nayles þat bcn withoute,

charter, we must know that the wicked Jews made him carry the wood from the house of judgment nearly to the mount; there, because of his extreme weakness, they forced a certain Simon of Cyrene to carry the cross. Some saintly and devout persons say that while he was carrying the heavy wood of the cross on his shoulders, his mother, nearly choked with grief, followed her son, hastening to see him, and she met him on the path in the field. There his mother cast such a painful look on her son, and the son on his mother, that both were so struck by their grief that they fell to the ground as if dead. And they say that this was the reason why the Jews forced Simon of Cyrene to carry the cross. Grievous was that sight when this mother saw her own son, whom she truly knew to be God, first being spat upon abominably, struck with fists, and most fiercely scourged, and now forced to carry the cross to his own death. Since on that cross the nail holes were farther apart than the members of his body, they put him on it lying flat on the ground and, tying strong ropes on his hands and feet, pulled his members so that, after the veins and tendons were broken, his arms and feet would reach to the nail holes. When he was thus nailed and stretched on the cross, they lifted him from the ground and let the body with the cross fall into a hole in the ground with a horrible thump. This pain was greater than all previous ones, as the saints say. Therefore Christ could rightly speak the words of Lamentations: "O all you who pass by the way," and so forth.

> Ah, you men that by me pass,
> Abide a while and look on me,
> Whether you find in any place
> Such sorrow as in me you see.

But all these aforementioned pains do not grieve him so much as the ingratitude of man whom he has loved so much and still does. Therefore, a devout person reproaches man in Christ's stead as follows:

> Man, behold what I suffer for you,
> If there is any pain like the one that torments me.
> To you I call who die for you.
> Behold the pains by which I am afflicted.
> Behold the nails with which I am pierced.
> Yet while my external suffering is so great,
> My inner lament is still more grievous,
> Because I find you so ungrateful.

> Byholde mon what I dree . . .

How þey me þorlenn to þys tre.
Of all my pyne haue I no doute
But ȝif vnkynde I fynde the.]

Circa locum passionis tercio est sciendum quod fuit in monte Calvarie,
60 sive Golgatha Syriace, quod locus clavi sive calvarie Latine dicitur. Qui
secundum Isidorum sic nominatur eo quod capita hominum dampnatorum ibidem
decollarentur. Ibi enim gratis locum sue passionis elegit. Nam sicut solent
homines ut communiter supra montes arma demonstrare, sicut fuit antiquitus
in monte Olimpo, cursus [eciam] et situs stellarum inspicere, et similiter
65 placita et brigas terminare—sic certe Christus remedium animarum nostrarum, quando in ligno super montem pependit, arma sue potencie demonstravit,
quibus ad plenum hostem humani generis ibidem prostravit. Cursus eciam
stellarum, corporum scilicet supracelestium, hoc est Patris et Filii et
Spiritus Sancti, apercius consideravit. Atque antiquum litigium inter homi-
70 nem et diabolum terminavit dicens, "Consummatum est," quasi diceret, iam
omnia consummata sunt que dicta sunt de me, ut vos hereditatem amissam
recuperare possetis, nam per me iam pax inter Deum Patrem et hominem peccatorem reformatur. Scitis enim quod quando milites tractant de pace, gladio-
rum, lancearum, et aliorum armorum ferreorum punctus versus se tenent.
75 Certe sic Christus, ut pacem inter Patrem et hominem faceret, punctus
lancee et ferri usque ad interiora cordis sustinuit, "et continuo exivit
sanguis et aqua," etc., ad nostram expiacionem.

---

1 rei] modi C.   2 in] *om* O.   4 illo] illa O.   6 autem] eciam O.   11 tempore] dieque
C.   14 eterna] *add* deo gracias C.   18 fecerunt] angariaverunt *before* quemdam O.
20 suum] *add* semel O.   25 proprium] *abbreviation for* propter C.M.R; ipsum W.
27 vidit] *om* C.O. *Text in* Et.C.etc.   34 Bene] cum C.   Trenorum] tunc C.   36–
39 A . . . me] *text from* R. *Verse 30, in* B3.E.Go1.Go2. L2.LC.R.Sp.V.W1.
47 clavos] claves C.   49 Set] *om* O.   tamen] est O.   50 Dum] *after* ingratum O.   51–
58 Byholde . . . the] *text from* R. *Verse 31, in* B3.E. Go2.L2.LC.R.Sp.W1.   77 etc.]
om O.

III.xii   QUA HORA, QUA ETATE, ET QUO TEMPORE CHRISTUS PASSUS EST

[T]ercio iam ostenditur qua hora, qua etate, et quo tempore hanc cartam
per suam passionem confirmavit. Unde pro ⟨primo⟩ sciendum quod hora nona
passus est, illo scilicet tempore quo homines [ut] communiter se reficiunt
et ad maius solacium se disponunt in pastu [f. 49v] et aliis solaciis
5 corporalibus. Et hec hora recte in meridie diei accidit, quando sol est in
maiori sua potestate. Si ergo anima devota ad Christum clamans dicat illud
Canticorum: "Indica michi ubi pascas, ubi cubes in meridie," revera respon-

Third, with respect to the place of his Passion, we must know that this
was on Mount Calvary, or Golgotha in Syrian. In Latin this means "the place of
the skull"; according to Isidore, it is so named because on it the heads of
condemned criminals were cut off. This he willingly chose as the place of his
Passion. For just as men commonly display arms on mountaintops—as they did
on Mount Olympus in ancient times—, and observe the course and position of the
stars, and further settle their legal business and quarrels there, thus did
Christ, the remedy for our souls, when he hung on the cross at the mountaintop, display the weapons of his power, with which he completely defeated there
the enemy of mankind. He further observed the course of the stars more openly,
that is, of the heavenly bodies, namely the Father, the Son, and the Holy
Spirit. And he settled the ancient strife between man and the devil when he
said, "It is fulfilled," as if saying: now all things are completed that have
been said of me, so that you can recover your lost inheritance, for now peace
between God the Father and sinful man is reestablished. You are aware that
when soldiers negotiate about peace, they turn the points of their swords,
lances, and other iron weapons toward themselves. Christ likewise, in order to
make peace between God the Father and man, suffered the iron point of a spear
to penetrate to his heart, and "at once blood and water flowed forth" for our
atonement.

10–12 *In* 17100; Chevalier 17928.   **13–14** Ps. 117.24.   **34–35** Lam. 1.12.   **43–50** By
Philip the Chancelor; see *Verses* p. 167.   **70** John 19.30.   **76–77** John 19.34.

III.xii   THE HOUR, AGE, AND SEASON OF CHRIST'S PASSION

In the third place, we now show in what hour, age, and season he confirmed
this charter through his Passion. On the first topic we must know that he
suffered at the ninth hour, that is, at the time when men commonly take a rest
and allow themselves some refreshment in food and other bodily comforts. This
hour rightly occurs at midday, when the sun is at its highest point. If a
devout soul calling to Christ says the words from Canticles: "Show me where
you feed, where you lie at midday," the Psalmist may answer that, as he was

dere bene potest quod ad Patrem recessurus primo genus humanum pavit mira-
culis et doctrinis, et postea discipulos propria carne et sanguine. Et hoc
10   fuit illud admirandum convivium in quo Christus et Iudas, Deus et diabolus,
vitulus et ursus simul comedebant; Ysaie 9: "Vitulus et ursus pascentur
simul." Set rogo, ubi cubat in meridie? Revera si sollerter considerare
velimus quomodo in meridie est estus et totus fervor diei, et ideo pastor animalium tunc temporis gaudet si posset locum amenum invenire ad cubandum.
15   Qui quidem locus tunc amenus dicitur si sit virens frondibus et floribus,
et precipue si ex uno latere sit aqua decurrens vel fons scaturiens et ex
alia arbores prominentes late ramos pretendentes cum foliis virentibus.
Talis enim locus valde delicatus est in estu, sicut patet de ⟨iuni⟩pero et
Helia, Regum 19, et de Iona et edere, Ione 3. Nota historias si placet. Et
20   precipue in estate deliciosum valde videtur sub umbra albe spine cubare,
nam ipsa ex floribus redolet et ex foliis umbram habet. Revera, karissimi,
post illam cenam pretactam perhennis memorie, in qua Christus semetipso
discipulos suos pavit, sequebatur una ferventissima meridies, videlicet in
die Parasceves, in qua maximus estus erat. Scitis enim quod videtur homini
25   maximus esse estus quando non potest sustinere vestes suas super se set
illas a se proicit. Set revera Christus illa die tantum estum sustinuit
amoris et caritatis quod pannis a se proiectis nudus pro salute nostra
voluit in cruce cubare [f. 50] et quiescere; Danielis 13: "Estus quippe
erat." Locus autem amenus et virens, quem pre ceteris elegit, erat lignum
30   crucis. Et certe locus ille ex uno latere habuit aquam fluentem quando
"unus militum lancea latus eius aperuit et continuo exivit sanguis et
aqua," Iohannis 19. Et ideo tunc temporis canit Ecclesia: "Vidi aquam
egredientem de templo a latere dextro," etc. Set tunc inclinavit Christus
capud suum sub umbra albe spine quando milites plectentes coronam de spinis
35   imposuerunt capiti eius, ubi supra. Hec hora erat in qua Christus non
tantum pavit vel eciam cubavit, verum eciam in qua mortem pro nobis sustinuit.

    Circa vero etatem in qua Deus passus est, sciendum quod fuit triginta
et trium annorum, in iuventute et in tenera etate. Et per consequens pena
40   gravior, nam quantum membrum tenerius, tantum in illo pena gravior probatur, sicut patet de oculo. Et adverte: Caro enim hominis est tenerior quam
caro bruti animalis, et inter homines caro femine tenerior est quam mascu-
li, et inter feminas tenerior est caro virginis quam corrupte. Set caro
Christi fuit de purissimis sanguinibus Virginis Benedicte assumpta et
45   propagata, et ipsemet in purissima virginitate usque ad mortem permansit,
quod satis experimentaliter probatur. Dicitur enim libro *De animalibus* quod
si caro alicuius scindatur post mortem et rubea inveniatur, signum proba-
tissimum virginitatis est; si autem livida, signum est corrupcionis. Set
Christus post mortem lanceatus, non tantum rubea aparuit eius caro, set ad
50   litteram sanguis emanavit. Unde de ista teneritudine et puritate dicitur

about to return to his Father, he first nourished mankind with his miracles and teaching, and then his disciples with his own flesh and blood. This was that wonderful banquet at which Christ and Judas, God and the devil, the calf and the bear, ate together; Isaiah 9: "The calf and the bear shall feed together." But I ask: where does he rest at midday? If we skillfully consider how midday brings the greatest heat of the day, it is at that time that a shepherd is glad to find a pleasant place for his rest. That place is called pleasant if it is lush with foliage and flowers, and especially if on one side there is some flowing water or a gushing wellspring and on the other tall trees spreading their branches wide with green foliage. Such a place is very delicious in summertime, as one may see from Elijah and the juniper in Kings 19, or from Jonah and the ivy in Jonah 3. Tell these stories if you wish. And in summertime one finds it particularly delightful to rest beneath the hawthorn, whose flowers give a sweet smell and its leaves shade. In the same way, beloved, after that banquet of eternal memory which we have mentioned, in which Christ fed his disciples with himself, there followed a very hot noon, namely on Good Friday, on which the greatest heat occurred. You know that it seems to be hottest when one cannot stand to have clothes on but throws them off. But Christ sustained such heat of love and charity on that day that he threw off his clothes and wanted to lie and rest naked on the cross for our salvation; Daniel 13: "For it was hot weather." The pleasant and lush place which Christ chose before all others was the wood of the cross. This place indeed had flowing water on one side—when "one of the soldiers opened his side with a spear and at once blood and water flowed forth," John 19. Therefore the Church sings at that time: "I have seen water come forth from the temple on the right side," etc. Then Christ laid his head in the shade of the hawthorn when the soldiers wove a crown of thorns and put it on his head, as we saw earlier. This, then, is the hour in which Christ not only fed but also rested, and in which he suffered death for us.

With respect to the age at which God suffered, we must know that he was thirty-three years old, in his youth and tender age. For this reason his suffering was even more painful, because the tenderer a part of our body is, the more painful is the suffering it experiences, as can be seen in the eye. And keep in mind that the flesh of man is tenderer than that of a wild animal, and among men the flesh of a woman is tenderer than that of a man, and among women, that of a virgin more so than that of a woman who has lost her virginity. But Christ's flesh was taken and formed out of the most pure blood of the Virgin, and he himself lived in the most pure virginity until his death. This is shown well by observation. The *Book on Animals* tells us that if someone's flesh is cut after death and found to be red, it is a sure sign of virginity; but if it is white, it is a sign that virginity has been lost. Now, when Christ was pierced with a lance after his death, his flesh not only looked red, but literally blood flowed forth from it. Therefore in Kings 23 is said of

Regum 23: "David sedet in cathedra sapientissimus inter tres, tenerrimus
quasi ligni vermiculus." David autem interpretatur manu fortis vel facie
decorus, et bene Christum signat. Iste enim sedet in cathedra, idest in
cruce. Unde Augustinus in quodam sermone: "Crux, inquit, Christi pacientis
55 facta est cathedra magistri docentis." [f. 50v] Sequitur: "Sapientissimus
princeps inter tres," idest tercius inter latrones quasi princeps latronum,
set tener sicut vermiculus ligni; Psalmista: "Ego sum vermis et non homo."
Et hic nota quod fuit tener in paciendo, set quam durus erit in iudicando!
    Fertur enim quod Salomoni erat avis dicta strucio habens pullum clau-
60 sum in vitrio vase, quem cum mater habere nequiret, tulit de deserto vermi-
culum quendam ex cuius sanguine vitro linito confractum est et sic pullum
liberavit. Spiritualiter iste Salomon est Deus Pater, cui erat quedam
strucio, idest Filius eius coeternus. Set hic Filius habuit pullum, scilicet genus humanum, quasi in vase vitrio, idest in inferno, inclusum. Videns
65 ergo strucio ista quod pullum suum habere nequiret, tulit de deserto vermi-
culum, hoc est, naturam humanam assumpsit de deserto huius seculi. Quo
facto sanguine illius nature assumpto dictum vas infernale linivit et
statim confractum est et pullus liberatus, prout canit Ecclesia:

        Pede conculcans tartara
70   Solvit a pena miseros.

    Circa vero tempus in quo Christus passus est, sciendum quod fuit in Qua-
dragesima, in qua ut communiter omnia animalia ad suam voluptatem magis
excitantur. Et ideo illud tempus magis ordinavit quam aliud pro sua passione, ut sic nos exemplo sui voluptatibus naturalibus et diversis per
75 penitenciam resistamus. Dicit enim Apostolus: "Omnis Christi actio nostra
est instructio." Et ideo dicitur Exodi 25: "Inspice et fac secundum exemplar quod tibi in monte monstratum est." Fertur enim in libro *De naturis
animalium* quod elephans viso sanguine acuitur ad prelium. Verum ut dicitur
Machabeorum 6, unde ante prelium ostendunt illis homines "⟨sanguinem uve⟩
80 et mori." Revera sic fidel⟨i⟩s, considerata per fidem et amantem memoriam
sanguinis Christi effusione, armari debet et acui in prelium contra diabolum, mundum, et carnem. Et certe sic certe bene tempus nostrum ordinamus.
Unde Galatarum 6: "Dum tempus habemus, operemur bonum ad omnes."

---

2 primo] prima C; *add* est O.   5 sol] *add* scilicet O.   8 potest] *add* psalmista O.   10 ad-
mirandum] mirandum O.   11 9] 4 O.   18 iunipero] ienupero C.   30 Et] set O.   35 hora
erat] est ergo hora O.   40 tantum] tanto O.   53 sedet] sedit O.   65 pullum suum] dictum
pullum O.   79 sanguinem uve] vivere C.M.W.   80 fidelis] fideles C.   82 certe] *add* si
O.

this tenderness and purity: "David sits in the chair, the wisest among the
three, most tender like a little worm of the wood." "David" means strong of
hand or beautiful of face and symbolizes Christ. For Christ "sits in the chair,"
namely the cross. Hence Augustine says in a sermon: "The cross of the
suffering Christ has become the chair of the teaching master." The scriptural
quotation then goes on: "The wisest among the three," that is to say, he was
the third among thieves, as if the prince of thieves, but as tender as a little
worm of the wood; according to the Psalmist: "I am a worm and not a man."
Notice that he was tender in his Passion; but how tough will he be in his
judgment!

It is reported that Solomon had a bird called ostrich, which had a chick
enclosed in a glass vessel. As the mother bird could not get to it, she fetched
a small worm from the desert whose blood she rubbed on the glass, which
then broke, and thus she freed her chick. Spiritually interpreted, Solomon is
God the Father, who had an ostrich, his coeternal Son. This Son had a chick,
namely mankind, which was so to speak enclosed in a glass vessel, namely hell.
When this ostrich perceived that it could not get to its chick, it fetched a
small worm from the desert, that is, Christ took human nature from the desert
of this world. He then took blood from this human nature and rubbed it on the
vessel of hell. The latter broke at once and the chick was set free. Therefore the Church sings:

> Treading down on hell he freed
> The suffering from their pain.

With respect to the season in which Christ suffered, we must know that
this was in Lent, during which season all animals normally are stirred up in
their lust. He ordained this season before any other for his Passion so that
by his example we might resist our various natural desires through penance.
For the Apostle says: "Every action of Christ serves for our instruction."
Wherefore it is said in Exodus 25: "Look and do according to the pattern that
was shown you on the mount." In the book *On the Nature of Animals* it is
reported that when an elephant sees blood, he is stirred to combat. For which
reason Maccabees 6 says that before a battle men show elephants "the juice of
the grape and the mulberry." In the same way, a faithful person should meditate in faith and loving memory on the shedding of Christ's blood and thereby
become armed and stirred to do battle against the devil, the world, and the
flesh. If we do this, we surely use our time well. As is said in Galatians 6:
"While we have time, let us work good to all men."

---

7 Cant. 1.6. **11–12** Isa. 11.7. **18–19** 1 Kings 19.3–8. **19** Jon. 4.5–6. **28–29** Dan.
13.15. **31–32** John 19.34. **32–33** Antiphon, see Legg, pp. 11 and 135. **51–52** 2

III.xiii DE QUIBUS CHRISTUS ACCUSABATUR ET QUOCIENS ILLUSUS EST

[M]odo autem quarto restat videre de quibus accusabatur ° [f. 51] ante passionem et quociens illusus. Unde sciendum est quod primo accusabatur quod tributum reddi Cesari prohibebat, secundo quia regem se dicebat, et tercio quia Filium Dei se faciebat. Set contra has accusaciones in Paras-
5 ceves in persona Christi ostenduntur tres ⟨ac⟩cusaciones dum canitur canti- cum illud: "Popule meus, quid feci tibi," etc. Ubi Christus exprob[r]at tria beneficia Iudeis crucifixoribus collata ante illa tempora, que sunt hec, videlicet liberacio ab Egipto, regimen in deserto, et plantator vinee in loco optimo, acsi Christus diceret: Accusas me de tributi reddicione—
10 pocius gracias agere deberes quia [liberavi te a tributo et servitute illa Egipciorum; accusas eciam quando me dixi regem—pocius gracias agere de- beres quia regaliter pavi te in deserto; accusas me tercio quia me Filium Dei dixi esse—pocius gracias agere deberes quia] te in vineam meam elegi et in loco optimo te plantavi ac filium et heredem regni te esse optavi.
15 Unde Bernardus: "O, inquit, bone Iesu, quam dulciter cum hominibus conver- satus es, quam magna et habundantissima eis largitus es, quam dura et aspera pro eis passus es, dura inquam verba, duriora verbera, set ad ulti- mum durissima crucis tormenta." Hec ille.
     Et nota quod Christus passus est opprobriose primo pro iniustis, unde
20 Petri 3: "Christus semel pro peccatis nostris mortuus est, iustus pro iniustis"; secundo ° ab iniustis, iuxta illud Iob 16: "Conclusit me Dominus apud iniustum," etc.; tercio cum iniustis, ut patet Matthei 15 cum dicitur: "Cum eo crucifixerunt duos latrones."
     Nec mirum ergo si gravis erat et contumeliosa passio sua, quia per
25 omnes sensus diffundebatur. Primo passus est in oculis quando lacrimatus est. Et revera iste lacrime erant doloris. Et ideo ascendit in altum, ut longius audiretur; fortiter clamavit ut nullus excusaretur, cuius clamori lacrimas addidit ut sibi compateretur. Alias autem dicitur quod bis lacri- matus est, scilicet in suscitacione Lazari, et ille fuerunt lacrime amoris;
30 unde quidam dixerunt de astantibus: "Ecce, quomodo amabat eum." Secundo super civitatem Ierusalem ex compassione sue future ruine. Unde narrat Iosephus quod biennio [f. 51v] ab imperatore Tito civitas Ierusalem obsessa est, ubi inter cetera mala que graviter obsessos perurgebant tanta fames

Sam. 23.8.   **54–55** Cf. Augustine, *Sermo 234* 2 (PL 38:1116).   **57** Ps. 21.7.   **59–62** See Thomas Cantimpratensis, *Liber de natura rerum* IX.44 (p. 309); the worm is called "thamur." Similarly in *Convertimini*, fol. 110v.   **69–70** From the hymn "Aurora lucis rutilat," stanza 2. Chevalier 1644.   **76–77** Exod. 25.40.   **77–78** Alexander Neckam, *De laudibus divinae sapientiae* IX.67–68.   **79–80** 1 Macc. 6.34.   **83** Gal. 6.10.

III.xiii   OF WHAT CHRIST WAS ACCUSED AND HOW OFTEN TAUNTED

It now remains, in the fourth place, to consider what Christ was accused of before his Passion and how often he was taunted. About this we must know that he was firstly accused of forbidding to render tribute to Caesar, secondly of calling himself king, and thirdly of making himself Son of God. Against these accusations are set three counter-accusations when the Church on Good Friday sings as if in the person of Christ: "My people, what have I done to you," etc. Here Christ reproaches the Jews who crucified him on account of three good deeds he had conferred on them before that time, which are: their liberation from Egypt, their guidance through the desert, and his planting the vineyard in an excellent place. It is as if Christ were saying: you accuse me about rendering tribute, but instead you should give thanks that I freed you from giving tribute and being slave to the Egyptians; you further accuse me of calling myself king, but instead you should give thanks that I fed you like a king in the desert; you accuse me thirdly of calling myself the Son of God, but instead you should render thanks that I have chosen you as my vineyard and planted you in an excellent place and wanted you to be my son and heir of the kingdom. Therefore Bernard exclaims: "O good Jesus, how sweetly you talked with men, how great and abundant gifts you gave them, and how hard and sharp pains you suffered for them. Hard were the taunts, harder the strokes, but hardest of all the torment of the cross."

Notice also that Christ suffered shamefully, in the first place for the unjust; hence Peter 3: "Christ died once for our sins, the just for the unjust." In the second place, he suffered from the unjust, according to Job 16: "God has shut me up with the unjust man." And in the third place, he suffered with the unjust, as is shown in Matthew 15: "With him they crucified two thieves."

No wonder, then, that his Passion was grievous and shameful, for it spread through all his senses. First, he suffered in his eyes, when he wept. Those were indeed tears of pain. And he climbed up high so that he might be heard farther; he cried out loud so that no one might excuse himself; and he added tears to his cry so that men should have compassion with him. Elsewhere he is said to have wept on two other occasions, namely when he raised Lazarus from death—and those were tears of love; wherefore some of the bystanders said:

ibi invaluit quod parentes a filiis et e contrario, viri ab uxoribus et e
35   contrario, cibum non tantum de manibus verum eciam de dentibus rapiebant.
Iuvenes autem etate forciores velud simulacra per vias oberrando pre fame
exanimes mortui ceciderunt. Illi eciam qui mortuos super mortuos sepeliebant, sepe et ipsi mortui super [eos] cadebant. Fetor[em] itaque cadaverum
non ferentes ex publico sumptu ipsa sepeliebant, set deficiente sumptu et
40   invalescente cadaverum multitudine, de muro illa precipitare compulsi sunt.
Titus vero civitatem circuiens, cum vidisset valles cadaveribus repletos et
totam patriam ex eorum fetore corruptam, manus suas cum lacrimis lavit et
ad celos respiciendo ait: "Deus, tu vides quia hoc non facio." Tanta eciam
fames ibi erat quod calciamenta cum corrigiis commedebant. Tandem secundo
45   anno Vaspasiani Titus Ierusalem cepit et captam subvertit, templumque
funditus destruxit. Et sicut Iudei Christum pro triginta denariis vendiderunt, sic et ipse Titus pro uno denario triginta vendidit Iudeos. Et prout
narrat id⟨em⟩ Iosephus, sic pro tunc nonaginta septem milia vendiderunt et
undecies centena milia interierunt. Nec mirum ergo si tot mala isti civita-
50   ti ventura presciens Christus ex compassione super illam flevit dicens:
"Si cognovisses et tu." Secundo passus est in auditu, tot opprobria, tot
eciam blasphemia[s] audiendo, quando vocabant illum "filium fabri," "menda-
cem," et "demonem [habentem]," et cetera huiusmodi. Tercio in odoratu, quia
magnum fetorem sentire potuit in monte Calvarie, ubi ut predicitur dampna-
55   torum cadavera putrida et feda fuerant proiecta. Quarto in gustu, quando
ipsi optulerunt ei [f. 52] acetum cum mirra et felle mixtum ut cicius per
acetum moreretur. Quinto in tactu, quia "a planta pedis usque ad verticem
capitis non fuit in eo sanitas."
       Circa autem suam illusionem est sciendum quod quatuor vicibus erat
60   illusus. Primo in domo Anne, ubi recepit sputa et alapas et oculorum vela-
cionem; unde Bernardus: "Vultum tuum, inquit, o bone Iesu, desiderabilem,
in quem desiderant angeli prospicere, sputis coinquinaverunt, manibus percusserunt, velo pro derisione cooperuerunt, nec amaris vulneribus peperce-
runt." Secundo in domo Herodis, qui eum fatuum [et] non sane mentis esti-
65   ma⟨ns⟩, quia sibi non respondit, pro derisione illum veste alba indui
precepit; unde in vestitu superbientes redarguit Bernardus in persona
Christi dicens: "Tu, inquit, homo es et habes sertum de floribus, et ego
Deus et homo coronam spineam; tu cyrothecas in manibus et calciamenta in
pedibus, et ego clavos defixos; tu eciam albis vestibus tripudias, et ego
70   pro te derisus ab Herode remissus fui ad Pilatum in veste alba; tu habes
latus apertum per vanam gloriam, et ego latus pro te fossum et lanceatum.
Et tamen reverte[re] ad me, dicit Christus, et ego suscipiam te." Tercio in
domo Pilati, quando milites clamide coccinea ipsum circumdederunt et coronam spineam super capud suum posuerunt et genibus flexis dixerunt, "Ave,
75   rex Iudeorum." Secundum autem Magistrum Historiarum, corona illa spinea

"Behold, how much he loved him"; the other time he wept over the city of Jerusalem, out of compassion for its coming destruction. Regarding the latter, Josephus tells us that Jerusalem was besieged by the emperor Titus for two years; among other sufferings which heavily afflicted the besieged citizens, such a great famine arose that parents tore away the food not only from the hands but even from the very teeth of their children, and vice-versa, and husbands from their wives, and vice-versa. Young men, the strongest in their age, walked by the ways like shadows and fell down dead, made lifeless by hunger. And those who buried the dead upon dead, themselves often fell dead on top of them. Unable to stand the stench of the corpses, they buried them at public expense, but when the public funds ran out and the number of corpses grew, they were compelled to toss them over the wall. When Titus, passing around the city, noticed the ditches filled with corpses and the entire land infected with their stench, he washed his hands with his tears and looking up to heaven said: "God, you see that I am not doing this." So great was the famine then that they ate their shoes with the strings. Finally, in the second year of Vespasian, Titus took Jerusalem and destroyed it and razed the Temple. And as the Jews had sold Christ for thirty denarii, so Titus sold thirty Jews for one denarius. As Josephus reports further, they then sold 97,000 Jews, and 1,100,000 perished. No wonder, then, that Christ in his foreknowledge that so much suffering was to befall this city wept over it out of compassion, saying: "If you but knew." Second, he suffered in his sense of hearing, when he heard so many taunts and blasphemies, as they called him "carpenter's son," "liar," "having a demon," and the like. Third, he suffered in his sense of smell, for he could smell the great stench on Mount Calvary, where, as we said earlier, the putrid and ugly corpses of condemned criminals had been thrown. Fourth, he suffered in his sense of taste, when they offered him vinegar mixed with myrrh and gall, that he might die sooner through the vinegar. And fifth, he suffered in his sense of touch, for "From the sole of his foot unto the top of his head there was no soundness in him."

With respect to his taunting we must know that he was taunted four times: first in the house of Annas, where he was spat upon, given blows in his face, and blindfolded; whence Bernard says: "Your lovable face, O good Jesus, which the angels desire to look upon, they stained with their spittle, struck with their hands, covered with a veil in derision, and did not spare to hurt with bitter wounds." The second time he was taunted in the house of Herod, who, judging him to be a fool and not of a sane mind because he gave him no answer, had him clothed in a white garment in order to have him scorned; whence Bernard, in the person of Christ, reproaches those who take pride in their clothing and says: "You are a man and wear a garland of flowers, and I am God and man and wear a crown of thorns; you have gloves on your hands and shoes on your feet, and I nails driven through them; you dance in white garments, and I was

erat de iunctis marinis, quorum acies non minus dura spina est et penetra-
tiva. Quarto in cruce, quando principes et sacerdotes illudebant ei dicentes illud Matthei 27: "Si rex Israel es, descende de cruce," etc. Unde
Bernardus: "Interim, inquit, pacienciam magis exibet, humilitatem commen-
80 dat, obedienciam implet, perficit caritatem." In hiis ergo quatuor gemmis
virtutum quatuor crucis cornua ornantur, quia [f. 52v] pro eminenciori
ponitur caritas superius, a dextris obediencia, a sinistris paciencia, set
humilitas, radix omnium virtutum, in profundo, nam ab ea omnia bona sancta
et perfecta procedunt.

---

1 accusabatur] *add* quod C.   5 accusaciones] excusaciones C.   8 et] *om* O.   12 me ter-
cio] *om* M.   16 habundantissima] *add* bona O.   21 secundo] *add* pro inimicis et C.
26 erant] fuerunt O.   35 de(2)] ab ipsis O.   38 eos] C *reads* supercadebant.   46 de-
struxit] subvertit O.   pro] *om* O.   48 idem] illud C.   50 Christus] *add* si O.   52 blas-
phemias] blasphemia C.M.   55 fuerant] fuerunt O.   56 ei] *om* O.   58 fuit] erat O.
63 cooperuerunt] operuerunt O.   65 estimans] estimavit C.   69 eciam] *add* in O.
73 clamide] clamidem C?   ipsum] illum O.   80 perficit] et proficit O.   81 eminenciori]
supereminenciori O.

III.xiv   FORMA ET VIRTUS CRUCIS

[Q]uinto ergo et ultimo iam videndum est de forma ipsius crucis et eius
virtute. Est ergo sciendum quod ipsa crux tunc temporis erat supplicium
dampnatorum, et crudelius et vilius quod poterat inveniri, ad modum thau
formata. Set revera crux Christi ex quatuor lignis specialiter fabricata.
5 Cuius pes erat cipressi, que nec aquis nec terris putrescit. Et ideo credentes Iudei Christum numquam depositurum de cruce, ideo cipressum pro
firmitate in terra fixerunt. Secundo cedrus erat longitudo crucis erecta,
que arbor est odorifera, habens calidam naturam, colorem aliqualem rubeum.
Unde propter eius suavem odorem illam in longitudinem posuerunt ne fetorem
10 crucifixi sentirent transeuntes. Talis enim, ut videtur, erat opinio Iudeorum pessimorum. Tercio latitudinem crucis in signum victorie de palma
construxerunt, que antiquitus erat [signum victorie. Nam secundum poetas
victores palma coronabantur. Quia ergo Iudei] credebant se Christum devi-
cisse et victoriam de eo habuisse, latitudinem crucis de palma posuerunt.
15 Quarto de oliva fecerunt tabulam, in signum pacis, credentes pacem inter
illos in eternum fore Christo crucifixo. In cuius figura legitur Genesis 8

scorned for your sake and sent from Herod to Pilate in a white gown; your side
is open through vainglory, and mine is cut and pierced for you. Yet return to
me (says Christ) and I shall receive you." The third time he was taunted in
the house of Pilate, when the soldiers wrapped him in a purple cloak and put a
crown of thorns on his head and with bent knees said, "Hail, King of the Jews."
According to the Master of the *Historia*, that crown of thorns was made from
water rushes, whose point is not any less hard and piercing than thorns. The
fourth time he was taunted on the cross, when the princes and priests mocked
him saying, as in Matthew 27: "If you are the king of Israel, come down from
the cross," etc. Whence Bernard says: "Meanwhile, he shows more patience,
commends humility, fulfills obedience, and practices charity." The gems of
these four virtues decorate the four points of the cross, for on the top is
placed charity, on the right arm obedience, on the left patience, but at the
bottom humility, the root of all virtues, from which all good things that are
perfect and holy derive.

The material of this chapter parallels largely the first part of the chapter on the Lord's Passion in *Leg. aurea*, pp. 224–227, except for lines 19–23, 31–51, and 75–77.   **6** From
the Improperia, sung on Good Friday; Legg, pp. 112–113.   **20–21** 1 Pet. 3.18.   **21–
22** Job 16.12.   **23** Matt. 27.38 or Mark 15.32.   **30** John 11.36.   **30–31** Luke 19.41–
44.   **31–49** Cf. Josephus, *De bello Judaico* VI.   **51** Luke 19.42.   **57–58** Isa. 1.6.
74–75 Matt. 27.29.   **75–77** Peter Comestor, *Hist. scholastica*, In evangelia, 168 (PL
198:1628).   **78** Matt. 27.42.   **79–80** Bernard, *In Resurrectione*, sermo 1, 3 (5:76).

III.xiv   THE FORM AND POWER OF THE CROSS

In the fifth and last place we must now speak of the form of this cross
and its power. We should know, then, that at that time the cross was the
punishment for condemned criminals, the most cruel and vile one that could be
found, formed in the shape of a T. Now, the cross of Christ was especially
built from four kinds of wood. Its foot was of cypress wood, which does not
rot in water or in the earth. Since the Jews believed Christ would never be
taken from the cross, they put its foot of cypress in the ground, for its
solidity. Second, its upright beam was of cedar, which is a sweet-smelling
tree and warm by nature, and somewhat reddish in color. They used this wood
for the upright because of its smell, so that passersby might not smell the
stench of the crucified. Such, as they say, was the thought of the wicked
Jews. Third, as a token of victory they made the crossbeam from a palm tree,
which in ancient times was a sign of victory. For according to the poets,
winners were crowned with palm. Therefore, since the Jews believed they had
overcome Christ and won the victory over him, they made the crossbeam of
palmwood. Fourth, they made a tablet of olive wood, in sign of peace, for they

quod revertens columba ad archam Noe ramum olive virentis in ore afferebat,
in signum, ut dicunt doctores, quod pax inter Deum et hominem erat reformata. De illis quatuor habentur tales versus:

20   Stipes cipresssi, cedrus quod tendit in altum,
        Palma transversa, titulum portavit oliva.

De ista ergo cruce figuram habemus Danielis 4 de arbore illa quam
vidit Nabugodonosor "in medio terre," cuius "altitudo ni- [f. 53] mia" quia
"proceritas eius" celos tangebat, cuius "aspectus erat usque ad terminos
25   terre, folia eius pulcherrima, et fructus eius nimius, esca universorum in
ea; subter quam habitabant animalia et bestie, in ramis eius conversabantur
volucres celi, et ex ea vescebatur omnis caro." Hec in textu. Spiritualiter
autem loquendo hec omnia faciliter de cruce exponi possunt. Ipsa enim crux
stabat in medio terre, et non tantum ad litteram, verum eciam spirituali-
30   ter. Videmus enim ad sensum quod illud quod est in medio se habet equaliter
ad extrema, unde omnibus in circuitu est commune. Revera sic ista crux in
qua Christus iuxta Psalmistam operatus est salutem in medio terre stat in
medio, ut ad illam fugiant Iudei et gentiles omnes, et non tantum iusti set
maxime peccatores. Cuius altitudo celos tangebat, nam ab inferno usque ad
35   celos protendunt rami sue virtutis, dum alterum spoliavit, alterum restau-
ravit.
        "Folia eius," idest verba Christi in cruce pendentis, "pulcherrima."
Quorum verborum primum fuit pietatis et misericordie, quando dixit illud
Luce 23: "Pater, dimitte illis," etc. Secundum, societatis et iusticie,
40   quando dixit latroni: "Hodie mecum eris in paradiso," quia sicut socii in
passione, ita et in consolacione. Tercium, amoris matris benedicte, quando
dixit: "Mulier, ecce filius tuus," et ipsam [Virginem] virgini commendavit,
quia "cum sancto sanctus eris," etc. Quartum fuit simplicitatis et innocencie, quando dixit: "Deus meus, Deus meus," etc. Quintum, amoris, desiderii,
45   et angustie, quando dixit: "Sicio," scilicet salutem humani generis. Sextum
fuit ° fortitudinis et perseverancie, cum dixit: "Consummatum est," scilicet opus redempcionis nostre. Septimum fuit perfecte obediencie, quando
dixit: "Pater, in manus tuas," etc.
        Sequitur in figura "et fructus eius nimis." Nam Christus esca et cibus est
50   omnium, hominum scilicet et angelorum. Nam ipse dicit Iohannis 6: "Caro
mea vere est cibus, et sanguis meus vere est potus," etc. Set "subtus [f.
53v] habitabant animalia," idest mundiales, qui non faciunt que sursum
sunt, set ad terram per cupiditatem inclinantur. "In ramis eius conversabantur volucres celi," idest religiosi terrena spernentes et per contempla-
55   cionem in supernis conversantes. Ista ergo arbor crucis lignum vite est;
"qui apprehenderit illam, beatus."

believed that with Christ's crucifixion there would be peace among them forever. A type of this occurs in Genesis 8, where we read that on its return to Noah's ark the dove brought a green olive branch in its beak as a sign, as the Fathers explain, that peace between God and man had been restored. About these four we have these verses:

> The foot of cypress wood, the upright trunk of cedar,
> The palm across, and olive bore the title.

Of this cross we find a type in Daniel 4, in the tree which Nebuchadnezzar saw "in midearth," which was "very tall" so that "its end" touched the sky; it "could be seen as far as the ends of the earth; its foliage was most beautiful, and it had much fruit, to feed all men on earth; beneath it lived beasts, and in its branches the birds of the sky; and all flesh ate from it." Thus in Holy Scripture. All these things can be interpreted with reference to the cross. For the cross stood in the middle of the earth, not only literally but also allegorically. For we can observe that what is in the middle is equidistant from the ends and thus belongs equally to all things around it. In this way the cross, on which according to the Psalmist Christ gained salvation in the midst of the earth, stands in the center, so that all the Jews and the Gentiles may flee to it, and not only the righteous but above all the sinners. Its height touched the sky, for the branches of its power extend from hell to heaven, since it has despoiled the former and restored the latter.

"Its leaves were most beautiful," that is, the words of Christ as he hung on the cross. His first word was one of pity and mercy, when he said, in Luke 23: "Father, forgive them," etc. The second was a word of fellowship and justice, when he said to the thief: "Today you shall be with me in paradise," for as they were fellows in their Passion, so too in their consolation. The third was a word of love for his blessed mother, when he said: "Woman, behold your son" and commended the Virgin to a virgin, because "with the holy you will be holy," etc. The fourth was a word of simplicity and innocence, when he said: "My God, my God," etc. The fifth was one of love, desire, and anxiety, when he said: "I thirst," namely for the salvation of mankind. The sixth was a word of strength and perseverance, when he said: "It is consummated," namely the work of our redemption. And the seventh was a word of total obedience, when he said: "Father, into your hands," and so forth.

In the biblical *figura* then follows: "And it had much fruit." For Christ is food and nourishment for all, for men as well as angels. He himself says in John 6: "My flesh is meat indeed, and my blood is drink indeed," etc. But "beneath it dwelled animals," that is, the worldly-minded who do not do the things above but are bent to the earth in their desires. "In its branches dwelled the birds of the sky," that is, the religious, who scorn earthly values

Circa enim virtutem istius crucis est sciendum, prout narrat Vincencius in *Speculo historiali*, si lupus vellet hominem invadere et homo ponat
signum aliquod inter eos, statim timet lupus fraudem, eo quod putat illud
60   erectum esse ad sui capcionem, et fugit. Revera sic diabolus, quando vidit
signum crucis erectum, statim fugit.

Et ideo narrat Gregorius in libro *Dialogorum* de quodam Iudeo [qui] per
patriam transiens a casu sero hospitabatur in quodam templo ydolorum. Qui
quamvis infidelis de virtute crucis cogitans, quam quasi clipeum habuerunt
65   Christiani contra diabolum et cetera mala, fecit sibi circulum in loco quo
iacebat undique signo crucis munitum. Tandem circa mediam noctem timens et
anxiatus vidit quamplures demones venientes de suis maleficiis compotum
reddituros. Quem cum percepissent accesserunt ipsum suffocare volentes, set
virtute sancte crucis ultra circulum accedere non audebant. Quo viso horri-
70   bili clamore dicebant: "Heu, heu, vas vacuum set signatum!" Unde ipse ad
fidem conversus ab episcopo in crastino baptizatus est.

Contigit eciam in conventu Fratrum Minorum Salopie quendam fratrem ad
mortem infirmari nomine Warinum ⟨Souȝth⟩, cui alius frater ministravit
dictus frater Thomas de Whitchirch. Cum ergo esset dictus infirmus fere in
75   ultimis et crux ad modum fratrum ante eum esset erecta, tremebunde suspexit
et pro lectore [f. 54] domus fortiter clamavit. Quod autem dictus servitor
audiens celeriter accurrit et causam clamoris quesivit et quid cum lectore
vellet interrogavit. Cui ille: "Nam intraverunt per fenestras et hostia
quasi infiniti demones et totam domum impleverunt, et cum sim simplissime
80   literature, ferventissime opponunt michi de Trinitate increata et fide
catholica, nec scio respondere. Et ideo pro lectore festinetis, ut me
adiuvet et pro me respondeat." Quo audito dictus servitor cum impetu crucem
deposuit et in manibus infirmi tradidit, et ait: "Ne timeas, quia si nes-
cias respondere, iste pro te optime respondebit quousque rediero." Et pro
85   lectore festinavit. Quo facto quasi in momento in risum altissimum prorupit. Unde eius servitor admirans velociter revertens causam tanti risus
subitanei ab eo quesivit. Cui ille: "Quamcito, inquit, istum responsalem
michi dedisti, quasi conclusi et confusi omnes festinantissime fugerunt. Et
in tantum festinant per fenestras et ostia fugere quod ut michi videtur
90   unusquisque collum super dorsum alterius rumpere non desistit." Et sic per
virtutem sancte crucis a temptacione demonum liber evasit.

Item pro virtute sancte crucis nota *Vitam sancti Cipriani*, et in
Dialogis et in *Vitas Patrum* quamplura mirabilia, et ideo hic pertransio.

Merito ergo adoranda est sancta crux, quia in omni necessitate protegit,
95   iuxta illud versus:

Per crucis hoc signum salvetur quodque benignum.
Et per idem signum fugiat procul omne malignum.

and meditate in contemplation on higher things. This tree of the cross, therefore, is the tree of life; "he who retains it is blessed."

With respect to the power of this cross we should know that, as Vincent
tells us in his *Mirror of History*, if a wolf wants to fall upon a man, and the
man places some sign between himself and the wolf, the wolf at once fears some
trick because he suspects that the sign is put up in order to catch him, and so
he flees. In the same way, the devil flees at once when he sees the sign of
the cross put up.

And Gregory in his book of *Dialogues* reports of a Jew who traveled through
his country and, as it was late, happened to stay overnight in a pagan temple.
Though he was an unbeliever, he thought of the power of the cross which Christians used as a shield against the devil and other evils; and he made for
himself a circle in the place where he lay and fortified it all around with the
sign of the cross. About midnight, he—filled with fear and anxiety—saw many
demons coming together to give an account of their evil deeds. As they noticed
him, they rushed to throttle him, but through the power of the cross dared not
come across the circle. When they perceived this, they cried with a horrible
shout: "Woe, you empty vessel, yet marked with the cross!" By this he was
converted to the faith and the next day baptized by the bishop.

Further, in the house of the Franciscans at Shrewsbury it happened that a
friar by the name of Warren South lay dying and was cared for by another friar
called Thomas of Whitchurch. As the sick man was near his end and a cross was
placed before him, as is the custom of friars, he looked about him with trembling and called loudly for the lector of the house. His aforementioned servitor heard this, came quickly to him, and asked him for the reason of his
calling and what he wanted the lector for. Warren said: "An almost infinite
number of demons have just come through the windows and doors and filled the
whole house; and since I have very little learning, they are pressing me very
hard with questions about the uncreated Trinity and about our Catholic faith,
and I don't know how to answer. Run for the lector that he may help and answer
for me!" On hearing this, the servitor took down the cross and thrust it
firmly into the sick man's hands, saying: "Don't be afraid; if you don't know
how to answer, this one will answer for you well till I return." And he ran
off for the lector. At this, the dying man almost instantly broke into loud
laughter. Then the servitor was amazed and returned quickly and asked him for
the reason of this sudden laughter. The sick man then said: "As soon as you
gave me this respondent, all the demons started to run away in great hurry as
if they were overcome and confounded. And they are rushing so much to get
through the windows and doors that it seems to me each one of them cannot help
breaking his neck on the back of an other." And thus he went free of the
demons' temptation through the power of the cross.

Regarding the power of the cross, see also the *Life of Saint Cyprian* and

Et hec de invidia et caritate ad presens dicta sufficiunt. Dicendum
est modo de aliis beneficiis caritative nobis manifestatis in suo ingressu
100   in [hunc mundum, progressu in] mundo, et egressu de mundo.

---

10 videtur] dicitur O.   **14** eo] illo O.   **35** sue virtutis] suas virtutes M.R.   **41** ita] sic
O.   **46** fuit] *add* scilicet C.   **48** etc.] commendo spiritum meum O.   **50** 6] *om* O.
52 faciunt] sapiunt M.R *both corr.*   **59** putat] credit O.   **60** vidit] videt O.   **62** narrat . . . in] narratur O.   **69** sancte] *om* O.   **70** dicebant] dixerunt O.   **71** crastino]
crastinum O.   **73** Souȝth] gurthi C. *Where the two friars are fully named, their names are
clearly* Warinus (Warren) South *and* Thomas de Whitchurch(e); gurthi *and* gouȝth (R.M)
are evident scribal corruptions.   **77** accurrit et] acurrens O.   **78** interrogavit] *om* O.
Nam] iam O.   **82** adiuvet] iuvet O.   **83–84** nescias] nescis O.   **88** fugerunt] fugiunt
O.   **89** fugere] effugere O.   **90** super] et O.   **91** sancte] *om* O.   **92** sancte] *om* O.   **96–
97** Per . . . malignum] *the second halves of the two hexameters reversed* O.

III.xv   DE CHRISTI INGRESSU IN HUNC MUNDUM

[S]cito de caritate Christi quam in sua morte benedicta generi humano
ostendit, ⟨est sciendum quod⟩ illam aliis modis [f. 54v] quampluribus nobis
misericorditer manifestavit, sicut patet hic per suum in hunc mundum ingressum, progressum, et egressum. Circa ergo primum, scilicet suum ingres-
5   sum qui patet in suo adventu et nativitate, est sciendum quod ipse naturam
nostram assumpsit propter multas raciones. Prima, quia prevaricator diabolus abstulit nobis Deum, necesse est ideo ut Christus reparator redderet
nobis illum. Secunda, quod quamvis humanitas Filii Dei d⟨e⟩cuit humiliari
ad penas in natura, tamen divina non potuit, eo quod natura divina immuta-
10   bilis est et permanens. Ergo oportuit quod in alia natura, puta humana,
penas pro nobis sustineret. Tercia, ut tanta esset humilitas in Christo
redemptore quanta fuit superbia in homine prevaricatore. Set hominis superbia tanta fuit ut vellet esse Deus; unde econtra tanta fuit Filii Dei
humilitas ut vellet fieri homo. Quarta, ad vitandum istud inconveniens,
15   quia si Deus non scivisset incarnari vel voluisset aut non potuisset,
videretur in illo fuisse ignorancia, invidia, aut inpotencia; quod absit
dicere aut sentire.
Et nota quod sicut mos est modernorum nobilium quod mortuo aliquo tali
quod nobilior dominus et eius sanguini propinquior primo faciet oblacionem
20   pro eo et eius scutum in altari offerret, sic spiritualiter loquendo.
Nobilis et valens valde erat primus parens, eo quod tamquam regem et imperatorem omnium terrenorum instituit Deus et omnia subiecit sub pedibus

many miracles in the *Dialogues* and the *Lives of the Fathers*; because of them I
now pass on. The holy cross therefore should rightly be worshipped, for it
protects us in every need, after these verses:

Through this sign of the cross may every good be protected,
And through the same sign let every evil flee far.

These things regarding envy and charity suffice for the moment. We now
turn to other benefits Christ has shown us through his charity, in his entrance
into this world, his journey through it, and his departure from it.

16–17 Gen. 8.11.   **22–27** Dan. 4.7–9.   **32** Ps. 73.12.   **39** Luke 23.34.   **40** Luke
23.43.   **42** John 19.26.   **43** Ps. 17.26.   **44** Matt. 27.46.   **45** John 19.28.   **46** John
19.30.   **48** Luke 23.46.   **50–51** John 6.56.   **56** Prov. 3.18.   **62–71** Gregory, *Dialogi*
III.7 (SC 260:279–284).   **72–91** The story also appears in a collection of tales in Leices-
ter, Wyggeston Hospital, MS 1.D.50/xiii/3/1, fol. 3v.   **96–97** Cf. *Prov* 21192. For an
English version, see Person, No. 35.

III.xv   CHRIST'S ENTRANCE INTO THIS WORLD

Since we have learned about the charity which Christ showed to mankind in
his blessed death, we should now understand that he showed it to us mercifully
in many other ways as well, as can be seen in his entrance into this world, his
journey in it, and his departure. With respect to the first, that is, his
entrance, which occurred in his advent and nativity, we must know that he took
our nature for many reasons. First, since the devil, the apostate, took God
away from us, it is necessary that Christ our restorer should give him back to
us. Second, although it was fitting that the human nature of the Son of God be
humbled to suffer natural pains, his divine nature could not do so, because
divinity is unchangeable and permanent. Therefore it became necessary that he
should suffer pain for us in his other nature, the human one. Third, so that
in Christ our redeemer there should be as great a humility as there was pride
in man when he first sinned. But man's pride was so great that he wanted to be
God; hence, in contrast, the Son of God's humility was so great that he wanted
to become man. Fourth, in order to avoid the following incompatibility: if God
had not known how to become man or had not wanted to or been able to, it would
seem that there would have been ignorance, envy, or powerlessness in him; which
it be far from us to say or think.

And notice that there is this custom among noblemen of our day: when one
of them dies, the most noble lord and closest relative will present the first
offerings for him and offer his shield at the altar. So is it also in the
spiritual realm. Our first parent was very noble and valorous, for God had set

eius. Qui tamen, cum esset mortuus, non habebat in terris ex omnibus pro-
pinquis et amicis qui iuste et digne scutum eius potuit portare et ibi in
25   altari offerre, eo quod inquinata hostia non potest inquinatos mundare. Et
ideo ex nimia caritate sua quam habuit ad nos venit Dei Filius tamquam
proximus sanguine et nostram naturam assumpsit sine peccati contagione, et
scutum [f. 55] Ade, nostri generis primi parentis, in altari optulit. Set
quia scutum deformatum per peccatum ° nimis indecens erat, ideo Christus
30   eius scutum ordinavit quod erat satis decens. Primus enim parens, scilicet
Adam, habuit scutum triangularem de superbia, avaricia, et concupiscencia.
Et ideo econtra Christus Dei Filius nostri honoris et salutis zelator
precipuus scutum pulcherrimum et decentissimum publice pro nobis optulit et
ostendit de humilitate, paupertate, et castitate. Et quia primus parens
35   scutum suum in arbore vetita appendit, ideo Dei Filius pro nostra salute
eius scutum in ligno crucis expandit, iuxta illud ecclesiastici cantus:
"Vexilla regis prodeunt," etc.
      Est eciam sciendum quod cicius Filius quam Pater aut Spiritus Sanctus
decuit incarnari, quamvis sint indivisa opera Trinitatis. Sicut patet de
40   tribus domicellis unam illarum induentibus, inter quas ut patet quicquid
facit una, facit et alia pro illa induicione; similiter et tercia, et tamen
una sola illarum trium induitur. Eodem modo dicendum est de Christi incarnacione. Quandoque enim ipsa incarnacio attribuitur Patri, sicut patet
secundum illud Apostoli: "Cum venerit plenitudo temporis, misit Deus Filium
45   suum in terris," etc. Quandoque Filio, sicut in evangelio: "Exivi a Patre
et veni in mundum." Quandoque Spiritui Sancto. Et tamen tantum Filius est
incarnatus. Et hoc propter multas raciones. Prima racio est ut per eandem
sapienciam qua mundum condidit, iterum per eandem mundum repararet. Set
hoc fuit per Filium; ergo, etc. Secunda, ut ille qui Filius erat in divinitate
50   foret in humanitate. Tercia, ne ⟨idem esset⟩ Pater et Filius, si Pater de
homine nasceretur, et ideo Filius incarnatus. Quarta, quod congruencius
mittebatur ille qui est ab alio quam ille qui est a nullo. Quinta, quod
ille qui dat dampni occasionem, dampnum dedisse videtur. [f. 55v] Set sic
de Filio in ruina hominis et non de Patre aut Spiritu Sancto; ergo, etc.
55   Exemplum ad hoc in figura Ione, ubi legitur quod orta tempestate in
mari dixit: "Si propter me orta est tempestas, mittite me in mari." Et
cecidit sors super eum, et eiectus absortus est a cete. In cuius ventre
tribus diebus et tribus noctibus legitur permansisse. In sacra enim scriptura due leguntur tempestates fuisse, quarum una orta est in celo inter
60   Deum et angelos malos, de quibus ad presens pertransio. Set secunda que in
terra est fuit tumor superbie ex vana cupiditate divine sapiencie, que
Filius Dei est. Promiserat autem serpens mulieri dicens: "Si comederitis,
eritis sicut dii scientes bonum et malum," Genesis 2. Cum ergo secundum
Magistrum *Sentenciarum* Patri appropriatur potencia, Filio sapiencia, et

him as king and emperor over the whole earth and put everything under his feet.
But when he died, there was no relative or friend on the whole earth who could
rightfully and worthily carry his shield and offer it on the altar, because a
defiled host cannot purify those who are defiled. Therefore, out of the great
love he had for us, the Son of God came as our closest relative and took our
nature upon himself without stain of sin, and he offered the shield of Adam,
first parent of our race, on the altar. But since in its deformity through sin
this shield had become too unfitting, Christ fashioned a shield for him that
was fully fitting. Our forefather, Adam, had a triangular shield of pride,
avarice, and concupiscence. In contrast, Christ, the Son of God, wholly zeal-
ous for our honor and salvation, offered for us and displayed publicly a most
beautiful and becoming shield which was made of humility, poverty, and chastity. And since our first parent hung his shield on the forbidden tree, the Son
of God displayed his shield for our salvation on the tree of the cross, according to the Church's hymn: "The king's banners go forth," etc.

  We must also realize that it was more fitting that the Son should become
man rather than the Father or the Holy Spirit, even though the works of the
Trinity are indivisible. This is seen in the group of three damsels who clothe
one among them: the gesture which one of them makes in the act of clothing is
repeated by the second and by the third likewise, and yet only one of the three
is being clothed. In the same way can one speak of Christ's incarnation. For
sometimes the incarnation is attributed to the Father, as in the words of the
Apostle: "When the fullness of time had come, God sent his Son to the earth,"
etc. Sometimes it is attributed to the Son, as in the Gospel: "I have gone
out from the Father and come into the world." And sometimes to the Holy
Spirit. And yet it was only the Son who became man, and this is so for many
reasons. The first is that through the same wisdom by which God created the
world, he would restore it again. But that was done through the Son; therefore, and so forth. The second reason is that he who was a son in his godhead
should be so likewise in humanity. The third is that Father and Son should not
be the same, which would be the case if the Father were to be born of man; and
so it is the Son who became man. Fourth, it was more fitting that he should be
sent who has his being from another than one who has his being from no one.
And fifth, because he who gives the occasion for damnation seems to have given
condemnation; but his pertains to the Son in the condemnation of man, not to
the Father or the Holy Spirit; therefore, etc.

  We have an example of this in the *figura* of Jonah. Here we read that when
a tempest rose at sea, he said: "If this storm has risen for my sake, throw me
into the sea." And the lot fell to him and he was cast out and swallowed by a
whale, in whose belly he is reported to have stayed for three days and three
nights. We read in Holy Scripture that there were two tempests: one arose in
heaven between God and the bad angels, which I pass over for the moment. But

65 Spiritui Sancto clemencia, ergo nec Pater occasio huius tempestatis nec
    Spiritus Sanctus, set Filius, qui utriusque sapiencia; ergo, etc. Dicit
    ergo Ionas iste, Christus scilicet Filius Dei, Deo Patri: "Si propter me
    est hec tempestas, mitte me in mari." Quod et factum est quando missus est
    in mundo, qui est mare magnum et spaciosum, in quo reptilia quorum non est
70 numerus; ubi tandem absortus est in ventre terre tribus diebus et tribus
    noctibus, ut satis patet scripturam intuenti. Patet ergo quod iuste cicius
    erat Filius incarnatus quam Pater aut Spiritus Sanctus.
        Circa quam incarnacionem multa mirabilia acciderunt. Primum testante
    Luce 2, virgo concepit et peperit filium. Item sicut habetur in Crisostomo
75 quod ista nocte nativitatis Christi magis super quodam monte orantibus
    stella quedam iuxta illos apparuit, que formam pueri pulcherrimi habebat,
    in cuius capite crux splendebat. Que magis alloquendo dixit ut in Iudeam
    pergerent et ibi puerum natum invenirent, qui dominus foret tocius crea-
    ture. Narrat eciam Eusebius in *Cronicis* quod ante nativitatem post mortem
80 Iulii Cesaris [f. 56] tres soles in celo apparuerunt, qui tandem in unum
    corpus solare redacti sunt, in signum future nativitatis illius in quo
    tria, scilicet divinitas, anima, et caro humana, insimul convenirent.
        Refert eciam Innocencius papa tercius quod imperator Octavianus toto
    orbe subiugato in tantum senatui placuit ut ipsum pro deo colere intende-
85 bant. Set prudens imperator se mortalem esse considerans nomen immortalita-
    tis noluit usurpare. Cum igitur in die nativitatis Christi Sibilla prophe-
    tissa fuisset adducta ad Capitolium (in quo loco iam Fratres Minores collo-
    cantur), ut per eius oracula ⟨disceret imperator⟩ si maior eo aliquando
    nasceretur, ecce in die medio circulus aureus circa solem apparuit et in
90 medio circuli virgo pulcherrima super quandam aram puerum gestans in gre-
    mio. Quo viso dixit Sibilla: "Hic puer maior te est. Ipsum ergo honorare
    oportet." Quo audito renuit imperator se deum vocari. Et statim eandem
    cameram in honore Beate Virginis et Christi filii eius pro ecclesia fecit
    fabricari, que usque in hodiernum diem dicitur Sancta Maria Ara Celi.
95   Item prout habetur in *Cronica* fratris Martini de Ordine Predicatorum,
    ipso die nativitatis Christi trans Tyberim de taberna emeritoria fons olei
    de terra emanavit ac per totum diem largissimo rivulo fluxit. Similiter
    dicitur ibidem tunc statim ut Maria Christum peperit corruit statua illa
    erea quam in Romiliano palacio Romulus posuerat dicens quod nusquam caderet
100 quousque virgo pareret. Item ibidem dicitur quod eodem anno quo Christus
    natus est tulit eum Ioseph in Egiptum, quo ingrediente corru[er]unt omnia
    ydola Egipti. Et sicut traditur, non fuit templum in Egipto in quo ydolum
    non corruit. Item ibi dicitur quod in *Libro Infancie Christi* fertur quod
    fugiente Maria cum filio Iesu et Ioseph in Egiptum et sub [f. 56v] una
105 palma recubuissent laborante matre eius pre fame, ad preceptum pueri Iesu
    palma se ad terram inclinavit, set eius fructibus collectis ad statum

the second takes place on earth; this was the swelling of pride from the vain
lust for divine wisdom, which is the Son of God. For the serpent had promised
the woman: "If you eat, you will be like gods, knowing good and evil," Genesis
2. But since according to the Master of the *Sentences* power is related to the
Father, wisdom to the Son, and mercy to the Holy Spirit, neither the Father nor
the Holy Spirit was the occasion or this tempest, but the Son, who is the
wisdom of both; therefore, etc. Thus this Jonah, that is, Christ the Son of
God, says to God the Father: "If this tempest is on my account, throw me into
the sea." This happened when he was sent into the large and wide sea of the
world, where there are reptiles without number, and where he finally was swallowed into the womb of the earth for three days and three nights, as anyone can
see who reads the Scripture. Therefore, it is evident that it was rightly the
Son rather than the Father or the Holy Spirit who became man.

At his incarnation occurred many miracles. The first was that a virgin
conceived and bore a son, as is witnessed by Luke 2. Further, as can be found
in Chrysostom, in the night of Christ's birth a star appeared to the Magi as
they were praying on a mountaintop; it had the shape of a beautiful child, on
whose head a cross was shining. The star addressed the Magi and told them to
go to Judea, where they would find a newborn child who would be the lord of all
creation. Also, Eusebius tells in his *Chronicles* that before the nativity,
after the death of Julius Caesar, three suns appeared in the sky, which yet
were gathered into one solar body, as a sign of the coming birth of him in whom
three things were joined together, namely godhead, a human soul, and human
flesh.

Further, Pope Innocent III reports that after the Emperor Octavian had
subdued the entire world, he pleased the senate so much that they wanted to
worship him as a god. But the emperor, who was prudent and judged himself but
mortal, did not want to usurp the title of immortality. Now, as on the birth-
day of Christ the prophetess Sibyl was brought to the Capitol (in which place
now the Franciscans have a church) so that through her prophesying the emperor
might learn whether anyone greater than himself would at any time be born,
behold at midday a golden ring appeared around the sun, and in the center of
the ring a most beautiful virgin on an altar who carried a child on her lap.
When the Sibyl saw this, she told the emperor: "This child is greater than
you; it is he, therefore, who should be honored." Hearing this the emperor
refused to be called a god. And he had that hall at once made into a church in
honor of the Blessed Virgin and her son, Christ, which still today is called
Santa Maria in Ara Celi.

Moreover, as can be found in the *Chronicle* of Friar Martin, of the Friars
Preachers, on the same day of Christ's birth a fountain of oil welled up from
the earth in a shop in Trastevere and flowed all day long in a broad streamlet.
It is likewise said in the same source that as soon as Mary gave birth to

pristinum se erexit. Ac eciam siciente Ioseph ibidem ex precepto pueri Iesu
arida terra fontem aque copiose produxit. Item narratur ibi quod versus
Egiptum cum in ore cuiusdam spelunce hospitati fuissent et de eadem spelun-
110   ca duo magni dracones sunt egressi, a quorum contuitu dum Beata Virgo et
Ioseph terrerentur, ad preceptum pueri Iesu cum omni mansuetudine capitibus
inclinatis deserta pecierunt. Unus eciam leo in ipso itinere adveniens
usque in Egiptum illis in obsequium servus fuit. Hec ibi.
			Preter autem hec miranda sunt et alia quamplura admiranda in nativi-
115   tate istius pueri benedicti. Tunc autem erat primitas ultimata, inmensitas
limitata, eternitas terminata, virginitas fecundata; item longitudo ⟨cur-
ta⟩, latitudo arta, altitudo yma, profunditas plana; item virgo generans,
Deus infans, aqua siciens, panis esuriens. O admiranda et superadmiranda
novitas Christi incarnacionis, cum in ventre Virginis simul coeunt lutum et
120   deitas, fictor et fictile, magestas et parvitas, altum et humile, limus et
subtilitas, firmum et fragile, virtus et infirmitas, vanum et utile. Quia
tunc ibi videbatur mons magnus in parvo milio, mare occeanum in vase modico, circulum descriptum in puncto parvulo, et sol absconditus erat sub
modio. Unde merito posset tunc Deus Pater dicere illud Apocalipsis: "Ecce,
125   nova facio omnia," etc.

---

2 est sciendum quod] et C.   3 hic] *om* O.   8 decuit] docuit C.R.   18 est] *add* adhuc O.
21–22 regem et imperatorum] rex et imperator O.   24 ibi] *om* O.   29 peccatum] *add* et
C.   31 triangularem] triangulum O.   48 condidit] condiderat O.   50 idem esset] illud
esset idem C.   52–53 quod ille] ut iste O.   77 magis] magos O.   86 igitur] ergo O.
88 disceret imperator] diceret imperatori C.   91 Sibilla] *add* imperatori O.   116 termi-
nata] temperata O.   116–117 curta] circa C.   120 deitas] divinitas O.   121 subtilitas]
sublimitas O.   125 etc.] *om* O.

III.xvi   DE TRIPLICI ADVENTU CHRISTI

[C]irca autem Christi adventum sive eius incarnacionem est sciendum quod
tripliciter venit: in ventrem Virginis, in mentem hominis, in fine exami-

Christ, the bronze statue fell over which Romulus had placed in his palace, saying it would never fall as long as a virgin did not have a child. In addition, it is also reported in the same place that in the same year that Christ was born Joseph took him to Egypt, and when he entered that country, all the idols of Egypt fell down. And as tradition has it, there was not a temple in Egypt with an idol that did not fall. The *Chronicle* further says that the *Book of the Infancy of Christ* reports that when Mary with her son, Jesus, and Joseph fled to Egypt and were resting beneath a palmtree, with Mary suffering much from hunger, at the bidding of the child Jesus the palmtree bent to the ground, but when they had picked its fruit, it straightened itself up again. And when Joseph was thirsty in the same place, at the bidding of the child Jesus the dry earth produced a rich wellspring of water. The *Chronicle* further tells us that when the Blessed Virgin and Joseph on their way to Egypt rested at the entrance of a cave and two large dragons came out of it, they were greatly frightened by their sight; but at the bidding of the child Jesus the dragons meekly bowed their heads and made for the desert. Also, a lion came along on the same way and served them obediently until they were in Egypt.

Besides these marvels there were many other miraculous things in the nativity of this blessed child. For then, what was first became last; what was infinite, limited; eternity, bound in time; virginity, made pregnant; further, length, made short; width, made narrow; height, made low; depth, made shallow; and further, a virgin, giving birth; God, an infant; the water, thirsty; and the bread, hungry. O admirable and miraculous novelty of Christ's incarnation, when in the womb of the virgin dust and divinity came together, the potter and his vessel, majesty and smallness, the high and the humble, slime and the sublime, the strong and the frail, power and weakness, the gainless and the useful. For then appeared a large mountain in a small millet, the ocean in a little dish; a circle was circumscribed in a tiny point, and the sun hidden under a bushel. At that moment, God the Father therefore could rightly say the words of Revelation: "Behold I make all things new."

---

37 Hymn for Vespers in Passiontide; Chevalier 21481. For English versions, see *Verses*, pp. 70 and 90.   **44–45** Gal. 4.4.   **45–46** John 16.28.   **56** Jon. 1.12.   **62–63** Gen. 3.5.   **63–65** Peter Lombard, *Sent.* I.xxxiv.3–4 (1:251–252).   **74** Cf. Luke 1.31.   **75–77** Ps.-Chrysostom, *Opus imperfectum*, hom. 2 (PG 56:637–678).   **79–82** Cf. *Leg. aurea*, p. 44.   **83–94** Ibidem, p. 44.   **95–113** Martin of Troppau, *Chronicon*, p. 408.   **124–125** Rev. 21.5.

III.xvi   CHRIST'S THREEFOLD COMING

With respect to Christ's coming or incarnation, we should know that he comes in three ways: into the Virgin's womb, into man's heart, and in the final

nis. Primo in ventrem [f. 57] Virginis: tunc in modum flaminis, Luce 2:
"Spiritus Sanctus super⟨veniet⟩." Secundo in mentem hominis: tunc in modum
5   fluminis, Ysaie 53: "Cum venerit quasi fluvius." Tercio in fine examinis:
tunc in modum fulguris, Matthei 24: "Sicut fulgur exiit ab oriente, sic
erit adventus filii hominis."
     Et nota quod in quolibet istorum adventuum premisit signum, litteras,
et nuncium. In primo autem adventu signa erant ros supra castra, rubus
10 _Moysi, vellus Gedeonis, et virga Aaron. Littera erat illud Ysaie: "Ecce,
virgo concipiet et pariet filium." Nuncius erat angelus Gabriel dicens:
"Ave, gracia plena. Ecce concipies et paries, et vocabis nomen eius Iesum."
     Set nota quod primum signum istum adventum signans, ut dicitur, erat
ros supra castra ad temperandum; de quo Numeri 11 dicitur: "Cum descendis-
15 set ros supra castra, descendit pariter et manna." Hec enim castra bene per
~ Virginis corpus designantur ac per eius animam et spiritus, in quibus
ordinata erant omnia ad istum filium benedictum recipiendum et servandum.
Et nota quod ros numquam descendit nisi quando tempus est serenum, hoc est,
neque nimis calidum neque nimis frigidum. Revera sic nec ista Virgo Maria
20 fuit nimis calida per avariciam neque nimis frigida per desperacionem,
neque nimis humida per carnalitatem neque nimis sicca per desi[di]ositatem.
Cuius serenitatis signum fuit quando ingressus est angelus ad eam, non
invenit ostium apertum, quia frequencias et colloquia hominum vitabat, ne
vel orantis turbaretur silencium vel eius castitatis turbaretur indicium.
25 Sancta enim erat Iudith, et oculorum suorum laqueo captus est Holofernes,
ut patet in historia.
     Signum secundum adventum Christi signans fuit vellus Gedeonis, de quo
Iudicum 6: pluvia descendit in vellus totam aream rigatur⟨a⟩. Nota historiam. [f. 57v] Illud autem vellus caro Virginis est, de quo Christus vesti-
30 mentum sue humanitatis [sumpsit. Et est hic advertendum quod vellus faciliter aquam bibit et de facili comprimendo] ⟨effundit illam⟩. Revera sic
Virgo benedicta aquam gracie de facili a Deo recepit ac ad nos suam transmittit. Numquam enim eius deficiet gracia, quia nunquam exhauriri potuit
eius misericordia. De isto ergo descensu dicit Psalmista: "Descendit sicut
35 pluvia in vellus." Unde Bernardus: "Celestis, inquit, aream rigaturus totum
velleri prius infundit, et mundum Dei Filius redempturus totum precium
contulit in Mariam." Ros enim totus in area et totus in vellere fuit, set
in nulla parte aree fuit totus sicut in vellere et stillicidia. Sic Deus
per Virginem distillat omne bonum gratuitum, cuius stillicidii pars supe-
40 rior est in celo per fruicionem, pars inferior est in terris erga nos per
gracie infusionem, ut graciam perditam per culpam nostram recuperemus, ut
sic res nobis perdita erit nobis salva. Deuteronomii 22 precipitur ut res
perdita sit aput inventorem donec qui perdidit veniens requiret eam. Set
revera gracia Dei a nobis perdita erat a lapsu primi parentis usque ad

judgment. First, into the Virgin's womb, like a breath; Luke 2: "The Holy
Spirit will come." Second, into man's heart, like a river; Isaiah 53: "When
he will come as a stream." And third, at the final judgment, like lightning;
Matthew 24: "As a lightning has come out of the east, so will the coming of
the Son of Man be."

And notice that in each of his comings he has sent before him a sign,
letters, and a messenger. The signs for his first coming were the dew on the
camp, the burning bush of Moses, the fleece of Gideon, and the rod of Aaron.
The letter was that verse of Isaiah: "Behold, a virgin shall conceive and bear
a son." And the messenger was the angel Gabriel saying: "Hail, full of grace.
Behold you will conceive and bring forth a son, and you will call his name
Jesus."

As I said, the first sign that indicated this coming was the dew upon the
camp sent as a relief; of it is written in Numbers 11: "When the dew fell upon
the camp, the manna also fell with it." This camp signifies the body of the
Virgin as well as her soul and spirit, in which everything was set in order to
receive and keep that blessed child. Notice that dew only falls when the
weather is fair, that is, when it is neither too hot nor too cold. Just so,
the Virgin Mary was neither too hot through avarice nor too cold through
despair, neither too humid in fleshly desires nor too dry in sloth. The sign
of her serenity was that, when the angel came to her, he did not find her door
open, for she avoided frequent get-togethers and chats, in order not to disturb
the silence of prayer or to attack the mark of her chastity. For Judith was
holy, and yet Holofernes was caught in the snares of her eyes, as we see in the
biblical story.

The second sign that indicated Christ's coming was the fleece of Gideon,
of which we read in Judges 6 that rain fell on the fleece drenching all the
area around it. Tell the entire story. That fleece is the flesh of the
Virgin, from which Christ took the clothing of his human nature. We should
note that a fleece easily soaks up water and, when it is squeezed, easily sheds
it again. In the same way did the Blessed Virgin easily receive the water of
grace from God, and she passes her grace on to us. Her grace will never be
wanting, for her mercy could never be exhausted. Regarding this falling of the
dew the Psalmist says: "He comes down like rain upon the fleece." Whence
Bernard says: "The heavenly dew that was to drench the area first soaked the
fleece, and God's Son, who was to redeem the world, gave the whole price in
Mary." For all the dew was on the ground and on the fleece, but on no part of
the ground was there so much dew and dropping rain as on the fleece. Thus God
lets every good of his grace drop down through the Virgin. The upper part of
this falling rain is in heaven, for our final enjoyment; the lower part is on
earth, where it comes to us by infusion, so that we may regain that grace we
have lost through our sin, and the thing we had lost will be saved for us. In

45   incarnacionem Christi Iesu, quod fuit per quinque milia annorum et ducentos
     excepto uno, secundum illud:

          Annis quingentis decies rursusque ducentis
          Unus defuerat cum Deus ortus erat.

     Set certe concepto Dei Filio illam invenit Maria, testante angelo Luce 2:
50   "Invenisti graciam aput Deum." Non ergo diffidimus set confidenter ad
     ill⟨a⟩m accedamus et sine murmure nobis illam liberabit.
        Tercium signum adventus Christi fuit rubus Moysi, de quo Exodi 3
     dicitur: Descendit angelus in flamma ignis et vidit Moyses quod rubus
     arderet et flamma non combureretur in rubo, ad signandum quod partus in
55   Virgine ut rubus illuminabatur [f. 58] set non comburebatur, quia virgini-
     tas Marie non violabatur.
        Et ideo de ea bene dicitur Apocalipsis 12: "Signum magnum aparuit in
     celo, mulier amicta sole et luna sub pedibus eius, et in capite eius corona
     stellarum duodecim." "Signum magnum aparuit in celo, mulier," etc. Spiri-
60   tualiter autem loquendo Beata Virgo erat signum nostre reconciliacionis,
     nostre liberacionis, nostre protectionis, nostre miseracionis, pii auxilii,
     et subvencionis. Et ideo h⟨e⟩c est quasi arcus positus in signum federis,
     Genesis 9, quod peciit Gedeon in signum velleris, ut patet supra. Et hec
     ideo est funiculus coccineus in fenestra Raab, Iosue 2. Et ideo hec est
65   illa virga aurea Assueri regis, Hester 4. Et ideo hec est "illa radix
     Iesse, que stat in signum populorum; ipsam gentes deprecabuntur." Set ipsa
     confert omne bonum, et ideo ipsa est signum peregrinantibus directivum,
     preliantibus protectivum, navigantibus confortativum. Et ideo non incongrue
     stella maris appellatur, quia sicut illa dirigit et rectificat in mari
70   navigantes, sic Beata Virgo dirigit in hoc mundo fluctuantes. Unde Bernar-
     dus in *Omelia super Missus est angelus*: "Si, inquit, insurgunt venti temp-
     tacionum, si incurras scopulas tribulacionem, respice stellam, invoca Ma-
     riam. Ipsam autem sequens non devias, ipsam rogans non desperas, ipsam
     cogitans non erras, ipsa te tenente non corruis, ipsa protegente non me-
75   tuis, ipsa duce non fatigaris, set ipsa propicia pervenis ad portum eterne
     salutis."
        Et nota quod inter omnia signa hoc signum describitur ut utile quia
     "signum," ut mirabile quia "magnum," ut sublime quia "in celo." Et ideo
     ipsa est primo signum dilectionem Dei ad hominem ratificans, tamquam
80   signum sigilli in cedula ratificat ibidem contenta. Et ideo de ea Genesis 9:
     "Archum [f. 58v] meum ponam in nubibus celi, et [erit] signum federis inter
     me et terram." Si enim consideremus istius formam, quomodo est de radiis
     solis generatum, colore ceruleo coloratum, ac contra nos arcuatum, possumus
     in ea tria erga nos considerare, scilicet caritatem, humilitatem, et pieta-

Deuteronomy 22 the law is given that a lost object should remain with its
finder until he who has lost it comes and asks for it. But God's grace had
been lost to us from the fall of our first parent until the incarnation of
Jesus Christ, that is, for 5,200 years minus one, according to the verse:

> Five hundred years ten times, and another two hundred added,
> That number but one year was the time when God became man.

But when she had conceived the Son of God, Mary found that grace again, as
the angel told her in Luke 2: "You have found grace before God." Therefore,
let us not lose faith but go to her with confidence, and she will deliver that
grace to us without murmur.

The third sign of Christ's coming was the burning bush of Moses, of which
is said in Exodus 3 that an angel descended in a flame of fire and Moses saw
that the bush was afire but the bush did not burn, to indicate that in the
Virgin, childbirth would light up like that bush but not burn, because Mary's
virginity was not violated.

Therefore it is well said of her in Revelation 12: "A great sign appeared
in heaven: a woman clothed with the sun, and the moon under her feet, and on
her head a crown of twelve stars." "A great sign appeared in heaven; a woman,"
etc. Spiritually speaking, the Blessed Virgin was the sign of our reconciliation, liberation, protection, commiseration, help, and subvention. Therefore,
she is, as it were, the rainbow set as a sign of covenant, Genesis 9, which
Gideon asked for in the sign of the fleece, as we saw earlier. And she is that
scarlet cord in Rahab's window, Joshua 2. And she is that golden scepter of
king Ahasuerus, Esther 4. And she is also that "root of Jesse, which stands
for an ensign of the people; her the Gentiles shall beseech." But she bestows
all that is good, and thus she is a sign which gives direction to pilgrims,
protection to warriors, and comfort to travelers at sea. Not unfittingly is
she thus called the star of the sea, because as that star directs and points
the right way to sailors, so the Blessed Virgin directs those who are rocked
back and forth in this world. Therefore Bernard says in a homily on *Missus
est angelus*: "If the winds of temptation rise, if you run onto the cliffs of
tribulation, look at the star, call upon Mary. Following her you will not go
astray, asking her you will not despair, thinking of her you will not fall into
error; if she holds you, you will not come to ruin; if she protects you, you
need not fear; if she leads, you will not tire; but if she is well disposed, you
will come to the harbor of eternal salvation."

And notice that among all signs this one is described as useful because
it is "a sign," marvelous because it is "great," and sublime because it is "in
heaven." Thus Mary is, first, a sign that guarantees God's love toward man, as
the sign of a seal on a document makes its contents valid. Therefore Genesis 9

85   tem. Expone ut scis. Est eciam ipsa secundo signum certificans ad modum
     signi paxilli: certificat viatores in semitis ne deviant. Sic ipsa pecca-
     tores dirigit ad portum; unde Ysaie 40 dicitur: "Levabit Dominus signum in
     nacionibus et congregabit dispersos Israel." Et tercio ipsa est signum °
     fortificans peccatores contra hostes ad modum signi vexilli in prelio;
90   Sapiencie 16 dicitur: "In brevi ad correctionem turbati sunt," scilicet
     peccatores superbi, "habentes signum salutis," scilicet Mariam.
        Et sequitur in auctoritate: "Mulier amicta sole." Si enim per solem
     intelligatur gracia, tunc aliquando fuit amicta sole in hac vita, quia
     totaliter impleta erat gracia; Luce 2: "Ave, gracia plena," quasi diceret
95   angelus sic: O Maria benedicta, Dei gracia es repleta, quod totaliter a
     triplici ve es elongata, videlicet primo a ve carnalis concupiscencie, a ve
     mundialis avaricie, a ve infernalis superbie. Quo contra dicitur de pecca-
     toribus obstinatis sine omni gracia illud Apocalipsis: "Ve, ve, ve habitan-
     tibus in terra," eo quod tales in tribus predictis sunt illaqueati. Secun-
100 do, si per solem intelligitur gloria, ⟨tunc⟩ certum est quod iam per solem
     amicta est in patria, ubi iam iuxta illud in Psalmo: "In sole posuit Deus
     tabernaculum suum." Si enim legatur de aliis sanctis quod "fulgebunt iusti
     sicut sol," quanto magis ipsa que solem carne induit, que solem mundo
     protulit, que solem sinu tenuit, in Christi incarnacione, in Christi partu-
105 ricione, in Christi nutricione.
        Sequitur in autoritate: "Et lunam sub pedibus eius," idest Ecclesia
     aut omnis creatura; "et in [f. 59] capite coronam stellarum duodecim," que
     sunt duodecim prerogativa beate Marie, videlicet sanctificacio in utero,
     salutacio ab angelo, humilitas obediens, castitas conveniens, item creduli-
110 tas perficiens, gracia reficiens, conceptus sine libidine, partus sine
     gravamine, item circa prolem misterium, de prole contemplacionis deside-
     rium, de prole singulare martirium, cum prole salutare dominium.
        [C]irca autem secundum adventum Christi, [scilicet] in mente hominis,
     est sciendum quod signa fuerunt secundum illud Psalmi: ° "Percussit pet-
115 ram," idest cor hominis fere obstinatum, "et fluxerunt aque et torrentes
     inundaverunt," scilicet confessionis et satisfactionis. De quibus satis
     patet parte 5; nota infra. Littere autem fuerunt illud Ioelis 2: "Converti-
     mini ad me in toto corde vestro." Set nuncius fuit Iohannes Baptista cla-
     mans: "Penitenciam agite," etc.
120   [C]irca autem tercium adventum, scilicet in fine examinis, signa sunt
     illa Luce 21: "Erunt signa in sole et luna et stellis." Ubi secundum
     Ieronimum in ann⟨a⟩libus Hebreorum quindecim sunt signa examinis illius,
     idest diei iudicii. Quorum primum est quod prima die eriget se mare cubitis
     quadraginta supra altitudinem moncium, stans in loco suo quasi murus.
125 Secunda die tantum descendet quod vix videri poterit. Tercia die belue
     marine apparentes supra mare horribilem dabunt rugitum usque ad celum.

says of her: "I will set my bow in the clouds of heaven, and it shall be the sign of a covenant between me and the earth." If we reflect on the form of the rainbow, how it is created by the rays of the sun, blue in color, and bent toward us, we can think of three things which Mary has toward us, namely, charity, humility, and pity. Explain this. Mary is, secondly, a roadsign which like a signpost directs travelers on their ways that they may not go astray. Thus she directs sinners to their haven; whence Isaiah 40 declares: "The Lord shall set up a standard unto the nations and shall assemble the fugitives of Israel." And thirdly, Mary is a sign that strengthens sinners against their enemies, as a standard does in battle; Wisdom 16: "They were troubled for a short time for their correction," that is, proud sinners, "having a sign of salvation," namely Mary.

And the quoted Scriptural passage continues: "A woman clothed with the sun." If we take "sun" to mean grace, then she was already clothed with the sun in this life, because she was totally filled with grace in accordance with the words of Luke 2: "Hai!, full of grace," as if the angel were saying: O blessed Mary, you are filled with God's grace, because you are totally detached from the triple woe—the woe of fleshly concupiscence, the woe of worldly greed, and the woe of devilish pride. The opposite is said in Revelation of obstinate sinners who are without any grace: "Woe, woe, woe to the inhabitants of the earth," for these are ensnared in the three evils mentioned. If, on the other hand, we take "sun" to mean glory, then it is certain that Mary is presently clothed with the sun in heaven, where now, according to the Psalm, "God has put his tabernacle in the sun." For if we read of other saints that "the just shall shine like the sun," how much more will this be true of her who has clothed the sun with flesh, who gave it to the world, and who held it at her breast in Christ's incarnation, birth, and nursing!

The quoted Scripture text further continues: "And the moon under her feet," that is, the Church or all creation; "and on her head a crown of twelve stars," which are the twelve prerogatives of blessed Mary: her sanctification in the womb, her being greeted by the angel, her obedient humility, suitable chastity, perfect trust, restorative grace, her conceiving without lust, giving birth without pain, her care for her son, her desire to contemplate her son, her unique martyrdom for her son, and her salvific rule with her son.

With respect to the second coming of Christ, namely into man's soul, we should know that its signs were the following, according to the Psalm: "He struck the rock," that is, man's heart that had been quite obstinate, "and the waters gushed out, and the streams overflowed," that is, of confession and satisfaction. For these matters, see below, part 5. But the letters were the words of Joel 2: "Turn to me with all your heart." And the messenger was John the Baptist calling: "Do penance," etc.

With respect to Christ's third coming, namely for the final judgment, its

Quarta die ardebit mare et omnes aque. Quinta die arbores et herbe dabunt
rorem sanguineum. Sexta die ruent omnia mundi edificia. Septima die petre
adinvicem collidentur. Octava die erit generalis terremotus per totum mun-
130   dum. Nona die terra planissime equabitur. Decima die exibunt homines de
cavernis nec valebunt loqui. Undecima die surgent ossa [f. 59v] mortuorum
et stabunt supra sepulcra. Duodecima die cadent stelle de celo secundum
quosdam. Decima tercia die morientur omnes viventes ut iterum resurgant.
Decima quarta die celum et terra ardebunt, idest superficies aeris et
135   terre. Et decima quinta die fiet celum novum et terra nova. Set utrum dies
isti quibus hec fient sint continui futuri an interpolati, ibidem non
exprimitur nec aliquis novit nisi solus Deus.
    Legitur eciam in *Cronicis* quod anno ab urbe condita 324 populus Roma-
nus solidam columpnam marmoream in foro statuerunt, super quam statuam
140   Iulii Cesaris stare fecerunt acsi deus adorandus fuisset. Qui tamen Iulius
in tota sui nobilitate et pompa tria signa recepit quasi premunitoria. Nam
centesimo die ante eius mortem fulmen cecidit ante statuam eius in foro et
de nomine et superscripcione litteram capitalem, scilicet I, abrupit.
Secundum signum erat quod nocte precedente diem obitus sui fenestre thalami
145   cum tanto strepitu aperte sunt ut Cesar de stratu suo exiliens ruituram
domum estimaret. Tercium signum erat quod eodem die obitus sui cum ad
Capitolium rediret, sunt ei littere oblate indices sue mortis iminentis.
Quas si statim legisset, de morte evasisset; set eodem die quo mortuus
fuerat, invente sunt in manu eius adhuc clause.
150   Spiritualiter sic est ex parte ista: Ut enim superbus et peccator
iudicium finale et mortem eternam bene evadat, triplex signum a Trinitate
benedicta recipit. Pater enim primo ostendit suam potenciam, secundo Filius
eius sapienciam, et tercio Spiritus Sanctus suam clemenciam. Primum ergo
signum Iulii Cesaris fuit in delecione capitalis littere sui nominis, per quam
155   litteram intelligo habundanciam diviciarum. Nam hoc precipuum est quod
facit hominem nomen habere in terris, scilicet divicie. Nemo enim nominatur
aut reputatur in populo, [f. 60] ut manifeste patet, nisi fuerit dives,
quia si queratur quis sit maior alicuius ville, statim respondetur quod
ille qui habet plures divicias, et sic preponitur aliis eciam si pessimus
160   fuerit. Patet ergo quod divicie sibi nomen inponunt, quia si dives non
esset, nomen non haberet nec nominatus tunc fuisset. Venit ergo Filius Dei
volens hominem salvare, cui sapiencia attribuitur, et dat sibi signum
primum eius divicias subtrahendo; illum in paupertatem deicit, ut sic
saltem qui per divicias a Deo recessit, per paupertatem redeat, ⟨quia ut
165   dicitur⟩ in Psalmo: "Pauper et inops laudabunt nomen tuum, Domine." In
cuius figura Danielis 4 legitur de Nabugodonosor qui propter suas divicias
equalem se Deo reputabat, set depositus et depauper⟨a⟩tus illum laudabat.
Nota historiam.

signs are those mentioned in Luke 21: "There will be signs in the sun and the
moon and the stars." According to Jerome, in the Annals of the Hebrews, there
are fifteen signs of his judgment, that is, fifteen days of judgment. The
first is that on the first day the sea will rise forty cubits above the highest
mountain and will stand in its place like a wall. On the second day it will
fall so that it can hardly be seen. On the third day sea-monsters will appear
on the sea and make a terrible roar that reaches to the sky. On the fourth day
the sea and all the waters will burn. On the fifth day the trees and herbs
will produce a blood-colored dew. On the sixth day all the buildings of the
world will fall. On the seventh day rocks will clash with each other. On the
eighth day there will be a general earthquake throughout the whole world. On
the ninth day the earth will be absolutely flattened. On the tenth day people
will come out of caves and will not be able to speak. On the eleventh day the
bones of the dead will rise and stand on their graves. On the twelfth day,
according to some, the stars will fall from the sky. On the thirteenth day all
living people will die so that they may rise again. On the fourteenth day the
sky and the earth will burn, that is, the surface of the air and of the earth.
And on the fifteenth day the sky and the earth will become new. But whether
the "days" on which these events will happen are to be continuous or at inter-
vals, the quoted source does not say, nor does anyone know except God alone.

We read in the *Chronicles* that in the year 324 after the founding of Rome,
the Roman people put up a solid marble column in the Forum, on which they
placed a statue of Julius Caesar, who was to be worshipped as a god. But at
the height of his dignity and pomp, Julius received three signs as a forewarn-
ing. For on the hundredth day before his death, a lightning bolt fell in front
of his statue in the Forum and struck off the inital letter, that is, the *J*,
from the inscription of his name. The second sign was that in the night before
his death the windows of his bedroom were flung open with such force that
Caesar rushed from his couch thinking his house was about to fall. And the
third sign was that on the day of his death, as he returned to the Capitol, he
was handed letters with warnings of his imminent death. If he had read them at
once, he would have escaped death; but on the day he died, they were found
still unopened in his hand.

Spiritually speaking, in the same way a proud and sinful person receives a
threefold sign from the Blessed Trinity that he may escape final judgment and
eternal death. For in the first place the Father shows his power, then the Son
his wisdom, and thirdly the Holy Spirit his mercy. The first sign given to
Julius Caesar was the deletion of the initial letter of his name, by which I
understand abundance of wealth. For the latter, that is, wealth, is what
primarily gives people a name on earth. For no one, as can be easily seen, has
a great name or reputation among the people unless he is rich. If you ask who
is the biggest person in some town, you will be told at once that it is so-and-

Secundum signum Iulii Cesaris erat tumultus ad eius camere fenestras,
170   sic quod ipse credidit domum suam esse ruituram. Moraliter hec camera est
corpus humanum, quod cum homo considerat se esse fortem, pulcrum, et
scientem, mox in superbia erigitur et alios per suam fortitudinem deprimit et
contempnit, et sic in viam mortis pedem ponit. Et ideo venit Pater celestis, cui potencia attribuitur, et illum revocat ad viam salutis et sibi dat
175   signum secundum, quando facit tumultum ad fenestras corporis sui, hoc est,
quando inmittit infirmitates in omnia membra et sensus suos, in tantum quod
ad terram per mortem credit totaliter cadere. Quo facto revera ut sepe per
fortitudinem corporalem a Deo recesserunt, per infirmitates revocantur.
Psalmista: "Multiplicate sunt infirmitates eorum et post[ea] accelerave-
180   runt." In cuius figura Machabeorum 2 capitulo 9 de Antiocho superbo habetur
quod pre superbia sibi videbatur fluctibus maris imperare. Dixit eciam se
Iherosolimam venturum et illam congeriem sepulcris Iudeorum facturum. Et
tamen cum sic a Deo humiliatus esset qui prius sidera celi attingere arbi-
trabatur, postea vermes [f. 60v] de eius corpore miserrimo scaturirent, et
185   propter fetorem sic ut nec alii tollerare non possent, ⟨ait⟩: "Iustum est
subditum esse Deo et non paria Deo sentire." Unde illud Hester 23: "Domine
Deus, in dicione tua cuncta sunt posita, et non est qui possit tue resistere voluntati," etc.

Tercium signum Cesaris erat quod littere sue mortis indices erant sibi
190   tradite, quas si legisset mortem evasisset. Et hoc est signum Spiritus
Sancti, cui attribuitur bonitas, qui tunc litteras nostre mortis nobis
tradidit cum sua gracia et bonitate sic consciencias nostras illuminat ut
legere possimus per veram confessionem peccata nostra, quibus mortem merui-
mus eternam, si velimus. Igitur, o peccator, iam considera in adventu Filii
195   [Dei] in carne quomodo opera Trinitatis sunt indivisa. Nam primo habes
signum Filii, qui sua sapiencia novit divicias tribuere et eripere. Habes
eciam signum Patris, qui novit sua potencia fortem facere et prosternere.
Et tercio habes signum Spiritus Sancti, qui vult sua clemencia peccata tua
ad memoriam reducere, et totum pro salute tua, quia secundum quod habetur
200   Iohannis 3: "Nisi signa et prodigia videritis, non credetis." Sic ergo
patent signa triplici⟨s⟩ Christi adventus ad iudicium, cuius adventus
littere scribuntur Apocalipsis ultimo: "Ecce venio cito et merces mea
mecum," etc. Set nuncii erunt Enok et Helias, qui tempore Antichristi
advenient.

205   Unde pro isto in carnem narratur de quodam imperatore Valerio, quod
olim sibi et suis proceribus prophetatum erat quod sibi talis filius nasceretur qui hostes regni sui strenue debellaret et suo imperio subiugaret.
Igitur cum imperatrix concepisset, dictus imperator cum suis proceribus
apud deos sacrificiis instabant diligencius sciscitantes si puer talis
210   esset pariendus quod alico signo evidenti illis innotescere posset. Quibus
tandem responsum est quod si puer ille nasceretur utraque manu clausa vel

so who has great wealth; and thus he is placed before anyone else even if he is
a scoundrel. Thus you see that wealth gives him a name; if he were not rich,
he would have no name or be mentioned in that case. Therefore the Son of God,
to whom we attribute wisdom, comes with the desire to save man and gives him
the first sign: he takes away man's wealth and casts him into poverty, so that he
who has perhaps abandoned God through his wealth may return through poverty, for as it is said in the Psalm: "The poor and needy shall praise your name,
Lord." A type of this is Nebuchadnezzar, of whom we read in Daniel 4 that in
his wealth he judged himself equal to God, but when he was deposed and made
poor, he praised him. Tell this story.

The second sign of Julius Caesar was the great noise at the windows of his
bedchamber, so that he thought his house was falling. In moral terms, this
chamber is the human body. When a man sees that he is strong, beautiful, and
learned, he soon becomes exalted in pride and puts down and scorns others in
his strength, and thus he puts his foot on the path of death. Then the heavenly Father comes, to whom we attribute power, and calls him back to the way of
salvation and gives him the second sign, when he raises a noise at the windows
of his body, that is, when he sends sickness to all his limbs and senses, to
the point that man thinks he is altogether falling to the ground in death.
Thereby it often happens that those who had turned away from God in their
bodily strength are called back to him through their sicknesses. The Psalmist
says: "Their infirmities were multiplied, and afterwards they made haste." As
a type, 2 Maccabees 9 proposes the proud Antiochus, who in his pride thought of
himself as commanding the waves of the sea. He also said he was going to go to
Jerusalem and turn it into a pile of graves for the Jews. And yet, when he was
so humbled by God—he who first thought he could reach the stars of the sky,
and afterwards worms crawled from his wretched body, and thus on account of
his stench not even other people could stand him—, he said: "It is just to be
subject to God and not to feel equal to him." Hence we read in Esther 23:
"Lord God, all things are in your power, and there is no one that can resist
your will," etc.

The third sign of Caesar was that he was handed letters with a warning of
his death; if he had read them, he would have escaped. This is a sign of the
Holy Spirit, to whom we attribute goodness; he hands us letters of our death
when he enlightens our consciences with his grace and goodness so that we can
read—through true confession, if we wish to do so—our sins for which we have
deserved eternal death. Therefore, O sinner, reflect now how in the coming of
the Son of God the workings of the Trinity are indivisible. For first you have
the sign of the Son, who in his wisdom knows how to give wealth and to take it
away. You also have the sign of the Father, who in his power knows how to make
strong and how to overthrow. And finally you have the sign of the Holy Spirit,
who in his mercy wants to bring your sins to your remembrance, and all for your
salvation, for as we read in John 3: "Unless you see signs and wonders, you do

aperta, quod non [f. 61] esset ille nobilis puer illis revelatus; set si
nasceretur manu dextra aperta et sinistra clausa, quod tunc esset ille.
Quod et factum est, quia natus est puer ille dextra manu aperta et sinistra

215   clausa. Moraliter ista revelacio seu prophetacio congrue puero Iesu potest
adaptari. Ipse autem prenunciatus erat a multis prophetis. Ysaias autem
dixit capitulo 7: "Ecce virgo concipiet et pariet filium." Et Matthei 1:
"Virgo in utero habebit et pariet filium," etc. Set puer iste Christus ad
modum istius pueri prophetati natus est dextra manu aperta et sinistra

220   clausa. Per quas operaciones eius intelligo, quia per dextram intelligo
opera prosperitatis et consolacionis, et per sinistram opera adversitatis
et tribulacionis. Natus [est] ergo puer Iesus dextra manu aperta, quia a
tempore sue nativitatis et ortus opera misericordie excercuit et pietatis
et consolacionis. Venit ipse misereri, parcere, et mederi contritis corde.

225   Set certe hec manus antiquitus erat clausa quando ulciones excercuit et
vindictas, set iam in eius nativitate est omnino aperta; Iob 14: "Operi
manuum tuarum porriges dexteram"; et Psalmista: "Aperiente te manum tuam,
omnia implebuntur bonitate." Et ideo iam clausa est manus sinistra, que est
ulcionis et vindicte, eo quod [totum tempus] presens tempus est misericor-

230   die. Set adverte quod summe ponderandum est. Dicit enim Psalmista: "Delectaciones in dextera tua usque in finem." Ad litteram: In fine mundi, idest
in iudicio, aperietur manus sinistra ulcionis et vindicte, quia tunc sta-
tuet bonos a dextris et malos a sinistris, tamquam per manum sinistram
puniendi. Quod utinam advert[er]ent potentes tyranni qui manum sinistram

235   tociens aperiunt simplices iniuste torquendo. Non sic, set cum Psalmista
dicamus Christo: "Salvum me fecit dextera tua, Domine."

---

4 superveniet] super me C.   **9** et] *om* O.   **14** dicitur] *om* O.   **17** servandum] serenata
O.   **24** turbaretur(2)] temptaretur M.W. *and others*.   **26** in historia] 1 capitulo R.M; capitulo 7 W.   **27** adventum] adventus O.   **28** rigatura] rigaturam C.M.   **29** illud] istud O.
quo] qua O.   **31** effundit illam] moriendo effundit C.   **35–36** Celestis . . . infundit]
garbled in C.O. *The quotation should probably read*: Celestis, inquit, ros aream rigaturus
se totum velleri prius infudit.   **50** diffidimus] diffidemus O.   **51** illam] illum C.   libera-
bit] libere dabit *corr* M.   **52** fuit] *om* O.   **62** hec] hic C.R.   **63** quod] quam O.   **71** an-
gelus] *om* O.   **80** 9] *add* dicitur O.   **82** de] ex O.   **85** ut scis] sicut placet M; *om* R.W.
88 signum] *add* fortissimum C.   **90** scilicet] *add* demones O.   **94** gracia(1)] *add* iuxta illud O.   **100** tunc] quod C.   **111** item] *om* O.   **114** Psalmi] *add* percussit petram et fluxerunt aque C.   **117** parte] particula O.   infra] *corr marg from* supra; supra O.
121 annalibus] annualibus C.   Hebreorum] *add* quod O.   **133** omnes] *add* homines O.
resurgant] surgant O.   **138** eciam] autem O.   **143** nomine et] nominis eius O.   **150** est]
om O.   **151** bene] *after* evadat O.   **164–165** quia ut dicitur] qui dicit C.   **167** de-
pauperatus] depaupertatus C.   **169** Secundum] *add* autem O.   **170** suam] *om* O.
172 superbia] superbiam O.   **178** recesserunt] recesserant O.   **180** 2 capitulo 9] *corr
marg from 8* C; 8 O.   **185** ait] actuum C.O.   **201** triplicis] triplicia C.   **203** mecum] *add*
est O.   **211** ille] iste O.   **212** ille] iste O.   **216** autem(1)] enim O.   **217** 1] 7 O.
223 sue] *om* O.   **224** Venit] *add* enim O.   **234** adverterent] advertent C; advertant W.

not believe." Thus, then, we see the signs of Christ's threefold coming to the judgment. The letter of this coming is written at the end of Revelation: "Behold, I come quickly, and my reward is with me," etc. And his messengers will be Enoch and Elijah, who will come in the time of Antichrist.

With regard to Christ's coming in the flesh, there is a story about a certain emperor Valerius. It was once prophesied to him and his noblemen that a son would be born to him who was to make war on the enemies of his kingdom and subject them to his rule. So, when the empress had conceived, the emperor and his noblemen solicited their gods with sacrifices and implored them eagerly that, should the boy to be born be the prophesied one, it would be made known to them by some clear sign. They finally received the answer that, if this boy were born with both hands either closed or open, it would not be the prophesied noble child; but if he were born with his right hand open and his left closed, then he would be the one. And this is what happened: a child was born with his right hand open and his left closed. Morally interpreted this revelation or prophecy may be rightly applied to the child Jesus. For he had been foretold by many prophets. Isaiah said of him, in chapter 7: "Behold, a virgin shall conceive and bear a son." And Matthew, in chapter 1: "A virgin shall be with child and bring forth a son." But the child Jesus was like that prophesied boy born with his right hand open and his left closed, by which I understand his works. For the right hand indicates works of prosperity and comfort, the left works of adversity and tribulation. Thus the child Jesus was born with his right hand open, because from the time of his birth on he did works of mercy, pity, and comfort. For he came to have mercy, to spare, and to heal the brokenhearted. In former times this hand had been closed, when he sent punishment and revenge, but now, in his birth, it has been fully opened; Job 14: "To the work of your hand you shall reach out your right hand"; and the Psalmist: "When you open your hand, all things will be filled with good." And thus his left hand is now closed, the hand of punishment and revenge, because all the present time is a time of mercy. But notice what must be most carefully weighed. The Psalmist says: "At your right hand are delights even to the end." Literally this means: "at the end of the world," that is, in the final judgment, will be opened his left hand of punishment and revenge, for then he will place the good at his right and the wicked at his left, as it were to be punished by his left hand. Oh that our powerful tyrants would pay heed to this, who so often open their left hand to the poor people and torture them unjustly! Let us not do so but say to Christ with the Psalmist: "Your right hand has saved me, Lord."

---

4 Luke 1.35.   5 Isa. 59.19.   6–7 Matt. 24.27.   10–11 Isa. 7.14.   12 Luke 1:28, 31. 14–15 Num. 11.9.   31 Cf. Jth. 9.13.   33 Judg. 6.36–40.   34–35 Ps. 71.6.   35– 37 Cf. Bernard, *In laudibus Virginis Matris*, hom. 2, 7 (4:25).   42–43 Perhaps Deut.

III.xvii   CHRISTUS VENIT IN TRIBUS MODIS

[f. 61v] Et nota quod Christus non tantum hiis tribus modis venit in
terris set istis similiter: primo venit ut medicus bonus ad nos sanandum,
secundo venit ut pia mater ad nos pascendum, tercio venit ut fortis miles
ad nos salvandum. Si spiritualiter infirmamur, habemus ipsum medicinam
5   preparantem; si spiritualiter esuriamu⟨s⟩, habemus ipsum per elemosinam
reficientem; si per hostes insidiamur, habemus ipsum defendentem et salvan-
tem.
　　Circa primum est sciendum quod contra infirmitates nostras spirituales
venit Christus tamquam bonus medicus ad nos sanandum. Et ideo Christus
10   facit sicut medicus talis. Nam condiciones ⟨inquirit⟩ infirmi et qualitatem
morbi, scilicet tangendo pulsum, videndo urinam. Sic Christus in visitacione peccatoris ipsum primo ad sui ipsius et proprii peccati cognicionem
sua gracia illuminat ut de [illis] conterendo caveat; Ieremie 3: "Vide vias
tuas et scito quid feceris." Secundo considerata infirmitate secundum
15   infirmantis exigenciam inponit sibi dietam et taxat, scilicet quibus uten-
dum et a quibus cavendum, hoc est, docet occasiones peccatorum vitare et
occasionibus virtutum adherere. Tercio dieta inposita et sic ordinata dat
syropum, electuarium, vel aliquid aliud tale econtrarium tali morbo et
ipsius expulsivum, hoc est, dat sibi contricionem de peccatis, que fit de
20   herbis amaris, sicut patet parte 5, capitulo 6; de qua dicitur: "Erit amara
pocio tua." Quarto, curato eo monet quod caveat a residivo et docet quomodo
vivere debeat eo quod ponit illum in bono proposito continuandi vitam
bonam. Item in multis aliis modis Christus ad modum infirmitatum corpora-
lium nos sanat, quia primo per contricionis sudorem, qui adquiritur per
25   laborem, qui est cogitacio de peccati vilitate et timore iudicii, etc.
　　⟨Secundo per minucionem confessionis; unde in Psalmo: "Libera me de sanguinibus, [f. 62] Deus," etc. Tercio per dietam ieiunii et satifactionis, quo

22.1–3. **47–48** *In* 1119. **50** Luke 1.30. **53–54** Cf. Exod. 3.2. **57–59** Rev. 12.1. **62–63** Gen. 9.12–13. **63** Judg. 6.36–40. **64** Josh. 2.18. **65** Esther 4.11ff. **65– 66** Cf. Isa. 11.1. **71–76** Bernard, *De laudibus Virginis Matris*, hom. 2, 17 (4:35). **81– 82** Gen. 9.13. **87–88** Isa. 11.12. **90–91** Wisd. 16.6. **94** Luke 1.28. **98–99** Rev. 8.13. **101–102** Ps. 18.6. **106–107** Rev. 12.1. **114–116** Ps. 77.20. **116–117** *FM* V.xi–xxvi. **117–118** Joel 2.12. **121** Luke 21.25. **121–137** The attribution is standard in medieval works; see William W. Heist, *The Fifteen Signs before Doomsday* (East Lansing: Michigan State College Press, 1952), pp. 23–34. The entire passage occurs also in *Legenda aurea*, pp. 6–7. **138–149** Martin of Troppau, *Chronicon*, p. 406. **165** Ps. 73.21. **166–167** Cf. Dan. 4.26–34. **179–180** Ps. 15.4. **180–185** 2 Macc. 9.8–10, 14. **185–186** 2 Macc. 9.12. **186–188** Esther 13.9. **200** John 4.48. **202–203** Rev. 22.12. **217** Isa. 7.14. **218** Matt. 1.23. **226–227** Job 14.15. **227–228** Ps. 103.28. **230–231** Ps. 15.11. **236** Ps. 137.7.

III.xvii   THREE MANNERS OF CHRIST'S COMING

And notice that Christ comes to the earth not only in those three but also in the following three manners. First he comes as a good physician to heal us, second he comes as a loving mother to nourish us, and third he comes as a strong knight to save us. If we are spiritually sick, we have him to prepare our medicine; if we are spiritually hungry, we have him to feed us with his alms; and if we are oppressed by enemies, we have him to defend and save us.

With respect to the first, we must know that for our spiritual sicknesses Christ comes as a good physician to heal us. Christ acts like a physician in the following way. A doctor investigates the condition of the sick person and the nature of his sickness by such methods as taking his pulse and inspecting his urine. Thus when Christ visits a sinner, he first enlightens him with his grace to understand himself and his own sin, so that he may repent of his sins and shun them; Jeremiah 3: "See your ways and know what you have done." Second, after diagnosing the sickness he gives the sick person a diet as he requires and prescribes what he should eat and what he should avoid; this means that Christ teaches to avoid the occasions of sin and to seek the occasions for practicing the virtues. Third, after he has prescribed and worked out a diet, he gives the sick person some syrup, an electuary, or some other medicine against this sickness to expel it; that is, Christ gives him contrition of his sins, which is made from bitter herbs, as is shown in part 5, chapter 6; of it is written: "Your drink will be bitter." Fourth, when the sick person is healed, he warns him against relapsing and teaches him how to live, so that he fosters in him a good intention to live a good life. Christ further heals us in many additional ways as if from physical illness: first through the sweat of contrition, which one gets into by hard exercise, namely by reflecting on the vileness of sin, on the fearful day of judgment, and so forth. Second, through the bloodletting of confession; whence the Psalm says: "Deliver me from blood,

secundum Ieronimum sanantur pestes corporis. Quarto per emplastrum sive
unctionem devote oracionis.⟩ Quinto per humorum superfluorum expulsionem,
30   que notatur in largicione elemosinarum, que fient de omnibus possessis et
maxime superfluis; Luce 11: "Date elemosinam et omnia munda erunt vobis."
Sexto per instigacionem mali consorcii et occasionem peccati, quia iuxta
Psalmistam: "Cum sancto sanctus eris," etc. Et septimo per adustionem
caritatis. De quibus omnibus nota particulis suis sufficienter, parte 5 de
35   caritate et parte 5 capitulo 5.
    Circa secundum est sciendum quod contra esuriem spiritualem venit
Christus ut pia mater ad nos pascendum. Nam ipse dicit Iohannis 6: "Ego sum
panis vivus qui de celo descendi." Et nota quod quinque sunt panes, quibus
quinque milia hominum pavit et adhuc nos pascit. Primus est panis pauperum
40   grossus et rud⟨i⟩s, quia ordeacius vel de pisis aut fabis, quo difficilime
vescuntur plures. Et est panis contricionis, qui valde durus est multis;
Psalmista: "Fuerunt michi lacrime mee panes die ac nocte." Set iste panis
in tribus frust⟨is⟩ dividetur, scilicet in dolore peccatorum preteritorum,
presencium, et futurorum. Secundus panis est confessionis; Psalmista: "Sur-
45   gite postquam sederitis qui manducatis panem doloris," quasi diceret: vos
qui habetis contricionem, moram nimis non trahatis set festinanter surgite
ad confessionem. Tres vero partes istius panis sunt: primo quod debet
comedi cum festinacione ne putrescat, secundo cum mundicia ne vilescat, et
tercio cum discrecione ne tepescat. Tercius panis est penitencie et satisfactio-
50   nis, de quo in Psalmo: "Cinerem tamquam panem manducab⟨am⟩." Quicquid
enim cineres tangunt, fit amarum. Sic ad tempus penitencia hic amarescit,
set alibi dulcessit. Et iste panis in tribus dividitur: in ieiunio, oracione, et elemosina. Nota ut supra. Quartus panis est perseverancia sine
residivacione; de [f. 62v] qua Ysaie 32: "Erit panis frugum terre uberrimus
55   et pinguis." "Uberrimus" autem dicit propter largam voluntatem satisfaciendi, set "pinguis" propter voluntatem continuandi et non residivandi. Et
iste panis dividitur in tr⟨ibus⟩, scilicet in compassione mortis Christi,
in consideracione proprii periculi, et in caucione futuri mali. Quintus
panis est eucaristie. Et est panis dominorum, [scilicet] eorum qui propriis
60   peccatis dominantur et illa castigant et domant. Et ideo hic est panis
[vite], de quo Iohannis 6: "Qui manducat hunc panem, vivet in eternum." Et
iste similiter in tribus dividitur: in cordis mundicia, in fidei constan-
cia, in boni operis perseverancia.
    Circa tercium est sciendum quod contra hostes nostros spirituales
65   venit Christus tamquam pugil et miles fortis ad defendendum, qui sunt caro,
mundus, et demon. De quorum insultu et quomodo vincuntur satis nota supra,
parte 5, capitulis 12, [13,] 14. Et qui vult hos tres hostes debellare,
oportet quod hec tria habeat, scilicet audaciam aggrediendi ne terreatur,
secundo astuciam ne decipiatur, tercio constanciam ne inficiatur. Unde de

O God," etc. Third, through the diet of fasting and penance, by which according to Jerome the illnesses of the body are cured. Fourth, through the plaster or ointment of devout prayer. Fifth, through draining excessive bodily fluids, which means giving alms from all our goods, primarily from those we own beyond our needs; Luke 11: "Give alms, and all things will be clean to you." Sixth, through the surgical removal of evil companionship and the occasion of sin, for according to the Psalmist: "With the holy you will be holy," etc. And seventh, through the cautery of charity. On all these matters you will find more in the respective sections of part 5 on love and part 5, chapter 5.

With respect to the second point we must know that for our spiritual hunger Christ comes like a loving mother to nourish us. He himself says in John 6: "I am the living bread that has come down from heaven." Notice that there are five loaves of bread with which he fed five thousand men and is still feeding us. The first is the coarse and simple bread of the poor, made of barley or peas or beans, which hardly feeds many. This is the bread of contrition, which for many people is too hard; as the Psalmist says: "My tears have been my bread day and night." But this loaf of bread will be broken into three bites, remorse for our sins of the past, the present, and the future. The second loaf is the bread of confession; the Psalmist says: "Rise after you have been sitting, you that eat the bread of sorrow," as if he were saying: you who are contrite, do not delay overlong but rise quickly to confess your sins. This loaf has three qualities: it must first be eaten in a hurry so that it does not mold, second with purity so that it does not become dirty, and third with discretion so that one does not lose one's appetite. The third loaf is the bread of penance and satisfaction, of which the Psalm says: "I ate ashes like bread." Whatever is touched by ashes turns bitter. In the same way, penance here in time tastes bitter, but elsewhere it is sweet. This, too, falls into three parts: fasting, prayer, and almsgiving. See above. The fourth loaf is perseverance without backsliding; of it Isaiah 32 says: "The bread of the grain of the land shall be most plentiful and fat." He calls it "most plentiful" because of its generous desire to make satisfaction, and "fat" because of its desire to persevere and not relapse. This loaf, too, has three parts: compassion with Christ's death, reflection on one's own danger, and caution about future evil. The fifth loaf is the bread of the Eucharist. This is the bread of masters, that is, of those who master their own sins and chastise and overcome them. And thus it is the bread of life, of which John 6 says: "He who eats this bread will live forever." And this is likewise divided into three parts: purity of heart, constancy of faith, and perseverance in good work.

With respect to the third point we must know that Christ comes like a champion and strong knight to defend us against our spiritual enemies, who are the flesh, the world, and the devil. On their attack and on how to overcome

70   Iulio Cesare narratur quod cum devicta regione Pontica triumphasset inter
     fercula, trium verborum tulit titulum dicens: "Veni, vidi, vici." Revera
     sic quicumque vincere voluerit oportet sicut ipse habuit in veniendo primo
     audaciam, quod notatur quando dixit Cesar "Veni," scilicet audacter ad bel-
     lum, quia iuxta Philosophum 3 *Ethicorum* audaces sunt prevalentes. Magnam
75   ergo audaciam habere deberes cum Filium Dei iam habes propugnatorem.
     Nam contra demonis maliciam superbie, ire, invidie ipse venit pro nobis ad
     bellum cum lorica caritatis, lancea mititatis, et galea humilitatis. Contra
     mundi avariciam venit super equum paupertatis, quasi super crucem. Contra
     carnis lasciviam venit cum gladio sobrietatis, calcaribus vivacitatis, et
80   cum scuto castitatis. [f. 63] Expone ut placet. Secundo, vide, scilicet
     prudenter, quia iuxta dictum beati Iob: "Inimici tui obsederunt tabernacu-
     lum tuum in giro." Set vide ne illis credas vel assencias quamvis tibi
     locuti fuerint placencia, quia pleni sunt dolo. Et ideo inter tot fures
     prudenter videte quomodo "caute ambuletis, quia dies mali sunt." Quod si
85   feceris, leviter dicere poteris tercium verbum, scilicet "Vici," per forti-
     tudinem et constanciam, scilicet mundi vanitatem, carnis voluptatem, et
     demonis malignitatem. Et hec ad presens de Christi incarnacione sufficiunt.

4–7 Si . . . salvantem] *after the following sentence* C.W.   **5** esuriamus] esuriamur C.
10 inquirit] querit C.   **15** infirmantis] infirmitatis O.   **20** Erit] erat O.   **23** in] *om* O.
Christus] *om* O.   **26–29** Secundo . . . oracionis] *In* C *the order of items 2–4 is 4–3–2.*
27 Deus] *add* deus salutis O.   **32** instigacionem] inscicionem R.W.   **40** rudis] rudus
C.M.   **43** frustis] frustris C.   **45** postquam sederitis] *om* O.   **50** manducabam] man-
ducabis C.   **52** panis] *om* O.   **57** tribus] tres C.   **66** quorum] quo O.   **72** habuit] *om* O;
other MSS have habeat *or* quod habeat.   **83** fures] fraudes O.   **84** videte] vide O.

III.xviii   DE CHRISTI PROGRESSU IN HAC VITA

     [C]irca autem Christi progressum sive peregrinacionem in hac vita, que
     fuit secundum Crisostomum *Super Mattheum* per annos triginta tres, et tantum
     quantum est ab eius nativitate usque ad Pascha. Unde dicit ipsum plenarie
     complevisse triginta annos quando venit ad ° baptismum. Et ita secundum eum
5   Christus vixit in huius peregrinacionis vita triginta et tribus annis cum
     dimidio. Secundum autem evangelium Christus vixit triginta duobus annis,

them you will find more in part 5, chapters 12–14. He who wants to fight these three enemies must have the following three virtues: boldness to attack so as not to be frightened, shrewdness so as not to be tricked, and constancy so as not to be corrupted. Whence the story is told of Julius Caesar that when he had subdued the region of Pontus and was celebrating his triumph at a banquet, he took the motto of three words, stating: "I came, I saw, I conquered." Thus, anyone who wants to overcome must, like Caesar, first be bold in coming, which is shown by Caesar's saying "I came," namely boldly to the war; for according to the Philosopher in Book 3 of the *Ethics*, the bold prevail. You should have great boldness, since you already have the Son of God as your champion. For he came to fight for us against the malice of the devil in pride, wrath, and envy, with his armor of charity, lance of mildness, and helmet of humility. Against the avarice of the world he came on his horse of poverty, as it were, on the cross. Against the lust of the flesh he came with the sword of soberness, the spurs of liveliness, and the shield of chastity. Explain this as you will. Second, "See," namely, with prudence, for according to blessed Job: "Your enemies have besieged your tabernacle around you." But see to it that you do not believe or give in to them, whatever pleasing things they may have told you, for they are full of trickery. Therefore, see prudently that among so many thieves "you walk with caution, for the days are evil." If you do so, you will easily be able to say the third word, "I conquered," namely the vanity of the world and the lust of the flesh and the wickedness of the devil through strength and constancy. And this much suffices for now about Christ's incarnation.

13–14 Jer. 2.23.   **20** *FM* V.vi–vii; also x, xii.   **20–21** Cf. Isa. 24.19.   **26–27** Ps. 50.16.   **28** Perhaps Jerome, *Adversus Jovinianum* II.11–13 (PL 23:313–316).   **31** Luke 11.41.   **33** Ps. 17.26.   **34–35** *FM*: perhaps III.x.146ff.; and III.v–xxvi.   **37–38** John 6.41.   **42** Ps. 41.4.   **44–45** Ps. 126.2.   **50** Ps. 101.10.   **54–55** Isa. 30–23.   **61** John 6.59.   **66–67** *FM* V.xxvii–xxxvii.   **70–71** Suetonius, *De vita Caesarum* I.37.   **74** Aristotle, *Ethica Nicomachea* III (1116a). The text should probably read *prevolantes*; thus in both the *Ethica vetus* (2:39) and Grosseteste's translation (3:192 and 4:423).   **81–82** Job 19.12.   **84** Eph. 5.16.

III.xviii   CHRIST'S PILGRIMAGE IN THIS LIFE

Christ's progress or pilgrimage in this life, according to Chrysostom on Matthew, lasted thirty-three years altogether, reckoning from his birth to Easter. Whence Chrysostom says Christ had completed thirty years when he came to be baptized. And in his view Christ lived in the pilgrimge of this life thirty-three and a half years. But according to the Gospel, Christ lived for thirty-two years and three months. For it says: "Jesus was beginning about

mensibus tribus. Di⟨c⟩it enim: "Iesus erat incipiens quasi annorum triginta," scilicet quando venit ad baptismum ante suam predicacionem; hoc est,
Christus inceperat tricesimum annum. Unde tredecim diebus eiusdem anni
10   peractis, eodem anno revoluto convertit aquam in vinum, et in sequenti
Pascha incarceratus est beatus Iohannes, et in alio Pascha decollatus est.
Unde secundum quod habetur in *Cronicis* Martini et eciam alibi, anno Domini
29 cepit Iohannes predicare baptismum penitencie, et anno 32 idem Iohannes
decollatus est. Ita quod secundum aliquos Iohannes erat senior Christo per
15   sex menses et ante eum predicavit per unum annum et ante eum mortuus est
per unum annum.
      Et nota quod in isto toto tempore peregrinacionis Christi in vita ista
multa signa caritatis nobis ostendit multipliciter, sicut patet in penis
temporalibus quas pro nobis et nostra erudicione sustinuit, cuiusmodi
20   fuerunt [f. 63v] esuries, sitis, calor, frigus, et huiusmodi. Similiter
plura opprobria et contumelias usque ad mortem, sicut patet manifeste
seriem evangeliorum consideranti. Quod autem vita Christi hic in terris
fuit quasi peregrinacio quedam ad sui exemplum nos inducens, patet multipliciter pro eo quod ad modum peregrini multis miseriis et penalibus, ut
25   dictum est, affligebatur, scilicet fame, siti, etc., iuxta illud Iob 13:
"Homo natus de muliere brevi vivens tempore, repletur multis miseriis,"
etc. Secundo quia a paucis vel quasi a nullis cognoscebatur. Unde ut patet
discipuli eius euntes in Emaus [ipsum non cognoverunt], Luce ultimo, dicentes: "Tu solus peregrinus es," etc. Tercio quia cum eo sicut cum peregrino
30   sepe iniuste agebatur, sicut patet quod ipsum demonium habere Iudei dicebant et tamquam trutannum populum seducentem reputabant. Quarto quia sicut
peregrinus multis periculis ac eciam morti frequenter exponebatur, per quod
in terris securam requiem non haberet, sicut patet in conspiracionibus
Iudeorum contra eum quando dixerunt quod populum seducebat et templum
35   destrueret, et cetera huiusmodi.
      Et nota quod in isto (scilicet Iesu) satis aperte patent signa pere-
grini, que sunt sclavonium, pera, baculus, capellum, solee ferrate, singulum, et gurda. Nam Christi sclavonium album, pelliceum, et depictum fuit
cutis sua, que pro nobis in tantum erat depicta et dilacerata quod "a
40   planta pedis usque ad verticem capitis non erat in eo sanitas"; Trenorum:
"Cutis mea denigrata est." Secundo habuit loco pere vulnus laterale, de quo
pro nostra salute exivit sanguis et aqua. Tercio, loco baculi, qui est
superius rotundum et *pomelee* vel aliquando transversus superius et inferius
satis acutum, [habuit lignum crucis,] ut patet in illius forma; vel iste
45   baculus potest esse lancea illa qua post mortem erat lanceatus. Quarto,
loco capelli super capud habuit coronam spi- [f. 64] neam. Quinto, pro
soleis ferreis et sirotecis habuit clavos ferreos in manibus et pedibus
satis acutos et duros. Sexto, pro cingulo habuit cordas, funiculos, et

the age of thirty years," that is, when he came to the baptism before he began
his preaching; that is to say, Christ had then begun his thirtieth year.
Therefore, after thirteen days of this year, one year later he changed water
into wine, and on the following Passover Blessed John was put in prison, and a
Passover later he was beheaded. Further, according to what can be found in the
Chronicles of Martin and elsewhere, John began to preach baptism for the forgiveness of sins in A.D. 29 and was beheaded in A.D. 32. That means, according
to some, that John was six months older than Christ and preached one year
before him and was killed one year before him.

Notice that during all this time of his pilgrimage in this life Christ
showed us in many ways many signs of his love. This is evident in the bodily
sufferings he sustained for us and for our instruction, such as hunger, thirst,
heat, cold, and the like; and similarly many reproaches and mistreatments
including death, as is quite evident when one considers the Gospel narrative.
That Christ's life here on earth was like a pilgrimage that invites us to
follow his example is clear in many ways from the fact that he was afflicted by
many miseries and pains like a pilgrim, as already said, that is, by hunger and
thirst and so forth, after the words of Job 13: "Man born of woman, living for
a short time, is filled with many woes," etc. Second, he was known to few or
hardly any. Thus, as we see, his disciples who went to Emmaus did not know
him, for they said, at the end of Luke: "Are you only a stranger," etc. Third,
people treated him unjustly, as they treat a pilgrim; for the Jews said he had
a demon and considered him a vagabond who was leading the people astray.
Fourth, like a pilgrim he was often exposed to many dangers and even death, so
that on earth he had no quiet rest; that is shown in the conspiracy of the Jews
against him when they accused him of misleading the people and destroying the
Temple, and other things of the same kind.

Notice also that in him one can clearly see the typical marks of a pilgrim, which are the pilgrim's robe, his bag, his staff, his hood, his nailed
sandals, his girdle, and his gourd. For Christ's robe was white, made of skin,
and painted—his skin, which was so painted and torn for our sake that "from
the sole of his foot unto the top of his head there was no soundness in him";
Lamentations: "My skin has become black." Second, for a pilgrim's bag he had
that wound in his side, from which water and blood issued forth for our salvation. Third, for the pilgrim's staff, which is round on the top and bears a
pommel or sometimes has a little crosspiece on top and is pointed at the
bottom, he had the wood of the cross, which has the same shape; or else the
pilgrim's staff could be that lance with which he was pierced after his death.
Fourth, for a hood on his head he wore a crown of thorns. Fifth, for nailed
sandals and gloves he wore iron nails in hands and feet that were very sharp
and hard. Sixth, for a girdle he had strings, ropes, and scourges with which
he was bound, pulled, and beaten in the most cruel way. And seventh, for a

flagella, quibus ligatus, tractus, et flagellatus erat durissime. Et septi-
50 mo, pro gurda offerebant sibi Iudei spongeam felle et mirra impletam. Et
sic patent signa eius peregrinacionis.
    Et notandum quod Christus sicut quilibet bonus Christianus duo fecit.
Primo, peregrinando debita sua solvit. Sic Christus generi humano infirmato
promiserat dicens: "Amen, dico vobis, veniam et curabo eum." Quod et fecit
55 ab infirmitate peccati, sicut supra proximo satis patet. Secundo, solutis
debitis et de domo et familia ordinat[is], testamentum condidit quando
animam suam legavit Deo Patri, discipulis pacem, ac paranimpho matrem,
iuxta illud Matthei 25: "Homo quidam peregre proficiscens vocavit servos
suos et tradidit illis bona sua, unicuique secundum propriam virtutem et
60 mercedem." Et nota quod propria virtus cuiuslibet est illud ad quod Deus
illum instituit. In signum quod racio cuiuslibet hominis debet ordinare
sensus suos, ad ea scilicet tantum [ad] que sunt a Deo instituta et non ad
alia, sicut oculos ad vigilandum, quia ille quasi ianitor anime; de cuius
custodia nota parte 7. Et ideo Matthei 25 dicitur: "Homo quidam peregre
65 proficiscens," etc., "ianitori precepit ut vigilet." Similiter aures ad audiendum bona, sicut verbum Dei; os ad Deum laudandum et proximum instru-
endum et non ad detrahendum. Istis ergo peractis et debito modo ordinatis,
non restat peregrino nisi amicis valedicere et iter suum arripere, quod
eciam fecit Christus quando ex hoc mundo ad sanctum Calvarie locum pergens
70 omnia temporalia reliquit et animam Deo Patri reddidit. Et nota quod omnia
[f. 64v] que fecit Christus aut in sua peregrinacione huius mundi sustinuit
fuerunt amore humani generis et ad eius consolacionem et informacionem.
    Et ideo si vere peregrini et eius sequaces esse velimus, oportet quod
habeamus, sicut et ipse habuit, primo sclavonium caritatis contra invidiam,
75 secundo capellum humilitatis contra superbiam, tercio peram largitatis
contra avariciam, quarto baculum mititatis contra iram, quinto soleas
vivacitatis contra accidiam, sexto singulum castitatis contra luxuriam,
septimo gurdam sobrietatis contra gulam, etc.

---

2 Mattheum] *add* plenarie O.   4 ad] *add* beatum C.   5 peregrinacionis vita] vite peregrinacione O.   7 Dicit] dixit C.   12 Unde] item O.   19 et] *add* pro O.   33 haberet]
habebat O.   36 scilicet Iesu] *om* O.   41 vulnus] *add* illud O.   44 habuit . . . crucis] *om*
C.O; *supplied from* E.   52 notandum] nota O.   56 ordinatis] ordinat C.R.W.   64 7] *add*
capitulo O. 25] 7 O.   66 Dei] *add* similiter O.   73 vere] veri O.

III.xix   DE CHRISTI EGRESSU DE HAC VITA

[C]irca autem Christi egressum ° de hac vita est sciendum quod ibi
similiter summe suam caritatem nobis ostendit, sicut patet in sua benedicta

gourd the Jews offered him a sponge soaked with gall and myrrh. Thus we see
the marks of his pilgrimage.

And notice that just like any good Christian Christ did two things.
First, by going on a pilgrimage he made good his vow. Christ had promised
mankind in its sickness: "Amen, I say to you that I shall come and heal him."
And he did heal us from the sickness of sin, as we saw just above. In the
second place, after settling his accounts and making the necessary dispositions
for his house and family, he set up his testament when he gave his soul to God
the Father, his peace to his disciples, and his mother to the bridesman, after
the words of Matthew 25: "A man going into a far country called his servants
and delivered to them his goods, to each according to his proper ability and
reward." And notice that the "proper ability" of any object is the purpose for
which God has created it. Consequently, man's reason must rule its senses only
toward the purposes for which they have been created by God and no others; thus
the eyes must be used for watching, for they are, so to speak, the doorkeepers
of the soul; concerning their guarding, see part 7. Therefore in Matthew 25 it
is said: "A man who was going into a far country," etc., "commanded the porter
to watch." Likewise, the purpose of the ears is to hear good things, such as
the word of God; and of the mouth, to praise God and to teach one's neighbor,
not to speak ill of him. After the pilgrim has done these things and put
everything in due order, nothing is left for him but to bid his friends farewell and start on his journey; Christ did this when, setting out from this
world to the holy place on Calvary, he left all earthly goods behind and
returned his soul to God his Father. And notice that everything that Christ
did or suffered on his pilgrimage in this world was for the love of mankind and
for its comfort and instruction.

Therefore, if we wish to be true pilgrims and followers of Christ, we must
have, as he did, a robe of charity against envy, a hood of humility against
pride, a bag of generosity against avarice, a staff of mildness against wrath,
sandals of liveliness against sloth, a girdle of chastity against lechery, and
a gourd of soberness against gluttony.

2–3 Cf. Chrysostom, *In Matthaeum*, hom. 10, 1 (PG 57:184).   **7–8** Luke 3.23.   **12–
14** Martin of Troppau, *Chronicon*, p. 408.   **26** Job 14.1.   **29** Luke 24.18.   **34–35** Cf.
Matt. 26.59–61.   **39–40** Isa. 1.6.   **41** Job 30.30 (cf. Lam. 4.8).   **54** Matt. 8.7.   **58–
60** Matt. 25.14.   **64** *FM* VII.ii.   **64–65** Cf. Mark 13.34.

III.xix   CHRIST'S EXIT FROM THIS LIFE

With respect to Christ's exit from this life, we must know that there,
too, he showed us his love most fully, as can be seen in his blessed Passion

passione et morte, similiter resurrectione, ascensione, et Spiritus Sancti
missione. De quibus breviter tractabitur consequenter. Set quia de eius
5   passione et morte superius satis diffuse est discussum, ideo hic levius
pertransitur.

Narrat tamen pro sua benedicta passione et morte Ovidius magnus de
bello Troiano quomodo rapta Helena, uxore Menelay, ab Alexandro filio
Priami, fuit prophetatum quod civitas Troianorum numquam caperetur quo-
10 usque Achilles mortuus esset, miles ille fortis. Quod cum mater eius audisset,
inter domicellas camere sue illum veste muliebri induit. Ulixes ergo hanc
propheciam intelligens se ad querendum Achillem preparavit. P⟨re⟩senciens
ergo eum inter mulieres absconditum, velut cautus mercator cum mercimoniis
suis ad usum dominarum spectantibus in decora classi cum armis militaribus
15 ⟨desuper⟩ positis ad castrum matris Achillis applicuit. Publicatis ergo
mercimoniis descendit mater cum domicellis in dictam navem illius mercimo-
nia considerare. Cum igitur unaquaque illarum que fuerunt [f. 65] sibi
accepta emisset, Achilles quasi instinctu naturali omnibus huiusmodi relictis ad arma accessit, scutum apprehendens hastamque fortiter vibrans. Quo
20 viso ipsum esse Achillem ex hoc Ulixes deprehendit. Unde velo navis appli-
cato cum illo affugit et ad bellum Troianorum deduxit. Mortuo igitur Achil-
le capta est civitas et obsides partis adverse libere sunt dimissi.

Spiritualiter per Alexandrum qui Helenam rapuit, filium Priami regis
Troianorum, intelligo diabolum, et per Helenam genus humanum a diabolo
25 raptum et captivatum. Per civitatem Troianam intelligo infernum. Set Achilles miles optimus Christus est, de quo prophetatum fuit quod genus humanum
numquam salvaretur quousque pro omnibus ipse moreretur. Unde Ulixes miles
providus et circumspectus, idest Spiritus Sanctus, de nostra salute sollicitus, navem oneravit diversis mercimoniis, idest Virginem Mariam omnibus
30 ornavit virtutibus. In quam descendit Achilles, Filius scilicet Dei quando
ex Virgine Maria carnem assumpsit. [Set tunc arma assumpsit] et fortiter
vibravit quando cum cruce, lancea, et clav⟨i⟩s pugnans captus est et occisus. Per cuius mortem statim capta est civitas inferni et eius obsides,
idest anime humane ibidem captivate et detente, libere sunt dimisse.

35 Unde in memoria illius passionis amor accendi deberet in corde cuiuslibet nostrum, sicut solet homo ignem accendere de lapide durissimo. Tunc
autem accipit homo lapidem cilicinum et illum ferro fortiter percutit, ex
quo scintilla egressa in materia sicca recipitur. Quo facto accenditur
filus sulphuratus, et sic ignis augmentatur. Revera sic homo qui vult ignem
40 caritatis accendere primo debet cor suum a voluptatibus desiccare et post
lapidem, Christum, menti incorporare, quomodo scilicet lancea ferrea, [f.
65v] spinis, clavis erat percussus et perforatus. Ipse enim "faciem suam
exposuit quasi petram durissimam" Iudeis ipsum percucientibus. Et statim
egredietur scintilla amoris et caritatis erga eum, teste Psalmista: "Et in

and death, and likewise in his resurrection, ascension, and the sending of the
Holy Spirit. Of these we shall treat briefly in the following; but since we
have already spoken fully of his Passion and death above, we will touch on
these only lightly.

In connection with his blessed Passion and death, the great Ovid tells
that in the Trojan War, after Helen, the wife of Menelaos, had been abducted by
Alexander, son of Priam, it was prophesied that the city of the Trojans would
never be captured until the strong knight Achilles were dead. When his mother
heard this, she put woman's clothes on him and hid him among her chambermaids.
Now when Ulysses heard of this prophecy, he set out himself to look for Achilles. Having an inkling that he might be hidden among the women, he sailed with
a splendid fleet to the castle of Achilles' mother as a diligent merchant with
merchandise for women's use, on top of which he had spread military gear. When
the merchandise was being advertised, Achilles' mother came with her maids into
his ship to inspect the wares. Now, as each of them bought what was fitting
for herself, Achilles by his natural instinct bypassed all the women's stuff
and went to the weapons, gripping a shield and brandishing a spear. From this,
Ulysses understood it was Achilles; he took hold of him, hoisted the sail, fled
away with him, and carried him to the Trojan War. And when Achilles had died,
the city was captured and the hostages of the opposing side were allowed to go
free.

Allegorically, by Alexander, son of Priam, the king of Troy, who carried
off Helen, I understand the devil, and by Helen mankind, which was carried off
and held captive by the devil. The city of Troy stands for hell. But Achilles, the foremost knight, is Christ, of whom it was prophesied that mankind
would never be saved until he died for all. Whence the provident and shrewd
knight Ulysses, that is, the Holy Spirit, in his care for our salvation loaded
a ship with all kinds of merchandise, that is, he embellished the Virgin Mary
with all the virtues. Into this ship Achilles entered, that is, the Son of God
when he took flesh from the Virgin Mary. And he grasped the weapons and
brandished them when he fought with cross, spear, and nails and was captured
and killed. Through his death the city of hell was taken at once, and its
hostages, that is, those human souls that were held captive there, were let go
free.

In memory of this Passion, love should be kindled in the heart of each one
of us, and this in the same way as one kindles fire with a hard stone. For in
that case one takes a flint and strikes it hard with iron, so that a spark
falls into some dry material. From that a sulphur thread is lit, and thus the
fire is kindled. In the same way, when one wants to kindle the fire of love,
one must first dry out one's heart of evil desires and then place a stone,
Christ, in one's mind, by remembering how he was struck and pierced with an
iron spear, thorns, and nails. For he "set his face as a most hard rock," to

45   meditacione mea exardescit ignis." Quo facto apponantur ligna crucis. Et
     sic ignis permaximus accenditur, amoris scilicet et caritatis.
       Et nota quod Christus mortem crucis magis elegit quam aliam propter
     duo: Illa enim ⟨mors, scilicet⟩ suspendium in ligno, infligitur propter
     duo, videlicet furtum et homicidium, quorum utrumque commisit primus pa-
50   rens. Furtum commisit eo quod furtive comedit contra Dei preceptum; et
     similiter homicidium, quia non tantum se ipsum occidit set totam suam
     posteritatem. Volens igitur Filius Dei pro omnibus satisfacere ut nos
     salvaret, mortem crucis elegit, que fuit mors turpissima, etc.

---

1 egressum] *add* sive peregrinacionem *interl* C.   12 Presenciens] persenciens C.   15 desuper positis] suppositis C.   17 igitur] ergo O.   25 captivatum] captivum O.   30 ornavit
virtutibus] oneravit virtutibus et ornavit O.   32 clavis] clavos C.   34 captivate] captive
O.   44 Psalmista] *add* qui dicit O.   Et] *om* O.   45 exardescit] exardescet O.   48 mors
scilicet] scilicet mors vel C.   50 Furtum] *add* autem O.   52 igitur] ergo O.   53 etc.] *om*
O.

III.xx   DE CHRISTI RESURRECTIONE

       [M]odo de eius benedicta resurrectione est aliquid breviter dicendum,
     que quasi videtur de sompno et non de vera morte fuisse, cum tamen veris-
     sime fuit. Est ergo advertendum quod sicut videmus quando aliquis magnus se
     reclinat tempore estivo ad dormiendum in meridie super lectum, primo fenes-
5   tre clauduntur et post ceteri aditus, per quos lumen intrare posset, sic
     per omnia Christus fecit in ligno crucis collocatus feria sexta in meridie.
     Fenestre mundi per quas lumen intrare solet clause fuerunt, quando scilicet
     "a sexta hora tenebre facte sunt super universam terram usque ad horam
     nonam," dum scilicet Christus rex universorum sompnum mortis super lectum
10   crucis suscipere dignabatur, ut patet Matthei 27. Set tunc quasi brevi
     sopore facto excitatus a Patre surrexit, sicut ipsemet per Psalmistam ait:
     "Ego dormivi et sompnum cepi et exurrexi quia Dominus suscepit me."
       Set quare ita cito surrexit potest racio multiplex [f. 66] assignari.
     Videmus enim inter dormientes de tota familia quod ille qui tenetur tardius
15   cubare et cicius surgere est ianitor, quia illius est diluculo ianuas
     aperire et alios excitare. Et ideo signanter discretus paterfamilias pere-
     gre profecturus "ianitori precepit ut vigilaret," ut habetur in evangelio.
     [Set Christus ianitor est Ecclesie sive hostiarius,] sicut dicit Augustinus
     super illud Iohannis: "Huic hostiarius aperit," etc. Et ideo, licet tardius
20   cubasset inter sanctos qui dormitum [mortis] in antiqua lege susceperunt,
     voluit tamen primo hostia aperire ut bonus ianitor et alios excitare. Et
     omnium sic dormiencium erat primus qui surrexit; Corinthiorum 15: "Christus
     surrexit primicie dormiencium." Alia causa fuit hec. Videmus enim quod

the Jews who persecuted him. Then a spark of love and charity for Christ will at once spring forth, as the Psalmist testifies: "In my meditation a fire shall flame out." After that one must lay to it the wood of the cross, and in this way a great fire will start to burn, a fire of love and of charity.

And notice that Christ preferred death on the cross to any other for two reasons. Death by being hung on the cross is inflicted for two crimes, theft and murder, both of which our first parent had committed. He committed theft when he stealthily ate against God's commandment; and he committed murder, for he killed not only himself but his whole posterity. Therefore, as the Son of God wanted to make satisfaction in all things so that he might save us, he chose death on the cross, which was the most shameful kind of death.

7–22 Ovid, *Ars am.* I.689ff.; see Tubach 43.   **42–43** Cf. Isa. 50.7.   **44–45** Ps. 38.4.

III.xx   CHRIST'S RESURRECTION

Now we must speak briefly of his blessed resurrection, which seemed more like an awakening from sleep than from true death, though it most certainly was the latter. Notice that we commonly see that when in summertime a nobleman lies down on his couch for a nap at noon, first the windows are closed and then any other openings through which the light might come in. In the same way, when Christ was placed on the wood of the cross at noon on Friday, the windows of the world, through which normally the light enters, were closed, namely when "it grew dark over the whole earth from the sixth to the ninth hour," when Christ, the king of all, consented to suffer the sleep of death on the couch of the cross, as is reported in Matthew 27. But after having, so to speak, taken a little nap, he was wakened by his Father and rose up, as he himself says through the Psalmist: "I have slept and taken my rest, and I have risen up because the Lord has protected me."

Many reasons can be given for his rising so soon. The person that among all who sleep in a household has to go to bed last and to rise first is the doorkeeper, for it is his job to open the doors at daybreak and to wake the others. Therefore the thoughtful master of the household who went on a journey very meaningfully "ordered the doorkeeper to watch," as we find it in the Gospel. But the doorkeeper or porter of the Church is Christ, as Augustine says in commenting on the words of John: "To him the porter opens," and so on. And thus, although he was the last to go to bed among the saints who fell into the sleep of death in the Old Law, he yet wanted like a good doorkeeper to be the first to open the gates and to wake the others. And thus, of all that were

ianitor quiescens in lecto, si amicum pulsantem ad ianuam audit, continuo
25   surgit eo quod amicus est. Set revera Christus vocem dilecti sui, scilicet
generis humani, indesinenter pulsantis audivit, propter quod diucius dormire noluit, tamquam si diceret: "Vox dilecti mei pulsantis, 'aperi michi,' " supple: non sinit me amplius dormire. Unde querenti a Christo causam
potissimam quare ita cito surrexit convenienter respondere potest et dicere
30   illud Canticorum 5: "Surrexi ut aperirem dilecto."
      Et ideo hic advertendum est pro illa admirabili resurrectione post tam
diram mortem quod ita erat de Christo secundum sentenciam cuiusdam doctoris
subtilis sermonem facientis super dictum thema Canticorum 5: "Surrexi ut
aperirem dilecto," sicut aliquando erat de bellatoribus antiquis. Ait ergo
35   sic: "Cum, inquit, varii sunt eventus belli, non semper illa pars que in
principio prosperatur consequetur victoriam. Imo cautela magna est interdum
fugam simulare, et precipue quando pars adversa cupida est prede." Unde
Sextus Iulius super Trogum Pompeyum libro 3, capitulo 10, narrat quod [f.
66v] Hanibal nobilissimus bellator et dux Cartaginensium aliquociens gratis
40   castra sua hostibus dimisit in predam et fugam simulavit ad tempus, set
post subito quasi superveniens hostes ⟨devicit⟩ et predam, quam amiserat,
eciam cum lucro recuperans exercitui distribuerat ut volebat. Revera sic
Christus fortis bellator et indeficiens in die Parasceves cum diabolo
prelium gessit. Videns ergo illum mirabiliter ad predam avidum et advertens
45   quod si ad tempus hostibus predam dimitteret, eam postea cum lucro recuperare posset, castrum illud nobilissimum corporis sui purissimo sanguine
virginali cementatum hostibus ad tempus concessit et fugam quasi similans
ad limbum patrum descendit. Et tunc more cuiusdam nobilis bellatoris, de
quo refert predictus Iulius libro eodem, capitulo 11, tantum rediit super
50   hostes uno die qua⟨ntum⟩ duobus diebus se simulaverat aufugisse, et sic
nobilem illam predam corporis sui benedicti die sue resurrectionis cum
lucro inmortalitatis recuperans eam sub sacramento velatam nobis curialis-
sime distribuit, ut merito dici potest illud Proverbiorum 31: "De nocte
surrexit deditque predam domesticis suis." Nec mirum quia hic est ille
55   fidelis amicus de quo in evangelio dicitur quod media nocte surgens dedit
petenti panes quotquot habuit necessarios. Nam ipse dat nobis corpus suum,
quod est panis vivus qui de celo descendit.
      Et nota quod secundum astrologos sol in firmamento per plura signa
discurrit a mense in mensem, inter que est quoddam signum quod Gemin⟨i⟩
60   vocatur, et hoc est spiritualiter signum federis et dilectionis Dei. In quo
signo Christus, qui est verus sol iusticie, potissime fuit die sue resurrectionis. Exemplum. Narrat enim Ovidius *Methamorphoseos* [f. 67] quod Gemini
erant duo fratres, quorum unus fuit mortalis et alius inmortalis. Set iste
secundus suam inmortalitatem partitus est fratri suo mortali eo quod tantus
65   esset inter eos amor et dilectio vera. Christus enim Filius Dei, qui est

asleep, he was the first to rise; Corinthians 15: "Christ is risen from the
dead, the first fruits of them that sleep." Another reason was this. When a
doorkeeper who is resting in his bed hears a friend knocking at the door, he
gets up at once because it is his friend. In the same way, Christ heard the
voice of his beloved, that is, of mankind who kept knocking without ceasing;
for which he would not sleep any longer, as if he were saying: "The voice of
my beloved knocking, 'Open me,' " add: it does not let me sleep anymore. Therefore, if one were to ask Christ for the true reason why he rose so soon, he
could answer fittingly with the words of Canticles 5: "I rose up to open to my
beloved."

With regard to this miraculous resurrection after such a painful death, we
may notice that in the opinion of a subtle doctor who preached on the quoted
theme from Canticles 5, "I rose up to open to my beloved," it was with Christ
just as it sometimes was with warriors of ancient days. This is what he says:
"Since the outcome of war is changeable, it is not always the party which is
successful in the beginning that wins the victory. Indeed at times it is a
great trick to pretend that one is fleeing, especially when the other side is
very eager for booty." Whence Sextus Julius in commenting on Trogus Pompey,
book 3, chapter 10, tells us that Hannibal, a noble warrior and general of the
Carthaginians, sometimes willingly left his castle as a booty in the hands of
his enemies and pretended for a while that he was fleeing; but suddenly he fell
on his enemies and overcame them and recovered the booty he had lost with even
greater gain, which he then distributed among his army as he wanted. In the
same way Christ, a strong and unfailing champion, as he did battle with the
devil on Good Friday, seeing that he was exceedingly eager for booty and aware
that, if he left his booty to the enemies for a while he could afterwards
recover it with gain, left the most noble castle of his body, which had been
built up from the most pure blood of a virgin, for a while in the hands of his
enemies and, as if pretending to flee, descended to the limbo of the forefathers. And then, like a noble warrior of whom Julius writes in chapter 11 of
the same book, he came back against his enemies on a day after he had pretended
to flee for two days, and recovering that noble booty of his blessed body on
the day of his resurrection with the gain of immortality, he has most courteously distributed it to us hidden in the sacrament. Of him can justly be
said what is written in Proverbs 31: "She has risen in the night and given a
prey to her household." It is no wonder that he is that faithful friend of
whom the Gospel says that he rose at midnight and gave him that was asking as
much bread as he needed. For he gives us his body, which is the living bread
that has come down from heaven.

Notice that according to the astronomers the sun in the sky passes through
various signs, month after month, among which is a sign called Gemini, and that
symbolizes the bond and love of God. In this sign was Christ, the true sun of

inmortalis secundum divinitatem et ex alia parte, scilicet [secundum] humanitatem, caro et frater noster est, partitus est nobis ex magna sui dilectione scilicet et amore suam immortalitatem. Cum prius mortalitati essemus subiecti, tamen per virtutem sui corporis benedicti, quod cotidie
70   sumimus, post diem iudicii erimus inmortales, si tamen rite sumendo transeamus in naturam eius, quem ad modum truncus convertitur in naturam surculi et non e contrario. Nam secundum Augustinum, si primi parentes stetissent in innocencia, per esum ligni vite fuissent inmortales. Sicut eciam nunc oportet corpus nostrum corrumpi propter cibum corporalem quem sumimus, sic
75   in paradiso erimus celesti inmortales propter cibum spiritualem quo ibidem nutriemur. Unde de isto cibo dicitur Iohannis 6: "Qui manducat hunc panem vivet in eternum."

Est eciam hic notandum quod non solum est corpus Christi benedictum panis set eciam caro delicatissima, prout habetur ibidem: "Panis, inquit,
80   quem ego dabo caro mea est." Et certe quia caro est, ideo merito preda dici potest generosa et venatica. Nam ut illa caro fieret tenera et delicata diutina venacione, sic voluit Christus fatigari et lacerari ut preda venatica diceretur. Que quidem preda fuit in craticula crucis sufficienter assata aut decocta. Quando experiri volumus utrum caro aliqua fuerit satis
85   assata aut decocta, parum illam comprimimus, et si nichil sanguinis exeat, dicitur quod satis est. Revera sic erat de carne Christi super craticulam crucis posita: cum ultima gutta sanguinis exivit aqua [f. 67v] in signum quod nichil crudum in illa remanserat. Unde figurative fuit iste agnus assandus, de quo Exodi 12: "Non comedetis ex eo crudum quid nec coctum
90   aqua, set tantum assatum igni." Similiter hec preda venacione Iudeorum capta bene figurabatur per cibum illum quem Iacob intulit Ysaac patri suo dicens: "Surge, comede de venacione mea," Genesis 26. In quo quidem festo sive cibo deceptus erat Ysaac in omni sensu preterquam in auditu. Revera sic est de illo cibo spirituali: quasi sumus decepti quoad omnem sensum
95   solo auditu excepto, ⟨nisi⟩ quantum per fidem edocemur.

Et nota quod sicut victores post bella gravia solent cum suis exultari et festa facere, revera sic Christus volens sue resurrectionis victoriam declarare. Ideo sue resurrectionis die nos de preda illa dulcissima sui corporis pascit et festum facit, ut sic cum eo simul letemur ac victores
100   esse videamur; Ysaie 14: "Letabuntur coram te sicut qui letantur in messe et sicut victores capta preda quando dividunt spolia."

Et nota quod fuit de Christo in sua resurrectione sicut est de viris religiosis quando minuti sunt sanguine. Vid⟨e⟩mus ergo quod inter illos talis consuetudo habetur quod, quando de gravi labore venerunt aut sanguine
105   minuuntur, tocius noctis quies illis conceditur, quando alii non vexati nec minuti media nocte surgere tenentur. Si quis ergo diligenter considerat, vi⟨debit⟩ quod Christus triginta tribus annis quibus in hoc mundo vixit

justice, particularly on the day of his resurrection. As an example, Ovid in his *Metamorphoses* tells the following story. The Gemini were two brothers, one mortal, the other immortal. But the latter shared his immortality with his mortal brother, so great was the true love and liking between them. Christ, the Son of God, did the same: being immortal in his divinity, and on the other hand, that is in his human nature, flesh and our brother, he shared his immortality with us out of his great liking and love. Though we were originally subject to mortality, by the power of his blessed body, which we receive daily, we shall yet be immortal after the day of judgment, if indeed by receiving him rightly we change into his nature, just as a stock is changed into the nature of the graft and not the reverse. For according to Augustine, if our first parents had remained firm in their innocence, they would have become immortal by eating from the tree of life. Just as now our body must become corrupted because of the bodily food we eat, so in the heavenly paradise we shall be immortal because of the spiritual food with which we shall be nourished there. Whence John 6 says of this food: "He that eats that bread shall live forever."

And we should notice further that not only is the blessed body of Christ our bread but also his most delicate flesh, as is said in the same place, John 6: "The bread that I will give is my flesh." And since it is flesh, it may rightly be called the flesh of a noble game. For just as game becomes tender and delicate through long hunting, so Christ wanted to be tired out and torn to pieces that he might be called game. That game was thoroughly broiled and cooked on the gridiron of the cross. When we want to try if a piece of meat is sufficiently broiled or cooked, we squeeze it a little, and if no blood comes out, we say that it is well done. This is what happened to Christ's flesh on the grill of the cross: with the last drop of blood water came out as a sign that nothing raw was left in it. Therefore he was figuratively that lamb of Exodus 12 which was to be broiled: "You shall not eat thereof anything raw, nor boiled in water, but only what has been roasted on the fire." Similarly, this prey captured in the hunt of the Jews is prefigured in the dish which Jacob brought his father, Isaac, saying: "Arise, eat of my venison," Genesis 26. In that feast or food Isaac was deceived in all his senses except his hearing. Thus it is also with this spiritual food: we are, as it were, deceived by it in all our senses with the exception of our hearing, unless we are taught by faith.

Notice that just as the winners after a fierce war usually celebrate and feast with their own, so Christ wanted to declare the victory of his resurrection. Therefore, on the day of his resurrection he feeds us with the sweet booty of his body and gives us a banquet, so that we may be happy with him and appear as winners; Isaiah 14: "They shall rejoice before you as they who rejoice in the harvest and as conquerors after taking a prey, when they divide the spoils."

continuis laboribus se afflixit, et non solum hoc set in utroque brachio
minutus fuit et ceteris membris, ut patet. Quid ergo mirum si per duas
110   noctes quievit et postea surrexit?
    Nota eciam quod Christus surrexit multis modis. Primo veraciter,
contra falsos et fictos qui in Quadragesima solum surgunt a peccatis [f.
68] suis propter famam et iudicium aliorum. Secundo surrexit velociter,
contra procrastinantes correctionem vite. Tercio indeficienter, contra
115   recidivantes. Et quarto patenter, contra illos qui nulli audent peccata sua
detegere set sic obstinantur.
    Et nota quod Christus post suam resurrectionem diversis locis et
personis se manifestavit, scilicet [primo] in orto ut ortolanus, secundo in
via ut peregrinus, tercio in cenaculo ut strenuus bellator, quarto iuxta
120   mare ut providus piscator, quinto in castro ut cautus i⟨o⟩culator. Primo
manifestavit se in orto, ubi aquam copiosam ad irrigandum suum viridarium
invenit. Que quidem [aque] lacrime fuerunt Marie Magdalene, cui post resurrectionem primo apparuit. Per quam aquam suum viridarium, idest animam
predicte Marie, irrigavit, cum prius fuit puteus abissi vilissimus. Qua sic
125   inde irrigata, Christus tamquam optimus ortolanus in illa plantavit primo
rosam caritatis, secundo lilium castitatis, tercio violam humilitatis,
quarto solsequium stabilitatis. Et nota quod solsequium naturaliter ad
ortum solis se aperit et ad occasum se claudit; sic fides Marie cum Christo
claudebatur, quia credebat eum mortuum quando erat mortuus, et cum Christo
130   ⟨non⟩ aperiebatur, quia ⟨non⟩ statim eum vivum credebat postquam surrexit.
Et ideo necesse fuit Christum illud solsequium sua gracia irrigare.
    Secundo dico quod Christus aparuit in via sicut peregrinus. Summa enim
recreacio et solacium est in via bonas narraciones audire. Et ideo Christus
narravit discipulis utilia et eciam mirabilia, compunctiva passionis, et
135   inflammativa dilectionis, que omnia satis patent Luce ⟨2⟩4 de discipulis
euntibus in Emaus. Tercio aparuit in cenaculo ut strenuus bellator, et hoc
trepidantibus pre timore discipulis, de quibus dicitur quod "erant congre-
gati in unum propter metum Iudeorum." Ad quorum solacium primo ostendit
pedes quibus vicerat peccata in- [f. 68v] feriora, scilicet gulam et luxu-
140   riam; secundo ostendit eis manus, quibus vicerat mundi prosperitatem et
adversitatem; tercio latus, quo eciam vicerat diaboli superbiam, iram, et
invidiam. Quarto et ultimo aparuit iuxta mare ut providus piscator, sicut
patet in evangelio unde dixit stans in litore: "Numquid pulmentarium habetis?" Et post dicitur: "Cum in terram ascendissent, viderunt prunas positas
145   et piscem superpositum." Quinto aparuit in castro ut cautus i⟨o⟩culator.
Tunc enim se ostendit plaudentibus, set quia eorum plausus de Christo
fuerat vanus, ideo insufflavit in pixidem, idest in eos, et statim disparuit, ut per hoc ostenderet eis eorum gaudium vanum fuisse.
    Et nota bene quod pro ista resurrectione secundum Palladium *De agri-*

And notice that in his resurrection it was with Christ as it is with religious when they have been let blood. For we see that among them it is the custom that, when they have done very hard work or are let blood, they are allowed to rest the whole night, whereas others that are not exhausted from labor or bloodletting are required to rise at midnight. Whoever considers it carefully will see that Christ took upon himself constant hard work for the thirty-three years that he lived in this world, and in addition he was let blood in both arms and other parts, as is evident. What wonder, then, if he rested for two nights before he rose?

Notice also that Christ rose in many ways. First, he rose truly, against those false and feigned Christians who rise from their sins only during Lent for the sake of their reputation and other people's opinion. Second, he rose quickly, against those who delay the amendment of their life. Third, he rose without fail, against those who slide back. And fourth, he rose openly, against those who dare not show their sins to anyone and thus become hardened in sin.

And notice further that after his resurrection Christ showed himself in different places and to different people, namely in the garden as a gardener, on the road as a pilgrim, in the supper room as a strong warrior, by the sea as a skillful fisherman, and in the castle as a cautious juggler. First he showed himself in the garden, where he found abundant water to water his park. These waters were the tears of Mary Magdalene, to whom he appeared first after his resurrection. Through this water he watered his park, that is, the soul of Mary Magdalene, which formerly had been a most vile cesspool. When it was thus watered, Christ like an excellent gardener planted first a rose of charity in it, then a lily of chastity, third a violet of humility, and fourth a sunflower of stability. Notice that the sunflower by its nature opens at sunrise and closes at sunset; in the same way, Mary Magdalene's faith closed with Christ, for she believed he was truly dead when he had died, but it did not open with Christ, for she did not right away believe that he was alive after he rose. Therefore it was necessary for Christ to water that sunflower with his grace.

In the second place I say Christ appeared on the road as a pilgrim. The best kind of recreation and comfort on a journey is to listen to good stories. For that reason Christ told his disciples useful and marvelous things that led to compassion and kindled their love. All this can be seen in Luke 24, concerning the disciples on the road to Emmaus. In the third place he appeared in the supper room as a strong champion, and he did so before his disciples, who were shaking with fear, of whom it is said that "they were gathered together for fear of the Jews." To comfort them he first showed them his feet, with which he had overcome the lower sins, that is, gluttony and lechery; secondly he showed them his hands, with which he had overcome the prosperity and the adversity of the world; thirdly he showed them his side, with which he had

150   *cultura* Christ⟨us⟩ cum vulneribus resurgens bene amigdalo comparatur, cuius
      natura est secundum eundem quod, si aliqua scriptura in illa scribatur et
      postea in terra plantetur, quod in foliis, fructu, et radice in posterum
      predicta scriptura apparebit. Unde secundum eum illius arboris fructus est
      cibus precipuus infirmorum. Revera iste fructus Filius Dei bene potest
155   dici, per cuius corporis viaticum infirmi per peccata ad vitam reducuntur
      eternam; Iohannis 6: "Qui manducat hunc panem, vivet in eternum." In isto
      ergo amigdalo corporis Christi quinque littere scripte fuerunt, scilicet
      quinque plage. Que littere possunt dici regis Assueri, quibus veteres
      littere Aman, idest diaboli, iniqui insidiatoris, corriguntur, cuius lit-
160   tere fuerunt male suggestiones per quas primos parentes in quinque sensibus
      peccatis fecit consentire. Set Assuerus, qui beatitudo interpretatur, idest
      Christus Filius Dei, per litteras vulnerum suorum eius litteras correxit et
      totaliter delevit dum potestate[m] diaboli per dicta vulnera in cruce
      depressit. Set iste amigdalus in terra plantatur dum Christus in sepulcro
165   terre ponitur iuxta illud [f. 69] evangelii: "Erit Filius Hominis in corde
      terre tribus diebus et tribus noctibus." Set certe tunc crevit quando
      ⟨Christus⟩ surrexit a mortuis, in quo tunc dicte littere apertissime appa-
      ruerunt. Et hoc bene patuit quando dixit Thome: "Videte manus meas et
      pedes," etc.
170   Item ad idem de quodam animali pantera nomine narratur, quod est
      animal mansuetum et pulcrum valde, eo quod variis coloribus est respersum.
      Cuius presencia omnibus animalibus est valde delectabilis preterquam draco-
      ni et pullis eius. Cum ergo comederit animal illud et fuerit saciatum,
      cavernam intrat, ubi tribus diebus et noctibus continue fertur dormire.
175   Tercio vero die evigilans clamorem magnum emittit, quem odor suavissimus
      commitatur. Cuius clamorem cum audierint animalia longe aut prope distan-
      cia, propter odoris suavitatem sibi occurrunt et secuntur, dracone tamen
      excepto, qui odio naturali illum cum pullis suis affugit et abscondit.
      Pantera autem iste propter suam mansuetudinem et pulcritudinem signat
180   Christum, qui de seipso ait illud Jeremie: "Ego quasi agnus mansuetus," et
      in Psalmo: "Speciosus forma pre filiis hominum." Postquam hic Christus
      comederit et saciatus fuerit penis et miseriis diversis in hoc mundo, post
      in caverna crucis et monumenti tribus diebus et noctibus dormivit. Cum ergo
      tercia die quasi a mortis dormicione evigilasset et demum surrexisset et
185   per suos predicatores vitam eternam proclamasset, cuncta animalia, idest
      diversa genera Christianorum, ipsum sequuntur, solo dracone, idest diabolo,
      cum pullis falsorum Christianorum et aliorum infidelium exceptis et sub
      terrena cupiditate absconditis.
          Ad idem eciam fertur quod natura leonis est quod cum leena peperit
190   catulum, generat illum mortuum et tribus diebus sic custodit, donec tercia
      die pater eius venerit et in faciem eius sufflaverit, cuius natura [f. 69v]

overcome the devil's pride, wrath, and envy. In the fourth and last place he appeared by the sea as a skillful fisherman, as can be found in the Gospel when he said on the shore: "Have you any meat?" And then follows: "As soon as they came back to land, they saw hot coals lying and a fish laid thereon." In the fifth place he appeared in the castle as a cautious juggler. For then he showed himself to those who applauded him, but since their applause was vain, he blew in his box, that is, on them, and at once disappeared, in order to show them that their joy was vain.

And notice that because Christ rose with his wounds he can well be compared to the almond, as Palladius describes it in his work *On Agriculture*. According to Palladius the almond has this characteristic that, if one writes something on it and then plants it in the ground, the writing will afterwards appear on its leaves, fruit, and root. Whence according to Palladius the fruit of this tree is excellent nourishment for the sick. This fruit may be said to be the Son of God, through whose body as viaticum those who are sick with sins are brought back to eternal life; John 6: "He that eats this bread shall live forever." On this almond, the body of Christ, were written five letters, that is, the five wounds. These may be said to be the letters of King Ahasuerus, by which the old letters of Haman, that is, of the devil, the instigator of mischief, are corrected. These letters were the evil suggestions through which the devil caused our first parents to consent to sin in their five senses. But Ahasuerus, whose name means blessedness and who stands for Christ, the Son of God, has through the letters of his wounds corrected and wholly erased the former letters when he suppressed the devil's power through his wounds on the cross. This almond is planted in the earth when Christ is laid in a tomb in the earth, according to the Gospel: "The Son of Man shall be in the heart of the earth for three days and three nights." But the almond started to grow when Christ rose from the dead, and then the aforementioned letters appeared in him most openly. This was quite evident when he said to Thomas: "Behold my hands and my feet," etc.

On the same subject we read further about an animal called panther, which is very meek and beautiful because it is sprinkled with various colors. Its company is very delightful to all other animals except the dragon and its offspring. When this animal has eaten its fill, it enters its cave, where it is said to sleep for three days and nights without interruption. But on the third day it awakens and gives forth a loud cry, accompanied by a most sweet odor. When the other animals hear this cry, whether they are far or near, they run toward it because of the sweet smell and follow it, with the exception only of the dragon, who flees from it with its offspring because of its inborn hatred and hides itself. This panther, because of its meekness and beauty, symbolizes Christ, who says of himself the words of Jeremiah: "I am like a meek lamb," and of the Psalm: "Beautiful above the sons of man." After Christ

catulus vivificatur. Sic omnipotens Pater Filium eius in cruce mortuum
tercia die eius flatu divinitatis a morte suscitavit, dicente Iob: "Dormi-
vit, inquit, leo et sicut catulus leonis suscitavit," scilicet a mortuis.

2–3 verissime] certissime O.   **6** Christus . . . collocatus] christo in ligno crucis collocato
O.   **23** surrexit] *add* a mortuis O.   **31** illa admirabili] ista mirabili O.   **36** consequetur]
consequitur O.   **41** devicit] divisit C.   **42** exercitui] *add* suo O.   **50** quantum] quam
C.R.W.   **53** merito] *add* de eo O.   **59** discurrit] decurrit O.   **59–60** quod Gemini vo-
catur] geminis M.R; gemima W.   **59** Gemini] geminus C.   **66** divinitatem] deitatem O.
68 scilicet] *om* O.   **79** ibidem] *add* iohannis capitulo 6 O.   **88** iste] ille O.   **89** quo] *om*
O.   **94** illo] isto O.   **95** nisi] ubi C.   **103** Videmus] videamus C.   ergo] autem O.
107 videbit] videlicet C.   **115** sua] *om* O.   **118** primo] *om* R.C.   **120** ioculator] iaculator C.   **122** aque] *om* C.W. Marie] *om* O.   **124** fuit] fuerit O.   **126** humilitatis] *add* et
O.   **127** stabilitatis] M *and others add the following*: et nota quod solsequium dicitur
quasi sequens solem sic fidelis debet sequi christum in omnibus factis suis.   **130** non(1)]
canc and marg vero C.   non(2)] *exp* C.   **132** sicut] ut O.   **135** 24] 34 C.R.   **143** unde]
quando O.   **145** ioculator] iaculator C.   **150** Christus] christi C.   **151** eundem] eum
O.   **167** Christus] dixit C.   **173** illud] istud O.   **175** Tercio] tercia O.   **177** tamen] tantum O.   **183** tribus . . . noctibus] *om* O.   **184** mortis] mortuis O.   demum] *om* O.

III.xxi   DE CHRISTI ASCENSIONE

[C]irca autem ascencionem Christi post eius benedictam resurrectionem
est aliquid breviter dicendum. Circa quod est advertendum quod nobis maximam dilectionem ostendit quando nostram naturam in tam sublimi loco pre
ceteris creaturis dignaretur collocare, scilicet ad dextram Patris in celo,
5 quasi per hoc innuens quod si veri fideles fuerimus et false nomen Christi
non usurpaverimus, sicut ipse supra omnem creaturam in nostra natura et nos
sequemur pre ceteris tamquam filii et heredes ab eo veraciter denominati
sine fine regnaturi. A Christo enim Christiani nominantur. Et ideo de sua
benedicta ascencione ante nos in nostra natura bene dici potest illud
10 Michee 3: "Ascendit iter pandens ante eos," quasi diceret: Christus sicut
bonus doctor et ductor nos precedit rectam viam nobis ostendens quomodo
sine devio illum sequemur.

had eaten his fill of divers pains and miseries in this world, he went to sleep in the cave of the cross and the tomb for three days and nights. But when he woke on the third day and rose, as from the sleep of death, and proclaimed eternal life through his preachers, all the animals followed him, that is, the various kinds of Christians, except the dragon, that is, the devil, and its offspring of false Christians and other unfaithful, who hide in earthly cupidity.

On the same topic it is said that it is the nature of the lion that, when the female gives birth to a cub, she brings it forth dead and keeps it thus for three days, until on the third day its father comes and breathes into its face, by whose breath the cub comes to life. In the same manner the omnipotent Father brought his Son, after he had died on the cross, back to life on the third day with his divine breath; as Job says: "The lion has slept, and like the cub of the lion he has raised," that is, from the dead.

8–9 Matt. 27.45.   **12** Ps. 3.6.   **17** Cf. Mark 13.34.   **18–19** Augustine, *In Iohannis evangelium* XLVI.3 (CC 36:399); on John 10.3.   **22–23** 1 Cor. 15.20.   **27–28** Cant. 5.2.   **30** Cant. 5.5.   **38–42** Frontinus, *Stratagemata* III.x.3–4.   **53–54** Prov. 31.15. **55–54** Cf. John 6.41ff.   **62–65** *Mythographus Vaticanus III* III.7; based on Ovid, *Met.* II.18.   **72–73** Probably Bede, as quoted in *Glossa* on Gen. 1.29–30 (CC 118A:30f.). **76–77** John 6.59.   **79–80** John 6.52.   **89–90** Exod. 12.9.   **92** Gen. 27.31.   **100– 101** Isa. 9.3.   **135–136** Cf. Luke 24.32.   **137–138** John 20.19.   **143–144** John 21.5. **144–145** John 21.9.   **145–148** For a story about a juggler, or rather trickster, who blows and makes people blow into a *pixis*, see *Tabula exemplorum*, p. 88 note 6, and No. 50. **149–154** Palladius, *De agricultura* II.xv.13.   **156** John 6.59.   **158–161** Cf. Esther 8. **165–166** Matt. 12.40.   **168–169** Luke 24.39.   **170–178** The same story and moralization in Brinton, Sermons 40, 56, and 107 (pp. 179, 258f., and 494). Cf. *Physiologus*, p. 124.   **180** Jer. 11.19.   **181** Ps. 44.3.   **189–192** Cf. Isidore, *Etym.* XII.ii.5.   **193– 194** Cf. Gen. 49.9.

III.xxi   CHRIST'S ASCENSION

With respect to Christ's ascension after his blessed resurrection, we must briefly say and call to mind that he showed his great love for us when he placed our nature in such an exalted place above any other creature, namely at the right hand of the Father in heaven. By this he let us know that if we are truly faithful and do not take the name of Christ falsely, we shall—just as he is above all creation in our nature—follow him before all others as his children and heirs, truly named after him, in order to rule without end. For Christians have their name from Christ. Therefore the words of Micah 3 can be applied to his blessed ascension before us in our nature: "He goes up opening the way before them," as if he were saying: Christ goes before us as a good teacher and leader, showing us the right way by which we shall follow him without going astray.

Et nota: quando via aliqua non est usitata, non sufficit solum quod
aliquis doceat nudo verbo per illam volentem transire, verum eciam cum
15   doctore indiget ductore. Set modo via celi ante Christi ascencionem non
fuit multum usitata, et ideo Christus non solum docuit viam illam verbo aut
signo, sicut multi faciunt protensa manu quamvis per eam non incedant,
sicut faciunt ypocrite, de quibus ⟨Mattheus⟩: "Dicunt et non faciunt"; set
Christus primo cepit facere et postea docere, precedens scilicet ante nos
20   viam quam docuit secundum illud Deuteronomii: "Dux itineris fuisti in conspectu eius."

Exemplum. Elephas autem secundum Solinum huius nature est quod si per
desertum a casu hominem vagabundum viderit, usque ad notas vias ducatum
prebet. Et secundum Ambrosium, si viderit hominem timere eum, a via di- [f.
25   70] vertit quousque sit ante eum, et sic precedit quousque ad viam rectam
perduxerit.

Ad idem eciam narrat Sextus Iulius de quodam duce Zenophilus nomine,
qui dum excercitum per ardua itinera incedere precepisset et illi murmuran-
do dixerunt facile esse sedentem precipere difficilia, statim equum ascen-
30   dens in dictis itineribus precessit alios animans ut eum constanter seque-
rentur. Revera sic fuit de Christo duce nostro. Ipse enim precessit nos per
viam penitencie ducens ad celum, iuxta illud Psalmi: "Ego custodivi vias
duras."

Avis enim ascendens sursum secura est ab ancupe doloso, et quanto
35   alcior tanto securior; set quamcito descendit ad terram ut quiescat vel ut
cibum capiat, tunc est in periculo ne forte illaqueatur. Et tamen verum est
quod non sentit laqueum dum comedit aut quiescit, set quando vellet recedere et ascendere, tunc primo se sentit illaqueatam et detentam. Revera sic in
proposito. Homo enim volans ad Deum per contemplacionem securus est, set
40   quamcito descendit ad terram, hoc est ad quietem deliciarum terrenarum, in
periculo est ⟨ne⟩ forte in peccato illaqueatur. Et tamen ibi quamdiu delicie
durant nullum sentit periculum aut laqueum, set quando a mundo vellet
recedere et ad Deum redire, tunc sentit laquea peccatorum ipsum detinencia,
iuxta illud Iob 18: "Tenebitur planta eius laqueo." Et ideo Christus
45   volens nos ab huiusmodi periculis precavere, ad modum aquile pullos suos
ascendere et volare docentis nos instruit; ⟨Deuteronomii 32⟩: "Sicut aquila
provocans ad volandum pullos suos," supple: sic Christus nos instruit periculis cavere.

Natura autem aquile talis est quod secum portat [escam] pro pullis
50   suis et ante eos gradatim, non subito nec statim, elevat se in sublimi
quantum posset, set primo iuxta eos prope volat, secundo aliquantulum supra
eos, et tercio ad suppremum ascendit. Revera sic in proposito. [f. 70v]
Quantum ad divinitatem Christus [est] esca nostra, per quam spiritualiter
pascimur et fovemur. Igitur ob nimium amorem nos instruit et docet gradatim

And notice: when a road is unknown, it is not enough for the would-be traveler to get verbal instructions, but with the teacher he also needs a leader. Now, before Christ's ascension the road to heaven was not much in use; therefore, Christ did not merely point it out with a word or sign, as many people do by pointing with their hand, even though they themselves never use that road, as hypocrites do, of whom Matthew says: "They say and do not do"; but Christ first began to do it himself and only afterwards to teach it, thus going before us on the way he taught, in accordance with the words of Deuteronomy: "You were the guide of its journey in its sight."

As an example: according to Solinus the elephant has this characteristic that, if by chance he sees a man wandering through the desert, he will lead him to some well-known road. And according to Ambrose, if the elephant sees that man to be in fear, he turns away from the road until he is in front of the man and then goes before him until he has led him to the right road.

On the same subject, Sextus Julius tells of a general named Zenophilus; when he commanded his troops to march through rough territory and they grumbled, saying it is easy for a man at rest to order difficult things, he at once got on his horse and went before them on the rough roads, encouraging them to follow him bravely. Thus it was likewise with Christ, our leader. For he went before us, leading us on the way of penance to heaven, according to the Psalm: "I have kept hard ways."

When a bird flies up high, it is safe from the deceitful fowler, and the higher it flies, the safer it is; but as soon as it comes down to the ground to rest or to catch some food, it is in danger of being ensnared. And yet it is true that this bird does not feel the snare while it is eating or resting; but when it wants to go back and fly up high, then it finds itself snared and held fast. The same is true in spiritual matters. When a man flies to God in contemplation, he is safe, but as soon as he comes down to the ground, that is, to rest in earthly delights, he is in danger of becoming ensnared in sin. And yet, as long as his delights there last, he feels no danger or snare; but when he tries to leave the world and return to God, then he feels the snares of sin holding him fast, according to the words of Job 18: "His sole shall be held in a snare." Therefore, since Christ wants us to beware of such dangers, he teaches us as an eagle teaches its young to rise up and fly; Deuteronomy 32: "As an eagle enticing her young to fly," add: thus Christ teaches us to beware of dangers.

It is the custom of an eagle, when he carries some food for his young, not to rise suddenly before them as high as possible but rather at first to fly close to them, then to fly somewhat above them, and thirdly to rise up high. In moral terms, in his divine nature Christ is our food, with which we are spiritually fed and nourished. Therefore, in his great love he teaches us to rise after him by steps. First through contemplation and prayer, wherein any

55 post illum ascendere. Et primo per contemplacionem et oracionem, ubi quili-
    bet devotus invenit refectionem spiritualem delicatissimam; ad quem gradum
    ipsemet Christus sicut bonus ductor primo ascendit, iuxta illud Matthei 34:
    "Ascendit in montem solus orare." Secundus gradus est per penitenciam,
    idest per passionem penitencie, quando scilicet homo ita elevatus est a
60 terrenis et carnalibus quod tantum in operibus penitencie gloriatur, iuxta
    illud Ad Galatas 6: "Michi autem absit gloriari nisi in cruce ⟨Domini
    nostri Iesu Christi⟩." Et certe hunc gradum similiter Christus ascendit,
    quando scilicet in cruce pro nobis elevatus est et mortem pro nobis subire
    voluit. Unde istam arborem ascendere oportet quod hoc fiat, eciam cum magno
65 labore "reptando manibus et pedibus" sicut fecit Ionathas post David, sicut
    habetur 1 Regum 14. Nota historiam. Sic enim fecit Christus ante nos,
    quando lignum crucis ascendit manibus et pedibus in illa affixis, ad quam
    si attingere poterimus, maximam contra inimicos securitatem inveniemus.
        Unde refert Gamaleel in *Historia Iherosolomitana* quod quedam naturalis
70 inimicicia est inter aquilam et serpentem. Et ideo aquila volens sibi et
    pullis suis securitatem previdere ponit nidum suum non deorsum in terra set
    superius in aliqua arbore vel rupe serpenti inaccessibili. Quod ⟨cum⟩
    avertit serpens, instinctu naturali ex opposito ascendit super aliquem
    montem altum, quando scilicet ventus dirigitur versus locum illum ubi pulli
75 latent, et ibi aerem secundum posse suum inficit ut sic per venenum missum
    in aere dictos pullos possit interficere. Set hanc maliciam supernaturali-
    ter presciens aquila lapidem quemdam querit, amatistus nomine, et illum in
    nido cum pullis ponit, cuius virtute pulli salvantur. Spiritualiter per
    istam aquilam Christus [f. 71] intelligi potest, qui supra human⟨u⟩m fertur
80 obtuitum. Set per illum serpentem intelligitur hostis antiquus; sicut ergo
    videmus, inter Deum et hunc serpentem fuerunt inimicicie ab inicio creacio-
    nis. Pulli autem in nido Christi sunt homines in hac vita, quos continue
    dictus serpens insidiatur ut interficiat. Volens ergo Christus pullis suis
    previdere locum securum et altum, in arbore quadam, idest in ligno crucis
85 in monte Calvarie, propter omnem securitatem nostram elegit. Si ergo ser-
    pens iste per malas suggestiones in mente per audita, dicta, aut facta
    aerem nostri intellectus per flatum elacionis et superbie infecerit, per quam
    pullos bonorum operum nostrorum interficeret, capiamus h⟨u⟩nc lapidem
    amatistum, idest Christum, in exemplum humilitatis omnimode, et contra
90 omnia mala per hoc salvemur.
        Tercius gradus fuit quando in celum videntibus discipulis ante nos
    ascendit, ubi certe tenet cibum illum delicatissimum pro nobis, scilicet
    corpus suum benedictum, per quem hic in enigmate set ibi facie ad faciem
    depascemur sine fine; Ieremie 49: "Ecce aquila ascendet et volabit et
95 expandet alas suas."
        Et nota: homo ascendens in sublimi potest a remociori videre quam

devout person finds the most delicate spiritual nourishment; to this step
Christ himself climbed first, like a good guide, according to Matthew 34: "He
went into a mountain alone to pray." The second step is through penance and
through the suffering of penance, that is, when a person has risen so high
above earthly and fleshly things that he finds his glory only in works of
penance, after Galatians 6: "God forbid that I should glory, save in the cross
of our Lord Jesus Christ." Certainly, Christ rose to this step in like fashion
when he was raised on the cross for us and wanted to undergo death for us.
Therefore it is necessary to climb this tree, and this is done by "creeping on
hands and feet" with great labor, as Jonathan did after David, as in 1 Kings
14. Tell this story. Christ did the same before us when he climbed on the
tree of the cross and was nailed to it with his hands and feet; if we can come
to this cross, we shall find absolute safety from our enemies.

Therefore Gamaliel in his *History of Jerusalem* reports that there is a
natural hostility between the eagle and the snake. Consequently, when the
eagle wants safety for himself and his young, he puts his nest not on the
ground but high up in a tree or on a rock which is out of the snake's reach.
But when the snake notices this, by its natural instinct it creeps up on some
high mountain that stands against the eagle's nest, and when the wind blows in
the direction of the nest where the young birds are hidden it poisons the air
as much as it can, so that it may kill the young birds with its poison released
in the air. But the eagle has some supernatural presentiment of such mischief
and looks for a certain stone called amethyst, which it puts in the nest
together with his young, by whose power the young birds are saved. Allegorically, by this eagle we may understand Christ, whose sight is said to be keener
than man's. But that serpent stands for our ancient enemy; as we see, there
has been enmity between God and this serpent from the beginning of creation.
The young birds in Christ's nest are men in this life, whom that serpent
constantly tries to kill. Therefore, in his care for his young, Christ chose a
safe place high up in a tree for our safety, namely in the tree of the cross on
Mount Calvary. But if this serpent has poisoned the air of our mind by its
breath of arrogance and pride and has blown evil suggestions into our mind
through things we hear, say, or do, through which it might kill the offspring
of our good works, then let us hold on firmly to this stone, Christ, as our
example of humility, and we shall be safe from all evils.

The third step was his ascension into heaven before us, with his disciples
looking on. There he certainly holds that most delicate food for us, his
blessed body, through which we shall be fed, here under a veil but there face
to face, in order to live without end; Jeremiah 49: "Behold the eagle shall
come up and fly and spread his wings."

And notice that when a person climbs onto a high place he can see farther
than those who remain below. Thus, when a person has overcome earthly and

inferius commorantes. Revera sic homo superatis terrenis et carnalibus et
in monte virtuose operacionis et humili contemplacione celestium constitutus potest videre a remotis ex omni parte que sunt bona et que sunt mala,
100   que fugienda et que amplectenda. Exemplum. Si enim respiciat ad orientem
sui ortus, ibi propriam miseriam satis intuetur; si ad occidentem sue
mortis, hoc idem prospiciet; si ad aquilonem, bene consideret iudicium et
penam inferni; si quarto ad aliam partem, scilicet austrum, respexerit, ibi
considerabit gloriam et gaudium beatorum. Et certe sicut per humilem con-
105   templacionem omnia predicta in monte devocionis [f. 71v] considerare optinebit, sic certe [in] valle cupiditatis et avaricie latens non tantum
istorum set eciam sui ipsius noticiam perdet, scilicet quomodo fuit in sui
primordio sperma vilissimum, in sui medio vas stercorum, et in sui termino
nichil aliud quam esca vermium. "Attendat ergo homo peccator," dicit Ber-
110   nardus, "sua primordia et erubescat, media et ingemiscat, ultima et contre-
miscat." Et ideo vocatur homo ab humo, quasi de vili materia, propter sui
humiliacionem; Iob: "Homo̦ natus de muliere brevi vivens tempore repletur
multis miseriis," etc. Ascende ergo, o homo, ad montem contemplacionis cum
Christo et considera quomodo homini existenti deorsum et inferius omnia
115   superiora videntur parva, scilicet sol et luna et huiusmodi. Considera e
contrario quomodo homini existenti superius in altissimo monte similiter
omnia inferiora videntur minima. Revera sic qui superius ascendunt ad Deum
per caritatem parum curant de terrenis, et e contrario, sicut patet intuenti. Set caveant homines, quia certe mundus ducit in invio et non in via
120   recta set erratice, ita quod numquam permittit hominem per rectum iter ad
celum, quantum in illo est, pervenire.
     Set ecce remedium quod numquam a via recta versus celum deviabis.
Oportet te facere sicut isti marinarii faciunt quando sunt longe in mari et
de nocte nescientes quo se divertere debent. Accipiunt autem parvum acum et
125   ponunt per medium parvi straminis, et tunc utrumque ponunt in vase cum
aqua, ut sic levitate straminis simul in aqua natent. Quo facto accipiunt
lapidem magnetem, cuius natura est ferrum attrahere, et vas illud cum dicta
acu et stramine circueunt ab extra, et semper lapidem sequitur ferrum
naturaliter. Quo facto quasi instantanee retrahit manum cum lapide, et tunc
130   ferrum velociter circuit quasi querens lapidem. Set quando natura lapidis
in ferro re- [f. 72] cepta consumitur, tunc natans requiescit versus orientem naturaliter et occidentem, et tunc sciunt ad quam partem divertere
debent. Revera sic in proposito. Ferrum istud ponderosum corpus humanum
signat, set leve stramen animam signat, ex cuius levitate corpus vivit.
135   Mare est mundus, set vas cum aqua est cor contritum. Si ergo fuerimus extra
viam versus celum, capiamus lapidem, scilicet Christum, et giramus bene
istud corpus, scilicet meditando iugiter de eius vilitate et fragilitate,
ut superius est dictum, et ⟨quam⟩ levis, pura, et perfecta in se est anima,

fleshly values and lives on the mountain of virtuous deeds in humble contemplation of heavenly things, he sees farther in all directions what is good and
what is evil, what is to be shunned and what is to be embraced. For example,
if he looks to the east of his birth, he will see his own wretchedness; if he
looks to the west of his death, he will see that there; if he looks to the
north, he will clearly see the judgment and the pain of hell; and if, lastly,
he looks to the south, he will see the future glory and the joy of the blessed.
And just as, in humble contemplation, he thus reflects on all these things on
the mountain of devotion, so a person that hides in the valley of cupidity and
avarice will lose the knowledge not only of these things but even of himself,
that is, how at his beginning he was vile sperm, in mid-life a vessel of dung,
and in his end nothing else but food for worms. "Let the sinner therefore
think of his beginnings and blush," says Bernard, "let him think of his mid-
life and sigh, and let him think of his end and tremble!" For this reason,
homo, "man," is so called from *humus*, "earth," that is, a vile matter, in order
to become humble; Job: "Man born of woman, living for a short time, is filled
with many miseries," etc. Therefore, climb up, man, to the mountain of contemplation with Christ and consider how to a person that lives below, all higher
things, such as the sun and the moon and so on, seem small. Consider, on the
other hand, how to a person that lives above, on a high mountain, similarly all
things below seem tiny. Thus, those who climb up high toward God in charity
care very little for earthly things, and vice-versa, as one can see. But let
men beware, for the world certainly leads us where there is no path, not on the
straight road but astray, so that it never lets a man come to heaven by the
right way, as much as this lies in its power.

But here is a remedy so that you will never stray from the right way to
heaven. You must do as sailors do when they are far at sea in the night
without knowing in which direction to sail. They take a small needle, put it
through the middle of a small piece of straw, and place both in a dish of
water, so that the needle and straw float in the water because of the lightness
of the straw. Next they take a magnetic stone, which naturally attracts iron,
and move it around the outside of the dish with the water and the straw, and
the iron needle always follows the stone by its natural impulse. Then they
suddenly withdraw the hand holding the stone, and the iron needle turns fast in
a circle as if it were seeking the stone. But when the magnetism which the
needle had received from that stone is spent, by the force of nature the needle
floats to rest pointing toward east and west, and then the sailors know in
which direction they must sail. In moral application, this piece of iron,
which is heavy, symbolizes man's body, but the light straw is his soul, by
whose light nature the body lives. The sea is the world, but the dish with
water is a contrite heart. If we have strayed from the way to heaven, let us
take that stone, Christ, and make our body turn around, namely by meditating

quia ex propria natura ipsum statim celum ascenderet nisi esset a pondero-
140   sitate impedita acus tui corporis. Quo facto retrahe manum, et statim
consideres orientem tue nativitatis, quomodo scilicet mundum intrasti,
sicut dictum est, et ubi erit occidens, scilicet quomodo per mortem transi-
bis. Et revera istis bene consideratis numquam per peccatum deviabis, iuxta
illud: "Memorare novissima tua et in eternum non peccabis."
145   Narrat autem inspector naturarum quod coturnix quando intendit transire mare explorat ventum ut cum illo volare possit, et si non possit uno
volatu transire, descendit in mare ut paulatim quiescere possit. Et tunc
elevat unam alam contra ventum, quia nisi sic fecerit, statim submergere-
tur. Sic nos qui mare tribulacionis huius mundi transire debemus, ex quo
150   non possumus uno volatu ad celum venire, oportet quiescere parum et expectare et unam alam elevare, scilicet affectionem nostram ad Deum vel ad
ventum Spiritus Sancti. Et tunc iuxta dictum Psalmiste: "Spiritus tuus
bonus deducet me in terram rectam."
Sic ergo patet quomodo Christus celum ascendit sicut bonus dux ante
155   nos et quomodo eum sequi possemus. Et nota, sicut patet ex serie evangelii,
quod Christus conversatus in terris quadrupliciter ascendit: in montem ut
sciolus informator [f. 72v] ad docendum quatuor scibilia; in navem ut
providus gubernator ad transeundum [maris] quatuor pericula; in Iherosolimam ut strenuus propugnator ad vincendum quatuor prelia; ad celi curiam ut
160   largus remunerator ad largiendum quatuor stipendia.
Primo dico quod Christus docuit in monte quatuor scibilia, que sunt
quatuor virtutes cardinales, videlicet iusticia, prudencia, temperancia, et
fortitudo, de quibus satis nota parte 5 locis suis.
Secundo, in navi transivit quatuor maris pericula, que sunt scopuli,
165   scirces, syrene, etc., de quibus eciam nota parte 5, capitulo 12. Et nota
quod quatuor de causis solent homines navem ascendere, scilicet ad diluvium
evitandum, [ad transfretandum, ad mercandum, ad piscandum. Primo ergo dico
ascendunt homines navem ad diluvium evitandum;] Genesis 8: "Inundaverunt
aque super terram," idest peccata. Peccatum autem solebat habere duas
170   ripas, scilicet timorem Domini et pudorem seculi; set modo aque peccatorum
per tales rivul⟨o⟩s dirivantur, quia iuxta dicta Osee 4: "Maledictum,
furtum, homicidium inundaverunt." Et ideo ab isto diluvio peciit liberari
Psalmista dicens: "Non me demergat tempestas aque." Secundo ⟨ascenditur⟩
navis ad transfretandum; Matthei 9: "Ascendit naviculam et transfretavit et
175   venit in civitatem suam." Sic et nos si volumus ad civitatem nostram pervenire supernam oportet hanc navem, scilicet fidem Ecclesie, ascendere, cuius
malus ⟨Christus⟩ est, quem "Deus exaltavit et dedit ei nomen quod est super
omne nomen." Et in Psalmo de Christo dicitur: "Dextera Domini fecit virtutum, dextera Domini exaltavit me." Cuius velum Maria dici potest, nam sicut
180   malus per velum, sic Christus per Mariam flectitur ad misericordiam et

rightly on its vile and weak nature, as we said earlier, and on how light, pure, and perfect in itself our soul is, because of its own nature it would at once rise to heaven were it not hindered by the heavy needle of your body. Then withdraw your hand, and you will at once direct your attention to the east of your birth, namely in what way you entered the world, as we have said, and to the west, namely in what way you will pass on in death. And indeed, once you have paid attention to these things, you will never go astray through sin, according to the words: "Remember your last end, and you shall never sin."

An observer of the nature of animals tells us that when the quail plans to cross the sea, it checks the wind so that it can fly with it, and if it cannot cross the sea in one flight, it comes down on the water in order to rest for a spell. And at that point it raises one wing against the wind; if it did not do so, it would at once drown. So should we act who must pass over the troublesome sea of this world. Since we cannot get to heaven in a single flight, it behooves us to rest and wait a while and to raise one wing, that is, our affection, to God or to the breeze of the Holy Spirit. And then, in the words of the Psalmist, "Your good spirit shall lead me into the right land."

Thus we see how Christ ascended to heaven before us as a good leader and how we can follow him. And notice that according to the Gospel narrative Christ ascended four times while he was on earth: on the mount, as a learned instructor to teach us four points; on the ship, as a skilled pilot to sail through the four perils of the sea; into Jerusalem, as a strong champion to win four tourneys; and to the court of heaven, as a generous recompenser to bestow four rewards.

First I say Christ taught four points on the mount, which are the four cardinal virtues: justice, prudence, moderation, and strength; they will be treated in part 5, in their respective chapters.

Second, he sailed on the ship through the four perils of the sea: rocks, sandbanks, sirens, and so forth, which are also discussed in part 5, chapter 12. And notice that men go aboard for four reasons: to escape from a flood, to sail across the sea, to do business, and to fish. In the first place, men go aboard in order to escape from a flood; Genesis 8: "The waters overflowed the earth," that is, their sins. Sin used to be contained between two banks, the fear of the Lord and worldly shame; but nowadays the waters of sin break through their banks in many streamlets, since according to the saying in Hosea 4 "cursing, theft, and killing have overflowed." Therefore, the Psalmist prayed to be delivered from this flood when he said, "Let not the tempest of water drown me." In the second place, one goes aboard in order to ferry across some body of water; Matthew 9: "He entered into a boat and passed over the water and came into his city." We too, if we wish to come to our eternal city, must go aboard this ship, namely the faith of the Church, whose mast is Christ, whom "God has exalted and given a name which is above all names." And in the

ducitur ad adiuvandum. Dicit enim Bernardus: "Cum, inquit, mater ostendit
filio pectus et ubera, filius Patri latus et vulnera, non poterit esse
repulsa ubi tot sunt amoris insignia." Ventus prosper sit devota ad matrem
Dei supplicacio. Rector est Spiritus Sanctus; et gubernaculum gracia divi-
185   na. [f. 73] Quibus bene dispositis per hanc navem ad portum salutis secure
deveniemus. Tercio ascenditur navis ad mercandum. Unde de anima devota
dicitur Proverbiorum ultimo: "Facta est quasi navis institoris de longe portans panem suum." Quando vero huiusmodi anima ad portum bonis virtutibus
advenerit, optime recipitur ac bonis patrie, scilicet gloria et honore,
190   adimpletur. Et ideo de tali anima dicitur ibidem: "Gustavit et vidit quia
bona est negociacio eius." Quarto ascenditur navis ad piscandum, sicut
patet de beato Petro, Iohannis ultimo. Sic nos debemus navem, idest doctrinam Ecclesie, ascendere ad piscandum peccatores de aquis peccatorum attra-
hendo verbo pariter et exemplo. Et nota quod Christus nostram naturam assu-
195   mens quodammodo navem ascendit ad piscandum naturam lapsam hominum
ad Dei Patris convivium preparandum. Et merito dicitur eius incarnacio quasi
cuiusdam navicule ascencio, quia leg⟨em⟩ nature tunc supergrediens et ipsam
totaliter sibi supponens, lucem limo, summa ymo, vermem Deo, iustum reo
eterno federe copulavit. In qua navicula habemus per oppositum ad navem
200   diaboli loco mali humilitatem altissimam, loco veli caritatem amplissimam;
habemus loco funiculi doctrine veritatem, loco gubernaculi iusticie equitatem °; habemus insuper in ista navicula corporis Christi tres ordines
remorum, quia ex una parte remum vite puritatis contra luxuriam, remum
victus parcitatis contra gulam, remum operis se⟨du⟩litatis contra accidiam;
205   ex alia parte remum humilitatis contra superbiam, remum paupertatis contra
avariciam, remum benignitatis contra invidiam. Et de istis omnibus satis
patet locis suis. Et nota quod sicut qui sunt in periculo maris ad salva-
cionem navis unusquisque sollerter occupatur—quia iste navem exonerat,
ille aquam exhaurit, iste rupturas obstruit, ille anchoram iacit, [f. 73v]
210   iste velum deponit, ille gubernaculum sumit—; sic spiritualiter. Ne iste
navis anime pereat, paupertas navem exonerat ne per divicias submergatur;
Thimothei 5: "Qui volunt divites fieri," etc., "cum mergunt hominem in
interitum." Secundo confessio aquam peccatorum exhaurit; Trenorum 2: "Ef-
funde sicut aquam cor tuum." Tercio contricio rupturas obstruit; Ecclesias-
215   tici 7: Hic obstruit foramina ⟨sensuum⟩ per que mors intrat. Quarto fides
anchoram iacit stabilitatis. Quinto humilitas velum deponit superbie. Et
sexto caritas omnia gubernat ⟨ipsa⟩, prout habetur 1 Corinthiorum 13:
"Omnia suffert, omnia potest, non emulatur, non inflatur," etc., sine qua
quicquid fecero nichil prodest.
220   Tercio principaliter ascendit Iesus Iherosolimam ut strenuus propugnator ad vincendum quatuor prelia, que sunt contra mundum, carnem, diabolum,
et propriam [voluntatem]. De quibus tribus primis nota parte [5] in fine,
et similiter principalibus particulis suis, puta ubi agitur de superbia,

Psalter it is said of Christ: "The right hand of the Lord has wrought
strength, the right hand of the Lord has exalted me." The sail of this ship
may be said to be Mary, for just as the mast is bent by the sail, so is Christ
through Mary bent to be merciful and to give us help. For Bernard says: "When
the mother shows her son her bosom and breasts, the son his Father his side and
wounds, there can be no refusal where there are so many tokens of love." Let
the favorable wind be our devout prayer to the Mother of God. The helmsman is
the Holy Spirit; and the rudder is divine grace. When all these are in good
order, we shall on this ship safely come to the harbor of salvation. In the
third place, one goes aboard for business. Therefore, at the end of Proverbs
it is said of the devout soul: "She is like the merchant's ship, bringing her
bread from afar." When such a soul arrives with good virtues in the harbor,
it is well received and is filled with the goods of her homeland, that is, with
glory and honor. And then it is said of her, as in the same place: "She has
tasted and seen that her traffic is good." In the fourth place, one goes
aboard in order to fish, as Blessed Peter did, at the end of the Gospel of
John. In the same way should we enter the boat, that is, the teaching of the
Church, in order to fish sinners from the waters of their sins, drawing them by
word and example. And notice that when Christ took our human nature he entered, as it were, a boat in order to catch man's fallen nature for the banquet
of God the Father. His incarnation can thus rightly be called a "going
aboard," for by overstepping the law of nature and subjecting it completely to
himself, he united in an eternal bond light and dust, height and depth, God and
worm, the just and the sinner. In this ship, in contrast to the ship of the
devil, we find as a mast the most profound humility, as a sail the most far-
reaching charity, as a rope the teaching of truth, as a rudder the equity of
justice. And above all, in this ship of Christ's body we find three orders of
oars: on one side the oar of a pure life opposed to lechery, the oar of restraint in food opposed to gluttony, and the oar of eager work opposed to sloth;
and on the other side, the oar of humility opposed to pride, the oar of poverty
opposed to avarice, and the oar of kindness opposed to envy. All these virtues
and vices are fully treated in their respective parts. And notice further that
in the peril of the sea every sailor is diligently busy about the safety of the
vessel, for one casts burdens overboard, another bails out water, this one
stops leaks, that one casts the anchor, one takes down the sail, and another
mans the helm. In the same way allegorically, lest the ship of the soul be
wrecked, poverty unburdens the ship so that it may not be drowned by wealth;
Timothy 5: "They who will become rich," etc., "drown man into destruction."
Second, confession bails out the water of sin; Lamentations 2: "Pour out your
heart like water." Third, contrition stops the leaks; Ecclesiasticus 7: he
stops the holes of our senses through which "death enters." Fourth, faith
casts the anchor of stability. Fifth, humility takes down the sail of pride.
And sixth, charity steers all these, as is said in 1 Corinthians 13: "It bears

parte 1; et ubi agitur de avaricia, parte 4; et ubi de concupiscencia,
225   parte 7. Set de quarto [prelio], scilicet [contra] propriam voluntatem,
nota parte [1] ubi agitur de superbia et humilitate.

Set quarto principaliter ascendit Iesus ad celi curiam ut largus
remunerator ad largiendum quatuor stipendia, que sunt vita sine morte, dies
sine nocte, sacietas sine esurie, gaudium sine fine.
230   Et nota quod Christus in sua benedicta ascencione ad maximum honorem
generis humani fecit ad modum ciconie. Ipse enim quando pulli avolaverunt
de nido quos prius tantum dilexerat, tactus dolore redit ad nidum et illum
terra implet. Revera sic Christus fecit. Eius autem pulli fuerunt angeli
lucentes. Qui cum per superbiam a nido celorum avolassent, quasi quodam
235   dolore tactus Deus ipse hominem de terra formavit ad locum illorum implen-
dum. In cuius signum Christus Filius Dei in humana [f. 74] natura primo
seisinam in celo accepit pro se et suis. Et hic nota cartam, ut supra.
Similiter nota narracionem de milite peregrino dicente: "Quem quesivi hic
inveni," etc.

---

5 Christi] christiani O.   **18** Mattheus] multi C.   **25** sic] tunc O.   **28** dum] cum O.
41 ne] nec C.   **46** Deuteronomii 32] matthei C.   **50** suis] *om* O.   sublimi] sublime O.
53 divinitatem] deitatem O.   est] *om* C.M.   **61–62** Domini . . . Christi] etc C.   **66** 14]
18 O.   **72** cum] tamen C.   **75** et ibi] ubi O   **77** presciens] presenciens O.   **79** hu-
manum] humanam C.   **83** ergo] igitur O.   **88** hunc] hanc C.   **89** amatistum idest] *om*
O.   **93** quem] quam M.W; quod R.   **96** nota] *add* quod O.   **99** potest videre] videt O.
106–107 optinebit] potest M; *om* R.W.   **109** ergo] igitur O.   homo] *om* O.   **132** tunc]
om O.   **133** debent] *om* O.   **134** signat(2)] *om* O.   **136** scilicet] *om* C.   **138** quam]
quamvis C.R.   **139** ipsum] ipsa O.   **171** rivulos] rivulas C.   dicta] dictum O.   **173** as-
cenditur] transgreditur C.   **174** Ascendit] *add* in O.   **177** Christus] duplex C.   **178–179**
Dextera . . . virtutem] *om* O.   **196** preparandum] *om* O.   **197** legem] legis C.W.   **201–**
202 equitatem] *add* etc C.   **204** sedulitatis] servilitatis C.   **209** ille . . . iacit] *om* O.
210 iste(2)] *om* O.   **212** etc. cum] *om* O.   **215** sensuum] secundum n.m C.R.
217 ipsa] propter ea C.   **218** etc.] *om* O.   **226** superbia] obediencia O.   **231** Ipse] ipsa
O.   **232** tactus] tacta O.   **234** avolassent] evolassent O.   **237** ut supra] *om* O.   **238** di-
cente] *om* R.W; scilicet M.   **239** etc.] *om* O.

III.xxii   DE SPIRITUS SANCTI MISSIONE

[C]irca missionem Spiritus Sancti ad nos a Patre et Filio, qui amor est
medians tam Patris quam Filii, sciendum est quod tunc eciam maxima caritas

all things, it can do all things, it does not envy, it is not puffed up," and
so on; whatever I do without it, it profits me nothing.

With respect to my third main point, Jesus went up to Jerusalem as a
strong champion in order to win four tourneys, namely against the world, the
flesh, the devil, and self-will. The first three will be discussed near the
end of part 5; they are likewise treated in the respective parts on their
related chief sins, that is, under pride in part 1, under avarice in part 4,
and under concupiscence in part 7. But for the fourth tourney, that against
self-will, see the discussion of pride and humility in part 1.

And with respect to my fourth main point, Jesus ascended to the court of
heaven as a generous recompenser in order to grant four rewards, namely: life
without death, day without night, fullness without hunger, and joy without end.

And notice that in his blessed ascension Christ conferred the greatest
honor on mankind in a way similar to the stork. For the latter, when its
offspring which it had formerly loved so much have left the nest, returns to
the nest in grief and fills it with earth. Indeed Christ did the same. His
offspring were the shining angels. When these had flown out of the nest of
heaven in their pride, God himself, as if in grief, formed man from earth in
order to fill their place. As a token of this, Christ the Son of God in human
nature took possession of heaven for himself and for his own. Notice his
charter discussed earlier, and similarly the story about the knight-pilgrim
that said, "Whom I have sought I have found here."

---

10 Mic. 2.13. **18** Matt. 23.2. **20–21** Ps. 79.10. **22–24** Solinus, *Coll. rerum memorabilium* XXV.6. **27–31** Frontinus, *Stratagemata* IV.vi.2. **32–33** Ps. 16.4. **44** Job
18.9. **46–47** Deut. 32.11. **58** Matt. 14.23. **61–62** Gal. 6.14. **65–66** 1 Sam.
14.13. **69–78** Cf. Vincent of Beauvais, *Speculum naturale* XVI.35 (1178), attributed to
"Jorath." **94–95** Jer. 49.22. **109–111** Bernard, *De diversis*, sermo 12, 1 (6.1:127).
112–113 Job 14.1. **144** Ecclus. 7.40. **145–149** The same story without source appears in Brinton, Sermon 76. **152–153** Ps. 142.10. **163** *FM* V.xv, xxxi, xxxiv, and xxxvii. **164–219** A close parallel appears in *GR* 17, pp. 308–310. **165** *FM* V.xxix.
168–169 Gen. 7.6. **171–172** Hos. 4.2. **173** Ps. 68.16. **174–175** Matt. 9.1. **177–
178** Phil. 2.9. **178–179** Ps. 117.16. **181–183** Arnaud de Bonneval, *De laudibus
Beatae Mariae Virginis* (PL 189:1726); see Wenzel, "A Latin Miracle with Middle English Verses," *Neuphilologische Mitteilungen*, 72 (1971), 77–85. **187–189** Prov.
31.14. **190–191** Prov. 31.18. **192** John 21.1–14. **206–207** *FM* VII, VI, V, I, IV,
and III, respectively. **212–213** 1 Tim. 6.9. **213–214** Lam. 2.19. **215** Cf. Jer. 9.21.
218 Cf. 1 Cor. 13.1–8. **222** *FM* V.xxvii–xxxvii. **223** *FM* chapters as indicated in
text. **237** *FM* II.vii, near end. **238–239** *FM* III.vii.60–70.

III.xxii THE SENDING OF THE HOLY SPIRIT

With respect to the sending of the Holy Spirit to us from the Father and
the Son, who is the love between Father and Son, we should know that in this

et dilectio generi humano est ostensa, eo quod in illa missione contra omne
malum summe remedium nobis advenit. Si enim consideremus intensum amo-
5   rem Iesu Christi Filii Dei benedicti erga nos, aperte videbimus quod omnia
fecit ad merchandum amorem hominis. Scivit enim Christus quod naturaliter
omnes homines diligunt munera et secuntur retribuciones. Et ideo dedit
primo homini corpus et animam racionalem super bruta et exterius omnia
habundancia, scilicet solem, lunam, et stellas, in ministerium sui. Et
10   tamen videtur quod maxima ingratitudo sit ex parte hominis, eo quod magis
dona quam datorem diligit secundum Augustinum: "Ac datorem ingrate dese-
rendo donis inhesit." Set certe adhuc circumscripta Christi Dei dilectio ac
circumspecta intime videri potest satis quod propter hoc adhuc non cessavit
Deus et dator iste Christus quin ad se hominem reducere conatur. Unde quia
15   naturaliter homo munera affectat, consideravit ergo et fecit seipsum donum,
ut sic ad nostrum amorem alliciendum simul esset et dator et donum, ut sic
donum diligamus et ipsum diligamus. Si datorem diligamus, in consimile
incidamus. Igitur hac eadem occasione, ut predictum est, prius misit Deus
Pater Filium suum in terris et dedit nobis eundem cum ipso Deo carnem
20   [assumentem], iuxta illud Iohannis: "Sic Deus dilexit mundum ut Filium suum
unigenitum daret." Ubi advertendum quod aliter natura humana per illud
donum ad amorem Dei erat inclinata quando Patri celesti exhennium nostre
nature in Filio suo transmisit, ut sic [f. 74v] amicicia per mutua munera
firmaretur. Quod quidem exennium fecerunt primi parentes, Adam cum sua
25   posteritate, qui in limbo tot annis fuerant ⟨incar⟩cerati. Tunc enim redempcionem Deo Patri optulerunt per quam pace sic facta plene reconciliati
fuerunt. Apparet igitur ⟨super⟩abundans amor et dilectio Dei Patris ad nos,
ut fiat continuacio mutui amoris inter ipsum et nos, quando iterum post
benedictam Filii sui ascencionem munus aliud eiusdem nature, scilicet Spi-
30   ritum Sanctum, nobis misit. Quod donum tam Patris quam Filii nominatur. Sic
enim canit sancta Ecclesia: "Qui Paraclitus diceris, donum Dei altissimi."
      Et ideo est hic advertendum quod Christus Deus, qui est caritatis
infinite, qui secundum Apostolum dilexit nos antequam essemus et ad vitam
preordinavit eternam, vidit quod a nostra beatitudine septem peccatis
35   mortalibus impedimur. Ideo in eius remedium septem dona nobis contulit, que
septem dona Spiritus Sancti dicuntur. Et adverte: Videmus autem de quocumque ab aliquo dilecto quod sua dilectio maxime apparet in donis, quia
secundum Gregorium probacio dilectionis est exhibicio operis. Revera sic in
proposito. Si velimus scire quis in Spiritu Sancto est dilectus, ecce
40   patebit quod ille est qui habet dona que Spiritus Sanctus confert dilectis
Ecclesie, ut sic certissimum argumentum sit quod qui illa dona habet,
similiter et Spiritum Sanctum habet. Et sunt hec septem dona, scilicet
sapiencia, intellectus, timor, concilium, sciencia, pietas, fortitudo.
      Et ista dona bene possunt esse illuminaciones anime septem ad melius

sending mankind was shown the greatest charity and love, because in it the supreme remedy for every ill has come to us. For if we consider the intense love which Christ, the blessed Son of God, has for us, we shall readily see that he did everything to purchase man's love. For Christ knew that all men naturally love gifts and go after rewards. Therefore he gave the first man a body and a rational soul (above what animals have) and abundant external gifts, such as the sun, the moon, and the stars, to serve him. Yet in this it appears how great man's ingratitude is, that he loves the gifts more than their giver— in Augustine's words, "ungratefully leaving the giver, he has become attached to the gifts." But this love on the part of Christ, our God, may still appear to be limited and considerate, because on account of it God and this giver, Christ, has still not ceased trying to call man back to himself. Therefore, since man by nature craves gifts, God took this into consideration and made a gift of himself, so that he would be at once giver and gift in order to draw our love, that we may love the gift and with it himself. If we love the giver, we meet what is exactly like him. Therefore, as we said earlier, God the Father first sent his Son to earth on that occasion and gave him to us when he took flesh with his divinity, according to the words of John: "God so loved the world that he gave his Only-Begotten Son." In this we must notice that on account of that gift human nature was differently inclined to love, when it sent to its heavenly Father a present of our nature in his Son, so that in this way friendship might be cemented through mutual gifts. This present was offered by our first parents, Adam and his offspring, who had been imprisoned in Limbo for so many years. For at that moment they offered God the Father the redemption, through which they were fully reconciled when peace had been made. Now, God the Father's overabundant love and affection toward us appears in the continuing exchange of love between him and us, when after the blessed ascension of his Son he sent us another gift of the same kind, namely the Holy Spirit. This is called a gift from both the Father and the Son, and the Church therefore sings: "You are called Paraclete, the gift from God the Most High."

Here we should note that Christ, who is God of unlimited love, who according to the Apostle has loved us before we existed and has foreordained us to eternal life, saw that we are kept from our bliss by the seven deadly sins. Therefore he gave us seven gifts against them, which are called the seven gifts of the Holy Spirit. And notice: We see by experience that if someone is loved by someone else, this love appears foremost in gifts, for according to Gregory the proof of love lies in open deeds. So it is also in our spiritual life. If we want to know who is beloved by the Holy Spirit, it evidently will be the person who has the gifts which the Holy Spirit gives to those he loves in the Church. Hence, it is safe to deduce that whoever has these gifts has the Holy Spirit. And the seven gifts of the Spirit are these: wisdom, understanding, fear, counsel, knowledge, piety, and strength.

45 videndum et operandum contra septem mortalia peccata que nos infestant. Nam
sicut ad sensum patet, illorum quorum noticiam haberi oportet sunt quedam
supra nos, quedam infra nos, quedam subter nos, quedam ante nos, quedam
post nos, quedam a dextris, et [f. 75] quedam a sinistris. Si ergo fueris
illuminatus ad cogitandum de illis rebus que sunt supra nos, scilicet de
50 gaudiis celi et beatorum, tunc incipis sapere et cogitare quam gloriosum et
quam iocundum est cum beatissimis spiritibus glorie conditoris assistere,
presentem Dei vultum cernere, etc. Et certe sic generatur in te donum
sapiencie, hoc est donum sapide sciencie, quod directe vadit contra peccata
ire; Proverbiorum 2: "Dominus dabit sapienciam et ex ore eius scienciam,"
55 scilicet benignitatis et iocunditatis contra iram et rancorem. Secundo
autem, si illuminatus fueris ad considerandum illa que sunt infra te,
scilicet propriam conscienciam et miserias humanas, tunc incipis habere
donum intellectus. Intelligere autem dicitur quasi intus legere. Et istud
donum bene vadit contra gulam. Gulosi autem, ut videmus, cum inebriati
60 fuerint omnem intellectum amittunt; et ideo contra hoc petit Psalmista: "Da
michi intellectum et scrutabor mandata tua." Si autem tercio illuminatus
fueris ad considerandum illa que sunt subtus te, scilicet tormenta inferni,
quam multa scilicet sunt, quam dura, et quam diuturna, tunc incipies habere
donum timoris, quia iuxta evangelium: "Timete eum qui potest et animam et
65 corpus perdere in ihehennam," scilicet timore filiali. ⟨Nam⟩ ille timor
facit hominem humilem et perfectum. Et istud donum vadit directe contra
peccatum superbie; Ecclesiastici 25: "Beatus homo ° cui donatum est habere
timorem Dei." Si vero quarto illuminatus fueris ad considerandum illa que
sunt ante te, scilicet mortem et iudicium, tunc adquires tibi donum conci-
70 lii. Quilibet autem talis frequenter mortem et iudicium precogitans vult
sibi ipsi consulere contra peccata ne subito in illis capiatur. Et istud
donum vadit contra luxuriam; ⟨Proverbiorum⟩ 12: "Qui tenent pacis concilia,
sequitur eos gaudium." Numquam anima pacificatur ubi corpus per luxuriam
coinquinatur; secundum ergo concilium Apostoli, [f. 75v] Corinthiorum 6:
75 "Fugite fornicacionem," etc. Si vero quinto illustratus fueris ad considerandum illa que sunt post te: commissa scelera et Christi beneficia in sua
incarnacione, passione, et resurrectione, etc., ut predicitur, que quamvis
fuerunt preterita, non tamen debent oblivisci (oblivio autem est proprie de
preteritis) set semper sunt in memoria retinenda—quod si feceris, tunc
80 adquiris donum sciencie, quod directe contra peccatum vadit invidie, que in
nullo beneficia recordatur set hominem excecat ne peccata commissa consideret. Contra quam dicitur Sapiencie 9: "Dedit illi scienciam sanctorum,"
scilicet ad recordandum Christi beneficia et propria delicta. Si autem
sexto illuminatus fueris ad considerandum [ea] que sunt a dextris, per que
85 ⟨pro⟩spera intelliguntur, et compati[tur] aliis qui sunt in angustiis et
illorum indigenciis condescendens, tunc adquiris donum pietatis, que bene

These seven gifts can well be considered seven illuminations of the soul, which make us see and act better against the seven deadly sins that attack us. For we can see that among the objects that we should have knowledge of, some are above us, others within, others below, others before, others behind, others to our right, and others to our left. So, if you have been enlightened in your reflection on the things that are above us, that is, on the joys of heaven and the blessed souls, then you begin to know and to meditate on how glorious and joyful it is to stand with the blessed spirits in the glory of our Creator, to behold directly God's face, and so forth. And then the gift of wisdom grows in you, that is, the gift of knowing and savoring, which directly opposes the sins of wrath; Proverbs 2: "The Lord shall give wisdom, and out of his mouth shall come knowledge," that is, of kindness and joy against wrath and anger. In the second place, if you have been enlightened to reflect on the things that are within you, that is, on your own conscience and human wretchedness, then you begin to have the gift of understanding. *Intelligere*, "to understand," means as it were *intus legere*, "to read inside." This gift opposes gluttony, for gluttons, as one can see, lose all their understanding when they are drunk; therefore, the Psalmist prays for help against it: "Give me understanding and I will search your commandments." If in the third place you have been enlightened to reflect on the things that are below you, that is, the torments of hell, how many they are, how hard, and how prolonged, then you will begin to have the gift of fear, for according to the Gospel: "Fear him," that is, with filial fear, "who can destroy both soul and body in hell." This kind of fear makes a person humble and perfect. And this gift directly opposes the sin of pride; Ecclesiasticus 25: "Blessed is the man to whom it is given to have the fear of God." If in the fourth place you have been enlightened to reflect on the things that are before you, that is, death and judgment, then you shall acquire the gift of counsel. For whoever thinks often of his coming death and judgment will provide himself against sins so that he may not be suddenly caught in them. This gift opposes lechery; Proverbs 12: "Joy follows them that take counsels of peace." The soul never attains peace where the body is stained by lechery; for according to the advice of the Apostle in Corinthians 6, "Flee fornication," etc. If in the fifth place you have been enlightened to reflect on the things that are behind you: the sins you have commmitted, and Christ's benefits of his incarnation, Passion, resurrection, and so on, as we discussed them earlier—but although they occurred in the past, they must not be forgotten (the act of forgetting belongs to things of the past) but must always be kept in memory—; if you do so, then you acquire the gift of knowledge, which directly opposes the sin of envy. This sin does not remember any benefits received from anyone but makes a person blind so that he does not consider the sins he has committed. Against it is said in Wisdom 9: "She gave him the knowledge of holy things," that is, to remember Christ's benefits and

vadit contra peccatum avaricie; Luce 6: "Date mutu⟨um⟩ nichil inde sperantes." Pietas, prout dicitur Ad Timotheum 4, "ad omnia utilis est, promissio-
nem habens vite que nunc est et future." Septimo, si fueris illustratus ad
90   considerandum ea que sunt a sinistris, per que intelligo adversa, cuiusmodi
sunt infirmitates, amissio bonorum, mors amicorum, etc., tunc cogitares
quod per angustias et tribulaciones regnum celorum adquiritur, et quod per
talem portam sancti patres, cuiusmodi sunt apostoli et martires, illud
intraverunt. Quod si fecerimus paciencia et exemplo eorum, tunc adquirimus
95   donum fortitudinis, que bene vadit contra accidiam; contra quod dicitur
Ysaie 40: "Dabo lasso virtutem, et hiis qui non sunt ° fortitudinem"; et
Psalmista: "Dominus dabit virtutem et fortitudinem plebi sue," etc.
    Expositor autem Virgilii super illud "Fillidis ignes" narrat quomodo
ipsa Fillis erat regina Tracie, que Demofontem [f. 76] revertentem de bello
100 Troiano in coniugium requisivit. Qui primo se in patriam iturum et post ad
illam reversurum fideliter repromisit. At illa, cum ipse nimium tardaret,
tacta dolore cordis laqueo se suspendit. Unde prout fabulatur, in arborem
amigdalinam foliis carentem est conversa. Quod cum predictus miles Demofons
intellexisset, ipsum truncum est amplexus, quo facto ipsa de trunco folia
105 pulcherrima emisit virencia. Regina illa Fillis animam signat Christianam,
que Demofontem, idest Christum, de bello mortis resurgentem, in coniugium
adoptavit. Cuius sponsalia in eius corporis suscepcione meruit. Set Christus se in patriam suam, idest celum, iturum et postea rediturum, hoc est
post eius ascencionem in Sancti Spiritus missione plenam coniugii iunctio-
110 nem, repromisit. Que quidem regina, idest anima Christiana, ob nimiam moram
Sancti Spiritus adventus laqueo inimici capitur, idest in peccato, et sic
vita spirituali privata in aridum truncum obstinacionis convertitur. Set
redeunte Christo et dato Spiritu Sancto, ut predicitur, quasi a sponso est
amplexata, ex cuius gaudio ad vitam redit et folia pulcherrima bonarum
115 virtutum emittit iuxta illud Iohannis: "Venit hora et nunc est quando
mortui audient vocem Filii Dei, et qui audierint vivent."
    Narrat Ovidius *Methamorphoseos* libro 3 prope finem de quadam virgine
nomine Athlanta, que cum a magnis in coniugium peteretur, omnibus hac
condicione apposita respondit quod siquis illam currendo vinceret, eius
120 coniugio potiretur. Quod audiens iuvenis quidam Ypomenes dictus, et secundum alios Adonydes, a Venere, dea amoris, tria poma aurea accepit et cum
illis ad locum certaminis pervenit. Cum ergo cum illa cucurrisset et ex
doctrina dicte dee primo, secundo, et tercio dicta poma ante virginem
proiecisset et illa capta pul- [f. 76v] critudine pomorum divertisset a
125 cursu, retardatur et vincitur. Et sic in coniugium [ab] Ypomene ducitur.
Moraliter hec virgo naturam signat humanam, que ideo cursu velocissima
dicitur quia numquam in eodem statu permanet, quia modo puer, modo iuvenis,
modo adolescens, modo senex, modo sanus, modo eger, modo dives, modo pauper

one's own faults. If in the sixth place you have been enlightened to reflect
on the things that are to your right, by which we understand prosperity, and
you have compassion on others who are hard pressed and you bend down to their
needs, then you acquire the gift of pity, which opposes the sin of avarice;
Luke 6: "Lend without hoping to gain anything thereby." As is written in the
Letter to Timothy, chapter 4: "Pity is profitable to all things, having promise of the life that now is, and of that which is to come." And in the seventh
place, if you have been enlightened to reflect on the things that are on your
left, by which I understand adversity, such as sickness, the loss of possessions, the death of friends, and the like, then you think that through hardships and tribulations one gains the kingdom of heaven, and that through this
door our holy fathers, such as the apostles and martyrs, have entered into it.
If we do this, in patience and by following their example, then we acquire the
gift of strength, which opposes sloth; against it is said in Isaiah 40: "I
will give strength to the weary and force to them that are not"; and the
Psalmist says: "The Lord will give strength and force to his people," etc.

The commentator on Virgil, where he treats the words "The fires of Phyllis," tells us that Phyllis was the queen of Thracia, who wanted Demophon as
her husband when he returned from the Trojan War. He promised her faithfully
that he would first go to his own country and then return to her. But when he
tarried too long, she hanged herself out of great grief and according to the
fable was changed into an almond tree without leaves. When the aforementioned
knight Demophon learned of this, he embraced this trunk, and as a result she at
once sent forth beautiful green leaves from the tree trunk. Queen Phyllis
stands for the Christian soul, who desired Demophon as her husband, that is
Christ, when he rose from the battle of death. She took her bridal gift in
receiving his body. But Christ promised her that he would go to his own land,
that is, heaven, and afterwards return, that is, by sending the Holy Spirit
after his ascension, and thus complete the marriage. But because of the delayed coming of the Holy Spirit, this queen, the Christian soul, is caught by
the snare of the enemy, that is, in sin. And therefore, deprived of her
spiritual life, she is changed into the dry trunk of obstinacy. But when
Christ returns and gives her the Holy Spirit, as was explained earlier, she is,
as it were, embraced by her spouse and in great joy comes back to life and
sends forth the beautiful leaves of good virtues, after the words of John:
"The hour comes and is now, when the dead shall hear the voice of the Son of
God, and they that hear shall live."

Near the end of Book 3 of his *Metamorphoses*, Ovid tells of a maiden by the
name of Attalanta. As she was desired by mighty men in marriage, she set for
all of them this condition that whoever defeated her in a race would gain her
in marriage. A certain youth named Hypomenes—by others called Adonis—heard
this and got three golden apples from Venus, the goddess of love, with which he

existit. De qua velocitate Iob 9 dicitur: "Dies mei ⟨velociores⟩ sunt
130   cursore," etc.; "pertransierunt quasi naves poma portantes." Set iste
Ypomenes Deus est, qui cursum istius virginis de peccato in peccatum impedire peroptat. In antiqua ergo lege primum pomum aureum proiecit, quando ex
Dei Patris potencia per eius signa, mirabilia, et prodigia que fecit erat
homo aliqualiter a peccato retardatus. Videns ergo Deus quod hoc non ob-
135   stante quamplures proni erant ad malum, ut notabilius eos retardaret secundum pomum tunc proiecit quando Filium incarnari instituit, per quod eos ad
eius amorem magis excita[vi]t. Set nondum perfecte, quia adhuc nec eius
apostoli perfecte Deum dilexerunt quousque tercium pomum, idest Spiritum
Sanctum, ad illos proiecit. Quod quidem pomum longius erat proiectum,
140   quando scilicet gracia Spiritus Sancti ultra Iudeam et in naciones diffusa
est; Ioel: "Effundam de spiritu meo super omnem carnem." Quo facto omnes in
amorem Dei victi [eum Christum] in coniugium eternum sunt po⟨t⟩iti. Dicit
ergo Christus Deus homini peccatori illud Canticorum 7: "Omnia poma ⟨nova⟩
et vetera, dilecte mi, servavi tibi."
145   Fingunt poete, sicut Esyodus et Oracius, quod deus Promotheus, postquam fecerat homines de luto, deam Minervam adiit, cuius auxilio celos
ascendit et adhibita facula ad rotam solis ignem extraxit et hominibus
demandavit. Moraliter iste deus Promotheus, qui [a] "providencia" dicitur,
Dei sapienciam signat, qui Christus est. ⟨Hic⟩ autem ⟨Minervam⟩, que et
150   Pallas dicitur, adiit, que eciam secundum fabulas semper [f. 77] virgo
manere asseritur, et signat Beatam Virginem Mariam, de qua Christus carnem
assumpsit, in qua celos ascendit eamque carnem tamquam faculam divinitate
lucentem rote solis adhibuit dum medius dextra sedit, et Spiritum Sanctum
visibiliter in specie ignis misit ⟨et suos in perfecta caritate reformavit,
155   ut merito de illo dicatur⟩ illud Jeremie: "De excelso misit ignem," idest
Spiritum Sanctum.
     Nota eciam si placet devotam narracionem de Spiritu Sancto ubi agitur
contra desperacionem de duobus sociis de banco, parte 2, capitulo 3.

---

5 Iesu] *om* O.   11 diligit] diligunt O.   25 incarcerati] macerati C.R.   27 superhabun-
dans] circumabundans C.   31 sancta] *om* O.   35 remedium] oppositum M.W; opposi-
cione R.   36 autem] *add* experimentaliter O.   37 aliquo] *add* magno O.   39 ecce]
ecclesie O.   48 et] *om* O.   51 quam] *om* O.   52 sic] tunc O.   65 Nam] vere C.
67 homo] *add* qui timet et C.   68 illuminatus] illustratus O.   72 Proverbiorum] *canc and*
marg parabola sa. 12 C.   77 et] *om* O.   78 fuerunt] fuerint O.   84 que] quam O.
85 prospera] aspera C.   87 mutuum] mutuo C.   90 que(2)] quam O.   91 cogitares]
cogitare C.   93 sunt] *om* O.   96 sunt] *add* fortes C.   102 fabulatur] fabulantur O.
105 pulcherrima] *add* continuo O.   110 idest] scilicet O.   nimiam moram] nimia mora
O.   120 potiretur] petiretur M.R; peteretur W.   125 ab] *om* C.R.   129 velociores] long-
iores C.   142 potiti] positi C.M.W.   143 nova] vana C.   149 Hic] hec C.M; *om* W.
Minervam] minerva C.O.   151 Mariam] *om* O.   152 divinitate] deitate O.   153 sedit]
consedit O.   154–155 et . . . dicatur] secundum C.   158 3] 4 O.

came to the place of trial. As he was racing with her and, on the advice of
Venus, cast the first, second, and third apple in front of the maiden, and she,
attracted by the beauty of the apples, diverted from the course, she was slowed
down and defeated. And thus she became Hypomenes' wife. Morally interpreted,
this maiden stands for human nature, which runs very fast, for it never stands
still; now it is a child, a youth, an adolescent, then an old man; now healthy,
then sick; now rich, then poor. Of this swiftness says Job 9: "My days are
swifter than a runner," etc.; "they have passed by as ships carrying apples."
But Hypomenes is God, who wishes to halt this maiden's racing from sin to sin.
He therefore cast the first golden apple in the Mosaic Law, when by the power
of God the Father man was somewhat slowed down in his sinning through the signs
and wonders God worked. But when God saw that nonetheless many were prone to
sin, he cast the second apple in order to slow them down even more and decreed
that his Son become man, whereby he challenged them to greater love. But even
this was not yet perfect, because not even the apostles as yet loved God
perfectly. Then at last he cast the third apple before them, that is, the Holy
Spirit. This apple was cast farther than the others, for the grace of the Holy
Spirit spread out beyond Judea and to the Gentiles; Joel: "I will pour out my
spirit upon all flesh." In consequence, they were all overcome for God's love
and gained Christ for their eternal spouse. For Christ, our God, says to
sinful man those words of Canticles 7: "All apples, the new and the old, my
beloved, I have kept for you."

Such poets as Hesiod and Horace claim that after the god Prometheus had
made men from mud, he approached the goddess Minerva, with whose help he
went up to heaven, put a torch to the disk of the sun, extracted fire from it, and
brought it to mankind. Morally interpreted, the god Prometheus, whose name is
derived from "providence," stands for God's wisdom, who is Christ. He approached Minerva, who is also called Pallas and according to the myths is
affirmed to have always been a virgin; she stands for the Blessed Virgin, from
whom Christ took flesh. In this flesh he ascended to heaven, and he put it,
like a torch shining with its divinity, to the disk of the sun when he sat to
the right hand of God; and then he sent the Holy Spirit visibly in the form of
fire and reformed his own children in perfect charity, so that of him the words
of Jeremiah are justly spoken: "From above he has sent fire," that is, the
Holy Spirit.

You may also, if you wish, tell the pious story concerning the Holy Spirit
and the two lawyer companions, in the section against despair, in part 2,
chapter 3.

20–21 John 3.16.   **31** Stanza 2 of the Pentecost hymn "Veni, Creator Spiritus";
Chevalier 21204.   **38** Gregory, *In Evangelia*, hom. 30, 1 (PL 76:1220).   **54** Prov. 2.6.
61–62 Ps. 118.115.   **64–65** Matt. 10.28.   **67–68** Ecclus. 25.15.   **72–73** Prov.

III.xxiii   DE BENEDICTA TRINITATE

[D]ict⟨o⟩ de caritate Christi erga genus humanum quoad eius incarnacionem, peregrinacionem, passionem, resurrectionem, ascensionem, ac Spiritus
Sancti missionem tam a Patre quam a Filio, iam de benedicta illa Trinitate
et unitate est aliquid breviter advertendum. Secundum ergo mentem sancti
5   Augustini 14 *De Trinitate*, mens humana est ipsa ymago Dei et similitudo
Trinitatis, que capax est eius. Ex quibus verbis accipio duo. Unum est quod
Trinitas potest cognosci, et aliud est quod Trinitas in anima in mente
potest recipi. Et ideo sollempnitatem de Trinitate propter ista duo facimus, ut scilicet Trinitatem benedictam melius cognoscamus et cognitam
10   amplius diligamus. Si igitur ipsam Trinitatem videre velimus, ipsam maies-
tatem perscrutari in se sicuti est non temptemus, quia Proverbiorum 2[5]
dicitur: "Qui [per]scrutator est mag[estat]is, opprimetur." Et ideo animam
nostram solummodo intueamur.
   Narratur enim iocose de quodam existente super ripam maris et pro scapha
15   proclamante. Quem cum nauta quidam interrogaverat quisnam esset, et
ipse respondisset: "Ut quid nomen meum queris cum nemo alius noticiam mei
habet?" dixit nauta ad socium: "Ecce vis mirum audire: Here is one come þat
no man wote." Et alius quasi de eo non curans set subridendo hoc modo
dixit: "Ye, þe deuyll in thynn eye, rowe forth þe boote." [f. 77v] Et sic
20   illum permittentes ad loca nociora remigabant. Spiritualiter per istas
nautas per mare remigantes in scapha intelligo animas hominum corpora
nostra tamquam scaphas in mari huius mundi remigantes, et per illum igno-
tum, benedictam Trinitatem, cuius noticiam aut nomen si queratur respondit
illud Exodi: "Quare queris nomen meum quod est mirabile?" quasi diceret: ad
25   noticiam mei, quomodo scilicet sum Deus trinus et unus, numquam in hac vita
nisi in enigmate et in fide Ecclesie deveniet homo, nec unde sum, unde
veni, aut quo vado aut ex quibus procedo, quia dicitur Ysaie 53: "Generacionem eius quis enarrabit?" quasi diceret, nullus. Ita enim ineffabilis
est processus Trinitatis benedicte quia secundum beatum Ambrosium *Contra*
30   *hereticos*: "Mens deficit, vox silet, non tantum hominis set et angelorum."
Cum ergo eius processus, quid scilicet sit aut unde sit, similiter de
Christo scire quomodo de virgine poterat nasci aut quomodo virgo et mater
esse posset, et cetera huiusmodi Dei misteriorum omnem sensum exsuperant,

12.20. **75** 1 Cor. 6.18. **82** Wisd. 10.10. **87–88** Luke 6.35. **88–89** 1 Tim. 4.8.
96 Cf. Isa. 40.29. **97** Ps. 67.36. **98–105** Servius, Commentary on Virgil, *Eclogues*
V.10. **115–116** John 5.25. **117–125** Ovid, *Met.* X.560–580. **129–130** Job 9.25–
26. **141** Joel 2.28. **143–144** Cant. 7.13. **145–148** Hesiod, *Works and Days* 54–105;
Horace, *Carmina* I.xvi.13ff. The actual source is Servius, Commentary on Virgil,
Eclogues VI.42, who mentions both classical authors. **155** Lam. 1.13. **156–157** *FM*
II.iii.101–136.

III.xxiii THE BLESSED TRINITY

After we have spoken of Christ's love for mankind that is shown in his
incarnation, pilgrimage, Passion, resurrection, ascension, and the sending of
the Holy Spirit from Father and Son, we must now say a few words of the Blessed
Trinity and Unity. In the thought of Blessed Augustine, in Book 14 of *On the
Trinity*, the human mind itself is an image of God and a likeness of the Trinity, which it is capable to receive. From these words I gather two things: one,
that the Trinity can be known, and the other, that the Trinity can be received
in the mind. Therefore we celebrate the feast of the Holy Trinity for these
two purposes, namely that we may know the Blessed Trinity better, and that
after knowing it we may love it more fully. But if we desire to see this
Trinity, we must not attempt to search its majesty as it exists in itself, for
in Proverbs 25 is said: "The searcher of majesty shall be overwhelmed."
Therefore, let us examine our soul alone.

There is a joke about someone who stood on the seashore and called for a
ferry. When a sailor asked him who he was, and he replied, "Why do you want to
know my name since nobody else knows me?" the sailor said to his companion:
"You want to hear something strange? Here is one come whom no one knows."
And the other, as if he did not care much for him, answered laughingly: "Yeah,
the devil in your eye. Row forth the boat!" And thus they left him and rowed
on to better-known places. Spiritually speaking, by these sailors that row their
boat on the sea I understand men's souls who row their bodies like boats on the
sea of this world; and by that unknown person, the Blessed Trinity. If one
asks for his name or any information about him, he will say those words of
Exodus: "Why do you ask for my name, which is marvelous?" as if he were
saying: in this life, man will never come to the knowledge of me, that is, that
I am God in Three and One, except darkly and in the faith of the Church—nor
whence I am, where I come from, where I go, or from which I proceed. For
Isaiah says in chapter 53: "Who shall declare his generation?" as if to say,
no one. For the procession of the Blessed Trinity is so ineffable that according to Blessed Ambrose in *Against the Heretics*, "the mind fails and the voice
is silent, not only of man but even of the angels." Since therefore the
knowledge of the Trinity, what it is and whence it is, and likewise the knowledge of how Christ could have been born of the Virgin or how she could be

permittamus i[s]ta stare cum fide vera Ecclesie et ad nociora naviculam
35 nostri intellectus remigemus et animam nostram tantum, que est ymago Trinitatis, intueamur.
     Et nota quod sol tanti splendoris est quod oculum excecat ipsum lim-
pide intueri volentem. Et ideo astrologi qui corpus solare in suo eclipsi
vel alias intueri volentes speculum ponunt in pelvim, et sic aqua coopertum
40 radiis solis obiciunt, et sic solis radios considerant, quamvis in quanti-
tate multipliciter pelvim exced⟨a⟩t et speculum. Et sic sine oculorum
lesione per ymaginem de ipso iudicant, set inperfecte quantum ad omnia.
Spiritualiter eciam loquendo benedicta Trinitas, que ⟨sol est⟩ nostre
intelligencie, tam resplendentis glorie et claritatis existit quod si in
45 eam sicuti est [f. 78] visum prefigere presumimus, oculos nostri intellectus excecat. Quia Ecclesiastici ⟨4⟩3 dicitur: "Sol triplex exurens cum
radiis suis excecat oculos." Et ideo istius veri solis inspectores, idest
prudentes theolog⟨i⟩, in quodam speculo aqua cooperto huius solis ymaginem
contemplantur. Per quod speculum animam humanam intelligo, quia sicut
50 speculum uniuscuiusque rei speciem in se recipit et omnibus rebus ad quas
se convertit assimilatur, sic anima humana capax est omnium ad que se
converterit per amorem. Unde istud speculum aqua gracie coopertum ac veri
solis radios ex opposito per amorem in se recipiens in eandem ymaginem
transformatur; Corinthiorum: "Gloriam Domini speculantes in eandem ymagi-
55 nem transformamur." Et propter hoc isti sancti doctores qui de Trinitate investigare desiderant, istud speculum intuentur; Corinthiorum 13: "Videmus nunc
per speculum in enigmate, tunc autem facie ad faciem." Ex quibus patet quod
illam parvam noticiam quam de benedicta Trinitate habere v⟨a⟩lemus non de
ipsa directe set per eius ymaginem, scilicet animam humanam, accipere
60 debemus, alioquin excecari faciliter poterimus, sicut de Sabellio, Arrio,
et multis aliis hereticis ante nunc accidit manifeste.
     Et sic, si Deum trinum et unum amare velimus, studeamus illum in
animam recipere, que capax est ac suum habitaculum est. Set quomodo? Videmus autem quod aliter accipit mariscallus regis hospicium pro domino suo
65 tempore pacis, in loco scilicet inhabitato et repleto, cuiusmodi sunt
civitates et ville, et aliter tempore guerre, in loco deserto et vasto. Nam
in locis bene edificatis non oportet aliquid edificare, set tantum ibi
ponitur signum armorum domini sui. Et sic ingressi habitant ibi. Set in
locis desertis, ubi super faciem campi morari coguntur, hoc modo [f. 78v]
70 ordinatur: nam campum marescallus in certas areas dividit, et cum unicuique domino ordinata fuerit certa porcio secundum eius statum, ibi statim
tentoria et alia habitacula eriguntur.
     Revera spiritualiter loquendo ipsa benedicta Trinitas, Deus et Dominus
noster, qui est "rex regum et dominus dominancium," duo regna possidet,
75 unum scilicet animarum sanctarum, quod est regnum pacis, et aliud animarum

virgin and mother, as well as the other mysteries of God thus pass all understanding, let us let these things stand, in the true faith of the Church, and
row forth the boat of our understanding to better known places and examine our
soul, insofar as it is the image of the Trinity.

Notice that the sun has such great brightness that it blinds the eye when
people want to see it clearly. Therefore, when astronomers want to observe the
sun in its eclipse or otherwise, they place a mirror in a basin, cover it with
water, and put it so as to reflect the sunbeams; and in this way they observe
the sunbeams, even though the sun by far surpasses the basin and mirror. In
this fashion they can without damage to their eyes study the sun by its image,
however imperfectly in every respect. Spiritually speaking, the Blessed Trinity, the sun of our understanding, has such a great brightness and clarity in
its glory that, if we dare direct our sight to it in order to see it in its
nature, it blinds the eyes of our understanding. For in Ecclesiasticus 43 it
is said: "The sun, burning three times as much with its beams, blinds the
eyes." Therefore students of this true sun, that is, prudent theologians, look
at its image in a mirror covered with water. By this mirror I understand man's
soul. For just as a mirror receives in itself the picture of any object and
thus becomes like the objects to which it turns, thus man's soul is able to
receive anything to which it turns in love. Therefore, when this mirror is
covered with the water of grace and receives in itself through love the beams
of the true sun against which it places itself, it becomes transformed into
that same image; Corinthians: "Beholding the glory of the Lord, we are transformed into the same image." For this reason, the holy doctors who desire to
investigate the nature of the Trinity examine that mirror; Corinthians 13:
"Now we see through a glass darkly, but then face to face." From this follows
that what little knowledge we are able to have of the Blessed Trinity we must
receive from it not directly but through its image, that is, man's soul. Otherwise we could easily become blind, as it manifestly happened to Sabellius,
Arius, and many other heretics before our time.

And thus, if we want to love the triune God, we must strive to receive him
in our soul, which is capable of receiving him and is his dwelling place. But
how? We observe that the king's marshal prepares quarters for his lord in one
way in time of peace, namely in an inhabited, built-up place, such as a city or
a town, and in a different way in time of war, namely in a deserted and open
place. For in built-up places there is no need to put up any buildings but
only to place his lord's escutcheon; and so they enter and dwell there. But in
deserted places, where they are compelled to rest on open ground, quarters are
prepared as follows. The marshal divides the field into areas, and after an
area is assigned to each lord according to his rank, then tents and other
dwellings are put up there.

In spiritual terms, the Blessed Trinity, our God and Lord, who is "king of

in hac vita existencium, quod est regnum belli. Unde in anima generaliter
loquendo quasi familiare hospicium suum ipsa benedicta Trinitas ab inicio
creacionis hominis accepit. In cuius signum ibi similitudinem armorum
suorum ⟨depixit⟩ quando dixit illud Genesis: "Faciamus hominem ad ymagi-
80   nem et similitudinem nostram." Nam sicut in benedicta Trinitate tres sunt
persone et tamen non est nisi unus Deus, ubi Patri potencia, Filio sapiencia, Spiritui Sancto clemencia attribuitur, sic correspondenter tres sunt
potencie in anima, scilicet memoria, intellectus, et voluntas, et tamen non
est nisi tantum una anima. Ymaginemur igitur quod anima humana est sicut
85   locus aptus in quo habitaculum sancte Trinitatis edificari possit. Quia in
animabus b⟨eat⟩orum iam habitat sicut in edificiis eternorum castrorum, in
quibus sunt omnes virtutes et gracie eternaliter confirmate. Set certe in
nobis non habitat nisi sicut in quodam campo deserto et vasto, eo quod
sumus in bello continuo. Ergo oportet quod campus anime nostre pro eius
90   recepcione quasi in tres areas et porciones dividatur, scilicet in memoriam
pro Patre, in intellectum pro Filio, et in voluntatem pro Spiritu Sancto.
Cum ergo ista benedicta Trinitas quasi in nostro bello nobiscum commorari
dignatur, et "non hic habemus manentem civitatem" in qua valeat honeste
recipi set tantum manet cuilibet homini sua porcio pro figendis [f. 79]
95   tabernaculis assignata, ideo secundum concilium Matthei 17 "faciamus hic
tria tabernacula." Que quidem tria tabernacula dici possunt tres virtutes
theologi[c]e, de quibus Ad Corinthios 13: "Nunc autem manent fides, spes,
et caritas, tria hec." Et causa quare iste virtutes tabernacula dici possunt est quia huiusmodi tabernacula non deserviunt nobis nisi tempore belli
100   et non pacis, nec eciam diu durant set aliquando vix una nocte vel duabus
ad plus; revera sic nec iste virtutes nobis non deserviunt nisi in bello
presentis vite. Et ideo videtur michi quod ista sunt [illa] tabernacula
pulcra de quibus Ysaie 54 dicitur: "Dilata locum tentorii et pelles tabernaculorum extende."
105   Si ergo de erectione istorum tabernaculorum loqui velimus, est breviter sciendum: primo in area nostre memorie erigendum est tabernaculum fidei
quantum ad Patris potenciam; secundo in area nostri intellectus erigendum
est tabernaculum spei quantum ad Filii sapienciam; tercio in area nostre
voluntatis erigendum est tabernaculum caritatis quantum ad Spiritus Sancti
110   clemenciam. Circa primum est advertendum quod si homo de articulis fidei
temptetur, melius refrigerium haberi non potest quam ad Patris potenciam.
Quia si queratur quomodo Deus potest esse homo, mater virgo, et huiusmodi,
respondeo quod Deus est infinite potencie et quod plus potest facere quam
nos intelligere. Ad hoc igitur tabernaculum contra huiusmodi temptaciones
115   curramus, et cito certe levamen inveniemus. Et nota quod istud tabernaculum
debet debite mensurari et solide collocari, ne scilicet sit nimis amplum
[nec nimis artum. Nam quidam illud habent nimis amplum,] nam cum hoc

kings and lord of lords," has two kingdoms: one of blessed souls, which is the kingdom of peace, and another of souls in this life, which is a kingdom of war. In general, the Blessed Trinity has, as it were, taken homelike quarters in the soul from the beginning of man's creation. To indicate that, he painted there a likeness of his escutcheon when he said in Genesis: "Let us make man to our image and likeness." For just as in the Blessed Trinity there are three persons and yet only one God, where to the Father is attributed power, to the Son wisdom, and to the Holy Spirit mercy, thus there are three corresponding faculties in the soul, namely memory, intellect, and will, and yet there is only one soul. Let us then imagine that the human soul is like a fitting place in which the dwelling of the Holy Trinity can be built. For in the souls of the blessed the Trinity already dwells as in the buildings of the eternal camps, in which all virtues and graces are confirmed forever. But in us the Trinity dwells only as in a deserted and open field, because we are engaged in an ongoing war. Therefore, in order to receive him it is necessary to divide the field of our soul as it were into three areas and shares, namely into memory for the Father, intellect for the Son, and will for the Holy Spirit. Since then the Blessed Trinity deigns to dwell with us, as it were in our own war, and since "we have here no permanent city" in which the Trinity can be worthily received, but everyman only has his plot, assigned to him to put up his tabernacles, therefore let us, according to the advice of Matthew 17 "make here three tabernacles." These three tabernacles can be said to be the three theological virtues, of which is written in Corinthians 13: "But now remain faith, hope, and charity, these three." The reason why these virtues can be called tabernacles is that such tabernacles serve us only in time of war, not in peace, nor do they last long but sometimes hardly for a night or two at the most. In the same way these virtues serve us only in the war of this life. Thus I think these are the beautiful tabernacles of which Isaiah 54 says: "Enlarge the place of your tent and stretch out the skins of your tabernacles."

If we are to speak about putting up these tabernacles, we must briefly indicate that first we have to build the tabernacle of faith in the lot of our memory, with respect to the power of the Father; second we have to build the tabernacle of hope in the lot of our intellect, with respect to the wisdom of the Son; and third we have to build the tabernacle of charity in the lot of our will, with respect to the mercy of the Holy Spirit. Concerning the first we must know that if someone is tempted with regard to the articles of faith, he can find no better comfort than in the Father's power. For if anyone questions how God can be man, a mother a virgin, and so forth, I answer that God has infinite power and can do much more than we can understand. Let us therefore hasten to that tabernacle against temptations of this type, and surely we shall quickly find relief. But this tabernacle must be duly measured and put up firmly, so that it may be neither too wide nor too narrow. For some have it

quod multi credunt que Ecclesia credit, mult⟨a⟩ eciam fatua credunt a latere;
cuiusmodi sunt sortilegi et nigromantici et huiusmodi. Et alii sunt qui
120   habent istud tabernaculum fidei nimis artum et strictum, scilicet qui
sequuntur hereses, similiter dicentes [f. 79v] Deum nullum hominem eternaliter velle dampnare, eo quod ita bene peccatorem suo precioso sanguine
redemit sicut et iustum, et huiusmodi.
      Contra quos Seneca sexto libro *Declamacionum*, capitulo 3, narrat quod
125   antiquitus talis erat lex, scilicet quod filius ancille hereditatem post
mortem patris participaret cum filio libere. Alia lex erat eciam quod
senior frater patrimonium divideret et minor eligeret. Accidit quod quidam
predives duos habuit filios, unum de libera et alium de ancilla. Mortuo
ergo patre, filius libere, qui erat senior, patrimonium sic divisit: posuit
130   autem ex una parte omne patrimonium et ex alia parte pauperem matrem fratris sui. Quo facto gratitudine ductus iunior, cui electio competebat,
matrem tantum elegit. Conquestus tamen est quod senior fraudulenter divisit. Respondit alius quod non, allegans legem quod si patrimonium elegisset
suum fuisset; cum ergo dimisso patrimonio matrem elegit, nulla sibi esse
135   facta iniuria. Revera sic in proposito. Dives iste Deus Pater est, qui
habet duos filios, unum scilicet de libera, Christum Filium [eius], et
alium de ancilla, scilicet hominem peccatorem, cuius mater terra est de qua
omnes nascimur et ad illam revertemur. Vult tamen Pater celestis ut omnes
cum Christo, si velimus, partem habeamus de hereditate celesti. Set lex est
140   quod senior [dividet et iunior eliget. Christus igitur, qui senior] est secundum Apostolum Romanorum 8, qui dicit: "Ipse sit primogenitus in multis
fratribus," sic dividit: Ponit enim ex una parte totum patrimonium, scilicet celeste gaudium, et ex alia parte carnales voluptates et terrena bona.
Si ergo homo, qui iunior est, matrem terre eligat, cum sit liberi arbitrii,
145   quid imputandum est Christo? Dico: certe nichil. Revera tunc respondeo:
Quando dicunt [Christum] neminem velle dampnare, concedo: ° illorum qui
saniorem partem eligunt et aliam [f. 80] dimittunt. Tunc ad argumentum
"Christus sanguinem fudit pro peccatore sicut pro iusto," concedo: de
peccatore contrito, et simpliciter nego de peccatore obstinato.
150   Si ergo, karissimi, in isto tabernaculo fidei velimus Patrem celestem
manere, oportet primo quod sit debite mensuratum, quia dicit Apostolus
Romanorum 12: "Non plus sapere quam oportet," etc., supple de fide, nec
minus quam oportet. Secundo oportet quod istud tabernaculum sit solide
collocatum, contra illos qui secundum Matthei 8 "ad tempus credunt et in
155   tempore temptacionis recedunt." Non sic, set iuxta concilium Ysaie 22 "vade
ad eum qui habitat in tabernaculo," scilicet ad Deum Patrem per solidam
fidem. Et certe tunc bene de te dicetur quod ibidem sequitur: "Excidisti in
excelso memoriale diligenter ⟨in petra⟩ tabernaculum."
      Secundum tabernaculum, scilicet spei, debet erigi in nostre intelli-

too wide, when they, together with many who believe as the Church believes, also believe many foolish things in error, as is the case with soothsayers and necromancers and such. Other people have this tabernacle of faith too narrow and tight, namely those who follow heresies and people who say that God will not condemn anybody for eternity because he has redeemed the sinner with his precious blood as well as the just person, and so forth.

Against such people Seneca tells us in Book 6 of his *Declamations*, chapter 3, that in olden times there was a law to the effect that the son of a servant woman would, after his father's death, share the inheritance with the son of a free woman. There was also another law that the older brother would divide the inheritance and the younger would take his choice. Now it happened that a very rich man had two sons, one by a free woman, the other by a servant girl. After the father's death the son of the free woman, who was the older, divided the inheritance as follows: on one side he put all the inheritance, and on the other the poor mother of his brother. At this, the younger brother, who had the right to choose, picked his mother only, as he was led by gratitude. However, he complained that the older brother had cheated in making such a division. But the other replied that this was not so and cited the law that, if the younger brother had chosen the goods, they would have been his; but since he picked his mother and not the goods, no injustice was done to him. If we apply this to the spiritual life, the rich man is God our Father; he has two sons, one by a free woman, who is Christ his Son, and another by a bondwoman, namely sinful man, whose mother is the earth from which we all are born and to which we shall return. However, our heavenly Father wants that we all, if we so wish, share with Christ in the heavenly inheritance. But there is a law that the older will divide and the younger will take his choice. Therefore, Christ, who is the older according to the Apostle who says in Romans 8: "That he might be the firstborn among many brethren," divides as follows: he puts the entire inheritance to one side, that is, the joy of heaven, and on the other side he puts fleshly delights and earthly goods. So, if man, who is the younger brother, picks his mother, the earth, since he has free will, what then is Christ to blame for? Certainly nothing whatsoever. Hence my answer to the saying quoted earlier is this: when these people claim that Christ will not condemn anybody, I agree that this is true of all who choose the better portion and leave the other alone. And with respect to the argument that "Christ has shed his blood for the sinner as well as for the just man," I agree that this applies to a sinner who is repentant, but not to one who is not.

Therefore, dearly beloved, if we wish that our heavenly Father stay in this tabernacle of faith, we must see to it, first, that it be duly measured, for the Apostle says in Romans 12: "Not to be more wise than it behooves," etc., add: regarding our faith, nor less than is necessary. Second, we must see to it that this tabernacle be put up firmly, in contrast to those who, in

160 gencie area, que est locus sapiencie Filio Dei deputatus. Filius enim Dei
      istud tabernaculum habet pro loco [suo], quia non sufficit quod tantum eius
      habeamus memoriam. Immo si inter personas divinas comparacionem facere
      liceret, quicquid fecit Filius, fecit et Pater et Spiritus Sanctus; set
      ultra hoc Filius est homo tantum illarum personarum et naturam humanam
165 assumpsit, in qua suo benedicto sanguine nos redemit et a peccato mundavit,
      ut merito de eo apud nos erigatur [eius] tabernaculum actualis et incensi-
      bilis intelligencie, que est locus et area sua. Psalmista: "Intelligite qui
      obliviscimini Domini," quasi diceret: Vos ingrati, pro quibus tanta feci,
      intelligite vulnera et angustias, verbera et iniurias que pro vobis susti-
170 nui, et confidenter sperate in me. Set timeo quod pluribus dicere potest
      Christus illud Psalmi: "Oblivioni datus sum tanquam mortuus a corde,"
      propter illorum ingratitudinem, quamvis in corporibus illorum [videatur]
      vivere, dum ita horribiliter per membra eius iurant; et cum indi- [f. 80v]
      guerint, ad eius auxilium clamant, set necessitate cessante apud illos
175 moritur, ut manifeste patet. Patet ergo quare intelligencia est locus
      tabernaculi Christi Filii Dei.
          Set iam rogo quare est spes tabernaculum eius? Respondeo: Cum enim
      speramus omnes venire ad celum, nullum colorem habemus ex meritis nostris
      aut spem, set [per] merita passionis [Christi]. Et ideo ibi erigamus illud
180 tabernaculum sibi, [et] quocienscumque nobis aliquid temptacionis occurre-
      rit, quasi scilicet merita nostra non sufficiant nobis pro regno celesti
      habendo, recurramus ad illud tabernaculum spei de meritis passionis Chris-
      ti, scilicet quod illa sufficiant, et revera omnem securitatem ibi invenie-
      mus iuxta illud Ysaie 4: "Tabernaculum erit in umbraculum diei ab estu et
185 securitatem a turbine et a pluvia."
          Et nota quod in erigendo [istud tabernaculum] duo sunt attendenda.
      Unum est quod non erigatur sine aliquo solido ligno cui innitatur, quia
      numquam tentorium aliquod extendi potest sine ligno; Iob 14: "Lignum habet
      spem"; sic nec aliquod tentorium spei sine ligno bonorum operum, iuxta
190 illud Psalmi: "Spera in Domino et fac bonitatem." Valde mirabile est spera-
      re quod aliter Christus concederet nobis celum quam matri sue et aliis
      sanctis, vel aliter quam ipsemet quesivit in terris. Set ipse per tribula-
      ciones et passiones sicut et ceteri sancti celum adquisivit; et tamen
      nichil de illis set tantum de gaudiis celi participare vellemus, cum tamen
195 "regnum celorum vim patitur." Et hic nota contra tales parte 5, ubi agitur
      de accidiosis satis, capitulo 3. Secundo in erigendo [tentorium], prout
      dicunt experti, attendendum est quod semper contra ventum erigatur et cum
      vento deponatur. Revera ventus iste significat adversitatem temporalem,
      cuiusmodi sunt mors, amissio bonorum, infirmitas, et huiusmodi. Cum ergo
200 ventus te agitaverit, tunc audacter [f. 81] tentorium spei erige. Set si
      ventus prosperitatis tecum sit et nullus ventus adversitatis contrarius

the words of Matthew 8, "believe for a while, and in time of temptation they
fall away." Let us not act thus, but after the counsel of Isaiah 22 "go to him
that dwells in the tabernacle," that is, to God the Father, in firm faith.
Then it will certainly be said of you what follows in the same passage: "You
have hewn out a monument carefully in a high place, in the rock a tabernacle."

The second tabernacle, that of hope, must be built in the lot of our
intellect, which is assigned to the wisdom of the Son of God. The Son of God
has this tabernacle as his dwelling place, because it is not enough only to
remember him. If one may make any comparison between the divine persons at
all: whatever the Son has done, the Father and the Holy Spirit have done as
well; but beyond this, of these three divine persons only the Son is man and
has taken a human nature, in which he has redeemed us with his blessed blood
and cleansed us from sin, so that his tabernacle of knowing him concretely and
in our mind may be rightly built within us, which is his proper dwelling place
and lot. The Psalmist says: "Understand these things, you who forget the
Lord," as if to say: you ungrateful ones, for whom I have done so much, understand the wounds and hardships, the blows and injuries I have suffered for you,
and confidently put your hope in me. But I fear that to many people Christ can
say the following words of the Psalm: "I am forgotten as one dead from the
heart," because of their ingratitude, even though he seems to be alive in their
bodies since they swear so horribly by his members; and when they have need,
they call for his help, but when their need is over, he dies in them, as can be
clearly seen. Thus it is manifest why our understanding is the place for the
tabernacle of Christ, the Son of God.

But I ask why is this tabernacle hope? I answer: While we all hope to
come to heaven, we have no color or hope from our own merits, but rather
through the merits of Christ's Passion. Therefore, let us build him this
tabernacle there, and whenever we run into any temptation, namely when we are
tempted to think that our merits may be insufficient for the heavenly kingdom,
let us take refuge in that tabernacle of hope built on the merits of Christ's
Passion, thinking that they will suffice us, and thus we shall find there
complete safety, according to the words of Isaiah 4: "There shall be a tabernacle for shade from the heat in daytime, and for safety from the whirlwind and
from rain."

And notice that in building this tabernacle two things need to be attended
to. One is that it must not be put up without some solid wooden pole for
support, for without a wooden pole one can never stretch out the tent; Job 14:
"A tree has hope"; thus, this tent of hope cannot be put up without a pole of
good works, according to the Psalm: "Trust in the Lord and do good." It is
very strange that someone hopes Christ would grant us heaven in any other way
than that by which he granted it to his mother and the other saints or by which
he sought it himself when he was on earth. But he himself as well as the other

sit, ⟨tunc⟩ timeas et non nimis istud tentorium erigere presumas. Unde con-
sulendum est quod nemo quantumcumque [bonus] in tantum presumat de Dei
misericordia quin aliquando timeat, nec aliquis quantumcumque malus, quin
205   aliquando speret. Et revera si sic istud tentorium paraverimus, nulli dubium quin contra omnia adversa iuvabit ille Filius; unde Thobie 13 dicitur:
"Confitere Domino in bonis et benedic Deum celorum, ut re[e]dificet in te
tabernaculum suum," scilicet recte spei sine presumpcione aut desperacione.
      Tercium tabernaculum, scilicet caritatis, erigendum est in area nostre
210   voluntatis, que est locus deputatus Spiritui Sancto. Ipse enim est caritas
et dilectio tam Patris quam Filii. Et ideo istud tabernaculum pro semper
durabit; ⟨Iob⟩ 5: "Scias quia pacem habebit tabernaculum tuum."
      Est autem hic notandum quod ad tabernaculum erigendum quatuor requi-
runtur, videlicet meremium, pannus, paxilli, et corde. Si ergo de isto
215   tentorio caritatis loqui velimus, timeo quod meremium non potest coniungi,
quod panni sunt lacerati, quod corde sunt false, fracte, et rupte, et quod
paxilli amittuntur. Et ideo numquam tale tentorium erigetur. Et nota quod
istius tabernaculi meremium dici possunt persone ordinate in caritate Dei
et proximi. Panni vero qui extenduntur super ligna [sunt] affectiones bone,
220   quibus desideras Deo honorem et obedienciam, et proximo que sibi competunt
et expediunt, [sicut] tibi ipsi. Paxilli sunt beneficia que quilibet pro
alio in necessitate facere tenetur; set corde verba amicabilia et educata
loquela. Set timeo quod Spiritus Sanctus ab illo tabernaculo expellitur et
iacet sub divo, sicut ipse conqueritur Ieremie 4: "Tabernaculum meum vasta-
225   tum est, omnes funiculi disrupti sunt, non est qui extendat [f. 81v] tentorium meum et erigat pelles me⟨a⟩s." Nam ligna tentorii, scilicet homines
qui in caritate esse debent, nolunt aptari, quia nec sunt coniuncti Deo per
humilitatem et obedienciam, nec proximo per benignitatem et amiciciam. Vix
enim tres in una civitate inveniuntur qui veraciter se mutuo diligunt, set
230   quilibet alium quasi continue inpugnat. Unde mirabile valde videtur quod
iam minor dilectio invenitur inter homines quam inter demones. Legimus
autem Luce 8 quod una legio demonum, scilicet sex milia sexcenti sexaginta
sex, in uno homine adinvicem habitabant, et tamen nullus eorum alium expu-
lit. Quomodo ergo sex tantum vicini caritative in una civitate sine inpug-
235   nacione habitare non possunt ex invidia? Similiter per istam invidiam panni
sunt totaliter lacerati, in tantum quod vix remanet una particula integra.
Unde hec est causa quare ex omni parte intrant ventus et pluvie falsitatis
et nequicie. Paxilli eciam beneficiorum fracti sunt et deperditi vel a
vermibus impietatis erga proximum corrosi et destructi. Corde eciam educa-
240   cionis per loquelam irrisionibus, contencionibus, et huiusmodi dirupte
sunt, vel saltem per verba falsa et ficta putride et corrupte, ut sic istud
tabernaculum Sancti Spiritus, quod per caritatem in voluntate hominis
regere deberet, prosternitur per invidiam et destruitur. Non sic, set istud

saints gained heaven through tribulations and sufferings; should we, then, want not to share in them but only in the joys of heaven while "the kingdom of heaven suffers violence"? With respect to such people see part 5, chapter 3, where I shall discuss the slothful. The second thing to attend to in putting up a tent, as the experts tell us, is that it must always be set up against the wind and taken down with the wind. This wind symbolizes worldly adversity, such as death, the loss of our belongings, sickness, and the like. Therefore, when this wind blows at you, bravely set up your tent of hope. But when there is a favorable wind of prosperity and no wind of adversity blows against you, then you must be cautious and not too eager to put up this tent. Therefore it is advisable that no one, however good he is, should trust so much in God's mercy that he does not sometimes fear; nor should anyone, no matter how evil he is, live without having some hope. If we then set up this tent in this way, God the Son will without doubt help us against all adversity; whence it is written in Tobit 13: "Give glory to the Lord for your good things and bless the God of heaven, that he may rebuild in you his tabernacle," namely that of true hope without presumption or despair.

The third tabernacle, that of charity, must be built in the lot of our will, which is the space assigned to the Holy Spirit. For he is charity and love of both Father and Son. And therefore this tabernacle will stand forever; Job 5: "You shall know that your tabernacle is in peace."

We must note that four things are required for building a tabernacle: timber, cloth, pegs, and ropes. Speaking of this tent of charity, I fear the timber cannot be joined, the cloth is tattered, the ropes are deceptive, broken, and in pieces, and the pegs are lost. Such a tent can never be set up. Notice that the timber of this tabernacle can stand for persons who are well ordered in their love for God and their neighbor. The cloth which is stretched over the poles are good affections with which one desires that God may receive honor and obedience, and one's neighbor whatever is fitting and useful for him, as much as oneself. The pegs are the good deeds which anyone is held to do for another in his need; and the ropes are friendly and uplifting words. But I fear that the Holy Spirit is driven out of this tabernacle and lies in the open, as he himself complains in Jeremiah 4: "My tabernacle is laid waste, all my cords are broken, there is none to stretch out my tent any more and to set up my curtains." For the tent poles, that is, people who should be charitable, do not fit together, because they are not joined to God in humility and obedience, nor to their neighbor in goodwill and friendship. Hardly three can be found in a city who truly love each other, but everybody fights someone else almost all the time. Therefore it is astonishing that among humans one finds less peace than among devils. For we read in Luke 8 that a legion of devils, that is, 6666, were dwelling together in one person, and yet none of them drove another one out. How, then, can a mere six neighbors not live charitably in

tabernaculum cum munda voluntate pro recepcione eius ⟨e⟩rigamus firmiter,
245 ut sibi dicere possimus illud Ysaie 33: "Oculi tui videbunt civitatem
Ierusalem opilentam, tabernaculum quod n⟨equa⟩quam transferri poterat, nec
auferentur clavi in sempiternum et omnes funiculi eius non rumpentur."
    Ista ergo tabernacula Patri et [f. 82] Filio et Spiritui Sancto parare
et erigere non cessemus, ut cum per mortem secundum dictum beati Luce 16
250 defecerimus, "recipiant nos in eterna tabernacula," que ipsi parabunt diligentibus se.
    Et hec de invidia et caritate Dei et hominis ad presens iam dicta suf-
ficiant. Et sic terminatur tercia pars principalis huius libelli.

---

1 Dicto] dicta C.   **4** sancti] beati M.R; *om* W.   **17** one] *om* R.M; *for the whole English
clause* M *gives*: hic venit huc quod nullus de eo scit; vel sic: iste ad tantam etatem venit et
tamen adhuc nemo nomine nec de eo aliquid scit.   **19** dixit] respondit O.   Ye . . . boote]
forte ipse est diabolus vel eius pedellus vel eius nuncius M.   **41** excedat] excedit C.
42 ymaginem] *add* solis O.   set] licet M.W; quamvis R.   **43** que] qui O.   sol est] solem
C.   **46** 43] 93 C.   **48** theologi] theologe C.   **50** et] *add* eciam M; *add* in R.W.   **58** vale-
mus] volemus C.   **62** Et sic] secundo O.   velimus] volumus M.W; *om* R.   **63** animam]
anima O.   **65** inhabitato] habitato O.   **70** campum marescallus] campus per marescallum
O.   dividit] ordinatur M; dividitur R; *om* W.   **75** sanctarum] beatarum O.   **79** depixit]
depixerit C.   **86** beatorum] bonorum C.R.   **90** porciones] proporciones M.W; *om* R.
92 ergo] igitur O.   **96** tria(2)] *om* O.   **97** 13] *add* dicitur O.   **98** et] *om* O.   **111** re-
frigerium] refugium M *corr.*   **117** nec . . . amplum] *om* C.O.   **118** multa] multi C.
123 et] *add* cetera O.   **126** eciam] *add* talis O.   **146** concedo] *add* opinionem C.
147 saniorem] seniorem R.W.   **158** memoriale] *corr* C; memoria O.   in petra] impetratur C.   tabernaculum] *corr* C; tabernaculi O.   **160** est . . . deputatus] sapiencie Filii
Dei deputatur O.   **166–167** incensibilis] incessabilis O.   **178** colorem] *thus* C.W *and
others*; valorem M; calorem R.   **179** illud] istud O.   **182** habendo] *om* O.   illud] istud
O.   **189** aliquod] istud O.   **192** quesivit] adquisivit O.   **199** sunt] est M; *om* R.W.
mors] *add* amicorum O.   **202** tunc] et sic C.   **206** ille] iste O.   **212** Iob] iohannis C.
habebit] habeat M.W; habebat R.   **223** illo] isto O.   **226** meas] meos C.   **231** dilectio]
pax O.   **235** ex] et O.   **238** beneficiorum] benefactorum O.   **240** per . . . conten-
cionibus] in loquela per irrisiones contenciones O.   **243** regere] erigi M.   **244** taber-
naculum] *om* O. erigamus] irrigamus C.   **246** nequaquam] numquam C.   **253** huius]
istius C.

one city without fighting and envy? Similarly, through the same envy the tent cloth is totally torn, so that hardly one small part of it remains whole. This is the reason why from all sides the wind and rain of deceit and wickedness come in. Likewise, the pegs of good deeds are broken and lost or gnawed and destroyed by the worms of pitilessness toward our neighbor. Also the ropes of uplifting speech have become broken through derision, strife, and the like, or perhaps have become rotten and useless through deceitful and feigned words, so that this tabernacle of the Holy Spirit, which should stand fast through love in man's will, is overthrown and destroyed through envy. Let it not happen thus, but let us instead build it up firmly with our pure will in order to receive him, so that we may be able to say to him the words of Isaiah 33, "Your eyes shall see Jerusalem, a rich city, a tabernacle that cannot be removed, nor shall its nails be taken away for ever, nor shall any of its cords be broken."

Let us therefore not cease from preparing and setting up these three tabernacles for the Father, Son, and Holy Spirit, so that, when we come to our death, according to the words of Blessed Luke 16, "they may receive us into everlasting tabernacles," which they prepare for those that love them.

And this discussion of envy and of the love of God and man should suffice for now. And thus ends the third main part of this book.

5–6 Cf. Augustine, *De Trinitate* XIV.viii.11 (CC 50A: 436) and passim.   12 Prov. 25.27.   24 Judg. 13.18.   27–28 Isa. 53.8.   46–47 Ecclus. 43.4.   55–54 2 Cor. 3.18.   56–57 1 Cor. 13.12.   74 Deut. 10.17, etc.   79–80 Gen. 1.26.   93 Hebr. 13.14.   95–96 Matt. 17.4.   97–98 1 Cor. 13.13.   103–104 Isa. 54.2.   124–135 Seneca, *Declamationes* VI.3.   141–142 Rom. 8.29.   152 Rom. 12.3.   154–155 Luke 8.13.   155–158 Isa. 22.15.   167–168 Ps. 49.22.   171 Ps. 30.13.   184–185 Isa. 4.6.   188–189 Job 14.7.   190 Ps. 36.3.   195 Matt. 11.12.   195–196 *FM* V.i, iii–iv.   207–208 Tob. 13.12.   212 Job 5.24.   224–226 Jer. 10.20.   232–233 Cf. Luke 8.26–39.   245–247 Isa. 33.20.   250 Luke 16.9.

PARS IV

De avaricia

IV.i QUID SIT AVARICIA

[E]xpeditus de particulis tribus spiritui maligno specialius deservi-
entibus, scilicet de superbia, ira, et invidia, que sunt fili⟨e⟩ diaboli
propinquiores, et etiam de virtutibus illis contrariis et eas expugnanti-
bus, scilicet humilitate, paciencia, et caritate; restat iam quarto per-
5 tractare de illis que mundo miserabili specialius deserviant, scilicet de
avaricia et cupiditate, et de virtutibus similiter [sibi] contrariis,
scilicet de contemptu mundi et voluntaria paupertate.

Circa avariciam ergo sic procedam: primo quid sit et quomodo diffinitur; secundo de eius proprietatibus et a quibus progreditur; tercio de
10 eius membris et quare iuste contempnitur.

Dico ergo primo quod avaricia secundum Augustinum *Super Genesim* est
qua quis aliquid appetit amplius quam oportet propter excellenciam et
quendam proprie rei amorem. Item avaricia (dicit ipse) est "am⟨or⟩ specialis pecunie et inmoderatus appetitus habendi." Que secundum Magistrum *Sen-*
15 *tenciarum* libro 2, distinctione 22, "non tantum est inmoderata pecunie
cupiditas set (dicit ipse) altitudinis et sciencie, cum supra modum sublimitas ambitur." Et nota quod huiusmodi avariciam hoc modo describit Inno-
cencius: "Avarus, inquit, naturaliter ad petendum est promptus, ad dandum
tardus, ad negandum frontuosus. Magnificat datum, vilificat dandum, dat ut
20 lucratur set non lucratur ut det, largus in [f. 82v] alienis, parcus in
propriis, gulam evacuat ut archam impleat, corpus extenuat ut lucrum ostendat. Et cum adipiscit quod optaverat, desiderat ampliora." Hec ille.

---

2 filie] filii C; filia W.   **5** deserviant] deserviunt O.   **13** amor] amator C.   **15** 22] 21 O.
20 lucratur] lucretur M.R.

PART IV

Avarice

IV.i THE MEANING OF AVARICE

After treating in three parts the vices that especially serve the evil spirit, namely pride, wrath, and envy—the direct offspring of the devil—, as well as the virtues that oppose and combat them, namely humility, patience, and charity; we now come, in the fourth part, to treat of those vices that are more directly in the service of the wretched world, namely avarice and cupidity, as well as their opposite virtues, namely contempt of the world and voluntary poverty.

With regard to avarice I shall proceed as follows: first I shall discuss what it is and how it is defined; second, its qualities and from whence it comes; and third, its members and why it is rightly despised.

First, then, I say that according to Augustine in his book *On Genesis* avarice occurs when one desires something more than befits its value and the love the object deserves. He says further that avarice is "in particular the love of money and the immoderate desire to possess." According to the Master of the *Sentences*, book 2, distinction 22, it is "immoderate desire not only for money but also for rank and knowledge, when one strives for a high position beyond measure." Innocent describes such greed as follows: "An avaricious person is naturally eager in grasping, slow in giving, and shameless in denying. He praises what is given and puts down what he should give; he gives in order to gain, but does not gain in order to give; he is generous with what belongs to others, but niggardly with his own; he avoids gluttony in order to fill his coffer, and he starves himself in order to show his wealth. And when he obtains what he had wished for, he wants even more."

11–14 Cf. Gregory, *In Evangelia*, hom. 16, 2 (PL 76:1136).   **15–17** Peter Lombard, *Sent*. II.xxi.5 (1:436).   **18–22** Innocent III, *De miseria* II.xvi.1 (p. 51).   **22** Ibidem, II.vi.1 (p. 43).

IV.ii   DE PROPRIETATIBUS AVARICIE: LABOR IN PERQUIRENDO

Circa autem proprietates a quibus progreditur est secundo sciendum quod iste sunt, scilicet: labor in perquirendo, timor in possidendo, et dolor in amittendo, ut patet in hiis versibus:

> Dives divicias non congregat absque labore,
5 > Nec tenet sine metu, nec desinit absque dolore.

Quod enim prima proprietas patet, sic probatur: Si enim loqui velimus de avaro et quantum laborem sustinet bona temporalia perquirendo, ad sensum videre poterimus quod nichil audibile, cogitabile, visibile, aut loquibile ymaginari potest quin huiusmodi avarus miserabili modo concupiscit, in
10 tantum quod numquam cessat de die ac nocte, sero an mane, itinerando, equitando, navigando, suis inordinatis imo miserabilibus oculorum concupiscenciis satisfacere, cum tamen sint in periculis maximis tam corporalibus quam spiritualibus. De qua Ecclesiastici 5 dicitur: "Avarus numquam implebitur peccunia." Nam sicut Bernardus: "Cum omnia creata a Deo suis
15 limitibus terminantur, sola avaricia finem non habet." Nam si lucratus fuerit totam terram, maria appetit; et si illud, mox aerea concupiscit. Et sic ascendendo finem non habet.

Et ideo bene dicitur ignis ille infernalis qui numquam dicit "sufficit." N⟨am⟩ ignis iste sic accenditur et inflammatur per ligna cupidita-
20 tis, rapacitatis, ⟨dis⟩censionis, et impietatis, et cetera huiusmodi, quod nequaquam ab aqua universa extingui ° potest.

Et ideo de illa avaricia sic inflammante narrat Beda *De gestis Anglorum* libro 3 quod cum semel sanctus Furseus exutus esset a corpore et ab angelis in altum [f. 83] deportatus, ad inferiora respiciens vidit vallem
25 terribilem et tenebrosam a quatuor igni[bu]s succensam, et cum interrogaret quid hec significarent, respondit angelus: "Vallis, inquit, tenebrosa mundus est, set quatuor ignes sunt quatuor peccata que mundum consumunt. Quorum primus est ignis mendacii, eo quod iam homines non implent quod in baptismo promiserunt, scilicet credere firmiter in Deum, munde vivere,
30 diaboloque et pompis eius abrenunciare. Secundus ignis est mundi cupiditas, propter quam amor celestium postponitur. Tercius est ignis discordie et discencionis, sicut patet in bellis et pugnis que propter mundum et eius avariciam tociens accenduntur. Set quartus est ignis impietatis, per quem simplices destruuntur." Est ergo hec mundi avaricia ignis inextinguibilis,
35 qui numquam dicit "sufficit." Unde versus:

> Cum sitim sedare possit tunc altera crescit.
> Crescit amor nummi cum ipsa pecunia crescit.

IV.ii   THE PROPERTIES OF AVARICE: HARD WORK IN ACQUISITION

With respect to the qualities from which avarice arises, we should know that there are three, namely: hard work in acquiring, fear in possessing, and pain in losing, as is shown in the following verses:

> Not without hardships great does a rich man gather his riches,
> Not without fear does he hold them, nor without pain are they lost.

The truth of the first quality can be shown as follows. Speaking of an avaricious person and the great hardships he endures in acquiring temporal goods, we know from experience that one cannot imagine anything audible, thinkable, visible, or speakable that an avaricious person does not in his wretched way crave to possess, so that he never ceases by day or night, early or late, to satisfy the disorderly, indeed wretched lust of his eyes, whether by journeying about or riding or sailing, whereby he places himself in the greatest physical as well as spiritual dangers. Of him is said in Ecclesiasticus 5: "The covetous man will never be satisfied with money." For as Bernard claims: "Whereas all created things have their limits set by God, avarice alone is without a limit." For when it has gained the whole earth, it wants the sea; and after that, it soon craves for what is in the air. And by rising thus it knows no limit.

Therefore, avarice may well be called that hellfire which never says "Enough!" For that fire is so much kindled and lighted with the sticks of covetousness, craving, strife, pitilessness, and other vices of this kind that it can never be quenched by all the water in the world.

Of this burning avarice Bede reports in book 3 of *The Deeds of the English* that at one time Saint Furseus left his body and was carried by angels to the depth of hell. There he saw an awesome, dark valley burning with four fires, and when he asked what these things meant, an angel replied: "The dark valley is the world, and the four fires are four sins which consume it. The first is the fire of lying, because people now do not fulfill what they promised in baptism, that is, to believe firmly in God, to live in purity, and to renounce the devil and his pomp. The second fire is worldly covetousness, by which the love of heavenly things is set aside. The third is the fire of discord and strife, as can be seen in wars and fights that are so often kindled for the sake of the world and its avarice. But the fourth is the fire of pitilessness, by which poor people are ruined." Thus the avarice of the world is an unquenchable fire which never says "Enough!" Hence the verses:

> One's thirst perhaps is quenched, but soon it comes anew.
> One's love of money grows the more one's riches grow.

Unde Bernardus: "Ancipiter, inquit, avis rapacissima est, tamen con-
tentus in aere, et lupus in silva, lucius in aqua, set miser homo omnibus
40   hiis rapa⟨cior⟩, quia terram et aerem et aquam si posset suis nutrimentis
spoliaret." "Et non tantum hoc (dicit Gregorius), imo petit celum. Quod si
ei daretur, vellet equari Deo et post, si posset, supra eum quereret." Et
revera per istam miserabilem pestem oriuntur tot pugne, tot bella, tot
clades, tot pericula, tot casus, et tot infortunia. Et non tantum hec, set
45   mediante avaricia destruitur in terris veritas et sciencia; Osee 4: "Non
est veritas, non est misericordia, non est iusticia, non est sciencia Dei
in terris," supple propter mundi avariciam, et per consequens habundant
falsitas, crudelitas, et fatuitas.
    Et ideo timendum est ne modernis [f. 83v] temporibus hominibus dici
50   posset quod quondam dictum erat et revelatum cuidam ⟨s⟩enatori Romano
querenti causam a deo suo quare tot miseriis infestabantur, sicut per
bella, pestilencias, et fames. Cui responsum erat quod iret ad portas
civitatis et diligenter inspiceret que ibi scripta inveniret. Qui cum ibi
accessisset, has literas sic invenit: SSS, PPP, RRR, FFF. Quarum intellec-
55   tum [cum] non intellexisset, iterum deum consuluit pro intellectu. Et hoc
modo sibi responsum fuit:

            Seculum sapienciam sustulit.
            Pax patrie perditur.
            Regnum Rome ruet,
60   Ferro, fame, flamma.

[Anglice:

            ⟨Oure⟩ wysdam þis world haþ byraft,
            Pes of londe is loste and lafte.
            þe kyndam of Rome betȝ for-lore
65   With swerd, hongur, and fuyre þer-fore.]

Nonne hiis diebus simili modo seculum cum eius cupiditate et avaricia veram
sapienciam abstulit ab hominibus? Credo quod sic. Et hoc tam in clero quam
eciam in populo. Quia si de clero [loquamur], videmus quod [tantum] nituntur temporalia adquirere quod pro illis habendis unus miser cuiuscumque
70   condicionis extiterit potest in falsitatibus et aliis miseriis iacere,
sicut in luxuria, symonia, et huiusmodi, eciam usque ad finem vite, qui
iuste ab illis per veram sapienciam graviter redargui ac corrigi deberet.
Si autem loquamur de populo, et maxime de regnorum gubernatoribus, cuiusmodi sunt iuriste, iusticiarii, et huiusmodi, qui in omni sapiencia et veri-
75   tate populum regere deberent, ibi eciam credo quod ordine retrogrado vadit

Whence Bernard says: "The hawk, which is a very rapacious bird, is yet content in the air; so is the wolf in the forest and the pike in the water. But wretched man is greedier than all these, because if he could, he would rob earth and air and water of their nourishment. And not only this, but beyond it he strives for heaven. If that were given to him, he would want to be God's equal, and after that, if it were possible, he would even seek to climb higher than God." Indeed, through this miserable pestilence arise so many fights, wars, clashes, dangers, tragedies, and mishaps. And not only do these things happen, but by means of avarice truth and knowledge are ruined on earth; Hosea 4: "There is no truth, there is no mercy, there is no justice, and there is no knowledge of God in the land," add: because of worldly avarice, and as a result deceit, cruelty, and folly abound.

Therefore we must fear that the same could be said to the people of our times that was once said and revealed to a Roman senator who asked his god why they were being troubled by so many miseries, such as wars, pestilences, and famines. In response he was told to go to the city gates and read carefully what he might find written there. As he arrived there, he found the letters SSS, PPP, RRR, FFF. Since he did not understand their meaning, he asked his god again for clarification. And he received this answer:

> The world has taken away wisdom.
> The country's peace is lost.
> The realm of Rome shall fall
> With the sword, hunger, and fire.

In English:

> Oure wysdam þis world . . .

Has not in our days the world with its covetousness and greed similarly taken away true wisdom from the people? I believe so. And this among the clergy as well as among the layfolk. Speaking of the clergy, we see them striving so much for temporal goods that in order to acquire these, a wretched person of whatever social rank can, to the very end of his life, lie in falsehood and other forms of wretchedness, such as lechery, simony, and the like, who by right should be firmly reproved and corrected by the clergy in true wisdom. But speaking of the lay people, and particularly of such leaders of the country as lawyers and judges and the like, who should rule the people in all wisdom and truth, I believe that here, too, the world is going backwards. It should be marching straight with wisdom in the direction of truth; but nowadays it goes astray through avarice and covetousness in the direction of falsehood and injustice.

mundus. Quia quod cum sapiencia a parte vera procedere deberet, iam per
avariciam et cupiditatem declinatur ad partem falsam et iniustam, etc.

Unde satis [patet quod] verum est quod seculum sapienciam sustulit. Et
hoc probatur per talem narracionem. Fertur quod quidam iudex a quodam
80 paupere, ut ipsum in [vera] causa iuvaret, bigam in precio suscepit, quia
forte peccunia caruit. Cuius adversarius venit et eidem iudici pro sua
causa falsa promovenda iuga boum maioris [f. 84] valoris dedit. Cum vero ad
discucionem cause pervenissent, iudex contra pauperem propter mundi lucrum
tenuit. Cui pauper: "Domine, inquit, domine, plaustrum male vadit." Et
85 iudex: "Nec mirum. Boves tam fortes sunt quod [illud] extra viam rectam
extraxerunt." Et ideo de talibus bene dici potest illud Ysaie 59: "Iusticia
longe stetit, quia corruit in platea veritas." Unde apud tales iam similiter verificatur illud Sapiencie 9: "Error tamquam lex custoditus est."

Tales enim vilissime errant dum bona simplicium tamquam per legem veritatis
90 tam laboriose colligere non cessant mala simulantes, qui prius per veram
scienciam et legem positivam delicta malorum haberent corrigere, scientes
quia "iustis non est [lex] posita" secundum iura.

Et ideo est de talibus sicut de quibusdam infantibus qui nullo modo
sciunt sonare hanc literam R set pro illa, ut communiter, accipiunt hanc
95 literam L. Qui si dicere deberent hoc nomen "Rogerum," dicunt "Logelum,"
et cetera huiusmodi. Revera sic in proposito. Iura enim omnia iudices,
advocatos, et huiusmodi informant per omnia defectus per veram sapienciam
corrigere. Set quod dolendum est, sicut pueri vertunt literam R in L quando
mala dissimulant corrigere et temporalia tam avide non cessant colligere.
100 De quibus Baruc 1 dicitur: "Colligerunt pec⟨cuniam⟩ secundum uniuscuiusque
⟨manus⟩." Et ita permittunt malos in suis erroribus inpunitos pertransire,
quia iuxta Psalmum "dextra eorum repleta est muneribus," nam "pecunie" et
donis "obediunt omnia."

Et ideo de talibus sicut trufando legitur ° de quodam vicario, qui cum
105 esset correptus a suo episcopo eo quod asinum suum sepulture tradidisset,
respondit: "Karissime, inquit, domine, nescitis quantum asinus meus in
testamento suo vobis legavit?" Qui cum respondisset, "Non"—"Certe, domine," ait, "quadraginta solidos." Quo audito respondit episcopus, "Requies-
cat in pace!" Patet ergo quomodo [f. 84v] seculum, hoc est bona seculi,
110 abstulit sapienciam.

Et certe hec est causa potissima quod iam secunda proposicio verificatur, scilicet quod "Pax patrie perditur," sicut manifeste patet. Nam cessante vera sapiencia et doctrina, nec invenitur vera pax in civitate vel
regno, familia vel domo, imo—quod peius est—nec [inter] patrem et filium,
115 matrem et filiam, quin unusquisque mortem alterius pro bonis temporalibus
habendis affectat. Nec mirum ergo si iusto Dei iudicio istud regnum ruat,
sicut actenus visum est, modo ferro, modo fame, modo flamma.

Therefore it is patently true that the world has taken away wisdom. This
is borne out by the following story. In order to help a poor man in his just
cause, a certain judge is said to have accepted a cart in payment, perhaps
because the man had no money. Then the poor man's adversary came and gave the
same judge a yoke of oxen of much greater value, in order to further his unjust
cause. As they came together to hear the case, the judge, for worldly gain,
decided against the poor man. Then the latter said: "My lord, the cart is
running poorly." And the judge replied: "No wonder. The oxen are so strong
that they have pulled it from the right road." To such people the words of
Isaiah 59 may well apply: "Justice has stood far off, because truth has fallen
down in the street." And about such men the saying of Wisdom 9 has come true:
"Error was kept as a law." For they err most shamefully when they unceasingly
and with such effort collect the goods of poor people as if in agreement with a
true law and invent some crime, they whose task it is to correct the crimes of
the wicked through true knowledge and the established law, knowing that "for
the just there is no law" according to the laws.

These people behave like some small children who cannot in any way pronounce the letter r but instead say l as a rule. If they should say "Roger,"
they pronounce it "Logel," and so forth. To the case in point: all the laws
require that judges and advocates and the like always correct failings with
true wisdom. But alas, like little children they turn r into l when they
pretend to *correct* failings and never cease in their greed to *collect* worldly
goods. Of them is said in Baruch 1: "They made a collection of money according to everyman's power." And thus they allow the wicked to continue with
impunity in their crimes, for according to the Psalm "their right hand is
filled with gifts," for "all things obey money" and gifts.

To them also applies a joke we read about a vicar. When he was censured
by his bishop for giving burial to his ass, he answered: "Dear lord, do you
not know how much my ass has left for you in his will?" As the bishop replied,
"No," the vicar said: "Forty shillings, to be sure." At which the bishop
answered: "May he rest in peace!" Thus it is evident how the world, that is,
the goods of the world, has taken away wisdom.

This is the strongest reason why the second pronouncement also has come
true, namely that "the country's peace is lost," as can be clearly seen.
Because once true wisdom and teaching are gone, no real peace is found in city
or realm, family or house, not even—what is worse—between father and son,
mother and daughter, for indeed each one desires the other's death in order to
gain his temporal goods. No wonder, then, that after the just judgment of God
this realm is falling, as we have seen, now by the sword, now by hunger, and
now by fire.

Let these people therefore pay attention to what is reported of a Parisian
lawyer of this kind. As was his habit, he once planned to take the stand

Attendant ergo tales quod narratur de quodam tali advocato Parisius
qui, ut semper consueverat, propter munera semel proposuit contra personas
120   innocentes et religiosas falso stare. Cuius nomen erat Iohannes vel Wilhelmus
Malemortis. Accidit ergo ut quadam die cameram suam intravit quo melius
raciones et cavillaciones veritati contrarias ad dampnum eorum proponeret.
Cumque in crastinum ad comparendum vocaretur nec inveniretur, socii eius
hostium camere fregerunt, et ecce ipsum subito a demone strangulatum inve-
125   nerunt et corpus eius totum redactum in pulverem, de cuius fetore multi
accedentes interierunt. Unde unus literatus de sociis metrice sic ait:

Morte cadunt subita mala mors simul et mala vita.

[Anglice:

þourgh ferly deth to-gedur arn fald
130   Bothe euel lyf and euel deth cald.]

Cui alius respondit metrice sic:

Hanc vitam vita, ne moriaris ita.

[I rede such lyf þou forsake,
Wyth suche deth lest þou be take.]

135   Et hic nota narracionem de illo falso iudice nomine Gayus, qui tandem
captus a demonibus horribiliter clamavit et sic dixit:

Heu, heu, ° prothdolor, sicut iudicavi sic iudicor!

[Anglice sic:

Alas, alas, þat I was boren,
140   For dome with dome I am forloren,]

quasi diceret: sicut false innocentes iudicavi propter munera, sic iuste
iam iudicor a Deo, qui per Psalmistam dicit: "Cum accepero tempus, ego [f.
85] iusticias iudicabo."
Unde de talibus qui sic circa t[empor]alia laborant bene dicitur illud
145   Ysaie 56: "A dextris et a sinistris accipiunt et [in] iniusticiam semper
esuriunt." Et tamen in fine verificatur illud Ecclesiastici 5: "Infirmitas
pessima quam vidi sub sole: divicie conservate in manu domini sui, quia
sicut nudus egressus est de utero matris sue, sic revertetur et nichil

falsely against innocent and religious people for the gifts he had received.
His name was John or William Malemorte. It happened that one day he entered
his chamber to prepare ruses and arguments contrary to the truth in order to
convict them. As on the following day he was called to appear and could not be
found, his companions broke the door of his chamber, and behold, they found him
strangled by a demon and his body totally reduced to dust, from whose stench
many people died when they came near. One of his companions who was literate
then said in verse:

> Both Evil Death and evil life
> Are felled at once in sudden death.

In English:

> þough ferly deth . . .

To whom the other responded in verse as follows:

> Avoid such life that thou not end
> Like he in such a death!

In English:

> I rede such lyf . . .

And remember the story of the false judge called Gayus, who finally was
caught by demons and cried out horribly and said:

> Alas, alas, what pain! I'm judged as I have judged!

In English thus:

> Alas, alas . . .

as if he were saying: as I have falsely sentenced the innocent for gifts, so am
I now rightly sentenced by God, who says through the Psalmist: "When I shall
take the time, I shall judge justices."

Therefore, of such people who work hard in this fashion for temporal goods
it is well said in Isaiah 56: "They take from right and left and always hunger
for injustice." But in their ending the words of Ecclesiasticus 5 will come
true: "The worst evil I have seen under the sun: riches kept to the hurt of
the owner. As he came forth naked from his mother's womb, so shall he return,

a⟨u⟩feret secum de labore." Et Ecclesiastici 4 scribitur: "Unus est et si
150 non habet filium nec fratrem, laborare tamen non cessat nec saciantur oculi
eius diviciis, nec recogitat in corde suo dicens, 'Cui laboro et fraudo
animam bonis?' In hoc quoque vanitas et afflictio spiritus pessima," etc.

---

19 Nam] non C.   **20** discensionis] excensionis C.   **21** extingui] *add* non C.   **25** ignibus]
ignis C.M.   **36** Cum] dum O.   **37** cum] quantum O.   **39** et] *om* O.   **40** rapacior]
rapacicior C; rapticior M; rapcior W.   **50** senatori] cenatori C.   **61–65** Anglice . . .
þerfore] *text from* R. *Verse 33, in* B1.B3.E.Go1.L1.LC.R.Sp.V.W1.   **62** Oure] pure R.
68 eciam] *om* O.   **70** aliis] ceteris O.   **77** etc.] *om* O.   **87–88** similiter] super *after* verificatur R.W; *om* M.   **88** 9] 19 O.   **91** positivam] positam *apparently* O.   **92** quia] quod
O.   iustis] iusto O.   **95** Logelum] logerum O.   **100** Colligerunt] collegerunt O.   pec-
cuniam] pcca C.O.   **101** manus] viam C; munus *corr* M.   **104** legitur] *add* sicut C.
114 inter] *om* C.M.   **116** iudicio] *add* si O.   **128–134** Anglice . . . take] *text from* R.
Verse 34, in B1.B2.B3.E.Go1.L2.LC.R.Sp.V.   **137** heu] *add* heu C.   **138–140** Anglice . . . forloren] *text from* R. *Verse 35, in* B1.B3.E.Go1.L2.L3.LC.R.Sp.V.W1.etc.
147 manu] malum R.   **149** auferet] afferet C.

IV.iii   TIMOR IN POSSIDENDO

Secunda proprietas avaricie est timor in possidendo. Unde Ieronimus:
"Avarus, inquit, semper insidiantes metuit; aspicit potenciorem se et putat
esse violentem; conspicit pauperem et putat esse furem; et sic (dicit ipse)
in possidendo numquam securus est." Unde legitur de timido avaro habente
5 uxorem sanctam et devotam, ad cuius instigacionem concessit ipse Deum
laudare pro bonis sibi collatis et ipsum sepius exorare. Accidit tamen quod
latenter avarus iste habuit in sua capella ollam quamdam subterraneam,
tabula coopertam, quam timore aliorum ibi abscondebat; super quam omni die
missam audiens genuflexit, hoc modo oracionem profundens: "Rogo te, Domine
10 Iesu Christe, ne permittas hanc ollam a me alienari neque me mori quousque
illam pecunia adimplevero totaliter." Tandem olla impleta in sua sanitate
mortuus est. Cum autem cito post uxor sua alium cepisset maritum, iuvenem
largum et lascivum, et illum eodem modo ad devocionem et oraciones insti-
gasset, accidit quadam die dum in dicta capella missam audiret et in eodem
15 oratorio supra dictam ollam genuflexisset, [f. 85v] clavus in tabula supra
ollam infixus illum ledebat in genu. Ipse autem gravatus arrepto securi
volens clavum corrigere extraxit tabulam et coopertorium olle predicte.
Quam cum impletam sic invenisset, ⟨s⟩ilenter genua flectens hoc modo oravit: "Rogo te, omnipotens Deus, ut numquam permittas hanc pecuniam a me
20 alienari neque me mori quousque ollam istam evacuavero et cum bona societate consumpsero." Quo facto duxit dies letos et ad peticionem spero devenit.

and he shall take nothing away with him of his labor." And in Ecclesiasticus 4 is written: "There is but one, and if he has no son or brother, he yet does not cease to labor, nor are his eyes satisfied with riches, nor does he reflect in his heart and say, 'For whom do I labor and defraud my soul of good things?' In this also is vanity and a grievous vexation of the soul," etc.

2–3 This pattern also in Innocent III, *De miseria* I.xv.3 (p. 21).   **4–5** *Prov* 6059 et al. **13–14** Eccles. 5.9.   **14–15** Cf. Innocent III, *De miseria* II.vi (pp. 43–44).   **22– 34** Tubach 2229, from Bede, *Hist. eccl.* III.19.   **36–37** Cf. Ovid, *Met.* III.415; and Juvenal, *Sat.* XIV.139.   **41–42** Cf. Ps.-Augustine, *Ad fratres in eremo* 48 (PL 40:1330). **45–47** Hos. 4.1.   **50–65** Tubach 1150; for further occurrences, see *Verses*, p. 170.   **79– 86** Tubach 2851; similarly Bromyard, "Advocati," A.XIV.4.   **86–87** Isa. 59.14. **88** Wisd. 14.16.   **92** 1 Tim. 1.9.   **100–101** Bar. 1.6.   **102** Ps. 25.10.   **102–103** Eccles. 10.19.   **104–109** Tubach 376; cf. Bromyard, "Dedicacio," D.IV.13, and Rutebeuf, *Testament de l'asne* (ed. Adolf Kressner, *Rustebuefs Gedichte*, Wolfenbüttel, 1885, pp. 109–113).   **118–134** Tubach 3002; for further occurrences, see *Verses*, p. 171.   **135– 140** See Wenzel, "The 'Gay' Carol and Exemplum," *Neuphilologische Mitteilungen*, 77 (1976), 85–91.   **142–143** Ps. 74.3.   **146–149** Eccles. 5.12–14.   **149–152** Eccles. 4.8.

IV.iii   THE FEAR OF POSSESSION

The second quality of avarice is the fear one has in possessing property. Jerome says on this: "An avaricious person is always afraid that people are laying plots for him. He sees a man who is stronger than himself and thinks he will be violent; he sees a poor man and thinks he is a thief. And thus he is never at rest in his possessions." On this point we read of a fearful miser who had a saintly and devout wife, to whose urging he yielded so far as to praise God for the goods he had received and frequently to make his petitions. It happened that this miser secretly kept a pot in the ground of his chapel, covered with a plank, which he was hiding there out of fear of other people. He knelt above this pot every day and heard Mass, pouring forth his prayers as follows: "I ask you, Lord Jesus Christ, do not let this pot be stolen from me, nor let me die until I have totally filled it with money." At last, when the pot was filled, the man died in his health. Soon thereafter his wife took another husband, a generous and lusty young man, and urged him in the same way to make his devotions and prayers. One day it happened that he was hearing Mass in the same chapel and was kneeling in the same oratory above that pot, when a nail from the plank over the pot hurt his knee. Bothered by it he took his knife in order to fix it and pulled up the plank and the cover of the pot. As he found it so full, he knelt down and silently prayed: "I ask you, Almighty God, that you never let this money be taken from me, nor let me die until I have emptied this pot and used it up in good fellowship." And he spent

Figura[m] eciam ad hoc, scilicet quem fructum reportat avarus de congrega-
cione diviciarum, habemus Iosue 7 de Achor qui concupivit aurum et abscondit, propter quod postea lapidatus est. Et ideo dicit Augustinus: "Qui,
25   inquit, terrenis inhiant, celestia contempnunt et utrisque carebit in
fine."
    Non est ergo timor ponendus in amissione temporalium, set tantum in
Deum, quia ut dicit Sapiens: "Inicium sapiencie timor Domini." Unde Beda:
"Timentibus, inquit, Deum vilescit gloria presens, flos iuventutis concul-
30   catur, generositas non reputatur. Si ergo sapis (dicit ipse), si cor habes,
si est tecum lumen oculorum, desine ea sequi que sequi miserum est." Hec
ille. Set hodie magis timent honore privari quam a Deo separari. Simul⟨a⟩nt
enim mortem pati pro Christo; pro seculo cotidie gratis mortem paciuntur.
Unde plus timent [amittere] bovem aut asinum quam illorum largitorem; unde
35   Psalmista: "Non est timor Dei ante oculos eorum." Unde narratur in *Vitas
Patrum* quod frater quidam quendam senem interrogavit quomodo venit timor
Domini in homine. Qui respondit: "Si, inquit, habeat homo paupertatem,
humilitatem, et non iudicet alterum, sic veniet in eo timor Domini." Hec
ille.
40   [Et] nota quod tantum iam moderni timent bona amittere quod propter
illum timorem veritas et iusticia conculcatur, in tantum quod non [f. 86]
audent facere veritatem aut iusticiam, verum eciam nec dicere. Unde iam est
sicut erat antiquitus apud Egipcios. Narrat enim Augustinus *De civitate
Dei*, libro 8, capitulo 5, quod olim Egipcii volentes deificare Ysidem et
45   Serapem hoc modo fecerunt. Statuerunt enim primo quod quicumque diceret eos
esse homines vel aliquid de eorum geneologia narraret, capite plecteretur.
Secundo, ut lex predicta nullum lateret, in omni templo in quo eorum ymagines ponebantur, semper iuxta eos stabat unum parvum ydolum habens digitum
labiis applicatum, ut per hoc faceret signum silencii omnibus illa templa
50   ingredientibus, per quod ab omnibus veritas taceretur. Revera modo consimili accidit inter modernos maiores. Quando enim iustificare et quasi deificare seipsos [volunt], ponunt quoddam ydolum coram ocul⟨i⟩s mundanorum ad
faciendum illis signum silencii, ut scilicet nullus audeat eorum voluntati
contradicere set quod dissimulentur eorum errores, per quod veritas tacea-
55   tur. Et si queras quod est istud ydolum, revera timor mundanus est quo
timent, si loquerentur veritatem, perdere bona temporalia. Et ideo iuxta
Psalmistam: "Non est in ore eorum veritas."
    Contra quos narrat Iulius Sextus libro 3, capitulo 1, quod Clearcus dux
Lacedomonium ducens semel excercitum perpendit quod ultra quam decebat
60   cepit excercitus ille adversarios timere. Unde convocatis omnibus dixit ad
eos: "Considerate, inquit, karissimi, quod plus est timendus imperator quam
hostis. Nam si hostes aggredimini, mors est vobis dubia; set si imperatorem
offenditis, mors est vobis certa." Spiritualiter imperator noster Christus

his days joyfully and, I guess, got what he had prayed for. We find a type of this, that is, of the fruit which a miser derives from gathering riches, in Achan of Joshua 7, who craved for gold and then hid it, for which he was later stoned to death. And therefore Augustine says: "Those who gasp for worldly goods scorn heavenly ones, and in the end they will not have either."

Therefore we should not have fear of losing temporal goods, but only of God, for as the wise man says, "the beginning of wisdom is the fear of the Lord." Whence Bede says: "To those who fear God, the glory of this life is worthless, the flower of youth is trodden down, nobility loses its esteem. Therefore, if you are wise, if you have a heart, if there is light in your eyes, stop following the things which it is misery to follow." But nowadays people are more afraid of losing their honor than of becoming separated from God. They do not want to suffer death for Christ, but they willingly suffer death for the world every day. They fear to lose an ox or an ass more than him who has given them those. Whence the Psalmist says: "There is no fear of God before their eyes." In the *Lives of the Fathers* it is reported that a brother asked a hermit how the fear of God comes into man. He answered: "If a man has poverty and humility and does not judge his fellow man, then the fear of the Lord will come to him."

Notice also that nowadays people are so afraid of losing their goods that on account of that fear truth and justice are trampled upon, to the point that they fail not only to do what is true and just, but even to say it. Therefore it is now with us as it formerly was with the Egyptians. Augustine in his *City of God*, book 8, chapter 5, tells us that in ancient times, when the Egyptians wanted to make Isis and Serapis into gods, they did as follows. First, they decreed that whoever stated that they had been human or told anything about their lineage would be beheaded. Second, in order for this law not to remain unknown to anyone, in every temple where their images were put there also stood next to them a small idol which held its finger to its lips, so as to give a sign of silence to all who entered these temples; and thus the truth was withheld from all. Something similar happens among the more powerful citizens today. For when they want to justify themselves and make themselves into gods, they place an idol before the eyes of worldlings to give them a signal of silence, that is, that none of them may dare to contradict their will but rather that their failings should be covered up; and by this the truth is hidden. If you want to know what this idol is: it is worldly fear, which makes them afraid that, if they were to speak the truth, they would lose their temporal goods. Therefore, after the Psalmist, "there is no truth in their mouth."

Against them Sextus Julius tells a story in book 3, chapter 1. Clearchus, the leader of the Lacedaemonians, as he once was leading his army, noticed that the army had begun to fear their enemies more than was reasonable. He called them all together and said to them: "My friends, keep in mind that you should

est, set humani generis hostis est mundus vanus et lubricus, qui quamvis
65 [pulchre] promittit, tamen vilissime decipit et in fine confundit, sicut
carnifex porco ostendit grana usque perduxerit ad macellum. Ibi cum [f.
86v] pervenerit et coram illo illa effuderit, quando in illa commedendo
magis delectatur, ab illo occiditur. Sic mundus ostendens avaro temporalia
tamquam delectabilia, et quando magis in illis delectatur, ab eo auferuntur
70 et sic morte decipitur ut patet. Unde quamvis iste mundus promittat in hac
vita corporis sanitatem, vite diuturnitatem, fortune prosperitatem, et
penitencie oportunitatem, invenies tamen ipsum falsum et decipientem. Expe-
rimento autem videmus tota die quod sanitas corporalis vertitur in infirmitatem, vite diuturnitas in temporis brevitatem, fortune prosperitas in
75 adversitatem, penitendi oportunitas in inpenitencie malignitatem. Unde de
sua falsitate ait Augustinus in sermone *De miserrima vita* dicens: "O,
inquit, vita presens non est hec via vera quam nobis ostendis, quia aliis
te ostendis longam ut perdas; aliis brevem ut dum penitere vellent de
peccatis non permittas; aliis latam ut faciant quod voluer⟨i⟩nt; aliis
80 angustam ut non possint benefacere." Hec ille.
S⟨atis⟩ ergo patet quod mundus et eius avaricia capitalis inimicus est
homini. Non est ergo ille timendus sicut imperator Christus. Et ideo iuxta
concilium Luce 13 "ne terreamini ab hiis," scilicet mundialibus, "set hunc
timete qui habet potestatem tam corpus quam animam mittere in gehennam,"
85 scilicet Christum Filium Dei.

---

3 violentem] violentum O.   **4** de] *add* quodam O.   **9** oracionem] oraciones O.
11 adimplevero] implevero O.   sanitate] sanctitate M.R.   **18** silenter] scilenter C.
21 spero] prospere M; ut spero R.   **32** Simulant] simulent C.M; silent W.   **34** amittere]
om C.M.W *and others*.   **41–42** non . . . dicere] *evidently a scribal emendation of a cor-*
ruption of non solum facere veritatem aut iusticiam omittunt verum eciam dicere. *The*
main verb must have been lost early in the tradition and is supplied by omittunt, timent,
metuunt, *or* formidant *(sometimes at the end of the sentence).*   **50** ab] *om* O.   **52** volunt]
om C.R.   oculis] oculos C; *add* aliorum O.   **66** Ibi] ubi O.   **70** sic] *om* O.   **75** malig-
nitatem] *add* etc O.   **76** miserrima] misera M.R; miseria W.   **79** voluerint] voluerunt
C.   **81** Satis] similiter C.

IV.iv   DOLOR IN AMITTENDO TEMPORALIA

Tercia proprietas avaricie est dolor temporalia amittendo. Unde Ieronimus: "Si, inquit, avarus pecuniam amiserit, in vehementissimo labitur
dolore. Si fures scilicet rapiant aut ignis ardeat, contristatus et dolens
dicit se raptum et combustum esse. Non enim dicit 'sua,' set 'se,' acsi
5 diceret, 'plus diligo mea quam me.' " Unde tales increpat beatus Bernardus
dicens: "Cur pecuniam tuam preciosiorem facis quam [f. 87] teipsum, cuius

fear your emperor more than your enemy. For when you attack the enemy, you may perhaps die; but if you offend your emperor, you will certainly die." Spiritually speaking, our emperor is Christ, but the enemy of mankind is this changeable and slippery world: although it makes beautiful promises, it deceives us in the most shameless way and ruins us in the end, just as the butcher offers a pig corn until he has led it to the market. When he gets there, he spreads the corn in front of it, and when the pig eats it with the greatest delight, it gets killed. In the same way, the world holds before an avaricious person its temporal goods that seem so delightful, and when he takes the greatest pleasure in them, the goods are taken from him and he is deceitfully killed. Therefore, even though the world may promise during this life health of the body, length of life, good fortune, and an opportunity to do penance, you will yet find it to be false and deceitful. By experience we see every day that bodily health turns into sickness, a long life into a short while, good fortune into bad, the opportunity to do penance into evil impenitence, and so forth. Therefore, in his sermon on this wretched life Augustine speaks of the world's falsehood as follows: "O present life, this is not the true way you show us, because for some you are long only to ruin them; for others short, so that when they want to repent of their sins, you do not let them; for some you are wide, so that they may do what they want; and for others you are narrow, so that they cannot do good."

Thus it is manifest that the world with its avarice is a major enemy to man. Therefore it must not be feared as much as our emperor, Christ. And according to the counsel given in Luke 13, "be not afraid of them," that is, of worldly people, "but fear him who has the power to cast both body and soul into hell," that is, Christ, the Son of God.

4–21 Tubach 3879 (unique); also in Bromyard, "Avaricia," A.XXVII.13.   23–24 Josh. 7.   28 Ecclus. 1.16.   35 Ps. 13.3.   43–50 Augustine, *De civ. Dei* XVIII.5 (CC 48:597).   57 Ps. 5.10.   58–63 Frontinus, *Stratagemata* IV.i.17.   76–80 Ps.-Augustine, *Ad fratres in eremo* 49 (PL 40:1332).   83–84 Luke 12.4.

IV.iv   PAIN IN LOSS

The third quality of avarice is the pain that comes from losing temporal goods. Jerome says: "When an avaricious person has lost his possessions, he suffers the most vehement pain. For when thieves rob or fire burns his property, he says with great sadness and grief, 'I have been robbed and burnt.' He does not say, 'my goods' but 'I,' as if he were saying, 'I love my goods more than myself.' " Therefore Blessed Bernard reproaches such people and says:

estimacio taxari non potest? Christus enim semel pro peccatis nostris
mortuus est, iustus pro iniustis, et tu preciosiorem facis animalium
congregacionem quam Christi redempcionem?" Hec ille. Et mirum est quod
10   homines tantum de amissione temporalium [tristantur] cum non sit nisi
quedam umbra aut fumus, prout ait beatus Augustinus in quodam sermone
dicens: "O, inquit, vita presens mundialis, que tantos decepisti et execca-
sti! Cum enim fugis, nichil es. Cum videris, umbra es. Cum exaltaris,
fumus es. Stultis quam dulcis, quam amara sapientibus. Qui, inquit, te
15   diligunt te non cognoscunt. Ipsi te contempnunt qui te intelligunt. Fuge
ergo (dicit Augustinus), sapiens, et curre, sapiens, quia sic erit vita tua
quasi aliena." Hec ille.

Unde fertur poetice quod antiquitus mundus sic depingebatur, scilicet
in specie muliebri sedens cum tribus capitibus coronatis et inscriptis. Nam
20   in fronte primi capitis scribebatur hoc verbum: "Promisi." Set in eius
corona sic: "Celum fecit fabulam." In fronte secundi capitis scribebatur
hoc verbum: "Derisi," set in eius corona: "Mare fecit statuam." In fronte
vero tercii capitis scriptum erat hoc verbum: "Dimisi," set in eius corona
sic: "Terra legit literam." Spiritualiter autem loquendo, ista mulier mundi
25   falsitatem significat, cuius tres facies sunt tres condiciones mundi felicitatis, que sunt hee: prosperitas, sagacitas, et falsitas. In facie ergo
prosperitatis scribebatur "Promisi." Set hec promissio fallit, quia, ut
dicit Seneca ad Lucillum, mundus non est nisi quasi unus saltus de loco ad
locum. Videmus enim quod saltans, ut lucretur plus de spacio quam socius, a
30   longe capit cursum, et in tantum nititur a longe saltare quod frequenter
excedit vires, unde necessario [f. 87v] a tergo cadit. Revera sic cupidi et
avari metas aliorum in tantum nituntur saltando et terrena adquirendo
excedere quod antequam compleverant intentum, per mortem subtrahuntur et
cadunt. Et ideo bene in eius corona scribebatur, "Celum fecit fabulam,"
35   quasi diceret: tota hec mundi f⟨elic⟩itas, in qua tantum confidis et quam
[tantum] perquirere peroptas, respectu beatitudinum celi non est nisi sicut
fabula vana respectu evangelii, quia secundum beatum Gregorium in communi
omelia unius martiris, si consideremus que et quanta sunt que nobis promittuntur in celis, vilescunt animo omnia que habentur in terris. Nam in
40   celestibus non est fabula vel fallacia, set certe terrena sicut umbra
pretereunt et sicut ioculator omni die fallunt et decipiunt.

Unde fertur de quodam ioculatore Ulfridus nomine qui multum anxie
penuriam et paupertatem ducebat. Cupiebat enim divicias ultra modum. Volens
ergo [diabolus] illum deludere, transfigurabat se in formam et personam do-
45   mine Fortune. Que sedens in quadriga cum maximo apparatu obvi⟨u⟩m habuit
dictum ioculatorem super divicias habendas multum cogitantem. Qui cum ab
ea requisitus fuit quid cogitaret et ipse veritatem dissimularet, dixit
illa: "Scio, karissime, scio quod de diviciis habendis nimis cogitas, eo

"Why do you hold your possessions more precious than yourself, whose value cannot be estimated? For Christ once died for our sins, the just one for the unjust, and you place a greater value on gathering animals than on Christ's redemption?" It is strange that people are so saddened by losing their temporal goods, which are nothing but a shadow or smoke, as Augustine says in one of his sermons: "O life in this world, you have deceived and blinded so many. When you pass, you are nothing. When you are looked at, you are a shadow. When you are exalted, you are smoke. So sweet to fools, so bitter to the wise. They who love you do not know you, and they who know you scorn you. Flee, then, and run, you who are wise, for thus your life will become a stranger."

The poets tell us that in old times the world was depicted in the form of a woman, sitting, with three crowned heads that bore inscriptions. On the first forehead was written, "I have promised," but on its crown, "Heaven has made a fable." On the second forehead was written, "I have laughed at," but on its crown, "The sea has made a statue." And on the third forehead was written, "I have abandoned," but on its crown, "The earth has read out a letter." Spiritually interpreted, this woman stands for the falsehood of the world, whose three faces are the three conditions of worldly happiness, namely: prosperity, shrewdness, and falsehood. On the face of prosperity, then, was written "I have promised." But this promise is false, for as Seneca says to Lucillus, this world is nothing but a jump from one place to another. When a person jumps, we see that in order to go farther than his companion he takes a long run before leaping, and he tries so hard to make a long jump that he often goes beyond his strength and necessarily falls on his back. In the same way, covetous and avaricious people try so hard to go beyond the marks of others in jumping and acquiring earthly goods that before they have reached their goal they are carried off by death and fall down. Therefore, it is quite rightly written on the crown of this first face, "Heaven has made a fable," meaning that all the happiness of this world, in which you trust so much and which you want to obtain so badly, is nothing more in comparison with the bliss of heaven than what an empty fiction is in comparison with the Gospel. For as Gregory says, in his common homily for a martyr, if we reflect on what and how great things are promised us in heaven, everything on earth becomes contemptible to our mind. For in the things of heaven there is no fable or lie; but the things of this earth certainly pass as a shadow, and like a juggler they trick and deceive us every day.

There is a story about a juggler named Ulfrid, who lived with great worry in need and poverty. He craved beyond measure to be rich. So, as the devil wanted to trick him, he transformed himself into the form and person of Lady Fortune. Sitting highly decorated in a chariot, she came to meet this juggler as he was deeply in thought about how he could get rich. She asked him what he was thinking about, but he tried to hide the truth. So she said: "I know, my

quod tantum penuria afficeris." Misericordia quasi mota anulum de manu
50 abstraxit et sibi tradidit dicens: "Obvium, inquit, habebis regem Attridem,
cui istum anulum trades pro signo et dices ei quod ex parte regine et
domine Fortune te ditet." Ille vero gracias agens processit in via et cito
post dicto regi obviabat. Quem cum flexis genibus adorasset, porrexit
anulum et fecit nuncium. Quem cum accepisset rex, mox peticioni regine ad-
55 [f. 88] quievit. Tradidit ergo sibi clamidem quandam sub tali condicione,
quod de clamide illa aut aliis diviciis sibi evenientibus nequaquam gloria-
retur. Quod si fecerit, mox ad pristinam paupertatem deveniret. Recepta
ergo clamide et cum reverencia et graciis regi Attride valedicto, rediit
domum indilate. Ubi divicias continuo habundanter invenit. Cogitans ergo
60 quadam die apud se quomodo in multis festis et conviviis fuisset, in quibus
multa beneficia ab amicis accepisset, voluit quasi modo aliqualis recompen-
sacionis et ipse convivium facere cum magnatibus et amicis. Quibus invita-
tis et de convivii statu omnibus ordinatis, ut seipsum decenter ornaret erga
adventum ipsorum cameram privatam sue domus ascendit et super honestam
65 robam dictam clamidem vestivit. Quo facto descendit in medio populi invita-
ti et ibi stetit. Cumque vidisset quod clames honestius se decebat, cepit
aliqualiter gloriari et in animo exaltari, et statim quasi in momento omnes
eius divicie cum clamide evanuerunt, ita quod oportuit invitatos ad propria
incenatos redire. Revera ad literam sic est. Domina enim Fortuna, que est
70 quasi mundi regina, omnes cupidos et avaros ad regem Attridem, idest
Christum, pro promocione transmittit mittens anulum, idest concupiscenciam
sine labore tum certo pro signo. Quod cum receperit, dat eis clamidem,
idest divicias, quibus quasi cum clamide cooperiuntur, dicens eis illud
Psalmi: "Divicie si affluant, nolite cor apponere," scilicet nimis, nam
75 quanto magis crescunt, tanto magis in oblivionem Dei eius sequaces inducunt. Set certe habitis illis, scilicet diviciis, statim obliviscitur [f.
88v] Deus; Ieremias: "Saturavi vos," scilicet diviciis, "et obliti estis
me." Quid ergo faciat Christus? Revera, quando magis de mundi clamide
gloriantur, omnia in momento aufert ab illis et nudos, sicut prius invenit,
80 illos derelinquit, sicut de Ulfrido actum est, de quo sic metrice dicitur
versus:

Ulfridus clamidem quam susceperat per Attridem
Servavit pridem, casus dedit, abstulit idem.

[þat mantel þe kyng to Vlfride lente,
85   With hap hit come, with hap hit wente.

Unde de illa domina Fortuna est antiquum proverbium sic canens:

dear, I know: you are in deep thought about how to get rich, because you suffer such great poverty." As if moved by pity she took a ring from her hand and gave it to him with these words: "You will meet King Attrides; give him this ring as a token and tell him that he should make you rich on behalf of Queen and Lady Fortune." The juggler thanked her and continued on his way, and shortly thereafter he met the king she had mentioned. After he had worshipped him on bent knees, he gave him the ring and the message. The king accepted the ring and granted the queen's petition. He gave the juggler a cloak with the condition that he must never be proud about that cloak or any other riches that might come to him; if he did that, he would at once return to his earlier poverty. The juggler took the cloak, worshipped and thanked the king, bade him farewell, and without delay went home. There he found at once an abundance of wealth. Now, one day he thought by himself how he had been at many feasts and banquets where he had received many good things from his friends; and he decided in return to give the noblemen and his friends a banquet. When they had been invited and all the preparations for the banquet had been made, he went up to a private chamber of his house in order to dress up properly for the party and put the cloak on top of his good clothes. After that he came down and stood in the midst of the invited crowd. When he saw how well that cloak suited him, he began to be somewhat proud and exult in his soul—and at once, in the twinkling of an eye, all his riches and the cloak were gone, and his guests had to go home without dinner. This story may be interpreted as follows. Lady Fortune, who is so to speak the queen of the whole world, sends all covetous and avaricious people to King Attrides, that is, Christ, for advancement, and she sends him a ring as a sure token, that is, concupiscence without hardship. When the king receives this, he gives them a cloak, that is, riches with which they are covered as with a cloak, and tells them the words of the Psalm: "If riches abound, set not your heart upon them," that is, not too much, for the more these riches grow, the more they cause those who pursue them to forget God. Yet indeed, once these riches are obtained, God is soon forgotten; Jeremiah: "I have filled you," that is, with riches, "and you have forgotten me." What, then, would Christ do? When those covetous people take great pride in the cloak of the world, he takes everything away from them in a moment and leaves them naked as he had found them before. Thus it happened to Ulfrid, of whom the following poem is said:

> Once Ulfrid had a cloak, received from King Attrides.
> It came to him by chance, by chance it went again.
>
> þat mantel þe kyng . . .

Whence there is an old proverb about Lady Fortune, which goes thus:

The lade dame Fortune is bothe frende and foo.
Of pore hoe maketh riche and ryche of pore also.
Hee turneth woo to wele and wele also to woo.
90   Ne trust noght to his word, þe whele turneth so.]

Non ideo est dolendum de amissione temporalium fortuitorum que modo
sunt modo non sunt, modo habundant modo deficiunt, prout ascendendo et
descendendo in rota illa a domina Fortuna [revoluta] de diversis depingitur. Quorum primus suppremus ait:

95   Rex presens regno, possum fore cras sine regno.

Secundus:

Heu michi, regnavi, quid prodest illud quod amavi?

Tercius:

Nuper dives ego. Vix mea membra tego.

100   Quartus:

Sum regnaturus cum sim miser moriturus.

[Pro illis quatuor signis domine Fortune dicitur sic primus Anglice:

Kynge I syt and loke aboute,
To-morn I may ben with-oute.

105   Secundus:

Wo is me, a kynge I was.
þis worlde I louede, but þat I las.

Tercius:

Nouȝth longe gon I was ful ryche,
110   But now is ryche and pore ylyche.

Quartus:

I shal be kynge, þat men schull se.
When þe wreche ded shal be.]

The lady dame Fortune is our friend and foe,
Poor people she makes rich, and rich men poor just so.
She turns woe into well, and well back into woe.
Trust not unto her word, her wheel turns ever so.

Therefore we must not grieve about the loss of temporal goods of fortune,
which now are here, now are gone, now abound, now fail, just as various people
are depicted as rising and falling on that wheel turned by Lady Fortune. The
first of them, sitting on top, says:

As king I rule; perhaps I lose my realm tomorrow.

The second:

Alas, I was a king. What use is what I loved?

The third:

Shortly ago I was rich; now hardly I cover my limbs.

And the fourth:

I shall be king when you, o wretch, will go to death.

For these four situations of Lady Fortune we can say in English as follows.
The first:

Kyng I syt . . .

The second:

Wo is me . . .

The third:

Nou3th longe gon . . .

And the fourth:

I shal be kyng . . .

Now, on the second forehead of the image of the world and its happiness
was written, "I have laughed at," as if the world were saying, "Whatever I

In secundo enim fronte ymaginis mundi et eius f⟨elic⟩itatis scribe-
115　batur "Derisi," quasi diceret mundus: "Quicquid tibi, o avare, promisi,
aperte decepi, ut est dictum. Et ideo quia in me nimium confidebas, te
derideo. Unde de te propter facta tua scriptura corone mee iam verificatur,
scilicet 'Mare fecit statuam.' " Per istud enim mare, quod est ⟨s⟩alsum et
amarum, intelligo peccati amaritudinem, quam, si bene consideramus hanc
120　scripturam, satis veracem inveniemus, eo quod post peccata non plus iuvat
mundus set dimittit peccatores quasi statuas mortuas et suffocatas, eo quod
mors homines male vite quasi statuam mortuam insequitur. Et ideo dicit
Salvator: "Dimitte mortuos sepelire mortuos suos." Ista ergo mors de iure
ad contemptum mundialium hominem excitaret, quia iuxta beatum Ieronimum
125　facile omnia contempnit [f. 89] qui se cogitat moriturum.

　　De quo habemus exemplum in natura de quodam serpente nomine pandera,
qui cum hominis pedem percusserit, mox eius venenum ad cetera membra
ascendit. Set contra illud efficax remedium invenitur, si homo per pedes
cicius suspendatur, propter quod ascensus veneni facilius impeditur. Revera
130　sic amor temporalium pedem affectionis in homine percutit quod statim ad
omnia membra corporis, ut avaricie serviant, se diffundit. Set huiusmodi
amor prohibetur quando homo cogitat quomodo premiis sibi suspenditur et
sic quasi per pedes intime cogitacionis suspenditur a temporalibus atque
reprimitur et ea facilius contempnit.

135　　Et ideo mortis memoria avaris frequenter nunciari deberet. Unde legitur
in *Historia [Bragmanorum]* quod Didimus didascalus Alexandro magno sibi
dicenti, "Doce me aliquid sapiencie plenum," respondit: "Si, inquit, vellem
a deo sensum acceptum tibi offerre, non habes unde tale munus reciperes.
Impleverunt animam tuam avide et inmoderate cupiditates. Quomodo ergo pos-
140　sem desiderio tuo satisfacere, quem totus mundus tibi serviens non potuit
adimplere? Et tamen, si omnia possideas, tandem tamen necesse est ut solum
de terra tantum habeas quantum vides me iacentem occupare." Iacuit tunc
Didimus sub arbore quadam inter herbas.

　　Igitur hanc terre mensuram diligenter considerare deberent avari, qui
145　tam avide temporalibus adherent. In cuius figura legitur Genesis quod Abra-
he, cui Deus habundanciam temporalium concessit, precepit ut terre sue
longitudinem et latitudinem, orientem et occidentem consideraret. Sic divites considerare deberent quod illorum origo de terra est, et quod ad illorum occasum et mortem illuc rever- [f. 89v] tentur. Cuius terre longitudo
150　vix tunc erit septem pedum, latitudo vero duorum. Respice ergo, avare,
terram ad quam redire necesse est in giro, de qua venisti, iuxta illud
metricum:

　　　Vertitur in giro natura sct ordinc miro.
　　　Unde dat hoc esse, dat ad illud redire necesse.

promised you, avaricious man, was done in open deceit, as has been declared. And since you trusted in me so much, I laugh at you. Therefore the inscription on my crown will come true as applying to you for your deeds: 'The sea made a statue.' " By this sea, which is salty and bitter, I understand the bitterness of sin. We shall find this to be the case when we reflect well on this inscription, because after we have sinned, the world no longer helps us but abandons sinners as if they were dead and lifeless statues, because death follows men of evil life as a dead statue. Therefore our Savior says: "Let the dead bury their dead." Thus, this death should rightly rouse man to scorn worldly values, for according to blessed Jerome, he who considers that he will die easily scorns everything.

We find an example of this in nature, in a serpent called pandera. When it bites man in the foot, its poison soon rises to the other parts of his body. An effective remedy against this is to hang this man up quickly by his feet, whereby the rising of the poison is easily prevented. In the same way, the love of temporal goods strikes man's foot of affection and at once spreads to the other members of his body so that they become slaves to avarice. But such love is countered when one reflects on how one loses one's reward; then a person is, as it were, suspended by the feet of his inner meditation and restrained from worldly goods and thus scorns them more readily.

Therefore, avaricious people should be frequently reminded to meditate on death. We read in *The History of the Brahmins* that, when Alexander the Great asked Didimus the teacher, "Teach me something that is full of wisdom," he replied as follows: "If I wanted to offer you some thought I had received from God, you do not have wherein to receive such a gift. For your soul is filled with greedy and immoderate desires. How, then, could I satisfy your desire, whom the whole world that serves you could not fill? And yet, if you possess all things, in the end you need to have only so much of the earth as you see me covering where I lie." Didimus was then lying in the grass under a tree.

This piece of earth all greedy persons should earnestly think about, those who cling so avidly to temporal goods. We find an allegory for this in Genesis when, after giving Abraham an abundance of temporal goods, God commanded him to look at the length and breadth, the east and the west, of his land. Thus, rich people should reflect that their origin is from the earth and that in their death they will return to it. This piece of earth will then hardly be seven feet long and two feet wide. Behold then, O avaricious man, the earth from which you came and to which which you must return in a circle, according to this verse:

Round in a circle turns nature, and that in marvelous fashion.
From where it gives us being, there it makes us return.

155 [Anglice:

> All monkyn tornth in well,
> And þat on wonder gyse.
> For wethen hit come, aȝeyn hit wente,
> To dwelle on all wyse.]

160   In tercio enim fronte mundi f⟨elic⟩itatis scribebatur, "Dimisi," et
bene, acsi diceret avaro: "Quando plus confidis in me, tunc dimitto te
nudum ut inveni." Unde bene in eius corona scribitur sic: "Terra legit
literam," quasi diceret: "Vade, tu avare, ad sepulcrum patrum tuorum, ubi
invenies satis bene quod terra literam legit, scilicet quod ad illam tu
165   redibis sicut patres tui." Unde cum istis bene concordat historia de trono
Salomonis, Regum, qui signat felicitatem mundi, qui habuit sex gradus, per
quos intelligo sex predictas scripturas.

---

8 animalium] temporalium M.R; alium W.   **10** tristantur] M *marg*; *om* C; curant R;
dolent W *marg after* temporalium.   **23** scriptum erat] scribebatur O.   **33** compleverant]
compleverint O.   **35** felicitas] falsitas C.   **36** tantum] *om* C.W.   **37** fabula] fallacia
R.W.   **43** ultra] supra O.   **44** deludere] illudere O.   **45** obvium] obviam C.   **47** fuit]
fuisset O.   dissimularet] dissimulasset O.   **51** istum] illum O.   **52** Fortune] *add* quod
O.   **54** rex] *om* O.   **57** fecerit] faceret O.   **66** et ibi stetit] et stetit *after* descendit O.
clames] clamis M.R; clavus R.   **70** quasi] *add* tocius O.   **72** tum] cum O.   Quod] quos
O.   **78** faciat] facit O.   **80** de] *add* isto M.W; *add* illo R.   **84–85** þat . . . wente] *text
from* R. *Verse 36, in* B1.B3.E.Go1.Jo.L2.LC.R.Sp.V.W1.   **87–90** The . . . so] *text
from* R. *Verse 37, in* B1.B3.D.E.Go1.Go2.Jo.L2.LC.R.Sp.V.W1.etc.   **91** ideo] ergo *after* est O.   **93** revoluta] *om* C.W.   **102–113** Pro . . . be] *text from* R, *where it occurs after* mortuos (*line 123*); *in some manuscripts each English couplet appears immediately
after its Latin source. Verse 38, in* B1.B3.E.Go1.Go2.Jo. L2.LC.R.Sp.V.W1.etc.
114 felicitatis] falsitatis C.   **118** salsum] falsum C.   **127** hominis pedem] hominem pede
O.   **132** prohibetur] *om* O.   sibi] *om* O.   **133** atque] *om* O.   **144** avari] *om* O.
146 precepit] *om* O.   **150** ergo] *add* o O.   **154** hoc] hec O.   **155–159** Anglice . . .
wyse] *text from* R. *Verse 39, in* B1.B3.E.L2. LC.R.W1.   **160** felicitatis] falsitatis C.
161 dimitto] *add* et M.R; *add* te et W.   **162** inveni] *add* derelinquo O.   **166** felicitatem]
falsitatem R.

IV.v   DE MEMBRIS AVARICIE: RAPINA

    [C]irca autem membra avaricie et cupiditatis que miserum hominem
errare faci[un]t a via veritatis et iusticie et ducunt ad viam iniquitatis
et miserie, est iam tercio advertendum quod specialiter sex sunt, scilicet
rapina, dolus, prodicio, usura, symonia, sacrilegium.
5   Circa autem rapinam est primo dicendum quod raptor est ille qui vi
simplices spoliat et bona eorum rapit acsi essent illius propria pred⟨a⟩;

In English:

> All monkyn tornth . . .

Finally, on the third forehead of the world and its happiness was fittingly written, "I have abandoned," as if the world were saying to the avaricious man: "When you trust in me most, I abandon you naked as I found you." Hence the fitting inscription on its crown: "The earth has read out a letter," as if it were saying: "Go, avaricious man, to the tomb of your fathers, where you will find that earth reads you a letter, namely that you will return to it as your forefathers did." With all this the story of Salomon's throne agrees well, which is told in the book of Kings and signifies the happiness of the world: it had six steps, by which I understand the six inscriptions I have mentioned.

6–9 Cf. Guerric d'Igny, *De resurrectione Domini*, sermo 2, 3 (PL 185:146).   **7–8** Cf. 1 Pet 3.18.   **12–17** Ps.-Augustine, *Ad fratres in eremo* 49 (PL 40:1332).   **38–39** Cf. Gregory, *In Evangelia*, hom. 37, 1 (PL 76:1275).   **42–69** The story also appears in Bromyard, "Avaricia," A.XXVII.61 (shortened) and Worcester Cathedral MS F.10, fol. 322v; see *Verses*, p. 173.   **74** Ps. 61.11.   **77–78** Cf. Bar. 4.8.   **82–83** No separate occurrence known.   **95–101** *In* 7251; *Prov* 10344.   **123** Matt. 8.22.   **125** Jerome, *Ep. 53* XI.3 (CSEL 54:465).   **136–143** Cf. Leo the Archpriest, *Historia de preliis*, p. 107. **145–147** Cf. Gen. 13.14–18.   **153–154** See *Verses*, p. 178.   **166–167** 1 Kings 10.18ff.

IV.v   THE MEMBERS OF AVARICE: THEFT

Now, in the third place, we turn to the members of avarice and covetousness, which cause wretched man to err from the way of truth and justice and lead him on the way of iniquity and misery. They are six in particular: theft, cheating, treachery, usury, simony, and sacrilege.

About theft we must first say that a thief is a person who despoils simple people by force and takes their goods as if they were his proper prey; Ecclesi-

Ecclesiastici 13: "Venacio leonis onager in heremo, sic pascua sunt divitum
pauperes." Et ideo tales sunt similes lupis rapacibus qui comedunt·argillam
ut ponderibus suis prosternant predam. Similiter pedem proprium mordet ut
10 sic magis iratus ad predam excitetur. Revera sic ° offensa divitum est
grave pondus pauperi, quia in eius spoliacionem et tormentum redundat;
Ezechielis 21: "Principes eius in medio eius quasi lupi rapientes predam."
Item sunt similes [f. 90] avibus rapacibus vilibus et degenerantibus. Magna
quippe ignobilitas est in ave generosa, que deberet aves silvestros ca-
15 pere, si alias domesticas venatur et illas dimittit. Revera sic potentes
qui [gladio] accinguntur ut tantum hereticos et infideles debellan⟨t⟩, si
domesticos pauperes spoliant et confundant. Set certe, sicut vulpes furtive
in lardario et superflue carnibus repletus non valens pre nimia ventris
replecione per foramen exire per quod intravit, aut necessario evomere
20 compellitur quod comedit aut a canibus capi, dilacerari, et occidi; revera
sic divites bona pauperum iniuste sicut latrones invadentes, aut eis oportet ⟨a⟩blata restituere aut a demonibus capi et occidi. Unde in *Prover-*
bi⟨is⟩ philosophorum narratur quod quidam sapiens filio suo dixit: "Ne te
decipiant divicie seculares, ⟨ut⟩ ⟨irretitus⟩ fallaciis secularibus peri-
25 culi et future mortis obliviscaris et tibi contingat sicut latroni domum
divitis latenter intranti. Qui cum illam plenam diviciis [invenerit],
stupefactus de diversis diversa, de preciosis preciosiora ad furandum
eligere curat et minus preciosa relinquere. Unde in eligendo tempus transit
et dies veniens quod facere vellet detegit. Excitati ergo homines furem
30 capiunt, ligant, incarcerant, et suspendunt." Revera sic avari curiosi sunt
circa terrena et solliciti, nunc congregando, nunc preciosiora depredata
thesaurizando, quousque mortis dies superveniens a demonibus capitur,
ligatur, et in inferno incarceratur; Thimothei 6: "Qui, inquit, volunt
divites fieri," scilicet ex rapinis, "incidunt in temptacionem et in laque-
35 um diaboli."
     Unde narratur de quodam tali in episcopatu Norwici qui fuit [f. 90v]
ballivus domini regis, qui ex consuetudine pauperes et simplices vexabat.
Habuit tamen uxorem bonam et sanctam ab omnibus dilectam. Tandem ambobus
mortuis, eorum filius et heres de statu eorum certum scire cupiens, ieiuni-
40 is et oracionibus intentus pro huiusmodi Deum exorabat. Quadam autem nocte
in spiritu raptus ductus est per angelum ad locum amenissimum, ubi matrem
in maximo gaudio iocundantem aspexit, dicens quod salvata esset et suppli-
cans quod similiter statum patris aspiceret. Et circumductus ad locum
t⟨eterrim⟩um vidit patrem suum in penis horribilibus vexatum. Quem cum de
45 statu suo fuisset allocutus, respondit pater: "Fili, inquit, Deus dereliquit me eo quod suos pauperes spoliavi et miseros reliqui, et hostis anti-
qus in hoc loco tenebrarum me suscepit, ubi semper cum bestiis diabolicis
et amentibus crucior, quia pauperum bestias iniuriose tractavi." Quod

asticus 13: "The wild ass is the lion's prey in the desert; so are the poor
devoured by the rich." Such men are like raging wolves who eat some loam so
that they can overthrow their prey with their weight. A wolf likewise bites
its own foot so that it may be roused to greater fierceness against his prey.
In the same way, the wrath of rich people is a heavy burden on the poor man,
for it results in his spoiling and torment; Ezekiel 21: "Her princes in her
midst are like wolves ravishing the prey." They are further like vile and
degenerate birds of prey. It is indeed a great vileness in a noble bird, who
should catch birds of the forest, if he chases after domestic fowl and leaves
the others in peace. Thus it is with powerful men who are girt with the sword
in order to fight heretics and pagans, if instead they spoil and ruin the poor
in their own country. But a fox who has secretly entered the larder and eaten
more than his fill so that in his fullness he cannot get out through the hole
by which he entered must either throw up what he has eaten or else be caught by
the dogs and torn to pieces and killed. In the same way, when the rich unjustly possess themselves of the goods of the poor, like thieves, they must
either restore what they have taken or else be caught by demons and killed.
Whence the *Proverbs of the Philosophers* tells of a wise man who said to his
son: "My son, beware that worldly riches do not deceive you, lest caught in
the net of worldly deceits you forget their danger and your future death and
you fare like the thief who secretly enters the house of a rich man. As he
finds it full of riches, he is dumbfounded and wants to choose and carry off
some of each and the most precious and leave the less precious behind. Thus he
wastes his time in choosing, and then the coming day reveals what he intended
to do. When the people are awake, they catch the thief, bind him, put him in
prison, and hang him." In the same way, avaricious people are full of care and
anxiety about earthly goods, now gathering, now hoarding the precious objects
they have stolen. But when the day of their death comes upon them, they are
caught by the demons, bound, and imprisoned in hell. Timothy 6: "They that
want to become rich," that is, through theft, "fall into temptation and into
the snare of the devil."

There is a story about such a person from the diocese of Norwich, who was
a reeve of our lord the king. He habitually tormented the poor and simple.
Yet he had a good and saintly wife who was beloved by all. When they both had
died, their son and heir wanted to know for sure in what state they were, and
he implored God for this favor with much fasting and prayer. One night, then,
he was carried off in the spirit and led by an angel to a most pleasant place,
where he saw his mother rejoicing in great happiness, saying she was saved and
praying that he would similarly see his father's way of life. Then he was led
about to a very dark place and saw his father tormented in horrible pains.
When he spoke to him about his state, his father answered: "My son, God has
abandoned me because I despoiled his poor and left them wretched, and the

audiens filius mundum reliquit et in paupertate et humilitate Domino servi-
50   ebat.
Ad idem narratur de tali bedello quod cum quadam die fugabat animalia
pauperum propter redditum domini sui ultra quoddam vadum, et ipse siccis
pedibus transire non poterat, puero suo dixit ut ipsum ultra aquam porta-
ret. Quem cum supra dorsum accepisset et usque ad profundam aquam portas-
55   set, dixit puer: "Magister, ultra modum ponderas, non possum amplius te
portare." [Cui ille:] "Nec mirum, inquit, quia innumerabiles portas maledictiones, et maxime virginum, viduarum, coniugatarum, religiosorum, et
ceterorum omnium." Quod audiens puer dixit se ad tot maledictiones perfe-
rendas inpotentem esse, et prostravit illum in aqua. Quo facto occurrit
60   quedam vacca nigra de grege [f. 91] quam tunc effugaverat et ipsum pedibus
conculcabat et cornibus viscera lacerabat. Et omnes alie bestie venientes
in minimis frustris ipsum dividebant, et facto horribili tonitruo demones
animam rapiebant.
Et nota quod inter omnes homines Anglici possunt Deo regraciari prop-
65   ter speciale privilegium quod habent. Dicitur enim quod in Hibernia et in
Wallia bene inveniuntur latrones qui vaccas, boves, et alia pecora vicino-
rum furantur, propter quod "latrones" aperte dicuntur. Set in Anglia—
laudetur Deus—non sic. Set quid? Revera, generos⟨i⟩ inter nos dicuntur
shaueldours et *ryfelours*. Tales enim frangunt thesauros mag⟨n⟩orum, as-
70   portant bona, abigant pecora, spoliant religiosos, nec inde conscienciam
habent, set summe gaudent quando abbatem, priorem, vel alium monachum
spoliare possunt, et dicunt: "Certe voluntas Dei fuit quod talis rusticus,
monachus, aut frater hodie nobis occurrit." Unde illis videtur quod quicquid fecerint, quod iuste faciunt et cum racione. Et ideo nichil faciunt
75   quin raciones satis apparentes per falsitatem quasi coloratas et depictas
pro se sciunt adducere.
Unde narratur de quodam tyranno talis condicionis nomine Dionisius
Siracusanus, de quo dicit Valerius Maximus ad Tiberium imperatorem quod
cum erat predo domesticus et sacrilegus pessimus, tamen quantumcumque
80   malum commiserit, semper factum suum scivit colorare et raciones apparentes pro se ostendere. Accidit ergo semel quod templum deorum intravit in
quo symulacra deorum colebantur, quia ita libenter templum quam alium
locum spoliavit. Quod cum introisset, invenit Iovem clamidem auream habentem, et statim ipsam de illo spoliavit et clamide lanea qua ipse utebatur
85   Iovem induit. Deinde ulterius procedens vidit Appolinem inber- [f. 91v] bem
sedentem et filium suum Eschulapium in eodem templo iuxta eum cum barba
aurea resedere. Quo viso statim barbam arripuit. Et ultra pertransiens
vidit alia symulacra manibus extensis coronas tenencia. Illas rapuit et
secum omnia asportavit. Cum ergo super hoc a templi custodibus argueretur,
90   respondit: "Non, inquit, miremini, quia ostendam racionem bonam pro omnibus

ancient fiend has taken me into this place of darkness, where I am continually punished by diabolical and mad beasts because I treated the beasts of the poor badly." When his son heard this, he left the world and served God in poverty and humility.

Another story is told about a reeve of the same kind who one day was driving animals of the poor that were his lord's revenue across a ford. When he himself could not get across on dry foot, he told his boy to carry him through the water. The boy took him on his back. As he was carrying him through the deepest spot in the water, he said: "Master, you are too heavy, I cannot carry you any further." And he replied: "No wonder, since you are carrying countless curses, and mostly from maidens, widows, married folk, religious, and all others." When the boy heard this, he said he was not strong enough to carry so many curses, and he let his master fall in the water. At that moment a black cow came up from the herd that he had been driving and trampled on him with her feet and tore his intestines with her horns. And then all the other animals came and tore him into small pieces, and with a terrible thunderclap demons carried off his soul.

Notice that among all people the English can be thankful to God for a special privilege they have. For it is said that in Ireland and in Wales one readily finds thieves that steal their neighbors' cows, oxen, and other cattle, for which they are openly called "thieves." But not so in England, God be praised. But what then? Among us, in fact, the noble are called *shaveldours* and *riflers*. They break into the treasures of the rich, carry off their goods, drive away their cattle, despoil the religious, and have no qualms of conscience about this but instead rejoice greatly when they can despoil an abbot, prior, or other monk, and they say: "Surely, it was God's will that we ran into this peasant or monk or friar today." Thus they imagine that whatever they do, they do with right and reason. And so they do nothing for which they cannot adduce what appear to be good reasons, whose falsehood, as it were, is colored and painted over.

There is a story about a tyrant of this sort named Dionysius of Syracuse, of whom Valerius Maximus reports to the emperor Tiberius that, as he was a thief in his own house and a sacrilegious person, whatever crime he committed, he always knew how to color his deed and to show apparent good reasons for it. It once happened that he entered a temple in which statues of the gods were worshipped—for he would rob a temple as gladly as any other place. As he entered, he found Jupiter with a golden cloak, which he at once took off and replaced with the wool cloak he himself was wearing. Going further he saw the beardless Apollo sitting there, and next to him, in the same temple, his son Aesculapius with a golden beard. When he saw the latter, he right away pulled off his beard. And going further, he saw other statues that were proffering golden crowns in their hands. Those he took away and carried them all with

que in hoc templo feci. Primo, inquit, Iovem non spoliavi set cum eo
clamidem commutavi. Scivi enim quod senex erat et debilis nature, et quod
aurum in hyeme frigidum est, in estate ponderosum, et pro neutro tempore
sibi valuit, set quod lanea ad utrumque tempus est apta, quia calida est
95   in hyeme et levis in estate. Quod autem postea a iuvene Esculapio barbam
dempsi, iuste feci, quia inconveniens et irracionabile michi videbatur et
est ut filius appareat barbatus et pater inberbis. Et quia pater eius
Apollo extitit inberbis, sibi similem [illum] feci propter verba aliorum.
Ulterius, quando tercio coronas de manibus symulacrorum accepi, bene feci,
100   quia quod michi sponte offerebatur gratanter recepi. Scitis enim (dicit
[ipse]) quod a diis dona petimus, et ideo stultum erat illa respuere que
eos videmus nobis gratanter offerre."
      Revera pro toto mundo sic est de istis potentibus raptoribus, qui
quantumcumque simplices spoliaverunt, semper tamen habent in promptu ali-
105   quam racionem et responsionem quasi veram apparentem. Nam ponamus primo
quod iuxta aliquem talem maneat aliqua vidua paupercula, que acram terre
loco clamidis habuerit sibi vicinam. Certe, velit nolit secum commutabit
pro alia terra minoris precii et valoris. Et tamen dicet quod multum pro ea
facit eo quod dat ei terram viciniorem et per consequens magis [f. 92]
110   conveniens pro se. Secundo, pono quod sit aliquis iuvenis mercator in
aliqua civitate extraneus et forte de pauperibus genitus, qui sit providus
et discretus, quem intelligo per barbam auream. Rogo quid eveniet? Revera,
ut communiter alii de antiqua stirpe illius civitatis statim incipient
[sibi] invidere dicendo: "Unde sibi tot divicias congregaret?" Et sic pro
115   posse ex pura invidia facient illum poni in aliquo officio per quod in
arriragio in brevi deveniet, per quod necessario bona sua perdet et pauper
deveniet. Et tamen dicunt quod hoc faciunt pro salute anime sue, ad deponendum suam superbiam in illo de novo inceptam et ostensam. Tercio, per
istas ymagines coronas tenentes intelligo religiosos, monachos, canonicos,
120   et huiusmodi possessionatos, quos tales tiranni vi et metu cogunt filios et
nepotes promovere, licet indigni fuerint, similiter dare eis inpensas ac
robas, quo⟨us⟩que ab illis fuerint promoti, et breviter totum lucrum
reputant quicquid ab eis quocumque modo poterunt extorquere. Unde si ab eis
queratur qua consciencia hoc faciunt, respondent quod licet eos recipere
125   que sponte sibi dantur. Et dicunt falsum, quia quicquid hoc modo recipiunt,
vi et metu extortum est.
      Exemplum: Si autem me suffocare temptares pro bonis meis et ego liben-
cius huiusmodi bona dimitterem et traderem tibi ut me sine maiori malo
liberum abire permitteres, numquid huiusmodi bona licite possideres? Certum
130   est quod non, quia esset rapina manifesta. Sic ergo patet quod huiusmodi
responsiones non valent quando excercetur potestas pro iusticia. [Unde
quidam dicit Anglice:

him. When he was reproached for this by the temple guards, he answered: "You must not be astonished, for I will give you a good reason for everything I have done in the temple. First, I did not rob Jupiter but merely exchanged cloaks with him. For I knew that he is old and weak, and that gold is cold in winter and heavy in summer and thus is of no help to him in either season, whereas wool is good for both seasons, for in winter it is warm and in summer light. That I next took off young Aesculapius's beard I did justly, for it seemed to me, and indeed it is, unfitting and unreasonable that the son should wear a beard and his father be beardless. And since Apollo, his father, is beardless, I made his son like him, according to the words of others. Finally, when in the third place I took the crowns from the hands of the statues, I did well, because I gratefully accepted what was freely offered to me. You know well enough that we ask the gods for gifts; and thus it would be foolish to reject what the gods offer us willingly."

This, for all the world, applies exactly to the powerful who are thieves, for however much they rob the poor, they always have an answer ready that is false but appears to be true. For let us assume, first, that next to such a person there lives a poor widow who, instead of the cloak, owns an acre of land next door. Surely, whether she likes it or not, she will have to exchange that for another piece of less price and value. And yet the powerful citizen claims that he is doing a lot for her by giving her land that is closer and therefore more convenient for her. Second, let us assume a young merchant lives in some city as a foreigner and was perhaps born of poor parents, who is provident and discreet, which I understand by the golden beard. What is going to happen, I ask you? Surely, as commonly happens, some people from old families in that city will at once begin to be envious of him and say: "How come he could gather so much wealth for himself?" And so, if it is in their power, out of sheer envy they will have him put in some job where he will soon fall in arrears, for which he will of necessity lose his goods and become poor. And yet they claim they are doing this for the salvation of his soul, to put down the pride that he felt or showed! And third, by those statues that were carrying crowns I understand religious, monks, canons, and other possessioners, whom those tyrants compel, by force and fear, to advance their sons and nephews, even if the latter are unworthy, and similarly to pay for their living expenses and clothes until they have gotten advancement; and they consider gain everything they can extort from them in whatever way. If one asks them with what conscience they do this, they answer that it is right for them to accept what is freely given. But in this they lie, because whatever they receive in this way has been extorted by force and fear.

As an illustration: if you tried to strangle me for my goods and I willingly gave and handed them over to you so that you might allow me to go free without any greater harm, would you own these goods by right? Certainly not,

Sithyn law for wyll bygynnyt to slakyn
And falsehed for ⟨sleythe⟩ is i-takyn,
135   Robbyng and reuyng ys holdyn purchas
And of vnthewes is made solas—
Engelond may synge "alas, alas!"]

---

5 dicendum] sciendum O.   **6** preda] predia C.   **9** ponderibus suis] ponderosius O.
10 sic] *add* est C.   **14** silvestros] silvestres O.   **16** debellant] debellantur C.   **22** ablata]
oblata C.   **22–23** Proverbiis] proverbio C.   **23** dixit] *add* fili cave B1.   **24** ut] aut C.
irretitus] hereticus C.   **32–33** quousque . . . incarceratur] qui mortis die superveniente a
demonibus capiuntur, ligantur, et in inferno incarcerantur *corr* R. *The sentence is
emended in various ways in the various groups.*   **43** statum] vitam O.   **44** teterrimum]
tartarium C.   **51** fugabat] fugaverat O.   **59** occurrit] accurrit R.W.   **65** in(2)] *om* O.
68 generosi] M.R.A (*from where it is quoted in the* New English Dictionary *under* shav-
aldour). *The reading is of importance for the dating of* Fasciculus morum; *see Frances A.
Foster, "Some English Words," in* Essays and Studies in Honor of Carleton Brown *(New
York, 1940), pp. 155–156. Variants are*: generose C.W.B1.Go1; *the phrase* generosi . . .
dicuntur: inter nos dicuntur tales, Co.Et. Go2; *om* B3. *The entire passage is omitted in*
B2.   **69** shaueldours et ryfelours] tales ribaldores et raptores M; schaildors ryflors R;
schaualdours rifoluris W.   magnorum] magistrorum C.   **78** dicit] refert O.   **79** et] ac
O.   **80** semper] *add* tamen O.   **82** quam] sicut O.   **84** ipse] ipsemet O.   **87** resedere]
residere O.   **94** tempus] *add* sibi M.R; *add* satis W.   **99** symulacrorum] simulacri O.
100 Scitis] satis O; *for the missing verb* M *supplies* patet *after* ipse.   **105** racionem et] *om*
O.   quasi] falsam et O.   **114** congregaret] potuit congregare O.   **119** tenentes] gestantes
O.   **122** quousque] quocienscumque C.   **131–137** Unde . . . alas] *text from* R. *Verse
40, in* B1.B3.D.Go1.Jo.L2.LC.R.Sp.V.W1.

IV.vi   DE PRODICIONE, DOLO, ET MENDACIO

[D]e prodicione autem et dolo et mendacio, que specialiter consistunt
in emendis et vendendis, est sciendum quod dolendum est quod vix sunt
mercatores moderni iam in aliquo [f. 92v] factum suum facere scientes nisi
fiat fraus, in emendo vituperando quod melius est, et in vendendo nimis
5   laudando quod peius est; et hoc sive mensurando sive ponderando sive quicquid aliud faciendo, ut sic propter lucrum tale false proximos decipiant.
Unde Psalmista: "Mendaces filii hominum in stateris ut decipiant." Et certe
quamvis credunt hoc modo alios decipere, magis tamen decipiuntur et ipsi,
quia quicquid in aliqua re per dolum et prodicionem atque mendacium sive
10   periurium operatum est, in die iudicii in conspectu omnium apercius ad
illorum confusionem revelabitur. Unde scriptum est Osee 7: "Revelata est
iniquitas Effraym et malicia Samarie, quia operati sunt mendacium." "Effraym" enim interpretatur crescens, et "Samaria," lana Domini. Et bene signat
mercatores in lanis et aliis diviciis crescentes, quorum iniquitas et dolus

for this would be open theft. It is therefore obvious that excuses of that
kind are not valid when force is used instead of justice. Whence someone says
in English:

> When law grows lax for power of will,
> And falsehood is taken to be good skill,
> When robbing and theft are called purchase,
> And vices are made into pleasant solace,
>   Then England can sing "Alas, alas!"

7–8 Ecclus. 13.23.   **12** Ezek. 22.27.   **33–35** 1 Tim. 6.9.   **36–50** Tubach 451.   **51–63** Tubach 510 (unique). A similar story in Bromyard, "Malediccio," M.I.1.   **69** In chronicles written during the early decades of the fourteenth century, the noun *shavel-dours* (and variants) designates "groups of landed gentry in the north of England who made flagrant raids in the years 1313–1319"; Frances A. Foster, "Some English Words from the *Fasciculus morum*," in: *Essays and Studies in Honor of Carleton Brown* (New York, 1940), p. 156. For such criminal gangs of nobles see also E. L. G. Stones, "The Folvilles of Ashby-Folville, Leicestershire, and their Associates in Crime, 1326–1347," *Trans. Royal Hist. Soc.*, fifth series, 7 (1957), 117–136.   **77–102** Tubach 4614, from Valerius, I.i.ext. 3. Also in Bromyard, "Rapina," R.I.22 (with moralization); Holcot, *In Sapientiam* lect. 176; Cambridge University Library, MS Kk.4.24, fol. 188 (with moralization).

IV.vi   TREACHERY, TRICKS, AND LIES

With regard to treachery and tricks and lies that occur particularly in
buying and selling, we should realize how deplorable it is that merchants in
our days can hardly carry out a single business transaction without fraud,
whether they degrade below its value what they want to buy, or extol beyond its
worth what they want to sell; and this when they measure or weigh or whatever
else they do, so that for the sake of gain they deceive their neighbors with
their falsehood. Hence the Psalmist says: "The sons of men are liars in their
scales, that they may deceive." But though they believe they deceive others in
this way, they are even more greatly deceived themselves, because whatever
mischief they have done through tricks and treachery and lies and perjury will
be revealed openly on Judgment Day in the sight of all to their own confusion.
Whence it has been written in Hosea 7: "The iniquity of Ephraim was discov-
ered, and the wickedness of Samaria, for they have committed falsehood." Ephraim means "growing" and Samaria, "the wool of the Lord," and it indicates

15 erga simplices emendo et vendendo in fine ° tamen coram Deo revelabitur.
    [Nam] quamvis hic in sua dolositate secundum Iob 21 "ducunt in bonis dies,"
    tamen propter suam prodicionem et dolum in fine quasi "in puncto ad inferna
    descendent."
       Unde advertant tales quod pro certo vita peccatoris bene linee compa-
20 ratur, cuius extrema sunt duo puncta, scilicet principium et finis, hoc est
    nativitas hominis et mors. Set nota: secundum philosophos, quicquid acce-
    peris inter puncta divisibile est, set cum ad punctum perveneris, non est
    ulterius aliqua divisio, quia tantum unitas manet. Sic in proposito.
    Quamcumque horam acceperis de vita peccatoris, scilicet quanta est, certum
25 est quod bene dividi potest, eo quod quanta est. Et causa est quia dummodo
    est quanta, hoc est alicuius temporis et quantitatis, potest peccator
    persistere, potest eciam penitere. Set certe cum venerit ad punctum, hoc
    est ad finem, tantummodo [f. 93] manet unitas, idest unum; in qua unitate,
    nisi se melius hic habuerit, "in puncto," ut dicitur, "ad inferna descen-
30 det." Et ideo peccatores nititur in presenti diabolus per prosperitates
    mundanas et delectaciones seducere, ut sic in puncto mortis a beatitudine
    seclusos secum trahat ad iehennam et penam.
       Desistant ergo a dolis, prodicionibus, mendaciis, et periuriis mer-
    catores, quia huiusmodi vita est sicut venenum aspidum insanabile, eciam
35 sibi ipsis plus quam aliis. Et nota quod venenum aspidis ignoranter quasi
    intrat, latenter penetrat, et tamen patenter interficit. Sic vita huiusmo-
    di proditoris, mendacis, et dolosi erga simplices: primo intrat ignoranter
    per veritatis simulacionem, set latenter penetrat per fraudulencie execuci-
    onem, quia ut dicitur Ieremie 9: "Sagitta vulnerans lingua eorum." Et certe
40 sic tandem patenter interficit quando occulte et mendaciter sic ponit
    insidias contra innocentes; Psalmista: "Locuti sunt adversum me lingua
    dolosa." Et alibi sequitur: "Disperdat Dominus universa labia dolosa et
    linguam magniloquam."

---

6 false] falso O. **9** in aliqua re] malicia O. **10** operatum] operata O. **15** et] *om* O.
fine] *add* occultetur C. **18** descendent] descendunt O. **23** aliqua] *om* O. **32** trahat]
pertrahat O. **34** aspidum] aspidis O. **36** patenter] potenter O. **37** mendacis] mendacii
after dolosi O. **40** patenter] potenter M.W; interdum R.

IV.vii   DE USURA

[C]irca autem usuram est tercio sciendum quod usurarius, quamvis ad
tempus mundana lucretur, in maximo tamen periculo est, et hoc primo quia
vendit pauperi proximo quod ex lege nature debet ei, scilicet subsidium in
necessitate. Exemplum: Fluvius vacuitatem fovee inveniens inde non per-

merchants who grow in wool and other riches, whose iniquity and tricks against the simple in buying and selling will yet be revealed before God in the end. For although here in their trickery "they spend their days in wealth," according to Job, yet in the end they will, because of their treachery and tricks, "at a point go down to hell."

Let such people therefore note that the life of a sinner can certainly be compared to a line, which terminates in two points, namely beginning and end, that is to say, man's birth and death. But notice that according to the philosophers the space between the end points is divisible, but when you come to the end point, no further division is possible, for then only a single unit remains. For our purpose: whatever hour in the life of a sinner you select, that is, an extent of time, this can certainly be divided because it is an extent of time. As long as there is an extent, therefore—that is, time and duration—, a sinner can either continue in his sin or he can repent. But when he comes to the point, that is, his end, only a single and indivisible unit remains; and in this single unit—unless he has here lived better—he will, as is said, "at a point go down to hell." Therefore, during this present life the devil tries to seduce sinners by worldly prosperity and pleasures, so that at the point of their death, when they are shut out from eternal bliss, he may carry them with him to hell and to pain.

Let merchants then give up their tricks, treachery, lies, and perjury, for such a life is like the incurable poison of asps, and more so for themselves than for others. Notice that the poison of an asp enters the body imperceptibly, spreads secretly, and yet kills it openly. Such is the lifestyle of one who betrays, lies to, and tricks the simple: first it enters imperceptibly by simulating the truth, but then it spreads secretly when deceit is carried out, for as is written in Jeremiah 9, "their tongue is a piercing arrow." And at last it certainly kills openly, when one sets hidden and deceitful traps for the innocent; as the Psalmist says: "They have spoken against me with a deceitful tongue." And elsewhere he continues: "May the Lord destroy deceitful lips and the tongue that speaks proud things."

---

7 Ps. 61.10.   **11–12** Hos. 7.1.   **16–18** Job 21.13.   **39** Jer. 9.8.   **41–42** Ps. 108.3.
42–43 Ps. 11.4.

IV.vii   USURY

In the third place, with respect to usury we should know that a usurer, though he gains worldly riches for a time, is yet in the greatest danger, and this first because he sells to his poor neighbor what he owes him freely by the law of nature, namely help in his need. By way of an example: when a river

5   transit donec illam impleverit. Et ideo Luce 6 dicitur: "Date mutuo nichil
inde sperantes," scilicet cum usura mundi, ubi nullum lucrum est set dampnum. Unde Augustinus: "Miser, inquit, homo, cur feneraris homini? Fenerare
Deo, et centuplum accipies et eciam vitam eternam." Et ecce quamvis super
hoc arguantur quod iniuste aliena recipiunt et contra prohibicionem Eccle-
10   sie, tamen ad restituendum flecti non possunt et per consequens [f. 93v]
[nec] a laqueo diaboli liberari, cum tamen aves que laqueum senciunt
po⟨cius⟩ dimittunt pedem vel alam ⟨quam⟩ non evadant; Ecclesiastici 10:
"Quomodo capiuntur pisses hamo?"
        Et nota quod "usura est ex mutuo pacto lucrum debitum et exactum. Non
15   tamen credo usuram committi si gratis oblatum gratis accipiatur; argumento
14, questione 4, *Usura*; Distinctione 18." Et ideo nisi sit acceptum et
extortum, non est usura. Set talis usura est duplex, quia una manifesta,
alia palleata. Manifesta est quando quis tradit pecuniam numeratam, ⟨ut⟩
monetam; vel ponderatam, ut es, aurum, argentum; vel aliquid mensuratum,
20   ut frumentum, vinum, oleum, tali pacto ut sibi detur aliquid ultra sortem.
Usura autem palleata habet sex species, quarum prima est circa pignora et
circa obsides. Circa pignora est quando quis granatam alterius habet pro
pignore et colligit [fructus] ultra sortem. Set ° circa obsides est quando
usurarius vivit de expensis obsidis vel non vult dare dilacionem obsidi
25   nisi prius aliquid sibi detur. Secunda species est circa empcionem et
vendicionem, quando scilicet usurarius emit aliquam possessionem longe
minori precio quam valeat, tali condicione quod venditor illam rehaber⟨e⟩
possit quando precium solvere voluerit. Si tamen quis vendiderit possessionem ali[qu]am tali condicione quod quantumcumque solvitur precium ab eo
30   vel herede suo illam rehabeat sine resistencia et dilacione, non est usura.
Et tunc potest emptor facere fructus suos sine periculo nisi in fraudem
usure facta sit empcio, ut quando ante terminum emit tali precio de quo
dubitari non potest quin melior sit. Possessio talis usura est. Tercia
species est circa consuetudines tacite facientes pactum, sicut accidit
35   inter fatuas mulieres et cum eis peccantes. Ibi autem ipsa consuetudo [f.
94] pactum facit ipsis tacentibus, et in isto casu palliant ipsi maliciam
usure bonitatis nomine, vocantes tales usuras "bonitates"; contra quos
Ysaie 5: "Ve qui dicitis malum bonum!" Quarta species est circa societatem,
cum quis scilicet tradit pecuniam suam alicui negociatori tali condicione
40   quod sit socius in lucro et non in dampno. Similiter cum quis tradit alicui
pauperi animalia sua tali condicione quod sint sibi salva numero et valore
quocumque casu eveniente, nisi in se sicut in recipiente suscipiat pericula
belli, incendii, et pestis, usuram committit. Quinta species est circa
penas. Que licet aliquando iuste fieri possunt, c⟨uiusmodi⟩ sunt iudicia-
45   les, hoc est a iudice posite et statute ad puniendum contumaciam credito-
ris, aut si sint pene convencionales, hoc est de consensu omnium parcium in

encounters an empty ditch, it does not flow past until it has filled it. And
so it is said in Luke 6: "Lend to one another without expecting anything from
it," that is, any worldly profit where there is no gain but only loss. Whence
Augustine says: "Wretched man, why do you lend with interest to another man?
Lend to God, and you will receive a hundredfold and even eternal life." Although usurers are accused of receiving other people's goods unjustly and
against the Church's prohibition, yet they cannot be directed to make restitution, and therefore they cannot escape the devil's noose, whereas birds when
they feel the noose would rather lose a foot or a wing than not escape; Ecclesiasticus 10: "How are fish taken with the hook?"

And notice that "usury is a gain which is owed and demanded by mutual
agreement. However, I do not believe usury occurs when something freely offered is freely received; see 14, question 4, *Usura*; and Distinction 18."
Therefore, unless some profit is accepted and extorted, it is not usury. But
usury itself is of two kinds: manifest and cloaked. Manifest usury occurs when
someone trades a commodity that can be counted, such as money; or can be
weighed, such as bronze, gold, or silver; or can be measured, such as wheat,
wine, or oil, with an agreement that he receive something back beyond its
original value. Cloaked usury has six different species. The first concerns
securities and hostages. Usury from securities occurs when one person holds
someone else's granary as a pledge and collects income from it. Usury from
hostages occurs when the usurer lives off a hostage's expenses or will not give
the hostage what he owes him unless he first receives something for himself.
The second kind concerns buying and selling, namely when a usurer buys some
good for a far smaller price than it is worth, on the condition that the seller
can have it back when he wants to pay the full price. But when someone sells
some good on the condition that whenever the price is paid by him or his heir
he will have it back without opposition or delay, then it is not usury. And
then the buyer may make some profit without danger, unless he has cheated, as
when he buys the good before the set term at a price that is undoubtedly less
than the object's value; this is usury. The third kind concerns customs that
implicitly constitute an agreement, as happens between foolish women and men
who sin with them. In this case, custom establishes a contract without an
explicit agreement, and they hide the evil of usury under the name of goodness
by calling such profits "bounties." Against these people is said in Isaiah 5:
"Woe to you that call evil good!" The fourth kind concerns partnership, namely
when someone gives his commodity to some merchant on the condition that he
shares his gains but not his losses. Similarly, when someone gives a poor man
his animals on the condition that they are his except for the number and value
of the animals he gives him, no matter what accidents may happen. If in this
case he does not accept for himself the risk of war, fire, or pestilence as the
recipient does, he commits usury. The fifth kind concerns penalties. These

ipso contractu apposite, ut saltem metu pene debitum certo die solvatur; et
in istis non committitur usura. Set quantum ad illos qui non intendunt [in
huiusmodi] penis ut cicius sibi solvatur set quod amplius sibi solvatur,
50   usura est. Sexta species est circa translacionem factam a re ad rem vel a
persona ad personam. A re ad rem, quando dives non accipit pecuniam a
paupere ultra sortem, set bene accipit quod operetur in vinea duobus diebus
vel tribus. A persona ad personam, ut quando ipsemet usurarius non accomo-
dat set facit amicum alium ad usuram accomodare, vel si ipsemet accomodet
55   decem denarios ut dentur ultra hoc quinque denarii pauperibus; quibus
pauperibus si talis tenetur, usura sibi est; si non tenetur illis, tunc
usur⟨a⟩ est illis et tene⟨n⟩tur restituere.
     Item usurarum alia est spiritualis et bona, de qua Luce 19: "Quare non
dedistis pecuniam ad mens⟨am⟩ ut ego veniens cum usuris utique exigissem
60   eam?" Alia est corporalis et iniqua, de qua [f. 94v] hic agitur. Et ista
est duplex, quia una est sortis et alia usurarum, secundum Raymundum paragrapho 2. Et hec ultima vocatur improbum fenus. Unde illam exercens fit
infamis ipso iure et eciam secundum leges; 3, questione 78, *Tria*, in fine.
"Secundum tamen iura canonica," ut Hostiensis dicit paragrapho *Quot sunt*,
65   "in utraque peccatum mortale committitur et infamia irrogatur: 6, questione
1, *Infamis*."
     Est tamen hic advertendum quod sunt aliqui casus in quibus licet
recipere ultra sortem, scilicet: Si laicus tenet violenter et iniuste
aliquod predium ecclesie, tunc potest clericus cui assignata est illa
70   ecclesia accipere ab eo illud predium et similiter recipere ultra sortem,
s⟨i⟩ hoc non faciat lucri causa set ut redimatur res Ecclesie de manu
laici. Item si fideiussor solverit usuras creditori, potest ea repetere a
debitore pro quo fideiussit, quia non sunt usure quantum ad fideiussorem
set vitacio dampni. Item racione mor⟨e⟩, verbi gracia: si enim michi
75   teneres ad centum solidos ad certum terminum et non vis solvere in termino,
ita quod oportet me recipere pecuniam sub usuris propter negocia me[a]
tractanda, tunc tu [teneris] michi solvere illas usuras, si ego solvi eas.
Et si non solvi, teneris tamen me liberare ab illa obligacione. Item racione dubii, verbi gracia: si quis dat tibi decem mensuras grani, vini, vel
80   olei, ut alio tempore totidem sibi grani, vini, olei mensure reddantur,
que licet tunc plus valeant, dum tamen utrum plus vel minus tempore soluci-
onis fuerint valiture verisimiliter dubitat, non debet propter hoc usurarius appellari. Racione eciam huius dubii excusatur qui pannos, granum,
vinum, aut alias huiusmodi merces vendit ut amplius [quam] tunc valeat
85   recipiat pro eisdem in certo termino, si tamen tempore contractus non
fuerit ea venditurus; si autem venderet ad terminum longe maiorem maiori
precio quam modo valet, usura est.
     [f. 95] Unde nota pro omnibus istis et aliis quod grat⟨is⟩ oblatum et

may sometimes be given justly, such as judicial punishments, which are set and given by a judge in order to punish the illegal harshness of a creditor; or else they may be contractual penalties, specified in a contract by the consent of all parties, so that out of fear of such a penalty a debt may be paid off by a certain date. In these cases there is no usury. But when such penalties are set with the intention not that some debt be paid in time but that the debt may be increased, then it is usury. The sixth kind concerns transfers from one object to another or from one person to another. A transfer of objects occurs when a rich man does not accept interest money from a poor man but rather has him work in his vineyard for two or three days. A transfer of persons occurs when the usurer does not lend himself but has some friend lend the commodity at profit, or when he himself lends ten pence on the condition that an additional five pence be given to the poor; if he has an obligation to support these poor, he commits usury; if not, then it is usury for them and they must make restitution.

There is, further, one kind of usury that is spiritual and good, which is spoken of in Luke 19: "Why did you not give my money into the bank, that at my coming I might have exacted it with usury?" and another kind that is material and evil, which we are dealing with in this discussion. The latter is again twofold: one species pertains to profit, the other to fraudulent usury, according to Raymundus in paragraph 2. This last kind is called outrageous interest. He who engages in it becomes disreputable by right and according to law: 3, question 7, *Tria*, at the end. "And according to canon law," as Hostiensis says in the paragraph *Quot sunt*, "in both kinds a mortal sin is committed and loss of one's good reputation is inflicted: 6, question 1, *Infamis*."

We must, however, observe that there are some cases in which it is licit to accept some gain beyond the principal. For example, when some layperson holds a church building by force and unjustly, the clergyman to whom the church is entrusted may receive from him the price of the church together with interest, if he does so not for the sake of gain but so that the church property may be bought back from lay possession. Further, if a pledge pays interest to the creditor, he may get it from the debtor for whom he has pledged, for this is not usury to the pledge but avoidance of loss. Usury is also licit by reason of delay. For instance, if you owe me a hundred shillings at a certain date and cannot pay me in time, so that I must receive the money with interest in order to carry out my own business, in that case you owe me payment of that interest, in case I have indeed paid it myself. If I have not paid it, you are still obligated to free me from my own obligation. Further, usury is licit in case of doubt. For instance, if someone gives you ten measures of grain, wine, or oil, so that at a later time the same amount of grain, wine, or oil may be given back to him, which at the later point is worth more, if he is at the moment of payment in genuine doubt whether their price would go up or down,

acceptum non inducit usuram, dum tamen non sit intencio corrupta, quia sola
90   spes sive intencio facit usuram. Qui ergo sub tali spe mutuant, quicquid
supra sortem acceperint, usura est. Secundum ergo Gregorium X in Concilio
Lugdunensi, capitulo "De usuris," stat quod nullus tal⟨e⟩s secum habitare
permittat set infra tres menses de terris suis expellantur. Qui vero contra
fecerit, si persona ecclesiastica fuerit cuiuscumque condicionis, et maxime
95   maiores, suspencionem incurrunt, minores vero persone excommunicacionem,
collegium autem et universitas interdicionem, laici vero omni privilegio
ce⟨s⟩sante per censuram ecclesiasticam compescantur. Et si tales ad penitenciam redire voluerint, donec de usuris plenarie sit satisfactum, non
debent suscipere communionem, nec debent recipi eorum oblaciones, nec sunt
100 in cimiterio sepeliendi. Si tamen (dicit Gregorius) suppetunt facultates
episcopo aut saltem sacerdoti parochiali coram fidedignis, sufficiens [cau-
cio] presteter de restitucione et exprimatur quantitas restitu⟨endorum⟩
quantum possibile est; quod si non fecerit, nullus eos ad confessionem seu
⟨ad absolucionem⟩ admittat, nec testamentis eorum intersit, et testamenta
105 sic facta nichil valent. Clericus eciam usurarius non ordinetur. Si vero
ordinatus est, aut desistat aut deponatur.

  Unde narratur de quodam usurario qui hoc modo multas congregabat
divicias, qui cum ad mortem infirmabatur et ab uxore ut testamentum conde-
ret fuisset sepius admonitus, constanter negavit, set fecit uxorem suam
110 iurare quod post mortem eius ligaret circa corpus eius de huiusmodi lucro
triginta marcas, quas in thesauro reposuisset, dicens ei: "Ne timeas pro
me. Quamcumque enim terram introiero, [f. 95v] si hanc pecuniam mecum
habuero, bene negociabor et caute." Sepulto ergo eo cum pecunia, cito post
venit curie legatus et hec audiens precepit sacerdoti qui eum sepelierat a
115 sepultura fidelium extrahi et in campum proici et comburi. Qui cum eius
familiaribus accessisset, in loco ubi denarii fuerant ligati invenerunt
bufones teterrimos corpus miserum et horridum corrodentes et vermes innumerabiles in braccale peccunie. Quo viso ignem apposuerunt, et multi illius
fetore interierunt.
120   Ad idem eciam narracio de eodem legato, magister Robertus nomine, cum
in sua visitacione apud Werdeley venisset et sibi idem intimatum fuisset de
quodam usurario nuper defuncto, quem cum exhauriri iussisset, amoto lapide
superiori viderunt corpus eius nigrum et fetidissimum, et quendam bufonem
supra eum sedere, qui tenuit ad os eius quasi eius nutrix nummos ardentes
125 et ipsum ad modum nutricis pavit cum illis. Quod cum vidissent, perteriti
fugerunt, et venerunt demones et corpus cum tumba asportabant, nec usquam
comparuit.

---

4 Fluvius] *add* autem O.   **11** liberari] *om* O.   **12** pocius] post C.R.W.   quam] quamvis
C.   **15** accipiatur] recipiatur M.R; *longer om* W.   **18** ut] vel C.   **22** granatam] grangiam
R.W.   **23** Set] *add* contra C.   **27** rehabere] rehaberi C.   **29** solvitur] solvatur O.

he must not be called usurer. For the same reason of doubt a person is excused
if he sells cloth, grain, wine, or other such merchandise with the condition
that he will receive more for them at a certain future date than their value is
at the date of sale, provided he did not actually sell them on the date of the
contract; but if he were to make a far future sale at a higher price than their
present value, this is usury.

Notice, then, that in all these and other cases, what is freely given and
freely accepted does not lead to usury, as long as there is no corrupt intention, for usury always rests upon such expectation or intention. Thus, whoever
loans money with such expectation, whatever profit he makes is usury. Therefore, according to the decree "On Usury" given by Gregory X at the Council of
Lyons, no one must allow such usurers to dwell with him but expel them from
his country within three months. Whoever acts otherwise, if he is a member of
the clergy of whatever rank, and especially if of a higher rank, incurs suspension; the lower clergy, excommunication; a college or university, interdict;
whereas laymen are to be curbed by ecclesiastic censure with the cessation of
all privileges. And when such usurers want to do penance, they must not
receive Communion until they have made complete satisfaction, nor must their
offerings be accepted, nor are they to be buried in the cemetery. If however,
says Gregory, they present goods to the bishop or their parish priest in the
presence of witnesses, an adequate security about their restitution should be
given and the amount to be restituted should be specified, inasmuch as is
possible; if such is not done, no one is to admit them to confession or absolution, nor may he be present at their making their last will, and the testaments
thus made have no validity. A cleric who is a usurer must not be ordained; and
if he is already ordained, he must either desist from usury or be deposed.

There is a story about a usurer who had in this fashion gathered great
wealth. When he was in his last sickness and was often admonished by his wife
to make his will, he always refused, but he made his wife swear that after his
death she would tie thirty marks from his profits on his body, which he had
placed in his treasure, telling her: "Do not be afraid for me. To whatever
country I travel, if I have this money on me, I shall make a good and careful
bargain." Shortly after he had been buried with the money, a legate came from
the Curia and, hearing all this, ordered the priest who had buried him to take
him out of the cemetery of the faithful and throw him in the open field and
burn him. Now, when the priest and his assistants came to him, they found in
the place where the money had been tied ugly toads that gnawed at his miserable
decomposing body and countless worms instead of an armband of money. When
they saw this, they burned him, and many died of the stench.

In the same vein it is reported of the same legate named Master Robert
that he once came to Verdely on his visitation. There he was told about a
usurer who had recently died. He ordered his body to be exhumed. When the
upper stone had been removed, they saw his black and stinking body and a toad

31 fraudem] fraude M.R; ? W.   **44** cuiusmodi] cicius C.M.W; *corr in* R.   **45** puniendum] puniendam O.   **49** sibi(2)] *om* O.   **57** usura] usurarius C.W.   tenentur] teneatur C; tenantur M.   **59** mensam] mensuram C; usuram M.   utique] *om* O.   exigissem] exegissem O.   **61–62** paragrapho] *om* O.   **66** Infamis] infames O.   **71** si] set C.   **73** ad] *add* ipsum O.   **74** more] mortis C.O *and other groups; text in source*.   **77** ego] *om* O.   **79** tibi] *om* O.   **79–80** mensuras . . . olei] solidos M; *om* R.W.   **84** quam] *om* C.M.W; *marg* R.   **86** maiorem] maiori M; *om* R.W.   **88** gratis] gratum C.   **92** tales] talis C.R.W.   **97** cessante] censante C.   **102** restituendorum] restitucionis C.   **104** ad absolucionem] oblacionem C.   **105** sic] aliter M.W; eorum R.   **107** congregabat] congregasset O.   **112** introiero] intravero O.

IV.viii   DE SYMONIA

[D]e symonia iam dicendum est, et primo quid sit. Secundum enim theologos et iuristas, ut communiter, dicitur quod "symonia est studiosa voluntas emendi vel vendendi spirituale"; vel spirituali annexum, quod additur pro iure patronatus, prohibetur vendi; Extravagantes "De iure patronatus,"

5   [*De iure*]. Dicunt enim quidam quod ius patronatus nullo modo vendi potest cum sit spirituali annexum, transire tamen potest cum universitate. Si[cut] quando quis emit villam, non emit tunc ius patronatus [illius], set illud ius tunc transit cum illa villa ad eius emptorem, sicut Abraham non emit ius sepulture in spelunca dupplici [f. 96] set totum agrum, cum quo transit

10   ad eum ius sepeliendi.

Et nota quod symonia dicitur a Symone mago, primo auctore huius sceleris in Novo Testamento, qui volebat emere graciam Spiritus Sancti a beato Petro, Actuum 8, sicud Gyesi in Veteri Testamento, Regum 5, vendidit sanitatem Naaman Syro et sanitatem ideo amisit. Et iste commisit symoniam

15   de post facto, quia precedens ad beneficium pravam int⟨o⟩rsit intencionem quasi bene posset. Unde venditor spiritualium proprie dicitur gyesiticus, set emptor symoniacus, usu tamen communi uterque symoniacus a dicto Symone.

Est autem advertendum quod triplex est munus quo committitur symonia inter homines, scilicet a manu, a lingua, ab obsequio. A manu, hoc est per ma-

20   num, committitur symonia per pecuniam (nomine autem pecunie intelliguntur omnia que habent homines in terris, sive mobilia sive immobilia); Causa 1, questione 1, *Sunt nonnulli*, in fine proxime questionis. Munus a lingua sunt favor, preces que fiunt pro indigno, quia tunc preces et huiusmodi succedunt loco precii. Si tamen fiant pro digno, non est symonia, dummodo ordi-

sitting on it, who, like a nurse, held burning coins to the dead man's mouth and fed him these. When they saw that, they fled in horror, and then demons came and carried the corpse with its coffin away, and he was nowhere seen again.

5–6 Luke 6.35.   **7–8** Cf. Augustine, *En. in Ps. 36* III.6 (CC 38:372–373).   **13** Eccles. 9.12.   **14–16** Raymundus, *Summa* II.vii.1 (p. 227). The canonical references are to Gratian II.14.3.4 (1:735) and Gratian I.18 (1:53–58).   **18–20** Raymundus, loc. cit.   **21–57** Almost verbatim in Peraldus, *Summa vitiorum* IV.ii.1, except for lines 28–33 and 42–43.   **38** Isa. 5.20.   **58–63** Raymundus, II.vii.2 (227).   **58–60** Luke 19.23.   **63** Gratian II.3.7. pars ii, 20, near end (1:526).   **64–66** Hostiensis, *Summa aurea*, V, "De usuris," 3 (1615). The reference is to Gratian II.6.1.17 (1:558).   **66–87** Raymundus, II.vii.3 (228–229).   **91–92** The reference is to the Council of Lyon, 1274.   **91** *Decretals* 5.5 (2:1081–82).   **107–19** Tubach 5054b (not 4889). Similarly in Bromyard, "Acquisicio," A.XII.31–32.   **120–127** Tubach 4889; very widespread.

IV.viii   SIMONY

Now we will speak of simony, and first of its nature. According to theologians and lawyers, it is commonly said that "simony is the eager desire to buy or sell something sprirtual"; or something attached to a spiritual value, which is added because the right of patronage is forbidden to be sold. Thus in Extravagantes, "On the right of patronage," *De iure*. Some authorities say that the right of patronage cannot be sold in any way, since it is attached to a spiritual value; but it can pass on with a university. Thus, when someone buys a village, he does not buy its right of patronage, but the latter passes on to the buyer together with the village, just as Abraham did not buy the burial right in the double cave, but the whole field, with which the burial right passed on to him.

Simony is so called after Simon Magus, the first originator of this crime in the New Testament, who wanted to buy the grace of the Holy Spirit from Blessed Peter, in Acts 8, just as Gehazi in the Old Testament, in Kings 5, sold health to the Syrian Naaman and thereby lost his own. He committed simony after the fact, because when he approached to receive a gift, he twisted his evil intention as if he could receive the gift by right. Hence, someone who sells spiritual values is properly called a Gehaziite, whereas the buyer is a simoniac. But in common usage both are called simoniacs, after the before-mentioned Simon.

Notice that the gift by which simony is committed among people is of three kinds: of hand, tongue, and service. Simony "of hand," that is, by hand, is committed by means of *pecunia*, "a commodity" (under the name of *pecunia* we understand everything men have on earth, moveable or unmoveable); Causa 1,

25 nator vel elector non habeat respectum ad preces set ad Deum et meritum
persone. Et nota quod nullus per se quantumcumque dignus potest petere
beneficium ecclesie habens curam animarum sine symonia. Beneficium tamen
simpliciter si indiget et sentit se dignum potest petere absque metu symonie. Munus vero ab obsequio est servitus indebite impensa, sicut si honeste
30 obsequeris inhonesto ut usurario vel tyranno; vel econtrario si inhoneste
honesto, ut si fias armiger alicuius pro aliquo spirituali. Nota tamen quod
huiusmodi obsequium est duplex, scilicet corporale et spirituale. [f. 96v]
In corporali autem obsequio et honesto licitum est, ut si quis vadat ad
curiam pro ecclesia vel serviat episcopo in licitis et honestis, dum tamen
35 sine pactione hoc facit. Si vero obsequium sit inhonestum, non potest. Si
autem fuerit tale obsequium spirituale, tunc illud non debet facere pro
beneficio, nisi tale officium sit tali beneficio inpositum. Verbi gracia:
alicui prebende impositum est hoc onus, scilicet quicumque habuerit illam,
legat in theologia vel cantet vel cantari faciat de Beata Virgine.
40   Et nota quod quinque sunt casus in quibus datur licite temporale pro
spirituali a manu. Primus, si gratis munus datur vel offeratur pro spirituali; 1, questione 1, *Quicquid*. Secundus, pro operibus spiritualibus ad
que non tenetur quis ex officio; 12, questione 2, *Carita⟨tis⟩ verb⟨a⟩*:
"Iustum, inquit, est ut illi consequentur stipendium qui pro tempore suum
45 comodare reperiuntur obsequium." Tercius est pro quibusdam operibus spiritualibus alicuius divitis, sicut si episcopus consecrat ecclesiam vel
visitat episcopatum, potest tunc exigere procuracionem debitam et modera-
tam; Extravagantes E, *Cum sit Romana*, et "De prescriptis," *Cum ex officio*.
Quarto, pro vita eterna et pro peccatorum remissione, cuiusmodi sunt elemo-
50 sine. Quinto, pro reddenda vexacione que sibi fit iniuste super spirituali
iure; Extravagantes, capitulo *Dilecte*.
    Et nota quod symonia committitur in ordine, quando quis scilicet
symoniace suscipit ordines; similiter quando quis symoniace adquirit beneficium vel intrat religionem. Et hic nota bene casus quos ponit Lincol-
55 niensis in *Templo*, et sunt extracta de *Penitenciali* magistri Roberti ⟨Fla-
meyn⟩. Et sunt isti: Primus est si aliquis tibi adquisivit ecclesiam vel
ordines vel habitum religionis te sciente vel ignorante, et postea te
percipiente possides, nisi re- [f. 97] signes. Secundus, si aliquod munus
accepisti, dedisti pro promocione tua vel alterius ad ordines vel ecclesiam
60 vel religionem. Tercius, si fecisti alicui obsequium tibi indebitum vel
indebite persone, ut per hoc haberes ecclesiam, ordines, vel habitum religionis. Quarto, si habes ecclesiam ex dono alicuius principis vel alterius
magistri cui pater tuus vel amicus fecit obsequia, et hoc scis. Quintus, si
contendas pro ecclesia et tamen tu scis nichil iuris habere et das adversa-
65 rio tuo pro suo iure corporale munus. Sextus, si vendidisti vel emisti ius
patronatus simpliciter per se et non cum alio corporali annexo. Septimus,

question 1, *Sunt nonnulli*, at the end of the question. A gift "of tongue" is favoritism or intercession made for an unworthy person, for such intercession and the like take the place of money. But if intercession is made for a worthy person, it is not simony, as long as the person who ordains or elects the candidate does not act out of regard for the intercession but rather for God and the merits of the candidate. And notice that no one, no matter how worthy he may be, can ask for himself for a church benefice that has the care of souls attached to it without incurring simony. But he may ask for a simple benefice without fear of simony, if he is in need and thinks he is worthy of it. A gift "of service," finally, is service that is undertaken inappropriately, as when one serves honorably a dishonorable person, such as a usurer or a tyrant; or conversely when one serves an honorable person dishonorably, as when one becomes someone's squire for a spiritual purpose. Such service, however, is twofold, bodily and spiritual. If the service is bodily and honorable, it is licit, as when someone goes to the Curia for his church or serves his bishop in licit and honorable business, as long as he does this without a contract. But if the service is not honorable, it cannot be licit. If on the other hand the service is spiritual, he must not render it for a benefice unless the service is a required part of the benefice. For instance, a prebend may have attached to it a required charge, that is, that he who holds the living must study theology, or say Mass daily, or have a Mass said in honor of the Blessed Virgin.

Notice also that in five cases a temporal gift can be given licitly "by hand" for something spiritual. First, if a gift is freely offered for a spiritual value; 1, question 1, *Quicquid*. Second, for spiritual acts to which one is not officially obligated; 12, question 2, *Caritatis verba*, which declares: "It is just that those should receive a stipend who are found to give their service on their time." The third is for any spiritual works of a rich person, as when a bishop consecrates a church or visits his diocese, he may ask for a licit and moderate compensation; Extravagantes E, *Cum sit Romana*, and in the title "On prescriptions," *Cum ex officio*. Fourth, for eternal life and for the remission of sins, as are alms. And fifth, in order to repay for any vexation that is suffered unjustly in carrying out the spiritual law; Extravagantes 1, *Dilecte*.

Notice further that simony is committed in holy orders when someone receives orders simoniacally; similarly when someone acquires a benefice or enters the religious life simoniacally. Mark well the cases which Grosseteste lists in his *Temple*, which are excerpted from the *Penitential* of Master Robert of Flamesborough. And they are: (1) If someone acquires a living for you or holy orders or the religious habit with or without your knowledge, and afterwards you come into possession with full knowledge, and you do not resign it. (2) If you have received or given any gift for your own or another person's

si ius patronatus dedisti episcopo et recepisti eam in usus proprios pro
collacione iuris tui. Octavus, si dedisti decem ut concederet rector tibi
pensionem suam post se. Nonus, si concessisti pencionem novam ut haberes
70   ecclesiam vel augmentum. Decimus, si dedisti decem prelato ut te non
visitet vel dedicet ecclesiam tuam. Undecimus, si iurasti conservare iura
ecclesie antequam posses in illam institui vel pro institucione dedisti
corporale munus vel accepisti. Duodecimus, si post ordinacionem, electio-
nem, beneficii collacionem, vel habitus [religionis] suscepcionem exactus
75   sub pretextu alicuius consuetudinis aliquid dedisti. Mala enim consuetudo
peccatum non minuit set auget; Extravagantes E, *Sicut pro certo*. Et tamen
si gratis et sine [ex]actione, set propter dilectionem ex beneficio collato generatam vel propter devocionem aliquid dedisti, non est symonia.
Decimus tercius, si commodasti decem patrono ut tibi conferat ecclesiam et
80   confert. Decimus quartus, si compelli⟨s⟩ aliquem ad solucionem pecunie pro
annuali vel tricennali, etc. Decimus quintus, si pro certa pecunia celebras divina ex condicione in ecclesia alicuius, puta pro quadraginta solidis; [f. 97v] si tamen pro alico quam pro certa pecunia, ut pro altari, non
[est] symonia, eciam si altare valeat quadraginta solidis. Et ⟨racio est⟩,
85   secundum dictum magistri Roberti Lincolniensis, quia ibi altare accipitur
nomine ecclesie, et iustum est ut qui servit altari, quod de altari vivat.
Set denarii recipiuntur nomine burse, et hoc maxime quando taxati sunt ad
certum numerum. Decimus sextus, si ex officio teneris ad aliquam missam vel
exequias vel simile, et tamen propter hoc exigis aliquid, symonia est.
90   Gratis tamen oblatum potes recipere. Si vero ad huiusmodi non tenearis et
desunt tibi sumptus, potes licite locare opera tua ad diem vel annum,
sicut faciunt conducticii sacerdotes; 1, questione 1, et Extravagantes, "Ne
prelati." Si autem habes sumptus aut teneris gratis celebrare aut cessare,
hoc tamen forte non esset symonia, cum non tenetur aliquis propriis stipen-
95   diis militare, secundum opinionem doctorum. Decimus septimus est, si cele-
brata una missa celebras aliam pro pecunia vel hominum adulacione, indistincte non evades dampnacionem. Decimus octavus, si emisti decimas ad te
prius non spectantes a laico sine licencia episcopi vel [alterius] superioris. Decimus nonus, si laicus ecclesiam ad firmam accepit, vel eciam cleri-
100 cus propter lucrum temporale principaliter, symonia est secundum opinionem
doctorum; argumento pro eis 1, questione 3, *Salvator*. Vicesimus est si
renunciasti beneficio tuo non existens patronus [eiusdem], ut conferes
alteri certe persone propter aliquod lucrum. Vicesimus primus, si das
ecclesiam pro alia sine licencia episcopi pro lucro. Vicesimus secundus, si
105 pro sciencia et pericia ministras episcopo coadiutor eius factus in causis
decidendis et aliis conciliis spiritualibus pro certa taxacione stipendio-
rum ex condicione. Officium enim tale spirituale est et ideo sine condicione et certa taxacione fieri licet. Et idem videtur de sacerdote [f. 98]

promotion to holy orders or a living or the religious life. (3) If you have given any inappropriate service, or have given service to an inappropriate person, in order thereby to acquire a living or holy orders or the religious habit. (4) If you hold a living as a gift from a prince or another master to whom your father or a friend of yours gave service, and you are aware of it. (5) If you compete for a living, knowing that you have no claim to it, and you give your opponent a tangible gift in exchange for his right. (6) If you have sold or bought the simple right of patronage by itself, not with any tangible benefit attached to it. (7) If you have given the right of patronage to your bishop and have received the benefice for your own use in return for your right. (8) If you have given ten marks so that the pastor would leave you his income after his death. (9) If you have given a new share in order to gain a living or some increase. (10) If you have given ten marks to a prelate so that he would not make his visitation or that he would dedicate your church. (11) If you have sworn to uphold the rights of a living before you could be installed in it, or if you have given or received a tangible gift for the installation. (12) If under the pretext of following established custom you have made any gift that was extorted from you for your ordination, election, the conferral of a benefice, or your entrance into the religious life. An evil custom does not diminish a sin but increases it; Extravagantes E, *Sicut pro certo*. If, however, you have made a gift freely and without any such pressure, out of love created by the benefice conferred on you, or out of devotion, this is not simony. (13) If you have given ten marks to a patron so that he would confer a living on you, and he does so. (14) If you compel someone to pay money for an anniversary or a triennial Mass and the like. (15) If you celebrate Mass in someone's church for a fixed sum of money as a condition, say for forty shillings. If, however, you do this for anything other than a fixed sum of money, say for the income from an altar, then it is not simony, even if the altar is worth forty shillings. The reason, according to the explanation of the said Master Robert of Lincoln, is that in this case the altar is received in the name of the church, and it is right that he who serves the altar should live by the altar. But money is received in the name of the purse, and especially so if it is specified by a certain amount. (16) If by virtue of your office you are required to say Mass or conduct a burial or the like and yet you demand to be paid for it, that is simony. A freely offered gift, however, you may accept. But if you are not required to give such service and you lack livelihood, then you can licitly hire out your work by the day or the year, as stipendiary priests do; 1, question 1; and Extravagantes, under the title "Prelates should not." But if you have your livelihood, you are held either to celebrate for free or not at all. Even in this case, however, it might perhaps not be simony since, in the opinion of some doctors, no one is obligated to do service at his own cost. (17) If after saying one Mass you say another for the

quem sibi adducat dives aliquis ut sibi celebret divina, secundum opinionem
110 Lincolniensis et alterius magistri Roberti. Vicesimus tercius, si dedisti
vel accepisti pro iudicio differendo vel celando iniuste vel pervertendo;
14, questione 5, *Non sane*. Vicesimus quartus, si forum ecclesiasticum ad
certam firmam posuisti vel aliquam iurisdictionem habentem aliquod spirituale annexum vel vicedominatum vel rerum aliarum ecclesiasticarum adminis-
115 tracionem; 1, questione 3, [*Salvator*]. Vicesimus quintus, si accepisti pro
alico sacramento ecclesiastico in quo gracia confertur. Hoc enim dicitur ad
differenciam matrimonii, in quo gracia non confertur, et ideo pro eo accipi
potest. Vicesimus sextus, secundum Raymundum, si accepisti munus pro intro-
nizacione episcoporum vel institucione canonicorum vel pro benedictione
120 abbatis vel pro sepultura vel pro danda absolucione vel iure decimarum vel
pro iusticia Ecclesie servanda. In omnibus hiis accipere pecuniam est
symonia, secundum doctores. Vicesimus septimus, si magister scolasticus
habens beneficium in ecclesia aliqua assignatum ut clericos ecclesie et
alios pauperes instruat et tamen ab eisdem aliquid exigerit et acceperit.
125 Si tamen huiusmodi beneficium non sufficit, competenter ° potest licite
accipere, moderate tamen, aliter non. Sponte vero oblata potest licite
accipere. Vicesimus octavus, [si] magister scolasticus pro die iure colendo
pecuniam acceperit a scolaribus ad eum colendum, vel concessisti istum
colendum pro pecunia, secundum Lincolniensem. Vicesimus nonus, si dedisti,
130 promisisti, vel aliquid accepisti pro licencia docendi, similiter symonia
est. Tricesimus, si presbiter parochialis prece aut precio, favore aut
consanguinitate celaverit episcopo publicum peccatum parochiani sui vel si
minus digne pe[ni]tentem a reconciliacione amoverit; Extravagantes E, *Nemo*.
Tricesimus primus, si presentatus ad ordines non habens titulum iurasti vel
135 promisisti te non inquietaturum ordin[ator]em vel [f. 98v] presenta⟨tor⟩em
ordinatus fuerit. Sine dispensacione domini pape in tali ordine non debet
ministrare. Ordinator vero ab ordinum collacione et presentator ab ordinum
execucione per triennium suspendantur; Extravagantes E, *Siquis ordinaverit*.
Tricesimus secundus, si habes ecclesiam tibi datam vel promissam tempore
140 rectoris eiusdem. Hic enim casus ponitur hoc loco licet non sit symonia,
quia tamquam symoniacus privandus est de beneficio illo, secundum doctores.
      De pena autem symoniaci distinguendum est, quia aut est symonia in
ordine suscepto aut in beneficio. Si in primo, non recipiet execucionem
set ipso iure est suspensus quoad se et quoad alios, sive sit occultum sive
145 manifestum, sicut notorius fornicator; Extravagantes "De symonia," *Can.ta*,
et 32 distinctione, [a.] 8. Et similiter sic intelligitur 1, questione 1,
Reperiuntur. Item punitur deposicione et infamia; 15, questione 3, *Sane*.
Nec pecuniam potest repetere, non quia alius bene recepit set quia iste
turpiter dedit; 14, questione 5, *Non sane*. Si autem symonia sit in benefi-
150 cio suscepto, tenetur ideo renunciare et restituere omnes fructus percep-

sake of money or human adulation, without question you will not avoid being damned. (18) If you have bought from a layman tithes that did not belong to you before, without license of your bishop or another superior. (19) If a layman accepts a living as a payment, or even a cleric, if he does so chiefly for the sake of temporal gain, this is simony in the opinion of the doctors; on this see 1, question 3, *Salvator*. (20) If you have renounced your benefice without being its patron, in order to confer it to someone else for the sake of gain. (21) If you exchange one living for another without permission from the bishop, for the sake of gain. (22) If you serve your bishop with your knowledge and skill as his coadjutor, in judging legal cases or in giving other spiritual advice, on the condition of a fixed amount of compensation. Such an office is a spiritual one and must therefore be carried out without any condition and fixed compensation. The same applies to a priest whom a rich person employs to say Mass for him, after the opinion of Grosseteste and the other Master Robert. (23) If you have given or accepted any gift for delaying judgment or unjustly hiding it or perverting justice; 14, question 5, *Non sane*. (24) If you have given as a payment the church court, or any jurisdiction that has any spiritual value attached to it, or the office of deputy, or any administration of other church goods; 1, question 3, *Salvator*. (25) If you have accepted any gift for any sacrament of the Church in which grace is conferred. The last qualification is made to set apart matrimony, in which grace is not conferred; and therefore a gift can be received for it. (26) According to Raymundus, if you have accepted a gift for the inthronization of bishops, the installment of canons, the blessing of the abbot, a funeral, giving absolution, the right of tithing, or to carry out ecclesiastic justice. To accept money for any of these is, in the teaching of the doctors, simony. (27) If a schoolmaster holds a benefice in some church assigned to him to teach clerics of the Church or the poor and still demands a gift from them and accepts it. However, if his benefice is not sufficient, then he may rightly accept a gift, but with moderation, not otherwise. What is offered him voluntarily, he can licitly accept. (28) If a schoolmaster has accepted money from his students to keep a legally established holiday, or if he has granted them a holiday for money, according to Grosseteste. (29) If you have given, promised, or received any gift for the permission to teach, it is similarly simony. (30) If on account of a request, a tangible gift, a favor, or consanguinity, a parish priest has hidden from his bishop a publicly known sin of his parishioner, or has removed from reconciliation someone who does penance less worthily; Extravagantes E, *Nemo*. (31) If at being presented for ordination without a title you have sworn or promised not to disturb the person who was to ordain or present you, and you were ordained. In such a state you cannot legally serve without dispensation from the lord pope. But the person who conferred the order must be suspended from giving holy orders, and the person who presented you from carrying out the

tos; 14, questione 6, *Si res aliena*. Symoniacus vero ordinator, beneficiator, aut mediator suspensus est quoad se si sit occultum, et quoad alios si sit manifestum. Et idem secundum Innocencium et Hostiensem dicitur de omnibus notoriis excommunicatis, depositis, et suspensis, quia ordines et
155 huiusmodi ab illis collatis officium non habent; 1, questione 3, *Ea que*. Si layci symoniaci sint, debent excommunicari. Symoniacus autem in religione, si ipso sciente commissa est symonia, sine spe restitucionis de suo monasterio repellatur et ad perpetuam penitenciam peragendam in loco regule arcioris retrudatur. Si vero arcior regula non inveniatur, debet mutari in
160 aliud monasterium eiusdem regule mutatis prioribus locis; [f. 99] Extravagantes ut supra. Si vero ipso ignorante commissa est symonia, postquam simpliciter renunciaverit potest dicto de novo recipi; argumento Extravagantes "De electione," *Bone memorie*. Hec *Summa confessorum*, libro 1, titulo "De symonia," questione 28, pro maiori parte.
165 Circa vero dispensacionem talium est distinguendum: circa ordinem quatuor casus in quibus prohibita est dispensacio, hoc est, non consuevit papa dispensare. Et patent casus per istos versus:

Si bis ordo detur sive baptismus repetatur,
Ut evertatur fidei ordo que petatur,
170 Vel si prestetur, utrumque Symon operetur,
Ut dispensetur spes irrita prorsus habetur.

Et tamen in hiis et in omnibus aliis potest dominus papa de plenitudine potestatis dispensare, ut patet 1, questione 7, *Sabi*, et "De consecracione," distinctione 4, *Eos qui bis*. Episcopus autem potest dispensare cum
175 symoniaco in ordine, si ipso [ordinato] ignorante sit commissa symonia, et ipsi episcopo non fuerit data pecunia, set suo collaterali ipso ignorante; aliter non. Set dominus [papa]; 1, questione 1, *Erga*. Et hoc idem potest episcopus cum symoniaco in beneficio suo cui adquiritur beneficium si eo ignorante symonia commissa sit eciam ut de novo ei conferatur beneficium,
180 cui si[bi] pure ac simpliciter resignaverit; Extravagantes E, "De symonia." Set hoc intelligendum est si episcopus hoc simpliciter ignoraverit. Item cum religioso si eo ignorante commissa est symonia, potest prelatus vel capitulum dispensare, dum tamen non sint participes symonie. Et tamen credo quod circa ordines dispensare non possunt, set episcopus, ut patet 8,
185 questione 25.
Contra igitur huiusmodi symoniacos narratur quod defuncto Innocencio papa quarto quidam cardinalis dormiens sibi videbatur quod fuerat in celis coram maiestate Dei sedentis pro tribunali, a cuius dextris stabat Beata Virgo, set a sinistris stabat quedam mulier nobilissima corpore [f. 99v] et
190 habitu decentissime ornata. Que exten⟨to⟩ brachio super manum sinistram deferebat quasi templum, in cuius fronte scribebatur quasi literis aureis

function of orders, for three years; Extravagantes E, *Siquis ordinaverit.* (32)
If you hold a church living that was given or promised you at the time while
its rector was still alive. This case is placed here even though it is not
simony, because according to the doctors you are still to be deprived of that
benefice as if you were a simoniac.

Concerning the punishment for simony, one must distinguish between simony
in receiving holy orders and in receiving a benefice. If the former was the
case, the simoniac will not receive the faculties to carry out holy orders but
is *ipso iure* suspended, he himself as well as the others involved, whether the
case was secret or open, just as if he were a notorious fornicator; Extravagantes, "On simony," *Tanta,* and Distinction 32, a. 8. And similarly in 1, question 1, *Reperiuntur.* A simoniac is further punished with deposition and loss
of good name; 15, question 3, *Sane.* Nor can he get his money back—not because
the other person received it legally, but because he gave it in violation of
the moral law; 14, question 5, *Non sane.* But if simony has occurred in receiving a benefice, he is held to renounce it and return all its income; 14,
question 6, *Si res aliena.* A person who has comitted simony in ordaining,
giving a benefice, or mediating is suspended in his own person if the case was
secret, and publicly if it was open. According to Innocent and Hostiensis, the
same applies to all well-known excommunicated persons and those that have been
deposed and suspended, because their orders and whatever else of this kind they
have conferred are not valid; 1, question 3, *Ea que.* Laymen that are simoniacs
must be excommunicated. In the case of a religious person who is a simoniac,
if simony was committed with his knowledge, he must be expelled from his
monastery without hope of restitution and relegated to a place with a harsher
rule, in order to do perpetual penance. If a more demanding monastic rule is
not available, he must be transferred to another house with the same rule, away
from his original house; Extravagantes, as quoted above. But if simony was
incurred without his knowledge, after a simple renunciation he may be admitted
to his house again; see Extravagantes, "On Election," *Bone memorie.* These
cases are taken from book 1 of the *Summa confessorum,* under the title "On
Usury," question 28, for the most part.

With regard to the dispensation of such people: there are four cases
concerning holy orders in which dispensation is forbidden, that is to say, the
pope usually does not give it. They are listed in the following verses:

> If baptism is repeated, or orders giv'n twice,
> If orders are requested out of their normal line,
> If either sacrament is giv'n for money gain—
> To hope for dispensation in these is wholly vain.

And yet even in these and all other cases can the lord pope give dispensation
out of the fullness of his power, as is found in 1, question 7, *Sabi,* and in

hoc verbum "Ecclesia." Coram autem Maiestate iunctis manibus et erectis
vidit dictum papam flexis genibus petens misericordiam, non iudicium. Cui
econtra predicta mulier nobilissima ait: "Domine, iuste iudex, rectum
195   redde iudicium. Modo enim accuso eum super tribus. Primo, cum in terris
Ecclesiam fundasses ac libertatibus eam fundasti, hic vero illam propter
lucrum temporale reddit ancillam, nobilissimam vilissimam. Secundo, cum in
terra eam fundasti ad salutem peccatorum et ut lucrifaceret animas miserorum, hic vero illam symoniace vivendo fecit illam mensam nummulariorum.
200   Tercio, cum illam fundasti in fidei firmitate et iusticia et veritate, iste
fidem per gestus et mores illam fecit vacillare, iusticiam subvertit,
fidem obumbravit. Iustum igitur iudicium michi redde." Ait ergo sibi
Deus: "Vade, maledicte, in ignem eternum," etc. Cum ergo dominus cardinalis
ex terrore evigilasset, quasi extra se raptus est in tantum ut servi eius
205   furiosum ipsum estimarent. Tandem mitigato dolore ita cepit narrare et
postea vitam suam ordinavit in melius.

---

7 illius] *om* C.W.   illud] *add* illud C.   8 illa] eadem O.   15 intorsit] intersit C.W.
34 episcopo] *add* vel alicui ecclesiastico O.   39 cantet] *add* cotidie O.   faciat] faciet M;
facit R.W.   41 datur vel] *om* O.   43 Caritatis] caritas C.R.   verba] verbis C.   54 quos]
add hic O.   55–56 Flameyn] lyncolniensis C; flauyn R; flaueyn W.   58 nisi resignes] *om*
O.   60 alicui] tibi M.W; *om* R.   70 ecclesiam] *add* novam O.   77 exactione] actione
C.R.   78 generatam] geratam O.   80 compellis] compellit C.   81 etc.] ut cetera
huiusmodi O.   84 racio est] ideo C.   91 desunt] deficit O.   101–104 Vicesimus . . . lu-
cro] *items 20–21 reversed* O.   120 abbatis] abbatum O.   125 competenter] *add* non C.
135 presentatorem] presentacionem C.   142 est(2)] *om* O.   143 in(2)] *om* O.   159 re-
trudatur] detrudatur M.W; detradatur R.   167 Et . . . istos] unde M.R; *om* W.   169 Ut]
sive ut M; vel R; cum W.   190 extento] extendente C; existente R.W.   193 papam] *add*
innocencium O.   194 Domine] *om* O.   196 libertatibus] literalibus M.W (*and most other
groups except* z); lateralibus R.   202 fidem] veritatem O.   obumbravit] *add* fidem O.
igitur] ergo O.   203 etc.] *add* qui preparatus est diabolo et angelis eius O.

"On Consecration," distinction 4, *Eos qui bis.* A bishop on the other hand can give dispensation in cases of simony in the conferral of orders, if the ordained person is ignorant that simony has occurred and the bishop himself was not given any money; or if his associate received any without his knowledge; otherwise not; but the lord pope may dispense in these cases: 1, question 1, *Erga.* In the same way, the bishop can give dispensation in cases of simony in receiving a benefice. If someone has committed such simony in ignorance, the benefice may be newly bestowed on him once he has resigned it to the bishop purely and simply; Extravagantes E, "On Simony." But one must understand that this is possible only if the bishop did not know about it. In case a religious person has incurred simony without his knowledge, his prelate or chapter can give dispensation, as long as they are not involved in the same case of simony. But I believe that the latter cannot give dispensation in cases of simony in holy orders, but only the bishop, as can be seen from 8, question 25.

Against simoniacs of this kind the following story is told. After the death of Pope Innocent IV, a cardinal while asleep seemed to be in heaven before God's majesty seated in judgment, at whose right stood the Blessed Virgin, and at whose left a woman of most noble figure and most splendidly clothed. She had her arm extended and, in her left hand, carried what seemed to be a temple on whose front the word "Church" was written, as it seemed in golden letters. Before God's majesty he saw Pope Innocent on bent knees, his hands joined and held up, asking for mercy, not judgment. Against him that noble woman was saying: "My lord and just judge, render a just judgment. For I now accuse him of three things. First, while you on earth founded your Church and endowed it with liberties, this man has made her a slave for the sake of temporal profit, and has rendered the noble one most despicable. Second, while you founded her on earth for the salvation of sinners and that she might gain merit for the poor souls, this man, by living in simony, has made her a table for moneylenders. Third, while you founded her in the strength of faith, justice, and truth, this man has caused that faith to totter through his actions and behavior, has subverted justice, and has cast a shadow over truth. Therefore, render a just judgment for my sake!" And God said to him: "Go to the eternal fire, O cursed one!" As the lord cardinal started out of his sleep, he was almost out of his mind so that his servants thought he was raving. But when his grief had finally abated, he began to tell them this vision and later reformed his life.

1–10 Raymundus, I.i.1 (3–4).   4–5 *Decretals* 3.38.16 (2:614–615).   8–10 Cf. Gen. 23:4–20.   11–17 Raymundus, I.i.3 (5–6).   12–13 Acts 8:18–19.   13–14 2 Kings 5:20–27.   18–22 Raymundus, I.i.4 (6).   21–22 Gratian II.1.1.114 (1:402–403).   22–29 Cf. Raymundus, I.i.7 (8).   29–31 Raymundus, I.i.4 (6), expanded with material also found in Grosseteste and Flamborough, see below.   31–39 Raymundus, I.i.6 (7–8).

IV.ix   DE SACRILEGIO

[C]irca sacrilegium est ultimo iam sciendum quod sacrilegium est sacre
rei violacio vel eiusdem usurpacio. Et ideo sacrilegium dicitur quasi sacri
ledium, idest sacrum ledens vel sacre rei lesio. Committitur autem sacrilegium tribus modis, quia asportando et iniuste usurpando aut sacrum de
5   sacro—hoc est res sacrata, cuiusmodi sunt calices, reliquie, et huiusmodi, de
loco sacrato, sicut de ecclesia—, aut sacrum de non sacro, aut non sacrum
de sacro. Secundum tamen Raymundum sacrilegium committitur aliquando
racione persone, ut cum quis verberat clericum vel personam religiosam—
[f. 100] 27, questione 4, *Quisquis*; aliquando racione loci, quando scilicet
10   emunitas ecclesiastica aut cimiterium violatur; et aliquando racione rei,
quando scilicet sacrata vel sacro usui deputata usurpantur—27, questione
4.
Est ergo sciendum quod aliquando sacrilegium est gravius peccatum
secundum Thomam et aliquando levius, quia "tanto gravius quanto res sacra in
15   quam peccatur maiorem habet sanctitatem." Unde gravius peccat quis iurando
contra personam sacram quam contra locum sacrum, quia sanctitas loci ordi-

40–51 Raymundus, I.i.5 (6–7).   **42** Gratian II.1.1.101 (1:394–395).   **43–45** Gratian II.12.2.45 (1:702).   **48** *Decretals* 5.3.10 (2:751) and 2.26.16 (2:388).   **51** *Decretals* 5.3.28 (2:758–759).   **52–141** The thirty-one cases that follow combine material from Grosseteste with material from Raymundus. For Grosseteste, see the edition of *Templum Dei* by Joseph Goering and Frank Mantello (Toronto, 1984), pp. 53–54. The sources are as follows: *FM* 1=G[rosseteste] 1; 2=G.2; 3=G.3; 4=G.4; 5=G.5; 6=G.7; 7=G.19; 8=G.10; 9=G.11; 10=G.15; 11=G.8; 12=?; 13=G.12; 14=G.13; 15=G.14 (with addition); 16=Raymundus, I.i.17 (19); 17=Raymundus, ibid.; 18=G.16; 19=G.18; 20=G.22; 21=G.23; 22=G.21 (with addition); 23=G.17; 24=G.20 (with addition); 25=Raymundus, I.i.16 (18); 26=Raymundus, ibid.; 27=Raymundus, I.iii.2 (30), and end of 3 (31); 28=Raymundus, I.iii.2 (30); 29=Raymundus, I.iii.4 (31); 30=Raymund, Raymundus, I.i.16 (18b); 31=?; 32=G.9.   **76** *Decretals* 5.3.39 (2:765).   **92–93** Perhaps Gratian II.1.1.23 (1:367–368); and *Decretals* 5.4 (2:767–768).   **101** Gratian II.1.3.8 (1:413–415).   **112** Gratian II.14.5.15 (1:742).   **115** Gratian II.1.3.8 (1:413–415).   **133** *Decretals* 5.3.14 (2:753).   **138** *Decretals* 5.3.45 (767).   **142–153** Raymundus, I.i.9 (9–10).   **145–146** Apparently, the first reference is to *Tanta* in *Decretals* 5.2.7 (2:750); the second, to Gratian I.32, pars iii (1:118–119).   **146–147** Gratian II.1.1.7 (1:359).   **147** Gratian II.15.3.4 (1:752).   **149** Gratian II.14.5.15 (1:742).   **151** Gratian II.14.6.1 (1:742–743).   **153–155** Hostiensis, *Summa aurea*, V, "De simonia," 10 (1500).   **155** Gratian II.1.3.5 (1:412).   **155–163** Raymundus, I.i.14 (14–15).   **162–163** *Decretals* 1.6.23 (2:66–68).   **163–64** John of Freiburg, *Summa confessorum* I.i ("De simonia").21–27.   **165–177** Raymundus, I.i.11 (12).   **173** I.e., *Saluberrimum*, Gratian II.1.7.21 (1:435).   **173–174** "De consecratione": Gratian III.4.118 (1:1398).   **177** Gratian II.1.1.110 (1:410).   **177–181** Raymundus, I.i.13 (13).   **180** *Decretals* 2.1.4 (2:240).   **181–185** Raymundus, I.i.14 (15).   **184–185** Reference unclear; see Raymundus I.i.12 (12–13).   **186–206** Cf. Tubach 4118. From Matthew of Paris, *Chronica majora*, ed. H. R. Luard, Rolls Series 57 (London: 1872–1883), 5:472.

IV.ix   SACRILEGE

Now, in the last place, with respect to sacrilege we must know that this is a violation or usurpation of a sacred object. Therefore *sacrilege* has its name from *sacri laedium*, that is, "hurting something sacred" or a deliberate harm done to a sacred object. Sacrilege is committed in three ways, by carrying off or unjustly usurping either something sacred from something sacred— that is to say, a sacred object, say a consecrated chalice, relics, or the like, from a consecrated place, say a church—, or something sacred from something nonsacred, or something nonsacred from something sacred. According to Raymundus, however, sacrilege is committed: sometimes with respect to a person, as when one strikes a cleric or a religious person—27, question 4, *Quisquis*; sometimes with respect to a place, as when the sanctity of a church or churchyard is violated; and sometimes with respect to an object, as when a consecrated object or one destined for sacred use is disappropriated—27, question 4.

One must further know that according to Thomas sacrilege is sometimes a grievous sin, sometimes a light one; its seriousness increases with the degree of sanctity the object has which is the occasion of the sin. Thus, cursing a

natur a sanctitate hominis. Et ideo gravissimum sacrilegium est quod committitur contra sacramentum eucaristie, quia illud continet ipsum Deum. Et
sic descendendo secundum dignitatem et sanctitatem personarum et aliarum
20   rerum sacrarum.

Unde sciendum secundum canones quod sacrilegii duplex est pena: alia
spiritualis, cuiusmodi est excommunicacio maior vel minor secundum quantitatem culpe, ut dictum est; alia pecuniaria. Que quidem pena qualis et
quanta sit et cui solvenda sit, tamquam pro sacrilegio commisso in personam
25   sacram quam in rebus sacris, habetur ubi supra, 27, questione 4, *Quisquis*,
et similiter *Si quis contumax*, et *Quisquis inventus*, et *Si quis deinceps*.

Unde contra huiusmodi sacrilegos Ecclesie [et] eius membris et ministris insidiatores narratur de quodam principe magno qui non tantum in
proximis pauperibus dum adhuc viveret ultra modum sevit, verum eciam super
30   omnia in Ecclesia Dei et eius servitoribus. Unde ipso mortuo quidam clericus in curia sua nutritus et per eum promotus vehementer de illo sollicita-
batur qui sic crudeliter vixerat, utrum dampnatus a⟨ut⟩ salvatus esset.
Accidit ergo quadam die dum ipse cum aliis per quoddam nemus transivit, in
quo dictus princeps venari consueverat, et dum sic cogitabat sollicite de
35   illo, ecce nubes densa super eos [venit], in qua densitate ipse a sociis
divisus est. Cum ergo socius quasi vagabundus deviaret, [f. 100v] habuit
obviam quendam sessorem in equo magno et nigro, qui dixit ei: "Si, inquit,
vis scire que desideras, cito ⟨de equo tuo descende et meum⟩ ascende,
qu⟨i⟩ ad hostium cuiusdam aule satis secure portabit te. Ubi cum veneris,
40   descende et talem cameram intra, et ibi videbis quod optas. Set si vis cum
vita evadere, statim ut audieris istius equi hinnitum et cornu sonitum,
ascende equum et fuge periculum." Et fecit omnia que preceperat. Cum ergo
dictam cameram intrasset, ibi vidit cathedram ignitam positam, in quam
imposuerunt duo demones miserum hominem omnibus doloribus agitatum, in
45   cuius capite posuerunt coronam ignitam. Quo facto intravit magnus cervus
cum cornibus acutissimis et a cathedra ipsum inpetuose proiciens cum cornibus totum corpus eius dilacerabat, et recessit. Set ipse per illos in
cathedra restitutus resedit. Et ecce, duo leporarii terribiles et nigri
venientes illum a cathedra iterum retraxerunt et mirabiliter laceraverunt.
50   Quibus egressis iterum in cathedra restituitur. Intravit ergo quidam iuvenis cum gladio evaginato acutissimo, et illum per coronam capitis de cathedra prostravit ad terram et gladium in corona usque ad cerebrum infixit, et
postmodum quasi radendo ipsam totaliter amputavit. Et cum ad pedes suos
ill⟨am⟩ proiecisset, statim festinus exivit. Cum ergo iterum in cathedra
55   fuerat miser iste positus, clericum respiciens dixit ei: "Ego, inquit, sum
ille quem tu queris." Sciscitante ergo clerico quid essent que vidit sic
ipsum cruciantem, respondit: "Corona, inquit, ignita quam sic in capite
gero plus ponderat de pena quam tota terra mundana. Et quia semper Ecclesi-

sacred person is more serious than cursing a sacred place, for a place derives
its sanctity from that of a person. Hence, the most grievous sacrilege is that
committed against the sacrament of the Eucharist, because it contains God
himself. And thus one can make a scale according to the dignity and sanctity
of persons and of other sacred objects.

Whence it must be known that according to canon law the penalty for
sacrilege is twofold: one is spiritual, such as the greater or lesser excommunication, according to the degree of guilt, as has been said; the other is
monetary. What kind and how much the penalty should be, and to whom it is to
be paid, whether for a sacrilege committed against a sacred person or against
sacred objects, can be found as indicated above in 27, question 4, *Quisquis*,
and similarly in the canons *Si quis contumax*, *Quisquis inventus*, and *Si quis
deinceps*.

To warn people who in this way sacrilegiously offend the Church and harm
its members and ministers, a story is reported about a great prince who, during
his life, not only raved against his poor neighbors but also, and especially
so, against God's Church and her servants. After his death a cleric that had
been brought up in his court and had been advanced by him, worried passionately
if the prince, who had led such a cruel life, was damned or saved. One day he
and others happened to pass through a forest in which his prince had used to
hunt, and as he was thinking of him with great concern, a thick cloud came over
them, in which he got separated from his companions. As he was wandering about
like a lost wayfarer, a rider on a large black horse came toward him and said:
"If you want to know what you desire, get off your horse quickly and climb on
mine, which will safely carry you to the door of some hall. When you get
there, dismount and enter that chamber, and you shall see what you desire. But
if you want to escape with your life, as soon as you hear this horse neigh and
a horn blow, get on the horse and flee from that danger." He did all as he had
been commanded. When he then entered the chamber, he saw a burning chair set
up, on which two devils put a wretched man who was tormented by all kinds of
pain and put a fiery crown on his head. When this was done, a large stag with
very sharp antlers entered, flung the man fiercely from the chair, and gashed
his whole body with his antlers. Then he disappeared. But the man was set
back into the chair by the two devils. And behold, two horrible black hunting
dogs came and pulled him again from his chair and tore him into many pieces.
When they had gone, he was once more placed on the chair. Then a young man
entered with a sharp sword drawn, pulled him by his hair from the chair, and
sank his sword into the top of his head to the brain, and then with a motion as
if he were shaving him cut off the top of his head completely. And after he
had flung the top at his feet, he quickly left at once. When the wretched man
was once again on his chair, he looked at the cleric and said: "I am the one
you are looking for." As the cleric wanted to know what those things were he

am Dei et clerum in odi⟨o⟩ habui, et ipsam toto conamine [f. 101] servum
60   feci et destruxi et coronam cuiusdam clerici quasi radendo contemptibiliter
amputavi, ideo coronatus sic in capite tantam sustineo penam. Similiter
quia aliquando in isto nemore in venacione fui, duos homines suspendi feci,
quia ultra voluntatem meam duos detinuerunt leporarios, ideo ab illis bis
in die torqueor. Quia eciam propter delectacionem venacionis missam et
65   officium divinum contempsi et omisi, ideo cervus iste in toto corpore sic
me lacerat et affligit. In quibus ergo delectacionem habui maiorem, merito
in hiis sic afflictus crucior." Et hiis dictis, audivit clericus equi
hinnitum et cornu sonitum, et statim equum ascendit et vix evasit. Nam ipso
velocius fugiente audivit demonum tumultus terribiles ipsum a tergo inse-
70   quentes. Filia autem predicti principis ista narravit cuidam religioso,
quorum nomina utilius credo tacere quam in palam exprimere, etc.

23 quidem] quedam O. 32 aut] an C. 37 obviam] obvium O. 38 de . . . meum]
super equum istum mecum C. 39 qui] quia C. 54 illam] illud C. 55 positus] *om* O.
59 odio] odium C. 67 audivit] *add* ipse O. 71 etc.] *om* O.

IV.x   QUARE AVARICIA CONTEMPNANDA EST

[O]stensis igitur avaricie proprietatibus et membris, restat modo
quarto videre quam iuste est contempnenda et quare. Et certe primo dico
quia voluntati divine et eius mandatis in omnibus contrariatur. Si enim
loquamur de primo Dei precepto, quod est istud: "Honora Deum tuum," scili-
5   cet per decimas, oblaciones, et primicias, et cetera huiusmodi, certum est
quod omnia tollit avaricia et per illam contrariatur. S⟨i⟩ de secundo, quod
est: "Sabbatum serva," videmus quomodo avarus propter lucrum temporale
violare illud non veretur. Tunc enim circuit de loco ad locum, de nundinis
ad nundinas cum mercimoniis suis. Si de tercio, quod est: "Honora patrem,"
10   quod facere tenemur non tantum in spiritualibus, verum eciam in temporalibus—set contra hoc vadit directe avaricia—, videmus quod propter hereditatem filius optat mortem patris, et [f. 101v] propter iocalia filia mortem
matris, et cetera huiusmodi. Si autem de quarto loquamur, scilicet "Non
accipies nomen Dei in vanum," patet quomodo avaricia ibi contrariatur in

had seen tormenting him thus, he replied: "The fiery crown which I wear on my
head is heavier in its pain than all this earth. And because I always hated
God's Church and the clergy, and oppressed and destroyed it as much as I could,
and because I once cut off the crown of a cleric in contempt as if I were
tonsuring him, I now suffer this punishment by being thus crowned in my head.
Likewise, once when I went hunting in this forest, I had two men hanged for
keeping two hounds against my will; for that I am now tortured by them in this
way twice daily. And because I scorned Mass and the divine office and failed
to attend because I loved hunting more, that stag now gashes and punishes me
thus in my whole body. In the things I delighted in most, I am now justly
tormented and punished." And when he had said this much, the cleric heard the
horse neigh and a horn blow, and he mounted the horse at once and hardly
escaped with his life, for as he was quickly flying away, he heard a terrible
tumult of demons following him from behind. The daughter of this said prince
told this story to a religious, whose names, however, I think it more helpful
to pass in silence than to mention openly.

1–3 Raymundus, I.xiii.1 (115).   7–12 Ibid., 2 (115).   9 Gratian II.17.4.21 (1:820).
11–12 Ibidem.   14–15 Thomas Aquinas, *Summa theologiae*, 2a–2ae, qu. 99, art. 3,
resp.   21–26 Raymundus, I.xiii.3 (115–116).   25–26 Gratian II.17.4.21–22 (1:820).
The first allegation should be II.17.4.7 (816).   28–71 Tubach 2621 (unique). Also in: MS
Royal 7.D.i, fol. 137v (wrongly analyzed as Tubach 2517); Bromyard, "Rapina," R.I.31;
MS Lambeth Palace 78, fol. 284–284v (probably copied from *FM*); *Speculum exemplorum* IX.206; Johannes Major, *Magnum speculum exemplorum*, "Paupertas," ex. 5
(p. 572).

IV.x   WHY AVARICE SHOULD BE SCORNED

After we have shown the qualities and members of avarice, it remains now,
in the fourth place, to see how this sin deserves to be scorned and why. Certainly, in the first place I say because it opposes in every respect God's will
and his commandments. For if we speak of God's first commandment, which is,
"Honor your God," namely with tithes, offerings, first fruits, and the like, it
is certain that avarice takes all these away and opposes them. If we speak of
the second, which is, "Observe the Sabbath," we see that an avaricious person
is not ashamed of violating it for the sake of temporal profit. For on that
day he goes from place to place, from market to market, with his wares. If we
speak of the third, which is, "Honor your father," which we are held to do not
only in spiritual but also in temporal matters, avarice goes directly against
it, too. We see that a son wishes his father dead on account of the inheritance, and a daughter wishes her mother dead for her jewelry, and so forth.
But if we speak of the fourth commandment, "You shall not take the name of

15 falsis assisoribus, causidicis, mercatoribus, quia tota die propter lucrum
temporale non tantum iurant imo horribiliter se periurant. Si de quinto,
quod est: "Non furtum facies," videmus quod tota die avari proximos spoliant et bona illorum furtive rapiunt. Si de sexto, quod est: "Non dices
falsum testimonium," satis patet quomodo contra illud similiter faciunt
20 isti causidici et advocati et cetera huiusmodi propter lucrum temporale. Si
de septimo, quod est: "Non occides," patet quod propter avariciam suscitantur tot pugne, tot bella, tot strages et homicidia, et quasi non pro alia
re nisi tantum pro mundi avaricia et cupiditate. Si de octavo, quod est:
"Non concupisces rem proximi tui," patet quomodo illi contrariatur avarus
25 eo quod hoc modo bona proximi concupiscit iuxta proprietatem quod omnia
cupit et numquam refundere vellet. Si de nono et decimo, que sunt: "Non
mechaberis, nec concupisces uxorem proximi tui," patet satis quod hoc
faciunt et ut frequenter plus propter bona illa[rum] quam propter amorem
quem habent ad corpora.
30   Et bene de talibus adduci potest illud Apocalipsis 13: "Et vidi de
mari," ait Iohannes, "bestiam ascendentem habentem septem capita et cornua
decem, et hec bestia similis erat pardo et pedes sicut ursi et os eius
sicut leonis." Revera, spiritualiter loquendo per istam bestiam bene intelligitur avaricia, cuius capita sunt rapina in magnatibus, furtum in latro-
35 nibus, usura in simplicibus, dolus in mercimoniis, infidelitas in artifi-
ciis, falsitas in iudiciis, symonia in ecclesiasticis. Set mare dicitur
mundus propter alia septem, videlicet propter laboris inquietu- [f. 102]
dinem, periculorum frequenciam, tribulacionum multitudinem, tumultus inquietudinem, corporum mortuorum eiectionem, tempestatum suscitacionem,
40 minorum a maioribus devoracionem. Versus:

> Bestia vasta maris istis septem capitaris:
> Fur, rapit, usura, mercandi noxia cura,
> Fraus in reddendis, t⟨itulus⟩ malus in repetendis,
> Et questus cleri turpis sub nomine veri.

45 In istis autem versibus aperte patent septem capita avaricie, cuius decem
cornua bene dici possunt decem predicte contrarietates decalogi. Se⟨quitur⟩
ergo: "Hec bestia similis erat pardo," propter pellis varietatem. Nam
pellis avari est varia mundi fortuna, sicut per rotam Fortune superius,
capitulo 2. Et hec bestia, scilicet avaricia, habuit "pedes ursi," scilicet
50 propter studiosam rapiendi calliditatem. Pedes enim ursi habent figuram
pedis hominis, scilicet animalis racionalis. Unde hec bestia cupiditatis et
avaricie facit studiose inquirere, racionari, et investigare quomodo bona
proximi possit rapere et inquirere et ad hoc ut videtur ponitur illorum
totus mentis effectus et affectus, quasi sunt duo pedes animalis raciona-
55 lis. Et aliquando huiusmodi perquirit fraudulenter et aliquando violenter

your God in vain," it is clear how avarice goes against it in false assessors, lawyers, and merchants, who for temporal profit not only swear but indeed forswear themselves horribly all day long. If we speak of the fifth, "You shall not steal," we see that the avaricious despoil the poor all day long and rob their goods like thieves. If of the sixth, which is, "You shall not give false witness," it is clear enough how lawyers and advocates and others like them similarly act against it for temporal profit. If of the seventh, which is, "You shall not kill," it is clearly because of avarice that so many fights, wars, slaughters, and killings arise, and hardly for any other reason than worldly avarice and covetousness. If we speak of the eighth commandment, which is, "You shall not covet your neighbor's good," it is clear that the avaricious person goes against it because he covets his neighbor's belongings in such a way that he covets them all and never wants to give any back. And if we speak of the ninth and tenth commandments, which are, "You shall not commit adultery, nor covet your neighbor's wife," it is obvious that avaricious people do precisely that, and often more for the wives' property than out of love for their bodies.

To such people may well be applied the words of Revelation 13: "And I saw," John says, "a beast coming up out of the sea, having seven heads and ten horns; and the beast was like a leopard, and its feet like the feet of a bear, and its mouth like that of a lion." Spiritually interpreted this beast signifies avarice, whose heads are oppression in overlords, theft in robbers, usury in the simple, trickery in commerce, unreliability in crafts, falsehood in lawsuits, and simony in churchmen. But the sea stands for the world, because of another seven properties, namely: the restlessness of hard work, the frequency of dangers, the multitude of tribulations, the unquiet of heavy motion, the ejection of dead bodies, the rising of tempests, and the devouring of the small fish by the big. In verse:

> The great beast from the sea you notice by these seven:
> Theft and oppression, usury, the harmful care in trading,
> Deceit in paying off, bad justice to make gains,
> The clergy's shameful greed, made to look like the truth.

These verses clearly list the seven heads of avarice, whose ten horns can be said to be the ten aforementioned opposites to the Ten Commandments. Scripture then continues: "This beast was like a leopard," because of its mottled hide. For the hide of an avaricious person is the mottled fortune of the world, symbolized by the wheel as we saw earlier, in chapter 2. And this beast, avarice, had the "the feet of a bear," namely on account of its eager shrewdness in grasping. For the feet of a bear look like human feet, that is, of a rational animal. Therefore, this beast of covetousness and avarice causes man eagerly to search, to reason, and to investigate how he can grasp and go after his

per potestatem. Et ideo habet "os leonis," idest os imperiale, lacerans et
devorans pauperes et per potenciam illos opprimens. Habet eciam bestia
ista potestatem diaboli ad faciendum virtutes et mirabilia, quia nichil
⟨cogitabile⟩ invenitur quin potest pecunia facere. Unde Oracius:

60   Et genus et formam regina peccunia domat.

Et ideo dicit Augustinus quod aliqui vocaverunt peccuniam deum Iovem, quia
sub eius ut fingunt potestate omnia sunt, libro 7 *De civitate*, capitulo
18.
    Et nota quod ita est de avaricia sicut de leone. Si enim offeras leoni her-
65 bam virentem [f. 102v] aut campum florentem, non tamen propter hoc illum
excitabis in concupiscenciam illorum, quia in natura non habet ut herbas
comedat. Set si ostendas ei carnes bovinas crudas, placet. Revera sic hic.
Si enim avaro de celesti dulcedine loquaris, ad eius concupiscenciam non
penitus excitatur. Si vero de temporalibus loquaris, mox applicat aurem et
70 multum delectatur.
    Secundo avaricia est contempnenda quia in omni parte sui deceptibilis
invenitur. Unde similis potest dici illis qui ludunt cum coreis in digitis.
Tales autem ubicumque ponunt digitum, credunt esse intra et tamen in fine
est extra. Sic avari, quanto magis mundo adherent, tanto mundana cicius
75 amittunt. Et ideo quamvis talibus dicitur illud Luce 12: "O anima, habes
multa bona, requiesce, comede," respondet tamen Psalmista dicens: "Relin-
quent alienis divicias suas, quia sepulcra eorum domus eorum in eternum."
Et huiusmodi temporalia bene assimilantur fluvio hyemali, qui quamvis
veniat cum impetu, [cito] tamen disparet. Et postquam transierit aqua
80 clara, tantum lutum horridum remanet. Sic temporalia quamvis fluunt in
principio habundanter, cito tamen defluunt. Que cum transierint delectacio
in illis prius habita, relinquitur tamen possessori culpa cum pena. Et ideo
tales similes sunt molendinariis, qui obstruunt aqua⟨s⟩ donec non poterunt
illas sustinere, set post propter superfluitatem oportet quod deriventur
85 velint nolint ad usus aliorum. Sic qui congregat divicias. Unde versus:

          Sic vos non vobis vellera fertis, oves;
          Sic vos non vobis nidificatis, aves;
          Sic vos non vobis mellificatis, apes.

Et nota quod est de mundo et avaro sicut de uno puero ludente cum
90 alio, quorum unus pomum alterius apprehendens in foveam [f. 103] cadit et
alius quasi dolens se fingit flere. Volens ergo ipsum iuvare et de luto
elevare, manum arripit cum pomo et illud sibi rapit. Quo habito socium
retrocadere permittit et ipsum deridendo aufugit. Revera sic avari temporalia colligendo adinvicem se associant et mutuo accipiunt et expendunt.

neighbor's goods; and he puts the entire longing and thought of his mind to
that purpose, which are, as it were, the two feet of his rationality. Thus he
seeks to make a profit, sometimes with fraud and sometimes with power and violence. And therefore he has "the mouth of a lion," the mouth of a royal animal, which tears to pieces and devours the poor and oppresses them with his
might. This beast further has power from the devil to work signs and wonders,
for there is nothing imaginable which money cannot do. Whence Horace says:

> Queen Cash with power rules both birth and beauty.

And in book 7, chapter 18, of *The City of God* Augustine reports that for that
reason some people called money the god Jupiter because, as they imagine, all
things are under his power.

And notice that avarice acts like a lion. If you offer a lion green grass
or a flowering field, you will not arouse in him any desire for these, because
it is not in his nature to eat herbs. But if you show him raw beef, that
pleases him. The same holds true here. If you talk to an avaricious person of
the sweetness of heaven, he will not get excited about that. But if you speak
of temporal gains, he soon lends you his ear and takes great delight.

Avarice must be scorned, secondly, because it is found to be deceitful in
every part of its being. Therefore it can be considered similar to those who
play with strings in their fingers. Wherever they put their finger, they think
it is in, and yet in the end it is out. This applies to avaricious people as well:
the more they cling to the world, the sooner they lose worldly goods. Thus,
though the words of Luke 12 are said to them: "O my soul, you have many
things, rest and eat," yet the Psalmist answers with: "They shall leave their
riches to strangers, for their sepulchers shall be their houses forever." Such
temporal goods can well be likened to a winter flood: though it comes with a
great rush, it yet disappears quickly, and when the clear water is gone, only
dirty mud remains. In the same way, although worldly goods flow abundantly
in the beginning, they soon ebb; and once the joy in having them that one first
experienced is gone, only guilt and punishment are left to their owner. Therefore such people are like millers: they dam up the water till they can no
longer hold it, but then when it overflows they have to let it go, willy-nilly,
for use by others. Thus it happens to people who gather riches. Hence the
verses:

> You sheep give wool, but not for yourselves.
> You birds build nests, but not for yourselves.
> You bees make honey, but not for yourselves.

Notice that the world deals with an avaricious person just as a boy does
who plays with another. One of them catches an apple from the other but falls

95 Set cum alter per mortem in foveam cadit, statim iuxta Psalmistam "diripi-
unt alieni labores suos." Set cum acceperint quod optaverunt, gaudentes
rem⟨e⟩ant et luctum quem pro morte finxerunt in gaudium convertunt; Ecclesiastici 12: "In oculis tuis lacrimabitur inimicus." Unde Ier⟨emie 9⟩:
"Unusquisque a proximo suo se custodiat, et in omni fratre non habeat
100 fiduciam, quia omnis amicus fraudulenter incedit, et vir fratrem suum
deridebit." Hec ille.
    Et ideo mundus facit sicut faber qui ferrum fere ignitum in vico
proicit, ut equitantes descendere faciat, per quod manus suas comburunt et
fedant. Et tamen illud amittunt pro quo descenderunt. Sic mundus proicit
105 temporalia ut capientes decipiat; Ysaie 30: "Ambulatis ut descendatis in
Egiptum." Et ideo de illis est sicut de columba qui ibi nidificat ubi
sepius pullos suos amittit; Osee: "Effraym quasi columba seducta."
    Tercio est mundi avaricia detestanda quia suos per omnia deturpat,
fedat, et inficit. Unde fertur quod quidam correptus a quodam sancto quod
110 mundi feditatem relinqueret et vite puritati se daret, qui [super] hoc
admirans respondit dicens:

        Mundus non mundat set mundus polluit omnes.
        Qui manet in mundo, quomodo mundus erit?

[Anglice sic:

115   þis worlde fyle ys and clansyt lyte.
        Of fylþe þerinne who may be quyte?]

quasi diceret: Ex quo Deus ipse mundum detestatur et tamen sine mundo
vivere non possumus, non mirum ergo cum omnia in illo sordescunt. S⟨et⟩
ego vivo in mund⟨o⟩. Quid ergo faciam? Qui respondit:

120   Nec Deus odit opes nec detestatur habentes, [f. 103v]
        Set qui divicias preposuere Deo.

[Anglice sic:

        The ryche ne rychesse God ne hatyth,
        But who-so for rychesse God forsakyth.]

125 Exemplum ad hoc: Videmus quod pueri qui gardinum alterius aut ortum
[furtive] intraverunt poma auferre, quod adinvicem decertant quis eorum
posset maiorem congeriem coadunare et in sinu abscondere; quorum alii socii
minus potentes exterius stant et clamant partem rogantes, set ipsi interius
hoc audire dissimulant, quia omnia soli vellent auferre. Set quid accidit?
130 Revera cum in capucio, sinu, et gremio undique fuerunt onerati et ianuam

into a ditch. The other pretends to weep in grief and then feigns wanting to
help him and pull him out of the mud; but as he grabs the hand that holds the
apple, he takes the apple away from him, lets his playmate fall back, and runs
away with laughter. In the same way, avaricious people group together in order
to gather worldly goods and take and spend them with each other. But when one
of them falls into the ditch through death, right away as the Psalmist says,
"strangers plunder his labors." And when they have obtained what they wanted,
they return happy and change the sorrow they feigned over his death into joy;
Ecclesiasticus 12: "An enemy weeps tears." Therefore Jeremiah 9: "Let everyone guard himself against his neighbor, and let him not trust in any brother of
his, for every friend walks deceitfully, and a man will mock his brother."

Thus the world does like a blacksmith who throws an almost glowing-hot
horseshoe in the road and thereby causes riders to dismount, so that they burn
and dirty their hands. And still they lose that for which they have dis-
mounted. In the same way, the world throws temporal goods in order to deceive
those who catch them; Isaiah 30: "You walk to go down into Egypt." They are
thus like the dove, who builds her nest where she frequently loses her young;
Hosea: "Ephraim is like a dove that has been deceived."

In the third place, the avarice of the world deserves our contempt because
it defiles, dirties, and poisons its followers in every way. There is a story
of someone who was admonished by a saint to leave the dirty world and give
himself to a pure life. He wondered about that and said:

> The world makes no one clean but rather stains us all.
> How then will he be clean who stays on in this world?

In English:

> þis world . . .

as if he were saying: "Since God himself despises this world, and yet we
cannot live without it, it is no wonder that all things in the world make us
dirty. But I live in the world. What then shall I do?" And the saint answered:

> Neither does God hate riches nor scorn those who possess them.
> But he hates those who put their riches before him.

In English:

> The ryche . . .

To give an example: We see that boys who have stolen into someone's garden
or orchard to carry off his apples vie with each other as to which of them can

exire proponunt, astat ibi ianitor contra illos paratus et eos de omnibus
collectis spoliat, verberat, et nudos tam pomis quam pannis ululantes et
flentes abire permittit. Spiritualiter autem illud gardinum sive ortum hic
mundus est, qui repletur pomis, ⟨idest⟩ bonis temporalibus; quem furtive
135   ingrediuntur avari, ut secundum posse eum spoliant. Et ideo inter [eos]
decertacio maxima est quis eorum maiorem numerum diviciarum colligere
posset et secum asportare. Extra vero stant pauperes ad ingrediendum, hoc
est ad huiusmodi lucrandum, inpotentes; partem et auxilium ab illis petunt,
set nichil optinent. Cum ergo isti undique onerati ex bonis temporalibus—
140   quia in domibus [et] cameris, silvis et pratis, cistis et loculis—exire
proponunt, ianitor, [idest] mors que nulli parcit, stat promptus illos
expectan⟨s⟩. Qui cum venerint credentes libere exire, statim eos spoliat
de omnibus que coll⟨e⟩gerunt. Unde eiulantes compelluntur abire. Si ergo,
dum interius in dicto gardino [fuerint], aliquid boni pauperibus fuerint
145   elargiti, revera tunc inde participare possunt cum gaudio sempiterno. Sin
autem, vacui a merito recedent ad penam cum dolore.

Consimile exemplum eciam ponit Anselmus *De similitudinibus*, de pueris
papiliones insequentibus quia sunt diversi coloris, puta aurei, argentei,
virides, et huiusmodi, et putant se rem preciosissimam apprehendere. [f.
150   104] Currentes ergo post illas nec ad pedes considerantes, pedes et tibias
cespitando ut communiter ledunt. Si vero ipsas apprehenderint, manus aperiunt et non habent nisi vermem mortuam cum fractis alis et manus vilissime
interius fedatas. Revera sic avari talem prosperitatem in auro et argento
et ceteris bonis videntes ipsa⟨m⟩ circumquaque per mundi partes insequun-
155   tur ut possideant, et hoc "per pericula fluminum, pericula latronum, pericula falsorum [fratrum]." Inter que cespitantes vulnerantur, mutilantur,
occiduntur, ut illam optineant. Que cum apprehenderint, morte superveniente-
te aperiunt manus consciencie et nichil ibi inveniunt nisi vermes consciencie, que nunquam morientur, excussis alis bonorum temporalium et aliis
160   necessario relictis. Unde Proverbiis dicitur: "Qui amat divicias, fructum
non capiet ex illis."

Unde pro omnibus istis predictis de mundi falsitate, quare iuste
detestatur, narratur in *Speculo historiali* quod in quadam civitate regionis
Romane erat talis lex edita quod quamvis aliquis pro culpa iudicialiter
165   esset dampnatus, si tamen talem amicum invenire posset qui cum eo locum
carceris seu aulam iudicis vellet intrare coram iudice et sufficienter
respondere pro tali dampnato, quod talis amicus reum illum propter suam
fidelitatem a morte salvaret. Contigit ergo ibidem quendam reum sic dampna-
tum tres habere amicos, quorum unum dilexit plus quam seipsum, alium sicut
170   seipsum, et tercium minus quam seipsum. Volens ergo istos in sua necessitate probare, accessit ad primum auxilium petens. Cui ille: "Fatue, inquit,
fecisti plus diligendo me quam teipsum. Nolo tamen me pro te ° tanto

gather and hide the most in his shirt. Some companions of theirs who are less strong stand outside and claim their share, but those inside pretend they do not hear them, for they want to carry off all for themselves. But what happens? Well, when they have filled up their hoods and shirts and pants and want to slip out at the gate, the gatekeeper stands there ready for them and takes all their gatherings from them, gives them a beating, and at last lets them get away without apples and clothes, howling and crying. Spiritually interpreted, this garden or orchard is this world, full of apples, that is, temporal goods, into which avaricious men steal to carry off as much as they can. And among them is the greatest rivalry as to which of them can grasp and carry with him the greatest amount of riches. Outside stand the poor, that is, those who are too feeble to enter, that is, to make a profit in this way; they ask for a share and for help from the others but get nothing. When these finally want to come out, loaded down with their temporal goods—that is, with houses and chambers, fields and forests, chests and purses—, the gatekeeper, that is Death, who spares no one, stands ready and waits for them. They think they can get by free, but he robs them of all they have gathered, and they are forced to go away howling. If, however, they have given some good to the poor while they were in that garden, then indeed they can keep it with everlasting joy. But if not, they will, devoid of any merit, go with grief to their punishment.

Anselm in his *Similitudes* gives a similar example of boys who chase after butterflies because these are of different colors, namely golden, silver, green, and so forth, and they believe they catch a most precious object. So they run after them and pay no heed to where they go, and stumble and often hurt their feet and legs. But when they have caught a butterfly, they open their hands and find but a dead worm with its wings crushed, and their palms awfully dirty. In the same way, avaricious men see great prosperity in gold and silver and other goods and chase after it through all the parts of the world to possess it, "through dangers in rivers, dangers from thieves, and dangers from false brethren." In these they stumble and are hurt, lose their limbs, and get killed, just in order to gain prosperity. But when they have acquired it, death comes upon them. Then they open the hands of their conscience and find nothing there but the worms of conscience which will never die, with the wings of worldly goods crushed and everything else by force left behind. Whence it is said in Proverbs: "He who loves riches will reap no fruit from them."

All these matters about the falseness of the world and why it is justly scorned are reflected in a story from the *Mirror of History*. In a city of the Roman region a law had been given that, although someone was legally condemned for his crime, if he could find a friend who was willing to go with him to jail or to the judge's hall before the judge and could answer sufficiently for the condemned man, then this friend would save the guilty man from death because of

periculo exponere. Set tantum tibi faciam: Hanc enim robam tibi dabo cum
qua teipsum cooperias et si potes defendas, et de cetero [f. 104v] discas
175   caucius negociari." Hiis dictis processit miser ille dolens et tristis ad
secundum amicum, quem sicut seipsum dilexerat, auxilium petens ab eo. Qui
breviter respondit quod hoc facere non potuit, set tantum pro eo faceret
quod ad locum iudicii secum iret, set nullo modo intraret, quia non audebat
propter horrorem. Quo audito ad tercium amicum accessit, quem minus dilexe-
180   rat, et illum solum amicum verum invenit. Nam ipse eum a morte coram iudice
liberavit.
        Spiritualiter autem loquendo, quotquot nascuntur in presenti habent
timere futurum Dei iudicium et sibi fideles amicos procurare ante tempus
mortis, quibus si necesse fuerit coram celesti iudice defendi valeant et
185   salvari. Set multi habent amicos similes predictis tribus, scilicet mundum,
parentes, et bona opera. Nam aliqui diligunt mundum plus quam se quando pro
seipsis, ut gloriam acquirant, nichil sustinere possunt, set pro mundo
cotidie quasi se exponere periculis diversis non verentur, nec aliquando
morti; qui tamen in extrema necessitate, quando ad tumulum ire secundum
190   cursum nature ° oportet, in nullo iuvabit, set omnino deficiet, excepto
quod robam parvi precii sibi concedit, quia vix cilicium aut linthiamen
antiquum laceratum et vile in quo sepeliendus poterit involvi. Secundo,
aliqui parentes sicut seipsos diligunt, sicut vir uxorem, et e contrario,
ut iustum est et natura docet. Set certe hoc non obstante nec illi quantum
195   possent pro deliberacione sui in necessitate extrema volunt laborare, set
vix tempore mortis ad locum sepulture quem evadere non po⟨ssun⟩t eiulando
et in oculis hominum quasi seipsos lacerando sequuntur, ubi sepulto corpore
dolor mitigatur, et sic domum sine lacrimis [festinant] indilate, nec
mortuum deplorant de cetero, set seipsos, dicentes: "Heu, heu, [f. 105]
200   iam sustentacionem perdidimus. Quid ergo faciemus?" Et non dicunt: "A,
Domine, quomodo possum animam eius de penis eripere?" Nichil ergo aliud
restat nisi accedere ad bona opera, que minus dilexeramus, que sunt oraciones, ieiunia, vigilie, elemosine, et huiusmodi, et revera illa salvabunt
[nos]; Tobie 4: "Si multum tibi fuerit, habundanter tribue," etc., quia
205   "elemosina a peccato liberat."
        Unde narratur de quodam qui post mortem cuidam amico apparens et, cum
ille quesisset qualiter cum eo erat, ex quo tam potens fuit in seculo,
respondit sic metrice:

            Sunt mea si qua dedi, fuerant mea si qua comedi.
210   Si qua remanserunt, nescio cuius erunt,

quasi diceret: Ea que dedi pro Deo, iam iuvant; ea que comedi, iuverunt;
set ea que remanserunt, quis potest capere, capiat, etc.

his faithfulness. It happened that such a condemned criminal had three friends; one of these he loved more than himself, the other as much as himself, and the third less than himself. Wanting to try them in his need, he approached the first for help, who said to him: "You have been foolish to love me more than yourself. I will not place myself into such danger for your sake. But I will do this much: I will give you this cloak with which you may cover and defend yourself if you can; for the rest, you must learn to act more cautiously." Upon these words the condemned man went grieving and sad to his second friend, the one he had loved as much as himself, and asked for his help. But this one replied curtly that he could not do it; he would do as much as go to the judge's place with him, but enter he would not—that he did not dare for great fear. Having heard this, the condemned man went to his third friend, the one he had loved less, and he found him alone to be a true friend, for he freed him from death before the judge.

Spiritually speaking, whoever is born into this world must fear God's coming judgment and find for himself true friends before his death, with whose help he can, if necessary, defend himself before his heavenly judge and be saved. But many have friends like the three I have described, namely the world, relatives, and good deeds. Some love the world more than themselves: they cannot endure any hardship for themselves so that they may gain eternal glory, but for the sake of the world they are not afraid to expose themselves daily to all sorts of dangers, sometimes even death. Yet this friend will give them no help whatever in their ultimate need, when they must go to their grave in the due course of nature, but it will then fail them, except that it grants them an inexpensive cloak, hardly more than an old cloth or a torn and dirty sheet, to wrap them for burial. Second, others love their kindred as much as themselves, as a husband loves his wife and vice-versa, which is right and according to nature. Nonetheless, even these will not make every effort they could to free them in their ultimate need. After their death they hardly follow them to the cemetery, which they cannot avoid, wailing and in the eyes of society as it were tearing themselves; but then, when the corpse has been buried, their grief abates and they quickly return home without tears, nor do they grieve for the dead any further, but only for themselves, saying: "Alas, alas, we have lost our support. What shall we do now?" But they do not say: "Ah, Lord, how can I help free his soul from its pain?" Therefore, nothing else remains but to turn to our good works, which we had loved less, such as prayers, fasting, vigils, almsgiving, and the like. They indeed will save us; Tobit 4: "If you have much, give abundantly," etc., because "alms free us from sin."

There is a story about someone who after his death appeared to his friend, and as the latter asked him how things were with him, since he had been a powerful man in life, he answered metrically:

[That Y ȝaf, þat ys myn.
þat I eet, þat was mynn.
215   That I lefte behynde me,
Who hit schall haue I con noȝt se.]

---

1 igitur] ergo O.   **6** Si] set C.W.   **26** et numquam] nec unquam O.   **27** nec] non O.
28 frequenter] frequencius O.   **43** titulus] tenet C; *variously corrupt in* O.   **45** decem]
om O.   **46–47** Sequitur ergo] set quare C.   **54** animalis] *om* O.   **57** pauperes] simplices
M.W; suum R.   **58** ista] *om* O.   **59** cogitabile] incogitabile C.   **62** sub] *om* O.   **69** au-
rem] aures O.   **76** respondet] respondit O.   **83** aquas] aquam C.   **84** deriventur] diri-
mentur O.   **85** Unde] *om* O.   **93** aufugit] affugit O.   **97** remeant] remaneant C.
98 Ieremie 9] ieronimus C.   **114–116** Anglice . . . quyte] *text from* R. *Verse 41, in*
B1.B3.E.L2.LC.R.Sp.W1.   **118** Set] si C.   **119** in mundo] inmunde C.M.   **122–**
124 Anglice . . . forsakyth] *text from* R. *Verse 42, in* B1.B3.E.L2.LC.R.Sp.W1.
130 fuerunt] fuerint O.   **134** idest] et C.   **135** eum] eam M.W; ea R.   **142** expectans]
expectantes C.M.   exire] transire O.   **143** collegerunt] colligerunt C.   **152** cum fractis]
confractis O.   **154** ipsam] ipsaque C.   **157** Que] quam O.   **172** teipsum] te O.   te] *add*
in C.   **190** nature] *add* ire C.   **193** diligunt] *om* O.   **196** possunt] potest C.   **199** mor-
tuum] mortem O.   **203** elemosine] *om* O.   **207** seculo] *add* qui O.   **208** metrice] *add* dicens O.   **212** etc.] *add* chache who so þat may B1.   **213–216** That . . . se] *text from* R.
Verse 43, in B1.B3.E.Go1.Go2.Jo.L2.LC.R.Sp.V.W1.

IV.xi   DE CONTEMPTU MUNDI

[A]d istud ergo vicium avaricie extirpandum iam procedit in medium
contemptus mundi, de quo pulcre et contra predictam huiusmodi avariciam
ait beatus Bernardus in quodam sermone *De adventu Domini*: "Filii, inquit,
Adam, avarum genus, ambiciosa gens, audite. Quid vobiscum cum terrenis
5   diviciis et gloria temporali? Aurum et argentum vestrum nonne terra rubea
sunt et alba, que solus error facit aut pocius reputat preciosa? Denique si
vestra sunt hec tollite vobiscum. Set homo (dicit ipse) 'cum interierit,
non sumet omnia neque descendet cum eo gloria domus eius.' " Hec ille.
Set nota quod iste mundi contemptus avaricie extirpator in tribus
10   consistit, videlicet in dominice passionis recordacione, in certe mortis
consideracione, in voluntarie paupertatis dilectione. De primo ergo pulcre
ait beatus Ambrosius in quodam sermone: "Circumspecta, inquit, pen⟨a⟩ in
cruce Christi, finem recipiat ambicio cupidi. A mundanis [f. 105v] se rebus
exuit, ut nullam mundus occasionem in eo inveniret per quam temporalia
15   diligeret. Et ideo sue maxime pene compaciendum est." Nam ipse Christus,
secundum beatum Gregorium super Iob, cum potuisset genus humanum aliter
quam per mortem suam salvasse, moriendo tamen redimere nos voluit a potestate diaboli per suum sanguinem benedictum, ut nobis compaciendi preberet
exemplum. Versus:

What I gave is mine, but what I ate has been.
If anything remains, it is I don't know whose,

as if to say: What I gave away for God's sake helps me now; what I ate helped
me once; but what is left over, let him have it who may.

That Y ʒaf . . .

30–33 Rev. 13.1–2.   **60** Horace, *Ep.* I.vi.37.   **61–62** Augustine, *De civ. Dei* VII.12
(CC 47:196).   **64–70** Ps.-Chrysostom, *Opus imperfectum*, hom. 31 (PG 56:792).   **75–
76** Luke 12.19.   **76–77** Ps. 48.11–12.   **86–88** *In* 18140; *Prov* 29560.   **95–96** Ps.
108.11.   **108** Ecclus. 12.16.   **99–101** Jer. 9.4–5.   **105–106** Isa. 30.2.   **107** Hos.
7.11.   **112–113** *Prov* 15647.   **120–121** *Prov* 17493a.   **147–153** Cf. Ps.-Anselm, *De
similitudinibus* 72 (PL 159:643–644).   **155–156** 2 Cor. 11.26.   **160–161** Eccles. 5.9.
163–181 Tubach 2216 or 2407. The tale of the Three Friends, represented also in *Everyman* as well as *King Lear*, occurs widely and in several variants. Bromyard, "Amicicia,"
A.XXI.5–7, for instance, contains three different versions.   **204–205** Tob. 4.9, 11.
209–210 *Prov* 30764. For additions, see *Verses*, p. 182.

IV.xi   THE CONTEMPT OF THE WORLD

In order to uproot this vice of avarice, contempt of the world now enters the
plain. Of it, and against the said avarice, Blessed Bernard speaks beautifully
in a sermon *On the Lord's Coming*: "Children of Adam, you greedy folk and
ambitious people, listen. What are worldly riches and temporal glory to you?
Are not your gold and silver but red and white soil, made precious—or rather,
considered to be so—only by mistake? If they are yours, take them with you!
But when a man 'has died, he will not take anything with him, nor will the
glory of his house go down with him.' "

This contempt of the world, uprooter of avarice, consists in three things:
memory of the Lord's passion, meditation on the certainty of death, and love of
voluntary poverty. Of the first, Blessed Ambrose says beautifully in a sermon:
"If he reflects intimately on Christ's suffering on the cross, an avaricious
man loses his ambition. He divests himself of worldly things, so that the
world will find no occasion in him by which he might love temporal goods.
Therefore we should have compassion with Christ's great suffering." For as
Blessed Gregory says in his commentary on Job, Christ could have saved mankind by another way than his death; but by dying he wanted to redeem us from
the devil's power through his blessed blood, that he might give us an example
of compassion. Hence the verses:

20   Nos sanguis mirus Christi dulcedine lavit
       Quos anguis dirus tristi mulcedine pavit.

Et de ista materia nota satis particula 3 de caritate.
    De secundo autem ait Augustinus: "Avaricie, inquit, morbus numquam
melius compescitur quam cum dies mortis premeditatur." Et ideo dicit beatus
25 Ieronimus: "Facile, inquit, contempnit omnia qui se cogitat moriturum et
omnia bona concessa mundo relinquenda." Unde Iob: "Dies, inquit, mei brevi-
abuntur et solum michi superest sepulcrum." Quod quidem sepulcrum satis est
strictum. Nam eius altitudinem cervix mencietur cum naso, pectus cum tergo
profunditatem, duo latera latitudinem, set longitudinem capud cum pedibus.
30   Et ideo ad mundane glorie extinccionem semper est mors ante oculos
mentis premeditanda. Unde pulcre ait Augustinus libro *De vera innocencia*,
capitulo ultimo dicens: "Divi⟨ci⟩is, inquit, flores, o a⟨v⟩are, et de
maiorum nobilitate te iactas. Exultas enim de patria, de pulcritudine
corporis, et de honoribus, que tibi ab hominibus deferuntur. Respice,
35 inquit, teipsum, quia mortalis et terra es et in terram ibis. Circumspice,
qui ante te similibus fulsere splendoribus. Ubi ergo sunt quos ambiebas
civium potentatus, ubi insuperabiles oratores, ubi satrape, ubi tyranni?
Nonne omnia pulvis, nonne favilla, nonne in paucis versibus eorum memoria
[f. 106] est?" Et sequitur: "Respice ergo sepulcra eorum et vide quis
40 dominus, quis servus, quis pauper, quis dives; discerne, si poteris, vinctum a rege, fortem a debili, pulcrum a deformi. Memor ergo (dict Augustinus) esto ita quod aliquando ne extollaris. Memor autem eris (dicit ipse)
si teipsum respexeris." Hec ille. "Memorare ergo novissima, et in eternum
non peccabis." Ipsa enim caute et inopinate ad modum furis hominem solet
45 invadere.
       Exemplum autem habere possumus de inimico persequente, nunc super
equum album, nunc super equum nigrum, ut caucius apprehendere possit,
equitat sic diversimode; et ideo si tibi non caveres, fatuum te esse ostende-
res. Revera sic quemlibet mundanum mors insequitur, nunc terminando diem
50 qui albus est, nunc noctem incipiendo qui niger est; Genesis 8: "Nox et
dies non requiescunt." De ista ergo materia quere supra, ⟨particula⟩ 1 de
humilitate.

---

2 huiusmodi] eius O.   **11** in certe] *apparently corr from* in incerte C; in certa O.
12 pena] penitencia C.   **23** autem] *add* bene O.   **29** profunditatem] latitudinem O.   lati-
tudinem] *om* O.   **32** Diviciis] divitis C.   avare] amare C.   **51** particula] capitulo C.

The wondrous blood of Christ has washed us in its sweetness,
Whom the dread serpent once fed with its sorrowful charm.

More on this subject can be found in part 3, on charity.

About the second aspect of the contempt of the world, Augustine says: "The illness of avarice can never be better stemmed than by thinking ahead of one's day of death." Therefore, Blessed Jerome says: "He who reflects that he will die and leave to the world all the goods that were granted to him, easily scorns everything." Whence Job exclaims: "My days will be shortened, and only the grave remains for me." This grave is very narrow, for its height reaches from our skull to the tip of the nose; its depth, from our breast to the back; its width, from one side to the other; and its length, from our head to our feet.

Thus, in order to quench worldly glory we must always hold our death before the eyes of our mind. Whence Augustine says beautifully in his book *On True Innocence*, in the last chapter: "O greedy man, you blossom with riches and boast of the nobility of your elders; you exult in your country, the beauty of your body, and the honors that are bestowed on you by others. Look at yourself, that you are mortal and dust and will go to dust. Look around you, at those who once shone in like splendor before you. Where then are the civil powers you strove for, where are the unsurpassable orators, the leaders, the tyrants? Is not all this dust and ashes, is not all their memory contained in a few verses?" And he continues: "Look, then, at their graves and see which is lord and which is slave, which is poor and which is rich; tell, if you can, the defeated from the king, the strong from the weak, the beautiful from the ugly. Keep this in mind, then, that you may not become proud. You will remember it once you have looked at yourself." "Remember, therefore, your last end, and you will never sin." For his end comes upon man quickly and unexpectedly like a thief.

We can find an illustration in an enemy that follows in pursuit: he rides in different ways, now on a white horse, now on a black one, so that he can catch us more surely; and if you do not take precautions, you will seem to be very foolish. In the same way, death pursues every worldling, now ending the day, which is white, now beginning the night, which is black; Genesis 8: "Night and day do not cease." See further on this matter above, in part 1 on humility.

3–8 Bernard, *In adventu Domini*, sermo 4, 1 (4:182).   **7–8** Ps. 48.18.   **16–19** Cf. Augustine, *De Trinitate* XIII.x.13 (CC 50A:399–400).   **23–24** Cf. comment in *Verses*, p. 148.   **25–26** See above, *FM* IV.iv.   **26–27** Job 17.1.   **32–43** Prosper, *Sententiae* 390 (PL 45:1897–98).   **43–44** Ecclus. 7.40.   **50–51** Gen. 8.22.   **51–52** *FM* I.xiii.

IV.xii   DE VOLUNTARIA PAUPERTATE

Circa vero paupertatem voluntariam, que est sicut fortis athleta
contra vicium avaricie, sic est procedendum: primo, quid sit et quomodo
diffinitur; secundo, a quibus illam sequi exemplum accipitur; tercio, que
mala eveniunt suis contemptoribus; quarto, que bona eveniunt suis amato-
5   ribus.

Primo dico quod paupertas voluntaria potest dici felix cupiditas qua
terrena et momentanea contempnuntur ut celestia et eterna adquirantur.
Istam ergo sequi habemus exemplum non tantum a Christo et aliis sanctis,
verum eciam ab infidelibus et paganis. Ipsam autem specialiter elegit
10   Christus in possessionem sibi et precipue amavit, ut ipsam amabilem nobis
ostenderet ad modum quo medicus bonus ° pocionem medicinalem prius gustat,
ut egrotus postea bibere non formidet. Et ideo eius exemplo sui eam specialiter elegerunt, ut apostoli, quando "relictis omnibus secuti sunt Dominum." Videmus autem quod [filius] mil⟨itis⟩ terren⟨i⟩ reputatur vecors si
15   renuat portare ar- [f. 106v] ma patris. Sic quilibet Christianus merito
dicitur vecors et infidelis qui vexillum timet portare patris sui regis
eterni. Quod vexillum signum est paupertatis quam ipse specialiter preele-
git. Nam cum ipse fuerat "rex regum et dominus dominancium," huiusmodi
tamen honore relicto pauper pro nobis fieri elegit. Quod bene ostendit
20   Crisostomus super Matheum in *Inperfecto*, omelia 3, super illud "Cum intrantes domum invenerunt," etc.: "Videamus, [inquit,] quid gloriosum magi
viderunt," etc. Nota in auctoritate. Ecce ergo regem degradatum et de
regno quasi depositum et mendicantem in terra aliena. Unde iam completum
erat in eo verbum regis in rota Fortune super solium sedentis, quod in
25   circulo circa eum conscribitur sic:

Regno, regnabo, regnavi, sum sine regno,

quasi diceret Christus: Quamvis eternaliter in celis regnavi, regno, et
regnabo, corporaliter tamen in terris sum sine regno, quia "regnum meum non
est de hoc mundo." Si enim queris palacium istius regis in terris, si
30   thalamum, si solium, vide quia iacet in presepio. Si queris comitivam et
familiam, ecce bovem et asinum. Si mensam, ecce lactis poculum. Si vestes
et ornamenta, ecce matris gremium. Si ministrallos, ecce pauperrima mater
illum foventem et iocundantem. Et ideo de eo bene dici potest illud Psalmi:
"Simul in unum dives et pauper," scilicet Deus et homo. De quo Ancelmus *De*
35   *sacramentis* ait quod ita pauper fuit in terris quod veniens non habuit ubi
nasceretur, nec natus propter boni inopiam ubi poneretur, nec transiens per
mundum ubi capud suum reclinaret, nec transiens de mundo unde nuditatem
suam tegeret, quia nudus pro nobis in cruce pependit. O ergo horrenda
insanies, que homines impedit ne hic Christum sequantur. Quibus Augustinus

IV.xii   VOLUNTARY POVERTY

With respect to voluntary poverty, which stands like a strong champion against the vice of avarice, I will proceed as follows: first I will discuss what it is and how it is defined; second, whom we can take as a model to follow; third, what evil consequences come to those who scorn it; and fourth, what good results come to those who love it.

First I say that voluntary poverty can be called a blessed desire by which earthly and transitory things are scorned so that heavenly and eternal goods may be gained. As as model to follow we have not only Christ and other saints, but even the infidels and pagans. Christ chose poverty especially as his possession and loved it above all, that he might show us how lovable it is, just as a good physician first tastes a medicinal potion so that his patient will not be afraid to drink it. And therefore, following his example, the apostles gave it special preference when they "left all things and followed the Lord." We see from experience that the son of an earthly knight is reputed degenerate if he refuses to carry his father's arms. Likewise any Christian is rightly called degenerate and faithless if he is afraid to carry the standard of his father, the eternal king. But this standard is the sign of poverty, to which he had given special preference. For though he had been "the king of kings and lord of lords," he yet left this honor and preferred to become poor for us. Chrysostom shows this well in Homily 3 of his *Imperfect Work on Matthew*, commenting on the passage "Entering the house, they found," etc. He says: "Let us see what glorious thing the Magi saw," etc. Note the entire passage. Behold then our king, as if he were demoted and deposed from his kingdom and become a beggar in a foreign country. Thus there was fulfilled in him the saying of the king who sits on a chair on the wheel of Fortune, written in a circle around him as follows:

I rule, I shall rule again, I once ruled, I am without kingdom,

as if Christ were saying: Though in heaven I have ruled from all time and continue and shall do so in the future, bodily here on earth however I am without kingdom, for "my kingdom is not of this world." If you seek this king's palace on earth, his bed, his throne—lo, he lies in a manger. If you seek his retinue and court—lo, an ox and an ass. For a banquet he has a cup of milk; for robes and ornaments, his mother's lap; for servants, his poor mother who nurses and comforts him. And thus the words of the Psalm can be said of him: "Both rich and poor together," namely God and man. Anselm in *On the Sacraments* says of him that he was so poor on earth that when he came, he had no place to be born in; when he had been born, there was no place where to put him, for lack of all goods; when he journeyed through the world, he had no place to lay down his head; and when he left the world, there was nothing with which to clothe

40   libro *Confessionum* bene ait: "Si, inquit, tu avare Christum in paupertate
     [f. 107] nolueris imitari, noli saltem adversari."
         Istam ergo paupertatem specialiter elegerunt apostoli et alii sancti,
     qui relictis temporalibus omnibus secuti sunt doctorem suum Christum.
     Videmus enim quod qui vult sequi currentem oportet se onus superfluum
45   deponere aut certe illum non attinget. Set iuxta Psalmistam [Christus]
     "exultavit ut gigas ad currendam viam," scilicet paupertatis; quem ergo si
     sequi volumus, oportet temporalia superflua deponere; unde Apostolus Ad
     Hebreos: "Deponentes omne pondus." Revera sic fecit beatus Petrus. Nam
     tantum post Christum festinavit quod cecidit ⟨iambe leue⟩, hoc est quod
50   elevatus tandem erat in cruce sicut Christus, pedibus tamen erectis et
     capite submisso. Bartholomeus eciam volens currere velociter ideo, ne
     pannis superfluis impediretur, tunicam dimisit, hoc est, excoriatus pellem
     reliquit propriam. Laurencius eciam Christum attingere volens onus pingue-
     dinis ne per illud impediretur a cursu super craticulam illud assari et
55   consumi permisit. Franciscus [eciam] calciatus ne impediretur ipsis abiec-
     tis et nudis pedibus velociter cucurrit. Et sic similiter alii sancti, qui
     iam cursum certaminum consummaverunt et Christum in celo apprehenderunt.
     Unde qui amaverunt Christum in vita sua eius paupertatem sequendo, ideo
     modo coronantur et accipiunt palmam, gaudium scilicet sempiternum possiden-
60   do. Videmus enim quod monete non apparet ymago nisi prius in cunagio
     feriatur mallio. Ecce sic nec in homine apparet Dei similitudo nisi prius
     feriatur tribulacionis baculo; Ecclesiastici 27: "Vasa figuli probat for-
     nax." In hoc fornace paupertatis ille sapientissimus aurifaber Christus
     similiter fabricat vasa glorie, idest animas sanctas in honorem.
65   Circa autem paupertatem philosophorum et aliorum paganorum infidelium,
     quomodo in vita extiterunt contemptores mundi et diviciarum, fertur diver-
     simode. [f. 107v] De Anaxagaro autem narratur in *Vitas philosophorum*, et
     accipitur a Valerio libro 8, quod cum ex diutina peregrinacione patriam
     repetisset possessionesque desertas vidisset, "Non essem, inquit, salvus
70   nisi ista perissent." De Dyogene philosopho eciam narratur a Satyro histo-
     riografo quod ipse pallio dupplici usus est propter frigus, peram pro
     cellaria habuit, secum portavit, clavam eciam gerebat ad corpusculi fragi-
     litatem qua iam senex membra sustentare solitus erat. Habitavit eciam in
     p⟨ort⟩arum vestibulis et in porticibus civitatum usquequaque profitens
75   verum et transeuncium abigens aut notans vicia que mores fedabant. Quodam
     [autem] tempore cum in usu potandi calicem ligneum gereret et vidisset
     pauperem manu concava bibere, calicem elisit in terra et fregit dicens:
     "Qua⟨m⟩diu homo stultus sarcinas habui supervacuas! Nescirem quod natura
     haberet poculum." Narrat eciam de eo Tullius libro 2 *Tuscullanarum questio-*
80   *num* quod moriens iussit se proici inhumatum. Cum ergo amici dicerent quod
     tunc a feris devoraretur, respondit: "Minimumque baculum quo eas abigare

his nakedness, for he hung naked for us on the cross. What terrible madness
that keeps men from following Christ in this! To them, Augustine says fittingly in his book of *Confessions*: "If you, greedy man, do not want to follow
Christ in his poverty, at least do not go against him!"

Such poverty the apostles and other saints chose especially when they left
all temporal possessions and followed their teacher, Christ. We see from experience that if one wants to follow someone who is running, one must take off
everything superfluous or else one will never catch up with him. But according
to the Psalmist, Christ "has rejoiced as a giant to run his way," namely that
of poverty. If we want to follow him, we must put away all superfluous temporal possessions; whence the Apostle says in Hebrews: "Laying aside every
weight." This is what Blessed Peter did. For he hurried so fast after Christ
that he fell *jambe levee*, "head over heels"; that is, in the end he was put on
the cross like Christ, but with his feet up and his head down. Bartholomew,
too, wanting to run so swiftly, took off his tunic so that he would not be
hindered by superfluous clothes, that is, he was flayed of his own skin. And
when Lawrence wanted to catch up with Christ, in order not to be slowed down by
any burden of fat, he allowed it to be fried and consumed on the grill. Likewise Francis, that he might not be hindered by his shoes, took them off and ran
swiftly on bare feet. And other saints did the same, who have already run
their course and have caught up with Christ in heaven. They who loved Christ
in their lives by following his poverty are now crowned and receive the palm,
namely in possessing eternal joy. We see from experience that the image on a
coin does not appear unless the ingot is first struck with a hammer. In the
same way, God's likeness in man does not appear unless man is first struck with
the staff of affliction; Ecclesiasticus 27: "The furnace tries the potter's
vessels." In this furnace of poverty, that wise goldsmith, Christ, likewise
produces vessels of glory, that is, holy souls for heavenly honor.

Concerning the poverty of philosophers and of other pagans outside the
Faith, many stories tell us how in their lives they scorned the world and its
riches. Of Anaxagoras we read in *The Lives of the Philosophers*, and this is
taken from book 8 of Valerius, that when he returned from a lengthy pilgrimage
to his country and found his possessions deserted, he said: "I would not be
safe if these had not perished." Of Diogenes, too, the historiographer Satyrus
reports that he wore a double blanket against the cold, had a gourd as his wine
cellar, and carried a rough stick with which the old man was wont to support
his weak body. He dwelled in the entranceway of gates and the porticoes of
cities, proclaiming the truth everywhere and pointing out the vices of those
who passed by which stained their good manners. As at one time he carried a
wooden bowl to drink from and saw a poor man drink from the hollow of his hand,
he dashed his bowl to the ground and broke it, saying: "How long have I
foolish man carried unnecessary burdens! I did not know that nature has given

possim iuxta me ponite." Cui responderunt: "Quid tunc facere poteris cum
non sencies?" Respondit: "Quid ergo ferarum laniatus michi non sencienti
obesse poterit?" quasi diceret: nichil. Secundum eciam predictum Satyrum,
85   cum seipsum in doleo torqueret set domum volubilem se habere letabatur.
Unde dolium propter frigus vertebat ad meridiem, ut ibi beneficio solis
congauderet. In estate vero propter calorem vertebat ad septentrionem. Et
ubicumque sol se inclinaverat, simul et Diogenes pretorium dolii divertebat
quiescens. Unde narrat Valerius de eo libro 4, capitulo 3, quod cum ad eum
90   sic in dolio versus solem sedentem accessit Alexander rex hortaretque ei
ut que sibi ab eo prestari vellet [f. 108] mendicaret. Qui respondit:
"Hoc, inquit, vellem pre ceteris, quod non stes inter me et solem." Per
illum Dyogenem quilibet nostrum intelligi potest, quia iuxta Psalmistam
"pauperes facti sumus." Vita presens est quasi dolium in quo manemus. Nam
95   sicut dolium est versatile de loco ad locum, sic vita presens de statu ad
statum. Nunc enim homo tristatur nunc letatur, nunc infirmatur nunc sanatur, iuxta illud Iob: "Numquam in eodem statu permanet." In isto ergo dolio
sedentes, idest in vita presenti manentes, semper nos vertere debemus ad
Christum, solem iusticie. Si ergo Alexander, idest mundus, venit querens
100 si aliqua voluerimus ab eo nobis prestari et suas divicias et vanitates
ostendat, hoc solum ab eo petere debemus quod non stet nec ponat obstaculum
temporalium momentaniorum inter nos et Christum, per quod ab eo seperari
possemus, dicentes cum Psalmista: "Providebam Dominum in conspectu meo
semper."
105   Fertur eciam a Ieronimo *Epistola 35* quod Crates Thebanus, homo quondam
ditissimus, cum ad philosophand⟨u⟩m Athenas pergeret, magnum auri pondus
abiecit, non putans se simul virtutes posse et divicias possidere, non plus
quam vicia et virtutes. Et ideo *Epistola 26* re⟨ci⟩tat de quodam philosopho qui multarum possessionum precium proiecit in pelagum dicens: "Abite,
110 male cupiditates, abite. Ego vos mergam ne submergar a vobis."
     Philosophi enim non reputabant bona mundi esse sua, et ideo nec ea
appetebant nec de amissione dolebant. Unde prout narrat Seneca Stibon
philosophus interrogatus n⟨unquid⟩ aliquid perdidisset, "Nichil, inquit.
Omnia mea mecum sunt." Et tamen patrimonium suum in predam cessar⟨a⟩t et
115 filios hostis Demetrius rapuerat. Habebat enim, ut dixit, secum vera bona,
puta sapienciam et paupertatem, in quibus non est manus iniectio. Que vero
dissipata fuerant, non reputabat sua, set adventicia [f. 108v] et fortunam
sequencia.
     Narrat Policraticus libro ⟨4⟩ quod cum Alexander Magnus gentem Brag-
120 mannorum debellare proposuisset, responderunt: "Quid erit homini satis cui
totus non sufficit mundus? Divicias enim non habemus quarum cupiditate nos
debeas expugnare. Omnia bona nobis communia sunt. Esca est nobis pro diviciis; pro cultibus et auro, vilis et rara vestis. Femine enim nostre non

us a cup!" And Cicero, in book 2 of the *Tusculan Disputations*, tells of him
that when he was dying he ordered to be thrown out without burial. When his
friends said that in that case he would be devoured by wild animals, he answered: "Then lay a small stick beside me so I can drive them off." They
replied: "But what can you do when you have no senses left?" And he: "So, if
I have no senses left, why should I worry about being torn by wild animals?" as
if to say: not in the least. According to the quoted Satyrus, he lived and
turned himself about in a tun and was happy to have a mobile home. For when it
was cold, he turned his tun to the south and enjoyed the warmth of the sun.
But in the heat of summer he turned it to the north. And wherever the sun went
on its course, Diogenes turned the opening of his tun and rested there. Valerius tells of him in book 4, chapter 3, that as he once was thus sitting in his
tun against the sun, King Alexander approached and encouraged him to ask for
whatever he would like to have from him. Diogenes answered: "There is one
thing I would like more than anything else: that you don't stand between me and
the sun." This Diogenes can symbolize anyone of us, for according to the
Psalmist, "we have become poor." Our present life is like a tun in which we
live. For as a tun can be turned from one position to another, so this life
changes from one state to another: now a man is sad, now happy; now sick, now
well; according to the words of Job: "He never continues in the same state."
While we sit in this tun, that is, while we are in this life, we must always
turn toward Christ, the sun of justice. Then if Alexander, that is, the world,
comes and asks us if we want him to give us anything and shows us his riches
and vain delights, we must ask him for only one thing: that he do not stand and
put the obstacle of temporal and passing pleasures between us and Christ, by
which we could be separated from him, and we must say with the Psalmist: "I
set the Lord in my sight always."

Also, in *Letter 35* Jerome tells that Crates of Thebes, a very wealthy man,
when he was traveling to Athens to study philosophy, got rid of a large amount
of gold, thinking that he could not possess virtues and riches at the same
time, any more than vices together with virtues. And in *Letter 26* he reports
of a philosopher who threw the wealth from his many possessions into the sea
with the words: "Go, evil desires, go. I drown you that I may not be drowned
by you."

For the philosophers did not believe that the goods of the world belonged
to them, and so they neither desired them nor grieved at their loss. Hence
Seneca tells of the philosopher Stilbo, who was once asked if he had lost
anything. "Nothing," he replied; "all that is mine is with me." And yet his
patrimony had fallen prey and his enemy Demetrius had captured his sons. But
as he said, his true possessions he had with him, namely wisdom and poverty, on
which no one can lay hand. But the things that had been scattered and taken he
did not reckon his own, but gifts of Fortune and chance.

ornantur ut placeant, quarum ornamentorum cultum pocius oneri deputant
125   quam honori, et eas ⟨n⟩es⟨c⟩iunt in augenda pulcritudine amplius affectare
quam quod nate sunt. Antra autem duplicem usum prestant, scilicet tegumen-
t⟨u⟩m in vita, et in morte sepulturam. Regem habemus non pro iusticia set
pro nobilitate conservanda. Quem ergo locum haberet vindicta, ubi nulla
iusticia?" Hiis ergo verbis motus, Alexander n⟨ull⟩am ratus victoriam si
130   eorum pacem turbaret, eos in quiete sua dimisit, et forte, si [contra]
eos bellum aggressu⟨s⟩ fuisset, minime prevaluisset, eo quod innocencia
facile non superatur a nocentibus. Hec ille.

Narrat eciam Valerius libro 4, capitulo 3, de Fabricio, qui dixit quod
illum locupletem faciebant non multa possidere set modica desiderare. Et
135   ideo dixit Aristoteles quod hoc tantum incomodum habet paupertas quod non
potest alios iuvare.

Circa autem mala que eveniunt contemptoribus voluntari⟨e⟩ pauperta-
t⟨is⟩ est sciendum quod ita contingit in fine de avaro divite et volunta-
rio paupere sicut de gallina et falcone. Falco autem in vita in pugno
140   portatur, in pertica collocatur, de carne recenti reficitur. Set gallina in
locis vilissimis sicut in fovea et sterquilinio et huiusmodi querit refectionem, in tugurrio locatur. Et tamen mortuo falcone in foveam proicitur,
et gallina assata coram rege et magnatibus in aulam defertur. [f. 109]
Revera simili modo dives hic in vita sua cibis delicatis reficitur, vesti-
145   bus preciosis induitur, et cetera huiusmodi. Set certe, ipso mortuo timendum est ne in foveam inferni proiciatur. Pauper vero cum difficultate et
tedio victualia adquirit, set ipso mortuo cum rege in aulam celorum et eius
sanctis illius anima defertur.

Exemplum Luce 16 de divite epulone et Lazaro pauperrimo. Et ideo
150   dicit Bernardus: "Pauper in pecunia, dives in consciencia, qui securius
iacet in tugurrio quam rex in forti castro, et tucius in palea quam rex in
purpura." Non timent dominos in rapina, predones non verentur, tranquilli
manent, [et] ubi divites laboriose vivunt, non habent quid tolli nisi suam
paupertatem. Quis rapere vellet quam pauci gratis admittunt? Item sicut
155   circa castri conservacionem deponitur terra ut fossa eius profundetur ne
hostes ad illud capiendum faciliter accedant, sic rex celestis de quacumque
anima fideli que est sicut Dei castrum, in quam per graciam debet habitare,
illam cingit fossa paupertatis contra hostes spirituales, quam super omnia
nititur diabolus implere terra avaricie et cupiditatis, ut sic ad illam ac-
160   cessum habeat forcius et caucius invadendam. Abacuc 1 dicitur: "Comporta-
bit aggerem et capiet eam." Tunc autem paupertatis contemptores de pauperibus cum dolore et tremore dicent illud Sapiencie 5: "Hii sunt quos aliquando habuimus in derisum et in similitudinem [improperii. Nos insensati vitam
illorum estimabamus insaniam et finem] illorum sine honore," etc. Et ideo,
165   ut dicitur Iob 2, "venit super nos indignacio," scilicet paupertas Christi.

Policraticus reports, in book 4, that when Alexander the Great threatened to make war against the people of the Brahmins, the latter replied: "What will suffice a man who is not satisfied with the whole world? We have no riches for which you might want to fight us in your greed. We share all property in common. For riches we have food, for wealth and gold, simple and vile clothes. Our women do not put on ornaments so that they might please, for they consider finery a burden rather than an honor, and they do not know how to use it to enhance the beauty with which they were born. Caves serve us for a double purpose, to give shelter in life and burial in death. A king we have, not to keep justice but our nobility. For what need is there for punishment where there is no injustice?" Moved by these words, Alexander did not consider it a victory if he were to disturb their peace and thus left them alone; if he were to attack them with war, he might perhaps not emerge as winner, because innocence is not easily overcome by people who do harm. So far *Policraticus*.

Further, Valerius tells us in book 4, chapter 3, of Fabricius, who said that what made him rich was not to possess many things but to desire only few. And therefore Aristotle said that poverty has only one disadvantage, that it cannot help others.

With respect to the evil consequences for those who scorn voluntary poverty, we must know that a greedy rich man and one who is voluntarily poor will have the same end as the hen and the falcon. For during his life the falcon is carried on the fist, sits on a perch, and is fed fresh meat; while the hen lives in the most vile places, such as ditches and dungheaps, seeks food of the same kind, and is put in a henhouse. But when they are dead, the falcon is tossed in a ditch, whereas the hen is roasted and brought before the king and his noblemen in the high hall. In the same way, during his life here a rich man is fed with dainty dishes, is clothed in precious garments, and so forth. But to be sure, when he dies, there is reason to fear that he may be thrown into the ditch of hell. A poor man, however, gains his living with hardship and vexation, but when he dies, his soul is brought before the king and his saints in the high hall of heaven.

We find an illustration in Luke 16, the story about Dives, who ate well, and Lazarus, who was extremely poor. Bernard says: "Poor in money but rich in his conscience, he rested more quietly in his hovel than the king in his strong castle, and more safely in the straw than the king in his purple." The poor do not fear the oppression of lords, they are not worried about thieves, they rest in tranquillity; and whereas the rich live in hardship, the poor have nothing that can be taken from them but poverty itself. Who would want to steal what few accept with pleasure? Further, in order to fortify a castle earth is dug up so that its moat is made deeper, that the enemy cannot easily capture it. The king of heaven acts with every faithful soul in like fashion, who is like God's castle in which he should live through grace. He surrounds it with the

Circa autem bona que pauperibus voluntariis evenerunt in fine est
quarto et ultimo sciendum secundum Bernardum qui ait: "In celo habundat
omnium rerum opulencia. Sola paupertas, hec species habundat in terris."
Set "nescivit homo precium eius." Hanc ergo venit Filius Dei querere, ut
170 sua estimacione illam faceret preciosam. Unde Corinthiorum 8: "Cum dives
esset," scilicet Christus, "factus est egenus pro nobis." Qui ergo erubescit [f. 109v] pauper[tat]em, erubescit se facere Deo similem. Distributor
autem elemosinarum inferius in cista ponit delicata et pinguia, et ⟨superi-
us⟩ grossiora. Ribaldi autem ex aviditate discrecionem non habentes pre-
175 currunt et de grosso pane porcionem accipiunt. Senes vero et humiles,
quorum est rerum exitus ex providencia metiri, gratis se subtrahunt expectantes in fine dulciora acceptura. Quod videntes alii dolent quod ita avidi
fuerunt, set supervacue, quia si iterum petant beneficium, vacui tamen
recedunt et eis dicetur: "Fare welle, þou hadde⟨st⟩!" sicut dictum erat
180 diviti, Luce 18: "Recepisti bona in vita tua." Et ideo ita facit [Christus]
de paupere sicut paterfamilias de nuncio pro negociis misso. Quando vult
quod redeat festinanter, tunc enim dat sibi parum de expensis, ut magis
domum festinet. Certe sic Christus pauperibus de rebus temporalibus ut ad
celestia sint expiditi et non impediantur. Et hoc est quod dicitur Ysaie
185 [51]: "Qui non habetis argentum, properate," scilicet ad celum, iuxta illud
Mathei 5: "Beati pauperes spiritu, quoniam ipsorum est regnum celorum."
    Ista ergo dicta de avaricia et cupiditate, de contempt⟨u⟩ mundi et
voluntaria paupertate ad presens sufficiunt.

---

11 bonus] add ad interl C.   **12** eam] illam O.   **14** militis terreni] miles (corr from militis) terrenus C.   **15** Christianus] qui filius dei appellatur O.   **17** Quod] add quidem O.
21 magi] magis O.   **22** in auctoritate] ibi auctoritatem O.   **30** vide] videte O.   **43** qui]
quando O.   **47** unde . . . Ad] om O.   **49** iambe leue] et titubavit ad crucem written into
blank space C; om M.   **55** Franciscus] sanctus franciscus B1; om E.Jo.L3.LC.Pe.
Madrid. All full manuscripts recorded.   **60** cunagio] cuneo O.   **61** Ecce] certe O.
70 ista] iste O.   **74** portarum] parcarum C.   **78** Quamdiu] quare diu C.   **81** Minimum-
que] minime sed O.   **81–82** abigare possim] abigam O.   **90** accessit] accessisset O.
91 que] si qua O.   **99** venit] venerit O.   **106** philosophandum] philosophandam C.
108 26] 56 O.   recitat] restat C.   **113** nunquid] ne C.   **114** cessarat] cessaret C.   **116**
quibus] que O.   **119** 4] 3 C.   **121** mundus] orbis O.   **124** quarum] quorum O.
125 nesciunt] vestiunt C.   **126** duplicem] add nobis O.   **126–127** tegumentum] tegu-
men tam C.   **129** nullam] naturam C.   si] sed O.   **130** eos . . . dimisit] om O.   contra]
om C.R.W.   **131** aggressus] aggressum C.   **137–138** voluntarie paupertatis] voluntariam paupertatem C.   **138** contingit] continget O.   et] add de O.   **149** Exemplum] exemplo O.   **173–174** superius] inferius C.   **179** haddest] hadde C; English om M.
181 pro] add arduo O.   **184** non] add per temporalia O.   **187** contemptu] contemptoribus C; conceptu W.   **188** paupertate] add in contrarium O.

moat of poverty against its spiritual enemies, which the devil tries above all
else to fill with the soil of avarice and covetousness, so that he can get to
it and invade it more quickly and easily. In Habakkuk 1 it is said: "He shall
cast up a mound and take it." And then those who have scorned poverty will say
with pain and trembling the words of Wisdom 5 about the poor: "These are they
whom we had some time in derision and for a parable of reproach. We fools
esteemed their life madness, and their end without honor," etc. Therefore, as
is said in Job 2, "indignation has come upon us," that is, the poverty of
Christ.

In the fourth and last place, with respect to the good results that come
to those who are willingly poor, we must know that Bernard says: "In heaven
abounds the wealth of all things; on earth, only poverty." But "man has not
known its value." The Son of God came to seek it, so that he might make it
precious by showing us its value. Hence Corinthians 8: "Though he was rich,"
that is, Christ, "he became poor for our sake." Therefore, whoever blushes at
poverty, blushes at making himself like God. The person who hands out alms
puts the more valuable and better pieces at the bottom of the chest and the
less valuable ones on top. Then vagabonds, who in their greed have no discretion, come running and take their share of coarse bread. But old and humble
people, who measure things prudently by their end result, willingly submit
themselves and hope to receive sweeter things in the end. When the others see
that, they grieve at having been so greedy, but in vain, for if they ask for
another boon, they will go empty and be told: "Farewell, you have had your
share." The same was said to the rich man in Luke 18: "You did receive good
things in your lifetime." And thus Christ deals with a poor man as the landlord does with a messenger sent on business. When he wants him to return in a
hurry, he gives him only little for his expenses, so that he will hurry home.
In the same way Christ gives the poor only little of temporal goods, that they
may be eager to hurry toward heaven and are not held back by temporal things.
For that reason it is said in Isaiah 51: "You who have no money, make haste,"
namely, toward heaven, according to the words of Matthew 5: "Blessed are the
poor in spirit, for theirs is the kingdom of heaven."

And for now this will suffice about avarice and covetousness, the contempt
of the world and voluntary poverty.

13–14 Luke 5.11.   **18** 1 Tim. 6.15.   **20–21** Matt. 2.11.   **21–22** Ps.-Chrysostom,
Opus imperfectum, hom. 2 (PG 56:641–642).   **26** Cf. *In* 16534; *Prov* 26495.   **28–
29** John 18.36.   **34** Ps. 48.3.   **35–38** Anselm, *Ep. de sacramentis Ecclesiae* 3
(2:241).   **43** Cf. Luke 5.11.   **46** Ps. 18.6.   **48** Heb. 12.1.   **57** Cf. 2 Tim. 4.7.   **62–
63** Ecclus. 27.6.   **67–70** Valerius, VIII.vii.ext.6.   **70–79** *Policraticus* V.17 (1:359),
from Jerome, *Adversus Iovinianum* II.14 (PL 23:316ff.). Both refer to "Satyrus."   **79–
84** Cicero, *Tusculanae disputationes* I.xliii.140.   **84–89** *Policraticus* V.17 (1:359).
89–92 Valerius, IV.iii.ext.4.   **94** Ps. 78.8.   **97** Job 14.2.   **103–104** Ps. 15.8.   **105–**

108 Jerome, *Ep. 58* 2 (CSEL 54:529). The story also occurs in John of Wales, *Breviloquium* II.2 and III.4; see *FM* V.xxxi.80–82.   **108–110** Jerome, *Ep. 118* 5 (CSEL 55:441).   **112–118** Tubach 3745a; from Seneca, *Ep. morales* IX.18.   **119–132** *Policraticus* IV.xi (1:270–271).   **133–134** Valerius, IV.iii.6.   **135–136** Aristotle, *Apophthegmata* 48 (ed. Heitz, 4.2:435).   **139–143** A very widespread simile, e.g.: Bromyard, "Paupertas," P.III.13; Holcot, *In Sapientiam*, lect. 64; Ross, *Middle English Sermons*, p. 239.   **149** Luke 16.19–31.   **160–161** Hab. 1.10.   **162–164** Wisd. 5.3–4.   **165** Job 3.26.   **167–168** Cf. Bernard, *In vigilia Nativitatis*, sermo 1, 5 (4:201).   **169** Job 28.13.   **170–171** 2 Cor. 8–9.   **180** Luke 16.25.   **185** Isa. 55.1.   **186** Matt. 5.3.

PARS V

De accidia

V.i   QUID SIT ACCIDIA

[C]ompleta autem particula 4 que mundo specialiter deservit, puta de
avaricia et cupiditate cum virtutibus sibi contrariis, restat iam quinto
pertractare de illis que a carne fetida et corrupta generantur sicut fere
pessime et dampnabiles, scilicet de accidia, gula, et luxuria, et de virtu-
5   tibus sibi contrariis, scilicet de occupacione sancta, abstinencia, et
continencia.

Circa accidiam sic procedam: primo, quid sit et quomodo diffinitur;
secundo, de eius proprietate et quibus comparatur; tercio, quare odiosa est
et iuste exsecratur. Primo ergo dico quod accidia est tedium boni sive
10   anxietas. Set diabolum tedet omne bonum, ergo non tantum carnis set eciam
sibi ad ministerium deputatur. Cuius proprietas est semper velle bene esse,
[f. 110] eciam cum Deo si posset regnare, et nullo modo occupari set in
omni tempore in desidia latitare.

Unde bene assimilatur cuidam servo de quo refert Petrus Alphonsus
15   libro *De sciencia clericali*. Cui cum precepisset magister suus de nocte ut
ianuas firmaret postquam ad lectum inisset, respondit: "Clause sunt,"
menciendo. Cum ergo de mane illum evigilasset, iussit ut illas aperiret;
respondens inquit: "Scivi quod illas hodie volebas esse apertas; ideo de
sero nolui illas claudere." Cum iterum sibi magister dixit: "Dies est,
20   surge, fac opus tuum," respondit: "Si dies est, da michi iantaculum!" Cui
magister: "Verecundia, inquit, tibi esset de nocte iantari." Et ille: "Si
nox est, permitte me quiescere." Revera sic est de istis pigris et accidio-
sis. Nichil enim eis inponi potest unde torporem et desidiam possent excu-
tere, quin ad libitum responsiones laterales adducere sciunt, et maxime si
25   aliquid pro Deo sustinere deberent, scilicet in ieiuniis, vigiliis, et
oracionibus, et huiusmodi. Primum enim non potest ne corpus nimis attenua-
ret, secundum propter debilitatem capitis et oculorum, nec tercium quia

PART V

Sloth

V.i WHAT SLOTH IS

After completing part 4 on the vice which especially serves the world, namely avarice and covetousness, together with the opposite virtues, we now come in the fifth place to treat those vices that spring from the stinking and corrupt flesh as its evil and damnable offspring, namely sloth, gluttony, and lechery, together with their opposite virtues, that is, holy activity, abstinence, and continence.

About sloth I shall proceed as follows: first I shall deal with what it is and how it is defined; second, with its characteristics and to what things it can be compared; and third, why it is harmful and rightly cursed. First, then, I say that sloth is boredom with respect to the good, or fearfulness. Now, to the devil, everything good is boring; therefore, this sin may rightly be said to serve not only the flesh but also the devil. Its characteristic is to want always to be at ease, even to reign with God if possible, and yet never to be busy but at all times to lie idle.

It can therefore be compared to a servant of whom Petrus Alphonsi speaks in his book *On Clerical Knowledge*. When his master ordered him at night to lock the doors after he had gone to bed, the servant replied, lying: "They are already shut." And when his master woke him in the morning to open the doors, he said: "I knew that you wanted them open; therefore I would not shut them last night." And when his master told him again: "It is day. Get up and do your work!" he replied: "If it is day, give me my dinner." Then his master said to him: "It would be a shame for you to eat at night [i.e., since you get hungry again in the morning]." And the servant came back with: "If it is night, let me go to sleep." Thus, indeed, it goes with lazy, slothful people. You cannot ask them for anything to cast off their torpor and laziness without their having excuses freely ready, especially if they ought to endure any hardship for God's sake, such as in fasting, vigils, prayers, and the like.

omnino "Pater Noster" et huiusmodi ignorat, et tamen si sciret, non potest
propter inflacionem lingue et labiorum.

30   Possunt tamen peroptime iuxta ciphum per totum diem et noctem ut
frequenter tales sedere, vigilare, et inutilia pertractare. Quos devote
arguit Bernardus in quadam meditacione dicens: "O, inquit, miser ingrate,
cur nichil sustinere possis pro me ex quo tot sustinui pro te? Dicis forte
capud doles vel arsuram cordis habes, que omnia forte ex superfluitate
35   evenerunt. Nonne capud habeo pro te coronatum et cor acutissima lancea
perforatum? Manus eciam et pedes in te a vermibus corroduntur ex humoribus
corruptis generatis, et ego habeo pro te utramque manum, utrumque pedem
acutissimis clavis perforatum et in ligno affixum. Habes eciam forte corpus
nudum et inedia maceratum? Cerne, [f. 110v] rogo, me nudiorem, macillencio-
40   rem, in patibulo spoliatum. Aliqui in te per verba insurgunt? Set quasi
omnes adversum me clamant: 'Crucifige, crucifige eum!' Aliqui tibi compaciuntur, set omnes me derident. Tu vero in ymo stas, ut sic aliqualiter confusio tua potest latere; set ego affligor in excelso, ut omnibus contemptibilis possim apparere et patere." Hec ille.

45   Unde tales bene comparantur trutannis contra solem tota die sedentibus
et nichil boni operantibus set ⟨onus⟩ bonarum occupacionum recusantibus. Et
ideo non sunt de numero eorum quos de labore terreno Christus vocavit ad
requiem dicendo illud Matthei 11: "Venite ad me omnes qui laboratis," etc.,
"et ego reficiam vos," scilicet gaudio eterno.

50   Item similes sunt cuculo, qui non fovet ova propria, set in alieno
nido ponit sua et ova comedit aliena. Sic certe de alieno labore accidiosus
reficitur, et quod alii duro labore et forti lucrabantur tales devorant
ociose; Psalmista: "Devorant pauperem in abscondito," hoc est, substanciam
de qua pauperes vivere deberent. Set ille est cibus qui perit et non
55   permanet in vitam eternam, ut dicit *Glossa* super Iohannem: "Cibus, inquit,
qui perit est panis ociosus quem comedunt ociosi nichil neque active neque
contemplative operantes." Unde Crisostomus super [Mattheum in] *Inperfecto*,
omelia 14, super illud "Panem nostrum cotidianum da," etc.: "Addidit,
inquit, 'cotidianum,' ut cibos luxuriosos compescat, ut scilicet quis
60   tantum manducet quantum racio exigit, non quantum lascivia impellit. Si
enim in uno convivio tantum expendas quantum sufficere poterit centum
hominibus moderate viventibus, non cotidianum cibum comedit set multorum."
Et ideo bene possunt dici tales vaspe vel apes degeneres, que non mellifi-
cant set mel consumunt; Psalmista: "Diripient alieni labores suos."

65   Tercio dico quod tales assimilantur aliquibus magnatibus qui vinaria
sua ita parce custodiunt quod nullibi ⟨participant⟩, [f. 111] set totum pro
heredibus conservant, ad quorum manus cum devenerint talia, sine modo aut
mensura devastant et consumunt. Sic in proposito multi hodie corpora sua
ociositati exponunt nichil boni operantes, quorum corpora cum ad heredes

The first of these a slothful man cannot undertake because it would weaken his body; neither can he undertake the second because he gets a headache or eye-ache; nor the third either because he does not know the Our Father and other prayers, and if he does, he gets a swollen tongue and lips.

And yet they are perfectly capable of sitting and waking by the cup all day long and all the night, as it frequently happens, and of uttering useless things. Bernard challenges such people in a devout meditation, saying: "O ungrateful lazybones, why can you not endure anything for me, who have endured so much for you? Perhaps you say your head hurts and you have heartburn, which probably come from eating too much. Do I not have my head crowned for you and my heart pierced with a sharp spear? Your hands and feet are being eaten by worms that come from your corrupt humors, and I have both hands and both feet pierced for your sake with sharp nails and have them stuck on the cross. Is your body naked and worn thin by fasting? Look at me, I pray, how I am even more naked, worn, and despoiled on the gibbet. Do people rise against you with words? But nearly everybody shouts against me: 'Crucify, crucify him!' On you, some people have pity, but of me all people make fun. You are lying low, so that your shame may be somewhat hidden; but I am tormented high up in the air, that I may appear openly contemptible to everyone."

Such slothful people may therefore be compared to bums who sit all day long in the sun and do no work but refuse the burden of any good activity. Therefore they do not belong to the number of those whom Christ called to rest from their earthly labor when he said, in Matthew 11: "Come to me, all you that labor, and I will refresh you," that is, with eternal happiness.

They are also like the cuckoo, who does not hatch its own eggs but puts them into the nest of another bird and eats the other bird's eggs. In this way the slothful person lives off other people's labor, and what others have gained by hard and painful work, he eats up in idleness; the Psalmist says: "They devour the poor man in secret," that is, the sustenance on which the poor should live. But that is food which perishes and does not last into eternal life, as the *Gloss* on John says: "The food that perishes is the bread which idle people eat who do no work in either the active or the contemplative life." Whence Chrysostom says in homily 14 of his *Imperfect Work on Matthew*, commenting on the words "Our daily bread": "He adds the word 'daily' to forbid luxurious food, so that we should eat only as much as our nature reasonably requires, not as much as our appetite craves. For if one spends as much on one dinner as might be enough for a hundred people who live modestly, one does not eat 'daily' food but food for many days." For this reason such people may well be called wasps or degenerate bees, which do not produce honey but consume it; as the Psalmist says: "Strangers will plunder his labors."

Third, I say that such people may be likened to certain noblemen who hold on to their vineyards so tightly that they share them with no one but preserve

70   devenerint, qui sunt vermes et serpentes, revera ibi sine modo et mensura
      illa vorabunt, secundum illud Ecclesiastici 10: "Cum moritur homo, heredi-
      tabit serpentes, bestias, et vermes." Et ideo tunc dabit invitus vermibus
      quod modo negat dare divinis obsequiis aut bonis operibus.
          Contra ergo tales bene narratur de quodam divite habente tres filios.
75   Volens autem scire quis eorum hereditatem suam dignius possideret, illam
      magis pigriori promisit. Quo audito dixit senior: "Pater, michi competit
      hereditas, nam ita piger sum quod, si iuxta ignem iacerem et illum viderem
      circa me undique dilatari, cicius pedes et tibias cremari permitterem quam
      illas ab igne retrahere vellem." Cui alius frater respondit: "Non sic, set
80   michi competit hereditas. Si enim iacerem in maxima pluvia et continue in
      oculis meis distillaret, cicius suffocarer quam faciem amoverem aut palpe-
      bras clauderem." Quo audito dixit tercius frater: "Mea, inquit, est iuste
      hereditas. Nam ita piger sum quod, si essem ductus ad suspendium et funus
      in collo meo circumderetur et gladium acutissimum haberem in manu, cicius
85   penderem quam cordam precin⟨d⟩ere vellem." Moraliter per primum fratrem
      intelligi potest luxuriosus, qui p⟨oc⟩ius in ardentissimis concupiscenciis
      consummari vellet quam pedes male affectionis inde retraheret. Per secundum
      intelligitur cupidus, qui cicius mallet excecari quam oculum mentis a
      cupiditate claudere, quia sicut stille continue cadentes excecant oculos
90   corporis, sic divicie oculos mentis. Per tercium intelligitur superbus vel
      in quocumque peccato alio homo captus et ligatus, qui pocius per funem male
      consuetudinis vellet ad infernum trahi et ibi [f. 111v] suspendi quam [per]
      gladium lingue in confessione liberari.
          Unde bene dicitur [illud] Proverbiorum 26: "Sicut ostium vertitur in
95   cardine, sic piger in lecto," scilicet perverse voluntatis, a quo exire non
      plus potest quam pissis in rethe vel avis in visco, eo quod ipsi in rete et
      visco diaboli circumvoluti undique sunt et ligati. Bene ergo dicitur piger
      "ostium in cardine," quia sunt nonulli quasi in lecto sompnolencie torpen-
      tes qui ultra tempus debitum plus appetunt in illo hinc inde revolvere et
100   in illo tepescere quam ad ecclesiam eundo missas et Dei officium audire. Et
      cum tarde surrexerint, plus festinant ad mensam quam ad ecclesiam. Quo ta-
      men cum venerint, supra prunas aut carbones ardentes videtur illis stare,
      et ideo minime ibi poterunt remanere, qui pocius stare deberent et morari
      quousque ab ecclesia fuerint redire licenciati. Quod fit quando missa [ter-
105   minatur] et a sacerdote dicitur: "Ite, missa est," quasi diceret: hec missa
      iam ad Patrem est transmissa, et ideo "ite," hoc est, in nomine Domini ad
      propria remeate.
          Sunt eciam aliqui tales qui nichil curant de missa nisi tantum ut
      panem sanctum habeant et aquam benedictam, et hoc sufficit, ut eis videtur.
110   Non enim attendunt quod corpus Christi quod sumit sacerdos non tantum pro
      se ipso facit, set pro omnibus [fidelibus qui ibi sunt vel esse vellent, si

it all for their heirs; but when the latter get these possessions into their hands, they waste and consume them without measure and reason. Thus, spiritually, many people today give their bodies over to idleness without doing any useful work, so that when their bodies come to their heirs, which are worms and snakes, the latter will eat them without measure and reason, according to the words of Ecclesiasticus 10: "When a man dies, he shall inherit serpents, beasts, and worms." And then he will, against his desire, give to the worms what he now refuses to give to divine worship or good deeds.

As a warning to such people there is a good story about a rich man who had three sons. As he wanted to know which of them was the worthiest to possess his heritage, he promised it to the laziest. When the oldest son heard this, he said: "Father, the heritage belongs to me, for I am so lazy that, if I were lying next to a fire and saw it spread all around me, I would rather let my feet and legs burn than draw them back from the fire." To whom the second brother replied: "Not so, but the heritage belongs to me. For if I were lying in a rainstorm and water were continuously dripping into my eyes, I would rather drown than move my head or close my eyelids." But when the third brother had heard this, he said: "Then the heritage is rightly mine, for I am so lazy that, if I were being led to the gallows with a rope around my neck and had a sharp sword in my hand, I would rather hang than cut the rope." By the first brother we can morally understand a lecher, who would rather be consumed in his burning lust than draw the feet of his evil affection from it. By the second we can understand the covetous person, who would rather go blind than close the eye of his mind to covetousness, because just as drops that fall constantly blind the eyes of our body, so do riches blind the eyes of our mind. And by the third we can understand a proud man, or anyone that is caught and bound in any other sin, who would rather be drawn to hell by the rope of evil habit and be hanged there than free himself in confession with the sword of his tongue.

Therefore it is well said in Proverbs 26: "As the door turns upon its hinges, so does the slothful upon his bed," that is, in the bed of his perverse desire, from which he cannot escape any more easily than a fish from the net or a bird from the lime, because he is completely wrapped up and bound by the net and lime of the devil. Hence a lazy person can well be called "a door upon its hinges," because many such people lie indolent in the bed of somnolence that they would much rather snuggle in its warmth beyond a reasonable time than go to church and attend Mass and God's service. And when at last they have got up, they hurry rather to the table than to church. If they should finally get there, it seems to them that they are standing on glowing coals, and so they can hardly stay there at all, whereas they really ought to remain until they are given leave to return home from church. This happens when Mass is over and the priest says, "Go, the Mass is ended," as if he were saying: this Mass has

quo modo possent; et quod specialiter pro omnibus] circumstantibus facit
mencionem in canone misse. Patet ergo quod qui interesse possunt et nolunt,
quod quantum in illis est ab illo beneficio privantur. Et sunt nonnulli qui
115   nec de pane sancto nec de aqua benedicta curant. Et forte causa est quia
virtutem illorum non agnoscunt.

---

7 Circa] *add* autem O.   **8** est] *om* O.   **11** ministerium] *add* iuste O.   **15** nocte] sero O.
17–18 iussit . . . inquit] ut illas aperiret respondit O.   **18** Scivi] *add* inquit O.   **19** Cum]
cumque O.   **21** iantari] iantare O.   **25** et] *om* O.   **31** sedere] *add* et O.   vigilare] *add*
vana O.   **32** Bernardus] christus O.   miser] piger O.   **33** Dicis] *corr in* C, *apparently
from* dices *to text*.   **44** possim] possum O.   **46** onus] usus C.   occupacionum] opera-
cionum O.   **54** deberent] debuerunt O.   **56** ociosus] *om* O.   **57** Mattheum] *om* C.R.
60 racio] racionalis O.   **66** sua] *add* et nemora O.   participant] percipiant C.   **68** devas-
tant] *add* illa M.W; *add* illi R.   **71** vorabunt] devorabunt O.   **75** autem] ergo O.
eorum] illorum O.   dignius] dignus O.   **76** magis] *om* O.   Pater] frater O.   **77** sum] *add*
ego O.   **81** faciem] capud O.   **83** funus] funis R.W.   **84** circumderetur] circumdaretur
O.   manu] *add* mea O.   **85** precindere] precingere C.   **86** pocius] prius C.   **96** in] de
O.   in(2)] a M; de R.W.   **109** sanctum] *om* O.   **115** sancto] *om* O.   nec de] vel O.

V.ii   DE VIRTUTE MISSE ET PANIS ET AQUE BENEDICTE

Et ideo iam considerandum est que sit virtus misse, panis, et aque benedicte. Set ut apercius hec intelligantur, primo videndum est de sacerdote
missam celebrante qualis esse debet; secundo, de forma et materia corporis
de qua fit sacramentum misse; et tercio, de virtute misse.
5   Est ergo sciendum quod sacerdos ad tam sacrum misterium deputatus
habebit ista quatuor: debet esse mundus, [f. 112] discretus, pius, et
iustus. Mundus autem debet esse a culpa quam in aliis est iudicaturus, quia
secundum Augustinum iudicat aliquando qui iudicandus est, seipsum condem-
nat. Cognoscat ergo seipsum primo et purget quod ab aliis iudicat purgan-
10   dum, et maxime antequam ad istud sacramentum sumere accedat, advertens
concilium Pauli: "Probet autem seipsum homo, et sic de pane illo edat et de
calice bibat. Qui autem manducat et bibit indigne, iudicium sibi manducat
et bibit." Et ideo debet sic in omni mundici[a] seipsum ornare, quod sibi
cedat ad salutem et aliis in exemplum. Secundo sacerdos debet esse discre-
15   tus, ut sciat circa sacramentum discernere et intelligere que pertinent ad
illud, quomodo tractabitur, quibus dabitur, et quibus negatur. Quod eciam
in aliis sit discretus, sicut in confessione, scilicet ut ibi sciat discernere de peccatis, quid veniale sit, quid mortale, et que penitencia cui-
[cum]que peccato convenit et sufficit, secundum qualitatem et quantitatem
20   illius. Unde Augustinus: "Caveat, inquit, sacerdos iudex spiritualis, ut
sicut non committit crimen nequicie, ita non careat ⟨munere sciencie⟩."
Tercio debet esse pius, maxime in confessione, ut scilicet diligenter

been sent to the Father; therefore, go, that is, in the Lord's name return to your homes.

There are also some people of this kind who do not care about the Mass except to get the blessed bread and holy water, and that, they think, is enough. They do not consider the fact that when the priest receives the Body of Christ, he does so not only for himself but for all the faithful who are present or who would want to be if they somehow could; further, that the priest explicitly mentions "all here present" in the canon of the Mass. It is therefore manifest that all who can be present and do not want to, lose the benefit of the Mass, as far as this lies in their power. And many do not even care about the blessed bread and water. Perhaps that is so because they do not understand their value.

15–22 Petrus Alphonsus, *De scientia clericali*, p. 38. Cf. Tubach 4288. **48–49** Matt. 11.28. **53** Hab. 3.14. **58–62** Ps.-Chrysostom, *Opus imperfectum*, hom. 16, 11 (PG 56:713). **64** Ps. 108.11. **71–72** Ecclus. 10.13. **74–85** Tubach 2896. **94–95** Prov. 26.14.

V.ii THE SPIRITUAL POWER OF THE MASS AND OF BLESSED BREAD AND HOLY WATER

Therefore we must now deal with the spiritual power of the Mass and of the blessed bread and water. That this may be understood more clearly, I shall first speak of the priest who celebrates Mass, what he should be like; second, of the form and the elements that belong to the sacrament of the Mass; and third, of the power of the Mass.

We should know, then, that the priest who is appointed to such a sacred mystery will have these four qualities: he must be pure, discreet, pious, and just. He must be pure from the sins which he is to judge in others, for according to Augustine, a man sometimes judges who himself is to be judged and condemns himself. He must therefore understand himself first and cleanse in himself what he judges must be cleansed in others. And especially so before he approaches to receive this sacrament, paying heed to the advice of Paul: "Let a man prove himself, and so let him eat of that bread and drink of the chalice. For he that eats and drinks unworthily, eats and drinks judgment to himself." And thus he must deck himself out in all purity, that it may be for his own salvation and as a good example to others. Second, a priest must be discreet, so that he can judge matters that concern this sacrament and understands what belongs to it, how it is celebrated, to whom it is given, and to whom it is refused. He must also be discreet in other things, such as confession, where he must know how to discern matters concerning sins, which is venial, which is mortal, and what penance belongs to each sin and is sufficient, according to

attendat peccatorum contricionem et modum, ut scilicet instruat ad confessionem et satisfactionem ante istius sacramenti suscepcionem, nunc confor-
25   tando peccatorem si desperet, nunc peccata inquirendo si erubescat, nunc
vitam et veniam pollicendo si se corrigat, nunc penas intollerabiles commi-
nando ne mortaliter peccet. Quarto debet esse iustus, considerando utrum
quis peccet casu an ex deliberacione, utrum ex se, per se, vel alterius suggestione; gravius enim punietur peccatum innatum quam seminatum. Debet
30   e⟨ciam⟩ attendere utrum quis ex sua malicia an ex coactione aut necessitate, quia sunt qui rapiunt et furantur compulsi egestate, et sunt qui rapiunt cupiditatis voragine. Et secundum hoc tenetur sacerdos suas penitencias
taxare.
      Circa [f. 112v] autem materiam et formam istius sacramenti est scien-
35   dum quod materia est panis et vinum. Unde Ambrosius libro *De sacramentis*:
"Sermone enim Christi hoc conficitur sacramentum, quia sermo Christi creaturam mutat. Et sic—hoc est, conversi⟨ve⟩ et non aliter—ex pane fit
corpus Christi. Et vinum cum aqua in calice missum fit sanguis consecracione Verbi celestis." Forma autem verborum ex quibus fit sacramentum dicit
40   Magister *Sentenciarum*, libro 4, distinctione 8, capitulo 4, sic: "Consecracio, inquit, quibus fuit verbis attende: que sunt 'Hoc est corpus meum,' et
iterum 'Accipite et bibite ex hoc omnes. Hic est sanguis meus.' Per reliqua
omnia que in missa dicuntur aut fiunt, laus Deo defertur." Dicit eciam
ibidem distinctione 2, capitulo 4, quod necessario vino admiscetur aqua,
45   per quam populus signatur qui per Christi passionem redemptus est. "Cum
igitur in calice vinum et aqua commiscetur, Christo populus adunatur et
credencium plebs in quem credit copulatur. Que copulacio aque et vini sic
miscetur in calice Christi, ut mixtio illa non possit separari. Nam si
vinum tantum quis offerat, sanguis Christi incipit esse sine nobis." Hec
50   ibi nota et plus satis.
      Et nota quod consecra⟨to⟩ Christi corpore plura mirabilia ibi conside-
rantur, iuxta illud Psalmi: "Memoriam fecit mirabilium suorum: escam dedit
timentibus se." Quorum mirabilium unum est quod ad verbum hominis una
substancia in aliam convertitur. Secundum est quod ad verbum unius sacerdo-
55   tis et non alterius hominis hoc fieri potest. Tercium est quod illud quod
fuit prius, postea non est, et tamen in nullo adnichilatur. Quartum est
quod multe substancie convertuntur in aliquid et illud non augmentatur.
Quintum [est] quod illud est de novo ubi prius non fuit, et tamen secundum
locum non mutatur. Sextum est quod idem corpus in numero sit simul in
60   infinitis locis. Septimum est quod magnum sub modica albedine continetur.
Octavum est quod tantum sit de isto corpore sub parte minima, quantum sub
tota. Nonum est quod totum corpus [f. 113] manducetur et non tangatur
dentibus. Decimum est quod aliqua quantitas dividatur et [tamen] contentum
sub una manet indivisum. Undecimum est quod multi [simul] cibum illum

its nature and gravity. Whence Augustine says: "Let a priest, who is a
spiritual judge, beware that as he does not commit the crime of sin, thus he
must likewise not lack the gift of knowledge." Third, he must be pious,
especially in confession, so that he pays careful attention to the sinners'
contrition and its form; he must instruct the sinner in making his confession
and satisfaction before he receives this sacrament, now by comforting him if he
despairs, now by asking about his sins if he is ashamed, now promising him life
and forgiveness if he amends himself, now threatening him with unbearable
punishment so that he does not commit mortal sin. And fourth, the priest must
be just and consider whether someone commits a sin by accident or deliberately,
whether of his own, by himself, or through someone else's suggestion. For a
sin that springs from a person's mind is more gravely punished than one planted
there. He must further discrimate whether someone has sinned of his own malice, or under constraint, or out of necessity, because some thieves steal
because they are forced by poverty, while others do so because they are en-
gulfed in covetousness. And according to such discrimination the priest must
determine the penances he imposes.

With respect to the elements and the form of this sacrament, we must know
that its elements are bread and wine. Ambrose says in his book *On Sacraments*:
"This sacrament is confected by the word of Christ, because the word of Christ
changes his creation. And in this way—that is, by conversion and not otherwise—the bread becomes the Body of Christ; and the wine mixed with water in
the chalice becomes his Blood, by the consecration of the Word from heaven."
The form of the words by which this sacrament is effected, the Master of the
Sentences announces as follows, in book 4, distinction 8, chapter 4: "Notice
the words by which the consecration is effected: they are, 'This is my Body,'
and again, 'Take and drink from it all. This is my Blood.' Everything else
that is said or done in the Mass is a matter of giving praise to God." And in
the same place, distinction 2, chapter 4, he says that necessarily water is
mixed with wine, to symbolize the people who are redeemed through Christ's
Passion. "For when wine and water are mixed in the chalice, the people is
united with Christ, and the mass of the faithful is joined to him in whom they
believe. This joining of water and wine in the chalice of Christ is a mixture
that cannot be separated. If someone were to offer only wine, the Blood of
Christ would come to be without us." Further discussion of the sacrament can
be found in the same place of the *Sentences*.

Notice that when the Body of Christ is consecrated, many miraculous things
can be found in it, according to the words of the Psalmist: "He has made a
remembrance of his wonderful works: he has given food to them that fear him."
One of these miracles is that at a man's word one substance is changed into
another. The second is that this comes about at the word of a single priest
and not of any other person. The third is that what existed before does not

65   accipiunt et tamen ille cibus integer persistat. Duodecimum est quod ac-
      cidencia existant in actus suos sine subiecto. Decimum tercium est quod
      vera caro Christi habet saporem panis. Decimum quartum est quod cibus cuius
      est nutrire corpus nutriat spiritum. Decimum quintum est quod cuius est
      incorporari cibanti sibi incorporat cibantem.

70   Et nota quod in isto sacramento benedicto ista sex considero: in
      figura rotunditatem, in pressura tenuitatem, in aspectu albedinem, in gustu
      dulcedinem, in una parte dulcis descripcio, in alia parte levis percussio.

          [Ronde in schapyng,
           þynne in þe bakyng,
75   Whyte in þe seyng,
           Swete in þe smackyng or tasting,
           On þe to halfe wel y-wrete,
           On þe toþer halfe þynne y-smete.]

      Primo dico quod videmus in isto sacramento in figura rotunditatem, in
80   signum quod simus rotundi ad omnes per amorem et caritatem; de qua nota
      supra, parte 3. Secundo, per pressure tenuitatem denotatur quod erimus
      tenues per penitenciam abstinencie; pro qua nota post, parte 6. Tercio, per
      albedinem in aspectu denotatur quod erimus puri et albi per castitatem et
      vite mundiciam; pro qua nota post, parte 7. Quarto, per gustus dulcedinem
85   denotatur quod nichil ibi loqui debemus nisi quod iustum, verum, et hones-
      tum est, contra detractores et huiusmodi; nota supra, parte 3. Quinto, per
      descripcionem crucis et nominis Iesu denotatur primo quod memoriter penes
      nos retineamus quomodo ille dulcissimus Iesus, qui salvator interpretatur,
      per virtutem et misterium crucis nos redemit et salvavit a potestate diabo-
90   li; unde de cruce nota supra satis, parte 3, de caritate, et de hoc nomine
      Iesu et de eius potestate similiter nota ibidem. Sexto, per levem percus-
      sionem denotatur quod erimus leves quasi nichil curando de istis terrenis,
      quod directe vadit contra avariciam et cupiditatem; pro quo nota supra
      parte 4, capitulo 1 et deinceps per totum. De isto nomine Iesu, [f. 113v]
95   quando scribitur Apocalipsis ultimo: "Veni, Domine Iesu," est sciendum
      quod tante virtutis et potestatis est quod sibi nullus potest resistere nec
      potest ipsum effugere. Est eciam t⟨err⟩or demonum, salus hominum, et gau-
      dium celestium ordinum; Philippensium 2: "In nomine Iesu omne genu flecta-
      tur, celestium, terrestrium, et infernorum," etc.

100   [C]irca autem virtutem et effectum misse est sciendum secundum Bernar-
      dum quod istud benedictum sacramentum est "egrotis medicina, peregrinan-
      tibus dieta, debiles confortat, valentes delectat, languorem sanat, sanitatem
      servat. Per illud eciam fit mansuecior ad correpcionem, paciencior ad laborem,
      ardencior ad amorem, sagacior ad cautelam, ad obediendum prompcior, et

exist thereafter, and yet it is in no way destroyed. The fourth is that many substances are changed into something, and yet the latter is not increased. The fifth is that it is newly where it was not before, and yet it has not changed place. The sixth is that the one Body is simultaneously in an unlimited number of places. The seventh is that such a great Body is contained in a small piece of whiteness. The eighth is that there is as much of this Body in the smallest part as there is in the whole. The ninth is that an entire body is eaten yet is not touched by teeth. The tenth is that a quantity is divided, and yet what is contained in it remains undivided. The eleventh is that many receive this food at the same time, and yet this food remains entire. The twelfth is that the accidentals continue to exist in their effects in the new substance. The thirteenth is that the true flesh of Christ tastes like bread. The fourteenth is that food whose function it is to nourish the body nourishes the spirit. And the fifteenth is that what usually becomes part of the person who eats it, here makes the person who eats it part of itself.

Notice further that I perceive six qualities in this blessed sacrament: roundness in its form, thinness in its molding, whiteness in its appearance, sweetness in its taste, a sweet inscription on one side, and a light compression on the other.

Ronde in schapyng . . .

First I say that in this sacrament we see roundness in its form, as a sign that we must be round to all people through love and charity; on this subject see above, part 3. Second, the thinnness of its molding indicates that we shall be thin through abstinence of penance; on which see later, part 6. Third, its whiteness indicates that we shall be pure and white in chastity and purity of our life; for which see part 7 below. Fourth, its sweetness indicates that we must not speak anything other than what is just, true, and honorable, in contrast to backbiters and the like; see above, part 3. Fifth, the impression of the cross and the name of Jesus indicates that we must always keep in mind how this sweet Jesus, whose name means "Savior," has redeemed us through the mystery and power of his cross and has saved us from the devil's power; about this cross see above in part 3 the chapter on charity, and about the name of Jesus and its power see similarly in a chapter of the same part. Sixth, its being compressed to a light weight indicates that we shall be light as if we had no care for earthly things, which is directly opposed to avarice and covetousness; on which see above, part 4, chapter 1 and following, through the whole part. Concerning the name of Jesus, as it is written at the end of Revelation: "Come, Lord Jesus," we should know that it has so much power and strength that no one can withstand or flee from it. For it is a terror to demons, salvation for men, and joy for the celestial ranks; Philippians 2: "In

105 ad graciarum actionem devocior." Hec ille. Item Augustinus, *De civitate Dei*,
     ait quod quocumque die quis devote missam celebraverit vel devote audierit,
     saltem si a peccato mortali immunis exstiterit, quod illa die conceduntur
     sibi cibaria necessaria, [levia colloquia dimittuntur,] iuramenta ignorata
     delentur. Illo eciam die lumen oculorum non amittetur, subito non morietur,
110 et si alias moriatur, pro communicato habeatur. Dum autem missam audierit,
     non senescit; quilibet passus eundo et redeundo ab angelis numeratur. Hec
     ille.
        Et nota similiter quod missa ex sua virtute animam pro qua specialiter
     celebratur a suo purgatorio refrigerat et alleviat, cetereque anime ibidem
115 existentes causa ipsius eciam alleviantur a penis suis, scilicet a tot quot
     competunt tante devocioni aut oracioni. Set quantum hoc fuerit, solus Deus
     novit. Si enim multi homines in domo tenebrosa fuerint, quorum unus tantum
     habeat candelam accensam in manu, certum est quod omnes alii participant
     cum eo de lumine. Si vero unusquisque eorum candelam teneat accensam, tanto
120 lucidiores erunt omnes in domo. Revera sic in proposito. Nam qui celebrat
     pro una [f. 114] anima, quasi unam lucernam tenet in manu unde omnes anime
     illuminantur in purgatorio, hoc est, de lumine illius misse omnes partici-
     pant, gracias illi anime referentes pro qua principaliter celebratur. Set
     quando sacerdos in generali dicit "Lux eterna luceat eis, Domine," etc.,
125 tunc quasi fa⟨culam⟩ ardentem accendit omnibus animabus, qua illuminantur
     penales tenebre et accenditur lux gracie. Unde patet quod quanto plures
     missas pro afflictis celebrat quis, tanto lumen animarum augmentat.
        Queri tamen solet utrum una missa magis prosit defunctis quam alia,
     quia omnis missa est pro defunctis, set non omnis missa est [de] defunctis.
130 Primum autem patet quia hostia, quando in tres partes dividitur, tunc una
     pars signat graciarum actionem que est pro sanctis, secunda signat oracio-
     nem que est pro vivis in terra,° set tercia propiciacionem signat que est
     pro defunctis afflictis in purgatorio. Unde quidam ponit tales versus:

        Pars est pro sanctis, pars illa pro sanctificandis.
135   Illa refert grates, supplicat illa Deo,

     quia tam pro vivis quam pro defunctis supplicamus, set pro sanctis ⟨tantum⟩
     gracias referamus. Et ideo illa sola missa est de defunctis in qua per
     omnes misse partes fit mencio de defunctis, sicut in introitu cum dicitur:
     "Requiem eternam dona eis," etc., et in Epistola et in Evangelio. Set sicut
140 dicunt, illa oblacio corporis Christi benedicti equivalet omnibus, et tamen
     ipsa devocio quam habet sacerdos dum offert eukaristiam Deo magis prosit
     uni quam alteri. Et per hoc patet quod sacerdos si promittat alicui celeb-
     rare pro anima alicuius amici sui, quod non solvit promissum suum nisi tan-

the name of Jesus every knee should bow of those in heaven, on earth, and in hell."

Concerning the effect and power of the Mass, we must first know that according to Bernard this blessed sacrament is medicine for the sick and daily food for pilgrims; it comforts the weak, delights those that are well, heals sickness, and preserves health. Through it one grows more meek under correction, more patient in hardship, more ardent in love, more shrewd in one's caution, more ready to obey, and more devout in thanksgiving. And Augustine says, in *The City of God*, that on the day one devoutly celebrates or hears Mass, especially if one is free from mortal sin, all necessary provisions are granted, idle words are forgiven, and forgotten oaths are canceled. On the same day one will also not lose one's eyesight and will not suddenly die, and even if one should die, one will be counted as having received the sacraments. And while one is hearing Mass, one does not grow older; and every step one takes in going to and returning from Mass is counted by angels.

Notice likewise that through its power a Mass lightens and decreases the purgatorial pains of a soul for which it is said in particular, and because of it the other souls in purgatory find a lightening of their pains, as much as such devotion or prayer can bring it. How much that might be, only God knows. If many people are together in a dark house and only one of them has a lighted candle in his hand, it is certain that all the others share his light. But if each one of them has a lighted candle, then all the people in that house will have so much more light. The same applies spiritually to our matter. The person who celebrates Mass for one soul holds, as it were, one lamp in his hand from which all other souls in purgatory gain some light, that is, they all share in the light of grace that comes from that Mass and give thanks to the one soul for whom the Mass is especially said. But when a priest says the Mass "May your eternal light shine upon them, Lord" in general, then he lights, as it were, a burning torch for all the souls, which illumines the darkness of their punishment and kindles the light of grace. Thus it is manifest that the more Masses one celebrates for the souls in purgatory, the more one increases their light.

Sometimes the question is raised whether one Mass is more useful to the dead than another, since every Mass is for the dead, but not every Mass is "of the dead." The first is the case, because when the Host is broken into three parts, one part symbolizes our thanksgiving for the saints, the second part our prayer for those living on earth, and the third part our sacrificial gift for the souls afflicted in purgatory. Hence the verses:

> One part is for the saints, another for those to be made such.
> The first one renders thanks, the second prays to God,

tum faciat quantum ad missam pro huiusmodi assignata[m] pertinet. Verumpta-
145   men si si⟨mplic⟩iter promittat pro anima alicuius celebrare, potest absolvi
a promisso quamcumque missam dicat.
      Unde narrat Gregorius libro *Dialogorum* de quodam [f. 114v] magnate in
Terra Sancta ab hostibus capto, qui cum diu in vinculis sic detineretur,
credens uxor eius ipsum esse mortuum pro eius anima omni die missas fecit
150   cantare. Unde quociens essent hostie sacre pro eo oblate, tociens solveban-
tur vincula eius. Cum ergo tandem domum reversurus uxori que evenerant
enarrasset, ipsa commemorans dies et horas quibus pro eo celebrare fecisset, cognovit eum eodem tempore a vinculis absolvi quo pro eo sacramentum
offerebatur.
155   Narratur eciam quod fuerunt duo religiosi multum se invicem diligentes, quorum unus devotus valde et alter aliqualiter dissolutus existebat.
Mortuo dissoluto apparuit quadam nocte in choro cum omni obscuritate socio
in sua devocione existente. Cum ergo ille pre timore dixisset, "Benedici-
te," respondit alius, "Dominus." Querens ergo quis esset et quomodo se
160   haberet, respondit socius suus: "Sum, inquit, in maximo purgatorio afflictus propter meas levitates. Set multum me iuvarent oraciones et misse, si
quis de me cogitare vellet et orare." Et hiis dictis disparuit. In crastino
autem socius ille devotus se disponens ad missam accessit. Et cum venisset
ad communionem, hiis verbis cum lacrimis devote pro socio Deum exorabat:
165   "Domine, inquit, Iesu, credo et ore confiteor nullum tam pium, misericor-
dem, ac remunerativum servis suis sicut te, Deum meum. Set nunc ita est
quod si quis a⟨ut⟩ Soldano Babilonie vel cuicumque alteri infideli fideliter in lege sua toto tempore vite sue servisset, et iste in carcere domini
sui socium ligatum haberet, et ad dominum accederet nichil aliud petens
170   post amorem domini sui pro toto servicio suo nisi liberacionem socii,
revera cito liberaretur. Set iam tibi servivi modo meo per tantum tempus
sicut scivi, quamvis non sicut debui, et socium meum [f. 115] habes in tuo
carcere purgatorii ligatum. Nichil ergo aliud peto a tua maxima misericordia et pietate pro toto servicio meo nisi socii mei deliberacionem. Et hanc
175   peticionem, si placet, michi concede." Et hiis dictis corpus Christi cum
omni reverencia sumpsit. Nocte vero sequente cum in devocione sua prostra-
tus orasset, apparuit sibi dictus socius cum inmensa claritate et illum
hiis verbis allocutus est: "Benedictus sis inter omnes socios. Nam per te a
pena sum deliberatus, et iam ad gaudium transio." Et statim disparuit.
180   Patet ergo quod maximum opus misericordie est hic captivos a vinculis
eripere, quorum penam sic per exempla perpendimus. Que quidem pena, scilicet purgatorii, secundum beatum Augustinum, omnes alias qualescumque in
centuplum excedit naturale⟨s⟩. De qua narrat venerabilis Beda *De gestis*
Anglorum, quod quidam paterfamilias in partibus Northhumbrorum vitam rcli-
185   giosam duxit. Tandem infirmitate correptus primo noctis tempore defunctus

because we pray for both living and dead, but for the saints we only give thanks. And therefore only that Mass is "of the dead" in which throughout all its parts mention is made of the dead, as, for instance, in the introit, when we say: "Give them eternal rest, O Lord," and so forth; and similarly in the readings of the Epistle and the Gospel. But as they say, the offering itself of the blessed Body of Christ is of equal value for all, and yet the particular intention a priest has when he offers the Eucharist up to God may bring greater benefit to one person than to another. From this it is clear that when a priest promises someone to celebrate a Mass for the soul of a friend, he does not make good his promise unless he does all that belongs to a Mass established for this purpose. If, however, he simply promises to say a Mass for someone's soul, the promise can be fulfilled by whatever Mass he says.

Gregory's *Dialogues* tells of a story about a nobleman who was captured by his enemies in the Holy Land. As he was held in fetters for a long time and his wife believed him to be dead, she had Masses sung for his soul every day. And every time the sacred Host was offered up for him, his fetters fell from him. When he finally returned home and told his wife what had happened, remembering the days and hours at which she had Mass celebrated for him, she recognized that he was freed from his fetters at the same time as the sacrament was being offered for him.

It is further reported that there were two religious who loved each other very much; one of them was very devout, the other somewhat dissolute. When the latter had died, he appeared one night rather darkly to his companion, who was praying in the choir. As he exclaimed in fear, "Bless us," the other replied, "O Lord." Then when he asked him who he was and how he was doing, his companion answered: "I am being afflicted with heavy pains in purgatory because of my levity. But prayers at Mass would help me greatly, if someone would think of me and pray." With these words he disappeared. On the following day, his friend disposed himself devoutly at Mass, and when he went to Communion, he devoutly prayed to God for his friend, with tears and in these words: "Lord Jesus, I believe and confess openly that no one is so compassionate, merciful, and ready to reward his servants as you are, my God. But now it is the case that if someone had faithfully served the Sultan of Babylon or any other infidel in his law during his whole life, and this person were to have a friend bound in his lord's prison and were to go to his lord asking, after his lord's love, for no other reward for all this service but the freedom of his friend, surely the latter would be quickly released. I have now served you in my own way for such a long time as well as I knew, even though not as well as I should, and my friend is bound in your prison of purgatory. Thus I ask for no other reward for my service from your great mercy and pity than freedom for my friend. Please grant me this petition." And after these words he received the Body of Christ with all reverence. In the following night, as he was praying

est. Set diluculo reviviscens, repente residebat. Quo viso omnes qui ibi
fuerant perterriti fugerunt excepta uxore, que plus ipsum diligebat. Quam
ipse consolabatur dicens: "Noli timere, quia iam vere a morte surrexi et
adhuc inter homines vivere permissus sum, ita tamen quod aliter quam antea
190   vixi vivam." Statimque ad oratorium perrexit ibique oracione facta mox
omnem substanciam in tres partes divisit, quia unam uxori, aliam filiis, et
terciam pauperibus erogavit. Ipse vero locum secrete mansionis ingressus
usque ad diem mortis sue in tantam penitenciam se constrinxit ut, si lingua
taceret, duricia quoque vite sue verum esse quod viderat exclamaret. Narra-
195   bat autem quomodo ab angelo ductus vidit tam paradisum iocunditatis et
glorie quam purgatorium afflictionis et pene quam eciam infernum, [f. 115v]
ut ibi patet, confusionis et miserie. Que omnia ut viderat, tam de gaudiis
quam de penis et tormentis, regi Alfrido, devotissimo tunc temporis super-
stiti, ac aliis ut converterentur ad Dei servicium studiosius enarravit.
200   Cum autem ipsemet frequencius aquam congelatam ingredi solebat, aliquando
usque ad lumbos, aliquando usque ad collum, et orare, et super hoc argueretur ab amicis, respondit se duriora vidisse; unde de duobus malis minus
malum eligendum esse. Hec Beda.
[C]irca vero panem et aquam benedictam est sciendum quod ambo ordinati
205   sunt contra diaboli potestatem et pro gracie recepcione. Unde quia in pri-
mitiva Ecclesia cotidie solebant homines communicari, et postea crescente
plebe institutum erat ut dominicis diebus communicarent, set adhuc magis
populo crescente ordinatum est ut ter in anno communicet, puta in Pascha,
Nativitate Domini, et Pentecosten, ideo propter hoc non quasi eukaristiam
210   set corporis Christi commemoracionem, quia tali die, idest die dominica,
dari soleba⟨t⟩ quibuscumque fidelibus, panis benedictus ordinatus est omnibus fidelibus die dominico distribui contra potestatem diaboli et pro corporis et anime, ut patet in sua benedictione, sanctitate et gracia. Aqua
vero benedicta, sicut patet in eius exorcismo, effugat demones, et ubicum-
215   que fuerit aspersa per invocacionem sancte Trinitatis, nulla demonum infestacio gravabit. Secundum autem aliquos tam panis ille quam aqua delent
venialia peccata et conferunt graciam.

---

6 et] *om* O.   **11** Pauli] iohannis evangeliste O.   **14** sacerdos] *om* O.   **14** negatur]
negetur O.   **19** et(2)] aut M.W; vel R.   **20** Augustinus] *add* ait O.   **21** munere sciencie]
vivere sancte C.   **23** instruat] instruatur M.W; *longer om* R.   **25** peccatorem] *om* O.
30 eciam] esse C; enim R.   sua] propria O.   **37** conversive] conversio C.   **41** fuit] fit R
and source.   **43** defertur] *add* hec ille O.   **44** aqua] *om* O.   **46** commiscetur] miscetur
O.   **47** plebs] *add* enim O; ei *source.*   **50** plus] plura O.   **51** consecrato] consecracio de
C; consecracio R.   **60** magnum] tam magnum corpus M.R; *longer om* W.   **69** cibanti]
add quod O.   **70** considero] *add* scilicet O.   **73–78** Ronde . . . y-smete] *text from* R.
Verse 44, in B1.B3.E.Go1.L2.LC.R.Sp.V.W1.   **80** quod simus] *om* O.   **82** 6] *add* capitulo O.   **84** 7] *add* capitulo O.   **85** loqui] sencire nec credere M; *om* R.W.   **86** 3] *add*

prostrated in great devotion, his friend appeared in a very bright light and
addressed him with these words: "Blessed may you be among all friends. I have
been freed from pain for your sake and now pass on to joy." And he disappeared
at once.

Thus it is manifest that it is a very great work of mercy in this life to
free captives from their bonds, of whose pain we can thus have some idea from
these examples. This pain, namely of purgatory, according to blessed Augustine, surpasses all natural sufferings a hundredfold. On this subject, the
Venerable Bede tells in his *Deeds of the English* of a landlord in Northumberland who led a very religious life. At last he fell sick and died in the first
part of the night. But at dawn he came back to life and suddenly sat up. At
this sight all who were present fled in great terror, except his wife, who
loved him very dearly. He comforted her and said: "Do not be afraid. I have
truly come back from the dead and am allowed to live still among men, but
otherwise than I have lived before." He at once went to the oratory, prayed,
and then divided all his property into three parts, one for his wife, one for
his children, and the third for the poor. He himself entered into a hidden
part of his house and mortified himself until his death in such great penance
that, if his tongue had been silent, the harsh manner of his life would have
proclaimed the truth of what he had seen. For he reported how he was led by an
angel and saw both the joy and glory of paradise and the torment and pain of
purgatory as well as the confusion and misery of hell, as one can find it in
Bede's book. All the things he had seen, the joys and the pains and the
torments, he reported to King Aldfrid, the most devout ruler of that time, and
to others, so that they might turn to serve God more eagerly. He himself often
used to step into ice-cold water, sometimes to his hips, sometimes to his neck,
and to pray thus; and when he was criticized for this by his friends, he
answered that he had seen worse things, and that of two evils one should choose
the lesser. So far Bede.

Regarding the blessed bread and water we must know that both have been
instituted against the power of the devil and for the reception of grace. In
the early Church people used to receive Communion every day, and later, when
the number of Christians increased, it was established that they should receive
Communion on Sundays. But as the number of Christians grew even further, it
was decreed that they should receive Communion three times per year, namely at
Easter, Christmas, and Pentecost. For this reason, not in place of the Eucharist but in commemoration of the Body of Christ, which formerly used to be given
to all the faithful on that day, that is, on Sunday, now the blessed bread has
been instituted to be given to all the faithful on Sunday, against the power of
the devil and for the sanctification and grace of body and soul, as can be seen
in its blessing. The holy water, on the other hand, as is shown in its exorcism, drives demons away, and wherever it is sprinkled about under invocation

capitulo O.   **91** ibidem] *add* capitulo O.   **97** terror] timor C.   **99** celestium …etc.] *om*
O.   **100** est] *add* primo O.   **106** audierit] *add* et O.   **110** autem] eciam O.   **122** illumi-
nantur] *add* alie O.   lumine] *add* gracie O.   **125** faculam] fasciculam C.M.W; fasciculum R.   **129** de] *om* C; pro M; *longer om* R.W.   **132** terra] C *has* quia . . .
referamus *(lines 136–37) here.*   **133** quidam ponit tales] *om* O.   **136** tantum] tunc C.
144 assignatam] assignata C.M.R; significata W.   **145** simpliciter] similiter C.   **147** narrat . . . Dialogorum] narratur O.   **151** evenerant] venerant O.   **161** et] *om* O.   **167** aut]
a C.M; in W.   **183** naturales] naturalem C.R.W.   **198–199** superstiti] superstes O.
208 in(2)] *om* O.   **209** Domini] *om* O.   **210** dominica] dominico O.   **211** solebat] solebant C.   **216** ille] iste O.

V.iii   DE ACCIDIA IN PRELATIS

Est autem advertendum quod non tantum illud vicium accidie in minoribus apparet set in maioribus sepe latere experitur, puta in prelatis Ecclesie et aliis illius Ecclesie ministris, qui frequenter nimis tepidi in sub-
ditorum supportacione et doctrina inveniuntur, set malum exemplum dando
5   satis vigiles et curiosi. Quos [f. 116] ideo Dominus vocat cecos, cum
Psalmista dicens: "Oculos habent et non videbunt," quasi dicat: oculos
sciencie habent et tamen neque peccatum proprium neque aliorum videre
volunt. De quibus Sapiencie 1 dicitur: "Excecavit eos malicia eorum"; unde
eciam et diabol⟨us⟩. Exemplum: Sicut aquila cum predam acceperit primo
10 eruit oculos illius quam tangat corpus ad comedendum, sic diabolus quosdam
prelatos cum ceperit in delectacionibus carnalibus primo oculos mentis
evellit, ne proprium videat defectum neque alienum. Unde Psalmista: "Nescierunt neque intellexerunt, in tenebris ambulant," etc. Et alibi: "Non est
qui faciat bonum, non est usque ad unum." Et ideo "ceci sunt duces ceco-
15 rum," Matthei 15. Et ideo, secundum Gregorium, "tot mortibus digni sunt
quot perdicionis exempla ad alios transmittunt"; unde Ezechielis 4: "Si non
annunciaveris, inquit, impio iniquitatem eius, ipse quidem in iniquitate
sua morietur, sanguinem eius de manu tua requiram." De talibus ergo dicitur
illud Matthei: "Dicunt et non faciunt. Aliis autem inponunt onera gravia et
20 inportabilia, digito autem suo nolunt ea movere." Et ideo tales sunt simi-

of the Holy Trinity, no attack of demons will grieve us. According to some, both this bread and the holy water delete venial sins and confer grace.

8–9 Ps.-Augustine, *De vera et falsa poenitentia* 20 (PL 40:1129).   **11–13** 1 Cor. 11.28.   **20–21** Ps.-Augustine, *De vera et falsa poenitentia* 20 (PL 40:1129).   **36– 39** Ambrose, *De sacramentis* IV.iv–v.14ff. (CSEL 73:52ff.); quoted by Peter Lombard, see the following note.   **40–43** Peter Lombard, *Sent.*. IV.viii.4 (2:282).   **44–49** Ibid., IV.xi.5 (2:301–302).   **52–53** Ps. 110.4.   **81** *FM* III passim.   **82** *FM* VI.iv–vi. **84** *FM* VII.xvii–xx.   **86** *FM* III.iii.   **90–91** *FM* III.xiv and vii.   **94** *FM* IV.x–xii. **95** Rev. 22.20.   **98–99** Phil. 2.10.   **101–105** Hugh of Strasburg, *Comp. theol. ver.* VI.15.   **106–111** This commonplace on "The Virtues of the Mass" or "Meeds of the Mass" was extremely widespread, in Latin and vernacular texts, both prose and poetry. It was attributed to various Fathers and Doctors of the Church. See A. Franz, *Die Messe im deutschen Mittelalter* (Freiburg, 1902; repr. Darmstadt, 1963), pp. 36–72; and *The Lay Folks Mass Book*, ed. T. F. Simmons, EETS 71 (London, 1879), pp. 366ff.   **124** From the Communion of the medieval funeral Mass; Legg, p. 433.   **139** Introit to the medieval funeral Mass; Legg, p. 431.   **147–154** Gregory, *Dialogi* IV.59 (3:196); Tubach 926. **155–179** Tubach 3388; also in Bromyard, "ors," M.XI.116.   **182–183** Cf. Ps.-Augustine, *De vera et falsa penitencia* XVIII.34 (PL 40:1127f.).   **184–203** Bede, *Hist. eccl.* V.12.   **204–217** On blessed bread, etc., see Joseph A. Jungmann, *The Mass of the Roman Rite*, trans. F. A. Brunner (New York, 1955), 2:325–329, 452–459.

V.iii   SLOTH AMONG THE CLERGY

Notice that this vice of sloth not only appears in people of lower status but can also often be found hiding in those of higher rank, namely in prelates and other servants of the Church, who are often found to be too lukewarm in supporting and teaching their subjects, but alert enough and attentive in giving a bad example. These the Lord calls "blind" when he says with the Psalmist: "They have eyes, but they shall not see," as if he were saying: they have the eyes of knowledge and yet do not wish to see their own sin or that of others. Of those is said in Wisdom 1 that "their own malice has blinded them," and the devil does likewise. As an example, just as the eagle, when he catches his prey, first pecks out its eyes before he touches its body to eat it, so the devil, when he has caught any prelates in fleshly delights, first plucks out the eyes of their mind so that they may not see their own or other people's fault. Whence the Psalmist says: "They have not known nor understood; they walk on in darkness," etc. And elsewhere: "There is none who does good, not a single one." Consequently, "the blind lead the blind," Matthew 15. And there-fore, according to Gregory, they are worthy to die as many deaths as they give examples of damnation for others; thus Ezekiel 4 says: "If you do not warn the wicked of his iniquity and he dies in it, I shall require his blood at your hand." And in Matthew it is said of such people: "They say and do not prac-tice. On others they lay heavy and unbearable burdens, but they will not move

les sacco pigmentarii qui bonum odorem refundit et tamen sibi feces retinet. Similiter eciam ioculatoribus qui probitates multas referunt et tamen
illa facere renuunt. Et similiter pauperibus contractis ante portam civitatis iacentibus, qui bonas habent linguas set cetera membra pessima. Unde
25 Ieronimus: "Qui bene docet et male agit, Deum instruit quomodo ipsum dampm-
nare debeat." Et Bernardus: "Miror, inquit, de prelatis cuius ordinis sunt,
qui in vestibus incedunt ut milites, in dignitate Ecclesie ut clerici, et
non pugnant ut milites, non predicant ut clerici. Unde (dicit ipse) cum
nullius ordinis sunt, ibunt ubi nullus ordo est set sempiternus horror in-
30 habitans." Crisostomus eciam super Mattheum, super illud "Super cathedram
Moy- [f. 116v] si": "Video, inquit, nonnullos in scola perversitatis residere qui elemosinas pauperum fidelium dumtaxat ut bene vivant conantur di-
ripere, qui ipsos in cultu dominico deberent informare et animas errancium
consolidare, qui magis de oblacionibus fidelium ventrem student pinguescere
35 quam animarum refectionem spiritualiter eis impendere; 'stipendium ergo
illorum est mors.' "
Cum ergo tales ad ecclesiam vel oratorium veniunt, nulla interveniente
devocione cum tedio et anxietate Dei officium sincopando ⟨ruminant⟩, per
quod Deum offendunt et seipsos a merito evacuant. Unde quedam anachorita
40 sancte vite semel narravit cuidam episcopo Wygornie de quodam sacerdote
tabernario et guloso, qui ibidem sedere solebat usque ad mediam noctem, diu
scilicet potare, et tarde cubare, et de mane nimis dormire et ad ecclesiam
dissolute venire, ibique indistincte officium psallere, sincopando et fes-
tinando in tantum quod uno versu semidicto a clerico alium inchoavit, et
45 sic de aliis similiter. Quod tandem admirans dicta domina Deo frequenter
supplicabat, ut aliquatenus ostenderet si eius obsequium Deo placeret. Unde
quadam nocte dum se oracioni dedisset, audivit vocem venientem et ei sic
Anglice loquentem:

Longe-slepars and ouer-lepers,
50 For-skippers and ouer-hippers,
I holde hem lither hyne.
I am not heryn,
Ne thay bith not myne.
But þey sone amende,
55 Thay shullen to hell pyne.

Et ideo contra tales dicitur in Psalmo: "In labore hominum non sunt, et cum
hominibus non flagellabuntur," quasi diceret: quia non laborant fideliter
in terris in Dei officio et aliis operibus virtuosis set in pigricia et
desidia torpescunt, ideo non [f. 117] flagellabuntur in penis purgatorii
60 cum ceteris hominibus salvandis, set pocius deputentur flagellis infernali-

them with their own finger." Therefore they are like the bag of a cosmetics
dealer which spreads a good smell yet contains excrement; and like storytellers
who tell of noble deeds yet refuse to do them themselves. And they are like
crippled poor people who lie at the city gate: they have good tongues, but
their other members are very poorly. Jerome thus says: "He who teaches well
and acts badly gives God a lesson how he should condemn him." And Bernard
says: "I wonder to what status prelates belong: they walk about in clothes
like knights and in ecclesiastical dignity like clerics, and yet do they neither
fight like knights nor preach like the clergy. Hence (says he), as they belong
to neither order of society, they will go to where there is no order but everlasting horror." And Chrysostom in his work on Matthew, commenting on the
words, "On the chair of Moses," says: "I see many sitting in the school of
perverseness who try to rob the alms of the faithful poor merely that they
themselves may live well, who should educate them in the worship of the Lord
and strengthen the souls of those who are going astray. They are more intent
upon filling their own stomach with the alms of the faithful than on giving
them spiritual food for their souls; 'their reward is death.' "

When such people come to the church or an oratory, they mumble through the
divine office without devotion but in boredom and with an anxious mind and clip
its words, whereby they offend God and deprive themselves of any merit. For
this reason, an anchoress of holy life once told the bishop of Worcester of a
priest who was a glutton and tavern-hunter, who used to sit there sometimes
till midnight, drink long and go to bed late, and in the morning he would over-
sleep and come to church in a state, and then he would mumble through the
office and swallow its words and hurry along, so that he would start a new
verse before his assistant had finished half of his own, and so on likewise
with the rest of his service. The anchoress was much astonished by this and
often asked God to show her if such service pleased him. Then one night, as
she was in prayer, she heard a voice come to her and say in English:

> Long-sleepers and prayer-leapers,
> Overskippers and word-clippers—
> Evil servants, I reckon well.
> Neither myself theirs
> Nor them mine do I tell.
> Unless they amend soon,
> They go to the pains of hell.

Therefore, against such people it is said in the Psalm: "They are not in the
labor of men, and they shall not be scourged like other men," as if to say:
since on earth they do not work faithfully in God's service and in other
virtuous deeds but rather lie torpid in sloth and laziness, they will not be

bus et eternis. Quam ergo iocundum erit in iudicio audire illud Matthei
⟨11⟩: "Venite ad me, omnes qui laboratis et onerati estis," scilicet in
bonis operibus, "et ego reficiam vos." Et quam durum audire illud Psalmi:
"Discedite a me, omnes qui operamini iniquitatem!" Versus:

65 Quantus erit luctus cum iudex dixerit "Ite,"
    Tantus erit fructus cum dixerit ipse, "Venite."

---

2 set] *add* eciam O. 9 diabolus] diaboli C. 17 eius] *om* O. 27 qui] quoniam O.
31 Moysi] *add* sederunt O. 38 ruminant] minuunt C. 41 solebat] *add* aliquando O.
43 dissolute] indissute M.W; indissolute R. 48 loquentem] dicentem O. 49–
55 Longe-slepars . . . pyne] *Verse 45, in* B1.B3.CC.E.Et.Go1.Go2. L2.L3.LC.R.Sp.V.
W1.W2. 57 quasi] acsi O. 62 11] 2 C. 64 iniquitatem] *add* unde O.

V.iv QUARE ACCIDIA SIT DETESTANDA

 Est igitur istud peccatum accidie odiosum et detestandum: primo,
[quia] dulcedinem devocionis tollit et destruit; Psalmista: "Omnem escam,"
scilicet devocionis, "abhominata est anima eorum," scilicet pigrorum. Secundo, quia nullum fructum bone conversacionis profert. Unde Gregorius ⟨33⟩
5 *Moralium*: "Infructuose, inquit, sunt arbores salicis, et tamen tante viri-
ditatis sunt ne arescere vix possunt." Sic accidiosi mundo virescunt carnaliter, set spiritualiter infructuosi arescunt; Osee 9: "Fructum nequaquam
faciunt." Tercio, quia quanto magis quiescit, tanto magis putrescit. Et
ideo bene comparatur aque putride. Natura enim aque est quod per motum et
10 cursum depuratur et in sua puritate conservatur, set per quietem putrescit
et corrumpitur et in vermes resolvitur. Revera sic ociosi putrescunt spiritualiter, quia singula vicia alia seriatim sibi addunt; unde Ezechielis 16:
"Hec fuit iniquitas Sodome, saturitas panis et ocium."
 Contra ergo istud vicium narratur de duobus militibus, quorum unus
15 strenuus erat et audax et alius vecors nimis. Isti tamen coniuraverunt quod
sicut fratres lucra in omnibus dividerent. Venientes ergo ad quandam civitatem ubi fuerat torneamentum proclamatum, cum ille miles vecors didisceret
quod pars adversa [fuerat] potencior, cepit timere languore simulato et
quiescens in lecto. Alter ad torneamentum perrexit, [f. 117v] ubi strenue
20 agens plures equos lucratus est. Quo facto rediit ad socium, querens de

scourged in the pains of purgatory with other people who will be saved, but instead will be handed over to the eternal scourges of hell. How joyful will it be to hear at the Judgment the words of Matthew 11: "Come to me, all you that labor and are burdened," namely in doing good deeds, "and I will refresh you." And how hard will it be to hear those words of the Psalm: "Depart from me, all you workers of iniquity!" Hence the verse:

> As great will be the grief when God our judge says, "Go,"
> As our joy will be when he says to us, "Come!"

---

6 Ps. 113.5; 134.16.   8 Wisd. 2.21.   **12–13** Ps. 81.5.   **13–14** Ps. 13.1, etc.   **14– 15** Matt. 15.4.   **15–16** Gregory, *Regula pastoralis* III.4 (PL 77:54).   **16–18** Ezek. 3.18.   **19–20** Matt. 23.3–4.   **25–26** Ps.-Chrysostom, *Opus imperfectum*, hom. 31 (PG 56:876).   **26–30** Bernard, *De consideratione* III.v.20 (3:447–448).   **30–31** Matt. 23.3.   **35–36** Rom 6.23.   **39–55** See Karl Reichl, *Religiöse Dichtung im englischen Hochmittelalter* (Munich, 1973), pp. 321–325.   **56–57** Ps. 72.5.   **62–63** Matt. 11.28. **64** Ps. 6.9.   **65–66** *Prov* 23647 and 30991a; an English verse rendition in "Unrecorded," No. 7.

V.iv   WHY SLOTH MUST BE SCORNED

This sin of sloth, then, is hateful and detestable, first, because it takes away and destroys the sweetness of devotion; as the Psalmist says: "Their soul," that is, of lazy people, "abhorred all manner of meat," that is, of devotion. Second, because it bears no fruit of a good life. Whence Gregory says, in book 33 of his *Moral Commentary on Job*: "Willow-trees bear no fruit, and yet they are so green that they can hardly grow dry." In the same way, slothful people look outwardly green before the world, but spiritually they are dry and bear no fruit; Hosea 9: "They yield no fruit." And third, because the more a slothful person is at rest, the more he rots. For this reason he can easily be compared to foul water. For as long as water moves and runs, it is naturally kept fresh and retains its freshness; but when it is stagnant, it turns foul and corrupt and grows vermin. In the same way, idlers grow foul spiritually, for they let every vice grow in them, one after the other; whence Ezekiel 16 says: "This was the iniquity of Sodom: fullness of bread and idleness."

To counter this vice, there is a story about two knights; one of them was strong and brave, the other a great coward. At one time they swore to each other that they would share all their winnings like brothers. Now, as they came to a city where a tournament had been proclaimed, when the cowardly knight had found out that the opposing party was more powerful, he grew fearful and

statu suo. Qui audiens torneamentum f⟨ini⟩tum et quod socius bene expedis-
set, capud suum erexit dicens: "Karissime frater, spero quod bene valeo si
haberem unam offam in vino." Qua accepta sanus factus est. Redientes ergo
versus domum ad locum ubi iter suum dividebatur, dixit miles vecors socio:
25 "Nosti, frater mi karissime, iuramentum et fedus inter me et te? Ex quo
ergo tu ad manerium tuum et ego ad meum pergam, iustum est ut lucrum
equorum qu⟨o⟩s in hoc torneamento lucratus es mecum participes." Cui miles:
"Karissime frater, nolo iuramento prestito contraire neque tibi falsus
esse. Et tamen scire debes quod duo in hoc torneamento lucratus sum, scili-
30 cet bonos equos et bonos ictus. Unde in fide qua teneor Deo et vobis, si
bonos equos omnino vultis mecum dividere, et ictus bonos dividetis." Et
extracto gladio cepit eum fortiter verberare. Spiritualiter autem loquendo:
Christus Filius Dei et nos fratres sumus, qui tantum nos dilexit quod
quicquid in vita sua lucrabatur in triginta duobus annis, nobiscum se
35 dividere repromisit. Set certe in hoc torneamento vite huius lucratus est
multam gloriam per angustias et tribulaciones diversas. Et ideo, si illam
gloriam secum participare velimus, oportet hic aliqu⟨id⟩ de pena sustinere,
quia aliter nequaquam suam gloriam nobiscum participabit, quia iuxta beatum
Gregorium in *Omelia unius martiris*: "Non coronabitur quis nisi qui legit-
40 time certaverit," etc.

---

4 33] in C; 23 R.   **6** ne] ut O.   **15** tamen] *add* semel O.   **17** didisceret] didicerat O.
21 finitum] factum C.   **24** domum] *add* simul O.   **27** quos] quis C.   **29** debes] debetis
O.   **36** multam] maximam O.   **37** aliquid] aliqua C.   **39** quis] *om* O.   **40** etc.] *om* O.

V.v   DE OCCUPACIONE SANCTA

[S]ed ad istud vicium expugnandum et extirpandum iam procedit in
medium vivacitas sive agilitas in honestis et bonis occupacionibus. Set
nota quod occupacio bona et honesta duplex est, scilicet activa et contemplativa, hoc est, temporalis et spiritualis. Primum patet in exterioribus
5 laboribus, quibus utuntur [f. 118] homines temporibus debitis ad diversa
necessaria, sicut arando, seminando, metendo, brixando, pandoxando, scin-
dendo, consuendo, edificando, et huiusmodi. Que quidem occupaciones temporibus debitis—quod dico contra illos qui violant dies sanctos per huiusmodi occupaciones et contra preceptum Dei, qui dicit "Sabbata sanctifica"—
10 sunt viriliter operanda propter tria. Nam primo temporibus debitis est
operandum viriliter propter aliarum creaturarum assimilacionem et imitacionem. Omnis enim creatura occupatur in aliquo ministerio; Psalmista: "Omnia

stayed in bed feigning some illness. The other went to the tournament, where
he fought fiercely and won many horses. After that he returned to his companion and inquired after his health. When the latter heard that the tournament
was over and that his companion had fared well, he lifted his head and said:
"Dearest brother, I think I shall be well if I have a sop of wine." He took it
and was healed. As they then were returning home together and came to the
place where their ways parted, the coward said to his companion: "Do you
remember, dearest brother, the oath and pact we made? As you now go to your
manor and I to mine, it is just for you to share with me the horses you have
won in the tournament." Then the brave knight replied: "Dearest brother, I
will not go against our oath nor be false to you. And yet you must know that I
have won two things in that tournament: good horses and good blows. Therefore,
upon the faith by which I am bound to God and to you, if you will share the
good horses with me, you shall also share the good blows." And he drew out his
sword and gave him a good beating. In spiritual terms, Christ, the Son of God,
and we are brothers; he loved us so much that whatever he gained in the thirty-
two years of his life, he promised to share with us. But truly, in the tournament of his life he won great glory through various sufferings and tribulations. Therefore, if we wish to share that glory with him, it is necessary for
us to endure here some of his suffering, for otherwise he will in no way share
his glory with us. For according to Blessed Gregory in his *Homily for One
Martyr*: "No one will be crowned unless he has fairly fought."

2–3 Ps. 106.18.   5–6 Gregory, *Moralia* XXXIII.v.11 (PL 76:676).   7–8 Hos. 9.16.
13 Ezek. 16.49.   14–32 Tubach 2965; also in Harley 7322 (fol. 40v); *Convertimini* (fol.
117); Holcot, Sermon 83.   39–40 2 Tim. 2.5; see Gregory, *In Evangelia*, hom. 37, 1 (PL
76:1275).

V.v   HOLY ACTIVITY

In order to overcome and uproot sloth, liveliness or busyness in honorable
and good works now enters the ring. But notice that holy and honorable activity is of two kinds, active and contemplative, that is, temporal and spiritual.
The first kind occurs in physical work which people undertake in due season and
for various necessary purposes, such as plowing, sowing, reaping, brewing,
baking, tailoring, sewing, building houses, and the like. These kinds of work
are to be undertaken "in due season"—and this I say in order to warn those who
violate the holy days by doing such work against God's commandment which says,
"Sanctify the Sabbath." This work should further be undertaken in a strenuous
manner for three reasons. First, one must work strenuously in due season in
harmony with and imitation of the other creatures. For every creature is
engaged in some task; as the Psalmist says: "All things serve you." But

serviunt tibi." Set nota quod duplex est ministerium, scilicet unum spirituale, de quo Apocalipsis 4 dicitur: "Requiem non habebant sancta animalia
15   dicencia, 'Sanctus, sanctus, sanctus,' " etc. Et aliud est corporale, quod
fit modo per creaturas superiores que sunt in celo, sicut sol, luna, et
stelle, de quibus Iob 38 dicitur: "Con⟨c⟩entum celi quis dormire faciat?";
modo per creaturas inferiores, de quibus dicitur: "Cunctis diebus terre se-
mentis frigus et estus, yemps et estas, dies et nox non requiescent," sci-
20   licet occupari ad Dei laudem in illis occupacionibus ad quas create sunt.
Merito ergo tenetur homo similiter operari ut ceteris creaturis similetur;
Corinthiorum 2: "Laboramus operantes manibus nostris."
    Secundo est viriliter operandum propter laboris occupacionem; Galata-
rum 6: "Opus bonum facientes non deficiamus. Tempore enim suo metemus non
25   deficientes." Sic enim fecit Christus, sicut patet, predicando, docendo,
etc., a nativitate usque ad mortem. In quo spacio, ut totaliter desidiam
auferret, nulla mollicies in manibus aut pedibus aut in quibuscumque aliis
sui corporis membris est inventa. Et ideo qui bene occupari recusant,
Christi discipuli se esse negant. "O," inquit Bernardus, "quam terribile
30   erit ociosis quando exquiretur quomodo tempus nostrum expendimus quod datum
est nobis [f. 118v] ad merendum! Quoniam (dicit ipse) totum tempus nostrum
ordinatum est ad veniam impetrandam, penitenciam agendam, graciam promeren-
dam, et gloriam ex misericordia Salvatoris consequendam. Quid ergo respon-
debitis in illa die quando exigetur a te in ictu oculi totum tempus vivendi
35   tibi impensum? Certe (dicit ipse), dicetur de te sicut de servo malo,
Matthei 22, 'At ille obmutuit.' " Et [tunc] secundum Gregorium sciencia sua
sibi non proderit, quia quando iuxta illam operari debuit illam amisit.
Unde Crisostomus super Mattheum ostendit quibus verbis arguet Dominus
ociosos in die iudicii dicens: "Ego propter vos factus sum homo, propter
40   vos alligatus, delusus, cesus, crucifixus, mortuus. Ubi est ergo tantarum
iniuriarum fructus? Ecce precium sanguinis mei dedi pro redempcione animarum vestrarum. Ubi est ergo servitus vester quem michi pro precio sanguinis
mei dedistis? Ego supra gloriam meam vos habui, cum essem Deus apparens
homo, et viliorem [me] omnibus rebus vestris fecistis. Que ergo iusticia
45   vel fides in vobis? Quis ergo accusabit vos ibi? Certe ipsa consciencia et
peccata; Sapiencie 4: 'Venient in cogitacione peccatorum suorum timidi, et
traducent illos ex adverso iniquitates illorum.' " Unde secundum beatum
Bernardum tunc illorum opera simul loquentur et dicent, "Tu nos egisti et
opera tua sumus. Non deseremus te, set semper tecum erimus et tecum ad
50   iudicium pergemus."
    Tercio viriliter laborandum est propter malorum vitacionem, quia ab opere
bono cessacio est immundarum cogitacionum introductio; unde Gregorius
⟨5⟩ *Moralium*: "Quanto securius ab internis actionibus cessant, tanto lacius
inmunde cogitaciones strepitum in se per ocium congregant," et frequenter

notice that such office is twofold. One is spiritual, which is spoken of in Revelation 4: "The holy animals did not rest saying, 'Holy, holy, holy,' " etc. The other is physical, which is done either by higher beings that are in the heavens, such as the sun, moon, and stars, of which Job 38 says: "Who can make the harmony of heaven sleep?" or by lower beings, of whom is said: "All the days of the earth, cold and heat, winter and summer, day and night shall not cease," that is, in being occupied about God's praise in those tasks for which they were created. Therefore man is rightly held to work in like fashion, so that he may be in harmony with other creatures; Corinthians 2: "We labor, working with our own hands."

Second, one must work strenuously in order to be kept occupied; Galatians 6: "In doing good, let us not fail. For in due time we shall reap, if we do not fail." Christ did this manifestly when he preached and taught and so forth, from his birth to his death. During that time there was no slackening of his hands or feet or other parts of his body, so that he avoided idleness completely. Therefore, people who refuse being well occupied confess that they are not disciples of Christ. "Oh," says Bernard, "how terribly will idlers fare when we are asked how we have spent our time that has been given us to gain merits! For our whole time is given us to pray for forgiveness, to do penance, to earn grace, and to obtain glory from the mercy of our Savior. What then will you answer on that day when you are required, in the twinkling of an eye, to give an account of the entire time of your life that was granted to you? Surely, then will be said of you as it was of that bad servant of Matthew 22: 'But he was silent.' " And according to Gregory his knowledge will not help him then, because he wasted it when he ought to have used it in his actions. Whence Chrysostom in commenting on Matthew shows with what words the Lord will accuse the idle on judgment day, when he says: "For your sake I became man, for your sake I was bound, scoffed, struck, crucified, and killed. Where then is my reward for so many sufferings? I gave my blood as price for the redemption of your souls. Where then is your service which you owe me for the price of my blood? I prized you more highly than my glory, since I was God yet appeared as a man, and you have made me more vile than anything of yours. What justice or faith, then, is in you? Who is it then that will accuse you there? Surely, your own conscience and your sins; Wisdom 4: 'They shall come with fear at the thought of their sins, and their iniquities shall stand against them to convict them.' " Wherefore, after Blessed Bernard, their deeds will then speak up all together and say: "You have performed us and we are your deeds. We will not leave you but be always with you and go with you to your judgment."

Third, one must work strenuously in order to avoid evil, for by desisting from good work we admit impure thoughts; whence Gregory says in book 5 of his *Moral Commentary*: "The more they rest from internal activity, the more do our

55 huiusmodi cogitaciones malas ad actum ducunt. Et ideo sicut aquilam alte
    volantem cadaver putridum facit descendere, sic hominem contemplantem cogi-
    taciones inmunde ad [f. 119] actum putridum et criminosum. Bene ergo ait
    Ieronimus ad Rusticum monachum: "Semper, inquit, aliquid boni operis faci-
    te, ne diabolus vos inveniat inocupatos" et ne ex ociositate aliquem aditum
60 ad animas diripiendas valeat invenire. Nam sic est de diabolo sicut de
    aliquo alium insequente quem nititur capere. Quia si lento passu incedat
    aut diu expectat, hostis eum cito invadit. Si vero expedite vadat, tunc
    frequenter hostis insidias evadere potest. Verbi gracia: Bestia silvestris
    cum a canibus venatur, si tunc retardet cursum aut in currendo aliquamdiu
65 expectat, cito et de facili capitur. Revera sic homo piger et accidiosus,
    dum in opere bono sompnolencia torpescit, a venatore diabolo cito capitur
    et cruciatur; Proverbiorum 23: "Desid[er]ia occidunt pigrum." Et iuxta
    consilium Apostoli Corinthiorum 14: "Omnia honeste et secundum ordinem
    fient in vobis," hoc est, in caritate et bona intencione, quia si aliter
70 fiant, stulta sunt et nullius utilitatis; si vero in caritate fiánt, sine
    merito nusquam recedant quocumque modo et tempore fiant.
        Unde narratur de quodam potente et divite set male vite et incomposi-
    te, qui tamen mediante gracia Spiritus Sancti transiens quodam die per
    quoddam nemus de sua miseria in peccatis cogitabat et quod vitam emendaret
75 et aliquid faceret. Inter alia bona unum specialiter elegit, scilicet quod
    cenobium pro bonis viris et religiosis ad Dei honorem construeret, ut pro
    se et suis tam in vita quam in morte intercessores haberet. Istis ergo
    precogitatis, gladium quo erat accinctus extraxit et modo suo cenobium
    precogitatum cum ecclesia et aliis edificiis mensuravit. Quo facto domum
80 rediit in sancta voluntate perdurans. Set a casu morte subitanea preventus
    in via moriebatur. Accedentes ergo spiritus tam boni quam mali, quis eius
    animam tolleret decertabant, allegan- [f. 119v] tes hinc inde mali mala,
    boni bona pro eo. Dixerunt autem boni angeli quod in ultima voluntate
    planxit peccata et illa deserere proposuit, in cuius signum dictum cenobium
85 in Dei honorem ordinavit. Cum ergo spiritus mali adhuc illud non esse con-
    structum asserebant, cor defuncti apperuerunt, ut videbatur, angeli boni ad
    confusionem aliorum. Et ecce in eius cordis medio quasi cenobium aureum
    cum omnibus pertinenciis quoad ecclesiam et aliis edificiis conspexerunt. Quo
    viso demones recedendo clamabant: "Heu nobis miseris, heu, quod in tam
90 parva hora amisimus ° per tantum tempus nostra opera laboriosa °!" Et hiis
    dictis sublato corpore ab angelis spiritus maligni recesserunt. Unde quali-
    tercumque se habuerit homo in vita, non desinet propter hoc exequi bona
    opera, quia in quacumque hora veraciter peccator ingemuerit de peccatis,
    "vita vivet et non morietur."
95   Est autem alia occupacio contemplativa et spiritualis, in qua omnes
    Christi fideles tenentur occupari, que in multis consistit, et specialiter

impure thoughts gather widespread tumult in them through idleness," and often they lead such evil thoughts to the deed. Therefore, just as a rotten corpse causes the high-flying eagle to come down, thus impure thoughts pull a contemplative to rotten and sinful action. And so Jerome says rightly to the monk Rusticus: "Always engage in doing something good, that the devil may find you busy and may not, because of your idleness, find a way to catch your souls." For with the devil it is just as it is with someone who follows another person whom he tries to catch. If the latter walks slowly or waits for a long time, his enemy soon falls upon him. But if he goes fast, he can often evade his enemy's pursuit. For instance, if a wild animal that is hunted by dogs slows down or hesitates some time on its run, it is caught quickly and easily. In the same way, when a lazy, slothful person grows languid with sleepiness in his good work, he soon gets caught and tortured by the devil, his hunter; Proverbs 23: "His desires have killed the slothful." Therefore, after the counsel of the Apostle in Corinthians 14: "Let all things be done decently and according to order among you," that is, with a good intention and charity, for otherwise they are foolish and of no use; but if they are done in charity, they will never leave you without merit, in whatever way and at whatever time they may be done.

There is a story about a powerful person who was rich but lived a bad, disorderly life. Yet one day, as he passed through a forest, by the grace of the Holy Spirit he reflected on how wretched he was in his sins and thought he should amend his life and do something good. Among various good works he chose one in particular, namely to build a house for good and religious men in God's honor, so that he might have intercessors for himself and his family both in life and in death. When he had thought about these things, he drew out the sword he was carrying and after his fashion drew a plan of the religious house he was thinking of with a church and other buildings. After that he returned home with these holy plans in his mind. But he happened to be overcome by sudden death and died on the way. Then both good and bad angels came and began to dispute which of them should take his soul, the bad angels reciting his evil deeds, the good angels his good ones. Now, the good angels said that with his last act of will he had wept for his sins and intended to leave them, in sign of which he planned the religious house in God's honor. But when the bad angels asserted that he had not yet build it, the good angels, as it seemed, opened his heart, in order to overcome the others. And lo, in the middle of his heart they found something like a golden house for religious with all that belongs to it, a church and other buildings. When the demons saw that, they drew back and shouted: "Woe to us wretches, woe! In such a short time we have lost what we had worked for so hard and so long!" With these words the body was taken away by the angels, and the evil spirits withdrew. Therefore, in whatever circumstances a person may find himself in his life, he should not for

in tribus, scilicet cordis contricione, oris confessione, et operis satisfactione; similiter in pugna contra mundum, carnem, et diabolum. Et nota
quod, quamvis Psalmista dicat: "Preoccupemus faciem eius in confessione,"
100 acsi apercius diceret: contra omnes alias occupaciones, in occupacione confessionis tamen teipsum, o peccator, occupari est necesse ante faciem sacerdotis qui ibi locum Dei occupat. Quia tamen hec occupacio est quasi quedam domina que nullo modo incedere potest sine duabus domicellis specialiter sibi assignatis, que sunt he⟨e⟩: contricio precedens et satisfactio
105 subsequens, ideo de contricione [esset] primo dicendum. Set tamen ad virtutem penitencie, ex qua predicte occupaciones contricionis, confessionis, et
satisfactionis oriuntur, est prius accedendum et aliquid in generali dicendum.

3 bona] sancta O.   9 Sabbata] sabbatum O.   17 Concentum] contentum C.R.W.   faciat]
faciet O.   21 similetur] assimiletur O.   27 aut(2)] *om* O.   28 est inventa] *om* O.
29 discipuli] discipulos R *corr.*   terribile] *add* ergo O.   43 Ego . . . habui] ego vos secundum gloriam meam habui O.   53 5] in C.   59 ne . . . inoccupatos] ut . . . occupatos
O.   65 facili] levi O.   67 23] *om* O. occidunt] occiderunt O.   Et] *add* ideo O.   75 alia]
que O.   85 in] ad O.   86 boni] *om* O.   90 amisimus] *add* quod C.   laboriosa] *add* per-
quirebat C.   100 contra] ante O.   104 hee] hec C.M.W.   105 subsequens] sequens O.

V.vi   DE PENITENCIA IN GENERALI

[f. 120] [C]irca quam est primo sciendum quod penitencia secundum
Augustinum est "mala preterita plangere et iterum plangenda non committere," hoc est, sic a peccato cessare quod voluntatem peccandi non habeat de
cetero. Hinc est quod Magister *Sentenciarum* libro 4 ait: "Penitencia est
5 gracia cum emendacionis proposito, cum commissa plangimus et odimus et
plangenda iterum committere nolimus," quia secundum Augustinum in *Solilo-*
quio, "inanis est penitencia quam sequens coinquinat culpa." "Nichil prodest homini ieiunare, orare, et alia pietatis opera facere nisi mens ab
iniquitate revocetur."
10   Et nota quod duo sunt tempora penitencie, scilicet temporaneum et
serotinum. Primum est ydoneum et congruum, ut scilicet tempore quo quis
peccat eo peniteat, vel dum sanus est et fortis, non quando infirmus et
debilis. Quia secundum Augustinum: "Si tunc penites quando peccare non
potes, peccata dimittunt te, non tu illa." Secundum non est ita congruum,
15   quia illud fit in fine vite, quando robur ad penitendum non suppetit. Et

that reason desist from doing good works, for in whatever hour a sinner is sorry for his sins, "he will live and not die."

There is another kind of activity, contemplative and spiritual, in which all Christians are held to keep themselves busy. This consists in many things, but especially in these three: contrition of heart, confession of mouth, and satisfaction in deed; and similarly in the fight against the world, the flesh, and the devil. And notice that although the Psalmist says, "Let us come before his presence in confession"—as if to say: before all other activities—, yet it is necessary for you, sinner, to be active in the presence of the priest, who in confession takes God's place. But this activity is like a noble lady who can in no way make her appearance without two ladies in waiting that are especially attached to her, namely contrition, who walks before her, and satisfaction, who follows her. Hence we must first speak about contrition. And yet before we do so, we must first consider what power penance has, from which the said three activities—contrition, confession, and satisfaction—derive, and say something about it in general.

---

9 Cf. Exod. 20.8.   **12–13** Ps. 118.91.   **14–15** Rev. 4.8.   **17** Job 38.37.   **18–19** Gen. 8.22.   **22** 1 Cor. 4.12.   **24–25** Gal. 6.9.   **29–36** Cf. Bernard, *De diversis*, sermo 17, 3 (6.1:152).   **36** Matt. 22.12.   **36–37** Perhaps Gregory, *In Evangelia*, hom. 9, 1 (PL 76:1106–1107).   **39–44** Ps.-Chrysostom, *Opus imperfectum*, hom. 49 (PG 56:919). **46–47** Wisd. 4.20.   **48–50** *Meditationes piissimae* II.5 (PL 184:488).   **53–54** Gregory, *Moralia* V.xxxi.55 (PL 75:709).   **58–59** Jerome, *Ep. 125* 11 (CSEL 56:130).   **67** Prov. 21.25.   **68–69** 1 Cor. 14.40.   **72–91** Tubach 3342.   **94** Ezek. 18.21.   **99** Ps. 94.2.

V.vi   ON PENANCE IN GENERAL

Concerning penance, then, we must first know that according to Augustine it means to weep for past sins and not to commit again what one weeps for, that is, so to abandon sin that one has no further desire for it. For this reason, the Master of the *Sentences* says in book 4: "Penance is grace with the intention to amend oneself, when we weep for our sins and hate them and do not want to commit again what we weep for," for according to Augustine in his *Soliloquy*, "that penance is in vain which is soiled by subsequent sin." "It avails man nothing to fast, to pray, and to do other works of piety unless he recalls his mind from evil."

Notice that there are two times of penitence, one timely and the other late. The first is fitting and suitable, namely when a person repents at the time he sins, or while he is healthy and strong, not sick and weak. For according to Augustine: "If you repent when you can no longer sin, your sins leave you, not you them." The second kind is not as suitable, for it is done at the end of one's life when one's strength may not suffice for doing penance.

tamen secundum Evangelistam: "Maius gaudium est in celo super uno peccatore
penitenciam agente," quamvis tempore serotino, "quam super nonaginta novem
non indigentibus penitencia." Exemplum: Dux autem in prelio illum militem
plus commendat qui post fugam conversus hostes in pre⟨l⟩io fortiter premit
20   quam illum qui numquam fugit nec umquam viriliter egit. Sic Christus peccatorem qui prius per malas diaboli suggestiones a bono inchoato fugit set
postea inde recedit et ab omni malo declinat ad bellum revertens et hostes
devincit. Item si homo ad totum victum suum non haberet nisi unum denarium,
qui quatuor continet quadrantes, si illum sapienter expenderet et iterum
25   per illum dives deveniret, multum laudaretur. Si vero ulterius tres partes
illius expenderet et quarta [f. 120v] remaneret, et inde totam substanciam
sive bene sive male expensam omnino recuperaret, adhuc magis laudaretur.
Revera sic in proposito. Per istum denarium intelligo vitam hominis que ex
quatuor etatibus constat, scilicet ex puerili, iuvenili, virili, et senili.
30   Set ut communiter tres prime etates predicte ab homine in vanitatibus
consumuntur. Si ergo in quarta etate et ultima sollicite sibi provideat et
in illa alia perdita recuperaret et dives in moribus [bonis] fieret, recte
laudandus censetur, quia non inchoantibus penitenciam set in illa fortiter
perseverantibus premium promittitur, quia scribitur: "Qui autem persevera-
35   verit usque in finem, hic salvus erit."
     Et nota quod quamvis sit aspera ad oculum, est tamen valde levis et
proficua quoad effectum. Unde refert Diascorides quod pionium appensum
circa colla puerorum non permittet eos cadere. Unde dicit se vidisse quemdam puerum circa cuius [collum] erat pionium appensum, et illo cadente
40   cedicit puer. Set iterum circa collum eius ligatum stetit puer. Spiritualiter per istud pionium, quod est nigrum exterius et interius habet nucleum
album, intelligo penitenciam veram, que quamvis [exterius] fuerit aspera et
quasi nigra et contemptibilis, habet tamen interius nucleum album, scilicet
virtutem penitencie, que tanta est ut dum aliquis fuerit in illa, non cadet
45   in peccatum mortale. Et si a casu suggestione diabolica ceciderit, secundum
Psalmistam tamen "Dominus supponit manum suam," scilicet dando graciam
resistendi illi et cum illa firmiter stare, quia "si ceciderit iustus, non
collidetur." De ista ergo penitencia sancta et meritoria bene ait Bernardus: "O, inquit, felix penitencium humilitas, tu vincis invi⟨nc⟩ibilem
50   quamcito, eciam tu tremebundum iudicem convertis in pium patrem."
     Et nota quod quatuor movent ad [f. 121] penitenciam, de quibus Bernar-
dus ait: "Nimis, inquit, durum est illud cor quod non emolli[un]t Dei beneficia, nec terrent inferni supplicia, nec alliciunt gaudia promissa, nec
castigant temporalia flagicia." Hec ille.
55   Item nota quod septem considero impedimenta [penitencie]. Primum est
pusillanimitas illam agg⟨redi⟩endi. Et tales similes sunt equo qui terretur
a trunco vel umbra. Secundum est pudor confitendi; et tamen, secundum

And yet, as the Evangelist says, "there is greater joy in heaven over one sinner who repents," even if late in life, "than over ninety-nine who do not need penitence." A general in battle has greater praise for a soldier who after first fleeing returns and presses hard upon his enemies, than for one who has never fled nor ever borne himself manly. So will Christ praise the sinner who has first, under the devil's evil suggestions, fled from the good he had begun, but then returns, leaves all evil behind, comes back into the battle, and overcomes his enemies. Likewise, if a man had only one penny (which has four farthings) for his needs and spends it so wisely that he becomes rich from it, he would deserve much praise. But if he had spent three parts of that penny and only one farthing were left, and if with that he were to recover his wealth totally, whether he had spent it well or badly, he would deserve even greater praise. Thus it is also in spiritual matters. By the penny I understand man's life, which consists of four ages: childhood, youth, manhood, and old age. But often a man's first three ages are spent in vain enterprises. Yet if he eagerly provides for himself in his fourth and last age and recovers the things he has lost and becomes rich in good manners, he is rightly worthy of praise, for the prize is not promised to those who begin a life of penance, but rather to those who firmly persevere in it; for it is written: "He that perseveres unto the end shall be saved."

Notice that although penance may be hard at first sight, it is yet very light and useful when one looks at its effect. Diascorides tells us that a peony tied around the neck of children keeps them from falling. He reports that he once saw a child around whose neck a peony had been tied; when the peony fell off, the child also fell, but when it was tied back on his neck, the child stood up again. Spiritually speaking, by this grain, which is black outside and has a white kernel within, I understand true penance. Although it is hard and, as it were, black and contemptible on the outside, it yet has a white kernel within, namely its effect, which is such that, if a person bears it, he will not fall into mortal sin. And if he should happen to fall, by the devil's suggestion, still "the Lord puts his hand under him," according to the Psalmist, namely by giving him grace to resist and thus with it to stand firm, for "if the just man were to fall, he shall not be bruised." About this holy and meritorious penance, therefore, Bernard says fittingly: "O blessed humility of the penitent, you quickly overcome the Invincible, and the awesome judge you turn into a loving father."

And notice that four reasons move a person to penitence, which Bernard mentions: "That heart is too hard which is not softenend by God's benefits, nor frightened by the punishments of hell, nor attracted by the promised joys, nor chastened by temporal mishaps."

Notice further that I count seven impediments to penitence. The first is pusillanimity in beginning it. Such people are like a horse that shies at a

Augustinum, pudor est maxima pars penitencie. Tercium est delectacio peccandi. Set caveat quia secundum Augustinum temporale est quod delectat, set
60   eternum quod cruciat. Quartum est spes diu vivendi. Set Dominus contra hoc
dicit: "Securis iam ad radicem arboris posita est," Matthei 3. Quintum est
desperacio graciam optinendi; set contra hoc dicit Dominus: "Quacumque hora
ingemuerit peccator, vita vivet." Sextum est timor recidivandi. Unde Augustinus de Christo: "Quando, inquit, cecidi, erexit me; et quando steti,
65   tenuit me; et quando ivi, duxit me," quasi diceret: ne timeas, homo, quia
in necessitate paratus est Dominus auxilium prebere. Septimum est confidencia in misericordia Dei. Set hoc est in Spiritum Sanctum peccare; unde
Gregorius: "Misericordiam Dei debemus erubescere, si eius iusticiam nolimus
formidare."
70   Et nota quod effectus penitencie est quod per eam homo absolvitur a
peccatis, restituitur Ecclesie, reconciliatur Christo, ditatur donis spiritualibus, de filio diaboli filius Dei efficitur. Per illam eciam paradisus
aperitur, angel⟨o⟩s letificat, amissa bona revocat, et penam eternam devitat. Et ideo iuxta concilium Evangelii qui sic dicit: "Penitenciam agite,
75   appropinquabit regnum celorum."

---

3 quod] ut M.R; et W.   6 nolimus] nolumus O.   15 suppetit] suppetat O.   19 prelio]
premio C.   25 laudaretur] *add* revera sic in proposito *canc* C.   38 colla] collum O.
41 pionium] granum O.   44 in] cum O.   49 invincibilem] invisibilem C.   52 emolliunt]
emollit C.W.   54 ille] bernardus O.   56 aggrediendi] aggerendi C.   59 caveat] caveant
O.   62 hoc] *om* O.   64 Christo] *add* ait O.   68 nolimus] nolumus M.W; no R.   73 an-
gelos] angelus C.

V.vii   DE CONTRICIONE

[C]irca autem partes pentiencie in speciali est modo dicendum, et
primo de contricione, que est eius prima pars integralis, de qua sic procedam: primo, quid sit contricio et quomodo adquiritur; secundo, de quibus
conterendum esse videtur; tercio, que mala eveniunt converti differentibus;
5   quarto, que bona eveniunt [f. 121v] vere conterentibus.
Est ergo contricio, prout habetur *De penitenciis*, distinctione 1,
"dolor voluntarie assumptus cum voluntate confitendi et satisfaciendi habi-

treetrunk or a shadow. The second is shame to confess; and yet, according to
Augustine, shame is the most important part of penitence. The third is pleasure in sinning. But let such people beware, for according to Augustine, what
delights us is temporal, but what torments us, eternal. The fourth is hope of
a long life. But against this the Lord says in Matthew 3: "Now the axe is
laid to the root of the tree." The fifth is despair of receiving grace. But
against this the Lord says: "At whatever hour the sinner groans, he shall
live." The sixth is fear to fall back into sin. With respect to this, Augustine speaking of Christ says: "When I fell, you helped me up; when I stood,
you held me firm; and when I walked, you guided me," as if he were saying: do
not be afraid, man, for God is ready to give his help in your need. And the
seventh impediment is overconfidence in God's mercy. But this is a sin against
the Holy Spirit; whence Gregory says: "We must blush before God's mercy, but
we should not fear his justice."

And notice finally that the effect of penitence is that through it man is
absolved from his sins, restored to the Church, reconciled with Christ, en-
riched with spiritual gifts, and from being a child of the devil made a child
of God. It further opens paradise, makes the angels happy, brings back goods
that had been lost, and wards off eternal pain. Therefore, after the counsel
of the Evangelist: "Do penance, for the kingdom of heaven is at hand."

2–3 A ubiquitous scholastic definition, frequently attributed to Augustine and perhaps
from Ps.-Ambrose, *Sermo 25* 1 (PL 17:655). **4–6** Peter Lombard, *Sent.* IV.xiv.3
(2:318). **6–9** Ibid., 2–3 (2:318–319). **13–14** Augustine, *Sermo 393* (PL 39:1715); cf.
Peter Lombard, *Sent.* IV.xx.1 (2:372). **16–18** Cf. Luke 15.7. **18–20** Gregory, *In
Evangelia*, hom. 34, 3 (PL 76:1248). **34–35** Matt. 10.22. **37–40** From Galen; see
Macer floridus, no. 49, lines 1617–1627 (ed. Louis Choulant, Leipzig, 1832). **46–
48** Ps. 36.24. **49–69** Almost identical in Hugh of Strasburg, *Comp. theol. ver.* VI.21.
49–50 Guerric d'Igny, *In quadragesima*, sermo II, 1 (PL 185:96). **52–54** Cf. Bernard,
De consideratione I.ii.3 (3:396). **58** Cf. Gratian, II.33.3.1.88 (1:1188). **59–60** Cf.
Ps.-Augustine, *Sermo 117 in app.* 3 (PL 39:1978). **61** Matt. 3.10. **62–63** Cf. Ezek.
18.21. **68–69** Perhaps based on Gregory, *Moralia* XVI.lxviii.82 (PL 75:1161). **70–74**
Almost identical in Hugh of Strasburg, *Comp. theol. ver.* VI.22. **74–75** Matt. 3.2, etc.

V.vii CONTRITION

Now we must deal with the parts of penance separately, and first with
contrition, its first integral part. I shall deal with it as follows: first, what
contrition is and how one acquires it; second, what one should be contrite
of; third, what evil results come to those who delay their conversion; and
fourth, what good effects come to those who are truly contrite.

As defined in distinction 1 of the section "On Penitence" in the *Decretum*,
contrition is "grief that is willingly borne with the intention to confess and

ta oportunitate," quia nisi illa huiusmodi voluntas habeatur, non contricio
set attricio nominatur; vel sic: "Contricio est dolor pro peccatis semper
10   puniens in se quod dolet amisisse."
       Et revera huiusmodi contricio multipliciter adquiritur. Nam primo
faciendum est quasi quoddam circinum de anima et corpore, cuius unus pes,
scilicet corporis, figatur in terra, et alius pes, scilicet anime, circum-
giratur per circumferenciam tocius vite humane, scilicet a nativitate
15   hominis usque ad eius mortem. Et sic facta discutere iuxta illud Psalmi:
"Recogitabo tibi omnes annos meos in amaritudine anime mee," hoc est, revolvere et cogitare debes quantum vixisti, quomodo tempus tuum expendisti,
quot bona dimisisti, quot mala commisisti, qualem societatem peccando
amisisti (quia Dei et Ecclesie), quibus adhesisti (quia diabolo et sociis
20   eius). Item cogitare debes ubi es, quia in hac valle miserie et lacrimarum
plena miseriis et infortuniis; ubi fuisti, quia in peccatis et aliis doloribus in conceptu et in partu; Psalmista: "In peccatis concepit me mater
mea." Si ergo in matrem aut in prolem conspicis, utrobique dolor et miseria: in tristicia parit mater, et cum luctu et eiulatu proles educitur,
25   quia, ut metrice dicitur:

       Tot clamant e vel a quotquot nascuntur ab Eva.

Unde Ieronimus: "Quis, inquit, det oculis meis fontem lacrimarum ut defleam
miseriam humani generis, progressum dampnabilem, dissolucionis egressum?
Consideraveram enim cum lacrimis de quo factus est [homo], quid faciat
30   homo, quid facturus sit homo. Sane formatus de terra, conceptus in culpa,
natus cum pena, et ideo magis lugendum est quam gaudendum." Hec ille.
       Considerandum est eciam quo devenies, [f. 122] quia ad iudicium terri-
bile pro minimo facto racionem redditurus, nesciens utrum odio vel amore
dignus fueris. Et [ideo] in *Vitas Patrum* dixit quidam senex cuidam homini:
35   "Vade et talem fac cogitacionem tuam sicut iniqui faciunt qui sunt in
carcere. Ipsi enim interrogant alios ubi est iudex et quando veniet, et in
ipsa expectacione suarum penarum plorant." Revera ita facere deberet quis-
cumque fidelis, animam scilicet suam obiurgare dicens: Ve michi, quomodo
habeo stare ante tribunal Christi, et quomodo sibi de actibus meis ibi
40   habeo respondere? Unde narratur ibidem quod Abbas Helias dixit fratribus
suis: "Tres res pre ceteris timeo: una est quando egressura est anima mea
de corpore, alia quando occursurus sum Deo, set tercia quando proferenda
fuerit contra me sentencia."
       Item considerandum est ubi non es, quia non in gloria, ad quam nemo
45   pertingere potest nisi per tormenta et lamenta, quod bene figuratur 2 Regum
3 quando ad Abner dixit David: "Non videbis faciem meam antequam adduxeris
michi Mychol, et tunc veniens videbis faciem meam." Michol autem interpre-

to make satisfaction when the opportunity arrives," for when this intention is not present, one cannot speak of contrition but only of attrition. Another definition is: "Contrition is grief for one's sins, which is always sorry for what it grieves to have lost."

Such contrition may be acquired in many ways. First, one should make, as it were, a pair of compasses of one's body and soul: one foot, namely one's body, should be stuck in the ground, and the other, that is, one's soul, should be drawn over the circumference of a man's whole life, from his birth to his death. And then you must examine your deeds, after the words of the Psalm: "I will recount to you all my years in the bitterness of my soul," that is, you must turn over in your mind and reflect on how long you have lived, how you have employed your time, how many good deeds you have failed to do, how many evil ones committed, what fellowship you have lost through sin (namely that of God and the Church), and who have become your companions (namely the devil and his followers). You must further reflect on where you are—in this vale of wretchedness and tears, so full of misery and unhappiness; and on where you have been—in sins and other pains at your conception and birth. The Psalmist says: "In sins did my mother conceive me." For if you look at a mother or at her offspring, in either place is pain and misery. A mother gives birth in pain, and her offspring is brought up in sorrow and weeping, because in the words of a verse,

All who are born of Eve cry out, Alas, our woe!

Whence Jerome says: "Who will give my eyes a fountain of tears that I may bewail the wretchedness of mankind, its damnable life and final dissolution? I had considered with tears what man is made of, what he does, and what he will do. Truly, he is made of earth, conceived in sin, and born with pain; and thus, there is more reason for sorrow in these things than joy."

And you must further reflect on where you will go—to that terrifying judgment where you will have to render an account of your least deed and will not know whether you are worthy of hatred or of love. Therefore in *The Lives of the Fathers* a hermit said to someone: "Go and make your thoughts like those of criminals in prison. For they ask others where the judge is and when he will come, and they weep in expectation of their punishment." Indeed, every faithful person should do thus, that is, admonish his soul earnestly and say: "Alas, how will I stand before Christ's judgment seat, and what can I answer him there for my deeds?" In the same book it is reported that Abba Elias told his brethren: "Three moments I fear above all else: when my soul will leave the body; when I shall meet God; and when the judgment will be pronounced against me."

You must further reflect on where you are not—in that glory to which no

tatur aqua ex omnibus, supple peccatis, quasi diceret Dominus: Non faciam
cum peccatoribus misericordiam aut amiciciam nisi per fletum et compunctio-
50   nem. Et ideo dicitur Ieremie 31: "In fletu venient et in misericordia
reducam eos." Si ergo hoc modo annos tuos recordatus fueris et facta tua,
cito percipies quod tu ipse es causa proprie miserie; quo facto statim ex
hoc verecundaberis et tibi occurret peccati detestacio; qua habita ad
cordis contricionem levissime devenies, per quam graciam divinam in omni
55   parte extorques, que quidem gracia secundum Augustinum arra est celestis
glorie.

   Est autem de Deo et homine peccatore sicut inter mercatores in nundinis et aliis mercacionibus. Videmus enim in talibus quod cautus mercator
quando vidit [f. 122v] proficuum suum in quibuscumque rebus et mercimoniis,
60   si voluntatem suam a venditore non poterit leviter adquirere nec cum illo
de illis concordare, tunc cautulose ducit eum ad tabernam et ibi facit eum
bene commedere et maxime bibere. Et quando vidit illum bene madefactum
optimo potu, tunc negocium suum proponit, et ut communiter ibi sic datis
arris intentum optinebit cicius. Ymaginemini hoc modo totam vitam nostram
65   quasi quasdam nundinas esse, quia sicut in nundinis est frequencia mult⟨a⟩
et concursus populi, apparatus multus et ornamenta diversa, merces varie et
celle diverse et multe, et tamen in brevi postmodum de tali loco omnia
distrahuntur et alibi deducuntur et totum tempus ibi expensum nisi quis
caucius de bonis suis ordinaverit amittitur emendo vel vendendo, nec in
70   tali loco aliquid remanet nisi sordes maiores quam alibi—revera sic in
vita ista videmus quasi in nundinis ornamenta diversa, pompam multiplicem,
sicut in pannis, equis, speciebus, etc. Set post modicum saltem in morte
omnia hec distrahuntur et evanescunt nec aliquid in loco illo apparebit
nisi sordes viciorum magis quam alibi, nisi quis melius tempus suum in vita
75   penitencie expenderit; Iob 27: "Dives cum dormierit, nichil secum auferet.
Aperietque oculos et nichil inveniet." Set iam advertite, quia ad istas
nundinas humane vite venerunt diversi mercatores sollempnes et magni nominis, scilicet Deus, diabolus, caro, et mundus. Deus enim proponit merces
suas optimas et preciosissimas homini peccatori, scilicet gloriam et graci-
80   am; diabolus vero peccatum et penam; set caro et mundus, quasi duo socii
participantes in lucro et dampno, proponunt voluptatem et cupiditatem.
Caute ergo oportet procedere si boni mercatores [f. 123] esse velimus. Nam
si cum tribus ultimis nos intromittamus, decipient nos in pugno, quia
quicquid proponunt, quamvis ad oculum delectabile videatur, in effectu
85   tamen non est nisi amaritudo, miseria, et dampnacio. Illos ergo caveamus et
ad primum, scilicet Christum, accedamus et videamus si cum eo pro mercibus
concordare possimus. Unde quamvis aliqualiter nobis videatur quod durus sit
in principio, nobis quasi resistens eo quod ipse dicit: "Non omnis qui
dicit 'Domine, Domine,' " supple: vel semel vel bis ⟨vel⟩ ter, "non intrabit

one can come without torments and wailing, as is prefigured in 2 Kings 3 when David said to Abner: "You will not see my face until you bring Michal to me, and then when you come, you shall see my face." Michal means "water from all" (add: sins), as if the Lord were saying: I shall not give sinners mercy and friendship unless they weep and have remorse. And therefore it is said in Jeremiah 31: "They will come with weeping, and I shall lead them back in mercy." If you, then, have remembered your years and your deeds in this fashion, you will soon understand that you yourself are the cause of your wretchedness. When this happens, you will at once feel shame and come to detest your sin. And with this you will easily come to heartfelt contrition, through which you will wrench grace from God, which according to Augustine is the pledge of heavenly glory.

The relationship between God and sinful man is like that among merchants at fairs and other businesses. For we observe that when a sharp merchant sees that he can make a profit in some transaction and merchandise but cannot get his will easily with the seller or agree with him, then he slyly takes him to a restaurant and makes him eat and, particularly, drink well. And when he finds him well lubricated, then he proposes his business deal; the two then make their pledges, and he gets easily what he has been wanting. In the same way imagine that our whole life is like a fair, for as at a fair there is a great crowd of people, much show and display, many kinds of merchandise, and lots of stands of all sorts; and yet, in a short while everything is taken away from such a place and carried somewhere else, and unless one has disposed of one's wares carefully, one loses all one's time that is spent there in buying and selling, nor is anything left in that place except more dirt than anywhere else. In the same way, just as at fairs we see much show and pomp in this life, such as can be found in clothes, horses, cosmetics, and so forth. But after a while, for sure, all of them are taken away by death and disappear, and in their place nothing will appear except the dirt of sins, which is greater than anywhere else, unless one has spent one's life better in doing penance; Job 27: "The rich man, when he sleeps, shall take nothing away with him. He will open his eyes and find nothing." But behold: to this fair of man's life several merchants have come who are stately and of great reputation, namely God, the devil, the flesh, and the world. God offers sinful man the best and most precious wares: grace and glory. The devil offers sin and punishment. But the flesh and the world, like two partners who share their profit and loss, offer lust and delight. If we want to be good merchants, we must proceed with due caution. For if we deal with the latter three, they will cheat us with a left, for though whatever they offer us may look pleasant to the eye, its end result is nothing but bitterness and misery and damnation. Let us therefore beware of them and go to the first merchant, that is, Christ, and see if we can come to an agreement with him about his wares. If he should seem to be hard to

90   in regnum celorum," propter hoc non dimittamus set ducamus illum ad taber-
      nam contricionis et [sibi] propinemus habundanter cibum et potum lacrima-
      rum, iuxta illud Psalmi: "Cibabis nos pane lacrimarum et potum dabis nobis
      in lacrimis in mensura." Et revera tunc cum sic biberit bene et arram
      cordis tui contriti acceperit, intentum sue gracie optinebis in presenti,
95   per quam ad promocionem et divicias eternas devenies, iuxta illud Psalmi:
      Si dederis "cor contritum et humiliatum," scilicet pro peccatis tuis, certe
      Deus non despiciet, set prout illud Psalmi dicit: "Tunc graciam et gloriam
      dabit Dominus," scilicet graciam in presenti bene vivere et gloriam in
      futuro.
100   Nichil enim tantum ab homine petit sicut cor, sicut patet Proverbiorum
      23 ubi dicit: "Fili, prebe michi cor tuum." Unde notandum est quod est de
      Deo sicut de falcone qui, cum ad predam volaverit et avem acceperit, si
      tunc cor avicule tantum sibi detur eo quod debitum eius est, bene contentus
      est et non plus curat nec petit. Revera sic Christus, postquam genus huma-
105   num quasi avem avolatam de campo inferni depredaverit, si cor hominis sibi
      detur non plus querit.
          Set a[d]verte: Videmus enim quod antequam cor avicule detur falconi,
      primo scinditur et quicquid sanguinis vel corrupcionis fuerit interius
      expellitur et bene [cum] aqua mundatur. Sic certe cor [f. 123v] hominis,
110   quod de iure Christo debetur, oportet quod primo bene mundetur per aquam
      lacrimarum [et] per cultellum acute contricionis in particulas scindatur,
      quia ipse dicit per Ioelis 2: "Scindite corda vestra," etc. Et si non
      habetis cultellum ad hoc aptum, formetur unus hoc modo. Primo enim materia
      calibis erit de capite lancee et clavorum per que latus Christi erat aper-
115   tum et duo manus et pedes perforati erant. Manubrium autem sit de lignis
      crucis indentatum. Virolla utriusque finis sit de corona asperrima qua
      coronabatur. Compactio, idest *cement*, qua scindulum manubrio coniungitur,
      sit amor ille in mente conglutinans; ista tamen asperrima pro te peccatore
      misero voluit sustinere. Cultellus ergo iste iam debet molari super corpus
120   illud benedictum, quod ita dure et crudeliter super crucem fuit molatum
      quod non remansit sane iunctura cum iunctura. Non enim videbatur miserrimis
      Iudeis sufficere illum occidere, set corpore illo benedicto se non exten-
      dente sufficienter ad foramina in cruce facta, nisi manus et pedes cum
      cordis traxissent quousque ad foramina pervenerunt, per quod diruptis
125   nervis et venis totum corpus dissolverunt. Quantumcumque autem acuitas
      istius cultelli tibi videtur obtusa et non satis acuta, debes illam dispo-
      nere et acuere super linguas pessimorum Iudeorum dicencium ipsum esse
      prophetam ⟨falsum⟩, demonium habentem, turbarum seductorem, et cetera hu-
      iusmodi; ut sic saltem discas improperia propter Deum sustinere, qui tanta
130   pro te sustinuit paciencier. Et si non habeas per quod poteris istum cultel-
      lum portare neque vaginam formare, accipe unam de coreo corporis Christi

bargain with at first—as if he were holding back from us, because he himself says: "Not everyone that says to me, 'Lord, Lord,' " add: once or twice or three times, "shall enter into the kingdom of heaven"—, let us not allow him to go away for that but rather take him to the tavern of contrition and treat him richly with the food and drink of our tears, after the words of the Psalm: "You will feed us with the bread of tears and give us for our drink tears in measure." And when he has drunk well and accepted the pledge of your contrite heart, you will receive his promise of grace in this life, through which you will come to profit and eternal wealth, after the words of the Psalm: if you give him "a contrite and humble heart," that is, for your sins, God will certainly not despise it, but as the Psalm says, "then the Lord will give his grace and glory," grace to live well in the present, and glory in the future.

For God desires nothing so much from man as his heart, as can be seen in Proverbs 23 when he says: "Son, give me your heart." Here we should notice that God acts just like a falcon: when the latter flies to its prey and catches a bird, if he then is only given the heart of a small bird, which is his due, he is well satisfied and cares or asks for no more. In the same way, after Christ has caught mankind as his prey from the field of hell, like a bird that had flown off, if only man's heart is given to him, he will ask for nothing more.

But take notice: we know from experience that before the heart of a small bird is given to the falcon, it is first cut into pieces, and whatever blood or corruption might be inside is taken out, and it is cleaned well with water. Thus, surely, man's heart, which by right belongs to Christ, must first be cleansed with the water of our tears and cut into pieces with the knife of sharp contrition, for he himself says through Joel 2: "Rend your hearts," and so forth. And if you do not have a knife for this purpose, make one in the following way. First, its steel blade shall be made from the spearpoint and the nails with which Christ's side was opened and his two feet and hands were pierced. Its hilt shall be inlaid with the wood of the cross. The boss at either end shall be from the sharp crown with which he was crowned. And the glue, that is, the *cement*, with which the blade is fastened to the hilt, shall be that love that spiritually binds together; for he wanted to suffer such bitter pains for your sake, wretched sinner. This knife must then be whetted on his blessed body, which was so fiercely and cruelly whetted on the cross that hardly any joints remained together. For the wretched Jews did not think it was enough to kill him, but when his blessed body would not reach the holes that had been drilled in the cross, they had to stretch his hands and feet with ropes until they came to the nail holes, whereby they broke his nerves and veins and tore his whole body apart. When this knife seems blunted and not sharp enough, you must sharpen it on the tongues of the wicked Jews who exclaimed that Christ was a false prophet who had a demon, a seducer of the

benedicti sic perforati et lanceati; nec oportet te ire ad alium vaginato-
rem ad illa depingenda, nam ubicumque aspexeris invenies rub[e]um sanguineum super [f. 124] album coreum. Et istam portare debes cum memoria funi-
135   culorum et cordarum quibus sic tractus erat et flagellatus. Si ergo iste
cultellus iuxta cingulum cordis tui debite fuerit appensus, certus sum quod
in sola passionis sue memoria cor durum incipiet in te pro peccatis conteri
et molliri.

      Et nota quod est de Deo et peccatore sicut de nutrice et puero. Ipsa
140   enim quando puer iacet in cunis et dormit, recedit ab eo et quasi pro tunc
non curat de eo. Set statim quando excitatur et ceperit lacrimari et clamare, continuo currens ⟨revertitur⟩ et illum ablactando demulcet et post
elevat et cum cantu in brachiis deportat. Revera sic Christus. Dum enim
homo in peccatis manet et iacet, quasi obstinatus dormit, certe quasi de
145   illo non curans recedit Christus. Set cum ad memoriam et penes se, ut
dictum est, deliberaverit quot bona dimisit et quot mala commisit, etc., et
ceperit flere pro peccatis et contristari, statim adest Christus ut nutrix,
promptissimus illum ablactans, modo ex una parte de mammilla gracie, modo
ex alia parte de mamilla pietatis et misericordie, dicens illud Regum 1:
150   "Non vadam donec ablactetur puer infans, et duca⟨m⟩ eum ⟨u⟩t appareat in
conspectu Domini." Et Osee 11 ait Dominus: "Ego quasi nutricius portabam
eos in brachiis meis."

      De ista ergo contricione sic adquisita, quante virtutis sit quod ipsa
quoque Dominum absentem cito reducit et delet peccatum et penam, narratur
155   de quadam muliere, de qua instigante diabolo pater suus prolem suscitave-
rat. Que postea ab alio lecatore dilecta in mortem patris sui consensit et
illum latenter occidit. Quapropter in peccatum desperacionis cecidit. Contigit ergo fratrem quendam predicare in quadam ecclesia ubi ipsa fuit de
Dei misericordia, que tam magna [f. 124v] est quod omnia peccata vere con-
160   tri⟨tis⟩ dimittit. Ex hoc compuncta et ad spem salutis reducta ultra se
continere non potuit set in medio omnium surrexit et stans a fratre quesivit si verum esset quod dixerat. Ipse ergo vera esse omnia per exempla et
narraciones probavit et affirmavit. Ait mulier: "Et ego, inquit, misera
tale facinus et tale commisi. Unde si verum sit quod dicis, misericordiam
165   Dei humilius deposco." Et nimio dolore pro peccatis compuncta cadens in
terram mortua est. Cum ergo homines de eius sepultura hesitassent, utrum
scilicet digna esset in loco sacro sepeliri an non, ecce vox audita est
dicens: "Sepelite eam honorifice, quia iam coronatur in gloria; ex nimia
enim contricione mortua est." Et hiis dictis evanuit. Unde pro peccatore
170   contrito de Dei misericordia confidente pulcre ait Bernardus super illud
Genesis: "Maior est iniquitas mea quam ut veniam merear": "Mentiris (inquit
Bernardus), o Chaym, quoniam sicut scintilla ignis in medio mari, sic misericordia Salvatoris super maliciam hominis"; Psalmista: "Miseraciones eius
super omnia opera eius."

crowds, and other things of this kind, so that you may learn to suffer such
reproaches for God's sake, who patiently suffered so much for you. And if you
have nothing to carry this knife in, such as a sheath, you must make one from
the leather of that blessed body that was thus pierced and cut; nor need you go
to a sheathmaker to have it painted, for wherever you look, you will find red
blood on the white leather. And this sheath you must carry remembering the
ropes and cords with which Christ was pulled along and scourged. If then this
knife is devoutly fastened on the belt of your heart, I am sure that your
hardened heart will begin to be sorry for your sins and become soft within you,
by the very remembrance of his Passion.

   And notice that the relationship between God and a sinner is like that
between a nurse and her child. When the child lies in its cradle and is
asleep, she leaves it and, as it were, takes no care of it for the time being.
But as soon as it wakes up and begins to cry and shout, she comes running back
and nurses it and then raises it up and carries it about in her arms singing to
it. So it is also with Christ. For when man remains in sin and, as it were,
lies hardened and asleep, then Christ leaves him as if he did not care for him.
But when the sinner remembers and, as I said, considers within him how many
goods he has lost and how many evil deeds he has done, and so on, and begins
to weep for his sins and grow sad, Christ is at once at his side like a nurse,
ready to nurse him, now from the one breast of grace and now from the other
of pity and mercy, saying the words of Kings 1: "I will not go till the child is
weaned and till I may carry him so that he may appear before the Lord." And in
Hosea 11 he says: "Like a foster father I carried them in my arms."

   How much power such contrition has to call back the Lord in his absence and
to cancel sin and punishment is shown in a story about a woman of whom, by
instigation of the devil, her own father had a child. Later on this woman was
loved by another lecher, agreed with him to kill her father, and did so secretly. For this she fell into the sin of despair. Then it happened that in some
church where this woman was present a friar gave a sermon about God's mercy,
which is so great that it forgives any sins of which one truly repents. At
this the woman was stung by remorse and led back to hope for salvation; she
could not contain herself but rose in the midst of the congregation and standing there asked the friar whether it was true what he had said. He confirmed
with stories and examples that all he had said was true. Then the woman said:
"I miserable wretch have committed such and such a crime. If what you say is
true, I most humbly ask for God's mercy." And pierced by great grief for her
sins, she at once fell to the ground and was dead. While the people there were
not sure what they should do about her burial, namely whether or not she was
worthy to be buried in hallowed ground, a voice was heard saying: "Give her an
honorable burial, for she is already crowned in glory. She has died from great
contrition." And with this the voice was gone. Therefore Bernard has some
beautiful words about the penitent sinner who trusts in God's mercy, as he com-

6 penitenciis] penitencia O.   **1**] 17 O.   **8** habeatur] *om* O.   **23** in(2)] *om* O. conspicis] conspiceris M.W; conspexeris R.   **26** Tot] omnes O.   **27** Ieronimus] *add* dicit O. **31** ideo] *add* in hiis O.   **39** stare] astare O.   **41** suis] *om* O.   **45** figuratur] figuratum est O.   **59** vidit] videt O.   proficuum] profectum O.   **65** multa] multus C.   **89** vel(3)] aut C.M.   **91** propinemus] proponemus O.   **96** tuis] *om* O.   **110** quod primo] prius quod O.   **118** in mente] inmense O.   **128** falsum] aut C; alium W.   **131** accipe] *om* O. **132** alium] aliquem O.   **133** rubium] rubum C.M.   **134** debes] debet O.   **142** continuo] continue O.   revertitur] revertat idest rockyth C.   **146** dictum] predictum O.   et] *om* O. **150** ducam] ducat C.M.W.   ut] et C.   **154** quoque] -met M.W.   **158** fratrem] predicatorem R.E.Jo.L3.LC; fratrem predicatorem group r.Sp; sacerdotem B4; sanctum hominem L1.groups t.z; *story om* group x. *All full manuscripts recorded.*   **160** contritis] contricionis C.W.   **163** probavit et] *om* O.   **165** Et] *add* statim O.   **170** confidente] *om* O.

V.viii   DE QUIBUS CONTERENDUM EST

[E]st autem nunc secundo advertendum de quibus conterendum est et quare videtur conteri. Ubi respondendum est: Primo propter Dei offensam quam peccator contra se graviter provocavit; unde Psalmista: "Usquequo, Domine, oblivisceris me in finem," etc.; "quamdiu ponam concilia in anima

5   mea," etc. Secundo propter diaboli servitutem, cui se subiugavit; I⟨ohannis⟩ 8 dicitur: "Qui enim facit peccatum, servus est peccati"; Petri 2: "A quo enim quis superatus est, servus eius factus est." De hoc dolebat Psalmista: "Dolor meus in conspectu meo semper." Tercio propter omnis boni amissionem quo diabolus ipsum spoliavit; Ecclesiastici 9: "Qui enim in uno

10   peccavit, multa bona perdidit"; Ruth 1: "Nolite me vocare N⟨o⟩emi, idest pulcram; set vocate Maram, idest [f. 125] amaram, quia amaritudine replevit me Dominus"; et subdit causam: "Egressa ⟨sum⟩ plena," [idest] meritis et operibus bonis, "et vacuam me reduxit Dominus." Quarto de bonorum naturalium vulneracione per quam impotens redditur anima; unde Psalmista: "Defe-

15   cit in dolore vita mea"; et causa: "quia infirmata est in paupertate virtus mea," quasi dicens: non solum exspoliatus set eciam vulneratus et secundum hoc impotens effectus sum et infructuosus Deo. Quinto timore pene iehennalis quam peccando meruit; Ecclesiastici 21: "In fine illorum," scilicet mortaliter peccancium; et Ad Romanos 6: "Stipendia autem peccati mors."

20   Unde Psalmista dolens ait: "Dolores inferni circumdederunt me, quia preocupaverunt me laquei mortis," scilicet peccata trahencia ad mortem. Et ideo ait Iob 10: "Dimitte me, Domine, ut plangam paululum dolorem meum." Sexto de amissione glorie; Ysaie 28: "Tollatur impius, ne videat gloriam Dei." Unde dolens ait Ieremie 10: "Transiit messis, finita est estas," hoc est

25   [tempus] ydoneum ad bene operandum, "et nos salvati non sumus," set gaudium eternum, quod Christus est, amisimus.

ments on the verse from Genesis, "My iniquity is greater than that I deserve pardon": "You lie, O Cain, for the mercy of our Savior is greater than man's mischief, as a spark is in the middle of the ocean." And the Psalmist declares: "His tender mercies are above all his works."

7–8 Raymundus, *Summa* III.xxxiv.8 (p. 443).   **9–10** Ps.-Augustine, *De vera et falsa poenitentia* VIII.22 (PL 40.1120).   **16** Isa. 38.15.   **22–23** Ps. 50.7.   **26** Innocent III, *De miseria* I.6 (p. 13).   **27–31** Ibidem, I.1 (p. 7).   **34–37** *VP* V.2 (PL 73:860).   **40–43** *VP* Appendix, 97 (PL 74:392).   **46–47** 2 Sam. 3.13.   **50–51** Jer. 31.9.   **75–76** Job 27.19.   **88–90** Matt. 7.21.   **92–93** Ps. 79.6.   **96** Cf. Ps. 50.19.   **97–98** Ps. 83.12.   **101** Prov. 23.26.   **112** Joel 2.13.   **150–151** 1 Sam. 1.22.   **151–152** Hos. 11.3.   **155–169** Tubach 2731 (and 2729, 2739). See Reichl, *Religiöse Dichtung*, pp. 160–162. The exemplum was also translated into English verse: see W. Heuser, *Anglia* 30 (1907), 200–205.   **171–173** Already used at *FM* II.iv.79–82.   **171** Gen. 4.13.   **173–174** Ps. 144.9.

V.viii   WHAT ONE MUST BE CONTRITE FOR

Now we must, in the second place, ask for what things and why we should be contrite. The answer is, first, because of the offense done to God, which provokes his heavy wrath against the sinner. Therefore the Psalmist says: "How long, O Lord, will you forget me until the end," etc.; "how long shall I take counsel in my soul," etc. Second, because of the sinner's slavery to the devil, under whose yoke the sinner has put himself; in John 8 it is said: "Whosoever commits sin is the slave of sin"; and in Peter 2: "By whom a man is overcome, he is his slave." At this the Psalmist grieved: "My sorrow is continually before me." Third, because of his losing all his good of which the devil has robbed him; Ecclesiasticus 9 says: "He who has offended in one, has lost many good things"; and Ruth 1: "Do not call me Noemi (that is, 'beautiful'), but call me Mara (that is, 'bitter'), because the Lord has quite filled me with bitterness"; and she gives as her reason: "I went out full," that is, of merits and good works, "and the Lord has brought me back empty." Fourth, because of the wound inflicted on his natural gifts, by which his soul is rendered weak. Whence the Psalmist says: "My life is wasted with grief"; and the reason for this is: "My strength is weakened through poverty," as if he were saying: I have been not only robbed but also wounded and thereby become feeble and fruitless for God. Fifth, because of the fear of hell pains which he deserves for his sins. Ecclesiasticus 21: "In their end [is the darkness of hell and pains]," that is, of those who commit mortal sin; and Romans 6: "For the wages of sin is death." For this reason the Psalmist laments and says: "The sorrows of hell have encompassed me, and the snares of death have prevented me," that is, the sins which draw me to death. And thus Job 10 says: "Suffer me, Lord, that I may lament my sorrow a little." Sixth, because of the loss of glory; Isaiah 28: "Let the wicked be taken away, that he may not see

Et nota quod Christus amittitur tribus modis. Primo per peccatorum multiplicacionem, scilicet inter illos qui peccata peccatis continue addunt, qui bene assimilantur latronibus qui, cum semel vel bis a suspendio
30   evaserint, plus semper et plus ad hoc inardescunt. [Unde Gregorius: "Peccatum quod per penitenciam non diluitur mox suo pondere ad aliud trahit."]
Secundo amittitur in mundana prosperitate; unde Augustinus: "Nequicia, inquit, mundi inpunita leticia, scilicet modo luxurie operam dare, spectaculis vagari, ebrietate ingurgitari, et cetera huiusmodi." Et notandum quod
35   absurdum est dicere quod huius mundi leticia que fit in coreis et cantilenis et huiusmodi in istis diebus solempnibus, que plus ad gulam, luxuriam, et ceteras miserias se excitant quam ad Dei laudem [f. 125v] et sanctorum, quod Deo placere non possunt, et tamen placere bene estimant quando magis huiusmodi superfluitatibus vacant. Quorum tamen opera sunt infructuosa,
40   sicut patet de labore ursi firmiter ligati, qui quamvis tota die terram pedibus conculcat donec fatigatus desistat, ad nichilum valet. Sic nec labores talium in choreis et aliis huiusmodi vanitatibus valent coram Deo, set ipsum in illis graviter offendunt. Tercio amittitur inter opera carnalia voluptuose delectacionis; Canticorum 3: "In lecto meo quesivi quem
45   diligit anima mea; quesivi et non inveni." Nec mirum si Christus, qui "inter lilia pascitur," si in carnis inmundicia non invenitur. Surge ergo, o peccator, de lecto voluptuositatis et vade ad presepium penitencie et asperitatis, et ibi eum cum pastoribus in lecto suo invenies pannis involutum. Abhorret enim Marie purissima virginitas prostibulum voluptatis, set
50   non abhorret eius profundissima humilitas stabulum paupertatis. Putasne ergo tu, peccator, quod dimittet matrem solam in stabulo et veniet tecum iacere in lecto fetido? Absit. Unde Bernardus: "Quomodo, inquit, o bone Iesu, inter cognatos meos, idest opera carnalia secundum *Glossam*, te inveniam qui inter tuos minime inventus es?" quasi dicat: nullo modo. Iob 28:
55   "Non invenitur in terra suaviter vivencium." Quarto amittitur in mundana ambicione; Osee 1: "In gregibus et armentis vadunt ad querendum Dominum, et non invenitur, quia ablatus est ab eis."
Si ergo queris, o peccator dolens de Christo dilecto, illud Canticorum: "Numquid quem diligit anima mea vidisti? Quesivi illum et non inveni."
60   Quesivi illum primo in oriente primarie nativitatis, set ibi nichil inveni nisi lamentacionem et lacrimas nascentis. Quesivi in occidente m⟨or⟩tis temporalis, [f. 126] et ibi nichil inveni nisi dolorem miseri morientis. Quesivi in aquilone pene infernalis, set nec ibi aliquid inveni nisi quendam horrorem inferni bullientis. Quesivi in meridie nepharie prosperitatis,
65   set ibi nichil inveni nisi abusiones et sarcinas colligentis. "Quesivi ergo illum et non inveni." Heu, heu, michi misero, quia in meridie inveni quem diligit caro mea, set nullibi invenio quem concupiscit anima mea. Heu michi! Quo abiit dilectus? Quid faciam? Quo me divertam? Anxior desiderio,

God's glory." And in Jeremiah 10 he says with grief: "The harvest is past, the summer is ended," that is to say, the proper season for good works, "and we are not saved" but have lost our eternal happiness, which is Christ.

Notice that one loses Christ in three ways. First, by multiplying one's sins. This holds true of those people that constantly add new sins to their old ones; they can well be likened to thieves who, if they have gotten off the gallows once or twice, fall ever more deeply in love with their criminal life. Whence Gregory says: "A sin which is not removed by penance soon draws one to another by its weight." Second, one loses Christ in worldly prosperity. Augustine says: "The mischief of this world is [to cultivate] unbridled pleasure, that is, to apply oneself eagerly to a life of luxury, to go to shows, to carouse in drunkenness, and the like." Notice that it is absurd to say that such worldly joy as is generated by dancing and singing and the like on holy days—activities which rouse people rather to gluttony, lechery, and similar wretched deeds than to the praise of God and his saints—can possibly please God; and yet they think they please him the more they devote themselves to such unwarranted activities. But their deeds are without fruit, like the "work" of a bear that is firmly tied up: even if he stamps the ground with his feet all day long until he is tired out, it amounts to nothing. In the same way, the efforts of such people in dances and other vain activities of this kind amount to nothing before God, but they offend him grievously thereby. Third, one loses Christ among deeds of fleshly delights; Canticles 3: "In my bed I sought him whom my soul loves; I sought and did not find him." It is no wonder if Christ, who "feeds among the lilies," is not found in fleshly impurity. Rise, then, O sinner, from the bed of lust and go to the manger of penance and hardship, and with the shepherds you will find him there in his bed, wrapped in swaddling clothes. Mary's most pure virginity shudders at the lustful brothel, but her meek humility does not shudder at the poor stable. Do you then think, O sinner, that Christ will leave his mother alone in the stable and come to lie with you in your stinking bed? Far from it! Therefore Bernard says: "How, O good Jesus, shall I find you among my relatives (that is, my fleshly deeds, according to the *Gloss*), you who could not be found at all among your own people?" as if to say: in no way. Job 28: "He is not found in the land of those who live in delights." Fourth, one loses Christ in worldly ambition; Hosea 1: "With their flocks and herds they go to seek the Lord, and he is not found because he has withdrawn from them."

If you, O sinner, therefore look with grief for Christ, your lover, saying with Canticles: "Have you seen him whom my soul loves? I have sought him and not found him"—I sought him first in the east of man's birth, but there I found nothing but the wailing and tears of the newborn. I sought him in the west of earthly death, and there I found nothing but the pain of a wretched person in death. I sought him in the north of hell pain, but even there I

fatigor laboricio, et tamen non desistam quousque dilectum invenero. "Indi-
70   ca ergo michi," o bone Iesu, illud Canticorum 1, "ubi pascas, ubi cubes in
meridie, ne vagari incipiam."
     Et nota hic quod bene huiusmodi anime contrite et dolenti referri
potest uno modo quod statim sequitur in Canticis: "Si ignoras," o anima
dolens, "egredere et abi post vestigia gregum," idest post ⟨facta⟩ sancto-
75   rum, et statim invenies ubi Christus dilectus tuus cubat in meridie, ⟨u⟩t
saltem ibi in l⟨ect⟩o ipsum invenire poteris, quia in cruce pro te. Si enim
sollerter considerare velimus quomodo in meridie diei est totus estus et
fervor diei, et ideo tunc temporis gaudet si locum amenum posset invenire
ad cubandum et quiescendum. Qui quidem locus tunc amenus dicitur si sit
80   virens frondibus et floribus, et precipue si ex uno latere habeat aquam
decurrentem vel saltem fontem scaturientem, et ex alia parte arbores ex-
crescentes et ramos late protendentes cum foliis virentibus. Et certe locus
talis valde est delicatus in estu, sicut patet de iunipero et Helia, Regum
19, et de Iona et edera, Ione 3. Et precipue eodem tempore anni ⟨delicio-
85   sum⟩ videtur sub arbore et umbra albe spine cubare, eo quod ipsa [f. 126v]
ex floribus redolet et ex foliis umbram amenam habet. Revera si de meridie
Christi quando quiescens cubavit loqui velimus, est sciendum quod ita fuit
dies ista ferventissima Parasceves, in qua maximum estum invenit. Exemplum:
Videtur enim homini maximus estus quando super se non potest sustinere
90   vestes suas set illas a se proicit. Set certe Christus in illa die tantum
estum sustinuit quod pannis proiectis nudus pro nobis pendere voluit et sic
quasi in cruce quiescere et cubare; Danielis 13: "Estus quippe erat." Locus
autem amenus et virens quem pre ceteris elegit fuit lignum crucis. Set
locus ille ex uno latere habuit aquam preterfluentem, quando prout Iohannis
95   19 "unus militum latus eius lancea aperuit, et continuo exivit sanguis et
aqua." Unde illo tempore canit Ecclesia: "Vidi aquam egredientem de templo
a latere dextro," etc. Et tunc reclinavit Christus capud suum sub umbra
albe spine quando milites plectentes coronam de spinis imposuerunt capiti
eius, ubi supra. Quod autem ille spine erant redolentes, nusquam audivi,
100 set magis credo quod verificabatur tunc temporis illud Ysaie 3: "Erit pro
suavi odore fetor."
     Si ergo, o anima dolens, devote contemplando quer⟨i⟩s dilectum quo
abiit, ubi pascat, ubi cubat in meridie, ecce tibi respondetur uno modo,
"Si ignoras, egredere et abi," etc., ut dictum est, et certe ibi illum
105 invenies. Alio modo responderi potest anime contrite querenti pro dilecto
Christo ubi querendus est et poterit inveniri: Egredere et quere cum Ioseph
et Maria, qui non cum canticis et tripudiis ipsum quesierunt, set cum
tristicia et dolore. Nec mirum, quando tantum iocale putabant perdidisse.
Et ideo ipso invento dixit Maria mater eius illud Luce 2: "Ego et pater
110 tuus dolentes querebamus te." Requirebant autem illum primo inter cognatos

found nothing but the horror of boiling hell. I sought him in the south of wicked prosperity, but there I found nothing but the insults and burdens of the man who gathers riches. Thus "I sought him and did not find him." Alas, woe to me, miserable wretch, in the south I found one whom my flesh loves, but nowhere did I find the one whom my soul desires. Alas, where has my beloved gone? What shall I do? Where shall I turn? I am driven with desire and worn out by fatigue, yet will I not rest until I have found my beloved. "Show me," therefore, O good Jesus, as in Canticles 1, "where you feed, where you lie at midday, lest I begin to wander."

And notice that to such a contrite and grieving soul I apply, in one way, the words that immediately follow in Canticles: "If you do not know," O grieving soul, "go forth and follow after the steps of the flocks," that is, after the deeds of the saints, and you will right away find where Christ, your lover, is resting at midday: there you will be able to find him on his bed, for he is on the cross for your sake. If we reflect earnestly, midday is the time of the greatest heat of the day, and at that hour one is glad to find a pleasant place where he can lie down and rest. That place is called pleasant if it is lush with foliage and flowers, and especially if it has running water or perhaps a gushing fountain on one side and tall trees with wide branches and green leaves on the other. Such a place, in truth, is most delightful in summertime, as can be seen in Elijah and his juniper (Kings 19) or in Jonah and the gourd (Jonah 3). And it seems to be delicious above all else to lie at this time of year in the shade of the hawthorn, for its flowers give a sweet smell and its leaves a pleasant shade. Now, if we want to speak of Christ's midday, when he lay and rested, we must know that it was that burning Good Friday, when he encountered the highest degree of heat. We realize this from the example of a person who throws off his clothes when it is so hot that he cannot bear to have his clothes on. Truly, such heat did Christ suffer on that day that he threw off his clothes and wanted to hang naked for our sake and thus, as it were, rest and lie upon the cross; Daniel 13: "For it was hot weather." The pleasant and lush place which he chose before all others was the wood of the cross. That place had running water on one side, for as John testifies in chapter 19, "one of the soldiers opened his side with a spear, and immediately there came out blood and water." Therefore the Church sings at this time: "I saw water issue forth from the temple on the right side," and so on. And Christ laid down his head in the shade of the hawthorn when the soldiers put the crown of thorns they had braided on his head, as we saw earlier. That these thorns gave a sweet smell I have never heard; rather, I believe, did then the words of Isaiah 3 come true: "Instead of a sweet smell there shall be a stench."

If you then, O grieving soul, in your devout contemplation look for your lover, where he has gone, where he feeds, where he rests at midday, lo, you

et notos, et non [f. 127] invenerunt. Et ideo: "Audi, filia," idest anima
contrita, "et vide et obliviscere populum tuum et domum patris tui," et
veni in Ierusalem, ubi eum invenies in scola humilitatis sedentem et docen-
tem. In qua quidem scola multi se illum querere simulant, [s]et revera
115   crucem querunt et non crucifixum, quia crucem denarii et non crucem Christi. Nec mirum quia, ut videmus, tot hiis diebus facit mirabilia crux denarii, eciam plura quam crux Christi facit ad oculum. Verbi gracia: Audivimus
autem quod crux Christi ex sua virtute fecit mutos loqui, claudos ambulare,
cecos videre, mortuos suscitare, et huiusmodi. Veniat ergo unus morte dig-
120   nus et signat bene cum hac cruce iudicem et alios sibi assistentes, et
statim ad vitam resuscitatur, quia bonus et fidelis est. Veniet eciam alius
habens causam satis veram et apertam in tota patria, et iudicem non signa-
verit nec advocatos ista cruce; devenient ita ceci quod nichil sue iusticie
videre possunt; et tamen redeat ipsemet cum alia causa falsissima in qua
125   nec Deus nec angelus, nec homo nec diabolus aliquem colorem iusticie discernere possit, et bene signet eos isto signo: optime videbit, vel si fuerit surdus, optime audiet, vel mutus, optime loquetur, vel eciam claudus,
statim gradietur, et sic de singulis. Set certe, a talibus non invenitur
Christus neque in loco in quo fetet "concupiscencia carnis" set in arto
130   presepio penitencie, neque in foro ubi fervet "concupiscencia oculorum," set
in secreto vere consciencie, neque in comitatu ubi regnat "superbia vite,"
set in templo, in scola humilitatis et sciencie. Et ideo iuxta illud Psalmi: "Querite Dominum et vivet anima vestra," scilicet cum Maria et Ioseph,
non cum avaris et voluptuosis, et superbis, set devote cum Magdalena lacri-
135   mando, sicut legitur Luce 7: "Maria stabat [f. 127v] ad monumentum foris
plorans."
      Item queres illum sicut homo ovem suam perditam, quia ovis dicitur
propter suam mansuetudinem, Ysaie 53: "Sicut ovis ad occisionem ductus
est"; et sicut mulier dragmam, Luce 15. Queramus ipsum ardenter ut fameli-
140   ci, quia ipse est panis vivus, Iohannis 6; sicut egrotus sanitatem, quia
sanitas in pane est, Malachie 3; et sicut cecus lumen, quia ipse est lux
mundi, Iohannis.
      Et nota quod ulterius tempus Christum querendi utiliter assignatur
tripliciter, scilicet dum dies est, dum prope est, dum vacat intendere.
145   Primo dico est Christus querendus dum dies est, quia in nocte raro invenitur; Canticorum 3: "Per noctem quesivi quem diligit anima mea, et non inveni." Et bene dicitur "per noctem," quia neque in nocte infidelitatis et
ignorancie, nec in nocte culpe, nec in nocte mortis; vita enim hominis est
quasi unus dies cuius occasus est mors. Secundo querendus est dum prope
150   est; Ysaie 9: "Querite Dominum dum inveniri potest, invocate eum dum prope
est." Iam enim ad ostium stat, ad modum pauperis pulsat, qui primo expulsus
parum se absentat, set iterum appropinquat; Canticorum 5: "Vox dilecti mei

will get one answer in the words, "If you do not know, go forth and follow,"
etc., as I have just explained, and you will certainly find him there. Another
answer that can be given to the contrite soul who asks for her beloved Christ,
where he must be sought and can be found, is this: Go out and seek with Joseph
and Mary, who did not seek him with songs and dancing but with sadness and
mourning. No wonder, since they thought they had lost such a jewel. And when
his mother, Mary, had found him, she said these words of Luke 2: "Your father
and I have sought you in sorrow." First they looked for him among their
relatives and acquaintances and did not find him. Therefore: "Hearken, daughter," that is, O contrite soul, "and see, and forget your people and your
father's home," and come to Jerusalem, where you will find him sitting and
teaching in the school of humility. Many pretend to be looking for him in this
school, but they seek the cross, not the Crucified—the cross on the penny, not
that of Christ. No wonder that in our days we see the cross on the penny work
so many miracles—in fact, more than the cross of Christ does, to all appearan-
ces. We have heard, for instance, that Christ's cross by its power often
caused the mute to speak, the lame to walk, the blind to see, the dead to rise,
and so forth. Now then, let one who is worthy to die come and make the sign of
this cross over the judge and his advocates, and he will at once rise to life,
for he is good and faithful. Let then another one come whose cause is just and
well known in the whole country, but who has not made this sign of the cross
over the judge and his advocates: these will turn so blind that they can see
nothing just in him. And yet, let him come back with another cause that is
most unjust, in which neither God nor his angel, neither man nor the devil, can
see any glimmer of right, and let him make this sign of the cross over them: he
who was blind will see perfectly, or if he was deaf, he will hear perfectly, or
if mute, be able to speak perfectly, or if lame, walk at once, and so on. But
in truth, such people do not find Christ: he is not found in the place that
smells with the "lust of the flesh" but rather in the narrow crib of penance,
nor in the marketplace where there is the "lust of the eyes" but rather in the
secret chamber of one's true conscience, nor in the fellowship where the "pride
of life" reigns but rather in the temple and in the school of humility and knowledge. And thus, according to the words of the Psalm: "Seek God, and your
soul shall live," namely with Mary and Joseph, not with the greedy, the lustful, and the proud, but with Magdalene in pious mourning, as we read in Luke 7:
"Mary stood outside the sepulcher weeping."

Seek him, further, as a man seeks his lost sheep, for Christ is called a
sheep for his meekness, Isaiah 53: "He was led as a sheep to the slaughter";
and as the woman in Luke 15 looks for her groat. Let us seek him passionately
as starving people do, for he is the bread of life, John 6; and as a sick man
seeks health, for in bread is health, Malachi 3; and as a blind man seeks
light, for he is the light of the world, according to John.

pulsantis, 'Aperite michi.' " Aperi ergo sibi dum prope est, ne forte declinat aut fugiat, et tunc dicas, "Quesivi et non inveni, vocavi et non res-
155   pondit michi"; set hoc erit in iudicio—nec mirum, quia ad hostium pulsavit
et sibi non respondisti. Tercio querendus est dum sibi vacat nobis intendere.
Modo enim secundum Psalmistam est "tempus miserendi eius," et ideo iam
"omnis qui petit accipit, et qui querit invenit, et pulsanti aperietur."
Set certe cum acceperit tempus ut iudicet, tunc non potest vacare nobis,
160   quia tunc solum erit tempus iusticie, etc.

5–6 Iohannis] ieremie C.   **7** enim] *om* O.   **10** Noemi] neemi C.   **12** sum] enim
C.M.W.   idest] *om* C.M.W.   **19** autem] *om* O.   **34** huiusmodi] similia O.   **34–38**
Et . . . possunt] *no manuscript presents a reading that is satisfactorily grammatical. Perhaps a clause has dropped out early in the textual history, or the sentence was faulty in the
author's draft, or* non *after* placere *is incorrect.*   **47** voluptuositatis] voluptatis O.
61 mortis] mentis C.   **74** facta] vestigia C.   **75** ut] et C.   **76** lecto] loco C.   **78** posset]
possit O.   **84–85** deliciosum] dilecto sicut C.   **88** ista] iste R.W; *apparently corr from*
iste M.   ferventissima] ferventissimus O. qua] quo O.   **94** prout] *add* testatur O.   **99**
ille] iste O.   erant] fuerunt O.   **102** queris] querens C.M.W.   dilectum] de christo dilecto O.   **111** idest] scilicet O.   **118** quod] *add* frequenter O.   **119** et] *add* cetera O.
127 eciam] *om* O.   **134** et] *om* O.   **137** queres] queras O.   **148** mortis] *add* nature O.
153–154 declinat] declinet O.   **160** etc.] *add* et non misericordie O.

V.ix   QUE MALA EVENIUNT CONTERI DIFFERENTIBUS

[C]irca autem mala que eveniunt conteri differentibus est iam tercio
sciendum quod primo dico Deo iniuriatur. Exemplum: [f. 128] Si enim aliquis
propriis sumptibus sibi domum magnam edificasset et alienata[m] precio
carissimo redemisset, si tunc sibi ad illius ostium pulsanti servus differ-
5   ret aperire aut omnino sibi introitum negaret, certum est quod domino suo

And notice lastly that the right time for seeking Christ is helpfully
described in a threefold way, namely: while it is day, while he is near, and
while he is waiting for us. First, I say, Christ must be sought while it is
day, for in the night he can rarely be found; Canticles 3: "I sought him by
night whom my soul loves and did not find him." "By night" is well said, for
he cannot be found either in the night of unbelief and ignorance, or in the
night of sin, or in the night of our natural death, for man's life is like one
day whose evening is death. Second, he must be sought while he is near; Isaiah
9: "Call upon him while he is near, seek the Lord while he may be found." For
now he is standing at the gate and is knocking like a poor man who after being
driven off first goes away for a little while but then comes again; Canticles
5: "The voice of my beloved knocking, 'Open to me.' " Open to him, then, while
he is near, so that he may not turn away and disappear and you will say, "I
sought him and did not find him; I called and he did not answer me": that will
be at the judgment, and it is no wonder, for he knocked at your gate and you
did not answer him. Third, he must be sought while he is waiting for us. For
according to the Psalmist, now is "the time for him to have mercy"; therefore,
"everyone who asks receives, and he who seeks finds, and he who knocks will
find the door open." But when the time has come for Christ to judge, then he
can no longer wait for us, for then is only the time of justice and not of
mercy.

3–5 Ps. 12.1–2.   **6** John 8.34.   **6–7** 2 Pet. 2.19.   **8** Ps. 37.18.   **9–10** Ecclus. 9.18.
10–13 Ruth 1.20–21.   **14–16** Ps. 30.11.   **18** Ecclus. 21.11.   **19** Rom. 6.23.   **20–
21** Ps. 17.6.   **22** Job 10.20.   **23** Cf. Isa. 26.10.   **24–25** Jer. 8.20.   **30–31** Gregory, *In
Ezech.* I.xi.24 (CC 142:179).   **32–34** Augustine, *Sermo 171* IV.4 (PL 38:935).   **44–
45** Cant. 3.1–2.   **46** Cant. 2.16; 6.2.   **55** Job 28.13.   **56–57** Hos. 5.6.   **59** Cant. 3.3,
2.   **69–71** Cant. 1.6.   **73–74** Cant. 1.7.   **83–84** 1 Kings 18.4.   **84** Jon. 4.5–6.
92 Dan. 13.15.   **95–96** John 19.34.   **96–97** Antiphon replacing the usual *Asperges* on
Easter Sunday; Legg, p. 135.   **100–101** Isa. 3.24.   **104** Cant. 1.7.   **109–110** Luke
2.48.   **111–112** Ps. 44.11.   **133** Ps. 68.33.   **135** John 20.11. Apparently, the text originally contained a reference to Mary Magdalene's weeping at the empty tomb as well as
her washing Christ's feet with her tears, Luke 7.37– 38.   **138–139** Isa. 53.7.   **139** Luke
15.8–10.   **140** John 6.48.   **141** Mal. 4.2?   **141–142** John 1.9.   **146–147** Cant. 3.1–
2.   **150–151** Isa. 55.6.   **152–153** Cant. 5.2.   **154–155** Cant. 5.6.   **157** Ps. 101.14.
158 Matt. 7.8.

V.ix   THE EVILS WHICH COME FROM DELAYING
CONTRITION

Now we turn, thirdly, to the evil consequences of delaying one's contrition. First I say such delay gives offense to God. For example: if someone
has built for himself a large house at his own expense and, after he had lost
it, has bought it back for a very high price, if then as he knocks at its gate

iniuriosus esset. Sic in proposito. Unusquisque vestrum iuxta illud Corinthiorum 6 templum Dei vivi est quod sua sapiencia condidit Deus, et conditum per diabolum alienatum suo precioso sanguine redemit; Petri 1: "Scientes quod non corruptibili auro vel argento set suo precioso sanguine,"
10   scilicet nos redemit. Set modo ad ostium cordis nostri pulsat; Apocalipsis
3: "Ecce ego sto ad ostium et pulso. Si quis ergo audierit, introibo ad
illum et cenabo cum illo." Qui ergo sibi aperire distulerint aut contempne-
rint aut pocius suo adversario aperint et contra illum tenent, certe ingrati sunt; Iohannis 1: "In propria venit et sui eum non receperunt." Et tamen
15   modo si quis gratanter aperiret, de levi omnia contra eum delicta remitteret.
Exemplum: Sicut enim puer quantumcumque irascitur pro pomo aut consimili, cito placatur, sic Christus quantumcumque offensus, offensam remittit
pro uno pomo. Quia sicut pro pomo offensus fuit, sic pro pomo cordis contriti remittit, et maxime si cito datur sine procrastinacione; Proverbiorum
20   3: "Ne dicas amico tuo, 'Vade et revertere, cras tibi dabo,' cum statim
possis dare."
     Unde contra tales procrastinantes converti ad Dominum videtur quod
diabolus ordinavit de eis dum adhuc viverent sicut quidam ducti curiositate
vel tenacitate ordinant de cultellis suis, quibus faciunt inscribi hec
25   verba: "Cras dabor, non hodie," ut sic per hanc scripturam cultelli colla-
cio semper procrastinetur in posterum et per consequens numquam detur. Isto
modo facit diabolus de talibus differentibus converti. Scribit enim in
cordibus, "Cras," etc., hoc est, facit eos semper [f. 128v] procrastinare
et numquam inchoare. Et ideo docet illos illam malam grammaticam et quod
30   semper dicunt "dabor," quia "dor" non dicitur nec est. Contra quos bene
loquitur Marcialis per totum epigrama ad Postumum sic dicens metrice:

          Cras te victurum, cras dicis, Postume, semper.
              Dic michi cras illud, Postume, quando venit?
          Quam longe cras illud, ubi est, aut unde petendum,
35   Cras illud quanti dic michi possit emi.
          Crede michi non est sapientis dicere 'vivam.'
              Ille sapit quisquis, Postume, vixit ⟨heri⟩.

Et alius sic:

          Noli per cras cras longas tibi ponere metas,
40   Nam cito per cras ⟨labitur⟩ omnis etas.

Unde Bernardus: "Iesu, inquit, Christo debes vitam tuam, quia ipse vitam
suam posuit pro vita tua et cruciatus amaras sustinuit penas, ne tu perpe-
tuas sustineres. Numquam procrastinat ipse tibi ministerium cursus syderum,
cel⟨orum⟩ beneficium, terre fructum, et huiusmodi innumerabilia."

the servant were to be slow in opening or were to deny him entrance altogether, he would certainly give his master great offense. The same applies to our case. According to the Apostle in Corinthians 6, each one of you is a temple of the living God, which God has built in his wisdom; and after it had been built and then alienated by the devil, God bought it back with his precious blood; Peter 1: "Knowing that not with corruptible gold or silver but with his precious blood," that is, he redeemed us. And now he is knocking at the gate of our heart; Revelation 3: "I stand at the gate and knock. If anyone hears, I shall come in to him and sup with him." Therefore, those who delay in opening or despise him or perhaps even open their heart to his enemy instead and keep it shut against him are certainly ungrateful; John 1: "He came unto his own, and his own did not receive him." And yet, if anyone would now open freely to him, he would easily forgive all sins committed against him. For example, just as a child, however often he gets angry on account of an apple or something like it, is quickly pacified, so does Christ, however often he is angered by being offended, forgive the offense for a small price. For as he was offended on account of an apple, thus he forgives for the apple of a contrite heart, and especially if it is given without delay; Proverbs 3: "Do not say to your friend, 'Go and come again; tomorrow I will give it to you,' if you can give it at once."

   It would therefore seem that with such people who procrastinate in return-ing to God while they are still alive, the devil deals as certain people deal with their knives, out of either refinement or miserliness—they have the words "Tomorrow, not today, shall I be given" engraved on them, so that on account of this inscription they will always postpone giving their knives and consequently not give them at all. In the same way does the devil deal with those who delay their penitence. He writes into their hearts, "Tomorrow," etc., that is, he causes them always to postpone and never to begin. And in that he teaches them bad grammar, so that they always say "I shall be given," because "I am given" is not said or in use. Against such people Martial speaks an entire epigram "To Postumus," saying in meter:

> Tomorrow you say you will live, "tomorrow" always, Postumus.
>   Tell me, Postumus, when does that "tomorrow" come?
> How far away is it then, where is it, where do I find it,
>   What price can it be bought for, that tomorrow, do tell me.
> Trust me, it is not wise always to say, "I shall live."
>   He is wise who has lived, Postumus, his yesterday.

And another verse declares:

> Don't set your goal with "tomorrow" into the far distant future.
>   For with tomorrow all time quickly passes away.

45   Secundo, sic differens converti dampnum facit proximo, quia sicut
     zizannia bono a⟨c⟩ puro semini commixtum, similiter spine et herbe nocive
     purissimo tritico in agro illud deformant et corrumpunt, [sic differentes
     per suum malum exemplum proximos corrumpunt] et ad consimilia trahunt;
     Ysaie 1: "Semen nequam et filii scelerati." Unde Crisostomus: "Quemadmo-
50   dum si colligas herbas de agro, triticum invalescit, sic si vicia pr⟨esci⟩ndan-
     tur, [iusticia] invalesc⟨i⟩t."
        Tercio, dampnum faciunt tam sibi ipsis quam aliis; Luce 5: "Gaudium
     est angelis Dei super uno peccatore penitenciam agente." Unde Bernardus
     super Cantica: "Gaudent, inquit, angeli in conversione et penitencia pecca-
55   torum sal[u]tem hominum sicientes. Lacrime penitencium vinum eorum." Ex
     quo relinquitur quod qui penitenciam et conversionem differunt, quantum in
     eis est gaudium ange- [f. 129] lorum minuunt et propriam salutem destruunt.
        In cuius signum patet Luce de filio prodigo, ubi pius pater hortabatur
     servos ad gaudendum pro conversione filii. Et adverte: Si autem esset civi-
60   tas amenissima omnibus bonis plena et malis vacua, que esset cito omnibus
     participanda, et esset tibi ianua aperta set cito claudenda, ne[c] scires
     quam cito, set ipsa clausa numquam ingredi posses, immo qui prius intrare
     ⟨n⟩oluisti in horrendum carcerem mittereris in perpetuum, ubi omne malum et
     nullum bonum—nonne pro stulto reputareris, immo demens, si ingressum
65   differres? quasi diceret, omni modo. Revera sic in proposito. Civitas autem
     hec [est] celum; Psalmista: "Gloriosa dicta sunt de te, civitas Dei."
     Carcer infernus est, set ianua penitencia; Actuum 14: "Per multas tribula-
     ciones oportet intrare regnum Dei." Sic enim Abraham, sic Ysaac, sic Iacob
     et Moyses ac omnes Deo placentes, et ipsemet Filius Dei per multas tribula-
70   ciones transierunt. Clausio ianue penitencie mors, que omnino incerta,
     iuxta illud: "Nichil est incercius hora mortis." Si ergo distuleris et
     exclusus fueris, de carcere inferni securus eris. Non est ergo differendum,
     set iuxta consilium Domini, Joelis 2, faciendum est, ut dicit: "Convertimi-
     ni ad me in toto corde vestro."
75   Refert enim Seneca *De naturalibus questionibus* libro 3 quod in corpo-
     ribus venenosis propter maliciam veneni et multam frigiditatem nullus
     vermis nasci potest; set si percussa fuerit fulmine, post dies paucos
     vermes producerent. Spiritualiter per illud corpus venenosum intelligo
     hominem in peccato mortali, qui tunc habet in se quasi venenum insanabile.
80   Totus enim mundus pro uno peccato mortali non satisfaceret. Et ideo talis
     lamentabiliter bene dicere potest illud Jeremie 15: "Factus est dolor meus
     perpetuus, plaga desperabilis renuit curari." Et ideo talis propter frigi-
     ditatem [f. 129v] [peccati] verme⟨m⟩ contricionis non potest producere, set
     si percuciatur in fulmine gracie Dei cito converti potest; Ieremie 31:
85   "Converte ° me et convertar," quasi diceret peccator: nichil quod in me est
     potest me convertere, set si tu, Domine, feceris quod in te est, statim

Whence Bernard says: "You owe your life to Jesus Christ, for he gave his life
for your own and suffered bitter pains and torments so that you should not
suffer in eternity. He never postpones the help you get from the course of the
stars, the beneficial influence of the heavens, the fruits of the earth, or
innumerable other things of this kind."

Second, the person who delays his penitence causes harm to his neighbor,
for just as tares crowd out and blight the good and pure seed with which they
are mixed, and as nettles and harmful weeds do the same to the pure grain in
the field, so people who delay their penitence corrupt their neighbors by their
bad example and draw them to similar evils; Isaiah 1: "Wicked seed and ungra-
cious children." Therefore Chrysostom says: "If you pull up the weeds in the
field, the grain grows strong; in the same way, if your vices are pulled out,
justice grows strong in you."

Third, they do harm to themselves as well as to others; Luke 5: "There is joy
before the angels of God over one sinner who does penance." Whence Bernard
says in his comment on Canticles: "The angels rejoice over the conversion and
repentance of sinners because they thirst for men's salvation. The tears of
penitents are wine to them." From this it follows that people who delay their
repentance and contrition diminish the joy of the angels, inasmuch as that lies
in them, and ruin their own salvation.

A token of this is the story of the Prodigal Son in Luke's gospel, when
his loving father admonished his servants to rejoice in the conversion of his
son. Think: if there were a most delightful city, full of all good things
without any evil, which would soon be shared by all, and the gate were open for
you but soon to be closed, but you did not know when, and after it had been
closed you would never be able to enter and in fact, since you would not enter
in time, you were to be thrown forever into a terrible dungeon where there
would be every misery and nothing good—would you not be reckoned a fool or
truly insane if you delayed your entrance? Surely, quite so. Spiritually
speaking: this city is heaven; whence the Psalmist says: "Glorious things are
said of you, O city of God." The dungeon is hell. But the gate is penitence;
Acts 14: "Through many tribulations we must enter into the kingdom of God."
In this way did Abraham, Isaac, Jacob, Moses, and all who pleased God, and
even the Son of God himself, enter through many tribulations. The closing of
the gate of penitence is death; it is entirely uncertain, after the saying: "Nothing is more uncertain than the hour of death." If you therefore delay and are
shut out, you can be certain of the dungeon of hell. Therefore, let us not
delay but act after the Lord's advice given in Joel 2 where he says: "Turn to
me with all your heart."

In book 3 of his *Questions on Nature*, Seneca reports that in poisonous
bodies no worm can come to life, because of the harmful poison and great
coldness; but when they are struck by lightning, they will generate worms after

convertar; tu autem dicis, "sine me nichil potestis facere." In cuius figura Actuum 9 patet de Paulo, qui cum per viam incederet, subito circumfulsit
eum lux de celo, et statim qui fuerat sevissimus peccator conversus factus
90   est fidelissimus predicator.

Set notandum est quod ad hoc quod Deus suam graciam peccatori infundat vult Deus quod homo ad hoc seipsum adiuvet et laboret. Quia secundum
Augustinum: "Qui, inquit, fecit te [sine te], non iustificat te sine te."
Quia licet Deus de potencia sua sine te hoc possit facere, tamen non vult.
95   Magis est autem Deo convertere peccatorem quam creare mundum. Et racio est,
quia in mundi creacione nullam resistenciam invenit sicut in homine. Necessario ergo requiritur quod peccator seipsum per preces humiles et alia bona
opera iuvat ad sui conversionem. Hoc enim vult Deus. Nam sicut corpus vivum
facilius de terra elevatur quam corpus mortuum, eo quod ad hoc ipsummet
100   corpus agit, sic certe homo mortuus per peccatum nolens se iuvare ad sur-
gendum numquam ad Deum convertetur.

Set timendum est quod est de multis sicut de quadam ave que vocatur
popeiaye, de qua dicitur quod est avis durissimi capitis. Et ideo quando
instruitur loqui, primo percutitur leviter cum virga in capite; quod non
105   senciens propter capitis duriciam, non curat. Quod videns magister suus
percutit illam gravius. Quod adhuc non senciens vel forte parum curans,
accipit magister virgam ferream et illam valde fortiter percutit, et sic
eius doctrinam recipit. Revera sic est de magistro nostro Christo, de quo
Matthei: "Magister, scimus quia verax es," etc. Si igitur [f. 130] secundum
110   suam doctrinam nec verbo nec opere voluerint homines se emendare nec ad
eum converti, quid facit? Certe, primo percutit eos leviter, quando scilicet
mittit eis infirmitates leves. Set quia peccatores sunt duri capitis et
durioris cervicis, unde modicum vel nichil curant de Deo, percutit eos
forcius quando mittit illis tribulaciones et adversitates, sicut in amis-
115   sione temporalium et huiusmodi. Et si adhuc se non correxerint, certe tandem percuciet eos virga ferrea per gravissimas persecuciones et infirmitates. Unde precepta sua et informaciones capiunt et sic propter suas indi-
gencias convertuntur; Psalmista: "Imple facies eorum ignominia, et querent
nomen tuum, Domine," etc.

---

3 alienatam] alienata C.O.   6 illud] *add* apostoli O.   7–8 conditum . . . alienatum] con-
dita . . . alienata O.   11 Ecce] *om* O.   18 uno pomo] parvo precio O.   23 ducti] *add* vel
O.   37 heri] erit C.   38 Et alius sic] alii versus *marg* M; *om* R.W.   40 labitur] delebitur
after omnis C.   43 procrastinat] procrastinavit O.   ministerium] misterium O.   44 celo-
rum] celestiorum C.   46 ac] aut C.   50 prescindantur] priscundantur C.   51 invalescit]
invalescunt C.   55 salutem] saltem C.M.W.   63 noluisti] voluisti C.W.   71 mortis] *om*
O.   73 ut] ubi O.   83 vermem] vermen C.   85 Converte] *add* ad C.R.   89 peccator]
persecutor O.   94 possit] posset O.   99 corpus] *om* O.   119 etc.] *om* M.W; et alibi multiplicate sunt infirmitates eorum postea acceleraverunt R.

a few days. In spiritual terms, by the poisonous body I understand a person who lies in mortal sin, who in this state has as it were an incurable poison in him. For the whole world could not make satisfaction for a single mortal sin. Therefore, such a person may well lament with Jeremiah 15: "My sorrow is become perpetual, my desperate wound refuses to heal." And thus he cannot bring forth the worm of contrition because of the coldness of sin. But when he is struck with the lightning bolt of God's grace, he will soon be able to convert; Jeremiah 31: "Convert me, and I shall be converted," as if the sinner were saying: there is nothing in me that can convert me; but if you, Lord, do what only you can do, I will at once be converted; for you say, "Without me you can do nothing." A type of this can be found in Paul, of Acts 9: as he was traveling on the road, suddenly a light from heaven shone all around him, and he who had been a fiercely raving persecutor was suddenly turned into the most faithful preacher.

But we must realize that in order to give the sinner his grace, God wants man to help himself and to labor for it. For according to Augustine, "he who made you without you does not justify you without you." For even though God by his power could do this without you, he yet does not wish to. It is a greater work for him to convert a sinner than to create the world. The reason for this is that in creating the world he found no resistance as he finds it in man. Therefore it is absolutely necessary that the sinner should help himself with humble prayers and other good works to gain his conversion. That is what God wants. As a live body can be lifted more easily from the ground than a dead one because the body itself helps in this, so a man who is dead through sin and does not want to help himself to get up will never be converted to God.

But it is to be feared that many people act like a bird called parrot—in English *popejaye*—who is said to have a very hard head. When he is being taught to speak, he first gets a light tap on the head with a rod; but since he does not feel it because his head is so hard, he pays no heed. When his master notices this, he hits him harder. And as the parrot still does not feel it or perhaps does not care, the master takes an iron staff and strikes him heavily, and then the bird learns his lesson. The same applies to our master, Christ, of whom is said in Matthew: "Master, we know that you are truthful," etc. For when people do not want to amend their words or deeds or turn to him according to his teaching, what does he do? Surely, first he gives them a light tap, namely when he sends them some minor illness. But since sinners have a hard head and an even harder neck, for which they pay little or no heed to God, he hits them harder in sending them tribulations and adversities, such as the loss of their worldly goods and the like. And if they still do not correct their lives, he certainly will at last strike them with an iron staff through heavy sufferings of persecution and illness. Then they accept his commandments and teaching and are converted because of their needs; as the Psalmist says: "Fill their faces with shame, and they shall seek your name, O Lord."

V.x   QUE BONA EVENIUNT VERE CONTERENTIBUS

[I]am est videndum que bona eveniunt vere conterentibus. Ubi sciendum
est quod primo misericordiam Dei et graciam extorquent, sicut superius
patet exemplum de mercatoribus in nundinis ductis ad tabernam. Unde sicut
modica pluvia magnum ventum ⟨s⟩edat, sic magnam iudicis iram vera contrici-
5   onis compunctio. Unde Crisostomus: "O, inquit, lacrima humilis, in oracione
est potencia tua, ante tribunal iudicis intrare non vereris, non est qui
[te] intrare vetat. Si semel intras, numquam sola vel vacua redibis, actuum
tuorum accusatoribus silencium ponis, iudicium ab ore iudicis rapis, plus
crucias diabolum quam pena infernalis. Quid plura? Vincis invincibilem et
10   ligas omnipotentem. Ploremus ergo coram Domino qui fecit nos, quia ipse est
prestabilis super maliciam." Hec ille. Sicut enim pugno tunditur pomum a
pueris ut succus extrahatur, sic debet peccator pomum sui pectoris per
veram contricionem tundere, ⟨u⟩t fructus vere penitencie subsequatur. In
cuius figura Luce 18 dicitur quod publicanus a longe stans [f. 130v] pectus
15   suum tundebat. Exemplum enim habemus de fil⟨a⟩trice paupercula accipiente
lanam ad philandum, que frequenter necessitate coacta, quia non habet unde
victitare vendit de lana; cum illam reportare deberet, ne pondus deficiat
lanam humectat. Revera sic nos debemus facere. Cum enim aliquando cogente
diaboli suggestione et carnali delectacione non lanam, non linum alienamus
20   a Deo set animam nostram ad eius similitudinem creatam, quam sua morte
preciosa redemit, unde si illam sibi restituere velimus, ne aliquod pondus
virtutis in illa deficiat, oportet illam bene per penitenciam et lacrimas
contricionis humectare. Unde Beda super Iudith in *Glossa*: "Lacrime, inquit,
pondera vocis habent, que imperant, non supplicant." Et Bernardus: "Luctu,
25   inquit, penitencie recuperamus perdita." In aqua autem turbida melius piscatur quam in clara. Sic in corde compuncto melius peccata capiuntur et
consumuntur; Psalmista: "Turbatum est cor meum intra me."
      Secundo, animam purgat. Videmus enim in magnis civitatibus quod quic-
quid fetidum est in domibus eicitur in platea, unde veniente pluvia in
30   aquam vel foveam deportatur. Sic quicquid fuerit fetidum in domo cordis,

6–7 1 Cor. 6.19. **8–9** 1 Pet. 1.18. **11–12** Rev. 3.20. **14** John 1.11. **20** Prov. 3.28. **25** Thus also in Holcot, Sermon 47. **32–37** Martial, *Epigrammata* V.58. **39–40** *Prov* 17109 and 17109a. **49** Cf. Isa. 1.4. **49–51** Ps.-Chrysostom, *Opus imperfectum*, hom. 8 (PG 56:678). **52–53** Luke 15.10. **54–55** Bernard, *Super Cant.* XXX.ii.3 (1:212). **58–59** Luke 15.22ff. **66** Ps. 86.3. **67–68** Acts 14.21. **71** A commonplace saying; see, for instance, Ps.-Anselm, *Meditationes* VII (PL 158:741), or *In* 16440. **73–74** Joel 2.12. **75–78** Seneca, *Naturales quaestiones* II.xxxi.2. **81–82** Jer. 15.18. **85** Jer. 31.18. **87** John 15.5. **88–90** Acts 9. **93** Augustine, *Sermo 169* xi.13 (PL 38:923). **109** Matt. 22.16. **118–119** Ps. 82.17.

V.x   THE GOOD EFFECTS OF TRUE CONTRITION

Now we turn to the good effects on those who are truly contrite. First, we must know that they wring mercy and grace from God, as we saw earlier in the example of the merchants at the fair who are taken to the tavern. Just as a little rain calms a heavy storm, so true compunction calms the heavy wrath of our judge. Therefore Chrysostom says: "O humble tear, in your prayer is power, you do not fear the judge's court, nobody forbids you to enter. Once you enter, you will never come out alone or empty-handed; you silence the accusers of your deeds, you take away the judge's sentence from his mouth, you torture the devil worse than hell pain. What more? You overcome the Invincible and bind the Almighty. Let us therefore weep before the Lord who made us, for he is greater than any wickedness." As children squeeze an apple in their fist that they may get its juice, thus should a sinner squeeze the apple of his heart through genuine contrition, so that the fruit of true penance may come from it. As a figure of this, we read in Luke 18 that the publican stood from afar and beat his breast. We find an illustration in a poor spinning woman who takes in wool for spinning. Often, as she is forced by her need since she has nothing for her livelihood, she sells some of the wool, and when she must take it back, she moistens it lest it be wanting in weight. Now, we should do the same. For sometimes, forced by the devil's suggestion and by carnal delight, we steal not wool or linen from God but our soul that was created in his likeness, which he has redeemed with his precious death. So, if we wish to give it back to him, lest any weight of virtue is missing in it, we must moisten it well through penitence and our tears of contrition. For this reason Bede says, in the *Gloss* on Judith: "Our tears have a weighty voice: they do not implore, they command." And Bernard declares: "Through penitential sorrow we regain what we have lost." One catches more fish in troubled than in clear water. Thus, sins are better caught and canceled in a heart that is contrite; as the Psalm says: "My heart within me is troubled."

Second, contrition purifies the soul. We observe that in large cities all the garbage is thrown out of the houses and into the square, and when the rain

eici debet ad plateam oris, et sic veniens unda lacrimarum totum proiciat
in foveam divine oblivionis; Ezechielis 18: "Impius si egerit penitenciam,
omnium iniquitatum eius non recordabor, dicit Dominus." Mulieres autem
paupercule mendicantes pueros quos gestant ad hostia divitum faciunt flere,
35   ut elemosinam cicius accipiant. Sic debemus nos compunctionem cordis et
lacrimas producere, ut Dei misericordiam cicius impetrare possemus. Et
certe ita pius est et misericors, quod dando quod petimus lacrimis recom-
pensat, sicut pia mater diligens tenere puerum, cum [f. 131] ipsum flentem
aspexerit, sibi compatitur et diu flere non permittit set manu propria ab
40   oculis suis lacrimas abstergit. Certe sic Christus, iuxta illud Apocalipsis
20: "Abstergit Deus omnem lacrimam ab oculis sanctorum," etc. Unde Bernardus: "Felices, inquit, lacrime quas pie manus Domini abstergunt."

Tercio, Deum effugatum per peccatum sane reducit, sicut patet superius
post cultellum contricionis de nutrice et puero dormiente.
45   Quarto, diabolum fallit et decipit. Exemplum enim: venaticus dum
bestiam insequitur, ipsa caute transit flumen, per quod canis eius vestigium amittit. Sic anima transeundo per flumen lacrimarum diabolum decipit, ne
eius vestigium ulterius inveniat.

Quinto, iter abbreviat versus celum. Ut enim frequenter ubi longum est
50   iter per terram, breve est per aquam; ⟨sic per aquam⟩ lacrimarum et contricionis semita compendiosa ad celum invenitur. Exemplum de Magdalene
contricione, Luce 7. Sic ergo patet effectus contricionis et quot bona facit.

Unde quidam metrice de lacrimis sic ait:

In lacrimis tria sunt que multis congrua prosunt:
55   Sunt lacrime salse, sunt clare, sunt et amare.
Clarificant clare, sal condit, purgat amarum.

Quasi dicat: Lacrime clare animam clarificant et mundant; lacrime salse
condunt, hoc est, abscondunt peccata; set lacrime amare animam purgant omnino a peccatis. Unde narratur in *Vitas Patrum* quod quidam senex pergens
60   per heremum cogitans de quodam peccato mortali vidit quendam demonem sub
arbore scribentem. Cumque interrogasset quid scriberet, respondit: "Peccata
hominum, ne lateant; et modo illud quod dudum cogitasti memoriter scribo."
Cum ergo de illo intime doleret et flendo amare Deo confiteretur, rediens
quesivit dicens: "Quid modo sentis?" Respondens inquit: "Michi mala fecis-
65   ti, quia [f. 131v] parva aqua calida omnem laborem meum delevit."

Historiam habemus ad hoc de rege Manasse, qui fuit filius Ezechie
prophete, secundum Ieronimum *De hebraicis questionibus*. Qui ita prophanus
erat quod cultum Dei destruxit et ydola coluit et construxit, eciam Ysaiam
° avum suum sibi contradicentem sarra lignea sarrari fecit. Qui eciam
70   secundum quod habetur in *Historiis scolasticis*, in fine 4 Regum, plate⟨as⟩
Ierusalem sanguine innocencium purpuravit. Qui tandem permissione divina

comes, it carries it to the river or a ditch. In the same way, whatever garbage
there is in the house of one's heart should be thrown out to the square
of one's mouth, so that the water of one's tears can carry it all away into the
ditch of God's oblivion; Ezekiel 18: "If the wicked does penance, I shall not
remember any of his sins, says the Lord." Poor beggar women carry their
children to the doors of the rich and make them cry, in order to receive alms
more readily. In the same way should we call forth heartfelt compunction and
tears, so that we can obtain God's mercy more readily. He certainly is so loving
and merciful that he grants us what we ask for with tears, just as a mother
who tenderly loves her child, when she sees him weep, has compassion and
does not let him cry for long but wipes the tears from his eyes with her own
hand. Thus does Christ, too, after the words of Revelation 20: "God shall wipe
away all tears from the eyes of the saints." Whence Bernard says: "Happy
the tears which the loving hands of the Lord wipe away."

Third, contrition brings God back to us when he has been driven away by
our sin, as we saw earlier in speaking of the nurse and her child, after dis-
cussing the knife of contrition.

Fourth, it cheats and deceives the devil. For example: When a hunting dog
pursues a wild animal, the latter shrewdly crosses a river, whereby the dog
loses its tracks. In the same way, by passing through the river of tears our
soul deceives the devil, so that he may no longer find its tracks.

Fifth, contrition shortens our way to heaven. Often a journey is long by
land but short by water. Thus, we can find a short road to heaven through the
water of tears and contrition. We have an example in the contrition of Magdalene, Luke 7. These, then, are the effects of contrition and its good consequences.

Someone made the following verses about tears:

> Three things there are in tears, of usefulness to many:
> For tears are salty, they are bright, and also bitter.
> Brightness makes clear, bitterness pure, their salt adds taste,

as if to say: bright tears make the soul bright and clean; salty tears add
taste, that is, they hide one's sins; and bitter tears cleanse the soul altogether from one's sins. There is a story in *The Lives of the Fathers* that a hermit who was wandering through the desert and thinking about some mortal sin
saw a demon beneath a tree in the act of writing. When he asked him what he
might be writing, he answered: "The sins of people, that they may not remain
hidden. And just now I am writing down what you were thinking a moment ago."
After the hermit grieved about this in his heart and confessed to God with
bitter tears, he returned and asked the demon again: "What do you perceive
now?" And he replied: "You have done me great harm, for a little warm water
has canceled all my labor."

propter peccata sua a rege Babilonie captus est et illuc ductus atque in
vase eneo perforatus missus et amoto igne nomina ydolorum que colebat
vocans nichil profuit. Recordatus ergo quod crebro a patre suo Ezechia
75   audierat quod sibi Dominus in tribulacione dixit: Cum invocaveris me in
tribulacione et conversus fueris, exaudiam te, mox idola sprevit et nomen
Domini Dei Israel invocavit. Quo facto quasi pro momentanea contricione
exaudivit eum Dominus et liberavit eum, et quasi in momento ad modum
Abacuc ad Danielem ad regnum suum restituit et reduxit.
80   Hoc eciam patet de sancto latrone qui in iuventute Christum fugientem
in Egiptum cum matre et patre optinuit et salvavit. Unde tandem captus
tempore mortis Christi et iuxta ipsum patibulo affixum de malefactis quasi
in momento conterens dixit: "Memento mei, Domine," etc. Cui remittens
Christus ait: "Amen, dico tibi, hodie mecum eris in paradiso." Ecce quam
85   levis contricio a morte liberat.
        Unde narrat Plinius de quodam animali nomine harpa quod faci⟨e⟩ homini
assimilatur. Quem tamen si in deserto casu invenerit, in illum irruit et
interficit. Cum ergo aquam pro potu invenerit et faciem suam in illa conspexerit, considerans quod suum similem [f. 132] interfecerit, mox confusus
90   et dolens desertum petit et ibi residuum vite in merore conducit. Revera
bestia ista homo peccator est, qui cum mortaliter peccaverit, per quod
ymaginem Dei, ad cuius similitudinem creatus est, in anima deformaverit et
in quantum in se est deleverit, statim ad fontem consciencie debet recur-
rere, ubi cum dictam similitudinem sic destructam conspexerit, ad desertum
95   penitencie debet festinare et ibi delictum commissum deflere; Psalmista:
"Exitus aquarum deduxerunt oculi mei."
        Narratur ergo de quodam sene per desertum transeunte colligendo her-
bas. Quem cum quidam iuvenis sibi obvians interrogasset de qua terra esset,
respondit: "De tali terra, inquit, ego sum in qua omnes fontes fetidi sunt
100 et corrupti." Et iuvenis: "Cuiusmodi homo es?" Et ille: "Pauper, inquit,
querens radices et herbas ad medicinam." Cum ergo quesisset quid cum herbis
vellet facere, respondit: "Quidam rex nobilis et potens michi tradidit filiam
suam custodiendam sub pena mortis. Que ingressa terram meam de quodam
fonte bibens unde propter feditatem aque et terre facta est leprosa. Et
105 ideo dum tempus habeo quero medicinalia, ut sanem eam et mortem evadam."
Moraliter rex iste Christus est, qui est rex regum, cuius filia est anima
fidelis, quia secundum Augustinum: "Si quis posset Deum videre in sua divinitate et animam humanam in sua puritate qua creata est, vere diceret quod
filia eius esset pre nimia similitudine." Hec ille. Senex autem iste est
110 corpus humanum, quod totaliter post peccatum primi parentis ° terra fetida
et corupta remansit, cui tamen pro custodia committitur anima. Quam cum
ipsa ingressa fuerit et suis factis quoquo modo assenserit, de suis aquis
corruptis bibit, unde sicut leprosa efficitur, quia secundum beatum Grego-

A biblical story to the same effect concerns King Manasseh, who according to Jerome's *Hebrew Questions* was the son of the prophet Hezekiah. He was so worldly that he uprooted God's worship and instead venerated and built idols, and further had Isaiah, his grandfather, sawed with a wood saw when he spoke against him. In addition, according to what the *Scholastic History* reports from the final section of 4 Kings, he stained the squares of Jerusalem with the blood of the innocent. But finally, because of his sins he was, with God's permission, captured by the king of Babylon and taken to that city; he was cast into a brass vessel, and when the fire was removed, he called upon the names of the idols he worshipped, but to no avail. Then he remembered that he had often heard from his father, Hezekiah, that the Lord had said to him in his tribulation: "When you call upon me in your tribulation and turn to me, I shall hear you." He at once scorned his idols and called upon the name of the Lord God of Israel. At this, in the instant of his contrition, the Lord heard him and set him free, in the same way as he had freed Habakkuk and Daniel, restored him at once to his kingdom, and brought him back.

The same is manifest in the Good Thief, who in his youth had protected and saved Christ with his mother and father on their flight into Egypt. When he was finally caught at the time of Christ's death and was hung on the gallows next to him, he repented of his misdeeds, as it were in the twinkling of an eye, and said: "Lord, remember me," and so forth. Christ forgave him and said: "Amen, I say to you, this day you shall be with me in paradise." Behold, how a little contrition sets free from death!

Pliny reports of an animal called harpy, whose face is like that of a man. When it finds a man by chance in the desert, it attacks and kills him. But then it comes to a watering place to drink and sees its own face in it and thinks it has killed one of its own kind; wherefore it becomes troubled and with grief seeks the desert and spends the rest of its life there in mourning. In truth, this wild animal is sinful man; when he has committed a mortal sin, by which he has deformed and, as far as possible, destroyed the image of God in his soul in whose likeness he was created, he should at once hasten to the wellspring of his conscience; when he sees there that likeness he has destroyed, he should hurry into the desert of penance and there bewail his misdeed. As the Psalmist says: "My eyes have sent forth springs of water."

Another story is told of an old hermit who wandered through the desert in search of herbs. When a young man met him and asked him what country he was from, he replied: "I am from a country where all the wellsprings are dirty and polluted." Then the young man said: "What kind of man are you?" And he: "A poor man looking for roots and herbs for medicine." But when the other asked what he was going to do with those herbs, he answered: "A powerful and noble king has given me his daughter to keep safe under pain of death. When she came to my country, she drank from a spring and, because of the polluted water and

rium tot pu- [f. 132v] pulas, tot vesiculas habet in facie quot viciis sub-
115 iacet. Quia ergo in vita ista est tempus ydoneum [salutis], herbas et radices, hoc est dignos fructus penitencie, querere debemus, nec oportet illas
querere in deserto, quia crescunt in orto nostro, scilicet in corpore proprio. Et si queratur que sunt iste herbe et radices, revera respondit quod
ille de quibus in principio istius capituli actum est pro contricione sani-
120 tatis adquirenda, scilicet quantum vixisti, quomodo tempus tuum expendisti,
quot bona dimisisti, quot mala commisisti, et cetera, prout ibidem numeran-
tur. Et hec de contricione ad tempus sufficiunt.

---

3 exemplum] in exemplo O.   **4** sedat] cedat C.R.   **6** ante] tuum regnum O.   intrare] *om*
O.   **7** actuum] viciorum M; amicorum R.W.   **13** ut] et C.   **15** filatrice] filiatrice C.W.
18 sic] *add* et O.   **37** lacrimis] lacrimas M.W *and others*.   **41** abstergit] absterget O.
etc.] *om* O.   **45** enim] canis R; bonum W.   **50** sic per aquam] s. C; *om* M; *text add marg*
W.   **64** Respondens inquit] qui respondit multa inquit O.   **66** hoc] *add* 2 paralipomenon
O.   **68** eciam Ysaiam] *add* et C; ysaiam eciam M.W; ysaiam et R.   **70** plateas] platee
C.O.   **78** eum(2)] *om* O.   **86** facie homini] faciei homini C.W; faciei hominis R.
88 aquam . . . invenerit] ad aquam pro potu venerit O.   **95** delictum] dictum O.   **97** col-
ligendo] collegit M; qui collegit R; qui colligit W.   **100** Cuiusmodi] cuius O.   **102** fa-
cere] *om* O.   **109** ille] augustinus O.   **110** parentis] *add* in C.   **111** Quam] quod O.
122 ad tempus] *om* O.

V.xi   DE CONFESSIONE: QUID EST

[N]unc ad partes confessionis attendendum est, qu⟨e⟩ bene potest dici
purgacio spiritualis infirmitatis. Unde sicut solent medici suis pacienti-
bus primo dare preparativa, postea purgativa, deinde dietam proficuam et
sanativam ordinare, sic spiritualiter egrotus primo preparat se per cordis
5   contricionem, postea purgatur per oris confessionem, set tercio eius dieta
ordinatur per operis satisfactionem. Set quia dictum est iam de contricione, modo de confessione dicendum est. Circa quam sic est procedendum,
scilicet ostendere primo quid sit confessio et quibus confitendum ordina-

soil, became leprous. Therefore, while I have time I seek for medicine that I may heal her and escape death." The moral meaning of this tale is that this king is Christ, the king of kings, whose daughter is the faithful soul, for according to Augustine, "if one could see God in his divine nature and the human soul in the purity in which it was created, one would surely say that she is God's daughter for its great likeness." But the old hermit is man's body, which after the sin of our first parents has become a totally dirty and polluted country; yet to its safekeeping is the soul entrusted. When the latter entered it and somehow consented to its deeds, she drank from its polluted water and thereby became so to speak leprous; for according to Gregory, she has as many boils and blisters in her face as she is subject to vices. But since this life is a fitting time to gain salvation, we must seek for herbs and roots, that is, worthy fruits of penance; and it is not necessary to look for them in the desert, because they grow in our own garden, that is, in our body. And if you ask what these herbs and roots are, I reply that they are those considerations of which I spoke at the beginning of this chapter, on how to gain contrition for the sake of one's health, namely: how much you have lived, how you have spent your life, how many good deeds you have failed to do, how many evil deeds you have done, and so forth, as I listed them there. And this much suffices on the topic of contrition.

5–11 The passage is quoted, with attribution to "Ieronimus in quadam epistula," and translated into English prose in Cambridge University Library, MS Ii.3.8, fol. 93v; see P.C. Erb, *MS* 33 (1971), 81.   **14–15** Luke 18.13.   **27** Ps. 142.4.   **32–33** Cf. Ezek. 18.21–22.   **41** Rev. 21.4.   **42** Ps.-Bernard, *Declamationes* XXXIV.40 (PL 184:459). **51–52** Luke 7.37–48.   **54–56** *In* 8958; *Prov* 11797a; Ridevall, *Fulgentius metaphoralis*, p. 93.   **66–69** Cf. 2 Chron. 33.1–20; 2 Kings 21.1–18.   **67** Jerome, *Quaestiones hebraicae*, on 2 Chron. 33.10 (PL 23:1466).   **69–79** Petrus Comestor, *Historia scholastica*, on 2 Kings 32–33 (PL 198:1414–1415).   **80–81** For this legend, see Aelred of Rievaulx, *Informatio ad sororem* 48 (PL 32:1466).   **83–84** Luke 23.42.   **86–90** Tubach 634.   **96** Ps. 118.136.   **97–105** Tubach 3026. From Etienne de Bourbon; see *Tabula exemplorum*, No. 98 and note.

V.xi   THE NATURE OF CONFESSION

Now we must turn to the individual parts of confession, which may be said to be the purgation of a spiritual sickness. As physicians usually give their patients first a prophylactic, then a purgative, and afterwards prescribe a helpful and healing diet, so a person who is spiritually ill first prepares himself by contrition of heart, then purges himself by confession of mouth, and thirdly regulates his diet by satisfaction in deed. Since we have already spoken of contrition, we now deal with confession and proceed by showing, first, what confession is and to whom one must confess; second, what it should

tur; secundo qualis debet esse et cuius virtutis inveniatur; tercio que
10   mala eveniunt illam differentibus; quarto que bona eveniunt ad illam festi-
nantibus.
       Est ergo confessio secundum Raymundum "coram sacerdote legittima pec-
catorum declaracio." Et dicit "declaracio" contra eos qui peccata occultant,
celant, aut excusant. "Peccatorum" dicit contra eos qui confitentur peccata
15   per abnegacionem, ut si reus fuerit delicti, dicit tamen excusando et
false, "non sum talis," aut qui sua bona facta occasione vane glorie recitat. De quibus Bernardus: "Multis modis fiunt excusacio- [f. 133] nes in
peccatis. Dicit enim aliquis se excusans, 'Non feci quid, aut saltem bene
feci, aut si male feci non tamen multum male, aut si multum male non tamen
20   mala intencione.' " "Coram sacerdote" dicit quia sacerdos tantum habet
potestatem solvendi et ligandi. Vel alio modo dicitur confessio quasi
"simul fassio," eo quod omnia peccata simul et semel fari debemus, et hoc
uni sacerdoti et non pluribus, quia aliter non est con-fessio set dimidia-
cio.
25   Et nota quod huiusmodi confessio solis sacerdotibus est facienda quia,
ut dictum est, habent potestatem solvendi et ligandi. Secundum tamen Augustinum tanta est virtus confessionis quod si deest copia sacerdotis, meretur
tamen ex voluntate veniam a Deo qui crimen confitetur socio. Hoc tamen
intelligo in necessitate et mortis articulo, quod non solum in infirmitate
30   intelligitur set eciam de quocumque alio periculo morti vicino, puta si
timeat hostem vel predonem, aut navigaturus periculose, et cetera huiusmodi. Tunc eciam potest simplex sacerdos absolvere a casibus reservatis,
condicionaliter tamen, ut si tale periculum evadat [quod iterum superiori
potestatem habenti confiteatur. Sic eciam debet confessus layco, si pericu-
35   lum evadat].
       Forte dicit aliquis: "Potestne aliquis alteri confiteri quam suo pro-
prio sacerdoti?" Dicunt autem ipsi et adducunt pro se decretalem *Omnis
utriusque sexus*, et similiter illud *De penitencia*, distinctione 6, *Placuit*,
quia ipse qui est prelatus tuus oportet reddere racionem pro anima tua, [et
40   non potest nisi facta tua] sciat; ergo, etc. Ad quod respondit Hostiensis
Summa que dicitur *copiosa*, rubrica "De confessionibus," *Patriarcha*, in
fine, ubi ponit tres proprios confessores et inmediatos cuiuslibet [homi-
nis], scilicet papam, diocesanum, et parochianum, cuiusmodi sunt rectores,
vicarii, et huiusmodi; "vel," dicit ipse, "quibus isti indulgent per licen-
45   ciam eciam sine litteris." Quod eciam patet in *Summa confessorum*, libro 3,
rubrica "De confessione," questione 38 in fine. Unde notandum quod per
⟨septem⟩ sacerdotum genera possunt aliquando homines confitendo absolvi.
Primo semper ab ipso papa, qui est capud omnium ecclesiarum. Secundo per
determinacionem superioris, ut episcopi [f. 133v] per determinacionem pape,
50   rectores, vicarii, etc., et maxime speciales penitenciarii per determina-

be like and what qualities it must have; third, what evil consequences come to those who delay it; and fourth, what good results it brings to those who hasten to it.

According to Raymundus, confession is the genuine showing of one's sins before a priest. He calls it a "showing," against those who hide, conceal, or excuse their sins. He further says, "of one's sins," against those who confess their sins by denial, as, for instance, when someone is guilty of a crime and excuses himself by saying falsely, "but I am not like this," or else he recites his good deeds and thereby derives an occasion for vainglory. Of such people Bernard says: "Excuses for one's sins are given in many forms. For example, someone excuses himself with: 'I didn't do it'; or, 'it's been for someone's good'; or, 'if I have done ill, it wasn't really bad, though'; or, 'if it was quite bad, I didn't mean to.' " And Raymundus says "before a priest," because only a priest has the power to loose and to bind. In a different way, confession means "saying together," because we must tell all our sins together at one time, and thus to one priest, not to several, for otherwise it is not a confession but a dis-membering.

Notice that such confession must be made only to priests, who, as I have already said, have the power to loose and to bind. Though according to Augustine, confession has such power that, if no priest is available, one can gain God's forgiveness if one desires it and confesses one's crime to one's [lay] companion. But this obtains only in an emergency or at point of death, the latter including not only sickness but also any other situation of mortal danger, such as an enemy attack or assault by thieves or danger at sea and the like. In such cases, a simple priest may also absolve from reserved cases, but only conditionally: if the penitent escapes from that danger, he must confess again to a higher authority who has the proper powers. The same applies to one who has made his confession to a layman, if he escapes from the dangerous situation.

Perhaps someone asks: "Can one confess to a priest other than his parish priest?" Such people refer to the decree *Omnis utriusque sexus* and to *De poenitentia*, distinction 6, *Placuit*. Since your parish priest must render an account for your soul and cannot do so unless he knows your deeds, therefore, etc. To this the *Summa* which is called "Copious" addresses itself in the section on confessions under the title *Patriarcha*, at the end. There it mentions that everyone has three priests that are related to him properly and immediately: the pope, the bishop, and the parish priest, such as the rector or his vicar and the like; "or," says the *Summa*, "to whomsoever these give a special license, even if not in writing." The same can be found in the *Summa of Confessors*, book 3, section "On Confession," question 38 near the end. We should therefore note that people may be absolved in confession by seven different kinds of priests. First and always by the pope himself, who is the head

cionem sui superioris, sicut pape et episcoporum. Tercio per licenciam
proprii sacerdotis potest alius discretus, honestus, et notus, cum tamen
licenciatus. Quarto, omnis sacerdos, ut dictum est, [in] mortis periculo.
Quinto, propter defectum proprii sacerdotis, sicut sunt peregrini a longe
55   constituti, vel si proprius sacerdos sit ydiota vel proditor confessionis
vel sollicitator ad peccata. Sexto, cum non inveniat aliquem sacerdotem qui
[habeat] auctoritatem absolvendi, tunc alius discretus et notus [in] ordine
et professione potest. Septimo, privilegiati, cuiusmodi sunt Fratres Predicatores et Minores, qui sunt [primo] licenciati et privilegiati per dominum
60   papam et eius concilium, ⟨et secundo⟩ recepti et licenciati ab episcopo in
diocesi sua. Unde a quocumque tali potest unusquisque confiteri ad libitum
s⟨ine⟩ requisicione vel licencia petita parochialis sacerdotis in parochia
sua et ultra, quia quantum potest parochialis in parochia sua propria,
tantum potest talis frater receptus sic vel licenciatus ab episcopo ibidem
65   et similiter per totum episcopatum, et similiter in pluribus, si ad plures
fuerit receptus.
    Qualis ergo debet esse sacerdos ad illud officium deputatus nota supra
parte 5, capitulo 2, de virtute misse.

---

1 que] quod C.W.   **10** eveniunt] *om* O.   **16** qui] que O.   **20** dicit] *om* M.W; dicitur R.
25 quia] qui O.   **33–35** quod . . . evadat] *om* C.R.W; quod casus reservatos confiteatur
personis ydoneis M; *the sentence in C.R.W is clearly incomplete; it is here completed
from* B1.   **37** decretalem] *add* illum O.   **39–40** et . . . tua] *om* C.W; *om with* sciat M.
42 confessores] sacerdotes O.   **44–45** licenciam] *add* specialem O.   **45** Quod] istud O.
47 septem] *thus all groups*; octo C, *see below at line 60*.   **58** et professione] et probate
religionis M; *om* R; et W.   **59** primo] *thus all groups*.   **60** concilium] *this spelling normal for* consilium *in* C; consilium O.   et secundo] 8° C.M.W *and* s.u.y; *longer om* R. *The
adopted reading seems demanded by the earlier* primo; *it occurs in group z (but* et similiter *in* Co).   **62** sine] suum C.   **63** quia] *add* A ware þe frere *marg* C.

V.xii QUALIS CONFESSIO DEBET ESSE, ET EIUS VIRTUS

[R]estat enim modo videre qualis debet fieri confessio ex parte tam
confessoris quam confitentis. Et nota quod ex parte confitentis erit integra et festina, [*hool and hyyng,*] vera et amara [*soþe and sorowyng*]. Primo
ergo dico quod confessio erit integra, ut scilicet uni tantum confiteatur
5   de omnibus peccatis et non partem uni et partem alteri. Parum enim valeret
si infirmus febrem suam alicui medico revelaret et eius pestem celaret ab
eo, sicut si nauta aliqua foramina obturaret et aliqua dimitteret. Et
a[d]verte: Dicunt enim multi quod in infirmo sudor universalis est signum
sanitatis, et e contrario sudor particularis, si tantum in pede, manu, [f.
10   134] vel capite, signum est mortis. Revera sic est in proposito. ⟨N⟩am
sicut sudor provenit ex interioribus humoribus superfluis et illicitis per

of all the churches. Second by delegation from a higher authority, such as the bishop by delegation of the pope, the rectors, vicars, and so on, and above all special penitentiaries by delegation from their superior, such as the pope and the bishops. Third, another priest who is discreet, honest, and well known may absolve with the permission of the parish priest if he has the proper license. Fourth, any priest can absolve at the point of death, as we have already said. Fifth, in case one's priest is unavailable, as when one is on a pilgrimage far from home, or in case one's priest is stupid or publicizes one's confession or stimulates penitents to sin. Sixth, when one cannot find a priest who has the necessary authority to absolve, then anyone in orders who is discreet and known can absolve. Seventh, priests with special privileges, such as Dominicans and Franciscans, after they have first received the required license and privilege from the lord pope and his council, and then have been accepted and licensed by the bishop in his diocese. Therefore, one may freely be shriven by any of these, without making a request or asking permission of one's parish priest, within one's parish and beyond. For whatever spiritual power a parish priest holds in his parish, the same is held by a friar who has been accepted and licensed by the bishop, in that parish and likewise throughout the diocese, and even in several dioceses, if he was accepted into several.

What qualities a priest must have who is given this office was dealt with earlier, in part 5, chapter 2, on the power of the Mass.

12–13 Raymundus, *Summa* III.xxxiv.13 (p. 447).   17–20 Bernard, *De gradibus humilitatis et superbiae* XVII.45 (3:51).   27–28 Ps.-Augustine, *De vera et falsa poenitentia* X.25 (PL 40:1122), repeated in Peter Lombard, *Sent.* IV.xvii.4 (2:351).   37–38 *Decretals* 5.38.12 (2:887).   38 Gratian III.4.3 (1:1244).   41–45 Hostiensis, *Summa aurea* (also known as *copiosa*) V.18 (1772).   45–46 John of Freiburg, *Summa confessorum* III.xxx.38.   46–66 On this passage, see Introduction, pp. 11–12.   68 *FM* V.ii.

V.xii   THE QUALITY OF A GOOD CONFESSION AND ITS POWER

Now we must see what confession should be like, both on the part of the priest and on the part of the penitent. On the part of the penitent, it must be integral and prompt, truthful and bitter:

Hool and hyyng,
Soþe and sorowynge.

First I say it must be integral: all sins must be confessed to one priest, not one part here, another there. It would not help very much if a sick man told his physician of his fever but kept still about his pestilence; or if a sailor

calorem naturalem expulsis, sic confessio de superfluis esse debet, que per
calorem divini amoris universaliter debent expelli. Refert enim Ysidorus de
quodam serpente nomine ydra habente capita septem, cuius natura est quod si
15   unum capud per se abscindatur, quod tria alia continuo succrescunt, nec
quovis modo interfici potest quousque omnia simul eius capita auferantur.
Revera sic [est] de peccatore qui forte habet in se septem mortalia peccata, que eciam capitalia dicuntur. Unde bene potest dici ydra serpens ille
venenosus habens septem capita, qui si confiteatur tantum unum peccatum
20   mortale ut sic illud caput abscindat, vel [forte] omnia preter unum, revera
propter illud unum dimissum paulatim succrescunt plura. Et si vult bene
purgari, oportet quod omnia simul tollat, ut possit dicere Domino illud
Psalmi: "Delictum meum cognitum tibi feci." Et certe tunc Deus remittit. In
cuius figura cum rex David adulterium cum Bersabee commisisset et cum super
25   hoc a propheta Nathan redargueretur, de throno concistorii descendit et
super terram sedit ac peccata sua coram omnibus confiteri non erubuit. Unde
propheta confestim audivit hec verba a Deo de illo: "Transtulit Dominus
peccatum tuum a te; non morieris."
      Secundo debet esse confessio festina, quia qui aliter facit similis
30   est ei qui ignem abscondit in sinum qui ipsum comburet, aut latronem in
domo qui ipsum spoliet. Cum ergo homo detegit, Deus tegit, et e contrario.
Unde dicitur Naum 3: "Revelabo pudenda," scilicet festinanter. Secundum
autem Innocencium tercium in quodam decretali, ubi ipse loquitur de Iudeis
et Saracenis: "Tria, inquit, sunt que malam remuneracionem reddunt hos[pi]-
35   tibus suis a quibus recipiuntur, et sunt ista, scilicet: mus in pera, ignis
in sinu, et serpens in gremio." Spiritualiter autem loquendo [f. 134v] mus
est superbia, que omnia bona primi angeli corrodit et ipsum demonem fecit.
Que quidem superbia sicut pessima mater peperit istas tres filias, scilicet
vanam gloriam, accidiam, et invidiam, quas misit ad primos parentes, et
40   ipse similiter bona illorum corrodebant. Postmodum vero hec mater cum
filiabus quasi totum mundum pene destruxerunt, iuxta illud Ioelis 1: "Residuum eruce comedit brucus, residuum bruci comedit locusta, et residuum
locuste comedit rubigo." Eruca enim crescit in oleribus et ea consumit, et
bene signat superbiam. Locusta autem dicitur quasi longa hasta, que eciam
45   quasi omnes percutit, [et] signat vanam gloriam. Brucus autem est fetus
locuste, qui antequam alas habeat omnia consumit ubi fuerit, et signat
invidiam. Set rubigo, que ferrum non ex[er]citatum corrumpit, signat accidiam. Secundo, per ignem in sinu intelligitur peccatum avaricie, quia quanto
plura incentiva apponuntur sibi, tanto plus inflamm⟨a⟩tur, et bene dicitur
50   ignis insaciabilis, quia non dicit "sufficit." Et tamen Proverbiorum 18
dicitur: "Cum defecerint lingna eius, tunc extinguetur." Tercio, per serpentem in gremio notatur luxuria, et ideo cavenda est eius vicinitas. Unde
Ieronimus: "Quis, inquit, umquam iuxta serpentem securus dormit? Mordere

stopped some holes in his vessels and left others open. And notice: many say that in a sick person a general sweat is a sign of health, but any partial sweating, such as on his foot or hand or head only, is a sign of death. The same goes for the topic under discussion. Just as sweat comes from humors within our body that are superfluous and bad and are driven out by our natural body heat, so should confession deal with superfluous things that must be completely driven out by the heat of divine love. Isidore speaks of a serpent called hydra who has seven heads; it has the characteristic that if one head is cut off, three others grow in its place at once, and it cannot be killed in any way until all its heads are cut off simultaneously. The same is true of a sinner who perhaps has seven deadly sins in him, which are also called the capital or head sins. He may well be called a hydra, that venomous serpent with seven heads, because if he confesses only one mortal sin, so that that head is cut off, or perhaps all of them except one, yet on account of the one remaining head several others eventually grow in their place. If he really wants to be cleansed, he must cut off all of them together, so that he can say to the Lord the words of the Psalm: "I have acknowledged my sin to you." Then God certainly forgives. A type of this is found in King David: when he had committed adultery with Bathsheba and was reproached for it by the prophet Nathan, he stepped down from his throne in the consistory, sat on the earth, and was not ashamed to confess his sins before all the people. For which reason the prophet at once heard these words from God about him: "The Lord has taken away your sin; you shall not die."

In the second place, confession must be prompt, for if you do otherwise, you are like one who hides fire in his bosom which burns him, or who hides a thief in his house who robs him. For when man uncovers, God covers, and vice-versa. Hence it is said in Nahum 3: "I shall uncover your shame," that is, swiftly. According to Innocent III, in a decree where he speaks of Jews and Saracens, "three things repay ill their hosts that receive them: a mouse in the satchel, fire in one's bosom, and a snake in one's lap." Spiritually speaking, the mouse is pride, which gnawed to bits all the goods the first angel possessed and made him a devil. This pride, like an evil mother, gave birth to three daughters: vainglory, sloth, and envy, which she sent to our first parents, whose goods they likewise gnawed to pieces. After that, this mother and her daughters destroyed almost the whole world, after the words of Joel 1: "What the cankerworm has left, the bruchus will eat, what the bruchus has left, the locust will eat, and what the locust has left, the rust will eat." The cankerworm grows on vegetables and consumes them, and thus symbolizes pride. The locust, whose name means *longa hasta*, "the far-reaching lance" which strikes everyone, symbolizes vainglory. The bruchus is the young locust before it has wings; it eats up everything where it is and thus symbolizes envy. And the rust, which destroys iron that is not being used, symbolizes sloth. Sec-

quandoque potest, tamen etsi non mordeat, timorem saltem sollicitat, quia
55   maius (dicit ipse) est perire non posse quam iuxta periculum non perisse."
De isto autem serpente Genesis 2: "Serpens erat callidior cunctis animanti-
bus terre," scilicet luxuria. Nam per illam fere omne genus hominum subpe-
ditatur. Nec aliud restat contra ista tria quam naturam cervi sequi, qui
postquam pugnando hauserit venenum, velocius properat ad fontem, ubi se
60   balneat, lavat, et refocillat. Revera sic nos ad confessionem oportet
festinare et ibi nos ab omni veneno peccati mundare; Psalmista: "Sicut
cervus desiderat ad fontes [f. 135] aquarum, ita desiderat anima mea," etc.
Et nota quod natura cervi est quando sagittatur, si evadere potest, [que-
rit] statim herbam bitonie, cuius natura est secundum medicos ferrum extra-
65   here, et sanatur. Sic tu, peccator, cum vulneratus fueris sagitta peccatorum, queras herbam betonie, hec est illa in qua est remedium idest sacerdotem contra peccatum. Ipse enim potest esse betonia tua; [Anglice: "He may
be þy bote and bete þy sinne."] Et sic sanaberis. Illud eciam debet fieri
cito propter multa incomoda que possunt evenire in medio tempore. Videmus
70   enim quamplures subtrahi de mundo multis modis mirabilibus et diversis, quia
quosdam per ignem, quosdam per aquam, quosdam per homicidium, quosdam subito, quosdam in lecto mortali, etc. Qui si in peccatis caperentur mortalibus, sine fine condampnarentur, quantumcumque dives, fortis, sciens, aut
pulcher, papa, episcopus, imperator, rex, dominus, aut servus. Et ideo iux-
75   ta concilium Sapientis, Ecclesiastici 5, "ne tardes converti ad Dominum et
ne differas de die in diem; subito enim veniet ira eius, et in tempore vindicte disperdet te."
   Unde narratur de quodam fatuo qui multum dominum suum dilexerat.
Considerans ergo illum iniuste vivere involutum peccatis multiplicibus,
80   cupiens illum ad correctionem festinare, finxit se infirmum et mittens pro
domino rogavit si sibi placuit quatinus condendo testamentum suum sibi
assistere dignaretur. Quo annuente hec tria legavit: Primo babellum suum
senescallo domini sui legavit tamquam maiori fatuo quem umquam vidisset,
dicens: "Domine mi, ille miser fatuus pauperes spoliat et multa mala com-
85   mittit ut te ditet et placeat. Set certe ex hoc non tantum animam propriam
dampnat, imo tuam, eo quod sic facere illum permittas. Dignus est ergo
babello tamquam maximus fatuus. Ego enim dictus sum fatuus et tamen nulli
noceo. Secundo, magnum discum meum, Anglice *bolle*, lego pincer- [f. 135v]
ne tu⟨o⟩ tamquam fortissimo potatori. Ipse enim numquam cessat a mane usque
90   ad vesperam et pluries usque ad mediam noctem cum intrantibus, ° exeuntibus,
ac eciam permanentibus ciphum levare et nimium potare °. Modo autem tercio
lego (inquit) animam meam diabolo ad infernum." Quod abhorrens dominus et
seipsum signans quare sic legavit causam querens. At ille respondens ait:
"Quia certus sum quod tu illuc ibis propter iniurias quas hic facis et
95   fieri permittis sine correctione; et quia semper hic tecum fui a nativita-

ond, by the fire in one's bosom we understand the sin of avarice; the more fuel
one puts to it, the more it gets kindled, and therefore it can rightly be
called an unsatiable fire because it never says, "Enough!" And yet it is
written in Proverbs 18: "When the wood fails, the fire will go out." Third,
by the snake in one's lap we indicate lechery, whose contact must therefore be
avoided. Whence Jerome says: "Who has ever slept safely beside a snake? It
can bite any time, and if it does not bite, it yet provokes fear, for it is
better not to be able to perish than not to have perished in the vicinity of
danger." Of this serpent is said in Genesis 2: "The serpent was more subtle
than all the beasts of the earth," which refers to lechery, for by it nearly
all mankind is dominated. Nothing else avails against these three except to
follow the natural behavior of the stag. After he has been infected with
poison in his fight, he quickly rushes to a wellspring, where he bathes and
washes himself and regains his strength. In the same say, we must hasten to
confession and cleanse ourselves there from all the poison of sin. As the
Psalmist says: "As the hart pants after the fountains, so my soul pants [after
you, God]." And notice that it is the nature of a stag, when he has been hit
by an arrow and can escape, to look at once for the herb betony, which according to the physicians has the power to extract iron, and he is healed. You,
sinner, must likewise look for this herb betony when you have been wounded by
the arrow of sins—which is the herb that gives help against your sin, namely a
priest. For he can be your betony; in English: "He can be your medicine and
mend your sin." And in this way you will be healed. But this must be done
quickly because of the many hindrances that can arise in the meantime. For we
observe that many people are taken from this world in astonishing and diverse
ways, some by fire, some by water, some by murder, some by sudden death,
some in their deathbed, and so forth. If they are taken in mortal sin, they will be
damned forever, no matter how rich, strong, knowledgeable, or beautiful they
were, or whether they were pope, bishop, emperor, king, lord, or servant.
Therefore, after the counsel of the wise man in Ecclesiasticus 5, "Delay not to
be converted to the Lord, and defer it not from day to day; for his wrath comes
all of a sudden, and in the time of vengeance he will destroy you."

There is a story about a fool who loved his lord much. Reflecting on how
wrongly his lord was living and how many sins he was involved in, and desiring
to prompt him to correct his life, the fool feigned being sick and, sending for
his lord, asked him please to be present at his making his last will. In the
lord's presence then he bequeathed three things. First, he gave his bauble to
the lord's seneschal, as to the greatest fool he had ever seen, saying: "My
lord, this wretched fool robs the poor and commits many evils in order to
enrich and to please you. But surely in this he not only damns his own soul
but yours as well, since you allow him to do so. Hence he is worthy of the
bauble as the greatest fool. For I am called a fool, and yet do no harm to

te, nec ibi te derelinquam." Cui dominus: "Non sic, Willelme, non sic; quia
pro certo meipsum corrigam." Et fatuus: "Ergo, inquit, sanus sum et lego
animam meam Deo et omnibus sanctis." Et sic reduxit dominu⟨m⟩ ad confessionem et vite correctionem.

100   Tercio debet confessio esse vera [et aperta]; Psalmista: "Ex voluntate
mea confitebor tibi"; et ideo, ut patet ad ⟨nostrum⟩ exemplum Iosue 7 [de
Achor, qui] dixit postquam de anathemate acceperat: "Vere, inquit, peccavi
coram Domino et sic feci et sic." Historiam eciam habemus ad hoc 2 Regum
ultimo de David, qui postquam [per] Ioab numerasset populum Israel contra
105   voluntatem Dei. Unde [Dominus] iratus [misit] ex sua electione pestilenciam
tribus diebus, in qua a Dan usque Bersabee ⟨septua⟩ginta milia virorum
mortui sunt. Quod videns David dixit ad angelum populum cedentem: "Ego
sum, inquit, qui peccavi; ego inique egi. Isti oves sunt, quid fecerunt? Vertatur, obsecro, manus tua contra me." Quibus dictis iuxta concilium prophete
110   Gaad optulit holocausta Domino, et propiciatus est Dominus.

Set est advertendum, quod dolendum est, quod multi hiis diebus non sic
faciunt, set fatue peccata sua excusant et in alios retorquent, et hoc
multis modis: aliquando per consue- [f. 136] tudinem, aliquando per societatem, aliquando Deo imputantes. Exemplum primi patet in istis periuranti-
115   bus qu⟨i⟩, si super hoc arguantur, respondent: "Libenter me corrigerem, set
sic sum assuetus ad huiusmodi iuramenta quod nullo modo me possum retra-
here." Et certe ista excusacio fatua est et falsa, primo quia auget culpam,
non minuit, secundo quia tu ipse ad illam pessimam consuetudinem te duxisti
et nullus alius—certum est, et ideo tu ipse reus es de culpa; tercio, pono
120   quod tu stares coram iudice et de furto, homicidio, aut ali⟨o⟩ huiusmodi
[fueris] accusatus, et diceres: "Certe, Domine, ita sum assuetus ad illa
quod me cohibere non possum"; rogo ⟨quam⟩ bene foret tibi responsio allocata? Certe, per illam teipsum dampnares.

Exemplum secundi, scilicet contra excusantes se per societatem: Quis
125   enim volens ire ad Terram Sanctam vel ⟨sanctum⟩ Iacobum aut Romam et se
associat ire volentibus ad Scociam, nonne fatuus diceretur? Tu enim proponis ire ad Terram Sanctam, idest ad celum. Quid ergo ad te tal⟨es⟩ [vis]
associare quos viam inferni per peccata conspexeris intrasse? Secundo, quomodo fatuus es qui minus caves periculum anime quam corporis! Exemplum:
130   Si enim videres aliquem intrare flumen et ibi submergi, certus sum quod
nulla societas te compelleret illum sequi. Revera multo minus ad peccata
quemcumque sequi deberes, si animam tuam diligeres sicut esset iuste dili-
genda. Unde falsa est hec excusacio, sicut fuit de Adam quando voluit
peccatum suum inponere uxori sue, ut patet Genesis 3: "Mulier, inquit, quam
135   dedisti michi sociam dedit michi, et commedi." Propter hanc excusacionem
dampnatus est ad mortem temporalem cum tota posteritate. Et revera si ipse
sicut David humiliter dixisset veniam petendo, "Ego sum qui peccavi," etc.,

anyone. Second, I bequeathe my large bowl to your steward as the strongest drinker. For he never ceases, from morning till evening and often until midnight, to raise the cup with all comers and goers and likewise with stayers and to drink overmuch. But in the third place, my soul I bequeathe the devil in hell." The lord shuddered, crossed himself, and wanted to know why he made such a will. And the fool said: "Because I am certain that you will go there for the injustices which you do here and allow to be done without correction. Here I have always been with you since my birth, and there I will not leave you." Then the lord said: "Not so, William, not so. I shall certainly correct my faults."—"Then I am well," said the fool, "and give my soul to God and to all the saints." And thus he led his lord back to confession and to the correction of his life.

In the third place, confession must be truthful and frank; as the Psalmist says: "With my will I shall confess to you." This is shown in an example for us by Achan, in Joshua 7, who said after he had received the curse: "Indeed I have sinned against the Lord and have done thus and thus." We find another biblical story to the same effect in the last chapter of 2 Kings, about David. After he had the people of Israel counted by Joab against God's will, the Lord became angry and sent, at David's choice, a pestilence of three days, in which seventy thousand men died from Dan to Beersheba. When David saw this, he said to the angel who was slaying his people: "It is I who have sinned; I have done wickedly. These are sheep, what have they done? Let your hand, I beseech you, be turned against me." After this, David offered the Lord burnt-offerings, after the counsel of the prophet Gad, and the Lord was reconciled.

But we must realize that unfortunately many people nowadays do not act in this way but rather excuse their sins foolishly and blame them on others, and this in different manners: sometimes they blame their own habit, sometimes society, and sometimes God. An example of the first kind may be found in people who perjure themselves; when they are reproached for this, they say: "I would gladly correct myself, but I am so used to swearing that I can in no way leave it." Surely, such an excuse is foolish and wrong, first because it increases rather than decreases one's sin; second because you yourself have brought yourself to the evil habit and no one else—therefore it is certain that you yourself are responsible for this sin—; and third: let us assume you are standing before a judge and have been accused of theft or murder or something else of the kind, and you were saying, "Certainly, my Lord, I am so used to these that I cannot abstain from them,"—what good would such an argument do you, I ask? Surely, with it you would condemn yourself.

As an example of the second kind, namely blaming one's sin on society: if someone wanted to travel to the Holy Land or Saint James or Rome and joined a group on its way to Scotland, would this person not be called a fool? Now, you propose to travel to the holy land, that is, heaven. Why then do you want to

neque ipse neque posteritas eius mortem gustasset. Tercio, [f. 136v] esto
quod sic coram iudice aliquo per societatem te ⟨ex⟩cusaveris, quid tibi
140   eveniret? Revera, suspendium.
        Tercio sunt aliqui, et precipue de peccato carnis, qui pessime se
excusant [peccatum] in Deum retorquentes. Nam quidam dicunt quod non possunt continere, et sic Deum de iniusticia accusant. Probacio: Si enim Deus
aliquid homini precepit quod non potest facere, iam esset iniustus et
145   crudelis. Similiter, si hominem dampnaret pro eo quod vitare non potest,
factum tiranni esset. Quidam sunt, et maxime muliercule, qu⟨e⟩ respondent
quando queritur ab eis quare sic fecerunt, scilicet quando venter [earum]
incipit tumescere et inflari, quod oportuit eas ita facere, nam predestinatum erat hoc eis ita ante tunicam vel camisiam. Set certe bene posset
150   [talibus] responderi sicut quondam quidam frater tali fornicarie respondit:
"Vere, filia," dixit ipse, "qui formavit istud sacculum, idest ventrem
tuum, pessimus cissor fuit, [for schamely hyt poket]." Set a talibus libenter scirem utrum voluntarie hoc fecerunt. Si sic, ergo potuerunt hoc non
fecisse. Probacio: Quia quod fit libere, sponte potest dimitti; ergo, etc.
155   Est ergo sciendum quod tales sic peccata sua palliantes assimilantur istis
falsis questionariis qui ostendendo reliquias suas ostendunt illas in
aliquo vase deaurato et lapidibus preciosis perornato, ac eciam in pannis
aureis et cericis involutas, ut saltem sic preciose appareant hominibus.
Que tamen, ut frequenter, si detegerentur aperte, non invenies nisi ossa
160   alicuius iumenti de fovea extracta, fetida et arida ac omni abhominacione
digna. Revera sic tales in confessione quando peccata sua deberent aperte
ostendere et veraciter, opponunt tot excusaciones, tot velamina, acsi
vellent facere de peccatis suis reliquias adorandas, cum tamen pessime
fetent coram [f. 137] Deo et angelis. Contra quos ait Augustinus: "Senten-
165   cia, inquit, criminum cum defenditur augetur. Facta scelera peccancium
tanto maiora incrementa suscipiunt quanto per defencionem multa tollerant."
Et ideo dicit idem: "Tu factor es tui peccati et defensor. Quomodo ergo
erit Deus liberator? Et ideo, ut ipse sit liberator, esto tu[i] accusator,"
et dic cum Psalmista: "Ex voluntate mea confitebor ei." Qui enim facit
170   invitus, non ipse facit, set de eo fit. Ideo Ecclesiastici 4 dicitur:
"Fili, conserva tempus et ne confundaris dicere verum pro anima tua."
        Unde narratur de quodam in carcere existente et sciente se non posse
liberari nisi prius tria verba veritatis secundum modum regionis diceret.
Ducto ergo coram iudice ait primo: "Sum hic," et respondit iudex: "Verum
175   est." Et ille secundo dixit: "Doleo quod veni huc." "Credo," inquit iudex,
"quod verum dicis." Et ille tercio ait: "Si semel evadere potero, numquam
gratis redibo." Et hiis dictis liberatus est, quia ter verum dixerat. Revera sic quilibet peccator in carcere diaboli ligatus per peccata liberari
non potest nisi tria verba veritatis diceret in confessione. Dicat ergo

join people whom you have seen enter the way to hell with their sins? Second, how foolish you are when you guard less against danger to your soul than to your body! For example: If you saw someone jump into a river and drown, I am sure no sense of fellowship would compel you to follow him. Much less then should you follow someone else into sin, if you love your soul as it should be loved by right. This excuse therefore is wrong, as was Adam's when he wanted to blame his wife for his sin by saying, in Genesis 3, "The woman, whom you gave me to be my companion, gave it to me, and I ate." For that excuse he was condemned to bodily death with all his offspring. If he had humbly said, "It is I who have sinned," and so forth, as David did, and asked for forgiveness, neither he nor his offspring would have tasted death. And finally, if you were to excuse yourself before some judge by thus blaming society, what would you get? The gallows, for certain.

Third, there are some people who wickedly excuse themselves by blaming God for their sin, especially their sin of the flesh. For some say they just cannot be continent, and thereby accuse God of injustice. Because if God has commanded man to do something which he cannot do, God would be unjust and cruel. And likewise, if he were to condemn man for what he cannot avoid, he would act like a tyrant. There are some pople, expecially young women, who, when they are asked why they did it when their belly begins to grow and swell, answer that they had to because it was foreordained for them "before tunic or shirt." But surely one could well reply to them as once a friar said to such a harlot: "Truly, my daughter, he who made that bag, your belly, this way was a terrible tailor, for it pokes out shamefully!" Further, I would simply ask them if they did this willingly. If so, then they could have not done it. Because, what one does freely can willingly be left undone; therefore, and so on. We should thus know that people who veil their sins in this fashion are like these false pardoners, who show their relics in some golden vessel that is decorated with precious gems, or else wrapped in cloths of gold and silk, so that they may look truly precious before the people. But as it often happens, when they open them up, you will find nothing but the bones from a farm animal that have been pulled out of a ditch, stinking and dried up and worthy of every abomination. In the same say, when such people ought to show their sins frankly and truthfully in confession, they put so many excuses around them like wrappers, as if they wanted to make of their sins relics to be worshipped, whereas in truth they stink horribly before God and his angels. Against such people Augustine says: "When the punishment for a crime is appealed, it grows worse. The evil deeds of sinners increase, the more they are tolerated by being excused." And therefore Augustine says: "You are the agent of your sin and its defender. How then will God free you from it? That he may free you, then, be an accuser of yourself and say with the Psalmist: 'With my will I shall confess to him.' For he who acts against his will does not act but is

180　primo "Sum hic," hoc est, sum hic humiliter et fideliter fatendo peccata
que commisi. Ego sum ille qui peccavi et non alius. Secundo dicat, "Doleo
quod huc veni," quasi diceret: doleo per veram cordis contricionem quod
talia commisi per que Deum offendi, unde huc venire oportet. Dicat tercio:
"Si semel evadere potero," etc., scilicet mundatus de commissis per virtu-
185　tem confessionis et contricionis, "numquam gratis huc redibo," quia pro
preteritis satisfaciam et cavebo a futuris. Et certe si sic feceris, a
carcere peccati liber evades.
　　　Quarto dico oportet quod confessio sit cum amara contricione, non cum
vana cachinnacione. De qua amaritudine quia sufficienter dictum est supra,
190　capitulo proximo de contricione, ideo hic leviter transeo.
　　　[f. 137v] Est tamen advertendum quod plures sunt condiciones et circumstancie tangentes peccata, que bene tam a confessore quam a confitente
oportet considerari. Et hec sunt, videlicet ut patet per versus:

　　　Quis, quid, ubi, quibus auxiliis, cur, quomodo, quando,
195　　　Quilibet observet anime medicamina dando.

Verbi gracia: Quando aliquis enim venit ad confessionem, debet confessor
considerare et ponderare primo quis est ille qui tale peccatum commisit, si
clericus aut laicus, dives vel pauper, senex aut iuvenis aut puer, quia
quanto status dignior, tanto lapsus gravior. Secundo debet considerare quid
200　sit peccatum in se et secundum quantitatem vel qualitatem procedere. Tercio, ubi commisit tale peccatum, ⟨ut si⟩ gracia exempli fuerit ⟨periurium⟩,
si in loco sacro vel non, et secundum hoc procedere. Quarto, quibus auxiliis tale peccatum committitur, quia sicut dictum est supra, quanto gradus
alcior, tanto delictum gravius. Quinto, cur hoc facit, aut ex propria
205　malicia aut necessitate et indigencia, sicut aliquando pauperes necessitate
compulsi furantur victualia et huiusmodi, quod non facerent si aliunde
haberent. Sexto, quomodo, vel hominem occidendo vel domos frangendo vel
ecclesias violando. Septimo, quando, hoc est, si in tempore sacro, puta
diebus festivis vel tempore missarum et huiusmodi. Et secundum hoc procede-
210　re debent absolvendo et penitencias inponendo. Et nota quod plures sunt
circumstancie peccatorum adhuc considerande et ponderande utrobique, ut
patet in hiis versibus:

　　　Quis, quid, ubi, quibus auxiliis, cur, quomodo, quando.
　　　Aggravat ordo, locus, persona, sciencia, tempus,
215　　　Sexus, condicio, numerus, mora, copia, causa,
　　　Et modus, et culpa, status alt⟨us⟩, lucta pusilla.

Expone ut placet.
　　　Si ergo ut dictum est fuerit confessio tua, revera tante virtutis est

acted on." Therefore it is said in Ecclesiasticus 4: "Son, observe the time
and be not ashamed to say the truth for your soul."

There is a story about someone who was in jail and knew that he could not
get free unless he would, after the fashion of that country, say three words of
truth. When he was led before the judge, he said the first, "I am here," and
the judge replied, "That is true." Then he said the second: "I regret that I
have come here."—"I believe," said the judge, "that you speak the truth."
And in the third place he said: "If I can get away, I'll never come back of my
own." And after these words he was set free, because he had spoken the truth
three times. In the same way, whatever sinner is bound by his sins in the
devil's prison cannot get free unless he says three true words in confession.
Let him then say first, "I am here," that is: I am here to confess humbly and
faithfully the sins I have committed. I am the one who has sinned, and no one
else. Second, let him say, "I regret that I have come here," as if to say: I
regret through true contrition of heart that I have committed such things by
which I have offended God, wherefore I have to come here. And third, "If I can
get away," and so on, that is: once I have been cleansed of my sins through the
power of confession and contrition, "I will never come back here of my own,"
for I will do penance for my past sins and beware of them in the future. If you
do thus, you will certainly go free of the prison of sin.

In the fourth place I say that confession must be accompanied by bitter
contrition, not by vain laughter. This bitterness I pass over now, for I spoke
of it sufficiently earlier, in the preceding chapter on contrition.

But we must realize that there are many conditions and circumstances
relating to sins which must be taken into consideration by both confessor and
penitent. They are, as shown in these verses:

> Who, what, where, with what help, and why and how and when—
> Check these when you try to give medicine to a soul.

For instance, when someone comes to confession, his confessor must consider
and weigh, first, who it is that comitted that sin: whether a cleric or a layman, a
rich person or a poor one, an old man, youth, or child, for the higher his
status, the more grave his fall. Second, he must consider the nature of the
sin and weigh its quantity and quality. Third, where the penitent has committed that sin: if, for instance, it was swearing, whether he did it in a holy
place or not, and weigh it accordingly. Fourth, with what help he has committed that sin, for as I have already said, the higher his rank, the more grievous his fault. Fifth, why, that is, whether out of his own wickedness, or
under compulsion, or in need, as poor people are sometimes compelled by their
need to steal food and such things, which they would not do if they otherwise
had what they needed. Sixth, how: whether by killing a man or breaking into
houses or violating churches. Seventh, when: if at a holy time, such as feast

quod, si plura commisisses quam aliquis [f. 138] vivens et omnia contra te
220   diabolus in libro confusionis reportasset, omnia delerentur et nomen tuum
cum iustis ascriberetur. Unde narratur in *Vita beati Bernardi* quod quidam
clericus multo tempore lubrice vixit set tamdem contritus ad sanctum virum
pro confessione accessit, et ita suam maliciam detestabatur quod in tantum
fletum prorupit quod nullo modo loqui potuit. Cuius contricionem attendens
225   sanctus precepit ut in cedula, ex quo loqui non potuit, peccata sua scriberet et sibi traderet. Quod et fecit. Cum ergo sanctus Bernardus illa legere
vellet, omnia deleta invenit. Si ergo in libro sancti peccata confessa et
contrita sic erant deleta, quanto magis scriptura diaboli. Et ideo hoc
[est] quod dicitur Ezechielis 13: "Convertimini et agite penitenciam ab
230   omnibus inquinamentis vestris, et non erit in vobis iniquitas."

---

3 hool . . . sorowyng] *the two English phrases together and introduced with* anglice
B1.W.—*Text from* R. *Verse 46, in* B1.B3.E.Go1.Jo.L2.L3.LC.Sp.V.W1.   **6** eius] illius
O.   **9** si] sicut O.   **10** Nam] iam C.   **12** debet] oportet O.   **15** continuo] continue O.
24 cum(3)] *om* O.   **27** Dominus] deus O.   **29** confessio] *om* O.   **33** quodam] quadam
O.   **36** et] *om* O.   **46** signat] designat O.   **49** inflammatur] inflammantur C.   **67–
68** Anglice . . . sinne] *text from* W. *See* Verses, *pp. 203–4. The English is rendered as*
nam potest extrahere a wlneribus anime sagittas peccatorum M.   **68** Illud] istud O.
69 possunt] possent M.R; W?   **70** enim] autem O.   multis] *om* O.   **81** sibi placuit]
placeret O.   **83** sui] *om* O.   **89** tuo] tue C.M.W.   **90** intrantibus] *add* et O.   **91** potare]
add non cessat C.   **92** diabolo] *om* O.   **93** respondens ait] respondit O.   **95** fieri] facere
O.   **97** meipsum] *om* M.W.; me R.   **98** dominum] dominus C.   **101** nostrum] verum
C.   **101–102** de . . . qui] *om* C.M.W.   **105** Dominus] *om* C.M.W.   misit] *om*
C.M.W.   **106** septuaginta] octoginta C.   **115** qui] quod C.   **118** illam] istam O.
120 alio] aliud C.M.W.   **121** illa] ista O.   **122** quam] non C.   **122–123** allocata] ad hoc
quod M; allegata R.   **125** sanctum] ad C.   **126** ad] versus O.   **127** ad(2)] *om* O. tales]
talibus C.   vis] *om* C.W.   **135** hanc] quam O.   **139** excusaveris] accusaveris C; ex-
cusares R.   **146** que] qui C.   **147** scilicet] *om* O.   **149** eis] illis O.   ita] *om* O.
151 sacculum] *add* hoc modo O.   idest] scilicet O.   **152** for . . . poket] *om* C; etc M;
text from R. See Verses, *pp. 205–206.* Set] secundo O.   **160** et] *om* O.   **162** opponunt]
apponunt O.   **164** quos] *add* bene O.   **167** idem] augustinus O.   **179** verba veritatis]
vera M.R; verba W.   **180** est] *add* ego O.   **193** ut . . . versus] *om* O.   **196** venit] venerit O.   **198** vel] aut O.   **201** ut si] et sic C.W; et si M.   periurium] parvi rei C.W; in re
M.   **203** committitur] fecit M; commisit R.W.   supra] *om* O.   **206** victualia] *add* focalia
O.   **208** in] *om* O.   **216** altus] alta C.   **225** precepit] *add* ei O.   **229** est] *om* C.R.
230 in] *om* O.

days or during Mass and the like. And then the confessor must proceed to absolve and give penances according to these circumstances. But notice that in both acts there are still several circumstances of sins that must be considered and weighed, such as are listed in the following verses:

Who, what, where, with what help, and why and how and when.
Orders add weight, as does place, and person, knowledge, and time,
Sex and complexion, number and time, occasion and cause,
Further its manner and shame, high status, too little grief.

Explain this as you see fit.

If then, as I have said, your confession is bitter, it has such power that, even if you had sinned more than any person alive and the devil were to write down all your sins against you in his book of condemnation, they would all be deleted and your name would be written with the just. For this reason, the *Life of Blessed Bernard* tells of a cleric who had been unchaste for a long time but at last repented and came to the saint to make his confession. He detested his wickedness so much that he broke into such violent weeping that he could not talk in any way. As the saint noticed his contrition, he asked him, since he could not talk, to write his sins on a slip of parchment and give that to him. This he did. But when Saint Bernard wanted to read it, he found everything deleted. If, then, sins that were confessed and repented were thus deleted in the book of a holy man, how much more will this be the case with the writing of the devil. Therefore, this is what is said in Ezekiel 18: "Be converted and do penance for all your iniquities, and your iniquity shall not be."

13–16 Isidore, *Etym.* XI.iii.34.   **23** Ps. 31.5.   **27–28** 2 Sam. 12.13.   **32** Nah. 3.5.
34–36 *Decretals* 5.6.13 (2:776).   **41–43** Joel 1.4.   **51** Prov. 26.20.   **53–54** Cf.
Jerome, *Contra Vigilantium* 16 (PL 23:368).   **55** Jerome, *Ep. 117* 3 (CSEL 55:426).
56–57 Gen. 3.1.   **61–62** Ps. 41.2.   **75–77** Ecclus. 5.8.   **78–99** For analogues to this
story, see Wenzel, "The Wisdom of the Fool," in *The Wisdom of Poetry. Essays in Early
English Literature in Honor of Morton W. Bloomfield*, ed. Larry D. Benson and Siegfried
Wenzel (Kalamazoo, Mich., 1982), pp. 225–240, 307–314.   **100–101** Ps. 27.7.   **102–
103** Josh. 7.20.   **103–110** 2 Sam. 24.   **134–135** Gen. 3.12.   **137** 2 Sam. 24.17.
164–166 Cf. Augustine, *En. in Ps. 139* 9 (CC 40:2017).   **167–170** Augustine, *En. in Ps.
68* I.19 (CC 39:916).   **169** Ps. 27.7.   **171** Ecclus. 4.23.   **172–177** Tubach 2233. The
story also occurs in Ross, *Middle English Sermons*, pp. 157–158, and British Library, MS
Harley 7322, fol. 36v.   **189–190** *FM* V.vii.   **194–195** *In* 16108 and also 16099–102;
Prov 25429a, 25431–32, 25338, and others.   **214–216** *In* 680; *Prov* 719.   **221–
226** Tubach 1202a.   **229–230** Cf. Ezek. 18.30.

V.xiii   QUE MALA EVENIUNT CONFITERI
DIFFERENTIBUS

[C]irca autem mala que eveniunt confiteri differentibus est sciendum
quod si copia sacerdotis ydonei haberi poterit et negligenter omittit, hec
inconveniencia sequuntur: Primo, talis iniuriatur Deo et ipsum contempnit;
secundo, oneri importabili se sub⟨i⟩cit; tercio, eternam penam sibi adqui-
5   rit. Precepit enim Dominus homini peccatori illud Luce 5: "Vade, ostende te
sacerdoti." Contrarium ergo faciens preceptum eius contempnit et per consequens ipsi s⟨umm⟩e iniuriatur. Exemplum: Si quis enim contra regem et eius
leges et precepta contra⟨ir⟩et unde iuste iudicium mortis subiret, si tunc
rex ex sua bonitate iudicium differret et illum ad satisfactionem expecta-
10   ret, necnon et de satisfaciendi facilitate ipsum cercionaret, nonne regi
iniuriosus et sibi ipsi dampnosus esset si ad satisfactionem venire differret? quasi dicat, omnino. Ita sic in proposito. Unde Gregorius in *Mora-*
libus: "Quisquis enim delinquit et vivit, idcirco [eum] divina dispensacio
tollerat ut ab iniquitate [f. 138v] compescat"; Romanorum ⟨2⟩: "Ignoras
15   quoniam Dei benignitas te adducit?" Item, quia tempus satisfaciendi non
ipsius offendentis, set Domini satisfactionem ⟨re⟩quirentis. Contrarium
ergo faciens Domino iniuriatur. Iudith 8 dicitur: "Posuistis vos tempus
visitacionis Domini et in arbitrio vestro diem constituistis ei. Et non est
ille sermo qui misericordiam provocet set pocius qui iram excitat et furo-
20   rem accendit." De quo conqueritur Salvator Apocalipsis: "Dedi sibi tempus
ut peniteret, et non vult." Patet ergo quod peccator qui ⟨tempus⟩ sibi
concessum a Deo ad merendum abutitur quod ipsum Deum manifeste contempnit et iniuriatur.

Set rogo quid dicemus de talibus qui ficte confitentur in Quadragesima
25   et statim post Pascha "sicut canis ad vomitum" sic et ipsi redeunt ad peccatum? Revera, quantum in illis est iterum Filium Dei crucifigunt. Probacio: Ipse enim Filius Dei pro peccatis nostris mortuus est ut nos offerret
Deo Patri mortificatos in carne, vivificatos autem spiritu. Set tales recidivantes quod ipse per mortem venerat mortificare gratis econtra nituntur
30   reviviscere; ergo etc.; Hebreorum 6: "Rursum crucifigentes Filium Dei."
Solent enim homines in odium arma habere quibus parentes eorum interfecti
sunt. Sic deberent homines peccatum pro quo primus parens et Christus
occisus est. Set timeo quod est iam de multis sicut de vipera. Volens
copulari cum lampreda, set non potest dum habet secum venenum, quod intel-
35   ligens in quodam loco secreto venenum suum evomit et sic copulatur ei, set
transacta copula venenum resumit. Revera sic multi volentes copulari Christo in Paschate evomant venenum in confessione, set postea redeunt ad illud
quod emiserunt; Proverbiorum 30: "Sicut canis qui revertitur ad vomitum,
sic inpudens qui iterat stulticiam suam."

V.xiii   WHAT EVILS COME TO THOSE WHO DELAY CONFESSION

With regard to the bad consequences of delaying confession we must know that, if a competent priest is available and one neglects to confess, the following evil consequences will occur: first, such a person offends and scorns God; second, he places himself under an unbearable burden; and third, he derives eternal punishment for himself. For the Lord has given sinful man this command of Luke 5: "Go and show yourself to the priest." If one therefore does the opposite, one scorns God's commandment and consequently gives him the greatest offense. For example: if one were to act against one's king and his laws and commands and thereby justly received the death sentence, and the king then out of his goodness deferred the sentence and expected one to make satisfaction and in addition granted one the opportunity to do so, would it not be an offense against the king and harmful to oneself if one delayed to make satisfaction? Surely so. The same is true in respect to confession. Whence Gregory says in his *Moral Commentary*: "If anyone sins and lives, God's tolerance allows him to live for the purpose of tearing him away from his iniquity"; Romans 2: "Do you not know that God's benignity leads you to penance?" Further, the time for making satisfaction is not set by the one who offends but by God who demands satisfaction. If one does the opposite, one offends God. In Judith 8 it is said: "You have set a time for the visitation of the Lord, and you have appointed him a day according to your judgment. This is not a word that may draw down mercy, but rather that may stir up wrath and enkindle indignation." Our Savior complains at this in Revelation: "I gave her a time that she might do penance, but she will not." Thus it is clear that a sinner who does not use the time God has given him to gain merits openly scorns and offends God.

But, I ask, what shall we say of those who pretend to confess in Lent and right after Easter return to their sin "as a dog returns to his vomit"? Verily, as much as it lies in them, they crucify the Son of God a second time. To prove this: the Son of God has died for our sins that he might offer us to God the Father dead in the flesh but alive in the spirit. But those who slide back try, on the contrary, to make alive again what he had come willingly to stifle through his death; therefore, etc.; Hebrews 6: "Crucifying again the Son of God." It is usual that people abhor the weapons with which their parents were killed. In the same way should all men hate sin, through which our first parent and Christ were killed. But I fear that nowadays many act like the snake that wants to copulate with the lamprey but cannot do it as long as it has its poison. When it understands this, it spits out its poison in some secret place, and then they copulate. But afterwards it takes its poison up again. In the same way, many who wish to be joined with Christ at Easter spit

40   Et nota: Licet utraque sit mala, [f. 139] scilicet peccare et post
confessionem recidivare, [ultimum tamen peius est] iuxta illud Petri 2:
"Melius est non cognoscere viam iusticie quam post agnicionem retrorsum
converti." Et ideo Ecclesiastici 2 dicitur: "Ve peccatori qui ingreditur
terram duabus viis." Due enim vie posite sunt coram homine, una scilicet

45   que ducit ad vitam—illa scilicet quam homo ingreditur cum adheret Deo per
bona opera, de qua scribitur: "Hec est via, ambulate in ea"—; alia est que
ducit ad mortem, de qua Proverbiorum 24: "Est via que videtur homini recta;
novissima autem eius ducunt ad mortem." Et istam viam ingreditur homo cum a
Deo recesserit et diabolo per peccatum inheret.

50   Unde notandum quod dolendum est iam de aliquibus sicut fuit de quodam
cane exeunte in quodam campo, de quo narratur quod cum audisset duo cornua
in diversis locis ad convivia invitancia, modo secutus est unum, modo
aliud, et sic tota die discurrens tandem nocte adveniente utroque convivio
privatus est. Revera sic est de multis qui in bonis diu stare non possunt.

55   Existunt autem hii in agro dum manent in hoc mundo, ubi duo cornua audiunt
ad diversa convivia invitancia, quorum unum invitat ad celum iuxta illud
Matthei 2: "Agite penitenciam, appropinquabit enim regnum celorum." Et
certe illud cornu multi audiunt et sequuntur dum peccata confitentur et
penitenciam agunt. Set postea audiunt aliud cornu quod invitat ad carnale

60   desiderium, cuius sonus est illud Sapiencie 3: "Venite, fruamur bonis que
sunt et utamur omni creatura ⟨in iuventute⟩, vino precioso et unguento
impleamur, et non pretereat nos flos temporis nostri." Istud autem cornu
multi audiunt et sequuntur dum opera penitencie dimittunt et ad peccata
redeunt, et sic per dupplicem viam vadunt per totam diem, idest vitam [f.

65   139v] presentem, et quietem in bono statu non invenient, sicut habetur
Ecclesiastici 3: "Cor ingrediens duas vias non habebit requiem." Et ideo
adveniente nocte mortis utroque convivio carebunt, quia cum anima exierit
de corpore, ad infernum descendunt celesti gaudio privati et a carnali
desiderio subtracti. Et ideo via sapiencie est quod homo, quando de statu

70   culpe profectus fuerit, ad illum non redire set in statu gracie firmiter se
tenere; unde illud Ecclesiastici 5: "Esto firmus in via Domini et in veritate sensus tui."

      Unde contrarium facientes, ut dictum est, quantum in ipsis est iterum
Deum crucifigunt. Et ideo bene assimilantur paralitico qui cito ridet et

75   cito post in fletum prorumpitur. Sic multi visa Christi passione aliquando
compaciuntur et compuncti peccata detestantur, set cito post cum aliqua
carnis delectacio eis surrexerit, mox sui Creatoris obliti iterum in dissolucionem prolabuntur. Unde Gregorius in quadam omelia: "Multi, inquit, sunt
cum verbum contra luxuriam audiunt, polluciones carnis de cetero perpetrare

80   non appetunt, verum eciam perpetratas erubescunt. Set mox ut carnis species
eorum oculis appareat, sic mens ad desiderium rapitur, acsi adhuc contra

out their poison in confession, but afterwards they return to what they have cast off; Proverbs 30: "As a dog that returns to his vomit, so is the fool that repeats his folly."

And notice that although both are evil: to sin, and after confession to slide back, yet is the latter worse, according to the words of Peter 2: "For it is better not to know the way of justice than after knowing it to turn back." And thus it is said in Ecclesiasticus 2: "Woe to the sinner who goes on the earth two ways." For two ways are put before man, one that leads to life—that is the one man takes when he clings to God by his good deeds, of which is written: "This is the way, walk in it"—; the other that leads to death, of which is said in Proverbs 24: "There is a way that seems good to a man; but its ends lead to death." This way one takes when one withdraws from God and clings to the devil by sin.

We should therefore notice that some people unfortunately act like a dog who went out into the field. He is said to have heard two horns from different sides inviting him to dinner. Now he ran after one, now after the other, and after he had run about all day long, when it got to be night at last he had neither dinner. The same way it goes with many who cannot follow a good life for long. As long as they live in this world, they are in a field where they hear two horns inviting them to different banquets. One invites them to heaven, according to Matthew 2: "Do penance, for the kingdom of heaven is at hand." Certainly, many hear this horn and follow it when they confess their sins and do penance. But then they hear another horn that invites them to fleshly delight, whose sound are the words of Wisdom 3: "Come, let us enjoy the good things that are present, let us use all creatures in our youth; let us fill ourselves with costly wine and ointments, and let not the flower of our age pass us by." Many hear this horn and follow it when they abandon their works of penance and return to their sins. And thus, throughout the whole day, that is, this life, they follow a double path and will find no rest in a good life, as is said in Ecclesiasticus 3: "A heart that goes two ways shall have no rest." So, when the night of death comes, they will fail to reach either banquet, for when the soul leaves the body, they go down to hell, deprived of the joy of heaven and pulled away from the delights of the flesh. Therefore it is the way of wisdom that, once one has come out of the state of sin, one does not return to it but rather remains firmly in the state of grace; hence the words of Ecclesiasticus 5: "Be steadfast in the way of the Lord and in the truth of your judgment."

And so, as I have said, people who do the opposite crucify God a second time, as much as it lies in them. They are much like a paralytic who easily laughs and then breaks into weeping. In the same way, when they see Christ's Passion, many people sometimes have compassion and, feeling remorse, detest their sins; but shortly afterwards, when some fleshly delight steals into them,

hec eadem desideria nichil sit deliberatum." Et sequitur: "Sepe enim contra
culpas compungimur, et tamen post fletum ad culpas redimus. In cuius figura
Balaam Israelitici populi tabernacula contemplandus flevit et eisdem in
85   morte similem fieri deposcit dicens: 'Anima mea moriatur morte iustorum, et
fiant novissima mea horum similia,' Numeri. Set mox ut hora compunctionis
transivit, in avaricie culpam exarcit. Nam propter promissa munera in
mortem populi concilium dedit, cuius morti se similem [fieri] prius peroptavit et [f. 140] quod planxerat oblitus [est] cum extinguere voluit quod
90   per avariciam ardebat." Hec ille. Tales ergo de morte Christi non compaciuntur, set sua peccata iterando Deum secundum posse iterum crucifigunt, et
ideo brutis animalibus peiores inveniuntur. Bos enim in prato si alterius
sanguinem aspexerit, statim quasi compaciendo magnum rugitum emittit, ut
sic alia animalia ad hoc faciendum provocet. Set peccator non sic, set
95   peccata peccatis addens et iterans mortem Christi et sanguinem renovare non
erubescit; Petri 1: "Agite penitenciam qualis agitur in Ecclesia," etc.
    Secundum autem malum quod homini confiteri differenti evenit est quod
oneri importabili se subicit. Exemplum in *Vitas Patrum* de illo quem vidit
beatus Arsenius tale onus lignorum colligentem quod levare non potuit, unde
100   quanto pluries [illud] levare temptavit et minus potuit, semper tamen plura
ligna apposuit, quousque ex nimio pondere oppressus cedidit. Cum ergo super
hoc beatus Arsenius miraretur, dixit sibi angelus: "Tales sunt peccatores
qui ad⟨dend⟩o peccata peccatis onus importabile colligunt et tamen plura
apponere non desistunt quousque ad mortem ab illis opprimuntur."
105   Et nota quod onera portantes tria solent considerare ad suum laborem
necessaria: oneris gravitatem, terrarum distanciam, et mercedis quantitatem. Quoad primum nota quod onus peccati ita est fastidiosum quod eius gra-
vitas si bene consideretur numquam ad portandum sumeretur. Nam tante ponde-
rositatis est quod celum una hora illud portare non poterit nec sustinere—
110   et tamen celum propter suam fortitudinem dicitur firmamentum—; Luce 10:
"Videbam Sathanam sicut fulgur de celo cadentem," et in Psalmo: "Sicut onus
grave gravate sunt super me," scilicet peccata. Quantum ad se⟨cund⟩um,
scilicet quamdiu [usquequo] onus portabat, [f. 140v] si bene consideraret,
⟨numquam illud⟩ ad portandum assumeret, quia nisi Deus de sua misericordia
115   de collo peccatoris deponat illud, portantem in infernum demergat, ubi in
pena sine fine remaneret; "laborabit in eternum et vivet adhuc in finem,"
etc. Simea enim cum duos fetus habeat, quando fugatur a venatoribus, quem
magis diligit inter brachia portat, set alium circa collum appendit. Cum
autem venator illam approximat, magis dilectum compellitur proicere, set
120   aliu⟨s⟩ in dorso velit nolit secum remanet. Unde pre gravedine eius et
pondere cum illo fetu capitur a venatore et detinetur et cathenatur. Revera
sic in proposito. Peccator habet duos fetus, scilicet bona temporalia, que
magis diligit et ideo illa quasi in brachiis amplexatur et deportat. Set

they forget their Maker and fall again into dissoluteness. Therefore, Gregory says in a homily: "Many, when they hear a warning against lechery, do not wish to commit any more unclean sins of the flesh but even are ashamed of those they have committed. But as soon as the beauty of the flesh appears before their eyes, their mind is drawn to desire, as if they had never made any decision against these desires." And he continues: "We are often deeply sorry for our sins, and yet after our tears we return to sin. As a type of this, Balaam wept when he looked at the tents of the people of Israel and begged that in his death he might become like them, saying in Numbers: 'Let my soul die the death of the just, and my last end be like them.' But as soon as the hour of his compunction was over, he burned in the sin of avarice. For because of the gifts that had been promised him, he gave his advice to bring death on the same people to whose death he had earlier wanted to become similar, and he forgot that he had wept when he did not want to extinguish what was burning through his greed." Such people have no compassion for Christ's death but, by repeating their sins, crucify God again, insofar as it lies within them, and thus they are found to be worse than brute animals. For if a bull in the field sees the blood of another bull, he at once gives a loud roar as if out of compassion, so that he incites other animals to do the same. But a sinner does not act like that; rather, by repeating his sins and adding new ones, he does not blush to cause Christ's death and bloodshedding again; Peter 1: "Do penance, as it is done in the Church," etc.

The second evil consequence of delaying one's confession is that one thereby places oneself under an unbearable burden. We find an example in *The Lives of the Fathers*, in the man whom Blessed Arsenius saw gather such a load of wood that he could not lift it. Every time he tried to lift it and could not do so, he put some more sticks on it, until at last he was crushed by the weight. As Blessed Arsenius marveled at that, an angel said to him: "Such are those sinners who add sins upon sins and gather an unbearable burden, and still they do not stop putting on more until they are crushed to death by them."

Notice that people who carry burdens usually consider three things that are necessary for their work: the weight of their burden, the distance they have to go, and the amount of their compensation. As to the first, notice that the burden of sin is so forbidding that, if only one considered well its weight, one would never stoop to carry it. For it is so heavy that heaven could not carry or bear it for a single hour—and yet heaven is called "firmament" because of its strength—; Luke 10: "I saw Satan like lightning falling from heaven"; and in the Psalm: "As a heavy burden they are become heavy upon me," that is, my sins. As to the second consideration, how far he is to carry the burden, if one were to consider this well, one would not want to take it up at all, for unless God in his mercy takes that burden from the sinner's neck, it will thrust its carrier into hell, where he will remain in torment without

fetus quem portat in dorso, quem minus diligit, est peccatum. Cum ergo
125 venator, idest mors, que omnes insequitur, venerit, compellitur terrena
proicere et mundo relinquere, set fetus peccati super dorsum pendens proicere non potest. Et ideo cum illo capitur et ligatur adeo ut cum illis ad
modum simee cachinnando et saltando in inferno modo suo ludit. Quantum ad
tercium, considerare debet que merces pro labore promittitur. Et respondet
130 Apostolus Romanorum 6: "Stipendia peccati mors." Si enim ligaretur aliquod
pondus ad collum hominis et esset bene alte in aere et ad terram caderet,
numquam profundius quam ad terram deveniret. Set si peccatum mortale in
collo dependeat et cum illo moriente cadat, non tantum ad terram deveniret,
imo usque ad infernum penetraret. Et ideo huiusmodi onus per confessionem
135 abiciamus et per penitenciam animam cum peccatis oneratam alleviamus. Dicit
enim Crisostomus omelia 3 in *Imperfecto*: "Confessionem, inquit, puta esse
digestionem [f. 141] inpuritatis et spurcicie que intus latent inclusa."
      Tercium malum quod evenit confiteri differentibus est adquisicio eter-
ne pene. Unde narrat Beda *De gestis Anglorum* libro 5, capitulo 13, de
140 quodam milite qui fuit cum Kynredo rege Merciorum, quem rex multum dilexit
quia probus in armis extiterat valde. Ad quem infirmatum cum rex venisset
hortans eum confiteri et penitere, respondit: "Non pro tunc," ne forte alii
dicerent quod fecerat pre timore mortis, set quod sanus voluerat. Igitur
morbo ingravescente, cum rex iterum intrasset ad illum informandum ut
145 prius, ipse miserabili voce clama[vi]t: "Quid huc venisti? Paulo ante te
intraverunt duo iuvenes pulcherrimi, quorum unus se posuit ad capud meum et
alius ad pedes, et unus illorum libellum michi parvissimum porrexit, in quo
omnia bona que umquam feci scripta erant satis pauca. Et codicem acceperunt, nichil michi dicentes recesserunt. Subito ergo postea exercitus demo-
150 num venit et domum implevit, quorum unus omnium terribilior protulit librum
horrende visionis et pondere importabilis, quem iussit michi deferri ad
legendum. In quo inveni omnia peccata mea, non solum que feceram opere vel
verbo, set eciam tenuissima cogitacione ° cogitavi, manifeste teterrimis
litteris. Dixitque ad iuvenes predictos: 'Quid hic facitis? Scitis autem
155 certissime quod hic noster est.' Et responderunt illi: 'Verum est, accipite
eum.' Quo dicto disparuerunt statim surgentes. Tunc duo demones cum duobus
vomeribus, *cultris*, ignitis percusserunt me, unus ad capud et alius ad
pedes, qui eciam modo cum maximo tormento eripiunt viscera mea. [f. 141v]
Cum ergo ad se invicem perveniant et vomeres sibi mutuo obviaverint, moriar
160 et ad infernum deducar." Et sic miser inconfessus in omni desperacione defunctus est.
      Consimiliter narratur de quadam virgine devota in reputacione omnium
et sancta, que tamen infirmitate preventa moriebatur. Post cuius sepulturam
accidit cito post quod iacente sacerdote confessore eius in ecclesia vocem
165 audivit in hiis verbis lugentem sic:

end; "he shall labor forever and live to the end," etc. When a monkey who has
two young ones flees from the huntsmen, she carries the one she loves more in
her arms and puts the other around her neck. But when the huntsman comes
close, she is forced to throw off the one she loves more, while the other
willy-nilly remains on her back. And because of its burden and hindrance, she
is caught by the huntsman together with her offspring and held fast and put on
a chain. As regards our subject: a sinner also has two young ones. The first
are his worldly possessions, which he loves more and therefore holds and carries in his arms, so to speak. But the young one that he carries on his back,
which he loves less, is his sin. Then, when the huntsman comes, which is
death, who pursues us all, he is forced to throw away his earthly goods and
leave them to the world; but his offspring of sin that hangs on his back he cannot throw off. And so he is caught with it and bound by the devil, who will
play with them in his fashion like a monkey, laughing and jumping about in
hell. As to the third consideration, he should reflect on what pay he is promised for his work. In answer the Apostle will say, Romans 6: "The wages
of sin is death." For if a weight were tied to a person's neck and he were
high up in the air and fell to the earth, he would not fall any lower than the
earth. But if a mortal sin hangs on his neck and he dies and falls with it, he
would not just fall to the earth but sink all the way to hell. Therefore, let
us cast off this burden through confession and lighten our soul that is weight-
ed down with sins by doing penance. For Chrysostom says in Homily 3 of his
Imperfect Work: "Think of confession as digesting the impurity and filth that
lie hidden enclosed in you."

The third evil consequence of delaying confession is gaining eternal
punishment. In book 5, chapter 13, of his *Deeds of the English*, Bede tells
about a knight who lived with Cynred, the king of the Mercians, whom the king
loved very much because he had been very brave in arms. When the knight was
sick, the king came to him and exhorted him to make his confession and repent;
but he replied, "Not yet," because he did not want other people to say he had
done it for fear of death; but he would do so when he got well. Then, as his
illness grew worse, the king came to him again to ask him as he had done
earlier. And the knight cried out with a miserable voice: "Why have you come
here? A short time before you, two very beautiful youths entered. One placed
himself at my head, the other at my feet, and one of them showed me a tiny book
in which all the good deeds were written that I have ever done—very few. Then
they took the volume and stepped back without saying anything to me. Right
afterwards came a crowd of demons and filled the house. One of them, who was
more terrifying than the rest, produced a book that was horrible to look at and
of unbearable weight, which he gave me to read. In it I found all my sins, not
only those I had done in deed and word but also those I have committed by the
slightest thought, written very clearly in very black letters. Then the demon

Allas, allas, þat I was borne,
Bothe life and soule I am for-lorne!

Ad que verba cum dictus sacerdos et eius confessor supra modum expavesceret
prima nocte, ° secunda et tercia nocte seipsum animans ad dictum clamorem
170 se exposuit, et ecce duos teterrimos et horribiles demones puellam gementem
ducere conspexit. Adiurans illam que esset, respondit: "Puella nuper de-
functa et tibi confessa." Et ille: "Cur dampnata es, cum ab omnibus devota
et sancta reputabaris?" Que respondit: "Solebam, inquit, contra matrem meam
insurgere et murmurare, et non credidi illud esse grave peccatum, cum tamen
175 sit directe contra Dei preceptum. De isto nolui confiteri, unde dampnata
sum ⟨e⟩t sic crucior sine fine."
    Et hic nota narracionem de illo qui eciam noluit confiteri, et quomodo
sibi Christus apparuit et extraxit sanguinem de vulnere et proiecit in
faciem suam. Nota narraciones hic ut placet. Istud eciam pensent qui tantum
180 confidunt in tribus verbis, scilicet "Miserere mei, Deus." Unde ad consummacionem vite emendacionem prolongant, et quia talis prolongacio Deo displicet, ideo gracia illorum verborum ab eis subtrahitur. Nemo autem sapiens
balsamum, vinum, aut pigmentum ponit in vase fetido et lutoso quousque bene
mundaretur interius [f. 142] maxime. Sic nec Deus suam graciam infundet in
185 corde hominis per peccatum fedo et polluto, quousque per confessionem bene
mundetur. Exemplum: Quando fenestra aperitur, sol intrat et totam domum
illuminat; sic cor quando per confessionem aperitur, transmittitur in illo
gracia Dei, unde omnes actus sui ad bene operandum illuminantur, et e
contrario.

---

2 negligenter omittit] negligitur O.   **3** ipsum] *om* O.   **4** subicit] subiecit C.   **5** Domi-
nus] deus O.   **7** summe] sentencie C.   **8** contrairet] contrariet C.   **12** Ita] *om* O.   **14** 2]
8 C.   **15** non] *add* est O.   **16** requirentis] adquirentis O.   **21** tempus] tantum C.   **23** et]
add ei O.   **27** nostris] *om* O.   **32** sunt] fuerunt O.   **41** ultimum . . . est] *blank* C; verum
tamen pocius est M; verumtamen est peius ⟨residivare *marg*⟩ W.   **47** recta] bona O.
50 notandum] *add* est O.   **61** omni] *om* O.   in iuventute] vivente C.   **64** viam] *add* presentem R.W; *add* presentem *canc* M.   **65** invenient] inveniunt M.R; invenint W.   **69** via
sapiencie] maxima sapiencia O.   **84** et] ac O.   **88** fieri] *om* C.M.W; *marg* R.   **103** ad-
dendo] adeo O.   **106** et] *om* O.   **110** firmamentum] *the apparent gap in the thought is
filled in group z as follows*: Genesis 3: Vocavitque Deus firmamentum celum; et tamen illud quamvis firmissimum et fortissimum erat, non potuit sustentare peccatum; unde Luce
10 Co.   **112** secundum] sensum C.   **114** numquam illud] nichil aliud C.   **116** adhuc in
finem] *om* O.   **119** autem] ergo O.   **120** alius] alium C.   **142** eum] ipsum O.
153 cogitacione] *add* quam C.   **156** demones] *add* surrexerunt O.   **157** ignitis] *add* et
O.   **164** vocem] *add* horribiliter O.   **166–167** Allas . . . for-lorne] *Verse 47, in*
B1.B3.CC.D.Et.Go1.Go2.Jo.L1.L2.L3.LC.R.Sp.V.W1.W2, *and elsewhere. To the separate occurrences listed in* Verses, *p. 187, add Greaves 54, fol. 96, and Harley 505, fol.
21v (analogue).*   **169** nocte] *add* et C.   **176** et] ut C.   **178** vulnere] *add* laterali O.
183 ponit] poneret O.   **186** mundetur] emundetur O.

said to those two youths: "What are you doing here? You know for sure that
this one is ours." And they answered: "Right; take him." With these words
they rose at once and disappeared. Then two demons struck me with fiery
plowshares, *culturs* in English, one at the head, the other at the feet, and
even now they are pulling out my bowels with the greatest torment. But when
they come together and their plowshares meet, I will die and be taken to hell."
And thus the wretched man died without confession in complete despair.

   There is a similar story about a virgin who was held to be devout and
saintly by everyone and who finally fell ill and died. Soon after her burial
it happened that the priest, her confessor, was lying in the church and heard a
horrible voice wailing in these words:

> Alas, alas, that I was born,
> For life and soul I now am lost!

As this priest, her confessor, was scared beyond measure by these words this
first night, in the following and the third night he took courage and confronted the shouting; and behold, he saw two very black and terrifying devils leading a maiden who was sighing. When he adjured her to tell him who she was,
she replied: "I am that maiden who has recently died and was shriven by you."
Then he said: "But why are you damned if you were held by all to be devout and
saintly?" And she replied: "I used to get angry and murmur against my mother,
but I did not think that was a grave sin, though it goes directly against God's
commandment. I would not confess that, and so I am now condemned and
tormented without end."

   Notice here also the story about the man who likewise did not want to make
his confession, and how Christ appeared to him, took blood from his wound,
and threw it in his face. You may tell further stories here, as you wish. Let
people weigh these things who put so much trust in the three words, "Have
mercy, God," and with that postpone their correction till the end of their
life. Since such postponement displeases God, the grace of those words is
taken from them. For no wise person would put balm, wine, or spice into a
dirty, muddy vessel before the dirt is completely washed out. Thus, God pours
his grace even less into a man's heart that is dirty and stained by sin, until
it be well cleansed in confession. As an example: when one opens a window, the
sun enters and lights up the whole house. In the same way, when one's heart is
opened in confession, God's grace is sent into it; and thus, all one's actions
are illuminated to bring forth good deeds, and the opposite happens if one does
not do so.

5–6 Luke 5.14.   **13–14** Gregory, *Moralia* XVII.vi.8 (PL 76:13).   **14–15** Rom. 2.4.
17–20 Jth. 8.13, 12.   **20–21** Rev. 2.21.   **25** Prov. 26.11; 2 Pet. 2.22.   **30** Heb. 6.6.

V.xiv   QUE BONA EVENIUNT VERE ET CITO CONFITENTIBUS

[C]irca autem bona que eveniunt cito et vere confitentibus dicit Crisostomus: "Confessio, inquit, cor emundat, sensus [illuminat, animam sanc-
tificat, et ad suscepcionem Christi preparat." Item secundum alios Deum]
homini manifestat; unde Augustinus: "Si nollem confiteri, non me absconde-
5   rem tibi set te michi." Item paradisum aperit; Augustinus: "O, inquit,
breve verbum 'peccavi,' quod portas paradisi aperit." Exemplum de David,
Magdalena, et sancto latrone, et huiusmodi. Item iram emollit divinam; unde
Glossa super illud Psalmi, "Delictum meum cognitum tibi feci": "O, inquit,
Deus tegit quod homo detegit. Si homo agnoscit, Deus ignoscit." Merito ergo
10 pessimi dicuntur qui tot bona torpente differunt et excludunt. Videmus enim
quod filii divitum non curant de laceratis vestibus, [ut nova possint habere, set illa dilacerant. Sic nec de peccatis aliquis in confessione aliquid conservare] curare debet, set illa per confessionem rumpere et dilace-
rare debet, ut sic virtutes novas et meritorias cito potest revestiri; unde
15 Romanorum 6 dicitur: "In novitate vite ambulemus."

     Et nota quod per confessionem gracia Spiritus Sancti anima humana
renovatur sicut alia terrena multipliciter renovantur. Verbi gracia: Primo
sicut gladius et calcaria per confricacionem, sic anima per contricionem et
confessionem; unde Machabeorum 4: "Ecce, contriti sunt inimici." Secundo,
20 sicut tempus transacta yeme in ortu florum et herbarum, sic anima spreta
vita veteri: tunc per confessionem abscondita panduntur et denudantur, et
flores novarum virtutum oriuntur; unde illud Ezechielis 36: "Dabo vobis cor
[f. 142v] novum et auferam a vobis cor lapideum de carne vestra." Tercio,
sicut serpens renovatur in angusto loco veterem exuviam sive pelle⟨m⟩
25 deponens, sic anima per confessionem veterem exuviam peccatorum exuendo;
Colossensium 2: "Expoliantes veterem hominem cum operibus suis induite

38–39 Prov. 26.11.   **42–43** 2 Pet. 2.21.   **43–44** Ecclus. 2.14.   **46** Isa. 30.21.   **47–48** Prov. 14.12.   **51–54** Tubach 1706. Also in *Convertimini*, fol. 96v.   **57** Matt. 3.2.   **60–62** Wisd. 2.6–7.   **66** Ecclus. 3.28.   **71–72** Ecclus. 5.12.   **78–90** Gregory, *In Evangelia*, hom. 15, 2 (PL 76:1132).   **85–86** Num. 12.10.   **98–104** *VP* III.38 (PL 73:763).   **111** Luke 10.18.   **111–112** Ps. 37.5.   **116** Ps. 48.9.   **130** Rom. 6.23.   **136–137** Ps.-Chrysostom, *Opus imperfectum*, hom. 3 (PG 56:650–651).   **139–161** Tubach 1501b–c; from Bede, *Hist. eccl.* V.13. Also in Harley 7322, fol. 105; Brinton, sermon 19; *Handlyng Synne* 4365–4510; etc.   **162–176** Tubach 1442.   **177–179** Tubach 2960. Also in Bromyard, "Dampnacio," D.I.22; Brinton, sermons 37 and 56; Mirk, *Festial*, pp. 91–92; Higden, *Ars componendi sermones*, ed. M. Jennings, p. 115; English *Gesta Romanorum*, p. 411; *Speculum laicorum* 136a; Bodleian Library, MS Bodley 649, fol. 26v; MS Greaves 54, fols. 85v–86v; Worcester Cathedral, MS F.126, fol. 31.   **179–180** See *FM* II.iv.48–55.

V.xiv   THE GOOD EFFECTS OF PROMPT AND TRUE CONFESSION

With respect to the good results of prompt and true confession Chrysostom says: "Confession cleanses one's heart, enlightens one's senses, sanctifies one's soul, and prepares one to receive Christ." And according to others, it reveals God to man; whence Augustine says: "If I were unwilling to confess, I would not hide myself from you, but rather hide you from myself." Further, confession opens paradise; Augustine says: "O short word 'I have sinned,' which opens the doors of paradise!" We find this exemplified in David, Magdalene, the Good Thief, and others. It also softens God's wrath. Whence the *Gloss* in commenting on the words of the Psalm, "I have acknowledged my sin to you," says: "Man uncovers and God covers. If man acknowledges his fault, God pardons." Therefore those who in their sloth defer and shut out so many good things are reckoned insane. We can observe that rich men's children do not care for old clothes but tear them, so that they can get new ones. In the same way, one must not care to save anything of one's sins when one makes one's confession but rather tear and pull them to pieces by confession, so that one may soon put on good and meritorious virtues. Therefore it is said in Romans 6: "Let us walk in newness of life."

And notice that in confession man's soul is renewed by the grace of the Holy Spirit in many different ways similar to other earthly things. First, just as a sword and spurs are made shining again by being rubbed, so also the soul by contrition and confession; whence Judas said in Maccabees 4: "Behold, our enemies are rubbed out." Second, just as when winter is gone a new season starts with flowers and grass springing up, so also the soul has its spring after it has cast off its old life through confession: what was hidden lies open, and the grass and flowers of new virtues spring forth from it; whence Ezekiel 36 says: "I will give you a new heart and will take away from you the

novum." Quarto virtutes renovantur per confessionem sicut aves nobiles
plumas veteres abiciendo, sicut aquila claritatem solis intuendo, et sicut
cervus hausto veneno aquam fontis degustando. Sic ergo satis apparet effec-
30   tus confessionis et que bona eveniunt per illam; unde Augustinus: "Qui per
vos peccastis, per vos erubescite," scilicet confitendo. Multum enim satisfactionis sue Deo optulit qui erubescendo nichil horum que commisit Dei
nuncio negat, scilicet sacerdoti.
      Unde narratur de quodam milite in partibus transmarinis habente uxorem
35   bonam et devotam, cum qua in omni amore, pace, et affectu maritali multo
tempore vixit. Tandem suggestione diabolica adamavit miles iste viduam
quandam iuxta illum manentem. Unde ipsa sibi consenciente clam in proprio
gardino sub quadam arbore pulcherrima adulterium commisit. Et ex tunc quasi
de propria uxore nichil curavit. Cito autem post factum [istud] accidit ut
40   quadam nocte miles ille cum propria uxore dormiret. Et ecce circa mediam
noctem cepit uxor eius fortiter cum eiulatu magno clamare. Cum ergo ipse
illam excitasset, causam tanti clamoris querens, respondit: "Territa, inquit, fui in sompnis," et rursum obdormivit domino suo adhuc vigilante. Et
ecce cito post cepit alcius clamare, et ille ipsam iterum evigilans ait:
45   "Quid tibi est? Volo omnino [f. 143] ut dicas michi sompnium tuum." Et
illa: "Videbatur, inquit, michi quod tu eras in gardino sub tali arbore, et
unus tyrannus veniens per medium corporis tui cum gladio acutissimo te
perforavit. Quod cum vidissem, de vita tua, quam summe super omnia dilexe-
ram, summe contristabar tam letale vulnus in domino meo conspiciens." Quo
50   audito avertit ille illud esse vulnus peccati anime ipsius. Et ait ille:
"Secure, inquit, iam dormies usque mane, quia in bono statu sum." Mane
autem facto dixit uxori sue: "Non habuisti bonam requiem nocte ista, et
ideo consulo ut missam audias et postea comedas et tunc dormitum vadas. Ego
hospites expectabo." Quod et factum est. Statim misit dominus pro confesso-
55   re suo, qui non multum distabat. Qui cum venisset, duxit illum sub arbore
predicta, ubi cum lacrimis excessivis una cum aliis dictum peccatum est
confessus. Et cum paratus esset gravissimam agere penitenciam, vid⟨ens⟩
confessor eius signa in eo nimie contricionis, pro omnibus peccatis suis
iniunxit sibi quinquies dicere Ave Maria, nec voluit sibi plura iniungere,
60   cum tamen ipse cum lacrimis multo graviora petivisset. Postea autem, cum
dictus miles et eius confessor eodem die in prandio sedissent, domina a
sompno excitata cum magno impetu aulam ingressa est, dominum suum frequenter et gaudenter osculans et amplexans. Cui ille: "Quid, inquit, tibi est?
Numquam in te tantam inpudenciam consideravi." Cui illa respondit: "Non
65   possum me continere pre gaudio, quia oblita sum dolorem pristinum quem
habui in visione nocte precedenti. Cum enim modo dormivi, vidi apertissime
ubi sub predicta arbore venit quidam medicus et posuit quinque flores in
vulnere tuo, unde [f. 143v] continuo sanatus es; et hec est causa leticie

stony heart out of your flesh." Third, as a snake renews itself by casting off
its old skin in a tight place, so the soul does too when it slips out of its
old skin of sins in confession; Colossians 2: "Stripping yourselves of the old
man with his deeds, put on the new." Fourth, in confession our virtues are
renewed like noble birds that shed their old feathers, or like the eagle when
it looks at the brightness of the sun, or like the stag that drinks water from
a wellspring when it has been infected with poison. In this way the effect and
good consequences of confession can be clearly enough seen. Wherefore Augustine says: "You who have committed sin of your own accord, blush of your own
accord," that is, by confessing your sins. For he who blushes and withholds
nothing of what he has done wrong before God's messenger, that is, the priest,
has already offered God a good deal of satisfaction.

There is a story about a knight from across the sea who had a good and
devout wife, with whom he lived a long time in great love, peace, and marital
affection. In the end, however, the knight, under the suggestion of the devil,
fell in love with a widow who lived close by. As she agreed with him, he
secretly committed adultery in his garden under a very beautiful tree. And
from that time on he hardly cared for his wife anymore. Soon after this it
happened that some night this knight was sleeping by his own wife. Then, about
midnight, his wife suddenly gave a loud, wailing cry. When he woke her up and
asked her for the cause of such a cry, she said: "I had a terrible dream" and
fell asleep again, while her husband remained awake. And behold, a little
while later, she cried out even louder, and he woke her again and asked: "What
is the matter with you? I want you to tell me your whole dream." And she
replied: "It seemed to me that you were in our garden under such and such a
tree, and a tyrant came and pierced you with a sharp sword through the middle
of your heart. When I saw that, perceiving such a deadly wound in my husband,
I became frightfully sad for your life, which I had loved more than anything
else." When the knight heard this, he realized that that was the wound of sin
in his soul. And he said: "You shall sleep quietly till morning, for I am
quite alright." But when it was morning, he said to his wife: "You have not
had a good rest last night. Therefore I suggest you go to Mass and then have
something to eat and go to bed again. I am expecting guests." When this was
done, the husband at once sent for his confessor, who did not live far away.
When he came, he took him under the tree mentioned before and there confessed
his aforesaid sin together with others, with an abundance of tears. And as he
was ready to do the most severe penance, his confessor, who saw the signs of
his very great contrition, gave him as penance for all his sins to say the Hail
Mary five times, nor did he want to give him any further penance, even though
the knight asked him with tears for a much harder one. Later on, as this
knight and his confessor were sitting together at table, his wife woke up from
her sleep and came rushing into the hall and kissed and hugged her husband

mee." Dictus autem miles veniens ad obsidionem castri de Kenelworth tempore
70 regis Henrici patris regis Edwardi illustrissimi pro parte regis istam
narracionem fratribus Coventrie narravit, rogans quod suis sermonibus pub-
licarent.

Narratur eciam de quadam muliere valde devota quadam die ad confessionem veniente, ubi omnia peccata sua ab infancia confitebatur, uno solo
75 excepto, quod pre pudore subticuit. Nocte igitur sequente, cum se sopori
dedisset, apparuit ei Iesus Christus cum stigmatibus apertis, ostendens ei
cor totaliter denudatum, sanguinolentum, et perforatum. Cui ille: "Cur
ergo, inquit, verecundaris ostendere michi cor tuum, quando non verecundor
tibi ostendere cor meum?" Et accipiens manum eius posuit in latus suum
80 dicens: "Accipe et tange cor meum." At illa statim compuncta evigilans
ostendit omnibus manus sanguinolentas et de peccato confitebatur. Unde in
signum quod peccatum fuit remissum manus ad pristinum statum redierunt. In
cuius figura de sancto Thoma Apostolo cui Christus dixit: "Affer manum tuam
huc et mitte in latus meum," etc. Proverbiorum 23 dicitur: "Fili, prebe
85 michi cor tuum," quasi diceret: ne diffidas, quia si dederis michi cor
tuum, dabo tibi meum cum omni misericorida et caritate.

---

7 et] *om* O.   10 pessimi] perversissimi M; amentissimi R; permansissimi W.   11 laceratis vestibus] vestimentis inveteratis O.   11–13 ut . . . conservare] *om* C.W; sed eas student lacerare et nova postulare sic eciam antiqua vestimenta malicie nullus conservare
marg M.   19 4] *add* dixit iudas O.   24 pellem] pellens C.   27 virtutes] *om* O.   37 il-
lum] eum O.   39 nichil] non O.   40 ille] iste O.   47 corporis] cordis O.   53 postea]
add aliquid M.R; *longer om* W.   55 suo] *add* fratre minore M.W(*add* scilicet); *also in*
y.B1.   57 videns] vidit C.   65 oblita] oblitus O.   70 Edwardi] *add* primi z.E.
71 fratribus Coventrie] canonicis Lychilfeld Go2.   Coventrie] conventus z.E.Et.L1.W2;
story om group r.x.Madrid. *All full manuscripts recorded.*   84 huc] *om* O.   etc.] et noli
esse incredulus sed fidelis O.   86 meum] *add* scilicet O.

V.xv   DE SATISFACTIONE QUA IUSTICIA

[T]actis de duabus partibus primis, scilicet de contricione et confessione, iam de tercia parte principali, scilicet de satisfactione, est dicendum. Circa quam est sciendum quod satisfactio uno modo potest dici virtus reddens unicuique quod suum est, alio modo, secundum Augustinum *De*
5 *ecclesiasticis dogmatibus*, est causas peccatorum excludere et ultra peccata
non iterare. Si ergo de primo modo satisfactionis loqui volumus, sic dico
quod satisfactio stat cum illa virtute cardinali que dicitur iusticia. [f.

again and again with great joy. He said to her: "What is the matter with you?
I have never seen you so silly." And she: "I cannot contain myself for joy,
for I have forgotten all the sorrow I had earlier in my dream of last night.
As I was sleeping now, I saw quite clearly how a physician came to that tree
and put five blossoms into your wound. Then you were well at once, and this is
why I am so happy." The knight of this story came to the siege of Kenilworth
Castle in the time of King Henry, the father of the most illustrious King
Edward, with the king's party, and he told this story to the friars of Coventry, asking them to make it known in their sermons.

There is another story about a very devout woman who came to confession
one day, where she confessed all the sins she had committed since childhood,
except one, which she held back for shame. In the following night, as she was
in profound sleep, Jesus Christ appeared to her with his wounds wide open and
showed her his heart, which was laid bare, bleeding and pierced. He spoke to
her: "Why are you ashamed of showing me your heart when I am not ashamed of
showing you mine?" And he took her hand and put it in his side, saying: "Take
and touch my heart." She woke up with great remorse and showed to all her
bloodstained hands and confessed that sin. For which, as a sign that her sin
was forgiven, her hands became as they had been before. A type of this is
Saint Thomas the Apostle, to whom Christ said: "Bring hither your hand
and put it into my side," and so forth. In Proverbs 23 it is said: "My son,
give me your heart," as if to say: do not distrust, for if you give me your heart,
I will give you mine, that is, with all my mercy and love.

2–3 Ps.-Chrysostom, *Opus imperfectum*, hom. 3 (PG 56:647).   5–6 Cf. *Ad fratres in
eremo* 30 (PL 40:1289).   8 Ps. 31.5.   8–9 Cf. Augustine, *En. in Ps. 31*, sermo ii.15
(CC 38:236).   15 Rom. 6.4.   19 1 Macc. 4.36.   22–23 Ezek. 36.26.   26–27 Col.
3.9–10.   30–31 Ps.-Augustine, *De vera et falsa poenitentia* X.25 (PL 40:1122).   34–
72 Tubach 1787 (unique). In MSS. Gol and V this and the following story are said to
come "de narracionibus fratris Rogeri de Burbache."   73–82 Tubach 2416, to which
many additions can be made, including: Bromyard, "Confessio," C.VI.58; Brinton, sermons 65, 86, and 88; Ross, *Middle English Sermons*, pp. 216–217; Mirk, *Festial*, pp. 90
and 95–96; *Speculum laicorum* 136.   83–84 John 20.27.   84–85 Prov. 23.26.

V.xv   SATISFACTION AS JUSTICE

After we have touched on the first two parts of penance, namely contrition
and confession, we now must speak of the third main part, namely satisfaction.
Regarding this, we should know that in one sense "satisfaction" means the
virtue which gives to each his own; in another sense, according to Augustine
in *On Church Dogma*, it means to shut out the causes of our sins and not
to repeat sins again. If we wanted to speak of satisfaction in the first sense,
I say that it is identical with the cardinal virtue called justice. In the second

144] Si vero secundo modo, sic est tercia pars penitencie, de qua hic ut in
suo loco agi deberet. Set ne ipsa satisfactio prout stat cum virtute iusti-
10   cia intacta transiret, primo de ipsa iusticia est aliquid dicendum.
        Est ergo advertendum quod "iusticia [est] virtutum preclarissima, et
in ipsa est omnis virtus," ut ait Philosophus 5 *Ethicorum*. Propter quod
dixerunt philosophi ipsam habere vultum aureum, ut ibidem commentator. De
eius partibus, que a beato Bernardo in *Sermone de Adventu* assignantur, est
15   primo sciendum quomodo antiqui ill⟨am⟩ ° observabant, et secundo quomodo
moderni illam contempnunt et fedant. Est ergo iusticia secundum Bernardum
virtus unicuique tribuens quod suum est, scilicet superiori obedienciam et
reverenciam, equali concilium et auxilium, ut sic concilio erudiatur ignorancia et auxilio iuvetur impotencia. Inferiori eciam debeatur custodia et
20   disciplina, ut scilicet in illo non regnet peccatum, set ut dignos faciat
fructus penitencie. Quibus omnibus debet adiungi verum iudicium. Que sunt
quasi septem columpne in domo sapiencie, Proverbiorum 9, prout exponit
Bernardus.
        Quod hec omnia antiquitus viguerunt tam in principibus rem publicam
25   iudicantibus quam in philosophis sapiencie et sciencie vacantibus, satis
patet ⟨librum⟩ *De nugis philosophorum curialium* intuentibus. Et primo de
obediencia et reverencia respectu superiorum. Cum autem princeps sit publica potestas et in terris quedam divine maiestatis ymago, prout dicitur
Policratico libro 4, ideo antiquitus sibi reverenter obedierunt et inobe-
30   dientes puniebantur. Unde narrat Augustinus 5 *De civitate Dei*, capitulo 18,
de quodam qui filium suum, pro patria tamen qui contra imperium suum
pugnaverat, licet vicisset, occidit, ne plus esset mali in exemplo imperii
contempti quam boni in gloria hostis occisi. Omnino enim vellent ut fierent
quod imperabant; quod si non fieret, licet melius facerent illi quibus
35   mandabant, [f. 144v] tamen eos puniebant in exemplum aliorum. Unde narrat
Agellius de quodam pontifice Crasso, qui cum obsidionem pararet, et esset
sibi necessaria trabes de qua faceret arietem, scripsit cuidam subdito ut
de duabus maiorem sibi mitteret. Et quia non misit prout mandaverat, set
aliam bono iudicio apciorem, detrahi iussit vestimenta et virgis multis
40   cedi. Si ergo tunc homines volebant sua imperia sic adimpleri et contempnentes puniebant tam acriter, quid mirum si Deus ecclesiarum leges et
precepta prelatorum vult observari, et precipue leges suas et mandata, cum
ipse sit "rex regum et dominus dominancium"? Unde de honore exhibendo
tam Deo quam Ecclesie et aliis superioribus, nota supra, parte 1, capitulo 6.
45   Quod autem auxilium et concilium prebuerunt antiqui [equalibus] patet
in hoc quod plus laborabant pro re publica quam pro salute propria. Unde
narrat Augustinus *De civitate Dei* et similiter Valerius libro 5 de Codro
rege Atheniencium, quod cum bellum instaret inter Athenienses et Polepo-
nenses et acceperunt in responsis quod illi essent futuri victores quorum

sense, however, it is the third main part of penance, whose proper place of
discussion is here. But that the former kind of satisfaction, which is identical with justice, may not be passed over altogether, we will first say some
words about justice itself.

We should realize, then, that justice is the most noble of all virtues,
and every virtue is contained in her, as the Philosopher says in book 5 of the
Ethics. For that reason the philosophers declared it to have a golden face, as
the commentator on the cited passage says. With respect to its parts, which
are given by Bernard in his *Sermon on Advent*, we must first see how the ancients cultivated it and second how our contemporaries scorn and defile it.
According to Bernard, justice is that virtue which gives to each what is his,
namely: obedience and reverence to one's superior, counsel and aid to one's
equal, so that by counsel his ignorance may be taught, and by aid his powerlessness be helped. And to one's inferior one owes watchfulness and discipline, so that no sin may reign in him, but rather that he may bring good
fruits of penance. To these should be added true judgment. And these are, as
it were, the seven columns in the house of wisdom, according to Proverbs 9, as
Bernard explains.

That all these virtues flourished in ancient times both among princes who gov-
erned the commonweal and among philosophers intent upon gaining wisdom and
knowledge, can be clearly seen by reading *The Trifles of Courtly Philosophers*.
First with regard to the obedience and reverence due to one's superiors: since
a prince holds public power and a certain likeness to the divine majesty here
on earth, as is explained in book 4 of *Policraticus*, the ancients obeyed him
with reverence and punished those who were disobedient. On this subject,
Augustine in book 5 of *The City of God*, chapter 18, tells of one who killed his
own son who was fighting for his country, even when he had been victorious,
because he had fought against his command; he did not want the evil that came
from the example of disobeying a command to outweigh the good of triumphing
over the slain enemy. Thus the ancients wanted absolutely that their orders be
carried out, to the point that if this was not the case, they would punish
those that had disobeyed as an example to others, even if those that had
received their orders had been more successful. Agellius in his book reports
of a certain priest Crassus that, when he prepared a siege and needed a beam to
build a battering-ram, he wrote to one of his subjects to send him the larger
of two beams. But this man did not send the beam Crassus had ordered but
instead another which in his judgment was better for the job. Crassus had his
clothes taken off and had him beaten with many rods. If, then, the people of
that time wanted their commands to be thus strictly fulfilled and punished thus
sharply those who did not obey, what wonder that God wants us to observe the
laws of the Church and the orders of our prelates, and above all his own laws
and commandments, since he is "the king of kings and lord of lords"? Concern-

50 dux occideretur. Quod audiens Codrus in habitu pauperis transivit ad hostes
    necemque ab eis per iurgium provocavit. Maluit enim mori dum viverent sui
    quam vivere suis superatis. Tantum enim diligunt rem publicam quod non
    fuerunt apud eos aliqui ad dignitates anelantes neque acceptores personarum.
    Unde de primo narrat Helymandus historiographus de quodam imperatore
55 quod cum ex senatore factus esset imperator et obsecrante ab eo senatu ut
    filium suum Augustum Cesarem vocaret, respondit: "Sufficere, inquit, debet
    quod ego ipse invitus regnaverim. Principatus enim non sanguini de- [f.
    145] betur, set meritis." Et ideo inutiliter regnat qui rex nascitur et non
    meretur; Ecclesiastici 17: "Noli querere fieri iudex nisi valeas," etc.
60 Contra eciam acceptores personarum et avariciam sectantes narrat Valerius
    libro 6 quod cum duo consules contenderent in senatu quis eorum in Hispa-
    niam mitteretur, respondit Scipio Emilianus omnibus suam sentenciam expec-
    tantibus: "Neutrum, inquit, istorum michi mitti placet, quia alter nichil
    habet et alteri nichil est satis," eque malam imperii magistram iudicans
65 inopiam et avariciam.
    Quod eciam tercium, scilicet disciplina et custodia, verissime apud
    eos vigebant dicitur *Policratico* libro 6, quod adeo Romanis profuit disci-
    plina ut totum orbem sue subiceret dicioni. Alexander enim exiguam manum
    militarem [suscepit] a patre set doctrinam qua orbem terrarum egressus
70 innumerum hostium copias fugit, ut ait de eo Vegecius libro 4. Debet enim
    princeps cum disciplina regere milites, ut ait Valerius libro 2. Ibi ponit
    ex⟨empla⟩ quare puniebant filios suos militarem disciplinam non obser-
    vantes. Aurelius enim filium suum quia preceptum suum non observavit inter
    pedites ⟨fungi⟩ coegit. Octavianus eciam filium suum ad gradum militarem
75 constitutum primo fecit exercitari ad cursum, ad saltum, ad usum natandi,
    iac[i]endi missilia et lapides manu et fundo; et filias eciam suas in
    lanificio instituit, ut si necessitas ingrueret, ⟨per artem⟩ sustentari
    possent. Et ideo Ecclesiastici 7 dicitur: "Si filii tibi sint, erudi illos";
    et sequitur: "Si filie tibi sint, serva corpus earum."
80 Quod eciam iudicium verum viguit apud eos narrat Valerius libro 6,
    quod cum quidam iudex male iudicasset, rex Cambices pellem eius de corpore
    extractam ⟨sedili suo iudiciario⟩ apposuit et filium eius in eo post eum
    iudicaturum sedere iussit, ut ipse [f. 145v] ad memoriam revocaret quod
    propter falsum iudicium sic punitus erat pater suus. Unde quidam metrista
85 ait:

        Sedens in cathedra iustus iudex stabilis sta.
        Sint tibi lucerna, lex, ius, pellisque paterna.
        A manibus re⟨sec⟩es munus, ab aure preces.

    Secundo autem narrat Valerius de Curio consule Romano, quod cum Samp-
90 nite sibi maximum pondus auri optulissent, ut pro voluntate eorum iudicium

ing the respect we are to show to God and his Church and to other superiors, see above, part 1, chapter 6.

That the ancients gave counsel and aid to their equals is shown in that they worked harder for the commonweal than for their private well-being. Augustine relates in *The City of God*, as does Valerius in book 5, about Codrus, the king of Athens, that when war was about to break out between Athens and the Peloponnesus, the Athenians received the prophecy that that party would be victorious whose leader was going to be killed. When Codrus heard this, he went disguised as a poor man to his enemies and provoked his own death in a brawl. For he would rather die so that his people might live, than live while his people were defeated. The ancients loved the commonweal so much that there were none among them who panted after public honors or were respecters of persons. Regarding the first, the historian Helinandus tells of an emperor who had risen to his position from being a senator and was then urged by the senate to call his son "Caesar Augustus." He replied: "It should suffice that I myself rule against my will. One ought not to become emperor because of one's blood but because of one's merits." Therefore, a person who is born a king but does not deserve it rules in vain; Ecclesiasticus 17: "Seek not to be made a judge unless you have the strength," and so forth. And against people who are respecters of persons and pursue greed, Valerius in book 6 relates that when two consuls disputed in the senate which of them should be sent to Spain, Scipio Aemilianus answered as everyone was waiting for his decision: "I am not willing to send either one of these, for the one has nothing, and to the other nothing is enough," thereby judging need and greed to be equally bad teachers in leadership.

That the third pair of virtues, that is, discipline and watchfulness, also flourished most truly among the ancients is shown by book 6 of *Policraticus*. To the Romans discipline was so useful that the whole world became subject to their rule. Alexander inherited only a small troop of soldiers from his father, but one well taught, with which he attacked the entire world and put a countless host of enemies to flight, as Vegetius says of him in book 4. For a prince must rule his soldiers with discipline, as Valerius says in book 2. There he gives examples of how they punished their sons if they would not keep military discipline. For Aurelius forced his son to serve in the infantry because he had not carried out his command. Octavian, too, made his son who was set on a military career first train himself in running, jumping, swimming, and throwing projectiles and stones by hand and slingshot; his daughters at the same time he made learn how to spin, so that they might be able to earn their living by this craft if need compelled them. Therefore it is said in Ecclesiasticus 7: "If you have sons, instruct them," and afterwards: "If you have daughters, have a care of their body."

That true judgment also flourished among the ancients, Valerius tells us in book 6. When some judge gave evil judgment, king Cambyses had him flayed,

dedisset, respondit se malle imperare super eos qui aurum habebant quam tantum super aurum eorum, quasi diceret: pro toto auro vestro verum iudicium
non dimittam, nec eos qui contra leges et iusticiam fecerint punire desistam.

95   Patet ergo quomodo verum iudicium et iusticia viguerunt apud antiquos,
iuxta illud Deuteronomii 6: "Iudices et magistros constitues in omnibus
partibus tuis ut iudicent populum iusto iudicio," hoc est, iuste reddere
cuique quod suum est. Unde Agellius describens Iusticiam dicit: "Iusticia
dici potest puella pulcra, in celum erecta, utroque oculo ceca, utraque
100   manu manca." Quasi diceret: Quilibet iudex iustus habet puellam pulcram,
scilicet intencionem rectam muneribus non corruptam. Cum enim intencio
iudicis per munera corrumpitur, illa tunc puella pulcritudinem et virginitatem amittit; contra quod Levitici 21: "Sordidam et repudiatam non accipi-
et," scilicet puellam. Debet eciam illa puella Iusticie stare in celum
105   erecta, in signum quod iudex in terris semper cogitabit iudicem se habere
in celis, ut secundum quod ipse iudicaverit, sive bene sive male, ab illo
iudicabitur. Unde Gregorius: "Tu, inquit, qui prees aliis, memento quod
tibi preest Deus." Tercio, puella erat ceca utroque oculo, in signum quod
iudex respectum non habebit a dextris, scilicet ad potestatem divitum vel
110   ad favorem amicorum, nec a sinistris, scilicet ad inopiam [f. 146] pauperis
vel ad odium inimici, set [sicut] ceca utroque oculo intencionis veritatem
iudicando habebit ad omnia sine accepcione aut respectu cuiusque rei aut
persone, iuxta Psalmistam: "Iusticia et iudicium preparacio sedis tue."
Quarto hec puella Iusticie in iudicio manca erat utraque manu, in signum
115   quod neque erit iudex a dextris nimis remissus nec a sinistris nimis auste-
rus, set ut de summo iudice dicitur in Psalmo: "Iustus Dominus [et] iusticias dilexit, equitatem vidit vultus eius," etc.
[E]t ista iusticia hiis effugit, quia prout habetur Ysaie 54: "Conver-
sum est retrorsum iudicium et iusticia longe stetit." Si enim loquamur de
120   superioribus, ⟨numquid⟩ manifeste depauperant et spoliant simplices et
propter dona maioribus parcunt, iuxta illud Sapiencie: "Munera excecant
oculos divitum"? Et ideo iam leges regni et civitatis bene comparantur tele
aranee, in qua capiuntur parve musce. Pro qua satis nota parte ⟨4⟩, capitulo 2. Si autem loquamur de inferioribus, nonne ipsi in quocumque statu fue-
125   rint contra voluntates superiorum recalcitrant et murmurant? Contra quod
nota parte 1 de humilitate et obediencia. Si de equalibus, nonne unusquisque alium persequitur ut destruat et confundat, unde tot invidie, rixe,
pugne, et homicidia suscitantur? Pro quo [nota] parte 2 de ira et parte 3
de invidia. Et ideo tales dicere bene possunt illud Sapiencie: "Erravimus a
130   via veritatis, et lumen iusticie non illuxit nobis." Et descripcio predicte
puelle Iusticie iam per tales corrumpitur et transformatur, quia secundum
illud Deuteronomii 23: "Non est inventa in puella virginitas." Et ideo

put his skin on the judge's seat, and made his son, who was to be judge after his father, sit on it, so that he would remember that his father had been thus punished because of his false judgment. Whence a poet has said:

> When you sit in this chair, be firm and just as a judge.
> Your lantern be the law, what's right, your father's skin.
> Keep from your hands the gift, and prayers from your ears.

Further, Valerius tells of the Roman consul Curius that, when the Samnites offered him a large amount of gold so that he might pass judgment in their favor, he replied that he would rather rule over the owners of gold than over their gold alone, meaning thereby: I will not abandon true judgment for all your gold, nor will I veer from punishing those who have acted against the laws and against justice.

Thus it is manifest how true judgment and justice flourished among the ancients, after the words of Deuteronomy 6: "You shall appoint judges and magistrates in all your tribes, that they may judge the people with just judgment," that is, to give in justice to each what is his own. Agellius describes Justice as follows: "She may be called a beautiful maiden, standing tall and reaching up to heaven, blind in both eyes, crippled in both hands." By this he means that every just judge has a beautiful maiden, that is, a right intention which is not corrupted by bribes. For when the judge's judgment is corrupted by bribes, that maiden loses her beauty and virginity. Against this, Leviticus 21 declares: "A defiled maiden or a woman that has been divorced he shall not accept." This maiden Justice must further stand tall and reach to heaven, as a sign that an earthly judge must always keep in mind that he has a judge in heaven, and that according to how he judges, whether well or badly, he himself will be judged. Therefore Gregory says: "You who rule others, remember that God rules you." Thirdly, the maiden was blind in both eyes, to show that a judge shall pay no attention on the right side to the power of the rich or the favor of friends, nor on the left side to the lack of means of the poor or the hatred of an enemy, but like a person who is blind in both eyes he shall, in giving judgment, have in every respect regard for the truth, without accepting anything or respecting any person, after the words of the Psalmist: "Justice and judgment are the preparation of your throne." And finally, this maiden Justice, in giving judgment, was crippled in both hands, meaning that a judge must be neither remiss on one hand nor too strict on the other, but as it is said of the highest judge in a Psalm: "For the Lord is just and has loved justice; his countenance has beheld righteousness."

But in our days such justice is overturned and put to flight, for as we find in Isaiah 54, "judgment is turned away backward, and justice has stood far off." For if we are to speak of the upper classes, do they not openly impover-

istorum ymago potest formari ad modum meretricis fornicarie cum oculis
vagis et manibus apertis et dissolutis, in signum quod iam iudices quasi
135 omnes oculos suos secundum Psalmistam "statuerunt declinare in terram,"
idest, circa terrena cupidi. Et ideo [f. 146v] qu⟨e⟩ ° manca deberet esse°,
iam manus protensas habet, quia "dextera eorum repleta est muneribus."

---

8 pars] *add* integralis O.   **14** beato] *om* O.   **15** illam] illud primo C; ibi W.   **21** Que]
add tunc O.   **24** antiquitus] *add* ergo O.   **26** librum] vel C; libro M.R; l W.   **29** Policra-
tico] in policraticon O.   **35** mandabant] *add* nichilominus O.   **36** Agellius] *add* libro
O.   **38** mandaverat] imperaverat O.   **44** et] quam O.   **49** acceperunt] acceperant O.
57 quod] ut O.   **69** doctrinam] *thus C.O and other groups; the source reads* doctam.
70 innumerum] *thus* C.M.W; innumeram (. . . copiam) R.   **72** exempla] extra C; exemplum R.   **74** fungi] confundi C.   **77** per artem] partem C.   **82** sedili . . . iudiciario]
sedile suum iudiciarie C.M(iusticiarii).W. *Perhaps originally* selle sue iudiciarie, *as in*
John of Wales.   **84** pater suus] *om* O.   **84–85** Unde . . . ait] *om* O.   **86** Sedens] sistens
O.   **88** reseces] receses C.   **89** autem] eciam O.   Sampnite] sampnute C.   **91** malle]
male O.   **98** cuique] unicuique O.   **98–99** Iusticia . . . potest] *om* O.   **108** puella] *om*
O.   **113** persone] *add* scilicet O.   **118** hiis] *add* diebus pervertitur et R.   **120** numquid]
inquit C.M.W.   **123** 4] 5 C.   **136** que] quia C.O; *add* iam C.   esse] *add* manus C.

ish and rob the simple and spare the wealthy for their gifts, according to the
words of Wisdom, "Gifts blind the eyes of judges"? For this reason, the laws
of the realm and of the city can nowadays be compared to spiderwebs in
which the little flies get caught. On this see further part 4, chapter 2. But
if we are to speak of the lower classes, do they not, whatever their status,
kick and grumble against the rule of their superiors? Against this vice, see
part 1 on humility and obedience. If we are to speak of the relations among
equals, does not everyone persecute someone else in order to destroy him and
bring him down? Hence arise all these cases of envy, strife, fights, and
killings. On this see part 2 on wrath and part 3 on envy. Such people could
well speak the words of Wisdom: "We have strayed from the way of truth, and
the light of justice has not shone upon us." And through such people the image
of the maiden Justice which I have described is corrupted and changed in our
days, for according to the words of Deuteronomy 23, "virginity is not found in
the maiden." For this reason, one could fashion an image of such people like a
whore with wandering eyes and open and dissolute hands, to indicate that nowadays nearly all judges, according to the Psalmist, "have set their eyes bowing
down to earth," that is, they are greedy for earthly goods. And she who ought
to be crippled now stretches out her hands, because "their right hand is filled
with gifts."

The following material in this chapter occurs verbally also in John of Wales, *Breviloquium*: lines 11–13 (prologue); 14–23, 26–30, 45–46, 64–84 (I.7); 30–35, 47–52, 54–
58, 60–65 (I.4).   **4–6** Gennadius, *Liber eccl. dogmatum* 24 (PL 42:1218).   **11–12** Aristotle, *Ethica Nicomachea* V.1 (1129b).   **14–23** Bernard, *In adventu Domini*, sermo iii,
4–7 (4:178–1181).   **22** Cf. Prov. 9.1.   **26** Apparently referring to John of Salisbury,
Policraticus.   **28–29** *Policraticus* VIII.17 (2:345).   **30–33** Augustine, *De civ. Dei*
V.xviii.2 (CC 47:151).   **36–40** Aulus Gellius, *Noctes Atticae* I.xiii.11–13.   **43** 1 Tim.
6.15, etc.   **44** *FM* I.ix–xi.   **47–52** Tubach 1136. Augustine, *De civ. Dei* XVIII.19 (CC
48:610); Valerius, V.vi.ext.1. Also in Brinton, sermons 80 and 104; Grisdale, *Three Middle English Sermons*, pp. 67–68.   **54–58** Tubach 421; reported in Vincent of Beauvais,
Speculum historiale X.69 (392), where the story is said to be about "Aelius Adrianus" and
attributed to "Helinandus lib. II."   **59** Ecclus. 7.6.   **61–65** Tubach 841. Valerius,
V.iv.2.   **67–70** *Policraticus* VI.14 (2:37).   **73–74** Valerius, II.vii.4.   **74–78** *Policraticus* VI.4 (2:13–14 and 15).   **78–79** Ecclus. 7.25.   **81–84** Tubach 2859. Valerius,
VI.iii.ext.3. The story and the following verses are very widespread, including: Bromyard, "Iudex," I.IX.36; Holcot, *In Sapientiam*, lectio 84; Higden, *Polychronicon*,
3:174.   **86–88** *In* 17466; *Prov* 27839; English translation in *IMEV* 1811.   **89–94** Valerius, V.iv.2.   **96–97** Deut. 16.18.   **98–100** Aulus Gellius, *Noctes Atticae* XIV.iv. Similarly in *Convertimini* 7; Holcot, sermon 92; *GR* 247.   **103–104** Lev. 21.14.   **107–108**
Cf. Gregory, *Moralia* XXI.xiv.21 (PL 76:202–203).   **113** Ps. 88.15.   **116–117** Ps.
10.8.   **118–119** Isa. 59.14.   **121–122** Ecclus. 20.31.   **123–124** *FM* IV.ii and v.
126 *FM* I.viii–xi.   **128–129** *FM* II and III, passim.   **129–130** Wisd. 5.6.   **132** Deut.
22.20.   **135** Ps. 16.11.   **137** Ps. 25.10.

V.xvi   DE SATISFACTIONE QUA PARS PENITENCIE

[C]irca autem satisfactionem que est tercia pars integralis ipsius
penitencie, de qua hic est dicendum, hoc modo intendo procedere, videre
scilicet primo quid sit et quomodo diffinitur; secundo que sunt eius species quibus adimpletur. Dico ergo prout superius dicitur quod satisfactio

5   secundum Augustinum et similiter secundum Rabanum *De naturis rerum* libro 5,
capitulo 8, est causas peccatorum et illorum suggestiones excludere et
ultra peccatum non iterare, set pro commissis secundum posse satisfacere.
Quamvis enim cum peccamus Deum offendimus ac postea per contricionem et
confessionem sibi reconsiliati sumus, non tamen sufficit sine satisfactione

10   et emenda. Est enim de Deo et peccatore sicut de duobus confligentibus ac
proinde discordantibus, set pace reformata, qui magis deliquit magis emen-
det. Modo ita est quod nos peccando contra Deum deliquimus et non e contrario, et ideo maiorem exigit emendam et iuste, scilicet pro peccato et culpa
satisfactionem. Et non exigit tamen ex sua caritate et curialitate t⟨an⟩tam

15   emendam correspondentem quantum deliquisti, set qualem equanimiter portare
potes, quia iuxta Psalmistam quod "pro nichilo dat terram desiderabilem."
Et ideo est de Deo sicut de puero cum quo de levi negociatur: imo si
habeat aliquam monetam, pro pomo extorquetur. Revera sic est in proposito.
Ante enim incarnacionem Christi nullus poterat facere cum Deo bonum forum,

20   quia quantumcumque darent, non poterant tamen quocumque modo celum
comparare, quia nec Iohannes Baptista nec ceteri patriarche aut prophete. Set
postquam Christus factus est puer humanam naturam sumendo, optimum forum
facere possumus cum illo et quasi puerum decipere; Psalmista: "Pro nichilo
salvos facies illos," scilicet [f. 147] modo peccatores, quia ut dicitur

25   Iohelis 2: "Prestabilis est super maliciam." Nunc ergo bonum est negociari
cum illo puero et per levem satisfactionem celum ab eo emere. Et ideo noli
expectare cum divite epulone tempus illud in quo maxima caristia erit aque,
scilicet post mortem, set sicut paratus est modo ad ignoscendum, ita parati
simus et prompti ad confitendum. Nam secundum beatum Anselmum: "Qui

30   invite facit, non ipse facit, set ⟨de⟩ eo fit," quasi diceret: si quis invite
confitetur aut pro peccatis compellitur ad satisfactionem, ipse tunc bonum
opus illud confessionis et contricionis non facit, quia diabolus illud
impedit et retardat, et ideo de eo tunc fit ° materia a d⟨iabol⟩o puniendi.
Est tamen hic sciendum quod sicut puer quamvis invite flendo et eiulando

35   pascitur cibo sibi competenti et nutritur nec tamen obicitur quin ille
cibus sibi cedit ad nutrimentum, sic quamvis homo aliquando quasi invite ad
confessionem et satisfactionem compellitur, si tunc in faciendo aliqualis
bona voluntas accreverit, certum est quod aliqualiter ad nutrimentum et
meritum spirituale facit, licet non totum. Dicit ergo Psalmista: "Ex volun-

40   tate mea confitebor illi," etc.

V.xvi   SATISFACTION AS A PART OF PENANCE

With respect to that kind of satisfaction which is the third main part of
penance, which must now be discussed, I intend to proceed as follows: first,
what it is and how it is defined; and second, what its parts are by which it is
carried out. As was said above, then, according to Augustine and similarly
Rabanus in book 5 of *The Nature of Things*, chapter 8: satisfaction means to
shut out the causes of sins and their suggestions and not to repeat sin any
more but to make satisfaction for what we have committed as much as it lies in
our power. For even if we offend God when we sin but afterwards have been
reconciled to him through contrition and confession, yet this is not enough
without our making satisfaction and bettering our ways. For the relation between God and sinner is like that between two parties who fight and hence are
at odds with each other: when peace has been made, the one whose fault is
greater shall make more reparation. Now, it is the case that in sinning we
have failed against God and not the reverse; therefore, he requires reparation
from us by right, namely satisfaction for our sin and our guilt. But out of love
and courtesy he does not demand as much reparation as might correspond to
your fault, but only as much as you can bear, for according to the Psalmist,
"he gives the desirable land for nothing."

God is like a child with whom one can strike an easy bargain: if the child
has some money, one can talk him out of it for an apple. Just so is it with
God. Before Christ's incarnation no one made a good business deal with God,
because whatever they would give him, they could in no way buy paradise with
it, not even John the Baptist or other patriarchs and prophets. But after
Christ has become a child by taking human nature, we can make a splendid
business deal with him and, as it were, trick him like a child. The Psalmist
declares: "For nothing you will save them," that is, sinners in the present
state, for as it is said in Joel 2: "He is ready to repent of the evil." Therefore it is a good thing to bargain with this child now and buy from him
heaven for a little satisfaction. Therefore, do not wait with the rich man
that ate well for the time when there will be a great lack of water, that is,
after death; but as God is now ready to pardon, so let us be ready and prompt
to make our confession. For according to Blessed Anselm, "he who does something unwillingly does not do it himself, but it happens to him," as if he were
saying: if anyone confesses unwillingly or is forced to make satisfaction for
his sins, he does not really do the good work of confession and contrition, for
the devil hinders and delays him in it; and thus he becomes an object for the
devil's punishment. But in this respect we should also realize that although a
child may eat good and nourishing food unwillingly with tears and screams, it
is still being nourished and the food does not lose its nourishing power; in the
same way, even though a person is sometimes compelled to make his confes-

14 tantam] totam C.   **20** celum] paradysum O.   **26** illo] isto O.   **30** de] ab C.   **33** fit] *add* scilicet C; *longer om* M.   diabolo] deo C; *longer om* M.W.   **35** ille] iste O.

V.xvii   DE SPECIEBUS SATISFACTIONIS: ORACIO

[C]irca autem species sive partes principales satisfactionis est sciendum quod sicut homo tripliciter peccat, scilicet corde, ore, et opere,
sic statuit Ecclesia pro penitencia triplex satisfactionis remedium in hiis
tribus consistens, scilicet in oracione, abstinencia, et elemosina, ut sic
5   i⟨st⟩e ternarius numerus et remedium peccatorum contra illum nephandum
ternarium diaboli numerum opponatur, quia oracio contra superbiam, abstinencia contra carnis concupiscenciam, elemosina contra avariciam opponatur.
Patet ergo quod iste sunt tres partes principales satisfactionis, ad quas
omnes alie species satisfactionis quasi secundarie [f. 147v] reducuntur.
10   Nam vigilie, peregrinaciones, discipline, et cetera huiusmodi opera carnem
affligencia ad abstinenciam et ieiunium reducantur; opera vero misericordie, cuiusmodi sunt vestire nudum, pascere esurientem, ad elemosinam; set
omnia alia spiritualia, cuiusmodi sunt sancte meditaciones, pie affectiones, etc., ad oracionem.
15   Nunc ergo de prima parte satisfactionis, scilicet oracione, est sciendum primo qualis debet esse oratio; secundo, que compellunt orare; tercio,
quociens sit orandum et qualiter; quarto, que bona confert oracio. Circa
primum est sciendum quod primo orandum est devote, ut scilicet intenta
cordis devocio ori sit omnino consona, quia alioquin manet reprobanda,
20   sicut qui alteri ore adulatur et aliud in corde machinatur. Unde Augustinus: "Oracio, inquit, cordis est, non labiorum, neque verba tantum depre-
cantis set devota intencio mentis." Nam alio modo orare vituperat Dominus
per prophetam, Ysaie 29: "Populus hic labiis me honorat, cor autem eorum
longe est a me." Unde inquit Bernardus: "Parum prodest orare et sola voce
25   clamare sine cordis intencione." Et ideo vulgaliter dicitur: "Vox in choro
et mens in foro." Vidua est [illa] oracio: manet enim derelicta sicut vidua
viro mortuo. Et ideo nota supra, parte 1, capitulo 4: "Non vox set votum."
Unde bene dicitur:

Vox est grata chori quando ⟨cor⟩ consonat ori.

sion and satisfaction against his will, but then by doing it he acquires a little goodwill for it, this certainly will help him a little toward his spiritual nourishment and merit, even though not entirely. Therefore the Psalmist says: "With my will I shall confess to him."

4–7 See *FM* V.xv.4–6.   16 Ps. 105.24.   23–24 Ps. 55.8.   25 Joel 2.13.   39–40 Ps. 27.7.

V.xvii   THE PARTS OF SATISFACTION: PRAYER

With respect to the members or chief parts of satisfaction, we should know that as a person sins in three ways, namely in heart, mouth, and deed, so has the Church established a threefold remedy of satisfaction as penance, consisting in the three practices of prayer, fasting, and almsgiving, so that this triad in the remedy for sins may be set against that cursed triad of the devil, for prayer is opposed to pride, fasting to fleshly lust, and alsmgiving to avarice. Thus it is manifest that these are the three chief parts of satisfaction, to which all other aspects of satisfaction can be reduced as secondary parts. For vigils, pilgrimages, scourging, and other acts that mortify our flesh in this way belong to abstinence and fasting; the deeds of mercy, such as clothing the naked and feeding the hungry, to almsgiving; and all other spiritual acts, such as holy meditations, pious desires, and so on, to prayer.

About the first part of satisfaction, that is, prayer, we must investigate how our prayer should be; what reasons compel us to pray; how often and in what way we should pray; and what good effects prayer brings. About the first we must know that we should, firstly, pray devoutly, so that the attentive devotion of our heart is in full agreement with the words in our mouth; otherwise prayer would be blameworthy, like a person who flatters someone with his mouth and plots against him in his heart. Therefore Augustine says: "Prayer is a matter of the heart, not of the lips; not so much the words of the person who prays as the devout attention of his mind." Any other way of praying, the Lord censures through his prophet, in Isaiah 29: "This people honors me with their lips, but their heart is far from me." Whence Bernard says: "There is little use in praying only with one's voice without the heart's attention." And thus it is commonly said: "The voice in the choir, the mind in the market." Such prayer is a widow: it is left behind like a widow after her husband's death. Notice also the verse cited above in part 1, chapter 4: "Not your voice but your vow." Whence it is well said:

That choir's voice is pleasing when heart agrees with mouth.

30   Similiter bene dicitur:

      Fructum preclarum faciant fontes lacrimarum,
      Nam merito fletus Deus occurrit tibi letus.
      Pectore ferventi dic laudes omnipotenti.
      Cum sis vir fortis, non stes ut formula mortis.
35   Gutture sic cantes manibus ut premia plantes.
         Non vox sola placet, set manus ipsa vacet.
      Carmina consueta cantans sit mens tua leta.
      Si non insit amor, mirabilis sit tibi clamor.
      [f. 148] Voci da votum, clamori cor dato totum.
40   Tunc exauditum tibi dat Deus ⟨omne⟩ petitum.

      Et nota [quod sic est] de devota oracione et indevota sicut de ense.
      Ipsa autem in quantum in se est eandem vim habet in manu fortis et in manu
      debilis, et tamen habet alium effectum quando valide et fortiter tractatur
      et vibratur et quando remisse. Revera sic oracio. Ipsa enim celos penetrat
45   quando cum devocione cordis emittitur, set non sic quando tepide fit et
      sine devocione, quia tunc parum prodest, et tamen sanctitas, quantum in se
      est, non augetur nec minuitur. Sciendum eciam quod non multum curatur de
      ydiomate orando, et tamen verba sacra et prophetica et evangelica, que sunt
      a Spiritu Sancto edita, vim maiorem habere creduntur quam alia, eciam si
50   non ab intelligentibus proferuntur, maxime si cum mentis affectione profe-
      runtur. Unde Augustinus libro *De spiritu et anima* dicit quod "oracio est
      conversio mentis in Deum per pium et humilem affectum." De qua Canticorum
      2: "Sonet vox tua in auribus meis," scilicet mentis affectu, quia quanto
      ⟨a⟩ffectus mentis profundior, tanto vox alcior est. "Brevis enim oracio"
55   cum tali ⟨a⟩ffectu, ut dicitur, "penetrat celum." Et nota quod pia oracio
      tante fortitudinis est quod non tantum celum penetrat verumptamen totum
      celi excercitum erumpit ac ipsum [Dominum] invadit et ligat. Et ideo sicut
      linea recta dicitur brevissima secundum Philosophum, que nec est obliqua
      per distractionem nec retorta per inconstanciam et ⟨desercionem⟩, sic ora-
60   cio talis celum penetrat nec ullam resistenciam invenire potest, set ipsum
      Deum vincit et flectit ad indulgenciam, sicut patet Exodi 32 de Moyse, quo-
      modo ipse orando humiliter Deum contra populum Israel devicit. Nota histo-
      riam.
      Secundo orandum est discrete, hoc est, quod nichil illicitum petamus
65   nisi quod licite concedi potest. Et ideo quidam bene dicit: [f. 148v]

      Non est donandum quicquid sit iure negandum.

And similarly:

> The fonts of our tears produce a noble fruit:
> In answer to your tears God gladly sends you help.
> With fervent heart your praises to th'Almighty sing.
> Since you are strong, you must not stand and look like Death.
> Sing thus as if your were planting reward with the hands of your voice.
> Nor does your voice alone please, but your hands too should help.
> Sing songs that are well known, and let your mind be glad.
> If love is not in it, you only make great noise.
> Give fervor to your voice, your whole heart to your cry.
> Then God will hear and grant you all that you have asked.

Notice that the difference between devout and undevout prayer can be seen in the comparison with a sword. Its inherent strength is the same in the hand of a strong person as in that of a weak man, and yet its effect is very different when it is drawn and brandished with valor and strength than when it is handled feebly. The same is true of prayer. When it is sent forth with heartfelt devotion, it pierces heaven, but not so when it comes from a lukewarm heart without devotion; in this case it is of little use, though its inherent holiness is neither increased nor diminished. We should also realize that the language of one's prayer does not greatly matter, though the holy words of prophets and the Gospels, which are inspired by the Holy Spirit, are believed to have greater power than others, even when they are uttered by people who do not understand them, and especially when they are uttered with the affection of one's mind. Therefore Augustine says in the book *On the Spirit and the Soul* that prayer is the mind's turning to God with pious and humble emotion. Of it is said in Canticles 2: "Let your voice sound in my ears," that is, with your mind's affection, because the deeper the affection of our mind is, the higher our voice reaches. For "a short prayer" that has such emotion "pierces heaven," as they say. And notice that pious prayer has such strength that it not only pierces heaven but defeats the entire army of heaven and overcomes and binds the Lord himself. According to the Philosopher, a straight line is said to be the shortest way, because it goes neither sideways through distraction nor crooked through inconstancy and evasion. Prayer of this kind pierces heaven and finds no resistance, but it overcomes God himself and bends him to be merciful, as can be seen in Exodus 32 from Moses, how in humble prayer he overcame God as he was fighting against the people of Israel. Tell this biblical story.

Second, we must be discreet in prayer, that is, not ask for anything that cannot be granted to us rightfully. As someone has fittingly expressed it:

Quod bene figuratur Matthei 20 de peticione matris filiorum Zebedei, cui respondit Dominus quasi ipsam corripiendo pro sua indiscreta peticione: "Nescitis quid petatis." Et ideo nichil petendum est, et maxime de tempora-
70 libus, nisi sub condicione a Deo, scilicet eo modo quo ipse Deus scit nobis expedire et proficere. Et ideo Ambrosius super illud Psalmi "Beati immaculati": "Dum, inquit, oras Deum, magna postula et eterna, non terrena et caduca"; et sequitur: "Noli orare pro pecunia, quia erugo est, nec pro possessione, quia terra est. Oracio enim talis ad Deum non pervenit, quia
75 nisi quod dignum suis ducit esse beneficiis, Deus non audit." Hec ille. Unde Bernardus super Mattheum: "Bene enim orat qui Deum orando querit; qui a terrenis ad superiora progreditur, virtutem curie superioris ascendit." Unde Dominus Iesus, ut oraret, solus in montem ascendit. Et sequitur: "Qui enim de diviciis et honoribus seculi vel de morte inimici oracionem facit,
80 in ymo iacens viles ad Deum mittit preces." In cuius figura patet Regum 3 quod Salomon qui huiusmodi non petivit set tantum sapienciam ad populum bene regendum, et ideo placatus Dominus illam sibi cum longitudine dierum concessit et abundanciam diviciarum, sicut satis ibidem patet. Unde Bernardus: "Sperare procul dubio possumus quicquid recte petimus."
85   Et nota quomodo Christus contra omnia mala in omni necessitate docet nos orare cotidie, dicens in Mattheo: "Sic, inquit, orabitis: Pater noster, qui es in celis, sanctificetur nomen tuum," supple: in nobis, ita quod per tuam graciam et auxilium simus vasa sancta et munda, contra luxuriam. "Adveniat regnum tuum," scilicet nobis pro terreno regno quod dimisimus,
90 contra cupiditatem et avariciam. "Fiat voluntas tua," pro qua [f. 149] voluntatem nostram contempnimus, contra superbiam. "Panem nostrum cotidianum," etc., hoc est necessariam sustentacionem, hoc est n⟨on⟩ nimis superfluam [nec nimis remissam], contra gulam. "Et dimitte nobis," etc., contra iracundiam. "Et ne nos inducas in temptacionem," scilicet carnalem, mundia-
95 lem, et maxime diabolicam, contra invidiam. "Set libera nos a malo," scilicet per opera misericordie et alia opera penitencie, contra accidiam.
    Tercio oracio debet esse fervens et lacrimosa; alioquin non potest facere fructum, secundum Bernardum, non plus quam terra sicca et arida. Et hoc bene vadit contra ypocritas qui orando unum simulant ore et aliud
100 intendunt corde, eo quod subito quasi in aspectu hominum orando lacrimas emittunt et statim a tergo in risus dissolutos dissolvuntur, ad modum quo trutanni mendicantes, cum viderint homines appropinquare, clamant et se simulant flere, ut sic dumtaxat uberiores elemosinas accipiant; set cum preterierint, in risum et frequenter in derisionem prorumpunt, ut patet
105 supra, parte 1, capitulo 4. Et ideo huiusmodi ypocritas pulcre redarguit Crisostomus super Mattheum in *Inperfecto* super illud "Ve vobis ypocrite qui similes estis sepulcris dealbatis": "Dic, inquit, ypocrita, si bonum est

Nothing can come as a gift that must be denied by right.

This is clearly figured in the prayer by the mother of the sons of Zebedee, in Matthew 20; the Lord answered her with, "You do not know what you ask," as if he were criticizing her for her indiscreet prayer. Therefore, we must not ask for anything from God, especially any temporal good, except on condition, that is to say, insofar as God himself knows what is expedient and useful for us. Hence Ambrose comments on the words "Blessed are the undefiled" of the Psalm: "When you pray to God, pray for great and eternal things, not for what is earthly and transitory." And he continues: "Do not pray for money, for it is rust, nor for possessions, for they are dust. Such prayer does not reach God, for God does not hear but what he considers worthy of his benefits." For this reason, Bernard comments on Matthew: "He prays well who in his prayer seeks God; as he progresses from earthly things to higher ones, he climbs to the power of the heavenly court." Hence the Lord Jesus went up by himself on a mountain to pray. And Bernard continues: "He who prays for money and worldly honors or the death of his enemy lies low and sends shameful prayers to God." As a type of good prayer, Solomon in Kings 3 did not ask for such things but only for the wisdom to rule his people well; and the Lord was well pleased with his prayer and granted him wisdom together with a long life and abundance of wealth, as one can find it plainly in that chapter. Therefore Bernard says: "We can hope beyond doubt to receive what we ask rightly."

And notice how Christ teaches us to pray daily against all evils in all our needs, when he says in Matthew: "Thus, therefore, shall you pray: Our Father, who art in heaven, hallowed be thy name," add: in us, so that through your grace and help we may be holy and clean vessels, against lechery. "Thy kingdom come," that is: to us, in place of the earthly kingdom which we have left behind, against avarice and covetousness. "Thy will be done," for we scorn our self-will, against pride. "Give us today our daily bread," that is, all that is necessary to sustain us, neither too much nor too little, against gluttony. "And forgive us," and so on, against wrath. "And lead us not into temptation," namely of the flesh, the world, and especially the devil, against envy. "But deliver us from evil," that is, through the deeds of mercy and other works of penance, against sloth.

Third, our prayer must be fervent and tearful; otherwise it cannot bear fruit, according to Bernard, any more than dry and barren land. This quality is opposed to hypocrites who pretend one thing in their mouth when they pray and mean another in their heart. Thus, when they pray, they quickly shed tears in the face of other people, but behind their backs they at once break into boundless laughter, like good-for-nothing beggars who cry out and pretend they are weeping when they see other people approach, in hope of getting greater

esse bonum et malum esse malum. Si primum, ut quid ergo non vis esse quod
vis apparere? Si secundum, scilicet si malum est esse malum, ut quid ergo
110   vis esse quod non vis apparere? Quod enim turpe est apparere, turpius est
esse, et quod formosum est apparere, formosius est esse. Ergo (dicit ipse)
aut appare quod es aut esto quod appares, quia manifestum malum non repre-
henditur a sapientibus dum insania estimatur." Hec ille.
Set rogo quid dicemus hiis diebus ex quo tot apparent [f. 149v] homi-
115   nes in exteriori et tamen in interiori sunt bestiis silvestribus peiores?
Revera, pro toto mundo videtur de talibus esse sicut isti pictores formant
aliquas ymagines que dicuntur *babewynes* in parietibus. Aliquas enim eorum
formant cum facie hominis et cum corpore leonis, aliquas eciam cum facie
⟨hominis⟩ et residu⟨o⟩ corporis asini, et alias cum capite hominis et cum
120   parte posteriori ursi. Et sic de singulis. Sic certe est de talibus ypocri-
tis, nam aliqui apparent exterius mundi et casti, set a tergo sunt equis
vel asinis luxuriosiores. Similiter alii apparent in facie et a parte ante
mites et pii ut homo, set a tergo sunt leonibus crudeliores verberando,
spoliando, mactando. Similiter alii apparent sobrii, et tamen propter
125   inmoderatam gulam quam exercent latenter sunt ursis fetidiores. Et sic de
singulis. Unde narratur de quodam papa nomine Benedicto, qui symoniace
intravit et, quamvis se sanctum simulaverat, pessime tamen vixit. Quo
mortuo cito post cuidam sibi familiari apparuit cum capite asini et corpore
ursi. Cum autem alius perteritus quisnam esset quesierat, respondit: "Ego,
130   inquit, sum ille papa Benedictus, eo modo tibi apparens quo vixi. Qui enim
quamvis totum studium meum sanctitate pr⟨e⟩tendebam, fuit c⟨irc⟩a luxuriam,
ideo capud asini porto, qui animal est luxuriosum. Et quia residuum cogita-
tus fuit circa ventrem et ciborum delicias, ideo corpus ursinum porto vel
gesto." Et hiis dictis disparuit. Unde Crisostomus in *[In]completo*, homelia
135   4, sic ait contra tales ypocritas: "Nescio, inquit, si homo es. Manifeste
possum ali⟨ud⟩ dicere cum enim calcitras ut asinus, saltes ut taurus, fre-
mas in mulieres ut equs, [f. 150] castrimargiam paciaris ut ursus, carnem
inpingues velud mulus, rapias ut lupus, irasceris ut serpens, percucias ut
scorpio, dolosus sis ut vulpes, venenum malicie observes ut aspis et vipe-
140   ra, et prelieris adversus fratres quemadmodum perniciosus demon." Hec ille.
"Qualiter ergo (dicit ipse) potero te inter homines numerare? Non video in
te talis nature carecteres. Quid enim feram te dicam? Set bestie ab una
harum maliciarum retinentur, tu autem simul omnes deferens longe ab earum
irracionabilitate incedis. Si vero demonem te dicam? Set demon neque ven-
145   tris servit tirannidi nec pecunias concupiscit. Cum ergo et feris et
demonibus malicias plures habeas, qualiter te hominem dicemus? Erubesce
ergo, ypocrita (dicit Crisostomus), appare quod es aut esto quod appares."
Hec ille.

alms; but when the people are gone, they break into laughter and often into derision, as we saw earlier in part 1, chapter 4. Therefore Chrysostom reproaches such hypocrites in his *Imperfect Work on Matthew*, in commenting on the words, "Woe to you, hypocrites, because you are like whited sepulchers": "Tell me, you hypocrite, if it is good to be good and bad to be evil. If the former is the case, why do you not want to be what you want to appear? If the latter, that is, if it is bad to be evil, why do you want to be what you do not want to appear? For what is shameful in appearance is even more shameful in reality, and what is beautiful in its appearance is even more beautiful in its being. Therefore, either be in truth what you appear to be, or appear as such as you are, for an open evil is not condemned by wise men, since it is judged to be insanity."

But what, I ask, shall we say when nowadays so many people appear to be human outwardly but inside are worse than wild animals? For all the world they seem to be like those images called *babewynes*, "grotesques," which painters depict on walls. Some of them they paint with a human face and the body of a lion, others with a man's face and the body of an ass, and others again with a human headd and the hind part of a bear, and so on. Surely, the same is true of hypocrites, for some of them appear in their face and front part to be mild and meek like a human person, but in their back part they are more cruel than lions through their habits of striking, robbing, and killing. Others likewise appear outwardly clean and chaste, but behind they are more lecherous than horses or asses. Others again appear to be sober, and yet on account of the unlimited gluttony which they indulge in secretly they are uglier than bears. And so forth. There is a story about a pope named Benedict who came into office by simony and lived a most evil life, even though he pretended to be a saintly person. Soon after his death he appeared to a member of his household with the head of an ass and the body of a bear. When this man asked him in great terror who he was, he replied: "I am Pope Benedict, appearing in the form in which I lived. For though I pretended to be entirely concerned with holiness, it was in reality all about lechery. Hence I carry the head of an ass, which is a lecherous animal. And because the remainder of my thoughts were spent on my stomach and delicious food, I have the body of a bear." And with these words he disappeared. Whence Chrysostom speaks against hypocrites in Homily 4 of his *Imperfect Work* as follows: "I do not know if you are human. Obviously I could say differently since you kick like an ass, jump like a bull, neigh at women like a horse, yearn for food like a bear, grow fat like a mule, ravage like a wolf, get angry like a snake, sting like a scorpion, are tricky like a fox, spit the poison of evil like an asp and viper, and fight against your brothers like a harmful demon. How, then, can I count you among humans? I do not find any human traits in you. What then? Can I call you a wild animal, if wild

5 iste] ille C.   **29** cor] vox C.   **40** omne] esse C.M.   **49** a] *om* O.   **54** affectus] effectus C.   **55** affectu] effectu C.   **59** desercionem] deseracionem C; discrescionem W.   **59–60** sic oracio] *om* O.   **90** pro qua] qua M; quia R.W.   **91** nostram] propriam O.
92 non] nec C.   **93** nobis] *add* debita nostra O.   **116** isti] ibi M.W; ubi R.   **117** Aliquas] aliquos O.   **119** hominis] leonis C.   residuo] residuum C.M.   alias] alios O.   **121–124** nam . . . mactandi] *the two sentences reversed* O.   **131** pretendebam] protendebam C.   circa] contra C.   **133** porto vel] *om* O.   **134** Incompleto] completo C.R.   **136** aliud] aliquid C.M.   calcitras] calcitres O.   **143** earum] illarum O.

V.xviii   QUE NOS COMPELLUNT AD ORANDUM

[S]ecundo compellimur ad orandum propter necessitatem. In tanta enim
p⟨auper⟩tate est homo quod quasi nichil boni habet, quia omnia consumit ad
le hasard. Et ideo pro auxilio necesse habet petere, quia Iacobi 1 dicitur:
"Si quis vestrum indiget sapiencia, postulet a Deo qui dat omnibus affluen-
5   ter." Secundo propter Christi liberalitatem. Ipse enim plus paratus est
dare quam tu audeas petere. Et ideo bene dici potest rex Assuerus, qui Hester parva petenti respondit: "Et si dimidium regni pecieris, impetrabis."
In eo autem fallit illud verbum rusticanum: "To a goode bidder goode wer-
nar," set eius contrarium verificatur, scilicet: "To goode bidder fre
10   yever." In cuius signum petere differentes redarguit Iohannis 16; dicit:
"Usque modo non petistis quicquam in nomine meo; petite et accipietis."
Tercio, propter advocati nostri in curia celorum [f. 150v] auctoritatem.
Ante enim ascencionem Domini nostri Iesu Christi talem advocatum non habuimus sicut modo, set iam tante auctoritatis est ibi advocatus noster Chris-
15   tus quod non solum quicquid ipse petit, set eciam quicquid in nomine eius
petitur impetratur; Iohannis 14: "Quicquid pecieritis in nomine meo, fiet
vobis. Petite ergo et accipietis."

2 paupertate] potestate C.   homo] *add* peccator O.   **8–9** To . . . wernar] *see* Verses, *pp.
204–205.*   **13** Domini . . . Iesu] *om* O.

animals have one of these evil characteristics each, while you have them all together and thus go far beyond their irrational natures? Or shall I call you a demon? But a demon does not serve the tyranny of the stomach, nor does he lust for money. Since you thus have more evils in you than wild beasts and demons, how shall we call you human? Blush, then, O hypocrite, and appear as what you are or else be in truth what you appear to be."

21–22 Isidore, *Sent.* III.vii.4 (PL 83:672). 23–24 Isa. 29.13 and Matt. 15.8. 27 *FM* I.vii.20–21. 29 *Prov* 34177b. 51–52 Ps.-Augustine, *De spiritu et anima* 50 (PL 40:816). 53 Cant. 2.14. 54–55 For the background and popularity of this saying, see Alford, *MP* 72 (1975), 390–391. *FM* seems to predate the passages with *brevis* listed by Alford. 61–62 Exod. 17.8–13. 66 *Prov* 17624. 67–69 Matt. 20.20–28. 71–72 Ps. 118.1. 78 Cf. Luke 9.28. 81–83 1 Kings 6–14. 86–95 Matt. 6.9–13. 105 *FM* I.vii.5–8. 106–107 Matt. 23.27. 107–113 Ps.-Chrysostom, *Opus imperfectum*, hom. 45 (PG 56:885). 126–134 Tubach 575; see Peter Damiani, *De abdicatione episcopatus* 3 (PL 145:428–29). 147 Ps.-Chrysostom, *Opus imperfectum*, hom. 45 (PG 56:885).

V.xviii   WHAT COMPELS US TO PRAY

In the second place, we are compelled to pray by our need. Man is in such poverty that he has almost nothing that is good, for he has wasted it all at *le hasarde*, at gambling. Therefore he must needs ask for help, for in James 1 it is said: "If any of you lack wisdom, let him ask it of God, who gives to all men abundantly." Second, we are compelled by Christ's generosity. For he is more ready to give than you dare ask. Therefore he could be said to be King Ahasuerus, who replied to Esther when she asked him for a small gift: "Even if you should ask for half of my kingdom, you shall obtain it." In Christ the popular proverb which says, "A good asker, a good refuser," fails to apply, whereas its opposite comes true, namely: "To a good asker a generous giver." To show this he reproved those who are slow in their prayers, when he said in John 16: "Hitherto you have not asked anything in my name; ask, and you shall receive." Third, we are compelled to pray because of the authority which our advocate wields in the court of heaven. Before the ascension of our Lord Jesus Christ we did not have such an advocate as we have now; but now our advocate, Christ, has such authority there that not only whatever he himself asks, but even what we ask in his name is granted; John 14: "Whatsoever you ask the Father in my name shall be given to you. Ask therefore and you shall receive."

4–5 James 1.5. 7 Esther 5.3. 11 John 16.24. 16–17 John 14.13.

V.xix   QUOCIENS ET QUALITER ORANDUM EST

[T]ercio est sciendum quod sepcies in die et nocte est devote orandum,
iuxta illud Psalmi: "Sepcies in die laudem dixi tibi." Et hoc quia "sepcies
in die cadit iustus," et ideo ut tociens possit resurgere, tociens orat, ut
per hoc semptemplici don⟨o⟩ Spiritus Sancti valeamus adimpleri et a septem
5   viciis capitalibus premuniri et defendi. Et similiter in memoria septem ho-
rarum Christi. Nam primo nocte media oramus, quia in hac hora Christus natus est, similiter a Iudeis captus est et illusus. Dicitur eciam in *Magis-
trali* quod media nocte infernum spoliavit large loquendo, scilicet ante
lucem mane surrexit, et hora prima apparuit. In hac eciam hora ad iudicium
10   venturus [esse] asseritur. In hac ergo hora laudes Deo persolvimus et ei de
eius nativitate, capcione, et patrum liberacione gracias agamus, et eius
adventum ad iudicium sollicite expectamus. Adduntur eciam laudes tunc matu-
tinales, quia illa hora Egipcio[s] in mari submersit, mundum creavit, et
resurrexit. Et ideo tunc laudes sibi referrimus, ne in mari huius mundi cum
15   Egipciis demergamur et ut pro nostra creacione et eius resurrectione sibi
gracias persolvamus. Hora autem prima Christus Pilato est presentatus et a
mortuo resurgens primo mulieribus apparuit, hoc est in prima hora diei. Et
ideo tunc sibi laudes persolvimus, gracias sibi resurgenti et [f. 151] ap-
parenti reddendo. Hora tercia Christus ad columpnam flagellatus est que, ut
20   in historiis habetur, adhuc vestigia cruoris ostendit. Et hac hora eciam
Spiritus Sanctus missus est sanctis apostolis. Hora sexta in cruce clavis
confixus est et tenebre facte sunt in universum mundum, ne sol in morte Domini sui ipsum crucifigentibus lucem preberet. Et in hac hora die ascencionis cum discipulis discubuit. Hora autem nona spiritum emisit, miles eius
25   latus ap⟨e⟩ruit, cetus apostolorum ad orandum convenire consuevit, Christus
celum ascendit, etc. Hora vesperarum Christus in cena sacramentum corporis
et sanguinis instituit, pedes discipulorum lavit, de cruce depositus et in
sepulcro collocatus est, similiter discipulis in habitu peregrino se manifestavit. Hora completorii Christus guttas sanguinis sudavit, in monumento
30   custoditur, et resurgens pacem discipulis nunciavit. Et ideo istis horis
laudes et gracias persolvimus.

Et nota quod communiter ad orientem adoramus, secundum Damascenum,
libro 4, capitulo 5, triplici racione: Primo ut patriam nostram nos requirere
ostendamus; secundo ut Christum crucifixum respiciamus; tercio ut advenien-
35   tem iudicem nos expectare ostendamus. Ait enim sic: "Dominus enim crucifixus ad orientem respiciebat, et ita adoramus ad ipsum respicientes. Et assumptus ad orientem sursum ferebatur, et ipsum apostoli adorabant, et ita
veniet quomodo viderunt eum euntem in celum. Ipsum ergo expectantes ad
ipsum orientem adoramus." Hec Damascenus.

V.xix HOW OFTEN AND IN WHAT WAY WE SHOULD PRAY

In the third place we must know that we should pray devoutly seven times by day and night, according to the words of the Psalm, "Seven times a day I have given praise to you." And this because "a just man falls seven times a day," and therefore he prays as often so that he may rise as many times; through this we can be filled with the sevenfold gift of the Holy Spirit and be fortified and protected against the seven capital vices. And similarly we pray seven times in memory of the seven hours of Christ. For first we pray at midnight, because in that hour Christ was born and likewise captured by the Jews and mocked. It is also said, in the *Magisterial Work*, that at midnight he harrowed hell, broadly speaking, that is to say, he rose in the morning before dawn and appeared at the first hour. Further, in this hour he is asserted to come for the judgment. In this hour, therefore, we render praise to God and thank him for his birth, capture, and the freeing of our forefathers, and eagerly wait for his coming to judgment. To this are then added Lauds at dawn, for in that hour he drowned the Egyptians in the Red Sea, created the world, and rose from death. And therefore we praise him in that hour so that we may not drown with the Egyptians in the sea of this world and to give him thanks for our creation and his resurrection. At Prime, that is, in the first hour of the day, Christ was presented to Pilate and, rising from the dead, first appeared to the holy women. And therefore we praise him at that time and give him thanks for his resurrection and appearance. At the third hour, Christ was scourged at the column which still today shows marks of his blood, as can be found in histories. And in the same hour the Holy Spirit was sent to the apostles. At the sixth hour, he was nailed to the cross and darkness came over the whole world, so that at the death of its lord the sun did not give its light to those who were crucifying him. And in the same hour he lay at table with his disciples on the day of the ascension. But at the ninth hour he gave up his spirit, a soldier opened his side, the group of the apostles used to gather for prayer, Christ ascended to heaven, and other events occurred. At Vespers, Christ instituted the sacrament of his holy Body and Blood at supper, washed the feet of his disciples, was taken from the cross and placed in the tomb, and also showed himself to his disciples clothed as a pilgrim. And at Compline, Christ perspired drops of blood, was guarded in the tomb, and after his resurrection announced his disciples his peace. And for this let us give him praise and thanks at these hours.

Notice also that usually we pray facing east, according to Damascene, book 4, chapter 5, and this for three reasons: first, to show that we seek our home; second, to look at Christ on the cross, and third, to show that we are waiting for the coming of our judge. For Damascene says as follows: "When Christ was

---

4 dono] dona C.   **7** est(2)] *om* O.   **10** esse] est M.W.   **17** mortuo] mortuis O.   sanctis]
om O.   **25** aperuit] apparuit C.   **30** horis] *add* sibi O.   **36** orientem] occidentem R.

V.xx   QUE BONA CONFERT ORACIO

[C]irca quartum, scilicet de oracionis utilitate et que bona confert
oracio, est sciendum quod primo ad superna desiderium ascendere facit, et
maxime si sit de- [f. 151v] vota et pro peccatis lacrimosa. Sicut vis
flamme ignis fumum in aere[m] facit ascendere, et ventus aquam attrahit a

5   mari que ad terre humectacionem postea habet descendere, sic et oracio
devota et lacrimosa a spiritu afflatur et sursum vehitur et iterum descendit, ut magis ac magis lav⟨e⟩t lacrimis contagia culpe; Psalmista: "Ascen-
ciones in corde suo disposuit in valle lacrimarum." In cuius figura legitur
de David, Regum 15, quod ascendit altitudinem montis "scandens et flens."

10 Et ideo dicitur Iob 23: "In amaritudine anime mee inmorabitur oculus meus."
Secundo, apud Deum graciam et virtutum efficaciam impetrat; unde Thobie 12
legitur quod angelus dixit ei: "Quando orabas cum lacrimis, optuli oracionem tuam Domino." In cuius eciam figura Regum 20 cum egrotasset Ezechias,
conversus ad parietem ⟨ad⟩orabat cum lacrimis et exauditus es[t]. Tercio,

15 ventos temptacionum deicit ad modum quo frequenter parva pluvia ventos et
tempestates cedat; Thobie 3: "Post tempestatem tranquillum facis, et post
lacrimarum fletus exultacionem mittis," quia secundum Gregorium, "dulciores
sunt lacrime penitencium quam delicie regum." De quo admirans Bernardus
ait: "Si enim tam pium est flere de te, o bone Iesu, dulcissimum est de te

20 gaudere." Et ideo dicit Augustinus: "Currebant michi lacrime et bene michi
erat cum illis."
   Fertur autem quod antiquis temporibus a commentatore Iuvenali Oracio
depingebatur ad modum hominis pulcherrimi habentis corpus igneum et capud
in celum erectum, super unam lanceam rectam et altissimam, cum quatuor

25 angelis illam supportantibus et rotul⟨u⟩m in manibus singulis tenentibus
codicem condiciones Oracionis continentem. In quorum primo rotulo scribebatur:

      Terris, igne, mari, ventis peto dominari.

crucified, he was facing west, and therefore we adore him this way by looking back at him. And when he was taken to heaven, he was carried upward to the east, and the apostles adored him; and he will come in the same way as they saw him go to heaven. Therefore, we pray to him expecting him from the east."

The substance of this chapter occurs similarly in *Leg. aurea*, pp. 847–849. **2** Ps. 118.164. **2–3** Prov. 24.16. **32–39** John Damascene, *De fide orthodoxa* IV.12 (PG 94:1136). **35** The textual confusion between East and West occurs also in manuscripts of Damascene; see the edition by Eligius M. Buytaert (St. Bonaventure, N.Y., 1955), p. 305.

V.xx   WHAT GOOD EFFECTS PRAYER HAS

With respect to the fourth point, namely the usefulness of prayer and its good effects, we should know that, first prayer causes in us a desire to rise to heavenly things, especially if it be made with devotion and tears for our sins. Just as the natural power of fire causes smoke to rise in the air, and as the wind draws water from the sea which later will fall to moisten the earth, so does devout and tearful prayer receive the breathing of the Spirit and is carried aloft and descends again to wash the stains of sin more and more with its tears. As the Psalmist says: "He has disposed in his heart to ascend by steps, in the vale of tears." A type of this is found in David of Kings 15, who climbed to the height of a mountain "going up and weeping." And in Job 23 it is said: "My eye shall abide in bitterness of my soul." Second, prayer gains for us grace and the power of virtues from God. Hence we read in Tobit 12 that the angel said to Tobit: "When you were praying with tears, I offered your prayer to the Lord." This is prefigured in Kings 20: when Hezekiah was ill, he turned to the wall, adored God with tears, and was heard. Third, prayer abates the winds of temptation, in the same way as a little rain often quiets winds and storms; Tobit 3: "After a storm you make a calm, and after tears and weeping you send joyfulness," because according to Gregory, "the penitent's tears are sweeter than a king's delights." Bernard spoke of this in amazement: "If weeping for your sake is such a lovely thing, O good Jesus, then rejoicing for your sake is most sweet." And for this reason Augustine says: "My tears flowed, and with them I was happy."

In ancient times, Prayer is said to have been depicted, by the commentator Juvenal, as a most beautiful man with a body of fire, his head lifted to heaven, leaning on a straight and tall lance, and supported by four angels who held scrolls in their hands which expressed the qualities of prayer. On the first was written:

Lands and fire, sea and winds I strive to rule.

[Anglice sic:

30   Fyre, watur, wynd and lond
            Y wylne to haue in my honde.]

In secundo: [f. 152]

            Vir, pete, sum presto; si plangas, cercior esto.

[Anglice sic:

35   Byd faste and Y come sone;
            Yf þow sorow, þe tyt þy bone.]

In tercio:

            Si petor, accedo; sin autem, inde recedo.

[Anglice sic:

40   Whyle þou bydde, redy Y am;
            When þou leuyst, Y go þe fram.]

Et in quarto:

            Adiuvo ferventer, non desero, pugno libenter.

[Anglice sic:

45   ⟨Smertly⟩ I helpe ⟨and noght⟩ forsake.
            Gladly Y fyȝt þe maystry to take.]

Spiritualiter autem loquendo Oracio in forma hominis depingebatur in signum
quod ipsa erit sicut homo racionalis; et erecta in signum quod orans superius in Deum totam spem ponit et non in homine, quia "maledictus homo qui
50   ponit spem in homine." Exemplum illius: Iudas Machabeus bellum aggressurus
contra multitudinem adversariorum suorum in Domino confortans, ut scilicet
in illo spem ponerent et non in homine, dixit: "Sicut fuerit voluntas in
celo, sic fiet." Item Oracio ponebatur super lanceam erectam in signum quod
nullo modo est tortuosa set ex omni parte cum equitate iusticie linealis ad
55   nullam partem declinans. Et non solum debet esse recta sine tortuositate
secundum legem et iudicium humanarum constitucionum, verum eciam omni modo

In English:

> Fire, water, wind, and land
> Firmly I wish to have in hand.

On the second:

> Pray, I am at your will; if you weep, you may be more sure.

In English:

> Fast you pray, and I come soon,
> If you are sorry, you get your boon.

On the third:

> If I am asked, I come, but leave as soon as you stop.

In English:

> As long as you pray, ready I'll be,
> But when you stop I go from thee.

And on the fourth:

> With fervor I help, I do not forsake, and gladly I fight.

In English:

> I eagerly help and not forsake,
> And gladly fight the crown to take.

In spiritual terms, Prayer is depicted in human shape to show that it must be rational like man; and upright, to show that when one prays, one puts one's hope entirely above, in God, not in man, for "cursed is the man who puts his trust in man." As an example of this: when Judas Maccabaeus was about to enter the war against a multitude of enemies, he comforted his troops with the Lord, that is, that they should put their hope in the Lord and not in man, saying: "As it is his will in heaven, so let it be done." Further, Prayer rested on a straight lance, to show that it is in no way crooked but everywhere straightforward with just equity and not partial in any way. It must be straight without crookedness, not only in accordance with the law and human legislation,

secundum conscienciam rectam et ordinatam secundum legem preceptorum Dei.
Item depingitur cum quatuor angelis, in signum quod angeli semper sunt
parati Deo preces recte ordinatas offerre. Exemplum Thobie 12 de angelo
60   Raphaele qui dixit: "Quando orabas optuli oracionem tuam Domino."
Et nota quod tantum quatuor depingitur habere angelos, ad designandum
quod ad hoc quod oracio fiat recta, exaudibilis, et perfecta, oportet quod
sit ex quatuor particulis consequentibus, quarum prima est quod orare
debemus tantum quod sit ad Dei voluntatem et expediens ⟨elementis⟩, ex
65   quibus et per que omnia inferiora bene vel male ordinantur et reguntur. Et
ideo in primo rotulo primi angeli scribebatur: "Terris, igne, mari," etc.
Exemplum de igne: Genesis ⟨9⟩, de Sodoma et Gomorra; et similiter Regum 2,
de Helia et duobus [f. 152v] principibus quinquagenariis, et qualiter
tercius princeps salvatus est per humilitatem oracionis. Exemplum secundo
70   de ventis et aere, Regum, quomodo per oracionem Helie in vindictam sceleris
populi per tres annos et sex menses ventus aere non erat madefactus, nam
per tantum tempus non pluit super terram, set postea per humilem oracionem
celum dedit pluviam et terra germen suum. Exemplum tercio de aqua patet in
Mari Rubro super Pharaonem et excercitum eius orante Moyse quomodo in illo
75   erant submersi. Et eciam prius patuit in diluvio. Et eciam secundum beatum
Orosium et Augustinum *De civitate Dei*, libro 16, capitulo 10, postea propter peccatum hominis multas provincias et partes provinciarum subvertit
diluvium parciale, scilicet Ogigi et Decalionis, quamvis non fuerit nisi
semel, scilicet tempore Noe, diluvium generale. Et ponit ibi exemplum:
80   Quodam tempore Cicropis regis Assiriorum factum est diluvium in orientali
plaga fere perveniens ad Egiptum. Et similiter nota quomodo aque converse
sunt in sanguinem tempore Pharaonis, ut patet Exodo. Similiter patet Regum
3 de aquis amaricatis per Heliseum dulcoratis.
Secunda particula pertinens ad oracionem est quod fiat cum lacrimis et
85   planctu ex dolore proprii commissi et reatus. Et ideo in secundo rotulo
secundi angeli scribebatur: "Vir, pete, sum presto," etc. Exemplum Regum 20
de Ezechia, ut patet supra, quomodo cum egrotasset conversus ad parietem
plorans et orans exauditus est. Exemplum eciam de Magdalena, et de beato
Francisco, quomodo in principio sue conversionis plangens et plorans cum
90   oracione dies annorum suorum, ex voce melliflua confortatus et certificatus
fuit. Et ideo de illis et huiusmodi aliis pro peccatis dolentibus dicitur
in Psalmo: "Recogitabo tibi omnes annos meos," etc., supple: quos in vanis
expendidi, propter quod [f. 153] annos eternos in mente habui, quos scilicet et quorum gloriam amisi, et ideo illos in mente contrita iugiter reti-
95   nui. Unde bene dicitur illud Ieremie 32: "In fletu venient et in misericordia reducam eos," [quasi diceret: venient ad me cum lacrimis devote orantes
et in misericordia reducam eos] bene conversantes.
Tercia particula ad oracionem pertinens est quod sit constans et
assidua. Et ideo scribitur in tercio rotulo: "Cum petor, accedo," etc.

but also in every respect in accordance with a conscience that is straightforward and formed by the law of God's commandments. Moreover, it is depicted with four angels, to show that the angels are always ready to carry rightly fashioned prayers to God. An example is the angel Raphael of Tobit 12, who said: "When you prayed, I offered your prayer to the Lord."

And notice that Prayer is depicted with only four angels to show that, in order to be straightforward, worthy to be heard, and perfect, prayer must have the following four aspects. The first is that we must pray only for what is in agreement with God's will and helpful to the elements by and through which all lower natures are well or badly formed and ruled. Therefore, in the scroll of the first angel was written: "Lands and fire, sea," and so on. Concerning fire, we find an example in Sodom and Gomorrah of Genesis 9, and similarly in Elijah and the two princes of fifty men in Kings 2, and how the third prince was saved by humble prayer. An example for wind and air occurs in Kings, how at the prayer of Elijah, in punishment for the crime of the people, wind and air was not moist for three years and six months, for all that time it did not rain on the earth; but afterwards, at his humble prayer, heaven yielded rain and the earth began to sprout. An example for water is the Red Sea, in which Pharaoh and his army were drowned when Moses prayed; and the same can be seen in Noah's flood. And later on, according to Blessed Orosius and Augustine, in book 16 of *The City of God*, chapter 10, a partial flood, namely that of Ogyges and of Deucalion, destroyed many provinces and parts of provinces because of man's sin, although a general flood had come only once, that is, in the time of Noah. And Augustine mentions as an instance the flood that occurred at the time of Cecrops, king of the Assyrians, on the eastern shore, reaching almost as far as Egypt. In the same way, notice how in the time of Pharaoh the waters were turned into blood, as we read in Exodus. Similarly in Kings 3, how the bitter waters were made sweet by Elisha.

The second aspect that belongs to prayer is that it must be made with tears and lament in grief for one's sin and fault. Therefore it was written in the scroll of the second angel: "Pray, I am at your will," and so forth. An example is Hezekiah of Kings 20, as we saw earlier: when he was ill, he turned toward the wall, wept and prayed, and was heard. Another example is Magdalene; and Blessed Francis, how in the beginning of his new life, as he wept and in prayer grieved over the days of his past life, he was comforted by a honey-sweet voice and strengthened in his resolve. Therefore, the words of the Psalm apply well to these and others who thus grieve for their sins: "I will recount to you all my years," and so forth; add: the years I have spent in vain endeavors, for which I have held the eternal years in my mind which I have lost with their glory, and therefore I have kept them firmly in my contrite mind. Hence it is said in Jeremiah 32: "They will come in weeping, and I will bring them back in mercy," as if God were saying: they shall come to me praying devoutly with tears, and I shall bring them back in mercy to lead a good life.

100 Exemplum de Iosue, quomodo ipso orante contra populum Amalech prevaluit
Israel, cessante illo prevaluit Amalech. Exemplum de Moyse, Exodi 17,
quomodo dum extensis manibus oravit, populus Israel prevaluit, set illis
depositis succubuit; propter quod filii Israel manus suas sustentabant.
Unde dicitur: "Multum valet oracio iusti assidua"; et Ad Thessalonicenses
105 5: "Orate sine intermissione."
Quarta particula oracionis est quod ipsa debet esse ardens et in fine
devota. Et ideo scribitur in quarto rotulo: "Adiuvo ferventer," etc. Exemplum Iosue, cui oranti sol et luna quamdiu voluit obedierunt. Exemplum
eciam Machabeorum 10 de Iuda Machabeo qui facta oracione bellum aggressus
110 est et auxilio duorum virorum de celo descendencium fultus victoriam optinuit mirabilem. Exemplum eciam Regum 6 de obsidione Samarie et fame et
dolore, et quomodo viri fugati sunt per supernalem excercitum grandem angelorum. Sic ergo hoc modo oracio iusta, humilis, et discreta debet esse, ut
scilicet nichil petatur nisi quod sit ad Dei voluntatem et salutem anima-
115 rum, ad modum quo quidam sanctus, ut patet in *Vitas Patrum*, solebat Deum
orare dicens: "Domine, sicut vis et scis, miserere mei." Et nota quod
quicquid dicitur supra in ⟨ista⟩ particula, capitulo 2, de effectu misse,
potest hic adduci et e contrario. Hec de oracione dicta sufficiunt ad
presens.

7 lavet] lavit C. **10** 23] 27 O. inmorabitur] morabitur O. **14** adorabat] et orabat C;
orabat R. **19** o] *om* O. **22** Iuvenali] iuvenalis M.W. **25** rotulum] rotulam C. **26–
27** scribebatur] *add* sic O. **29–46** Anglice . . . take] *material in brackets supplied from
R. Verse 48, in* B1.B3.Go1.Go2.Jo.L2.L3.LC.R.Sp.V.W1. **42** Et in] *om* O. **43** fer-
venter] frequenter R.W. **45** Smertly . . . noght] i helpe anon R. **53** fiet] fiat O.
60 orabas] *a later hand has added* cum lacrimis C. **64** elementis] clementer C.R.W.
66 etc.] O *complete the line as above, 28.* **67** igne] *add* primo O. 9] primo C.
82 tempore] *om* O. **88–89** beato Francisco] sancto francisco Sp; *om* groups x and y.E.
Jo.L3.LC; *manuscript defective* L1. *All full manuscripts recorded.* **91** aliis] ceteris O.
dolentibus] *add* bene O. **95** 32] 31 O. **100** de] *om* O. **101** Israel] *add* sed O.
104 Unde] *add* bene O. **113** Sic] sit O. debet esse] *om* O. **114** scilicet] *add* quod O.
117 ista] prima C; quinta M.

V.xxi   DE IEIUNIO

[I]am enim de abstinencia et ieiunio, quod est [f. 153v] secunda pars
satisfactionis contra carnales insultus penitus esset dicendum, set quia de
illo postea particula 6 post vicium gule satis diffuse tractabitur, ideo

The third aspect of prayer is that it must be constant and eager. Therefore it was written on the third scroll: "When I am asked, I come," and so
forth. As an example, when Joshua prayed against the people of Amalek, Israel
prevailed, but when he stopped, Amalek prevailed. Another example is Moses, in
Exodus 17, how as long as he was praying with uplifted hands, the people of
Israel prevailed, but when he let his hands sink, the people succumbed; and for
this reason the children of Israel supported his hands. Therefore it is well
said that "the eager prayer of the just is of great help"; and at Thessalonians
5: "Pray without ceasing."

The fourth aspect of prayer is that it must be fervent and for a pious
purpose. Therefore it was written on the fourth scroll: "With fervor I help,"
and so forth. We find an example in Joshua, to whom sun and moon obeyed as
long as he wanted while he was praying. Another example is Judas Maccabaeus,
in Maccabees 10, who began the battle after he had prayed and won a miraculous
victory with the help of two men who came down from heaven. A further example
is the siege, hunger, and grief of Samaria, in Kings 6, and how the men were
put to flight by a large troop of angels from above. Let your prayer, then, be
just, humble, and discreet in this way, that nothing be asked for except what
is according to God's will and for the good of souls, in the way a saintly
person used to pray to God as is found in *The Lives of the Fathers*: "Lord,
have mercy on me as you see fit and want it." All that was said earlier about
the good effects of the Mass, in chapter 2 of this part, can be applied here
also; and conversely the bad consequences for people who do not pray. This
much about prayer is sufficient for now.

7–8 Ps. 83.6. **9** 2 Sam. 15.30. **10** Job 17.2. **12–13** Tob. 12.12. **13–14** 2 Kings
20.1–6. **16–17** Tob. 3.22. **19–20** Ps.-Bernard, *Lamentatio in Passionem Christi* 3
(PL 184:771). **20–21** Augustine, *Confessiones* IX.vi.14 (CC 27:141). **22–47** Tubach
3896; add Harley 7322, fol. 155v (with English verses). **49–50** Jer. 17.5. **52–53** 1
Macc. 3.60. **60** Tob. 12.12. **67** Gen. 19.24. **67–69** 2 Kings 1.9–15. **70–73** 1
Kings 17. **74–75** Exod. 14. **75** Gen. 8. **75–81** Augustine, *De civitate Dei* XVIII.x
(CC 48:601). **81–82** Exod. 7. **82–83** 2 Kings 2.19–22. **87–88** 2 Kings 20.1–6.
88 Luke 7.38ff. **89–91** For example, Bonaventure, *Legenda sancti Francisci* III.6
(8:511). **92** Isa. 38.15. **95–96** Jer. 31.9. **101–103** Exod. 17.8–13. **104** James
5.16. **105** 1 Thess. 5.17. **108** Josh. 10.13. **109–111** 2 Macc. 10.15–38. **111–113**
2 Kings 6. **115–116** Cf. *VP* III.207 (PL 73:806). **117** *FM* V.ii.100–203.

V.xxi FASTING

We should now speak about abstinence and fasting, which form the second
member of satisfaction, which is set against the attacks of our flesh. But
since these will be dealt with at length later on, in part 6, after the vice of

quod illud sit athleta fortis gulam extirpans, totum hic causa brevitatis
5 pertranseo.

---

2 contra] *add* scilicet O.   **4** totum] ideo O.

V.xxii   DE ELEMOSINA

[C]irca terciam partem satisfactionis, scilicet de elemosina, cum ipsa
tante virtutis sit quod opera meritoria in suo statu custodit et alia consimilia introducit remuneranda, ⟨ideo⟩ de illa ad presens dicendum est, et
videndum primo quid sit elemosina et de quibus facienda, secundo quibus
5 comparatur et quibus eroganda, tercio que illam impediunt, quarto que bona
per illam eveniunt.

Est ergo primo sciendum quod elemosina est opus pietatis ad omnia valens, que ubicumque in sua indigencia confortat et sublevat. Et ideo secundum Augustinum hoc modo aliter diffinitur: "Elemosina, inquit, est res
10 sancta que auget presencia, dimittit peccata, vitam elongat, separat a diabolo, sociat Deo, et angelos vocat in auxilium." Et nota secundum quod habetur *Summa confessorum*, libro 3, titulo "De hospitalitate ordinandorum,"
questione 2, et accipitur a Thoma in *Summa*, questione 32: "Quedam elemosine
sunt corporales, que scilicet exercentur per septem opera misericordie, que
15 sunt esurientem pascere, sicientem potare, vestire nudum, recolligere hos-
pitem, visitare infirmum, redimere captivum, sepelire mortuum." Unde versus:

Visito, poto, cibo, redimo, tego, colligo, condo.

Quedam eciam sunt spirituales elemosine, et sunt iste: ignorantem docere,
20 dubitanti consulere, consolari tristem, corrigere peccantem, offendenti
remittere, onerosos portare, et pro omnibus orare. Unde versus:

Consule, castiga, solare, remitte, fer, ora.

Et nota quod elemosine corporales faciende sunt de propriis [f. 154] iuste
et legitime adquisitis et non de rapinis aliorum illicitis et inhonestis,
25 ut patet in *Summa confessorum*, libro 2, titulo 8, rubrica "De illicitis
adquisitis," ut sunt de furtis, usuris, rapinis, meretriciis, et ceteris
huiusmodi.

[D]e secundo vero, scilicet quibus comparatur elemosina et quibus eroganda est, primo est sciendum quod tria in elemosine dacione sunt conside-
30 randa, scilicet iustum, ordo, et intencio. Iustum autem, ut sit de iusto et

gluttony, which they uproot like a strong champion, I will now bypass them for
the sake of brevity.

---

3 *FM* VI.iv–vi.

V.xxii   ALMSGIVING

And so we turn to the third part of satisfaction, namely, almsgiving,
which has such great power as to preserve our meritorious deeds in their status
and to introduce others like them which will gain us reward. About it we must
investigate, first, what almsgiving is and from what things alms should be
given; second, to what it can be compared and to whom alms may be given;
third, what things prevent it; and fourth, what good consequences it has.

First, then, we should know that almsgiving is a work of compassion which
is useful in all sorts of ways; it comforts and helps wherever there is need.
Therefore, another definition according to Augustine goes as follows: "Almsgiving is a holy work which increases present merits, forgives sins, prolongs
life, separates us from the devil, joins us to God, and calls his angels to our
help." And according to the *Summa for Confessors*, book 3, under the title
"On the hospitality of people who are to be ordained," question 2 (and this is
taken from Thomas's *Summa*, question 32): "Some alms are bodily and are
practiced by the seven works of mercy, namely: to feed the hungry, give drink
to the thirsty, clothe the naked, house the stranger, visit the sick, redeem the
captive, and bury the dead." Hence the verse:

I visit, feed, give drink, redeem, clothe, shelter, bury.

Other alms are spiritual, and they are: to teach the uneducated, give counsel
to people who are in doubt, console the sorrowing, correct the sinner, forgive
those who offend, support those who are burdened, and pray for all. Hence the
verse:

Counsel, punish, console, forgive, support, and pray.

And notice that bodily alms must be given from one's own property that has been
justly and legally acquired, not from what has been taken illegally and dishon-
estly from others, as is stated in the *Summa for Confessors*, book 2, title 8,
under the rubric "On illegal gains," by such means as theft, usury, extortion,
prostitution, and the like.

On the second point, to what things alms can be compared and to whom they
may be given, we must first understand that when we give alms, three things

de proprio, ut predictum est, et non de illicito adquisito. Unde si hoc
dubitatur utrum bona possint licite rapi ab avaro, usurario, vel a ceteris
huiusmodi ut inde daretur elemosina aut non, respondit Raymundus quod non.
Item dicit quod mala non sunt facienda ut inde eveniant bona quecumque: 30,
35   questione 1, *Nosce*. Et ideo de talibus dicit Augustinus, 14, questione 5:
"Forte, inquit, huiusmodi cogitacio diaboli calliditate suggeritur. Nam si
totum tribuat circa elemosinas quod tali modo abstulit, addit pocius peccatum quam minuat, quia aufert sibi copiam restituendi. Numquam enim dimittitur peccatum nisi restituatur ablatum."
40   Secundo considerandus est ordo, ut scilicet primo elemosinam [incipi-
at] a seipso et postea ° proximo ⟨faciat⟩. Scribitur enim Matthei 7 et Luce
6: "Ipocrita, eice primo trabem de oculo," etc. Et Ecclesiastici 30: "Miserere anime tue placens Deo." Super quod dicit Magister *Sentenciarum*, libro
4, distinctione 15: "Si enim aliqui ex una parte elemosinas largiuntur et
45   ex alia in diversis peccatis involvuntur, credentes virtute huiusmodi elemosinarum inmunes persistere, quoad omnia sciant se delusos iuxta illud
Psalmi: 'Qui diligit iniquitatem, odit animam suam.' [Set (ait ipse) qui
odit animam suam,] non est misericors set crudelis. Ergo, etc. Ex quibus
omnibus datur intelligi quod in peccatis mortalibus permanentes etsi elemo-
50   sinas lar- [f. 154v] gas faciunt, non tamen per illas satisfaciunt, quia
inordinate agunt dum elemosinas suas a seipsis non incipiunt, nec proprie
[dicitur] elemosina tale opus dum sibimetipsis crudeles existunt, non
placentes Deo. Ergo non dicenda est ista peccati satisfactio, quam quis
agit pro peccato uno et perdurat in alio." Hec ille.
55   Tercio circa elemosinas considerandum est quia oportet quod fiant
intencione recta, hoc est, propter Deum et non propter vanam gloriam.
Scribitur enim Ad Galatas 5: "Non efficiamini inanis glorie cupidi." Nam
valde venenosum est ventus inanis glorie, qui sua malicia fructus bonorum
operum evellit, ne ad maturitatem perveniant. Non enim potest homo de bonis
60   operibus inde gloriam querere, set mercedem retribucionis eterne. Unde
Gregorius in *Moralibus*: "Quasi, inquid, est latrunculus appetitus humane
laudis qui recto itinere gradientibus ex latere iungitur ut ex occultis
educto gladio trucidetur." Est ergo ventus venenosus eo quod opera nostra
suo flatu occidit, ne nobis proficiant ad ⟨mercedem⟩; Ecclesiastici 5:
65   "Quid prodest ei qui laborat in vanum," quasi dicat, nichil. Ne ergo ille
ventus bona nostra opera destruat, dirigamus illa ad Deum solum, ut ipse a
vana gloria nos preservat.
Exemplum autem refert Plinius, quod aquila in altum nidificat, cuius
pullis insidiatur serpens nomine pa⟨ri⟩as. Qui videns se non posse propter
70   altitudinem ad pullos ascendere, trahit se naturali instinctu ad partem
venti et venenum emittens ⟨illum⟩ inficit. Et sic per ventum et aerem
infectum pullos occidit. Quo comperto aquila instinctu naturali mirabilem

should be considered, namely their justness, order, and intention. Their justness: so that alms be taken from one's legal property, as has already been said, and not from illegal gains. Therefore, if anyone questions whether any goods may be legally taken from an avaricious man, a usurer, or someone else of this kind, with the intention of using them for alms, Raymundus replies, No. He also explains that one may not do evil with the intention that some good may come from it; see 30, question 2, "Know." And about such people Augustine says, as cited in 14, question 5: "Such a thought is probably suggested by the devil's cunning. For if a man gives everything he has taken away in this fashion as alms, he adds to his sin rather than diminishing it, for he deprives himself of the wherewithal for making restitution. For sin is never forgiven unless what has been taken away is restored."

In the second place we must consider the right order of giving alms: a person must first give alms to himself and only then to his neighbor. For in Matthew 7 and Luke 6 it is written: "You hypocrite, cast out first the beam from your own eye," and so forth. And in Ecclesiasticus 30: "Have pity on your own soul, pleasing God." On which the Master of the *Sentences* says in book 4, distinction 15: "If someone on the one hand gives alms and on the other involves himself in various sins, in the hope that he would remain guiltless by virtue of these alms, he should know that he is totally mistaken, according to the words of the Psalm: 'He that loves iniquity hates his own soul.' Now, he who hates his soul is not merciful but cruel; therefore, etc. From this we are given to understand that people who live in mortal sins, even if they give generous alms, do not make satisfaction thereby, because they act against the right order since their alms do not begin at themselves; nor can such action be rightly called almsgiving, since they are cruel to themselves and do not please God. Therefore it cannot be called satisfaction for sin when one does so for one sin and continues to commit another."

In the third place, we must consider that alms be given with the right intention, namely for God's sake, not for vainglory. For in Galatians 5 it is written: "Do not become desirous of vain glory." The wind of vainglory is very harmful; in its mischief it casts down the fruits of our good works, so that they do not come to full ripeness. For man cannot gain glory from his good works, but the reward of eternal retribution. Whence Gregory says in his *Moral Commentary*: "The desire for human praise is like a thief who secretly joins those who travel on a straight way, that he may pull his dagger in secret and murder them." And it is a poisonous wind because it kills our good works with its breath, so that they have no power to bring us reward; Ecclesiasticus 5: "What does it profit him that he labors in vain [*read* for the wind]," as if to say: nothing. So that this wind may not destroy our good works, let us direct them to God alone, and he will keep us from vainglory.

As an example, Pliny reports that the eagle builds his nest on high, for

adhibet cautelam. [f. 155] Nam statim querit lapidem quendam gagates dictum
et ponit in nido in illa parte qua ventus stat et flat, qui sua virtute
75 venenum repellit, et sic pulli salvantur. Moraliter per aquilam istam, que
ardui volatus et acuti visus est, intelligitur quilibet bonus Christianus,
cuius vita et desiderium a terrenis debet elevari in altum versus celum, ut
dicere possit cum Apostolo: "Nostra conversacio in celis est." In qua
altitudine conversacionis debet pullos bonorum [operum] producere. Quod
80 cum fecerit, statim serpens ille antiquus, scilicet diabolus, veneno malicie et invidie accensus nititur illa per apposicionem alicuius peccati
mortalis intoxicare et interficere. Set forte propter vite eminenciam talis
boni viri intentum non valet implere. Dicit enim beatus Gregorius: "Mentem,
inquit, in altum fixerat, propterea hostis ad eum rumpere non valebat." Quo
85 viso vadit serpens ille et temptat illos per ventum inficere venenatum, dum
laudem humanam et vanam gloriam illis commendat. Que si ad intencionem
hominis pervenerit, ut scilicet propter appetitum huiusmodi laudis bona
opera faciat, mox morientur pulli bonorum operum quoad meritum. Quid ergo
est faciendum? Revera accipiendus est lapis [iste] Christus, de quo Corin-
90 thiorum: "Petra autem erat Christus," et ponendus est in[ter] ipsa opera et
ventu⟨m⟩ vane laudis et glorie °, ut scilicet opera nostra tantum dirigamus
ad Deum, [et] certe tunc vivent opera illa et nobis eveni⟨e⟩nt ad meritum
vite eterne, quia qualis fuerit intencio, tale et opus reputabitur. Unde
Bernardus: "Intencio, inquit, tua operi tuo nomen inponit."
95 Similiter enim habetur in proprietatibus rerum et naturis animalium:
strucio talis nature [f. 155v] est quod numquam ponet ova nisi quando viderit Pliades in celo oriri. Ubi nota quod isti Pliades sunt ille septem
stelle vicinitate ⟨coniuncte⟩ et tactu omnino disiuncte. Que secundum exposicionem Gregorii in *Moralibus* signant sanctos qui in diversis temporibus
100 mortui sunt et sic quasi disiuncti, et tamen eadem intencione, quia propter
Christum et fidem mortui sunt, et sic [quasi] coniuncti inter se. Quasi ad
modum istius avis, quando debemus opera bona producere, omnino dirigamus
intencionem ad Pliades, idest ad i⟨nten⟩cionem et premium sanctorum patrum,
qui sunt quasi stelle fixe in celo, scilicet quomodo Deus eis contulit pro
105 operibus suis, ut sic illorum imitacione opera nostra omnino pro Deo et non
pro laude et gloria humana faciamus, iuxta illud Apostoli Ad Corinthios:
"Quicquid facitis, omnia in gloriam Dei facite."

---

3 ideo] et C. 3–4 et videndum] videndo M.R; *om* W. 4 elemosina] *om* O. 12 titulo]
add scilicet O. 20 peccantem] peccatorem O. 24 legitime] licite O. 25 ut] prout O.
in] *om* O. 26 ut] cuiusmodi O. 30 et] *om* O. sit] scilicet . . . fiat O. 40–41 incipiat]
om C.O *and elsewhere; text* r.t.z *and source.* 41 postea] *add* a C.M.W. faciat] a proximo C; *om* W. 46 delusos] delusi O. 55 quia oportet] *om* O. 64 mercedem] virtutem
C. 69 parias] panas C.W. 71 illum] nidum C; illos *corr* W. et(3)] sive per O.

whose young ones a snake named parias lies in ambush. When the latter understands that it cannot get to the young eagles because of the height, it moves
by its natural instinct in the direction from which the wind blows and poisons
it by emitting its venom. And in this way it kills the young eagles through
the poisoned wind or air. When the eagle finds this out, through his own
natural instinct he takes a marvelous countermeasure. For he looks for a stone
called agate and puts it in his nest on the side from which the wind blows; by
its natural power the stone repels the poison, and thus the young eagles are
safe. In moral terms, by the eagle, who is strong in flight and of keen
eyesight, we may understand any true and good Christian, whose life and desire
should be raised high from earthly things toward heaven, so that he may say
with the Apostle, "Our homeland is in heaven." In that high homeland he must
bring forth the offspring of good works. When he has done that, the old
serpent, the devil, stirred by the poison of malice and envy, tries at once to
poison and kill the eagle's offspring by bringing some mortal sin to it. But
perhaps he cannot carry out his intention on account of the lofty life of such
a person. For Blessed Gregory says: "He had fixed his mind on high, therefore
the enemy could not break him." When the serpent perceives this, it goes and
tries to infect them with poisoned wind by holding before them human praise and
vainglory. When these enter a man's will, that is, when he does his good works
out of desire for such praise, the offspring of his good deeds will soon die as
far as their meritoriousness is concerned. What, then, is to be done? Indeed,
we should take that stone which is Christ, of whom is said in Corinthians, "the
rock was Christ," and put it between our good deeds and the wind of praise and
glory, so that we orient our deeds only toward God; then certainly our deeds
will live and will bring us the reward of eternal life, because any deed will
be weighed according to what has been its intention. Whence Bernard says:
"Your intention gives your deed its name."

As we find in treatises on the properties of things and the nature of animals, it is characteristic of the ostrich not to lay eggs until it has seen the
Pleiades rise in the sky. The Pleiades are seven stars joined very closely together in space without touching each other. After the explanation of Gregory
in his *Moral Commentary*, they symbolize the saints who have died in different
ages and therefore do not touch each other, so to speak, but who yet died with
the same intention, namely for Christ and the faith, and are thus, as it were,
joined closely together. Therefore, when we must bring forth our deeds, we
should like the ostrich direct our attention wholly to the Pleiades, that is,
to the intention and reward of the holy fathers, who are like fixed stars in
the sky, that is to say, we should attend how God has rewarded them for their
deeds, so that in imitating them we may carry out our deeds entirely for God's
sake and not for human praise and glory, after the words of the Apostle to the
Corinthians: "Whatsoever you do, do all to the glory of God."

76 bonus Christianus] verus christianus et bonus O.   **91** ventum] ventus C; venenum M.
glorie] *add* repellitur C.   **92** evenient] eveniant C.   **95** Similiter] sicud O.   **98** con-
iuncte] coniunctione C.O; *text as in source.*   **99** in] *om* O.   **102** modum] *add* ergo O.
avis] animalis O.   **103** intencionem] imitacionem C.

V.xxiii   QUIBUS ELEMOSINA COMPARATUR—1

[C]omparatur autem elemosina semini propter multa. Et primo quia ad
modum boni seminis debet terre bone et convenienti, idest bonis ⟨pau⟩peri-
bus, commendari, iuxta illud Thobie: "Vade, adduc amicos de tribu nostra
timentes Deum, ut epulentur nobiscum." Et tamen quia in moderno populo
5   tales difficulter reperiuntur, ideo faciendum est sicut facit agricola non
habens bonam terram: ipse enim iacit [semen] in terram quam habet. Sic et
nos; quia si non inveniantur boni pauperes, tamen elemosina danda est
talibus qui in nomine Christi Iesu elemosinam petunt, et hoc intendendo
sustentacionem nature et non fomentum culpe, Thobie 3: "Omni petenti te
10   tribue." Et nota quod non omnes sunt boni pauperes. Unde Beda: "Pauper,
inquit, spiritu beatus est, qui si clamet Dominus exaudit: pauper a crimine, pauper a viciis, pauper eciam in quo nichil mundi huius invenitur."
Et ideo dicit Augustinus: "Si di- [f. 156] ves, inquit, habet facultates et
in hiis non extollitur set pocius in humilitate deprimitur, inter pauperes
15   tunc numeratur. Et e contrario si pauper habet facultates nullas et tamen
ex cupiditate inordinata inflatur, talis inter divites reprobos dampnatur."
Secundo, ad modum seminis debet esse elemosina in terra non seminata
seminari, scilicet inter pauperes et non inter divites; Ecclesiastici 8:
"Noli fenerari homini diciori te, quia si feceris quasi perditum habes." Et
20   ideo dicit Bernardus: "Misericordiam de pauperibus habeatis, ut ad ⟨iudici-
um⟩ secure veniatis." Quia secundum beatum Gregorium terrena servando
amittimus, set pauperibus largiendo servamus. Et iuxta concilium Augustini
aperi manum tuam pauperi, ut tibi Christus ap⟨eri⟩at ianuam celi. Cuius
contrarium fecit dives ille qui micas panis Lazaro negavit et [ideo], quia
25   nichil propter Deum erogare voluit pauperi, nichil meruit. Unde ipse in
pena tortus misericordiam petens dicit illud Luce 16: "Pater Abraham,
miserere mei." Mox sibi responsum erat: "Fili, recordare quod recepisti

12–22 John of Freiburg, *Summa confessorum* III.   **13** Thomas Aquinas, *Summa the-ologiae* 2a–2ae, qu. 32, art. 2.   **18** *In* 20647; *Prov* 33805.   **22** As at 18.   **25–26** John of Freiburg, *Summa confessorum* II.viii.   **33** Raymundus, *Summa* II.viii.7 (p. 249).
34–35 Raymundus refers to Gratian II.1.1.27, *Non est putanda* (1:369–370).   **35–39** Augustine as quoted in Gratian II.14.5.3 (1:739).   **42** Matt. 7.5; Luke 6.42.   **42–43** Ecclus. 30.24.   **44–54** Peter Lombard, *Sent.* IV.xv.5–6 (2:330–331).   **47** Ps. 10.6.   **57** Cf. Gal. 5.26.   **61–63** Gregory, *Moralia* IX.xxv.37 (PL 75:879).   **65** Eccles. 5.15.   **68–94** On the stone *gagates* see Pliny, *Hist. naturalis* X.iv.12 and XX-XVI.xxxiv.142. The same story and moralization in *GR* 37.   **78** Phil. 3.20.   **90** 1 Cor. 10.4.   **94** Cf. Ambrose, *De officiis* I.xxx.147 (PL 16:66), quoted in Peter Lombard, *Sent.* II.xl (1:557).   **96–97** Similarly in *Convertimini*, fol. 105v.   **97–101** Gregory, *Moralia* XXIX.xxxi.67–68 (PL 76:515).   **107** 1 Cor. 10.31.

V.xxiii   TO WHAT THINGS ALMS CAN BE COMPARED—1

Alms can be compared to seed for many reasons. First, like good seed they must be entrusted to good and fitting soil, that is, to the deserving poor, according to Tobit: "Go and bring friends from our tribe that fear God, to feast with us." And since in modern society it is difficult to find such, we must do as the farmer does when he has no good soil: he casts his seed on such land as he has. So should we do, too. For if we cannot find deserving poor, then let us give our alms to those who ask for it in the name of Jesus Christ, with the intention of helping nature and not of nourishing sin, as at Tobit 3: "Give to everyone that asks you." Notice that not all the poor are deserving. Whence Bede says: "The 'poor in spirit' are blessed, those whom God hears when they call out: who are poor in crime, poor in vices, and poor in the sense that nothing of this world is found in them." And thus, Augustine says: "If a rich person has wealth but is not proud of it but rather becomes humble, then he is counted among the poor. And if, on the contrary, a poor man has no pos-sessions but swells with disorderly desires, he is condemned with the rich that are rejected."

Second, like seed, alms must be sown in land that has not been seeded before, that is to say, among the poor, not the rich; Ecclesiasticus 8: "Do not lend to a man who is richer than yourself; if you do so, count it as lost." And therefore Bernard says: "You shall have mercy from the poor, so that you may come to your judgment safely." For according to Blessed Gregory, by trying to keep earthly goods we lose them, but by giving them to the poor we keep them. And after the advice of Augustine, "open your hand to the poor so that Christ may open the door of heaven to you." The rich man of the Gospel acted contrariwise when he denied Lazarus a few crumbs of bread; and so, as he would spend nothing on the poor man for God's sake, he deserved nothing. Therefore he was tormented in pain and asked for mercy, saying the words written in Luke

bona in vita tua," etc. Unde Gregorius: "Quid est, inquit, quod Dominus
Deus de divite et paupere verbum faciens nomen pauperis dicit, nomen divi-
30   tis non dicit, nisi quod Dominus humiles novit et approbat, superbos vero
ignorat? Et ideo dicit illis: 'Amen, dico vobis nescio vos.' Dicit enim de
divite: 'Homo quidam,' etc., set de paupere ait 'Lazarus nomine,' acsi
aperte diceret: humilem et pauperem scio, set divitem nescio nec superbum."
      Et nota quod dives ille fuit in vita cupidus in adquirendo, excedens
35   in expendendo, et avarus in retinendo. Unde post mortem penas coresponden-
tes sustinuit. Quod primo erat cupidus patet [f. 156v] cum dicitur: "Homo
quidam erat dives," ita scilicet ex spoliis, rapinis, et aliis illicitis,
et pro istis sustinuit mendicitatis et extreme paupertatis inopiam, quod
bene patuit quando guttam aque miserrime petebat. Multe enim misere fuerunt
40   ille epule et aride atque ⟨s⟩alse, ubi tantum siciebat. Nec mirum, quia
fuerunt sine aqu⟨a⟩ misericordie, de qua dicitur: "Sicut aqua extinguit
ignem, sic elemosina extinguit peccatum." Quod eciam secundo erat excedens
in expendendo patet ibidem cum dicitur: "Et induebatur purpura et bisso."
Bissus enim levis et suavis est, set purpura pungens et aspera. Igitur eius
45   indumentum erat de purpura et bisso, quia interius pungebatur consciencia,
quamvis exterius delectabatur in vestura. Set revera contra istam pompam
sustinuit extreme vilitatis abiectionem, quia ut patet ibidem "sepultus
erat in inferno." In alio autem cimiterio eius sepulturam non elegit, et
ideo iustum fuit ut ibi sepeliretur; Ysaie 24: "Pepigimus fedus cum morte,
50   et cum inferno pactum fecimus." S⟨et⟩ ibi non induebatur purpura et bisso,
set vermibus et tineis, iuxta illud Ysaie 14: "Detracta est ad inferos
superbia tua; concidit cadaver tuum; subter te sternetur tinea, et operimentum tuum erit vermis." Tercio erat avarus in retinendo, quod patet ibi:
"Epulabatur cotidie splendide," hoc est per se sine societate convenienti,
55   quia nullos servorum Dei habere voluit qui omnia largitur, set miseros
peccatores. Et ideo contra delicias has tormentorum sustinuit acerbissimam
varietatem, tam per ignem quando dixit "crucior in hac flamma" quam per
famem quando guttam aque peciit et nemo illi dabat.
      Et nota quod [f. 157] merito denegata fuit illi misericordia propter
60   multa. Primo, quia ipse misericordiam in vita prius receperat iuxta illud:
"Recepisti bona in vita tua." Osee 2: "Misereor ei qui fecit misericordiam"; *Glossa*: "Indignum est enim Deum ei esse propicium qui crudelis est in
proximum." Secundo denegata fuit ei misericordia quia misericordiam non
fecerat, quia vulgariter dicitur: "Hoc facies alii quod tibi vis fieri."
65   Dicit forte aliquis huiusmodi avarus illum excusans quod tot erant ibi
mendicantes quod non sufficiebat sibi omnibus elemosinam dare; set contra
hoc dicitur in evangelio illo singulariter sic: "Erat quidam," et non
multi. Vel quod non petebat; set contra hoc dicitur "mendicus," et per
consequens petens elemosinam sicut pauper. Vel quod non cognovit eum;

16: "Father Abraham, have mercy on me." To which the reply was: "Son, remember that you received good things in your lifetime," and so forth. On this, Gregory comments: "Why is it that the Lord God, when he speaks of the rich and the poor man, mentions the poor man's name, but not that of the rich man, other than that the Lord knows and acknowledges the poor, but does not recognize the rich? Thus he says to them: 'Amen, I say I do not know you.' For he refers to the rich man as 'a certain man' and so on, but to the poor man as 'named Lazarus,' as if he were saying explicitly: the humble and poor I know, the rich and proud I do not."

Notice also that during his life this rich man was greedy to gain, too free in spending, and miserly in keeping his goods for himself. Therefore he suffered corresponding punishments after his death. That he was, first, greedy can be seen in the words "There was a certain rich man," rich, that is, from his robbing and plundering and other lawless acts; and for these he suffered the punishment of begging and of extreme poverty, as can be seen when in his misery he asked for a drop of water. For the dishes where he was suffering such thirst were miserable and dry and salty. No wonder, for they had no water of mercy, of which is written: "As water quenches fire, alms quench sin." That he was, second, too free in his spending can be seen in the same passage where it says: "He was clothed in purple and fine linen." For fine linen is light and soft, but purple is pricking and rough. Therefore his garment was of purple and fine linen because inside he was pricked by his conscience, whereas on the outside he took bodily pleasure in his clothes. But for such pomp he suffered being thrown into extreme lowness, for as can be seen in the Gospel text, "he was buried in hell." He chose not to be buried in any other cemetery, and so it was just that he should be buried in hell; Isaiah 24: "We have entered into a league with death, and we have made a covenant with hell." There he was no longer clothed in purple and fine linen but rather with worms and moths, according to the words of Isaiah 14: "Your pride is brought down to hell; your carcass is fallen down; under you the moth shall be strewed, and worms shall be your covering." Third, he was miserly in keeping things for himself. This can be seen in the words, "He feasted sumptuously every day," that is, by himself without fitting society, for he did not want to have God's servants with him to whom he could give his goods, but only wretched sinners. Against these pleasures he suffered a variety of bitter torments, both through fire, when he said "I am tormented in this flame," and through hunger, when he asked for a drop of water and no one gave him any.

And notice that he was denied mercy deservedly for several reasons. First, because he had already received mercy in his life, as seen in the words: "You did receive good things in your lifetime." Hosea 2: "I have mercy on him who has been merciful"; and the *Gloss* comments: "It is not right that God should be merciful to someone who is cruel to his neighbor." Second, he was

70   contra quod dicitur quod "Lazarus dicebatur." Vel quod non expectabat;
      contra quod dicitur ["iacebat"; tamen nimis longe et non habebat per quem
      sibi mitteret; contra quod dicitur] quod iacuit "ad ianuam." Vel quod
      trutannus erat et laborare pro prandio potuit; contra quod [dicitur] "ulce-
      ribus plenus." Vel ⟨non⟩ comedisset de cibariis [meis]; contra quod "cupi-
75   ens saturari." Vel quia nimis preciosa petebat; contra quod "micas que
      cadebant de mensa." Ex quibus patet quod nullam excusacionem habuit sibi
      misericordiam denegare; Ecclesiastici 28: "In hominem similem sibi non
      habet misericordiam." Tercio denegata fuit sibi misericordia quia tempus
      misericordie pertransierat. Tempus enim presentis vite est tempus miseri-
80   cordie; unde Psalmista: "Tempus miserendi eius quia venit tempus." Set
      tempus future vite erit tempus iusticie; Psalmista: "Cum accepero tempus,
      ego iusticias iudicabo." Quarto, quia indebito modo misericordiam peciit.
      In cuius peticione quinque verba inutilia notantur, quorum primum fuit ver-
      bum adulacionis quando dicit "Pater Abraham." Patrem vero adulando vocat
85   illum, cuius numquam antea [f. 157v] voluit esse filius. Secundum verbum
      fuit presumpcionis, ibi: "Mitte Lazarum." Magna enim presumpcio erat quod
      ab eo voluit serviri cui numquam servire dignabatur, cum tamen servicium
      non meretur habere qui illud negat impendere. "Filius enim Dei non venit
      ministrari set ministrare." Non enim peciit ut duceretur ad Lazarum, set ut
90   Lazarus duceretur ad eum. Unde Petrus Ravennatensis: "Adhuc, inquit, dives
      ille maliciam suam non deserit quod non se ad Lazarum duci postulat, set
      Lazarus ad ipsum. Optat enim Lazarum de gremio patris ad infernum, de solio
      sublimi ad abissum duci, qui tamen minimum servientem ad illum mittere
      noluit dum ad portam iacebat ulceribus putrefact⟨u⟩s." Tercium verbum fuit
95   desperacionis, quando dixit "ut intinguat." Iuste enim desperabat, et ideo
      quasi stillam misericordie postulabat. Unde Crisostomus: "Qui in preciosis
      excellit in culpa, vilissima perit in pena." Quartum fuit inpaciencie et
      murmuracionis, quando dixit "crucior in hac flamma," acsi diceret: Dominus
      dure me punit nimis. Non enim recognoscebat humiliter quod iuste culpe sue
100   debebatur, sicut latro qui ait Luce 23: "Nos, inquid, iuste digna factis
      recipimus." Quint⟨um⟩ verbum fuit carnalis affecionis, ibi: "Habeo quinque
      fratres."
         Per ista iam dicta patet salvacio humilium pauperum et reprobacio super-
      borum divitum. Et ideo iuxta Apostolum, "dum tempus habemus, operemur
105   bonum," etc., maxime ad indigentes, ut ipsi opera nostra coram summo iudice
      faciant meritoria. Et nota quod secundum legem caritatis tenentur divites
      pauperibus subvenire, sicut ipsi e contrario [f. 158] tenentur pro ipsis
      orare. Dicit enim Apostolus: "Alter alterius onera portate," etc. Et certe
      quicumque sic fecerit, perfecta caritas in illo esse probatur, "quia Deus
110   caritas est, et qui manet," etc. Et hic nota narracionem quomodo cecus
      claudum portavit ad participacionem, et econtra claudus docuit viam ceco.

denied mercy because he had not been merciful, for the common proverb says: "Do to others as you want to have it done to you." Now, someone who is similarly avaricious may want to excuse the rich man and say that there were so many beggars around that he did not have enough to give alms to all of them. But against this objection, the Gospel uses the singular and says, "there was a certain beggar," not many. Another objection is that no one was asking for alms; but against this the Gospel says, "a beggar," and consequently he was asking for alms as a poor man does. Or else, that the rich man did not know the beggar; against which the Gospel says, "he was called Lazarus." Or else, that the beggar was not waiting for alms; against which the Gospel says, "he lay." Or else, that the beggar was far away, and the rich man had no one to send alms to him; against which the Gospel says that he lay "at his gate." Or else, that the beggar was a good-for-nothing and could have worked for his food; but against this the Gospel says, "full of sores." Or else, that he would not eat of the rich man's food; but against this the Gospel says, "he desired to be filled." Or else, that he was asking for alms that were too costly; but against this the Gospel says, "the crumbs that fell from the table." From all this it can be seen that the rich man had no excuse for denying Lazarus his mercy; Ecclesiasticus 28: "He has no mercy on a man like himself." Third, he had to be denied mercy because the time for mercy had expired. For the time for mercy is the time of our present life; as the Psalmist says: "It is time to have mercy on him, for the time has come." But the time of the future life will be a time of justice; the Psalmist: "When I take a time, I shall judge justices." Fourth, because he asked for mercy in an unbecoming way. In his prayer can be found five useless expressions. The first was an expression of flattery when he said "Father Abraham." He flatteringly calls him "father" to whom he has never before wanted to be a son. The second was an expression of presumption, namely, "send Lazarus." For it was very presumptious to want to be served by him whom he was never willing to serve; for no one deserves to receive service who refuses to give it himself. "For the Son of God has not come to be ministered unto but to minister." The rich man did not ask to be led to Lazarus, but that Lazarus be led to him. On which Petrus of Ravenna comments: "The rich man still does not abandon his wickedness, insofar as he is asking, not that he be led to Lazarus, but that Lazarus be led to him. He wishes that Lazarus be sent from his father's bosom to hell, from his throne on high to the abyss, he who did not even want to send his lowliest servant to Lazarus while he was lying at his gate rotting with ulcers." The third expression was one of despair, when he said, "that he may dip." For he was then rightly despairing of mercy, and thus begged, as it were, for a drop of it. Whence Chrysostom says: "He who stood high in splendor during his sinful life will perish in the most abject punishment." The fourth expression was one of impatience and grumbling, when he said, "I am

Revera sic divites, qui sunt quasi ceci in spiritualibus, tenentur suppor-
tare pauperes, qui nichil habent unde sustentantur aut suppodiantur nisi
per elemosinas. Et econtra pauperes, qui sunt perspicui visus in spiritua-
115 libus, tenentur divites viam versus participacionem celi docere ac pro
illis Deum iugiter orare. Et sic alter alterius onus supportans adimplebit
legem Christi.

---

2 pauperibus] operibus C.W.   **5** difficulter] difficiliter O.   **8** in] *om* O.   **15** facultates
nullas] *om* O; *apparently a scribal emendation after loss of* non *before* habet (*present in*
R.M).   **20–21** iudicium] deum C.   **23** aperiat] appareant C.   **35** et] *om* O.   **36** dicitur]
add ibidem O.   **40** salse] false C.W.   **41** aqua] aque C.   **46** exterius] *add* corporaliter
O.   **50** Set] scilicet C.   **74** non] quod C.   **78** denegata] deneganda O. sibi] ei O.
80 unde] *om* O.   **93** duci] deduci O.   **94** putrefactus] putrefactis C.   **95** desperabat] *add*
de misericordia O.   **100** ait] dixit M.R; dicit W.   **101** Quintum] quinto C.   **114** ele-
mosinas] *add* suas O.

V.xxiv   QUIBUS ELEMOSINA COMPARATUR—2

Tercio comparatur elemosina semini quia sicut semen ante oculos semi-
nantis seminatur et non a tergo, sic homo ante oculos suos debet elemosinam
facere et non a tergo co[n]fidendo nimis in parentibus relictis et executo-
ribus. Tales enim ut communiter mortuos a tergo decipiunt, et cicius fre-
5 quenter domestici quam ignoti. Quia unusquisque, puta uxor, filius, filia,
neptis, nepta, et huiusmodi, sibi appropriant bona defuncti, et sic anima a

tormented in this flame," as if he were saying: the Lord is punishing me too hard. He did not humbly acknowledge that he deserved this punishment justly for his guilt, as the thief did when he said, in Luke 23, "We have justly received the due reward for our deeds." And the fifth expression was one of carnal love, namely: "I have five brothers."

In what we have said can be seen how the poor who are humble are saved, and how the rich who are proud are reproached. Therefore, following the Apostle, "let us do good while we have time," and so forth, particularly to the needy, that they may make our deeds meritorious before the highest judge. Notice that according to the law of charity the rich are held to support the poor, just as the poor on the other hand are held to pray for their benefactors. For the Apostle says: "Bear one another's burdens," and so on. Whoever does so, surely in him perfect charity is proven to reside. For, "God is charity, and he who abides in charity," and so on. Note here the story in which a blind man carried a lame one to a banquet and, in exchange, the lame man taught the blind which way to go. In the same manner, the rich, who are as it were blind in a spiritual way, are held to support the poor, who have nothing to sustain and support them except their alms. In exchange, the poor, who spiritually have a clear sight, are held to teach the rich the way to the banquet of heaven and to pray to God for them. In this manner, one carries another's burden and fulfills the law of Christ.

3–4 Tob. 2.2.   **9–10** Luke 6.30.   **13–16** Cf. Augustine, *En. in Ps. 48*, sermo 1, 3 (CC 38:552).   **19** Ecclus. 8.15.   **21–22** Gregory, *In Evangelia*, hom. 4, 5 (PL 76:1092). **26–28** Luke 16.24–25.   **28–33** Gregory, *In Evangelia*, hom. 40, 3 (PL 76:1305). **31** Matt. 25.12.   **32** Luke 16.19–20.   **36–37** Luke 16.19.   **41–42** Ecclus. 3.33. **43** Luke 16.19.   **47–48** Luke 16.22.   **49–50** Isa. 28.15.   **51–53** Isa. 14.11.   **54** Luke 16.19.   **57** Luke 16.24.   **61** Luke 16.25.   **61–62** Hos. 2.23.   **64** Cf. Whiting D.274. **67–102** Luke 16.19–28.   **77–78** Ecclus. 28.4.   **80** Ps. 101.14.   **81–82** Ps. 74.3.   **88– 89** Matt. 20.28.   **90–94** Petrus Chrysologus, *Sermo 122* 4 (CC 24A:734).   **100– 101** Luke 23.41.   **104–105** Gal. 6.10.   **108** Gal. 6.2.   **109–110** 1 John 4.16.   **110– 111** Tubach 690; add: Bromyard, "Caro," C.II.9; Brinton, sermon 26.

V.xxiv   TO WHAT THINGS ALMS CAN BE COMPARED—2

Alms can be compared to seed for a third reason: just as seed is sown in front of the sower and not at his back, so must a person give alms in front of himself and not at his back by relying too much on his relatives, successors, and executors. For these frequently deceive the dead behind their backs, and it is more often members of one's household than strangers that do so. For each and every one: wife, son, daughter, grandchildren, and so on, take the

bonis meritoriis relinquitur supervacua. Et iuste, quia noluit seipsum
iuvare quando potuit. [Et ideo vulgariter dicitur:

> Who-so woll noȝt when he may,
> He schall noȝt when he woll.

10

Ideo bene dicitur in Anglico:

> When þou þy lyfe vp-holdyste,
> þynke wan þou arte oldyste,
> And do gode at þe ȝate.
> When þou with deth vnboldeste,
> ⟨þou schall noȝt yf þou woldest,⟩
> For þan is al to late.]

15

Unde narratur de quodam in extremis laborante et amissa loquela, dixit
uxor eius ancille sue: "Heu michi quod cito morietur! Et ideo statim sume
tibi ulnam unam et dimidiam de panno lineo ad consuendum." Que respondit:
"Nimis parum est, quia homo magne stature est. Adde ergo qua[r]terium
unum." Dixit illa: "Ut quid pro putrifactione nimis consumemus?" Quod audiens infirmus resumpto spiritu cum tumultu ait: "Sic, domina, sic curtam fac
michi camisiam et brevem." Cui illa: "Tace, fatue, nescis propositum meum
quare hoc feci. Novi quod grandis [f. 158v] restat tibi via et prolixa, et
ne forte in luto te illam fedare contingat, hoc feci."

20

25

Ad idem eciam narratur veraciter de quodam divite qui pre nimia infirmitate testamentum suum ad plenum condere non v⟨a⟩lebat, set omnia bona sua
in manibus duorum sacerdotum de parochia et unius laici vicini sui reliquit. Cumque post eius mortem isti tres bona sua considerarent, videntesque
ibi vasa argentea, unus eorum dixit: "[Indigeo calice. Dentur ergo michi
hec vasa argentea,] et ego fideliter pro anima eius cantabo." Cui alter
ait: "Et ego nuper in villam hanc veni nec adhuc provisus sum. Dentur ergo
michi hec utensilia, et ego similiter pro anima eius cantabo." Ad hec
respondit laicus: "Et ego animalibus indigeo pro aratro et biga. Dentur
ergo boves michi et equi." Quo audito indignati sacerdotes dixerunt: "Tu
pro anima eius quid facies cum sis laicus? Nos sumus sacerdotes et pro
anima eius cantabimus, tu vero non sic." Quibus irrisorie [ille] dixit: "Si
vos pro anima illius cantare velitis ad hoc quod bona sua habeatis, in
nomine Domini canite, et ego tripudiabo, quia revera quicquid feceritis,
vobiscum de bonis hiis participabo." Unusquisque ergo sapiens de bonis suis
disponat in vita sua. Nota pro illa materia supra, parte 1 °. Nota illud
[quod] vulgariter dicitur in versibus:

30

35

40

dead person's possessions for themselves, and thus his soul is left quite
without good deeds that will bring him eternal reward. And this is only just,
because he would not help himself when he could. Hence the common proverb:

> He who will not when he can,
> He shall not when he will.

And it is well said in English:

> When you your life uphold,
> Reflect on when you're old,
>   And do good at your gate.
> For when in death you're weak,
> You won't get what you seek,
>   For then all is too late.

There is a story about someone who lay dying and had lost his speech. His
wife said to her maid: "Woe to me, he will soon be dead! Take now an ell and
a half of linen cloth to sew his winding-sheet." The maid replied: "That is
too little, he is a big man. Add another quarter." Then the wife said: "Why
should we sew that much for the rot?" When the sick man heard this, his
strength returned and he said in great anxiety: "O lady, do you make my shirt
so short?" And she to him: "Shut up, you fool, you don't know why I have done
this. I know that you have a long and hard way to go, and I have done this so
you won't get your shirt dirty in the mud."

On the same subject there is a true story about a rich man who was unable
to make his last will completely because of his great illness; so he left all
his goods in the hands of two priests from his parish and one layman, a neighbor of his. When these three inspected his possessions after his death and saw
that there were silver vessels, one of the priests said: "I need a chalice.
Let me have these silver vessels, and I shall faithfully sing Mass for his
soul." The second then said: "I have recently come to this parish and am as
yet unprovided. Let me have these household goods and I will likewise sing
Mass for his soul." Then the layman replied: "And I need farm animals for my
plow and cart. Let me, then, have the oxen and horses." When the priests
heard this, they grew indignant and said: "What are you going to do for this
soul, you who are a layman? We are priests and will sing for his soul. But
you cannot do that." To whom he replied with derision: "If you want to sing
for his soul so you can have his goods, in God's name sing, and I shall dance.
For whatever you do, I will have my share of his goods with you." Therefore,
whoever is wise, let him dispose of his goods while he is alive. See further

Dum vivis vivunt, moriens moriuntur amici.

45   Mors facit immemores quos vita tenebat amicos.

Post mortis morsum vertit dilectio dorsum.

Finita vita, finit amicus ita.

---

6 neptis] *add* et O.   **8–17** Et . . . late] *text from* R.   Who-so . . . woll] *See* Verses, *pp.*
191 and 205.   When . . . late] *Verse 49 in* B1.B3.Go2.L2.LC.R.W1.   **16** þou . . .
woldest] *om* R; *text from* B3.   **28** valebat] volebat C.   **31–32** Indigeo . . . argentea] *om*
C.O; *text supplied from* B1.   **38** dixit] respondit O.   **39** illius] eius O.   **42** 1] *add* c. C;
add capitulo 3 M.   **43** quod] *om* C.W.

V.xxv   QUE ELEMOSINAM IMPEDIUNT

Circa autem impedimenta elemosine est sciendum quod ipsa sicut bonum
semen ne fructificet septempliciter impeditur. Nam primo sicut granum
seminatum impeditur crescere et fructificare quando non bene cooperitur,
ventis et volucribus exponitur, revera sic elemosina sive granum boni
5   operis impeditur quando vento [f. 159] humane laudis et superbie exponitur
[et] non cooperitur terra humilitatis. Talis enim elemosina non fructificat
eo quod paleam boni operis dat Deo et granum mundo. Contra quod Matthei 5
dicitur: "Attendite, ne iusticiam vestram faciatis coram hominibus," et
Ecclesiastici 29: "Conclude elemosinam in sinu pauperis." Set certe de
10   multis dici potest illud Aggei 1: "[Seminastis] multum," idest opera multa,
"et intulisti[s] parum." Et subdit ⟨causam⟩ dicens quia "qui merces congregavit, misit eos in sacculum pertusum." Qui autem ponit denarios in sacculum pertusum, bene scit quando ponit set nescit quando perdit, et tamen °
simul ponit et perdit °. Sic qui dat elemosinam vel aliquod bonum opus
15   facit propter superbiam et mundi laudem, bene scit quando facit, set non
percipit quando per⟨dit⟩, quia simul et semel facit et perdit.
     Secundum impedimentum est econtra quando granum nimis profunde infigi-
tur in terra, ita quod germen non potest exire. Sic elemosina, in qua com-
pas⟨sio⟩ et nutrimentum proximi consistit per avariciam. Nam quando avari-
20   cia terram terre accumulat et [per] nimium illius amorem elemosin⟨a⟩, in
qua compas⟨sio⟩ et nutrimentum proximi est, non potest exire ad auxilium
pauperum, impeditur eius fructus et per consequens perdit amorem celestium.
Et nota iuxta illud Apostoli Philippensium 3: "Que michi fuerunt lucr⟨a⟩,"
[scilicet] ⟨secundum⟩ mundum, "hec arbitratus sum propter Christum detri-
25   menta"; Matthei 8: "Quid prodest homini si universum mundum lucretur,
anime," etc., quasi dicat, nichil. Unde dicit Gregorius: "Quid, inquit,

on this subject above, in part 1. And notice what is commonly said in these verses:

>Your friends will live as long as you, and with you they die;
>Your death makes those forget whom your life kept as your friends.
>After the bite of death their love turns its back on you.
>   When life is done, done is your friend as well.

18–26 Tubach 4356; add: Bromyard, "Executores," E.VIII.13.   **27–41** Perhaps Tubach 1933. The same story as here also in Bromyard, "Executores," E.VIII.8.   **42** *FM* I.xiii–xiv.   **44–45** *Prov* 6780, 15149, 4583.   **46–47** *Prov* 22027.

V.xxv   WHAT THINGS HINDER ALMSGIVING

With respect to the obstacles to almsgiving, we should know that, as good seed is prevented from bearing fruit, almsgiving is prevented in seven ways. For first, a grain that has been sown is prevented from growing and producing fruit when it is not well covered and thus exposed to wind and the birds. In the same way, alms or the grain of a good deed is stunted when it becomes exposed to the wind of human praise and of pride and is not covered with the soil of humility. Such alms do not produce fruit because they give to God the straw of a good deed, and the grain to the world. Against such people it is said in Matthew 5: "Take heed that you do no do your justice before men," and in Ecclesiasticus 29: "Shut up alms in the heart of the poor." But surely the words of Haggai 1 may be said of many people: "You have sowed much," that is, many deeds, "and brought in little." And he adds the reason for this by saying that, "he that has gathered wages put them into a bag with holes." He who puts coins in a bag with holes knows when he puts them in but does not know when he loses them, and yet he puts them in and loses them at one and the same moment. In the same way, he who gives alms or does some good deed out of pride or for worldly praise knows well when he does this but does not notice it when he loses it, for he does it and loses it at one and the same moment.

The second obstacle occurs when, in contrast, the seed is laid too deep in the soil, so that its sprout cannot come up. In this fashion, alms, in which lie compassion and nourishment for our neighbor, are hindered by avarice. For when avarice heaps earth upon earth, and because of its great love alms, in which is compassion and nourishment for our neighbor, cannot come up to help the poor, then their fruit does not develop and consequently they lose the love of heaven. Notice the words of the Apostle in Philippians 3: "The things that were gain to me," that is, things of the world, "these I have counted loss for

confert homini si per amena loca ducatur ad suspendium? Aut quid prodest
homini si per divicias ad infernum ducatur?" quasi dicat, nichil. Unde
Ecclesiastici 29 dicitur: "Perde pecuniam propter amicum et fratrem et non
30   abscondas illam sub lapide in perdicionem." Et nota quod bene dicit "perde
pecuniam," quia sicut semen quod in terra iacitur perdi videtur et tamen
postea multi- [f. 159v] plicatur, sic semen elemosine quando datur indigen-
ti videtur perdi, set postea tamen crescit in infinitum, [quia] a morte
liberat et non permittit in tenebras pertransire.
35   Tercium inpedimentum est ad modum gelu nimium constringens. Nam sicut
in grano nuper seminato nimium gelu illius calorem naturalem extinguit,
cuius caloris beneficio germinant herbe et concrescunt, sic per invidiam
per gelu signatam destruitur naturalis calor caritatis, sine qua semen boni
operis non proficit. Corinthiorum ⟨13⟩: "Si tradidero corpus meum ut ar-
40   deam, caritatem autem non habuero, nichil sum." Set quod dolendum est, hiis
diebus "superabundat malicia et refrigescit caritas multorum." Set de hac
caritate et invidia nota supra, particulis suis.
Quartum impedimentum est spinarum et veprium ac saxorum multitudo, per
que non incongrue ira designatur et odium, que in corde hominis bonum semen
45   paciencie impediunt. Unde Luce 8: "Semen cecidit inter spinas, et simul
exorte spine suffocaverunt illud." De qua nota supra particula sua.
Quintum impedimentum seminis est carencia pluvie et terre siccita⟨s⟩,
per quod indevocio et necligencia designatur quoad accidiam; Luce 8: "Aliud
cecidit supra petram," scilicet supra cor durum, "et natum aruit quia non
50   habebat humorem," scilicet devocionis. Et ideo de talibus bene dicitur Regum 19: "Facti sunt velud semen agri," etc., "arefactum est antequam veniat
ad maturitatem." Sic in proposito. Antequam opera pigri veniant ad perfectionem, boni scilicet finis, arescunt et non fructificant. Et h⟨i⟩c esset
dicendum de illis qui numquam humectant terram cordis sui per aquam contri-
55   cionis; set quere supra particulis suis.
Sextum impedimentum est fimi superflui apposicio, [f. 160] que frequenter herbas producit nocivas et germen totum necant, ad modum quo vinea
naturaliter quanto plus stercorizatur tanto cicius corrumpitur. Et bene
signat gulam, que quanto plus de cibariis superfluis attribuit carni, tanto
60   vicia anime nutrit nociva que animam necant et virtutes meritorias auferunt. Subitus autem ymber et nimis impetuose cadens arva subvertit et semen
submersit. Revera sic cibus inmoderatus animam subruit et in infernum de-
mergit. Set pluvia que desursum serotinus descendit terram humectat et
semen fructificare facit. Sic secundum Augustinum cibus in moderacione
65   sumptus animam reddit sobriam.
Septimum impedimentum est frequens conculcacio transeuncium, per quod
signatur peccatum luxurie; Ysaie: "Posuisti in terram corpus tuum et quasi
viam transeuntibus." De illo ergo impedimento Luce 8 dicitur: "Aliud ceci-

Christ"; and Matthew 8: "What does it profit a man if he gains the whole world," and so on, as if he were saying: nothing. On this, Gregory comments: "What good is it for a man to be led to the gallows through pleasant places? Or what good does it do a rich man if he is led to hell through riches?" as if he were saying, none. Therefore Ecclesiasticus 29 says: "Lose your money for your friend and your brother and do not hide it under a stone to be lost." And notice that the text says, "lose your money," for just as seed seems to be lost when it lies in the earth, and yet afterwards it multiplies, so the seed of alms seems to be lost when it is given to a needy person, and yet afterwards it grows toward infinity when it frees us from death and does not let us fall into darkness.

The third obstacle shrinks our alms as frost does. For just as in a newly sown grain too much frost extinguishes the natural heat through which herbs sprout and grow, so the natural heat of charity, without which the seed of a good deed is of no profit, is destroyed by envy, which is symbolized by the frost. Corinthians 13: "If I should deliver my body to be burned but have no charity, it profits me nothing." But it is to be lamented that in our days "iniquity abounds and the love of many grows cold." But on this love and on envy see above, in their respective sections.

The fourth obstacle is the multitude of thorns and brambles and rocks, which not unfittingly symbolize anger and hatred. These work against the good seed of patience in man's heart. Whence it is said in Luke 8: "Some seed fell among thorns, and the thorns growing up with it choked it." See further on this above in the part on wrath.

The fifth obstacle for this seed is lack of rain and drought of the soil, by which we may understand lack of devotion and the negligence of sloth; Luke 8: "Some fell upon a rock," that is, on a hard heart, "and as soon as it had sprung up, it withered away because it had no moisture," that is, of devotion. To such people, the words of Kings 19 apply well: "They became like seed of the field," etc.; "it withered before it came to maturity." In terms of our comparison: before the deeds of a lazy person reach the perfection of a good ending, they wither and bring no fruit. And here we should speak of those who never moisten the soil of their heart with the water of contrition. But look for these matters above in their respective sections.

The sixth obstacle comes from giving too much fertilizer, which often produces harmful weeds and thereby kills all the young sprouts, just as, in the way of nature, the more a vineyard is fertilized, the sooner it is ruined. This symbolizes gluttony: the more unnecessary food it gives our body, the more it feeds the harmful vices of our soul, which kill the soul and take away its meritorious virtues. A sudden rain which falls too violently ruins the fields and drowns the seed. In the same way, taking food beyond measure ruins our soul and drowns it in hell. But the rain which falls lightly in the evening

dit secus viam et conculcatum est," scilicet a transeuntibus. Et nota quod
70 quidam gratis apperiunt corda sua pravis cogitacionibus que bona opera seminata conculcant et [ad] actum malum alliciunt. Et ideo hic esset agendum
de malis cogitacionibus, set quere supra particula prima de superbia cordis.

Igitur amoveamus huiusmodi impedimenta et actui caritatis et elemosine
75 nos disponamus, atque ad ea que pertinent ad semen bonorum operum bene
seminandum oculum cordis habeamus. Et sunt multe condiciones ad bene seminandum. Prima est quod antequam iac⟨i⟩atur in terram, necessaria est diligens preparacio terre, quia si sit infructuosa, debet primo comburi igne
contricionis et postea arari vomere confessionis. Et nota: sicut enim terra
80 quando aratur, illa que profundius iacet superius evertitur, sic revera in
confessione faciendum est. Nam illa que interius latent in corde debent
superius everti et per confessionem expelli. [f. 160v] Set forte dicit
aliquis: "Non sum bonus paterfamilias, et quamvis essem, pauper sum et
aratrum non habeo nec pertinencia ad illud. Quid ergo faciam ut terra
85 cordis mei bene colatur et seminetur et in posterum bonos fructus et uberes
producat?" Revera respondeo, et quamvis fuerint [dies] festivales, tamen ad
modum illius terre pro amore Dei optimum aratrum tibi accomodabo cum pertinenciis suis. Aratrum autem in se erit bona voluntas bene operandi et
continuandi. Cuius scindibulum, scilicet *cultur* et *share*, erunt dolor et
90 contricio pro peccatis. Sex autem boves erunt quinque sensus cum bona
memoria, que terram optime arabunt, scilicet bene discuciendo per omnes
sensus cum bona memoria quid, quantum, quomodo, cur, ubi, et quare tale
peccatum commisisti, prout patet supra, capitulo 7, modo scilicet per talem
sensum, puta per visum, modo per sensum talem, puta auditum, etc. Postea
95 debent trunci et male herbe eradicari et tunc apponi alia terra fertilis et
pinguis, scilicet terra que Anglice vocatur *marle*, hoc est vera et iusta
penitencia pro tali peccato et tali. Et tunc seminemus semen bonorum operum. Et ne forte cum creverint illis inmisceant se alie herbe nocive mala-
rum cogitacionum aut, quod absit, oper⟨um⟩, debent cum furculo et hamo
100 acuto abscindi et proici, que sunt remorsus consciencie et detestacio
culpe. Postea tempore suo fructum productum metes et insimul colligando
colliges in diversas congeries per iugem continuacionem, et tunc duces
garbas ad horreum pure consciencie, in quo bladum verberabitur per frequens
exercicium penitencie. Et certe, si sic feceris, habebis in die festo de
105 terra tua in aula celesti panem leticie et potum gaudii. Ecce aratrum
spirituale cum suis pertinenciis. [f. 161] Et ne aliquid necessarium defi-
cere videatur, servus ille qui illud a tergo tenebit erit spes future
glorie, set puer cum virga stimulata, Anglice *a goode*, erit timor pene.
Iuxta ergo concilium Osee: "Seminate in veritate iusticiam, non in vanita-
110 te," idest pro humana laude, set tantum propter Deum, et tunc bonos fructus

moistens the earth and makes the seed produce fruit. Thus, according to Augustine, does food taken in measure render our soul sober.

The seventh obstacle comes when bypassers frequently trample on it, which symbolizes the sin of lechery; Isaiah: "You have laid your body on the ground and as a way for those who pass by." Of this obstacle it is said in Luke 8: "Some fell by the wayside and was trodden down," that is, by those who pass by. Notice that some people freely open their hearts to evil thoughts that trample on the good deeds that have been sown there and lure them into sinful deeds. Therefore, we now ought to deal with evil thoughts; but for this subject see above in part 1, on pride of the heart.

Let us therefore remove these obstacles and dispose ourselves for acts of charity and almsgiving and direct our heart's eye to those things which relate to sowing the seed of good deeds well. This calls for a number of different conditions. First, before the seed is cast on the soil, the latter must be carefully prepared; if it is sterile, it must first be burned with the fire of contrition and then be plowed with the plowshare of confession. And notice: when the earth is plowed, what lies deeper is thrown up on top. We must do likewise in confession, for what is hidden at the bottom of one's heart must be turned up and cast out through confession. Now, perhaps someone will say: "I am not a good householder, and even if I were, I am poor and have neither plow nor what goes with it. What then shall I do to cultivate the soil of my heart so that it will receive good seed and later produce a good and rich harvest?" To him I reply: Even if it were a feast day, for the love of God I will make you a superb plow with all that goes with it for this particular soil. The plow itself will be your goodwill to work well and to persevere. Its blade, that is, *coulter* and *share*, will be the grief and contrition for your sins. The six oxen will be your five senses plus your memory, which are to plow your soil well, namely by examining all your senses and your memory as to what, how much, in what way, why, where, and with what help you have committed a sin, as I have explained earlier, in chapter 7—now with one sense, perhaps your sight, then with another, perhaps you hearing, and so forth. Next you must pull out stubs and bad weeds and put on it some soil that is rich and fertile, called *marl* in English, which is true and just penance for this and that sin. And then let us sow the seed of good works. But that no harmful weeds of evil thoughts or—God help us—evil deeds may grow up intermingled with them, those must be cut out with a hoe and a sharp harrow—that is, remorse of conscience and hatred of sin—and be thrown away. Then, when the right time has come, you will reap the harvest and bind it in sheaves by persevering in good work, and you will take the sheaves to the barn of good conscience where the crop is threshed in frequent penitential exercises. And if you do all this, you will certainly, on the feast day in the hall of heaven, have the bread of gladness and the drink of joy from your land. This, then, is the spiritual plow with

colligetis, aliter vero non. Quia si elemosinas feceris pro laude et gloria
mundana, sicut faciunt ypocrite ambiciosi, "amen dico tibi recepisti mercedem tuam." Et ideo facienda est tantum propter Christum, et hoc voluntarie,
quia dicitur:

115   Non doni cultum set dantis respice vultum,

quia "hillarem datorem diligit Deus."
    Fertur enim in *Gestis Romanorum* quod quidam predives palacium constru-
ere volens de sub terra in quodam sarcophago cuiusdam antiquitus sepulti
iuxta ossa sua quatuor anulos invenit sic inscriptos. Nam in primo scribe-
120   batur sic:

    Quod expendi habui.

In ⟨secundo⟩:

    Quod donavi habeo.

In ⟨tercio⟩:

125   Quod servavi perdidi.

In quarto:

    Quod negavi punio.

    [þat Y spende þat Y had.
    þat Y ȝeue þat Y haue.
130   þat Y kepte ys lost fro myne.
    For ⟨þat⟩ I warnyt now Y pyne.]

Moraliter autem loquendo, prima particula est de se satis plana, scilicet
"quod expendi habui." Nam illa que in vita expendi circa victum et vestitum
et huiusmodi, ex illis solacium et beneficium tunc habui. Set pro secunda
135   circumscripcione, ⟨que est "quod donavi habeo," in quadam glossa Ad Galatas
9 dicitur: "Dare, inquit, elemosinam non est perdere set ad tempus seminare, ut in futuro plus habeatur." Unde Gregorius 18 *Moralium*: "S⟨umm⟩e,
inquit, expedit elemosinam dare, nam terrena omnia que servando omittimus,
largiendo servamus; patrimonium enim retentum perditur, set permanet ero-
140   gatum. Diu autem cum rebus nostris esse non possumus, quia aut nos illas
moriendo deseruimus aut ille nos viventes deserunt pereundo. Agendum est
ergo (dicit Gregorius) nobis ut illas absolute perituras modo pereuntem

all that goes with it. And lest anything necessary may seem to be lacking, the servant who will have it behind him is the hope of future glory. But the boy with the rod to drive the oxen—the *goad* in English—will be the fear of punishment. After the counsel of Hosea, "sow justice in truth and not in vanity," that is, not for human praise but only for God's sake, and then you will gather a good harvest, not otherwise. For if you have given alms for the sake of human praise and worldly glory, as ambitious hypocrites do, "Amen, I say to you, you have received your reward." Therefore, alms must be given for Christ's sake alone, and with goodwill, for it is said:

Do not regard the worth of a gift but the giver's face,

because "God loves a cheerful giver."

The Deeds of the Romans tells a story about a very rich man who, when he wanted to build a palace, found in the ground in a sarcophagus of someone who had been buried there a long time before, besides his bones, four rings with the following inscriptions. On the first was written: "What I have spent I have had." On the second: "What I have given I have." On the third: "What I have kept I have lost." And on the fourth: "What I refused I now suffer for." In English:

þat Y spende þat Y had . . .

In moral terms, the first inscription, namely "What I have spent I have had," is fairly clear of itself. For what I have spent on food and clothes and such during my life, from that I have had my comfort and benefit. But regarding the second inscription, namely "What I have given I have," a gloss on Galatians 9 explains: "When we give alms, we do not lose anything but sow in time, so that we may gain from it in the future." Whence Gregory says in book 18 of his *Moral Commentary*: "To give alms is of the greatest advantage, for any earthly goods that we might lose by trying to keep, we keep by giving them away; an inheritance that is held on to is lost, but if it is distributed, it remains ours. We cannot always be with our possessions, for either we leave them when we die, or they leave us by perishing while we are still alive. We should then act in a way by which we compel these possessions—which we will lose either way—to yield more than such transitory reward." Regarding the third inscription, which was, "What I have kept I have lost," Chrysostom comments on Matthew: "If you keep your riches, you have already lost them, for they are of no avail to your salvation but rather help to condemn you forever." Therefore Blessed Augustine says in Sermon 5 of his work *On the Lord's Words*: "If you have money, spend it. By spending your money you increase justice." And he continues: "If you praise a man for selling lead and buying gold, why do you not praise one who changes money into justice?" And regarding the fourth

cogamus transire mercedem."⟩ Pro tercia vero circumscripcione, ⟨scilicet
"quod servavi perdidi," ait Crisostomus super Mattheum: "Si servas, inquit,
145   divicias iam perdidisti, quia tibi non proficient ad usum salutis, set ad
interitum dampnacionis." Et ideo beatus Augustinus *De verbis Domini* sermone
5 ait: "Si habes pecuniam, eroga. Erogando pecuniam auges iusticiam." Et
sequitur: "Si illum laudas qui vendidit plumbum et adquirit aurum, quare
non laudas eum qui pecuniam mutat in iusticiam?"⟩ [f. 161v] Pro quarta
150   scriptura, que fuit "quod negavi punio," est sentencia Salvatoris quod
homines qui in hac vita negant opera pietatis et misericordie quod in
tremendo iudicio punientur illius voce terribili: "Ite, maledicti, in ignem
eternum." Quid, ergo, credis eveniet illis qui non [tantum] elemosinam
negan⟨t⟩ pauperibus, verum eciam pro suis vanitatibus et transitoriis in
155   victu et vestitu, equitatu, ac eciam pro edificiis construendis et cetera
huiusmodi habendis spoliant pauperes? quasi dicat: vox predicta et ultra,
si posset. Et ideo tales redarguendo Hugo de Sancto Victore: "Ampla, inquit, sibi reges edificant palacia, set domus eorum sepulcra illorum in
eternum. Turres firmas in summis moncium locant, vallem aggere, muro cin-
160   gunt, [montes] non suis manibus set pauperum spoliis transferunt, solo enim
imperio circumductis fluminibus hostium vires excludunt. Nichil tamen horum
morti contradicere potest." Et sequitur: "Episcopi eciam domos non impares
ecclesiis magnitudine construunt, depictos delectantur [f. 162] thalamos
habere, vestiunt ibi ymagines preciosis ⟨co⟩lorum indumentis, et pauper
165   sine vestibus incedit ac vacuo ventre clamat ad hostium. O, inquit, mira
delectacio Troiana! Gestat mira paries pictus purpura et auro vestitos, et
Christianis negantur veteres panni!" Et sequitur: "Grecorum exercitui dantur arma, victori clipeus aureus datur auro splendens, pauperi autem ad
hostium clamanti non porrigitur panis. Si verum fatear (dicit ipse), spoli-
170   antur sepe pauperes ut vestiantur lapides et lingna." Hec ille. Et ecce ad
huiusmodi non confert Deus divicias, set secundum beatum Gregorium "omnipotens Dominus largiendo terrena suadet celestia." Et ideo in persona Christi
dicit Augustinus: "Da michi ex eo quod dedi tibi de meo. Quero [da,] et
reddam. [Habuisti,] inquit, me largitorem; me ergo facito debitorem." Unde
175   quidam:

> Fac quod Christus amat cum pauper ad hostia clamat:
> Impartire sibi quod dedit ante tibi.

Ipse enim est minimus in nomine Christi petens. Set Christus in Mattheo:
"Quod uni ex minimis meis fecistis, michi fecistis," etc.

---

10 Seminastis] *om with blank* C.M; *om* W.   **11** intulistis] intulisti C.W.   causam] tamen
C.   **12** eos] eas R.M; *om* W.   **13** tamen] *add* quod C.   **14** perdit] *add* bene scit C.   vel]
aut O.   **16** perdit] perdidit C.   **18–19** compassio] compascitur C.   **20** elemosina] elemosinam C.   **21** compassio] compascitur C.   **23** lucra] lucri C.   **24** secundum] sicud

inscription, which read "What I refused I now suffer for," we have the declara-
tion of our Savior that people who in this life refuse deeds of compassion and
mercy will be punished at the fearful judgment by his awesome words: "Go, you
cursed, into everlasting fire." What, then, do you think will happen to those
who not merely refuse giving alms to the poor but in fact rob the poor in order
to get their transitory pleasures in food, clothing, horses, buildings, and the
like? Surely they will hear the words just quoted, and what follows them. In
reproaching such people Hugh of Saint Victor says: "Kings build large palaces
for themselves, but their houses are tombs forever. They put strong towers on
hilltops; they surround them with moat, rampart, and wall; they transfer mountains not with their hands but with the spoils of the poor, for by their command alone they have water flow around them to ward off the troops of enemies.
And yet, nothing of all this can withhold death." And Hugh continues: "Bishops, too, build themselves houses that are not unlike churches in size. They
love to have painted beds. They dress up images in precious and colorful
garments. And the poor man goes without clothes and cries at their gate with
an empty stomach. Oh wonderful Trojan delight! Their splendid walls have
pictures clothed in purple and gold, and Christian people are denied even some
old rags!" And he continues: "The Greek army is given arms, the victor a
golden shield shining with gold. But the poor man who cries at the gate does
not get a rag. To tell the truth, their poor are often robbed so that stone
and wood may be dressed up." But lo, God does not grant riches for such use,
but according to Blessed Gregory, "the Almighty Lord grants earthly goods to
draw us to heavenly ones." And therefore Augustine says in the person of
Christ: "Give me, for I have given you from what is mine. Give, I ask, and I
shall give it back to you. You have had me as your giver; let me therefore
become your debtor." Whence someone says:

> Do what Christ will love when the poor man cries at your door:
> Share with him what he has earlier shared with you.

For this is "the least one" who asks in Christ's name, as Christ says in
Matthew: "What you did to one of the least of my brethren, you did to me."

---

8 Matt. 6.1.   **9** Ecclus. 29.15.   **10–12** Hag. 1.6.   **23–25** Phil. 3.7.   **25–26** Matt.
16.26.   **29–30** Ecclus. 29.13.   **39–40** 1 Cor. 13.3.   **41** Cf. Matt. 24.12.   **42** *FM*
III.vi–xxiii and i–v.   **45–46** Luke 8.7.   **46** *FM* II.ii–iii.   **48–50** Luke 8.6.   **51–52** 2
Kings 19.26.   **55** *FM* V.vii–x.   **67–68** Isa. 51.23.   **68–69** Luke 8.5.   **72–73** *FM*
I.iii.   **93** *FM* V.xii.   **109–110** Hos. 10.12.   **112–113** Cf. Matt. 6.2, etc.   **115** *Prov*
17520; cf. 17442.   **116** 2 Cor. 9.7.   **117–131** Tubach 4175; see also *Verses*, pp. 29–32.
Further occurrences in Holcot, sermon 64; Dublin, Trinity College MSS 347, fol. 405v,
and 667, fol. 64v.   **137–143** Gregory, *Moralia* XVIII.xviii.28 (PL 76:52).   **144–
146** Cf. Ps.-Chrysostom, *Opus imperfectum*, hom. 15 (PG 56:719–720).   **147–149** Augustine, *Sermo 61* iii.3 and iv.4 (PL 38:410).   **152–153** Matt. 25.41.   **157–170** Hugh of
Saint Victor, *De claustro anime* I.1 (PL 176:1019).   **171–172** Gregory, *In Evangelia*,

C.O. **26** dicit] *om* O. **28** homini] diviti O. **30** abscondas] abscondes O. **38** sig-
natam] designatam O. **39** 13] 8 C.W. meum] *add* ita O. **47** siccitas] siccitatis C.O.
48 designatur] intelligitur O. **53** hic] hoc C.R.W. **68** illo] isto O. **71** ad] *om* C.W.
76–77 ad . . . seminandum] *om* O. **77** iaciatur] iaceatur C. **87** illius] istius O.
94 sensum(2)] *om* O. **96** scilicet . . . Anglice] vulgariter M; anglice R.W. **98** inmis-
ceant] intermisceant O. **99** operum] opera C. **117** enim] autem O. **122** in secundo] in
tercio C; *om* O. **124** in tercio] in secundo C; *om* O. **126** in quarto] *om* O. **128–**
131 þat . . . pyne] *text from R. Verse 50, in* B1.B3.C.Co.E.Go2.Jo.L2.LC.R.Sp.W1.
131 þat] *om* R. **135–149** que . . . iusticiam] C *reverses the second and third inscrip-*
tions, as above. **137** Summe] sine C.R.W. **139–140** erogatum] irrogatum O.
154 negant] negantes C. **164** colorum] telorum C. **166** mira] *om* O. **175** quidam] *add*
ait sic O.

V.xxvi QUE BONA PER ELEMOSINAM EVENIUNT

[R]estat modo ultimo videre de effectu elemosine, scilicet que bona
per illam eveniunt. Et est sciendum secundum quod superius in eius diffinicione dicebatur: ipsa elemosina dimittit peccata, auget presencia, separat
a diabolo, et sociat angelis. Et ideo iuxta concilium Luce 14: "Cum facis
5 cenam, noli vocare amicos," etc., "set voca pauperes et debiles, et beatus
eris." Narratur de quodam episcopo nomine Odone, quomodo in caristia docuit
dare elemosinam, promittens sic facientibus centuplum accepturis. Quod cum
audisset quidam [f. 162v] devotus et dives credens dictis suis, tradidit
viginti libras pauperibus distribuendum et cirographum pro promissis acce-
10 pit. Cum ergo cito post eius mortem venisset uxor sua cum liberis ad Odonem
episcopum cum dicto cirographo debitum ⟨viri petens⟩, duxit illos ad eius
monumentum, et facta oracione cum illud apperuisset, ecce defunctus iacuit
vultu placido acsi dormisset, quandam cartam pulcherrimam in manu tenens
sigillo signatam aureo. Quam cum de manu sua statim accipere non possent,
15 facta iterum oracione acceptam cartam ap⟨e⟩ruerunt, quam litteris aureis
sic conscriptam invenerunt: "Sciant presentes et futuri quod ego talis pro
pecunia quam pro disposicione episcopi Odonis in usus pauperum distribui
centuplum ante mortem meam accepi in hoc seculo, scilicet in plena remissione
peccatorum meorum, et secundum eius promissum vitam eternam in futuro."
20 Sic eciam patet de elemosina quid sit et de quibus facienda, quibus
comparatur et quibus eroganda, que illam impediunt et que bona inde eveniunt. Et ideo hic nota narraciones et alia et dilata ut placet. Et nota quod
plura que dicta sunt superius de avaricia possunt hic allegari. Unde h⟨e⟩c
iam de elemosina et eius partibus ad presens dicta sufficiunt.

11 viri petens] vi repetens C. **15** acceptam] accepta O. aperuerunt] apparuerunt C.
17 disposicione] *add* domini O. **22** et(3)] *om* O. **23** hec] hic C.

hom. 32, 6 (PL 76:1237).   **173–174** Thus also in Peraldus, *Summa vitiorum* IV.iv.7.
176–177 *Prov* 8659.   **179** Matt. 25.40.

V.xxvi   WHAT GOOD EFFECTS COME FROM ALMSGIVING

In the last place we must now speak of the effect of almsgiving, that is,
the good results that come from it. And according to what was said earlier
when we discussed its definition, we must know that almsgiving forgives sins,
increases our current merits, separates us from the devil, and joins us with
the angels. Therefore, after the counsel of Luke 14, "when you make a dinner,
do not call your friends," etc., "but call the poor and the weak, and you shall
be blessed." There is a story about a Bishop Odo, how during a famine he
taught to give alms, promising to all who did so that they would receive a
hundredfold reward. A certain pious rich man heard this and believed the
bishop's words. He gave twenty pounds for distribution among the poor and
received a promissory note for it. When he died shortly afterwards, his wife
and children went to Bishop Odo with this promissory note and asked for what
he owed to her husband. The bishop took her to her husband's grave and, after
saying a prayer, opened it. There was the dead man lying, with a peaceful face
as if asleep, and held a beautiful charter in his hand sealed with a golden
seal. As they could not at once take it out of his hand, they prayed again,
then took the charter and opened it. In it they found the following written
with gold letters: "Let all present and future know that for the money I gave
to Bishop Odo to be distributed for the use of the poor I have received a
hundredfold return before my death in this world, namely the full remission of
my sins, and in the future, as he had promised, eternal life."

Thus, then, it is manifest what almsgiving is, from what we should give alms,
to what things these can be compared, to whom they should be given, what
obstacles prevent them, and what their good effects are. You may tell here
other pious tales and things and amplify them if you wish. Notice also that
many things I said earlier about avarice can be cited here as well. But this
much will be enough about almsgiving and its aspects.

4–6 Luke 14.12–14.   **6–19** Tubach 176; add: Bromyard, "Elemosine," E.III.48.

V.xxvii   DE PUGNA CONTRA MUNDUM

[D]icto aliqualiter contra vicium accidie de occupacione spirituali
quantum consistit in penitencia et eius partibus, scilicet in contricione,
confessione, et satisfactione, et illarum partibus, ulterius de illa occupacione est dicendum quantum consistit in pugna contra tres hostes princi-
5   pales, qui sunt mundus, caro, et diabolus, quos oportet debellare per
fidem, spem, et caritatem, similiter per prudenciam, [f. 163] temperanciam,
et fortitudinem. Unde de istis primo est videndum quomodo per dictos hostes
debellamur, secundo quomodo per dictas virtutes eis resistere possumus,
sternere, et vincere; cuius processus reddendo singula singulis clarius
10 legenti apparebit.

Est ergo advertendum, secundum beatum Gregorium, quod isti tres hostes
hoc modo nos infestant. Nam primo mundus et caro nituntur [ad] peccata allicere, set diabolus cum illis totaliter nititur subvertere. Caro autem
querit suavia, mundus preparat ligna, diabolus mittit incendia. Caro ligat
15 ad voluptatem, mundus impellit ad vanitatem, diabolus trahit ad iniquitatem. Caro eciam est hostis domesticus suadens suavia, quia luxuriam et voluptatem, per quas deprimit nos in⟨f⟩ra nos. Mundus est hostis sophisticus
suadens inania, quia avariciam et cupiditatem, cum quibus trahit nos extra
nos. Set diabolus est hostis occultus suadens pessima, quia superbiam,
20 iram, et invidiam, cum quibus erigit nos supra nos. Et tamen, secundum
Bernardum, hoc modo mercedem retribuunt suis servitoribus, quia caro dat
suis quasi momentaneam voluptatem, mundus transitoriam dignitatem, set diabolus eternalem captivitatem. Tot igitur et tantis inimicis nos obpugnanti-
bus est viriliter resistendum et constanter debellandum, ut victoriam
25 habeamus.

[C]irca autem mundi adversitatem est sciendum quod ipsa nos multipliciter impugnat, et primo undique pericula opponens. Unde propter eius
inquietudinem et amaritudinem non inmerito mari comparatur. Unde Crisostomus omelia 33 in *Inperfecto*: "Mare, inquit, mundus est ubi aque salse
30 s⟨unt⟩ propter iniquitates, ubi dominantur potestates et diversa pericula
spirituum certamina." Sicut enim assidua est in [f. 163v] mari tempestas,
sic in mundo, nam alterutrum se comedunt, sicut in mari pisses forciores
devorant infirmiores; Abacuc 1: "Facies hominis quasi pissis maris." De
isto ergo mari ait beatus Ambrosius in sermone confessoris communi dicens:
35 "Navigantibus enim nobis per hoc mare magnum et spaciosum, in quo reptilia
quorum non est numerus," etc., usque "agone luctantur." In quo quidem mari
navis principalis est cupiditas, cui adherent tria genera scapharum, scilicet mercatorum, piscatorum, et piratarum. In prima enim navigant mercatores
cupidi, qui nituntur alios decipere emendo et vendendo. In secunda autem
40 navigant homines curiales, scilicet qui morantur in curiis istorum magnorum
nec fluctuantes piscari desistunt nunc per dona, nunc per promissa ad bona

V.xxvii   THE BATTLE WITH THE WORLD

After we have spoken about spiritual activity, the virtue opposed to the
vice of sloth, insofar as it consists in penance and its parts, that is, contrition, confession, and satisfaction, with their respective divisions, we must
now further treat of that spiritual activity which consists in the battle
against our three main enemies, that is, the world, the flesh, and the devil,
which we must combat with faith, hope, and charity, and likewise with prudence,
temperance, and fortitude. Concerning this matter, we must first investigate
how we are being attacked by these three enemies, and second how we may withstand, prostrate, and defeat them through the said virtues. The development of
this matter, matching the single enemies with the respective virtues, will
become clear as you read on.

We must, then, realize that according to Blessed Gregory these three
enemies beset us in the following way. First, the world and the flesh try to
lure us to sin, but the devil tries to ruin us completely with their help. For
the flesh seeks what is soft, the world prepares the wood, and the devil brings
fire to it. The flesh binds us to pleasure, the world pushes us to vanities,
and the devil draws us to iniquity. Further, the flesh is our domestic foe who
persuades us to seek softness, by lechery and carnal pleasure, by which it
pushes us below ourselves. The world is a sophist, a tricky foe who persuades
us to seek vain things, by avarice and covetousness, with which he draws us
outside ourselves. But the devil is a secret enemy who draws us to the worst,
namely to pride, wrath, and envy, with which he lifts us above ourselves. And
yet, according to Bernard, these enemies give their servants their reward in
the same way, for the flesh gives its followers, as it were, a momentary
pleasure; the world, transitory rank and worthiness; but the devil, eternal
capitivity. These many and great enemies who beset us must be opposed with
manly resistance and fought with constancy, so that we may gain the victory.

With respect to the adversity of the world, we must know that it besets us
in many ways, and first by setting up dangers for us everywhere. Therefore it
is fittingly compared to the sea, because of its restlessness and bitterness. In
Homily 33 of his *Imperfect Work*, Chrysostom says: "The world is a sea whose
waters are salty because of its injustices; in it power prevails, and many
dangers, and struggle among spirits." As in the sea, so in this world storms
are frequent; and one eats another, as in the sea the stronger fish devour the
weaker ones; Habakkuk 1: "The face of man is like the fish of the sea." Of
this sea Blessed Ambrose speaks in his common sermon for a confessor as follows: "As we sail on this large and wide sea, in which there are numerous
reptiles," and so on, to "they fight in their battle." The major ship in this
sea is covetousness, accompanied by three kinds of boats, namely those of
merchants, fishermen, and pirates. In the first sail greedy merchants, who try
to cheat others in their buying and selling. In the second sail courtiers,

temporalia ascendere. In tercia vero navigant magni domini raptores et
iniusti, qui simplices spoliant et eorum bona asportant. In quibus eciam
navibus sunt tria genera recium, quorum unum est in quo portantur palee,
45   cum [quo] piscantur qui non cessant ista vana et transitoria, que iuste
paleis comparantur, adquirere tam avide. Aliud genus est per quod capiuntur
avicule, et in illo aucupant qui in altum per inanem gloriam nituntur
ascendere et tamquam avolare. Tercium genus est per quod capiuntur pisses,
cum [quo] piscantur luxuriosi qui pisses tam magnos quam parvos, scilicet
50   uxores, viduas, virgines, et coniugatas, destruunt et confundunt. Quorum
navium gubernatores sunt huiusmodi operatores.

Est eciam mundus forum deceptorium. Nam sicut proprium est fori ut in
eo omnia vendantur et emantur, ubi eciam vendentes et ementes se invicem
[f. 164] decipiant, sic in mundo ostenduntur diversa concupiscibilia vena-
55   lia, quorum mercatores fere non est qui faciat bonum—"non est usque ad
unum," iuxta Psalmum. Item sicut locus fori sive nundinarum modo est popu-
losus, multimodis bonis refertus, gaudiosus, et gloriosus, et in modico cum
quilibet redit ad propria, quidam cum lucro, quidam cum dampno, confestim
fit quasi locus desertus, turpis, fedus, et contemptuosus—revera sic est
60   de mundo. Unde illud fit Sapiencie 5: "Quid nobis profuit superbia aut
diviciarum iactancia? Quid inde nobis contulerunt? Omnia transierunt velud
umbra, et tanquam navis que pertransit aquam fluctuantem, ci[to ut] preter-
ierit, non [videtur]."

Et ideo, ut videtur, bene tercio comparari potest diluvio generali
65   tempore Noe, quod totum mundum occupavit et submersit nisi quos in archam
Noe recepit. Revera sic mundi cupiditas et miseria omnes quasi submersit,
quia ut habetur Ieremie 6, "a minori usque ad maiorem omnes avaricie student, et a propheta usque ad sacerdotem omnes faciunt dolum." Nec est qui
eius diluvium potest evadere nisi submergatur aut perimatur, nisi quis ad
70   archam crucis Christi ligneam voluerit confugere; Sapiencie 10: "Cum aqua
deleret terram, sanavit sapiencia, per contemptibilem lignum iustum guber-
nans." Expone ideo ut ait Crisostomus: "Maria fuit desponsata fabro ligna-
rio, quoniam Christus, sponsus Ecclesie, per lignum crucis salutem omnium
operaturus erat in medio terre." Unde illud Proverbiorum capitulo 3: "Lig-
75   num vite est; qui apprehenderit, beatus."

Quod autem lignum crucis convenienter comparatur arche Noe, et e contrario, satis declarat Augustinus De civitate Dei, capitulo 26, dicens:
"Iam vero, [inquit,] quod Noe homini iusto et, sicut [f. 164v] de illo
veridica scriptura loquitur, in sua generacione perfect⟨o⟩—non utique
80   sicut proficiendi sunt cives civitatis Dei in illa inmortalitate qua equa-
buntur angelis Dei, set sicut esse possunt in hac peregrinacione perfecti—
imperat [Deus] ut archam, in qua cum suis, cum uxore, filiis, et nuribus,
et cum animalibus que ad illum ex precepto Dei in archam ingressa sunt,

those who reside in the courts of the great, who while they float on this sea never stop fishing for temporal goods and higher positions, now with gifts and now with promises. In the third boat sail great lords who oppress and are unjust, who rob the lower classes and carry off their goods. In these ships are three kinds of nets. One is the kind in which one carries straw; this is used by those who never cease from eagerly grabbing at vain and transitory goods, which can rightly be compared to straw. Another kind is that with which one catches birds; this is used by people who want to rise up high in vainglory and fly like birds. And the third kind is that with which one catches fish; it is used by lechers, who catch and kill big fish and little fish, that is to say, wives, widows, virgins, and betrothed. People who act this way are the pilots of these ships.

This world is likewise a treacherous marketplace. It is in the nature of a marketplace that everything is sold and bought there and that the sellers and buyers cheat each other; in the same way, in this world many desirable things are offered for sale, among whose merchants there is hardly one who does good — "no, not one," as the Psalm says. Also, as a marketplace or a fair is now filled with people, stocked with all sorts of goods, joyful, and magnificent, and in a little while everyone goes back to his home, one with profit, another with loss, and the place at once becomes deserted, ugly, dirty, and contemptible. Just so does it happen with the world. Whence the words of Wisdom 5: "What has pride profited us, or what advantage has the boasting of riches brought us? All those things are passed away like a shadow, and as a ship that passes through the waves; as soon as it is gone by, it is no longer seen."

And so, I believe, the world can thirdly be compared to the universal flood of Noah's time, which covered the whole world and drowned everything except those whom Noah had taken into his ark. Thus has the world's covetousness and misery drowned everyone, for as we read in Jeremiah 6, "from the least to the greatest, all are given to covetousness; from the prophet to the priest, all practice deceit." There is none who can escape the world's flood without drowning or perishing except he who will flee to the wooden ark of Christ's cross; Wisdom 10: "When water destroyed the earth, wisdom healed it again, directing the course of the just by contemptible wood." Explain this after Chrysostom: "Mary was espoused to a carpenter, because Christ, the spouse of his Church, had, through the wood of the cross, worked salvation for all in the midst of the earth." Hence the words of Proverbs 3: "It is the tree of life; he that retains it is blessed."

That the wood of the cross can be fittingly compared to Noah's ark, and vice-versa, Augustine shows clearly in chapter 26 of *The City of God*, where he says: "Now God commands that Noah be saved from the vast flood by the ark in which he entered at the Lord's command with his family, his wife and sons and daughters-in-law, Noah, a just man and, as Scripture says of him truthfully,

liberaretur a diluvii vastitate. Procul dubio figura est peregrinantis in
85 hoc seculo civitatis Dei, hoc est Ecclesie, que fuit salva per lignum in
quo pependit mediator Dei et hominum, homo Christus Iesus. Nam et mensure
ipsius longitudinis, latitudinis, et altitudinis signant corpus humanum, in
cuius veritate ad homines prenunciatus est venturus et venit." Et sequitur:
"Humani corporis quippe longitudo a vertice usque ad vestigia sexies tantum
90 habet quam latitudo, que est ab uno latere usque ad alterum latus, et
decies tantum quam altitudo, cuius altitudinis mensura est in latere a
dorso usque ad ventrem, velud si iacentem hominem meciaris suppinum se[u]
pronum, sexies tantum longius est a capite usque ad pedes quam latus a
dextra in sinistram vel e contrario, et decies quam altus a terra. Unde
95 facta est archa trecentorum in longitudine cubitorum et quinquaginta in
latitudine et triginta in altitudine, ad modum corporis humani. Et quod
ostium in latere accepit, profecto est illud vulnus quando latus crucifixi
lancea perforatum est. Hac quippe a⟨d⟩ illum venientes ingrediuntur, quia
inde sacramenta manarunt, quibus credentes muniuntur. Et quod de lignis
100 quadratis fieri iubetur undique stabilem vitam sanctorum signat, que quocumque verteris quadrum stabit," vel supple: [f. 165] signare satis congrue
potest quatuor partes ligni crucis. Et sequitur: "Quoniam non solum in
inferioribus mansiones habere archam voluit verum eciam in superioribus, et
hec dixit bicamerata. Et in superioribus superiorum, et hec appellavit
105 tricamerata, vel ab ymo versus sursum tria construeret habitacula. Possunt
hec intelligi tria illa que commendat Apostolus, que sunt fides, spes, et
caritas." Hec Augustinus. Quia vero parte supra satis tractatur de mundo,
ideo hic causa brevitatis leviter transio.

---

3 illa] ista O.   9 sternere] prosternere O.   17 infra] intra C.   30 sunt] scilicet C.R.
42 temporalia] add et dignitates O.   45 cum quo] cum C; et cum ⟨isto avari⟩ M; et cum
W.   47 aucupant] occupant ⟨se superbi⟩ M; aucupantur R.   48 tamquam] add aves
R.W.   60 fit] om O.   62–63 et . . . videtur] the quotation appears in different abbreviated forms O.   79 perfecto] perfecta C.   87 ipsius] ipse M.W; ipsa (mensura) R.   al-
titudinis] add eius O.   98 ad] ac C.   103] archa O.   105 construeret habitacula] tercia
consurgeret habitacio O.

V.xxviii   DE FIDE

[C]ontra ergo istum hostem, scilicet mundum, et eius insultum audacter
iam primo accedit fides ut illum ⟨expugnet⟩ et devincat, iuxta illud Iohannis canonica sua prima, capitulo 5: "Hec est victoria que vincit mundum,

perfect in his generation—not, however, with that perfection with which the citizens of the city of God are to progress in that immortality in which they are like the angels, but rather insofar as they can be perfect in this present pilgrimage. Beyond doubt, for those who make their pilgrimage in this world this is a prefiguration of the city of God, that is, the Church, who was saved by the wood on which the mediator between God and men hung, the man Jesus Christ. For the measurements of its length and width and height stand for the human body, as he was in truth foretold to come and has come." Then Augustine continues: "The length of a man's body from his head to his footsoles is six times his width, measured from one side to the other, and ten times his depth, measured on the side from his back to his stomach. If you measure a man stretched out on the ground, whether he is on his back or his stomach, his length from head to feet is six times the distance from his right side to his left or vice-versa, and ten times his elevation from the ground. For this reason, the ark was built at a length of three hundred cubits, a width of fifty, and a depth of thirty, just like the human body. The door in its side surely is that wound which the side of the Crucified received when it was pierced with a lance. Through it those enter who come to it, for from it the sacraments flowed forth by which the faithful are cleansed. And that it was ordered to be built from squared beams on all sides symbolizes the stable life of the saints, for wherever you turn a cube, it will stand firm," or add: it may fittingly symbolize the four parts of the wood of the cross. And Augustine continues: "He wanted the ark to have rooms not only on its lower but also on its upper level, and these he called 'second stories'; and further on an even higher level, which he called 'third stories,' so that Noah was to build three levels of rooms from the bottom to the top. By this we may understand the triad which the Apostle recommends, namely faith, hope, and charity." Since I have dealt with the world further in an earlier part, I now move on for the sake of brevity.

11–25 A compilation of commonplaces; see Wenzel, "The Three Enemies of Man," *MS* 29 (1967), esp. 53ff.   29–31 Ps.-Chrysostom, *Opus imperfectum*, hom. 39 (PG 56:846).   33 Hab. 1.14.   55–56 Ps. 13.1.   60–63 Wisd. 5.8–9.   67–68 Jer. 6.13.   70–72 Wisd. 10.4.   72–74 Ps.-Chrysostom, *Opus imperfectum*, hom. 1 (PL 56:630–631).   74–75 Prov. 3.18.   78–107 Augustine, *De civitate Dei* XV.xxvi.1 (CC 48:493–494).   79 Cf. Gen. 6.9.

V.xxviii   FAITH

Against this enemy, the world, and its attack, faith now bravely enters the field to fight and overcome it, after the words of 1 John 5: "This is the victory which overcomes the world, our faith." Concerning this faith we must

fides nostra." Circa hanc fidem est sciendum primo quid sit et in quibus
5   consistit, secundo [de] eius effectu quomodo mundum expugnat et prosternit.
Est ergo fides secundum Apostolum, Ad Hebreos 2, "substancia rerum sperandarum, argumentum non apparencium." In qua quidem diffinicione fides dicitur "substancia," idest fundamentum substans edificacioni spirituali, quod
est gracia et gloria, quia per hanc inhabitat nos Spiritus Sanctus quasi
10   arra celestium bonorum. Ipsa namque fides facit iam aliqualiter res speran-
das in nobis subsistere per graciam, et tandem faciet per gloriam, quia
ipsa est primus habitus virtutum, tempore quamvis non natura. Dicit eciam
"sperandarum," quia fides per assensum facit in nobis subsistere res spe-
randas. Dicitur eciam "argumentum," idest arguens mentem, quia fides probat
15   de non apparentibus et inclinat intellectum ad credendum ea que non apparent. Et ideo dicitur pocius argumentum [quam] conclusio. Secundum enim
Magistrum *Sentenciarum* distinctione 23, capitulo 8: "Hoc veraciter dicitur
credi [f. 165v] quod non valet videri. ⟨Nam credi iam non potest quod
videri potest.⟩" Et ponit exemplum dicens: "Thomas, inquit, aliud vidit et
20   aliud credidit, quia hominem vidit et Deum confessus est." Unde secundum
eum fides est virtus qua creditur quod non videtur. Dicitur eciam "fides
est rerum non apparencium" eo quod ipsa sua luce et veritate manifestat ea
que non apparent, tam preterita quam futura, sicut per fidem credimus
resurrectionem mortuorum, iudicium futurorum, etc., ut satis patet tam in
25   cimbolo Consilii Niceni quod cantatur in missa quam eciam in cimbolo Atha-
nasii quod dicitur "Quicumque vult," et maxime in communi cimbolo apostolorum, quod omnibus Christi fidelibus exponitur ad docendum.
     In quo si respectus habeatur ad eos qui illud cimbolum ⟨e⟩diderunt,
tunc articuli sunt duodecim, secundum numerum apostolorum. Si vero conside-
30   ramus que radicaliter sunt credenda, tunc articuli sunt quatuordecim,
quorum septem spectant ad divinitatem et septem ad Christi humanitatem. Et
hec bene figurantur in septem stellis Apocalipsis et in septem candelabris
aureis, in quorum medio Filius Hominis ambulat. Septem ergo que pertinent
ad divinitatem: Primus articulus est credere in unum Deum, secundus est
35   Patrem esse Deum; que duo notantur ibi: "Credo in Deum Patrem omnipotentem." Et istos duos articulos posuit beatus Petrus. Et convenienter, quia
eius fides virebat pre ceteris, et ideo in fide pre ceteris apostolis
commendatur a Christo sibi dicente illud Matthei 16: "Tu es Petrus, et
super hanc petram edificabo Ecclesiam meam," quam scilicet per fidem con-
40   fessus es. Tercius est Filium esse Deum, ibi: "Et in Iesum Christum, Filium
eius unicum, Dominum nostrum." Quia ergo credimus quod ipse Dominus Deus
ponit nobis manum in auxilium, munus in premium, [f. 166] et minas in
supplicium, ideo in eum speramus. Et hunc articulum posuit Andreas, et hoc
convenienter propter spem vite eterne. Ipse fuit discipulus beati Iohannis
45   Baptiste audiens ipsum de Christo predicantem; ipse ex tunc Christum seque-

investigate, first, what it is and in what it consists, and second how it works
to fight and prostrate the world. According to the Apostle in Hebrews 2, faith
is "the substance of things to be hoped for, an argument for things that do not
appear." In this definition, faith is called a "substance," that is, the foundation *sub-stans*, "underlying," the spiritual building, which is grace and
glory, for through it the Holy Spirit dwells within us as an earnest of the
heavenly goods. This faith causes the things we hope for to be partially
present in us already now through grace, and in the future it will do so
through glory, because faith is the first habit of the virtues, though only
according to the order of time, not in its nature. The Apostle speaks of
"things to be hoped for," because through our assent faith causes the things
we hope for to exist in us. It is likewise called *argumentum*, that is to say,
arguens mentem, "convincing our mind," because it proves the existence of
what cannot be seen and inclines the intellect to believe in what lies outside the
experience of our senses. Therefore it is called "argument" rather than "conclusion." For according to the Master of the *Sentences* in distinction 23,
chapter 8, "that is truly said to be an object of belief which cannot be seen.
For what one can see cannot be an object of belief." And he gives an example
and says: "Thomas saw one thing and believed another, for he saw a man and
confessed him to be God." Hence, according to the same, faith is the virtue by
which we believe what we do not see. Faith is further said to be "of things
that do not appear," because by its light and truth it makes things manifest
that otherwise are hidden, both past and future; thus, through faith we believe
in the resurrection of the dead, the future judgment, and so on, as can be
found in the Nicean Creed, which is sung at Mass, as well as in the Athanasian
Creed, which begins with "Whoever wants," and above all in the common
Apostles' Creed, which is taught and explained to every Christian.

If we attend to the authors of this creed, there are twelve articles, the
number of the apostles. But if we consider the fundamental subject matter of
our belief, then there are fourteen articles, of which seven relate to Christ's
divinity and seven to his humanity. These are prefigured in the seven stars in
Revelation and in the seven gold candelabra in whose midst the Son of Man
walks. Of the seven that relate to Christ's divinity, the first states that we
believe in one God, and the second, that God is our father. These two are
expressed in the sentence: "I believe in God, the Father, the Almighty," and
they were given by Blessed Peter, and fittingly so, because his faith was
stronger than that of the others and was singled out from that of the other
apostles as Christ said to him in Matthew 16, "you are Peter, and on this rock
I will build my Church," that is, which you have confessed through your faith.
The third article declares that the Son is God, when it states: "And in Jesus
Christ, his only Son, our Lord." Since we believe that the Lord God offers us
a hand in aid, a gift in reward, and a threat in punishment, we put our hope in

batur. Quartus articulus est credere Spiritum Sanctum esse Deum, ibi:
"Credo in Spiritum Sanctum." Nam ipse spiritus pietatis est et compassionis
qui pie infundit activis opera misericordie, ac eciam per suam consolacionem reddit hominem mitem et invictum, et ideo vocatur Paraclitus, idest,
50   consolator. Nam ipse "Deus tocius consolacionis est, qui consolatur nos in
omni tribulacione nostra." Et hunc articulum posuit Bartholomeus, et bene,
nam ipse interpretatur suspendens aquas, in signum quod ipse Spiritus
Sanctus suspendit aquas tribulacionis et angustie. Qui in tantum istum
Apostolum reddebat invictum quod vinci non potuit, quamvis pro amore eius
55   vivus excoriatus fuit. Sic ergo patet quod isti quatuor articuli sunt de
unitate divine essencie et trinitate personarum. Quintus articulus est
credere remissionem peccatorum hiis qui sunt in Ecclesia, quod notatur ibi:
"Sanctam Ecclesiam catholicam, sanctorum communionem, remissionem peccatorum." Et hunc articulum posuit Symon, qui interpretatur obediens et perse-
60   verans, quia ad hanc remissionem numquam pervenitur nisi per humilitatem et
in bonis perseveranciam, iuxta illud Matthei: "Qui perseveraverit usque in
finem," etc. Sextus est mortuorum resurrectio vel resuscitacio, quod patet
ibi: "Carnis resurrectionem." In ista enim resurrectione erit maxima mutacio, quia ex carne corruptibili et mortali fiet incorruptibilis et inmorta-
65   lis; que quidem mutacio erit ad maximam gloriam bonis, et ad maximam miseriam malis. Hunc articulum posuit [f. 166v] Thadeus, qui c⟨o⟩rculum interpretatur, quasi cor colens, quia sic ille corda barbarorum coluit quod eius
resurrectionis ad gloriam esse meretur. Septimus est bonorum remuneracio,
sub quo eciam comprehenditur malorum punicio; ibi: "Vitam eternam. Amen."
70   Quem posuit Mathias, qui interpretatur donatus, scilicet pro Iuda qui
seipsum tradidit ad mortem eternam. Iuste dicitur datus, quia gloria eterna
non venditur nec est aliquis qui habeat unde emat, set illa per Christum
sine precio datur, iuxta illud Psalmi: "Pro nichilo salvos facies illos,"
scilicet fideles in te confidentes. Et isti tres ultimi articuli ad divini-
75   tatem pertinent eo quod virtute Dei fit remissio peccatorum, que est anime
iustificacio, et corporum resuscitacio atque corporis et anime glorifica-
cio.
     Alii sunt septem articuli qui ad Christi humanitatem pertinent. Quorum
primus est credere Iesum Filium Dei conceptum fuisse de Spiritu Sancto, et
80   secundus est credere quod idem Filius natus est de Maria Virgine. Qua[m]
quidem concepcione[m] et eciam nativitate[m] caritas Christi erga genus
humanum pre ceteris operabatur iuxta illud Apostoli: "Propter nimiam caritatem qua dilexit nos misit Filium suum in similitudinem carnis peccati."
Set istos duos posuit Iacobus Minor, qui eciam frater Domini appellatur. Et
85   bene frater Domini dicitur propter nimiam similitudinem quam habuit pre
ceteris; similiter quia ad modum Christi "vinum et ciseram non bibit" nec
carnes comedit, set in omni persecucione viriliter restitit, propter quod

him. This article was given by Andrew, and fittingly so, because of his hope
for eternal life. Andrew was a disciple of Blessed John the Baptist, whom he
heard preaching of Christ; and from that point on he followed Christ. The
fourth article declares that the Holy Spirit is God, when it says: "I believe
in the Holy Spirit." This is the spirit of piety and compassion, who lovingly
infuses works of mercy into people who follow the active life, and who also
through his consolation renders man mild and strong, for which he is called
Paraclete, that is, consoler. For he is "the God of all consolation who
comforts us in all our tribulation." And this article was given by Bartholomew, whose name means "suspending the waters," in token that this Spirit
suspends the waters of tribulation and anxiety. He rendered this apostle so
strong that he could not be overcome, even when he was flayed alive for his
love. In this way, then, it is clear that these four articles refer to the
unity of God's being and to the trinity of persons. The fifth article states
our belief in the remission of sins for those who belong to the Church, when it
says: "The holy Catholic Church, the communion of saints, the forgiveness of
sins." This article was given by Simon, whose name means "obedient" and "persevering," because one can never come to this remission of sins except through
humility and perseverance in good works, after the words of Matthew: "He who
perseveres unto the end," etc. The sixth article declares the resurrection of
the dead, in the words: "The resurrection of the body." In this resurrection
a tremendous change will take place, for our corruptible and mortal flesh will
become incorruptible and immortal; this change will bring the greatest glory to
the good, and the greatest wretchedness to the wicked. This article was given
by Thaddeus, whose name means *corculum*, "little heart," as if to say *cor
colens*, "worshipping the heart," because he cherished the hearts of barbarians
so much that it helped him to the glory of the resurrection. The seventh
article states the rewarding of the good, which also implies the punishment of
the wicked; and it says: "Life everlasting. Amen." This was given by Mathias,
whose name means "given," because he was given in the place of Judas, who
handed himself over to eternal death. And he is rightly called "given," because eternal life is not for sale, nor can anyone buy it, but it is given without
money and freely by Christ, according to the words of the Psalm: "For
nothing you will save them," that is, the faithful who trust in you. These
last three articles belong to Christ's divinity because it is by virtue of his
divinity that sins are forgiven (which is the soul's justification), that our
bodies shall rise, and that body and soul will be glorified.

The other seven articles relate to Christ's humanity. In the first we
believe that the Son was conceived by the Holy Spirit, and in the second, that
the same Son was born of the Virgin Mary. His conception and birth was foremost a deed of his love for mankind, after the words of the Apostle: "For his
exceeding charity with which he loved us, he sent his Son in the likeness of

in fine lapidatus est. Tercius est credere Filium Dei pro nobis mortuum in
cruce, quod notatur ibi: "Passus sub Poncio Pilato, crucifixus, mortuus, et
90   sepultus." [f. 167] Et hunc articulum posuit Iohannes. Et iuste, quia ipse
plus vidit de Christi passione quam aliquis alius, et ideo scripcit de
Christi matris recommendacione et de Christi lanceacione. Et eciam addidit
in suo evangelio pre ceteris quod Christus dixit "Sicio," scilicet salutem
animarum, et similiter alia que nullus alius evangelista vidit. Unde in
95   fine [sue] passionis dicit: "Qui vidit, testimonium perhibuit," etc. Quartus et undecimus est credere Filium Dei descendisse ad inferos secundum
animam, ibi: "Descendit ad inferna, tercia die resurrexit a mortuis." Et
hunc articulum posuit beatus Thomas, et bene, quia ipse erat niger [primo]
propter incredulitatem sive infidelitatem, [quod notatur ibi: "Descendit ad
100   inferna," et postea candidus per confessionis fidelitatem,] quod notatur
quando dixit: "Tercia die," etc. Et iste in Yndia predicavit. Quintus et duodecimus est credere sanctam Ecclesiam catholicam, sanctorum communionem.
Cuius articuli duplex potest esse sensus. Unus est: Credo Ecclesiam militan-
tem, que iam adheret Deo per contemplacionem, esse assumendam ad Eccle-
105   siam triumphantem, ubi adherebit Deo per claram visionem. Et hoc est quod
oramus in canone misse dicendo: "Supplices te rogamus, omnipotens Deus,
iube hec perferri per manus sancti angeli tui in sublime altare tuum," etc.
Non enim oramus quod ille species panis portetur in illud altare sublim⟨e⟩,
quia illuc numquam deveniet, nec oramus quod verum corpus Christi quod
110   semper ibi est illuc deportetur, set quod veritas tocius Ecclesie que per
illud sacramentum significatur in celum deportetur. Et hoc propter illius
convenienciam. Nam sicut panis ex quo fit eucharistia fit ex multis granis,
et vinum ex quo fit sanguis ex multis racemis, sic Christi Ecclesia adunatur ex multis fidelibus. [f. 167v] Et ideo oramus quod ista veritas Eccle-
115   sie finaliter in celum deportetur. Est autem communis modus loquendi iste,
quia si videam ymaginem alicuius, statim dicam "istum diligo vel odio," non
tamen pro ipsa ymagine, set pro ipso significato per ymaginem, scilicet pro
amico vel inimico. Sic in proposito. Aliter eciam intelligitur articulus
iste, "Credo in sanctam Ecclesiam," etc., idest, credo illam Ecclesiam cum
120   sanctis communicare, que maxime fit per virtutem contemplacionis. Et istum
articulum posuit Mattheus, qui de peccatore vocatus est in discipulum
Christi, sicut Ecclesia militans collecta de peccatoribus fiet Ecclesia
triumphans. Iste enim Mattheus predicavit in Macedonia. Sextus et decimus
tercius est credere Christum ascendisse ad Patris equalitatem, ibi: "Ascen-
125   dit ad celos, sedet ad dextram Dei Patris," etc. Christus enim in sua
ascensione attendebat gaudium et depellebat timorem, quia sedet ad dextram
Dei Patris, et ibi est summa pax et eterna concordia. Et ideo congrue hunc
articulum scripsit Iacobus Maior, frater s⟨cilicet⟩ Iohannis Evangeliste,
qui huius ascencionis et ad dexteram cessionis maxime desideravit esse

sinful flesh." These two articles were given by James the Less, also called "brother of the Lord." He is fittingly called "brother of the Lord" because he was very much like him, more than anyone else. In addition, like Christ he "did not drink wine or strong drink," nor did he eat meat; and he persevered manly in every persecution, for which he was stoned in the end. The third article affirms that the Son of God died for us on the cross, as it is said in the words: "Suffered under Pontius Pilate, was crucified, died, and was buried." And this article was given by John, and fittingly so, because he witnessed more of Christ's Passion than anyone else and thus wrote about Christ's entrusting his mother to him and his being pierced with a lance. And further, he adds in his gospel to what the other evangelists report, that Christ said "I thirst"—namely, for the salvation of souls—and other things which no other evangelist saw. For this reason he says at the end of his account of the Passion: "He who saw it has given testimony," and so on. The fourth and eleventh article affirms that the Son of God descended into hell, with respect to his soul, saying: "He descended into hell, the third day he rose from the dead." This article was given by Blessed Thomas, and fittingly so, because he was first black on account of his incredulity or lack of faith, which is shown in "He descended into hell," and afterwards white in the faith of his confession, which is shown when he said, "On the third day," and so on. Thomas preached in India. The fifth and twelfth article affirms our belief in the holy Catholic Church, the communion of saints. This article can carry a twofold meaning. One is this: I believe that the Church Militant, which now is united to God through contemplation, will be taken into the Church Triumphant, where it will be united with God through direct vision. For this reason we pray in the canon of the Mass as follows: "We humbly beseech you, Almighty God, let these gifts be carried by the hands of your holy angel," and so on. We do not pray that the particular form of bread be carried to the altar on high, for it could never travel there; nor do we pray that the true Body of Christ may be carried there, because it is there always; but we pray that the truth [*read* unity?] of the whole Church, as it is symbolized in this sacrament, be carried to heaven. And this is fitting, for just as the bread which becomes the Eucharist is made out of many grains, and just as the wine which becomes the Blood of Christ is made from many grapes, so is Christ's Church gathered together from many believers. We therefore pray that this true Church may in the end be carried to heaven. It is a common way of speaking that when I see someone's picture, I say at once "I love him" or "I hate him," referring not to the picture but to him who is depicted by it, that is, my friend or enemy himself. The same holds true of the matter under discussion. The second way to understand this article "I believe in the holy Catholic Church," etc., is that the Church is in communion with the saints, which happens above all by virtue of contemplation. This article was given by Matthew, who was called

130   particeps, ut patet in eius matris peticione dicentis: "Dic ut sedeant hii
      duo filii," etc. Iste predicavit in Hispania. Septimus et decimus quartus
      est credere quod Filius Dei est venturus iudicare vivos et mortuos. Nam
      Christus venturus ad mundum resplendebit per sapienciam qua inter bonos et
      malos iuste iudicabit, et sicut lapis crisolitus emittit scintillas de ore
135   suo, idest ardencia iudicia et horribilia contra malos iuxta illud Psalmi:
      "Ignis in conspectu eius exardescit," etc. [Hunc articulum posuit beatus
      Philippus,] et bene secundum sui nominis interpretacionem. Interpretatur
      enim os la⟨mpad⟩is, signans quod in [f. 168] iudicio de ore suo fulgur et
      ignem ad modum la⟨mpa⟩dis emittet. Et iste apostolus predicavit in Galilea,
140   scilicet Philippus qui hunc articulum posuit.
         Sic ergo patent articuli fidei per duodecim apostolos ordinati. Que
      quidem fides propter eius constanciam et soli⟨ditat⟩em non incongrue nomi-
      natur primus lapis in fundamento Ecclesie Christi, lapidi iaspidi compara-
      ta, cuius natura talis invenitur: videlicet, semper virescit, fugat fantas-
145   mata, reddit tutum inter pericula, luxuriam cohibet, morbos sanat. Revera
      sic fides semper viret in stabilitate nec marcessit pro quacumque tribula-
      cione seu persecucione. Et Petri 5 dicitur: "Adversarius vester diabolus
      tamquam leo rugiens circuit querens quem devoret; cui resistite fortes in
      fide," etc. Secundo [fides] fugat fantasma[ta] errorum ac heresim; Actuum
150   15: "Fide purificans corda eorum." Tercio reddit tutum inter pericula, et
      ideo assimilatur scuto, dicente Apostolo: "Accipite scutum fidei." In quo
      scuto depingi non incongrue possunt arma illustrissimi regis Anglie. Ipse
      enim, ut videtis, gestat scutum de ⟨minio⟩, idest *goules*, cum tribus leo-
      pardis transeuntibus de auro puro. Et bene per illud scutum de *goules*
155   intelligo ardentem [amorem] et caritatem, per quam accendimur ad intensam
      fidem et credulitatem in Deum et articulis prescriptis. Per tres leopardos
      potest intelligi benedicta Trinitas, in qua cunctis aliis abiectis creden-
      dum est; et per aurum divinitatem istius Trinitatis. Nam sicut ita purum
      aurum est in minori leopardo sic[ut] in maiori, et e contrario, sic ita
160   purus Deus et verus est una persona in benedicta Trinitate sicut alia, et e
      contrario. Set isti leopardi sunt transeuntes ad denotandum quod non nimis
      studiose debemus nos intromittere, discutere, et disputare quomodo tres
      persone possunt esse unus [f. 168v] Deus et cetera huiusmodi ad fidem
      pertinencia, ne forte ad incredulitatem et heresim deducemur sicut pluries
165   auditum est de aliis, set transeundo unde et firmiter credere tenemur prout
      Ecclesia Dei credit et docet. Quarto fides luxuriam cohibet, sicut patet de
      Magdalena cui dixit Christus: "Fides tua te salvam fecit." Quinto, morbos
      sanat, iuxta illud Matthei: "Signa eos qui crediderint hec sequentur: in
      nomine meo demonia eicient," etc., "supra egros man⟨us⟩ imponent, et bene
170   habebunt," etc. Et maxime contra morbum ydropicum, idest contra avariciam,
      nam avarus est sicut ydropicus, quia quanto plus bibit, tanto plus sitit;

from a sinful life to become Christ's disciple, just as the Church Militant is gathered together from sinners and will become the Church Triumphant. Matthew preached in Macedonia. The sixth and thirteenth article affirms that Christ rose to assume an equal position with his Father: "He ascended into heaven, sits at the right hand of the Father," etc. For in his ascension Christ rose to joy and cast down fear, for he sits at the right hand of God the Father, where there is the greatest peace and eternal harmony. For this reason, this article was fittingly given by James the Greater, the brother of John, who deeply desired to share Christ's ascension and sitting at God's right hand, as we learn from his mother's petition when she said: "Say that these my two sons may sit," etc. James preached in Spain. And the seventh and fourteenth article affirms that the Son of God will come to judge the living and the dead. For Christ will come into the world shining in his wisdom with which he will judge the good and the evil with justice; and like the chrysolite, he will send forth sparks from his mouth, that is, burning and horrible judgments against the wicked, according to the words of the Psalm: "A fire shall burn before him," etc. This article was given by Blessed Philip, and fittingly so after the meaning of his name, which is "the mouth of the lamp," for in his judgment Christ will send forth lightning and fire from his mouth like a lamp. And Philip, who formulated this article, preached in Galilee.

These, then, are the articles of faith as they were established by the twelve apostles. This faith is not unfittingly called the first stone in the foundations of Christ's Church, because of its stability and firmness. It can be compared to the jasper, which has these qualities: it is always green, it drives away phantasms, it keeps one safe in dangers, it prevents lechery, and it heals sicknesses. In the same way, faith is always green in its stability and never wilts in any tribulation or persecution whatever. Therefore it is said in Peter 5: "Your adversary, the devil, goes about like a roaring lion, seeking whom he may devour; resist him, strong in faith," and so forth. Second, our faith puts the phantasms of errors and heresies to flight; Acts 15: "Purifying their hearts by faith." Third, it keeps us safe among dangers, and therefore it is compared to a shield by the Apostle when he says: "Take the shield of faith." In this shield may be fittingly depicted the arms of the most illustrious king of England. For as you know, he carries a shield of red, *goules*, with three leopards rampant of pure gold. By the shield in *goules* I understand the fervent love and charity which inflame us to have an intense faith and belief in God and the articles mentioned above. By the three leopards we may understand the Blessed Trinity, in whom we must believe after casting off all other idols. And by the gold I understand the divine nature of this Trinity. For this gold is as pure in the smallest leopard as it is in the largest, and vice-versa; thus God is purely and verily in one person of the Blessed Trinity as he is in another, and vice-versa. These leopards are ram-

ita ipse quanto plus habet, tanto plus appetit [temporalia]. Unde illud Ad Hebreos: "Sancti [per fidem] vicerunt regna," idest, per illam divicias regnorum contempserunt.

---

2 expugnet] repugnat C.	8 edificacioni] edificio O.	14 eciam] ergo O.	18–19 Nam . . . potest] iam non potestque videri C.O; *text from* B1, *thus also in source.* 21 eciam] *add* quod O.	22 rerum] *om* O.	28 ediderunt] condiderunt C.	29–30 consideramus] consideremus O.	34 in] *interl* C; *om* O.	44 convenienter] *add* primo O. 46 credere] *om* O.	52 nam] *om* O.	ipse(2)] iste O.	53 Sanctus] *om* O.	61 Qui] *add* autem O.	62 resurrectio vel resuscitacio] resuscitacio M.R; resurreccio W.	66 Hunc articulum] et hunc O.	corculum] circulum C.	73 precio] *add* et libere O.	75 Dei] deitatis O.	79 fuisse] *om* O.	80 credere] *om* O.	85 quam habuit] inter eos O.	92 addidit] addit O.	93–94 scilicet . . . animarum] *om* O.	94 evangelista] apostolus M; *om* R.W. 99–100 quod . . . fidelitatem] *text from* R; M.W *have eyeskip* ibi . . . notatur.	103 est] iste O.	107 in . . . tuum] *om* O.	108 ille] iste M.W; ista R.	sublime] sublimi C. 119 illam] istam O.	120 istum] hunc O.	124 credere] *om* O.	125 ad . . . Patris] *om* O.	128 scilicet] sancti C.	Evangeliste] *om* O.	130 ut] quod O.	132 credere] *om* O. 133 venturus] *add* est O.	resplendebit] *add* ut O.	136 exardescit] exardescet M.R; ardesset W.	136–137 Hunc . . . Philippus] *om* C (*see below, line 140*).W. *Text from* R. M *reads* paulus *for* philippus.	138 lampadis] lapis C.	suo] *om* O.	139 lampadis] lapidis C. apostolus] *om* O.	140 scilicet . . . posuit] *om* O.	141 duodecim] christi O. 142 soliditatem] sollicitudinem C.	148 tamquam . . . devoret] etc M.R; *om* W. 149 etc.] *om* O.	153 minio] auro C.	idest] *om* O.	154 bene] *add* nam O.	165 tenemur] *om* O.	169–170 supra . . . etc.] *om* O.	169 manus] manent C.	170 ydropicum] ydropisis O.	171 est] *om* O.	quia] *om* O.

# V.xxix	QUOMODO FIDES MUNDUM VINCIT

[M]odo videndum est quomodo hec fides mundum vincit et debellat. Ubi sciendum quod primo vicit mundum errantem per vie directionem. Ipse mundus quasi continue deviat ad illicita instigando. Nec mirum, quia "in tenebris est et in tenebris ambulat." Et ideo Osee 4 scribitur: "Non est veritas in
5	terra," ergo crudelitas; "non est sciencia," ergo fatuitas; et sequitur: set est (supple: in terra) "maledictum, mendacium, homicidium, furtum, adulterium," etc. Non ergo est mirum si mundus erret. Unde Augustinus: "Omnis, inquit, labor hominis vacuus est sine fide." Est ergo fides secundum eum cognicio rerum que non videntur. Deus autem invisibilis est, et
10	tamen perfecte credendo videri potest, dum scilicet fides Ecclesie sine fictione firmiter tenetur, ut patet de articulis predictis et corpore Christi in altari. Et bene ait Iesus Matthei 10: "Beati qui non viderunt et [f. 169] crediderunt"; *Glossa* ibi: "Per veram fidem, ait Christus, me vident qui perfecte in me credunt." Unde Bernardus omelia 16: "Fides,

pant, to indicate that we must not be too eager to investigate, discuss, and dispute how three persons can be one God and other aspects of our faith, so that we may not be led into disbelief and heresy as it has often happened to some people, but we should leap beyond and firmly believe as God's Church believes and teaches. Fourth, faith prevents lechery, as can be seen in Magdalene, to whom Christ said: "Your faith has made you whole." And fifth, it heals sicknesses, according to what is said at the end of Matthew: "These signs shall follow them that believe: in my name they shall cast out devils," and so on; "they shall place their hand on the sick, and these shall be healed," etc. Faith avails especially against the illness of dropsy, that is, against avarice. For a man who suffers from dropsy, the more he thirsts, the more he drinks; so does an avaricious person desire more and more temporal goods, the more he already has. Hence the words of Hebrews: "By their faith the saints conquered kingdoms," that is, through their faith they scorned the riches of earthly realms.

3–4 1 John 5.4. 6–7 Heb. 11.1. 17–21 Peter Lombard, *Sent.* III.xxiii.7 (2:145). 25–27 The Nicean Creed is found in the missal (e.g., Legg, p. 211), the Athanasian Creed in the breviary: Procter and Wordsworth, eds., *Breviarium ad usum insignis ecclesiae Sarum* (Cambridge, 1879–1886), 2.46–48; for the Apostles' Creed, see the following discussion. 38–39 Matt. 16.18. 50–51 2 Cor. 1.4. 61–62 Matt. 10.22. 73 Ps. 55.8. 82–83 Eph. 2.4 and Rom. 8.3. 86 Luke 1.15, from Lev. 10.9. 93 John 19.28. 95 John 19.35. 106–107 Legg, p.223. 130–131 Matt. 20–21. 136 Ps. 49.3. 147–149 1 Pet. 5.8–9. 150 Acts 15.9. 151 Eph. 6.16. 167 Matt. 9.22. 168–170 Mark 16.17–18. 173 Heb. 11.33.

V.xxix   HOW FAITH OVERCOMES THE WORLD

Now we must investigate how this faith fights against and overcomes the world. We should know, then, in the first place, that it overcomes the world's misguidance by putting us on the right way. The world almost constantly leaves its way to urge us on to forbidden actions, and it is no wonder, because "it is in darkness and walks in the dark." Therefore it is written in Hosea 4: "There is no truth in the land," but rather cruelty [*read* credulousness?]; "there is no knowledge," but rather foolishness; and it continues: "Cursing, lying, killing, theft, adultery," add: are in the land, and so forth. No wonder, then, that the world goes astray. Augustine says: "All man's efforts are empty without faith." Thus according to him faith is the knowledge of things that are not seen. God is invisible, and yet through perfect belief he can be seen as long as one firmly holds the Church's faith without feigning, as is manifest from the articles discussed earlier and the Body of Christ on the altar. Jesus says in Matthew 10: "Blessed are they that have not seen and

15   inquit, attingit inaccessa, deprehendit ignara, comprehendit inmensa, et
     apprehendit novissima." Et tamen iuxta Apostolum Iacob: "Fides sine bonis
     operibus mortua est."
         Secundo fides vincit mundum sterilem per fructuum virtutum multiplica-
     cionem. Quod autem mundus de se sterilis est, patet Regum 2, [ubi dicitur]
20   quod aque Iericho "pessime sunt et terra sterilis." Iericho enim interpre-
     tatur luna, que crescendo et decrescendo continue mutatur. Et bene signat
     mundum quia sterilis est et volubilis; Ecclesiastici 5: "Qui amat divicias,
     fructum non capiet ex eis." Set contra hoc Ad Hebreos 10 dicitur: "De fide
     terra sterilis virtutem seminis in concepcione accepit."
25   Tercio vincit mundum mortificantem per operis vivificacionem. Est enim
     mundus quasi mare mortuum, in qua non vivit aqua. Nec mirum, quia non
     ⟨descendit⟩ de eo nisi favilla. Set certe illu⟨m⟩ fides vivificat, quia
     quicquid meriti, quicquid vite et beatitudinis in mundo invenitur, ex fide
     procedit. Et nota quod mundus mari bene comparatur propter eius pericula,
30   que in hiis versibus continentur:

         Sunt scopul⟨i⟩, sirtes, syrene, Scilla, Caribdis,
         Atque bitalassus metuenda pericula ponti.

     Sunt autem scopul⟨i⟩ saxa prominencia, ad que si navis collidatur, frangi-
     tur. Sic in mundo sunt scandala, propter que dimittit homo opera peniten-
35   cie. Et ideo corpus, quod est navis anime, frangitur dum a fortitudine
     vigoris ignavia laxatur. Sirtes autem sunt loca ubi est inequalitas fundi,
     quando scilicet in alico loco est aqua profundissima et statim iuxta est
     alius locus vadosus aut aqua nulla [f. 169v] set zabulum tantum. Sic est in
     mundo. Nam unus habet bonorum superfluitatem et alius nimium defectum et
40   calamitatem, quo contra Proverbiorum 30 dicitur: "Divicias et paupertates
     ne dederis michi, set tantum," etc. Syrene autem sunt monstra ⟨mari⟩na, que
     ut dicitur dulcedine sui cantus nautas ad se attrahunt et submergunt. Sic
     mundus per voluptates et vanas delicias quamplures decipit; Ysaie 13:
     "Syrene in delubris voluptatis." Est tamen sciendum quod poete fingunt
45   syrenas fuisse tres sorores transformatas, ex parte virgines et ex parte
     volucres, alas habentes et ungulas, quarum una voce, alia tibiis, et tercia
     lira canebant, que illectos navigantes suo cantu et melodia in naufragium
     trahebant. Secundum tamen veritatem fuerunt meretrices que transeuntes
     ducebant ad egestatem, ut dicit Ysidorus. Que ideo dicitur ipsas alas
50   habuisse et ungulas sicut aves, quia amor volat et vulnerat. In fluminibus
     ⟨eciam⟩ dicuntur commorasse, quia fluctus venerem [pro]curat, hoc est,
     habundancia rerum, que per fluctus designatur, luxuriam generat. Est eciam
     Scilla ingens saxum habens multa capita prominencia, ad que naves collisi
     aut fluctus horrendum faciunt strepitum. Propter quod dicitur fabulose
55   Scilla latrare. Sic in mundo sunt multi latratus, quia iurgia, contencio-

have believed"; and the *Gloss* comments: "Christ says, 'they who believe in me wholly see me in true faith.' " Whence Bernard says in Homily 16: "Faith attains to what is above one's reach, it perceives what is unknown, grasps what is beyond measure, and sees what is to come in the future." And yet, according to the Apostle, "faith without works is dead."

In the second place, faith overcomes the world's sterility by producing manifold fruit of virtues. That the world of itself is sterile can be seen from Kings 2, where it is said that the waters of Jericho are very bad and its soil sterile. Jericho means "the moon," which constantly changes by waxing and waning. And thus it well symbolizes the world, because the latter is sterile and changeable; Ecclesiastes 5: "He who loves riches shall reap no fruit from them." But against this is said in Hebrews 10: "Through faith the sterile earth [*read* Sarah] received strength to conceive seed."

In the third place, faith overcomes the world's deadliness by bringing man's works to life. For the world is like the Dead Sea, whose water does not live. And this is no wonder, because nothing comes from it but hot ashes. But faith brings life to it, for whatever merit, life, and beauty are found in the world come from faith. And notice that the world can be compared to the sea because of its dangers, which are summarized in the following lines:

> Hidden rocks and sandbanks, sirens, Scylla, Charybdis,
> Currents of pitch are the dangers at sea to be feared.

First, the hidden but large rocks: if a ship runs against them, it breaks. In the world, these are the scandals, on whose account one refrains from doing works of mercy and of penance. And then one's body, which is the ship of the soul, is broken when through idleness it relaxes the tone that comes from a strenuous life. Sandbanks are places where the depth of the water changes: in one place the water is very deep, and right next to it is a shallow place or no water at all but only sand. The same is true of the world, for one person has an abundance of goods, while another suffers want and misfortune, against which is said in Proverbs 30: "Give me neither riches nor poverty, but only," etc. The sirens are sea monsters who are said to attract sailors by their sweet song and then drown them. In the same way does the world deceive many with its pleasures and vain delights; Isaiah 13: "Sirens in the temples of pleasure." Notice that the poets say the sirens were three sisters who had been transformed and were partially maidens, partially birds with wings and claws; one of them used to sing, the second played a flute, and the third played a lyre; and when they had lured sailors with their song and music, they would bring them to shipwreck. But in reality they were whores who used to lead passersby into poverty, according to Isidore. Thus, they are said to have had wings and claws like birds because their love flies and wounds. They are further said to dwell in streams because water gives birth to Venus, that is to say: rich possessions,

nes, ire, rixe. Secundum tamen Ysidorum *Ethimologiarum* libro 11, capitulo
4, "poete fingunt Scillam vetulam fuisse quandam cum caninis latrantem
capitibus." Caribdis est locus voraginosus et vertiginosus, ubi naves
transeuntes ad se attrahit et deglutit. Qui bene avariciam designat, [f.
60   170] que plures in mari huius mundi ad se trahit, quia secundum Ieremie 8
"a minore usque ad maximum omnes sequuntur avariciam." In hoc tamen sunt
Caribdis et avaricia dissimiles quia Caribdis ter in die aquas absorbet et
ter evomit et sic fluctus erigit, set avarus quod semel absorbet numquam
gratis evomit set tenacissime retinet et astringit. Dicit tamen Hugo quod
65   ista Caribdis fuit vetula quedam voracissima, que quia boves Herculis
furabatur, a Iove fuit fulminata et in mari precipitata, ubi adhuc antiquas
fingitur ipsam exercere voracitates et rapinas. Quod quidem figmentum bene
avaricie competit, que voracissima invenitur, eciam labores bovum, scilicet
fructus terre et frumenta, rapit et abscondit. Et ideo non tantum fulminata
70   a deo Iove set eciam maledicta a Deo Iesu Christo et expulsa de celo. Unde
illud Proverbiorum 11: "Qui abscondit frumenta in tempore, maledicetur in
populis." Bitalassus vero est locus bituminosus et limosus, in quem cum
navis impingit, propter limi eius tenacitatem exire non potest. Sic in mundo
est ut communiter conversacio hominum limosa et societas quamplurimum
75   infecta, quam cum quis intraverit, vix exire valebit, quia ut dicitur: "Qui
tetigerit picem, inquinabitur ab ea."
     Set revera ista pericula huius maris, idest mundi, satis secure per-
transit homo in fide radicatus. Nam talis homo proprium corpus habet pro
navi in quo commercia portat preciosissima, scilicet animam cum suis poten-
80   ciis et graciis tam naturalibus quam infusis; que iuste preciosa dicuntur
eo quod Christi sanguine precioso redempta, ut dicitur Petri 1: "Non cor-
ruptibilibus auro et argento," etc. In quo quidem navi racio est nauta, que
regit corpus in mundo [f. 170v] sicut nauta navem in mari. Iste igitur
nauta racionis sedet in parte posteriori, hoc est, debet recordari de
85   miseria sui ortus pertransiti et respicere ad partem anteriorem considerando miseriam sue mortis. In illo eciam navi malum est spes, lignum transversum est solida fides de cruce Christi, et velum caritas. Tam cito ergo
[hoc] mare ab ista navi pertransitur, quamcito vita labitur. Set nota quod
nullus existens in navi percipit quamcito ipsa currit, nisi qui in lignum
90   vel aliud inmobile in terra oculum figit. Sic nullus percipit quamcito ista
vita currit nisi oculum mentis per fidem veram in lignum crucis et mortem
Christi fixerit; quod si fecerit, illesus transibit et salvus, iuxta illud
Matthei: "Fides tua te salvum fecit," quia prout Ad Hebreos: "Sancti per
fidem vicerunt."

---

5 crudelitas] *thus* C.M.W; creduliter R; incredulitas B1.   12 Matthei] iohannis M.R; *om*
W.   15 attingit] *corr to* accingit(?) C.   16 Iacob] *om* O.   23 De] *om* O.   24 terra] *thus*

which are symbolized by streams of water, produce lechery. Scylla is a
huge rock with many cliffs jutting out from it. Ships and waves that are
thrown against them make a fearful noise, and for that reason in the fables
Scylla is said to bark. In the same way there is much barking in the world,
namely arguments, strife, anger, and fights. Yet Isidore says in book 11 of
his *Etymologies*, chapter 4: "The poets imagine that Scylla was an old woman,
barking, with heads of dogs." Charybdis is a deep whirlpool that draws passing
ships into it and swallows them. It fittingly symbolizes avarice, which in the
sea of the world similarly draws many people to itself, for in Jeremiah 6 it is
said: "From the least to the greatest, all are given to covetousness." But
Charybdis and avarice differ insofar as Charybdis swallows the water three
times a day and throws it up again and thereby makes the waves rise and fall;
but the avaricious person never gives willingly back what he has once swallowed, but rather holds on to it and clutches it most tightly. Hugh reports that
this Charybdis was a voracious old woman who for stealing the oxen of Hercules
was struck by Jove with a thunderbolt and flung headlong into the sea. There
she is still imagined to engage in her former robbing and devouring. This
image fits avarice very well, for this vice also is found to be most voracious
and to steal and hide the labors of oxen, that is, the fruit and harvest of the
earth. It was therefore not just struck with a thunderbolt from the god Jupiter but cursed by the true God, Jesus Christ, and expelled from heaven. Hence
it is said in Proverbs 11: "He who hides grain during a famine shall be cursed
among the people." A current of pitch, finally, is a spot in the sea that is
thick with tar; when a ship gets stuck in it, it cannot get out again because
of the stickiness. Likewise, in the world human intercourse is frequently
thick and muddy, and society sticky, so that once one has gotten into it, one
can hardly get out. Hence the saying: "If you touch pitch, you will get
dirty."

But the man who is rooted in faith passes safely through these dangers of
the sea, that is, of this world. Such a man has his own body for his ship, in
which he carries a most precious merchandise, namely his soul with its powers,
both the natural ones and those that have been infused; it is rightly called
precious because it has been redeemed with the precious blood of Christ, as is
affirmed in Peter 1: "Not with corruptible gold and silver," etc. In this
ship, the captain is our reason, who rules our body in this world as a captain
steers his ship in the sea. Reason, our captain, sits at the stern, which means
that he must remember the wretchedness of his beginning, the way he has
come, and must look toward what lies ahead, thinking of the misery of his
death. The mast in this ship is hope, the crossbeam is firm faith in the cross
of Christ, and the sail is charity. We sail over this sea as quickly as our
life passes. But note that no one on board a ship realizes how fast it runs
unless he keeps his eye on some wood or something else that stands still on
the land. In the same way, no one realizes how fast our life passes unless he

C.O; sara r,t,z *and source*.   **27** descendit] scitur C.   illum] illud C.   **31** scopuli] scopule
C.M.   **33** scopuli] scopule C.   **41** set tantum] *om* O.   marina] in arena C.   **51** eciam] et
C; autem R.   procurat] curat C.W; creat (?) M.   **66–67** antiquas fingitur] antiquitas
fingit R.B1.   **70** Deo . . . Christo] christo domino O.   **74** quamplurimum] plurium O.
79 quo] *corr* C; qua O.   **83** igitur] ergo O.   **86** illo] isto M.W; ista R.   **93** Matthei] *add*
15 O.   prout] *add* dicitur O.   **94** vicerunt] *add* regna operati sunt iusticiam etc O.

V.xxx   QUI FIDEM IMPUGNANT

[S]et istam fidem inpugnant et [sibi] contrariantur, quod dolendum
est, hiis diebus tam homines quam mulieres qui contra ordinacionem Dei et
Ecclesie diabolo instigante quod propriissimum est Deo omnium Creatori
attribuunt creaturis, scilicet futura contingencia scire et predicere,
5   sanitatem et infirmitatem cum fictis carminibus inponere et destruere.
Cuiusmodi sunt qui dicuntur incantatores, qui artem suam verbis excercent,
Anglice *tilsters*, qui cum carminibus et aliis miseriis suis sanitatem
promittunt. Unde quando stomachus alicuius ex nimia superfluitate cibi et
potus aggravatur et infirmatur, dicunt quod "mater cecidit," et tunc opor-
10   tet quod aliqua vetula misera tali arte imbuta adducatur ad fricandum
ventrem et latera. Que ut frequenter magis obest quam prodest, et maxime
spiritualiter, eo quod huiusmodi [f. 171] artes inhibite sunt. Et ideo in
talibus considerandum est utrum naturaliter videatur si tales effectus
possint causari an non, quia si non, consequens est quod pertine[n]t ad
15   artem demoniacam. Ex quo manifestum est quod ⟨natura efficaciam naturalem⟩
habere poterit, ut patet per Augustinum ° 12 *De civitate Dei*, c. Dicit
tamen Raymundus hic quod aliquis vel aliqua colligens herbas medicinales
vel huiusmodi faciens cum simbolo aut oracione dominica aut talia scribit
in cartis et ponat super aliquem infirmum, ut sic in illis tantum Deus
20   Creator omnium honoretur, non reprobatur dummodo nulla alia supersticiosa
misceantur, ut patet 26, questione 5, *Non liceat*, et questione 7, *Non
observetis*. Et dicit ipse: "Securum est quod huiusmodi faciens sit discretus, probatus in fide, bone vite et bone fame, et quod nullo modo infundat
oraciones huiusmodi super pomum, pirum, cingulum, aut consimilia, set
25   tantum super infirmitatem, iuxta illud Matthei ultimo: 'Super egros manus
inponent,' supple in nomine Domini nostri Iesu Christi, 'et bene habebunt,' " ut patet questione 2, *Utrum observaciones*.
Sunt eciam alii qui syromantici dicuntur, et sunt illi manuum inspec-

keeps the eye of his mind in true faith steadily on the wood of the cross and
on Christ's death; if he does so, he will go through life safe and without
harm, according to the words of Matthew 15: "Your faith has made you whole,"
for as it is written in Hebrews: "The saints conquered by their faith," etc.

3–4 1 John 2.11.   **4–7** Hos. 4.1–2.   **8** Cf. Augustine, *Sermo 8* X.11 (PL 38:72).   **12–
13** John 20.29.   **14–16** Bernard, *Super Cantica* LXXVI.iii.6 (2:258).   **16–17** James
2.17.   **19–20** 2 Kings 2.19.   **22–23** Eccles. 5.9.   **23–24** Heb. 11.11.   **40–41** Cf.
Prov. 30.8.   **44** Isa. 13.22.   **45–51** Isidore, *Etym.* XI.iii.30–31.   **56–58** Ibidem, 32.
61 Jer. 6.13.   **71–72** Prov. 11.26.   **75–76** Ecclus. 13.1.   **81–82** 1 Pet 1.18.   **93** Matt.
9.22.   **93–94** Heb. 11.33.

V.xxx   PEOPLE WHO GO AGAINST THE FAITH

But, alas, in our days both men and women attack and go against this faith
when they, contrary to the rule set by God and the Church and under the impulse
of the devil, attribute to creatures what belongs to God alone, the Creator of
all, namely the ability to know and predict future events and to bring health
and sickness by laying on made-up charms. To this kind belong witches, in
English *tilsters*, who carry out their craft with words and promise to bring
healing with their charms and other wretched contrivances. For instance, when
somebody's stomach is heavy and sick because he has eaten and drunk too much,
they say "his mother has fallen," and then it is necessary to call in some
wretched old woman who knows this craft to rub his stomach and sides. Often
this does more harm than good, especially in spiritual terms, because skills of
this sort are forbidden. Therefore, in such cases one must inquire whether or
not such effects may be caused naturally, because if they are not, then it
follows that they are the result of some diabolical skill. Which proves that
nature could have a natural effect, as Augustine declares in book 12 of *The
City of God*. But Raymundus says on this issue that if a man or woman gathers
medicinal herbs or something of this kind and does so reciting the Creed or the
Lord's Prayer or writes these on a piece of paper which he places on the sick
person, so that by doing this he only honors God, the Creator of all things,
there is no reproach in this as long as nothing else of a superstitious character gets mixed in with it; thus in the *Decretum*, 26, question 5, *Non liceat*,
and question 7, *Non observetis*. And Raymundus says: "It is safe if the person
who does this is discreet, tried in faith, of a good life and good reputation,
and if in no way prayers of this kind are spoken over an apple, pear, belt, or
the like, but only over the sickness, according to the words at the end of
Matthew: 'They shall lay their hands upon the sick,' add: in the name of our
Lord Jesus Christ, 'and they shall recover,' " as is evident from question 2,
Utrum observaciones.

tores qui per lineamenta earum dicunt se futura contingencia scire et
30   predicere, quot viros talis mulier habebit et quot uxores talis vir, quomodo eciam talis est ad dignitatem promovendus et talis in patibulo suspen-
dendus. Que omnia falsa sunt et ab arte diaboli collecta et ficta, eo quod
in futuris contingentibus iudicium certum dari non potest nisi a Deo. Alii
autem sunt qui coniectores dicuntur, et sunt interpretatores sompniorum,
35   qui scilicet in talibus nimis credunt, cum tamen in rei veritate ut communiter ⟨e⟩veniunt ex aliqua causa naturali intrin- [f. 171v] seca, verbi
gracia: si enim complexio fuerit habundans ex humore frigido, tunc talis
communiter sompniabit de aquis, pluviis, nivibus, et huiusmodi. Quibus
propositis respondent tales coniectores quod venient in promptu tribulacio-
40   nes et angustie. Si autem complexio sua fuerit calida et sicca, tunc naturaliter sompniabit de igne, de luminaribus, cereis, et candelis. Set illis
propositis dicunt quod mors veniet in promptu. Que omnia falsa sunt, vana,
et supersticiosa. Et idem patet de illis qui credunt in primis donis, qu⟨e⟩
dicuntur *yerysyeftis* et *handselles*, per que credunt melius vel peius expe-
45   dire in die, ebdomoda, et mense et anno. Sunt et alii dicti arioli, ab aris
nominati, qui eciam precibus et sacrificiis faciunt artem suam, qui eciam
alio modo dicuntur ymaginarii et ydolatre, ydolas colentes ut sibi respondeant de futuris per oblaciones. Alii eciam ⟨phitonici⟩ sive specularii
dicuntur, quorum ars est inspicere in speculis, pelvibus, et unguibus
50   politis, et huiusmodi, [in quibus] vident ut dicunt mirabilia. Sunt eciam
alii nigromantici a nigredine dicti, sive vultuosi, et tales in circulis
demones suscitant ut ad quesita respondeant. Et similiter in cera et alia
molli materia componunt effigies hominum ad interficiendum eos. Ubi nota:
de peregrino queratur qui visitavit beatum Petrum quomodo salvatus fuit ab
55   uno tali. Sunt eciam alii qui dicuntur sortilegi, dicti a "sors, sortis,"
qui per sortem faciunt artem suam, sicut patet de *ragemonn* et festucis
contrahendis. Et similiter mathematici, scilicet qui per stellas sciunt
divina predicere. Versus:

Doctrinam mathesis notat, set divina[re] mathesis,

60   [et cetera huiusmodi.]
Set rogo quid dicendum est de talibus miseriis et supersticiosis [f.
172] qui de nocte dixerunt se videre reginas pulcherrimas et alias puellas
tripudiantes cum domina Dyana choreas ducentes dea paganorum, que in
nostro vulgari dicitur *elves*? Et credunt quod tales possunt tam homines quam
65   mulieres in alias naturas transformare ⟨et⟩ secum ducere apud *eluenlond*,
ubi iam, ut dicunt, manent illi athlete fortissimi, scilicet Onewyn et Wad
et ceteri. Que omnia [non] sunt nisi fantasmata et a maligno spiritu illis
demonstrata. Nam cum diabolus animam alicuius talis ad talia credendum

Others there are who are called palm readers, who look at one's hand and say
they can know and predict future events from the lines in one's palms, such as: how
many husbands such and such a woman will have, or how many wives a man,
how one person will be promoted to a high rank and another be hanged on the
gallows. But all this is false and made up and gathered by demonic art,
because there is no certain knowledge about future events except from God.
There are others, called soothsayers, and they interpret dreams; they have an
extraordinary faith in dreams, whereas in reality dreams usually are caused by
some natural and intrinsic factor; for instance, if someone is cold by his
physical constitution, he will normally dream of water, rain, snow, and the
like. But the soothsayers interpret such dreams as foreshadowing imminent
tribulations and anxieties. But if he has a hot and dry temper, he will
naturally dream about fire, lights, tapers, and candles. But the soothsayers
tell him that death will come soon. All of this is false, vain, and superstitious. And the same is true of people who believe in first gifts, which are
called *year's gifts* or *hansels*, by which they believe they will fare better or
worse in the particular day, week, month, and year. Others are called *arioli*,
from *ara*, "altar," because they practice their craft with prayers and sacrifices; they are otherwise also known as image-worshippers or idolaters, who
worship images and make offerings to them so that they might receive an answer
about the future. Others are called *phitonici* or *specularii*, whose art it is
to look into mirrors, bowls, polished fingernails, and the like, in which they
claim they see marvelous things. Others again are necromancers, so called from
nigredo, "blackness," or else "grimacers"; these raise devils in their circles
that are expected to answer their questions. Likewise they make figures of
people in wax or some other soft material in order to kill them. Notice the
story of a pilgrim who visited Blessed Peter, by whom he was saved from one of
this kind. Others there are who are called *sortilegi*, from *sors*, "lot," who
practice their art by casting lots, such as the *ragman* and drawing straws. And
there are *mathematici*, astrologers, who can foretell God's plans by the stars.
Hence the verse:

> *Máthesis* is a science, but the art to predict, *mathésis*.

And there are yet others of this sort.

But I ask, what shall we say of those superstitious wretches who claim
that at night they see the most beautiful queens and other girls dancing in the
ring with Lady Diana, the goddess of the heathens, who in our native tongue are
called *elves*? And they believe that these can change both men and women into
other beings and carry them with them to *elvenland* where there are already, as
they say, those strong champions like Onewynn and Wade and others. All this is
nothing but phantoms shown them by a mischievous spirit. For when the devil

subiugavit, seipsum aliquando transformat, modo in formam angeli, modo in
70 formam hominis, modo mulieris, modo aliarum creaturarum, modo equos,
modo pedes, modo eciam in torneamentis et hastiludiis, modo ut dictum est in
choreis et aliis ludis. Per que omnia animam talis miseri sic per credu-
litatem captivatam multipliciter deludit, ut talia credant et enarrent.
Quod beatus Paulus asserere non audebat quando raptus erat usque ad tercium
75 celum, set dicit: "Sive in corpore sive extra corpus, nescio; Deus scit."
Revera de istis sicut de supradictis omnibus dico aperte sicut patet
in *Decretis* 26, questione 5, *Episcopi*, quod qui in talibus credunt vel
pertinaciter docent, maxime postquam veritatem audierint, quod infidelissi-
mi sunt et paganis deteriores. Unde tam illa quam huiusmodi omnia et singu-
80 la secundum omnes doctores catholicos maledicta sunt a Deo et sancta eius
Ecclesia quater in anno. Et non tantum hoc, set omni die a communitate tota
ministrorum Ecclesie sancte. Dicit enim Psalmista: "Maledicti qui declinant
a mandatis tuis." Set mandatum Dei est: "Non habebis deos alienos." Ergo
contra illud facientes sunt maledicti, cuiusmodi sunt huiusmodi incredules
85 eo quod laborant iura propria Salvatoris ceteris [f. 172v] creaturis false
attribuere. Scribitur enim Ysaie 10: "Anima que declinaverit ad magos vel
ariolos," etc., "ponam faciem [meam] contra eam et interficiam illam de
medio populi"; quod Actuum 1 dicitur: "Non enim vestrum est nosse tempora
vel momenta que Pater posuit in sua potestate."
90 Et nota quod lex est in multis provinciis quod siquis in carcere
poneretur per regem vel principem, ⟨si tunc⟩ arte aliena aut ingenio carcerem frangat et evadit, quod ex tunc quantumcumque fuerit iustus vel innocens seipsum facto illo reddit reum et culpabilem, et ideo post hoc maiori
plectitur pena. Moraliter enim loquendo carcer Dei infirmitas est sive alia
95 quecumque tribulacio, in qua nos rebelles sua iusticia occulta sive manifesta pro delictis affligit et castigat. Set hunc carcerem nituntur ⟨e⟩va-
dere et infringere qui per sortilegium et illicita carmina querunt illicita
sue infirmitatis remedia, et ideo gravius pro hiis merito punientur et
forte ad mortem, prout patet Regum 1 de rege Ochosia qui spreto Deo ° vivo
100 et vero consuluit deum Accharon. Similiter Saul in angustia positus consuluit Phitonissam, propter quod secundum aliquos tam ipse quam filius eius
Ionathas in bello cadebant et regnum datum est David. Nam Sauli dixerat
Samuel, Regum 28: "Cras enim tu et filii tui mecum eritis." Unde Exodi 22
dicitur et precipitur: "Non pacieris maleficos vivere," quasi diceret: quia
105 opera Creatoris, scilicet de futuris contingentibus, creaturis attribuunt,
merito sunt detestandi. Quod optime patet sic.
Narrat enim Malmesbury libro 6 *De gestis Anglorum* de quadam muliere
apud Berkeley maleficiis consueta, que dum quadam die circa coniuraciones
occuparetur, corniculam quamdam quam in [f. 173] cibo nutrierat audivit
110 more suo insolito crocitantem et miro modo garrientem. Quo audito cecidit

has subdued someone's soul into believing these things, he transforms himself,
now into an angel, now into a man or a woman, now into other creatures, now
[on] horses, now [on] foot, sometimes even at tournaments and jousts, sometimes, as I have said, at dances and other games. By all of these he deludes
in many ways the soul of a wretch whom he has captivated through his credulity,
so that he will believe and recount all this. Blessed Paul did not dare to
tell about similar things after he had been carried up to the third heaven, but
instead said: "Whether in the body or out of the body, I do not know; God
knows."

So, indeed, of these people and all the others mentioned above I say
openly what can be found in the *Decretum* 26, question 5, *Episcopi*, that those
who believe in such things or obstinately teach them, especially after they
have heard the truth, are most faithless and worse than heathens. Wherefore
these and all other superstitious beliefs and practices are, according to all
the doctors of the Church, cursed by God and his holy Church four times a year.
And beyond this they are cursed every single day by the entire community of the
servants of Holy Church. For the Psalmist says: "Cursed are they who decline
from your commandments." But God's commandment is: "You shall have no other
gods." Therefore, those who act against this commandment are cursed, and this
applies to such people of wrong belief as we have seen, who are at pains
falsely to attribute to creatures what by right belongs to our Savior alone.
For it is written in Isaiah 10: "I will set my face against the soul that has
gone aside after magicians and soothsayers," etc., "and I will cut him off out
of the midst of his people." For in Acts 1 it is said: "It is not for you to
know the times or moments which the Father has put in his own power."

And notice that there is a law in many regions that if someone is put in
jail by the king or prince and breaks jail and escapes by his cleverness or
some outside help, he thereby renders himself guilty, even if he had been
guiltless and innocent before, and in consequence is given a greater punishment. Morally speaking, God's prison is some illness or some worldly tribulation, in which he touches and chastises us rebels for our crimes with his
justice, whether in secret or openly. But people who seek for forbidden reme-
dies for their illness by means of soothsaying and forbidden charms try to
break and escape from this jail; and therefore they will justly be punished
more grievously for these acts, perhaps even with death, as it evidently happened to Ahaziah, in Kings 1, who scorned the living and true God and instead
consulted the god of Ekron. In a similar way, when Saul was in great straits
he consulted the witch of Endor, for which act, according to some writers, both
he and his son Jonathan fell in battle and the kingdom was given to David; for
in Kings 28, Samuel had said to Saul: "For tomorrow you and your sons shall be
with me." Whence it is said and commanded in Exodus 22: "You shall not suffer
wizards to live," as if to say: since they attribute the works of the Creator,

cultellus de manu eius ac simul vultus palluit, et concidit et producto
gemitu profundo: "Hodie, inquit, audiam et accipiam aliquid grande." Et
hiis dictis intravit quidam nuncius obitum filii sui et familie ruinam
exponens. Que statim pre angustia in lecto decubuit usque ad mortem saucia-
115 ta, et superstites liberos suos, unam monacham et alium monachum, pernici-
bus incitavit epistolis, quibus advenientibus dixit: "Nunc quia ad finem
vite mee propero et demones habeo exactores in pena quos per sortilegia et
alia maleficia hactenus suasores habui in culpa, vos ergo per materna
viscera rogo ut saltem al⟨levi⟩are temptetis tormenta. Et cum mortua fuero,
120 hoc modo corpus meum servate: Primo insuite corpus in corio cervino, deinde
ponite in tumulo lapideo, operculo ferreo et plumbeo constringite, et super
hec omnia lapidem tribus cathenis ferreis magni ponderis circumdate. Et
psalteria quinquaginta per tres noctes et eiusdem numeri missas de die pro
me cantari faciatis, que forsan adversariorum concursus levigent et resis-
125 tent. Et si tribus noctibus ibidem secure iacuero, quarto die infodite
matrem vestram humo, quamquam verear ne terra me recipiat suis finibus que
tociens gravata fuit sortilegiis." Et hiis dictis expiravit. Cum ergo omnia
ut preceperat facta fuissent, pro dolor nil pie lacrime liberorum value-
runt, nil vota, nil preces, tanta erat circa eam demonum potestas. Nam
130 primis duabus noctibus, cum chori clericorum psalmos circa eius corpus [f.
173v] concreparent, demones ostium ecclesie obturatum ingenti clausura
leviter distringentes duas extremas cathenas fregerunt, media vero que erat
quasi laboriosius obturata [illibata] duravit. Tercia ergo nocte circa
gallicantum horribili strepitu demonum adveniencium nonnulla fundamenta
135 monasterii visa sunt moveri. Unus ergo demonum vultu terribilior et statura
eminencior ianuas ecclesie maiori vi concussas in fragmenta deiecit. Diri-
guere clerici metu, steterunt quique non valentes aufugere. Ille ergo
demon, ut videbatur, arroganti gestu ad tumulum lapideum accessit et ibidem
invocato et acclamato eiusdem mulieris nomine ut surgeret imperavit. Qua
140 respondente: "Nequeo pre vinculis," respondit demon: "Solveris, inquit, set
malo tuo." Quo dicto mox cathenam ut stuppam disrumpens operculum tumbe
pede excussit et apprehensam coram omnibus extra ecclesiam traxit, ubi pre
foribus equs nigerrimus horribiliter ⟨hinn⟩iens videbatur aculeis ferreis
per totum dorsum repletus, super quem misera imposita mox ab oculis intuen-
145 cium cum tota [demonum] multitudine disparuit numquam deinde visa. Ipsa
tamen audiebatur fere per quatuor miliaria clamando ac miserabiliter inpre-
cando. Hec ibi.
     Ad idem eciam patet 4 libro *Dyalogorum* de quodam nequam excommunicato
in ecclesia sepulto et a demonibus foras eiecto. Caveant ergo omnes tales,
150 quia secundum beatum Augustinum 26, questione 7, tam huiusmodi malef⟨ici⟩a
observantes quam attendentes, docentes, consencientes, credentes, et ad domum taliter accedentes aut int⟨rodu⟩ctos interrogantes sciant se a Christi

namely future events, to his creatures, they are rightly to be rejected. This
is quite manifest from the following account.

In his *Deeds of the English*, William of Malmesbury reports of a woman that
practiced witchcraft near Berkeley. One day, as she was busy with her incanta-
tions, she heard her raven, whom she had reared up with her own food, croak in
an unusual way and chatter in a strange fashion. When she heard this, her
knife fell from her hand and she turned all pale in the face, and she fell down
and gave a heavy sigh, saying: "Today I shall hear and receive something important." At these words a messenger entered and announced the death of her
son and the ruin of his family. She at once lay down in her bed in great
anxiety, hurt to death. Then she hastily sent by letter for her remaining
children, one a nun, the other a monk, and when they arrived, she said to them:
"I am quickly coming to the end of my life, and the demons who so far have
helped me in sin, by my soothsaying and witchcraft, will now carry out my
punishment. As I am your mother, I ask you to do everything to lessen my
torments. When I am dead, you must keep my body as follows: first, sew me in
the hide of a stag; then put me in a stone coffin with a lid of iron and lead;
and on top of this put a rock wound with three iron chains of great weight.
Then you must have fifty psalters said for me for three nights, and fifty
Masses per day, which perhaps will lighten and hold back the attacks of my
enemies. If I lie safe this way for three nights, then you can put your mother
in the ground on the fourth day, although I fear that the earth may not accept
me anywhere because I have so often burdened it with my witchcraft." And with
these words she died. Everything was done as she had ordered, but alas!
neither the pious tears of her children nor the offerings nor the prayers
availed anything, so great was the devils' power over her. For in the first
two nights, as the choirs of clerics let their prayers resound round her body,
the devils easily pulled open the church door that had been heavily barred and
broke the two outer chains, while the one in the middle, which was more heavily
wrought, remained intact. But in the third night at cockcrow the very foundations of the monastery could be seen to shake with the horrible noise of the
devils when they came. One of them, with a terrifying face and taller than the
rest, kicked the church doors with great force and broke them down in pieces.
The clerics stood absolutely stiff with fear and could not flee. Then that
devil went to the stone tomb, as it seemed with haughty steps, and there called
out the woman's name, ordering her to rise. She answered: "I can't, because
of the chains," but he replied: "You shall be freed, but for your own evil."
With these words he right away broke the chain as if it were a string, kicked
the lid aside with his foot, and grabbed the woman and pulled her outside the
church in the sight of everybody. There, outside, appeared a black horse which
gave an awesome neigh and had its whole back full of iron needles. The wretched woman was put on that and soon disappeared from everybody's sight with the

fide apostatasse et suum baptismum prevaricasse, [f. 174] per quod iram Dei
ac eius inimiciciam incurrisse, nisi ecclesiastica doctrina emendati per
155   penitenciam Deo reconcilientur. Et quod si talis fuerit clericus, deponendus [est] et in monasterio detrudendus; si laicus, excommunicandus. Et si
notorium sit, eucaristia cum ceteris [beneficiis] Ecclesie deneganda et
pena secundum canones Extravagancium *De sortilegiis*, quadraginta dierum
inponenda.
160   Nota eciam quod omnes tales pro hereticis iudicantur. Nam hereticus
secundum beatum Augustinum est qui falsam opinionem de fide gignit et in
illa perseverat et pertinaciter defendit; vel secundum Ieronimum, qui
sacram scripturam aliter intelligit, docet, ac pertinaciter defendit quam
Spiritus Sancti sensus flagitat. Et nota quod numquam aliquis hereticus
165   censendus est nisi qui in illa perseverat et illam pertinaciter defendit.
Et talis secundum Raymundum, sive occultus sive manifestus, ipso iure est
maiori excommunicacione excommunicatus. Et talis cuiuscumque condicionis
sit, eciam si papa fuerit, deponendus est. Easdem eciam excommunicaciones
incurrunt omnes illorum fautores, receptores, et in illis credentes.
170   Bene ergo deberent propter periculum excommunicacionis omnes tales ab
huiusmodi maleficiis et interdictis desistere. Est ergo excommunicacio a
qualibet licita communione actu separacio, et talis excommunicacionis due
sunt species, quia una maior, alia minor. Prima separat omnino a sacramentis et ab ingressu ecclesie, et a communione fidelium. Set nota quod nus-
175   quam est aliquis excommunicandus nisi propter peccatum mortale, nec maior
excommunicacio infligenda nisi pro contumacia tantum et contemptu; set minor pro contumacia et aliis culpis. Et nota quod timenda est excommunicacio
tum quia ipsa est quasi [f. 175] gladius spirtualis separans animam a Deo
sicut gladius materialis separat animam a corpore, tum quia talis excommu-
180   nicatus est quasi ab hostibus captus et Dei auxilio omnino destitutus, tum
quia privatus communione fidelium et ab omnibus bonis que fiunt in Ecclesia.
Nota quod communicans cum excommunicatis magno periculo se exponit, et
primo in semetipso, quia non cavet sibi ab eo qui habet morbum contagiosum.
185   Secundo in excommunicato, eo quod sibi aufert remedium mortis, scilicet
confusionem, ex cuius metu deberet conteri et corrigi; Ecclesiastici 4
dicitur: "Est confusio adducens gloriam." Tercio peccat in illo pro quo
excommunicacio fit, quia aufert sibi rem suam. Et quarto in Deum, quem in
ministro suo spernit et contempnit; Luce 10: ["Qui vos spernit, me sper-
190   nit." Per istud legitur in figura Exodi 10] quod "tenebre horribiles facte
sunt in universa terra Egipti," in signum separacionis illorum a Deo; set
"ubicumque fuerunt filii Israel, lux erat." Unde hos ab illis divisit
tamquam lucem a tenebris, in signum quod nulla debet esse communicacio
bonorum ad malos et precipue excommunicatos; unde Genesis 1 dicitur: "Divi-

whole crowd of devils and was never seen again. However, she was heard howling and cursing miserably at a distance of nearly four miles.

A similar story appears in book 4 of the *Dialogues*, of an excommunicated wretch who had been buried in the church and was cast out of it by devils. Therefore, let all such people take heed, because according to Blessed Augustine in the *Decretum* 26, question 7, both those who practice witchcraft of this kind and those who are present at it, teach, consent, or believe in it, go to the house of such practitioners or put questions to the spirits that have been raised—all these must be aware that they have fallen away from faith in Christ and have violated their baptismal vow; and by this they have incurred God's anger and his enmity, unless enlightened by the Church's teaching they become through penitence reconciled with God. If such a person is a member of the clergy, he is to be deposed and placed in a monastery; if he is a layman, he is to be excommunicated. And if his case is well known, he is to be denied the Eucharist and other benefits of the Church and is to receive a penance of forty days, according to the canons *De sortilegiis* in the *Extravagantes*.

Notice further that all such offenders are judged to be heretics. For according to Blessed Augustine, a heretic is a person who generates a false teaching about the faith, perseveres in it, and defends it tenaciously; or according to Jerome, it is a person who understands and teaches Holy Scripture, and who tenaciously defends such teaching, in a sense that differs from what the sense of the Holy Spirit requires. But notice that no one is to be considered a heretic unless he perseveres in his false belief and defends it tenaciously. Such a person, whether he remains hidden or is openly known, is automatically excommunicated by the Great Curse, according to Raymundus; and whatever his station may be, he is to be deposed, even if he were the pope. The same excommunications extend to all who protect, shelter, and believe in such heretics.

Therefore, it would be well if all such people desisted from witchcraft and other such forbidden practices because of the danger of excommunication. Excommunication means the actual separation from any kind of permissible communion, and it has two kinds, the greater and the lesser. The first excludes a person totally from receiving the sacraments, from permission to enter a church, and from contact with the faithful. But notice that no one is ever excommunicated unless it be for some mortal sin, nor must the greater excommunication be applied except in case of obstinacy and contempt. The lesser excommunication is for obstinacy and other sins. Excommunication must be feared, both because it is a sharp spiritual sword that separates the soul from God just as a bodily sword separates the soul from the body, and because an excommunicated person is, as it were, captured by his enemies and totally without God's help, and further deprived of the communion of the faithful and of all the good that is available in the Church.

195   sit Deus lucem a tenebris." Ad idem eciam figuram habemus Paralipomenon de
      Iosaphat rege Iuda, qui quia communicavit cum impio rege Achab, Israel
      periculum mortis incurrit, et post prophetam audire a Deo meruit qui "impio
      prebens auxilium," etc., "idcirco iram Domini merebaris." In Novo Testamen-
      to, Matthei silicet 18, precepit Dominus quod ille qui monitus ab Ecclesia
200   Ecclesiam audire contempneret, esset "tamquam ethnicus et publicanus," qui
      fuerunt a Deo reprobati.
         Igitur huiusmodi supersticiosa sunt omnino fugienda, et ad veram fidem
      est festinandum. Ipsa enim vitam eternam adquirit iuxta illud Iohannis 11:
      "Qui credit in me, eciam si mortuus fuerit, vivet." Et quod probatur [f.
205   174v] verum, ipsa est carta Christianorum habendi et tenendi libere et qui-
      ete regnum celorum, quia sicut qui fideliter habet cartam alicuius domini
      sibi iuste concessam super aliqua terra vel tenemento, quamdiu ille fideli-
      ter faciat servicium suum domino, debite tenetur eum dominus salvare et
      warantizare pro quibuscumque aliis. Ita quamdiu fideliter tenemus fidem
210   nostram in carta simboli contentam, nec illa ibi conscripta diminuimus nec
      augmentamus aliter quam Spiritus Sanctus docet, contra omnes inimicorum
      insultus Christus Dominus noster warantizabit nos et pro servicio nostro
      regnum celorum prestabit. Et sic patet quomodo vera fides mundum vincit et
      celum adquirit.

---

14 possint] possunt O.   pertinent] pertinet C.R.   **15** natura . . . naturalem] nullum effectum C; nullam efficaciam naturalem R.   **16** Augustinum] *add* di C.   **17** herbas medi-
cinales] herbam medicinalem O.   **26** nostri] *om* O.   **31** dignitatem] dignitates O.
36 eveniunt] est veniunt C.   **39** quod] *add* sibi M.R; *add* si W.   venient] evenient M.W;
eveniunt R.   **41** igne] *add* similiter M.W; *add* sicut R.   **43** que] qui C.   **45** et] in O.
48 phitonici] prohibitonici C.   **50** politis] pollicis O (*not all clear*).   **56** qui] *add* scilicet
O.   **59** divinare] divina C.M.W.   **62** dixerunt] dicunt O.   **64** dicitur] *all four manuscripts have* dr.   **65** vel] et C.   **67** non] *om* C.W.   **71** eciam] *om* O.   **73** captivatam]
captivam O.   **79–80** et singula] *om* O.   **83** deos alienos] deum alienum O.   **84** in-
credules] increduli O.   **88** enim] *om* O.   **91** si tunc] set tunc C, *with* tunc *canceled*.
92 evadit] evadat M.R; vadat W.   **94** Moraliter enim] sed moraliter M.W; sic moraliter
R.   **95** quecumque] *add* mundi O.   **96–97** evadere] invadere C.   **99** Deo] *add* et C.
110 crocitantem] cornicantem O.   **114–115** sauciata] saucia O.   **118** ergo] *om* O.
119 alleviare] alienare C.   **120** corpus(2)] me O.   **121** ponite] *add* me O.   **123** et
eiusdem] eiusque O.   **125** ibidem] hoc modo O.   **127** fuit] *om* M.W; est meis R.
129 potestas] potencia O.   **133** obturata] operata O.   **143** hinniens] inhiens C.   **146–
147** inprecando] deprecando O.   **147** ibi] ille O.   **150** maleficia] malefacta C.   **152** in-
troductos] interdictos C.M(?).   **178–204** gladius . . . probatur(204)] *on fol. 175, with
signe de renvoi at end of fol. 174. The the text continues fols. 174v–175v.*   **198** prebens]
prebes O.   **203** est] *om* O.   **205** verum] *see note at line 178.*   **208** faciat] facit O.   **212**
noster] *om* O.   nos] *om* O.   **213** prestabit] dabit O.

Notice that someone who communicates with an excommunicated person exposes himself to great danger. First to himself, because he does not protect himself against a person who has an infectious disease. Next he harms the excommunicated person also, because he takes from him the remedy for his death, that is, his social stigma that should lead him to repentance and correction; in Ecclesiasticus 4 it is said: "There is a shame that brings glory." Third, he sins against him for whose sake the excommunication occurs, for he robs him of his own. And fourth, he sins against God, whom he scorns and despises in his minister; Luke 10: "He who despises you, despises me." As a type of all this, we read in Exodus 10 that "horrible darkness came over all the land of Egypt," to indicate their separation from God; but "wherever the children of Israel dwelt, there was light." Thus God separated the Israelites from the Egyptians as light from darkness, as a sign that there must be no communion between the good and the wicked, and especially the excommunicated; for in Genesis 1 it is said: "God divided the light from the darkness." We have another type of the same in Jehoshaphat, the king of Judah, in Chronicles: when he communicated with the godless king Ahab, Israel was in danger of death, and then deserved to hear the prophet from God, because "by helping the ungodly," etc., "you deserved the wrath of God." And in the New Testament, namely in Matthew 18, the Lord commanded that a person who after being admonished by the Church refuses to listen should be "as a heathen and publican," which were people rejected by God.

Therefore, we must altogether flee from such superstitions and hasten to the true faith, for it brings us to eternal life, after the words of John 11: "He who believes in me, even if he were dead, will live." In proof of this, faith is a charter for Christians to have and to hold the kingdom of heaven freely and in peace. If anyone holds in good faith a charter given to him rightfully by his lord, over some piece of land or fief, as long as he serves his lord faithfully, the lord is held to keep and protect him from all others. In the same way, as long as we keep our faith that is contained in the charter of the Creed and neither take away nor add anything to what is written there, in opposition to what the Holy Spirit teaches us, our Lord Christ will protect us against all the attacks of our enemies and will for our service grant us the kingdom of heaven. Thus it is manifest how true faith overcomes the world and gains heaven.

On the background of this chapter and analogous treatments, see G. R. Owst, "Sortilegium *in English Homiletic Literature of the Fourteenth Century,* in *Studies Presented to Sir Hilary Jenkinson*, ed. J. C. Davies (London, 1957), pp. 272–303. **15–16** Perhaps Augustine, *De civ. Dei* XII.25 (CC 48:381). **17–27** Raymundus, *Summa* I.xi.3 (pp. 104–105) and marginal gloss. **21–22** Gratian II.26.5.3 (1:1027–28) and II.26.7.16 (1:1045–46). **25–27** Mark 16.18. **48–50** On this kind of superstition, and the reading

V.xxxi   DE PRUDENCIA CONTRA MUNDUM

[R]estat ergo ostendere quomodo sibi similiter per prudenciam est
obviandum et resistendum. Circa quam hoc modo est procedendum: ostendere
primo quid sit; secundo, in quibus consistit; tercio, quomodo antiquitus
viguit. Est ergo prudencia secundum Tullium in *Secunda rhetorica*, libro 2,
5   rerum bonarum malarumque sciencia. Et ista prudencia in tribus consistit:
in memoria preteritorum, in intelligencia presencium, et in providencia
futurorum. Unde de tribus istis eius partibus exponi potest illud Exodi 15:
"Filii Israel ambulaverunt tribus diebus per solitudinem." Isti ergo filii
interpretantur "videntes Deum," ad designandum quod illi qui in so⟨li⟩tudi-
10   ne huius mundi per bonam et providam scienciam et discucionem trium predictorum ambulaverunt per tres dies, idest per tria tempora predicta, Deum in
fine videre merebuntur.
        Si ergo ad memoriam facta preterita reducere velimus, quomodo, si bene
an male, vixerimus, oportet librum consciencie diligenter revolvere. Ubi
15   notandum est quia qui super aliquem [f. 175v] librum incorrectum sine
cespitacione et defectu legere voluerit, necessario ad lucem habet oculum
dirigere, mediante qua poterit scripturam et litteras bene discernere et
videre. Si vero oculum ad tenebras advertat, secure non leget nec communiter bene, quantumcumque fuerit litteratus. Set modo ita est quod quilibet
20   nostrum habet pro libro conscienciam propriam, in qua omnia preterita opera
sive bona sive mala conscribuntur—set certe, ut timeo, multa plura mala
quam bona. De quo Danielis 4 dicitur: "Iudicium sedit et libri aperti
sunt." Lux ergo necessario adquiritur ad hunc librum perlegendum. Set illa

unguibus politis ("polished fingernails") rather than *unguibus pollicis* ("thumbnails"), see the autobiographical account in John of Salisbury, *Policraticus* II.28 (1:164); and G. L. Kittredge, *Witchcraft in Old and New England* (Cambridge, Mass., 1929), p. 185. **59** A mnemonic verse indicating the lexical difference between *máthesis*, "mathematical knowledge," and *mathésis*, "divination." It can be found in various forms; e.g., *Brito metricus* 1166 (ed. L. W. Daly, Philadelphia, 1968); Hugh of St. Victor, *Didascalicon* II.4 (PL 172:753); Eberhard of Bethune, *Graecismus* X.210 (ed. J. Wrobel, Breslau, 1887). See also *Policraticus* I.9, note on line 19 (1:49). **75** 2 Cor. 12.2, 3. **77–79** Gratian II.26.5.12 (1:1030–31). **82–83** Ps. 118.21. **83** Exod. 20.3. **86–88** Lev. 20.6. **88–89** Acts 1.7. **99–100** 2 Kings 1. **100–103** 1 Sam. 28.19. **104** Exod. 22.18. **107–147** Tubach 2461, from William of Malmesbury, *De gestis regum Anglorum* II (ed. W. Stubbs, Rolls Series, London, 1887–1889, 1:253). **148–149** Gregory, *Dialogi* II.xx-iii.4–5 (2:206–208) and IV.lii–liv (3:176–180). **150–155** Augustine as quoted in Gratian II.26.7.16 (1:1045–46). **158–159** *Decretals* 5.21.1 (2:822). **160–169** Raymundus, *Summa* I.v.1–6 (pp. 38–41). **160–162** Augustine, *De utilitate credendi* I.1 (CSEL 25:3). **162–164** Cf. Hilarius, *De Trinitate* II.Num. 8 (PL 10:51–52). **187** Ecclus. 4.25. **189–190** Luke 10.16. **190–192** Exod. 10.22. **194–195** Gen. 1.4. **196–198** 2 Chron. 19.2. **199–200** Matt. 18.17. **204** John 11.25.

V.xxxi HOW PRUDENCE FIGHTS AGAINST THE WORLD

Now we must show how the world is likewise to be countered and withstood by prudence. In this I will proceed as follows: I will show, first, what prudence is; second, what it consists in; and third, how it flourished among the ancients. According to Cicero in book 2 of his *Second Rhetoric*, prudence is the knowledge of good and evil. This virtue consists in three aspects: memory of what is past, understanding of what is present, and foresight of what is to come. To these three parts can be applied the words of Exodus 15: "The children of Israel marched three days through the wilderness." "Children of Israel" means "those who see God" and designates those who, after marching with a good and careful understanding and discernment of the aforesaid things in the wilderness of this world for three days, that is, for the three time periods mentioned above, will in the end merit to see God.

If we, then, wish to bring our past deeds back to memory in order to see how we have lived, whether well or badly, we must carefully leaf through the book of our conscience. For this purpose we must consider that whoever wishes to read an uncorrected book without stumbling and fault must needs turn his eye to the light, in which he will be able to distinguish and see the writing and the letters clearly. But if he keeps his eye in the dark, he will usually not read well and with certainty, no matter how well educated he may be. But now it is the case that instead of a book we all have our conscience, in which all our past deeds are written, the good as well as the bad ones—though I fear more of them bad than good. To this conscience Daniel 4 refers by saying: "Judgment sat and the books were opened." It is, therefore, necessary to have

lux lex Dei est, iuxta illud Proverbiorum 6: "Mandatum lucerna, et lex
25 lux." Ut ergo sciamus in isto libro quid sit corrigendum et quid non, que
eciam sit bona littera et que non, idest que opera sunt meritoria et que
non, oportet quod vertamus folia istius libri et quod oculum mentis ad
lucem legis Christi dirigamus, intente scilicet cogitando que sunt precepta
Dei, que concilia, que prohibencia, et cetera huiusmodi, et quomodo ista
30 observamus aut omisimus. Et certe tunc clare poterimus cognoscere que sunt
corrigenda et que non, et per confessionis abrasionem, in qua lingua pro
cultello habetur, mala corrigere valeamus. Pro isto nota supra particula de
preceptis, similiter de contricione et eciam de confessione.
    Circa secundam partem prudencie, intellectiva presencium, est sciendum
35 quod tempus presens est tempus gracie et misericordie, in quo preterita
sunt corrigenda et futura precavenda. In quo eciam insidiatur homo ab
inimicis quasi continue, qui sunt mundus, de quo satis nota supra particula
4 in principio et infra, et similiter in particula ista, capitulo proximo.
Alius inimicus est caro, de qua [f. 176] nota aliqualiter proximo capitulo
40 sequente, et maxime particula 7; similiter supra ubi agitur de accidia, et
post ubi agitur de gula, que carnis filie sicut luxuria dicuntur. Tercius
hostis est diabolus, qui instigat ad superbiam, iram, [et] invidiam, de
quibus nota supra particulis 1, 2, et 3 locis suis, et hic post, capitulo
15. Ab istis ergo est summe precavendum in presenti ne nos seducant ut
45 nituntur.
    Circa terciam partem prudencie, que est providencia futurorum, scili-
cet de morte et iudicio, nota supra: [particula 1, et] parte 4 capitulo 5
de morte; de iudicio vero nota supra particula 1. De isto tamen iudicii die
ait Augustinus: "O, inquit, homo, quid ages, quid dices cum contra te
50 loquitur consciencia, te accusabunt elementa, crux Christi, et passio, et
Christus per vulnera ligabit, cicatrices loquentur, et claves conquerentur?
Revera (dicit ipse Augustinus) angustie erunt undique, nam peccata ibi
erunt accusancia, inde demonia nunciancia, intus urens consciencia, extra
mundus ardens, subtus horrendum chaos inferni patens, supra iudex iratus,
55 et 'vix iustus salvabitur.' Homo ergo peccator sic deprehensus qua parte se
vertet? Latere erit inpossibile, et apparere intollerabile." Et ideo ait
Ieronimus: "Quociens, inquit, diem illum considero, toto corpore contremis-
co. Unde sive comedo, sive bibo, sive aliquid aliud facio, semper videtur
in auribus meis sonare et canere tuba illa terribilis: 'Surgite, mortui,
60 venite ad iudicium!' Quis ergo pavor ille, quis⟨ve⟩ pudor erit, o anima
mea, dum dimissis omnibus quorum tibi presencia tam iocunda fuerunt, scilicet tam gratus aspectus, cohabitacio tam familiaris, sola ingrediens °
incognitam regionem, ubi occurrencia tibi turmatim [f. 176v] ruere teterri-
ma illa monstra videbis? Quis tibi in tante necessitatis articulo succur-
65 ret? Quis te ducet? Quis te consolabitur? Quis te tuebitur a rugientibus

light to peruse this book. But this light is the Law of God, according to the words of Proverbs 6: "The Lord's commandment is a lamp, and his Law a light." Now, in order to know what in this book must be corrected and what not, which letters are right and which are not—that is, which of our deeds are meritorious and which are not—, it is necessary to turn the leaves of this book and to direct the eye of our mind to the light of Christ's law, by earnestly reflecting on what God's commandments are, his counsels, his prohibitions, and so forth, and how we have either kept or neglected them. Then we will certainly be able to discern clearly what needs to be corrected and what not, and we can correct the errors through the erasure of confession, in which our tongue is used as a pen knife. On this matter see above, in the part about the commandments, and likewise on contrition and confession.

With respect to the second part of prudence, which is the understanding of what is present, we must know that the present time is a time of grace and mercy, in which we should correct past sins and take precautions against future ones. Also, at this time man is continuously beset by his enemies: first the world, of which I have said enough above in part 4 at the beginning and later, as well as in the present part, the preceding chapter. The second enemy is our flesh, on which something may be found in the following chapter, and especially in part 7; likewise above, in the section devoted to sloth, and later in that on gluttony, which like lechery can be called daughters of the flesh. The third enemy is the devil, who urges us to pride, wrath, and envy, on which see above parts 1, 2, and 3, respectively, and also chapter 15 below in the present part. Against these we must take strong precautions in the present time, that they may not lead us astray as they always try to do.

With respect to the third part of prudence, that is, foresight of what is to come, namely death and judgment, see above, part 1 and part 4, chapter 5, on death; and part 1 above on judgment. Concerning the day of judgment, Augustine says: "O man, what will you do and say when your conscience speaks against you, when the elements accuse you, together with Christ's cross and Passion, when Christ proves his case with his wounds, when his scars speak and the nails lament? Indeed, there will be anxiety everywhere, for on one side will be your sins to accuse you, on the other devils to denounce you, within you your burning conscience, without the whole world in flames, at your feet the horrible chaos of hell gaping wide, and above you your wrathful judge. 'Scarcely the just man will be saved.' Where then shall a sinful man turn who has been thus caught? To hide will be impossible, and to come into the open unbearable." Therefore, Jerome says: "Whenever I think on that day, I tremble all over. Whether I eat or drink or do anything else, that terrible trumpet always seems to sound in my ears and say, 'Rise, you dead, and come to your judgment.' What will then be your dread, what your shame, O my soul, when you must leave all the things whose presence was so joyful, a pleasing sight or friendly company,

preparatis ad escam? Fili mi, '⟨memorare⟩ hec novissima et in eternum non
peccabis.' " Et sequitur: "Adam post unius pomi gustum abscondit se; nos
ergo quo ibimus?" Quasi diceret: omnino nescimus.

[Q]uomodo autem illa prudencia apud antiquos viguit, satis patet in
70   diversis locis. Qui plus de prudencia, que est ut dicitur bonorum malorum-
que sciencia, quam de toto mundo reputabant. Unde narrat Valerius libro 7
quomodo Themistodem philosophum consuluit unice filie pater, utrum scilicet
eam pauperi ornato sciencia et virtutibus an locupleti et parum probato in
talibus collocaret nubendo. Cui philosophus: "Malo, inquit, virum indigen-
75   tem pecunia quam pecuniam indigentem dominum." Carentem autem sciencia
et virtutibus, scire uti rebus non estimavit. Et ideo ait commentator 1 *Ethi-*
corum: "Prudencia, inquit, per se est desiderabilis, que valet et est
utilis ad multa." Unde Proverbiorum 3: "Beatus vir qui invenit sapienciam
et affluit prudencia." Et ideo eius gracia philosophi mundum et pecuniam
80   abiciebant. Unde narrat Valerius quod Crates Thebanus quondam ditissimus
cum ad philosophandum pergeret, magnum pondus auri abiecit non estimans
se mundi divicias simul et virtutes possidere. Et ideo Proverbiorum 18 bene
dicitur: "Quid stulto divicias habere, cum sapienciam emere non possit?"
Quasi diceret, nichil.
85   Patet ergo quod mundus nos invadens per fidem et prudenciam viriliter
conculcatur.

---

2 et] *add* sibi O.   **6** et] *om* O.   **9–10** solitudine] sollicitudine C.   **15** librum] *see note on line xxx.178.*   **22** quo] qua O.   **29** prohibencia] prohibentes O.   **34** intellectiva] que est intelligencia O.   **47** particula . . . et] *om* C.W.   **52** Augustinus] *om* O.   **60** quisve] quis vero C.   **62** ingrediens] *add* ruina in C.   **65** te(3)] *om* O.   **66** Fili mi] filioli mei O.   memorare] nota C.   **75** dominum] domino R.   **77** inquit] *om* O.   **85** quod] quomodo O.

V.xxxii   DE PUGNA CUM CARNE

[S]equitur modo de pugna cum carne, que difficilior pugna est aliarum.
Omnis enim pugna [f. 177] ⟨aliquorum⟩ hostium ab ipsa provenire et originem
attrahere videtur experimentis. Quia sicut omnia flumina a mari effluunt et

and you will go by yourself into an unknown land where you will see black monsters come rushing in crowds against you? Who will come to your aid in such great need? Who will lead you? Who will give you comfort? Who will guard you against those roaring monsters ready to devour you? O my children, 'remember these last things, and you will not sin in eternity.' Adam hid himself after merely tasting an apple; but we, where shall we go?" As if to say: we have no idea.

How much this prudence flourished among the ancients can be seen in various places. They valued prudence—the knowledge of good and evil, as I said earlier—more highly than the whole world. Valerius in book 7 narrates how the father of an only daughter consulted the philosopher Themistocles on whether he should give her in marriage to a poor man who possessed knowledge and virtues, or rather to a rich man who had been little tried in such things. The philosopher answered: "I would rather have a man without money than money without a master." For he reckoned that a man who lacked knowledge and the virtues did no know how to make use of his possessions. Therefore the commentator on the first book of the *Ethics* says: "Prudence is desirable in itself, because it is capable and useful for many things." Hence in Proverbs 3: "Blessed is the man that finds wisdom and is rich in prudence." For her sake the philosophers renounced the world and money. Valerius tells us that when Crates of Thebes, a very rich man, went to study philosophy, he threw away a large amount of gold, thinking that he could not possess riches and virtues together. And therefore it is said in Proverbs 18: "What does it avail a fool to have riches, seeing that he cannot buy wisdom?" as if to say: nothing.

Thus it is manifest how the world that besets us can be manfully overcome through faith and through prudence.

4–5 Cicero, *De inventione* II.liii.60.   **8** Exod. 15.22.   **22–23** Dan. 7.10.   **24–25** Prov. 6.23.   **32–33** *FM* III.vii and V.vii–xiv.   **37–38** *FM* IV.iv and V.xxix.   **39–41** *FM* V.xxxii, VII passim, V.i, and VI passim.   **43–44** *FM* I–III and V.xxxv.   **47–48** *FM* I.xiii and IV.xi; I.xiv.   **49–56** Cf. Ps. Bernard, *De interiori domo* XXII.46 (PL 184:531); also in Anselm, *Meditatio 1* (3:78–79).   **55** 1 Pet. 4.18.   **57–60** Ps.-Jerome, *Regula monacharum* 30 (PL 30:417), based on Jerome, *Ep. 66* 10 (CSEL 54:660).   **66–67** Ecclus. 7.40.   **71–76** Valerius, VII.2.ext.9.   **78–79** Prov. 3.13.   **80–82** Jerome, *Ep. 58* 2; see *FM* IV.xii.105–108. The story occurs in John of Wales, *Breviloquium* II.2 and III.4.   **83** Prov. 17.16.

V.xxxii   THE BATTLE AGAINST THE FLESH

Now follows the battle against our flesh, which is more difficult than the others; for to those experienced in such matters it seems that every battle against the other enemies stems and takes its origin from this one. For just

ad illud refluunt, sic a primis motibus carnis omnes temptaciones proveni-
5   unt. Et ideo secundum Bernardum diabolus plus confidit in operibus carnis
quam in propriis viribus, quia plus nocet hostis domesticus quam ignotus,
iuxta illud vulgare dictum: "Inimici hominis domestici eius." Et ideo
errant qui dicunt primos motus a suggestione diabolica provenire, cum ipse
sit omnino ignarus de cogitacionibus humanis n⟨isi⟩ inde aliquem motum
10   exterius percipit. Unde narratur in *Vitas Patrum* quod quidam sanctus quesivit a diabolo si sciret cogitaciones hominum. Et ille respondit quod sic.
Volens ergo vir sanctus ipsum probare dixit: "Cogito nunc; dic michi quid
est." Qui cum dixisset et ad⟨iu⟩ratus fuisset quomodo hoc scivisset, [res-
pondit]: "Quando, inquit, labia tua movebantur in cogitando, statim per
15   illum motum cogitaciones cordis tui percepi." Per quod satis patet quod
carnis suggestio forcius inpugnat et facilius devincit. De qua postea
particula 7 satis patebit.

---

1 aliarum] ceterarum O.   **2** aliquorum] occultorum C.   **3** experimentis] expertis O.
9 nisi] nec C.W.   **11** ille] *om* O.   **12** ipsum] illum O.   **13** adiuratus] admiratus C.M;
longer om W.

V.xxxiii   DE SPE CONTRA CARNEM PUGNANTE

[C]ontra hunc hostem spes se opponit fortiterque pugnans reportat triumphum. Est ergo spes "certa expectacio future beatitudinis ex Dei gracia
et meritis propriis proveniens," secundum Magistrum *Sentenciarum*. Et ideo
dicit ipse: "Sine meritis aliquid sperare non est spes set presumpcio dici
5   potest." Et nota quod sicut fides ita spes de invisibilibus est. In hoc
tamen differunt quod fides est de preteritis et futuris, spes autem de futuris tantum; fides eciam de bonis et malis est, spes vero de bonis tantum;
fides eciam de bonis tam sibi quam aliis, set spes de [f. 177v] propriis
bonis tantum. Et nota quod spes prout viatorum, hoc est in vita illa exer-
10   cicium, sic est in certitudine opinionis ut dictum est. Spes autem illorum
qui sunt in purgatorio et in limbo est in certitudine sciencie. Set spes
que fuit in beato Stephano quando vidit celos apertos, et in Paulo qui
dixit: "Scio cui credidi et certus sum," et similiter que fuit in Adam ante
peccatum, fuit in certitudine visionis, magis tamen debilis quam est in ce-
15   lo. [Ex quibus patet quod in celo] non est spes set omnium bonorum habitudo
simul et tota possessio. Unde ibi nichil est futurum quod speretur. Et nota
quod licet sanctis adhuc sit futura resurrectio corporum secundum rem, tamen presens est secundum cognicionem.
    Et nota quod effectus spei multiplex est. Quorum unus est quod liberat

as the water of all the rivers comes from the sea and flows back to it, so do
all temptations proceed from the first stirrings of the flesh. Hence, according to Bernard, the devil relies more heavily on the deeds of the flesh than on
his own powers, for an internal enemy is more harmful than a stranger, according to that common proverb, "A man's enemies are his inmates." Therefore
those are wrong who say the first stirrings come from the devil's suggestion,
because he is quite ignorant of a man's thoughts unless he perceives an external change caused by them. In *The Lives of the Fathers* there is a story about
a holy man who asked a devil if he knew men's thoughts. He replied that he
did. Then the holy man wanted to try him and said: "I am thinking. Tell me
what it is about." The devil told him; and when he was conjured to tell how he
knew that, he answered: "When you were thinking, your lips moved, and from
that movement I at once knew the thoughts of your heart." This shows us
clearly how forcefully the suggestive power of the flesh attacks us and how
easily it can overcome us. We will say more about this later in part 7.

5–6 Cf. *Meditationes piissimae* XIII.35 (PL 184:504).   **7** Cf. Whiting E.97.   **10–**
15 Tubach 4844; cf. Augustine, *De eccl. dogmatibus* 48 (PL 42:1221).   **17** *FM* VII.i–
xvi.

V.xxxiii   HOW HOPE FIGHTS AGAINST THE FLESH

Against this enemy stands hope, who repels him with force and carries the
victory. Hope is "the certain expectation of gaining future bliss, based on
God's grace and one's own merits," according to the Master of the *Sentences*.
And he says further: "To hope for anything without any merit of one's own is
not hope but can be called presumption." Notice that just like faith, hope is
about invisible things. But they differ in that faith deals with matters both
past and future, whereas hope deals only with future ones. Also, faith is
concerned with good as well as evil things, but hope only with good ones.
Faith is about things that are good for oneself and for others, but hope is
only about what is good for oneself. And notice that insofar as hope is held
by people on their pilgrimage through this life, it has the certainty of belief,
as was said in the definition. But the hope of souls in purgatory and in limbo
has the certainty of knowledge. Whereas the hope that was in Blessed Stephen
when he saw the heavens open, and in Paul when he said, "I know whom I
have believed, and I am certain," and similarly in Adam before his fall, had
the certainty of vision, although it was weaker than it is in heaven. And from
this it follows that in heaven there is no hope but the instantaneous, present,
and complete possession of all good things; there will be nothing to come in
the future for which one can only hope. And notice that although for the

20   a tribulacione, sicut patuit de Susanna et Daniele in lacu misso; unde
     Psalmista: "In te speraverunt et liberasti eos." Spes autem eciam confor-
     tat, sicut patuit de sanctis Machabeis, quos mater "sub uno diei tempore
     conspiciens mori, bono animo ferebat propter spem quam in Deo habebat."
     Exemplum eciam de David rege qui Goliam devincens ait: "Tu venis ad me cum
25   gladio et hasta, ego autem in nomine Domini," quasi diceret cum Psalmista:
     "Si exurgat adversum me prelium, in hoc ego sperabo," scilicet in auxilio
     et in nomine Domini. Et alibi: "In Deo speravi, non timebo quid faciat
     michi homo." Et ideo Proverbiorum 22 dicitur: "Appone ad doctrinam cor
     tuum, ut sit in Domino fiducia tua." Set prodolor de desperantibus conque-
30   ritur Salvator Ysaie 36 dicens: "Super quid habes fiduciam qui recessisti a
     me?" quasi dicat Dominus: si de me desperatis, in quo sperare proponitis?
     Unde Augustinus: "Non enim nostrorum vulnerum multitudo in desperacionem
     nos deprimant, [f. 178] quoniam maior est potencia medici quam magnitudo
     langoris. Attende ergo, homo (dicit ipse), de qua terra factus es, quia in
35   universo mundo unius talis terre pugillatum non invenies." Figuli enim de
     terra meliori et tenaciori vasa faciunt, que si in aliquo frangantur, nullo
     ingenio modo quo prius redintegrantur. Set homo factus de terra si peccando
     in aliquo mortali crimine quasi frustris dissolvatur, adhuc tamen per unam
     spem in Domino cum virtute contricionis et confessionis reintegratur, et
40   forte melius quam prius. Est ergo in Domino sperandum, non tamen in spe
     peccandi, quia "maledictus homo qui peccat in spe." Unde de desperacione
     nota supra, particula 2, capitulo 6, et similiter de Dei misericordia.

---

8 bonis] *add* est O.   **9–10** exercicium] existencium B1.   **16** futurum] futurorum O.
20 unde] *om* O.   **23** Deo] domino O.   **37** modo quo] ut M.R; *longer om* W.   **38** aliquo . . . crimine] M.e (?) M.W; me R.   tamen] *om* O.

V.xxxiv   DE TEMPERANCIA CONTRA CARNEM
PUGNANTE

    [V]iso vero quomodo spes vera hostem carnis succumbit, iam videndum
est quomodo virtus temperancie idem facere non desistit. Et nota quod
temperancia secundum Macrobium libro 1 est nichil appetere [penitendi], in
nullo legem moderacionis excedere, set sub iugo racionis cupiditatem do-
5   mare. Item temperancia est racionis [in] libidinem atque in non rectos

saints the resurrection of their bodies still remains in the future as a material event, it is already present to them in their knowledge.

The effect of hope is manifold. One is to free us from tribulation, as is
shown in Susanna and in Daniel in the lions' den; as the Psalmist says: "They
have hoped in you, and you have delivered them." Further, hope gives us comfort, as can be seen in the holy Maccabees: their mother saw them die in the
course of one day, yet she bore it well on account of the hope she had in the
Lord. There is also the example of King David, who overcame Goliath and said:
"You come to me with a sword and a spear, but I in the name of the Lord," as if
he were saying with the Psalmist: "If a battle should rise up against me, in
this I will have hope," that is, in the help and the name of the Lord. And
elsewhere: "In God I have put my trust, I will not fear what man may do
against me." Hence it is said in Proverbs 22: "Apply your heart to my teaching, so that your trust may be in the Lord." But alas, the Savior complains at
people who despair, in Isaiah 36: "In what do you trust, who are revolted from
me?" as if he were saying: if you despair of me, whom else do you propose to
set your hope on? Hence Augustine declares: "The large number of our wounds
must not put us in despair, for the power of our physician is greater than our
sickness. Keep in mind, O man, of what earth you were made, for in the whole
universe you will not find a single handful of such earth. Potters make their
vessels from better and firmer soil, but if those break, they cannot by any art
be restored to what they were before. But man, who is made of earth, if by
sinning against me he becomes, as it were, broken into bits, he can still be
mended again through one act of hope in the Lord with the power of contrition
and confession, and perhaps become even better than before." Therefore, we
should hope in the Lord, but not sin at the same time, for "cursed is the man
who sins in hope of forgiveness." About despair, and likewise about God's
mercy, see above, part 2, chapter 6.

2–9 Peter Lombard, *Sent.* III.xxvi.1–3 (2:159–160).   13 2 Tim. 1.12.   20 Dan. 13 and
6.   21 Ps. 21.5.   22–23 2 Macc. 7.20.   24–25 1 Sam. 17.45.   26 Ps. 26.3.   27–
28 Ps. 55.5.   28–29 Prov. 22.17–19.   30–31 Isa. 36.5.   32–35 Cf. Augustine, *En. in
Ps. 102* 5 (CC 40:1454–55).   42 *FM* II.iv passim.

V.xxxiv   HOW TEMPERANCE FIGHTS AGAINST THE FLESH

After we have seen how true hope subdues our enemy the flesh, we must now
see how the virtue of temperance unceasingly does the same. According to
Macrobius, in book 1, temperance means to desire nothing for which one will be
sorry and not to go beyond the right measure but to bridle one's desire with
reason. Further, temperance means the firm and just rule of reason over one's

impetus animi frena et moderata dominacio. Cuius partes sunt continencia,
clemencia, et modestia, secundum Tullium, *Rhetorica prima*, libro 2.
    Ubi est notandum quod continencia dicitur triplex. Uno modo prout est
cohibicio gule et luxurie, de quibus nota post, particulis 6 et 7. Alio
10   modo prout est cohibicio cupiditatis et avaricie, de quibus nota supra,
particula 4, capitulo 5. Et tercio prout est cohibicio elacionis et superbie, de quibus nota supra, particula 1.
    Secunda autem pars est clemencia, que est temperancia animi in potes-
tate ulciscendi vel lenitas superioris ad inferiorem, [f. 178v] ut ait
15   Seneca libro 2 *De clemencia*. Et nota quod ista clemencia quadrupliciter
dicitur. Primo in compaciendo affectualiter aliorum infortuniis, et de illa
loquitur Valerius libro 5 dicens: "Marcus, inquit, Marcellinus capt⟨i⟩s ab
eo Syracusan⟨i⟩s, cum esset in arce constitutus et fortunam opulentissime
urbis tunc afflicte cerneret ex alto et casum lugubrem, fletum cohibere non
20   potuit." Similiter nec Cesar, ut dicitur ibidem, cum capud Pompey aspexis-
set, pias lacrimas dedit. Et ideo dicit Orosius de Alexandro Darium inter-
fectum ac cathenis aureis ligatum inveniente. Quod eciam patet Regum 1 de
David lugente mortem Saulis inimici eius. Alio modo dicitur clemencia in
remittendo malefacta, eciam quamvis gravia. De qua Valerius ubi supra ait
25   quod Pompeius erga regem Armenie quamvis multa contra Romanos gesserat,
ipsum tamen vinctum in conspectu suo supplicem iacere non est passus, set
benignis verbis recreatus diadema quod abiecerat capiti reponere iussit et
in pristinum fortune habitum restituit, eque pulcrum iudicans vincere regem
et facere. Similiter et Paulus consul, ut dicitur ibidem, cum audisset
30   quendam captivum ad se adduci, sibi occurrit et volentem ad genua procum-
bere dextra sua ipsum allevavit eumque proximum sibi sedere fecit dicens:
"Si enim deicere hostem egregium est, non minus laudabile et infelicis
scire misereri." Sic enim docet Virgilius libro 6 *Enoydos*, et recitat
Augustinus libro 5 *De civitate Dei*, capitulo 13, versus:

35   Tu rege⟨re⟩ imperio populos R⟨oma⟩ne memento.
          Hee tibi sunt artes pacisque inponere mores: [f. 179]
          Parcere subiectos et debellare superbos.

Hoc eciam docet natura brutorum, iuxta illud versus:

          Parcere prostratis est nobilis ira leonis.
40   Tu quoque fac simile, quisquis dominaris in orbe.

Et alibi Ethnicus sic dicit per versus:

desires and the uncontrolled stirrings of one's heart. Its parts, according to
Cicero in book 2 of his *First Rhetoric*, are continence, clemency, and modesty.

Continence has three meanings. One is the virtue that controls gluttony
and lechery, of which I shall speak later, in parts 6 and 7. The second controls covetousness and avarice, of which I have spoken earlier, in part 4,
chapter 5. And the third controls overbearing and pride, of which see above in
part 1.

The second part of temperance is clemency, which is the moderation of
one's mind with respect to one's power of revenge, or else leniency on the part
of a superior toward his inferior, as Seneca says in book 2 of *On Clemency*.
Notice that such clemency has four aspects. The first is to feel compassion
with other people in their misfortunes. Of this speaks Valerius in book 5 when
he says: "When Marcus Marcellinus had captured Syracuse and, from his castle,
saw the misfortune and sad fall of that rich city in its affliction, he could
not refrain from weeping." Similarly, as is written in the same book, when
Caesar saw Pompey's head, he shed tears of compassion. Orosius tells us the
same about Alexander when he found Darius killed and bound with chains of gold.
And the same can be seen in David, who mourned at the death of his enemy Saul,
in Kings 1. Another aspect of clemency is to forgive evil deeds, even grave
ones. Of this speaks Valerius in the passage cited above, where he says that
although the king of Armenia had done the Romans much harm, yet Pompey would
not suffer him to lie bound and on his knees before him, but instead restored
him with benign words and had the crown he had cast off his head replaced in
order to reinstate him in his former fortune, judging it to be equally fair to
overcome a king and to make one. Similarly, as is narrated there also, when
the consul Paulus heard that a captive was being brought to him, he went toward
him, raised him with his right hand as he was about to fall to his knees, and
made him sit next to himself, saying: "If it is a great thing to overcome an
enemy, it is no less praiseworthy to know how to have pity on one in his
misfortune." Virgil teaches the same in book 6 of the *Aeneid*, and Augustine
quotes the passage in *The City of God*, book 5, chapter 13:

> But Roman thou, do thou control
> The nations far and wide;
> Be this thy genius, to impose
> The rule of peace on vanquished foes,
> Show pity to the humbled soul,
> And crush the sons of pride.

The nature of wild animals teaches us the same, according to the following
lines:

E[s]t piger ad penas princeps, ad premia velox.
Quique dolet quociens cogitur esse ferox.

Tercio modo dicitur clemencia dando indiguis bona. De qua narrat Valerius
45   libro ⟨5⟩ quod cum Cartaginencium legati ad captivos redimendos venissent
in urbem, protinus hiis sine pecunia reddidit mille marcas septingintos et quadraginta. "Tantum hostium exercitum dimissum, tantam pecuniam conceptam,
tot iniuriis veniam datam legatos obstupuisse arbitror ac secum dixisse: 'O
munificencia gentis Romane, deorum benignitati equanda!' " Quarto modo di-
50   citur clemencia in condescendo subditis. Nichil enim ita trahit principes
caros suis militibus sicut benignitas clemencie. Unde in *Gestis Romanorum*
legitur de Troiano imperatore quod cum arguerunt eum amici quod in omnes
[ultra] quam deceret esset communis, respondit se velle esse imperatorem
qualem quisquis privatus optasset. De Alexandro eciam dicit Valerius quod
55   cum in tempestate duceret exercitum, milit⟨e⟩m confectum senio et frigore
obstupefactum conspexit. Unde ipse sedens in sublimi prope ignem, protinus
surrexit et manibus suis primum militem in sua sede collocavit.
Pro illa igitur clemencia nota supra de Christi misericordia erga
peccatores, particula 2. In ipso enim multo excellencior erat hec virtus
60   quam in aliis principibus. Nam quantumcumque eum aliquis offenderet, [f.
179v] si peniteat et se emendat, statim pacificatur. In cuius figura dixerunt viri Samarie ad Benadab dominum suum ab Achab rege Israel victum et
effugatum, secundum illud Regum 20: "Reges Israel clementes sunt. Ponamus
ergo saccos in lumbis nostris et funiculos in capitibus nostris et egredia-
65   mur ad eum. Forte salvabit animas nostras." Moraliter isti reges sunt Pater
et Filius et Spiritus Sanctus, unus Deus tamen, quia ita clemens vult esse,
et propter penam non timeatur set propter clemenciam cicius adametur. De
quo Ione 4 dicitur: "Scio quia tu es Deus clemens et misericors." Si ideo
istum offendimus, ponamus saccos in lumbis nostris, per quos intelligo
70   penitenciam. Exemplum: Sicut enim iste domine mortuis maritis pulcris et
nobilibus non utuntur robis, coloratis et preciosis, set veste nigra et
vili in signum tristicie et doloris, sic quilibet peccator amittens Christum per peccatum: quoniam autem et dominus et sponsus eius fuerat dulcissi-
mus qualis numquam alius erat, debet robam tristicie et penalitatis vesti-
75   ri, sicut fecit rex Ninive, Ione 3. Et non tantum hoc set eciam ponamus
funiculos in capitibus nostris, hoc est, reddamus nos humiliter Deo et faciamus nobis funiculum de tribus cordulis, scilicet de contricione, confessione, et satisfactione, et certe "salvabit animas nostras."
Tercia pars prudencie est modestia, que dicitur "sciencia earum rerum
80   que aguntur aut dicuntur loco suo collocandarum," ⟨ut⟩ ait Tullius libro 1
De officiis. Unde de modestia Titi imperatoris legitur quod in morte sua

The noble lion in his wrath still spares the fallen.
You do the same when all the world is your dominion.

And elsewhere the heathen poet says:

A prince is slow to punish, quick to give reward,
And grieves whenever he is forced to show his fierceness.

The third kind of clemency is to give to the needy. Valerius writes in book 5
that when the legates from Carthage came without money to the City to ransom
their captives, he gave them at once 1740 marks. "I suppose the legates were
dumbfounded at the release of so many enemies, the gift of so much money, and
the forgiveness for such great harm, and said among themselves: 'O munificence
of the Roman people, equal to the bounty of the gods!' " The fourth aspect of
clemency is to stoop to one's inferiors. Nothing makes princes as dear to
their soldiers as such benign clemency. Thus we read in *The Deeds of the
Romans* that when his friends reproved the emperor Trajan for making himself
more common to everyone than he should, he answered that he wanted to be the
kind of emperor that the last foot soldier might desire. And of Alexander
Valerius reports that when he was leading his army in a storm, he noticed a
soldier exhausted with old age and stiff with cold. Whereupon Alexander, who
had been sitting above near the fire, got up at once and with his own hands
placed the soldier in his seat.

Concerning this clemency, see also Christ's mercy toward sinners discussed
above in part 2. In him this virtue was far more outstanding than in other
princes. For however much someone might offend him, if he is sorry and cor-
rects himself, Christ is at once reconciled. As a type of this: when Ben-hadad
had been defeated and put to flight by Ahab, the king of Israel, his men said
the following words of 3 Kings 20 to him: "The kings of Israel are merciful.
So let us put sackcloth on our loins and ropes on our heads and go out to him.
Perhaps he will save our lives." In moral terms, the "kings of Israel" are the
Father, Son, and Holy Spirit, one God, who wants to be so clement that he is
not feared for his punishment but rather loved for his clemency. Of whom Jonah
4 says: "I know that you are a gracious and merciful God." If we, then, have
offended him, let us put sackcloth on our loins, by which I understand penance.
Just as, for example, women in our society do not wear beautiful, expensive,
colorful, and precious clothes when their husbands have died, but rather a
black and simple dress as a sign of their sadness and mourning, so should any
sinner do the same when he has lost Christ through sin. For as Christ had been
his most beloved lord and spouse, such as no other had ever been, he should put
on a robe of mourning and grief, as did the king of Nineveh according to Jonah

non recoluit ullum factum quod esset puniendum excepto uno, quod tamen
nulli innotuit, eo quod omnia modeste egit prout erant agenda.
     Ad has ergo partes temperancie pro carnis domacione reduci possunt
85 ille partes quas ponit [f. 180] Macrobius libro 1 dicens: "Temperancia[m],
inquit, sequntur verecundia, abstinencia, honestas, moderacio, parcitas,
sobrietas." De quibus nota locis suis, etc.

---

1 vero] autem O.   **2** temperancie] *add* hoc O.   **5** in] *om* C.M.   **7** et] *om* O.   **16** illa] ista
O.   **17** captis] captus C.O.   **18** Syracusanis] syracusanus C.O.   **24** eciam] et O.
34 versus] *om* O.   **35** regere] regens *corr* C.   Romane] racione C.   **38** versus] *om* O.
39 est] sit (scit) O.   **41** sic] *om* O.   per versus] *om* O.   **45** 5] 15 C.   **52** arguerunt] ar-
guerent O.   **53** ultra] *om* C.M.   **55** militem] militum C.   **61** emendat] humiliaverit
M.R; humiliaverat W.   **65** reges] *add* israel M.w; *add* simul R.   **67** et] quod R.B1; ut
Co.Et.Go1.   **73** quoniam] quando O.   **80** ut] ubi C.R.W.   **81** imperatoris] *add* dicitur et
O.   **87** etc.] *om* O.

V.xxxv   DE PUGNA CONTRA DIABOLUM

     [S]equitur autem tercio de antiqui hostis inpugnacione, idest diaboli,
qui multipliciter humano generi se reddit gravem et nocivum, videlicet sex
modis: Primo a facie, quando scilicet nititur nos a bono revocare; secundo
a tergo, quando scilicet ad aliqua terrena desideria que dimisimus suadet
5   redire; tercio a dextris, quando scilicet nos in prosperitate facit super-
bire; quarto deorsum, quando nos manifeste instigat et intemptat. Unde
Augustinus: "Intemptator, inquit, malorum est diabolus et non missor";
Isaie: "Ego ⟨creavi⟩ fabrum sufflantem prunas." Mirandum est ergo quod a
brutis animalibus non di⟨sc⟩amus, cum ipsa naturaliter hostes suos fugiunt et
10 abhorrent, ut agnus lupum, avis aquilam, columba ancipitrem, et huiusmodi.
     Et nota quod diabolus hominem invadens quinque facit sicut solent
homines facere quando volunt quiescere et dormire. Nam ne quies turbetur
per tumultum, primo ostium camere claudit, secundo lumen extinguit, tercio

3. And not only this, but let us further put ropes on our heads, that is, give ourselves humbly to God and make a rope of three cords, namely from contrition, confession, and satisfaction; then he will certainly "save our lives."

The third part of prudence is modesty, which is said to be the knowledge of what one should do and say in the right place, as Cicero says in book 1 of *On Offices*. Hence we read about the modesty of the Emperor Titus that, when he was dying, he could not think of anything that ought to be punished except one deed; but that was not known to anyone because he always did things modestly, just as they should be done.

To these parts of temperance, which are necessary in ruling our flesh, can be reduced the parts of the virtue which Macrobius enumerates in his first book when he says: "Temperance is followed by shamefacedness, abstinence, propriety, restraint, sparingness, and soberness." These branches are treated in their respective places.

The following material in this chapter occurs also almost verbatim in John of Wales, *Breviloquium*: lines 3–7 (III.1); [the division of 8–12] (III.2); 13–21, 23–57 (III.5); 79–87 (III.6).   **3–5** Macrobius, *In somnium Scipionis* I.viii.7.   **5–7** Cicero, *De inventione* II.53.   **9** *FM* VI–VII.   **10–11** *FM* IV.xii.   **12** *FM* I.   **13–15** Seneca, *De clementia* II.iii.1.   **17–20** Valerius, V.i.4.   **20–21** Valerius, V.1.10.   **21–22** Paulus Orosius, *Historiae* III.17 (PL 31:831–32).   **22–23** 2 Sam. 1.11–12.   **24–29** Valerius, V.i.9.   **29–33** Valerius, V.i.8.   **35–37** Virgil, *Aeneis* VI.851–53, and Augustine, *De civ. Dei* V.xii.2 (CC 47:144).   **39–40** *Prov* 20668.   **42–43** Ovid, *Ex Ponto* I.ii.123–24.   **44–49** Valerius, V.i.1.   **51–54** Thus verbatim in John of Wales, see above.   **54–57** Valerius, V.i.ext.1.   **59** *FM* II.iv.   **61–65** 1 Kings 20.31.   **68** Jon. 4.2.   **75** Jon. 3.6.   **79–81** Cicero, *De officiis* I.xl.142.   **81–83** *Policraticus* III.14 (1:230).   **85–87** Macrobius, *In somnium Scipionis* I.viii.7.

V.xxxv   THE ATTACK OF THE DEVIL

In the third place, we turn to the attack of our ancient foe, the devil. He makes himself grievous and harmful to mankind in six different ways: first, from the front, by trying to make us swerve from our good intention; second, from behind, by persuading us to return to the earthly desires we have given up; third, from the right side, by stirring us to feel proud in prosperity; fourth, from below, by inciting and tempting us openly. Whence Augustine says: "The devil does not send us evil but tempts us to do it"; and Isaiah: "I have created the smith that blows the coals." It is astonishing that we should not learn from wild animals: they naturally flee and shrink from their enemies, as the lamb from the wolf, the bird from the eagle, the dove from the hawk, and so forth.

Notice that when the devil attacks man, he does five things similar to what people do when they want to take a rest and sleep. For in order not to have

fenestras obstruit, quarto familiam quiescere precipit, quinto fetencia
15   expellit. Revera sic diabolus. Nam primo ostium anime claudit quando os
obturatur ne ipsum diabolum qui intus est per peccatum per aperturam confessionis inquietetur. In cuius figura Machabeorum 5 dicitur quod obstruxit
portam civitatis ne Iudas, idest confitens, transiret ad confessionem. Et
nota quod os hominis ne confiteatur diabolus obstruit quinque digitis,
20   quorum primus est pudor confitendi, secundus complacencia peccati, tercius
spes vite longioris, quartus timor perse- [f. 180v] verandi in bono, quintus desperacio venie, gracie, et misericordie. Secundo lumen extinguit
divine cognicionis, quando sic hominem excecat ne cognoscat peccati sui
vilitatem et dampnacionem; unde Sapiencie 2 dicitur: "Excecavit eos malicia
25   eorum." Et nota quod sicut homo de facili magnum pondus levat in aqua nec
sentit illius naturalem ponderositatem quousque ad siccum pervenerit, sic
quamdiu delectacio que velud aqua cito transit durat, non sentit peccator
eius ponderositatem, set certe illa cessante satis bene sentit. Tercio
fenestras obstruit ne sol intret aut eius radii, quando quinque sensus
30   obturat ne Christus, qui est verus sol iusticie, aut eius gracia aut misericordia, que sunt eius radii, ad animam illuminandam intrent. Et hoc maxime facit quando aures ob⟨t⟩urat ne verbum Dei audiat homo, et os ne per
illud peccatum agnoscat. Et certe hic est ille demon de quo Matthei 8, qui
reddit hominem mutum et surdum, quem Dominus curavit ponens digitum in
35   auriculam eius in memoriam quinque plagarum. Nota historiam. Quarto familiam quinque sensuum compescat quando illos bene operari non sinit. Optat
enim summe in domo manere ocio vacante. Unde legitur quod intravit hominem,
hoc est domum corporis sui, quando invenit scopis peccatorum mundatam,
idest vacuatam a virtutibus. Qu⟨int⟩o fetores expellit, quando aufert
40   homini odorem peccati ne illum senciat aut peccatum intelligat. Fetidi enim
et ebrii non senciunt fetorem. Unde narratur in *Vitas Patrum* de quodam
sancto sene ut corpora mortuorum sepeliret transeunte, cui comitabantur
quidam angelus et quidam iuvenis lascivus. Cum ergo ad qu⟨oddam corpus⟩
fetidum pervenissent et senex nares ob- [f. 181] turasset, ait angelus:
45   "Quare hoc corpus non sepelis?" Et ille: "Non possum, inquit, pro fetore."
Cui angelus: "Quantum fetet corpus illud in oculis tuis, tantum et multo
amplius fetet iuvenis iste peccator in conspectu Dei."
       Est ergo diabolus hominem invadendo tamquam adulator qui primo delec-
tabilia loquitur, ut postea caucius decipiat. Similiter sicut ille qui
50   muscas capere proponit primo ollam melle linire facit °. Et similiter sicut
piscator qui ut pisses decipiat hamo abscondito escam [pro]ponit. Est eciam
sicut aquila qui oculos prede primo eruit et postea totum corpus dilacerat.
Unde Crisostomus omelia 50 in *Inperfecto*: "Intrans, inquit, in hominem
(supple diabolus) non statim ducit ad peccatum, set prius quempiam delectat
55   malis et desideria carnis alligat et postea ducit ad peccatum et furatur

one's rest disturbed by noise, one first closes the door of the room, then extinguishes the light, thirdly shuts the windows, fourthly tells the household to keep quiet, and fifthly casts out anything that smells bad. The devil does the same. First he closes the door of the soul by stopping man's mouth so that the devil, who is within through sin, may not be disturbed by its being opened in confession. As a type, it is said in Maccabees 5 that the people barred the gate of the city so that Judas, whose name means "confessing," might not pass on to confession. Notice that in order to prevent a person from confessing his sin, the devil stops his mouth with five fingers: shame to confess, pleasure in sinning, the hope of a long life, fear to be unable to persevere in a good life, and despair of gaining forgiveness, grace, and mercy. Next, he extinguishes the light of the knowledge of God, by making man so blind that he does not see the vileness of his sin and his damnation, as is said in Wisdom 2: "Their own malice has blinded them." And notice that in water one can lift a heavy weight easily, nor does one feel its normal weight until one is outside the water; in the same way, a sinner does not feel the weight of his delight— which passes as quickly as water—as long as it lasts, but when it is gone he certainly notices how heavy it is. Third, he shuts the windows so that the sun or its rays may not enter, by stopping a man's five senses so that Christ, who is the true sun of justice, or else his grace and mercy, which are its ray, cannot come in to enlighten him. This he does especially by stopping man's ears so that he may not hear God's word, and his mouth so that he may not acknowledge his sin through it. This is surely that demon of whom Matthew 8 says that it caused that man to be deaf and dumb whom the Lord healed by putting his finger in his ear, in memory of his five wounds. Explain this story. Fourth, he makes his household of the five senses be quiet by not allowing them to be active. For he wants above all else to be absolutely idle in his house. Therefore we read that the devil entered man, that is, the house of his body, when he found it swept with the broom of sins, that is, emptied of virtues. And fifth, he casts out bad smells by taking from man the smell of sin, so that man can no longer smell or notice sin. For people who are dirty or drunk have no sense of smell. In *The Lives of the Fathers* there is a story about a holy desert father who went about burying the bodies of the dead and was accompanied by an angel and a lecherous young man. When the desert father came to a body that smelled very badly and he stopped his nose, the angel asked him: "Why are you not burying this body?" He replied: "I cannot, for its stench." Then the angel said: "As much as this body smells to your senses, so much and even more does that sinful young man smell before God."

When the devil wants to invade man, he behaves like a flatterer, who begins by telling a person delightful things so that he can later deceive him more craftily. Or he acts like a man who plans to catch flies and smears honey on a pot. Or else like a fisherman who deceives the fish by hanging bait on

vestimenta virtutum, ⟨aurum intellectus⟩, argentum divinorum eloquiorum,
linthiamina graciarum, ceter[ar]umque virtutum divicias tollens mendicum
facit et nudum." Et Bernardus in quadam meditacione ait: "Hic est, inquit,
qui iugiter machinatur malum, ⟨argute⟩ loquitur, artificiose suggerit,
60   callide decipit, motus inflat illicitos, venenatas cogitaciones inflammat,
movet bella, nutrit odia, incitat gulam, inducit luxuriam, desideria carnis
instigat, peccati occasiones parat, et mille nocendi artibus corda hominum
temptare non cessat." Hec ille.
     Et nota quod ipse precipue solitarios temptat. Exemplum de Eva, quam
65   solam existentem primo aggressus est, Genesis 3. Item Regum 17 de Goliath
petens certamen singulare. Item de Christo existente in deserto, Matthei 4.
Unde Crisostomus omelia 13: "Nos adinvicem continue congregare debemus,
ne facile capiamur [f. 181v] a diabolo, quia tunc maxime instat ubi viderit
solitarios." Exemplum: Sicut avis non congregatim volans cito ab ancipitre
70   capitur, et acies dispersa ab hostibus suffocatur, atque animal brutum
extra armentum cicius strangulatur a lupo, sic solitarius a diabolo.
     Unde narratur in *Vitas Patrum* de quodam adolescente qui quasi invito
patre monachabat. Qui sancte conversante vix post ab abbate optinens licenciam heremum petebat, quem duo monachi conducebant qui in via nimio estu
75   fatigati dormire coacti sunt. Et ecce aquila veniens illos ali⟨s⟩ excitavit
et recessit aliqualiter ab eis. Qui evigilantes dixerunt socio: "Angelus
tuus est. Sequere eum." Quibus valedictis illum sequebatur. Post autem
horas tres divertit aquila ad dexteram partem sequentis et statim disparuit. Qui illuc respiciens vidit tres arbores palmarum fontemque aque ac
80   speluncam modicam, et ait: "Ecce, locus quem preparavit michi Dominus."
Et morabatur ibi annis sex solitariam vitam ducens. De eius autem conversa-
cione sancta diabolus invidens quodam die sibi apparuit in similitudine
cuiusdam abbatis. Quo viso timens procidit ad pedes eius et adoravit. Cum
ergo didicit diabolus quod per sex annos ibi fuisset, respondit: "Cogitavi
85   hic manens quod vicino habitares quod irem ad te hominem Dei tecum de nostrarum animarum salute conferre. Et hac de causa, quia nichil hic profici-
mus in cellis sedentes eo quod corpus Christi non sumimus." Et sic illum
excitavit ultra ad tria miliaria exire quasi ad quoddam monasterium habens
presbiteros, ut corpus Christi sumer⟨et⟩. Quo cum perduxisset, disparuit.
90   Cum autem a fratribus cognovit quod diabolus esset, facta communione cum
fratribus ad cellam [f. 182] rediit. Cui in brevi aparuit diabolus in
habitu seculari sibi nuncians mortem patris et matris et quod pater sibi
totam hereditatem dimisisset et omnia sua bona. Et sic eum ad seculum reduxit vivente patre et de exitu graviter illum arguente. Cum ergo non multum
95   post in fornicacionem et alia vicia quamplurima incidisset, tandem inpeni-
tens vitam hanc miserrime consummavit.
     Nota eciam hic narracionem pro diaboli temptacione que habetur in *Vita*

his hook. Or further like the eagle who first pecks out the eyes of his prey
and then tears its body to pieces. Hence Chrysostom says in Homily 50 of his
Imperfect Work: "When he (that is, the devil) enters into a person, he does
not at once lead him to sin but first lets him take pleasure in sin and binds
him with carnal delight; then he leads him to sin and robs the clothes of his
virtues, the gold of his understanding, the silver of God's words, the linen of
his graces, and the riches of his other virtues, and thus leaves him a naked
beggar." In one of his meditations Bernard says: "This is the one who engi-
neers evil smoothly, who speaks cleverly, suggests craftily, deceives smartly,
who breathes into us illicit stirrings and kindles poisonous thoughts, who
stirs up war, fosters hatred, spurs on to gluttony, induces lust, instigates
the desires of the flesh, prepares the occasions for sin, and never desists
from tempting men's hearts with a thousand harmful skills."

Notice that he tempts especially those who live alone. An example is Eve,
whom he approached first when she was by herself, in Genesis 3. Another is
Goliath, who asked for single combat, in Kings 17; and similarly Christ when he
was alone in the desert, Matthew 4. For this reason, Chrysostom says in Homily
13: "We must constantly keep company with others so that we may not be lightly
captured by the devil; for he attacks most keenly where he sees people living
by themselves." Other examples are: the bird who does not fly in a flock is
quickly caught by the hawk; or when an army is scattered it gets wiped out by
its enemies; or a beast outside its herd is more readily strangled by the wolf.
In the same way, people in the solitary life become more easily a prey to the
devil.

There is a story in *The Lives of the Fathers* about a young man who became
a monk against his father's will. As he led a holy life, he soon went into the
desert with his abbot's permission. Two monks led him on the way, but they
were so exhausted by the heat that they had to rest and sleep. Then, lo, an
eagle came, woke them with his wings, and then stood a little back from them.
When the companions woke up, they told the monk: "It is your angel; follow
him"; and he took his leave and followed the eagle. After three hours the
eagle flew to the right of the monk who was following him and then disappeared.
The monk looked after him and saw three palmtrees, a spring, and a small cave,
and said: "Lo, the place which the Lord has prepared for me." And there he
lived in solitude for six years. Now, as the devil was envious of his holy
life, he appeared to him one day in the likeness of an abbot. When the monk
saw him, he fell at his feet in fear and worshipped him. As the devil learned
that he had been there for six years, he said: "As I live close by, I thought
that since you are my neighbor I would come to you, a man of God, and talk with
you about the salvation of our souls. The point is that we make no progress
sitting here in our cells because we do not partake of the Body of Christ."
Thus he blinded him into traveling more than three miles to a monastery where

beati Andree, quomodo quidam demon in specie cuiusdam mulieris pulcherrime
quemdam episcopum temptavit in die sancti Andree, cuius festum omni anno
100   devote celebrabat, et quomodo veniente sancto Andrea in specie peregrini ad
portam elemosinam petente proposuit tres questiones. Prima hec: "Quid est
minus spacium in quo Deus facit maius miraculum?" Et ipse respondit: "In
facie hominis." Remisit aliam proponens questionem utrum alcius esset celum
quam terra. Respondit quod terra, propter Christi humanitatem. Tercio
105   adiecit, quantum distabat celum a terra. Qui cum respondisset ipsum melius
scire eo quod diabolus erat et de celo ad terram et eciam ad infernum
cadendo mensus fuisset, disparuit, et sic episcopum ab eius temptacione
liberavit.

   Item nota narracionem in *Vitas Patrum* de diabolo cui quidam senex
110   obviabat in veste cribrata, ubi in quodam nodo pendebat ampulla. Asseruit
in qualibet fuisse special⟨em⟩ decoctio[nem] pro diversis peccatis; in una
pro superbia, in alia pro ira, et sic de singulis.

   [E]st autem de diabolo hominem invadente et ad plus instigante sicut
de venatore pullos tigridis furanti inventos. Venator autem ille sibi tria
115   specula pro- [f. 182v] vidit magna et rotunda et vadit ad locum ubi pulli
commorantur. Cum ergo mater illorum perrexerit pro alimento querendo,
venator illos capit et fugit. Set timens adventum matris cum sit animal velo-
cissimum et forte, unum speculum proicit in via. Ad quod cum ipsa venerit
et similitudinem in illo viderit, credit pullos [secum] habere. Set postea
120   sciens se deceptam venatorem persequitur. Et ille secundum speculum, similiter et tercium in via proiciens ipsam ut prius decipit et sic occidendo
pullos illesus ab ea trans⟨i⟩t.

   Moraliter per istud animal tam forte et velox cum pullis suis intelligitur homo cum operibus virtuosis. Venator autem diabolus est, qui continue
125   "circuit querens quem devoret." Ipse semper nititur furari pullos bonorum
operum. Set homo est ita fortis quod contra voluntatem peccare per diabolum
co⟨g⟩i non potest. Exemplum: Si enim aliquis applicaret gladium ad pectus
alterius nec plus posset nocere, si tunc alius gratis curreret super gladium et se interficeret, certum est quod ipsemet sui interitus causa fuerit
130   principalis, quamvis alius occasionalis. Revera sic diabolus non potest
plus facere nisi offerre et applicare delectabilia ad sensus. Unde si homo
huiusmodi admittat, ipsemet est causa sui interitus. Set quid facit diabolus contra hominem tam fortem? Revera utitur cautelis. Nam quando homo
redit ad se cogitans de vita sua mala et de bonis operibus que incaute
135   omiserat, cepit dolere. Statim proicit sibi primum speculum, hoc est, facit
sibi unam racionem: "Tu es iuvenis et ideo adhuc potes stare in peccato et
in senectute satis tempestive te corrigere." Ex cuius suggestione frequenter homo subtrahitur a bono. Set si [f. 183] talis homo cogitet apud se
quod iuvenes moriuntur sicut senes, dicens apud se: "Hic non morabor, set

there were priests, so that he could receive the Body of Christ. And when he had led him there, he disappeared. Now, when the monk learned from the brethren that it was the devil, he received communion there and then returned to his cell. But a short while later the devil appeared to him again in secular clothing and reported the death of his father and mother, and that his father had left him the whole inheritance and all his possessions. And so the devil led him back to the world while his father was yet alive and criticized him sharply for leaving him. And not long afterwards he fell into fornication and many other sins, and at last he ended his life without repentance.

Notice here also a story about the devil's temptation which is found in *The Life of Blessed Andrew*. A demon tempted a certain bishop in the form of a very beautiful woman on the day of Saint Andrew, whose feast day the bishop used to celebrate devoutly every year. Also, when Saint Andrew arrived at the gate in the form of a pilgrim asking for alms, he put to him three questions. The first was: "What is the least thing in which God works the greatest miracle?" He answered, "In man's face." Then he asked another riddle and question, whether the sky was higher than the earth. He answered that it was the earth, because of Christ's human nature. And as the third question he added, how far heaven was from the earth. Then he answered that he knew this one quite well because he was the devil and had measured the distance when he fell from heaven to earth and further to hell; and with this he disappeared and left the bishop free of temptation.

Notice also the story in *The Lives of the Fathers* about a devil who met a desert father. He wore a garment full of holes, in each of which hung a vial, and he claimed that in each vial was a special potion for a different sin: one for pride, another for wrath, and so forth.

When the devil invades man and tries to stir him to sin, he acts like a hunter who tries to steal a tiger's cubs. Such a hunter takes three large round mirrors with him to the place where the cubs are. When their mother goes out in search of food, the hunter grabs the cubs and flees. But as he fears the mother's return, who is a very swift and strong animal, he places one mirror in her way. When she comes to it and sees her image in it, she believes her cubs are with her. But as she finds out that she has been deceived, she pursues the hunter. Then he puts the second and third mirrors similarly in her way to deceive her as before; and so he kills the cubs and gets away without harm.

Morally interpreted, this strong and swift animal and her cubs stand for man and his virtuous deeds. The hunter is the devil, who constantly "goes about seeking whom he way devour," for he is always trying to carry off the cubs of good deeds. But man is so strong that he cannot be forced by the devil to sin against his will. For example, if one person were to put a sword against another's chest without being able to do him any real harm, and the

140 adhuc pullos bonarum virtutum insequer," statim proic⟨it⟩ aliud speculum
dicens: "Tu es satis potens et omnia habes ad votum. Unde si Deus foret
tibi offensus, non fieret ita bene tecum." Si ergo tunc cogitaverit penes
se quod "divites moriuntur sicut et pauperes, ergo sic non possum manere,
set ultra pullos virtutum sequ⟨ar⟩," statim diabolus proicit tercium specu-
145 lum dicens: "Cogita de misericordia Dei, nam illi qui quondam erant peccatores maiores in terris, sicut Petrus, Paulus, et Magdalena cum ceteris,
modo alciores regnant in celis." Et sic facit hominem dormire in peccatis
et tandem finaliter interire.
Modo restat ostendere quod ille raciones non concludunt. Quarum prima
150 fuit: "Tu es iuvenis, ergo," etc. Contra quam ait Bernardus: "Non est,
inquit, aliquid in mundo quod ita accelerat ⟨iudicium⟩ sicut peccatum." Et
ideo ait Psalmista: "Non dimidiabunt dies suos," supple peccatores. Et
posito quod possent vivere diu eciam usque ad mille annos, adhuc quanto in
malo diucius permanent, tanto magis ⟨iudicium⟩ aggravant et suam penam
155 accumulant. Exemplum de sagittante, qui quanto alcius et forcius sagittam
trahit, tanto gravius percutit et vulnerat. Quod eciam secunda racio non
valet, scilicet "Tu es dives," probat beatus Gregorius dicens: "Continuus
successus temporalium bonorum divine reprobacionis est indicium." Exemplum de medico qui dat infirmo ⟨de quo desperat⟩ omnia que appetit aut placent
160 sibi. Quod autem tercia racio non valet, que fuit: "Cogita de misericordia
Dei," probat ille qui ait: "Maledictus homo [f. 183v] qui peccat in spe."
Et hic nota supra capitulum de misericordia Dei et de desperacione satis et
alia ut placet.

2–6 sex . . . intemptat] *all MSS read* sex. M *has the following marginal addition*: a sinistris quando in adversis blasvemare et resistere facit; de sursum quando in beneplacitis et
celestibus(?) facit gloriare et presumere(?) iactare. *Group z reads the first three ways as C
and then continues*: quarto a sinistris quando facit hominem de adversitate nimium murmurare; quinto a sursum quando facit hominem de bono opere nimium gloriari; sexto a deorsum quando nos manifeste instigat et intemptat. **5** facit] movet O. **8** creavi] teram
C.O; *text* B1 *and source*. **9** discamus] differamus C.M.W. suos] *om* O. **24** unde] *om*
O. **28** satis bene] *om* O. **32** obturat] obdurat C. **39** Quinto] quando C.R.W. **42** co-
mitabantur] comitabatur O. **43** quoddam corpus] quendam C. **46** multo] *om* O.
50 proponit] *add* et O. facit] *add* et postea viscum C. sicut] *om* O. **56** aurum intel-
lectus] ut aurum vitemus et C. **57** ceterarumque] ceterumque C.M.W. **59** argute] argu-
mentive C. **67** Nos . . . debemus] oportet nos adinvicem continue congregari O.
75 alis] alios C; animalis W. **77** illum] illam R.W. **83** timens] *add* alius O. **85** ma-
nens] *add* iuxta O. quod] quia O. **86** hac de] hec O. **89** sumeret] sumeretur C.
94 de] *add* suo O. arguente] corripiente O. **96** miserrime] *om* O. **100** veniente] adveniente O. **102** spacium] *om* O. facit] fecit O. respondit] respondens O. **104** Re-
spondit] qui respondens O. **106** et(2)] *om* O. **111** specialem decoccionem] specialis
decoctio C. **122** transit] transiit C; pertransit O. **124** virtuosis] *add* sive viciosis O.
127 cogi] conari C.M.W. **131** sensus] *add* nostros O. **135** omiserat] comiserat O.
138 subtrahitur] retrahitur M.W; trahit se R. **140** proicit] proiciens C. **142** fieret] foret

other then rushed onto the sword and killed himself, certainly the second person would be the principal cause of his death, even if the first were responsible for providing the occasion. In similar fashion, the devil cannot do any more than offer and hold up pleasing objects to our senses. If man accepts the offer, he himself is the cause of his death. But what does the devil do against man who has this much power? Well, he uses tricks. For when man comes to himself and thinks of his evil life and the good deeds which he had failed to do in his negligence, he begins to be sorry. Then the devil quickly puts the first mirror before him, that is, he rationalizes with him: "You are still young and may live in sin a little longer; when you are old, you can correct yourself fast enough." Such a suggestion often causes a man to withdraw from the good. But if he then thinks by himself that young people die as fast as old ones, he says: "I won't stay here but still follow my cubs of good virtues." Then the devil puts up the second mirror and says: "You are strong enough and have everything at your will. If God were angry with you, things would not go so well for you." If he then thinks within himself that, "The rich die just as the poor; therefore I cannot remain here, but I will follow the cubs of my virtues," the devil at once puts up the third mirror and says: "Think of God's mercy, for those who once were the greatest sinners on earth, such as Peter, Paul, Magdalene, and others, now reign the higher in heaven." And thus he causes man to sleep in his sins and finally to perish.

   We now need to show that these arguments are invalid. The first was: "You are still young; therefore," and so on. Against this Bernard says: "Nothing in the world hastens judgment as much as sin does." Therefore, the Psalmist declares: "They shall not live out half their days," add: the sinners. Even if we assume that they could live as long as a thousand years, still the longer they lead an evil life, the heavier their judgment will be, and the greater their punishment. This is like shooting with bow and arrow: the more one draws the arrow, the more heavily it strikes and wounds. That the devil's second argument, "You are rich," is equally invalid is shown by Blessed Gregory when he says: "A continuous success in temporal matters is a sign of divine reprobation." An example for that we find in the physician who gives his patient everything he craves for or that pleases him, when he despairs of his recovery. And that the third argument, namely, "Think of God's mercy," is also invalid, is proven by him who says: "Cursed is the man who sins in hope." On this matter you can find more above in the chapter on God's mercy and on despair.

7 Cf. James. 1.13.   8 Isa. 54.16.   17–18 Perhaps 1 Macc. 5.47.   24–25 Wisd. 2.21.
33–35 Mark 7.31ff.   37–38 Matt. 12.43–45.   41–47 Tubach 2559, from *VP* VI.18 (PL 73:1014).   53–58 Ps.-Chrysostom, *Opus imperfectum*, hom. 51 (PG 56:925).   58–63 *Meditationes piissimae* XIII.35 (PL 184:505).   65 Gen. 3.1–5.   65–66 1 Sam. 17.8.   66 Matt. 4.1–10.   67–69 Chrysostom, *In Matthaeum*, hom. 13, 1 (PG 57:209).

O. **144** sequar] sequatur C.   **146** Petrus] *add* et O.   et] *om* O.   cum ceteris] etc O.
147 modo] iam O.   **149** ille] iste O.   **151** iudicium] in deum C(?).M.W(?).   **154** iudi-
cium] in deum C(?).M.W(?).   **158** bonorum] *om* O.   **159** de quo desperat] desperato
C.   **160** sibi] *om* O.   autem] eciam O.

V.xxxvi   DE CARITATE CONTRA DIABOLUM PUGNANTE

[C]ontra ergo hunc hostem caritas constanter se opponit et devincit,
que secundum Augustinum est dulce vinculum quo sola mens ligatur, cuius
dulcedo tanta est quod si eius minima gutta in infernum caderet, tota eius
amaritudo in dulcedinem verteretur. Unde de ea pulcre ait Hugo *De laude*
5   *caritatis*: "O, inquit, caritas, magnam vim habes. Tu enim sola Deum trahere
potuisti ad terram. O ergo, quam forte est vinculum tuum, quo et Deus ligari potuit et homo ligatus vinculis tuis vincula iniquitatis disrupit." Ista
ergo caritas consistit in dilectione Dei, sui, et proximi, ita quod Deus
diligatur supra [omnia; et postea anima propria supra omnia; et postea
10   anima proximi supra] omnia temporalia; et tandem amicum in Deum, et inimicum propter Deum. Et certe tunc bene ordinatur caritas in homine iuxta
illud Canticorum 2: "Ordinavit in me caritatem."
Fertur autem in *Gestis Romanorum* quod cum semel a diis suis fuit
quesitum quamdiu civitas illa in sua nobilitate duraret, responsum erat
15   quod tamdiu ROMA litteris transversis apud eam maneret. Vertas autem hanc
dictionem ROMA et tunc habebis AMOR, quasi diceret: quamdiu verus amor
durat apud vos, n⟨umquam⟩ corruet civitas vestra set capud et domina omnium
aliarum permanebit, et e contrario; destructo enim amore, et civitas illa
destruetur. Quo audito depinxerunt ymaginem Amoris ad modum puelle pulcher-
20   rime habentis capud discoopertum et hillarem vultum, omnibus pretendens
pomum gestans in manu sic inscriptum: "Longe et prope," quasi diceret:
verus amor numquam deficit sive homo longe et a remotis [f. 184] partibus
fuerit sive prope. In pectore vero dicte ymaginis scribebatur "Vita et
mors," quasi diceret: verus amor numquam deficiet neque in vita neque in
25   morte. Quo facto sibi per ordinem hec quatuor offerebant: Primo aquilam,
que alcius volat, in signum quod Deus super omnia ut predicitur sit diligendus. Secundo offerebant leonem, qui forte animal est, in signum quod
peccatis resistendo teipsum fortissime diligis. Tercio optulerunt olivam
virentem, in signum quod sicut arbor illa numquam marcessit, sic nec amor
30   tuus erga proximum in caritate Dei. Et quarto pavonem, cuius natura est
quod in maiori eius pompa glorians de pulcritudine pennarum suarum, quando
scilicet pronior est ad vindictam, set cum tunc aspiciat pedes, tota sua
pompa ac appetitus vindicte cessat; in signum quod quamvis in corde contra
inimicum exaltatus fueris vindictam optans, si tunc oculum cordis ad pedes
35   et terram defixeris, intime scilicet cogitans quod terra es sicut ipse, mox

72–96 *VP* V.24 (PL 73:897–900). **97–108** Cf. *Leg. aurea*, pp. 20–21. **109–112** *VP*
III.61 (PL 73:769). **113–122** A widespread tale, from Ambrose, *Exameron* VI.iv.21
(PL 14:265). **125** 1 Pet. 5.8. **152** Ps. 54.24. **162–163** *FM* V.xxxv and II.iv.

V.xxxvi   HOW CHARITY FIGHTS AGAINST THE DEVIL

Against this enemy, charity opposes herself firmly and overcomes it.
According to Augustine, it is the sweet bond which binds the mind, and its
sweetness is so great that if the smallest drop of it fell into hell, all
hell's bitterness would turn into sweetness. Hugh, in *The Praise of Charity*,
speaks of it beautifully: "O charity, you have great power. You alone could
draw God to earth. Oh how strong is your bond, by which even God could be
bound, and man, once he was bound with your bonds, has broken the bonds of
sin." This charity consists in loving God, oneself, and one's neighbor, so
that God is loved above all things, and after him our own soul above all other
things, and then the soul of our fellow man above all earthly goods, and
finally our friend in God and our enemy for God's sake. Then is charity surely
well ordered in man, according to the words of Canticles: "He set in order
charity in me."

In *The Deeds of the Romans* it is reported that once when the gods had been
asked how long the City would last in its glory, they answered: "As long as
the name ROMA with its letters reversed remains with the City." Reverse the
word ROMA and you will get AMOR, as if the oracle were saying: as long as true
love endures among you, your city will never fall but remain the head and queen
of all others. And conversely, when love is destroyed, the City too will be
destroyed. When they heard this, they painted an image of Love, like a beautiful maiden, with her head bare and a joyful face, offering to all an apple in
her hand on which was written, "Far and near," as if to say that true love
never fails, whether one is far away or near. On the breast of this image was
written, "Life and death," to indicate that true love will never fail in life
or in death. And then they offered her these four: first an eagle, who flies
higher than other birds, to show that, as was said earlier, we must love God
above anything else. Next they offered a lion, who is a strong animal, to show
that you should love yourself most strongly by resisting sin. In the third
place, they offered a green olive tree, to show that as this tree never withers,
so must your charitable love for your fellow man not diminish. And in
the fourth place they offered a peacock, whose characteristic is as follows:
when in its glory it takes pride in its feathers—that is, when it is ready to
work vengeance—, if it then looks at its feet, all its glory and desire for
revenge goes away; and this indicates that however incensed you might be
against your enemy and thirst for revenge, if you then direct the eye of your

perversa voluntas cessabit et inimicum diliges propter Deum, qui pro inimicis suis Patrem orabat dicens: "Pater, ignosce illis, quia nesciunt quid
faciunt." Et nota quod si caro pavonis cocta et ad plenum assata fuerit,
cito tamen post, puta in biduo aut triduo, cruda invenitur, in signum quod
40 quamvis coctus aut assatus fueris per ignem ire et vindicte erga inimicum,
propter tamen Christum emollir⟨i⟩ debes usque ad sanguinis effusionem, qui
propter te in cruce sanguinem suum effudit. Et certe si sic feceris, tunc
gestas coronam de quadrifolio fidelis amoris.

[þow loue God ouer all þing.
45 Syþyn þy selfe withowte synnyng.
Syþyn þy frende as kynd þe teche.
þan þy foo withouten wreche.]

Habita ergo hac caritate dictum hostem levissime devinces. Nichil enim
est quod tantum timet sicut caritatem, secundum Hugonem super *Regulam*
50 *sancti Augustini*, ubi dicit sic: "Si enim [f. 184v] distribuerimus totum
quod habemus, hoc non timet diabolus quia ipse nichil possidet. Si ieiuna-
verimus, hoc non timet, quia cibum non capit. Si vigilaverimus, inde non
terretur, quia sompno non utitur. Set (dicit ipse) si caritate coniungimur,
inde vehementer expavescit, quia hoc solum tenemus in terra quod ipse in
55 celo servare contempsit." Hec ille. Unde apud poetas fuit antiquitus solempne proverbium: "Amor vincit omnia, quia vincit Pana." Pana autem apud
eos fingebatur Deus omnium vel Deus tocius, quem t⟨amen⟩ fingunt ipsi poete
captum et devictum amore Syrynge, cuiusdam puelle pulcherrime, ad modum
quo dicimus Filium Dei devictum amore humane nature. Unde de caritate
60 Christi erga genus humanum nota satis parte 3, capitulo 4.
Patet ergo quomodo pre ceteris hec est forcior et maior. Quod tali
poe⟨si⟩ confirmare potestis. Fertur autem quod versus orientem in Lernia
pal⟨u⟩de erat quidam serpens qui solo flatu omnem infecit aerem. Unde
homines transeuntes intoxicabantur. Cum ergo semel quidam pastor serto
65 coronatus et illesus pertransisset, et alius didicerat quod virtute illius
serti sic evasit, idem rapuit, et statim pastor mortuus est. Quod audiens
Mercurius a raptore sertum abstulit et ad pastorem mortuum accessit, in
cuius ore flores illius singillatim imposuit. Et sic tandem virtute unius a
morte surrexit. Moraliter in vita, mundi palude, manet serpens gravis huma-
70 ni generis hostis precipuus, scilicet diabolus, ex cuius flatu et malicia
omnes quasi per illum transeuntes inficiuntur. Quod advertens vir iustus
sertum sibi facit de optimis floribus bonarum virtutum, quarum virtute [f.
185] ab eius malicia et veneno ill⟨es⟩us pertransit. Quod si casu sertum
amiserit vel a se ablatum fuerit, per quod quasi spiritualiter moritur,
75 venit Mercurius, Christus Filius Dei, et dictum sertum reducit et diversis

heart to the ground and to your feet, thinking within yourself that you are earth as he is, then your wrong desire will go away and you will love your enemy for God's sake, who prayed to God for his enemies, saying: "Father, forgive them, for they do not know what they are doing." Notice also that the peacock's flesh, though it has been cooked and fully broiled, shortly afterwards, namely in two or three days, is found to be raw again, as a sign that although you have been cooked or broiled in the fire of wrath and vengeance against an enemy, yet for Christ's sake you should become soft to the point of shedding your blood, for he has shed his blood on the cross for you. If you do this, then indeed you wear a crown of the quatrefoil of true love:

> Love God above all other things,
> Yourself next without sin,
> And next your friend as nature wants,
> Your en'my then without sting.

If you have this love, you will overcome your enemy the devil most easily. For he fears nothing so much as charity, according to Hugh in his comment on *The Rule of Saint Augustine*, where he says: "If we were to give away all we have, the devil is not afraid of that because he owns nothing. If we were to fast, he does not fear that either, because he takes no food. Nor if we were to wake is he afraid of that, because he does not use to sleep. But if we are joined in charity, of that he is violently afraid, because we have on earth the only thing which he refused to keep in heaven." For this reason, the ancient poets had a renowned saying: "Love conquers all, for love conquers Pan." Pan, among them, was held to be "the god of all" or "the god of everything." Yet the ancient poets imagine him as captured and overcome by his love for Syrinx, a most beautiful maiden, in the same way as we say the Son of God was overcome by his love for human nature. On Christ's charity toward mankind see part 3, chapter 4.

Therefore it is clear how among all the virtues charity is the strongest and greatest. This you can prove by the following poetic fable. It is said that in the swamp of Lerna in the East there was once a serpent who with its breath alone infected all the air so that men who passed by were poisoned. Now when once a shepherd who wore a wreath on his head passed by without getting hurt, and another shepherd understood that he had escaped the danger by virtue of that wreath, he took the wreath from him and the first shepherd died at once. When Mercury heard this, he took the wreath from the thief and went to the dead shepherd, into whose mouth he put flowers from it one by one. And thus he at last rose from death by the virtue of a single flower. In spiritual terms: In the swamp of this world lives the dangerous serpent, the foremost enemy of mankind, namely the devil, by whose breath and malice nearly all who

floribus illius per os cordis reficit illum, quia modo floribus humilitatis, modo floribus pietatis, modo floribus castitatis, et cetera huiusmodi.
Si vero ad plenum per illos flores non revixerit, iterum apponit flores
fidei et spei, et si nec tunc revixerit, tandem apponit flores caritatis,
80   ex cuius contactu statim ad vitam revertetur, eo quod ipsa caritas sit maioris virtutis omnium aliarum virtutum, iuxta illud Corinthiorum 13: "Nunc
autem manent fides, spes, caritas, tria hec; maior autem horum est caritas."
Et nota quod per huiusmodi caritatem leviter diabolum vincunt et a se
85   expellunt, et hoc quadrupliciter. Primo cordis contricione et lacrimarum
effusione, sicut mastivus de coquina aqua calida; Psalmista: "Contribu-
la⟨s⟩ti capita draconis in aquis multis." Sic enim eiecti erant de Magdalena septem demonia, idest septem peccatorum mortalium incitamenta, ut patet
Luce 7. Secundo enim deicient fumo devocionis ex consideracione dominice
90   passionis. Non enim audet diabolus ibi remanere ubi vidit vexillum eius a
quo devictus est, ad modum quo naturaliter solent homines odisse arma illa
quibus parentes aut amici interfecti sunt. Et hic nota supra parte de
nomine Iesu. Tercio, per opera penitencie et carnis afflictione, sicut
ribaldus eicitur de hospicio magnatis; Proverbiorum 21: "Virga discipline
95   effugabit illam." Quarto, per ieiunium, sicut lupus per famem a ⟨nemore⟩;
Matthei 18: "Hoc genus demoniorum non potest eici nisi in oracione et
ieiunio." Et quinto per invocacionem nominis divini, sicut per incantacio-
nem eicitur coluber de caverna; Matthei ultimo: "In nomine meo demonia
eicient."

---

12 2] *om* O.   **15** tamdiu] dummodo O; *add* hec diccio O.   **16** tunc] istam M; *om* R; ista
W.   **17** numquam] nos C.   **20** et] *om* O.   **22** partibus] *om* O.   **28** diligis] diliges O.
33 in(2)] *om* O.   **37** orabat] exorabat O.   **41** emolliri] emollire C.   **42** effudit] fudit O.
44–47 þow . . . wreche] *text from R. Verse 51, in* B1.B3.Go1.Go2.Jo.L2.LC.R.Sp.
V.W1.   **50** sancti] beati M.W; *om* R.   **52** timet] metuit O.   **57** tamen] tm C; *om* R.
59 quo] *add* nos O.   **61–83** Patet . . . caritas] *the whole passage had already been used
in III.vi; om in* R *with reference* usque ad finem.   **62** poesi] poet. C.M; poete.   **63** pa-
lude] pallide C; palide M.W.   **66** evasit] evasisset M.W.   **73** illesus] illius C.   **75** et(2)]
add de M.W.   **84** vincunt] vincent O.   **85** expellunt] expellent O.   quadrupliciter] quin-
tupliciter R.   **86–87** Contribulasti] contribulanti C.R; conturbasti R; conturbati W.
88 incitamenta] *om* O.   **95** nemore] venatore C.   **96** potest eici] eicitur O.   **99** eicient]
add et hic nota de nomine iesu O.

pass by are infected. A just man who notices this makes for himself a wreath of the finest flowers of good virtues, by whose virtue he passes without being hurt by the devil's malice and poison. But if he perchance loses this wreath or it is taken from him, so that he as it were dies spiritually, Mercury comes, namely Christ, the Son of God, and brings the wreath back and heals him with its different flowers through the mouth of his heart, now with flowers of humility, now of piety, now of chastity, and thus with all the others. When he then has not yet fully revived through their virtue, he again gives him the flowers of faith and hope, and if he still does not come back to life, he finally gives him flowers of charity; as soon as he is touched by them, he returns to life, for charity has greater power than all the other virtues, according to Corinthians 13: "But now remain faith, hope, and charity, these three; but charity is the greatest of them."

And notice that through such charity they will easily overcome the devil and expel him from themselves, and this in four ways. First, by heartfelt contrition and the shedding of tears, as the mastiff is driven from the kitchen with hot water. The Psalmist says: "You crushed the heads of dragons in many waters." In this way the seven demons were cast out of Magdalene, that is, the urges of the seven deadly sins, as can be seen in Luke 7. Second, they will cast out the devil with the smoke of their devotion, by meditating on the Lord's Passion. For the devil does not dare remain where he sees the banner of him by whom he was defeated, just as men naturally hate the weapons with which their relatives or friends were killed; see above on the name of Jesus. Third, he is cast out through works of penance and mortification of the flesh, just as a bum is thrown out of a nobleman's household; Proverbs 21: "The rod of correction shall drive it away." Fourth, he is cast out through fasting, just as a wolf is driven from the wood by hunger; Matthew 18: "This kind of demons cannot be cast out except by prayer and fasting." And fifth, the devil is cast out through invoking God's name, as a snake is driven from a cave by an incantation; Matthew, near the end: "In my name they shall cast out demons."

2–7 See above, III.vi.22–31.   5–7 Hugh of St. Victor, *De laude caritatis* (PL 176:974).   12 Cant. 2.4.   13–19 Tubach 4123 (unique).   19–25 This image with inscriptions occurs also in: Bromyard, "Gratitudo," G.IV.9; Bromyard, *Distinctiones* (MS Bodley 859, fol. 109); and elsewhere. See B. Smalley, *English Friars and Antiquity in the Early Fourteenth Century* (Oxford, 1960), p. 180, n. 1; F. Saxl, "A Spiritual Encyclopaedia of the Later Middle Ages," *JWCI* 5 (1942), 100 and illustrations.   37–38 Luke 23.34.   43–47 The verses and the image of *quadrifolium amoris* were already used in III.ix.52–56.   50–55 Hugh of St. Victor, *Expositio in regulam beati Augustini* 1 (PL 176:883); from Gregory, *In Ezechielem*, hom. 1, viii.7 (CC 142:105).   55–83 Already used in III.vi.32–60. See notes to that chapter.   60 *FM* III.vi.   86–87 Ps. 73.13.   87–89 Luke 8.2.   92–93 *FM* III.vii.   94–95 Prov. 22.15.   96–97 Matt. 17.20.   98–99 Mark 16.17.

V.xxxvii   DE FORTITUDINE CONTRA DIABOLUM PUGNANTE

[A]d istum hostem igitur devincendum sicut domina ca- [f. 185v] ritas
iam accedit virtus fortitudinis, que secundum Macrobium libro 1 est "⟨ani-
mum⟩ s⟨uper⟩ metum agere nichilque nisi turpia timere, fortiter tollerare
adversa et prospera." Cuius extrema sunt audacia et pusillanimitas, ut
5   patet ex diffinicione 3 *Ethicorum* in fine, ubi dicit sic in opposito:
"Fortitudo, inquit, est habitus medio modo se habens circa timores et
audacias pacienter sufferens." Et nota quod aliquando videntur aliqui in
principio adversorum nimis temerarii, audaces, et presumptuosi, sicut erat
beatus Petrus, qui primo dixit Christo: "Si oportuerit me mori tecum, non
10   te negabo," et tamen paulo post imminente Christi passione unius ancille
voce perterritus ter Dominum suum negavit. Similiter et "relicto eo omnes
fugerunt," sola Beata Virgine per triduum permanente fortiter in fide. De
talibus ergo bene dicitur:

Acriores in principio franguntur in fine.

15   Et ideo iuxta consilium Sapientis: "Qui se existimat stare, videat ne
cadat," etc.
Set hic nota quod quidam sunt fortes corpore tantum, que fortitudo
frequenter magis obest quam prodest, sicut patet in istis hastiludiantibus,
luctantibus, et huiusmodi, ubi pro ⟨parva⟩ vana gloria exponunt se extremis
20   periculis. Contra quos Ysaie 1: "Fortitudo vestra quasi favilla stuppe." Et
tamen fortes spiritu non sunt, quia nichil pro Deo et propria salute sustinere possunt. Et certe huiusmodi fortitudo non est virtus, set pocius debi-
litas spiritus et occasio viciorum. Contra quod Corinthiorum: "Quando in-
firmor," scilicet corpore, "tunc forcior sum," scilicet mente; "nam virtus
25   in infirmitate perficitur." Verumptamen si una alteri copuletur, laudabili-
or est condicio. Qualis fuit David qui dicebat: "Fortitudinem meam ad te
custodiam," scilicet, ante adventum inanis glorie illam confirmavi.
Et certe huiusmodi fortitudo reddit hominem magna- [f. 186] nimum, pacientem, perseverantem. Magnanimum quidem corde, ore, opere, que patent
30   in detestando vilitatem, in profitendo veritatem, et in aggrediendo ardui-
tatem. Exemplum autem magnanimitatis, scilicet in detestando vilitatem,
ponit Seneca in quadam epistola dicens: "Est, inquit, proprium hominis
habere excelsum et gloriosum spiritum querentem ubi honeste vivat, non ubi
tutissime." Per quod patet quod maxime debet homo dedignari subici vilibus
35   et maxime peccatis; unde alibi dicit idem Seneca: "Si, inquit, scirem deos
ignoscituros et homines ignoraturos, ego peccare dedignarer quia," ut ait
Epistula 48, "ad maiora natus sum quam ut sim mancipium corporis mei."
Hec ille. Exemplum secunde magnanimitatis, silicet in profitendo veritatem,

V.xxxvii   HOW FORTITUDE BATTLES AGAINST THE DEVIL

In order to overcome this enemy, as Lady Charity does, the virtue of
strength also comes to our aid, which according to book 1 of Macrobius is the
courage to act in danger without fear, to dread nothing but shameful things,
and to bear bravely with ill as with good fortune. Its opposite extremes are
foolhardiness and cowardice, as one can see from the definition given at the
end of book 3 of the *Nicomachean Ethics*, where its author says: "Strength is
the habit that lies in the middle between fear and foolish bravery, enduring
all things patiently." Notice that sometimes people appear to be very coura-
geous, brash, even presumptuous at the beginning of their misfortune, as Peter
was when he first said to Christ, "If I had to die with you, I will not deny
you," and yet a little while later, when Christ's Passion was threateningly
close, he denied his lord three times, frightened to death by a word from a
servant girl. In the same way, "they all left him and fled," except for the
Blessed Virgin, who remained firm in her faith during the three days. Of such
people it is well said:

Those who are keenest at start yet break in the end.

Therefore, according to the counsel of the wise man, "He who thinks that he is
standing, let him take heed lest he fall," and so forth.

But notice that some people are strong only in their bodies. This kind of
strength is often more a spiritual disadvantage than an advantage, as one can
see in people who fight in tournaments or wrestle and the like, where they expose themselves to extreme dangers for the sake of a little vainglory. Against
them it is said in Isaiah 1: "Your strength shall be as the ashes of tow."
And yet these are not strong in the spirit, for they cannot suffer anything for
God and their own salvation. This kind of strength surely is not a virtue but
rather a spiritual weakness and an occasion for sin. Against such people it is
said in Corinthians: "When I am weak," namely in the body, "then am I more
powerful," namely in my spirit, "for power is made perfect in infirmity." But
when both kinds of strength are joined together, then a man's state is most
praiseworthy. David was such a person, who said: "I will keep my strength to
you," that is: I have established it before the coming of vainglory.

Such strength surely makes a person magnanimous, patient, and persevering.
Magnanimous in his heart, mouth, and deed, because he will scorn everything
base, profess the truth, and bravely tackle difficult tasks. An example of
magnanimity in scorning what is base is given by Seneca in a letter where he
says: "It is proper for a man to have a high-minded and noble spirit that
seeks where he may live in honor rather than in the greatest security." Therefore a person must refuse absolutely to subject himself to baseness and especially to sin. For this reason Seneca says elsewhere: "Even if I knew that

patet eo quod cicius antiqui maluerunt dicendo veritatem mori quam tacita
40   veritate vivere. Unde Valerius libro 6 narrat de quadam muliere inmerito
dampnata a Philippo rege temulento, que dixit: "Provocarem ad Philippum,
set ad sobrium." Qua voce excussit ei crapulam et coegit facere sibi sentenciam iustiorem causa diligencius inspecta. Idem eciam narrat de quadam
muliere pro incolumitate Dionisii tyranni orante, omnibus aliis eius mortem
45   optantibus. Qui cum quesisset ab ea quo merito sui hoc fecisset, respondit:
"Cum puella essem et haberem gravem tyrannum, eo carere cupiebam. Quo
interfecto gravior arcem occupavit, set et eius mortem optavi. Quo eciam mortuo, tercium inportuniorem habere cepimus. Timens ergo ne si tu assumptus
fueris cum omnium predictorum pessimus es, deterior te succedat." Exem-
50   plum tercie magnanimitatis, scilicet in arduorum aggressione, satis patet in
istis sanctis patribus, martiribus, confessoribus, virginibus, qui propter
Christum et fidem mori non timebant, etc.
[f. 186v] Secunda pars virtutis fortitudinis est paciencia, que secundum Tullium, *Prima rhetorica* libro 2, est honestatis aut utilitatis causa
55   rerum arduarum voluntaria perpessio. Et huiusmodi paciencia in hiis quatuor
specialius consistit, scilicet in sustinencia contumeliarum in verbis, in
longanimi perpessione penarum in corporibus, in remissione iniuriarum in
molestacionibus, et in moderacione disciplinarum in correctionibus. [Exem-
plum primi libro 3 *De nugis philosophorum* de Augusto Cesare, cui cum quidam
60   diceret: "O tyranne!" pacienter respondit dicens: "Si esset, non diceres."]
Item ibidem narratur quod Aristopus cuidam sibi maledicenti respondit: "Ut
tu lingue tue, sic ego aurium mearum dominus sum," quasi diceret: sicut tu
potes lingua tua mala loqui, sic ego pacienter auribus meis audire possum.
Ibidem e⟨ciam⟩ legitur quod Anticanes respondit cuidam sibi maledicenti:
65   "Facile est in me maledicere, et ego didici maledicta contempnere." Item
libro 5 *De nugis philosophorum* dicitur quod Alcibiade Socratem interrogante
quare uxorem suam iurgiosam non cohercebat, respondit: "Cum, inquit, talem
domi perpetior, insuesco et excercitor ut ceterorum iniuriam facilius
feram, et ideo illam domi molestam sustineo." Secundo paciencia consistit
70   in penarum perpessione in corporibus, sicut satis patuit in sanctis martiribus, quibus propter spem future glorie mors, que est ultimum terribilium,
erat desiderabilis. Item eciam patuit antiquis temporibus, prout recitat
Valerius libro 6 de Theodoro Cyreneo quem cum Lis[i]machus misisset cruci-
figi respondit: "Terribile hoc fuit purpuratis tuis. Ossa mea autem nichil
75   interest ° humi an in sublimi putrescere." Idem eciam narrat libro 3 de
Cleonide nobili Sp⟨artan⟩o, qui cum trecentis civibus tantum pugnavit cum
Xerse rege Persarum pro libertate paterno, quos alacri animo exhortatus est
ipso prandente dicens: "Commilitones mei, prandete tamquam [f. 187] apud
inferos cenaturi," quasi diceret: nichil restat nisi mors; ideo pacienter
80   sustinete. Hec ille. Tercio paciencia consistit in iniuriarum remissione.

the gods would forgive me and that men would never know about it, I would still refuse to sin because," so he says in *Letter 48*, "I was born for greater things than to be the slave of my body." An example of magnanimity in professing the truth can be found in that the ancients would rather die for telling the truth than live by hiding it. Hence Valerius, in book 6, reports of a woman who was unjustly condemned by King Philip as he was intoxicated. She said: "I would challenge Philip, but when he is sober." With this word she brought him back to soberness and forced him to give her a more just judgment after examining her case more carefully. The same writer tells of a woman who prayed for the well-being of the tyrant Dionysius when everyone else was asking for his death. As Dionysius asked her for what reason she did so, she replied: "When I was a girl and lived under a harsh tyrant, I wanted to be rid of him. When he died, another one took his castle who was even harsher, and again I wished for his death. Now when this one was dead, we got an even more cruel one. So now I am afraid that if you, who are the worst of the ones we have had, are taken away, another may follow who is even worse." And an example of the third kind of magnanimity, that is, in tackling difficult tasks, can be easily found in our holy fathers, martyrs, confessors, and virgins, who were not afraid to die for Christ and their faith.

The second aspect of the virtue of strength is patience; according to Cicero, in book 2 of the *First Rhetoric*, it is the voluntary endurance of hardships for the sake of honor and usefulness. Such patience consists espe-cially in four things: in sustaining verbal offenses, in the long-suffering endurance of bodily pains, in forgiving one's injuries and harm, and in being lenient when giving punishment. An example of the first occurs in book 3 of *The Philosophers' Trifles*: when someone said, "O you tyrant!" to Caesar Augus-tus, he patiently replied with: "If I were a tyrant, you would not tell me so." In the same book it is reported that Aristoppus replied to someone that was cursing him: "As you are master of your tongue, so am I of my ears," meaning: as you can speak evil with your tongue, so can I hear it patiently with my ears. And we read further in the same book that Anthicanes replied to one who was cursing him: "It is easy to curse me, and I have learned to scorn curses." And in book 5 of *The Philosophers' Trifles* it is said that when Alci-biades asked Socrates why he did not chastise his shrewish wife, he answered: "As I suffer from her at home, I get used and ready to bear the offenses of others abroad more easily, and thus I bear with my shrewish wife at home." The second aspect of patience, the suffering of pains, can be found in the holy martyrs, to whom death, the last of all fearful things, was desirable because of their hope for future glory. Such virtue also appeard in ancient times, as Valerius reports in book 6 about Theodore of Cyrene: when Lysimachus ordered him to be crucified, he said: "This may be terrible for you in your purple, but my bones do not care whether they rot in the earth or on the gallows." The

Unde Cithoro de laude Cesaris ait quod nichil solet Cesar oblivisci nisi
iniurias. Et secundum Augustinum, *Epistula 5*, non solum obliviscitur sapiens iniuriarum set negat illas sibi illatas. Unde Seneca libro 3 *De ira*
narrat de Socrate quod cum iret per civitatem et esset c⟨ola⟩pho percussus,
85 nichil amplius fertur dixisse nisi quod molestum esset quia nescirent homines quando cum galea aut sine deberent prodire. Ibidem eciam dicitur de Di-
ogene causam agente cum Lentulo, et ipse attracta saliva in fronte eius
⟨media⟩ quantum poterat spuisset, paciencter faciem abstersit dicens: "Af-
firmabo, inquit, omnibus, o Lentule, falli eos qui te os habere negant."
90 Quarto paciencia in disciplinarum moderacione in correctionibus. Unde Valerius libro 4 ait quod Architas Tarentinus cum advertisset eius rura per
negligenciam villici corrupta et deperdita, intuens illum: "Supplicium,
inquit, sumpsissem a te nisi essem iratus." Maluit enim ipsum inpunitum
dimittere quam propter iram iniuste gravius punire. Ista ergo de fortitudi-
95 ne et paciencia et huiusmodi quamplura nota in *Breviloquio* Valensis, nota
supra, parte 4, capitulo satis.
    Tercia autem pars virtutis fortitudinis est perseverancia, que secun-
dum Tullium *Prima rhetorica* est in racione boni constituta stabilis et
perpetua permansio. Et per hanc fit homo immobilis, ut non frangatur adver-
100 sitatibus nec extollatur in prosperitatibus nec terreatur comminacionibus
nec flectetur ⟨pro⟩missionibus. Unde secundum expositorem Boecii *De consolacione Philosophie*, philosophi antiquitus posuerunt duo dolia in limine
domus dei Iovis, de quibus utroque op⟨orteba⟩t intrantes bibere vinum
amarum et aliud dulce. Moraliter hec domus mundus est, duo [f. 187v] dolia
105 prosperitas et adversitas, de quibus necesse est ubicumque mundum intrantes
gustare. Quam ergo necessaria est perseverancia ostendit Crisostomus dicens: "Tolle, inquit, perseveranciam, nec obsequium mercedem habet nec
beneficium gracias nec laudem." Quia secundum Bernardum perseverancia est
summi regis filia singularis, virtutum finis, et consummacio. Matthei 8
110 dicitur: "Qui ⟨autem⟩ perseveraverit usque in finem," supple in bono, "hic
salvus erit," et per consequens per illam diabolum vincit.
    Ex predictis ergo satis patet de accidia et eius contrario, scilicet
de occupacione sancta, similiter de bello spirituali contra mundum, carnem,
et diabolum, de quibus iam dicta ad presens sufficiunt. Et sic terminatur
115 quinta pars huius libelli.

---

1 igitur] ergo O.   **2–3** animum] omnium C.   **3** super] sic C.R.W; sine M.   **5** ubi] ut
O.   **19** parva] una C.   **27** ante] *om* O.   **28–31** magnanimum . . . arduitatem] *in M and
W arranged as a schema of three coordinated triads; but the following development shows
that the second and third triads* (ore in profitendo . . . , opere in detestando . . .) *also
apply to* magnanimum *rather than to* pacientem *and* perseverantem *respectively.*   **30** et]
om O.   **32** quadam] *om* O.   **35** idem] *om* O.   **38** secunde] similiter O.   **52** etc.] *om* O.

same writer tells in book 3 of the noble Spartan Leonidas, who with his three hundred citizens fought against Xerxes, king of the Persians, for the freedom of his country; he exhorted his troops with cheerful heart, saying: "Eat, my comrades, as if you were dining in the underworld," as if to say: nothing is left but death, therefore endure it with patience. The third aspect of patience is the forgiveness of our injuries. Cicero, in his praise of Caesar, says that Caesar used to forget nothing except his injuries. And according to Augustine in *Letter 5*, a wise man not only forgets his injuries but denies that he ever received any. Thus, Seneca in book 3 of *On Anger* tells of Socrates that, when he was walking through the city and received a blow in his face, he reportedly said nothing further than that it was tedious not to know when one should go out with a helmet. In the same book we read that when Diogenes conducted a lawsuit against Lentulus, the latter spat as hard as he could in the middle of his face; Diogenes patiently wiped his face and said: "I shall affirm before everybody, O Lentulus, that those are mistaken who declare you have no mouth." And the fourth aspect of patience is to be lenient in giving punishment. Valerius in book 4 says that Archytas of Tarent, when he realized that his fields were ruined and destroyed through the negligence of his steward, looked at him and said: "I would give you a hard punishment if I were not so angry." For he would rather let him go unpunished than punish him severely in unjust anger. This and more material on strength and patience and the like can be found in the *Breviloquium* by John of Wales, and also above, part 4.

The third aspect of the virtue of strength is perseverance; according to Cicero in his *First Rhetoric*, this is the virtue of remaining firm and stable in pursuit of the good. Through it, a person becomes unmoveable so that he is neither broken by adversity nor made proud by prosperity, and neither frightened by threats nor bent by promises. According to the commentator on Boethius's *Consolation of Philosophy*, in ancient times two vats were placed at the threshold of the temple of Jupiter, and all who entered had to drink from both, some bitter wine as well as some sweet. Morally interpreted, this temple is the world, and the two vats are prosperity and adversity, from both of which it behooves all who come into this world to drink. How much, then, it is necessary to have perseverance, Chrysostom shows us when he says: "Take perseverance away and obedience will have no merit, nor will a good deed get thanks or praise." For according to Bernard, perseverance is the unique daughter of the king on high and the end and consummation of the virtues. And in Matthew 8 it is said: "He who perseveres unto the end," add: in the good, "he shall be saved," and therefore he overcomes the devil through perseverance.

Thus we have learned about sloth and its opposite virtue, namely holy activity, and likewise about the spiritual combat against the world, the flesh, and the devil, of which enough has now been said. And thus ends part 5 of this book.

57 longanimi] longanima O.   **58** et] *om* O.   **61** quod] *om* O.   **64** eciam] et C.
68 ceterorum] *add* fore M.W; fero R; foris B1.   **70** in corporibus] *om* O.   **75** interest]
add et C.   **76** Spartano] sportaneo C.   **77** Xerse] exerse O.   paterno] paterna R; patrie
B1.   **78** ipso prandente] *om* O.   **83** illas] eas O.   **84** colapho] calopho C.   **88** media] in
eo C.   **89** Lentule] lentille O.   **90** in correctionibus] *om* O.   **94** iniuste] iuste M.R; iusto
W.   **99** immobilis] *corr from* immortalis C; immortalis O; immobilis B1.   **101** promis-
sionibus] commissionibus C.   **103** oportebat] optabant C; oportebant W.   **110** autem] ait
C.

The following material in this chapter occurs also almost verbatim in John of Wales, *Breviloquium*: lines 2–7, [28–29], 29–49 (IV.1); 53–69 (IV.3); 69–70, 71–79 (IV.4); 80–89 (IV.5); 90–94 (IV.6). **2–4** Macrobius, *In somnium Scipionis* I.viii.7. Some MSS add here definitions from *Ad Herennium* and Cicero's *De inventione*. **6–7** Aristotle, *Ethica Nicomachea* II.3 (1105a). **9–10** Matt. 26.35. **10–11** Matt. 26.69–75. **11–12** Matt. 26.56. **15–16** 1 Cor. 10.12. **20** Isa. 1.31. **23–25** 2 Cor. 12.10. **26–27** Ps. 58.10. **35–36** This quotation is often, as here, coupled with the following and attributed to Seneca; e.g., Chaucer, *Parson's Tale* 144–45 and its source, Raymundus, *Summa* III. xxxiv.9 (p. 443); Roger Bacon, *Moralis philosophia*, ed. F. Delorme and E. Massa (Zurich, 1953), p. 56. **37** Seneca, *Ep. morales* LXV.21. **40–43** Valerius, VI.ii.ext.1. **43–49** Ibidem, ext.2. **54–55** Cicero, *De inventione* II.53. **59–61** *Policraticus* III.14 (1:227). **61–62** Ibidem (1:223–24). **64–65** Ibidem (1:224); the text combines several separate quotations from *Policraticus*. **66–69** Ibidem, V.10 (1:327). **73–75** Valerius, VI.ii.ext.3. **76–80** Ibidem, III.ii.ext.3. **81–82** Cicero, *Oratio pro Q. Ligario* 35, cited by Augustine, *Ep. 138* II.9 (PL 33:529). **84–86** Seneca, *De ira* III.xi.2. **86–89** Ibidem, III.xxxviii.2. **91–94** Valerius, IV.i.ext.1. **95** See above, headnote to this chapter. **96** The reference must be to *FM* IV.vi–vii. **98–99** Cicero, *De inventione* II.53. **101–104** Boethius, *De consolatione Philosophiae* II, pr. 2, 13 (CC 94:20). **107–108** Bernard, *Ep. 129* 2 (7:323). **108–109** Bernard, *De diversis* XLI.10 (6.1:251). **110–111** Matt. 10.22.

PARS VI

De gula

VI.i   DE GULA

[C]ompleta autem particula 5 de accidia, que est prima filia carnis,
et de occupacione sancta eius contraria ac illam extirpante cum suis membris, restat iam sexto pertractare de domina Gula, secunda filia carnis,
primo, et secundo de contrario, scilicet de abstinencia. Circa autem vicium
5   gule sic consequenter intendo procedere: primo, quid sit gula et quomodo
diffinitur; secundo, que sunt eius species ex quibus cognoscitur; tercio,
quare contemptibilis est et iuste contempnitur.
   Est autem gula secundum Hugonem *De sacramentis*, libro [2, parte] 13,
capitulo 2, "immoderatus appetitus edendi," quam necessario evacuare opor-
10   tet si virtutes meritorias affectamus. Dicit enim *Glossa* super Matthei 4:
"In pugna Christi primo contra gulam agitur, quia nisi prius hec refrene-
tur, frustra contra alia vicia laboratur."

VI.ii   DE SPECIEBUS GULE

Eius autem species in hiis versibus connotantur:

   Prepropere, laute, nimis ardenter, studiose.
   Sic Ionathas, populus, Sodomita, Seyrque sacerdos.

Prima species est prepropere, hoc est, tempore indebito et extra horam,
5   sicut fecit Ionathas, de quo Regum 14, pro quo maledictionem patris incurrit et morti addictus est. [f. 188] Nec tamen ultra comedit nisi quod
summitate virge in melle intinxit. Quid ergo de gulosis dicendum est qui

PART VI

Gluttony

VI.i THE NATURE OF GLUTTONY

After completing part 5 on sloth, the first daughter of the flesh, and its opposite virtue which uproots her, that is, holy activity and its members, we now turn in part 6 to Lady Gluttony, the second daughter of the flesh, and then to her opponent, Abstinence. Concerning the vice of gluttony I plan to proceed as follows: first to see what it is and how it is defined; second, what its branches are by which it can be recognized; and third, why it is contemptible and how it is rightly to be scorned.

According to Hugh in *On the Sacraments*, book 2, part 13, chapter 2, gluttony is "the intemperate desire to eat," of which we must necessarily rid ourselves if we wish to gain meritorious virtues. For the *Gloss* says on Matthew 4: "Christ's first battle is against gluttony, for unless we bridle this vice first, we struggle in vain against the others."

---

9 Hugh of St. Victor, *De sacramentis* II.xiii.1 (PL 176:526). **11–12** *Glossa ordinaria* on Matt. 4.2 (5:15v.E).

VI.ii THE KINDS OF GLUTTONY

Gluttony's branches are listed in the following lines:

> Too soon, too rich, too eagerly,
>   And food too well prepared:
> Thus Jonathan, the Israelites,
>   Sodom, and Seyr the priest.

The first branch is eating too soon, that is, at an improper time or other than the set hour. Thus did Jonathan, in Kings 14, and thereby incurred his father's

diebus abstinencie ieiunia frangunt, et hoc non tantum bis vel ter in die,
set de vespere usque ad mediam noctem? Revera iuxta propheciam Ysaie 5
10   merces talium est hec: "Ve, ve, qui surgitis mane ad ebrietatem sectandam et
vinum potandum usque ad vesperam." Istud ergo "ve" hortatur precavendum
Ecclesiasticus: "Cogitavi in corde meo abstrahere vinum a carne mea." Nam
per nimiam gulam vini adquiritur corporis corrupcio. Nam ° corpus corrumpit
quicquid infunditur, sicut vas corruptum liquorem reddit ° fetidum aliqua-
15   tenus e⟨i⟩ infusum, quod per exitum gustus aperte probatur; Ioelis 2:
"Ululate qui bibitis vinum in dulcedine; perit enim ab ore vestro." Inde
enim est quod plus fetet os gulosi quam maximus fimarius, iuxta illud
Apocalipsis 9: "Ascendit fumus pute⟨i⟩ abissi ut fumus fornacis magne." O
quam abhominabile et mirabile quod voluptas gutturis, que tanti hodie
20   estimatur, vix duorum digitorum habet latitudinem, nec durat delectacio
nisi quantum durat transitus ille! Unde Proverbiorum 23: "Ne intuearis
vinum quando fla⟨v⟩escit cum splenduerit in vitro; ingreditur enim blande"
° —ecce pacificus ingressus—"set in fine mordebit ut coluber," etc.
      Secunda species est nimis laute pasci, sicut fuit de populo Israel, ut
25   patet Numeri 11, ubi dicitur quod cum haberent in deserto copiam manne omne
delectamentum habentis, adhuc optabant substanciam carnis, porra, ⟨pepo-
nes⟩, et huiusmodi. Et ideo de istis Psalmista ait: "Adhuc esce eorum [f.
188v] [erant] in ore ipsorum, et ira Dei ascendit super eos."
      Tercia species est nimis ardenter et nimis avide comedere, sicut fe-
30   cerunt Sodomite, quorum ruina ab ocio et nimi⟨a⟩ habundancia incepit. Unde
ex hoc proprie accidit crapula, scilicet quando quis sumit plus quam possit
bene et congrue digerere. Per quod contingit frequenter vomitum facere;
Ysaie 28: "Omnes mense eorum replete sunt vomitu."
      Quarta species gule est nimis studiose cibaria preparare, sicut fecit
35   Seyr aut Esau, de quo Genesis 25 legitur quod propter edulium lentis vendidit primogenita sua, quod avidissime comedit.
      Et tamen iuxta Psalmistam tales "famem pacientur ut canes." Unde Iero-
nimus: "Voluptas, inquit, habita famem non saturitatem parit." Et hoc est
quod dixit filius prodigus: "Fame pereo," Luce 10. Ad litteram enim verum
40   est de illo qui se inebriat vespere, quod necessario siciet in sequenti
mane; unde Proverbiorum 23 dicitur: "Quando evigilabo et rursus vina repe-
riam?" etc. Deinde scitit [usque] ad prandium nisi prius bibat. Idem eciam
accidit de esurie. In prandio enim non cessat esuries, eo quod non habet
que vellet vel preparata ut vellet. Unde Augustinus: "Ubicumque enim caro
45   querit refectionem, invenit defectionem." Nam etsi habuerit quantum ad
cibaria que, quanta, et qualia optat, tunc deficiet sibi venter aut saccus.
Et nota quod nulla racione potest talis esse sine fame. Nam ex defectu
famis, quando venter eius nimium repletur, tunc oportet ire spaciatum, ut
sic esuriat et famem querat et quasi ⟨venatur⟩; Ecclesiastici 28: "Noli

curse and was condemned to death, and yet he did not eat anything more
than what little honey he had gotten with the tip of his staff. What then
shall we say of those gluttons who break their fast on days of abstinence and
eat not only twice or three times a day but from evening till midnight? Indeed, according to the prophecy in Isaiah 5, their reward is this: "Woe to you
that rise up early in the morning to follow drunkenness, and to drink till the
evening." Against this "woe" Ecclesiastes warns us as follows: "I thought in
my heart to withdraw wine from my flesh." For too much wine leads to the
body's ruin. The body ruins whatever one puts into it, just as a bad container
gives the liquid poured into it a bad smell, as one can clearly experience by
its aftertaste; Joel 2: "Mourn, all you who drink sweet wine; for it is cut
off from your mouth." For that reason the mouth of a glutton reeks worse than
the biggest dungheap, according to Revelation 9: "The smoke of the bottomless
pit arose as the smoke of a great furnace." Oh how abominable and astonishing
it is that the lust of the palate, which nowadays is held in such esteem,
hardly extends over two fingers' breadth and lasts just as long as it takes
food to pass by it! Hence Proverbs 23: "Look not upon the wine when it is
yellow, when it shines in the glass; it goes in pleasantly"—behold, a peaceful
beginning—"but in the end it will bite like a snake."

The second branch is eating food that is too rich, as the people of Israel
did. This can be seen in Numbers 11, where it is reported that although they
had plenty of manna in the desert, full of all delight, they still hankered
after meat, leeks, cucumbers, and the like. And therefore the Psalmist says of
them: "As yet their meat was in their mouth, and the wrath of God came upon
them."

The third branch is eating too eagerly and too avidly, as the Sodomites
did, whose destruction began with their idleness and an overabundance of food.
From this branch comes overindulgence, that is, taking more food than one can
easily and naturally digest. This vice frequently leads to vomiting; Isaiah
28: "All their tables are full of vomit."

The fourth branch of gluttony is to prepare one's food too elegantly, as
Seyr did, or else Esau, of whom we read in Genesis 25 that he sold his birth-
right for a dish of lentils, which he ate most eagerly.

And yet, according to the Psalmist, such people suffer hunger like dogs.
Hence Jerome says: "When our desire is fulfilled, it does not lead to satiety
but to more hunger." It is for this reason that the Prodigal Son said: "I
perish with hunger," Luke 15. This is literally true of a person who gets
drunk at night: the next morning he will naturally be thirsty. Whence it is
said in Proverbs 23: "When shall I awake and find wine again?" And thereafter
he suffers thirst until dinner unless he drinks before that. The same also
applies to hunger; for hunger does not cease when one is eating, because one
does not get what one wants or as one wants it prepared. Therefore Augustine

50 avidus esse in omni epulacione." Cuius aviditatis signa sunt hec: avide
sumere cibum, tremore manuum arripere ciphum, frustrum tenere in manu aut
bolum, et effusio vultus hinc inde super cibum, sorbere inmasticatum.
　　[f. 189] Et revera tales sunt, ut dicit Apostolus Ad Ephesios 3,
"quorum deus venter est, et gloria in confusione." Et adverte: Solent enim
55 antiquitus homines diis suis templa construere, altaria erigere, ministros
ad serviendum ordinare, sacrificia immolare, thura concremare, et oraciones
fundere. Revera sic ad propositum templum sive ecclesia dei ventris et gule
est coquina. Campane in illa sonantes sunt pueri coquorum assaturam procla-
mantes ac cocturam et huiusmodi. Altare est mensa. Calix cum phialis est
60 ciphus cum ollis et tancardis. Ministri sunt ipsimet socii. Sacrificia sunt
pecudes immolate et similiter carnes assate et cocte. Fumus incensi est
sapor et odor ciborum. Oracio vero duplex: una autem ante saturitatem est
hec: "Utinam dupplicem ventrem haberem!" et alia post, quando venter fere
rumpitur, et est hec: "A, bely, mercy, bely, mercy!"
65 　　Set forte dicis: "Cuius figure est iste deus ventris et gule?" Revera,
ut videtur, bene potest formari et depingi cum capite porci primo, nam
sicut porcus in omnibus fedis capud et os ponit, sic gulosi omnia volunt
temptare, quia modo vinum, modo servisiam, modo medonem, et frequenter,
velud sus, feces calidatas. Secundo depingitur cum ventre sanguissuge,
70 cuius natura est quod cicius frangitur quam saciatur. Et ideo, ut videtur,
in ventre eorum est ignis ille "qui numquam dicit 'sufficit'" set omnia
consumit, Proverbiorum 30. Et tercio depingitur cum posteriore parte asini,
qui est animal luxuriosissimum, in signum quod luxuria est finis et conclusio gule. Et de luxuria una aliam sequitur sicut uxor virum. Quia cum tales
75 fuerint inebriati, tunc oportet visitare prostibula et omnem angulum ville
circa mulieres tam uxoratas quam solutas, nec curant nisi ut vilissima
eorum libido compleatur. Et sic generant hanc prolem ⟨male⟩dictam: litigium, fur- [f. 189v] tum, mendacium, homicidium, periurium, contemptum
Dei, et necligenciam sui. Quorum autem angelus diabolus, "et sunt potentes a
80 seculo viri famosi," Genesis 6. Unde congrue dicitur Ieremie 5: "Saturavi
eos et mechati sunt." "Quamdiu," ut dicit Ieronimus, "Eva in paradiso
abstinuit se, virgo fuit. Quamcito preceptum Domini comedendo de vetito
violavit, corrupcionem sensit." Et hoc est quod dicit Augustinus: "Minus,
inquit, nobis nocet princeps extorquendo pecuniam quam venter suscipiendo
85 escam," supple voluptuose. Ipse enim extorquendo nos alleviat, iste vero
suscipiendo nos inflat et inflammat. Et qui vult temptacionibus carnis
resistere, faciat sicut cocus providus facit quando olla bullit. Ipse vero
ne pinguedo exeat, materiam ignis retrahit. Sic tu materiam luxurie retrahe, idest superfluitatem ciborum. Vel sicut facit nutrix quando vult puerum
90 ablactare, ponit super mammillam aliquod amarum. Sic qui luxuriam vult
resecare, amaritudinem abstinencie adhibeat, etc.

says: "Wherever our body seeks refreshment, it finds something lacking." For
even if we have gotten the food we want, in the right quantity and kind, our
stomach or sack will still fail us. Such a person can in no way suffer to go
without hunger. For when he is not hungry because his stomach is too full, he
must go for a walk in order to get hungry and to look for hunger as if he were
hunting for it. Ecclesiasticus 28: "Be not greedy in any feasting." The
signs of such avidness are as follows: reaching for food greedily, snatching
the cup with trembling hands, holding a morsel or cake in one's hand, glaring
at the wine this way and that, and swallowing one's food without chewing it.

Indeed, as the Apostle says in Ephesians 3, these are the people "whose
god is their belly, and whose glory is in their shame." And notice that in
ancient times people used to build temples for their gods and erect altars for
them, ordain ministers for their worship, bring sacrifices, burn incense, and
offer up prayers. Applying this to our topic, we can say that the temple or
church of the god of the belly and of gluttony is the kitchen. The bells
ringing in it are the kitchen boys who call out what roast or cooked dish is
served. The altar is the dining table. Their chalice with its vials is the
bowl with cups and tankards. The priests are their boon companions; their
sacrifices, the slaughtered beasts and their roasted and boiled flesh; their
incense, the smell and savor of the food. And they have two prayers: one
before they are full, which goes, "Oh, if only I had two stomachs!" the other
when their belly nearly bursts: "Ah, belly, have mercy; belly, mercy!"

But perhaps you say: "What does this god of the belly and of gluttony
look like?" Well, it seems that he may be imagined and depicted first with the
head of a pig, for just as a pig pokes its head and snout into everything, even
the garbage, so gluttons want to try everything—now wine, now beer, now mead,
and often like a pig the stale dregs. Second, he may be depicted with the body
of a leech, whose characteristic it is to burst rather than be satisfied. And
thus it seems that in the gluttons' belly is that fire which never says
"Enough!" but devours everything, according to Proverbs 30. And third, he may
be depicted with the hindquarter of an ass, which is a very lecherous animal,
to indicate that the end and result of gluttony is lechery; for one follows the
other as a woman follows her man. When such people are drunk, they must visit
the brothel and every corner of the village in search of women, both married
and single, and they do not care where they may fulfill their shameful lust.
And then they bring forth this cursed offspring of quarreling, theft, lies,
manslaughter, perjury, contempt of God, and neglect of themselves. Their angel
is the devil, and they are "the mighty men of old, men of renown" referred to
in Genesis 6. Therefore, Jeremiah 5 says fittingly: "I fed them to the full,
and they comitted adultery." "As long as Eve in paradise was abstinent,"
Jerome says, "she was a virgin. But as soon as she broke the Lord's command by
eating the forbidden fruit, she experienced corruption." And for this reason

Narratur eciam de quodam qui attente rogabat diabolum pro expedicione
unius. Qui respondit: "Si feceris quod peto a te, iuvabo." Cum ergo ipse
spopondisset facturum, ait diabolus: "Elige tibi unum ex istis: utrum velis
95 suspendi, vel concumbere cum matre, vel occidere patrem, vel semel inebriari." Qui cum cogitasset ebrietatem esse peccatum levius, illam concessit.
Iste ergo quadam die ivit ad tabernam ut pactum compleret, et inebriatus
est. Veniens ergo domum et matrem fessam super lectum conspexit, illam
violenter oppressit. Superveniens ergo pater at illum graviter corripiens,
100 illum occidit. Mox clamor attollitur et homicida capitur, et incontinenti
ad suspendium ducitur. Ecce quot peccata ex ebrietate oriuntur.
[f. 190] Merito ergo illam vitare debemus, non tantum propter pericula
illam sequencia, verum eciam propter penam ad quam ducit. Exemplum nota
supra de divite epulone, parte 5, ubi agitur de elemosina, capitulo 11. Set
105 forte dicit [ali]quis: "Oportet me comedere et bibere, quia aliter vivere
non possum, eo quod naturale est. Quomodo cibum aut potum vitare possum?"
Revera respondeo: Bene autem volo quod eciam comedas et bibas, set adverte
quod tanta sit necessitas quantam ostendis; quia licet non posses vitare,
vivere tamen potes—et eciam melius—si non excedas. Et ideo consulo ut
110 comedas sicut racio docet, non sicut venter appetit. Quia si permittas
ventrem dominari, ad miseriam et confusionem te ducet. Exemplum de istis
heredibus qui omnia expendunt in tabernis et coquinis, quos non oportet
diabolum temptare sicut temptavit Christum dicens, "Dic ut lapides isti
panes fiant," eo quod ipsi ex lapidibus castrorum et aliorum edificiorum
115 illa vendendo in pane et vino et aliis cibis et potibus voluptuose consumunt. Unde tandem miserrime et quasi fame moriuntur. In cuius figura Regum
2 legitur quod Naas Amonites, cum Iabes Galaad obsedisset et illi ab eo
fedus petissent, respondit: "In hoc, inquit, feriam vobiscum pactum ut
eruam vobis oculos dextros." Iste enim Naas signat deum ventris qui super
120 gulosos imperare dedignatur nisi eruat oculos racionis eorum, et non tantum
illos verum eciam oculos corporis, quia ad litteram ut pluries tantum comedunt et bibunt quod lumen oculorum amittunt, ac eciam pedes et capud cum
memoria et intellectu, etc.

---

2 Prepropere] propere O.   **4** Prima] *add* autem O.   prepropere] propere O.   **6** quod] *add*
in O.   **7** intinxit] tinxit O.   **11** vinum] *om* O.   **12** Ecclesiasticus] ecclesiastes O.
13 Nam] *add* igitur C.   **14** reddit] *add* corruptum C.   **15** ei] est C.   **18** putei] M *corr*
from puteus; puteus C.R.W.   **22** flavescit] flammescit C.   blande] *add* ut quidem delectacio diu duraret desiderabit longum guttur ut grus C.   **26–27** pepones] pipionis pavones
C.   **30** nimia] nimis C.   **36** quod] quam O.   **37** pacientur] paciuntur O.   **42** etc.] *om*
O.   **46** quanta] quantum O.   **48** famis] *add* quia O.   **49** venatur] venenatur C.
53 Ephesios] philippenses M.W.   **55** altaria] *add* sibi O.   **73** luxuria] iuxta O.   **74** una]
add enim O.   **76** nisi ut] ubi O.   **77** maledictam] benedictam C.   **92** rogabat] rogavit

Augustine says: "A lord who extorts our money does us less harm than our stomach when it takes food," add: greedily. By robbing our money the former makes us light, but by taking food the latter swells us up and inflames us. Therefore, whoever wants to resist the temptations of the flesh must do as the circumspect cook when the pot is boiling: lest the broth boil over, he pulls out some of the firewood. In the same way, you must reduce the fuel for lechery, that is, your abundance of food. Or else, when a nurse wants to wean a child, she puts something bitter on her nipples. In the same way, whoever wants to reduce the lust of his flesh must give it the bitterness of abstinence, and so forth.

There is a story about someone who earnestly prayed to the devil for success in some enterprise. The devil said to him: "If you do what I ask, I will help you." When the man had promised him that, the devil said: "Choose one of the following: to be hanged, or to sleep with your mother, or to kill your father, or to get drunk once." Thinking that drunkenness was a very small sin, he chose that. So, one day he went to a bar to fulfill his promise and got drunk. But coming home, when he saw his mother lying tired out on her bed, he raped her. As his father surprised him and chastised him severely, he killed him. Soon an outcry arises and the murderer is caught, and at once he is led to the gallows. Lo, how many sins come from drunkenness!

We must therefore rightly avoid it, not only because of the dangers that come from it, but also because of the punishment to which it leads us. Notice the case of the rich man who dined splendidly, in the section above on almsgiving, part 5, chapter 11. But perhaps someone objects: "I have got to eat and drink, for that is natural, and otherwise I cannot live. How could I possibly go without food and drink?" To that I reply: of course I want you to eat and drink, but be sure that your need for food is as great as you make it out to be; for while it is true that you cannot go without food, you certainly can live—and even better—if you do not eat more than necessary. Therefore I advise you to eat as reason teaches, not as your stomach desires. For if you give your stomach the upper hand, it will lead you to misery and confusion. We see an example in those people who spend all their inheritance on bars and the kitchen; they do not need to be tempted as Christ was when the devil said to him, "Command that these stones be made bread," because they change the stones of their castles and other buildings by selling them for bread and wine and other food and drink which they consume lustily. And in the end they die in great wretchedness as of hunger. As a type of this we read in Kings 2 that when Nahash the Ammonite laid siege to Jabesh-Gilead and they asked for a truce, he replied: "On this condition will I make a covenant with you, that I may pluck out your right eyes." Nahash stands for the god of the belly, who will not deign to rule over gluttons unless he tears out their eyes of reason,

O.   **95** vel(3)] aut O.   **98** conspexit] *add* statim instigante dyabolo O.   **106** possum(2)]
potero O.   **108** vitare] *om* O.   **109** tamen] *om* O.   ut] quod O.   **113** temptavit] fecit O.
117 2] 11 M.W; 21 R.   **120** imperare] *add* non *exp* C; *add* non M.W.

VI.iii   QUARE GULA EST CONTEMPTIBILIS

[E]st ergo istud peccatum detestandum propter predicta ac eciam plura
que producit. Ex isto igitur primo generatur spiritualis intelligencie
oblivio; Osee 13: "Saturati sunt et elevaverunt cor suum, et obliti sunt
mei." Unde [f. 190v] Augustinus: "Si modum inmoderate excedis, si precioso
5   potu te ingurgites, quantaslibet laudes lingua resonat, vita blasphemat."
Et Ieronimus: "Qui luxuriatur, vivens mortuus est, et qui inebriatur, mortuus et sepultus est," quia "racionis vile sepulcrum est ebrietas." Nam illa sepulcrum est quasi quedam submersio spiritualis, in qua enim aliquociens
quemquam sepeliri est submergi. Et ideo talis nimietas, ex quo spiritum
10   infatuat et sic inhebetat, subiectum stultum reddit.
   Secundo gula est detestabilis eo quod est divini contemptus terribilis
provocacio. Ab illis enim despicitur Deus. Ancipiter enim famelicus cum a
domino suo reclamatur, confestim omnibus dimissis ad ipsum venire festinat,
set non saturatus; similiter et homo abstinens. Set gulosus diebus eciam
15   festivis clamorem ecclesie aut campanarum pulsaciones audire contempnit,
quando cicius petit tabernam quam ecclesiam, [cicius] mensam quam missam,
cicius ut cibis superfluis ingurgitet ventrem quam ut cibis spiritualibus
impleat mentem. Et ideo, ut predicitur, bene dicitur venter eorum deus,
quia secundum Augustinum hoc ab homine colitur quod pre ceteris diligitur.
20   In hoc ergo quod ventrem tantum honorant, deterior est quam ydolatria paganorum. Pagani enim honores impendunt auro, argento, lapidibus preciosis, et
huiusmodi, set gulosus honorat ventrem, qui est vilissimum sterquilinium et
feda latrina. Unde merito dici possunt peregrini diaboli. Exemplum: Pere- ·
grini enim Dei vadunt ad sanctos, ut usum membrorum perditorum recipiant.

and not only them but their bodily eyes as well, for they often eat and drink
so much that they literally lose their eyesight as well as their feet and head
with their memory and reason.

2–3 On these verses see Introduction, pp. 5–11.   **5–7** 1 Sam. 14.   **10–11** Isa. 5.11.
12 Eccles. 2.3.   **16** Joel 1.5.   **18** Rev. 9.2.   **21–23** Prov. 23.31–32, and cf. 1 Sam.
16.4 and 1 Kings 2.13.   **25–27** Num. 11.4–9.   **27–28** Ps. 77.30.   **30** Cf. Ezek.
16.49.   **33** Isa. 28.8.   **35–36** Cf. Gen. 25.27–34.   **37** Ps. 58.7.   **38** Cf. Jerome on
Hos. 4.10–12 (CC 76:42) and on Eccles. 2 (PL 23:1076).   **39** Luke 15.17.   **41–
42** Prov. 23.35.   **44–49** The Augustine quotation and its context also in Peraldus,
Summa vitiorum II.i.6.   **49–50** Ecclus. 37.32.   **54** Phil. 3.19.   **54–57** Hugh of Folieto,
De claustro anime II.19 (PL 176:1072).   **71** Prov. 30.16.   **79–80** Gen. 6.4.   **80–
81** Jer. 5.7.   **81–83** Cf. Ps.-Augustine, *Sermo 144 in app.* 1 (PL 39:2026), said of
Adam.   **92–101** Tubach 1816. The story occurs with summarizing verses in Latin and
English in MS Harley 2316, fol. 15.   **104** *FM* V.xxiii.24–102.   **113–114** Matt. 4.3.
117–119 1 Sam. 11.1–2.

VI.iii   WHY GLUTTONY IS TO BE SCORNED

This sin, then, is worthy to be despised for the evil consequences I have
just mentioned, as well as for others. For from it comes, first of all, that
we forget our spiritual knowledge; Hosea: "They were filled and lifted up
their heart, and they have forgotten me." Hence Augustine says: "If you go
beyond the reasonable measure, if you gorge yourself with costly drink, your
life denies whatever praises your tongue sings." And Jerome: "Whoever lives
in luxury is dead in his life; and whoever is drunk is dead and buried, for
drunkenness is the base grave of our reason." Drunkenness is a grave as if it
were a drowning of the spirit; to bury someone in it is to drown him. Hence by
stupefying and weakening the mind such excess renders a man a fool.

In the second place, gluttony is to be detested because it is a terrible
provocation of God's contempt. For God is despised by gluttons. When a hungry
hawk is called back by his master, he at once leaves everything and hurries to
him; so does a person who is abstinent. But a glutton scorns to listen to the
appeal of the Church or the ringing of the bells on feast days, as he goes to
the tavern instead of the church, seeks his table instead of the altar, and
crams his belly with an abundance of dishes instead of his mind with spiritual
food. Therefore, as we said earlier, their belly is fittingly called their
god, for according to Augustine man worships what he loves before all else.
Insofar as they give such great honor to their belly, their worship is even
worse than pagan idolatry. For the pagans pay homage to gold, silver, precious
stones, and the like, but a glutton pays homage to his belly, which is a most
vile dunghill and a dirty cloaca. Whence they may rightly be called pilgrims
of the devil. God's pilgrims travel to certain saints that they may regain the

25   Set gulosi ad tabernam peregrinantur, ut sensum ibi amittant ac usum mem-
     brorum que[m] prius habuerunt. Nam illuc perdunt visum, gressum, cerebrum,
     et omnia membra racionis. Et ideo de illis bene ait Sapiens Proverbiorum
     23: "Cui ve, cuius patri ve, cui rixe, cui fovee, cui sine causa vulnera,
     cui suf- [f. 191] fossio oculorum? Nonne hiis qui morantur in vino et
30   student in calicibus epotandis?" Et sequitur: "Vinum autem blande ingredi-
     tur, set in novissimo mordebit ut coluber, et sicut regulus venena diffun-
     det."
         Tercio est detestabilis quia est iterate esuriei inmoderacio; Osee 4:
     "Comedent et non saturabuntur." Et Psalmista: "Famem, inquit, paciuntur ut
35   canes." Et vocatur illa infirmitas bolismus, idest caninus appetitus, qui
     numquam fere saciatur; Proverbiorum 31: "Iustus comedet et replet animam
     suam, venter autem impiorum insaciabilis." Merito ergo cavenda et vitanda
     est.
         Narratur de quodam ceco provid⟨um⟩ valde ductorem habente, qui in
40   omnibus magistrum suum bene duxit in quibus sibi voluit consentire. Euntes
     ergo semel per viam, contigit cecum esurire. Rogat ergo ductorem ut undique
     respiceret ut forte locum perciperet ubi manducare possent. Respondit puer
     quod non erat hora comedendi et quod multum impediret eos si tali hora a
     via declinarent, ex quo multum haberent ire, et addidit viam esse tortuo-
45   sam, unde nisi illum caucius duceret, faciliter cespitare posset et illum
     ledere. Cum ergo puero adquiescere nollet set ductorem oculos girare compu-
     lisset, interim cespitavit, ita quod fere fregit sibi collum. Venientes ad
     locum prandii ubi eis dabatur [crudus] et insanus cibus set delectabilis,
     premunivit illum puer ne ex illo commederet. Et ille: "Habeo, inquit,
50   optimum stomachum," et sic nimis avide devorans se ipsum confundit. Morali-
     ter per istum cecum intelligo voluntatem hominis sive appetitum, qui nichil
     cognoscit nisi per virtutem intellectivam. Ductor eius ratio est, que hanc
     voluntatem ducit in via versus celum. Omni autem die si meritorie profici-
     at, expedit se de una dieta. Tunc ergo voluntas mane esurit [f. 191v]
55   quando ante horam debitam comedere appetit. Si ergo pro tunc importune
     compellat racio[nem] cogitare et providere nimis sollicite quid comedendum,
     quid bibendum, revera quando racio circa huiusmodi giratur et occupatur,
     voluntas quasi cecus in absencia ductoris cespitat. Similiter, quando est
     hora comedendi, si contra consilium racionis in qualitate aut quantitate
60   nimis comedat, seipsum intoxicat. Non ergo excusari potest homo de gula
     dicendo, "Nescio quid, quale, aut quantum michi comedere expedit," quia in
     omnibus si velit adquiescere, racio sibi dictabit.
         Narrat eciam Alexander De naturis rerum quod erat quidam comes illus-
     tris in armis et strenuus et sanguine generosus, qui cotidie epulabatur
65   splendide sicut dives epul⟨o⟩, de quo Luce 15 ut supra, parte 5, capitulo
     11, tractatur. Cui successit filius optimus, pauperum solacium, viduarum et

lost use of their members. But gluttons make their pilgrimage to the tavern so
that they may there lose their senses and the former use of their members; for
there they lose their sight, their ability to walk, their brain, and the use of
the other parts of their reason. Therefore the wise man says well of them, in
Proverbs 23: "Who has woe? whose father has woe? who has contentions? who
falls into pits? who has wounds without cause? who has red eyes? Is it not
those that pass their time in wine and study to drink off their cups?" And he
adds: "For wine goes in pleasantly, but in the end it will bite like a snake
and will spread abroad poison like a basilisk."

In the third place, gluttony is to be detested because it leads to even
greater hunger; Hosea 4: "They shall eat and not be filled." And the Psalmist
says: "They shall suffer hunger like dogs." That disease is called bolismus,
a dog-like appetite which hardly ever gets quenched; Proverbs 31: "The just
man eats and fills his soul, but the belly of the wicked is insatiable."
Therefore, gluttony must justly be guarded against and avoided.

There is a story about a blind man who had a very circumspect guide, who
would guide his master well as long as he would agree with him. Once as they
were walking along, the blind man got hungry. He asks his guide to look around
if perhaps he could find a place for them to eat. The boy replied that it was
not yet time to eat and that it would slow them down very much if they went off
the road just then, for they still had a long way to go; and he added that the
road was very uneven, so that unless he guided him carefully, he might easily
stumble and get hurt. As the blind man would not listen to the boy but in-
sisted that he cast his eyes all about him, he stumbled and nearly broke his
neck. Then they came to an eating-place where they were given delicious but
raw and unhealthy food; so the boy warned the blind man not to eat any of it.
But he said: "I have a first-class stomach" and ate greedily and so made himself sick. Morally interpreted, the blind man stands for a man's will or appetite, who has no understanding except by way of his intellectual faculty. The
guide is his reason, which leads this will on the way toward heaven. Every day
that it walks with spiritual profit, it advances as much on its journey. But
the will gets hungry in the morning when it wants to eat before the set time.
If it then compels reason to think and cast about too eagerly what it should
eat and what it should drink—when in other words our reason revolves around
and busies itself with such matters—, then our will stumbles like the blind
man when his guide is absent. Similarly, if at the meal hour it acts against
the counsel of reason by not eating the right kind or amount of food, it
poisons itself. A man can therefore not excuse his gluttony by saying, "I
don't know what kind of food and how much is good for me to eat," for his
reason will clearly instruct him in every respect, if he will only listen to it.

Alexander in *On the Nature of Things* reports that once there was an
illustrious count, strong in arms and of noble blood, who ate splendidly every

orphanorum refugium. Qui sepius sepulcrum patris cum devocione et lacrimis visitare consuevit. Cum ergo quadam die quamplures proceres ad convivium convocasset et cum illis ante prandium dictum sepulcrum visitasset, spiritu
70 Dei iussit lapidem ammoveri. Et ecce vidit bufonem teterrimum collum patris pedibus amplectantem. Quo viso cum lacrimis [clamans] ait: "O pater mi, quam solempnes epule per hoc collum in stomachum descenderunt. Set heu, qualis inhoneste crapule remuneracio!" Et hiis dictis et lapide reposito, mundum reliquit et paupertati et abstinencie totaliter se dedit. Unde
75 ⟨Ecclesiastici⟩ 10 dicitur: "Cum dormierit homo, hereditabit bestias, serpentes, et vermes." Ad litteram enim dicitur quod de corpore humano post mortem nascuntur tria genera vermium: de capite enim et collo nascitur bufo, de spina dorsi scorpio, et [de] ventre et stomacho gurgullo.

Et nota [f. 192] quod gulosus nititur omnes sensus inebriare. Delecta-
80 tur enim visus in claritate vini ac pulcritudine aliorum ciborum et potuum, tactus vero in potuum frigiditate et ciborum caliditate, gustus in sapore, nasus in odore. Et quia nichil est in calice quod posset auditum delectare, ideo assumit liram et tympanum, per que miserabiles appetitus in voluptatis aviditate acuit. Et tamen per hec omnia anima miserabilis post vitam con-
85 funditur. Et nota ad litteram quod qui de sero se inebriat os habet fetidum de mane. Et ideo bene sepulcro comparatur iuxta illud Psalmi: "Sepulcrum patens est guttur eorum." Nota eciam quod ⟨caro⟩ hominis potest dici terra pessima et fetidissima. Ceteris autem terris apponuntur stercora ut fructificent, set econtra terra corporis hominis appositis cibariis delicatissi-
90 mis nichil fructificat nisi stercora, et quanto preciosiora sunt cibaria, tanto ad secessum perveniencia sunt viliora. Nota eciam secundum Augustinum quod ebrietas aufert memoriam, dissipat sensum, confundit intellectum, concitat libidinem, involvit linguam, corrumpit sanguinem, omnia membra debilitat, et omnem salutem exterminat. Unde Gregorius: "Ebrietas, [in-
95 quit,] est blandus demon, dulce venenum, suave peccatum, quam qui habet, se non habet; quam qui facit, non tantum facit peccatum set totum est peccatum, quia attrahit sibi omnia peccata." Et ideo Apostolus ad mensuram instigans ait Ad Romanos 12: "Non plus sapere quam oportet sapere," etc. De qua quidam sic metrice ait:

100   Sicut ad omne quod est mensuram ponere prodest,
         Sic sine mensura deperit omne quod est.

---

2 igitur] ergo O.   3 13] *om* O.   8–9 aliquociens quemquam] aliquem O.   10 sic inhebetat] hebetat O.   13 omnibus] ceteris O.   14 set . . . saturatus] *om* O.   26 quem] que C.W.   27 omnia] cetera O.   34 paciuntur] pacientur O.   37 cavenda et] *om* O.˙   39 pro-

day, like the rich man of Luke 15, of whom we spoke above in part 5, chapter 11. He was succeeded by his son, a very good person, comfort of the poor and refuge of widows and orphans. He often used to visit his father's tomb with devotion and tears. Now, as one day he invited many noble citizens to a banquet and before dinner visited his father's tomb with them, inspired by God's spirit he had the tomb slab removed. And behold, there was a very black toad clasping his father's throat with its feet. When he saw that, he cried out with tears: "O my father, what splendid banquets went through this throat into your stomach. But alas, what vile reward for your overindulgence!" Having said this and replaced the slab, he left the world and gave himself completely to a life of poverty and abstinence. Therefore it is said in Ecclesiasticus 10: "When a man dies, he will inherit beasts, serpents, and worms." They say that after death three kinds of vermin are literally born of a human body: a toad from his head and throat, a scorpion from his spine, and a weevil from his body and stomach.

    And notice that a glutton strives to inebriate all his senses. For his sight is charmed by the splendor of the wine and the beautiful sight of other food and drink; his touch, by chilled drinks and hot food; his taste, by their savor; his smell, by their aroma. And since there is nothing in a glass that might appeal to his ear, he takes the lyre and the tambourine with which he goads his wretched appetite into hot desire. And yet, through all these his wretched soul will come to ruin after this life. Notice that it is literally true that a person who gets drunk at night has bad breath next morning. Therefore he can well be compared to a sepulcher, after the words of the Psalm: "Their throat is an open sepulcher." Notice also that man's body can be called an absolutely worthless and ugly piece of land. For other pieces of land are given dung so that they may produce fruit; but when the land of man's body, in contrast, has been given the most dainty food, it produces no fruit but dung, and in fact, the more precious the food is, the more vile what goes down the privy. And notice further that according to blessed Augustine drunkenness takes away one's memory, blurs the senses, confuses the mind, stirs up lust, ties the tongue, poisons the blood, weakens all the limbs, and destroys one's health altogether. Hence Gregory says: "Drunkenness is a smiling fiend, a sweet poison, a soft sin; who has it loses himself; who engages in it does not only commit a sin but becomes completely sinful, because it draws all other sins to itself." Therefore the Apostle admonishes us to keep the right measure when he tells us, in Romans 12, "not to be more wise than it behooves," and so on. Of this subject someone has said in verse:

    As it is useful to take all things with due measure,
        So all things will perish if taken without it.

vidum] provido C. **51** istum] hunc O. **56** racionem] racio C; racioni M. **64** et] *om*
O. **65** epulo] epulio C; epulone M. ut] et O. **75** Ecclesiastici] actuum C. **87** caro]
terra C. **90** nichil] nec O. **91** secundum] *add* beatum O.

VI.iv   A QUIBUS ABSTINENDUM EST

[A]d hoc ergo vicium extirpandum iam procedit sobrietas et abstinencia
ut audax athleta illud [f. 192v] constanter aggrediens. Quam pulcre commen-
dans et describens ait Augustinus: "Abstinencia, inquit, tota est utilis et
formosa. Salvat enim memoriam, acuit sensum, sincerat mentem, dirigit vul-
5   tum, integritat pudorem, mitigat vicium, exornat cerebrum, expedit linguam,
explicat sermonem, confirmat sanguinem, nutrit medullam, contempnit libidinem, recreat corpus, propagat senectutem." Hec ille. De qua sic procedam:
primo, a quibus est abstinendum; secundo, de differencia abstinencie;
tercio, de eius utilitate.
10   Circa primum est sciendum quod a tribus est specialiter abstinendum.
Primo a superfluitate cibi et potus, de qua capitulo de gula supra proximo
satis dictum est. Secundo abstinendum est de mala societate. Vulgariter
enim dicitur: "Qui tangit picem, inquinabitur ab ea." Et ideo ait Psalmista: "Cum sancto sanctus eris," etc. Et ideo Sapiencie 2: "Dicunt impii de
15   viro iusto, abstinet a viis nostris tamquam ab inmundiciis." Et Proverbiorum 4 dicitur: "Ne delecteris in semitis impiorum, nec tibi placeat malorum
via. Fuge ab ea et non transeas per eam." Et Ecclesiastici 7: "Discede ab
iniquo et discedant a te mala." Tercio abstinendum est a peccatis et viciis; Tymothei 5: "Teipsum castum custodi. Noli adhuc aquam bibere, set modi-
20   co utere vino." Ubi *Glossa*: "Vult, inquit, Deus prudenter serviri ne nimie-
tate abstinencie debiliores ad bene operandum fiant homines et post medico-
rum suffragia requirant." Unde Bernardus: "Holocaustum, inquit, de rapina
facit qui corpus suum inmoderate affligit, scilicet aliqua egestate ⟨cibi
(supple necessarii)⟩ aut penuria somnpni." Et Seneca: "Hanc vitam sanam
25   tene, ut scilicet tantum corpori indulgeas quantum est valetudinis." Quia,
ut dicit Gregorius, dum caro plus restringitur, ad execu- [f. 193] cionem
boni operis enervatur. In cuius figura Numeri 30 dicitur: "Si voverit
mulier et iuramento se constrinxerit ut per ieiunium ac ceterarum rerum
abstinenciam affligit animam suam, in arbitrio viri sui erit." Sic penitens
30   in arbitrio discreti sacerdotis, ut per se tantam penitenciam aut tam

3–4 Hos. 13.6.   **4–5** Augustine, *En. in Ps. 146* 2 (CC 40:2122).   **6–7** Jerome, *Ep. 69* 9 (CSEL 54:696).   **7** This commonplace is, in Peraldus, *Summa vitiorum* II.i.5, attributed to "Rabanus."   **19–23** Peraldus, *Summa vitiorum* II.i.3.   **28–32** Prov. 23.29–32. **34** Hos. 4.10.   **34–35** Ps. 58.7.   **36–37** Prov. 13.25.   **39–50** Also in MS Harley 7332, fol. 44v.   **63–74** Tubach 4880; also in Bromyard, "Mors," M.XI.121. The same motif occurs in the tales about usurers in *FM* IV.vii.107–127.   **65–66** *FM* V.xxiii.24–102. **75–76** Ecclus. 10.13.   **86–87** Ps. 5.11.   **92–94** Also in Peraldus, *Summa vitiorum* II.ii.1.   **94–97** Ibidem.   **98** Rom. 12.3.   **100–101** *Prov* 29566.

VI.iv   FROM WHAT WE MUST ABSTAIN

To uproot this vice, soberness and abstinence steps forward like a brave champion and attacks it firmly. Augustine praises and describes this virtue beautifully when he says: "Abstinence is all useful and beautiful. For it preserves our memory, sharpens the wit, keeps the mind firmly set, composes the features, guards integrity, weakens any propensity to vices, strengthens the brain, frees the tongue, generates eloquence, cleanses the blood, nourishes the marrow, depresses lust, refreshes the body, and leads to a healthy old age." In treating it I will proceed as follows: first, I will discuss from what things one must abstain; second, of the different kinds of abstinence; and third, of its usefulness.

With respect to the first point, we must know that one is to abstain from three things in particular: first from taking too much food and drink, of which I have said enough in the preceding chapter. Second, we must abstain from bad companionship. For the popular proverb says: "He who touches pitch gets dirty." And the Psalmist declares: "With the holy, you will be holy," and so forth. And Wisdom 2: "The wicked say of the just man: 'He abstains from our ways as from filthiness.'" And in Proverbs 4 it is written: "Take no delight in the paths of the wicked, neither let the way of evil men please you. Flee from it and do not pass on it." And in Ecclesiasticus 7: "Depart from the unjust, and evils will depart from you." And third, we must abstain from sins and vices; Timothy 5 advises: "Keep yourself chaste. Do not still drink water, but use a little wine." On which the *Gloss* comments: "God wants that people serve him with prudence so that they do not, through their excessive abstinence, become too weak to do good deeds and afterwards need medical help." Whence Bernard says: "A person who mortifies his body without moderation, that is, by depriving himself of food (add: which he needs) or sleep, makes a burnt offering from stolen goods." And Seneca advises: "Observe this rule for a healthy life: that you grant your body as much as it needs for its well-being." For as Gregory says, when our flesh is held in too strict bonds, it grows too weak to carry out its good work. This rule is prefigured by what is said in

asperam accipiat, aut eciam ipse sacerdos iniungat, quod desperando illam
non deserat, sicut stultus est qui iumentum suum sic onerat quod sub illo
cadat et illum amplius non portat. Unde legitur in *Vitas Patrum* quod quidam
frater interrogabat abbatem Pastorem dicens: "Feci grande peccatum. Volo
35 ergo per triennium penitere." Cui abbas: "Multum est." Et ille: "Iubes
quadraginta dies?" Et senex: "Multum est. Set credo quod si ex toto corde
penituerit homo et non apposuerit iterum peccare, quod triduanam penitenciam suscipiet Deus, qui dicit, 'Nolo mortem peccatoris set ut magis con-
vertatur et vivat.' " Et ideo Ecclesiastici 4 dicitur: "Sapiens cor et in-
40 telligibile abstinet a peccatis." Unde hanc abstinenciam approbat Bernardus
dicens: "Tunc preclara est apud Deum abstinencia, cum animus a viciis ieiunat. Quid enim prodest corpus attenuari abstinencia si animus intumescat
superbia?" Et Ambrosius: "Quid enim prodest ieiunare visceribus et luxuriari veneribus, abstinere cibis et errare peccatis?" quasi diceret, nichil,
45 set pocius nocet. Unde Augustinus dicit: "Qui a cibis abstinent et numquam
male agere desistunt, demones imitantur, quibus carnalis cibus non est set
iniquitas semper inest." Et ideo Gregorius dicit: "Qui se ab alimentis abstinet sectando iusticiam, a culpa ieiunat," etc.

---

1 hoc] istud O.   **5** integritat] integrat O.   **12** de] a O.   **14** ideo] *add* sapiens ait O.
18 discedant] discedent O.   **23–24** cibi . . . necessarii] supple sibi necessaria C.
37 peccare] *add* ut penitenciam agat O.   **44** veneribus] venatibus O.   **47** inest] *om* O.
dicit] ait O.   **48** etc.] *om* O.

VI.v   DE DIFFERENCIIS ABSTINENCIE

[C]irca differenciam abstinencie est sciendum quod illa est multiplex
iuxta illud ⟨metricum⟩: [f. 193v]

Abstinet eger, egens, cupidus, gula, symea, virtus.

Quia hee sunt differencie abstinencie. Nam aliquando abstinet eger, quia
5 non potest comedere vel propter medicinam; Matthei 9: "Venient dies quando
auferetur ab eis sponsus, et tunc ieiunabunt." Aliquando abstinet egens,

Numbers 30: "If a woman has vowed and bound herself by oath to afflict her
soul by fasting or abstinence from other things, it shall depend on the will of
her husband." Similarly a penitent must subject himself to the judgment of a
discriminating priest, so that he may set for himself just so much penance, or
such a hard one, or else that the priest may enjoin just so much penance on
him, that he will not despair and give it up; as it would be foolish for a man
to put such a load on his beast of burden that it breaks down under it and
cannot carry it any further. In *The Lives of the Fathers* we read that a
brother was asking Abbot Pastor, "I have committed a great sin; I want to do
three years' penance for it." The abbot replied: "It is too much." And the
brother said: "Then will you give me forty days?" And the desert father: "It
is too much. But I believe that if a person is sorry with his whole heart and
intends not to sin again, if he then does penance, God will accept a penance of
three days, for he says: 'I do not desire the death of the sinner but rather
that he turn from his way and live.' " And thus it is said in Ecclesiasticus 4:
"A wise heart which has understanding will abstain from sins." Bernard approves of this kind of abstinence and says: "That abstinence is excellent
before God when one's mind fasts of vices. For what good does it do to weaken
our body with abstinence if our mind at the same time swells with pride?" And
Ambrose: "What good is it to fast in one's bowels and delight in one's hunt,
to abstain from food and wander about in sins?" meaning: it is no good at all,
but rather does harm. And Augustine says: "People who abstain from food but
never stop doing evil are followers of demons, who do not use fleshly food but
always practice wickedness." And therefore Gregory says: "He who abstains
from food and follows a life of justice fasts from sin."

---

13 Cf. Ecclus. 13.1.   **14** Ps. 17.26.   **14–15** Wisd. 2.16.   **16–17** Prov. 4.14–15.
17–18 Ecclus. 7.2.   **19–20** 1 Tim. 5.22.   **20–23** *Glossa ordinaria* on 1 Tim. 5.22
(6:221.A).   **24–25** Seneca, *Ep. morales* VIII.5.   **27–29** Num. 30.14.   **33–39** *VP*
V.x.40 (PL 73:920).   **38–39** Ezek. 33.11.   **39–40** Ecclus. 3.32.   **41–43** In Peraldus,
Summa virtutum III.v.11.6, attributed to Jerome.   **43–44** Ps.-Augustine, *Sermo 146 in*
app. 1 (PL 39:2029).   **45–47** In Peraldus, loc. cit., attributed to Isidore.

VI.v   DIFFERENT KINDS OF ABSTINENCE

With respect to the different kinds of abstinence, we have the following
verse:

> The sick man fasts, the needy, and the miser,
> As does the glutton and the ape, and also true virtue.

These are the various form of abstinence. For sometimes a sick person abstains
because he cannot eat, or he does so as a cure; Matthew 9: "The days will come

quia non habet quod comedat; Matthei 15: "Dixit Iesus discipulis suis:
'Misereor super turbam, quia non habent quod manducent.' " Aliquando cupidus, ut postea plura rapiat; Ecclesiastes 5: "Vir cui donavit Dominus
10   divicias et scienciam non tribuit potestatem ut comedat." Moraliter autem
loquendo, tales fame fere periunt ⟨u⟩t divicias congregant. Et eciam ad
litteram, ut patet. Aliquando eciam abstinent gulosi, et hoc primo ut
post[ea] avidius comedant, et certe tales preveniunt vigiliam dei ventris.
Isti enim diu ieiunant, set tunc querunt cibaria magis delicata de quibus
15   ma⟨gis⟩ comed⟨u⟩nt quam aliis temporibus, duobus diebus extra ieiunium. Et
certe tales tantam graciam faciunt deo ventri acsi darent sibi duos obulos
pro uno denario, quod credo non facerent Iudeo aut Saraceno. Et secundo
isti gulosi ieiunant sic quod per tres dies plus comedunt quam si non
ieiunarent. Nam die ieiunii precedente dicunt: "Comedamus hodie fortiter,
20   cras enim ieiunabimus." In die sequente ieiunium dicunt: "Hodie oportet
forcius comedere propter ieiunium hesternum." Set ipsomet die ieiunii
omnino excedere nituntur ne forte fame deficerent in sero. Et certe tales
defraudant deum suum eo quod pro duobus obulis non reddunt [nisi] denarium.
Contra quos dicitur Ysaie 15: "Nolite ieiunare [sicut] usque ad hanc diem."
25   Aliquando abstinent symee, idest ypocrite, ut laudentur, et illud ieiunium
est ⟨van⟩itatis. Luce 18 dicitur de Phariseo: "Ieiuno bis in sabbato," cum
tamen vix per annum ieiunant unum tantum diem sabbati. [f. 194] De quibus
satis nota supra, parte 5, capitulo 10, et parte 1, capitulo 4. Et ideo de
illis dicitur Matthei 6: "Cum ieiunatis, nolite fieri [sicut] ypocrite,
30   tristes." ⟨Set⟩ sexto et ultimo ieiunant virtuosi, ut inde meritum capiant.
Et illud tantum valet. De quo dicitur 1 Petri 1: "Administrate in fide
vestram virtutem, in virtute autem conscienciam, in consciencia vero abstinenciam." Et sic patent differencie.

---

2 metricum] quidam metricus ponit tales versus C.   11 ut] et C.   14 diu] dupliciter(?)
M; duo M.   15 magis] maius C. comedunt] comedant C.   17 non] *om* O.   secundo] tercio R.W.   21 ipsomet] ipsimet O.   23 duobus] tribus O.   26 vanitatis] pravitatis C.
27 diem sabbati] sabbatum O.   30 Set] etc. C.

VI.vi   DE UTILITATE IEIUNII ET ABSTINENCIE

[D]e utilitate vero veri ieiunii et abstinencie ait Leo papa, de
ieiunio decimi mensis dicens: "In omni, inquit, tempore et vita huius
seculi ieiunia contra peccata nos faciunt forciores. Ipsa enim concupiscen-

when the bridegroom will be taken away from them, and then they will fast."
Sometimes a needy person abstains, because he has no food; Matthew 15: "And
Jesus said to his disciples: 'I have compassion on the crowd, because they
have nothing to eat.'" Sometimes a greedy person abstains, in order to grab
more later on; Ecclesiastes 5: "The man to whom God has given riches and
knowledge, God has not given him power to eat." Morally speaking, such
people nearly perish with hunger in order to gather riches; but they also do so
literally, as one can easily observe. Sometimes even gluttons abstain. This
they do first in order to eat more eagerly afterwards; such people anticipate
the vigil of the god of the belly. For they fast for a long time, but then
search for more dainty food and eat of it more than at other times, two days
for each fast day. Surely, such people are so generous to the god of their
belly as if they were giving him two dollars for one dime, which I believe is
not what they would give to a Jew or Saracen. And secondly, these gluttons
fast in such a way that over three days they eat more than if they were not
fasting at all; for on the day before their fast they say, "Let us eat plenty
today, for tomorrow we shall be fasting"; and on the day after their fast they
say, "Today we must eat more because of yesterday's fast." But on the very
fast day they tend to consume more lest they be overcome by hunger in the
evening. But surely these cheat their God, for instead of two dollars they
give him only a dime. Against them are spoken the words of Isaiah 15: "Do not
fast as you have done until this day." Sometimes also apes abstain, that is to
say, hypocrites, in order to be praised, and that is the fasting of vanity. In
Luke 18 the Pharisee is reported to say: "I fast twice on the Sabbath," whereas in fact they fast hardly a single Sabbath in the whole year. On these hypocrites see further above, in part 5, chapter 10, and part 1, chapter 4. Concerning them it is said in Matthew 6: "When you fast, be not as the hypocrites, sad." But the sixth and last group of people who fast are the just,
and they do so in order to gain merit. This is the only valid kind of abstinence. Of it is said in 1 Peter 1: "Minister in your faith virtue; in virtue,
knowledge; and in knowledge, abstinence." Thus the different kinds of
abstinence are clear to see.

---

3 *In* 210; *Prov* 222a. **5–6** Matt. 9.15. **7–8** Matt. 15.32. **9–10** Eccles. 5.18. **24** Isa.
58.4. **26** Luke 18.12. **28** *FM* V.xvii.97–147 and I.vii.5–38. **29–30** Matt. 6.16.
31–33 2 Pet. 1.6.

VI.vi   THE USEFULNESS OF FASTING AND ABSTINENCE

With respect to the usefulness of true fasting and abstinence, Pope Leo
says, in speaking of the fast of the tenth month: "In every time and life of
this world, fasting makes us stronger against sins. For it overcomes our

cias vincunt, temptaciones repellunt, superbiam inclinant, iram mitigant,
5 et omnis bone voluntatis effectus ad maturitatem tocius virtutis emittunt."
Unde Bernardus in *Sermone de Quadragesima* ait: "Ieiunium non solum est
ablucio peccatorum, set eciam extirpacio viciorum, et non solum optinet
veniam, set eciam meretur graciam." Item Augustinus: "Ieiunium, inquit,
purgat mentem, carnem spiritui subicit, cor facit tribulatum et humiliatum,
10 quod Deus non spernit." Hec ille. In cuius figura Moyses ieiunando quadraginta diebus cum Domino loquitur familiariter, ut patet Exodo. Similiter
Helias quadraginta diebus ieiunando perrexit ad montem Dei Oreb cum Domino locuturus, Regum 19. Similiter Hester post ieiunia invenit graciam coram
rege Assuero, ut patet Hester. Similiter apostoli orantes et ieiunantes
15 Spiritum Sanctum acceperunt, ut patet Actuum 1.
    Et ⟨ista de⟩ gula et abstinencia ad presens iam dicta sufficiunt, et
sic terminatur sexta pars principalis huius libelli.

---

7 ablucio] absolucio O; abolitio *source*.   **15** acceperunt] susceperunt O.   **16** ista de] de
ista C.   **17** pars] particula O.

fleshly desires, drives back temptations, bends down our pride, softens anger, and leads every stirring of goodwill in us to the full maturity of virtue." Therefore Bernard says in his *Sermon on Lent*: "Fasting not only brings forgiveness for sins but also uproots our vices; it not only gains mercy but also deserves grace." And Augustine likewise: "Fasting purifies the mind, places the flesh under the rule of the spirit, and makes a heart troubled and humble, which God does not scorn." As a type of this, Moses fasted for forty days and talked with the Lord intimately, as is seen in Exodus. Likewise, Elijah fasted for forty days and then went to Horeb, the mountain of God, to talk with the Lord, Kings 19. Further, Esther after her fasting found grace before King Ahasuerus, as we see in Esther. And finally, the apostles prayed and fasted before they received the Holy Spirit, as seen in Acts 1.

This much suffices about gluttony and abstinence for now, and thus ends the sixth part of this book.

1–5 Leo the Great, *Sermo 15* 2 (PL 54:175).   **6–8** Bernard, *In quadragesima* sermo 6, 1 (4:368).   **8–10** Augustine, *Sermo 73 in app.* 1 (PL 39:1887).   **10–11** Exod. 34.28. **12–13** 1 Kings 19.1–8.   **13–14** Esther 3–5, esp. 3.16.   **14–15** Cf. Acts 2.13–15.

PARS VII

De luxuria

VII.i   DE LUXURIA

[U]ltimo iam sequitur pertractare de luxuria, que tercia filia carnis
est et pessima, cum suis membris. Ipsa autem tamquam publica meretrix cum
nullo veretur commisceri; unde merito execrabilis iudicatur. Secundo de
eius contrario, scilicet de continencia et puritate cum suis membris. Circa
5   [f. 194v] luxuriam primo sic intendo procedere: primo, quid sit et quomodo
diffinitur; secundo, de eius occasionibus [et ex quibus oritur]; tercio,
que sunt eius species illam consequentes; quarto, quare illam execrantur
Dominum timentes.
   Circa primum est sciendum quod a diversis diversimode diffinitur. Qui-
10   dam enim dicunt primo sic: "Luxuria est anime perverse amantis corporeas
voluptates neclecta temperancia." Secundo alius sic: "Luxuria est inconti-
nencia corporis ex pruritu carnis nascens vel originem habens." Tercio per
alium sic: "Luxuria est concubitus desiderium supra modum et contra racionem effluens." Quarto, Bernardus: "Luxuria est sitis ebria, deflacio momen-
15   tanea, amaritudo eterna; lucem odit, tenebras appetit, totam hominis depre-
datur mentem." Hec ille.

---

9 diversimode] *add* sic O.

VII.ii   DE OCCASIONIBUS LUXURIE: VISUS

[C]irca autem eius occasiones est sciendum quod secundum quosdam
quinque sunt occasiones inducentes in hoc versu contente:

   Visus et alloquium, contactus et oscula, factum.

Part VII

Lechery

VII.1 THE NATURE OF LECHERY

Now, in the last place, we pass on to deal with lechery, the third and worst daughter of the flesh, and its members. Like a public whore, this vice is not ashamed to lie with anybody; whence it is rightly deemed to be accursed. Following it, we will deal with its opposite virtue, namely continence and purity, and its members. Concerning lechery I plan to proceed as follows: first, I will discuss what it is and how it is defined; second, its occasions and from where it originates; third, the species that follow it; and fourth, why those who fear God curse it.

On the first point we should know that lechery is variously defined by various authors. Some say: "Lechery is the failure to observe moderation in a soul that perversely loves bodily pleasures." Another author says: "Lechery is bodily incontinence which is born of or has its origin in the itching of our flesh." Yet another definition is this: "Lechery is the desire to have sex which rises beyond measure and against reason." And a fourth definition, according to Bernard, declares: "Lechery is drunken thirst, a momentary outburst, eternal bitterness; it shuns the light, seeks darkness, and entirely plunders man's mind."

VII.ii THE OCCASIONS OF LECHERY: SIGHT

With regard to the occasions of lechery we should know that according to some authors there are five occasions that lead to this vice; they are listed in the following verse:

Sight and speech, touching and kisses, finally the deed.

Circa primum est sciendum secundum Augustinum quod concupiscencia ocu-
5   lorum est vana et curiosa cupiditas experiendi visa per carnem. In cuius
figura Genesis 38 legitur quod cum uxor Pharaonis oculos misisset in Ioseph, illum statim concupiscens ait: "Dormi mecum." Nota historiam. Idem
eciam patet Regum 11 de rege David et Bersabee. Nota historiam. Ideo magis
timendus est visus talis inordinatus quam hostium vibratus gladius, imo
10   magis quam basiliscus qui, nisi prius hominem videat, ipsum non interficit.
Set econtra dicit Ysidorus quod mulier, sive videat sive videatur, et visum
et videntem interficit. Et ideo Ecclesiastici 9 dicitur: "Averte faciem
tuam a muliere compta." Et sequitur: "Speciem mulieris aliene multi admirati sunt, et reprobi facti sunt." Unde Gregorius: "Deprimendi sunt, inquit,
15   oculi a lascivia suarum voluptatum, qui sunt quasi quidam raptores ad
culpam. [f. 195] Non enim (dicit ipse) Eva lignum tetigisset nisi prius
incaute in illud respexisset."

Et nota quod tres assignantur cause quare visum inordinatum restringere debemus. Primo quia oculi veloces valde sunt ad nocumentum anime.
20   Propter quod predonibus comparantur; Trenorum 4: "Oculus meus depredatus
est animam meam." Et ideo ait Augustinus: "Impudicus oculus impudici cordis
est nuncius, quia frequenter cordi mala et feda denunciat," puta carnales
voluptates et similia. Quibus a corde receptis, et cor ipsa ad portam oris
transmittit discucienda per verba luxuriosa, que prolata et discussa ut
25   communiter ad actum tendunt. Exemplum: sicut enim per fumum qui de domo
exiit cognoscitur quod ignis est intus, sic per verba luxuriosa exterius
cognoscitur quod ignis luxurie latet interius. Unde narrat Ambrosius libro
3 *De virginitate* de quodam adolescente gentili mire pulcritudinis; cum
percepisset se sua pulcritudine mulierum oculos sollicitare, vultum stigma-
30   tibus exaravit. Maluit enim deformem facie esse quam causam libidinis aliorum. Narrat eciam Boecius *De consolacione* de quadam meretrice speciosissi-
ma, quam videntes discipuli Aristotelis super eius pulcritudinem admirati
illam Aristoteli deduxerunt. Qua visa dixit: "O, inquit, fatui! Si, inquit,
linxeos oculos haberetis, quam turpe esset ° quod tam pulcrum esse vide-
35   tur!" Concludit ergo Philosophus quod hominem natura pulcrum non facit set
infirmitas oculorum; Proverbiorum 3: "Fallax gracia et vana est pulcritudo."

Secundo debemus visum restringere eo quod a remociori nocent quam alii
sensus. Gustus enim et tactus sunt eorum que sunt inmediata, set visus non
40   sic, set eorum ⟨que mediate⟩ consistunt. Unde Seneca: "Sagittarii et balis-
tarii, qui per oculum diriguntur, magis timentur." Unde Seneca: [f. 195v]
"Intelligendum, inquit, est partem innocencie esse cecitatem. Hinc enim
oculi adulterium demonstrant, hinc incestum considerant, hinc domum quam
concupiscis. Incitamenta sunt viciorum et duces scelerum." Hec ille. Prop-
45   ter quod quidam oculos inimicos suos vocant pessimos. Unde narratur in

With regard to the first, we must know that according to Augustine the "lust of the eyes" is our vain and curious desire to experience carnal sights. As a type of this, we read in Genesis 38 that when the wife of Pharaoh cast her eyes on Joseph, she at once lusted for him and said, "Come to bed with me." Expound the story. The same can be seen in Kings 11 with respect to King David and Bathsheba. Tell their story. Therefore, such disorderly looking must be feared more than the brandished sword of our enemies, indeed more than the basilisk, who does not kill a person unless he sees him. In contrast, as Isidore says, a woman, whether she looks or is looked at, kills both the one who looks at her and the one she has looked at. Hence it is said in Ecclesiasticus 9: "Turn your face away from a woman who is dressed up." And afterwards: "Many have admired the beauty of another man's wife and have become reprobate." Whence Gregory says: "Our eyes must be turned aside from the unbridled enjoyment of what gives them pleasure, for they draw us forcefully to sin. Eve would not have touched the tree if she had not first looked at it without caution."

Notice that three reasons can be given why we must restrain our undisciplined sight. First, our eyes are very quick to harm our soul. For that reason they are compared to thieves; Lamentations 4: "My eye has wasted my soul." And therefore Augustine says: "A shameless eye is the messenger for a shameless heart; it often announces evil and ugly things to the heart," that is to say, carnal desires and the like. When these are admitted into the heart, the latter sends them to the mouth to take audible form in lecherous words, and when these have been pronounced and broadcast, they often lead to a lecherous deed. As an example: by the smoke that issues from a house one knows that there is a fire inside; in the same way, by lecherous words that are spoken one recognizes that the fire of lechery is hiding inside. In book 3 of *On Virginity*, Ambrose reports of a young nobleman who was strikingly beautiful that, when he realized that his beauty attracted the eyes of women, he disfigured his face with wounds, for he preferred having a deformed face to becoming an occasion for lust to other people. Boethius, too, in *The Consolation of Philosophy*, tells of a most attractive whore whom Aristotle's disciples, when they saw her and admired her beauty, brought to their master. But seeing her Aristotle said: "Oh you fools! If you had the eyes of a lynx, how vile would that be which seems so beautiful!" Therefore the Philosopher concludes that it is not nature that makes a person beautiful but weakness in the eyes that behold him; Proverbs 3: "Favor is deceitful, and beauty is vain."

In the second place, we must bridle our sense of sight because it is struck from farther away than our other senses. For taste and touch respond to things in direct contact, but not so our sight, which is affected by objects through some intermediary. Therefore Seneca says: "Archers and artillerymen are feared more because they are guided by their eyesight." Hence he says:

Vitas Patrum quod cum quidam senex cum alio fratre laudabili vita vineam
excolendam intrasset, accidit ut unus ramunculus oculum eius evulsit. Quod
videns socius contristatus valde flevit. Quod videns senex ait: "Ne doleas,
frater, set pocius gaude, quia pessimum inimicum amisi. Duos enim capitales
50 prius habui, set iam—laudetur Deus—unum perdidi. Si vero ambos perdidis-
sem, de salute anime satis securus essem."
   Et nota quod inter omnia que ad custodiendum innocenciam sunt necessaria precipue videtur custodia oculorum. Exemplum: Quando enim inter duo
regna aliqua guerra suscitatur, tunc loca que sunt in marchiis precipue de-
55 bent muniri, et maxime infirmiora loca, [ut] patet. Sic inter regnum anime,
ubi princeps est recta racio, et regnum mundi, cuius princeps est diabolus,
⟨est⟩ continuum bellum in bonis hominibus °. Et sensus nostri ad regnum
anime pertinent, set ea que movent ad delectacionem et motus illicitos ad
regnum mundi pertinent. Set isti sensus, ut videtur, sunt quasi in marchia
60 duorum regnorum. Ergo super sensus istos debet esse diligens custodia. Set
inter omnes sensus visus est infirmior, quia minimo pulvere confundi potest
ac vento. Ergo ibi custodia precipue est necessaria, et ad hoc videtur ipsa
natura nos monere. Nam Philosophus 13 *De animalibus* capitulo 7 dicit quia
natura oculi creata est ex humiditate, quod ideo summe indiget diligenti
65 custodia. Unde naturaliter omne animal claudit oculum ne aliquid extrinse-
cum in illum cadat, et maxime homo. [f. 196] Dicitur ergo Numeri 15: "Non
sequamur cogitaciones nec oculos per res varias fornicantes."
   Tercio debemus visum restringere quia usus eorum valde necessarius est
et per consequens abusus valde timendus. Licet enim valde sit lingua cor-
70 rupta, tamen longo tempore includi potest et sic cessando ab eius usu impediri; set oculi non ⟨cessant⟩ videre quantum in eis est, ergo nec peccare;
⟨Petrus⟩: "Oculos habentes plenos adulterio." Unde et de Alexandro narrat
Vigesius libro 6 quod cum virgo quedam nimie pulcritudinis tradita esset ei
cuidam principi prius desponsata, summa abstinencia pepercit ut nec illam
75 aspiceret set ad sponsum remisit. Hec ille. Unde Ecclesiastico dicitur:
"Oculo nequius quid creatum est?"
   Et ideo refrenandi sunt oculi ab illicitis aspectibus, eo quod sunt
quasi due partes corporis nostri quibus si dominetur diabolus similiter
esset dominus tocius corporis, sicut qui occupat dominum portarum castri de
80 residuo securus est. Unde Iob 31: "Pepigi fedus cum oculis meis," etc. Narratur de quodam sancto ancillis Dei in via occurrente, quibus visis extra
viam divertit. Cui abbatissa: "Tu, inquit, si perfectus monachus es, sic
non respexisses ut sic agnosceres quod femine eramus." Unde per hoc patet
quod visus omnino est refrenandus.

---

6 misisset] iniecisset O.   **27** quod . . . luxurie] ignis luxurie qui (que W) O.   **30** facie]
corr from faciei C; faciei O.   **32** pulcritudinem] pulcritudine O.   **34** esset] *add* in natura

"We must understand that innocence consists partially in blindness. It is one's eyes that point to adultery, that look at incest or the house one desires. They goad us on toward vices and lead us to crimes." For this reason some call their eyes their worst enemies. There is a story in *The Lives of the Fathers* about a hermit who went to cultivate his vineyard with another brother of praiseworthy life. It happened that a small branch pierced his eye. When his companion saw that, he grew sad and wept a great deal. But the hermit said to him: "Do not grieve, brother, but rather rejoice, for I have lost a grievous enemy. I have had two main enemies and now, God be praised, I have lost one. If I had lost both, I could be quite sure of my soul's salvation."

Notice also that among all the things that are necessary for the protection of one's innocence, guarding one's eyes is the foremost. To illustrate: if war breaks out between two countries, places along the border have to be fortified, and especially weak places, as is evident. Thus, within good people there is a constant war between the realm of the soul, whose prince is right reason, and the realm of the world, whose prince is the devil. Our senses are part of the realm of the soul, but what moves them to delight and to illicit stirrings is part of the realm of the world. But these senses, so to speak, lie on the border between the two realms. Therefore they must be diligently guarded. Now, among all our senses sight is the weakest, for it can be ruined by the least bit of dust and wind. Therefore its safeguarding is particularly necessary. Nature itself seems to admonish us to do that. For the Philosopher says, in chapter 7 of book 13 of *On Animals*, that since the eye is made of liquid, it needs to be guarded most diligently. For this reason every living being closes its eye so that no foreign object may fall into it, and this is especially true of man. Therefore it is said in Numbers 15: "Let us not follow our thoughts and eyes that go astray after divers things."

In the third place, we must bridle our sense of sight because we need it so very much, and consequently its misuse is much to be feared. For if our tongue is evil, it can be kept shut up for a long time and prevented from misuse by not being used at all; but our eyes, as far as it lies in their power, cannot refrain from seeing and hence from sinning; as Peter says: "Having eyes full of adultery." Vegetius in book 6 tells us that Alexander was given an extremely beautiful maiden who had earlier been betrothed to some prince. Alexander observed the greatest degree of abstinence in that he did not even look at her and sent her back to her husband. Whence it is said in Ecclesiasticus: "What is created more wicked than an eye?"

Therefore, our eyes must be restrained from illicit looks, because they are, as it were, two parts of our body which, if the devil rules over them, he will likewise be lord over our whole body, just as when one holds the master of the castle gates, one can be sure of the rest of the castle. Therefore Job 31 says: "I made a covenant with my eyes," and so on. Of some saint it is

non crederetis C; *add* videretis M.—*C's reading seems to be unique, perhaps a scribal attempt to make sense of the syntax (cf. M) in light of the following sentence.* **35** Philosophus] philosophia M.W; plurima R.   **40** que mediate] inmediate C.   **44** concupiscis] concupiscas O.   ille] seneca O.   **56** est] *om* O.   **57** est] et C.   hominibus] *add* suscitat C.   **60** istos] *om* O.   **62** ad] *om* O.   **63** 13] 12 M.W; *om* R.   **68** usus] visus O.   eorum] illorum O.   **71** cessant] cessantes C.M.W.   **72** Petrus] per C.R.W; proverbiorum M.— B1.Co. Et.Go1.Go2 *have some form of* 2 Petri 2.   **73** nimie] eximie O.   ei] *om* O.   **78** partes] *corr to* porte M.   **79** castri] *add* et O.   **82** monachus] *add* nos O.

VII.iii   COLLOQUIA

[S]ecunda occasio luxurie est in colloquiis impudicis. Unde illud: "Corrumpunt bonos mores colloquia prava," et maxime quando fiunt colloquia inter hominem vanum et mulierem impudicam, iuxta illud Proverbiorum 7: "Mulier cum ornatu meretrico irritivit iuvenem multis sermonibus, et blan-
5   dimentis labiorum contraxit illum." Et Proverbiorum 9: "Mulier stulta et clamosa sedet in foribus domus sue vocans transeuntes per viam"; et multi voci eius obediunt, dicentes illud Psalmi: "Paratus sum et non sum turbatus." Nam quamvis prius in bona volun- [f. 196v] tate fuerunt, tamen auditis colloquiis et confabulacionibus earum sicut inconstantes devincuntur
10   omnino carnem sequentes et non spiritum. Et nota quod multi [sunt] qui quamvis in via ad celum ducente fuerint penitenciam agendo, levi tamen instigacione deviare possunt et dicunt in animo suo: "In via hac ulterius non vadam set revertar in terram in qua natus sum," Numeri 10, quasi dicat: penitenciam ac viam consciencie dimittam et ad carnis desideria
15   redibo. Caro enim est terra de qua nati sumus, quia secundum Evangelistam "quod natum est ex carne, caro est."
Et de talibus sicut de quodam monstro marino nomine ⟨lolligo⟩, cuius natura est quod quandoque habet societatem cum avibus et quandoque cum pissibus. Unde cum aquas et pisses fastidierit, alis pennigeris se levat in
20   aerem, ubi cum avibus ethera scandit. Cum ergo flatus ventorum sustinere non potest, ad aquas cogitur redire, et sic ibi labitur in profundum. Revera spiritualiter loquendo sic est de pluribus hominibus qui omnino instabiles dici debent, eo quod modo se in profundum voluptatum inmergunt, et cum illis saciati fuerint, fingunt se erigere per ieiunia et oraciones
25   et huiusmodi opera penitencie. Set cum senciunt modicum ventum temptacio-

reported that he met some nuns on his way and that, when he saw them, he went off the road. Then the abbess said to him: "If you were a perfect monk, you would not have looked at us in this way to find out that we were women." This shows us that our sight must be bridled altogether.

3 *In* 20651; *Prov* 33816, 33818–19, etc.   **6–7** Gen. 39.7.   **10** Isidore, *Etym.* XII.iv.6. **12–13** Ecclus. 9.8.   **13–14** Ecclus. 9.11.   **14–17** Gregory, *Moralia* XXI.ii.4 (PL 76:190).   **20–21** Lam. 3.51.   **21–22** Augustine, *Ep. 211* 10 (PL 33:961).   **27–31** Cf. the same story from Valerius, in *FM* VII.xviii.62–66.   **31–36** Boethius, *De consolatione Philosophiae* III, pr.8, 10 (CC 94:48).   **36–37** Prov. 31.30.   **40–44** Also in Peraldus, *Summa vitiorum* III.ii.4, but the first image is not attributed to "Seneca."   **63–64** Aristotle, *De animalium generatione* V.1 (779b); *De anima* 3 (425a.4); *De sensu* 2 (438a.5 ff.).   **66–67** Num. 15.39.   **72** 2 Pet. 2.14.   **72–75** Tubach 138.   **76** Ecclus. 31.15. **80** Job 31.1.   **81–83** *VP* V.62 (PL 73:872).

VII.iii   LECHERY IN CONVERSATION

The second occasion for lechery lies in unchaste conversation. Hence the saying: "Evil conversation corrupts good manners," especially if it takes place between a vain man and a shameless woman, according to the saying of Proverbs 7: "In her harlot's attire the woman entangled the young man with many words and drew him away with the flattery of her words." And in Proverbs 9: "A foolish and clamorous woman sits at the door of her house, calling those that pass by the way"; and many follow her voice, saying these words of the Psalm: "I am ready and am not troubled." For even if before they had had a good intention, after they hear their talk and chatter, they are overcome in their lack of steadfastness and follow their flesh every way rather than their spirit. Notice that many people who by doing penance have been on the way that leads to heaven can yet go astray with a little seduction and tell themselves: "I will not go further in this way but return to the country where I was born," Numbers 10, as if to say, I will leave penance and the way of conscience, and will return to the desires of the flesh. For the flesh is the country where we all were born, for according to the Evangelist, "what is born of the flesh is flesh."

Such people are like a sea creature called flying fish, whose nature it is to live sometimes with the birds and sometimes with the fish. Thus, when it gets bored with the water and the fish, it lifts itself on feathered wings into the air, where it flies up high with the birds. But when it cannot stand the wind's blowing, it is forced to return to the water, and thus it sinks into the depth. Spiritually speaking, the same applies to many people who must be said to be totally unstable, because now they submerge themselves in the depth of their desires, and when they are sated, they pretend to rise up through fasting

nis, hoc est verba inpudica et ad peccata allectiva, mox in pristinam
miseriam relabuntur. Unde de talibus Psalmista ait: "Ascendunt usque ad
celos et descendunt usque ad abissos." Unde Proverbiorum 5 dicitur: "Favus
distillans labia meretricis, etc.; novissima eius amara et quasi gladius
30   biceps," hoc est binos capiens in pena, videlicet lecatorem et meretricem.
Merito ergo est fedum alloquium fugiendum. Unde de illo nota supra, parte
1, capitulo 3 de superbia oris.

---

1 illud] *add* apostoli O.   **2** fiunt] *add* huiusmodi O.   **4** meretrico] meretricio R.   **17** Et]
add ideo O.   lolligo] bolingo C; lollico R.W.   **19** fastidierit] fastiderit O.   **25** senciunt]
senserint O.   **27** Unde de talibus] de quibus O.   **31** de] pro O.

VII.iv   TACTUS

[T]ercia occasio luxurie est tactus, de quo Ad Corinthios 7: "Bonum
est viro non tangere mulierem." Et causa assignatur ⟨Proverbiis⟩: "Qui
tangit picem," etc. Et ideo Crisostomus: [f. 197] "Sicut, inquit, ligatur
latro ut suspendatur, sic peccator amplexibus mulieris ad infernum duci-
5   tur." Et ideo Ecclesiastici 9 dicitur: "Cum muliere aliena non sedeas, nec
accumbas cum ea super cubitum." Quod bene perpendebat sacerdos ille de quo
in *Dialogis* dicitur quod ante ordinacionem sacerdotalem habuit concubinam,
quam postea relinquens quasi sororem habebat caste vivendo. Qui cum usque
ad mortem egrotasset et ipsa illum palpare voluisset, utrum spiritus eius
10   recessisset an non, dixit: "Recede a me, mulier, et tolle ⟨paleam⟩. Adhuc
viget igniculus." Unde illud Proverbiorum 6: "Numquid quis potest abscondere ignem in sinu suo ut vestimenta eius non ardeant?" quasi dicat, nullo
modo.
Cum igitur ex predictis patet quod luxuria sit quasi ignis, sic ergo
15   contra eam quasi contra ignem materialem triplex remedium apponendum est
cum ceperit exardescere, scilicet aque infusio, lignorum subtractio, aut
sui ipsius elongacio. Verbi gracia: si enim olla iuxta ignem ebulliat, ne
effundatur quod in ea continetur, tunc enim unum istorum trium fieri consuevit, quia vel aqua frigida infunditur, vel de lignis subtrahitur, vel
20   ipsa olla ab igne elongatur. Revera sic qui peccato luxurie temptatur, ad
litteram valet aqua frigida super te proiecta, vel saltem spiritualiter
recurras ad aquam lacrimarum vel ad aliam huiusmodi penitenciam, sicut
subtrahendo aliquam porcionem cibi vel potus. Et precipue illa cibaria
retrahenda sunt que ipsam luxuriam incitant, cuiusmodi sunt forcia vina
25   acuti saporis et huiusmodi, que sunt nutrimenta luxurie sicut ligna ignis.
Vel tamdem elongant se totaliter ab ipsa luxuria et eius occasionibus;
Corinthiorum 6: "Fugite fornicacionem." Ut dicit Ambrosius: "Cum aliis

and prayers and other such works of penance. But as soon as they feel a little
breeze of temptation, that is, unchaste words that entice them to sin, they
soon fall back into their former wretchedness. Of these the Psalmist says:
"They mount up to the heavens, and they go down to the depths." And Proverbs
5: "The lips of a harlot are like a honeycomb dropping, and her end is bitter
and as a two-edged sword," that is, always catching two in its punishment,
namely, the lecher and the whore. Thus it is right to flee from dirty conversation. See further on this topic above, in part 1, chapter 3, on pride of the
mouth.

---

2 1 Cor. 15.33.   **4–5** Prov. 7.10, 21.   **5–6** Prov. 9.13–15.   **7–8** Ps. 118.60.   **12–**
13 Num. 10.30.   **16** John 3.6.   **27–28** Ps. 106.26.   **28–30** Prov. 5.3.   **31–32** *FM* I.iv.

VII.iv   LECHERY IN TOUCHING

The third occasion for lechery is touching; of it is said in Corinthians
7: "It is good for a man not to touch a woman." The reason for this is given
in Proverbs: "He that touches pitch," and so forth. Therefore Chrysostom
says: "Just as a thief is bound in order to be hanged, so is a sinner carried
to hell in the arms of a woman." And thus it is said in Ecclesiasticus 9: "Do
not sit with another man's wife, nor lie on the bed with her." These words
were well heeded by that priest who in the *Dialogues* is reported to have had a
mistress before his ordination, from whom he afterwards detached himself,
living with her chastely like brother and sister. When he fell sick unto death
and she wanted to touch him to see whether he was still alive, he said: "Step
back, woman, and take the straw away. The spark is still glowing!" Hence the
words in Proverbs 6: "Can a man hide fire in his bosom, and his garments not
get burned?" as if to say: certainly not.

Since it is clear from what has been said that lechery is like fire, we
must therefore apply a threefold remedy against it when it begins to burst into
flame, just as if it were a material fire, namely: pour on water, withdraw the
wood, and step back from it. For instance, if a pot is boiling on the fire,
one does one of these three so that the contents of the pot may not boil over:
one either pours on some cold water, or takes some of the firewood away, or
takes the pot itself off the fire. In the same way, when one is tempted by the
sin of lechery, it is helpful literally to pour cold water over oneself, or
else spiritually to have recourse to the water of one's tears or some other
penitential practice, such as withdrawing a little of one's food and drink.
And especially those foodstuffs are to be withdrawn which kindle lust in us,
such as strong and spiced wines and the like, which nourish lechery as wood
nourishes a fire. Or finally one must detach oneself completely from lechery
and its occasions; Corinthians 6: "Fly fornication." As Ambrose says: "Other

nempe potest expectari viciis conflictus, set hanc fugite ne appropinquat,
quia melius quam [f. 197v] [per fugam] dimitti non potest." Exemplum habe-
30   mus Genesis 39 de Ioseph, cui cum dixit domina sua, uxor scilicet Putipha-
ri, "Dormi mecum," relicto pallio in manu eius fugit. Unde Augustinus:
"Mundus, inquit, et mulieres non melius quam fugiendo vincuntur." Et Gregorius: "Contra luxuriam fugam arripe si vis victoriam optinere." Et iterum
ait Augustinus: "Numquid aliquis mortalium iuxta viperam securum capit
35   sompnum, que etsi non percuciat, certe solicitat? Securius ergo (dicit
ipse) est non perire posse quam iuxta periculum non perisse."

Et nota quod quantumcumque pulcher sit flos, si tamen multum manibus
tractetur, marcessit. Sic certe est de virginitate. Alba eciam spina licet
pulcherrimos habeat flores superius, subtus tamen portat spinas acutissi-
40   mas. Revera sic mulieres quantumcumque fuerint ornate et pulcre, tanto
magis pungunt. Isidorus autem *Ethimologiarum* libro 12 narrat, et accipit a
Plinio, quod in mari Indico est quedam pissis dictus torpedo, quia facit
corpora torpescere illum viventem tangencia. Ipsa enim naturaliter a longe
quamvis fuerit et procul, si tamen hasta vel virga attingatur, pedes tamen
45   ad cursum velocissimos facit torpescere. Tantum enim virus visus est in ea
eciam ut membra corporis facit arida. Consimile ⟨eciam⟩ exemplum narratur
libro *De naturis rerum* de quadam pisse narchos dicta, cuius natura est quod
si filo rethis tangatur aut hamo, quod eciam totum corpus stupescere facit
nisi cicius abrumpatur. Revera sic est de carnali delectacione, que si vel
50   sola cognicione vel assensu teneatur, ⟨totam mentem⟩ reddit ° invalidam et
ad spiritualia inpotentem, nisi cicius auferatur, iuxta illud Levitici:
"Omnis qui tetigerit eam, inmundus est." Et ideo dicitur Trenorum 4: "Abite
et nolite tangere."

Et nota: vulgariter enim dicitur, "Bene pugnat qui bene fugit." Et [f.
55   198] certe sic est qui occasionem peccati devitat. Unde Albertus super
librum *Ethicorum*, ubi recitat quod Elena filia Priami fuit pulcherrima
mulier, propter quod sapientes dixerunt quod non fuit cum ea communicandum
set omnino a concupiscenciis eius abstinendum et per consequens ab eius
societate fugiendum. Eos ⟨ap⟩probat idem Albertus dicens et probans quod
60   melior est victoria quam fuga. Et hoc ostendit tali exemplo. Gorgonius,
inquit, fuit pulcherrimus hominum et pessimus in tantum quod sua pulcritudo
homines transeuntes inmobiles reddebat, hoc est, ita pulcher erat quod
quando aliquis vidit eum, propter eius pulcritudinem quasi staret delectabiliter acsi inmobilis videretur. Quos sic eum respicientes ex sua malicia
65   interficiebat. Quod cum quidam iuvenis strenuus et fortis considerasset,
illum interficere cogitavit. Deliberans tamen penes se quod si eum respice-
ret caperetur eius pulcritudine sicut alii; unde aversa facie illum occidit. Moraliter per istum Gorgonium intelligo mulieres comptas ornatas ad
libidinem provocantes, quarum si flammas pessimas extinguere proponis et

vices you can confront and do battle with, but this one you must flee and not let come near, because there is no better way of overcoming it than flight." We have an illustration in Joseph, in Genesis 39: when his lady, Potiphar's wife, said to him, "Come to bed with me," he left his cloak in her hand and fled. Therefore Augustine says: "The world and women cannot be overcome any better than by flight." And Gregory declares: "Against lechery you must take to flight if you want to have the victory." And Augustine again says: "Can any mortal sleep safely beside a viper, which even if it does not sting will certainly vex him? It is safer to be unable to perish than not to have perished in the presence of danger."

Notice how beautiful a flower is, but when it is touched by many hands, it wilts. This certainly applies to virginity. Also, the hawthorn has many beautiful blossoms in open view, yet underneath it carries very sharp thorns. Women are just like that: the more decked out and beautiful they are, the more sharply they sting. In book 12 of his *Etymologies* Isidore reports, as he takes it from Pliny, that in the Indian Ocean there is a fish, the electric ray, which is called *torpido* because it makes the bodies of those who touch it torpid. Even when it is far away, if it is merely touched with a spear or stick, it naturally causes even the swiftest feet to grow slack. For its poison is so strong that it causes the members of one's body to dry up. A similar example can be found in the book *On the Nature of Things*, concerning a fish called *narchos*, "crampfish," whose property it is to numb one's whole body if it is touched by the string of a net or a fishhook, unless one at once breaks it. The same applies to carnal delight: if it is as much as touched by one's thought or assent, it renders one's whole mind feeble and impotent to grasp spiritual things, unless it is at once put aside, after the words of Leviticus: "Everyone who has touched her is unclean." And therefore it is said in Lamentations 4: "Go away and do not touch."

Notice the popular saying: "Who flees well fights well." Surely this applies to a person who avoids the occasion for sin. Albertus in his comment on the *Nicomachean Ethics* narrates that Helen, the daughter of Priam, was the most beautiful woman; for this reason the wise men said that one should not hold company with her but instead abstain from desiring her altogether and thus flee her company. Albertus approves of this view, saying and proving that victory is better than flight. And this he shows by the following example. Gorgon was the most beautiful of men and yet the most evil because his beauty rendered people immobile when they passed by, that is, he was so beautiful that if someone saw him, he stood still with delight and thus appeared to be immobile. And then Gorgon out of wickedness killed those who were thus looking at him. When a strong and brave youth noticed that, he thought to kill him. But he reflected that if he were to look at him, he would be captivated by his beauty like all the others; therefore he killed him with his face turned away.

70 devincere, iuxta consilium Psalmiste "averte oculos tuos ne videant vanitatem," quasi diceret, averte omnino ab occasionibus illicitis, ut scilicet
   non videas concupiscibilia nec audias turpia. Et ideo ⟨Ioannes⟩ in suo
   Policratico, libro 4, capitulo 3, ait quod Iulius Cesar dixit in bello
   corpora hominum vulnerari, set in pace voluptatibus devinci. Unde signanter
75 dixit poeta quando querebat quare Egistus factus est adulter: "Causa,
   inquit, est inpromptu quia desidiosus erat." Nam sicut aqua non mota ex se
   putrescit, sic ociositas est causa peccati, et maxime libidinis. In cuius
   figura rex David quamdiu bella excercuit, non incidit in adulterium; et
   quando ocio domi vacabat, cum Barsabee adulteratus est et commisit homici-
80 dium.

---

2 Proverbiis] *canc and add marg* ecclesiastici 8 C.   **3** tangit] tetigerit O.   Crisostomus]
add ait O.   **8** relinquens] *add* et O.   **10** paleam] *apparently corr to* palliam C.   **14** igi-
tur] ergo O.   **22** vel] aut O.   **23** vel] et O.   **28** appropinquat] appropinquet O.   **30–**
31 Putiphari] pharaonis O.   **42** quedam] quidam O.   quia] eo quod O.   **45** ea] eo O.
46 eciam] enim C.   **47** quadam] quodam O.   **48** stupescere] obstupescere O.   **49** vel]
om O.   **50** cognicione] cogitacione M.R; coge W.   totam . . . reddit] coram mente reddit eam C.   **57** mulier] mulierum O.   **59** approbat] reprobat C.W.   **71** averte] *add* te
M.   **72** Ioannes] ieronimus C.M.

VII.v   OSCULUM

[f. 198v] [Q]uarta occasio luxurie est osculum. Unde Beda: "Qui, inquit,
meretricem deosculatur, pulsat inferni ianuam." Set certe delectantibus in
signo cum facto patefacta est ianua. Et ideo oscula meretricis comparantur
osculo Iude, quo Christum vendidit et ipsum Iudeis tradidit. Sic meretrix
5 mediantibus osculis animam hominis demonibus vendit, et eciam tradit dicens: "Accipite et ducite eum caute, ne forte resipiscat donec factum
consummat."
   Unde narratur quod quidam litteratus legens in scripturis acerbitatem
penarum iehenne rogavit Deum ut in vita presenti aliquid ex huiusmodi
10 levibus peccati signis, puta osculis, visibus, tactibus, et huiusmodi,
ostenderet, si aliquod peccatum ex illis emanaret. Unde cum multum circa
hoc laborando orasset, venit ad eum quidam dicens: "Veni et vide quid
postulas," et duxit eum in quoddam viridarium ubi vidit formam hominis et
mulieris valde terribiles se invicem amplectantes et deosculantes. Qui

To interpret morally: by this Gorgon I understand women who are dressed up and decked out to provoke lust; if you plan to extinguish and overcome their evil flames, "turn away your eyes that they may not see vanity," after the advice of the Psalmist, meaning: turn completely away from illicit occasions, so that you may not see what rouses lust or hear shameful things. For this reason, John in his *Policraticus*, book 4, chapter 3, says that according to Julius Caesar, in war men's bodies are wounded, but in times of peace they are killed by soft pleasures. Therefore the poet says meaningfully, when he asked why Aegisthus had become an adulterer:

> The cause is plain—he was a slothful man.

For just as stagnant water rots of itself, so does idleness generate sin, and particularly lust. As a type of this, King David did not fall into adultery as long as he engaged in warfare; but when he gave himself to idleness at home, he slept with Bathsheba and afterwards committed murder.

1–2 1 Cor. 7.1.   **2–3** Ecclus. 13.1.   **5–6** Ecclus. 9.12.   **6–11** Gregory, *Dialogi* IV.xii.3 (3:50).   **11–12** Prov. 6.27.   **27** 1 Cor. 6.18.   **27–29** Peraldus, *Summa vitiorum* III.iv.1 also has this quotation as well its context (lines 14–31).   **30–31** Gen. 39.7.   **34–36** Jerome, *Ep. 117* 3 (CSEL 55:425–426). Already quoted at *FM* V.xii.53–55.   **41–46** Isidore, *Etym.* XII.vi.45.   **47–49** Alexander Neckam, *De naturis rerum* II.44 (p. 156).   **52** Lev. 15.20.   **52–53** Lam. 4.15.   **55–60** Albertus Magnus, *Ethica* II.ii.11 (7:193).   **60–68** Ibidem, I.vii.2 (7:108).   **70–71** Ps. 118.37.   **73–74** *Policraticus* IV.3 (p. 244).   **75–76** Ovid, *Remedia amoris* 161–162.

VII.v   KISSING

The fourth occasion for lechery is kissing. Bede says: "He who kisses a whore is knocking at the door of hell." Surely, if one takes delight in the sign, the door is opened with the deed. Therefore the kisses of a whore can be compared to the kiss with which Judas sold Christ and betrayed him to the Jews. In the same way a whore sells and betrays a man's soul through her kisses to the demons, saying: "Take him and lead him along cautiously, lest he gets wise before completing the deed."

A story is told that a learned man who had been reading in Scripture about the harshness of hell pains asked God to show him in this life something about such light signs of sin as kisses, looks, touches, and the like, whether any sin had come from them. When he prayed for this with great intensity, someone came to him and said: "Come and see what you are asking for," and led him into a garden. There he saw the horrible-looking shapes of a man and a woman embracing and kissing each other, who then with a terrifying howl seemed to melt

15   tandem emisso horribili ululatu quasi cera liquescere videbantur. Deinde ad
     pristinam formam redeuntes, iterum ut prius liquefacti sunt. Cui ait ductor
     suus: "Isti, inquit, quos vidisti tales fuerunt dum viverent in huiusmodi
     delectantes. Et quia osculis et amplexibus quociens poterant adulterio
     delectabantur ardore, licet ab inmunda violacione corporea inmunes reman-
20   sissent, quia tamen sine confessione et penitencia de consensu peccandi
     decesserunt, dampnati sunt," etc.

---

15 horribili] horrido M.R; horrida W.   **21** etc.] *om* O.

VII.vi   FACTUM

     [Q]uinta occasio luxurie patet ex ipso facto, de quo Ad Galatas 4:
     "Manifesta sunt opera carnis, que sunt inmundicia," etc. Contra que preci-
     pitur Deuteronomii 3: "Expedite precedite absque uxoribus, pueris, aut
     iumentis." Notandum quod uxor ista est [f. 199] caro, cui nubet qui eam
5   fovet inmoderate et diligit. Cui liberi sunt delectaciones noxie et illici-
     ta desideria. Et iumenta sunt opera carnis et facta bestialia. Igitur hec
     tria—uxor, parvuli, et iumenta—recludenda sunt in civitate munita, que
     eciam arcenda sunt ab anima bene instructa ne nobiscum pergant ad prelium.
     Nam qui ista tria secum habent non sunt expediti set pocius impediti.
10   Solinus enim *De mirabilibus mundi* dicit quod si hyena aliquod animal ter
     lustraverit, quod ultra se movere non potest. Ista hyena est caro, que
     illos ter lustrat quos hiis tribus alligavit. Et ideo Iosue 1 dicitur:
     "Uxores vestre et filii et iumenta manebunt; vos autem transite armati,"
     acsi diceret: carnales consensus, delectaciones, et opera includatis per
15   opera penitencie, et armati bonis virtutibus contra vicia procedatis. Et
     certe si sic feceritis, verificatur illud de vobis Deuteronomii 7: "Non est
     apud te sterilis utriusque sexus." Nam quando spiritus dominatur carni,
     uterque tunc sexus fertilis est et bonos fructus virtutum profert. Et e
     converso quando caro dominatur spiritui, tunc uterque sterilis quoad bonos
20   mores redditur. Dicit enim Plinius quod si capra olivam lambat, reddit eam
     sterilem. Capra autem hec, que secundum Philosophum fetens est et inmunda,
     cuius fetus posterior naturaliter est peior priore, signat carnem, cuius
     concupiscencie et facta quanto plures fuerint tanto fetidiores et peiores
     inveniuntur. Oliva autem est mens humana, quam tunc caro lambit quando sibi
25   blandiendo eius robur attrahit. Et ideo non mirum si fructificare non per-
     mittat. Unde Ieremie 22: "Scribe virum istum sterilem."
         De ista ergo carne et eius operibus dicitur Apocalipsis 13: "Vidi
     aliam bestiam [f.199v] ascendentem de terra habentem cornua duo et loqueba-
     tur ut draco." Spiritualiter autem loquendo ista bestia est carnis concu-

like wax. After a moment they returned to their former shape and then melted again as before. Then his guide explained: "What you have seen are people who took delight in such things while they were alive. And since they engaged in kisses and embraces with adulterous passion whenever they could, even though they refrained from unchaste possession of each other's bodies, as they died without confession and repentance of having yielded to sin, they are damned."

1–2 Bede, *Super parabolas Salomonis* 22 (PL 91:1004).

VII.vi   THE SEX ACT

The fifth occasion of lechery clearly lies in the sex act itself, of which it is said in Galatians 4: "The works of the flesh are manifest, which are uncleanness," etc. Against them is given the commandment of Deuteronomy 3: "Go well prepared, without your wives, children, and cattle." Notice that "wife" here means the flesh, to which one is married when one pampers and loves it immoderately. Her "children" are harmful delights and forbidden desires. And the "cattle" are the deeds of the flesh and animal-like acts. Therefore, these three—wife, children, and cattle—are to be locked up in a fortified city, meaning they are to be reined in by the well-taught soul so that they do not go forth with us into battle. For whoever has these three with him is not well prepared but rather burdened down. Solinus in *The Marvels of the World* says that when the hyena has looked at an animal three times, the latter cannot move. This hyena is our flesh; it looks three times at those whom it binds to the aforementioned three. And therefore it is said in Joshua 1: "Your wives and children and cattle shall remain; but you pass over armed," as if to say: leave your fleshly desires and pleasures and works behind through the deeds of penance, and go forward against the vices armed with good virtues. If you do that, surely the words of Deuteronomy 7 will come true of you: "No one shall be barren among you of either sex." For when the spirit rules over the flesh, both sexes are fertile and bring forth the good fruit of virtues. Conversely, when the flesh rules over the spirit, both become sterile with respect to good habits. For Pliny says that when a goat licks an olive-tree, it renders it barren. The goat, which according to the Philosopher is a bad-smelling and unclean animal, and smells worse behind than in front, symbolizes the flesh, whose lusts and deeds are found to be ever more ugly and evil the more often they occur. But the olive-tree is man's mind; it is licked when the flesh with its fondling draws off its strength. Thus it is no wonder if the flesh does not allow it to yield fruit. Hence it is said in Jeremiah 22: "Write this man barren."

30   piscencia que de terra carnis nostre oritur, habens duo cornua, scilicet
      gulam et luxuriam, que non apparent terribilia set magis delusoria. Et ideo
      similia cornibus agni lascivi quia provocant ad lasciviam, et tamen in fine
      producunt ad insolenciam. Set ista bestia "loquebatur sicut draco." Draco
      enim de ore suo emittit flatum infectivum; sic caro provocat ad huiusmodi
35   loquendum. Unde vix est aliquis quin carnis lascivia infectetur et venene-
      tur, sicut patet in varietate vanitatum, modo in victu, modo in vestitu,
      modo in gestu, modo in affatu, modo in cantu, modo in ingressu et huiusmodi
      carnalibus miseriis confusionem inducentibus. Expone ut placet.
           Et nota quod preter quinque istas occasiones luxurie sunt alie sugges-
40   tiones vetularum, que multos tam homines quam mulieres a proposito conti-
      nencie et mundicie faciunt resilire, que pronube nuncupantur. Quarum opus
      opus diaboli est. Opus enim diaboli est super omnia operam dare, hoc est
      diligenciam, ut homines in peccatum deiciat et demergat. Cum ergo in per-
      fectis ipse diabolus arte propria prevalere non potest, huiusmodi pronubas,
45   idest vetulas, arte miserie infectas inmittit nuncias, que animas hominum
      et mulierum ad carnis peccata alliciunt. Ex quo patet quod potenciores sunt
      in malis quam ipse diabolus, et ideo magistra diaboli dici potest; de
      quibus bene dicitur Proverbiorum 16: "Indignacio regis nuncius mortis." Si
      ergo David interfici illum iussit qui prospera videbatur nunciare, ut patet
50   Regum 1 de morte Saulis, quid credis facturus est supernus David, idest
      Christus, illis qui quasi infernalia nunciant incendia? quasi diceret,
      David rex interficere non potuit nisi temporaliter, [f. 200] set Christus
      eternaliter; ergo, etc. Et ideo tales vetule maledicte sorores dici possunt
      serpentis Evam decipientis. Serpens autem, secundum Bedam, vultum habet
55   virgineum, et signat tales vetulas a diabolo electas ad animas decipiendas.
      De quibus Ioelis 1 dicitur: "Puellam vendiderunt pro vino." Set iuxta
      Psalmum: "Fel draconum vinum earum, et venenum aspidum insanabile."
           Et advertite. Si enim predicator verbi Dei unam animam tantum in vita
      sua lucraretur, multum faceret, eo quod talis anima C[h]risti sanguine re-
60   dempta plus valet quam omnia mundi bona. Unde si una talis vetula omnibus
      diebus suis nullum malum faceret aliud nisi ut unam animam perderet, nimis
      faceret. Si ergo nullum sacrificium tantum placet diabolo sicut perdicio
      animarum, ergo cum huiusmodi vetule huiusmodi faciunt, nullum peccatum est
      maius peccato vetularum, ut manifeste patet. Sicut natura falconis nobilis
65   est superius ascendere, et tamen per decepcionem aucipis illum invadentis
      sepe ad inferiora allicitur, et hoc per aliquam columbam super terram
      deceptorie positam ad illum alliciendum, sic aucupe inferni decipiuntur
      iuvencule per viam castitatis ascendentes, mediantibus talibus vetulis ad
      hoc assignatis.
70   Unde narratur de quadam iuvencula pudiciciam adamante et a quodam
      clerico tamen adamata contra voluntatem et inpudice. Cum ergo clericus ille

Concerning the flesh and its works it is written in Revelation 13: "I saw another beast coming up out of the earth, and he had two horns and spoke like a dragon." In spiritual terms, this beast is fleshly concupiscence, which rises from the earth of our flesh and has two horns, namely gluttony and lust, which do not look very terrifying and yet are quite deceptive. They are like the horns of a wanton lamb, because they invite to wantonness and yet in the end lead to insolence. This beast "spoke like a dragon." The dragon sends from his mouth poisonous breath; in the same way, the flesh stirs us to talk in this fashion. Hence there is hardly anyone who does not follow or hunt after wantonness in some manner, as can be seen in the variety of vanities, be it in food or clothing or gestures or speech or song or one's way of walking and similar wretched customs of the flesh that lead to damnation. Develop this point as you see fit.

And notice that in addition to these five occasions of lechery there are further the solicitations of old women called go-betweens, who cause many men and women to retreat from their good intention to live in continence and cleanness. They do the devil's work. For the devil's work is, above all, to strive with all diligence to cast people into sin and drown them. Now, when the devil himself cannot achieve this in people of great moral strength by his own ruses, he sends these go-betweens, full of wretched tricks, as his messengers to lure the minds of men and women into the sins of the flesh. Thus we can see that they are more powerful in evil than the devil himself and may be called the devil's coaches. Of them it is well said in Proverbs 16 that "the wrath of a king is the messenger of death." If David ordered to kill the man who seemingly brought good news, namely Saul's death, in Kings 1, what do you think the heavenly David, that is, Christ, will do to those who, as it were, bring news of the fires of hell? Surely: King David could only inflict temporal death, but Christ can give eternal death; therefore, etc. Hence those cursed old women may be called sisters of the serpent that deceived Eve. According to Bede, the serpent has the face of a maiden, and this stands for those go-betweens that have been chosen by the devil to deceive our souls. Of them is said in Joel 1: "The girl they have sold for wine." But after the Psalm, "their wine is the gall of dragons, and the venom of asps, which is incurable."

Observe the following: If a preacher of God's word were to win a single soul in all his life, he would do a great thing, because that soul, redeemed with the blood of Christ, is worth more than all the goods of the world. Therefore, if one of those go-betweens were to do no other evil in all her days than ruin a single soul, she would do a lot. But since no sacrifice pleases the devil as much as the ruin of souls, therefore—since this is what these go-betweens do—no sin is greater than theirs, as is plain to see. It lies in the nature of a noble falcon to fly up high, and yet he is often lured by the fowl-

de sua voluntate erga illam expedire non posset, cautelam adinvenit et
talem vetulam clam consuluit. Que cum ab eo fuisset allocata, catellam
quandam accepit et per duos dies aut tres a cibo retraxit. Quo facto quarto
75   die illam pavit pane nigro et cenapio acidissimo, ex cuius fortitudine
humores et lacrime ab eius oculis eruperunt. Quam tunc assumpsit et ad
domum [f. 200v] puelle pervenit. Ipsa autem querente causam lacrimarum
catelle, vetula quasi dolens et mesta respondit: "Heu michi, filia, heu! De
illa enim materia ulterius propter Deum loqui ne attemptes!" Cum ergo ad
80   modum mulierum ipsa magis temptabatur causam rei scire, tandem quasi fictis
lacrimis hec misera respondit: "Ista, inquit, catella quam sic lacrimantem
consideras filia mea karissima dudum extiterat ab uno clerico maledicto
nimium dilecta. Quam cum ad eius amorem verbis vel donis allicere non
poterat, pre dolore mortuus est. Unde iratus Deus vindictam assumpsit et
85   filiam meam in hanc formam catelle convertit, sic continue lacrimantem et
de stulticia eius condolentem." Quo audito expavit puella dicens: "Heu
michi, mater karissima, quid faciam? Nam in eodem statu et casu sum posita.
Tuum ergo consilium deposco." Cui illa: "Si, inquit, vivere optas, festinanter iuvenem illum voca et eius voluntatem per omnia imple." Quod et
90   factum est, et sic puellam decepit. Unde bene dicitur illud de talibus:
"Inveni mulierem morte amariorem," quasi diceret, mors naturalis simul et
semel nisi unum capere [non] potest, set talis misera tres simul confundit,
quia seipsam et duos alios.

---

1 luxurie] *add* nimis O.   **6** opera . . . facta] facta . . . opera O.   **7–8** que eciam] quod
M.W; quasi diceret R.   **12** 1] *om* O.   **35** lascivia] *corr from* lasciviam C; lasciviam
M.W; lascivia R; *add* aliquo modo O. infectetur] insectetur M.W; inflectetur R.   **35–**
36 venenetur] venatur M; venenatur R; venetur W.   **38** inducentibus] ducentibus O.
45 inmittit] *corr from* emittit C; emittit O.   **50** idest] scilicet O.   **66** aliquam] *add* anti-
quam O.   **83** vel] nec O.   **84** poterat] potuit O.   **89–90** et factum est] est factum O.
90 de talibus] *om* M.W; de ea R.   **91** naturalis] naturaliter O.

VII.vii   DE SPECIEBUS LUXURIE: FORNICACIO

Circa autem species huius vicii est sciendum quod plures sunt. Quarum
prima fornicacio dici potest, que detestabilior dicitur homicidio aut
rapina, eo quod illa substancialiter non sunt mala sicut fornicacio. Exemplum: Aliquis enim potest velle aliquem occidere meritorie, sicut iudex
5   amore iusticie, et similiter aliquis bonum alienum rapere in summa necessitate. Set nullus potest scienter fornicari quoquo modo nisi mortaliter

er's trick to come down, namely by means of some pigeon craftily set on the ground to lure him. In the same fashion, young women who climb up high on the way of chastity are tricked by the fowler of hell by means of such go-betweens that are assigned to this job.

For this we have a story about a young woman who loved her chastity but was loved unchastely and against her will by a cleric. As the cleric could make no headway in having her to his will, he thought of a ruse and secretly consulted such a go-between. When the latter had been hired by him, she took a bitch and starved it for two or three days. Then, on the fourth day, she fed it black bread and very sharp pepper, which made water and tears burst from its eyes. Then she took the bitch and went to the maiden's house. When the girl asked about the cause of the bitch's tears, the old dame answered, as if sad and grieving: "Alas, my daughter, woe to me. For God's sake, don't ask any further about this matter!" But when, like a woman, the girl was tempted even more to know the cause, the wretched dame at last answered with pretended tears: "This bitch you see thus crying once was my beloved daughter and was deeply loved by a cursed cleric. When he could not lure her with words or gifts to love him, he died of grief. But God in his anger took vengeance and changed my daughter into the shape of this bitch who is constantly weeping and mourning for her folly." When the girl heard this, she got frightened and said: "Alas, dear mother, what shall I do? For I am in the same case and condition. I implore you to give me your advice." Then she answered: "If you want to live, call the young man quickly and do his will in everything." That is what happened, and thus she tricked the girl. Wherefore it is well said: "I have found a woman more bitter than death," as if to say: in the course of nature, death can only catch one person at a time, but that wretched dame ruined three at once—herself and two others.

---

2 Gal. 5.19.   3–4 Deut. 3.19.   10–11 Pliny, *Hist. nat.* VIII.xliv.106.   13 Josh. 1.14.
16–17 Deut. 7.14.   20–21 Pliny, *Hist. nat.* VIII.lxxvi.204.   26 Jer. 22.30.   27–
29 Rev. 13.11.   48 Prov. 16.14.   49–50 2 Sam. 1. 13–16.   54–55 Petrus Comestor,
Hist. scholastica on Gen. 3 (PL 198:1072), also referring to Bede.   56 Joel 3.3.
57 Deut. 32.33.   70–90 Tubach 661.   91 Eccles. 7.27.

VII.vii   THE BRANCHES OF LECHERY: FORNICATION

As to the branches of this vice, there are several. The first may be said to be fornication, which is said to be more detestable than homicide or violent theft because the latter are not as evil in their substance as fornication is. For example, it is possible that someone wants to kill someone else by right, as does a judge out of love for justice; and likewise someone may steal someone else's goods out of great need. But no one can knowingly fornicate in any

peccat; ergo, etc. Et ideo ut patet Numeri 25, cum fornicatus esset Israel
cum filiabus Moab, iussit Dominus [f. 201] illorum principes suspendi. Et
ideo est sciendum quod licet fornicacio sit illicitus cohitus, ⟨speci⟩ali-
10   ter tamen intelligitur in usu viduarum aut meretricum vel concubinarum. Set
hoc nomine meretricum non debent mulieres appellari nisi ille tantum que se
universaliter omnibus exponunt, et hoc propter lucrum, nec aliquem abnegare
volunt.
      Unde propter eos qui dicunt simplicem fornicacionem non esse peccatum
15   mortale eo quod actus naturalis est, sunt hec tria per ordinem ostendenda,
videlicet primo ipsam absolute esse inhibitam, secundo omnino fuisse prohi-
bendam, tercio a Domino diabolicam nominatam. Primum autem patet, quod
simplex fornicacio absolute est inhibita, ex verbis que Deuteronomii 23
dicuntur: "Non est meretrix de filiabus Israel." Et Exodi ⟨2⟩4: "Non forni-
20   caberis." Et Ad Corinthios 6: "Fugite fornicacionem." Et Ad Galatas 5:
"Manifesta sunt opera carnis, que sunt fornicacio," etc. Et sequitur: "Qui
talia agunt, regnum Dei non possidebunt." Et sic patet primum.
      Secundum eciam patet, quod fornicacio omnino est prohibenda, quatuor
de causis. Prima est hec: propter pacem humani generis, quia si liceret
25   cuilibet qualibet uti, frequenter rixe, contenciones, odia, homicidia, et
multa plura quam modo sunt in mundo fierent. Secunda causa: propter crebram
prolis interfectionem. Nam matres proli providere non valentes nec auxilium
a patribus habentes sepe illam suffocant. Tercia racio est ut homo se
humiliaret preponendo voluntatem Dei amori carnali et precepta eius custo-
30   dire, quia ad diligendum Deum super omnia tenetur homo ex primo mandato
precipiente, "Diliges Dominum Deum tuum ex toto corde tuo," etc. Similiter
Deus precipit simpliciter et non condicionaliter dicens, "Non mechaberis."
Quarta est ut industria hominis et racio ceteris animalibus preponeretur.
[f. 201v] Set modo ita est quod sunt alique aves quarum talis est castitas
35   quod una uni tantum adheret, ut patet in turturibus. Cum ergo non minor
debet esse racio castitatis hominis quam turturis, iuste unus vir uni
mulieri coniugio adherere deberet. Indecens enim est ut carnalior sit homo,
qui preter carnem spiritum habet racionalem, quam avis, que solum carnem
habet, etc.
40   Tercium eciam patet, quod fornicacio vicium diabolicum est et sic a
Domino iudicatur, eo quod primo a diabolo proposita est, dicente illud Genesis 3: "Cur precepit vobis Deus ne comederetis ex omni ligno?" Qui eciam
modo cotidie suadet miseris quos per luxuriam sibi illaqueat et alliciat.
Patet ergo per hoc quod hoc peccatum omnino fugiendum est.
45   Unde narratur, et ab Ovidio accipitur, quod quidam iuvenis He⟨ro⟩
nomine puellam quandam Landam nomine multum adamavit. Cum ergo ipse
semel ad eam in quadam turre residentem per mare navigavit de nocte et ipsa
lucernam super murum posuisset ut illa visa directe regeret iter suum, orta

other way than by committing a mortal sin; therefore, etc. And thus, as can be seen in Numbers 25, when Israel had fornicated with the daughters of Moab, the Lord commanded their princes to be hanged. Therefore, we must understand that while fornication is any forbidden sexual intercourse, it particularly refers to intercourse with widows, prostitutes, or concubines. But the term "prostitute" must be applied only to those women who give themselves to anyone and will refuse none, and that for monetary gain.

People who claim that simple fornication is not a mortal sin because it is a natural act have to be shown the following three arguments in order: first, that it is absolutely forbidden; second, that it must be completely rejected; and third, that it has been called "diabolical" by the Lord. First, then, that simple fornication is absolutely forbidden is manifest from the commandments, as in Deuteronomy 23: "There shall be no whore among the daughters of Israel"; and Exodus 24: "Thou shalt not commit fornication"; and Corinthians 6: "Flee fornication"; and Galatians 5: "The works of the flesh are manifest, which are fornication," etc.; and the text continues: "They who do such things shall not obtain the kingdom of God." Thus the first argument is manifest.

The second point also, that fornication must be completely rejected, can be seen from four reasons. The first is: for the sake of peace in human society, for if everybody could freely sleep with anyone, frequent struggles would arise, strife, hatred, homicide, and many more evils than are now in the world. The second reason is the frequent killing of offspring, for mothers who cannot provide for their children or get no help from their fathers often stifle them to death. The third reason is that man should humble himself before God by placing God's will and the keeping of his commandments before his own carnal love, for man is held to love God over all things by the first commandment, which states: "Thou shalt love the Lord thy God from thy whole heart," etc. Similarly, God gives a simple command without qualifications when he says, "Thou shalt not commit adultery." The fourth reason is that man's diligence and reason should be higher than that of all other animals. But now it happens that some birds are so chaste that each mates only with one other, as is the case with turtledoves. Since the degree of chastity in humans must not be inferior to that of turtledoves, it is just that one man should be united to one woman in marriage. For it is quite shameful that a human person, who besides his flesh has a rational spirit, should be more fleshly than a bird, who has only flesh.

Also the third point, that fornication is judged by the Lord to be a diabolical vice, can be easily seen from the fact that it was first suggested by the devil when he said in Genesis 3: "Why has God commanded you that you should not eat from every tree?" He still persuades wretched people every day and binds and lures them to himself by means of lechery. It is therefore evident that this sin must be fled altogether.

tempestate extinguitur lucerna. Quo facto submergitur iuvenis, et puella
50   pre dolore precipitatur. Puella autem hec est anima racionalis ad ymaginem
Dei facta. Quam quidam iuvenis, qui a "iuvando" dicitur, adamavit, et
signat corpus humanum, quod datum est anime ad iuvamen. Inter que amor
naturalis est satis magnus, ut apparet, et maxime ex parte corporis, eo
quod corpus sine anima vivere non potest, set anima in turri residet undi-
55   que potenciis et virtutibus murata. Istam ergo lucernam racionis corpori in
mari huius mundi naviganti, qui sicut mare modo fluit modo refluit, anima
porrigit. Set orta tempestate carnalis concupiscencie, per consensum statim
lumen racionis extinguitur et corpus per mortem submergitur. Anima eciam
propter peccatum corporis precipitatur, [f. 202] ut sic ipsa cum Psalmista
60   dicat: "Veni in altitudinem maris et tempestas demersit me."

   Et ideo, ut videtur, iam propter istud peccatum tam commune verificantur quatuor contradictoria, [scilicet:

     That lawe hath noo ry3te,
     þat trewþe hath no my3t,
65   þat wysdom is foly,
     And holynysse is trechery.]

Primum patet de lege et precepto Dei, quando dicitur simpliciter "Non
mechaberis," quomodo illa "non habet iusticiam," eo quod non tenetur nec
observatur quando dicunt simplicem fornicacionem non esse mortale peccatum,
70   cum tamen sit directe contra preceptum Domini, ut patet. Non enim precipit
Deus particulariter "Non accipias illam uxorem aut illam monialem aut illam
viduam," set generaliter precipit quoad omnes dicens, "Non mechaberis," hoc
est, nullam mulierem [accipies] sine licencia Dei et Ecclesie. Set forte
dicit aliquis, "Nonne mulieres pro hominibus ordinate sunt, et e contra-
75   rio?" Revera respondeo quod eodem modo ordinantur boves pro aratro [et]
equi pro biga. Set capias bovem aut equum proximi sine licencia et suspen-
deris secundum eciam legem Dei et mundi. In lege enim Dei precipitur "Non
furtum facies," et in lege mundi ordinatur quod huiusmodi fures suspendantur. Si ergo propter rem temporalem [talem] penam portabis, quanto magis si
80   animam Christianam Christi sanguine redemptam a via pudicicie ad vilissimam
fornicacionem abduxeris. Et ideo dico quod illa excusacio pessima est.

   Set rogo quomodo se excusant ille iuvencule quando queritur ab eis
quare sic fecerunt quando venter incipit tumescere et inflari? Revera, ut
communiter respondent quod necessario oportuit eas ita facere, eo quod
85   illis predestinatum erat ab inicio et ante tunicam suam aut rochetam. Set
certe econtra talibus responderi potest sicut fecit quidam sapiens cuidam
mulieri sic repondenti: "Vere, filia (dixit ipse), vere, quicumque illud
formavit malus scissor fuit, *for hit schamely pokith.*" Patet ergo quod

There is a story, and it derives from Ovid, that a young man by the name
of Hero was deeply in love with a girl called Leander. One night he sailed
across the sea to her as she was sitting in a tower, and she had placed a lantern on the wall that he might see it and take his course by it. But a storm
arose and extinguished the light. Then the youth drowned, and the girl in her
grief threw herself into the sea. This girl stands for the rational soul which
has been made in God's image. A *iuvenis*, "youth," loved her, so named from
iuvare, "to help"; he stands for the human body, which is given to the soul for
its help. Between the two there is a very strong natural love, as it seems,
particularly on the part of the body, for the body cannot live without the
soul; but the soul sits in a tower, walled in on all sides by natural faculties
and virtues. Now, the soul holds up the lantern of reason for the body which
sails on the sea of this world, which ebbs and flows like the sea. But when
the storm of fleshly concupiscence arises, the light of reason gets blown out
through the consent of one's will, and the body drowns in death. On account of
the body's sin the soul, too, is flung down and can therefore say with the
Psalmist: "I am come into the depth of the sea, and a tempest has overwhelmed
me."

Thus it seems to me that because of this sin which is common, the following four paradoxes have now become true, namely:

> That law has no right,
> Truth has no might,
> Wisdom is folly,
> And holiness is treachery.

The first can be seen with respect to God's law and commandments; for the
simple prohibition "Thou shalt not commit adultery" nowadays "has no right,"
that is, it is not held or observed when people say that simple fornication is
not a mortal sin, although it goes directly against the Lord's commandment, as
is obvious. For God did not give this commandment in a particularized form:
"Do not sleep with this wife or this nun or this widow," but he gave a general
commandment covering all women when he said, "Thou shalt not commit adultery," that is, you shall not take any woman without permission from God and the
Church. But perhaps someone will say, "Aren't women made for men, and vice-
versa?" To that I answer that in the same way oxen are made for the plow and
horses for the cart. But take your neighbor's ox or horse without his permission, and you will be hanged according to the law of both God and the world.
For God's law commands: "Thou shalt not steal"; and secular laws decree that
such thieves should be hanged. If one therefore is to suffer such a penalty on
account of some temporal object, how much greater will the punishment be if one
has led a Christian soul, redeemed with Christ's blood, from the way of chaste-

tales pessime se excusant quando dicunt quod necessario sic oportuit esse
90   [f. 202v] et quod aliter non potest esse, eo quod peccatum suum in ipsum
Deum retorquent dicendo quod non possunt continere, et sic Deum accusant de
iniusticia. Probacio: Si autem Deus precipit homini facere quod non potest,
tunc esset crudelis exactor et tyrannus. Similiter, si dampnat pro eo quod
vitari non potest, manifestam iniusticiam faceret. Set hoc est falsum.
95   Ergo, etc. Vellem ergo scire utrum tales mulieres voluntarie huiusmodi peccata commiserint aut vi aut metu fuerint cognite. Si primum, ergo potuerunt
hoc non fecisse. Probacio: quia quod fit libere, libere potest dimitti;
ergo ipsemet tunc sunt in culpa et Deus immunis. Si secundum, scilicet quod
ad hoc vi fuerunt coacte, dico quod illud fit maximi meriti nec aliquid
100   contra virginitatem. Exemplum de beata Lucia, que suis tortoribus respondit
illam vi ad lupanar trahere et opprimere volentibus: "Numquam (dixit ipsa)
inquinatur corpus meum nisi consensu mentis." [Ergo,] etc.
        Secundum eciam iam patet verificatum, scilicet that ⟨trewth⟩ hath no
myght, de Sampsone fortissimo, Iudicum, cuius fortitudo per mulierem quasi
105   nulla facta est. Tercium eciam patet, scilicet that wisdome is foly, de
Salomone rege sapientissimo propter mulieres ydolatriam committente, per
quod stultus factus est. Quartum similiter patet in David rege sancto, scilicet that holynes ys trechery, quem propter suam sanctitatem elegit Deus
iuxta cor suum quando Uriam dolose fecit interfici propter Bersabee, uxorem
110   eius.
        Est eciam contra illos adhuc arguendum qui peccatum suum retorquent in
Deum dicendo quod propter eorum carnis fragilitatem se non posse continere.
Nam contra tales dicitur Genesis 4 de peccato: "Sub te erit appetitus tuus,
et tu dominaberis illius." Non enim dixit Deus quod peccatum dominaretur
115   homini, licet hodie sic fiat, et ideo tales quasi mendacium Deo imponunt.
Unde Ieronimus: "Sit maledictus qui dicit Deum precepisse impossibile. Nam
iuxta [f. 203] Apostolum Ad Corinthios, 'Deus fidelis est et non permittit
hominem temptari supra id quod potest,' hoc est, ulterius quam, si velit,
resistere valeat." Unde ibidem Ieronimus tales redarguit dicens: "O, in-
120   quit, prophana temeritas! O vesanorum insania illorum qui Deum dupplici
sciencie ignorancia contempnitis, scilicet quod Deus nescit et quod nesciat
misereri, quasi qui imposuerit mandatum quod impleri non potest. ⟨Pro⟩
nephas! Iniquitatem enim iusto inponunt et crudelitatem pio, acsi nos, quod
suspicari sacrilegium est, salvos ° non faceret set pocius ad penam deputa-
125   ret." Hec ille. In qua auctoritate insinuat Ieronimus illos esse blasphe-
matores qui dicunt se non posse continere. Ipsi enim Deo inponunt, ut supra
dictum est, iniusticiam, ignoranciam, et impietatem. Et ideo ait Seneca:
"O, ⟨sinite⟩, inquit, excusantes, quia nemo peccat invitus." Et Augustinus:
"Non enim peccat in eo quis quod vitare non potest. Nam peccatum est adeo
130   voluntarium quod, si non sit voluntarium, non est peccatum." Quia ergo ante

ness to vile fornication! Therefore I say that that excuse is absolutely worthless.

And, I ask you, how do those young women excuse themselves when one asks them why they have done it when their belly begins to swell and grow? Indeed, they often reply they had to do it by necessity, for it had been preordained for them "before their shirt or gown." But surely, against such excuses one may answer as a wise man once did who said to a woman that excused herself in this way: "Truly, my daughter, whoever made that bag was a bad tailor, for it pokes out shamefully." Thus it is obvious that such people give very poor excuses when they say that it had to be this way by necessity and could not be otherwise, because in saying that they cannot be continent they blame God for their sin and thereby accuse God of injustice. To prove this point: if God commands a man to do something of which he is incapable, he would be cruel in his demand and a tyrant. Likewise, if he condemns a person for what cannot be avoided, he would do an obvious injustice. But this conclusion is not true; therefore, etc. Hence, I would want to know if women in such a situation have committed sins of this kind voluntarily or if they had intercourse by violence or out of fear. In the first case, they were able not to commit the sin; for what one does freely, one can freely leave undone. Therefore, they themselves bear the guilt and God is not responsible. In the second case, that is, if they were forced to it, I say that such a deed has brought them great merit and is no stain on their virginity. For this we have the example of Blessed Lucia, who said to her torturers as they wanted to drag her by force to the brothel and violate her: "Never will my body be stained unless I consent to it in my mind." Therefore, etc.

The second paradox, namely that "truth has no might," has also come true in the strong Samson, of the Book of Judges, whose strength was reduced to nothing by a woman. Likewise the third, that "wisdom is folly," can be seen in King Solomon, who despite his great wisdom committed idolatry for the sake of women, through which he became insane. And the fourth paradox, that "holiness is treachery," is found in the holy King David, whom God chose after his heart on account of his holiness: he had Uriah treacherously killed for the sake of his wife, Bathsheba.

People who blame their sin on God by saying that they are incapable of continence because their flesh is weak should be further answered as follows. Against them Genesis 4 declares with regard to sin: "Your lust for it shall be under you, and you shall have dominion over it." God did not say that sin would reign over man, even though nowadays this is the case; hence people who make these excuses make God a liar. Therefore, Jerome says: "Cursed be he who says God has commanded what is impossible. For according to the Apostle in Corinthians, 'God is faithful and does not allow a man to be tempted above what he is capable,' that is, further than he is able to resist if he wants to."

hominem vita et mors proponuntur, et homo habet liberum arbitrium utrum
velit eligere vitam an mortem—nemo potest impedire mortem, ° tamen bene
potest homo retardare—, unde si mortem eligat, non est Deo imputandum,
secundum illud Ecclesiastici 15: "Apponit tibi aquam et ignem. Ad quod
135 volueris, porrige manum tuam. Ante hominem bonum et malum, vita et mors;
quod placuerit ei, dabit illi." Si ergo ignem luxurie elegerit homo, [que]
corpus et animam usque ad consummacionem devorat, et aquam continencie et
puritatis dimiserit, constat quod in nullo est Deo inputandum.

Item quero ab illo qui dicit se non posse continere, per quem cogitur
140 ad fornicandum, utrum per diabolum vel per mulierem [f. 203v] aut per
carnem propriam. Si dicat "per diabolum," contra: Dicit enim Gregorius:
"Hostis, inquit, ille timendus non est qui vincere non potest nisi permissus," scilicet a carne. Set diabolus est huiusmodi. Probacio: secundum
⟨enim⟩ Bernardum "diabolus ° plus confidit de adiutorio carnis quam in pro
145 priis viribus eo quod magis nocet hostis domesticus quam ignotus"; ergo,
etc. Si dicat "per mulierem," contra: Mulier enim est sub potestate viri et
non e contrario. Et per consequens, cum ipse ei dominatur, magis cogit eam
quam e contrario. Sequitur ergo quod malicia carnis proprie et non per
alium deducitur homo ad fornicandum. Item quero a tali: "Si vis continere
150 aut non potes? Si vis et non potes, ergo infidelis est Deus, qui patitur te
temptari ultra posse tuum. Si autem potes et non vis, ergo omnino inexcusa-
bilis es et nullo modo potes excusari," etc.

---

7 peccat] peccent M.W; peccet R.   9 sit] *add* omnis M.W; omnino R.   9–10 specialiter]
spiritualiter C.R.   19 dicuntur] dicitur O (*with different antecedents for* verbis *and* que).
24] 34 C.   39 etc.] *om* O.   40 est et sic] *om* O.   45 Hero] hep C.O.   62–66 scilicet . . . trechery] *text from* R. *Verse 52, in* B1.B3.CC.Co.Go1.Go2.Jo.L2.L3.LC.R.Sp.
W1.V.   85 suam] *om* M.R; meam W.   87 mulieri] muliercule O.   90 precipit] precepit
O.   96 commiserint] commiserunt O.   103 trewth] strengthe C.   105 scilicet] *om* O.
119 ibidem] idem O.   120 insania] infamia M.R; infama W.   121 contempnitis] con-
tempnatis M.W *and many others*; condempnatis R.   122 Pro] per C.   124 salvos] *add*
nos C; *add* vos M.   non] *interl* C; *om* O.   125 qua] *add* quidem O.   128 sinite] invite C;
mute M?; mite W?   excusantes] excusatores O.   129 quis] *om* O.   131 proponuntur] apponuntur O.   132 mortem] *add* quin homo potest bene eligere quod vult sive vitam sive
mortem ymo nec deus iuste C (*unique*).   144 enim] *before* secundum C.   diabolus] *add*
enim C.   149 Si] *interl for* non *exp* C; non M.W; aut non R.   152 etc.] *om* O.

Hence Jerome reproaches people who excuse themselves in this way and says, in the same place: "Oh impious temerity! Oh mad insanity of those who scorn God for a twofold failing, namely that he does not know and that he cannot have pity, as if he had given a commandment which cannot be observed. How monstrous! They accuse the one who is just of iniquity, the one who is full of pity, of cruelty, as if—which it is a sacrilege even to think—he were not saving us but rather condemning us to pain." In this quotation Jerome suggests that those who say they cannot be continent blaspheme against God. For, as I said earlier, they accuse God of injustice, lack of knowledge, and want of pity. Therefore says Seneca: "Oh, stop, you who excuse yourselves; nobody sins against his will." And Augustine: "One does not sin in what one cannot avoid. For sin is so voluntary that, if it is not voluntary, it is no sin."
Since life and death are put before man, and man has a free choice whether he wants to take life or death—no one can avoid death; yet man can well delay it—, therefore, if he chooses death, he must not blame God for it. According to the words of Ecclesiasticus 15: "He sets water and fire before you; stretch forth your hand to whichever you will. Before man is good and evil, life and death; whatever pleases him, he will give him." Therefore, if man chooses the fire of lechery, which totally devours body and soul, and lets go the water of purity and continence, it is obvious that he can in no way blame God for it.

    And I further ask the person who claims he is incapable of being continent: by whom is he compelled to commit fornication, by the devil, or by a woman, or by his own flesh? If he says "by the devil," the counterargument is that Gregory declares: "That enemy is not to be feared who cannot win except by our permission," which refers to our flesh. But the devil is of this kind. According to Bernard, the devil relies more on the cooperation of our flesh than on his own powers, because an enemy who belongs to one's household causes more harm than an outsider; therefore, etc. If a person says he is compelled "by a woman," the counterargument is that woman is under man's power and not vice-versa. Therefore, since man rules over woman, he compels her, rather than the other way around. Therefore, it follows that a man is led to commit fornication by the wickedness of his own flesh and not through anyone else. And further I ask a person who thus excuses himself: "Do you want to be continent or are you not capable of it? If you want to and are not capable of it, God is unfaithful because he allows you to be tempted beyond your capacity. But if you are capable and do not want to, then you are entirely without excuse."

7–8 Cf. Num. 25.1–4.   19 Deut. 23.17.   19–20 Exod. 34.15.   20 1 Cor. 6.18.   21–22 Gal. 5.19, 21.   31 Deut. 6.5.   32 Exod. 20.14.   42 Gen. 3.1.   45–50 Ovid, *Heroides* XVIII.   60 Ps. 68.3.   67–68 Exod. 20.14.   82–88 See above, *FM* V.xii.146–152.   100–102 Cf. *Leg. aurea*, p. 31.   104–105 Judg. 16.   106–107 1 Kings 11.   107–110 2 Sam. 11.   113–144 Gen. 4.7.   111–130 Verbally in Peraldus, *Summa*

VII.viii   STUPRUM

[S]ecunda species luxurie est stuprum, et est illicita defloracio
virginum. Quod eciam valde detestandum est. Nam sicut patet Genesis 34,
propter hoc peccatum cum Sychem, filius Emor, Dynam deflorasset, cum patre
interfectus est et cum toto populo urbis. Similiter quia bonum virginitatis
5   sic amissum est irrecuperabile, sicut vas vitreum fractum non potest red-
integrari; Psalmista: "Factum est cor meum tamquam vas perditum." Refert
enim Orosius libro 4 quod Hanibal, dux Cartaginencium, quamvis ita probus
fuerat quod in signum victorie de divitibus Romanorum interfectis et eorum
digitis extractis tres modios anulorum aureorum Cartaginem miserat, ipse
10 tamen sic armis invectus, prout recitat Valerius libro 4, ex incendio luxurie capitur et expugnatur. Et ideo racionabiliter concludit Carnotensis
quod principatus quem corrumpit luxuria diu stare aut durare non potest,
etc.

---

13 etc.] *om* O.

VII.ix   ADULTERIUM

[T]ercia species luxurie est adulterium, quod est accessus illicitus
"ad alterius thorum." Et hoc eciam dividitur in duas species, scilicet
quando coniugatus adulteratur cum soluta, vel uxorata cum [f. 204] coniuga-
tis. Cuius discrimen primo patet ex hoc quod est contrarium communi sacra-
5   mento matrimonii quod Deus in paradiso in statu innocencie instituit. Et
similiter ipse Christus innocens sub ordine tali dignatus est nasci, quod
non tantum sub virginali candore verum eciam sub coniugali honore, ut sic
illud sacramentum quasi dignissimum ostenderet, et eo amplius huic sacramento ⟨contraire⟩ quisque desisteret, sub pena gravi, quia Levitici 20
10 dicitur: "Si mechatus fuerit quis cum uxore alterius et adulterium perpe-
traverit, morte moriatur et mechus et adultera." Et similiter Numeri 5
scribitur: "Quia declinasti a viro tuo atque polluta es et concubuisti cum
viro altero, hiis maledictionibus subiacebis: Det tibi Deus maledictionem,

vitiorum III.vi.1, with the same quotations. **117–118** 1 Cor. 10.13. **129–130** Augustine, *De vera religione* XIV.27 (PL 34:133–134). **134–136** Ecclus. 15.17–18. **142–143** Cf. Peraldus, *Summa vitiorum* III.vi.2. **144–145** See above, *FM* V.xxxii.5–6, from *Meditationes piissimae*.

VII.viii   VIOLATING A VIRGIN

The second branch of lechery is violating, that is, unlawfully deflowering, a virgin. This is much to be detested. For as can be seen in Genesis 34, when Shechem, the son of Hamor, deflowered Dinah, he and his father and the entire population of the town were killed for this sin. Likewise, once the good of virginity has thus been lost, it is irrecoverable, just as a glass vessel cannot be made whole again once it has been broken; whence the Psalmist says: "My heart is become like a vessel that is destroyed." Orosius tells in book 4 that Hannibal, the leader of the Carthaginians, though he was such a great champion that, as a sign of his victory, he had sent to Carthage three measures of gold rings taken from the fingers of rich Romans that had been killed, yet after being undefeated in battle he was, as Valerius reports in book 4, captured and overcome by the fire of lechery. And the Chartrian concludes from this reasonably that a prince's reign cannot stand for long or remain if it is corrupted by lechery.

2–4 Gen. 34. **6** Cf. Ps. 30.13. **7–9** Orosius, *Historiae* IV.16 (PL 31:894). **10–11** Valerius, IX.ext.1. **11–12** Perhaps *Policraticus* VIII.vi (p. 260).

VII.ix   ADULTERY

The third branch of lechery is adultery, which is the unlawful approaching of another man's marriage bed. It can be divided into two species, namely adultery between a married and a single person, and adultery between two married persons. That adultery is a crime is obvious from the fact that, first, it goes against the common sacrament of marriage which God instituted in paradise in the state of innocence. Moreover, Christ himself in his sinlessness deigned to be born in wedlock—not only in the purity of virginity but also in the honorable state of matrimony—that he might show how eminently worthy this sacrament is. And that one should more earnestly refrain from violating this sacrament, he laid the offense under a grave penalty, for in Leviticus 20 it is said: "If a man has defiled another man's wife and committed adultery, let them be put to death, both the adulterer and the adulteress." And in Numbers 5 it is similarly written: "Since you have gone away from your husband and have

exemplumque sis cunctorum in populo; putrescere faciat femur tuum, et
15 cunctus uterus tuus disrumpatur."
   Refert enim Alexander *De naturis rerum* quod erant quondam due ciconie,
quarum femina super ova in nido sedit ad producendum pullos, masculus vero
in patriam volavit, ut sibi et illi cibum quereret. Interim accidit quod
illa in nido dimissa cum aliis ciconiis adulterata est. Quo facto instinctu
20 nature ne masculus rediens fetorem adulterii sentiret, lavit se in quodam
fonte qui erat ante cuiusdam militis portam. Et cum sic fecisset bis vel
ter, et miles illud factum considerasset, fontem iussit obstrui. Cum ergo
illa more solito veniret ut in illo se lavaret nec potuit, inmunda ad nidum
rediit. Cuius fetorem cum masculus de sero rediens persensisset, ipsam
25 quasi vindicta adulterii totaliter dilaceravit. Revera, spiritualiter loquendo sic est de Deo et anima humana quam Deus assumpsit sibi sponsam,
iuxta illud ⟨Osee⟩: "Sponsabo te michi in fide." Hanc ergo dimittit hic
Deus quasi in nido mundi ad producendum bona opera. Nec oportet illam nisi
ut bene agat de victualibus sollicitari, eo quod ipse Deus [f. 204v] omnium
30 indigenciam supplebit, iuxta illud Ysaie: "Discite bene facere," etc.,
qu⟨ia⟩ "si volueritis et audieritis me, bona terre comedetis." Set misera
anima cum ceteris miseris adulterans, iudicium timens lavat se in fonte
penitencie. Que penitencia ante portam confessoris est; de qua porta loquitur Psalmista dicens: "Hec porta Domini; iusti intrabunt in ea." Ante quam
35 portam debet esse fons penitencie et aqua contricionis. Post cuius locionem
fetor peccati totaliter recedit. Unde et Deus eciam peccata dissimulat;
Sapiencie 2: "Misereris omnium quoniam potes, et dissimulans peccata hominum propter penitenciam." Unde frequenter, quia Deus sic misericordiam
prestat, misera anima in peccatis recidivat. Et dum sic more solito lavari
40 vellet per penitenciam, sepe impeditur per subitam [vindictam], eo quod
fons contricionis per militem mortis obturatur. Et ideo bene ait homini
peccatori Ecclesiastici 15: "Ne tardes converti ad Dominum," etc.; "subito
enim veniet ira eius, in tempore vindicte disperdet te."
   De huiusmodi eciam vindicta quantum ad fornicarios legitur in *Vita*
45 *beati Germani episcopi* quod in terra de qua oriundus fuit mansit quidam
draco ingentissimus, in quo diabolum latere dicebatur, qui ibidem tam
homines quam bestias igne infernali innumerabiliter consumpsit. Cum ergo
conquesti homines essent illius regionis episcopo predicto Germano super
hac peste, compassione motus quadam hora matutina in oracione persistens
50 partes quas gravare solet nocturno tempore vidit, ipsum igne totum fumigan-
tem in quodam cimiterio non longe ab eo descendere. Ille vero locum bene
considerans illuc cum multitudine cleri et populi festinabat et orantibus
omnibus venit ad quendam tumulum, cuius summitas omnino flammis erat combustum. Et ut cognovit quod ibi esset, exhumavit terram usquedum veniret ad
55 quoddam corpus horridum et [f. 205] fetidum in duabus partibus divisum, in

been defiled and have lain with another man, these curses shall light upon you: May the Lord make you a curse and an example to all among his people; may he make your thigh rot, and may your womb burst asunder."

In his book *On the Nature of Things* Alexander reports that once there were two storks; the female sat on her eggs in the nest to hatch them, and the male flew about the country to seek food for himself and his mate. It so happened that while she was left behind in her nest she committed adultery with other storks. Out of her natural instinct then, lest her husband on his return should notice the smell of adultery, she washed herself in a spring that was in front of the gate of a knight. After she had done so twice or three times, the knight, who had noticed this, had the spring closed off. When she came as usual to wash herself but could not, she returned to her nest unclean. Upon his return at night, her mate perceived her smell and tore her completely to pieces in revenge for her adultery. This applies spiritually to God and man's soul, which God has taken to himself as his spouse, according to the words of Hosea: "I will espouse you to myself in faith." God leaves her here, as if in the nest of this world, so that she may bring forth good works. She does not need to worry about her livelihood, only about living a good life, because God himself will supply all her needs, after the words of Isaiah: "Learn to do well," etc., because "if you are willing and listen to me, you shall eat the good things of the land." But the wretched soul commits adultery with other wretches, and when she becomes afraid of the judgment, washes herself in the fountain of penance. This penance is in front of the door of the confessor, of which the Psalmist speaks as follows: "This is the gate of the Lord; the just shall enter into it." In front of this door must be the wellspring of penance and the water of contrition. After she washes herself, the stench of sin disappears totally. Hence God, too, covers up our sins; Wisdom 2: "You have mercy upon all because you can do all things, and you overlook the sins of men because of their repentance." Now it frequently happens that since God offers such mercy, the wretched soul relapses into sin. And when she wants to wash herself through penance as usual, she is often prevented from doing so by sudden vengeance, because the wellspring of contrition is closed off by the knight of death. Therefore, as Ecclesiasticus 15 fittingly speaks to sinful man: "Do not delay to turn to the Lord," etc., "for his wrath shall come of a sudden, and in the time of vengeance he will destroy you."

Concerning this vengeance that comes to fornicators, we read in the *Life of the Blessed Bishop Germanus* that in his native country there lived an enormous dragon, in whom the devil was said to lie hidden; he destroyed countless people as well as animals with hellfire. When the people of that region had complained about this pest to Bishop Germanus, he was moved by compassion and, as he was in prayer at early dawn, he saw the region which the dragon used to haunt at night, and the dragon itself in smoke and fire descending in a ceme-

cuius medio iacebat ille verendus draco. Quem continuo in nomine sancte
Trinitatis adiurans causam tante rei patenter quesivit. Cui draco: "Tibi,
inquit, resistere non possum quin dicam. Michi data est potestas hominibus
nocere et ° eorum bestiis [ac] inmediate vindictam sumere de hiis qui in
60   peccato mortali volvuntur, et maxime qui carnali commixtione ° contra [Dei]
disposicionem polluuntur. Et quoniam in partibus istis magis ⟨regnat hoc
peccatum adulterii, incestus, et huiusmodi⟩, ideo talem in eis persecucionem divina permissione infero. Cum ergo de tantis malis perpetratis fatigatus fuero, quietem hic assumo, quia hec est requies quam precipue elegi.
65   Hec enim mulier dum vixit erat adultera et in adulterio sine emendacione
deprehensa, et ideo in inferno in nostra societate moratur eius anima. Et
quia corpus suum divisit in adulterio, dans unam partem scilicet marito et
alteram adultero, ideo sic in duabus partibus dividitur, inter quas quasi
in suavi stratu requiesco." Quo dicto adiuratus a viro Dei ut inde recede-
70   ret et ulterius hominibus non noceret, erexit capud cum corpore et evola-
vit, igne infernali in corpore relicto, unde statim in pulverem redacta
est, ex cuius fetore multi de circumstantibus perierunt.
        Committitur autem adulterium alio modo, licet non ita dampnabile,
sicut dicit Ieronimus, quando scilicet suarum coniugum adulteri sunt pro-
75   prii mariti non affectantes proles set tantum libidinem, non ut Deus per
generacionem honoretur set ut voluptas exinde perficiatur. Unde Esdre 2
dicitur: "Multi dementes facti sunt propter suas uxores et servi facti
sunt," supple peccati, propter illas.
        Et ideo propter magnitudinem huius sceleris inmediate post prohibicio-
80   nem homicidii et ante prohibicionem furti ponitur, de quo Clemens querendo
ait: "Quid, inquit, in [f. 205v] omnibus peccatis adulterio gravius? Secundum in peccatis tenet locum," hoc est in prohibicione. Homicidio comparatur
quia, inquit, vir et mulier sunt una caro. Qui alicui uxorem aufert, idem
est acsi proprium virum auferret. Superat autem furtum eo quod in furto
85   attractatur [res] irracionalis, set in adulterio res racionalis, que est
melior omni terrena substancia. Unde illud Proverbiorum 6: "Non est grandis
culpa cum quis furatur ut repleat animam esurientem"; et sequitur: "Qui
ergo adulter est propter cordis inopiam, perdet animam suam."

---

9 contraire] communicari(?) C.   **11** moriatur] moriantur M.R; morientur W.   **22** illud]
om O.   **26** sibi] *add* in O.   **27** Osee] c C.   **31** quia] que C.   **32** miseris] viris M; viciis
R.W.   **38** Unde] *add* ut O.   **40** vellet] *om* M.W; solet R.   **59** et] *add* de C.   **60** com-
mixtione] *add* hoc . . . huiusmodi C (*from the following sentence*).   Dei] *om* C.R.W.
61–62 regnat . . . huiusmodi] regnant huiusmodi peccata C.   **70–71** evolavit] avolavit
O.   **74** coniugum] coniugium O.

tery close by. He marked the place and hurried there with a crowd of clergy
and laymen and, as all were praying, went to a grave whose top had been completely burned by fire. In order to find out what was there, he dug up the
earth until he came to a corpse that was horrid, evil-smelling, and split into
two parts, between which that fearsome dragon was lying. He conjured him at
once in the name of the Holy Trinity and asked him to tell them openly the
cause of all this. Said the dragon: "I cannot resist telling you the truth.
I have been given power to do harm to the people and their animals and to take
immediate vengeance on those who live in mortal sin, especially those who
pollute themselves with sexual intercourse against God's dispensation. And
since in these parts the sin of adultery, incest, and the like is very widespread, I inflict this punishment on them by divine permission. But when I am
tired out by so many evils, I take my rest here, for this is the resting place
I have chosen above all. For while this woman was alive, she was an adulteress
and was caught in adultery without amending her life; for that reason, her soul
dwells in hell in our company. And since she divided her body in adultery,
giving one half to her husband and the other to her lover, she lies thus split
into two parts, between which I take my rest as on a soft couch." After these
words he was conjured by the man of God to leave that place and harm the people
no longer, whereupon he lifted his head and body and flew off, leaving infernal
fire behind in the woman's body, which immediately disintegrated to dust, from
whose stench many of the bystanders died.

Adultery can also be committed in another way, as Jerome says, though this
is not as worthy of damnation, namely when husbands become adulterers with
their own wives, using sex not for procreation but for their lustful pleasure
alone—not in order to honor God by the work of creating new life but in order
to get pleasure from it. Whence it is said in Esdras 2: "Many have lost their
minds because of their wives and have become slaves," add: to sin, on their
account.

Thus, because of its gravity, this sin is placed immediately after the
prohibition against murder and before that against theft. In raising the question, "What is more grievous among all sins than adultery?" Clement says:
"Adultery holds the second place among the sins, that is, in their prohibition.
It is like manslaughter because husband and wife are one flesh: he who takes
someone's wife from him, does the same as taking her husband away. It is worse
than theft, because in theft an irrational object is taken, but in adultery a
rational being, who is better than any earthly object." Hence the words of
Proverbs 6: "The fault is not so great when a man has stolen in order to fill
his hungry soul"; and further: "But he that is an adulterer, for the folly of
his heart shall ruin his own soul."

10–11 Lev. 20.10.   **12–15** Num. 5.20–22.   **16–25** Alexander Neckam, *De naturis rerum* 64 (p. 112). Cf. Tubach 4640 and 3073.   **27** Hos. 2.20.   **30–31** Isa. 1.17, 19.

VII.x   INCESTUS

[E]st autem quarta species luxurie hiis annexa que incestus nuncupa-
tur, que est consanguinearum vel affinium abusus. Cuius magnitudo patet
tribus modis. Primo per penam in lege taxatam, nam Levitici 18 dicitur:
"Omnis anima que fecerit quippiam de abhominacionibus istis, de medio
5   populi peribit." Et ibi loquitur specialiter de incestu et peccato contra
naturam. Secundo quia per hoc vicium, ut patet Ad Corinthios 5, Apostolus
tradidit huiusmodi Sathane cruciandum. Tercio eciam patet eius magnitudo
per mala que ipsum secuntur. Parit enim homicidium, ut patet 1 Regum 12 de
Amon, qui sororem suam corrupit, quapropter ab Absolone fratre suo occisus
10   est. Nota historiam. Similiter hoc vicium reddit hominem cani similem, qui
in opere illo consanguinitatem in nullo servat.
   Et nota: sub hac specie continetur luxuria clericorum et religiosorum, quorum peccatum magis considerandum est. Unde Bernardus: "Ubi est maioris
doni gracie transgressor, ibi maiori subiacebit penitencie." Similiter et
15   culpe. Et nota quod illorum tria aggravant delictum. Primum est voti frac-
tio. Due enim circumstancie solent aggravare peccatum rapine, scilicet
preciositas rapti et magnitudo eius—magis autem dampnificatur proximus
tunc—et eius sanctitas, et tunc non solum committit furtum set eciam
sacrilegium. Castitas autem quam clericus promittit sacros ordines reci-
20   piendo, au- [f. 206] fert illam fornicando, et ideo irrecuperabilis est;
Ecclesiastici 26: "Omnis ponderacio non est digna continentis anime."
Secundum est quod clericus est de familia Dei et de eius expensis vivit. Si
ergo ille de bonis Dei luxuriatur, tamquam proditor ab eius servicio expellendus est. Unde Bernardus: "Ve, inquit, qui ambulant in carne, quia Deo
25   placere non possunt." Unde ad magis illorum dispendium votum frangunt et
per consequens maiorem penam incurrent, quia melius est votum non vovere
quam vovere et gratis illud frangere. Tercium est quia ipsi populum decipiunt, de quorum elemosinis vivunt et illorum intercessores se esse promittunt, set promissa minime aut saltem in peccatis et inmunde implent. Unde
30   Gregorius: 'Nos, inquit, de patrociniis Ecclesie vivimus et inde comedimus
et bibimus.' Si tacemus pro illis orare, profecto (dicit Bernardus) eorum
peccata comedimus et bibimus." Hec ille.
   Circa autem luxuriam religiosorum sub specie incestus contentam notandum quod quinque specialiter sunt illud peccatum aggravancia. Quorum pri-
35   mum patet ex hoc quod legitur Genesis 7 hec fuisse causa diluvii. Si ergo, ut
ibi habetur, tantum Deo displicuit quod filii Dei filias hominum in uxores

34 Ps. 117.20. 37–38 Wisd. 11.24. 42–43 Ecclus. 5.8–9. 44–72 Tubach 4252.
74–76 Jerome, *Adversus Iovinianum* I.49 (PL 23:281). 77–78 3 Esd. 4.26. 81–
82 Ps.-Clement, *Ep. 1 ad Iacobum* (PG 1:466–467); cf. Lombard, *Sent.* IV.xxxviii.2.10
(2:481). 86–88 Prov. 6.30–32.

VII.x   INCEST

The fourth branch of lechery is connected with the previous ones; it is
called incest, which means sexual intercourse with a person related by blood or
spiritual kinship. How grave this sin is can be seen in three ways. First, by
the punishment established for it in the Law; for in Leviticus 18 it is said:
"Every soul that commits any of these abominations shall perish from the midst
of the people." In this passage Scripture speaks specifically of incest and
the sin against nature. Second, according to Corinthians 5, the Apostle has
given people who sin in this fashion over to Satan for punishment. Third, its
gravity is further seen in its evil consequences. For it leads to manslaughter, as we find in Amnon, in 1 Kings 12, who corrupted his sister, for which he
was killed by his brother Absalom. Tell the entire story. Similarly, this
vice makes a man like a dog, who pays no attention to his blood relationship
when it comes to sex.

Notice that this branch comprises lechery among clerics and religious.
Their sin is more grievous than that of other people; therefore Bernard says:
"Where there is a greater gift of grace, the transgressor is liable to greater
punishment"; and the same is true of his guilt. Notice also that the sin of
people in this state is made more grievous by three reasons. The first is that
they break their vow. Two circumstances can aggravate the sin of theft, namely
the value of what is stolen and its size—for one's neighbor suffers greater
harm in this case—and also its sanctity, for in the latter case a thief does
not merely commit theft but also sacrilege. Now when a cleric commits a sexual
sin, he loses that chastity which he had promised to maintain when he received
holy orders, and it is thus irrecoverable; Ecclesiasticus 26: "No price is
worthy of a continent soul." The second reason is that a cleric belongs to
God's household and lives on its budget. If he then commits lechery with the
goods of God, he is to be expelled from his service like a traitor. Whence
Bernard says: "Woe to those who walk in the flesh, for they cannot please
God." Therefore, when they break their vow, they bring greater harm upon themselves and consequently incur a greater penalty, because it is better not to
make a vow than to make it and then break it voluntarily. The third reason is
that they deceive the people on whose alms they live and for whom they promise
to pray; but they hardly fulfill their promises at all or do so in a state of
sin and uncleanness. Therefore Gregory says: "We live off the Church's patrimony and receive from it our food and drink. If we do not pray in return,
indeed we eat and drink the people's sins."

acceperunt, quantum displicere sibi creduntur tales qui cum illis fornican-
tur! Secundum patet per apostasiam. Si quis habitum religionis dimittit
temerarie, apostata dicitur. Cum virtus castitatis sit magis substancialis
40   religionis quam habitus, videtur et certum est quod magis aggravat apostasia castitatis quam apostasia habitus. Unde Proverbiorum 6: "Homo apostata vir inutilis est." Tercium gravamen est quod patet ex hoc quod diabolus
tantum studet precipitare virum religiosum, eo quod plus gaudet de lapsu
unius talis quam multorum aliorum.
45   Unde narratur in *Vitas Patrum* quod cum quidam sanctus transiens vidit
supra portam civitatis unum tantum diabolum sedentem, set supra [f. 206v]
abathiam quasi innumerabiles. Cum ergo ex parte Dei a diabolo quesisset
causam, respondit: "Homines, inquit, civitatis quasi omnes michi subduntur,
et ideo pauci ad eius custodiam sufficiunt. Set in abathia omnes boni sunt,
50   et ideo ibi vix multi possunt prevalere." Idem eciam patet ex hoc quod cum
semel diabolus suum capitulum tenuisset et omnes demones punisset, quamvis
infra biduum vel triduum bellum, homicidia, adulteria, et cetera huiusmodi
procurassent, eo quod ita parum fecissent in tanto tempore; cum ergo tandem
unus dixit quod in triginta annis vix religiosum ad fornicacionem deduxe-
55   rat, a sede descendit et ipsum tamquam valenciorem coronatum ibidem collocavit.
      Quartum patet ex hoc quod ita graviter legitur Dominum punisse in claustro
commissum peccatum. Quorum primum claustrum fuit in celo ⟨ubi⟩ ipsemet
Deus fuit abbas, et ideo quia aliqui ibi de conventu contra illum conspira-
60   bant, absque spe venie condempnati sunt. Secundum claustrum fuit in paradiso terrestri, in quo eciam a Deo loci illius abbate expulsi sunt Adam et
Eva tamquam inobedientes nec ibi stare potuerunt, set cum tota posteritate
dampnati erant. Tercium claustrum fuit in principio Ecclesie, in quo beatus
Petrus fuit abbas, ubi qui proprietarii esse voluerunt, sicut Symon magus,
65   morte subita perierunt; similiter idem patet Actuum 5 de Anania et Saphira.
      Quintum aggravans luxuriam religiosorum patet ad litteram per hoc quod
vita claustralis est vita angelica, iuxta illud dictum Ieronimi: "In carne
enim preter carnem vivere, nature humane non est set angelice." Ergo claustralis homo ut angelus est; [Malachie 2: "Angelus Domini est." Si autem
70   angelus est,] aut bonus est aut malus. Si bonus, propositum; si malus,
diabolus est. Unde Ieronimus: "Professus, inquit, Christiane religionis aut
est angelis equalis aut demonibus compar," etc.

---

12 nota] *add* quod O.   **13–14** Ubi . . . penitencie] ubi est magis donum gracie, transgressor ibi maiori subiacebit pene O, *the reading shared by the other groups (with* maius
instead of magis *in groups* u, x, z).   **14** penitencie] pene O.   **15** delictum] peccata (*after*
illorum) M.W; peccatum (*after* illorum) R.   **44** multorum] plurimorum O.   **54** triginta]
tribus O.   **58** ubi] unde C.   **66** Quintum] tercium M.R; quartum W.   **70** est(2)] *om* O.
71 est] *om* O.   **72** demonibus] diabolis M; diabolus R.W.

With regard to sexual sins of the religious, which fall under incest, we should know that this sin is made more grievous for five reasons in particular. The first can be found in the fact that, as we read in Genesis 7, this was the cause of the Flood. If, as is written there, it displeased God so much that the sons of God took the daughters of men as their wives, how much must those fear to displease him who commit fornication with them! The second reason derives from the notion of apostasy. A person is called an "apostate" when he audaciously abandons his religious habit. But the virtue of chastity belongs more intimately to the religious life than the habit; therefore it is plain that abandoning chastity is much more grievous than abandoning one's habit. Hence it is said in Proverbs 6: "An apostate is an unprofitable man." The third aggravating factor is that, obviously, the devil tries very hard to bring a religious person to a fall, since he rejoices more over the fall of one religious than over that of many other people.

In *The Lives of the Fathers* we are told that a desert father saw only one devil sitting above the city gate, but an almost countless number on the monastery. When he asked, in God's name, for the reason, the devil replied: "The people of the city are almost all subject to me, and therefore few demons are needed to watch them. But in the monastery everyone is good, and therefore even a large number of demons can hardly prevail there." The same lesson is found in the story about the devil once holding chapter and punishing all the other demons for having done so little, although in two or three days they had caused wars, homicides, adultery, and other crimes; but when one demon finally reported that in thirty years he had just managed to lead one religious to fornication, the devil stepped down from his throne and placed that demon on it as being more worthy than himself.

The fourth reason for the sin's gravity is, as we read, that God punished sin that is committed in the cloister more severely. The first cloister was in heaven, where God himself was the abbot. As some inmates of that monastery revolted against him, they were condemned without hope of forgiveness. The second cloister was in the earthly paradise, from which Adam and Eve were expelled by God, the abbot of that place, because they had been disobedient and could not stay any longer but were condemned with all their offspring. The third cloister was the early Church, in which Peter was the abbot; those who wanted to hold possessions in it, like Simon Magus, died a sudden death; and the same happened to Ananias and Sapphira, in Acts 5.

The fifth reason which makes lechery among the religious more grievous is that, literally, the cloistered life is the life of angels, after the saying of Jerome: "To live in the flesh outside the flesh is not proper to human nature but to that of the angels." Therefore, a cloistered person is like an angel; Malachi 2: "He is the angel of the Lord." But if he is an angel, he is either a good or a bad one; if he is good, he is as the name indicates, an angel; if

VII.xi   SODOMIA

[f. 207] [Q]uinta et ultima species luxurie est illa diabolica contra
naturam, que sodoma dicitur. Quam horrore accepto transeo, aliis relinquens
exponendam.

Narrat autem expositor Virgilii quod cum Greci Yliam vastarent, idest
5   Troiam, quod illic invenerunt filiam Priami nomine Cassandram in templo
Minerve, cuius pulcritudine captus Ilax miles strenuus virginem [vi] oppressit. Propter quod factum Minerva dea pudicicie vindictam in illum talem
exercuit: Cum autem versus terram propriam rediret, commota sunt elementa
in mari et mare velocissime turbavit et de sublimi fulgura et chorusca-
10   ciones emisit, navemque contra rupem illisit, ita quod ipse cum omnibus
ibidem fulminatus interiit. Per istam Cassandram sub Iliace oppressam
intelligo ad literam mulierem quamcumque contra voluntatem Dei et Ecclesie
cum quocumque lecatore fornicariam. Per Minervam deam pudicicie Christum
intelligo. Quid ergo mirum si Christus vindictam excerceat in tales qui
15   eius preceptum contempnentes non tantum in simplicem fornicacionem set in
tam vile peccatum contra naturam abhominabile et innominandum se involvunt?
quasi dicat: nullum.

Expresse autem hanc figuram habemus Genesis 19 de Sodoma et Gomorra,
que sunt quinque civitates regionis illius. Igne et sulphure desuper caden-
20   tibus non tantum homines et animalia interfecerunt, imo aperiente terra os
suum omnes vivos absorbuit. Per quod certum est quod propter dictum peccatum in infernum eternaliter perierunt. In cuius indicium manifestissimum
usque in hodiernum diem ibidem manet mare mortuum, in quo nichil vivum
inmergi potest neque manere; et totum ex iusta vindicta in detestacionem
25   tanti peccati. Et ut dicitur libro *De naturis rerum* quod si lucerna accensa
in hoc mare proiciatur, supernatat nec mergi potest donec extin- [f. 207v]
guatur, in signum quod nichil vivum in luce gracie ad actum illum pro
quibus tanta vindicta facta est involvitur. Cuius eciam testimonium, ut
dicunt naturales et similiter plures moderni qui viderunt quod cum crescunt
30   in margine illius maris poma visu exterius pulcherrima, si in tempore matu-

he is bad, he is a devil. Therefore Jerome says: "A professed Christian monk
is either like an angel or like a devil."

4–5 Lev. 18.29.   **6–7** 1 Cor. 5.5.   **8–10** 2 Sam. 13.1–29.   **13–14** In Peraldus, *Summa
vitiorum* III.ii.8, attributed to "Gregorius" ("scientiae donum").   **21** Ecclus. 26.20.
24–25 Cf. Peraldus, *Summa vitiorum* III.ii.8.   **35** Cf. Gen. 6.2.   **41–42** Prov. 6.12.
64–65 Cf. Acts 8.9–24.   **65** Acts 5.1–11.   **67–68** Paschasius Radbertus, *Ep. ad
Paulam et Eustochium* 5 (PL 30:126).   **69** Mal. 2.7.   **71–72** Also in Peraldus, *Summa
vitiorum* III.ii.9.

VII.xi   SODOMY

The fifth and last branch of lechery is the diabolical sin against nature
called sodomy. I pass it over in horror and leave it to others to describe it.

The commentator on Virgil reports that when the Greeks were devastating
Ilion, that is, Troy, they found there the daughter of Priam, by the name of
Cassandra, in the temple of Minerva. The good knight Ajax was so overcome by
her beauty that he raped the maiden. For that deed Minerva, the goddess of
chastity, took the following revenge on him: when he was sailing back to his
homeland, she stirred up the elements on the sea and the sea itself violently
and sent lightning bolts and flashes from above, whereby she tossed the ship on
a rock so that he and all his companions perished in the tempest. This Cassandra raped by Ajax symbolizes any woman who engages in sex with any fornicator against the will of God and his Church. Minerva, the goddess of chastity,
stands for Christ. What wonder, then, if Christ takes vengeance on those who
scorn his commandment by getting involved, not just in simple fornication but
in that vile and abominable sin against nature that is not to be named? To be
sure, it is no wonder at all.

An explicit type of this occurs in Genesis 19, in Sodom and Gomorrha,
which are five cities of that region. Not only did fire and sulphur falling
from above kill people and animals, but the earth opened its mouth and swallowed all the living. Thus it is certain that on account of the said sin they
perished forever in hell. As an open sign the sea there remains dead even in
our days; no living being can submerge or remain in it; and it is all for just
revenge in horror of such a sin. As it is said in the book *On the Nature of
Things*, if a burning light is thrown into this sea, it floats on the surface
and cannot drown until it is put out, as a sign that nothing alive that is done
in the light of grace for those for whose sake such vengeance was taken is of
any use. And a further testimony, according to writers on natural history and
several moderns who have observed this with their own eyes, is that while the
apples that grow on the shore of that sea are most beautiful to look at, when
they are ripe and are cut open they give forth a sulphurous smoke and dusty

ritatis frangantur, fumum sulphureum et favillam terream emittunt. Revera
sic est de lecatoribus pessimis dictis fetiditatibus datis, qui quamvis
pulcritudinem exterius in corpore preferunt, sicut poma virida et pulcra,
quanto magis ad maturitatem etatis accedunt, tanto detestabiliorem favillam
35   ad modum sulphuris in concupiscenciis fetide ardentem emittunt. Unde Augustinus: "Tantum detestabatur Deus hoc vicium quod illud ante incarnacionem
videns in natura humana fieri, fere desiit incarnari." Et ideo cum noluit
cuiquam angelorum aut hominum execucionem huius pene committere, set sibi
ipsi vindictam illius reservavit, iuxta illud: "Michi vindictam, et ego
40   retribuam."

---

8 sunt] *om* O.   **19** que sunt] quasi scilicet M.W; quas et R.   **27** illum] illis O.   **35–**
36 Augustinus] secundum augustinum O.

VII.xii   LUXURIA EST DEO INIURIOSA

[M]odo ultimo videndum est quare Deum timentes vicium luxurie cum speciebus omnibus detestantur. Dicit enim Gregorius: "Cum, inquit, cetera
vicia tantum corpus maculant, hoc vicium solum corpus et animam fedat."
Detestantur ergo iuste propter quinque causas: primo quia Deo iniuriosum,
5   secundo quia angelis odiosum, tercio quia proprio subiecto perniciosum,
quarto quia nocet proximo, quinto quia obsequium diabolo.
Primum autem patet ex hoc quod homines huius seculi qui persone hono-
rabiliores reputantur magnum dedecus cernunt cum filie eorum fornicentur.
Quanto magis contumeliam faciunt regi celesti qui animam humanam, eius
10   filiam, fornicari compellunt, qui quasi templum Dei reputatur; Corinthiorum
3: "Nescitis quod templum Dei estis vos?" Et sequitur: "Qui ergo templum
Dei violaverit, disperdet illum Dominus." Et [f. 208] ideo Deus in humana
anima tamquam in templo glorificandus est. Set timeo, o Deus, iuxta illud
Psalmi quod "venerunt gentes in hereditatem tuam et polluerunt templum
15   sanctum tuum."
Narrat autem Seneca libro 6 *Declamacionum*, capitulo 8, quod antiquitus
lex erat talis quod mulieres in templo dee Veste ministrantes forent caste.
Set aliquando contigit quod una litterata earum scripsit talem versum:

Felices nupte, moriar quia nubere dulce.

20   [þat ys mery to be a wyfe.
Dye Y woll and lese my lyfe.]

ashes. The same applies to those evil lechers who are devoted to the aforementioned abhorrent sins: though they show great external beauty in their body, like green and beautiful apples, the riper they grow, the more they give forth a sickening ash in their lust that burns and smells like sulphur. Therefore, according to Augustine, "God hated this vice so much that, seeing it being committed by men before his incarnation, he almost refrained from becoming a man." And thus God did not want to entrust any angel or man with the execution of this punishment but kept its vengeance for himself, after the words: "Revenge is mine, and I will repay."

4–11 Servius on *Aeneidos* II.414.   **18–21** Gen. 19.1–25.   **25–28** Cf. Peraldus, *Summa vitiorum* III.ii.3.   **28–31** Josephus, *De bello Judaico* IV.8; Solinus, *Coll. rerum memorabilium* XXXV.8; Augustine, *De civ. Dei* XXI.v.1 (CC 48:765); and many other authors.   **36–37** In Peraldus, *Summa vitiorum* III.ii.3, attributed to "auctoritas."   **37–40** Innocent III, *De miseria* II.xxv.1 (p. 58).   **39–40** Rom. 12.19, quoting Deut. 32.35.

VII.xii   LECHERY IS OFFENSIVE TO GOD

Finally, we must see how those who fear God hate the sin of lechery with all its branches. Gregory says: "The other vices stain only the body [*read* soul?], but this one corrupts both body and soul." It is thus rightly hated for five reasons: because it offends God, is hateful to the angels, ruins the person who commits it, harms one's fellowman, and makes man obedient to the devil.

The first point is manifest in the fact that people of this world who are held to be very respectable find it greatly dishonorable when their daughters engage in fornication. How much greater dishonor, then, do those bring on the king of heaven who force the human soul to commit fornication, the soul who is God's daughter and, so to speak, is held to be his temple! Corinthians 3 asks: "Do you not know that you are the temple of God?" and continues: "But he who violates the temple of God, him the Lord will destroy." Therefore God should be glorified in the human soul as if in a temple. But, O God, I fear that, in the words of the Psalm, "the heathens are come into your inheritance, they have defiled your holy temple."

In book 6, chapter 8, of his *Declamations* Seneca reports that in ancient times there was a law that women who were ministering in the temple of the goddess Vesta had to be chaste. Sometime it happened that one of them who was educated wrote the following verse:

Happy are brides! I would die because marriage is sweet.

Quo percepto accusatur tamquam incesta, et hoc probatur in ipsa. Nam quia
ipsa nupcias affectat, predicat illas esse felices. Item in hoc quod dicit
"moriar," videtur illam affirmare eas consecuturas quas affectat. Item
25   queritur utrum iurat expertis nupciis vel inexpertis. Si primo, sequitur
quod est incesta. Si secundo, mendosa est, et per consequens ⟨indigna⟩
ministrare in templo tante dee. Secundum vero Ysidorum *Ethimologiarum*
libro 8, capitulo 11, ista dea Veste fuit ipsa terra, que variis vestita est
herbis, plantis, et arboribus, et ceteris huiusmodi. Et bene potest signi-
30   ficare naturam nostram terream, que transfertur in templum summum, idest in
celum, ubi deificatur in Christo. Et certe ista dea et domina non vult
habere ministros nisi castos. Quid ergo dicam de illis qu⟨i⟩ non tantum
cogitant in corde set eciam exprimunt ore quam dulce sit peccatum luxurie,
et tota die de illa materia feda locuntur? Vix enim est aliquis popularis
35   qui scit loqui aut tractare vel cantus insolentes ⟨componere⟩ nisi de illa
materia carnali. Quero ergo an tu qui dicis et cantas te velle desiderium
carnis habere, an dicis verum an non? Si verum, iuxta vocem Domini Matthei
5 iam mechatus es in corde tuo, et per consequens non es dignus ministrare
in templo Dei set omnino expellendus. Unde Apostolus Ad Ephesios 5: "Scito-
40   te intelligentes quoniam omnis fornicator aut inmundus aut avarus, quod est
ydolorum servitus, [f. 208v] non habebit hereditatem in regno Christi et
Dei." Si non dicis verum, tunc mentiris, quod est magnum dedecus et
peccatum, et maxime in viro perfecto, cuiusmodi est clericus cuiuscumque
ordinis, dignitatis, vel status. Et non solum mentiris, verum eciam alios
45   trahis ad peccatum tuo malo exemplo et verbis lascivis et inhonestis. Unde
Apostolus Corinthiorum 15 dicit: "Corrumpunt bonos mores colloquia mala,"
et per consequens a communione templi talis est expellendus.

---

4 Destestantur] detestatur O.   10 qui] que O.   14 et] *om* O.   20–21 þat . . . lyfe] *text
from* R. *Verse 53, in* B1.B2.Go1.Go2.L2.L3.LC.R.Sp.V.W1.   24 quas] quod O.
26 indigna] indignam C; indigit M; indiget W.   27 vero] autem O.   29 et] *om* O.
huiusmodi] *om* O.   30 summum] *om* O.   31 ubi] *add* quodammodo O.   dea et] *om* O.
32 qui] que C.   33 in] *om* O.   35 tractare] trufare O.   componere] tractare C.   36 car-
nali] *om* O.   et cantas] *om* O.   36–37 desiderium . . . habere] luxuriari O.   37 ve-
rum(2)] sic O.   37–38 vocem . . . 5] apostolum ephesiorum 5 O.   38 es . . . minis-
trare] ministrandus M.W; ministraturus R.   39–42 Unde . . . Dei] *om* O (*see preceding
sentence*).   42 dicis . . . mentiris] ergo mentitus es O.   42–43 est . . . peccatum] grave
peccatum O.   44 ordinis . . . status] condicionis O.   Et] item O.   45 tuo . . . inho-
nestis] et excitas O.   46 mala] prava O.   47 talis . . . expellendus] *om* O.

VII.xiii   LUXURIA EST ANGELIS ODIOSA

[S]ecundo luxuria est angelis odiosa. Quod probatur tali narracione:
Quidam clericus lubricus cum semel in theatro sedisset et diabolum coniu-

Merry it is to be a wife:
I would die and lose my life!

As this becomes known, she is accused of incest, and this is proven against her
as follows. She pronounces brides to be happy because she herself desires to
be married. Further, by saying "I would die" she seems to affirm that married
women obtain what she desires. And further, the question is raised whether she
is thus swearing from the experience of marriage or without such experience.
In the former case, it follows that she is incestuous. In the latter case, she
is a liar; consequently, in either case she is unworthy to minister in the
temple of the goddess. According to Isidore in his *Etymologies*, book 8, chapter 11, this goddess Vesta was earth herself, which is *vestita*, "clothed," with
different herbs, plants, trees, and so forth. She thus symbolizes our earthly
nature, which is taken into the highest temple, that is, to heaven, where it is
made godlike in Christ. Certainly, this goddess will have only chaste servants. What then shall I say of those who not only think in their heart but
pronounce with their mouth how sweet the sin of lechery is, and who engage all
day long in dirty talk on this subject? For hardly anyone enjoys popularity
unless he knows how to speak or jest or compose offensive songs on this subject. I ask then: you who are saying and singing that you want to make love to
a girl, do you mean it or not? If you do, then according to the Lord's word in
Matthew 5 you have already committed adultery in your heart, and consequently
you are not worthy to serve in God's temple but are altogether to be cast out.
Hence the Apostle says in Ephesians 5: "Know you this and understand, that no
fornicator, or unclean, or covetous person (which is a servant of idols) has
inheritance in the kingdom of Christ and of God." If you do not mean it, you
are lying, and that is a grave shame and sin, especially in a man of perfect
life, as a cleric should be of whatever order, rank, or status. In addition,
you are not only lying but you also draw others to sin with your bad example
and lewd and shameful words. Hence the Apostle says in Corinthians 15: "Evil
conversations corrupt good manners." And consequently you are to be expelled
from the communion of the temple.

2–3 Cf. 1 Cor. 6.18 and *Glossa ordinaria* on this verse; also Nicholas de Lyra (6:41v.G);
and Innocent III, *De miseria* II.xxi.1 (p. 55).   **11–12** 1 Cor. 3.16–17.   **14–15** Ps.
78.1.   **16–27** Seneca, *Declamationes* VI.8.   **27–29** Isidore, *Etym.* VIII.xi.61.
38 Matt. 5.28.   **39–42** Eph. 5.5.   **44** 1 Cor. 15.33.

VII.xiii   LECHERY IS HATEFUL TO ANGELS

In the second place, lechery is hateful to the angels. This is proven by
the following tale. Once a lecherous cleric was sitting inside his magic

rasset ut veniret et eius voluntatem perficeret, qui a longe stans respondit dicens: "Non possum pre fetore tue libidinis propius accedere. Set
5 cessa per triduum, et faciam quod placuerit tibi." Quo audito doluit ille
et vitam correxit. Sic ergo patet quod angelis malis est odiosum. Quod idem
patet de bonis angelis in illa narracione in *Vitas Patrum* de angelo corpora
mortuorum cum quodam sene sepeliente. Nec de fetore illorum horrebat sicut
senex, set transeunte quodam iuvene luxurioso, nares suas obturavit dicens
10 quod in centuplum plus fetebat coram Deo et angelis quam quodcumque aliud
cadaver corruptum. Set quod dolendum est, hunc fetorem ipsi luxuriosi non
senciunt, eo quod naturaliter inter fetentes fetor non sentitur. Unde illud
Ioelis: "Computruerunt iumenta in stercore suo." Unde dicit Gregorius: "Iumenta, inquit, in stercore putrescere est homines brutales in fetore luxu-
15 rie vitam finire." Unde Psalmista: "Disperierunt in Endor, facti sunt ut
stercus terre." Unde Gregorius: "Endor, inquit, est fons generacionis vel
oculus naturalis," et bene significat voluntatem humanam que operi carnali
et generacioni deservit, et non sequitur racionem set sensualitates. Et
ideo tales propter [f. 209] sui vilitatem bene compara⟨n⟩tur stercori
20 terre, etc.

---

1 odiosa] odiosum O.   4 propius] *om* M; proprius R.W.   11 fetorem] dolorem idest
fetorem M; dolorem R.W.   13 Unde] ut O.   16–17 vel . . . naturalis] *om* O.   17 voluntatem humanam] naturam O.   18–20 et(2) . . . etc.] cui comparatur propter sui vilitatem
(utilitatem M.W) O.   19 comparantur] comparatur C.

VII.xiv   LUXURIA EST PROPRIO SUBIECTO PERNICIOSA

[T]ercio est illud peccatum detestabile quia est proprio subiecto
perniciosum. Et hoc satis probatur in hoc quod sibi aufert tam bona temporalia quam et spiritualia, super tollit seipsum et seculi honorem. De bonis
temporalibus patet Luce 15 de filio prodigo, de quo supra parte 1, capitulo
5 6. De illo eciam legitur quomodo luxuriose bona sua dissipavit et post pre
fame porcos pascebat. Unde Augustinus *De civitate Dei* libro 3, capitulo 5:
"Hec, inquit, fercula appellantur, quorum celebratur convivium quo velud
su[i]s epulis demonia inmunda pascebantur." Nam luxuriosus fit magnum
ferculum demonibus quo ipsi pascuntur. De bonis eciam spiritualibus patet
10 per hoc quod dicitur Proverbiorum ⟨2⟩9: "Qui nutrit scortum, perdit substanciam," scilicet spiritualem, idest celum. Quod eciam tollit homini seipsum patet Osee 9: "Fornicacio, vinum, et ebrietas auferunt cor." Amans
enim amore fatuo non habet cor suum, set ipsum frequenter amittit. Propter
ergo huiusmodi amorem, ut patet Regum 12, Amon interfectus est quia corru-

circle and conjured the devil to come and do his will. But the devil stood far
off and said: "I cannot come any closer because of the stench of your lust.
But stop for three days and I will do what you please." When the cleric heard
this, he experienced great grief and amended his life. Thus we see how hateful
this sin is to evil angels. The same can be seen to be true of good angels in
the tale from from *The Lives of the Fathers* in which an angel was burying
bodies of the dead with a desert father. The angel was not as much stunned by
their stench as the desert father was; but when a lecherous young man walked
by, he stopped his nose saying that he stank a hundred times worse before God
and his angels than any decomposing corpse. But it is to be feared that
lechers themselves cannot smell this stench, because it is natural that an evil
smell is not felt among people who produce it. Hence the words of Joel: "The
beasts have rotted in their dung." On which Gregory comments: "Beasts rotting
in their dung signify bestial people who end their life in the stench of
lechery." Hence the Psalmist: "They perished at Endor, they became like dung
of the earth." And Gregory comments: "Endor means 'the fountain of procreation' or 'the natural eye,' " and signifies man's will that is busy about the
work of the flesh and of procreation and does not follow reason but its
sensual pleasure. Therefore, such people are, on account of their baseness,
compared to the dung of the land.

2–6 Tubach 956 (description not exact).   **7–11** Tubach 2559.   **13** Joel 1.17.   **13–
15** Gregory, *In Evangelia*, hom. 31, 5 (PL 76:1229).   **15–16** Ps. 82.11.   **16–18** Also in
Peraldus, *Summa vitiorum* III.i.3, following a quotation from Gregory.

VII.xiv   LECHERY IS HARMFUL TO THE PERSON WHO
COMMITS IT

In the third place, this sin is to be detested because it ruins the person
who commits it. This is shown sufficiently in that it robs him of his temporal
as well as spiritual possessions; but above all it deprives him of himself and
of his worldly honor. The loss of temporal possessions is shown in the Prodigal Son of Luke 15 (see above, part 1, chapter 6), of whom we read that in his
loose living he wasted his goods and then for hunger herded the swine. In book
3, chapter 5, of *The City of God* Augustine comments as follows: "These are
called 'dishes' because a banquet is given whose food, as it were, nourishes
unclean demons." For a lecher becomes a great dish for demons, who feed on
him. The loss of spiritual goods is shown in the words of Proverbs 29: "He
who maintains a harlot squanders away his substance," that is, his spiritual
possession, namely heaven. That this sin further deprives a man of himself is
shown in Hosea 9: "Fornication, wine, and drunkenness take away the heart."

15   pit Thamar, sororem suam. Unde Ieronimus: "Cotidie, inquit, sanguis mecho-
     rum funditur et adulteria dampnantur." Quod eciam mundi honorem aufert
     homini patet Genesis 49 de Ruben primogenito Iacob, qui prior in donis et
     maior imperio esse debuerat. Cui tamen dixit pater eius Iacob: "Non cres-
     cas, quia ascendisti cubile patris tui et maculasti stratum eius."
20   De vindicta ergo illius peccati narratur, et a multis testificatur, de
     quodam luxurioso qui in festivitate Omnium Sanctorum cum sua concubina
     iacens opus illud execrabile perpetravit. Cum ergo illa de solempnitate
     festi ipsum premunisset, ipse cum magna protervia respondit: "Quid ad
     sanctos de me? Propter eos non dimittam." Et ecce, vindicta ante finem
25   illius operis ambo a diabolo suffocati sunt. In crastino autem a vicinis
     inventi sunt insimul [f. 209v] coniuncti ut canes horribiles et fetentes,
     quibus nemo pre fetore poterat appropinquare. Ligabant ergo pedes eorum ad
     caudas equorum et extracti sunt extra villam et proiecti in quandam foveam
     fetidam et ibidem dimissi, ubi quasi in momento igne infernali consumpti
30   sunt.

---

3 et] eciam M.R; *om* W.   4 quo] *add* nota O.   10 29] 19 C.   22 perpetravit] impetravit
O.   25 autem] *om* O.   26 ut] quasi O.   28 extra villam] *om* O.   et] eciam O.   28–
29 proiecti . . . ibidem] in quadam fovea fetida O.

VII.xv   LUXURIA PROXIMO NOCET

     [Q]uarto est illud vicium detestabile quia nocet proximo. Quod vero
     patet [primo] per hoc quod qui datur huic vicio, nullam fidem quasi servat,
     sicut patet Regum de David et Uria; similiter Regum 12 de Amon et Thamar
     sorore sua. Similiter ex hoc patet quod pluribus aufert hereditatem suam,
5   sicut patet de filio prodigo, Luce 15, de quo nota supra. Et ideo Eccle-
     siastici 23 dicitur: "Omnis mulier relinquens virum suum peccabit, statuens
     heredem ex alieno matrimonio." Et ideo Deuteronomii 23 dicitur hoc modo
     pro talibus: "Si puella desponderit viro et invenerit eam ⟨aliquis⟩ in civitate
     et concubuerit cum ea, secundum legem uterque educetur extra civitatem et
10   lapidibus obruetur: puella, quia non clama[vi]t quia erat in civitate; et
     vir, quia violavit uxorem proximi sui." Spiritualiter hec puella virgo
     desponsata est anima viri vel mulieris voto continencie Christo copulata.
     Adulter autem est caro nostra, que continue sollicitat corpus ad peccatum.
     Si ergo homo sibi assenserit et ad Deum non clamaverit, ad portam civita-
15   tis, idest ad locum iudicii finalis, per quam omnes egredientur, lapidibus

For a man who is foolishly in love does not possess his own heart but frequently loses it. On account of such love, as is shown in Kings 12, Amnon was
killed because he lay with his sister Tamar. Whence Jerome says: "Every day
the blood of adulterers is shed and adultery is condemned." Finally, that this
sin deprives a man of worldly honor is seen in Genesis 49 in Ruben, the firstborn of Jacob, who ought to have been the first in gifts and command. But his
father Jacob said to him: "You shall not grow because you went up to your
father's bed and defiled his couch."

With respect to the vengeance that befalls this sin, there is the report,
witnessed by many people, of a lecher who committed this revolting deed with
his concubine on the feast of All Saints. When she warned him that it was a
very solemn feast day, he answered her with great impudence: "What do I have
to do with the saints? I'll certainly not give it up for their sake." But lo,
in punishment they were both strangled by the devil before completing the act;
and on the following day they were found by their neighbors joined together
like a couple of dogs, horrible to see and to smell, and nobody could go near
them for the stench. Then the neighbors tied their feet to the tails of
horses, and they were pulled out of their village and cast into a dirty pit and
left there, where they were immediately consumed by fire from hell.

4–5 *FM* I.ix.   **7–8** Augustine, *De civitate Dei* II.4 (CC 47:37).   **10–11** Prov. 29.3.
12 Hos. 4.11.   **14–15** 2 Sam. 13.1–29.   **15–16** Also in Peraldus, *Summa vitiorum*
III.i.2.   **17–19** Gen. 49.4.   **20–30** Tubach 155.

VII.xv   LECHERY IS HARMFUL TO ONE'S NEIGHBOR

In the fourth place, this vice is to be detested because it harms one's
fellow man. This is shown, first, by the fact that he who engages in this vice
hardly ever keeps faith, as we can see in David and Uriah, in the Book of
Kings; and in Amnon and his sister Tamar, in Kings 12. Likewise, the vice robs
many of their inheritance, as was the case with the Prodigal Son of Luke 15;
see above. Therefore it is said in Ecclesiasticus 23: "Every woman that
leaves her husband commits sin, because she brings an heir from another marriage." And in Deuteronomy 23 it is decreed, with respect to such sinners:
"If a girl is married to a man and someone finds her in the city and lies with
her, according to the Law both shall be brought outside the city and be stoned
to death: the girl because she did not cry out, though she was inside the city,
and the man because he violated his neighbor's wife." In spiritual allegory,
this betrothed maiden is the soul of a man or a woman who is married to Christ
by a vow of continence. The adulterer is our flesh, which constantly urges the
body to sin. If, then, a person yields to it and does not cry to God for help,

obru⟨etur⟩ una cum carne sua. Et ideo, si velis iuvari, clama, quia dicit
Psalmista: "Ad Dominum cum tribularer clamavi," etc.

---

7 heredem] hereditatem O.   8 aliquis] cum aliquo C.   10 obruetur] obruentur O.
16 obruetur] obruentur C.   17 etc.] *om* O.

VII.xvi   LUXURIA EST OBSEQUIUM DIABOLO

[Q]uinto est luxuria detestanda quia obsequium est diabolo. Et hoc
patet per hoc quod legitur in quadam glossa super Leviticum ubi dicitur
quod cum demones de omni peccato gaudent, precipue tamen gaudent de forni-
cacione et ydolatria, [f. 210] quia in illis tam corpus quam anima macula-
5   tur, et diabolus habet ibi forum vilissimum, quia pro momentanea quasi
delectacione lucratur binos et binos semper. Unde sicut gaudet mercator
quando cum uno denario lucratur quatuor, [sic diabolus] quando cum una
delectacione vel uno genere peccati, scilicet luxuria, lucratur plures
animas. Et nota quod cetera peccata quasi hami sunt diaboli, set hoc peccatum
10 est magnum suum rethe, cum quo piscatur clerum cum populo, pauperem cum
divite, iuvenem cum sene, dominum cum servo, dominam cum ancilla, matrem cum filia; unde Abacuc 1 dicitur: "Totum in hamo suo levabit et in rethe
congregavit."
Nota eciam quod diabolus ut hominem alliciat ad hoc peccatum, facit ad
15 modum fabri. Qui cum non potest ducere ferrum ad libitum, ad ignem ponit et
fortiter sufflat. Sic diabolus quando non potest hominem ducere ad libitum
suum, primo accendit ⟨circa⟩ illum ignem voluptatis, et hoc quatuor modis:
primo flatu oris, idest propria suggestione; secundo flatu follium, idest
suggestione ve⟨tul⟩arum, ut patet supra, capitulo 3; tercio per apposicio-
20 nem pinguedinis, idest gulositatis et ebrietatis; et quarto per vicinitatem
alterius ignis, quia sicut domus combusta accendit aliam, sic voluptas
unius voluptatem alterius. Quibus accensis ducit eos ad libitum, et cum
malleolis suggestionum diversarum super incudem cordis indurati et obstina-
ti format de illis quicquid placet, quia modo luxuriam, modo gulam, modo
25 accidiam, modo invidiam. Set tandem apertissime eosdem deludendo decipiet.
Et ideo, ut michi videtur, est ad litteram de diabolo homines seducen-
te sicut antiquitus sole[ba]t esse de gobelino. Antiquitus autem pluries
audivi quod homines qui solebant ire de nocte pro amasiis suis habendis [f.
210v] et aliis voluptatibus complendis, quod ut pluries accidit casus iste:
30 Quando vero inceperunt iter suum versus aliquem locum precogitatum, quod
quasi subito quadam acrisia seducti circuierunt erratice per totam noctem

the soul will be stoned to death together with her flesh, at the gate of the
city, that is, in the place of the Last Judgment, through which all men will
pass. Thus, if you want to receive help, cry out; for the Psalmist says: "In
my trouble I cried to the Lord."

---

3 2 Sam. 11.   **3–4** 2 Sam. 13.1–29.   **5** Luke 15.11–32; cf. *FM* VII.xiv.4.   **6–7** Ecclus. 23.32.   **8–11** Deut. 22.23–24.   **17** Ps. 119.1.

VII.xvi   LECHERY RENDERS SERVICE TO THE DEVIL

In the fifth place, lechery is to be detested because it renders service
to the devil. This is proven by a gloss on Leviticus which declares that while
the demons rejoice at any sin, they are particularly happy over fornication and
idolatry, because in these sins both body and soul are stained; and in this sin
the devil does his vile business best because for a little passing delight he
always gains two souls at once. As a merchant is happy when he can make a
profit of four dollars out of one, so can the devil win several souls with one
moment of pleasure or with a single type of sin, namely lechery. Notice also
that other sins are like the devil's fishhooks, but this one is a big net, with
which he catches cleric and layman, poor and rich, young and old, master and
servant, lady and maid, mother and daughter; hence it is said in Habakkuk 1:
"He will lift them all up with his hook and will gather them into his net."
    Notice also that in order to lure a person to this sin, the devil acts
like a blacksmith. Since the latter cannot shape iron at will, he puts it in
the fire and blows on it hard. In the same way, when the devil cannot lead a
person after his will, he first lights the fire of lust around him, and this in
four ways: first, by blowing with his mouth, that is, by the stirrings from
that person's own flesh; second, by puffing his bellows, that is, by the
allurements of go-betweens, as we saw earlier in chapter 3; third, by putting
some rich fuel in the fire, namely that of gluttony and drunkenness; and
fourth, by placing a second fire near it, because just as one house that is in
flames sets another one on fire, so does the lust of one person stir that of
another. And when the devil has thus set them on fire, he can bend them at his
will, and striking with the hammers of different suggestions on the anvil of
their hardened and obstinate heart he shapes them to whatever form he pleases:
now into lechery, now into gluttony, now into sloth, and now into envy. And
finally he deceives them quite openly.
    Therefore, it seems to me that when the devil seduces a person he acts
literally as the goblin did in former times. For in the past I have often
heard that the following frequently happened to men who used to go at night to
see their lovers and gratify other desires. When they set out on their way to

aliquod nemus vel manerium, semper credentes in recto itinere transire.
(Est autem acrisia quedam species ⟨cecuciei⟩, qua scilicet homo credit
videre quod non videt, idest unam rem pro alia.) Set tandem lucescente
35   aurora diei perceperunt se nichil proficisse in via quam principaliter
intendebant. Unde cum sic quasi attoniti et cogitativi considera[ba]nt se
esse delusos, ⟨audierunt⟩ iuxta se quendam strepitum acsi esset derisio
cuiusdam invisibilis, qui secundum aliquos est quidam demon qui vulgariter
dicitur *Gobelyn*. Revera sic est in proposito. Nox enim illa [in] qua plures
40   vadunt est vita carnalis, scilicet accidie, gule, luxurie, ad quam plures
per cautelas diaboli deducuntur. Cum ergo hanc viam ceperit homo, statim
recedit a Deo, qui est verus sol et dies claritatis et mundicie. Quod
videns diabolus, statim se exhibet ductorem illius ducens illum in giro,
modo ad gulam, modo ad luxuriam, modo ad periuria, modo ad homicidia,
45   modo ad ⟨cetera⟩ vicia que ex carnali voluptate generantur, iuxta illud Psalmi:
"In circuitu impii ambulant." Et sic facit eos vagari modo predicto quousque totam noctem istius tenebrose vite consummaverunt. Cum ergo tunc quasi
subito aparu[er]it aurora, que est tempus iudicii, quod erit quasi aurora
vite eterne, tunc primo audient iuxta se diabolum qui eos decepit aperte
50   ipsos deridentem; Ecclesiastici 12: "Tanquam pueris dedisti iudicium in
derisum."
     In quo quidem iudicio circumquaque op- [f. 211] probria et comminacio-
nes durissimas cernent anime misere sic seducte. Nam primo ante eas audient
voces angelorum clamancium et dicencium: "Surgite, mortui, venite ad iudi-
55   cium." Secundo a tergo audient propria facta clamancia: "Curramus et accu-
semus eius flagicium." Tercio audient clamorem proprie consciencie dicentis: "Feram contra te testimonium." Quarto a dextris audient strepitus demonum insultancium et horribiliter clamancium: "Vendicemus servos nostros."
Quinto a sinistris audient clamorem electorum dicencium: "Iuste iudex,
60   vindica te in tuos contemptores," quia iuxta illud [Psalmi]: "Letabitur
iustus cum viderit vindictam." Sexto subtus se audient infernum bullientem
clamantem et dicentem: "Descendite, o miseri, quia hic finaliter volutabi-
mini in pena." Septimo et ultimo supra se audient vocem iudicis irati dicentis: "Ite maledicti in ignem eternum." Clamores quos audient patent in
65   hiis versibus:

         Surgite defuncti, modo iudicis ira patebit;
             [iste est clamor angelorum ante.]
         Iam cernent cuncti tua facta nilque latebit;
             [iste est peccatorum retro.]
70   Conscia sum puncti minimi, nil teste carebit;
             [iste est proprie consciencie intra.]
         Tu michi servisti, meus es, dabo quod meruisti;
             [iste erit demonum a dextris.]

some assigned place, they wandered all night long in a circle around a grove or
a manor house as if suddenly led astray by some illusion, thinking all the time
they were proceeding on a straight path. (An illusion is a kind of blindness,
in which one believes one sees something one does not really see, that is, one
object instead of another.) But when at last dawn came, they realized that
they had made no progress on the way they originally planned to go. And as in
their astonishment and wonder they reflected that they were being deceived,
they would hear a noise close by that sounded like the laughter of some invisible being. According to some, this is a demon popularly called Goblin. All
this applies to the moral life. The night in which many people walk is their
carnal way of life, namely the way of sloth, gluttony, and lechery, into which
many people are led by the tricks of the devil. For when a man sets out on
this way, he at once abandons God, who is the true sun and the day of brightness and purity. When the devil sees this, he immediately offers himself as a
guide to such a person, leading him around in a circle, now to gluttony, then
to lechery, to perjury, to manslaughter, and to the other sins that spring from
fleshly lust, after the words of the Psalm: "The wicked walk round about."
And in this fashion he causes them to wander about in the said manner, until
they have spent the whole night of their shady life. And when suddenly dawn
breaks, that is, the time of judgment, which is the dawn of eternal life, only
then will they for the first time hear the devil close by laugh at them openly,
who has deceived them; Ecclesiasticus 12: "As to children you have given a
judgment to mock them."

   In that judgment, the wretched souls that have been thus seduced will
encounter the most severe reproaches and threats all around them. First, they
will hear before them the voices of angels who cry out: "Rise, you dead, and
come to your judgment." Second, from behind they will hear their own deeds
calling out: "Let us run and present his vile deeds." Third, they will hear
the cry of their own conscience: "I shall give witness against you." Fourth,
on their right they will hear the shouting of demons that hurl insults and
dreadful cries: "Let us lay claim on our own servants." Fifth, on the left
they will hear the call of the elect: "Rightful judge, take vengeance on those
that have scorned you"; for according to the words of the Psalm, "The just
shall rejoice when he sees the revenge." Sixth, below them they will hear hell
boiling and crying out: "Come down, wretches, for here you shall toss forever
in your pain." Seventh and last, above them they will hear the voice of their
angry judge saying: "You cursed ones, go into the eternal fire." These voices
that they will hear are listed in the following verses:

> Rise, O dead, for now the judge's wrath will show
> —this is the cry of the angels before us.
> Now all will see your deeds and nothing will be hidden
> —this of our sins behind us.

O Deus, hec signa tua puniat ulcio digna;
75   [iste erit sanctorum a sinistris.]
Hos, horrende chaos, ostende, vorare reos hos;
          [iste erit inferni subtus.]
O maledict⟨a⟩ cohors, sit semper in igne tibi sors!
          [ista erit vox iudicis superius.]

80   Unde pro omnibus istis dicitur illud Matthei 24: "Mittet angelos suos cum
tuba magna," scilicet in testimonium contra malos, "et eos congregabit a
quatuor ventis," scilicet ad dictas comminaciones et iudicium audiendum. Et
sic miser peccator exiit condempnatus, et "diabolus stet a dextris eius,"
ut dicit Psalmista.
85   Merito ergo est hoc peccatum detestandum ex quo sequitur tale et
tantum supplicium. Luxuria eciam [f. 211v] facit homini multa mala que in
hiis verbis continentur:

Corpus debilitat, animas et corpora fedat.
Et carnem frangit ciciusque senescere cogit.
90   Famam tollit, opes, animam, vim, lumina, vocem.
Polluit, adnichilat, necat, eripit, orbat, acerbat.

Et hec de luxuria ad presens sufficiunt.

---

1 est] prestat M; *om* R.W.   **7** quatuor] decem O.   sic diabolus] *om* C; *longer om* W.
quando] *om* O.   **8** delectacione . . . lucratur] voluptate M.R; *longer om* W.   **9–10** pec-
catum] *om* O.   **10** suum] *om* O.   **11** dominum . . . servo] *om* O.   **17** circa] supra C.
19 vetularum] vestiarum C.   **23** malleolis] martellis O.   **25** eosdem] eos O.   **27** autem]
enim O.   pluries] puerulus M; puerilus R; parvilis W; *add* ut O.   **28** quod] de M; qui R.
homines] hominibus O.   habendis] querendis O.   **30** vero] enim O.   **33** cecuciei] cecita-
tis acuciei C.   **35** perceperunt] perpendebat M; perpendebant R.W.   proficisse] per-
fecisse O.   **37** audierunt] et audiebant C.   **45** cetera] certa C.   **47** istius] *om* M.R; et
W.   **53** eas] eos O.   **55** curramus] currite O.   **67–79** iste . . . superius] *Evidently in the*
archetype the glosses (i.e, lines beginning with iste *or* ista) *were written next to the re-*
spective hexameters. This arrangement is preserved in M.   **68** cernent] cernunt O.
76 Hos] os M; *line om* W.   **78** maledicta] maledicte C; maledicti W.   **81** tuba] *add* et
voce O.   **83** sic] cum M.W; tunc R.   miser peccator] miseri anima M.W; misera anima
R.   condempnatus] condempnata O.   et] iuxta illud psalmi O.   **84** ut dicit Psalmista] *om*
O.   **85–91** ex quo . . . acerbat] quod tot mala requirit O.—*The additional material also*
occurs in group z and E. Line 3 of the verses should probably read: Famam tollit, opes,
sensum furiosa libido. Femina corpus, opes, animam, vim, lumina, vocem.   **92** Et] *om*
O.   ad presens] *om* O.

Conscious I am of my least deed, no witness is wanting
—this of our conscience within us.
You've served me well, now you are mine, I give what you've earned
—this of the devils on the right.
O God, let your just vengeance punish now these faults
—this of the saints to the left.
Open your mouth, O horrible hell, to swallow these sinners
—this of hell below.
O cursed cohort, your fate shall be in fire forever
—and this the voice of the judge above us.

To all these voices relate the words of Matthew 24: "He shall send his angels with a great trumpet," that is, in witness against them, "and he shall gather them from the four winds," that is, to hear the threats I have mentioned as well as their judgment. And thus the wretched soul leaves condemned, and after the words of the Psalmist, "the devil shall stand at her right hand."

Thus, this sin which leads to so much pain deserves indeed to be detested. In addition, lechery causes man many other injuries, which are listed in the following verses:

It weakens the body, and further it dirties both body and soul.
It breaks our flesh and renders us old before our time.
It robs good name, our wealth, soul, strength, eyesight, and voice,
And stains, wipes out, kills, wastes, deprives, and roughens them.

And this much suffices about lechery for now.

2–4 Peraldus, *Summa vitiorum* III.i.2 ("glossa super Lucam"). **12–13** Hab. 1.15.
19 *FM* VII.vi.39–93. **46** Ps. 11.9. **50–51** Wisd. 12.25. **52–84** The six points from which voices come at the Last Judgment form a widespread commonplace in meditative literature; see, for example, Anselm, *Meditatio 1* (3:78–79). For English metrical versions see Carleton Brown and Rossell Hope Robbins, eds., *The Index of Middle English Verse* (New York, 1943), items 2500 and 3218. **60–61** Ps. 57.11. **80–82** Matt. 24.31. **83** Ps. 108.6.

VII.xvii   DE CASTITATE

[C]ontra autem hoc vicium cum suis miseriis atque membris se offert
domina Castitas sive Continencia tamquam illius contraria et expugnatrix ad
modum quo pugil in duello socium aggreditur, nec mutilando, excecando,
occidendo dimittit donec illud verbum odiosum, scilicet "reddo me crimino-
5   sum," Gallice ⟨c⟩reaunt, dixerit. Sic continencia luxuriam aggreditur et
devincit. De qua sic intendo procedere: primo, quid sit et cui comparatur;
secundo, a quibus et quomodo adquiritur; tercio, de eius effectu et quomodo
terminatur.

Est autem continencia contra carnis voluptatem racionis frena et mode-
10   rata dominacio. Que eciam secundum Macrobium libro 1 est virtus reprimens
motus illicitos ad carnalem concupiscenciam. Cuius natura est, prout virtus
dicitur, nichil appetere quod legem moderacionis videtur excedere, set sub
iugo racionis cupiditatem carnis domare et eius concupiscenciam superare.
Nam secundum commentatorem 7 *Ethicorum*, qui superat concupiscencias
15   continens est, et qui superatur ab eis incontinens dicitur.

[C]omparatur autem bene hec virtus cuidam herbe que dicitur agnus castus. De qua dicit Albertus *De vegitabilibus*, libro 6, capitulo 5, quod ipsa
in estate floret, folia eciam et fructus producit, atque gaudet radice et
succo. Unde secundum eum tale nomen portat eo quod eius folia et fructus
20   [f. 212] et flores efficacissima sunt ad conservandam castitatem et continenciam, que si sparsa fuit in domibus vel in lectis, eundem effectum habent et retinent. Unde si moraliter de hac herba loqui velimus, ⟨l⟩ignum
crucis dominice bene dici potest. Cuius fructus est agnus castus et inmacu-
latus, Iesus Christus, de quo dicitur Trenorum 11: "Ego quasi agnus qui
25   portatur ad victimam." Cuius folia sunt eius dulcia verba in cruce, de
quibus supra parte 3, capitulo 13, vel dira vulnera et cicatrices. Set
fructus eius gracie et beatitudin⟨e⟩s. Que omnia, si in domibus animarum
nostrarum aut earum lectulis et cubiculis fuerint aspersa et continue per
iugem devocionem observata, puram continenciam ibi nutrire non deficient.
30   Et sicut antiquitus sacerdotes et virgines deo consecrate virtute illius
herbe concupiscencias superabant pudiciciam observando, sic nos virtute
ligni sancte crucis diabolum inimicum continue precipuuum devincemus.
Unde Ysaie dicitur: "Emitte agnum, Domine, dominatorem terre," etc.

Comparatur eciam continencia flori lilii propter eius puritatem; Can-
35   ticorum: "Sicut lilium inter spinas, sic amica mea inter filias." Et nota
quod bene lilio comparatur. Nam natura lilii est quod cum integra manet et
non fracta, odorem suavissimum diffundit, set fracta et attrita qualiter-
cumque fetorem pessimum emittit. Revera sic virginitas integre conservata
Deo et angelis fit placens et odorifera, set per voluptates contrita et
40   fracta pessime fetet et olet, sicut supra capitulo proximo de angelo et

VII.xvii   THE VIRTUE OF CHASTITY

Against this vice and its wickedness, Lady Chastity or Continence presents herself as its opponent and uprooter. Just as a champion in individual combat attacks his opponent and does not desist from trying to cut him to pieces, blind him, and kill him until he speaks that hateful word "I surrender"—*creaunt* in French—, so does continence attack and overcome lechery. I intend to discuss continence as follows: first, what it is and to what things it can be compared; second, by whom and how it may be acquired; and third, what its effects are and to what rewards it leads.

Continence is the bridle and measured rule of reason over the lust of the flesh. And further, according to Macrobius in book 1, it is the virtue that represses illicit stirrings to fleshly lust. Insofar as continence is a virtue, its character is not to desire anything that may go beyond the rule of moderation, but to control the fleshly appetite under the yoke of reason and to overcome the concupiscence of the flesh. For according to the commentator on book 7 of the *Nicomachean Ethics*, he who rules his base desires is continent, whereas he who is ruled by them is called incontinent.

This virtue can be compared to a herb called *agnus castus*, "tutsan" or "Saint John's wort." In his work *On Plants*, book 6, chapter 5, Albertus writes that this herb blossoms in summer, brings forth leaves and fruit, and delights in its root and juice. According to that author, it has that name because its leaves, fruit, and blossoms are most efficacious in preserving chastity and continence; even if they are strewn over the house or beds, they retain their effectiveness. If we want to interpret this herb morally, it may easily stand for the wood of the Lord's cross, whose fruit is *agnus castus*, the chaste and immaculate lamb, Jesus Christ, of whom is said in Lamentations 11: "I am as a lamb that is carried to be a victim." Its leaves are his gentle words on the cross, of which see above, part 3, chapter 13; or else his wounds and scars. But its fruit are his graces and blessings. If all these are sprinkled in the dwellings of our souls and their beds and couches and are constantly kept in mind through true devotion, they will not fail to nourish purity and continence in us. Just as in ancient times priests and virgins who were consecrated to their god used this herb to rule over their base desires and preserve their chasteness, so shall we always overcome our enemy, the devil, especially by virtue of the wood of the holy cross. Hence Isaiah says: "Send forth, O Lord, the lamb, the ruler of the earth," etc.

Continence can also be compared to the lily on account of its purity; Canticles 2: "As the lily among thorns, so is my love among the daughters." This comparison is very fitting, for by its nature the lily spreads a very sweet smell as long as it remains fresh and unbroken, but when it is broken and crushed in any way, it smells very bad. In the same fashion, unspoiled vir-

sene probatum est corpora sepeliendo. Et Ecclesiastici 34 dicitur: "Quasi
lilium date odorem." Set nota quod istud lilium [f. 212v] dicitur esse
"inter spinas," scilicet quando aliquis vel aliqua ⟨continens⟩ inter carnales peccatores commoratur. Videmus enim in arbore spinosa folia pulcra et
45 flores, et tamen occulte spine acutissime pungentes. Sic certe contingit in
istis lubricis. Ipsi enim ostendunt verba suavia et levia ad decipiendum,
set sub illis acutissime peccatorum punctiones ponuntur, ex quibus folia
lilii castitatis lacerantur.
      Et nota quod in lilio sex sunt folia candida, sex virtutes designancia
50 que virginitatem custodiunt illibatam. De quibus tres tangere sufficit,
scilicet honestas in loquendo, sobrietas in vescendo, raritas in ludendo.
Primum igitur folium lacerat loquacitas feditati adiuncta, de qua nota
supra, capitulo 2, et parte 1, capitulo 3. De qua ait Seneca: "A verbis
enim turpibus abstinete, quia licencia inpudiciciam ⟨nutrit⟩." Et Proverbi-
55 orum 7: "Ecce mulier occurrit ei ornatu meretricio, preparata ad capiendas
animas, garrula et vaga." Secundum folium est sobrietas. Inpossibile autem
est castitatem inveniri ubi regnat ebrietas, quia Proverbiorum 28 dicitur:
"Luxuriosa res est vinum." Et Ad Ephesios: "Nolite inebriari vino in quo
est luxuria," supple causaliter. Tercium folium est raritas in l⟨ud⟩endo,
60 hoc est, subtractio sufficiens ab istis ludis levibus et dissolutis. Exemplum Genesis 34 de Dyna, filia Iacob, que cum egrederetur "ut videret mulieres regionis illius," corupta est a filio Emor, Sychem. Et illud folium
similiter lacerat dissolutus modus cantandi et ludendi; Corinthiorum 15:
"Corrumpunt bonos mores colloquia prava."
65   Et ideo certe quia virginitas inter huiusmodi spinas crescit, de
facili leditur. Que tamen in seculo nimis habundant, quia revera iste
vacantes cornuum, caudarum, et [f. 213] aliarum vestium mulierum sunt
maxime cause libidinis. Et tamen secundum modum patrie mulier honeste indui potest sine peccato, nec ex hoc est reprehensibilis nisi in quantum super-
70 fluitas et causa mali superhabundare videtur. Dicitur enim de Beata Virgine
quod inter cetera opera puritatis quod ita raro loquebatur quod non invenitur in Evangelio ipsam nisi quatuor personis locutam fuisse, scilicet cum
filio, cum angelo, cum Elizabeth, et in nupciis cum Iohanne et ministris.
Sic pro virginitate servanda debemus loqui, primo cum Filio in oratione;
75 cum angelo, idest sacerdote, in confessione; cum Elyzabeth, idest sancta
muliere, in consolacione; et cum Dei ministris in postulacione. Unde ait
Augustinus: "Omnes, inquit, puellas et virgines equaliter ignora aut equaliter dilige, et vide ne sub eodem tecto cum muliere manseris, nec in pris-
tina castitate confidas." "Quia (dicit ipse) [ubi] cum mulieribus ⟨verius⟩
80 tabernaculi est cohabitacio, non facile tolitur peccati delectacio." Et
ponit exemplum: "Adamas, inquit, inter mallium et ferrum non frangitur, et
tamen hircino sanguine dissipatur. Sic (dicit ipse) vir aut mulier fortis,

ginity is pleasing and sweet-smelling to God and his angels; but when it has
been crushed and broken by lust, it has a terrible stench, as was proven
earlier, in the preceding chapter, in the tale about the angel and the desert
father who were burying the dead. And thus it is said in Ecclesiasticus 34:
"Yield a smell as the lily." But notice that this lily is said to be "among
thorns," namely when a continent man or woman lives among people involved
in sins of the flesh. On a thorn bush we see beautiful leaves and flowers, yet
underneath sharp pricking thorns are hidden. This is certainly the case in
people who are given to lechery; they offer sweet and light words which deceive, but underneath are the sharp pricks of their sins with which they tear
the leaves of the lily of chastity.

Notice that a lily has six white petals, which symbolize the six virtuous
practices that keep virginity unspoiled. It is sufficient to comment on three
of them: honesty in speech, sobriety in eating, and detachment in play. The
first petal is torn by chatter which is close to bawdy talk; on that, see
above, chapter 2, and part 1, chapter 3. Seneca says of it: "Abstain from
shameful words, for licentiousness nourishes unchasteness." And Proverbs 7:
"And behold, a woman meets him in harlot's attire, prepared to deceive souls,
talkative and wandering." The second petal is sobriety. It is impossible to
find chastity where drunkenness rules, for in Proverbs 28 it is said: "Wine is
a luxurious thing"; and in Ephesians: "Do not get drunk with wine, in which is
lechery," that is, deriving from it as its cause. And the third petal is detachment in play, that is, the necessary withdrawal from frivolous and dissi-
pated entertainments. We have an example in Dinah, the daughter of Jacob, in
Genesis 34: when she went out to see the women of that region, she became corrupted by Shechem, the son of Hamor. This petal is also torn by dissolute ways
of singing and playing; Corinthians 15: "Wicked conversations corrupt good
manners."

Therefore, since virginity grows among such thorns it certainly can easily
be damaged. Such thorns abound in this world, for too much attention paid to
women's "horns," "tails," and other articles of clothing is a great source for
lust. And yet a woman can dress herself decently according to the custom of
her country without committing a sin, nor is there anything reprehensible in
this unless it is a matter of superfluous fashion and hence a source for evil.
It is said of the Blessed Virgin that, among the other aspects of her purity,
she spoke so little that in the Gospel she is found to have spoken to only four
persons, namely her son, the angel, Elizabeth, and John and the servants at the
marriage [of Cana]. We should do likewise in our talks in order to guard our
virginity, namely speak first with the Son of God, in prayer; with the angel,
that is, with the priest, when we go to confession; with Elizabeth, that is,
with a saintly woman, for consolation; and with God's servants in prayer.
Therefore, Augustine says: "Either ignore or love all girls and maidens equal-

qui tribulacione non frangitur, in sanguine, hoc est in peccato Veneris,
levius resolvitur et dissipatur." Unde Ieronimus: "Non es, inquit, David
85 sanctior, non es Salomone sapiencior, non Absalone pulcrior, non Sampsone
forcior." Et tamen omnes isti a mulieribus fuerunt decepti. "Libido ferreas
mentes emollit. Si ergo (dicit Ieronimus) pudiciciam queris, feminam quam
videris bene conversantem dilige." Sic enim fecerunt antiqui. Ipsi autem
super omnia pudiciciam venerabantur. Unde Ieronimus *Contra Iovinianum* nar-
90 rat quod antiquitus imperatores, consules, et senatores Romani et ceteri in
⟨c⟩urribus [f. 213v] triumphantes, quando alicui virgini obviabant, magnum
honorem sibi dederunt, acsi in sua virginitate aliquid beatitudinis perspe-
xissent. Et ideo secundum aliquos hec est per quam angelis homines assimilantur, quia angelis cognata est virginitas. Et ideo in signum dilectionis
95 et honoris ad virginitatem elegit Christus virgo esse, de virgine nasci, et
baptizari.

Narrat ergo Ieronimus de continencia trium viduarum post mortem mari-
torum. Quarum prima nomine Machia offerentibus sibi virum respondit se non
invenire virum qui se propter se duceret set forsan propter sua. Erat enim
100 ⟨de⟩formis set dives. Secunda autem nomine Valeria respondit primum virum
semper in mente vivere, et ideo alium superinducere non posset. Set tercia
nomine Anania respondit se virum alium nolle accipere quacumque causa, quia
si esset bonus, semper timeret illum perdere sicut primum perdiderat; si
vero malus esset, semper doleret quod post tam bonum virum malum haberet.
105 Comparatur autem tercio continencia cuidam lapidi vocato terribulus,
de quo legitur libro *De naturis rerum* quod huiusmodi lapides sunt in quodam
monte orientis, et sunt lapides ignifiri masculus et femina. Quorum natura
est, quamdiu sunt ab invicem, ignis non accenditur; cum ergo simul appropinquaverint, mox ignis accenditur, in tantum ut omnia ardeant que sunt
110 circa illos in monte. Revera sic in homine continencia observatur quamdiu
separatur a consorcio mulieris et e contrario. Si tamen simul appropinquaverint, saltem mala voluntate accenduntur et puritas continencie suffocatur. Item idem est de duobus lapidibus si invicem collidantur quantumcumque
duris, scintille ignis exeunt. Nec mirum ergo si in fragili genere humano
115 cum invicem appropinquaverint, si ignis luxurie educatur. Unde Ieronimus:
[f. 214] "Non potest, inquit, cum Deo habitare qui feminarum accessibus
deputatur. Prothdolor (dicit ipse) quod pro momentanea delectacione se
obligat homo ad eterna supplicia." [Unde quidam sic Anglice ait:

Who-so leuyth in flescly wyll
120   And hit ne woll noȝt lete,
Aftur hym schall like ille
þat he so þowte hym so swete.

ly, and see to it that you do not stay with a woman under the same roof, nor
rely on your earlier chastity. For when one lives with women in the same
dwelling, sinful delight is not easy to avoid." And he gives this example: "A
diamond cannot be broken between the hammer and the anvil, and yet it dissolves
with the blood of a goat. Thus a strong man or woman who does not break in
tribulation dissolves and perishes most easily with blood, that is, in sexual
sin." For this reason Jerome says: "You are not holier than David, nor wiser
than Solomon, nor more beautiful than Absalom, nor stronger than Samson.
Yet all these were deceived by women. Lust rules minds of steel. If you seek
chasteness, love a woman whom you see living a good life." For that is what
the ancients did: they worshiped chasteness above all else. Jerome reports in
his work *Against Jovinian* that when in ancient times Roman emperors, consuls,
senators, and others who rode in a triumphal chariot met with a virgin, they
would do her great honor, as if they saw some blessing in her virginity. And
according to some authorities, through this virtue men become like angels,
because virginity is closely related to the angels. Therefore, as a sign of
his love and reverence of virginity, Christ chose to be a virgin, to be born of
a virgin, and to be baptized by a virgin.

Jerome tells us about the continence which three widows observed after the
death of their husbands. The first, by the name of Marcia, when people were
offering her a new husband, answered that she did not find a man who wanted to
marry her for herself but rather for her possessions; for she was ugly but
rich. The second, called Valeria, said her first husband would always live in
her mind, and thus she could not take another in his place. But the third, by
the name of Annia, said she would not take another husband for any reason
whatsoever, for if he were good, she would always be afraid of losing him as
she had lost her first husband; and if he were bad, she would always be sorry
to have a bad husband after such a good one.

In the third place, continence can be compared to a stone called *terribulus*. The book *On the Properties of Things* tells us that such stones are on
some mountain in the East; they are igniferous and are either male or female.
It is their property that when they are by themselves, they produce no fire;
but when they are brought closely together, their fire is soon kindled, so that
everything around them on that mountain begins to burn. In the same way, a man
keeps his continence as long as he keeps himself from being near a woman, and
vice-versa. But when they come close together, they are soon lighted by evil
desire and their purity quickly fades away. Further, if two stones, however
hard they may be, are struck together, sparks of fire leap out of them. No wonder
then that when two people, whose human nature is much weaker, come close
together, the fire of lechery breaks forth. Therefore Jerome says: "No one can
dwell with God who is attached to the companionship of women. Alas, that for a

Lechery woll þy sowle spylle
þat is so vn-to-mete.
125   Whan þi body lyþe in erþe stille,
þe sowle mote all be bete.]

---

1 atque membris] *om* O.   **4–5** reddo . . . Gallice] *om* O.   **5** creaunt] greaunt C.   **10–11** virtus . . . concupiscenciam] alterativum O.   **12** quod] puniendum aut O.   videtur] *om* O.   **13** carnis] *om* O.   eius] carnis O.   **15** dicitur] *add* secundum illum O.   **18** radice] caduco O.   **19** succo] sicco M.   **20** conservandam] producendum O.   **21** que] *add* eciam omnino O.   fuit] fuerint O.   vel in] aut O.   **21–22** habent et] *om* O.   **22** lignum] signum C.   **23** dominice] *om* O.   castus et] *om* O.   **24–25** Iesus . . . victimam] qui coram tondente eum sicut ovis obmutescebat O.   **25–26** eius . . . dira] christi O.   **27** beatitudines] beatitudinis C.   **31** observando] conservando R.M; conservanda W.   **32** sancte] *om* O.   **33** terre] *add* de petra O.   **41** 34] 39 M.R; 29 W.   **43** continens] timens C.   **52** igitur] autem O.   **54** nutrit] mittit C.   **59** ludendo] loquendo C.W; legendo M.   **71** opera] *add* sue O.   **73** Iohanne] iohannis O.   et] cum O.   **75** idest(2)] *add* cum O.   **79** ubi] *om* C; vir R.   verius] ultimi C; vermis W. *The correct reading apparently is* unius.   **82** aut mulier] sine muliere O.   **85** non] nec O.   **86** mulieribus] muliere O.   decepti] *add* quoniam dicitur O.   **87** emollit] domat O.   **91** curribus] turribus C.W.   obviabant] occurrebant O.   magnum] *om* O.   **100** deformis] indeformis C.   **114** scintille . . . exeunt] quod ignis exit O.   **118–126** Unde . . . bete] *text from* R.   *Verse 54, in* B1.B3.Go1.L2.LC.R.V.W1.

VII.xviii   A QUIBUS CONTINENCIA ADQUIRITUR

[C]irca autem modum adquirendi veram scienciam continencie et quomodo, facta antiquorum vicia spernencium virtutesque sequencium nos sequi necessario oportet. Prout ergo continencia superius diffinitur tam contra superbiam quam eciam contra cupiditatem et luxuriam, est sciendum quod omnibus
5   illis modis antiqui illam observabant. Unde de continencia superbie: Eo quod dominari arroganter non appetebant, set rem publicam regere cupiebant, ideo ad laudem Iulii Cesaris narratur quod numquam suis militibus dixit "Ite!" set "Venite!" affirmans quod labor participatus cum principe vel duce fuit minor. Item de eodem, libro 1 *De nugis philosophorum* narratur
10 quod cum quidam veteranus quadam die periclitaretur coram iudicibus Cesaris, mittebat ad Cesarem ut adesset ad eum iuvandum. Cui Cesar dedit bonum advocatum. Et ille: "O Cesar, inquit, te periclitante in bello Asiatico nullum vicarium quesivi pro me, set pro te ego ipse pugnavi." Et hiis dictis loca vulnerum detexit que pro Cesare ibi receperat. Erubuit igitur
15 Cesar et ad iudicium venit. Verebatur enim non tantum superbus set ingratus videri.

    Summus autem imperator omnium, Christus Dei Filius, per quem reges

momentary delight man should give himself over to eternal pains." Hence someone says as follows in English:

> Who always will follow his fleshly will
>> And never from it retreat,
> Hereafter it shall please him ill
>> What once he thought so sweet.
> Lechery your soul shall spill
>> Lest within bonds it stay.
> When your body lies in dust so still
>> Your soul for all will pay.

10–13 Macrobius, *In somnium Scipionis* I.viii.7. **14–15** Cf. Aristotle, *Ethica Nicomachea* VII.1 (1145). **17–19** Albertus Magnus, *De vegetabilibus* VI.i.5 (10:164). Albert
says, "gaudet calido vehementi et sicco temperato." **24–25** Jer. 11.19. **33** Isa. 16.1.
35 Cant. 2.2. **40–41** *FM* VII.xiii.6–11. **41–42** Ecclus. 39.19. **53** *FM* VII.iii and
I.iv. **55–56** Prov. 7.10. **58** Prov. 20.1. **58–59** Eph. 5.18. **61–62** Gen. 34.1–2.
64 1 Cor. 15.33. **77–79** Jerome, *Ep. 52* 5 (CSEL 54:423). **79–80** Ps.-Jerome, *Ep. ad
Oceanum de vita clericorum* 5 (PL 30:289). **84–86** Jerome, *Ep. 52* 5 (CSEL 54:423).
86–88 Cf. Ps.-Jerome, *Ep. ad Oceanum* 3–4 (PL 30:289). **90–93** Jerome, *Adversus
Iovinianum* I.41 (PL 23:283). **97–104** Ibidem, I.46 (PL 23:288). Tubach 3180 and
3181. **116–118** Ps.-Jerome, *Ep. ad Oceanum* 4 (PL 30:289).

VII.xviii EXAMPLES OF CONTINENCE

If we seek the way to gain a true knowledge of continence and how, it is
neccessary to imitate the deeds of the ancients who scorned vices and followed
virtues. Continence was earlier defined as the virtue opposed to pride as well
as to cupidity and lechery, and we should point out that the ancients kept this
virtue in all these apects. First with regard to continence against pride: because they did not desire to be lords in arrogance but rather wished to govern
for the common good. It is reported in praise of Julius Caesar that he never
said to his soldiers "Go!" but always "Come!" showing thereby that a hardship
shared with the prince or leader was less burdensome. Likewise in book 1 of
The Philosophers' Trifles there is a story that one day when a veteran soldier
was in trouble with the judges of Caesar, he sent for Caesar to be present to
help him. Caesar gave him a good advocate. But he said: "O Caesar, when you
were in trouble in the war in Asia, I did not look for a replacement but
battled myself for you." And with these words he laid bare the places of the
wounds he had received there for Caesar's sake. Then Caesar blushed and came
himself to the judgment; for he was ashamed to appear not only proud but also
ungrateful.

regnant, etsi numquam ad hominem venisset neque nostram naturam assumpsis-
set, non tamen propter hoc superbus aut ingratus visus esset. Non superbus,
20   quia nemo dicere posset quod imperator aut superbus esset aut ingratus
⟨qui⟩ contemptibilem robam servi induere ⟨vellet⟩; nec ingratus, quia numquam apud Deum tam meruerat homo quod vice grati- [f. 214v] tudinis eius ei
tantum beneficium conferre debuerat, sicut incarnari personaliter, mortem
pati. Set ex sua profundissima humilitate gratis ad hominem venit, et qui
25   fuerat Deus absconditus, per incarnacionem venit in publicum, homo factus
iuxta illud Baruc: "In terra visus est et cum hominibus conversatus est."
Et non tantum ho⟨c⟩, set cum homo iusto Dei iudicio periclitaretur propter
peccata, non solum sibi advocatum dedit set ipsemet in eius advocacionem
personaliter venit, secundum illud Ioannis canonica 1, capitulo 2: "Advoca-
30   tum habemus apud Patrem, Iesum Christum."
Consimile exemplum narrat Seneca, libro 3 *De ira*, de rege Antigono,
qui cum audisset nocte quadam quosdam milites sibi mala omnia inprecantes
⟨eo⟩ quod illos duxerat in tale iter et locum, accessit ad eos; qui maxime
in sua paciencia audit eos. Cum ergo ignorarent a quo adiuvarentur, dixit
35   ad eos: "Nunc maledixistis Antigono, cuius vicio in has miserias incidis-
tis. Set nunc bene optate ei, qui vos ex hac voragine duxit." O mira humilitas! Non enim dedignatus est descendere laborantibus. Et mira paciencia
et humilitas, quia non indignatur sibi maledicentibus, etc.
[D]e continencia cupiditatis quomodo apud antiquos viguit satis patet.
40   Nam antiqui principes et reges non propter lucrum temporale regnare optabant, set tantum propter rei publice utilitatem et custodiam. Unde narrat
Valerius libro 3 de consule Sipione, qui cum accusaretur apud senatum de
pecunia, respondit: "Cum, inquit, totam Affricam potestati subiecerim,
nichil inde quod meum diceretur detuli propter cognomen" (vocabatur enim
45   Sipio Affricanus quia Affricam devincebat), quasi diceret: nichil adoptavi
in auro et argento [f. 215] et huiusmodi, nisi ut Affricam sub dominio Romano subicerem. Idem narratur de Fabio Lucio cui cum per legatos a Sampni-
tibus erant dona missa, omnia remisit sue continencie beneficio sine pecunia predives, sine usu familie habunde comitatus, quia locupletem illum
50   faciebat non multum possidere set pauca desiderare. Narratur eciam ibidem
de Quinto Tuberone, ⟨cui⟩ consulatum gerenti cum gentes Etheolorum vasa
argentea magno pondere et exquisita fabrica per legatos misissent quia
retulerant se vasa fictilia vidisse in mensa eius, iussit eos abire cum
saracenis ne continencie tamquam paupertati succurrendum esse putarent.
55   [A]d propositum iam de continencia castitatis contra libidinem similiter quomodo illa apud antiquos viguit, quod satis notum est Maximianum ac
Policraticon legentibus ⟨cum⟩ ceteris antiquorum voluminibus de castitate
tractantibus. Unde Valerius libro 1 narrat quod Cornelius Sipio missus in
Hispaniam, eo momento quo castra intravit, edixit ut omnia que voluptatis
60   causa operata ibi essent auferentur. Unde et mille milia scotorum ab exer-

Even if the greatest emperor of all, Christ the Son of God, through whom all kings rule, had never come to man or taken our human nature, he would still for that matter not appear poor or ungrateful. He was not proud, for no one could call an emperor proud or ungrateful who wanted to put on the shabby robe of a servant; nor could he be called ungrateful because man had never earned so much merit before God that God was obligated in gratitude to give man a great gift in return, such as personally to become man for him and to suffer death. But out of his deep humility Christ came freely to man; and he who before had been a hidden God became visible to all through his incarnation, when he was made man, after the words of Baruch: "He was seen upon earth and conversed with men." And not only this, but as man was threatened by God's just judgment on account of his sins, he did not just give him an advocate but came personally as an advocate to man's help, according to 1 John 2: "We have an advocate with the Father, Jesus Christ."

A similar example is given by Seneca in book 3 of *On Wrath*. When King Antigonus some night heard some soldiers curse him because he had led them in that particular way and place, he went to them and listened in great patience. As they did not know who was helping them, he said to them: "You have just cursed Antigonus, through whose fault you have gotten into this mess. But now you must wish him well, because he has pulled you out of it." What wonderful humility: he did not disdain to lower himself to those who were suffering hardships. And what wonderful patience and humility, for he was not angry with those who cursed him!

Continence in the desire for acquisition flourished likewise among the ancients. For the ancient princes and kings did not want to reign for temporal gain but only for the benefit and protection of the commonweal. Therefore Valerius tells us in book 3 of the consul Scipio, who, when he was accused of misappropriation before the Senate, said: "When I had subjected all Africa to the power of Rome, I took nothing from there that could be said to be mine except my surname" (for he was called Scipio the African, because he had defeated Africa), as if to say: I have not taken any gold or silver or the like for myself, except that I have subjected Africa to the Roman rule. It is also reported that when gifts were sent from the Samnites through messengers, Fabricius Luscinus sent them all back, for in his continence he was wealthy without money and abundantly attended without a retinue, because what made him rich was not to posses many things but rather to desire few. And further, in the same source it is stated that when Quintus Tubero was consul and the Aetolians sent through their messengers silver vessels of great weight and exquisite workmanship, because they had reported seeing only earthen ones on his table, he ordered them to leave with their burdens lest they thought they were to support him in his poverty.

Turning now to the continence of chastity which is opposed to lust: how it similarly flourished among the ancients is well known to the reader of Valerius

citu leguntur abisse. Noverat enim vir industris quod voluptas enervat et
effeminat libidinosos. I⟨d⟩em eciam libro 4 de continencia visus contra
luxuriam narrat de quodam adolescente [Spurna], qui cum esset excellentis-
sime pulcritudinis, ne feminarum oculos sollicitaret, oculorum decorem
65   vulneribus diffudit atque visum exaravit, mallens deformem faciei esse quam
causa libidinis aliorum, ut patet supra, capitulo 3, etc. Consimile eciam
exemplum narrat Valerius ibidem de mira continencia Zenocratis, quomodo
apud Athenas scorta quedam cum iuvenibus spopondit eius continenciam corum-
pere. Cum ergo [f. 215v] [nocte] ad eum venisset et iuxta eum cubuisset nec
70   aliquo modo eum ad actum libidinosum eum excitare potuisset, iuvenibus qui
cum ea spopondissent eam deridentibus respondit non de statua vel trunco set
de homine se pignus posuisse. Vocavit enim Zenocratem statuam propter eius
immobilem continenciam.
De continencia autem o[s]culorum libro 3 *De nugis philosophorum* legi-
75   tur de quadam muliere cuius maritus summe reprobatus esset a multis de fetore oris et dencium, eo quod anelitum fetidum haberet. Qui tandem uxorem
suam increpavit eo quod sibi non premunivit eum de tali defectu ut adqui-
reret medicinas, respondit dicens: "Hoc, inquit, fecissem nisi credidissem
omnium hominum ora sic olere." Ex quo verisimile fuit quod ipsa os alterius
80   viri numquam tetigisset, etc.

---

1 continencie] *add* a quibus O.   2 nos] *om* O.   5 observabant] suffocabant O.   6 regere]
add et augere O.   10 iudicibus] *add* regis O.   14 receperat] susceperat O.   igitur] ergo
O.   18 regnant] *add* qui O.   20 aut ingratus] *om* O.   21 qui] quia C; licet R.   vellet]
nollet C.R; non (*interl*) vellet M; *om* W.   23 incarnari] *add* pro eo O.   24 qui] *add* prius
O.   27 hoc] homo C.W.   33 eo] eos C.   36 O] *om* O.   38 etc.] *om* O.   45 devincebat]
devincerat O.   47 Idem] *add* eciam O.   49 comitatus] communicatus(?) O.   50 multum]
multa O.   51 cui] B1; cum C.O.   54 saracenis] sarecenis R; sarasenis W; sarcinis B1.
56–58 quod . . . tractantibus] C *here follows group z and E, whose text has been used to
expand C's* legent. *and* tractant. *meaningfully*; valerium maximum ac policraticon leg-
entem cum ceteris voluminibus antiquorum satis est nota M *and similarly* R.W.   57 cum]
in C.   62 Idem] item C.   65 diffudit] diffundit O.   66 3 etc.] 2 O.   69 ad eum venisset]
venisset M; advenisset R.W.   70 aliquo modo] in aliquo O.   **70–71** eum . . . deriden-
tibus] illum labefecisset, propter illam dicti iuvenes deridissent O.   71 vel trunco] *om*
O.   72 se] *om* O.   74 osculorum] oculorum C.R.   **74–75** legitur] *om* M.W; narratur
R.   75 cuius] quod cum O.   a multis] *om* O.   **76–78** Qui . . . medicinas] et ipsam in-
culpasset quod eum non monuerat de hoc querere medicinam O.   78 credidissem] crede-
rem O.   79 hominum] virorum O.   Ex quo] *om* O.   verisimile] *add* autem O.   80 etc.]
hec libro 3 de nugis philosophorum O.

VII.xix   QUOMODO CONTINENCIA ADQUIRITUR

[U]t ergo hanc continenciam adquiramus, exemplo predictorum a tactibus
inpudicis, colloquiis perversis, verbis lascivis, et gestis inhonestis

Maximus, *Policraticus*, and other volumes of ancient writers on chastity. Thus, Valerius in book 1 tells us that when Cornelius Scipio was sent to Spain, the moment he entered a fortress he would command that everything which was done there because of carnal lust should be abandoned. As a result a million whores are said to have left the army. For that hard-working man knew that lust makes people weak and soft. With respect to the continence in one's sense of sight that opposes lust, he likewise reports, in book 4, of a youth by the name of Spurna. Since he was outstandingly beautiful, he destroyed his sensual beauty with wounds and ruined his face, so that he would not attract women's eyes, because he would rather have an ugly face than become a cause of lust to others, as we saw above in chapter 3, etc. Valerius gives a similar example in the same book, namely the marvelous continence of Xenocrates. A whore of Athens made a wager with some youths that she would break his continence. When she came to him at night and lay down beside him, she could not rouse him to lust in any way. Now, as those youths who had made the wager derided her for that, she replied that she had not made her bet about a statue or treetrunk but about a man—she called Xenocrates a statue because of his unshakeable continence.

With respect to continence in kissing, there is a story in book 3 of *The Philosophers' Trifles* about a woman whose husband was once sharply reproached by many people for the bad smell of his mouth and teeth, for he suffered from halitosis. When he reproved his wife for not warning him about it so that he might get some medicine, she answered: "I would certainly have told you so, but I thought that all men's mouths smell that way." She had obviously never tasted another man's mouth!

The following material in this chapter occurs also almost verbatim in John of Wales, *Breviloquium*, on temperance: lines 7–16, 31–54 (III.4); 58–80 (III.30).   **7–9** *Policraticus* IV.iii (1:244).   **9–16** Ibidem, III.14 (1:228); E. Woelfflin, *Caecilii Balbi De nugis philosophorum quae supersunt* (Basel, 1855), p. 13.   **26** Bar. 3.38.   **29–30** 1 John 2.1. **31–36** Seneca, *De ira* III.xxii.3.   **42–47** Valerius, III.vii.1.   **47–50** Ibidem, IV.iii.5. **50–54** Ibidem, IV.iii.7.   **58–62** Ibidem, II.vii.1.   **62–66** Ibidem, IV.v.ext.1.   **66** *FM* VII.ii.27–31.   **67–73** Valerius, IV.iii.ext.3.   **74–80** Woelfflin, *Caecilii*, p. 13, from Jerome, *Adversus Iovinianum* I.27 (PL 23:287). Also in *Policraticus* III.13 (1:216–217).

VII.xix   HOW TO ACQUIRE CONTINENCE

In order to acquire the virtue of continence, we must, after the example of the cited men and women, abstain from immodest touching, immoral conversa-

oportet abstinere et obsequiis honestis omnino vacare, superfluitatem ciborum et potuum que precipue ad libidinem excitativa videntur contempnere, et
5 asperitatem penitencie diligere. Narrat eciam Boicius *De consolacione*,
libro 4, de Ulixe, qui cum redisset de bello Troiano cum suis militibus,
applicuit in quandam insulam ubi hospitatus est in quadam domo cuiusdam
mulieris mage et venenose. Qui in formas bestiarum omnes sunt convers⟨i⟩,
Ulixe excepto. Dederat autem sibi Mercurius florem album et precepit ei ut
10 omnino florem illum secum deferret nec dimitteret, set ab lesione munde
custodiret. Ex cuius virtute salvus evasit, ut ibi dicitur. Moraliter flos
ille virginitas dici potest, quam qui non habueri[n]t, per cogitaciones,
verba, et facta illicita fiunt [f. 216] frequenter bestiales. De qua virginitate dicit Alexander in *Epistula ad Bragmannos*, quam nota supra, particu-
15 la 4, capitulo 5: "Virginitas, inquit, est flos aliarum virtutum."
Unde videmus quod flos quantumcumque fuerit pulcher, si frequenter
tangatur marcescit atque omnino perdit tam eius pulcritudinem quam odorem.
Revera sic flos virginitatis tactibus et amplexibus pollutus amittitur. Et
ideo sicut flos ille non conservatur inter manus set inter spinas, sic
20 virginitas inter spinas asperitatis et penitencie mundius conservatur. Unde
Ieronimus in suo *Exameron*: "Flos, inquit, rose ante peccatum caruit spinis,
set iam inter illas et stipites spinosas melius crescit." Revera sic virginitas. Ante ° peccatum non erat necessarium ut per penitencias homo se
affligeret, set iam omnino oportet, quia alioquin non cresceret neque fruc-
25 tum faceret. Quia secundum beatum Augustinum castitas inter delicias periclitatur. Et ideo ait Bernardus: "Humilitas, inquit, et castitas in tantum
se mutuo diligunt ut ex humilitate plures meruerunt conservare virginitatem, sicut Beata Virgo."
Et expertum est rosas magno tempore custodiri inclusas in vase ad quas
30 aer seu ventus intrare non potest. Sic certe virginitas in terra humilitatis inclusa, ubi ventus ambicionis et superbie nullo modo intret, optime
custoditur. Set si quis propriis meritis mundiciam ascribit, mox ventus
inanis glorie subintrat, et sic certe iuxta dictum beati Iacobi, "Flos eius
decidit et decor vultus deperiit."
35 Secundum autem Vigecium *De re militari*, quando una pars dimicancium
potest subtrahere alimenta cibi ne accedant ad aliam partem, in brevi adversarios devincet. Revera bellum continuum est inter carnem et spiritum,
nam caro petit vo- [f. 216v] luptatem, set spiritus pudiciciam et castitatem. Si ergo iuxta imperium racionis retraxeris a carne superfluitatem
40 ciborum ac potuum, leviter ipsum devinces.
Unde narrat Claudianus *De raptu Prosorpine*, libro 6, et eciam Ovidius,
Metamorphoseos, libro 9, quod Anche⟨u⟩s gigas de terra genitus talem habuit
de dono matris condicionem quod quandocumque et pro quocumque se senserit
debilitatum, si ad terram caderet, ad pristinam fortitudinem erat renovatus

tion, lewd words, and shameful gestures, and devote ourselves fully to honorable behavior, reject above all superfluous food and drinks that seem to excite us to lust, and love self-mortification. In book 4 of *The Consolation of Philosophy*, Boethius reports that when Ulysses was returning from the Trojan War with his soldiers, he landed on an island and stayed there as a guest in the house of a woman who was skilled in the use of witchcraft and poison. They were changed into the shapes of animals, all except Ulysses. For Ulysses had been given a white flower by Mercury, which he was to carry with him at all times and not to lose, but to protect from all harm. And through its power he remained whole, as Boethius has it. Morally interpreted this flower can be said to represent virginity; people who do not have it often become like animals through unlawful thoughts, words, and deeds. Of this virginity, Alexander says in his *Letter to the Brahmins*: "Virginity is the flower of all other virtues." On this letter, see above, part 4, chapter 5.

One can see that no matter how beautiful a flower is, if it gets frequently touched, it withers and loses both its beauty and its aroma altogether. In the same way, the flower of virginity is lost by unchaste touching and hugging. Therefore, just as a natural flower cannot remain fresh in people's hands but only among thorns, just so is virginity kept fresh among the thorns of self-denial and penance. For that reason Jerome says in his *Hexameron*: "Before the Fall, the rose blossom had no thorns; but now it grows well among them and among prickly branches." The same applies to virginity. Before the Fall, it was not necessary for man to engage in penitential practices; but now he must do so indeed, for otherwise he would not grow or bear fruit. For according to Augustine, among delights chastity is in grave danger. And Bernard says: "Humility and chastity love each other so much that many have been able to preserve their virginity and chastity because of their humility, as did the Blessed Virgin."

Experience shows that roses can be preserved for a long time if they are enclosed in a vase in which air or wind cannot enter. Thus can virginity also be best preserved if it is enclosed in the soil of humility, where the wind of ambition and pride enters in no way. But if someone attributes cleanness to his own merits, the wind of vainglory soon enters, and then certainly, after the saying of Blessed James, "his flower has fallen off, and the beauty of his face has perished."

According to Vegetius in his book *On Military Skill*, when one party in a war manages to keep supplies from reaching their opponents, they will soon defeat them. There is constant warfare between the flesh and the spirit, for the flesh desires gratification, but the spirit, modesty and chastity. If one therefore follows the rule of reason and withholds superfluous food and drink from the flesh, one will easily defeat it.

Hence Claudian narrates in book 6 of *The Rape of Proserpine*, as does Ovid

45 et forcior surrex⟨it⟩. Quod cum Hercules miles fortis et strenuus cum eo
    pugnans intellexisset, ipsum terram prohibuit lanceam tenens ad pectus, ubi
    illum tam fortiter strinxit donec moreretur. Moraliter loquendo iste An-
    che⟨u⟩s carnem signat que ad literam de matre terra generatur, quia terra
    est et in terram revertetur. Unde quociens se ad terrena seu carnalia
50 inclinat, magis forcior et contumax contra animam insurgit. Set hic Her-
    cules miles fortis, hoc est homo perfectus et racione ductus, hoc conside-
    rans, illam terram prohibet, idest carnales voluptates et terrenas cibi,
    potus, et huiusmodi ab ea retrahit. Et sic eam stringens brachiis amoris
    Christi ad pectus bone voluntatis levissime domat et vincit eciam usque ad
55 mortem, sicut fecerunt patres antiquitus, puta Benedictus, Bernardus, Fran-
    ciscus, Dominicus.
        Nullum enim castrum tam forte quin leviter capitur si ei victualia
    subtrahuntur. Nec ignis tam fervens quin per subtractionem lignorum extin-
    gui potest. Revera nec tam magnus ardor libidinis quin sedatur per subtrac-
60 tionem superfluitatis ciborum ac potuum, iuxta illud Proverbiorum 26: "Cum
    defecerint ligna, extinguetur ignis." Et nota quod vehementissimum signum
    gracie et dilectionis Dei erga hominem est quando quis nititur carnem
    propriam per penitencias domare ac per asperitates infir- [f. 217] mitatis,
    angustie, et tribulacionis pro eius amore pacienter tolerare. Neminem enim
65 affligit Deus nisi filios quos tenerrime diligit. Quia ipse ait Apocalipsis
    3: "Quos amo, arguo et castigo."
        Exemplum: Est enim de Deo et homine quem diligit sicut de puero luden-
    te cum troco. Trocus autem sicut videmus est latus superius et strictus
    inferius. Cum ergo puer ludit cum eo, non ponit latitudinem ad terram set
70 strictitudinem, et tunc flagellando percutit illum. Et sic per flagellacio-
    nem erectus tenetur ne cadat. Tacente vero flagello parum dormit, ut dicunt
    pueri, et cito super latus cadens iacet mortuus. Revera sic est de Deo et
    homine. Homo enim iustus et bonus latitudinem habet superius dum contempla-
    tur quam latum, quam magnum sit regnum Dei et eius potencia et gaudium; set
75 est strictus inferius dum bene considerat brevitatem vite sue, de qua
    Iacobi 4 dicitur: "Que est vita nostra?" [et] statim respondit: "Vapor ad
    modicum parens." Sic artus est homo inferius dum nil terrenum querit nisi
    necessarium, iuxta illud Sapiencie: "Divicias aut paupertates ne dederis
    michi, set tantum victui meo tribue necessaria." Set homo sic stans ad Deum
80 erectus, cito potest cadere si permittatur paululum dormire propter vite
    sue lubricitatem. Nam inimici eius ad eum prosternendum sunt semper in
    promptu, qui sunt caro, mundus, et demon. Isti sunt qui temptacionum aquas
    in itinere hominis proiciunt ut cadat. Nam sicut trocus non potest bene
    stare in terra aquatica et lutosa, sic nec homo in aqua temptacionis nisi
85 auxiliante Deo; Trenorum 4: "Lubricaverunt vestigia vestra in itineribus
    platearum." Que quidem aque sunt de quibus dicitur Osee 4: "Furta, menda-

in book 9 of the *Metamorphoses*, that the giant Antaeus, who was born of the
earth, had this characteristic inherited from his mother that, whenever and for
whatever reason he became weak, if he fell down to the earth, he would become
renewed to his original strength and rise up even stronger. When Hercules, a
strong and brave knight, noticed this as he was struggling with him, he kept
him away from the earth by holding a lance against his chest and squeezed him
so tightly that he died. In moral terms, Antaeus stands for the flesh which is
literally born of Mother Earth, for it is earth and to earth it will return.
For this reason, whenever it bends down to things of the earth or the flesh, it
rises stronger and more rebellious against the soul. But when the strong
knight Hercules—that is, a perfect man who is led by his reason—notices that,
he keeps his flesh away from the earth, that is, he withdraws from it the
fleshly and earthly pleasures of food, drink, and the like. And thus he easily
tames it by squeezing it with his arms of the love of Christ against his chest
of goodwill, and so defeats it to its death. This is what the fathers of old
did, such as Benedict, Bernard, Francis, and Dominic.

No castle is so strong that it cannot be easily taken if its provisions
are cut off. Nor is any fire so hot that it cannot be quenched by withdrawing
the wood. In the same way, no lust burns so hot that it cannot be stilled by
withdrawing unnecessary food and drink, according to the words of Proverbs 26:
"When the wood fails, the fire will go out." Notice that it is a very strong
sign of God's grace and his love toward man when someone tries to tame his own
flesh in penance and to bear the torments of sickness, anxiety, and tribulation
patiently for the love of God. For God does not chastise anyone but his children whom he loves most tenderly. He himself has said in Revelation 3: "Such
as I love, I rebuke and chastise."

A likeness of God's love for man is the child who plays with a top. As we
see, a top is wide above and narrow below. When a child plays with it, he does
not place the wider part on the ground but the narrower, and then spins it with
his whip. And in this way, by being whipped, the top is kept upright and does
not fall. But when the whipping stops, the top "goes to sleep," as children
say, and soon it falls on its side and "lies dead." The same is true of God's
relationship with man. For a just and good man has his width above, when he
contemplates how wide and great God's kingdom is, and its power and joy; but
below he is narrow, when he meditates on the shortness of his life, of which is
said in James 4: "What is your life?" and the answer is given immediately: "A
vapor which appears for a little while." Thus, a man is narrow below when he
seeks for no earthly good other than what he needs, according to the words of
Wisdom: "Give me neither riches nor poverty, give me only what is necessary to
my life." But a man who thus stands upright toward God can soon fall if he allows himself to go to sleep in the slipperiness of his life. For his enemies,
namely the flesh, the world, and the devil, are always ready to overthrow him.

cia, adulteria, etc., inundaverunt super terram." Hec enim impediunt hominem ne diu stare possit in bono. Set Deus, ne cadat, [f. 217v] apponit
flagellum abstinencie, paupertatis, et infirmitatis, etc., quod si taceret,
90   cito in peccatum homo caderet sicut mortuus. Unde Augustinus in quodam
sermone: "Si, inquit, angustia venerit, tempus petimus penitendi. Si misericordia respexerit, abutimur paciencia que pepercit. Vix (dicit ipse)
illata plaga preteriit et iam non recolit mens ingrata que protulit." Patet
ergo quod ubi Deus flagellat, signum est amoris; Thobie: "Acceptus eras
95   Deo. Necesse ergo fuerit ut temptacio pro⟨ba⟩ret te."
    Est eciam aliud remedium pro conservacione virginitatis et continencie
quam retractio cibi et potus, scilicet considerare iugiter quod caro illa
que tantum te ad libidinem provocat quasi tempore incognito ex sua fragilitate in cineres revertetur. Exemplum libro *De animalibus*, ubi dicitur quod
100   corvus si nidificaverit in arbore aliqua et licet posuerit ova, potest
tamen impediri ne pullos producat. Nam ponantur cineres vitri inter arborem
et corticem, et quamdiu ibi fuerint cineres, ille numquam pullos producet.
Corvus autem iste, qui cadaveribus pascitur animalium, signat carnem. Set
secundum Philosophum homo est arbor ⟨ever⟩sa, in qua tunc corvus carnis
105   nidificat cum caro tua istas libidinosas voluptates affectat. Cuius ova
sunt hec: accidia, gula, luxuria. Accipiatur ergo vitrum et redigatur in
cineres, hoc est, considera humanam naturam et cogites quam cito per mortem
in cineres redigitur. Et hos cineres proprie fragilitatis per iugem memoriam mortis pone inter amaram corticem mortis et arborem vite tue, quomodo
110   s⟨cilicet⟩ in brevi anima a corpore separatur, nesciens quo tendet. Et
certe dum illi cineres ibi iacuerint, numquam infestacio carnis prevalebit
nec pullos predictos producet, quia Ecclesiastici 7 dicitur: "Memorare
novissima [f. 218] [tua] et in eternum non peccabis."
    Et nota quod signa mortis secundum beatum Ieronimum sunt hec: Quando
115   nasus frigescit, facies pallescit, oculi tenebrescunt, aures surdescunt,
nervi et vene rumpuntur, cor in duas partes dividitur. Nichil vilius nec
abhomina[bi]lius cadavere mortuo. In domo non permittitur ne eius fetore
familia moriatur. In aere non suspenditur ne aer inficiatur. In aqua non
proicitur ne illa corrumpatur. Set quid? Revera terra foditur et in terram
120   proicitur [et] tamquam venenum mortiferum, ne amplius compareat, a terra
cooperitur. [Unde quidam Anglice sic dicit:

When þe hede quakyth
And þe lyppis blakyth
And þe nose sharpyth
125   And þe senow stakyth
And þe brest pantyth

It is they who throw the water of temptation on a man's path to make him fall. For just as a top cannot readily stand up on ground that is wet and muddy, so can a man not stand in the water of temptation unless God helps him; Lamentations 4: "Our steps have slipped in the ways of our streets." These waters are those of which Hosea 4 speaks: "Theft, lying, adultery, and so forth, have overflowed the earth." These prevent a man from standing firm in the good for long. But God keeps him from falling by applying the whip of abstinence, poverty, sickness, and the like. If a man then were to "go to sleep," he would soon fall into sin as if dead. Therefore, Augustine says in a sermon: "When some worry has come, we ask for time to do penance. If mercy looks upon us favorably, we abuse the patience that has spared us. The blow that has struck is hardly past, and already our ungrateful mind does no longer remember what it has suffered." Therefore it is manifestly a sign of his love when God strikes us; Tobit: "You were acceptable to God. Therefore it was necessary that temptation should try you."

There is another remedy to preserve virginity and continence besides the withdrawal of food and drink, namely the attentive reflection that the same flesh which urges you so much to lustful pleasure will for its frailty at an unknown time return to dust. An illustration of this is given in the book *On Animals*, where it is said that although the raven builds his nest in a tree and lays all his eggs there, he can yet be kept from bringing forth his young. One must place potash between the tree and its bark, and then, as long as the potash is there, the raven will not bring forth his young. This raven, who feeds on animals' carrion, stands for our flesh. According to the Philosopher, man is like an upside-down tree; in it the raven builds his nest when your flesh longs for these lustful pleasures. His eggs are these: sloth, gluttony, and lechery. Take, then, glass and reduce it to ashes; that is, examine human nature and reflect on how soon it returns to ashes through death. And put these ashes of your own frailty through attentive meditation on death between the bitter bark of death and the tree of your life, namely by reflecting on how soon your soul is separated from your body, without knowing where it will go. As long as these ashes lie there, the urging of your flesh will surely have no power, nor will it ever bring forth any offspring; for in Ecclesiasticus 7 it is said: "Remember your last end, and you will never sin."

And notice that according to Blessed Jerome the signs of death are as follows: the nose grows cold, the face turns pale, the eyes darken, the ears grow deaf, nerves and veins snap, and the heart is split in two. There is nothing more base or abominable than a corpse. It is not allowed to stay in the house, lest the people there should die of its stench. It is not hung up in the air, lest it should infect it. It is not thrown into water, lest it should pollute that. What then? To be sure, the earth is dug up and it is

And þe breþe wantyþ
And þe teþe rately3t
And þe þrote roteliþ
130 And þe sowle is wente owte
þe body ne tyt but a clowte.
Sone be it so stekenn
þe sowle all clene ys for3etenn.]

Satis ergo patet [quomodo] ad observanciam puritatis valent tam cibo-
135 rum abstinencia quam eciam mortis memoria. Ipsa enim caro ut hostis fortissimus est contra spiritum, cuius malicias bonum est fugere, quia non est
bonum pugnare de prope cum hoste ⟨qui⟩ a proximitate ⟨sibi sumit⟩ vires.
Set talis est luxuria. Nam corpus nostrum quod erat prius pacificum convertitur in hostem maleficum. Unde si princeps aliquis pugnare timeret cum
140 hostibus quando credit quod in exercitu suo sunt multi proditores qui
velint hostes iuvare quando bellum vel conflictus cepit imminere, ponit eos
in forti custodia vel in fronte belli vel aciei, ut cicius destruantur. Sic
revera homo pugnaturus contra luxuriam in bello spirituali sciens quod
semper tres fortes hostes et inimici, scilicet caro, mundus, et diabolus,
145 sunt quasi proditores ad ipsum decipiendum parati. Et ideo deberet ponere
ante oculos suos et expellere ab eo illorum delectaciones; quibus superatis
victoriam habeat et triumphum.

Exemplum: Sicut autem castrum faciliter capitur mortuo ianitore et
hostibus introductis, sic devicta carne, que ianitor est luxurie, per quam
150 ceteri hostes, hoc est [f. 218v] omnes carnis motus illiciti, introducun-
tur, castrum anime, idest mundicia vite per quam celum rapitur, facillime
capietur. Et sicut castrum bene muratum et nulla parte confractum securitatem dat inhabitantibus, sic corpus humanum continencia bene munitum omnes
voluptates expellit et anime securitatem prestat contra omnes hostes. Unde
155 pro facili devincit expugnacionem istorum hostium, scilicet carnis, mundi,
et demonis.

Narrat enim Techel *De naturis lapidum* quod quando in iaspide invenitur
homo sculptus, in manu una scutum tenens et in altera gladium, serpente⟨m⟩-
que sub pedibus, quod tunc lapis ille contra omnes inimicos habet virtutem.
160 Lapis autem iste Christum signat. Petra autem erat Christus qui pro nostra
defensione tam gladium quam scutum tenet in manibus et serpentem sub pedibus. Si ergo caro nos infestat, capiamus de manu eius gladium penitencie et
asperitatis, cum quo carnales affectiones dividemus et resecabimus; Deuteronomii 22: "Gladius meus devorabit carnes." Qui quidem gladius formabitur
165 ex tribus partibus penitencie, que sunt contricio, confessio, et satisfactio, ita quod scindolum—Anglice *the blade*—illius gladii sit vera confessio de omnibus commissis; Apocalipsis 3: "De ore eius procedit gladius ex

cast there and covered with earth like deadly poison, so that it may not be
seen anymore. Whence someone has said in English:

> When the head trembles,
> And the lips grow black,
> The nose sharpens,
> And the sinews stiffen,
> The breast pants,
> And breath is wanting,
> The teeth clatter,
> And the throat rattles,
> The soul has left,
> And the body holds nothing but a clout—
> Then will the body be thrown in a hole,
> And no-one will remember your soul.

Thus it is sufficiently clear how abstinence from food as well as meditation on death are powerful means to preserve purity. For our flesh stands like
a very strong enemy against our spirit, and it is a good thing to flee its
malice, for it is not a good idea to engage in close combat with an enemy who
grows stronger as he gets nearer to us. Lechery is just such an enemy; for our
body, which before was at peace, turns into a mischievous fiend. If a prince
were afraid to fight against his enemies when he believes there are many traitors in his army who are willing to help his enemies as soon as the battle
begins to get rough, he places them under a strong guard or else in front of
the battle or army, so that they may be quickly destroyed. In the same way must
a man act who is to fight spiritually against lechery. Knowing that three
strong enemies—the world, the flesh, and the devil—are always ready to deceive him like traitors, he should put these before his eyes and expel their
delights from himself, so that, when they have been defeated, he may have the
victory and triumph.

Another illustration: a castle is easily taken once the gatekeeper has
been killed and its enemies have gained entrance. In the same way, once the
flesh has been defeated, which is the gatekeeper of lechery and allows all the
other enemies to enter, namely the unlawful stirrings of the flesh, then the
soul's castle, that is, purity of life through which heaven is seized, will be
quite easily captured. And as a castle that is well fortified with walls and
unbroken at any point gives its inhabitants safety, so does the human body, if
it is well fortified by continence, expel lustful desires and give the soul
safety against all its enemies. In this way it easily overcomes the attack of
these three enemies, the flesh, the world, and the devil.

In his book *On the Property of Stones*, Techel reports that when one finds

utraque parte acutus." Secundo, *le hilte*—quod est ferrum transversum
servans manus, idest opera, a lesione—erit humillima contricio de preteri-
170   tis ex una parte et de presentibus ex alia parte. Set *le pomell*, quod est
corpus rotundum et solidum, erit solide satisfactionis circumquaque de
omnibus commissis preteritis, presentibus, et futuris quoad voluntatem. Et
nota quod ibi studiosius est rebellandum ubi gravior viget pestis. Set non
est peior pestis quam familiaris hostis, cuiusmodi est caro. Ideo sibi
175   omnino est resistendum. [f. 219] Narrat *Policraticus* quendam populum regem
suum magnaliter laudasse eo quod strenue inimicos suos debellasset et
vicisset; respondit se victorem non esse donec unum prosterneret hostem
ceteris forciorem. Requisitus ergo quisnam esset, respondit: "Caro propria." Magnum ergo imperium superat qui carnem domat. Unde Seneca: "Dabo
180   tibi imperium; impera tibi." Unde Ad Corinthios 9: "Sic pugno, non quasi
aerem verberans, set castigo corpus meum," etc.

   Secundo, si mundus te infestat, capias scutum paciencie a Christo,
iugiter considerans quomodo per pacienciam ipse mundi tyrannos devicit dum
equo animo sine murmure tot genera pertulit tormentorum usque ad mortem.
185   Quod vero scutum sic formabitur: Scutum autem in se erit purpureum, cum
leone argenteo *rampaunte* in medio, ac in pectore unam rosam de minio, idest
gowles, gestante. Spiritualiter per istud scutum purpureum [intelligo lignum crucis, quod est de] Christi sanguine dispersum et effusum. In cuius
medio leo *rampaunt* est corpus Christi benedictum; de quo Apocalipsis:
190   "Vicit leo de tribu Iuda." Set hic leo est argenteus, et bene, eo quod argentum est metallum inter cetera purum et clarum et signat Christi humanitatem purissimam. Que quidem Christi humanitas est coronata corona aurea,
idest divinitate. Set illa rosa in pectore est illud vulnus laterale, per cuius
medium hoc scutum erat perforatum per quandam lanceam *de felony*. Que
195   tamen omnia pro nobis paciencter sustinuit. Unde narrat Virgilius quod antiquus ⟨mos⟩ forcium erat quod quando in bello moriebantur, quod terram
mordebant ne ex inpaciencia aliquid turpe proferrent. Et ideo iuxta concilium Sapientis, "Sume scutum inexpugnabile," hoc est scutum paciencie,
quod nullum genus tormentorum potest penetrare.
200   Devictis ergo [f. 219v] ° hiis duobus hostibus, scilicet carne et
mundo, revera tercius hostis, puta diabolus, accedere non audebit, set
quasi disperso auxilio et exercitu ad fugam compellitur, quod si redierit,
certe omne robur et malicia quasi pro nichilo sub pedibus virtutum calcabi-
tur et confundetur. Sic ergo patet quomodo virtute illius lapidis Christi
205   hostes nostros singulos devincere valemus. Unde Gregorius: "Non potest
prevalere cordis angustia vel mundi molestia ubi tanti auxiliatoris est
presens potencia." Et Bernardus: "Quantumcumque, inquit, seviat tribulacio,
non putes te derelictum si memineris illud scriptum: 'Cum ipso sum in
tribulacione,' " scilicet ⟨cum⟩ Iesu Christo, quia in omni tribulacione et

a man sculpted in a jasper who holds a shield in one hand and a sword in the other, with a serpent beneath his feet, that jasper has power against any enemy. This precious stone stands for Christ, for Christ was a rock, who holds both sword and shield in his hands in our defense, and a serpent beneath his feet. When our flesh stirs against us, we should take the sword of penance and mortification from his hand, with which we shall divide and cut up our carnal desires; Deuteronomy 22: "My sword shall devour flesh." This sword is fashioned out of the three parts of penance, which are contrition, confession, and satisfaction. The blade of this sword is true confession of all our misdeeds; Revelation 3: "From his mouth came out a sharp two-edged sword." Second, the hilt, which is the cross-piece that protects the hands, that is, our deeds, from being hurt, is humble contrition of past deeds on one side, and of present deeds on the other. But the pommel, a round and solid knob, is the firm satisfaction we must make for all our sins, those of the past and the present, as well as those of the future by an act of good intention. Notice that one must fight back the harder where some evil flourishes more powerfully. But there is no greater evil than an internal enemy, such as is our flesh. Therefore, our flesh must be withstood most strongly. *Policraticus* reports that some people praised their king greatly because he had firmly fought against his enemies and overcome them. He replied that he would not be victorious until he were to cast down an enemy that was stronger than all the others. When they asked him who that was, he replied: "My own flesh." Therefore, he who tames his flesh rules over a large empire. Whence Seneca says: "I will give you an empire: rule yourself!" And in Corinthians 9: "I fight, not as one beating the air, but I chastise my body."

In the second place, if the world attacks you, take the shield of patience from Christ and reflect attentively how through his patience he overcame the tyrants of the world when he suffered so many kinds of torments with equanimity and without murmur, even unto death. This shield will be fashioned as follows: the shield itself will be purple, with a silver lion rampant in the middle, wearing a red rose, that is, in *goules*, on its chest. Allegorically, by this purple shield I understand the wood of the cross, which is besprinkled and totally covered with the blood of Christ. The lion rampant in its middle is Christ's blessed body, of which is said in Revelation: "The lion of the tribe of Judah has prevailed." But this lion is of silver, and fittingly so, because silver is a metal which is above all clean and bright and symbolizes the most pure human nature of Christ. Christ's human nature wears a golden crown, divinity. But the rose on the lion's chest is that wound in his side, with which this shield was pierced by the lance of a felon. All these things Christ suffered for us patiently. Virgil tells us that among the strong champions of old it was the custom, when they died in battle, to bite the dust, so that they might not speak any dishonorable word in their suffering. Therefore, after the

210 angustia succurrit nobis eius presencia. Verbi gracia: Si deviamus, habemus
eum ab errore revocantem; si spiritualiter infirmamur, habemus ipsum medicinam preparantem; si esuriamus, habemus eum largissime reficientem; si
temptacionibus tribulemur, habemus ipsum consolantem; si per peccatum car-
ceri diaboli mancipamur, habemus ipsum liberantem; si ab hostibus insi-
215 diamur, habemus ipsum respicientem. Que omnia et eorum exposicionem quere
supra, particula 3, capitulis 17, 20, et 21. Ex quibus liquet quod bellum
spirituale contra hos aggredi non debemus formidare set fortiter dimicare.
Quod si fecerimus, puritatem consciencie faciliter adquirere valeamus.

---

1 tactibus] tactis O. **2** lascivis et] *om* O. inhonestis] *om* O. **7** quadam] *om* O. **8** Qui]
que cum sibi et suis de suis veneficiis propinasset O. formas] *add* diversarum O. con-
versi] converse C. **9** et . . . ei] *om* O. **10** florem illum] *om* O. lesione] illesione M; il-
lisione R.W. **11** ut ibi] ubi sic O. **18** pollutus] pollutis O. **19** conservatur] servatur
O. **23** Ante] antequam C.M. **27–28** conservare virginitatem] conservacionem virginitatis et castitatis O. **29** Et] *add* nota O. expertum] *add* autem R.W. quas] quod
O. **37** devincet] devincent C. **40** ipsum] illum O. **42** Ancheus] ancheas C. **45** sur-
rexit] surrexerit C. **47–48** Ancheus] ancheas C. **55–56** Franciscus, Dominicus] *add*
etc M; et alii R; franciscus W. Franciscus] *om* Go1.L2.L3.LC.R.V; *story om* group x.M;
manuscript defective Jo.L1; *add* nicholaus z. *All full manuscripts recorded.* **69** Cum]
quando O. **78** aut] et O. **80** potest cadere] cadet O. paululum dormire] *om* O.
85 vestra] nostra O. **93** protulit] pertulit O. **95** fuerit] fuit M.R; *om* W. probaret] pro-
curet C. **98** ex] pro nimia O. **102** ille] illi M.W; vitri R. **104** eversa] onerosa C.
110 scilicet] *thus in* r, u, z *and anticipated in* R; si C.O. **121–133** Unde . . . forȝetenn]
text from R. *Verse 55, in* B1.B3.Go1.L2.LC.R.Sp.V.W1. **137** qui] quia C. sibi sumit]
cibi sunt C.—*The sentence gave the scribes much trouble, apparently because an abbreviation of* sumit *(thus in groups u and z) was misread as* sunt. **139** si] sicut M.R.
141 bellum vel] *om* O. **141–147** ponit . . . triumphum] sic debet homo pugnam timere
cum luxuria, eo quod corpus nostrum ad modum proditoris in pugna ita contra nos erit.
Que si devicta fuerit, alii duo hostes, scilicet mundus et demon, faciliter quasi devincuntur
O. **148** mortuo] occiso O. **149** introductis] *add* revera O. **151–152** mundicia . . .
capietur] celum capitur O. **155** istorum] *add* trium O. scilicet] *om* O. **157** enim] *om*
O. **158–159** serpentemque] serpentesque C. **161** tenet] *add* ipse O. **165** tribus] *om*
O. **166** Anglice *the blade*] *om* O. **169** a lesione] ab illesione M.R; ab ulucione W.
174 hostis] amicus M.W; inimicus R. **175–176** quendam . . . laudasse] quod (*om*
R.W) cum (*om* M.W) quidam (*om* M) regem suum laudassent O. **181** etc.] *om* O.
182 scutum] *add* de collo O. a Christo] christi O. **186** medio] *add* cum corona aurea
R. **187–188** intelligo . . . de] *om* C.O.—*Only in group r, but obviously required by the
sense of this passage. Group z omits* per *and reads* est crux sancta christi . . . **190** Set]
scilicet M.R; si W. est] *om* O. **196** mos] modus C; mors W. **200** ergo] *add* ergo C.
205 hostes] *add* et O. **209** cum] in C. **210** Si] *add* aliquid M.W; *add* aliquando R.
212 eum] ipsum M.W; ipse R. **215** quere] nota O. **216** capitulis . . . 21] capitulo M;
capitulo 3 R.W. **217** hos] hostes M; hostes hos R; hostes quos W. **218** valeamus] valeamus O.

advice of the wise man, "take an invincible shield," that is, the shield of patience, which no kind of torment can pierce.

And when these two enemies, the flesh and the world, have been defeated, the third, that is, the devil, will truly not dare come near us, but will be forced to flee because his helpers and his troops have been dispersed. Should he come back, all his strength and mischief will certainly be trodden under the feet of the virtues and be confounded as if they were nothing. And thus it is manifest how by the power of this precious stone of Christ we are able to overcome our enemies, one by one. Whence Gregory says: "Our heart's anxiety and the world's tribulation cannot prevail where the power of such a strong helper is present." And Bernard: "However violently tribulation may rage, do not think of yourself as abandoned if you remember this word: 'I am with him in tribulation,' " that is, with Christ Jesus, for his presence helps us in every trial and tribulation. For instance: if we go somewhat astray, he is with us to call us back from our wandering; if we are spiritually sick, he is with us to prepare some medicine; if we are hungry, he is with us to refresh us most generously; if we are troubled by temptations, he is with us to comfort us; if we are locked up in the devil's jail through our sin, he is with us to set us free; if we are beset by our enemies, he is with us to keep watch. For all these matters and their explanation, see above, part 3, chapters 17, 20, and 21. From this it is patent that we must not be afraid to enter into the spiritual battle against these enemies, but rather fight bravely. If we do so, it will be easy for us to acquire purity of mind.

6–11 Boethius, *De consolatione Philosophiae* IV, m. 3 and preceding prose.   **14–15** *FM* IV.iv.135–143.   **15** Cf. Ailred of Rievaulx, *De institutione inclusarum* 32 (PL 32:1462).   **25–26** Bernard, *De conversione ad clericos* XXI.37 (4:113).   **33–34** James 1.11.   **35–37** Cf. Vegetius, *Epitoma rei militaris* III.3 and 9 (pp. 69 and 87).   **41–47** Tubach 267; Claudian, *De raptu Proserpinae,* II, praef., 41, and Ovid, *Met.* IX.183–184.   **60–61** Prov. 26.20.   **66** Rev. 3.19.   **76–77** James 4.15.   **78–79** Prov. 30.8.   **85–86** Lam. 4.18.   **86–87** Cf. Hos. 4.2.   **94–95** Tob. 12.13.   **99–102** Also in *GR* 46.   **112–113** Ecclus. 7.40.   **114–121** For the "Signs of Death" commonplace, see *Verses*, pp. 197–199. Already used in *FM* I.xiii.28–35.   **157–159** Techel, 1; ed. Pitra, vol. III, p. 336. Also in Vincent, *Spec. naturale* VIII.77. Group z attributes this to "Conches."   **164** Deut. 32.42.   **167–168** Rev. 1.16.   **180–181** 1 Cor. 9.26–27.   **190** Rev. 5.5.   **195–197** Servius on *Aeneidos* XI.418.   **198** Wisd. 5.20.   **208–209** Ps. 90.15.   **216** The references seem to be to images of Christ as knight or fighter: *FM* III.xvii.64ff., xx.136–142, and xxi.220–226.

VII.xx   DE EFFECTU CONTINENCIE

[D]e effectu continencie et eius fine iam ultimo est advertendum quod
vere continentes Christum secuntur ad celorum regna, iuxta illud Apocalipsis 14: "Virgines enim sunt et secuntur agnum," idest Christum, "quocumque
ierit." Unde Augustinus libro *De bono virginitatis*: "Quo, inquit, ire
5   putamus hunc agnum quo eum nemo sequi vel audeat vel valeat nisi vos, [f.
220] scilicet virgines? Quo eciam putamus eum ire, in quos saltus vel
prata, ubi credo sunt gaudia virginum Christi? Nam sunt aliis alia set
nullis talia. In hoc ergo sequamini agnum quia agni caro utique virgo est.
Merito ergo sequ⟨amini⟩ illum virginitate cordis et corporis quocumque ie-
10   rit." Et sequitur: "Multa, inquit, ad illum imitandum omnibus proponuntur,
set virginitas carnis non omnibus. Non enim habent quod faciant quod virgines sunt, in quibus iam factum est ut virgines non sunt. Itaque agnum ceteri fideles qui virginitatem corporis amiserunt secuntur, set non quocumque
ierit ille set quousque ipsi poterunt possunt preterquam in decore virgini-
15   tatis. Ipse dicit: 'Beati pauperes,' quasi diceret: imitamini illum qui
propter vos factus est pauper cum tamen esset dives. 'Beati mites,' quasi
diceret: imitamini illum qui dixit, 'Discite a me quia mitis sum,' " etc. Et
sic enumeratis multis aliis sequitur: "Qui imitantur in hiis, agnum secuntur. Quod eciam coniugati possunt. Set ecce agnus ille graditur itinere
20   virginali. Quomodo ergo post illum ibunt qui hoc amiserunt quod nullo modo
percipiunt? Vos ergo post eum virgines eius et propter hoc unum, scilicet
virginitatem, quocumque ierit sequimini eum."

    Et nota quod virgines pre ceteris sanctis Christum secuntur propter
diversas earum prerogativas. Primo quia virginitas comitatur primariam
25   hominis creacionem. Nam homo creatus erat de terra virginea, et Eva sine
commixtione. Secundo quia comitatur paradisi recuperacionem. Primus enim
homo qui paradisum recuperavit fuit Helias, et ille erat virgo. Tercio,
quia comitatur tocius mundi dominacionem. Verbi gracia: virginitas enim
celos clausit, mortuos suscitavit, Iordanem divisit, Danielem et pueros
30   liberavit. Quarto virgi- [f. 220v] nitas est comes reparacionis. Christus
enim reparator noster erat virgo et natus de virgine. Quinto quia victoria
est antique corrupcionis. Sola enim virginitas vincit carnis corrupcionem.
Sexto quia est transcensio status mundani, quia secundum beatum Augustinum
"in carne preter carnem vivere terrena vita non est set celestis." Septimo
35   quia est equacio status angelici. Angelis enim semper virginitas est cognata. Merito ergo virginitas pre ceteris virtutibus Christum sequitur et
famulatur, ut domicella libera et principalis nullo officio forinseco aut
rudi occupata set crines et capud domini sui lavit et abluit, et sic
multipliciter gaudenter deservit.
40   Et ideo iuste sibi premia conceduntur in celis, ubi contra capitalia

VII.xx   THE END EFFECT OF CONTINENCE

Now we finally turn to the consequences and end effect of continence and
should notice that those who are truly continent follow Christ to the kingdom
of heaven, after the words of Revelation 14: "They are virgins and follow the
Lamb," that is, Christ, "wheresoever he goes." For that reason, Augustine says
in his book *On the Value of Virginity*: "Where do we think this Lamb is going,
where no one dares or can follow him except you, that is, virgins? Where do we
think he is going, to what pastures or meadows, where I believe the joys of the
virgins of Christ are? Others have other joys, but none have joys like these.
In this let us follow the Lamb, for his flesh is that of a virgin. Let us therefore truly follow him in the virginity of our heart and body, wherever he
may go." And Augustine continues: "Many things are possible for all who
want to imitate him, but virginity of the body is not within reach of all. For
those who have lost their virginity can do nothing to be virgins. Therefore,
those faithful who have lost bodily virginity follow the Lamb, but not wherever
he may go, but where they are able to follow without the special beauty of
virginity. He himself says, 'Blessed are the poor,' so as to say: follow him
who for your sake has become poor though he was rich. 'Blessed are the meek,'
as if to say: follow him who has said, 'Learn from me for I am meek.' " In the
same way Augustine lists the other beatitudes, and then continues: "Those who
imitate him in these matters follow the Lamb. This is within reach also of
married people. But lo, that Lamb walks on the path of virginity. How then
can those walk after him who have lost what they cannot regain in any way?
You, therefore, go after him specifically as virgins and follow him wherever he
might go on account of this alone, namely virginity."

And notice that virgins follow Christ in a way that is superior to other
saints because of several prerogatives they have. First, virginity went with
the original creation of man, for man was made from virgin soil, and Eve was
created without admixture of any other matter. Second, virginity accompanies
the recovery of paradise; the first human to recover paradise was Elijah, and
he was a virgin. Third, virginity accompanies the rule over the whole world;
for instance, it closed heaven, it revived the dead, it parted the Jordan, and
it set David and the young men free. Fourth, virginity is the companion of our
restoration; for Christ, who has restored us, was a virgin and was born of a
virgin. Fifth, virginity is the victory over our former corruption; for it
alone overcomes the corruption of the flesh. Sixth, virginity transcends our
condition in this world; for according to Blessed Augustine, "to live in the
flesh outside the flesh is not an earthly way of life but a heavenly one."
Seventh, virginity is equal to the status of angels; for it is always akin to
the angels. Therefore, virginity rightly follows and ministers to Christ before all other virtues, just as the chief maid, who is not a slave, does not do

septem beatitudines conceduntur, ut patet Matthei 5. Primo autem Christus
dicit superbis: "O superbi, qui parem habere noluistis, set in tumore et
arrogancia permansistis, ecce nunc in celo 'beati pacifici,' etc." Secundo:
"O iracundi, qui credidistis quod vita micium sit insania, modo in celo
45   videte quia 'beati mites.' " Tercio: "O invidi et detractores, qui credidistis misericordiam nichil fuisse, ecce iam in celo 'beati misericordes.' "
Quarto: "O cupidi et avari, qui credidistis quod vita pauperum fuisset
insania, iam ergo cognoscite et videte quia 'beati pauperes,' etc." Quinto:
"O accidiosi, qui credidistis quod penitencia esset insania, iam ergo
50   agnoscite et videte quia 'beati qui lugent.' " Sexto: "O gulosi, qui contempsistis abstinenciam, ecce modo 'beati qui esuriunt et siciunt,' etc."
Septimo et ultimo: "O luxuriosi, qui mundiciam contempsistis, ecce modo
quia 'beati mundo corde, quoniam ipsi Deum videbunt.' "
     Et ideo vos peccatores obstinati de mundis et virtuosis in extremo die
55   [f. 221] dicetis illud Sapiencie 15: "Hii sunt quos aliquando habuimus in
derisum et in similitudinem improperii. Nos insensati vitam illorum estimabamus insaniam et finem illorum sine honore. Set ecce iam quomodo inter filios Dei computati sunt, et inter illos sors illorum est." Et ideo Gregorius de gaudiis celi loquens ait: "In celesti, inquit, patria divicie si
60   diligantur ibi adquiruntur ubi perire non possunt, honor adquiritur ubi
nullus indignus honoratur, salus adipiscitur ubi nichil obesse saluti
invenitur, vita adquiritur ubi nichil mori potest, ubi eciam nichil obest,
nichil superfluum, nichil deficit, [nichil] exterius quod appetitur, nichil
interius quod fastiditur, set cives angelici mirantur in illum quem prospi-
65   ciunt, quo frui magis siciunt." Idem eciam Gregorius dicit in omelia communi unius martiris: "Si consideremus, karissimi, que et quanta sunt que
nobis promittuntur in celis, vilescunt animo omnia que habentur in terris."
Et sequitur: "Que lingua dicere aut quis intellectus capere sufficit ill⟨a⟩
superne felicitatis, quanta sunt gaudia angelorum choris interesse, cum
70   beatissimis spiritibus presencie Conditoris assistere, vultum Dei cernere,
incircumscriptum lumen videre, nullo mortis metu affici, set incorupcionis
munere letari?" Item Bernardus: "Tanta ibi est iocunditas et suavitas quod
si non liceret nisi per unius hore spacium ibi moram habere, omnes dies
istius vite pleni deliciis [pro nichilo] computarentur." Cui comparare omnes
75   delicias aliunde dolor est, omnis iocunditas meror, omne dulce amarum, omne
decus fetidum, omne quodcumque aliud quod delectari posset molestum est,
cum Dei bonitas et potencia omnia mundi gaudia infinite excedunt. Et ideo,
[f. 221v] secundum Gregorium, ⟨ibi⟩ diversa mirabilia sunt que nusquam in
hac vita videbantur, scilicet iuventus sine senectute, decor sine deformi-
80   tate, vita sine morte. Ibi satis sine sollicitudine, gaudium sine fine,
dies sine nocte. Item ibidem sunt dignitates iste: carmina non deficiunt,
premia non desinunt, regnum non amittitur. Ibi eciam est pax sine discor-

any coarse work outside the house but washes and dries the hair and head of her
lord and thus serves him in many ways with great joy.

Thus virginity rightfully receives its reward in heaven, where seven blessings are granted against the capital vices, as can be seen in Matthew 5.
Christ says first to the proud: "O you proud ones, who did not want to have
any equal but always lived in pride and arrogance, behold now in heaven 'blessed are the peacemakers,' etc." Second: "O you wrathful, who thought the life
of the meek was folly, now see how in heaven 'blessed are the meek.' " Third:
"O you envious and backbiters, who thought that mercy amounted to nothing,
behold, now in heaven 'blessed are the merciful.' " Fourth: "O you covetous
and avaricious, who thought that the life of the poor was nonsense, now understand and see that 'blessed are the poor,' etc." Fifth: "O you slothful, who
thought that doing penance was insane, now realize and see that 'blessed are
they who mourn.' " Sixth: "O you gluttons, who despised abstinence, behold
now that 'blessed are they who hunger and thirst,' and so forth." And finally,
in the seventh place: "O you lechers, who scorned cleanness, behold now
that 'blessed are the pure of heart, for they shall see God.' "

And thus, at the Last Judgment you hardened sinners will say those words
of Wisdom 5 with reference to the pure and virtuous souls: "These are the ones
whom we once held in derision and for a parable of reproach. We fools esteemed
their life madness and their end without honor. But behold how they are now
numbered among the children of God, and their lot is among the saints." And
speaking of the joys of heaven, Gregory says: "In our heavenly home, the
wealth we love is acquired where it cannot perish, honor is gained where no
unworthy person is honored, health is obtained where nothing exists that may
destroy it, life is gained where nothing can die. There is, further, no too
much or too little, no external good one desires, nor any internal good one
gets bored with; there the angelic citizens behold in wonder the one they see,
and thirst to enjoy him more." The same Gregory writes further in his common
homily on a martyr: "If we consider, dearly beloved, what and how great the
things are that we are promised to gain in heaven, all things on earth become
worthless to our mind." And he continues: "What tongue can tell, what mind
can grasp what great joys of heavenly bliss there are: to sing with the choirs
of angels, to share the glory of our Creator with the blessed spirits, to
behold God's face, to see the light without bounds, to be free from any fear of
death, and to rejoice in the gift of everlasting wholeness?" Bernard likewise
says: "There the joy and sweetness is so great that, if one could be there for
only one hour, all the days of one's life, even if they were full of pleasure,
would count as nothing. In comparison with that bliss, all other pleasures are
pain, all joy sadness, all sweetness bitter, all beauty ugly, everything else that
might give pleasure burdensome, for God's goodness and power transcend all
these infinitely." And therefore, after Gregory, in heaven there are several

dia, voluntas sine iniuria, sine mendacio iusticia, et sine oblivione memoria."
Unde secundum Bernardum: "Festinemus ad illum locum tuciorem, ad por-
85 tum suaviorem, ad gaudium uber⟨ius⟩, ubi habitemus sine metu, habundemus
sine defectu," etc. Dicit eciam idem Bernardus in quadam meditacione: "Ibi
est summum bonum et summa felicitas, summa iocunditas, perfecta caritas,
eterna securitas, et secura eternitas. Ibi est vera leticia, plena sciencia, omnis plenitudo, omnis pulcritudo, et omnis beatitudo, etc. Unde
90 versus:

> Est ibi pax, pietas, bonitas, lux, virtus, honestas,
> Gaudia, leticia, dulcedo, vita perhennis,
> Gloria, laus, requies, amor, concordia dulcis.

Sic patet quod cum Deo beatus erit, in cuius consciencia peccatum inventum
95 non fuerit; videbit Deum ad voluptatem, habebit eum ad voluntatem, et fruetur ad iocunditatem; in eternitate vigebit, in veritate fulgebit, in bonitate gaudebit. Sic habebit permanendi eternitatem, cognoscendi facilitatem,
et requirendi felicitatem. Cuius siquidem erit illius civitatis sancte beatitudo, cuius angeli sunt cives, Deus Pater templum, Filius eius splendor,
100 Spiritus Sanctus caritas. O sancta civitas, celestis mansio, secura patria,
totum continens quod delectat, populus sine murmure, incole quieti, homines
nullam indigenciam habentes. De [f. 222] ista civitate dicit Psalmista:
'Gloriosa dicta sunt de te, civitas Dei. Sicut letancium omnium habitacio
in te.' " Ad quam civitatem et delectabilem habitacionem perducat nos Iesus
105 Christus, rex, dulcor, et decus illius sanctissime civitatis. Amen.
Et hec de luxuria et eius opposito, scilicet continencia, ad presens
iam dicta sufficiunt. Et sic terminatur iste libellus.

Finis sermonum fit hec collectio morum.

---

7 gaudia] *add* propria O.   **9** sequamini] sequimur C.   **14** possunt] aut M; *add* ire R.
17 etc.] *om* M.W; et humilis corde R.   **22** eum] illum O.   **27** Helias] ennoc R.
29 clausit] clausos aperuit R.—B1 *reads* clausos aperuit, *the other representative MSS*
clausit.   **35** equacio] recepcio M.R; decepcio W.   **37** domicella] thalamita O.   **38** domini sui] domine sue R.   **40** conceduntur] concedit O.   contra] *add* vicia M.W; *add*
septem vicia R.   **41–42** ut . . . superbis] a christo qui ait primo O.   **43** nunc] *om* O.
etc.] *om* O.   **48** iam . . . et] modo O.   etc.] *om* O.   **49** qui] quia O.   esset] fuisset O.
58 illos] sanctos O.   **62** invenitur] timetur O.   **63** nichil] *om* O.   deficit] defluit O.   ap-
petitur] appetatur O.   **64** angelici] angeli O.   mirantur] *add* nichil deficiunt O.   quem]
qui O.   **68** illa] illius C.   **70** presencie] glorie O.   assistere] *add* presentem O.   **74** is-
tius] sue O.   pleni] plene O.   pro nichilo] *om* C.M.W.   **76** est] *om* O.   **77** mundi
gaudia] *om* O.   excedunt] excedit O.   **78** ibi] ideo C.   **80** Ibi] *om* O.   **81** Item . . . iste]

miracles which were never seen in this life, namely: youth without old age, beauty without decay, life without death. There is fullness without want, joy without end, day without night. Further, there are the following gifts of honor: songs do not end, rewards do not cease, possessions are not lost. And there is peace without discord, pleasure without hurt, justice without fail, and memory without forgetting." Therefore, according to Bernard, "let us hasten to the place that is safer, to the harbor that is sweeter, to the joy which is fuller, where we shall dwell without fear, in abundance without any want," and so forth. The same Bernard says further, in one of his meditations: "There is the highest good and the greatest happiness, the greatest joy, perfect love, eternal safety, and a safe eternity. There is true cheerfulness, complete knowledge, every fullness, every beauty, and every bliss," and so on. Hence these verses:

> Peace there is, and deep-felt love,
>> Goodness, light, virtue, honor.
> All joys and happiness we find,
>> Sweetness, and life eternal.
> Glory, praise, rest, and love there are,
>> And sweet oneness of hearts.

Thus it is clear that the person in whose conscience no sin is found will be blessed with God; he will see God to his pleasure, have him at his will, and enjoy him in bliss; he will live in eternity, shine in truth, and rejoice in goodness. In this way he will have eternity of being, ease of understanding, and the happy fulfillment of his searching. His will be the blessedness of that holy city whose citizens are the angels, whose temple God the Father, whose splendor God's Son, and whose love the Holy Spirit. O holy city, heavenly dwelling place, safe home, containing every delight, a people without murmuring, dwellers at rest, individuals without any want. Of this city the Psalmist says: "Glorious things are said of you, city of God. In you is the dwelling of all who rejoice." May he bring us to this city and delightful dwelling place, Jesus Christ, the king, sweetness, and beauty of that most holy city. Amen.

And these things about lechery and its opposite virtue, continence, suffice for now. Thus this book is finished.

This collection of moral matters is [for?] the end of sermons.

3–4 Rev. 14.4.   **4–22** Augustine, *De sancta virginitate* XXVII.27–XXIX.29 (PL 40:410–412).   **27** Cf. 2 Kings 2.11.   **28–30** The references are, evidently, to Eve, Elijah, Joshuah, Daniel, and the three youths in the fiery oven.   **34** Cf. above, *FM* VII.x.67–68.   **41–53** Matt. 5:3–9.   **55–58** Wisd. 5.3–5.   **66–72** Gregory, *In Evan-*

om O.   deficiunt] desinunt O.   **82** desinunt] deficiunt O.   Ibi eciam est] *om* O.
84 Unde secundum] secundum ergo O.   illum] *om* O.   **85** uberius] ubertatis C.
86 etc.] *om* O.   **86–105** Dicit . . . Amen] *this long expansion in C also occurs in group z and E*; ad quod gaudium nos perducat qui sine fine vivit et regnat amen O (M *omits* nos *and* amen).   **107** Finis . . . morum] *Also in* M.W.B3.B4.Et.Go1.Pe.W2, *all reading* est *instead of* fit.

gelia, hom. 37, 1 (PL 76:1275).   **72–74** Cf. Augustine, *De libero arbitrio* III.xxv.77 (PL 32:1308–09).   **78–84** Cf. Ps.-Augustine, *Ad fratres in eremo*, sermo 65 and 67 (PL 40:1351, 1353); *Soliloquia* 35 (PL 40:894).   **86–104** *Meditationes piissimae* IV.11 (PL 184:492).   **103–104** Ps. 86.3, 7.

Bibliography of Sources Cited

Albertus Magnus. *Opera omnia*, ed. A. Borgnet. 38 vols. (Paris, 1890–1899).

Alexander Neckam. *De naturis rerum* [and] *De laudibus divinae sapientiae*, ed. Thomas Wright, Rolls Series 34 (London, 1863).

Ambrose. *Exameron*, ed. Carl Schenkl. CSEL 32.1 (Vienna, 1896).

Anselm of Canterbury, *Opera omnia*, ed. F. S. Schmitt, 6 vols. (Seckau, Rome, and Edinburgh, 1938–1961).

Aristotle. *Ethica Nicomachea*, trans. H. Rackham. Second edition. Loeb Library (Cambridge, Mass., 1934).

Aristotle. *Ethica Nicomachea*, ed. R. A. Gauthier, in *Aristoteles latinus*, ed. L. Minio-Paluello, XXVI.1–3, 5 vols. (Leiden and Brussels, 1972–1974).

Aristotle. *Meteorologica*, trans. H. D. P. Lee. Loeb Library (Cambridge, Mass., 1952).

Augustine, Saint. *De civitate Dei*, ed. B. Dombart and A. Kalb. CC 47–48 (Turnhout, 1955).

Augustine, Saint. *Confessiones*, ed. Lucas Verheijen. CC 27 (Turnhout, 1981).

Augustine, Saint. *Contra Faustum*, ed. Joseph Zycha. CSEL 25.1 (Vienna, 1891).

Augustine, Saint. *Enarrationes in Psalmos*, ed. E. Dekkers and J. Fraipont. CC 38–40 (Turnhout, 1956).

Aulus Gellius. *Noctes Atticae*, trans. John C. Rolfe. Loeb Library (Cambridge, Mass., 1927).

Bede. *Historia ecclesiastica*, ed. Roger Mynors and Bertram Colgrave (Oxford, 1969).

Bernard of Clairvaux. *Opera*, ed. J. Leclercq and H. Rochais. 7 vols. (Rome, 1957–1974).

Boethius. *De consolatione Philosophiae*, ed. Ludwig Bieler. CC 94 (Turnhout, 1957).

Bonaventure, Saint. *Opera omnia*, ed. Patres Collegii a S. Bonaventura. 10 vols. in 11 (Quaracchi, 1881–1902).

Brinton, Thomas. *Sermons*, ed. Sister Mary Aquinas Devlin. 2 vols. Camden Third Series, 85–86 (London, 1954).

Bromyard, John. *Summa praedicantium*, British Library, MS Royal 7.E.iv. Quoted by alphabetical article; thus, the reference " 'Rapina,' R.I.5" is to paragraph 5 (as marked in the margins of this manuscript) of the article on "Rapina," which is the first entry under letter *R*.

Caesarius of Arles. *Sermones*, ed. G. Morin. CC 103–104 (Turnhout, 1953).

Chartham, William. *Speculum parvulorum*, London, Lambeth Palace, MS 78.

Chevalier, Ulysse. *Repertorium hymnologicum*, 6 vols. Analecta Bollandiana, Subsidia hagiographica 4 (Louvain and Brussels, 1892–1921).

Cicero. *De inventione*, trans. H. M. Hubbell. Loeb Library (Cambridge, Mass., 1949).

Convertimini, London, British Library, MS. Royal 7.C.i. See *Catalogue of Romances in the Department of Manuscripts in the British Museum*, vol. 3, ed. J. A. Herbert (London, 1910), pp. 116–136.

Decretum, *see* Gratian.

Disticha Catonis, ed. Marcus Boas (Amsterdam, 1952).

Dives and Pauper, ed. Priscilla H. Barnum. EETS 275 and 280 (London, 1976–1980).

English *Gesta Romanorum*: Sidney Herrtage, ed., *The Early English Versions of the Gesta Romanorum*. EETS, ES, 33 (London, 1879).

Francis, Saint. *Opuscula*, ed. Caietanus Esser. Bibliotheca franciscana ascetica medii aevi 12 (Grottaferrata, 1978).

Frontinus, Sextus Frontinus. *Stratagemata*, ed. Gotthold Gundermann (Leipzig, 1888).

Geoffrey of Monmouth. *Historia regum Britanniae*, ed. Acton Griscom (London, 1929).

Glossa ordinaria. In *Biblia . . . una cum glosa ordinaria et litterali moralique expositione Nicolai de Lyra*, 6 parts in 5 vols. (Basel, 1500–1502). Cited by volume, folio, and section as marginally marked.

Gratian. *Decretum* [and] *Decretalium collectiones*, in *Corpus iuris canonici*, ed. Emil Friedberg, 2 vols. (Leipzig, 1879; repr. Graz, 1959). In identifying references to medieval canon law, I use the following system: Gratian I = *Decretum* pars 1 (the distinctiones); Gratian II = *Decretum* pars II (the causae); Gratian II.33.3 refers to causa 33, quaestio 3, the long tract "De poenitentia"; Gratian III = *Decretum* pars III (i.e., "De consecratione"). This material forms vol. 1 of Friedberg's edition. The *Decretals* are found in vol. 2.

[Gregory the Great, Saint.] Grégoire le Grand. *Dialogus*, ed. Adalbert de Vogüe. 3 vols. SC 251, 260, 265 (Paris, 1978–1980).

Gregory the Great, Saint. *Homiliae in Hiezechihelem prophetam*, ed. Marcus Adriaen. CC 142 (Turnhout, 1971).

Grimestone, John de. Commonplace book of preaching materials, in Edinburgh, Advocates' Library MS 18.7.21. References are to the items as listed by Edward Wilson, *A Descriptive Index of the English Lyrics in John of Grimestone's Preaching Book*. Medium Aevum Monographs, n.s., 2 (Oxford, 1973).

Grisdale, D. M. (ed.). *Three Middle English Sermons from the Worcester Chapter Manuscript F.10* (Leeds, 1939).

[*Handlyng Synne*]. *Robert of Brunne's "Handlyng Synne,"* ed. Frederick J. Furnivall. EETS 119 and 123 (London, 1901).

Hesiod. *The Homeric Hymns*, trans. Hugh C. Evelyn-White. Revised edition. Loeb Library (Cambridge, Mass., 1936).

Higden. Ranulf. *Polychronicon*, ed. Churchill Babington and J. R. Lumby. 9 vols. Rolls Series 41 (London, 1865–1886).

Holcot, Robert. *In Sapientiam*, edition of Hagenau 1494 (repr. Frankfurt, 1974); the numbering of the *lectiones* in this more easily accessible reprint differs slightly from that found in manuscripts.

Holcot, Robert. *Moralitates*, in Holkot, *In librum Sapientiae* (Basel, 1586), pp. 708–750.

Holcot, Robert. *Sermones*, Cambridge, Peterhouse MS 210.

Horace. *Odes, Epodes*, trans. C. E. Bennett. Loeb Library (Cambridge, Mass., 1968).

Hostiensis, Henricus de Segusio cardenalis. *Summa aurea* (Venice, 1674; repr. Turin, 1963).

Hugh of Strasburg. *Compendium theologicae veritatis*, in Albertus Magnus, *Opera omnia*, ed. A. Borgnet, vol. 34 (Paris, 1895).

Innocent III. *De miseria humane conditionis*, ed. Michele Maccarrone (Lugano, 1955).

Isidore. *Etymologiarum sive originum libri XX*, ed. W. M. Lindsay. 2 vols. (Oxford, 1911).

Jerome, Saint. *Epistulae*, ed. Isidor Hilberg. CSEL 54–56 (Vienna, 1910–1918).

John Cassian. *De institutis coenobiorum*, ed. M. Petschenig. CSEL 17 (Vienna, 1888).

John of Freiburg. *Summa confessorum* (Augsburg, 1476).

John of Salisbury. *Policraticus*, ed. Clement C. J. Webb. 2 vols. (Oxford, 1909).

John of Wales. *Breviloquium*, in Aristotle, *Secreta secretorum, with Liber de regimine regum et principum vel dominorum*, etc. (Cologne, ca. 1472). Goff A-1047.

Josephus. *De bello Judaico*, trans. H. St. J. Thackeray. Loeb Library, 2 vols. (Cambridge, Mass., 1927–1928).

Legenda aurea, ed. Th. Graesse, third edition (Breslau, 1890; repr. Osnabrück, 1969).

Legg, J. Wickham (ed.). *The Sarum Missal* (Oxford, 1916).

Leo the Archpriest. *Historia de preliis*, in *Der Alexanderroman des Archipresbyters Leo*, ed. Friedrich Pfister. Sammlung mitellateinischer Texte 6 (Heidelberg, 1913).

Liebeschütz, *see* Ridevall.

Macrobius. *Opera*, ed. F. Eyssenhardt (Leipzig, 1868).

Martial. *Epigrammata*, trans. W. C. A. Ker. Loeb Library, 2 vols. (Cambridge, Mass., 1968).

Martin of Troppau, *Chronicon pontificum et imperatorum*, ed. Ludwig Weiland. MGH, Scriptores XXII (Hanover, 1872), pp. 377–475.

Mirk, John. *Festial*, ed. Theodor Erbe. EETS, ES, 96 (London, 1905).

Mythographus Vaticanus III, in *Scriptores rerum mythicarum Latini tres Romae nuper reperti*, ed. Georg Heinrich Bode. 2 vols. (Celle, 1834).

Ovid. *The Art of Love*, trans. J. H. Mozley. Loeb Library (Cambridge, Mass., 1939).

Ovid. *Metamorphoses*, trans. Frank J. Miller. Loeb Library (Cambridge, Mass., 1916).

Ovid. *Tristia, Ex Ponto*, trans. A. L. Wheeler. Loeb Library (Cambridge, Mass. 1924).

Palladius. *Opus agriculturae*, ed. Robert H. Rodgers (Leipzig, 1975).

Paschasius Radbertus. *De corpore et sanguine Domini*, ed. Beda Paulus. CC, Continuatio mediaevalis, 16 (Turnhout, 1969).

Peraldus, Guillelmus. *Summae virtutum et vitiorum* (Lyons, 1668).

Person, Henry A. (ed.). *Cambridge Middle English Lyrics*, revised edition (Seattle, 1962).

Peter Lombard. *Sententiae in IV libris distinctae*, ed. Patres Collegii S. Bonaventurae Ad Claras Aquas, 2 vols. (Grottaferrata, 1971–1981).

Petrus Alphonsus. *De scientia clericali*, ed. Alfons Hilka and Werner Söderhjelm. Acta Societatis scientiarum Fennicae, XXXVIII.4 (Helsingfors, 1911).

Petrus Chrysologus. *Collectio sermonum*, ed. Alexander Olivar. CC 24 and 24A–B (Turnhout, 1975–1982).

Physiologus, ed. Francis J. Carmody (Paris, 1939).

Pliny. *Historia naturalis*, trans. H. Rackham et al. Loeb Library, 11 vols. (Cambridge, Mass., 1944–1963).

Policraticus, see John of Salisbury.

Raymundus of Pennaforte. *Summa de poenitentia et matrimonio* (Rome, 1603; repr. Farnborough, Hants., 1967).

Ridevall, John. *Fulgentius metaforalis*, ed. Hans Liebeschütz (Leipzig, 1926).

Ross, Woodburn O. (ed.). *Middle English Sermons*. EETS 209 (London, 1940).

Seneca. *Declamationes*: ed. H. J. Müller, *L. Annaei Senecae patris Scripta quae mansuerunt* (Vienna, 1887).

Seneca. *De clementia*, in Seneca, *Moral Essays*, trans. John W. Basore, vol. 1. Loeb Library (Cambridge, Mass., 1928).

Seneca. *Naturales quaestiones*, trans. Thomas H. Corcoran. Loeb Library (Cambridge, Mass., 1971–).

Servius Grammaticus. *In Vergilii carmina commentarii*, ed. Georg Thilo, 3 vols. (Leipzig, 1878–1887; repr. Hildesheim, 1961).

Solinus. *Collectanea rerum memorabilium*, ed. Th. Mommsen, second edition (Berlin, 1958).

Speculum laicorum, ed. J. Th. Welter (Paris, 1914).

Suetonius. *The Lives of the Caesars*, trans. J. C. Rolfe, 2 vols. Loeb Library (Cambridge, Mass., 1913–1914).

Tabula exemplorum secundum ordinem alphabeti, ed. J. Th. Welter (Paris, 1926).

Techel ("Cethel"). *De lapidibus*, ed. J. B. Pitra, *Spicilegium Solesmense*, vol. 4 (Paris, 1855), pp. 335–37.

Thomas Aquinas, Saint. *Summa theologiae*, ed. Petrus Caramello. 4 vols. (Turin, 1948).

Thomas Cantimpratensis. *Liber de natura rerum*, ed. H. Boese (Berlin, 1973).

Thorndike, Lynn. *A History of Magic and Experimental Science during the First Thirteen Centuries of our Era*, 2 vols. (New York, 1923).

Tubach, Frederic C. *Index Exemplorum: A Handbook of Medieval Religious Tales*. FF Communications 204 (Helsinki, 1969). Quoted by item number.

Valerius Maximus. *Factorum et dictorum memorabilium libri*, ed. C. Kempf (Leipzig, 1888).

Vegetius. *Epitoma rei militaris*, ed. Carl Lang. Second edition (Leipzig, 1885).

Vincent of Beauvais. *Speculum quadruplex* (Douai, 1624; repr. Graz, 1964–1965).

Virgil. *Aeneid*, trans. H. R. Fairclough, 2 vols. Loeb Library (Cambridge, Mass., 1934–1935).

Whiting, Bartlett Jere, and Helen Wescott Whiting. *Proverbs, Sentences, and Proverbial Phrases from English Writings Mainly before 1500* (Cambridge, Mass., 1968).

INDEX